BRADFORD'S CROSSWORD SOLVER'S DICTIONARY

D0243106

Collins
An imprint of HarperCollins*Publishers*

fifth edition 2003

© Anne R. Bradford 1986, 1993, 1997, 2000
This edition © Anne R. Bradford, 2003

The Author hereby asserts her moral rights to be identified as the author of this work.

first edition published by Longman; second, third and fourth editions published by
Peter Collin Publishing Ltd

HarperCollins Publishers
Westerhill Road, Bishopbriggs, Glasgow G64 2QT
Great Britain

www.collins.dictionaries.com

Collins® is a registered trademark of HarperCollins Publishers Limited

ISBN 0-00-716922-1

A catalogue record for this book is available from the British Library

Computing support and typesetting by Thomas Callan

Printed and bound in Great Britain by Clays Ltd, St Ives plc

Author's preface

Every word has a definition – an identity. If it has only one definition we can look at it and know it for what it is, but some words are like cut stones with many facets; they can mean different things according to the way in which we use them. These are the words which add spice to the cryptic crossword puzzle – the setter plays with them and tries to deceive his solvers into believing he means what he does not. They are the basis of puns and word-play. Introduced to crossword puzzles at an early age, it soon became clear to me that some words are beloved of setters – rivers Po and Dee; the town of Diss in Norfolk; the diocesan 'see' of Ely. These and many more quickly became familiar, but now and again the odd one would elude the memory. It seemed logical then to write these down, and by a natural progression to start to turn the normal dictionary inside out – if 'flummery' is defined as a blancmange, then why not list it under 'blancmange' alongside other words which can be defined as such? Not a new idea, of course, but why stop at synonyms? There are words which have recognised associations with other words – descriptive words or words with literary connections, foreign words, archaic words, technical words and even folkloric words – all highly collectable. And so this crossword dictionary began to evolve. Every puzzle I have laid hands on in the past forty-five years has been scrutinised, the clues broken down into definitions and cryptic parts; words indicating anagrams, reversals, puns, etc. all carefully recorded and stored.

This fifth edition brings it up to date, but the work continues, and I wish all who use this book the satisfaction that comes with completing a challenging puzzle.

A.R.B. 2003

Solving crossword clues

Crossword puzzles tend to be basically 'quick' or 'cryptic'. A 'quick' crossword usually relies on a one or two-word clue which is a simple definition of the answer required. As has been stated, many words have different meanings, so that the clue 'ball' could equally well lead to the answer 'sphere', 'orb' or 'dance'. The way to solve 'quick' crosswords is to press on until probable answers begin to interlink, which is a good sign that you are on the right track.

'Cryptic' crosswords are another matter. Here the clue usually consists of a basic definition, given at either the beginning or end of the clue, together with one or more definitions of parts of the answer. Here are some examples taken from all-time favourites recorded over the years:

1. *'Tradesman who bursts into tears'* (**Stationer**)

Tradesman is a definition of stationer. Bursts is cleverly used as an indication of an anagram, which into tears is of stationer.

2. *'Sunday school tune'* (**Strain**)

Here Sunday is used to define its abbreviation S, school is a synonym for train, and put together they give strain, which is a synonym of tune.

3. *'Result for everyone when head gets at bottom'* (**Ache**) (used as a 'down' clue)

This is what is known as an '& lit' clue, meaning that the setter has hit on a happy composition which could literally be true. Everyone here is a synonym for each, move the head (first letter) of the word to the bottom, and the answer is revealed, the whole clue being the definition of the answer in this case.

4. *'Tin out East'* (**Sen**)

In this example, tin, implying 'money', requires its chemical symbol Sn to go out(side) East, or its abbreviation, E, the whole clue being a definition of a currency (sen) used in the East.

5. *'Information given to communist in return for sex'* (**Gender**)

Information can be defined as gen; communist is almost always red, in return indicates 'reversed', leading to gen-der, a synonym for sex.

6. *'Row about no enclosure of this with sardines'* (**Tin-opener**)

Row is a synonym for tier, about indicates 'surrounding', no enclosure can be no pen, leading to ti-no pen-er, and another '& lit' clue.

7. *'Cake-sandwiches-meat, at Uncle Sam's party'* (**Clambake**)

Meat here is lamb, sandwiches is used as a verb, so we have C-lamb-ake, which is a kind of party in America. Uncle Sam or US is often used to indicate America.

8. *'Initially passionate meeting of boy and girl could result in it'* (**Pregnancy**)

Initially is usually a sign of a first letter, in this case 'p' for passionate + Reg (a boy) and Nancy (a girl), and another clever '& lit'.

With 'cryptic' clues the solver needs to try to analyse the parts to see what he or she is looking for – which word or words can be the straight definition, and which refer to the parts or hint at anagrams or other subterfuges. Whilst it would be unrealistic to claim total infallibility, practice has shown that in most crosswords some 90% of the answers are to be found in this work.

Anne R Bradford

How to use the dictionary

This dictionary is the result of over forty-five years' analysis of some 300,000 crossword clues, ranging from plain 'quick' crosswords requiring only synonyms to the different level of cryptic puzzles. Therefore the words listed at each entry may be connected to the keyword in various ways, such as:

− a straightforward synonym

− a commonly-associated adjective

− an associated or proper noun

− a pun or other devious play on words

Keywords are listed alphabetically; in cases where the heading consists of more than one word, the first of these words is taken to be the keyword, and in cases where the end of a word is bracketed, the material up to the opening bracket is taken to be the keyword. Keywords marked with the symbol ▶ refer the user to other entries where additional information may be found. Keywords marked with the symbol ▷ give leads to anagrams and other ploys used by crossword setters. If the keywords found in the clue do not lead directly to the required answer, the solver should look under words given as cross-references to other entries. These are indicated by the symbol ➤, with the cross-referenced word shown in capitals.

As a completely innovative feature for this new edition, some entries have been divided into two parts − a general entry similar to the standard entries which appear elsewhere, and a panel entry which contains a list of more specific or encyclopedic material. So, for example, the entry 'Artist(ic)' includes not only a list of general words connected with 'Artist' or 'Artistic' in some way, such as 'Bohemian', 'Cubist', 'Fine' and 'Virtuoso', but also a panel with the heading 'Artists' containing a list of the names of specific artists, such as 'Bellini', 'Constable', and 'Rembrandt'. For added help, the words in these panels are arranged by length, with all three-letter words grouped together in alphabetical order, then all four-letter words, then all five-letter words, and so on.

About the Author

Anne Bradford's love of words began to make itself evident even in her schooldays, when, as Head Girl of her school, she instituted a novel punishment – instead of making rulebreakers write lines, she had them write out pages from a dictionary, on the grounds that this was a more useful exercise. Little did she know this was soon to be her own daily routine!

In time, crosswords became a magnificent obsession for Anne. All lovers of crosswords can understand the irresistible lure of solving them, but Anne's interest went much deeper than most people's, and when she stopped work in 1957 to have her first child, she found herself starting to note down answers to particularly tricky clues as an aid to memory, in case she should come across them again in another puzzle. It was from this simple beginning that this crossword dictionary evolved.

Over the space of 25 years, Anne continued to build on her collection of solutions, analysing every crossword clue as she solved it and adding it to her steadily growing bank of entries. This unique body of material eventually reached such proportions that she had the idea of offering it to her fellow crossword-solvers as a reference book, and since then, the book has gone from strength to strength, providing valuable help to countless cruciverbalists over a number of editions.

Anne Bradford continues to devote time each day to solving crosswords, averaging some 20 a week – both quick and cryptic – and still avidly collects new solutions for her Crossword Solver's Dictionary at a rate of around 150 a week, compiling each solution by hand (without the use of a computer!) This latest edition therefore includes much new material, gleaned by a true crossword lover who not only solves crosswords but, as an active member of the Crossword Club, can offer the user an insight into the mind of a cunning crossword compiler.

The Crossword Club

If you are interested in crosswords, you might like to consider joining the Crossword Club. Membership is open to all who enjoy tackling challenging crosswords and who appreciate the finer points of clue-writing and grid-construction. The Club's magazine, Crossword, contains two prize puzzles each month. A sample issue and full details are available on request.

The Crossword Club
Coombe Farm
Awbridge
Romsey, Hants.
SO51 0HN
UK

email: bh@thecrosswordclub.co.uk
website address: www.crosswordclub.demon.co.uk

A a

A, An Ack, Adult, Ae, Alpha, Angstrom, Argon, D, Ein, Her, If, L, One, Per, They

A1 Tiptop

AA Milne

Aardvark Ant-bear, Ant-eater, Ground-hog

Aaron's Rod Hagtaper

Aba, Abba Patriarch

Abacus Counter, Soroban

Abaft Astern, Sternson

Abalone Ormer, Paua

Abandon(ed), Abandonment Abnegate, Abort, Amoral, Apostasy, Back down, Cancel, Castaway, Corrupt, Decommission, Defect, Derelict, ➤ DESERT, Desuetude, Discard, Disown, Dissolute, Ditch, Drop, Dump, Elan, Expose, Flagrant, Forhoo(ie), Forlend, Forsake, Gomorra, Immoral, Jack(-in), Jettison, Jilt, Loose, Louche, Maroon, Old, Orgiastic, Profligate, Quit, Rat, Renounce, Reprobate, Scrap, Shed, Sink, Strand, Waive, Wanton

Abase Degrade, Demean, Disgrace, Grovel, ➤ HUMBLE, Kowtow, Lessen

Abash Daunt, Discountenance, Mortify

Abate(ment) Allay, Appal, Decrescent, Diminish, Lyse, Lysis, Moderate, Reduce, Remit, ➤ SUBSIDE

▷ **Abate** may indicate a contention

Abattoir Knackery, Slaughterhouse

Abbey Abbacy, Bath, Buckfast, Cloister, Downside, Fonthills, Fountains, Glastonbury, Je(r)vaulx, Medmenham, Melrose, Nightmare, Northanger, Priory, Tintern, Westminster, Whitby, Woburn

Abbot Aelfric, Archimandrite, Brother, Friar

Abbreviate, Abbreviation Abridge, Ampersand, Compendium, Condense, Curtail, ➤ SHORTEN, Sigla

ABC Absey

Abdicate Cede, Disclaim, Disown, Resign

Abdomen Belly, C(o)eliac, Epigastrium, Gaster, Hypochondrium, Paunch, Pleon, ➤ STOMACH, Tummy, Venter

Abduct(ed), Abduction Enlèvement, Kidnap, Rapt, Ravish, Shanghai, Steal

Aberdeen Granite City

Aberrant, Aberration Abnormal, Aye-aye, Deviant, Idolon, Perverse

Abet(tor) Aid, Back, Candle-holder, Second

Abeyance, Abeyant Dormant, Shelved, Sleeping, Store

Abhor(rent) ➤ DETEST, ➤ HATE, Loathe, Shun

Abide Dwell, Inhere, ➤ LAST, Lie, Live, Observe, Remain, Stand, Tarry

Abigail Maid, Masham

Ability Aptitude, Calibre, Capacity, Cocum, ➤ COMPETENCE, ESP, Facility, Faculty, Ingine, Lights, Prowess, Savey, Savv(e)y, Skill, Talent

Abject Base, Craven, Grovel, Humble, Servile, Slave

Abjure Eschew, Forswear, Recant, Renege, Reny

Ablaze Afire, Ardent

Able Ablins, ➤ ADEPT, Aiblins, Apt, Capable, ➤ COMPETENT, Fere, Seaman, Yibbles

Abnormal(ity) Anomalous, Atypical, ➤ DEVIANT, Dysfunction, Ectopic, Erratic, Etypical, Freakish, Odd, Preternatural, ➤ QUEER, Sport, Unnatural, Varus

Aboard On

Abode Domicile, Dwelling, Habitat, ➤ HOME, Lain, Libken, Midgard, Remain

Abolish, Abolition(ist) Annihilate, Annul, Axe, ➤ BAN, D, Delete, Destroy, Eradicate, Erase, Extirpate, John Brown, Nullify, Repeal, Rescind

Abomasum Read

Abominable, Abominate, Abomination Bane, Cursed, ➤ HATE, Nefandous, Nefast, Revolting, Snowman, Vile, Yeti

Aborigine, Aboriginal Adivasi, Aranda, Autochthon, Binghi, Boong, Buck, Bushmen, Carib, Evolué, Gin, Gurindji, Indigenous, Jacky(-Jacky), Kamilaroi, Koori, Lubra, Maori, Mary, Motu, Myall, Piljantjatjara, Pre-Dravidian, Sakai, Sican, Siwash, Truganini, Vedda(h)

Abort(ion), Abortive Apiol, Cancel, Ecbolic, Miscarry, Moon-calf, Slip, Sooterkin, Teras, Termination

Abound(ing) Bristle, Copious, Enorm, Rife, Teem

About A, Almost, Anent, Around, C, Ca, Circa, Circiter, Concerning, Encompass, Environs, Going, Near, Of, On, Over, Re, Regarding, Soon at

▷ **About** may indicate one word around another

Above Abune, Over, Overhead, Overtop, Owre, Sopra, Superior, Supra-, Upon

Abracadabra Cantrip, Heypass

Abrade, Abrasive Carbanado, Carborundum®, Chafe, Emery, Erode, File, Garnet paper, ➤ GRATE, Rub, Sand, Scrape, Scrat

Abraham Lincoln, Urite

Abreast Alongside, Au courant, Au fait, Beside, Level, Up

Abridge(ment) Audley, Compress, Condense, Cut, Digest, Dock, Epitome, Pot, Shorten, Trim

Abroad Afield, Away, Distant, Forth, Out, Overseas

▷ **Abroad** may indicate an anagram

Abrogate Abolish, Repeal, Replace

▷ **Abrupt** may indicate a shortened word

Abrupt(ly) Bold, Brusque, Curt, Gruff, Offhand, Premorse, Prerupt, Short, Staccato, Terse

Abscess Gumboil, Impost(h)ume, Ulcer, Warble

Abscond Absqatulate, Decamp, Desert, Elope, Flee, Leg-bail, Levant, Welch

Abseil(ing) Dulfer, Rappel

Absence, Absent(ee), Absent-minded(ness) Abs, Abstracted, Away, Distant, Distracted, Distrait, Exile, Hookey, Mitch, Scatty, Skip, Truant, Vacuity, Void, Wool-gathering

Absolute(ly) Bang, Complete, Dead, Downright, Implicit, Ipso facto, Just, Mere, Mondo, Plumb, Quite, Real, Sheer, Total, Unmitigated, Unqualified, Utter, Veritable, Very

Absolve Clear, Exculpate, Excuse, Pardon, Shrive

Absorb(ed), Absorbent, Absorbing, Absorption Assimilate, Autism, Blot, Consume, Desiccant, Devour, Digest, Dope, Drink, ➤ ENGROSS, Imbibe, Ingest, Intent, Merge(r), Occlude, Occupy, Porous, Preoccupation, Rapt, Sorbefacient, Spongy, Unputdownable

Absquatulate Skedaddle

Abstain(er), Abstemious, Abstinence, Abstinent Band of Hope, Celibacy, Chastity, Continent, Desist, Eschew, Forbear, Forgo, Maigre, Nazarite, Nephalism, Rechab(ite), Refrain, Resist, Sober, Temperate, TT

Abstract(ed), Abstraction Abrege, Abridge, Academic, Appropriate, Brief, Deduct, Digest, Discrete, Epitome, Essence, Metaphysical, Musing, Notional, Précis, Prepossessed, Prescind, Resumé, Reverie, Stable, Steal, Summary, Tachism

Abstruse Deep, Esoteric, Obscure, Recondite

Absurd(ity) Alician, Apagoge, Fantastic, Farcical, Folly, Inept, Irrational, Laputan, Ludicrous, Nonsense, Paradox, Preposterous, Ridiculous, Silly, Solecism, Stupid, Toshy, Whim-wham

Abundance, Abundant A-gogo, Bounty, Copious, Flood, Flush, Fouth, Fowth, Fruitful, Galore, Lashings, Mickle, Mine, Mint, Oodles, Opulent, Over, Plenitude, Plenteous, ➤ PLENTIFUL, Pleroma, Prolific, Replete, Rich, Rife, Routh, Rowth, Sonce, Sonse, Store, Tallents, Teeming, Uberous

Abuse Assail, Billingsgate, Blackguard, Flak, Fustilarian, Fustil(l)irian, Hail, Insult, Invective, Limehouse, Maltreat, Miscall, ➤ MISTREAT, Misuse, Obloquy, Opprobrium, Philippic, Rail, Rampallian, Rate, Rayle, Revile, Satire, Scarab(ee), Scurrilous, Slang, Slate, Sledging, Snash, Solvent, Tirade, Vilify, Violate, Vituperation

Abut Adjoin, Border, Touch

Abysm(al), Abyss Avernus, Barathrum, Barranca, Chasm, Deep, Gulf, Swallet, Tartarean, Tartarus

AC Current, Erk

Acacia Bablah, Boree, Brigalow, Gidgee, Gidjee, Koa, Mimosa, Mulga, Myall, Sallee, Shittim, Wattle

Academic(ian) A, Della-Cruscan, Don, Erudite, Fellow, Hypothetic(al), Immortals, Literati, Master, Pedantic, PRA, RA, Reader, Rector

Academy Athenaeum, Dollar, Loretto, Lyceum, Military, Sandhurst, Seminary, St Cyr, West Point

Acanthus Blankursine, Ruellia

Accelerate, Acceleration, Accelerator Antedate, Betatron, Bevatron, Collider, Cyclotron, Festinate, G, Gal, Gun, Hasten, Increase, Linac, Linear, Rev, Speed, Stringendo, Synchotron

Accent(ed), Accentuate Acute, Beat, Breve, Brogue, Bur(r), Circumflex, Cut-glass, Doric, Drawl, Enclitic, Enhance, Grave, Hacek, Intonation, Kelvinside, Long, Macron, Martelé, Morningside, Mummerset, Nasal, Orthotone, Oxford, Oxytone, Pitch, Rhythm, Stress, Tittle, Tone, Twang

Accentor Dunnock

Accept(able), Acceptance, Accepted A, Accede, Admit, Adopt, Agree, Allow, Approbate, Bar, Believe, Buy, Can-do, Common, Consent, Cosher, Done, Grant, Kosher, Obey, On, Pocket, Putative, Stand, Swallow, Take, Tolerate, U, Wear

Access(ible) Avenue, Card, Come-at-able, Credit, Door, Entrée, ➤ ENTRY, Fit, Ingo, Key, Passe-partout, Password, Random, Recourse, Remote, Sequential, Spasm, Wayleave

Accessory, Accessories Abettor, Addition, Aide, Ally, Ancillary, Appendage, Appurtenance, Attribute, Bandanna, Bells and whistles, Cribellum, Findings, Staffage, Trappings, Trimming

Accident(al) Adventitious, Bechance, Blowdown, Blunder, Calamity, ➤ CHANCE, Circumstance, Contingency, Contretemps, Crash, Disaster, Fall, Fluke, Hap, Hit and run, Mischance, Mishap, Promiscuous, Rear-ender, Shunt, Smash, Smash-up, Spill, Stramash, Wreck

Accidie Acedia, Sloth, Torpor

Acclaim Accolade, Applaud, Brava, Bravo, Cheer, Eclat, Fame, Fanfare, Hail, Kudos, Ovation, Praise, Salute

Accolade Award, Honour, Palm, Token

Accommodate, Accommodation Adapt, B and B, Bedsit, Berth, Board, Botel, Bunkhouse, Camp, Chalet, Compromise, Crashpad, Flotel, Gaff, Gite, Grace and favour, Homestay, Hostel, Hotel, House, Lend, Loan, Lodge, Lodgement, Motel, ➤ OBLIGE, Parador, Pension, Quarters, Rapprochement, Recurve, Room, Sorehon, Stabling, Stateroom, Steerage, Storage, Wharepuni

▷ **Accommodating** may indicate one word inside another

Accompany(ing), Accompanied (by), Accompaniment, Accompanist Accessory, Alberti, And, Attend, Chaperone, Chum, Concomitant, Consort, Continuo, Descant, ➤ ESCORT, Harmonise, Herewith, Obbligato, Obligate, Obligato, Trimmings, Vamp

Accomplice Abettor, Aide, ➤ ALLY, Collaborator, Confederate, Federarie, Partner, Shill, Stale

Accomplish(ed) Able, ➤ ACHIEVE, Arch, Attain, Clever, Complete, Done, Effect, Master, Over, Perform, Polished, Realise, Ripe, Savant

Accord(ingly), According to After, Agree, Ala, Allow, As per, Attune, Chime, Consensus, Give, Grant, Harmony, Jibe, Meet, Sort, Thus

According to nature SN

Accost Abord, Approach, Greet, Hail, Importune, Molest, Solicit, Tackle

Account(s) AC, Audit, Battels, Behalf, Bill, Cause, Charge, Chronicle, Current, Deposit, Discretionary, Enarration, Expense, Explain, Exposition, Ledger, Long, Memoir, Narration, Procès-verbal, Reason, Recital, Regest, Register, ➤ REPORT, Repute, Resumé, Sake, Suspense, Swindlesheet, Tab, Tale, Thesis, Version

Accountant Auditor, CA, Cost, Hyde, Liquidator, Reckoner, Vestry-clerk

Accredit Attribute

Accumulate, Accumulation Adsorb, Aggregate, ➤ AMASS, Augment, Backlog, Collect, Gather, Hoard, Lodg(e)ment, Pile, Uplay

Accuracy, Accurate(ly) Bang-on, Cocker, ➤ CORRECT, Dead-on, Fair, Fidelity, Minute, Precise, Right, Spot-on, True, Word-perfect

Accursed Argued, Sacred

Accusation, Accuse(d) Allege, Arraign, Attaint, Bill, Blame, Censure, Challenge, Charge, Criminate, Denounce, Dite, Gravamen, Impeach, Incriminate, Panel, Suspect, Tax, Threap, Threep, Traduce, Wight, Wite, Wyte

Accustom(ed) Acquaint, Attune, Enure, General, Habituate, Inure, Wont, Woon

Ace(s) Basto, Dinger, ➤ EXPERT, Jot, Master, Mournival, One, Quatorze, Spadille, Spadill(i)o, Spot, Tib, Virtuoso, Wonderful

Ache, Aching Aitch, Die, Long, Mulligrubs, Nag, Otalgia, Pain, Stitch, Yearn, Yen

Achieve(ment) Accomplish, Acquisition, Attain, Come, Compass, ➤ EFFECT, Exploit, Feat, Fulfil, Gain, Hatchment, Realise, Satisfice, Statisfy, Stroke, Succeed, Triumph, Trock, Troke, Truck

Acid(ity) Abietic, Abscisic, Acrimony, Acrylic, Acyl, Adipic, Alanine, Alginic, Amide, Amino, Aquafortis, Aqua-regia, Arachidonic, Arginine, Ascorbic, Asparagine, Aspartic, Auric, Barbituric, Benzoic, Boric, Bromic, Butanoic, Butyric, Capric, Caproic, Caprylic, Carbamic, Carbolic, Carbonic, Carboxylic, Caro's, Cerotic, Chloric, Chromic, Cinnamic, Citric, Citruline, Citrulline, Citydylic, Corrosive, Creatin(e), Cresylic, Crotonic, Cyanic, Cyclamic, Cystine, Decanoic, Deoxyribonucleic, Dichromic, Dicraboxylic, DNA, Dodecanoic, Dopa, Drop, Ellagic, Erucic, Etchant, Ethan(edi)oic, Fatty, Ferricyanic, Ferrocyanic, Ferulic, Folacin, Folic, Formic, Fulminic, Fumaric, Fusidic, Galactosamine, Gallic, Gibberellic, Glucoronic, Glutam(in)ic, Glycine, Glycolic, Guanine, Guanylic, HCL, Heptadecanoic, Hippuric, Histidine, Hyaluronic, Hydrazoic, Hydriodic, Hydrobromic, Hydrochloric, Hydrofluoric, Hypochlorous, Indoleacetic, Indolebutyric, Iodic, Isoleucine, Itaconic, Lactic, Lauric, L-dopa, Leucin(e), Lewis, Linoleic, Linolenic, Lipoic, LSD, Lysergic, Lysine, Maleic, Malic, Malonic, Meconic, Metaphosphoric, Methacrylic, Methanoic, Methionine, Mucic, Muramic, Muriatic, Myrostic, Nalidixic, Niacin, Nicotinic, Nitric, Nitrous, Nonanoic, Nucleic, Oleic, Orcin(ol), Ornithine, Osmic, Oxalic, Palmitic, Pan(to)thenic, Pectic, Pelargonic, Pentanoic, Peracid, Perchloric, Periodic, Permanganic, Persulphuric, PH, Phenol, Phenylalanin(e), Phosphoric, Phosphorous, Phthalic, Picric, Polyadenalic, Polybasic, Proline, Propanoic, Propenoic, Proprionic, Prostacyclin, Prostaglandin, Prussic, Pteroic, Pyro, Pyrogallic,

Pyroligneous, Pyruvic, Quinic, Racemic, Reaction, Rhodanic, Ribonucleic, Ricinoleic, RNA, Saccharic, Salicylic, Sarcolactic, Sassolite, Sebacic, Selenic, Serine, Sialic, Silicic, Solvent, Sorbic, Sour, Stannic, Stearic, Suberic, Succinic, Sulphonic, Sulphuric, Tannic, Tart, Tartaric, Taurocholic, Telluric, Thiocyanic, Thiosulphuric, Threonine, Tiglic, Titanic, Trona, Tryptophan, Tungstic, Tyrosine, Uric, Valeric, Valine, Valproic, Vinegar, Vitriol, Xanthic, Xylonic

Acknowledge(ment) Accept, Admit, Allow, Answer, Avow, Confess, Grant, Mea culpa, Nod, Own, Receipt, Recognise, Respect, Righto, Roger, Salute, Ta, Touché, Wilco

Acme Apex, Apogee, Climax, Comble, Crest, Peak, Summit, Top, Zenith

Acolyte Nethinim, Novice, Server, Thurifer

Acorn(s), Acorn-shell Balanus, Glans, Mast, Rac(c)ahout, Valonia

Acoustic(s) Harmonics, Sonics

Acquaint(ance), Acquainted Advise, Cognisant, Enlighten, Familiar, ➤ INFORM, Knowledge, Nodding, Notify, Tell, Versed

Acquiescence, Acquiescent Accept, Bow, Conform, Resigned, Roger, Wilco

Acquire, Acquisition Acquest, Earn, Ern, Gain, ➤ GET, Land, Obtain, Procure, Purchase, Steal, Take-over, Usucap(t)ion

Acquit(tal) Assoil, Cleanse, Clear, Exonerate, Free, Loose, Loste, Pardon

Acre(s) A, Area, Hide, Rival, Rood

Acrid, Acrimony Bitter(ness), Empyreuma, Rough, Sour, Surly

Acrobat(ic)s Equilibrist, Gymnast, Ropedancer, Splits, Trampoline, Tumbler

Acropolis Citadel, Parthenon

Across A, Ac, Athwart, Opposite, Over, Through

Act(ing), Action A, Antic, Assist, Assumpsit, Auto, Barnstorm, Behave, Bit, Business, Camp, Campaign, Case, Cause, Come, Conduct, Coup, Daff, Deal, ➤ DEED, Delaying, Deputise, Direct, Do, DORA, Double, Enclosure, Epistasis, Excitement, Exert, Exploit, Feat, Feign, Forth-putting, Function, Histrionic, Impersonate, Improbation, Incident, Industrial, Lance-jack, Litigate, Measure, Method, Movement, Mum, Partypiece, Pas, Perform(ance), Personate, Play, Pp, Practice, Pretence, Procedure, Process, Qua, Reflex, Replevin, Represent, Riot, Rising, Routine, Sasine, Scenery, Serve, Simulate, Stamp, Stanislavski, Statute, Steps, Suit, Synergy, Test, Thellusson, Thing, Treat, Trover, Turn, Twig, Uniformity, Union, Vicegerent, War, Windlass

Actinium Ac

Actinon An

Activate Arm, Goad, Spark, Spur, Stur, Styre, Trigger

Active, Activist, Activity A, Alert, At, Athletic, Brisk, Busy, Cadre, Deedy, ➤ DIY, Do(ing), Dynamited, Ecowarrior, Effectual, Energetic, Energic, Extra-curricular, Floruit, Fluster, Go-go, Goings-on, Hum, Hyper, Leish, Licht, Live, Mobile, Motile, Nimble, Ongo, Operant, Play, Rambunctious, Sprightly, Springe, Spry, Voice, Wimble

Actor(-like) Agent, Alleyn, Artist, Ashe, Barnstormer, Benson, Betterton, Burbage, Cast, Character, Company, Diseur, Donat, Gable, Garrick, Gielgud, Guiser, Ham, Hamfatter, Heavy, Histrio(n), Jay, Juve(nile), Kean, Luvvie, MacReady, Mime, Mummer, Olivier, Performer, Player, Playfair, Roscian, Roscius, Savoyard, Sim, Stager, Strolling, Super, Thespian, Tragedian, Tree, Tritagonist, Trouper, Understudy, Wolfit

Actress Bankhead, Duse, Ingenue, Pierrette, Siddons, Soubrette, Terry, West

Actual(ity), Actually De facto, Entelechy, Literal, Live, Material, Real, Real-life, True, Very

Acumen Insight

Acupressure Jin shin do, Shiatsu

Acute Astute, Dire, Fitché, ➤ INTENSE, Keen, Quick-witted

Adage Aphorism, Gnome, Maxim, Motto, Paroemia, Proverb, Saw, Saying, Truism

Adam Bede, Delved

Adamant Inexorable, Obdurate, Rigid, Unbending

Adapt(er), Adaptable, Adaptor Bushing, Ecad, Reorient, Tailor, Timeserver, Versatile

Add(ed), Addendum Accrue, Adscititious, ➤ APPENDIX, Attach, Cast, Coopt, Dub, Ech(e), Eik, Eke, Elaborate, Embroider, Enhance, Fortify, Insert, Lace, Reckon, Score, Spike, Sum, Summate, Tot(e), Total

Addict(ion) Abuser, Acidhead, Buff, Devotee, Etheromaniac, Fan, Fiend, Freak, Hophead, Hype, Jones, Joypopper, Junkie, Mainliner, Mania, Need, Pillhead, Pillpopper, Pothead, Shithead, Slave, Space-cadet, Speedfreak, User, Wino

Addison Spectator

Addition(al) Accession, Addend, Additive, Adscititious, Adulterant, Also, And, Annexure, (As an) in, Braata, Codicil, Corollary, Eik, Eke, Encore, Epithesis, Etc, Extender, ➤ EXTRA, Extramural, ➤ IN ADDITION, Increment, Makeweight, Monkey, New, Odd, On, On top, Other, Padding, Paragog(u)e, Parergon, Plus, PS, Rider, Ripieno, Spare, Suffect, Suffix, Supplementary, Thereto, Top-up, Verandah

Address, Address system Accommodation, Accost, Adroit, Allocution, Apostrophe, Apostrophise, Appellation, Art, ➤ ATLAS, Ave, Bub, Buster, Call, Compellation, Dedication, Delivery, Den, Diatribe, Direction, Discourse, Election, Epilogue, Epirrhema, Esquire, Gettysburg, Hail, Home, Lecture, Ode, Orate, Parabasis, Poste-restante, Prelection, Rig, Salute, Sermon, Speech, Stance, Tact, Tannoy®, Tuan, Valedictory, Wambenger, Y'all

Adelphic Adam

Adept Able, Adroit, Dab, Deacon, Don, ➤ EXPERT, Fit, Handy, Mahatma

Adequate Condign, Does, Due, Egal, Equal, Ere-now, Passable, Proper, ➤ SUFFICIENT, Tolerable, Valid

Adhere(nt), Adhesive Allegiance, Ally, Araldite®, Bond, Burr, Child, Cling, Conform, Cow Gum®, Dextrin, Disciple, Epoxy, Follower, Glue, Guebre,

Gum, Hot-melt, Jain(a), Mucilage, Partisan, Resin, Sectator, Servitor, Sticker, Supporter, Synechia, Waterglass

Adjacent, Adjoining Bordering, Conterminous, Contiguous, Handy, Nigh

Adjective Epithet, Gerundive

Adjourn(ment) Abeyance, Delay, ➤ POSTPONE, Prorogate, Recess, Rise, Suspend

Adjudicate, Adjudicator Judge, Jury, Referee, Try, Umpire

Adjunct Addition, Aid, Rider

Adjust(able), Adjustment Accommodate, Adapt, Attune, Coapt, Dress, Ease, Fit, Gang, Gauge, J'adoube, Modify, Modulate, Orientate, Prepare, Reduce, Regulate, Scantle, Sliding, Suit, Tram, Trim, True, Tune, Tweak

▷ **Adjust** may indicate an anagram

Adjutant Aide, Argala, Officer, Stork

Adler Irene

Administer, Administration, Administrator Adhibit, Anele, Apply, Arrondissement, Bairiki, Control, ➤ DIRECT, Dispence, Dispense, Executive, Intendant, Intinction, ➤ MANAGE, Regime, Registrar, Run, Secretariat, Steward

Admirable, Admiration, Admire(d), Admirer Clinker, Clipper, Conquest, Crichton, Esteem, Estimable, ➤ EXCELLENT, Flame, Fureur, Ho, Iconise, Idolater, Laudable, Partisan, Regard, Ripping, Toast, Tribute, Venerate, Wonder

Admiral Adm, Anson, Beatty, Beaufort, Benbow, Blake, Bligh, Boscawen, Butterfly, Byng, Byrd, Drake, Effingham, Fisher, Hood, Hornblower, Howard, Jellicoe, Keyes, Marrowfat, Navarch, Nelson, Raeder, Red, Rodney, Spee, Sturdee , Togo, Vanessa, Van Nieman, Van Tromp, White

Admission, Admit(ting), Admittance Access, Agree, Allow, Avow, Concede, ➤ CONFESS, Enter, Entrée, Entry, Estoppel, Grant, Ingress, Initiate, Intromit, Ordain, Owe, Own, Recognise, Tho(ugh), Yield

Admonish, Admonition Chide, Lecture, Moralise, Rebuke, ➤ SCOLD, Tip, Warn

Ado Bother, Bustle, Fuss

Adolescent Developer, Grower, Halflin, Juvenile, Neanic, Teenager, Veal, Youth

Adonais Keats

Adonis Pheasant's Eye

Adopt Accept, Affiliate, Assume, Embrace, Espouse, Father, Foster, Mother

Adoration, Adore Homage, Love, Pooja(h), Puja, Revere, Venerate, Worship

Adorn(ed), Adornment Attrap, Banderol, Bedeck, Bedight, Bejewel, Caparison, Clinquant, Deck, Dight, Drape, Embellish, Emblaze, Emblazon, Embroider, Enchase, Equip, Festoon, Flourish, Furnish, Garnish, Grace, Graste, Ornament, Riband, Tattoo, Tatu, Tinsel

Adrenaline Epinephrin(e)

Adroit Adept, Dextrous, Expert, Skilful

Adulate, Adulation Flatter(y), Praise, ➤ WORSHIP

Adullam Cave

Adult Amadoda, Grown-up, Man, Mature, Upgrown, X

Adulterant, Adulterate Cut, Debase, Impurify, Lime, Mix, Multum,
➤ POLLUTE, Sophisticate, Weaken

Adulterer, Adultery Avoutery, Cuckold, Fornication, Francesca,
Lenocinium

Advance(d) A, Abord, Accelerate, Anabasis, Ante, Approach, Assert,
Charge, Develop, Extreme, Fore, Forge, Forward, Get on, Grubstake,
Haut(e), Impress, Imprest, Incede, Late, Lend, ➤ LOAN, March, Mortgage,
Overture, Pass, Piaffe, Posit, Postulate, Precocious, Prefer, Prest, Process,
Progress, ➤ PROMOTE, Propose, Propound, Ripe, Rise, Sub, Submit,
Tiptoe

Advantage(ous) Accrual, Aid, ➤ ASSET, Avail, Batten, Benefit, Bisque, Boot,
Edge, Emolument, Expedient, Exploit, Favour, Fruit, Gain, Grouter,
Handicap, Handle, Head-start, Help, Interess, Interest, Lever(age), Odds,
One-up, Percentage, Plus, Privilege, Prize, Purchase, Salutary, Strength,
Toe-hold, Use, Van, Whiphand

Advent(ist) Coming, Shaker

Adventure(r), Adventuress Argonaut, Assay, Buccaneer, Casanova,
Conquistador, Emprise, Enterprise, Escapade, ➤ EXPLOIT, Filibuster, Gest,
Lark, Mata Hari, Mercenary, Merchant, Picaresque, Picaro, Risk, Routier,
Rutter, Swashbuckler, Vamp, Voyage

Adversary Cope(s)mate, Enemy, Foe

Adverse, Adversity Calamity, Cross, Down, Harrow, Misery, Reversal,
Setback, Untoward, Woe

Advert(ise), Advertisement Ad, Allude, Bark, Bill, Circular, Classified,
Coign(e), Coin, Commercial, Copy, Display, Dodger, Flysheet, Hype,
Jingle, Madison Avenue, Mailshot, Noise, ➤ NOTICE, Parade, Placard, Plug,
➤ POSTER, Promo, Promote, Promulgate, Prospectus, Puff, Quoin, Refer,
Sky-write, Splash, Stunt, Subliminal, Teaser, Throwaway, Tout, Trailer,
Trawl

Advice Conseil, Counsel, ➤ GUIDANCE, Guideline, Information, Invoice,
Opinion, Read, Recommendation, Re(e)de

Advise(d), Adviser, Advisable Acquaint, CAB, Counsel, Egeria, Enlighten,
Expedient, Genro, Induna, Inform, Instruct, Mentor, Oracle, Peritus,
Prudent, ➤ RECOMMEND, Tutor, Urge, Wise

Advocate(d) Agent, Argue, Attorney, Back, Devil's, Exponent, Gospel,
Lawyer, Move, Paraclete, Peat, Peddle, Pleader, Pragmatist, Preach,
Proponent, Syndic, Urge

Aerial Aeolian, Antenna, Dipole, Dish, Ethereal, Loop, Parabolic, Yagi

Aerobatics Stunt

➤ **Aeroplane** see AIRCRAFT

Aerosol Atomiser, Mace®

Aesir Loki

Aesthetic Arty, Tasteful

Affable Amiable, Avuncular, Benign, Suave, Urbane

Affair(s) Amour, Business, Concern, Current, Effeir, Effere, Event, Fight, Go, Indaba, Intrigue, Matter, Pash, Pidgin, Pi(d)geon, Ploy, Relationship, Res, Romance, Shebang, Subject, Thing

Affect(ed), Affectation, Affection(ate) Air, Alter, Breast, Camp, Chi-chi, Concern, Crazy, Endearment, Euphuism, Foppery, Hit, Ladida, Lovey-dovey, Mimmick, Minauderie, Minnick, Minnock, Mouth-made, Phoney, ➤ POSE, Poseur, Precieuse, Preciosity, Pretence, Prick-me-dainty, Spoilt, Stag(e)y, Storge, Susceptible, Sway, Tender, Twee, Unction, Unnatural

Affiliate, Affiliation Adopt, Associate, Merge, Unite

Affinity Bro, Kin(ship), Penchant, Rapport, Tie

Affirm(ative), Affirmation Assert, Attest, Maintain, Predicate, Protestation, Uh-huh, ➤ VERIFY

Affix(ed) Append, Ascribe, ➤ ATTACH, Connect, Fasten, On

Afflict(ed), Affliction Asthma, Cross, Cup, Curse, Disease, Furnace, Harass, Hurt, Lumbago, Molest, Nosology, Palsy, Persecute, Pester, Plague, Scourge, Smit, Sore, ➤ SORROW, Stricken, Teen, Tene, Tic, Tribulation, ➤ TROUBLE, Unweal, Visitation, Woe

Affluence Abundance, Fortune, Opulence, Wealth

Afford Bear, Manage, Offer, Provide, Spare

Affray Brawl, Fight, Mêlée, Scuffle, Skirmish

Affront Assault, Defy, Facer, ➤ INSULT, ➤ OFFEND, Outrage, Scandal, Slight, Slur

Afghan Dard, Hound, Kaf(f)ir, Pakhto, Pakhtu, Pashto, Pashtu, Pathan, Pushto(o), Pushtu

Afloat Abroach, Adrift, Natant

Afoot Astir, Up

Aforesaid Above, Same

Afraid Adrad, Alarmed, Chicken, Fearful, Funk, Rad, Regretful, Scared, Timorous, Windy, Yellow

Africa(n) Abyssinian, Akan, Angolan, Ashanti, Baganda, Bambara, Bantu, Barbary, Barotse, Basotho, Basuto, Beento, Bemba, Berber, Biafran, Bintu, Black, Boer, Botswana, Cairene, Carthaginian, Congolese, Cushitic, Damara, Dinka, Duala, Dyula, Efik, Ethiopian, Eve, Fang, Fanti, Fingo, Flytaal, Fula(h), Galla, Gambian, Ganda, Gazankulu, Grikwa, Griqua, Gullash, Hamite, Hausa, Herero, Hottentot, Hutu, Ibibi, Ibo, Igbo, Kabyle, Kaffer, Kaf(f)ir, Kenyan, Khoikhoi, Kikuyu, Kongo, Lango, Lesotho, Liberian, Libyan, Lowveld, Lozi, Luba, Luo, Maghreb, Maghrib, Malawi, Malian, Malinke, Mande, Mandingo, Masai, Mashona, Matabele, Mende, Moor, Moroccan, Mossi, Mozambican, Munt(u), Mzee, Namibian, Namu, Negrillo, Negro, Nguni, Nilot(e), Nubian, Nuer, Nyanja, Oromo, Ovambo, Pedi, Pondo, Rastafarian, Rhodesian, San, Shilluk, Shluh, Shona, Somali, Songhai, Sotho, Sudanese, Susu, Swahili, Swazi, Temne, Tiv, Tonga, Transkei, Transvaal, Tshi, Tsonga, Tswana, Tuareg, Tutsi, Twi, Venda, Voltaic, Wolof, X(h)osa , Yoruban, Zairean, Zulu

Afrikaan(s), Afrikaner Crunchie, Mynheer, Taal, Volk

After(wards) About, At, Behind, Beyond, Eft, Epi-, ➤ LATER, On, Past, Rear, Since, Sine, Subsequent

Afterbirth Sooterkin

▷ **After injury** may indicate an anagram

Aftermath Consequence, Mow(ing), Rawing, Rawn, Rowan, Rowen, Rowing, Sequel(a)

Afternoon A, Arvo, PM, Postmeridian, Undern

Afterpiece, Afterthought Addendum, Codicil, Epimetheus, Exode, Footnote, Note, PS, Supplement

Again Afresh, Agen, Anew, Back, Bis, De novo, Ditto, Do, Eft, Eftsoons, Encore, Iterum, More, Moreover, Over, Re-, Recurrence, Reprise, Than, Then

Against A, Anti, Beside, Con, Counter, Gainsayer, Into, Nigh, On, Opposing, To, V, Versus

Agape Feast, Hiant, Ringent, Yawning

Agate Chalcedonyx, Moss, Murr(h)a, Onyx

Agave Henequen, Lily, Maenad, Maguey

Age(d), Ages, Aging Ae, Aeon, Aet, Alcheringa, Antique, Archaise, Azilian, Calpa, Century, Chellean, Cycle, Dark, Day, Doddery, Eld, Eon, Epact, Epoch(a), Era, Eternity, Generation, Gerontic, Golden, Grey, Heroic, Hoar, Hore, Ice, Iron, Jazz, Jurassic, Kaliyuga, Kalpa, La Tene, Lias, Maglemosian, Mature, Middle, Millennium, Neolithic, New, Of, Oligocene, Paleolithic, Passé, Period, Phanerozoic, Progeria, S(a)eculum, Saros, Senescence, Silver, Space, Stone, Villanovan, Yellow, Yonks, Yug(a)

Agency, Agent Agitator, Ambassador, Art, Bailiff, Barm, Bond, Broker, BSI, Catalyst, Cat's paw, Cause, Commis, Comprador(e), Consul, Customs, Del credere, Delcredere, Doer, Double, Emissary, Environment, Envoy, Enzyme, Estate, Factor, Fed, Finger, Flack, Free, G-man, Go-between, Hand, Hirudin, Influence, Institorial, Instrument, Kinase, Legate, Literary, Man, Means, Medium, Mole, Mutagen, Narc, Narco, Ninja, -or, Order paper, Pinkerton, Procurator, Proxy, Rep(resentative), Resident, Runner, Salesman, Secret (service), Setter, Sleeper, Solvent, Spy, Syndic, Tass, Teratogen, Travel, Vakeel, Vakil, Voice

Agenda Business, Programme, Remit, Schedule

Aggie Agnes, Ines, Nessa, Nesta

Aggravate Annoy, Inflame, Irk, Needle, Nettle, Provoke, Try, Vex

Aggregate, Aggregation Ballast, Congeries, Detritus, Etaerio, Granulite, Gravel, Omnium, Ore, Sum, Total

Aggression, Aggressive, Aggressor Attack, Belligerent, Bullish, Butch, Defiant, Enemy, Feisty, Foe, Gungho, Hawk, Invader, Militant, On-setter, Pushing, Rambo, Rampant, Shirty, Truculent, Wild

Agile Acrobatic, Deft, Lissom(e), Nifty, Nimble, Quick, Spry, Supple, Swank

Agitate(d), Agitation, Agitator Activist, Ado, Agitprop, Betoss, Boil, Bolshie, Bother, Chartist, Churn, Commotion, Commove, Convulse, Demagogue, Discompose, Distraught, ➤ DISTURB, Doodah, Ebullient,

Emotion, Excite, Extremist, Fan, Ferment, Firebrand, Flurry, Fluster, Flutter, Frenzy, Fuss, Goad, Heat, Hectic, Jabble, Lather, Militant, Panicky, Pedetic, Perturb, Poss, Pother, Rattle, Restless, Rouse, Ruffle, Seethed, Sod, Stir(-up), Swivet, Tailspin, Taking, Tew, Tizzy, Toss, Tremor, Trepidation, Trouble, Turmoil, Tweak, Twitchy, Welter, Whisk, Ytost

▷ **Agitate** may indicate an anagram

Agley Awry, Unevenly

Aglow Alight, Tipsy

▶ **Agnes** see AGGIE

Agnostic Laodicean

Ago Lang syne

Agog Athirst, Eager, Keen

Agony Ache, Anguish, Ecstasy, Heartache, ➤ PAIN, Torment, Torture

Agree(ing), Agreed, Agreement Accede, Accept, Accord, Acquiescence, Allow, Amen, Analog(ue), Analogy, Apply, As one, Assent, Assort, Atone, Aye, Bilateral, Bipartite, Bond, Champerty, Chime, Closing, Coincide, Comart, Community, Compact, Comply, Comport, Concert, Concord(at), Concur, Conform, Congree, Congruent, Consension, Consensus, ➤ CONSENT, Consonant, Contract, Contrahent, Cotton, Covenant, Dayton Accords, Deal, Deign, Done, Entente, Equate, Escrow, Fadge, Gatt, Handfast, Indenture, Jibe, League, Mercasur, Net Book, Nod, Okay, Pact, Placet, Rabat(te), Right(o), Right on, Roger, Sanction, Schengen, Side, Sort(ance), Specialty, Sponsion, Square, Suit, Sweetheart, Sympathy, Synchronise, Synesis, Syntony, Tally, Threshold, Trade, Treaty, Uh-huh, Union, Unison, Unspoken, Wilco, Yea, Yes

Agreeable Amene, Harmonious, Pleasant, Sapid, Sweet, Well-disposed, Willing, Winsome

Agriculture, Agricultural(ist) Arval, Geoponic, Georgic, Inari, Permaculture, Smallholding, Tull

Aground Ashore, Beached, Sew, Stranded

▷ **Ague(ish)** may indicate an anagram

Ah Ach, Ay

Ahead Anterior, Before, Foreship, Forward, Frontwards, Onward, Up

Aiblins Perhap, Perhaps, Yibbles

Aid(s), Aide Accessory, Adjutant, Assist, Decca, ➤ DEPUTY, Galloper, Grant, Help, Key, Legal, Lend-lease, Monitor, Optophone, PA, Relief, Serve, Slim, Succour, Support, Visual

Ail(ment) Affect, Afflict(ion), Complaint, Croup, Disease, Malady, Narks, Pink-eye, Pip, Sickness

Aim Approach, Aspire, Bead, Bend, End, Ettle, Eye, Goal, Hub, Intent, Level, Mark, Mission, Object, Plan, Plank, Point, Purpose, Reason, Sake, Seek, Sight(s), Target, Tee, Telos, Train, View, Visie, Vizy, Vizzie

Aimless Drifting, Erratic, Haphazard, Random, Unmotivated

Air(s), Airer, Airy Aerate, Aerial, Aero, Allure, Ambiance, Ambience, Aquarius, Arietta, Atmosphere, Attitude, Aura, Bearing, Calypso, Canzona, Canzone, Cavatina, Dead, Demaine, Descant, Ditty, Draught, Dry,

Emphysema, Ether(eal), Expose, Fan, Filmy, Front, Gemini, Heaven, Horse, Inflate, Libra, Lift, Liquid, Look, Lullaby, Madrigal, Manner, Melody, Mien, Nitre, Ozone, Parade, Pneumatic, Radio, Screen, Scuba, Serenade, Serenata, Serene, Shanty, Side, Sky, Slipstream, Solo, Swank, Thin, Trigon, ➤ TUNE, Vent, Ventilate, Wake, Wind

Airborne Ab

Aircraft, Airship Aerodyne, Aerostat, Auster, Autoflare, Autogiro, Autogyro, Aviette, Avion, Biplane, Blimp, Brabazon, Camel, Canard, Chaser, Chopper, Comet, Concorde, Convertiplane, Crate, Dirigible, Doodlebug, Fixed-wing, Fokker, Galaxy, Glider, Gotha, Harrier, Heinkel, Helicopter, Hunter, Hurricane, Interceptor, Jumbo, Jump-jet, Kite, Lancaster, Liberator, Messerschmitt, Microlight, MIG, Mirage, Monoplane, Mosquito, Moth, Oerlikon, Ornithopter, Orthopter, Parasol, Penguin, ➤ PLANE, Ramjet, Rigid, Scramjet, Semi-rigid, Sopwith, Sopwith Camel, Spitfire, SST, STOL, Stratocruiser, Stratotanker, Stuka, Sweptwing, Swing-wing, Tankbuster, Taube, Taxiplane, Trident, Tri-jet, Triplane, Tube, Turbo-jet, Turbo-prop, Turboramjet, Viscount, VTOL, Zeppelin

Aircraftsman, Airman AC, Aeronaut, Erk, Fokker, Kiwi, LAC, RAF

Aircraftswoman Penguin, Pinguin

▶ **Airfield** see AIRPORT

Airlift Thermal

Airline, Airway Aeroflot, Anthem, BAC, BEA, Duct, Larynx, Lot, SAS, S(ch)norkel, TWA, Weasand(-pipe), Windpipe

▶ **Airman** see AIRCRAFTSMAN

Airport Drome, Entebbe, Faro, Gander, Gatwick, Heliport, Idlewild, Kennedy, Landing strip, Lod, Luton, Lympne, Orly, Runway, Shannon, Stansted, Stolport, Vertiport, Wick

Air-raid Blitz, Mission

Air-tight Hermetic, Indisputable, Sealed

Aisle Gangway

Aitch Ache, Aspirate, H

Ajax Loo

Aka Alias

Akin Alike, Cognate, Congener, Kindred

Alarm Alert, Arouse, Bell, Bleep, Caution, Dismay, False, Fricht, Fright, Ghast, Larum, Panic, Perturb, Rouse, Siren, Smoke, Startle, Tirrit, Tocsin, Warn, Yike(s)

Alas Ah, Alack, Ay, Eheu, Ha, Haro, Harrow, Io, Lackadaisy, Lackaday, O, Oh, Ohone, O me, Waesucks, Waly, Well-a-day, Wellanear, Wel(l)away, Woe

Alaskan AK, Sourdough

Alban Berg

Albanian Arna(o)ut

Albatross Alcatras, Golf, Gooney(-bird), Omen, Onus

Albeit Tho(ugh)

Albert Chain, Chevalier, Consort, Hall, Herring, Slang

Album Looseleaf, Record

Albumen, Albumin Chalaza, Glair, Mucin, Myogen, Protein, Ricin, White

Alchemic, Alchemist, Alchemy Adept, Brimstone, Faust(us), Hermetic(s), Multiplier, Orpiment, Paracelsus, Quicksilver, Sal ammoniac, Sorcery, Spagyric, Spagyrist, Witchcraft

Alcides Hercules

Alcohol(ic) Acrolein, Aldehyde, Bibulous, Booze, Borneol, Catechol, Cetyl, Chaptalise, Cholesterol, Choline, Citronellol, Cresol, Diol, Dipsomaniac, Drinker, Ethal, Ethanol, Ethyl, Farnesol, Feni, Fenny, Firewater, Fusel-oil, Geraniol, Glycerin(e), Grain, Hard, Inebriate, Inositol, Isopropyl, Jungle juice, Lauryl, Linalool, Mahua, Mahwa, Mannite, Mannitol, Mercaptan, Mescal, Methanol, Meths, Mow(r)a, Nerol, Phytol, Propyl, Rotgut, Rubbing, Sorbitol, Sphingosine, Spirits, Spirits of wine, Sterol, Tincture, Wino, Xylitol

Alcove Apse, Bay, Bole, Dinette, Lunette, Niche, Recess, Tokonoma

Alcyonarian Sea-feather

Aldehyde Acrolein, Aldol

Alder Fothergilla

Alderman Bail(l)ie, CA

Alderney CI, Cow

Ale, Alehouse Audit, Barleybree, Beer, Humpty-dumpty, Lamb's wool, Light, Morocco, Nappy, Nog, Nogg, October, Purl, Real, Stout, Swats, Tiddleywink, Tipper, Whitsun, Wort, Yard, Yill

Alert Arrect, Astir, Attentive, Aware, Gleg, Gogo, Intelligent, Qui vive, Red, Scramble, Sharp, Sprack, Sprag, Stand-to, Vigilant, Volable, Wary, Watchful

Alewife Gaspereau

Alexander, Alexandrine Alex, Arius, Macedonian, Pope, Sandy, Sasha, Sawn(e)y, Selkirk, Senarius

Alfalfa Lucern(e), Luzern

Alfred Dreyfus, Garnet, Jingle

Alfresco Barbecue, Plein-air

Alga(e) Anabaena, Blanketweed, Chlorella, Conferva, Desmid, Diatom, Dulse, Heterocontae, Isokont, Jelly, Nostoc, Pleuston, Pond scum, Prokaryon, Protococcus, Seaweed, Spirogyra, Star-jelly, Stonewort, Ulothrix, Ulotrichales, Valonia, Volvox, Zooxanthella

Algebra Boolean, Linear, Quadratics

Algerian Kabyle, Nimidian

Algonquin Innu

Alias Aka, Epithet, Moni(c)ker, Pen-name, Pseudonym

Alibi Excuse, Watertight

Alien(ate), Alienation A-effect, Amortise, Disaffect, Ecstasy, Estrange, ET, Exotic, External, Foreign, Forinsecal, Fremd, Hostile, Martian, Metic, Outlandish, Philistine, Repugnant, Strange(r)

Alight Alowe, Availe, Detrain, Disembark, Dismount, In, Lambent, Land, Lit, Perch, Pitch, Rest, Settle

Align Arrange, Associate, Collimate, Dress, Juxtapose, Marshal, Orient

➤ **Alike** see LIKE

Aliquot Submultiple

Alive Alert, Animated, Breathing, Extant, Quick

Alkali(ne), Alkaloid Antacid, Apomorphine, Base, Bebeerine, Berberine, Betaine, Borax, Brucine, Capsalcin, Codeine, Colchicine, Emetin(e), Ephedrine, Gelsemin(in)e, Guanidine, Harmaline, Harmin(e), Hyoscine, Lobeline, Lye, Narceen, Narceine, Nicotine, Papaverine, Piperine, Potash, Quinine, Reserpine, Rhoeadine, Scopolamine, Soda, Sparteine, Thebaine, Theobromine, Theophylline, Tropine, Veratrin(e), Vinblastine, Vincristine, Yohimbine

All A, ➤ ENTIRE, Entity, Finis, Omni, Pan, Quite, Sum, ➤ TOTAL, Toto, Tutti, Whole

Allah Bismillah, God

Allay Calm, Lessen, Quieten, Soothe

Allegation, Allege Assert, Aver, Claim, Obtend, Plead, Purport, Represent, Smear

Allegiance Faith, Foy, Loyalty

Allegory, Allegorical Apologue, Fable, Mystic, Myth, Parable

Allergy Atopy, Aversion, Bagassosis, Hives

Alleviate Allege, Calm, Mitigate, Mollify, Palliate, ➤ RELIEVE, Temper

Alley Aisle, Blind, Bonce, Bowling, Corridor, Ginnel, Lane, Laura, Marble, Passage, Tinpan, Vennel, Walk, Wynd

Alliance Agnation, Axis, Bloc, Cartel, Coalition, Combine, Compact, Federacy, ➤ LEAGUE, Marriage, NATO, Syndicate, Union

Alligator Al(l)igarta, Avocado, Cayman

Allocate, Allocation Allot, Earmark, Placement, Ration, Share, Zone

Allot(ment), Allow(ance), Allowed, Allowing Admit, Affect, Alimony, Allocation, Although, Aret(t), Assign, Award, Batta, Beteem(e), Budget, Charter, Cloff, Confess, Cor(r)ody, Diet, Discount, Dole, Enable, Entitle, Excuse, Feod, Grant, House-bote, Husbandage, Indulge, Latitude, Legit(imate), Let, Licit, Luit(en), Mag, Palimony, Parcel, Pension, ➤ PERMIT, Pittance, Plot, Portion, Quota, Ratio, Ration, Rebate, Rood, Sanction, Sequel, Share(-out), Shrinkage, Sizings, Stint, Stipend, Suffer, Tare, Teene, Though, Tolerance, Tolerate, Tret, Weighting, Yield

Allotment-holder Cleruch

➤ **Allow** see ALLOT

Alloy Albata, Alnico®, Amalgam, Babbit, Bell-metal, Billon, Brass, Britannia metal, Bronze, Cermet, Chrome(l), Compound, Constantan, Cupronickel, Duralumin®, Electron, Electrum, Gunmetal, Invar®, Kamacite, Latten, Magnalium, Magnox, Marmem, Mischmetal, Mix, Monel®, Nicrosilal, Nimonic, Nitinol, Occamy, Oreide, Orichalc, Ormolu, Oroide, Osmiridium, Paktong, Pewter, Pinchbeck, Platinoid, Potin, Shakudo, Shibuichi, Similor,

Solder, Spelter, Steel, Stellite®, Tambac, Terne, Tombac, Tombak, Tutenag, Zircaloy, Zircoloy
▷ **Alloy** may indicate an anagram
All-right A1, Assuredly, Fit, Hale, Hunky(-dory), OK, Safe, Tickety-boo, Well
All-round Overhead, Versatile
Allspice Jamaica pepper
Allude, Allusion Hint, Imply, Innuendo, Mention, Refer, Reference, Suggest
Allure, Alluring Agaçant(e), Charm, Circe, Decoy, Glam, Glamour, Magnet(ic), SA, Seduce, Seductive, Tempt, Trap, Trepan, Vamp
Ally, Allied Accomplice, Agnate, Aide, Alley, Alliance, Backer, Belamy, Cognate, Colleague, Dual, German(e), Holy, Marble, Marmoreal, Partner, Plonker, Related, Taw, Unholy
Almanac Calendar, Clog, Ephemeris, Nostradamus, Whitaker's, Wisden, Zadkiel
Almighty Dollar, God, Jehovah, Omnipotent
Almond Amygdal, Emulsion, Jordan, Marchpane, Marzipan, Orgeat, Praline, Ratafia, Sugared, Valencia
Almost Anear, Anigh, Most, Near, Nigh(ly), Ripe, Une(a)th, Virtually, Well-nigh, Welly
Alms Awmous, Charity, Dole, Handout
Aloe Agave, Pita
Alone Hat, Jack, Lee-lane, Onely, Secco, Separate, Single, Singly, Sola, Solo, Solus, Unaccompanied, Unaided, Unholpen
Along, Alongside Abeam, Aboard, Abreast, Apposed, Beside, By, Parallel
Aloof Abeigh, Apart, Cool, Detached, Distant, Hou inch, Indrawn, Mugwump, Offish, Remote, Reticent, Stand-offish, Toffee-nosed, Unapproachable
Alpaca Paco
Alphabet ABC, Brahmi, Braille, Cyrillic, Devanagari, Estrang(h)elo, Futhark, Futhorc, Futhork, Glagol, Glagolitic, Glossic, Grantha, Hangul, Horn-book, ITA, Kana, Kanji, Katakana, Kufic, Manual, Nagari, Og(h)am, Pangram, Phonetic, Pinyin, Romaji, Roman, Signary, Syllabary
Alpine, Alps Bernese, Cottian, Dinaric, Gentian, Graian, Laburnum, Lepontine, Matterhorn, Transylvanian, Tyrol
Also Add, And, Eke, Item, Likewise, Moreover, Too, Und
Altar, Altar-cloth, Altarpiece Dossal, Dossel, Polyptych, Retable, Shrine, Tabula
Alter Adapt, Adjust, Bushel, Change, Correct, Customise, Evolve, Falsify, Lib, Modify, Modulate, Mutate, Recast, Revise, Transpose, Up-end, ➤ VARY
Altercation Barney, Brawl, Fracas, Row, Words, Wrangle
Alternate, Alternating, Alternation, Alternative Boustrophedon, Bypass, Exchange, Instead, Metagenesis, ➤ OPTION, Ossia, Other, Rotate, Solidus, Staggered, Systaltic, Tertian, Variant

▷ **Alter(native)** may indicate an anagram
▷ **Alternately** may indicate every other letter
Althaea Mallow, Malva
Although Admitting, Albe(e), All-be, But, Even, Howsomever, Whereas, While
Altitude Elevation, Height
Alto Countertenor
Altogether Algate(s), All-to-one, Completely, Entirely, Holus-bolus, Idea, In all, Nude, Nudity, Purely, Slick, Tout, Uncut, Wholly
▷ **Altogether** may indicate words to be joined
Altruistic Heroic, Humane, Philanthropic, Selfless, Unselfish
Aluminium, Alumino-silicate Al, Bauxite, Sillimanite, Stilbite
Alumnus Graduate, OB
Always Algate(s), Ay(e), Constant, E'er, Eternal, Ever(more), Forever, I, Immer, Sempre, Still
Amalgamate Coalesce, Consolidate, Fuse, Merge, Unite
Amalthea Cornucopia
Amarylli(d)s Leocojum, Lily, Polianthes
Amass Accumulate, Assemble, Collect, Heap, Hoard, Pile, Upheap
Amateur(s) A, AA, Armchair, Beginner, Corinthian, Dilettante, Diy, Ham, Inexpert, L, Lay, Novice, Tiro, Tyro
Amatory Eros, Erotic, Fervent
Amaze(d), Amazement, Amazing Astonish, Astound, Awhape, Cor, Criv(v)ens, Dumbfound, Flabbergast, Gobsmack, Goodnow, Grace, Incredible, Magical, Monumental, O, Open-eyed, Open-mouthed, Perplex, Poleaxe, Pop-eyed, Stagger, Stupefaction, Stupendous, Thunderstruck
Amazon Ant, ATS, Brimstone, Britannia, Dragon, Hippolyta, Orellana, Penthesilea, Thalestris, Tupi, Virago
Ambassador Diplomat, Elchee, Elchi, Eltchi, Envoy, HE, Internuncio, Ledger, Legate, Leiger, Minister, Nuncio, Plenipo, Plenipotentiary
Amber Lammer, Ligure, Resin, Succinum
Ambience Aura, Milieu, Setting
Ambiguous, Ambiguity Amphibology, Cryptic, Delphic, Double, Enigmatic, Epicene, Equivocal, Loophole, Weasel words
Ambition, Ambitious Aim, Aspiring, Careerism, Drive, Emulate, Goal, Go-getter, High-flier, Keen, Office-hunter, Purpose, Pushy, Rome-runner
Amble Meander, Mosey, Pace, Saunter, Stroll
Ambrose Emrys
Ambrosia(l) Beebread, Fragrant, Odorant, Ragweed, Savoury
Ambulance, Ambulance-men Blood-wagon, Pannier, Van, Yellow-flag, Zambu(c)k
Ambulatory Stoa
Ambush(ed) Ambuscade, Bushwhack, Embusque, Latitant, Lurch, Perdu(e), Trap, Waylay

Amelia Bloomer
Ameliorate Amend, Ease, Improve, Remedy
Amen Ammon, Approval, Inshallah, Verify
Amenable Putty
Amend(ment) Alter, Change, Expiate, Fifth, Redress, Reform, Repair, Restore, ➤ REVISE, Satisfy
▷ **Amend** may indicate an anagram
Ament Catkin, Idiot
America(n) Algonki(a)n, Algonqu(i)an, Am, Caddo, Cajun, Carib, Chicano, Chickasaw, Copperskin, Digger, Doughface, Down-easter, Federalist, Flathead, Fox, Gringo, Interior, Jonathan, Latino, Mistec, Mixtec, Norteno, Olmec, Paisano, Salish, Stateside, Statesman, Statist, Tar-heel, Tico, Tupi, US(A), Yankee, Yanqui
Americium Am
Amiable Friendly, Genial, Gentle, Inquiline, Sweet, Warm
Amid(st) Among, Atween, Between, Inter, Twixt
Amide Asparagine
Amino-acid Dopa, Tyrosine, Valine
Amiss Awry, Ill, Up, Wrong
Ammonia(c) Amide, Amine, Choline, Ethylamine, Hartshorn, Oshac
Ammonite Serpent-stone
Ammunition Ammo, Bandoleer, Bandolier, Buckshot, Bullets, Chain-shot, Dum-dum, Grape(shot), Grenade, Round, Shot, Slug, Tracer
Amnesia Fugal, Fugue, Lethe
Amnesty Oblivion
Among Amid(st), In, Within
Amorous(ly) Casanova, Erotic, Fervent, Lustful, Smickly, Warm
Amorphous Formless, Shapeless, Vague
Amount Come, Dose, Element, Figure, Levy, Lot, Number, Pot(s), Price, Quantity, Quantum, Span, Stint, Throughput, Whale, Wheel
Amour Affair(e), Intrigue, Love
Ampersand Tironian sign
Amphetamine Benny, Benzedrine, Speed
Amphibian, Amphibious Amb(l)ystoma, Amtrack, Anura, Axolotl, Batrachian, Caecilia, Caecilian, Desman, Eft, Frog, Guana, Hassar, Mermaid, Mudpuppy, Newt, Olm, Proteus, Rana, Salamander, Salientia, Seal, Tadpole, Urodela(n), Urodele, Weasel
Amphipod Sand-screw, Shrimp
Amphitheatre Bowl, Coliseum, Colosseum, Ring, Stage
Ample Bellyful, Copious, Enough, Generous, Good, Large, Opulent, Profuse, Rich, Roomy, Round, Uberous, Voluminous
Amplifier, Amplify Booster, Double, Eke, Enlarge, Hailer, Laser, Loud hailer, Maser, Megaphone, Push-pull, Solion, Transistor, Treble
Amulet Abraxas, Charm, Churinga, Fetish, Greegree, Grigri, Grisgris, Haemon, Pentacle, Periapt, Phylactery, Sea-bean, Talisman, Tiki, Token

Amuse(ment), Amusing(ly) Caution, Cottabus, Disport, Diversion, Divert, Divertimento, Drole, Droll, Game, Gas, Giocoso, Glee, Hoot, Killing, Levity, Light, Occupy, Pleasure, Popjoy, Priceless, Rich, Scream, Slay, Solace, ➤ SPORT, Tickle, Titillate

Amy Johnson, Robsart

▶ **An** see A

Ana(s) Story, Teal

Anabaptist Abecedarian, Dipper, Dopper, Hutterite, Knipperdolling

Anableps Four-eyes

Anachronism Archaism, Solecism

Anaconda Water boa

Anacreon Te(i)an

Anaemia Aplastic, Cooley's, Favism, Haemolytic, Pernicious, Sickle-cell, Thalassaemia

Anaesthetic, Anaesthetise, Anaesthetist Analgesic, Avertin®, Benzocaine, Bupivacaine, Chloroform, Cocaine, Epidural, Ether, Eucain(e), Freeze, Gas, General, Halothane, Jabber, Ketamine, Lignocaine, Local, Metopryl, Morphia, Novocaine, Number, Opium, Orthocaine, Procaine, Stovaine, Trike, Urethan(e)

Anagram Jumble

Anal Proctal, Tewel

Analgesic Bute, Codeine, Disprin, Ketamine, Menthol, Morphia, Pethidine, Phencyclidine, Quina, Salicin(e), Sedative

Analogous, Analogy Akin, Corresponding, Like, Parallel, Similar

Analyse(r), Analysis Alligate, Anagoge, Anatomy, Assess, Breakdown, Construe, Emic, Eudiometer, Examine, Fourier, Harmonic, Parse, Process, Qualitative, Quantative, Quantitative, Rundown, Scan(sion), Semantics, Sift, Spectral, Systems, Test

▷ **Analysis** may indicate an anagram

Analyst Alienist, Jung, Psychiatrist, Shrink, Trick cyclist

Anarchist, Anarchy Black Hand, Bolshevist, Chaos, Kropotkin, Provo, Rebel, Revolutionary, Trotskyite

Anathema Ban, Curse, Execration, Oath, Warling

Anatole, Anatolian France, Hittite

Anatomy, Anatomist Bones, Framework, Herophilus, Histology

Ancestor, Ancestral, Ancestry Adam, Avital, Descent, Extraction, For(e)bear, Gastraea, Humanoid, Lin(e)age, Parent, Proband, Profectitious, Progenitor, Propositus, Roots, Sire, Tree

Anchor(age) Atrip, Bower, Cell, Deadman, Drag, Eremite, Grapnel, Hawse, Hermit, Kedge, Killick, Killock, Laura, Mud-hook, Nail, Ride, Roads(tead), Root, Scapa Flow, Sheet, Spithead, Stock

Anchorite Recluse

Anchovy Fish, Pear

Ancient Antediluvian, Archaic, Auld-warld, Early, Gonfanoner, Historic, Hoary, Iago, Immemorial, Lights, Neolithic, Ogygian, ➤ OLD(EN), Old-world, Primeval, Primitive, Pristine, Ur, Veteran

Ancient city Carthage, Ur

Ancillary Adjunct, Secondary, Subservient

And Als(o), Ampassy, Ampersand, Amperzand, Ampussyand, Besides, Et, Furthermore, 'n', Plus, Und

Andalusite Macle

Andiron Chenet, Dog, Firedog

Andrew(es) Aguecheek, Lancelot

Androgynous Epicene

Android Automaton, Golem, Robot

Anecdote(s) Ana, Exemplum, Story, Tale, Yarn

Anemometer Wind-sleeve, Windsock

Angel(s) Abdiel, Adramelech, Apollyon, Archangel, Ariel, Arioch, Asmadai, Azrael, Backer, Banker, Beelzebub, Belial, Benefactor, Cake, Cherub, Clare, Deva, Dominion, Dust, Eblis, Falls, Gabriel, Guardian, Hierarchy, Host, Investor, Israfel, Ithuriel, Lucifer, Power, Principality, Raphael, Record(ing), Rimmon, Seraph, Spirit, St, Throne, Uriel, Uzziel, Virtue, Watcher, Zadkiel, Zephiel

Angela Brazil

Angel's wings Begonia

Anger, Angry ➤ ANNOY, Bristle, Choler(ic), Conniption, Cross, Dander, Dudgeon, Enrage, Exasperation, Face, Fury, Gram, Heat, Horn-mad, Incense, Infuriate, Iracund, Irascible, Ire, Kippage, Livid, Mad, Monkey, Moody, Nettle, Pique, Radge, Rage, Rampant, Ratty, Renfierst, Rile, Roil, Rouse, Sore, Steam, Tantrum, Tarnation, Teen(e), Tene, Vex, Vies, Waspish, Waxy, Wrath, Wroth, Yond

Angina Sternalgia

Angle(d), Angular Acute, Altitude, Argument, Aspect, Axil, Azimuthal, Canthus, Cast, Catch, Chiliagon, Coign, Complementary, Conjugate, Contrapposto, Corner, Cos, Critical, Deidre, Diedral, Diedre, Dihedral, Elbow, Elevation, Ell, Fish, Fish-hook, Fork, Geometry, Gonion, Hade, Hip, In, L, Laggen, Laggin, Mitre, Oblique, Obtuse, Parallax, Pediculate, Perigon, Piend, Pitch, Plane, Quoin, Radian, Rake, Re-entrant, Reflex, Right, Sally, Sine, Sinical, Solid, Steeve, Steradian, Supplementary, Sweepback, Trotline, Vertical, Viewpoint, Washin, Weather

Angler Peterman, Rodster, Walton, Wide-gab

Anglesey Mona

Anglican(s) CE-men, Conformist, Episcopal

Anglo-Catholic High-church

Anglo-Indian Topi-wallah

Angora Goat, Mohair, Rabbit

Angst Dread

Anguish(ed) Agony, Distress, Gip, Gyp, Hag-ridden, Heartache, Misery,
➤ PAIN, Pang, Sorrow, Throes, ➤ TORMENT, Torture, Woe

Angus Aberdeen

Animal(s) Acrita, Anoa, Armadillo, Atoc, Bag, Bandog, Barbastel, Beast,
Bestial, Brute, Cariacou, Carnal, Chalicothere, Coati, Creature, Criollo,
Critter, Ethology, Fauna, Felis, Gerbil, Herd, Ichneumon, Jacchus, Jerboa,
Kinkajou, Klipdas, Mammal, Marmoset, Marmot, Menagerie, Moose,
Noctule, Oribi, Parazoon, Pet, Protozoa, Pudu, Quagga, Rac(c)oon,
Rhesus, Sensual, Sloth, Stud, Tarsier, Teledu, Urson, Waler, Xenurus,
Yapock, Zerda, Zoo

Animal-catcher Utricularia

Animate(d), Animation Activate, Actuate, Arouse, Biophor, Ensoul, Excite,
Fire, Hot, Inspire, Live, Morph, Mosso, Rouse, Spritely, Verve

Animosity Enmity, Friction, Hostility, Malice, Pique, Rancour

Ankle Coot, Cuit, Cute, Hock, Hucklebone, Knee, Malleolus

Ankle(t), Ankle covering Cootikin, Cuitikin, Cutikin, Gaiter, Jess

Anna, Anne, Annie Boleyn, Hathaway, Laurie, Oakley, Page, Pavlova,
Sewell, Sister

Annal(s) Acta, Archives, Chronicles, Register

Annex(e) Acquire, Add, Affiliate, Attach, Codicil, Extension, Subjoin

Annihilate Destroy, Erase, Exterminate, Slay

Anniversary Birthday, Feast, Jubilee, Obit, Yahrzeit

Annotate, Annotator Comment, Interpret, Note, Postil, Scholiast

Announce(r), Announcement Banns, Bellman, Biil(ing), Blazon, Bulletin,
Communiqué, Decree, Divulgate, Gazette, Herald, Hermes, Inform,
Intimate, Meld, Newsflash, Post, Preconise, Proclaim, Promulgate,
Pronunciamente, Publish, Release, ➤ REPORT, Speaker(ine), State,
Trumpet

Annoy(ance), Annoyed, Annoying Aggravate, Aggrieve, Anger,
Antagonise, Badger, Bother, Bug, Bugbear, Chagrin, Disturb, Drat, Fash,
Fleabite, Frab, Fumed, Gall, Harass, Hatter, Hector, Hip, Huff, Hump,
Incense, Irk, ➤ IRRITATE, Miff, Mischief, Molest, Nag, Nark, Nettle,
Noisome, Peeve, Pesky, Pester, Pipsqueak, Pique, Rankle, Rats, Resentful,
Ride, Rile, Roil, Rub, Shirty, Tiresome, Tracasserie, Try, Vex

Annual, Annuity Book, Etesian, ➤ FLOWER, Half-hardy, Hardy, Pension,
Perpetuity, Rente, Tontine, Yearbook, Yearly

Annul(ment) Abolish, Abrogate, Cashier, Cassation, Dissolution, Irritate,
Negate, Repeal, Rescind, Reversal, Revoke, Vacatur, ➤ VOID

Annular Toric

Anodyne Balm, Narcotic, Paregoric, Sedative

Anoint(ing) Anele, Cerate, Chrism, Embrocate, Grease, Hallow, Nard,
Smear

▷ **Anomaly** may indicate an anagram

Anon Again, Anew, Later, Soon

Anonymous Adespota, Anon, A.N.Other, Faceless, Grey, Impersonal,
Somebody, Unnamed

Anorak Wonk

Another Extra

Answer(ing), Answer(s) Acknowledge, Amoebaean, Ans, Antiphon, Because, Comeback, Crib (sheet), Defence, Echo, Key, Lemon, Light, No, Oracle, Rebuttal, Rebutter, Rein, Rejoin(der), Repartee, Reply, Rescript, Respond, Response, Retort, Return, Riposte, Serve, Sol, Solution, Solve, Verdict, Yes

Ant(s), Anthill Amazon, Army, Bull(dog), Carpenter, Colony, Driver, Dulosis, Emmet, Ergataner, Ergates, Fire, Formic, Formicary, Myrmecoid, Myrmidon, Nasute, Neuter, Pharaoh, Pismire, Sauba, Soldier, Termite, Thief, Velvet, White, Wood

Antacid Magnesia, Peptic

Antagonist, Antagonize Estrange, Peare, Peer

Antarctica Graham land

Ant-bear Tamanoir

Ante Bet, Punt, Stake

Ant-eater Aardvark, Echidna, Edental, Manis, Numbat, Pangolin, S(e)ladang, Spiny, Tamandu, Tamandua, Tapir

Antelope Addax, Antilope, Blackbuck, Blaubok, Blesbok, Bloubok, Bluebuck, Bongo, Bontebok, Bubal(is), Bushbuck, Chamois, Chikara, Dikdik, Duiker, Duyker, Dzeren, Eland, Elk, Gazelle, Gemsbok, Gerenuk, Gnu, Goral, Grysbok, Hartbees, Hartebeest, Impala, Inyala, Kaama, Kid, Klipspringer, Kob, Kongoni, Koodoo, Kudu, Lechwe, Madoqua, Nagor, Nilgai, Nilgau, Nyala, Nylghau, Oribi, Oryx, Ourebi, Pale-buck, Pallah, Prongbuck, Pronghorn, Puku, Pygarg, Reebok, Reedbuck, Rhebok, Sable, Saiga, Sasin, Sassaby, Serow, Sitatunga, Situtunga, Steenbok, Steinbock, Stemback, Stembok, Suni, Takin, Thar, Topi, Tragelaph, Tsessebe, Waterbuck , Wildebeest

Antenna Aerial, Dipole, Dish, Horn, Sensillum, TVRO

Anterior Anticous, Earlier, Front, Prior

Anthelmintic Worm

Anthem Hymn, Introit, Isodica, Marseillaise, Motet(t), National, Psalm, Responsory, Song, Star Spangled Banner, Theme, Tract

Anthology Album, Ana, Chrestomathy, Digest, Divan, Florilegium, Garland, Pick, Spicilege

Anthony Absolute, Adverse, Trollope

Anthrax Sang

Anthropoid Sivapithecus

Anthropologist Mead

Anti Against, Agin, Con, Hostile

Anti-aircraft AA

Anti-bacterial, Antibiotic Actinomycin, Bacitracin, Bacteriostat, Cephalosporin, Cloxacillin, Colistin, Doxorubicin, Doxycycline, Drug, Erythromycin, Gentamicin, Gramicidin, Griseofulvin, Interferon, Interleukin, Kanamycin, Lincomycin, Lineomycin, Methicillin, Mitomycin, Neomycin, Nystatin, Opsonin, Oxacillin, Oxytetracycline, Penicillin,

Polymixin, Rifampicin, Rifamycin, Spectinomycin, Streptomycin, Streptothricin, Terramycin®, Tetracycline, Tyrocidine, Tyrothricin, Wide-spectrum

Antibody Agglutinin, Amboceptor, Antitoxin, Blocker, Isoagglutinin, Lysin, Monoclonal, Precipitin, Reagin

Antic(s) Caper, Dido, Frolic, Gambado, Hay, Prank, Shenanigan, Stunt

Anti-carlist Queenite

Anticipate, Anticipation Antedate, Augur, Await, Drool, ➤ EXPECT, Forecast, Foresee, Forestall, Foretaste, Hope, Intuition, Prevenancy, Prolepsis, Prospect, Type

Anticlimax Bathos, Deflation, Letdown

Anticline Upwrap

Anticlockwise Dextrorse, Laevorotatory, Widdershins, Withershins

Anticoagulant C(o)umarin, Heparin, Hirudin, Prostacyclin, Warfarin

Anticyclone High

Antidote Adder's wort, Alexipharmic, Angelica, Antivenin, Bezoar, Contrayerva, Cure, Emetic, Guaco, Mithridate, Nostrum, Orvietan, Remedy, Ribavirin, Senega, Theriac(a), (Venice)-Treacle

Anti-freeze Lagging

Anti-imperialist Guelf, Guelph

Antimacassar Tidy

Antimony Sb, Stibium

Anti-parliamentarian Poujadist

Antipathy Allergy, Aversion, Detest, ➤ DISLIKE, Enmity, Repugnance

Anti-perfectionist Cobden

Antipodean Abo, Antarctic, Antichthon, Enzed, Underworld

Antipope Novatian(us)

Anti-protectionist Cobden

Antiquated, Antique, Antiquarian Ancient, Archaic, A(u)stringer, Bibelot, Curio, Dryasdust, FAS, Fogram(ite), Fog(e)y, Fossil, Old-fangled, Ostreger, Relic

Anti-reformer Obscurant

Anti-revolutionary White

Anti-Roman Ghibel(l)ine

Anti-royalist Whig

Anti-semitic Pamyat

Antiseptic Acriflavine, Carbolic, Cassareep, Creosote, Disinfectant, Eupad, Eusol, Formaldehyde, Guaiacol, Iodine, Phenol, Sterile, Thymol, Tutty

Anti-slavery Free-soil, Wilberforce

Anti-smoker ASH, Misocapnic

Antisocial Hostile, Ishmaelitish, Misanthropic

Antithesis Contrary, Converse, Opposite

Anti-three Noetian

Antitoxin Antibody, Antivenin, Guaco, Serum, Vaccine

Anti-union Secesher

Antler(s) Bosset, Horn, Rights, Staghorn, Surroyal, Tine
Ant-proof Bilian
▶ **Anus** see ANAL
Anvil Bick-iron, Block, Incus, Stiddie, Stithy
Anxiety, Anxious Angst, Brood, Care(ful), Cark, Concern, Disquiet, Dysthymia, Fanteeg, Fantigue, Fantod, Fraught, Grave, Heebie-jeebies, Hypochondria, Inquietude, Jimjams, Jumpy, Reck, Restless, Scruple, Solicitous, Suspense, Sweat, Tension, Twitchy, Unease, Unquiet, Upset, Uptight, Worriment
Any Arrow, Ary, Some
Anybody, Anyone One, Whoso, You
Anyhow Anyway, Leastways
Anything Aught, Oucht, Owt, Whatnot
▷ **Anyway** may indicate an anagram
Apache Arizona, AZ
Apart Aloof, Aside, Asunder, Atwain, Beside, Separate
Apartheid Racism, Verkrampte
Apartment Ben, Condominium, Digs, Duplex, Flat, Insula, Mansion, Paradise, Penthouse, Pied-a-terre, Quarters, Room, Simplex, Solitude, Suite, Unit
Apathetic, Apathy Accidie, Acedia, Incurious, Languid, Lethargic, Listless, Lobotomized, Pococurante, Torpid
Ape(-like), Apeman Anthropoid, Barbary, Big-foot, Catarrhine, Copy, Dryopithecine, Gelada, Gibbon, Gorilla, ➤ IMITATE, Magot, Mimic, Orang, Paranthropus, Pongo, Proconsul, Simian, Simulate, Yowie
Aperient Cascara, Laxative, Senna
Aperitif ➤ DRINK, Pernod®
Aperture Balistraria, Chink, Hole, Osculum, Spiracle, Window
Apex Acme, Culmen, Keystone, Knoll, Knowe, Summit, Vortex
Aphid Ant-cow, Phylloxera
Aphorism Adage, Epigram, Gnome, Proverb, Sutra
Aphrodisiac, Aphrodite Cytherean, Erotic, Idalian, Paphian, Philter, Philtre, Spanish fly, Urania, Yohimbine
Aplomb Assurance, Cool, Equanimity, Poise, Sangfroid, Serenity
Apocryphal Spurious, Tobit
Apograph Roneo®
Apollo Belvedere, Pythian, Sun
Apology Excuse, Justifier, Mockery, Oops, Pardon, Scuse
Apostate Citer, ➤ HERETIC, Pervert, Rat, Recreant, Renegade, Runagate, Turncoat
Apostle, Apostolic Cuthbert, ➤ DISCIPLE, Evangelist, Johannine, Jude, Matthew, Pauline, Spoon, Twelve
Apostrophe, Apostrophise Elision, O(h), Soliloquy, Tuism
Apothegm Dictum, Maxim, Motto

Appal(ling) Abysmal, Affear(e), Dismay, Egregious, Frighten, Horrify, Piacular, Tragic

▷ **Appallingly** may indicate an anagram

Apparatus Alembic, Appliance, Autoclave, Chemostat, Coherer, Colorimeter, Condenser, Cosmotron, Davis, Device, Eprouvette, Equipment, Eudiometer, Exciter, Fixings, Gadget, Golgi, Graith, Incubator, Instrument, Jacquard, Kipps, Kymograph, Masora(h), Multi-gym, Retort, Rounce, Scintiscanner, Scuba, Set, Snorkel, Sphygmograph, Still, Thermopile, Tokamak, Tromp(e), Whip-and-derry

Apparel Attire, Besee, ➤ COSTUME, Garb, Raiment, Wardrobe, Wardrop

Apparent(ly) Ap, Detectable, Ostensible, Outward, Overt, Plain, Prima facie, Semblance, Visible

▷ **Apparent** may indicate a hidden word

Apparition Dream, Eidolon, Fetch, Ghost, ➤ ILLUSION, Phantom, Shade, Spectre, Visitant, Wraith

Appeal(ing) Ad, Beg, Cachet, Catchpenny, Charisma, Charm, Cri de coeur, Cry, Entreat, Entreaty, Epirrhema, Fetching, Invocation, It, O, Oomph, Plead, SA, Screeve, Solicit, SOS, Suit

Appear(ance) Advent, Air, Apport, Arrival, Aspect, Broo, Brow, Burst, Compear, Debut, Emerge, Enter, Eye, Facade, Facies, Far(r)and, Farrant, Fa(s)cia, Feature, Garb, Guise, Habitus, Hue, Image, Kithe, Kythe, Loom, ➤ MANNER, Mien, Occur, Ostensibly, Outward, Person, Phase, Phenomenon, Physiognomy, Presence, Prosopon, Represent, Rig, Rise, Seem, Semblance, Show, Spring, Superficies, Theophany, View, Visitation, Wraith

Appease(ment) Allay, Calm, Danegeld, Mitigate, ➤ MOLLIFY, Munichism, Pacify, Placate, Propitiate, Satisfy, Soothe, Sop

Appendage Adjunct, Aglet, Allantois, Aril, Arista, Cercus, Codpiece, Ctene, Fang, Flagellum, Hanger-on, Lobe, Lug, Paraglossa, Pedipalp, Stipel, Suffix, Swimmeret, Tail, Tentacle, Ugly, Uropod, Uvula

Appendix Addendum, Apocrypha, Codicil, Grumbling, Label, Pendant, Pendent, Rider, Schedule, Vermiform

Appetite, Appetitive, Appetize(r) Antepast, Antipasto, Aperitif, Appestat, Bhagee, Bhajee, Bulimia, Bulimy, Canapé, Concupiscence, Concupy, Crudités, Dim-sum, Entremes(se), Entremets, Flesh, Hunger, Limosis, Malacia, Meze, Nacho, Orectic, Orexis, Passion, Pica, Polyphagia, Relish, Tapa(s), Titillate, Twist, Yerd-hunger, Yird-hunger

Applaud, Applause Bravo, ➤ CHEER, Clap, Claque, Eclat, Encore, Extol, Hum, Kentish fire, Olé, Ovation, Praise, Root, Ruff, Tribute

Apple Alligator, Baldwin, Balsam, Biffin, Blenheim orange, Bramley, Charlotte, Codlin(g), Cooker, Costard, Crab, Custard, Discord, Eater, Granny Smith, Greening, Jenneting, John, Jonathan, Leather-coat, Love, Mammee, Medlar, Nonpareil, Pearmain, Pippin, Pomace, Pome(roy), Pomroy, Pyrus, Quarantine, Quarenden, Quar(r)ender, Quarrington, Redstreak, Reinette, Rennet, Ribston(e), Ruddock, Russet,

Seek-no-further, Snow, Sops-in-wine, Sturmer, Sugar, Sweeting, Thorn, Toffee, Windfall, Winesap

Apple juice Malic

Apple-picker Atalanta

Applicant Postulant

Application, Apply, Appliance(s) Address, Adhibit, Appeal, Appose, Assiduity, Barrage, Blender, Devote, Diligence, Dressing, Exercise, Foment, Implement, Inlay, Lay, Lotion, Ointment, Petition, Plaster, Poultice, Put, Resort, Rub, Sinapism, Stupe, Truss, ➤ USE, White goods

Appliqué Hawaiian

Appoint(ee), Appointment Advowson, Assign, Berth, Date, Delegate, Depute, Designate, Dew, Due, Executor, Induction, Installation, Make, Name, ➤ NOMINATE, Nominee, Office, Ordain, Position, Post, Posting, Rendezvous, Room, Set, Tryst

▷ **Appointed** may indicate an anagram

Apportion(ment) Allocate, Allot, Mete, Parcel, Ration, Share, Weigh

Apposite Apt, Cogent, Germane, Pat, Pertinent, Relevant, Suitable

Appraise, Appraisal Analyse, ➤ EVALUATE, Gauge, Judge, Tape, ➤ VALUE, Vet

Appreciate, Appreciation Acknowledgement, Cherish, Clap, Dig, Endear, Esteem, Gratefulness, Increase, Prize, Realise, Regard, Relish, Rise, Sense, Thank you, Treasure, ➤ VALUE

Apprehend, Apprehension Afears, Alarm, Arrest, ➤ CATCH, Fear, Grasp, Insight, Intuit, Perceive, See, Take, Trepidation, Uh-oh, Unease, Uptake

Apprehensive Jumpy, Nervous, Uneasy

Apprentice(ship) Article, Cub, Devil, Garzone, Improver, Indent(ure), Jockey, Learner, L, Lehrjahre, Novice, Noviciate, Novitiate, Printer's devil, Pupillage, Trainee, Turnover

Approach(ing) Abord, Access, Accost, Advance, Anear, Appropinquate, Appulse, Avenue, Close, Come, Converge, Cost(e), Drive, Driveway, Fairway, Feeler, Gate, Imminent, Line, Near, Nie, Overture, Pitch, Procedure, Road, Run-up, Verge

Appropriate Abduct, Abstract, Annex, Apposite, Apt, Asport, Assign, Bag, Borrow, Collar, Commandeer, Commensurate, Confiscate, Convenient, Due, Embezzle, Expedient, Fit, Germane, Good, Happy, Hijack, Hog, Jump, Just, Meet, Nick, Pilfer, Pocket, Pre-empt, Proper, Right, Seize, Sequester, Sink, Snaffle, Steal, Suit, Swipe, Take, Timely, Trouser, Usurp

Approval, Approve(d) Adopt, Allow, Amen, Applaud, Attaboy, Aye, Blessing, ➤ COUNTENANCE, Credit, Dig, Endorse, Homologate, Hubba-bubba, Imprimatur, Kitemark, Laud, Nod, Okay, Olé, Orthodox, Plaudit, Rah, Ratify, Rubber-stamp, Sanction, Stotter, Thumbs-up, Tick, Tribute, Yes, Zindabad

Approximate(ly), Approximation Almost, Circa, Close, Coarse, Estimate, Guess, Imprecise, Near, Roughly

Apricot Mebos

April Apr

Apron Barm-cloth, Bib, Blacktop, Brat, Bunt, Canvas, Dick(e)y, Ephod, Fig-leaf, Gremial, Pinafore, Pinny, Placket, Stage, Tablier, Tier

Apse Concha, Exedra, Niche, Recess, Tribune

Apt(ly) Apposite, Appropriate, Apropos, Ben trovato, Capable, Evincive, Fit, Gleg, Happy, Liable, Prone, Suitable, Tends

Aptitude Ability, Bent, Faculty, Flair, Gift, Skill, Talent, Tendency

Aqua(tic) Euglena, Flustra, Lentic, Lotic, Regia, Zizania

Aqualung Scuba

Aqueduct Canal, Channel, Conduit, Hadrome, Xylem

Arab(ian), Arabia Abdul, Algorism, Ali, Baathist, Bahraini, Bahrein, Bedouin, Druse, Druz(e), Effendi, Fedayee(n), Gamin, Geber, Hashemite, Himyarite, Horse, Iraqi, Jawi, Lawrence, Mudlark, Nabat(h)ean, Omani, PLO, Rag(head), Saba, Sab(a)ean, Saracen, Semitic, Sheikh, UAR, Urchin, Yemen

Arachnid Podogona, Ricinulei, ➤ SPIDER

Arbiter, Arbitrator ACAS, Censor, Daysman, Judge, Ombudsman, Ref(eree), Umpire

Arbitrary Despotic, Random, Wanton

Arboreal, Arbour Bower, Dendroid, Pergola, Trellis

Arc Azimuth, Bow, Carbon, ➤ CURVE, Flashover, Fogbow, Halo, Octant, Quadrant, Rainbow, Reflex, Trajectory

Arcade Amusement, Burlington, Cloister, Gallery, Loggia, Triforium

Arcadia(n) Idyllic, Sylvan

Arcane Esoteric, Obscure, Occult, Orphism, Recherché, Rune, Secret

Arch(ed) Admiralty, Arblaster, Arcade, Archivolt, Arcuate, Camber, Chief, Coom, Counterfort, Crafty, Cross-rib, Crown-green, Ctesiphon, ➤ CUNNING, Curve, Elfin, Embow, Espiegle, Fallen, Fornicate, Fornix, Gill, Gothic, Hance, Haunch, Hog, Horseshoe, Instep, Intrados, Keel, Keystone, Lancet, Leery, Lierne, Marble, Ogee, Ogive, Order, Parthian, Pectoral, Portal, Proscenium, Roach, Roguish, Saucy, Soffit, Span, Squinch, Trajan, Triumphal, Vault, Zygoma

Archaeological, Archaeologist Carter, Dater, Dig, Evans, Layard, Leakey, Mycenae, Petrie, Pothunter, Wheeler, Woolley

Archangel Azrael, Gabriel, Israfeel, Israfel, Israfil, Jerahmeel, Michael, Raguel, Raphael, Sariel, Satan, Uriel

Arch-binder Voussoir

Archbishop Anselm, Augustine, Cosmo, Cranmer, Davidson, Dunstan, Ebor, Elector, Hatto, Lanfranc, Lang, Langton, Laud, Metropolitan, Primate, Temple, Trench, Tutu, Whitgift

Archdeacon Ven

Archduke Trio

Archer Acestes, Bow-boy, ➤ BOWMAN, Cupid, Eros, Hood, Philoctetes, Sagittary, Tell, Toxophilite

Archetype Avatar, Model, Pattern

Archibald, Archie, Archy Ack-ack, Cockroach, Oerlikon, Rice, Roach

Archilochian Epode

Archipelago Alexander, Antarctic, Azores, Bismarck, Camaguey, Fiji, Japan, Kerguelen, Malay, Marquesas, Sulu, Svalbard, Tierra del Fuego

Architect(ure), Architectural Arcology, Baroque, Bauhaus, Brutalism, Byzantine, Churrigueresque, Composite, Corinthian, Creator, Decorated, Designer, Doric, Entablature, Federation, Flamboyant, Gothic, Ionic, Jacobean, Landscape, Mission, Moderne, Neoclassical, Norman, Palladian, Perpendicular, Planner, Plateresque, Prostyle, Romanesque, Saxon, Tectonic, Tuscan

ARCHITECTS

4 letters:	Soane	Columbo	Vitruvius
Adam	Utzon	Gropius	**10 letters:**
Kent	**6 letters:**	Lutyens	Inigo Jones
Nash	Casson	Venturi	Mackintosh
Shaw	Chevel	Vignola	Trophonius
Webb	Foster	**8 letters:**	Van der Rohe
Wood	Nissen	Bramante	**11 letters:**
Wren	Repton	Hawkmoor	Abercrombie
5 letters:	Spence	Palladio	Butterfield
Gaudi	Street	Piranesi	Le Corbusier
Inigo	Wright	Saarinen	**12 letters:**
Nervi	**7 letters:**	Vanbrugh	Brunelleschi
Pugin	Behrens	**9 letters:**	
Scott	Bernini	Macquarie	

Architrave Epistyle, Platband

Archive(s) Muniment, PRO, Records, Register

Archon Draco

Arch-villain Ringleader

Arctic Estotiland, Frigid, Hyperborean, In(n)uit, Inupiat, Polar, Tundra

Ardent, Ardour Aflame, Aglow, Boil, Broiling, Burning, Fervent, Fervid, Fiery, Flagrant, Heat, Het, ➤ HOT, In, Mettled, Mettlesome, Passion(ate), Perfervid, Rage, Spiritous, Vehement, Warm-blooded, Zealous, Zeloso

Arduous Uphill

Are A

Area Acre, Are, Bailiwick, Belt, Bovate, Broca's, Carucate, Catchment, Centare, Centiare, Centre, Curtilage, Dec(i)are, Dedans, Development, Disaster, District, Endemic, Extent, Farthingland, Gau, Heartland, Hectare, Hide, Husbandland, Imperium, Karst, Landmass, Lathe, Latitude, Lek, Locality, Manor, Milieu, Morgen, Mush, No-go, Orb, Oxgang, Oxgate, Oxland, Patch, Place, Pleasance, Plot, Precinct, Province, Quad, Quadrat, Quarter, Range, Refugium, ➤ REGION, Retrochoir, Rood, Sector, Shire, Terrain, Territory, Theatre, Tie, Tract, Tye, Yard, Zone

Arena Circus, Cockpit, Dohyo, Field, Maidan, Olympia, ➤ RING, Stadium, Tiltyard, Venue

Argent Ag, Silver

Argentina RA

Argon Ar

Argonaut Acastus, Jason, Lynceus, Meleager, Nautilus

Argot Flash, Idiom, Jargon, Lingo, Shelta

Argue, Argument Altercation, Antistrophon, Argie-bargie, Argle-bargle, Argy-bargy, Bandy, Beef, Brush, Case, Casuism, Choplogic, Conflict, Contend, Debate, Deprecate, Diallage, Difference, Dilemma, Dispute, Elenchus, Elenctic, Enthymeme, Eristic, Exchange, Expostulate, Forensic, Free-for-all, Generalisation, Logic, Logomachy, Moot, Ob and soller, Ontological, Paralogism, Patter, Pettifog, Plead, Polemic, Premiss, Quibble, Quodlibet, Rammy, Ratiocinate, ➤ REASON, Remonstrate, Run-in, Sophism, Sorites, Spar, Stickle, Syllogism, Theme, Thetic, Tiff, Trilemma, Wrangle, Yike

Argyle Argathelian

Aria Ballad, Cabaletta, Melody, Song

Ariel Pen

Arise Appear, Develop, Emanate, Emerge, Upgo, Wax

Aristocracy, Aristocrat(ic) Blood, Boyar, Classy, Debrett, Duc, Elite, Eupatrid, Gentry, Grandee, High-hat, Junker, Nob, Noble, Optimate, Patrician, Tony, U-men, Upper-crust, Well-born

Aristotle Peripatetic, Stagirite, Stagyrite

Arithmetic(ian) Algorism, Algorith, Arsmetrick, Cocker, Euclid, Logistic, Modular, Sums

Ark(wright) Chest, Noah

Arly Thicket

Arm(ed), Arms Akimbo, Arsenal, Bearing, Brachial, Branch, Cove, Crest, Embattle, Equip, Escutcheon, Fin, Firth, Frith, Halbert, Hatchment, Heel, Heraldic, Inlet, Jib, Krupp, Limb, Loch, Member, Olecranon, Quillon, Radius, Ramous, Rotor, SAA, Small, Tappet, Tentacle, Timer, Transept, Tremolo, Ulnar, ➤ WEAPON, Whip

▷ **Arm** may indicate an army regiment, etc.

Armadillo Dasypod, Dasypus, Pangolin, Peba, Pichiciago, Tatou(ay), Xenurus

Armenian Haikh

Armistice Truce

Armour(ed) Ailette, Armet, Barbette, Beaver, Besagew, Bevor, Brasset, Brigandine, Buckler, Byrnie, Camail, Cannon, Casspir, Cataphract, Chaffron, Chain, Chamfrain, Chamfron, Chausses, Corium, Cors(e)let, Couter, Cuirass, Cuish, Cuisse, Culet, Curat, Curiet, Cush, Defence, Fauld, Garniture, Gear, Genouillère, Gere, Gorget, Greave, Habergeon, Hauberk, Jack, Jambeau, Jazerant, Jesserant, Lamboys, Loricate, Mail, Male, Mentonnière, Nasal, Panoply, Panzer, Pauldron, Petta, Placcat, Placket, Plastron, Plate, Poitrel, Poleyn, Pouldron, Sabaton, Secret, ➤ SHIELD, Solleret, Spaudler, Tace, Tank, Taslet, Tasse(t), Thorax, Tonlet, Tuille, Vambrace, Vantbrass, Visor, Voider, Weed

Armpit Axilla, Oxter

Armstrong Satchmo

Army Arrière-ban, BEF, Church, Colours, Confederate, Crowd, Federal, Fyrd, Golden (Horde), Horde, Host, IRA, Land, Landwehr, Legion, Line, Military,

Militia, Multitude, Para-military, Red, SA, Sabaoth, Salvation, Sena, Service, Soldiers, Standing, Swarm, TA, Territorial, Volunteer, War, Wehrmacht

▷ **Army** may indicate having arms

Aroma(tic) Allspice, Aniseed, Aryl, Balmy, Coriander, Fenugreek, Fragrant, Odorous, Pomander, Spicy, Vanillin, Wintergreen

Around About, Ambient, Circa, Near, Peri-, Skirt, Tour

▷ **Around** may indicate one word around another

Arouse, Arousal Alarm, ➤ EXCITE, Fan, Fire, Incite, Inflame, Must(h), Needle, Provoke, Stole, Urolagnia, Waken

Arrange(r), Arrangement Adjust, Array, Attune, Bandobast, Bundobust, Concert, Concinnity, Design, Dispose, Do, Edit, Engineer, Foreordain, Formation, Grade, Ikebana, Layout, Marshal, Modus vivendi, Orchestrate, Orchestration, Ordain, ➤ ORDER, Ordnance, Organise, Pack, Pattern, Perm, Permutation, Plan, Prepare, Prepense, Quincunx, Redactor, Regulate, Run, Schedule, Scheme, Set, Settle, Sort, Stow, Straighten, System, Tactic, Taxis, Transcribe

▷ **Arrange** may indicate an anagram

Arras Tapestry

Array(ed) Attire, Bedight, Deck, Herse, Marshal, Muster, Panoply

Arrear(s) Aft, Ahint, Backlog, Behind, Debt, Owing

Arrest(ed), Arresting Abort, Alguacil, Alguazil, Ament, Apprehend, Attach, Attract, Blin, Bust, Caption, Capture, Cardiac, Catch, Check, Citizen's, Collar, Hold, Knock, Nab, Nail, Nip, Pinch, Pull, Restrain, Retard, Riveting, Round-up, Run-in, Sease, Seize, Stasis, Stop, Sus(s)

Arrival, Arrive, Arriving Accede, Advent, Attain, Come, Get, Happen, Hit, Inbound, Influx, Johnny-come-lately, Land, Natal, Nativity, Reach, Strike

Arrogance, Arrogant Assumption, Bold, Bravado, Cavalier, Cocksure, Disdain, Dogmatic, Effrontery, Haughty, Haut(eur), High, Hogen-mogen, Hoity-toity, Hubris, Imperious, Morgue, Overweening, Presumption, Proud, Side, Surquedry, Toploftical, Uppity, Upstart

Arrogate Appropriate, Assume, Claim, Impute, Usurp

Arrow, Arrow-head Acestes, Any, Ary, Bolt, Dart, Filter, Flechette, Missile, Pheon, Pointer, Quarrel, Reed, Sagittate, Shaft, Sheaf

Arrowroot Kuzu, Maranta, Pia

Arsenal Ammo, Armo(u)ry, Depot, Magazine, Side

Arsenate, Arsenic(al), Arsenide As, Erythrite, Realgar, Resalgar, Rosaker, Salvarsan, Scorodite, Skutterudite, Smaltite, Speiss, Zarnich

Arson(ist) Firebug, Pyromania

Art(s), Arty, Art school, Art style Abstract, Ars, Bauhaus, Bloomsbury, Bonsai, Chiaroscuro, Clair-obscure, Clare-obscure, Clip, Cobra, Commercial, Conceptual, Constructivism, Craft, Cubism, Cunning, Dada, Daedal(e), Deco, Decorative, Dedal, De Stijl, Diptych, Earth, Ekphrasis, Environmental, Es, Expressionism, Fauvism, Feat, Fine, Finesse, Flemish, Fugue, Futurism, Genre, Guile, Impressionist, Jugendstil, Kano, Kinetic, Kitsch, Knack, Mandorla, Mannerism, Martial, Minimal, Montage, Mystery,

Nabis, Neoclassical, Neo-impressionism, New Wave, Norwich, Nouveau, Optical, Orphism, Performance, Performing, Perigordian, Plastic, Pop, Postimpressionism, Postmodern, Pre-Raphaelite, Primitive, Psychedelic, Quadratura, Quadrivium, Relievo, Sienese, ➤ SKILL, Still-life, Surrealism, Synchronism, Tachism(e), Tatum, Tenebrism, Toreutics, Trecento, Trivium, Trompe l'oeil, Trouvé, Virtu, Visual, Vorticism

▷ **Art** may indicate an -est ending

Artefact Neolith, Xoanon

▷ **Artefact** may indicate an anagram

Artemis Selene

Artemus Ward

Artery Aorta, Carotid, Coronary, Duct, Femoral, Iliac, Innominate, M1, Pulmonary, Route

Artful Cute, Dodger, Foxy, Ingenious, Quirky, Sly, Subtle, Tactician

Arthropod Limulus, Tardigrade, Water-bear

Artichoke Cardoon, Jerusalem

Article(s) A, An, Apprentice, Column, Commodity, Definite, Feature, Indefinite, Indenture, Item, Leader, Paper, Piece, Pot-boiler, Sidebar, Specify, The, Thing, Thirty-nine, Treatise, Ware

Articulation, Articulate(d) Clear, Coudé, Diarthrosis, Distinct, Eloquent, Enounce, Express, Fluent, Gimmal, Gomphosis, Hinged, Jointed, Jymold, Lenis, Limbed, Lisp, Pretty-spoken, Pronounce, Schindylesis, Trapezial, Utter, Vertebrae, Voice

Artifice(r), Artificial Bogus, Chouse, Dodge, Ersatz, Factitious, Finesse, Guile, Hoax, In vitro, Logodaedaly, Man-made, Mannered, Opificer, Pretence, Prosthetic, Pseudo, Reach, Ruse, Sell, Sham, Spurious, Stratagem, ➤ STRATEGY, Synthetic, Theatric, ➤ TRICK, Unnatural, Wile, Wright

Artillery Battery, Cannon, Fougade, Fougasse, Guns, Mortar, Ordnance, Pyroballogy, RA, Rafale, Ramose, Ramus, Train

Artiodactyl Camel, Chevrotain, Deerlet

Artisan Craftsman, Joiner, Journeyman, Mechanic, Pioner, Pyoner, Workman

Artist(ic) ➤ ARTISTS, Bohemian, Cartoonist, Colourist, Cubist, Dadaist, Daedal(e), Decorator, Deccie, Etcher, Fine, Gentle, Gilder, ICA, Impressionist, Limner, Linear, Maestro, Master, Miniaturist, ➤ MUSICIAN, Nazarene, Oeuvre, Orphism, ➤ PAINTER, Pavement, Paysagist, Piss, Plein-airist, Primitive, RA, Romantic, Screever, ➤ SCULPTOR, Sien(n)ese, Tachisme, Trapeze, Trecentist, Virtuose, Virtuoso

Artless Candid, Ingenuous, Innocent, Naive, Open, Seely

Arturo Toscanini

Arum Acorus, Green-dragon, Lily, Taro

As Aesir, Als, Arsenic, Coin, Eg, Forasmuch, Kame, Qua, Ridge, 's, Since, So, Thus, Ut, While

As above US

Asafoetida Hing

ARTISTS

3 letters:
Arp
Cox
4 letters:
Cuyp
Dadd
Dali
Doré
Etty
Goya
Hals
John
Klee
Lely
Miró
Moor
Opie
Phiz
5 letters:
Aiken
Appel
Bacon
Bosch
Corot
Crome
Degas
Dulac
Dürer
Ensor
Ernst
Fauve
Hoare
Hooch
Klimt
Leech
Léger
Lippi
Lotto
Lowry
Manet
Monet
Munch
Orpen
Redon
Rodin
Seago
Steen
Steer

Tatum
Watts
6 letters:
Boudin
Braque
Callot
Claude
Derain
D'Orsay
Friend
Fuseli
Giotto
Greuze
Guardi
Haydon
Ingres
Knight
Le Nain
Millet
Renoir
Ribera
Rivera
Romney
Rothko
Rubens
Seurat
Sisley
Stubbs
Tissot
Titian
Turner
Warhol
7 letters:
Apelles
Audubon
Bellini
Bernini
Bonnard
Breugel
Bruegel
Cézanne
Chagall
Chardin
Cimabue
Collier
Courbet
Cranach
Da Vinci

El Greco
Epstein
Gauguin
Hobbema
Hockney
Hogarth
Holbein
Hoppner
Kneller
Matisse
Millais
Morisot
Morland
Murillo
Nattier
Picasso
Pissaro
Poussin
Prudhon
Raeburn
Raphael
Rouault
Sargent
Sickert
Spencer
Tiepolo
Uccello
Utamaro
Utrillo
Van Dyke
Van Gogh
Van Eyck
Vermeer
Watteau
Zeuxian
Zoffany
8 letters:
Barbizan
Breughel
Brueghel
Daubigny
Eastlake
Headfast
Kirchner
Landseer
Leonardo
Magritte
Masaccio

Mondrian
Nevinson
Perugino
Piranesi
Reynolds
Rousseau
Topolski
Veronese
Whistler
9 letters:
Beardsley
Bonington
Canaletto
Carpaccio
Constable
Correggio
Delacroix
Die Brucke
Donatello
Fragonard
Gericault
Giorgione
Grunewald
Hiroshige
Rembrandt
Sternfast
Velasquez
10 letters:
Alma-Tadema
Botticelli
Burne-Jones
Guillaumin
Madox Brown
Rowlandson
Signorelli
Tintoretto
12 letters:
Gainsborough
Lichtenstein
Michelangelo
Winterhalter
14 letters:
Jackson Pollock
15 letters:
Hieronymus
    Bosch
Toulouse-Lautrec

As before Anew, Ditto, Do, Stet

Asbestos Amiant(h)us, Amosite, Chrysolite, Crocidolite, Earthflax, Fireproof, Rockwood

Ascend(ant), Ascent Anabasis, Climb, Dominant, Escalate, Gradient, Pull, Ramp, Rise, Sclim, Sklim, Slope, Up, Upgang, Uphill, Uprise, Zoom

Ascertain Determine, Discover, ➤ ESTABLISH, Prove

Ascetic Agapetae, Anchor(et), Anchorite, Ancress, Austere, Dervish, Diogenes, Encratite, Eremital, Essene, Fakir, Faquir, Hermit, Jain(ite), Monk, Nazarite, Nazirite, Sad(d)hu, Stylite, Sufic, Therapeutae, Yogi(n)

Ascidian Chordate, Urochordate

Asclepiad Stapelia

Ascribe Assign, ➤ ATTRIBUTE, Blame, Imply, Impute

Asdic Sonar

As far as Quoad

As good as Equal, Tantamount

Ash(es), Ashy Aesc, Aizle, Cinders, Cinereal, Clinker(s), Easle, Embers, Kali, Pallor, Pearl, Pozz(u)olana, Prickly, Rowan, Ruins, Sorb, Tephra, Urn, Varec, Wednesday, Witchen, Yg(g)drasil(l)

Ashamed Abashed, Embarrassed, Hangdog, Mortified, Repentant, Shent

Ashore Aland, Beached, Grounded, Stranded

Ash-pan Backet

Asia(n), Asiatic Balinese, Bengali, Cantonese, E, Evenki, Ewenki, Gook, Hun, Hyksos, Indian, Korean, Kurd, Lao, Malay, Mongol, Naga, Negrito, Nepalese, Pushtu, Samo(y)ed, Shan, Siamese, Sogdian, Tamil, Tibetan, Turanian, Turk(o)man

Asia Minor Anatolia, Ionic

Aside Apart, By, Despite, Private, Separate, Shelved, Sotto voce

Asinine Crass, Dull, Idiotic, Puerile, Stupid

Ask Beg, Beseech, Cadge, Demand, Desire, Entreat, Enquire, Evet, Implore, Intreat, Invite, Newt, Petition, Prithee, Pump, Quiz, Request, Rogation, Seek, Solicit, Speer, Speir, Touch

Askance Asconce, Askew, Oblique, Sideways

Askew Agee, Aglee, Agley, Ajee, Aslant, Awry, Crooked, Skivie

Asleep Dormant, Inactive, Napping

Asparagus Asperge, Sparrow-grass, Spear, Sprue

Aspect Angle, Bearing, Brow, Face, Facet, Facies, Feature, Look, Mien, Nature, Outlook, Perfective, Perspective, Side, ➤ VIEW, Visage, Vista

Aspersion Calumny, Innuendo, Libel, Slander, Slur, Smear

Asphalt Bitumen, Blacktop, Gilsonite®, Pitch, Uinta(h)ite

Aspirant, Aspirate, Aspiration, Aspire Ambition, Breath, Buckeen, Challenger, Desire, Dream, Ettle, Goal, H, Hope(ful), Pretend, Pursue, Rough, Spiritus, Wannabe(e)

Ass Buridan's, Burnell, Burro, Cardophagus, Chigetai, Clot, Couscous, Cuddie, Dick(e)y, Donkey, Dziggetai, Funnel, Golden, Hemione, Hemionus, Hinny, Jack, Jenny, Kiang, K(o)ulan, Kourbash, Kourmiss, Kouskous, Kumiss, Kurbash, Kyang, Liripipe, Liripoop, Moke, Neddy, Nitwit, Onager, Quagga, Sesterce, Simp, ➤ STUPID PERSON

Assail Assault, Batter, Bego, Belabour, Bepelt, Beset, Bombard, Impugn, Oppugn, Pillory, Ply, Revile

Assassin(ate), Assassination Booth, Brave, Bravo, Brutus, Casca, Frag, Gunman, Highbinder, Hitman, Killer, Ninja, Sword, Thuggee, Tyrannicide

Assault Assail, Assay, Attack, Battery, Bombard, Hamesucken, Indecent, Invasion, Mug, ➤ RAID, Stoor, Storm, Stour, Stowre

Assay Cupel, Examine, Proof, Test

Assemble, Assembly Agora, Audience, Ball, Bundestag, Chapter, Chatuaqua, Cho(u)ltry, Co, Collation, ➤ COLLECTION, Comitia, Company, Conclave, Concourse, Congeries, Congress, Consistory, Constituent, Convene, Conventicle, Convention, Convoke, Cortes, Council, Court, Curia, Dail Eireann, Dewain, Diet, Divan, Donnybrook, Ecclesia, Eisteddfod, Erect, Feis(anna), Folkmoot, Force, Forgather, Gather(ing), Gemot(e), Gorsedd, Group, Headstock, Hoi polloi, Kgotla, Knesset, Landtag, Legislative, Levee, Majlis, Make, Mass, ➤ MEETING, Mejlis, Moot, Muster, National, Panoply, Parliament, Patron, Pattern, Plenum, Pnyx, Powwow, Presence, Quorum, Rally, Rechate, Recheate, Repair, Resort, Sanhedrin, Sanhedron, Senate, Skupshtina, Sobranje, Soc, Society, Stort(h)ing, Synedrion, Synod, Thing, Tribunal, Troop, Unlawful, Volksraad, Wapens(c)haw, Wapins(c)haw, Wappens(c)haw, Wardmote, Weapon-s(c)haw, Witan, Witenagemot, Zemstvo

Assent Accede, Acquiesce, Agree, Amen, Aye, Comply, Concur, Nod, Placet, Sanction, Yea, Yield

Assert(ing), Assertion Affirm, Allege, Constate, Contend, ➤ DECLARE, Ipse-dixit, ➤ MAINTAIN, Pose, Predicate, Proclaim, Protest, Thetical

Assess(ment) Affeer, Appraise, Estimate, Evaluate, Gauge, Guesstimate, ➤ JUDGE, Levy, Measure, Perspective, Rating, Referee, Scot and lot, Tax, Value, Weigh

Asset(s) Advantage, Capital, Chattel, Fixed, Goodwill, Intangible, Liquid, Plant, Property, Resource, Talent, Virtue, Wasting

Assiduous Attentive, Busy, Constant, Diligent, Studious, Thorough

Assign(ation), Assignment Allocate, ➤ ALLOT, Apply, Aret, Ascribe, Attribute, Award, Date, Dedicate, Duty, Errand, Fix, Grant, Impute, Point, Quota, Refer, Transfer, Tryst

Assimilate(d) Absorb, Blend, Digest, Esculent, Fuse, Imbibe, Incorporate, Merge

Assist(ance), Assistant Acolyte, Adjunct, Aid(e), Ally, Alms, Attaché, Busboy, Cad, Collaborate, Counterhand, Counter-jumper, Dresser, Facilitate, Factotum, Famulus, Feldschar, Felds(c)her, Gofer, ➤ HAND, Help, Henchman, Legal aid, Offsider, Omnibus, Relief, Reinforce, Second, Server, Servitor, Sidesman, Stead, Subsidiary, Suffragan, ➤ SUPPORT, Usher

Assize Botley, Circuit, Oyer

Associate, Association Accomplice, Affiliate, Alliance, Ass, Attach, Bedfellow, Brotherhood, Cartel, Chapel, Chum, Club, Cohort, Combine, Compeer, Complice, Comrade, Confrère, ➤ CONNECT, Consort(ium), Co-partner, Correlate, Crony, Enclisis, Fellow, Fraternise, Gesellschaft, Guild, Hobnob, Intime, Join, Kabele, Kebele, League, Liaison, Member, Mix, Moshav, Pal, Partner, Press, Relate, Ring, Round Table, Sidekick, Sodality, Stablemate, Symbiosis, Syndicate, Toc H, Toenadering, Trade, Union, Word

Assort(ed), Assortment Paraphernalia, Various
▷ **Assorted** may indicate an anagram
Assuage Allay, Appease, Beet, Calm, Ease, Mease, Mitigate, Mollify, Slake, Soften
As such Qua
Assume, Assuming, Assumption Adopt, Affect, Arrogate, Attire, Axiom, Believe, Don, Donné(e), Feign, Hypothesis, Lemma, Occam's Razor, Posit, Postulate, Preconception, Premise, Premiss, Presuppose, Pretentious, Principle, Putative, Saltus, Suppose, Surmise, Take
▷ **Assumption** may mean attire
Assure(d), Assurance Aplomb, Aver, Belief, Calm, ➤ CERTAIN, Confidence, Confirm, Earnest, Gall, Guarantee, Pledge, Poise, Warranty
Assuredly Indeed, Perdie, Verily, Yea
Astatine At
Astern Abaft, Apoop, Rear
Asteroid Ceres, Eros, Hermes, Hygiea, Juno, Pallas, Star, Starfish
Astir Afoot, Agate, Agog
Astonish(ed), Astonishing, Astonishment, Astound Abash, Admiraunce, Amaze, Banjax, Bewilder, Confound, Corker, Crikey, Daze, Donnert, Dum(b)found, Dumbstruck, Flabbergast, Gobsmack, Open-eyed, Open-mouthed, Phew, Rouse, Singular, Stagger, Startle, Stupefaction, Stupefy, Stupendous, Surprise, Thunderstruck, Wow
Astray Abord, Amiss, Errant, Lost, Will, Wull
Astride Athwart, Spanning, Straddle-back
Astringent Acerbic, Alum, Catechu, Gambi(e)r, Harsh, Kino, Rhatany, Sept-foil, Severe, Sour, Styptic, Tormentil, Witch-hazel
Astrologer Archgenethliac, Chaldean, Culpeper, Faust, Figure-caster, Genethliac, Lilly, Moore, Nostradamus, Soothsayer, Starmonger, Zadkiel
Astronaut Cosmonaut, Gagarin, Glenn, Lunarnaut, Spaceman, Spacer
Astronomer, Astronomy Almagest, Aristarchus, Bessel, Bradley, Brahe, Callipic, Cassini, Celsius, Copernicus, Eddington, Encke, Eratosthenes, Eudoxus, Flamsteed, Galileo, Hale, Halley, Herschel, Hewish, Hipparchus, Hoyle, Hubble, Huggins, Jeans, Kepler, Laplace, Leverrier, Lockyer, Lovell, Meton, Omar Khayyam, Oort, Planetology, Ptolemy, Radio, Reber, Roche, Schwarzschild, Sosigenes, Tycho Brahe, Urania
Astrophel Penthia
Astute Acute, Canny, Crafty, Cunning, Downy, Perspicacious, Shrewd, Subtle, Wide, Wily
As usual Solito
As well Additionally, Also, Both, Even, Forby, Too
Asylum Bedlam, Bin, Bughouse, Frithsoken, Funny-farm, Girth, Grith, Haven, Institution, Magdalene, Refuge, Retreat, Sanctuary, Shelter, Snake-pit
Asymmetric(al) Lopsided, Skew
At Astatine, In, To

Atahualpa Inca
At all Ava, Ever, Oughtlings
At all events Algate
Atavistic Reversion, Throw-back
Atheist Doubter, Godless, Infidel, Sceptic
Athenian, Athene Attic, Cleruch, Pallas, Pericles, Solon, Timon
Athlete, Athletic(s) Agile, Agonist, Blue, Coe, Discobolus, Field, Gymnast,
   Jock, Leish, Miler, Milo, Nurmi, Olympian, Pacemaker, Runner, Sportsman,
   Sprinter, Track
Athodyd Ram-jet
Athwart Across, Awry, Oblique, Traverse
Atlantic Pond
Atlas Linguistic, Maps, Range, Silk
▷ **At last** may indicate a cobbler
Atmosphere Aeropause, Air, Ambience, Aura, Chemosphere, Elements,
   Epedaphic, Ether, F-layer, Geocorona, Ionosphere, Lid, Magnetosphere,
   Mesosphere, Meteorology, Miasma, Ozone, Thermosphere, Tropopause,
   Troposphere, Upper, Vibe(s)
Atoll Bikini, Eniwetok, Male, Motu
Atom(ic), Atoms Boson, Electron, Excimer, Gram, Ion, Iota, Isobare,
   Isotone, Isotope, Ligand, Molecule, Monad, Monovalent, Muonic, Nuclide,
   Particle, Pile, Radionuclide, Side-chain, Steric, Substituent
At once Ek dum, Holus-bolus, Immediate, Instanter, Presto, Statim, Swith,
   Tight, Tit(e), Titely, Tyte
Atone(ment) Aby(e), Acceptilation, Appease, Expiate, Redeem,
   Redemption, Yom Kippur
Atop Upon
▷ **At random** may indicate an anagram
Atrocious, Atrocity Abominable, Brutal, Diabolical, Flagitious, Heinous,
   Horrible, Monstrous, Outrage, Vile
Atrophy Degeneration, Marasmus, Sweeny, Wasting
▷ **At sea** may indicate an anagram
Attach(ed), Attachment Accessory, Adhesion, Adhibition, Adnate,
   Adnation, Adscript, Affix, Allonge, Bolt, Bro, Byssus, Covermount,
   Devotement, Devotion, Distrain, Glue, ➤ JOIN, Obconic, Pin, Snell, Stick,
   Tie, Weld
Attack(ing) Access, Airstrike, Alert, Anti, Apoplexy, Asperse, Assail, Assault,
   At, Batten, Bego, Belabour, Beset, Bestorm, Blitz(krieg), Bodrag(ing),
   Bombard, Bordraging, Bout, Broadside, Bushwhack, Camisade, Camisado,
   Campaign, Cannonade, Charge, Clobber, Counteroffensive, Descent,
   Diatribe, Feint, Fit, Flèche, Foray, Get, Handbag, Ictus, Impugn, Incursion,
   Inroad, Invade, Inveigh, Lampoon, Lese-majesty, Maraud, Mug, Offensive,
   Onding, Onrush, Onset, Onslaught, Oppugn, Pillage, Predacious,
   Pre-emptive, Push, Quart(e), Raid, Rough, Savage, Seizure, Sic(k), Siege,
   Snipe, Sortie, Storm, Strafe, Strike, Swoop, Thrust, Tilt, Vilify, Vituperate,
   Wage, Warison, Wolf-pack, Zap

Attain(ment) Accomplish, Arrive, Earn, Fruition, Get, Land, Reach

Attempt Bash, Bid, Burl, Crack, Debut, Effort, Endeavour, Essay, Go, Mint, Nisus, Seek, Shot, Shy, Stab, Strive, ➤ TRY, Venture, Whack, Whirl

Attend(ance), Attendant Accompany, Apple-squire, Await, Batman, Bearer, Be at, Behold, Cavass, Chaperone, Chasseur, Corybant, Courtier, Custrel, Entourage, Equerry, Escort, Esquire, Famulus, Footman, Gillie, Harken, Hear, ➤ HEED, Hello, Holla, Iras, Kavass, ➤ LISTEN, Maenad, Marshal, Mute, Note, Outrider, Page, Panisc, Panisk, Paranymph, People, Presence, Pursuivant, Respect, Roll-up, Satellite, Second, Sowar, Steward, Trainbearer, Turn-out, Valet, Varlet, Visit, Wait, Watch, Whiffler, Zambuck

Attention, Attentive Achtung, Assiduity, Court, Coverage, Dutiful, Ear, Gallant, Gaum, Gorm, Heed, Mind, Notice, Present, Punctilio, Qui vive, ➤ REGARD, Tenty, Thought

Attenuate, Attenuation Lessen, Neper, Rarefy, Thin, Weaken

Attest Affirm, Certify, Depose, Guarantee, Notarise, Swear, ➤ WITNESS

Attic Bee-bird, Garret, Greek, Koine, Loft, Mansard, Muse, Salt, Solar, Soler, Sollar, Soller, Tallat, Tallet, Tallot

Attila Etzel, Hun

Attire Accoutre, Adorn, Apparel, Clobber, ➤ DRESS, Garb, Habit

Attitude Air, Aspect, Behaviour, Demeanour, Light, ➤ MANNER, Mindset, Nimby, Pose, Posture, Sense, Stance, Tone

Attorney Advocate, Counsellor, DA, Lawyer, Proctor, Prosecutor

Attract(ion), Attractive Attrahent, Bait, Becoming, Bewitch, Bonny, Catchy, Charisma, ➤ CHARM, Cheesecake, Clou, Crowd puller, Cute, Cynosure, Dipolar, Dish(y), Draught, ➤ DRAW, Duende, Engaging, Entice, Epigamic, Eye-catching, Eyeful, Fanciable, Fascinate, Feature, Fetching, Fox(y), Gravity, Heartthrob, Hunky, Inducement, Inviting, It, Loadstone, Lodestone, Looker, Lure, Luscious, Magnes, Magnet(ism), Mediagenic, Meretricious, Photogenic, Picturesque, Pull, Sematic, Sexpot, Sideshow, Slick, Soote, Stotter, Striking, Studmuffin, Taking, Taky, Tasteful, Weber, Winning, Winsome, Zaftig, Zoftig

Attribute Accredit, Allot, Ap(p)anage, Ascribe, Asset, Credit, Gift, Impute, Lay, Metonym, Owe, Refer, Shtick

Attune Accord, Adapt, Temper

Atypical Aberrant

Aubergine Brinjal, Brown Jolly, Egg-plant, Mad-apple

Aubrey Beardsley

Auburn Abram, Chestnut, Copper, Vill(age)

Auction(eer) Barter, Bridge, Cant, Dutch, Hammer, Outcry, Outro(o)per, Roup, Sale, Subhastation, Tattersall, Vendue

Audacious, Audacity Bold, Brash, Cheek, Der-doing, Effrontery, Face, Hardihood, Indiscreet, Insolence, Intrepid, Neck, Nerve, Sauce

Audience, Auditorium Assembly, Court, Durbar, Gate, House, Interview, Pit, Sphendone, Tribunal

Audiovisual AV

Audit(or) Accountant, Check, Ear, Examine, Inspect, Listener

Auditory Acoustic, Oral
Audrey Hoyden
Augment(ed) Boost, Eche, Eke, Increase, Sch, Supplement, Swell, Tritone
August Awe-inspiring, Grand, Imperial, Imposing, Lammas, Majestic, Noble, Solemn, Stately, Stern
Augustine, Augustus Austin, Hippo, John
Auk Guillemot, Ice-bird, Roch, Rotch(e)
Aunt(ie) Agony, Augusta, Beeb, Giddy, Naunt, Sainted, Tia
Aura Aroma, Mystique, Nimbus, Odour, Vibrations
Aureole Coronary, Halo, Nimbus
Auricle Ear, Otic
Aurora Eos, Leigh, Matutinal
Auspice(s) Aegis, Patronage
Auster S-wind
Austere, Austerity Astringent, Bleak, Dantean, Hard, ➤ HARSH, Moral, Plain, Rigour, Stern, Stoic, Stoor, Strict, Vaudois, Waldensian
Austin Friar
Australia(n) Alf, Antipodean, Aussie, Balt, Banana-bender, Bananalander, Billjim, Canecutter, Cobber, Currency, Darwinian, Digger, Gin, Godzone, Gumsucker, Gurindji, Koori, Larrikin, Myall, Norm, Ocker, Oz, Pintupi, Roy, Sandgroper, Strine, Wallaby, Yarra-yabbies
Austrian Cisleithan, Tyrolean
Authentic(ate) Certify, Echt, Genuine, Honest, Notarise, Official, Real, Sign, Test, True, Validate
Author(ess) Anarch, Auctorial, Inventor, Me, Parent, Volumist, Wordsmith, ➤ WRITER
▷ **Author** may refer to author of puzzle
Authorise(d), Authorisation Accredit, Clearance, Empower, Enable, Exequatur, Imprimatur, Legal, Legit, ➤ LICENCE, Official, OK, Passport, ➤ PERMIT, Plenipotentiary, Sanction, Sign, Stamp, Warrant
Authority, Authoritarian, Authoritative Canon, Charter, Circar, Cocker, Commission, Commune, Crisp, Dominion, Ex cathedra, Expert, Gravitas, Hegemony, Inquirendo, Jackboot, Licence, Magisterial, Mandate, Mastery, Name, Oracle, Permit, ➤ POWER, Prefect, Prestige, Pundit, Remit, Right, Rod, Say-so, Sceptre, Sircar, Sirkar, Source, Warrant
Autobiography Memoir
Autocrat(ic) Absolute, Caesar, Cham, Despot, Neronian, Tsar, Tyrant
Autograph Signature
Autolycus Scrapman
Automatic, Automaton Android, Aut, Browning, Deskill, Instinctive, Machine, Mechanical, Pistol, Reflex, Robot, RUR, Zombi
Auto-pilot George
Autopsy Necropsy
Auto-suggestion Coueism
Autumn(al) Fall, Filemot, Leaf-fall, Libra, Philamot

Auxiliary Adjunct, Adjuvant, Adminicle, Aide, Be, Feldsher, Have, Helper, Ido

Avail(able) Benefit, Dow, Eligible, Going, Handy, On call, Open, Pickings, ➤ READY, Serve, Use, Utilise

Avalanche Deluge, Landfall, Landslide, Landslip, Lauwine, Slide, Slip, Snowdrop

Avant-garde Modernistic, Spearhead

Avarice, Avaricious Cupidity, Golddigger, Greed, Money-grubbing, Pleonexia, Sordid

Avatar Epiphany, Incarnation, Rama

Avaunt Away, Go

Avenge(r) Eriny(e)s, Eumenides, Goel, Kurdaitcha, Punish, Redress, Requite, ➤ REVENGE, Wreak

Avenue Alley, Arcade, Channel, Corso, Cradle-walk, Hall, Mall, Passage, Vista, Way, Xyst(us)

Aver Affirm, Asseverate, Depose, Swear, Vouch

Average Adjustment, Av, Batting, Dow Jones, Mean, Mediocre, Middle-brow, Middling, Moderate, Norm, Par, Run, Soso, Standard

Averse, Aversion Against, Antipathy, Apositia, Disgust, Distaste, Hatred, Horror, Opposed, Phobic, Scunner

Avert Avoid, ➤ DEFLECT, Forfend, Parry, Ward

Aviary Volary

Aviator Airman, Alcock, Bleriot, Brown, Earhart, Flier, Hinkler, Icarus, Johnson, Lindbergh, Pilot

Avid ➤ EAGER, Greedy, Keen

Avifauna Ornis

Avignon Pont

Avocado Aguacate, Guac(h)amole, Pear

Avocet Scooper

Avoid(er), Avoidance Ba(u)lk, Boycott, Bypass, Cop-out, Cut, Dodge, Duck, Elude, Escape, Eschew, Evade, Evitate, Evite, Fly, Forbear, Gallio, Hedge, Miss, Parry, Prevaricate, Scutage, Secede, Shelve, Shun, Sidestep, Skirt, Spare, Spurn, Waive

Avoirdupois Size, Weight

Avow(ed) Acknowledged, Affirm, Declare, Own, Swear

Await Abide, Bide, Expect, Tarry

Awake(ning) Aware, Conscious, Conversion, Fly, Rouse, Vigilant

Award Academy, Accolade, Addoom, Allot, Alpha, Aret(t), Bafta, Bestow, Bursary, Cap, Clasp, Clio, Crown, Emmy, Exhibition, Grammy, Grant, Medal, Meed, Mete, Oscar, Palme d'or, Premium, Present(ation), ➤ PRIZE, Scholarship, Tony, Trophy, Yuko

Aware(ness) Alert, Cognisant, Conscious, Conversant, ESP, Est, Hep, Hip, Informed, Liminal, Onto, Panaesthenia, Prajna, Presentiment, Samadhi, Scienter, Sensible, Sensile, Sensitive, Sentience, Streetwise, Vigilant, Wot

Away Absent, Afield, Apage, Avaunt, By, For-, Fro(m), Go, Hence, Off, Out, Past

▷ **Away** may indicate a word to be omitted

Awe(d) Dread, D(o)ulia, Fear, Intimidate, Loch, Overcome, Popeyed, Regard, Respect, Reverent, Scare, Solemn

Awe-inspiring Numinous

Awful(ly) Alas, Deare, Dere, Dire, Fearful, Horrendous, O so, Piacular, Terrible

▷ **Awfully** may indicate an anagram

Awkward Angular, Bumpkin, Complicated, Clumsy, Corner, Crabby, Cubbish, Cumbersome, Embarrassing, Farouche, Fiddly, Fix, Gauche, Gawky, Handless, Howdy-do, Inconvenient, Inept, Lanky, Loutish, Lurdan(e), Lurden, Mauther, Mawr, Nasty, Ornery, Perverse, Refractory, Slummock, Spot, Sticky, Stroppy, Stumbledom, Swainish, Uneasy, Ungainly, Wry

Awl(-shaped) Brog, Els(h)in, Nail, Stob, Subulate

Awn(ing) Barb, Beard, Canopy, Ear, Shade, Velarium

Awry Agley, Askew, Cam, Kam(me), Wonky

Axe Abolish, Adz(e), Bill, Celt, Chop(per), Cleaver, Eatche, Gisarme, Gurlet, Halberd, Halbert, Hatchet, Ice, Jethart-staff, Labrys, Mattock, Partisan, Palstaff, Palstave, Piolet, Retrench, Sax, Sparth(e), Sperthe, Spontoon, Thunderbolt, Tomahawk, Twibill

Axiom Adage, Motto, Peano's, Proverb, Saw, Saying

Axis Alliance, Anorthic, Anticous, Axle, Caulome, Chital, Cob, Columella, Hinge, Modiolus, Myelon, Optic, Pivot, Polar, Rachis, Spindle, Sympodium, X, Y, Z

Axle, Axle-shoulder Arbor, Axis, Fulcrum, Hurter, Journal, Mandrel, Mandril, Pivot

Ay I

Aye Eer, Ever, Yea, Yes

Ayesha She

Azo-dye Para-red

Aztec Nahuatl

B b

B Bachelor, Black, Book, Born, Boron, Bowled, Bravo

Babble(r) Blather, Chatter, Gibber, Haver, Lallation, Lurry, Prate, Prattle, Runnel, Tonguester, Twattle, Waffle

Babel Charivari, Confusion, Din, Dovercourt, Medley

Baboon Ape, Bobbejaan, Chacma, Dog-ape, Drill, Gelada, Hamadryas, Mandrill, Sphinx

Baby(hood) Bairn, Blue, Bub, Bunting, Duck, Grand, Infant, Jelly, Neonate, Nursling, Pamper, Papoose, Preverbal, Sis, Small, Sook, Suckling, Tar, Test tube, Tot, Wean

Babylonian Mandaean, Semiramis, Sumerian

Bacchantes Maenads

Bacchus Ivied

Bachelor BA, Bach, Benedict, Budge, Celibate, En garçon, Pantagamy, Parti, Single, Stag

Bacillus Comma, Germ, Micrococcus, Virus

Back(ing), Backward Abet, Accompany, Addorse, Again, Ago, Anticlockwise, Antimacassar, Arear, Arrière, Assist, Baccare, Backare, Bankroll, Buckram, Consent, Defender, Dorsal, Dorse, Dos, Ebb, Empatron, Encourage, Endorse, Finance, Frae, Fro, Gaff, Help, Hind, Historic, La-la, Late, Notaeum, Notal, Notum, On, Patronise, Poop, Pronotum, Punt, Rear(most), Retral, Retro(grade), Retrogress, Retrorse, Return, Rev, Ridge, Root, Shy, Spinal, Sponsor, Stern, ➤ SUPPORT, Sweeper, Tail, Telson, Tergum, Third, Thrae, Tonneau, Ulu, Uphold, Verso, Vie, Vo, Wager

▷ **Back(ing)** may indicate a word spelt backwards

Back and forth Boustrophedon

Backbiter, Backbiting Catty, Defame, Detract, Libel, Molar, Slander

Backbone Chine, Grit, Guts, Mettle

Backchat Lip, Mouth, Sass

Backer Angel, Benefactor, Patron, Punter, Seconder, Sponsor

Backfire Boomerang

Backgammon Acey-deucy, Lurch, Tick-tack, Tric-trac, Trick-track, Verquere

Background Antecedence, Fond, History, Horizon, Setting, Ulterior

Backhander Payola, Reverso

Backroom Boffin, Boy, Moor

Backslide(r), Backsliding Apostate, Lapse, Regress, Relapse, Revert

Backwash Rift

Backwater Bogan, Ebb, Retreat, Slough, Wake

Backwoods Boondocks, Boonies, Hinterland

Backyard Court, Patio

Bacon Danish, Essayist, Flitch, Francis, Gammon, Lardo(o)n, Pancetta, Pig, Pork, Rasher, Roger, Spec(k), Streaky, Verulam

Bacteria, Bacterium Aerobe, Bacteriological, Bacilli, Botulinum, ➤ BUG, Campylobacter, Chlamydia, Clostridia, Cocci, Culture, Detritivore, Diplococcus, Escherichia, ➤ GERM, Gonococcus, Gram-negative, Gram-positive, Intestinal flora, Klebsiella, Listeria, Lysogen, Meningococcus, Microbe, Mother, MRSA, Packet, Pasteurella, Pathogen, Prokaryote, Proteus, Pus, Rhizobium, Rickettsia, Salmonella, Schizomycete, Septic, Serotype, Serum, Shigella, Spirilla, Spirochaete, Spore, Staph, Staphylococcus, Strep(tococcus), Streptobacillus, Streptomyces, Superbug, Treponemata, Vibrio, Vinegar-plant, Yersinia

Bad(ly), Badness Addled, Chronic, Crook, Defective, Diabolic, Dud, Duff, Egregious, Execrable, Faulty, Heinous, Ill, Immoral, Inferior, Injurious, Lither, Mal, Naughty, Nefandrous, Nefarious, Nice, Off, Ominous, Oncus, Onkus, Piacular, Poor, Rank, Ropy, Scampish, Scoundrel, Sinful, Spoiled, Turpitude, Useless, Wack, Wick, ➤ WICKED

▷ **Bad(ly)** may indicate an anagram

Badge Brassard, Brooch, Button, Chevron, Cockade, Crest, Emblem, Ensign, Epaulet, Episemon, Fáinne, Flash, Garter, Gorget, ID, Insignia, Kikumon, Mark, Mon, Rosette, Scallop, ➤ SIGN, Symbol, Token, Vernicle, Wings

Badger ➤ ANNOY, Bait, Bedevil, Beset, Brock, Browbeat, Bug, Bullyrag, Cete, Dassi(e), Ferret, Gray, Grey, ➤ HARASS, Hassle, Hog, Honey, Hound, Nag, Pester, Plague, Provoke, Ratel, Ride, Roil, Sow, Teledu, Wisconsin

Bad habit Cacoethes, Vice

Badinage Banter, Chaff, Raillery

Bad luck Ambs-ace, Ames-ace, Deuce-ace, Hoodoo, Jinx, Jonah, Shame, Voodoo

Bad-tempered Carnaptious, Curmudgeon, Curnaptious, Curst, Grouchy, Grum(py), Irritable, Moody, Patch, Splenetic, Stroppy

Bad woman Harridan, Loose, Mort

Baffle(d), Baffling Anan, Balk, Bemuse, Bewilder, Confound, Confuse, Elude, Evade, Floor, Flummox, Foil, Fox, Get, Hush-kit, Mate, Muse, Mystify, Nark, Nonplus, Pose, Puzzle, Stump, Throw, Thwart

Bag(s), Baggage Alforja, Allantois, Ascus, Amaut, Amowt, Ballonet, Besom, Bladder, Body, Bulse, Caba(s), Caecum, Callet, Capture, Carpet, Carrier, Carryall, Cecum, Cly, Cod, Cool, Corduroy, Crone, Crumenal, Cyst, Daypack, Dilli, Dilly, Dime, Diplomatic, Ditty, Doggy, Dorothy, Duffel, Dunnage, ➤ EFFECTS, Excess, Flannels, Follicle, Galligaskins, ➤ GEAR, Gladstone, Grip, Holdall, Ice, Impedimenta, Jelly, Jiffy®, Kill, Lithocyst, Marsupium, Minx, Mixed, Nap, Net, Overnight, Oxford, Pantaloons, Pochette, Pock(et), Pockmanky, Pockmantie, Poke, Port(manteau), Portmantle, Portmantua, Pot, Pouch, Purse, Rake, Reticule, Ridicule, Rucksack, Sabretache, Sac(cule), Sachet, Sack, Saddle, Satchel, Scrip, Scrotum, Shopper, Slattern, Sleeping, Sponge, Sporran, Stacks, Strossers, Survival, Tea, Tote, ➤ TRAP, Trews, Trollop, Trouse(r), Udder, Unmentionables, Utricle, Valise, Vanity, Wallet, Weekend, Win

Bagatelle Bauble, Fico, Trifle, Trinket

Bagpipe Chorus, Cornemuse, Drone, Musette, Pibroch, Piffero, Skirl, Sourdeline, Uillean, Zampogna

Bahamas BS

Bail(er), Bailment Bond, Ladle, Mainpernor, Mainprise, Mutuum, Scoop

Bailey Bridge, Ward

Bailiff Adam, Bandog, Beagle, Bum, Factor, Foud, Grieve, Huissier, Hundreder, Hundredor, Land-agent, Nuthook, Philistine, Reeve, Shoulder-clapper, Shoulder-knot, Steward, Tipstaff, Water

Bairn Baby, ➤ CHILD, Infant, Wean

Bait Badger, Berley, Brandling, Burley, Capelin, Chum, Dap, Decoy, Entice, Gentle, Harass, Hellgram(m)ite, Incentive, Lobworm, Lug(worm), Lure, Mawk, ➤ RAG, Ragworm, Teagle, Tease

Bake(r), Baked, Baking Alaska, Batch, Baxter, ➤ COOK, Fire, Kiln-dry, Roast, Scorch, Shirr

Baker's daughter Own

Baker Street Irregular

Balance(d) Account, Beam, Counterpoise, Counterweight, Equate, Equilibrium, Equipoise, Equiponderate, Even, Gyroscope, Gyrostat, Isostasy, Launce, Libra, Librate, Meet, Otolith, Peise, Perch, Peyse, Poise, ➤ REMAINDER, Remnant, Residual, Rest, Scale, Spring, Stand, Steelyard, Symmetry, ➤ TOTAL, Trial, Trim, Tron(e)

Balcony Circle, Gallery, Loggia, Mirador, Moucharaby, Porch, Sundeck, Tarras, Terrace, Veranda(h)

Bald(ing), Baldness Alopecia, Apterium, Awnless, Barren, Calvities, Coot, Crude, Egghead, Fox-evil, Glabrous, Hairless, Madarosis, Open, Peelgarlic, Pilgarlic(k), Pollard, Psilosis, Slaphead, Smoothpate, Tonsured

Balderdash Drivel, Flapdoodle, Nonsense, Rot

Baldmoney Emeu, Meu, Spignel

Bale Bl, Bundle, Evil, Pack, Truss

Baleful Evil, Malefic, Malignant

➤ **Balk** see BAULK

Balkan Albanian, Bulgarian, Macedon, Rumanian, Serb, Vlach

Ball(s) Aelopile, Aelopyle, Aeolipile, Aeolipyle, Agglomerate, Alley, Ally, Ammo, Aniseed, Beach, Bead, Beamer, Bobble, Bolus, Bosey, Bouncer, Break, Caltrap, Caltrop, Cap, Cherry, Chinaman, Clew, Clue, Cotill(i)on, Cramp, Croquette, Crystal, Cue, Curve, Daisy-cutter, ➤ DANCE, Delivery, Dollydrop, Eolipile, Eolipyle, Eolopile, Eolopyle, Falafel, Felafel, Gazunder, ➤ GLOBE, Glomerate, Googly, Gool(e)ys, Goolies, Grub, Gutta, Gutter, Hank, Hop, Inswinger, Ivory, Knur(r), Leather, Leg-break, Lob, Long-hop, Marble, Masque(rade), Medicine, Minié, Moth, Nur(r), O, Off-break, Off-spin, Outswinger, Overarm, Pakora, Pea, Pellet, Pill, Poi, Pompom, Prom, Puck, Quenelle, Rissole, Rover, Rundle, Seamer, Sliotar, Sneak, Sphere, Spinner, Testes, Thenar, Tice, Witches, Wood, Yorker

Ballad(ist) Bab, Bothy, Bush, Calypso, Carol, Lay, Lillibullero, Lilliburlero, ➤ SONG, Torch-song

Ballast Kentledge, Makeweight, Stabiliser, Trim, Weight

Ball-boy Dry-bob

Ballerina Coryphee, Dancer, Pavlova

Ballet, Ballet movement, Ballet-system Bolshoi, Checkmate, Développé, Écarté, Firebird, Giselle, Kirov, Laban

Ballet-interlude Divertimento

Balloon(ist) Aeronaut, Aerostat, Airship, Bag, Barrage, Billow, Blimp, Bloat, Dirigible, Dumont, Fumetto, Hot air, Lead, Montgolfier, Pilot, Rawinsonde, Weather, Zeppelin

Ballot Election, ➤ POLL, Referendum, Suffrage, Ticket, Vote

Ballot-box Urn

Ballpoint Bic®, Biro®

Balm(y) Anetic, Arnica, Balsam, Calamint, Fragrant, Garjan, Gilead, Gurjun, Lemon, Lenitive, ➤ MILD, Mirbane, Myrbane, Nard, Oil, Opobalsam, Ottar, Redolent, Remedy, Soothe, Spikenard, Tolu, Unguent

Balmoral Bonnet

Baloney Bunk, Hooey

Balsam Canada, Copaiba, Copaiva, Nard, Peruvian, Resin, Spikenard, Tamanu, Tolu(ic), Touch-me-not, Tous-les-mois, Turpentine

Balt Esth, Lett

Bamboo Whangee

Bamboozle(d) Cheat, Dupe, Flummox, Hoodwink, Mystify, Nose-led, Perplex, Trick

Ban Abolish, Accurse, Anathema, Black(ing), Censor, D-notice, Debar, Embargo, Excommunicate, For(e)say, For(e)speak, Gate, Moratorium, No, Prohibit, Proscribe, Taboo, Tabu, Veto

Banal Corny, Flat, Hackneyed, Jejune, Mundane, Platitudinous, ➤ TRITE, Trivial

Banana(s) Abaca, Hand, ➤ MAD, Musa, Plantain, Scitamineae, Split, Strelitzia

Band(s) Alice, Ambulacrum, Anadem, Armlet, Barrulet, Belt, Border, Braid, Brass, Brassard, Brassart, Caravan, CB, Channel, Cingulum, Circlet, Citizen's, Clarain, Cohort, Collar, Collet, Combo, Company, Corslet, Coterie, Crew, Elastic, Endorse, Enomoty, Facia, Falling, Fascia, Fasciole, Ferret, Ferrule, Filament, Fillet, Frieze, Frog, Frontlet, Galloon, Gamelan, ➤ GANG, Garland, Garter, Gasket, Gaskin, Geneva, Gird, Girth, ➤ HOOP, Hope, Iron, Jazz, Jug, Kitchen, Label, Laticlave, Mariachi, Massed, Myrmidon, Noise, One-man, Orchestra, Orchestrina, Pack, Parral, Parrel, Parsal, Parsel, Pass, Patte, Pipe, Plinth, Purfle, Puttee, Retinaculum, Rib, Ribbon, Rigwiddie, Rigwoodie, Rim, Ring, Robbers, Rubber, Rymme, Sash, Scarf, Screed, Scrunchie, Scrunchy, Sect, Shallal, Shash, Shoe, Snood, Steel, Strake, Strap, Stratum, String, Stripe, Swath(e), Tambu-bambu, Tape, Tendon, Throat-latch, Tie, Tippet, Torques, Tourniquet, Train, Troop, Troupe, Turm, Tyre, Unite, Vinculum, Virl, Vitrain, Vitta, Wanty, Weeper, Welt, With(e), Wristlet, Zona, Zone

Bandage Bind, Capeline, Dressing, Fillet, Ligature, Lint, Pledget, Roller, Scapula, Sling, Spina, Suspensor, Swaddle, Swathe, T, Tape, Truss, Wadding

Bandicoot Pig-rat

Bandit Apache, Bravo, Brigand, Desperado, Fruit-machine, Klepht, Moss-trooper, Outlaw, Pirate, Rapparee, ➤ ROBBER, Turpin

Bandsman, Band-leader Alexander, Bugler, Conductor, Maestro, Miller, Wait

Bane Curse, Evil, Harm, Poison

Bang(er) Amorce, Big, Cap, Chipolata, Clap, Cracker, Crock, Explode, Flivver, Fringe, Haircut, Heap, Implode, Jalopy, Maroon, Rattletrap, Report, Sausage, Sizzler, Slam, Thrill, Wurst

Bangle Anklet, Armlet, Bracelet, Kara

Banish(ment) Ban, Deport, Depose, Exile, Expatriate, Expel, Extradition, Forsay, Maroon, Ostracise, ➤ OUTLAW, Relegate, Rusticate

Banjo Ukulele

Bank(s) An(n)icut, Asar, Backs, Bar, Bay, Bk, Blood, Bluff, Bottle, Brae, Brim, Bund, Camber, Cay, Central, Chesil, Clearing, Cloud, Data, Depend, Deposit, Dogger, Down, Dune, Dyke, Earthwork, Escarp, Gene, Giro, Glacis, Gradient, Gradin(e), Hele, Hill, Jodrell, Left, Levee, Link, Merchant, Mound, Nap, Nore, Overslaugh, Parapet, Piggy, Rake, Ramp, Rampart, Reef, ➤ RELY, Reserve, Rivage, Riverside, Rodham, Row, Sandbar, Shallow, Shelf, Side, Slope, Sperm, Staithe, Sunk, Terrace, Terreplein, Tier, Vault, World

Banker Agent, Financial, Fugger, Gnome, Lombard, Medici, ➤ RIVER, Rothschild, Shroff

Banknote Greenback

Bankrupt(cy) Break, Broke, Bung, Bust, Cadaver, Carey Street, Crash, Debtor, Deplete, Duck, Dyvour, Fail, Fold, Insolvent, Receivership, Ruin, Rump, Scat, Sequestration, Skatt, Smash

▷ **Bankrupt** may indicate 'red' around another word

Bank System Giro

Bann(s) Out-ask

Banner Banderol(e), Bandrol, Bannerol, ➤ FLAG, Gumphion, Labarum, Oriflamme, Sign, Streamer

Banquet Beanfeast, Dine, Feast, Junket, Spread

Banquette Firestep

Bant Diet, Reduce

Banter Badinage, Borak, Chaff, Dicacity, Dieter, Jest, ➤ JOKE, Persiflage, Picong, Rag, ➤ RAILLERY, Rally, Ribaldry, Roast, Tease

Bantu Bosotho, Herero, Sotho, Tutsi, X(h)osa

Bap Bread, Roll, Tommy

Baptise(d), Baptism, Baptist Affusion, Amrit, Christen, Dip, Dipper, Dopper, Dunker, Illuminati, Immersion, Sprinkle, Tinker

Bar(s) Angle-iron, Anti-roll, Astragal, Bail, Ban, Barrelhouse, Baulk, Beam, Bierkeller, Bilboes, Billet, Bistro, Blackball, Blacklist, Block(ade), Bloom, Bolt, Boom, Bottega, Brasserie, Buffet, Bull, But, Buvette, Café(-chantant), Café-concert, ➤ CAGE, Came, Cantina, Capo, Capstan, Colour, Counter, Cramp(on), Crow, Crush, Dive, Double-tree, Espresso, Estop(pel), Except, Exclude, Fen, Fid, Flinders, Forbid, Foreclose, Forestall, Gad, Gemel, Grate, Grid, Hame, Handspike, Heck, ➤ HINDRANCE, Horizontal, Hound, Impediment, Ingoes, Ingot, Ingowes, Inn, Inner, Judder, Juice, Karaoke, Kickstand, Knuckleduster, Latch, Let, Lever, Line, Local, Lounge, Macron, Mandrel, Mandril, Measure, Milk, Mousing, Mullion, No-go, Norman, Obstacle, Onely, Orgue, Overslaugh, Parallel, Pile, Pinch, Pole, Prohibit, Pub, Public, Putlog, Rabble, Rack, Rail, Ramrod, Rance, Randle-balk, Randle-perch, Randle-tree, Restrict, Rib, Risp, Rod, Roo, Rung, Salad, Saloon, Sans, Save, Saving, Scroll, Semantron, Shaft, Shanty, Shet, Shut, Singles, Skewer, Slot, Snack, Snug, Spacer, Spar, Speakeasy, Sperre, Spina, Spit, Sprag, Stancher, Stanchion, Stave, Sternson, Stick, Stirre, Stretcher, Stripe, Swee, T, Tael, Tap(-room), Tapas, Taphouse, Tavern(a), Temple, Toll, Tombolo, Tommy, Torsion, Tow, Trace, Trangle, Transom, Trapeze, Triblet, Vinculum, Ward, Whisker, Wine, Z, Zed, Zygon

Barabbas Robber

Barb(ed) Bur(r), Fluke, Harl, Herl, ➤ HOOK, Jag(g), Jibe, Pheon, Prickle, Ramus, Tang, Vexillum

Barbados, Barbadian Bajan, Bim(m)

Barbara Allen, Major

Barbarian, Barbaric Boor, Fifteen, Foreigner, Goth, Heathen, Hottentot, Hun, Inhuman, Lowbrow, Outlandish, Philistine, Rude, Savage, Tatar(ic), Tartar

Barbary Ape, Roan

Barbecue Braai vleis, Cook-out, Flame-grill, Grill, Hangi, Hibachi, Roast, Spit

Barbel Beard

Barber Epilate, Figaro, Scrape(r), Shaver, Strap, Todd, Tonsor, Trimmer

Barbiturate Goofball

Bard Ariosto, Griot, Heine, Meat, Minstrel, Muse, Ossian, Scald, Scop, Skald, Taliesin

Bare, Bare-headed Adamic, Aphyllous, Bald, Barren, Blank, Bodkin, Cere, Décolleté, Denude, Hush, Lewd, Marginal, Moon, ➤ NAKED, Open, Plain, Scant, Sear, Stark, Uncase, Uncover, Unveil

Barefoot Discalced, Unshod

Barely Hardly, Just, Merely, Scarcely, Scrimp

Bargain(ing) Barter, Chaffer, Champerty, ➤ CHEAP, Collective, Coup, Deal, Dicker, Find, Go, Haggle, Higgle, Horse-trade, Huckster, Option, ➤ PACT, Plea, Scoop, Snip, Steal, Trade, Trock, Troke, Truck, Wanworth, Wheeler-dealing

Barge Birlinn, Bucentaur, Budgero(w), Butty, Gabbard, Gabbart, Galley-foist, Hopper, Intrude, Jostle, Keel, Lighter, Nudge, Obtrude, Pra(a)m, Ram, Scow, ➤ SHIP, Trow, Wherry

▷ **Barge** may indicate an anagram

Bargee, Bargeman Keeler, Legger, Lighterman, Ram, Trow

Barium Ba, Witherite

Bark(ing) Angostura, Ayelp, Azedarach, Bass, Bast, Bay, Bowwow, Calisaya, Canella, Caribbee, Cascara, Cascarilla, Cassia, China, Cinchona, Cinnamon, Cork, Cortex, Cusparia, Honduras, Kina, Kinakina, Latration, Liber, Myrica, Peel, Pereira, Peruvian, Quebracho, Quest, Quillai, Quina, Quinquina, Rind, Salian, Sassafras, Scrape, ➤ SHIP, Skin, Tan, Tap(p)a, Totaquine, Waff, Waugh, Woof, Wow, Yaff, ➤ YAP, Yelp, Yip

Bar-keeper, Barmaid, Barman Advocate, Ale-wife, Bencher, Hebe, Luckie, Lucky, Tapster, Underskinker

Barley Awn, Bear, Bere, Bigg, Hordeum, Malt, Pearl, Truce, Tsamba

Barmecide, Barmecidal Imaginary

Barn Bank, Byre, Cowshed, Dutch, Grange, Skipper, Tithe

Barnaby Rudge

Barnacle Acorn, Cypris, Goose(neck), Limpet

Barometer Aneroid, Glass, Statoscope, Sympiesometer, Torricellian tube, Weatherglass

Baron B, Corvo, Drug, Munchausen, Noble, Thyssen, Tycoon

Baronet Bart

Baronne Dudevant Sand

Baroque Gothic, Ornate, Rococo

▷ **Baroque** may indicate an anagram

Barrack(s), Barracking Asteism, Boo, Cantonment, Casern(e), Cat-call, Garrison, Heckle, Irony, Quarters

Barrage Balloon, Fusillade, Heat, Salvo

Barred Banned, Edh, Trabeculated

Barrel(-stand) Bl, Butt, Cade, Capstan, Cascabel, Cask, Clavie, Drum, Hogshead, Keg, Kibble, Morris-tube, Organ, Pièce, Run(d)let, Tan-vat, Thrall, Tierce, Tun, Vat, Wood

Barrel-organ Apollonicum, Hurdy-gurdy

Barren Addle, Arid, Badlands, Blind, Blunt, Clear, Dry, Eild, ➤ EMPTY, Farrow, Hirstie, Jejune, Sterile, Unbearing, Waste, Wasteland, Wilderness, Yeld, Yell

Barricade, Barrier Bail, Barrage, Bayle, Block, Breakwater, Cauld, Cheval de frise, Chicane, Cordon (sanitaire), Crash, Crush, ➤ DAM, Defence, Drawgate, Dyke, Fence, Fraise, Gate, Hedge, Hurdle, Mach, Obstruct, Rail(-fence), Rampart, Restraint, Revetment, Roadblock, Sonic, Sound, Spina, Stockade, Tollgate, Turnpike, Turnstile, ➤ WALL

Barrister Advocate, Attorney, Counsel, Devil, Lawyer, Rumpole, Serjeant(-at-law), Silk, Templar, Utter

Barrow Dolly, Handcart, Henge, How, Hurley, Kurgan, Molehill, Mound, Pushcart, Tram, Trolley, Truck, Tumulus

Barrow-boy Coster, Trader

Bar-tail Scamel, Staniel, Stannel

Barter Chaffer, Chop, Dicker, ➤ EXCHANGE, Haggle, Hawk, Niffer, Sco(u)rse, Swap, ➤ TRADE, Traffic, Truck

Basalt Diabase, Toadstone, Traprock, Wacke

Base(ness) Adenine, Alkali, Bed, Beggarly, Billon, Bottom, Caitiff, Camp, Codon, Cytosine, Degenerate, Degraded, Dog, Down, E, Erinite, ➤ ESTABLISH, Floor, Foot, Foothold, Footstall, Found, Fundus, Guanine, Harlot, Ignoble, Infamous, Install, Lewis, ➤ LOW, ➤ MEAN, Nefarious, Nook, Partite, Patten, Platform, Plinth, Podium, Premise, Ptomaine, Purin(e), Pyrimidine, Pyrrolidine, Radix, Rascally, Rests, Ribald, Root, Rosaniline, Servile, Shameful, Shand, Sheeny, Socle, Soda, Staddle, ➤ STAND, Station, Substrate, Ten, Thymine, Torus, Triacid, Turpitude, Unworthy, Uracil, Vile

Baseball Nine

Baseless Idle, Unfounded, Ungrounded

Base-line Datum

Basement Bargain

Bash Belt, Clout, Go, Hit, Rave, Shot, Slog, Strike, Swat, Swipe

Bashful Awed, Blate, Coy, Modest, Retiring, Shamefast, Sheep-faced, Sheepish, ➤ SHY

Basic(s), Basis ABC, Abcee, Alkaline, Aquamanale, Aquamanile, Crude, ➤ ESSENTIAL, Fiducial, Fond, Fundamental, Ground(work), Gut, Integral, Intrinsic, Logic, Nitty-gritty, No-nonsense, Primordial, Principle, Radical, Rudimentary, Spit-and-sawdust, Staple, Substance, Underlying, Uracil

Basilisk Cannon, Lizard

Basin Aquamanale, Aquamanile, Artesian, Benitier, Bidet, Bowl, Canning, Catch, Cirque, Corrie, Cwm, Dish, Dock, Doline, Donets, Foxe, Geosyncline, Great, Impluvium, Lavabo, Laver, Minas, Monteith, Pan, Park, Piscina, Playa, Porringer, Reservoir, Scapa Flow, Slop, Stoop, Stoup, Tank, Tidal

Bask Apricate, Revel, Sun, ➤ WALLOW

Basket, Basket-work Baalam, Bass, Bassinet, Bread, Buck, Cabas, Calathus, Canephorus, Car, Cesta, Cob, Coop, Corbeil(le), Corbicula, Corf, Creel, Cresset, Dosser, Fan, Flasket, Frail, Gabian, Hamper, Hask, Junket, Kago, Kajawah, Kipe, Kit, Leap, Maund, Mocock, Mocuck, Moses, Murlain, Murlan, Murlin, Osiery, Pannier, Ped, Petara, Pitara(h), Pottle, Punnet, Rip, Scull, Scuttle, Seed-lip, Skep, Skull, Trug, Van, Wagger-pagger(-bagger), Waste(-paper), Wattlework, Whisket, Wicker(-work), Will(e), Wisket

Basket-bearer Canephor(a), Canephore, Canephorus

Basket-maker Alfa, Cane, Halfa, Wicker

Basque Euskarian

Bass Alberti, Ale, Alfie, B, Continuo, Deep, El-a-mi, Fish, Low, Ostinato, Serran

Bast Liber

Bastard, Bastard-wing Alula, Base, By-blow, Git, Illegitimate, Mamzer, Mongrel, Momzer, Sassaby, Side-slip, Slink, Spuriae, Spurious, Whoreson

▷ **Bastard** may indicate an anagram

Baste Enlard, Sew, Stitch, Tack

Bastion Citadel, Lunette, Moineau

Bat(ter), Bats, Batting, Batsman, Batty Aliped, Ames, Assail, Barbastelle, Baton, Blink, Chiroptera, Close, Cosh, Crackers, Dad, Die Fledermaus, Eyelid, Flittermouse, Grace, Hatter, Haywire, Hit, Hobbs, Hook, Horseshoe, In, Ink mouse, Kalong, Language, Leisler, Man, Mastiff, Maul, May, Mormops, Myopic, Nictate, Nictitate, Night, Nightwatchman, Noctilio, Nora, Opener, Pinch-hit, Pipistrel(le), Poke, Pummel, Racket, Racquet, Ram, Rearmouse, Reremice, Reremouse, Roussette, Ruin, Sauch, Saugh, Serotine, Sledge, Stick, Stonewall, Striker, Swat, Vampire, Vespertilionid, Viv, Whacky, Willow, Wood

Batch Bake, Bunch

Bath(room) Aeson's, Bagnio, Bain-marie, Bed, Blanket, Bubble, Caldarium, Cor, En suite, Epha, Foam, Hammam, Hip, Hummaum, Hummum, Jacuzzi®, Laver, Mik vah, Mustard, Piscina, Plunge, Sauna, Sitz, Slipper, Spa, Steam, Stew, Stop, Tepidarium, Therm, Tub, Turkish, Tye, Whirlpool, Wife

Bathe, Bathing Balneal, Balneation, Balneology, Bay(e), Beath, Bogey, Bogie, Dip, Dook, Embay, Foment, Immerse, Lave, Lip, Skinny-dip, Souse, Splash, Stupe, ➤ SWIM, Tub, ➤ WASH

Batman Valet

Baton Mace, Rod, Sceptre, Staff, Truncheon

Batrachian Frog, Toad

▷ **Bats, Batting** may indicate an anagram

Battalion Bn, Corps, Troop

Batten Fasten, Tie

Batter(ed) Bombard, Bruise, Buffet, Decrepit, Pound

Battery Artillery, Drycell, Field, Henhouse, Nicad, Pra(a)m, Solar, Troop, Voltaic, Waffle

Battle, Battleground Action, Affair, ➤ BATTLES, Ben, Clash, Cockpit, Combat, ➤ CONFLICT, Encounter, Engagement, Field, ➤ FIGHT, Fray, Front, Joust, Royal, Sarah, Sciamachy, Skiamachy, Spurs, Stoor, Stour, Stowre, Theatre, Wage, ➤ WAR

Battle-axe Amazon, Bill, Gorgon, Halberd, Ogress, Sparth(e), Termagant, Termagent, Turmagant, Turmagent

Battlement Barmkin, Crenellate, Merlon, Rampart

Battle-order Phalanx

Battleship Carrier, Destroyer, Dreadnought, Gunboat, Man-o'-war, Potemkin

Bauble Bagatelle, Gaud, Gewgaw, Trifle

Bauhaus Gropius

Baulk Demur, Gib, Hen, Impede, Jib, Shy, Thwart

Bavardage Fadaise

Bawdy Raunchy, Sculdudd(e)ry, Skulduddery

Bawl Bellow, Gollar, Howl, Weep

BATTLES

3 letters:
Kut
Ulm
4 letters:
Alma
Ivry
Jena
Laon
Loos
Mons
Nile
Zama
5 letters:
Accra
Alamo
Allia
Arcot
Arras
Boyne
Bulge
Crecy
Issus
Lewes
Marne
Parma
Sedan
Somme
Ypres
6 letters:
Actium
Argyle
Arnhem

Camlan
Cannae
Maldon
Naseby
Senlac
Shiloh
Varese
Verdun
Vigrid
Wagram
Wipers
7 letters:
Aboukir
Alamein
Beaches
Britain
Bull Run
Cambrai
Colenso
Coronel
Corunna
Dunkirk
Flodden
Flowers
Glencoe
Jutland
Lepanto
Magenta
Marengo
Nations
Picardy
Plassey

Salamis
Warburg
8 letters:
Ardennes
Blenheim
Borodino
Bosworth
Clontarf
Culloden
Edgehill
Flanders
Hastings
Inkerman
Marathon
Navarino
Omdurman
Philippi
Poitiers
Ragnarok
Saratoga
Talavera
Waterloo
9 letters:
Agincourt
Balaclava
Caporetto
Gallipoli
Otterburn
Oudenarde

Pharsalia
Ramillies
Sedgemoor
Solferino
Theomachy
Trafalgar
Worcester
10 letters:
Armageddon
Austerlitz
Bunker Hill
Camperdown
Gettysburg
Lundy's Lane
Stalingrad
Steenkerke
11 letters:
Bannockburn
Hohenlinden
Marston Moor
Prestonpans
Thermopylae
Wounded Knee
12 letters:
Flodden Field
13 letters:
Bosworth Field
Passchendaele

Bay Ab(o)ukir, Arm, Baffin, Bantry, Bark, Bell, Bengal, Bight, Biscay, Bonny, Botany, Broken, Byron, Cardigan, Chesapeake, Cove, Covelet, Creek, Daphne, Delogoa, Discovery, Dvina, False, Fleet, Frobisher, Fundy, Galway, Georgian, Glace, Golden, Green, Harbour, Hawke's, Herne, Horse, ➤ HOWL, Hudson, Inlet, James, Jervis, Laura, Laurel, Lobito, MA, Manila, Massachusetts, Narragansett, Niche, Oleander, Oriel, Pegasus, Pigs, Poverty, Recess, Red, Roan, Shark, Sick, Sligo, Suvla, Tampa, Tasman, Thunder, Tralee, Ungava, Vae, Voe, Waff, Wash, Yowl

Bayonet Jab, Skewer, Stab

Bazaar Alcaiceria, Emporium, Fair, Fete, Market, Pantechnicon, Sale, Sook, Souk

BBC Auntie

Be Exist, Live

Beach Bondi, Coast, Ground, Hard, Lido, Littoral, Machair, Miami, Plage, Sand, Seaside, Shingle, Shore, Strand, Waikiki

Beachcomber Arenaria

Beacon Belisha, Fanal, Lightship, Need-fire, Pharos, Racon, Radar, Radio, Signal

Bead(s) Aggri, Aggry, Baily's, Ballotini, Bauble, Blob, Bugle, Chaplet, Crab-stones, Drop, Droplet, Gadroon, Gaud, Moniliform, Ojime, Paternoster, Poppet, Poppit, Prayer, Rosary, Tear, Wampum(peag), Worry

Beadle Apparitor, Bederal, Bedral, Bumble, Herald, Paritor, Verger

Beak AMA, Bailie, Bill, Cad, Cere, Coronoid, Gar, JP, Kip(p), Magistrate, Master, Metagnathous, Mittimus, Nasute, Neb, Nose, Pecker, Prow, Ram, Rostellum, Rostrum

Beaker Cup, Goblet

Beakless Erostrate

Beak-shaped Coracoid

Beam(ing) Arbor, Balance, Bar, Boom, Bowstring, Breastsummer, Bressummer, Broadcast, Bum(p)kin, Cantilever, Carling, Cathead, Collar, Deck, Girder, Grin, Hammer, Herisson, Holophote, I, Irradiate, Joist, Ke(e)lson, Laser, Lentel, Lintel, Manteltree, Needle, Outrigger, Particle, Pencil, Principal, Purlin, ➤ RAFTER, ➤ RAY, Rayon, Refulgent, Rident, Ridgepole, Rood, Scantling, Searchlight, Shaft, Shine, Sleeper, Smile, Solive, Stanchion, Stemson, Sternpost, Streamer, Stringer, Summer, Support, Tie, Timber, Trabeate, Trabecula, Transom, Trave, Trimmer, Truss, Universal, Viga, Yard

Beamish Galumphing, Nephew

Bean(s) Abrus, Adsuki, Arabica, Berry, Black, Black-eye, Borlotti, Broad, Bush, Butter, Cacao, Calabar, Castor, Cocoa, Coffee, Cow-pea, Fabaceous, Fava, Flageolet, French, Frijol(e), Garbanzo, Gram, Haricot, Harmala, Head, Horse, Jack, Jumping, Kidney, Lablab, Lentil, Lima, Locust, Molucca, Moth, Mung, Nelumbo, Nib, Noddle, Ordeal, Pichurim, Pinto, Runner, Snap, Soy(a), String, Sugar, Tonga, Tonka, Tonquin, Urd, Wax, Winged

Beanfeast ➤ PARTY, Spree, Wayzgoose

Bear(er), Bearish Abide, Andean, Arctic, Baloo, Balu, Beer, Bigg, Breed, Brook, Brown, Bruin, Brunt, ➤ CARRY, Churl, Cinnamon, Coati-mondi, Coati-mundi, Demean, Dree, Ean, ➤ ENDURE, Engender, Exert, Fur-seal, Gonfalonier, Grizzly, Hack, Ham(m)al, Have, Hold, Honey, Humf, Hump(h), Jampani, Keb, Koala, Kinkajou, Kodiak, Koolah, Lioncel(le), Lionel, Lug, Mother, Nandi, Owe, Paddington, Panda, Polar, Pooh, Rac(c)oon, Rupert, Russia, Sackerson, Seller, Shoulder, Sit, Sloth, Spectacled, Stand, Stay, Stomach, ➤ SUFFER, Sunbear, Sustain, Targeteer, Teddy, Teem, Thole, Throw, Tolerate, Tote, Undergo, Upstay, Ursine, Whelp, Wield, Woolly, Yield

Bearberry Manzanita

Beard(ed) Arista, Awn, Balaclava, Barb, Beaver, Charley, Charlie, Confront, Defy, Face, Five o'clock shadow, Fungus, Goatee, Hair(ie), Hairy, Hear(ie), Imperial, Kesh, Mephistopheles, Outface, Peak, Rivet, Stubble, Vandyke, Whiskerando, Whiskery, Ziff

Beardless Callow, Clean, Tahr, Tehr

▷ **Bearhug** may indicate Teddy or similar around a word

Bearing(s) Air, Amenaunce, Armorial, Aspect, Azimuth, Babbitt, Ball, Behaviour, Bush, Carriage, Deportment, Direction, E, Endurance, Gait,

Hatchment, Manner, Mascle, Mien, N, Nor, Pheon, Port, Presence, Reference, Relevant, S, Tenue, Thrust, W, Yielding
▷ **Bearing** may indicate compass points

Beast(ly) ➤ ANIMAL, Arna, Behemoth, Brute, Caliban, Caribou, ➤ CREATURE, Dieb, Dragon, Dzeren, Gayal, Genet, Grampus, Hippogriff, Hog, Hy(a)ena, Jumart, Kinkajou, Lion, Mammoth, Marmot, Mastodon, Mhorr, Oliphant, Opinicus, Oryx, Panda, Potto, Quagga, Rac(c)oon, Rhytina, Rother, Sassaby, Steer, Sumpter, Tarand, Teg, Theroid, Triceratops, Wart-hog, Whangam, Yahoo, Yak, Yale, Zizel

Beat(er), Beaten, Beating Anoint, Arsis, Athrob, Bandy, Bang, Baste, Bastinado, Batter, Battue, Belabour, Belt, Bepat, Best, Blatter, Bless, Cadence, Cane, Chastise, Clobber, Club, Clump, Conquer, Cream, Cuff, Curry, Debel, ➤ DEFEAT, Ding, Donder, Dress, Drub, Excel, Fatigue, Faze, Feague, Feeze, Fibbed, Flagellate, Flail, Flam, Float, Flog, Floor, Flush, Fly, Fustigate, Hollow, Horsewhip, Ictus, Inteneration, Knock, Knubble, Lace, Laidie, Laidy, Lambast(e), Larrup, Lash, Laveer, Lay, Lick, Lilt, Lounder, Mall, Malleate, Mersey, Nubble, Outclass, Outdo, Outflank, Outstrip, Paik, Palpitate, Pash, Paste, Pommel, Pound, Prat, Pug, Pulsate, Pulse, Pulsedge, Pummel, Pun, Quop, Raddle, Ram, Ratten, Resolve, Retreat, Rhythm, Ribroast, Round, Rowstow, Ruff(le), Scourge, Scutch, Slat, Smight, Smite, Soak, Sock, Strak, Strike, Swinge, Systole, Taber, Tabor, Tabrere, Tachycardia, Tact, Tala, Tattoo, Thesis, Thrash, Thresh, Throb, Thud, Thump, Thwack, Tick, Tired, Top, Torture, Tricrotic, Trounce, Tuck, Tund, Verberate, Vibrate, Wallop, Wappend, Welt, Wham, Whip, Whisk, Whitewash, Wraught, Ybet, Yerk, Yirk
▷ **Beaten-up** may indicate an anagram

Beat it Skedaddle, Vamo(o)se

Beatitude Macarism

Beau Admirer, Blade, Brummel, Cat, Damoiseau, Dandy, Flame, Geste, Lover, Masher, Nash, Spark, Tibbs

Beaufort Scale, Windscale

Beaut(y) Advantage, Belle, Camberwell, Charmer, Colleen, Corker, Dish, Glory, Houri, Hyperion, Lana, Monism, Picture, Pride, Pulchritude, Purler, Sheen, Smasher, Stunner

Beautiful, Beautify Bonny, Bright, Embellish, Enhance, Fair, Fine, Ornament, Pink, Smicker, Specious, To kalon

Beauty spot Patch, Tempe, Tika

Beaver Beard, Castor, Eager, Grind, Oregon, Rodent, Sewellel

Because (of) As, Forasmuch, Forwhy, Hence, In, Inasmuch, Sens, Since

Beckon Gesture, Nod, Summons, Waft, Wave

Become, Becoming Apt, Besort, Decent, Decorous, Enter, Fall, Fit, Flatter, Get, Go, Grow, Happen, Occur, Seemly, Suit, Wax, Worth

Bed(ding), Bedstead Air, Allotment, Amenity, Apple-pie, Arroyo, Base, Bassinet, Berth, Bottom, Box, Bunk, Caliche, Camp, Carrycot, Channel, Charpoy, Cill, Cot(t), Couch(ette), Cradle, Crib, Cul(t)ch, Day, Divan, Doona, Doss, Duvet, Erf, Filter, Flying, Four-poster, Futon, Gault,

Greensand, Hammock, Inlay, Kang, Kip, Knot, Layer, Lilo®, Litter, Mat, Matrix, Mattress, Nap, Nest, Nookie, Pad, Paillasse, Pallet, Palliasse, Pan, Parterre, Pavement, Plant, Plot, Procrustean, Quilt, Retire, Roost, Sack, Scalp, Shakedown, Sill, Sitter, Sleep, Sofa, Stratum, Stretcher, Tanning, Test, Thill, Trough, Truckle, Trundle, Wadi, Wady, Ware, Water, Wealden

Bedaub Cake, Deck, Smear

Bed-bug B, B flat, Chinch, Flea, Louse, Vermin

Bedchamber, Bedroom Boudoir, Chamber, Cubicle, Dormer, Dorm(itory), Dorter, Ruelle, Ward

Bedcover Palampore, Palempore

Bedeck Adonise, Adorn, Array, Festoon

▷ **Bedevilled** may indicate an anagram

Bedjacket Nightingale

Bedlam Chaos, Furore, Madness, Nuthouse, Tumult, Uproar

Bed-rest Dutch-wife

Bee Athenia, Bumble, Carpenter, Cuckoo, Deseret, Drone, Drumbledor, Dumbledore, Group, Hiver, Honey, Humble, Killer, King, Lapidary, Leaf-cutter, Mason, Queen, Solitary, Spell, Spell-down, Swarm, Worker

Beech Hornbeam, Mast, Tree

Bee-eater Merops

Beef(y) Baron, Bleat, Brawny, Bresaola, Bull(y), Bullock, Carpaccio, Charqui, Chateaubriand, Chuck, Complain, Corned, Filet mignon, Groan, Grouse, Hough, Jerk, Liebig, Mart, Mice, Mousepiece, Muscle, Neat, Ox, Pastrami, Peeve, Porterhouse, Rother, Sauerbraten, Sey, Silverside, Sirloin, Stolid, Stroganoff, Tournedos, Tranche, Undercut, Vaccine

Beefeater Billman, Exon, Gin, Oxpecker, Warder, Yeoman

Bee-glue Propolis

Beehive Alveary, Ball, Gum, Skep

Beelzebub Devil

Beer Ale, Alegar, Bantu, Bitter, Bock, Chaser, Drink, Entire, Export, Gill, Ginger, Granny, Grog, Heavy, Kaffir, Keg, Kvass, Lager, Lambic, Lush, Malt, March, Middy, Mild, Mum, Near, Nog, October, Pils(e)ner, Pint, Pony, Porter, Root, Saki, Scoobs, Sherbet, Skeechan, Small, Spruce, Stingo, Stout, Swanky, Swats, Swipes, Switchel, Taplash, Tinnie, Tipper, Tshwala, Tube, Wallop, Zythum

Beer garden Brasserie

Bee's nest Bink

Beet Blite, Chard, Fat-hen, Goosefoot, Mangel(wurzel), Spinach

Beetle Ambrosia, Anobiid, Asiatic, Bacon, Bark, Batler, Bee, Blister, Bloody-nosed, Boll weevil, Bug, Bruchid, Bum-clock, Buprestidae, Buprestus, Burying, Bustle, Buzzard-clock, Cabinet, Cadelle, Cane, Cantharis, Carabus, Cardinal, Carpet, Carrion, Chafer, Christmas, Churchyard, Cicindela, Click, Clock, Cockchafer, Cockroach, Coleoptera, Colorado, Coprophagan, Darkling, Deathwatch, Dermestid, Devil's coach-horse, Diving, Dor(r), Dor-fly, Dumbledore, Dung, Dyticus, Dytiscus, Elater, Elytron, Elytrum, Firefly, Flea, Furniture, Glow-worm,

Goldsmith, Goliath, Gregor, Ground, Hammer, Hangover, Hercules, Hop-flea, Hornbug, Huhu, Humbuzz, Impend, Japanese, Jewel, June, Khapra, Ladybird, Ladybug, Lamellicorne, Larder, Leaf, Leather, Longhorn, Longicorn, Mall(et), Maul, May-bug, Meloid, Oakpruner, Oil, Overhang, Pinchbuck, Potato, Project, Protrude, Rhinoceros, Roach, Rosechafer, Rove, Scarab(ee), Scavenger, Scurry, Sexton, Skelter, Sledge(-hammer), Snapping, Snout, Spanish fly, Spider, Stag, Tenebrio, Tiger, Toktokkie, Tortoise, Tumble-bug, Tumble-dung, Turnip-flea, Typographer, Vedalia, VW, Water, Weevil, Whirligig, Wireworm, Woodborer, Wood-engraver

Beetle-crushers Cops

Befall Happen, Occur

Before(hand) A, Advance, Ante, Avant, By, Coram, Earlier, Early, Ere, Erst(while), ➤ FORMER, Or, Pre, Previously, Prior, Pro, Sooner, Till, To, Until, Van, Zeroth

Before food Ac

Befriend Assist, Cotton, Fraternise, Support

Befuddle Bemuse, Inebriate, Stupefy

Beg(gar), Beggarly, Begging Abr(ah)am-man, Ask, Badgeman, Beseech, Besognio, Bey, Bezonian, Blighter, Blue-gown, Cadge, Calendar, Clapper-dudgeon, Crave, ➤ ENTREAT, Exoration, Flagitate, Fleech, Gaberlunzie, Gangrel, Hallan-shaker, Implore, Impoverish, Irus, Jarkman, Lackall, Lazar(us), Lazzarone, Lumpenproletariat, Maund, Mendicant, Mump, Niggardly, Palliard, Panhandle, Pauper, Penelophon, Penniless, ➤ PLEAD, Pled, Pray, Prig, Prog, Ptochocracy, Rag, Randie, Randy, Ruffler, Sadhu, Schnorr(er), Screeve, Scrounge, Shool(e), Skelder, Skell, Solicit, Sue, Supplicate, Thig(ger), Toe-rag, Touch, Undo, Whipjack

Beget Gender

Beggar rule Ptochocracy

Begging bowl Clackdish, Clapdish

Begin(ning), Begun Ab ovo, Alpha, B, Cause, Clapdash, Commence, Daw, Dawn, Debut, Embryo, Enter, Exordium, Fall-to, Genesis, Germ, Go, Inaugural, Inception, Inchoate, Incipient, Incipit, Initial, Initiate, Intro, Lead, Learn, Logos, Nascent, Onset, Ope(n), Ord, ➤ ORIGIN, Outbreak, Pose, Prelim(inary), Seed, Set, ➤ START, Startup, Takeoff, To-fall, Yearn

Beginner Author, Black, Deb, Greenhorn, L, Learner, Neophyte, ➤ NOVICE, Primer, Rookie, Tenderfoot, Tiro, Tyro

Begone Aroint, Aroynt, Avaunt, Scram, Shoo, Vamo(o)se

Begonia Elephant's-ear(s)

Begorrah Bedad, Musha

Begrudge Envy, Resent

Beguile(r) Charm, Coax, Divert, Ensnare, Flatter, Gull, Intrigue, Jack-a-lantern, Wile

Behalf For, Part, Sake

Behave, Behaviour Act, Conduct, Convenance, Decorum, Demean, Do, Etepimeletic, Ethics, Horme, ➤ MANNER, Nature, Netiquette, Noblesse oblige, Obey, Praxeology, Quit, React, Response, Strong meat, Tribalism

Behead Decapitate, Decollate

Behind(hand) Abaft, Aft(er), Ahind, Ahint, Apoop, Arear, Arere, Arrear, Astern, Beneath, Bottom, Bum, Buttocks, Croup, Derrière, Fud, Late, Overdue, Prat, ➤ REAR, Slow, Tushie

Behold(en) Affine, Ecce, Eye, Indebted, La, Lo, Look, Observe, See, View

Beige Greige, Tan

Being Cratur, Creature, Ens, Entia, Entity, Esse, Essence, Existence, Human, Man, Metaphysics, Mode, Nature, Omneity, Ontology, ➤ PERSON, Saul, Soul, Subsistent, Substance, Wight

Bejabers Arrah

Belch Boak, Boke, Brash, Burp, Emit, Eruct, Rift, Spew, Yex

Belcher Foulard, Handkerchief, Toby

Beldam(e) Crone, Hag, Harridan, Scold

Belfry Campanile, Tower

Belgian Flemish, Walloon

Belief, Believe(r), Believed, Believing Accredit, Ativism, Bigot, Buy, Conviction, Credence, Credit, Creed, Cult, Culture, Deem, Deist, Doctrine, Doxastic, Doxy, Dukkha, Faith, Formulism, Gnostic, Heterodoxy, Hold, Holist, Idea, Islam, Ism, Ludism, Manichaeism, Messianist, Methink, Notion, ➤ OPINION, Ovist, Pantheism, Persuasion, Physicism, Pluralism, Presumption, Religion, Reputed, Seeing, Solfidian, Superstition, Tenet, Theist, Think, Threap, Threep, Trinitarian, Trow, Trust, Ubiquitarianism, Unitarian, Wear, Wis(t)

Belittle Cheapen, Decry, Depreciate, Derogate, Discredit, Disparage, Humble, Slight

Bell(s) Angelus, Ben, Bob, Bow, Bronte, Cachecope, Canterbury, Carillon, Chime, Crotal, Curfew, Daisy, Diving, Division, Gong, Grandsire, Jar, Low, Lutine, Passing, Pavilion, Peal, Peter, Pinger, Ring, Roar, Sacring, Sanctus, Tailor, Tantony, Tenor, Tent, Tintinnabulum, Toll, Tom, Triple, Tubular, Vair

Bell-bird Arapunga, Campanero

Belle Beauty, Starr, Toast, Venus

Bell-founder Belleter

Bellicose, Belligerent Chippy, Combatant, Gung-ho, Hostile, Jingoist, Martial, Militant, Truculent, Warmonger

Bellow(s) Buller, Holla, Holler, Moo, Rant, Rave, Roar, Saul, Thunder, Troat, Tromp(e), Trumpet, Windbag

Bell-ringer, Bell-ringing Bob, Campanology, Changes, Clapper, Course, Grandsire, Hunting, Quasimodo, Rope, Sally, Tocsin, Toller

Belly Abdomen, Alvine, Bag, Beer, Bunt, Calipee, Celiac, Coeliac, Kite, Kyte, Pod, ➤ STOMACH, Swell, Tum(my), Venter, Wame, Weamb, Wem(b), Womb

Belonging(s) Apply, Appurtenant, Chattels, Effects, Inhere, Intrinsic, Paraphernalia, Pertain, ➤ PROPERTY, Relate, Traps

Beloved Alder-lief, David, Dear, Esme, Inamorata, Joy, Lief, Pet, Popular, Precious

Below Beneath, Inf(erior), Infra, Nether, Sub, Under, Unneath

Belt(ed) Baldric(k), Band, Bandoleer, Bandolier, Baudric(k), Bible, Black, Cartridge, Chastity, Clitellum, Clobber, Commuter, Conveyor, Copper, Cotton, Crios, Equator, Fan, Gird(le), Girt, Inertial, Kuiper, Judoka, Larrup, Life, Lonsdale, Mitre, Orion, Orogenic, Polt, Pound, Roller, Safety, Sam Browne, Sash, Seat, Speed, Stockbroker, Storm, Strap, Surcingle, Stratosphere, Suspender, Swipe, Taiga, Tear, Tore, Tract, Van Allen, Wanty, Webbing, Wing, Zodiac, Zone, Zoster

Belt up Sh

Belvedere Gazebo, Mirador

Bemoan ➤ LAMENT, Mourn, Sigh, Wail

Bemuse Infatuate, Stonn(e), Stun, Stupefy, Throw

Ben Battle, Hur, Jonson, Mountain, Nevis, Spence

Bench Banc, Bink, Counter, Court, Cross, Exedra, Form, Knifeboard, Magistrates, Pew, Rusbank, ➤ SEAT, Settle, Siege, Stillage, Thoft, Thwart, Treasury, Trestle

Benchmark Yardstick

Bend(er), Bending, Bends Angle, Arc, Arch, Articular, Bight, Binge, Buck(le), Bust, Camber, Carrick, Chicane, Circumflect, Corner, Crank(le), Cringe, ➤ CROOK, Curl, Curve, Diffraction, Dog-leg, Elbow, Engouled, Epinasty, Es(s), Falcate, Fawn, Flex(ural), Flexion, Flexure, Fold, Geller, Geniculate, Genu, Genuflect, Grecian, Hairpin, Hinge, Hook, Horseshoe, Hunch, Inflect, Knee(cap), Kneel, Knot, Kowtow, Mould, Nutant, Ox-bow, Plash, Plié, Ply, Recline, Reflex, Retorsion, Retortion, Retroflex, Riband, S, Scarp, Souse, Spree, Spring, Stave, Stoop, Swan-neck, Twist, U, Ups(e)y, Uri, Wale, Warp, ➤ YIELD, Z

▷ **Bendy** may indicate an anagram

Beneath Below, Sub, Under, Unworthy

Benedict(ine) Cluniac, Dom, Eggs, Olivetan, OSB, Tironensian, Tyronensian

Benediction Blessing, God-speed

Benefactor Angel, Backer, Barmecide, Carnegie, Donor, Maecenas, ➤ PATRON, Promoter

Benefice, Beneficial, Beneficiary, Benefit ➤ AID, Avail, Behalf, Behoof, Behove, Boon, Boot, Charity, Collature, Commendam, Commensal, Devisee, Dole, Donee, Endorsee, Enure, FIS, Fringe, Incumbent, Inure, Invalidity, Living, Ménage, Neckverse, Pay, Perk, Perquisite, Portioner, Postulate, Prebend, Profit, Sake, Salutary, Sanative, Sinecure, Spin-off, Stipend, Supplementary, Unemployment, Use, Usufruct

Benevolence, Benevolent Charitable, Clement, Humanitarian, Kind, Liberal, Philanthropy

Benighted Ignorant

Benign Affable, Altruistic, Gracious, Kindly, Trinal

Benin DY
Benito Duce, Mussolini
Benjamin Franklin
Bennett Alan, Phil
Bent Akimbo, Bowed, Brae, Coudé, Courb, Crooked, Curb, Determined,
   Dorsiflex, Falcate, Fiorin, Flair, Habit, Heath, Inclination, Ingenium, Intent,
   Leant, Peccant, Penchant, Ply, Reclinate, Redtop, Scoliotic, Talent, Taste
▷ **Bent** may indicate an anagram
Bent grass Fiorin, Redtop
Bentham Utilitarian
Benzine Kinone, Phene, Toluene, Toluol
Bequeath, Bequest Bestow, Chantr(e)y, Demise, Endow, Heirloom,
   ➤ LEAVE, Legacy, Mortification, Pittance, Transmit, Will
Berate Censure, Chide, Jaw, Reproach, Scold, Slate, Vilify
Berber Almoravide, Kabyle, Riff, Tuareg
Bereave(d), Bereavement Deprive, Loss, Mourning, Orb, Sorrow, Strip,
   Widow
Berg Alban, Floe
Bermuda Shorts
Bernard Levin, Shaw
Bernini Baroque
Berry Allspice, Bacca, Cubeb, Fruit, Goosegog, Haw, Pepo, Pimento,
   Pottage, Rhein, Rhine, Sal(l)al, Slae, Sloe, Sop, Tomatillo
Berserk Amok, Baresark, Frenzy, Gungho, Rage
Berth Anchorage, Bunk, Cabin, Couchette, Dock, Moor, Seat, Space
Beryl Aquamarine, Emerald, Heliodor, Morganite, Silica
Beryllium Be
Beseech Beg, Crave, Entreat, Implore, Invoke, Obsecrate
Beset Amidst, Assail, Assiege, Badger, Bego, Environ, Harry, Perplex,
   Scabrid, Siege
Beside(s) Adjacent, Alone, And, At, Au reste, Else, Forby, Moreover, Next,
   On, Withal
Besiege(d) Beset, Best(ed), Blockade, Gherao, Girt, Invest, Obsess, Plague,
   Surround
▷ **Besiege** may indicate one word around another
Besmirch Smear, Soil, Sully
Besom Cow, Kow
Besot(ted) Dotard, Infatuate, Intoxicate, Lovesick, Stupefy
Bespangle Adorn, Gem
Bespeak, Bespoken Address, Bee, Beta, Engage, Hint
Best A1, Ace, Aristocrat, Beat, Choice, Cream, Creme, Damnedest, Deluxe,
   Elite, Eximious, Finest, Flower, Foremost, Greatest, Ideal, Optima, Outdo,
   Outwit, Overcome, Peak, Peerless, Pick, Pink, Plum, Purler, Ream, Super,
   The, Tiptop, Top, Topper, Transcend, Wale
Bestiary Physiologus

Best man Paranymph
Bestow Accord, Bequeath, Donate, ➤ GIVE, Impart, Present
Bestride Cross
Bet, Betting System A cheval, Ante, Back, Banco, Double, Flutter, Gaff,
 Gamble, Go, Hedge, Impone, Lay, Long shot, Martingale, Mise, Note,
 Pari-mutuel, Perfecta, Pip, Punt, Quadrella, Quinella, Ring, Risk, Saver, Set,
 Spec, Sport, Stake, Tattersalls, Tatts, Totalisator, Totalise, Tote, Treble,
 Triella, Trifecta, ➤ WAGE(R), Yankee
Betel Catechu, Pan, Pawn, Siri(h)
Betimes Anon, Early, Soon
Betise Solecism
Betray(al), Betrayer Abandon, Abuse, Belewe, Cornuto, Desert, Divulge,
 Dob, Double-cross, Giveaway, Grass, Judas, Renegade, Renege, Rumble,
 Sell, Sellout, Shop, Sing, Sinon, Stab, Traditor, Traitor, Treachery, Treason,
 Turncoat
Betroth(ed), Betrothal Assure, Engage, Ensure, Espouse, Fiancé(e),
 Pledge, Subarr(h)ation
Better Abler, Amend, Apter, Bigger, Buck, Cap, Fairer, Gambler, Gamester,
 Imponent, Improve, Meliorate, Mend, Outdo, Outpoint, Preponderate,
 Punter, Race-goer, Reform, Superior, Surpass, Throw, Top, Turfite, Worst
Between Amid, Bet, Betwixt, Inter, Interjacent, Linking, Mesne, Twixt
Bevel Angle, Cant, Oblique, Slope, Splay
Beverage Ale, Cocoa, Coffee, Cordial, Cup, ➤ DRINK, Nectar, Tea
Bevy Flock, Group, Herd, Host
Beware Cave, Fore, Heed, Mind, Mistrust
Bewilder(ed), Bewilderment Amaze, Baffle, Buffalo, Confuse,
 Consternation, Daze, Flummox, Mate, Maze, Mystify, Perplex, Stun,
 Taivert, Will, Wull
Bewitch(ing) Charm, Delight, Enchant, Ensorcell, Glam(orous), Hex, Jinx,
 Obeah, Obiah, Strike
Beyond Above, Ayont, Besides, Farther, Outwith, Over, Thule, Trans,
 Ulterior
Bias(ed) Angle, Bent, Discriminatory, Imbalance, One-sided, Partial, Parti
 pris, Partisan, Penchant, Predilection, ➤ PREJUDICE, Prepossess, Skew,
 Slope, Tendency, Warp
Bib, Bibulous Apron, Beery, Feeder, Pout, Tope, Tucker
Bibelot Objet d'art
Bible Alcoran, Alkoran, Antilegomena, Apocrypha, Authority, AV, Avesta,
 Bamberg, Book, Breeches, Coverdale, Cramer, Cromwell, Douai, Douay,
 Family, Gemara, Geneva, Gideon, Good book, Goose, Gospel, Hexapla,
 Itala, Italic, King James (version), Leda, Mazarin(e), Midrash, Missal,
 Murderer, NT, Omasum, OT, Pentateuch, Peshito, Peshitta, Peshitto,
 Polyglot, Psalter, Revised Version, ➤ RSV, RV, Scriptures, Septuagint,
 Stomach, Talmud, Tanach, Tantra, Targum, Taverners, Tyndale, Vinegar,
 Vulgate, Whig, Wyclif(fe), Zurich
Biblical scholar Rechabite, USPG, Wycliffe

Bibliophagist, Bibliophile Bookworm

Bicker Argue, Bowl, Brawl, Coggie, Dispute, Tiff, Wrangle

Bicycle, Bike Bone-shaker, Coaster, Dandy-horse, Draisene, Draisine, Hobby, Mixte, Moped, Mount, Mountain, Ordinary, Pedal, Penny-farthing, Raleigh®, Roadster, Safety, Scooter, Spin, Tandem, Velocipede

Bid(der), Bidding system Acol, Apply, Call, Canape, Command, Contract, Declare, Double, Gone, Invite, Misère, Nod, NT, ➤ OFFER, Order, Pass, Pre-empt, Proposal, Puffer, Redouble, Summon, Take-over, Tell, Tender, Vied

Biddy Gammer

Biennial Trieteric

Bier Hearse, Litter

Big Beamy, Bulky, Bumper, Burly, Cob, Enormous, Fat, Ginormous, Gross, ➤ LARGE, Loud, Massive, Mighty, Obese, Skookum, Slockdoliger, Slockdologer, Soc(k)dologer, Sogdolager, Sogdoliger, Stonker, Thumping, Tidy, Vast, Whacker, Whopper

Bigamy, Bigamist, Bigamous Bluebeard, Diandrous

Bigot(ed) Chauvinist, Dogmatist, Fanatic, Hide-bound, Intolerant, Racialist, Wowser, Zealot

Bigshot, Bigwig Cheese, Nob, Oner, Oneyer, Oneyre, Swell, ➤ VIP

Bijou Doll-like

➤ **Bike** see BICYCLE

Bikini Atoll, Tanga

Bile, Bilious(ness) Cholaemia, Choler, Gall, Icteric, Melancholy, Scholaemia, Venom

Bilge Leak, Pump, Rot, Waste

Bilingual Diglot

Bill(y) Ac(c), Accompt, Account, Act, Ad, Addition, Barnacle, Beak, Becke, Budd, Buffalo, Can, Carte, Chit(ty), Cody, Coo, Coronoid, Dixy, Docket, Double, Exactment, Fin, Finance, Goat, Hybrid, Invoice, Kaiser, ➤ LAW, Lawin(g), Legislation, Liam, Liar, List, Measure, Menu, Neb, Ness, Nib, ➤ NOTE, Notice, Poster, Private, Programme, Public, Reckoning, Reform, Remanet, Rhamphotheca, Rostral, Rostrum, Score, Shot, Sickle, Silly, Sparth(e), Sperthe, Spoon, Sticker, Tab, Tomium, Treasury, Willy

Billet Berth, Casern, Chit, Coupon, Note, Quarter

Billet doux Capon, Valentine

Billiards, Billiards player, Billiards stroke Bar, Cueist, Jenny, Massé, Pool, Potter, Pyramids, Snooker, Whitechapel

Billion Gillion, Milliard, Tera

Bill of sale Bs

Billow Roil, Roller, Rule, Surge, Swell, Wave

Bin Bing, Box, Container, Crib, Hell, Receptacle, Snake-pit, Stall, Wagger-pagger, Wheelie, Wheely

Binary ASCII

Bind(er), Binding Adherent, Akedah, Apprentice, Astrict, Astringent, Bale, Bandage, Bandeau, Bandster, Bias, Bibliopegist, Brail, Calf, Chain, Cinch, Clamp, Colligate, Complain, Cord, Cummerbund, Deligation, Drag, Edge, Embale, Enchain, Engage, ➤ FASTEN, Fetter, Galloon, Gird, Girdle, Grolier, Hay-wire, Hold, Incumbent, Indenture, Iron, Keckle, Lash(er), Leash, Ligament, Ligature, Mail, Marl, Morocco, Muslin, Obi, Obligate, Oblige, Oop, Organdie, Oup, Parpen, Pinion, Raffia, Restrict, ➤ ROPE, Roxburghe, Sheaf, Strap, Stringent, Stygian, Swathe, Syndesis, Tether, Thirl, Thong, Three-quarter, Tie, Tree-calf, Truss, Twine, Valid, Whip, Withe, Yapp, Yerk, Yoke

Bindweed Bearbine, Convolvulus, With(y)wind

Bing Crosby, Go, Heap

Binge Bat, Beano, Bend(er), Blind, Carouse, ➤ DRINK, Drinking-bout, Party, Riot, Soak, Souse, Spree, Toot, Tout

Bingo Beano, Housey-housey, Lotto, Tombola

Binocular(s) Glasses, OO, Stereoscope

Biochemical DNA

Biographer, Biography Boswell, CV, Hagiography, History, Life, Memoir, Plutarch, Potted, Prosopography, Suetonius, Vita

Biologist, Biology Cladistics, Mendel, Phenetics

Bioscope Kinema

Birch Birk, Cane, Cow, Flog, Hazel, Kow, Larch, Reis, Rice, Rod, Silver, Swish, Twig, Whip, Withe

Bird Al(l)erion, Bertram, Brood, Damsel, Doll, Early, Flier, Fowl, Gal, ➤ GIRL, Grip, Hen, Left, Pecker, Pen, Poultry, Quod, Raptor, Roaster, Sis, Skirt

BIRDS

2 letters:	4 letters:	Huma	Pyot
Ka	Aves	Ibis	Rail
3 letters:	Barb	Iynx	Rhea
Ani	Chat	Jynx	Roch
Auk	Cirl	Kagu	Rook
Boo	Cobb	Kaka	Ruff
Cob	Coly	Kite	Ruru
Emu	Coot	Kiwi	Rype
Fum	Crax	Knot	Shag
Jay	Crow	Kora	Smee
Kae	Dodo	Lark	Sora
Kea	➤ DUCK	Loon	Swan
Maw	Dove	Lory	Taha
Mew	Emeu	Lyre	Teal
Moa	Erne	Mina	Tern
Nun	Eyas	Monk	Tody
Owl	Fung	Myna	Tuli
Pea	Gled	Otis	Weka
Pie	Guan	Pavo	Wren
Ree	Guga	Pawn	Xema
Roc	Gull	Pern	Yale
Ruc	Hawk	Piet	Yite
Tit	Hern	Pink	**5 letters:**
Tui	Huia	Pown	Agami

Ardea	Reeve	Coucal	Parrot
Ariel	Rifle	Cuckoo	Parson
Avian	Robin	Curlew	Pavone
Bennu	Rotch	Cushat	Peahen
Booby	Ryper	Darter	Peewee
Bosun	Saker	Dikkop	Peewit
Capon	Scape	Dipper	Pernis
Colin	Scart	Drongo	Petrel
Colly	Scaup	Duiker	Phoebe
Crake	Scops	Dunlin	Pigeon
Crane	Scray	Duyker	Plover
Diver	Serin	Elanet	Pouter
Egret	Shama	Evejar	Progne
Finch	Sitta	Falcon	Puffin
Fleet	Skart	Fulmar	Pukeko
Galah	Snipe	Gambet	Pullet
Glede	Solan	Gander	Queest
Goose	Soree	Gannet	Quelea
Goura	Spink	Garuda	Quoist
Grebe	Sprug	Gentle	Redcap
Heron	Squab	Gentoo	Reeler
Hobby	Stare	Godwit	Roller
Homer	Stilt	Gooney	Scamel
Isaac	Stint	Goslet	Scarth
Junco	Stork	Grakle	Scaury
Kight	Swift	Hagden	Scraye
Liver	Sylph	Hagdon	Sea-cob
Lowan	Terek	Haglet	Sea-mew
Macaw	Tewit	Hermit	Seapie
Madge	Topaz	Hoopoe	Shrike
Manch	Twite	Houdan	Simara
Mavis	Umber	Jabiru	Simorg
Merle	Umbre	Jacana	Simurg
Mimus	Urubu	Jaegar	Siskin
Monal	Veery	Kakapo	Skarth
Murre	Vireo	Kotuku	Smeath
Mynah	Wader	Lanner	Soland
Nandu	Whaup	Leipoa	Sorage
Nelly	Widow	Linnet	Strich
Noddy	Wonga	Lintie	Sultan
Ornis	Yaffa	Loriot	Sylvia
Ousel	**6 letters:**	Lourie	Tailor
Ox-eye	Aquila	Lungie	Takahe
Peggy	Avocet	Magpie	Tarcel
Pekan	Avoset	Martin	Tassel
Pewit	Bantam	Menura	Tewhit
Picus	Barbet	Merlin	Tom-tit
Piper	Bishop	Merops	Toucan
Pipit	Bittor	Missel	Towhee
Pitta	Bittur	Mistle	Trogon
Poaka	Bonxie	Monaul	Turaco
Poker	Boubou	Mopoke	Turbit
Potoo	Brolga	Mossie	Tyrant
Prion	Bulbul	Motmot	Tystie
Quail	Chough	Musket	Verdin
Quest	Chukar	Nandoo	Walker
Quist	Condor	Oriole	Waxeye
Raven	Corbie	Osprey	Weaver

Whidah	Hacklet	Skylark	Bobolink
Whydah	Hadedah	Snow-cap	Bob-white
Willet	Hagbolt	Spadger	Buln-buln
Woosel	Hagdown	Sparrow	Caracara
Yaffle	Halcyon	Squacco	Cargoose
Ynambu	Hemipod	Staniel	Cheewink
Yucker	Hoatzin	Stinker	Chirn-owl
Zoozoo	Humming	Sturnus	Cockatoo
7 letters:	Ice-bird	Sunbird	Curassow
Anhinga	Jacamar	Swallow	Dabchick
Antbird	Kamichi	Tanager	Didapper
Apteryx	Kestrel	Tarrock	Dip-chick
Babbler	Killdee	Tattler	Dobchick
Bécasse	Kinglet	Teacher	Dotterel
Bittern	Lapwing	Teuchat	Estridge
Bittour	Leghorn	Tiercel	Fauvette
Bluecap	Limpkin	Tinamou	Fernbird
Blue-eye	Manakin	Titlark	Fish-hawk
Blue jay	Maribou	Titanis	Flamingo
Bluetit	Martlet	Titling	Gambetta
Boobook	Mesites	Tokahea	Gang-gang
Bullbat	Minivet	Totanus	Garefowl
Bunting	Oilbird	Touraco	Garganey
Buphaga	Ortolan	Tumbler	Greenlet
Bush-tit	Oscires	Tweeter	Grosbeak
Bustard	Ostrich	Vulture	Guacharo
Buzzard	Pandion	Vulturn	Hackbolt
Cacique	Peacock	Wagtail	Hangbird
Cariama	Pelican	Warbler	Hangnest
Chewink	Penguin	Waxbill	Hawfinch
Coal-tit	Phoenix	Waxwing	Hazelhen
Cole-tit	Pickmaw	Whooper	Hemipode
Colibri	Piculet	Widgeon	Hernshaw
Corella	Pinnock	Wimbrel	Hoactzin
Cotinga	Pintado	Witwall	Hornbill
Courlan	Pintail	Woosell	Killdeer
Courser	Pochard	Wren-tit	Kingbird
Cow-bird	Pockard	Wrybill	Kiskadee
Creeper	Poe-bird	Wryneck	Landrail
Crombec	Poy-bird	Yang-win	Lanneret
Cropper	Quetzal	**8 letters:**	Laverock
Dinorus	Rasores	Aasvogel	Longspur
Dottrel	Redpoll	Accentor	Lorikeet
Dovekie	Redwing	Adjutant	Magotpie
Dunnock	Regulus	Aigrette	Megapode
Emu-wren	Rooster	Alcatras	Mire-drum
Fantail	Rosella	Altrices	Morepork
Fern-owl	Rotchie	Amadavat	Murrelet
Figbird	Ruddock	Aquiline	Notornis
Finfoot	Sakeret	Arapunga	Nuthatch
Flicker	Sawbill	Avadavat	Ovenbird
Frigate	Scooper	Barnacle	Oxpecker
Gobbler	Scourie	Bellbird	Paradise
Goburra	Sea-mell	Blackcap	Peetweet
Gorcrow	Simurgh	Bluebird	Percolin
Goshawk	Sirgang	Blue-wing	Petchary
Grackle	Sitella	Boatbill	Pheasant
Grallae	Skimmer	Boattail	Philomel

Podargus	Albatross	Phalarope	
Poorwill	Aylesbury	Pictarnie	
Puffbird	Baldicoot	Porphyrio	
Quarrian	Baltimore	Ptarmigan	
Quarrion	Beccaccia	Razorbill	Marsh-robin
Rainbird	Beccafico	Salangane	Meadowlark
Rallidae	Bergander	Sandpiper	Noisy miner
Redshank	Blackbird	Sapsucker	Nutcracker
Redstart	Blackhead	Scansores	Pettichaps
Reedling	Bower-bird	Sea-turtle	Pettychaps
Reed-wren	Brambling	Secretary	Pratincole
Rice-bird	Broadbill	Seedeater	Quaker-bird
Rifleman	Bullfinch	Sheldrake	Racket-tail
Ringtail	Campanero	Shoveller	Rafter-bird
Riroriro	Cassowary	Skunk-bird	Rhampastos
Sandpeep	Chaffinch	Solitaire	Rhinoceros
Scolopar	Chickadee	Spoonbill	Roadrunner
Screamer	Coachwhip	Standgale	Sanderling
Shake-bag	Cockatiel	Stonechat	Sandgrouse
Shoebill	Cormorant	Storm-cock	Shearwater
Silktail	Corncrake	Sugarbird	Sheathbill
Skua-gull	Cross-bill	Swart-back	Sicklebill
Snowbird	Currawong	Sword-bill	Silverbill
Stanniel	Dowitcher	Talegalla	Spatchcock
Struthio	Estreldid	Thickhead	Stone-snipe
Surfbird	Fieldfare	Thick-knee	Tanagridae
Swiftlet	Fig-pecker	Thornbill	Tropicbird
Tantalus	Fire-crest	Trochilus	Wattlebird
Tapacolo	Fledgling	Trumpeter	Whisky-jack
Tapaculo	Francolin	Turnstone	Whisky-john
Teru-tero	Friarbird	Volucrine	Wonga-wonga
Thrasher	Frogmouth	Water-rail	Woodpecker
Thresher	Gallinule	Wind-hover	Woodpigeon
Throstle	Gerfalcon	Xanthoura	Yaffingale
Titmouse	Gier-eagle	**10 letters:**	Yellowlegs
Tom-noddy	Goldcrest	Aberdevine	Yellowyite
Toucanet	Goldfinch	Bluebreast	**11 letters:**
Tragopan	Goosander	Bluethroat	Apostlebird
Trembler	Grenadier	Bubbly-jock	Bokmakierie
Troopial	Guillemot	Budgerigar	Bristlebird
Troupial	Helldiver	Butter-bump	Gnatcatcher
Umbrette	Heronshaw	Chiff-chaff	Grallatores
Umbrella	Icteridae	Demoiselle	Honey-sucker
Water-hen	Impundulu	Dickcissel	Humming-bird
Wheatear	Jack-snipe	Didunculus	Ichthyornis
Whimbrel	Kittiwake	Dollarbird	Java sparrow
Whinchat	Lintwhite	Ember-goose	Leatherhead
Whipbird	Mallemuck	Eyas-musket	Mockingbird
Whitecap	Merganser	Fly-catcher	Moss-bluiter
White-eye	Mollymawk	Fringillid	Moss-cheeper
Woodchat	Mousebird	Goatsucker	Nightingale
Woodcock	Nutjobber	Gobemouche	Pied wagtail
Woodlark	Olive-back	Greenshank	Plantcutter
Woodwale	Ossifraga	Hen-harrier	Reed-warbler
Yoldring	Ossifrage	Honey-eater	Scissortail
9 letters:	Pardalote	Honey guide	Snowbunting
Accipiter	Peaseweep	Kingfisher	Stone-curlew
Aepyornis	Peregrine	Kookaburra	Storm petrel

Stymphalian	Drongo-shrike	Stormy petrel	
Thunderbird	Flowerpecker	Throstle-cock	
Tree-creeper	Honey creeper	Whippoorwill	
Whitethroat	Peppershrike	Willy wagtail	
Woodcreeper	Ring-dotterel	Yellow-hammer	**14 letters:**
Woodwarbler	Sage-thrasher	Yellow-yowley	Manx shearwater
Yellow-ammer	Sedge-warbler	**13 letters:**	Tawny frogmouth
12 letters:	Serpent-eater	Archaeopteryx	**17 letters:**
Bronze-pigeon	Standard-wing	Oyster-catcher	Pectoral
Drongo-cuckoo	Stonechatter	Willow warbler	sandpiper

▷ **Bird** may indicate a prison sentence

Bird-catcher Avicularia, Fowler, Papageno

Bird-like Hirundine, Sturnine

Bird's nest(ing) Caliology, Monotropa, Soup

Bird-watcher Augur, Twitcher

Birkenhead F.E.Smith

Birmingham Brum(magem)

Birth Burden, Congenital, Delivery, Drop, Extraction, Genesis, Jataka, Lineage, Nativity, Origin, Parage

Birthday Anniversary, Genethliac

Birthmark Blemish, Mole, Mother-spot, Naevus, Stigmata

Birthright Heritage, Mess, Patrimony

Birthwort Aristolochia

Biscuit Abernethy, Bath-oliver, Bourbon, Butterbake, Charcoal, Cookie, Cracker, Cracknel, Crispbread, Dandyfunk, Digestive, Dunderfunk, Fairing, Flapjack, Florentine, Garibaldi, Gingersnap, Hardtack, Kiss, Lebkuchen, Macaroon, Marie, Mattress, Nut, Oliver, Osborne, Parkin, Perkin, Petit four, Pig's ear, Poppadom, Poppadum, Pretzel, Ratafia, Rusk, Shortbread, Sweetmeal, Tack, Wafer, Zwieback

Bisexual AC/DC, Freemartin

Bishop Aaronic, Abba, Aidan, Ambrose, Bench, Berkeley, Bp, Cambrensis, Cantuar, Chad, Coverdale, Diocesan, Dunelm, Ely, Eparch, Episcopate, Eusebian, Exon, Golias, Hatto, Henson, Latimer, Lord, Magpie, Metropolitan, Norvic, Odo, Ordainer, Patriarch, Peter, Piece, Polycarp, Pontiff, Prelate, Priest, Primate, Primus, Proudie, RR, Sleeve, Suffragan, Titular, Tulchan, Weed

Bismarck Otto

Bismuth Bi

Bison Bonas(s)us, Buffalo, Ox, Wisent

Bit(s) Baud, Cantle(t), Chad, Cheesecake, Chip, Crumb, Curb, Curn, Drib, Excerpt, Fraction, Haet, Hate, Ion, Jaw, Jot, Mite, Modicum, Morsel, Mote, Mu, Nit, Ort, Ounce, Pelham, Peni, Penny, ➤ PIECE, Port, Rap, Rare, Ratherish, Scintilla, Scrap, Section, Shaving, Shiver, Shred, Smidgen, Snaffle, Snatch, Snippet, Soupcon, Spale, Speck, Splinter, Spot, Suspicion, Tad, Tait, Tate, Threepenny, Trace, Unce, Whit

Bite(r), Biting, Bitten Caustic, Chelicera, Chew, Eat, Engouled, Erose, Etch, Gnash, Gnat, Hickey, Hickie, Incisor, Knap, Masticate, Midge, Molar,

Mordacious, Mordant, Morsel, Morsure, Nibble, Nip(py), Occlude, Pium, Rabid, Remorse, Sarcastic, Sharp, Shrewd, Snap, Tart

Bitter(ness) Absinth, Acerb, Acid, Acrimonious, Ale, Aloe, Angostura, Bile, Caustic, Eager, Ers, Fell, Gall, Keen, Marah, Maror, Myrrh, Pique, Rancorous, Rankle, Resentful, Sarcastic, Sardonic, Snell, Sore, Spleen, Tart(aric), Venom, Verjuice, Virulent, Vitriolic, Wersh, Wormwood

Bittern Boomer, Bull-of the-bog, Butterbump, Heron, Sedge, Siege

Bittersweet Dulcamara

Bitumen Albertite, Asphalt, Blacktop, Gilsonite®, Maltha, Mineral tar, Pissasphalt, Pitch, Tar, Uintaite

Bivalve Clam, Cockle, Mollusc, Muscle, Mussel, Oyster, Pelecypod, Piddock, Razorshell, Scallop, Whelk

Bivouac Camp

Bizarre Antic, Curious, Eccentric, Exotic, Fantastic, Gonzo, Grotesque, Odd, Off-the-wall, Outlandish, Outré, Pythonesque, Queer, Strange, Surreal, Weird

Blab Babble, Gossip, Squeal

Black(ness), Blacken(ing), Black-out Amadoda, Atramental, B, BB, Bess, Blae, Boong, Carbon, Charcoal, Cilla, Coloured, Coon, Cypress, Darkie, Darky, Death, Denigrate, Dinge, Dwale, Ebon(y), Eclipse, Ethiop, Fuzzy-wuzzy, Geechee, Gladwellise, Graphite, Heben, Hole, Ink(y), Ivory, Japan, Jeat, Jet, Jim Crow, Kohl, Lepidomelane, Malign, Market, Melanic, Melano, Moke, Moor, Muntu, Myall, Negritude, Negro, Niello, Niger, Nigrescent, Nigritude, Obliterate, Obscure, Outage, Oxford, Piceous, Pitch, Platinum, Pongo, Prince, Pudding, Quashee, Quashie, Raven, Sable, Sambo, Scab, School, Sericon, Sheep, Slae, Sloe, Solvent, Sombre, Soot, Sooterkin, Spode, Spook, Stygian, Swart(y), Swarth(y), Tar, Uncle Tom, Weeds

Blackball Ban, Exclude, Pip, Reject

Blackberry Acini, Bramble, Mooch, Mouch

Blackbird Crow, Jackdaw, Ousel, Raven

Black eye(d) Half-mourning, Mouse, Shiner, Susan

Blackguard Leg, Nithing, Raff, Revile, Rotter, Scoundrel, Sweep

Blackhead Comedo

Black hole Collapsar

Blackjack Billie, Billy, Cosh, Flag, Sphalerite, Tankard, Truncheon, Vingt(-et)-un

Blackleg Fink, Scab, Snob

Black magic Goety

Blackmail(er) Bleed, Chantage, Chout, Exact, Extort, Ransom, Strike, Vampire

Blackout ARP, Eclipse, Faint, Swoon

Black Sea Pontic

Black sheep Neer-do-well, Reprobate

Blacksmith Brontes, Burn-the-wind, Farrier, Forger, Harmonious, Shoer, Vulcan

Blackthorn Sloe

Bladder(y) Balloon, Blister, Cholecyst, Cyst, Hydatid, Isinglass, Sac, Sound, Urinary, Utricle, Varec(h), Vesica, Vesicle

Blade Acrospire, Bilbo, Brand, Brown Bill, Cleaver, Co(u)lter, Cutlass, Dandy, Espada, Faible, Foible, Forte, Gleave, Gouge, Guillotine, Hydrofoil, Lance, Leaf, Man, Mouldboard, Oar, Palmetto, Peel, Propellor, Rachilla, Rapier, Razor, Rip, Rotor, Scimitar, Scull, Skate, Spade-bone, Spatula, Spatule, Spear, Spoon, Stiletto, Stock, ➤ SWORD, Symitar, Toledo, Vane, Vorpal, Web

Blame Accuse, Censure, Condemn, Confound, Decry, Fault, Guilt, Inculpate, Odium, Rap, Reproach, Reprove, Stick, Thank, Twit, Wight, Wite, Wyte

Blameless Innocent, Irreproachable

Blanch Bleach, Etiolate, Scaud, Whiten

Blancmange Carrageen, Flummery, Mould, Shape, Timbale

Bland Anodyne, Mild, Pigling, Sleek, Smooth, Suave, Unctuous

Blandish(ment) Agremens, Agrement, Cajole, ➤ COAX, Flatter, Treacle, Wheedle

Blank Cartridge, Empty, Erase, Flan, Lacuna, Mistigris, Planchet, Shot, Space, Tabula rasa, ➤ VACANT

Blanket Afghan, Bluey, Chilkat, Counterpane, Cover, General, Kaross, Mackinaw, Manta, Obscure, Overall, Poncho, Quilt, Rug, Saddle, Sarape, Security, Serape, Shabrack, Smog, Space, Stroud, Wagga, Wet, Whittle

Blare Horn, Trumpet

Blarney Cajolery, Flattery, Nonsense, Sawder, Taffy

Blasé Worldly

Blaspheme, Blasphemous Abuse, ➤ CURSE, Defame, Profanity, Revile

Blast(ed) Blight, Blore, Blow, Bombard, Dang, Darn, Dee, Drat, Dynamite, Explode, Fanfare, Flaming, Flurry, Fo(e)hn, Gale, Gust, Parp, Pryse, Rats, Scarth, Scath(e), Sere, Shot, Sideration, Skarth, Tantara, Toot, Tromp(e), Trump(et), Volley

Blatant Flagrant, Hard-core, Noticeable, Strident, Vulgar

Blather Baloney, Gabble

Blaze(r) Beacon, Bonfire, Burn, Cannel, Conflagration, Firestorm, ➤ FLAME, Flare, Glare, Jacket, Low(e), Lunt, Palatinate, Race, Ratch, Star, Sun, Tead(e)

Bleach(er) Agene, Blanch, Chemic, Chloride, Decolorate, Etiolate, Keir, Kier, Peroxide, Whiten, Whitster

Bleak Ablet, Bare, Blay, Bley, Dour, Dreary, Dreich, Raw, Wintry

Bleary Blurred, Smudged

Bleat Baa, Blat, Bluster

Bleed(er), Bleeding Cup, Ecchymosis, Epistaxis, Extravasate, Fleam, Haemorrhage, Leech, Menorrh(o)ea, Menorrhagia, Metrorrhagia, Milk, Purpura, Root-pressure

Bleep Earcon, Pager

Blefuscudian Big-endian, Little-endian

Blemish Birthmark, Blot, Blotch, Blur, Botch, Defect, Flaw, Mackle, Mark, Mote, Naevus, Scar, Smirch, Spot, Sully, Taint, Tash, Vice, Wart, Wen

Blench Flinch, Recoil, Wince

Blend(ing) Amalgam, Coalesce, Commix, Contemper, Contrapuntal, Counterpoint, Electrum, Fuse, Go, Harmonize, Hydrate, Interfuse, Interlace, Liquidise, Meld, Melt, ▸ MERGE, Mingle, Mix, Osmose, Portmanteau, Scumble, Sfumato, Synalepha

▹ **Blend** may indicate an anagram

Blenny Eel-pout, Gunnel, Shanny

Bless(ed), Blessedness, Blessing Amen, Approval, Asset, Beatitude, Benedicite, Benediction, Benison, Benitier, Bensh, Bismillah, Boon, Brachah, Brocho, Consecrate, Cup, Damosel, Darshan, Elysium, Ethereal, Felicity, Gesundheit, Gwyneth, Holy (dam), Kiddush, Luck, Macarise, Mercy, Mixed, Sain, Saint, Sanctify, Sanctity, Urbi et orbi, Xenium

Bless me Lawk(s)

Blight Afflict, Ague, Bespot, Blast, Destroy, Eyesore, Rot, ▸ RUIN, Rust, Shadow, Viticide, Wither

Blighter Cuss, Perisher, Varment, Varmint

Blimey Coo, Cor, Crimini, O'Riley, Strewth

Blimp Airship, Colonel

Blind(ness), Blind spot Amaurosis, Amblyopia, Artifice, Austrian, Beesome, Bisson, Blend, Blotto, Carousal, Cecity, Chi(c)k, Cog, Concealed, Dazzle, Eyeless, Feint, Festoon, Gravel, Hemeralopia, Hood, Jalousie, Legless, Mole, Meropia, Nyctalopia, Onchocerciasis, Persian, Persiennes, Pew, Prestriction, Rash, Roller, Scotoma, Seel, Shade, Shutter, Stimie, Stimy, Stymie, Sun, Snow, Teichopsia, Typhlology, Venetian, Word, Yblent

Blindfish Amblyopsis

Blindfold Bandage, Hoodwink, Muffle, Seal, Wimple

Blindworm Anguis

Blink(er), Blinkered, Blinking Bat, Bluff, Broken, Flash, Haw, Idiot, Insular, Nictate, Owl-eyed, Owly, Twink, Wapper, Wink

Bliss(ful) Beatitude, Bouyan, Composer, Delight, ▸ ECSTASY, Eden, Happy, Ignorance, Married, Millenium, Nirvana, Paradise, Rapture, Sion, Tir-na-nog, Valhalla, Walhalla, Wedded

Blister(ed), Blistering Blab, Blain, Bleb, Bubble, Bullate, Epispastic, Herpes, Pemphigus, Phlyctena, Scorching, Tetter, Vesicant, Vesicle

Blitz Attack, Bombard, Onslaught, Raid

Blizzard Buran, Gale, Snowstorm, Whiteout

Bloat(er) Buckling, Puff, Strout, Swell, Tumefy

Blob Bead, Bioblast, Drop, Globule, O, Spot, Tear

Bloc Alliance, Cabal, Cartel, Party

Block(ade), Blockage, Blocked Altar, Anvil, Ashlar, Atresia, ➤ BAR, Barricade, Barrier, Brake, Breeze, Brick, Briquette, Building, Bung, Bunt, Catasta, Choke, Chunk, Clint, Clog, Clot, Cloy, Compass, Congest, Constipated, Cyclopean, Cylinder, ➤ DAM, Dead-eye, Debar, Dentel, Dentil, Die, Dit, Electrotint, Embolism, Encompass, Euphroe, Fipple, Hack-log, High-rise, Hunk, Ileus, Impasse, Impede, Impost, Ingot, Insula, Interrupt, Interclude, Investment, Jam, Lingot, Lodgment, Log-jam, Lump, Ministroke, Mutule, Nog, Oasis®, Obstacle, ➤ OBSTRUCT, Occlude, Oppilate, Pad, Page, Parry, Pile-up, Plinth, Pre-empt, Prevent, Ram, Scotch, Sett, Siege, Stalemate, Stap, Starting, Stenosis, Stimie, Stimy, Stone, Stonewall, Stop, Stumbling, Stymie, Tamp, Thwart, Tower, Tranche, Trig, Triglyph, Uphroe, Upping-stock, Writer's, Zinco, Zugzwang

Blockbuster Epic

Blockhead Jolterhead, Mome, Nitwit, Noodle, Stupid

Bloke Beggar, Chap, Cove, Fellow, Gent, Man, Oik

Blonde Ash, Cendré, Fair, Goldilocks, Platinised, Platinum, Strawberry, Tallent, Towhead

Blood(y) Ancestry, Bally, Blue, Blut, Claret, Clot, Cruor, Cup, Ecchymosis, Ensanguine, Epigons, Factor, ➤ GORE, Haemal, Ichor, Introduce, Kin, Knut, Menses, Nut, Opsonin, Parentage, Persue, Pigeon's, Plasma, Platelet, Properdin, Pup, Race, Rare, Red, Rh negative, Rh positive, Ruby, Sang, Serum, Show, Stroma, Toff, Welter

Blood disease, Blood-poisoning Hypinosis, Isch(a)emia, Pyaemia, Spanaemia, Thalassemia, Toxaemia, Uraemia

Bloodhound Lime, Lyam, Sleuth, Spartan

Bloodless Anaemic, Isch(a)emic, Wan, White

Blood-letter Leech, Phlebotomist, Sangrado

▶ **Blood-poisoning** see BLOOD DISEASE

Blood-pressure Hypertension, Hypotension

Blood-sport Hunting, Shooting, Venery

Blood-sucker Asp, Dracula, Flea, Gnat, Ked, Leech, Louse, Mosquito, Parasite, Reduviid, Sponger, Tick, Vampire(-bat)

Bloom(er), Blooming Anthesis, Bally, Blossom, Blow, Blush, Boner, Dew, Error, Film, Florescent, Flowery, Flush, Gaffe, Glaucous, Heyday, Knickers, Loaf, Miscalculation, Out, Pruina, Rationals, Reh, Remontant, Rosy, Underwear

▷ **Bloomer** may indicate a flower

Blossom Blow, Burgeon, Festoon, Flourish, Flower, May, Orange, Pip

Blot Atomy, Blob, Cartel, Delete, Disgrace, Eyesore, Obscure, Smear, Smudge, Southern, Splodge, Splotch

Blotch(y) Blemish, Giraffe, Monk, Mottle(d), Spot, Stain

Blotto Legless

Blouse Choli, Garibaldi, Gimp, Guimpe, Middy, Sailor, Shirtwaist, Smock, Tunic, Windjammer

Blow(er) Appel, Bang, Bash, Bat, Bellows, Biff, Billow, Blip, Bloom, Brag, Breeze, Buckhorse, Buffet, Burst, Calamity, Clap, Clat, Claut, Clip, Clout, Clump, Conk, Coup, Cuff, Dad, Daud, Dev(v)el, Dinnyhayser, Dint, Douse, Dowse, Estramacon, Etesian, Facer, Fan, Gale, Grampus, Gust, Haymaker, Hit, Hook, Ictus, Impact, Insufflate, Karate, Kibosh, Knuckle sandwich, KO, Lame, Lander, Lick, Lounder, Muff, Neck-herring, Northerly, Noser, Oner, One-two, Paik, Pash, Phone, Piledriver, Plague, Plug, Plump(er), Polt, Pow, Puff, Punch, Purler, Rattler, Rats, Rib-roaster, Sas(s)arara, Scat, Settler, Sideswipe, Side-winder, Sis(s)erary, Skiff, Skite, Skyte, Slat, Slog, Slug, Snot, Sock, Sockdolager, Sockdologer, Southwester, Spanking, Spat, Spout, Squander, Stripe, Stroke, Strooke, Stunning, Supercharger, Swash, Swat, Swinger, Telephone, Thump, Thwack, Tingler, Tootle, Trump(et), Upper-cut, Waft, Wallop, Wap, Waste, Welt, Whammy, Whample, Whang, Whap, Wheeze, Wherret, Whiffle, Whirret, ➤ WIND, Winder, Wipe, Wuther

Blown-up Elated, Enlarged, Exploded

Blow-out Binge, Bloat, Exhale, Feast, Feed, Flat, Lava, Nosh-up, Snuff, Spiracle, ➤ SPREAD

Blowpipe Hod, Peashooter, Sarbacane, Sumpit(an)

Blub(ber) Cry, Fat, Snotter, Sob, Speck, ➤ WEEP, Whimper

Bludgeon Bully, Club, Cosh, Cudgel, Sap

Blue(s) Abattu, Accablé, Adult, Anil, Aquamarine, Azure, Beard, Berlin, Bice, Bleuâtre, Blow, Bottle, Butterfly, C, Caesious, Cafard, Cambridge, Cantab, Celeste, Cerulean, Clair de lune, Cobalt, Coomassie, Copenhagen, Cornflower, Cyan, Danish, Danube, Dejected, Dirty, Disconsolate, Doldrums, ➤ DOWN, Duck-egg, Eatanswill, Eggshell, Electric, Facetiae, Firmament, Fritter, Gentian, Germander, Glum, Hauyne, Hump, Indecent, Indigo, Indol(e), Iron, Isatin(e), Lapis lazuli, Lavender, Lewd, Lionel, Low, Mazarine, Methylene, Midnight, Monastral®, Mope, Morose, Murder, Nattier, Naughty, Navy, Nile, Oxford, Peacock, Perse, Petrol, Phycocyon, Porn, Powder, Prussian, Rabbi, Ribald, Riband, Right, Ripe, Robin's egg, Royal, Sad, Sapphire, Saxe, Saxon(y), Scurrilous, ➤ SEA, Shocking, Sky, Slate, Smalt(o), Smutty, Sordid, Splurge, Squander, Stafford, Steel, Stocking, Teal, Tony, Tory, Trist, True, Trypan, Turnbull's, Ultramarine, Unhappy, Verditer, Watchet, Wedgwood®, Welkin, Woad, Zaffer, Zaffre

▷ **Blue** may indicate an anagram

Bluebell Blawort, Blewart, Campanula, Harebell

Bluebottle Blawort, Blewart, Blowfly, Blowie, Brommer, Brummer, Cop, Cornflower, Fly, Policeman

Blue-legged, Bluestocking Basbleu, Carter, Erudite, Hamburg(h), Mrs Montagu, Précieuse, Sheba

Blueprint Cyanotype, Draft, Plan, Recipe

▶ **Bluestocking** see BLUE-LEGGED

Bluff(ing) Blunt, Cle(e)ve, Cliff, Clift, Crag, Fake, Flannel, Frank, Hal, Headland, Height, Hoodwink, Kidology, Pose, Precipice, Steep, Trick

Blunder(er), Blundering Betise, Bévue, Bish, Bloomer, Blooper, Boob, Bull, Bumble, Clanger, Clinker, Cock-up, Err, Faux pas, Floater, Flub, Fluff,

Gaff(e), Goof, Howler, Inexactitude, Irish, Josser, Malapropism, ➤ MISTAKE, Mumpsimus, Slip, Solecism, Stumble, Trip

Blunt(ed), Bluntly Abrupt, Alleviate, Bate, Bayt, Brusque, Candid, Deaden, Disedge, Forthright, Hebetate, Mole, Morned, Obtund, Obtuse, Outspoken, Pointblank, Rebate, Retund, Retuse, Roundly, Snub, Straight-out, Stubby

Blur(ring) Cloud, Confuse, Fog, Fuzz, Halation, Mackle, Macule, ➤ SMUDGE, Stump, Tortillon

Blurb Ad, Puff

Blush(ing) Colour, Cramoisy, Crimson, Erubescent, Erythema, Incarnadine, ➤ REDDEN, Rouge, Ruby, Rutilant

Bluster(er), Blustery Arrogance, Bellow, Blore, Hector, Rage, Rant, Rodomontade, Roister, Sabre-rattler, Squash, Swagger, Vapour, Wuthering

Boar Barrow, Calydonian, Erymanthian, Hog, Pentheus, Sanglier, Sounder, Tusker

Board(s), Boarding Abat-voix, Admiralty, Banker, Beaver, Billet, Bristol, Bulletin, Cheese, Chevron, Collegium, Committee, Contignation, Counter, Dart, Deal, Directors, Diving, Draft, Embark, Embus, Enter, Entrain, Fare, Fascia, Featheredge, Fibro, Flannelgraph, Gibraltar, Hack, Hawk, Hoarding, Idiot, Kip, Lag, Ledger, Lodge, Malibu, Notice, Otter, Ouija, Palette, Pallet, Panel, Particle, Pension, Planch(ette), Scaleboard, Plank, Ply(wood), Quango, Sandwich, Sarking, Screed, Shelf, Shingle, Side-table, Sign, Skirting, Sounding, Stage, Strickle, Stringboard, Surf, ➤ TABLE, Theatre, Trencher, Wainscot, Wobble

▷ **Board** may refer to chess or draughts

Boarder Interne, PG, Roomer

Boarding house Digs, Lodgings, Pension

Boast(er), Boasting Big-note, Blow, Blew, Blowhard, Bluster, Bobadil, Bounce, Brag, Braggadocio, Breeze, Crake, Crow, Fanfaronade, Gas, Gascon(nade), Glory, Hot air, Jactitation, Line, Ostent(atious), Prate, Rodomontade, Scaramouch, Skite, Swagger, Swank, Tall, Thrasonic, Vainglory, Vaunt, Yelp

Boat Canal, Dragon, Eight, Four, Foyboat, Gravy, Hooker, Jolly, Lapstrake, Launch, Lymphad, Mackinaw, Monohull, Narrow, Outrigger, Pair-oar, Pedalo, Pont, Puffer, Sailer, Sauce, Shallop, ➤ SHIP, Skiff, Slogger, Swing, Tender, Torpid, Vaporetto, ➤ VESSEL, Weekender

Boater ➤ HAT, Punter, Straw

Boatman Bargee, Charon, Cockswain, Coxswain, George, Gondolier, Harris, Hoveller, Phaon, Voyageur, Waterman, Wet-bob

Boat population Tank(i)a

Boat-shaped Carina, Scaphoid

Boatswain Bosun, Serang, Smee

Bob Acres, Beck, Curtsey, Deaner, Dip, Dock, Dop, Duck, Float, Hod, Hog, Jerk, Page-boy, Peal, Plumb, Plummet, Popple, Rob, S, Shingle

Bobbin Reel, Shuttle, Spindle, Spool

Bobble Pompom

Bobby Bluebottle, Busy, Copper, Flatfoot, Patrolman, Peeler, Pig,
➤ POLICEMAN

Bobby-dazzler Dinger, Stunner

Bock Stein

Bode Augur

Bodice Basque, Bolero, Bustier, Chemise, Chemisette, Choli, Corsage, Gilet,
Halter, Jirkinet, Liberty, Plastron, Polonie, Polony, Spencer, Tucker

Bodkin Eyeleteer, Needle, Poniard, Stilet(to)

Body, Bodies, Bodily Administration, Amount, Anatomic, Astral, Barr,
Board, Bouk, Buik, Buke, Bulk, Cadaver, Cadre, Carcase, Carcass, Carnal,
Caucas, Centrosome, Chapel, Chapter, Chassis, Chondriosome, Clay,
Coccolite, Cohort, Column, Comet, Committee, Contingent, Cormus,
Corpor(e)al, Corps, Corpse, Corpus, Corse, Cytode, Detail, Earth, Flesh,
Frame, Fuselage, Gazo(o)n, Golgi, Goner, ➤ GROUP, Hull, Inclusion, Lich,
Like, Lithites, ➤ MASS, Militia, Moit, Mote, Mummy, Nacelle, Nucleole,
Nucleolus, Pack, Personal, Phalanx, Pineal, Plant, Platelet, Platoon, Politic,
Posse, Purview, Quango, Relic(t), Ruck, Senate, Solid, Soma, Soredium,
Sound-box, Soyle, Spinar, Spore, Squadron, Square, Staff, Statoblast, Stiff,
Syndicate, Tagma, Testis, Thallus, Torse, Torso, Trunk, Turm, Ulema,
Wolffian

▷ **Body** may indicate an anagram

Body builder Steroid

Bodyguard Amulet, ➤ ESCORT, Gentleman-at-arms, House-carl, Minder,
Praetorian, Protector, Retinue, Schutzstaffel, ➤ SHIELD, SS, Triggerman,
Varangian, Yeomen

Body segment Arthromere, Metamere

Boer Afrikaner, Kruger

Bog(gy) Allen, Can, Carr, Clabber, Fen, Gents, Glaur, Hag, Lair, Loo, Machair,
Marsh, Mire, Morass, Moss(-flow), Mud, Muskeg, Peat, Petary, Quag,
Serbonian, Slack, Slade, Slough, Spew, Spouty, Stodge, Sump, Vlei,
Washroom, WC, Yarfa, Yarpha

Bog(e)y Boggart, Bug(aboo), Bugbear, Chimera, Eagle, Mumbo jumbo,
Nis(se), Par, Poker, Rawhead, Scarer, Spectre, Troll

Boggle Astonish, Bungle, Demur, Hesitate, Perplex, Shy

Bog-trotter Tory

Bogus Counterfeit, Fake, False, Histrionic, Phoney, ➤ SHAM, Snide,
Snobbish, Spoof, Spurious

Bohemian Arty, Beatnik, Gypsy, Hippy, Mimi, Taborite, Trustafarian

Boil(er), Boiled, Boiling point Anthrax, Blain, Botch, Brew, Bubble, C,
Coction, Cook, Cree, Dartre, Decoct, Ebullient, Feruncle, Foam, Furuncle,
Gathering, Hen, Herpes, Kettle, Leep, Ligroin, Pimple, Poach, Poule, Rage,
Reflux, Samovar, Seethe, Simmer, Sod, Sore, Stew, Stye, Tea-kettle

Boister(ous) Gilp(e)y, Gusty, Hoo, Knockabout, Noisy, Rambunctious,
Randy, Riotous, Rorty, Rough, Stormy, Termagant, Turbulent, Wild

Bold(ly), Boldness Assumptive, Brash, Brass, Bravado, Bravery, Bravura, Brazen, Caleb, Crust, Daredevil, Defiant, Derring-do, Diastaltic, Familiar, Free, Gallus, Hardihood, Heroics, High-spirited, Impudent, Intrepid, Malapert, Mature, Outspoken, Parrhesia, Pert, Plucky, Presumptive, Rash, Risoluto, Sassy, Temerity, Unshrinking

Bole Stem, Trunk

Bolivar Liberator

Bollard Cone, Kevel

Bolshevik Communist, Maximalist, Soviet

Bolster Cushion, Pillow, ➤ PROP

Bolt Arrow, Cuphead, Dash, Dead, Eat, Elope, Flee, Gobble, Gollop, Gorge, Gulp, Latch, Levant, Levin, Lightning, Lock, Missile, Pig, Pintle, Ragbolt, Rivet, Roll, Scoff, Slot, Snib, Sperre, Thunder, Toggle, U, Wolf

Bolus Ball

Bomb(er), Bombing Atom, Attack, B, Blockbuster, Borer, Buzz, Carpet, Cluster, Cobalt, Daisycutter, Deterrent, Doodlebug, Egg, Fission, Flop, Fragmentation, Fusion, Greek fire, Grenade, H, Hydrogen, Lancaster, Land-mine, Letter, Liberator, Logic, Megaton, Mills, Minnie, Mint, Molotov cocktail, Mortar, Nail, Napalm, Neutron, Nuclear, Nuke, Parcel, Petar, Petard, Petrol, Pineapple, Pipe, Plaster, Plastic, Prang, Ransom, Robot, Shell, Smoke, Stealth, Stick, Stink, Stuka, Tactical, Terrorist, Time, Torpedo, Turkey, V1, Volcanic

Bombard(ment) Attack, Battery, Blitz, Cannonade, Drum-fire, Mortar, Pelt, Shell, Stone, Stonk, Strafe, Straff

Bombardon Tuba

Bombast(ic) Euphuism, Fustian, Grandiose, Magniloquence, Orotund, Pomp, Rant, Timid, Tumid, Turgent

Bombay Nasik

Bombay duck Bum(m)alo

▶ **Bomber** see Bomb

Bonanza Luck, Windfall

Bonaparte Boney, ➤ NAPOLEON, Plon-plon

Bond(age) Adhesive, Agent, Assignat, Bail, Cedula, Cement, Chain, Compact, Connect, Copula, Corporate, Duty, Escrow, Flemish, Gilt, Hyphen, Ionic, James, Knot, Liaise, Ligament, Link(age), Manacle, Mortar, Nexus, Noose, ➤ PLEDGE, Rapport, Shackle, Starr, Thral(l)dom, ➤ TIE, Valence, Vinculum, Yearling, Yoke

Bond(s), Bondsman Bail, Bearer, Consols, Coordinate, Covalent, Covenant, Dative, English, Ernie, Esne, Fetter, Fleming, Flemish, Geasa, Granny, Income, Junk, Pair, Premium, Recognisance, Relationship, Revenue, Running, Serf, Slave, Stacked, Thete, Treasury, Vassal

Bone(s), Bony Acromion, Anableps, Apatite, Astragalus, Baculum, Calcaneus, Cannon, Capitellum, Carina, Carpus, Catacomb, Centrum, Chine, Clavicle, Cly, Coccyx, Coffin, Columella, Condyle, Coracoid, Coral, Costa, Crane, Cranium, Dentary, Diaphysis, Dib, Dice, Endosteal, Ethmoid, Femur, Fetter, Fibula, Fillet, Funny, Ganoid, Gaunt, Haunch, Horn,

Humerus, Hyoid, Ilium, Incus, Innominate, Involucrum, Ischium, Ivory, Jugal, Knuckle, Lamella, Luez, Luz, Malar, Malleolus, Malleus, Manubrium, Mastoid, Medulla, Membrane, Metacarpal, Metatarsal, Napier's, Nasal, Navicular, Occipital, Olecranon, Omoplate, Orthopaedics, Os, Ossicle, Parietal, Patella, Pecten, Pelvis, Pen, Percoid, Perone, Phalanx, Pisiform, Premaxilla, Pubis, Pygostyle, Quadrate, Rachial, Rack, Radialia, Radius, Relic, Rib, Sacrum, Scaphoid, Scapula, Sclere, Sesamoid, Skeleton, Skull, Sphenoid, Splint, Squamosal, Stapes, ➤ STEAL, Sternebra, Sternum, Stirrup, Suboperculum, T, Talus, Tarsus, Temporal, Tibia, Tot, Trapezium, Triquetral, Trochanter, Trochlea, Ulna, Vertebrae, Vomer, Wish, Wormian, Zygomatic

Bone-head Capitellum, Capitulum

Bonehouse Ossuary

Boneshaker Dandy-horse, Draisene, Draisine

Bonfire Bale-fire, Beltane, Blaze, Clavie, Pyre

Boniface Inn-keeper, Landlord, Taverner

Bonne-bouche Cate

Bonnet Balmoral, Bongrace, Cap, Cornette, Cowl, Easter, Glengarry, Hood, Hummel, Hummle, Kiss-me, Mobcap, Mutch, Poke, Toorie

Bonny Blithe, Gay, Merry, Sonsy, Weelfar'd

Bonsai Saikei

Bonus Bounty, Bye, Dividend, Hand-out, Lagniappe, No-claim, ➤ PREMIUM, Reward, Scrip, Spin-off, Windfall

Boob Gaffe, Nork, Simpleton, Stumer

Booby Dunce, Hick, Patch, Patchcocke, Patchoke, ➤ STUPID

Boojum Snark

Book(ish), Books, Bookwork Academic, Acts, Album, Amos, Antilegomena, Antiphonary, Apocalypse, Apocrypha, Atlas, Audio, B, Backlist, Baruch, Bestiary, Bible, Black, Blue, Bodice-ripper, Breviary, Caxton, Chrestomathy, Chron(icles), Classic, Commonplace, Compendium, Cookery, Corinthians, Course, Cyclopedia, Dan(iel), Deuteronomy, Diary, Dictionary, Digest, Directory, Domesday, Doomsday, Eccles, Edda, Ench(e)iridion, Encyclopedia, Engage, Enter, Eph, Ephesians, Erudite, Esdras, Ezek(iel), Esther, Exercise, Exeter, Exodus, Ezra, Facetiae, Folio, Gal, Galatians, Genesis, Good, Gradual, Gradus, Grimoire, Grolier, Guide, Hag(gai), Haggadah, Haggadoh, Hagliographa, Hardback, Heptameron, Herbal, Hitopodesa, Hosea, I Ching, Imprint, Incunabula, Isaiah, Issue, Jashar, Jasher, John, Joshua, Jude, Jud(ges), Kells, Kings, Lam(entations), Ledger, Leviticus, Lib, Liber, Libretto, Literary, Log, Luke, Macc, Manga, Manual, Mark, Martyrs, Matthew, Micah, Missal, Monograph, Mook, Nahum, NT, Numbers, Octavo, Octodecimo, Omnibus, Open, Orarium, Order, Ordinal, OT, Page-turner, Paperback, Paralipomena, Passionary, Pedantic, Penny dreadful, Pharmacopoeia, Philemon, Philippians, Phrase, Pica, Plug, Porteous, Portesse, Potboiler, Primer, Proverbs, Psalms, Psalter, Publication, Quair, Quarto, Quire, Ration, Reader, Remainder, ➤ RESERVE, Responsorial, Revelations, Rom,

Romans, Script, Scroll, Sextodecimo, Sibylline, Sir, Sixteenmo, Snobs, Softback, Statute, Studious, Study, Sus, Sutra, Tablet, Text(ual), Thriller, Title, Titule, To-bit, Tome, Triodion, Twelve Tables, Twelvemo, Vade-mecum, Veda, Vercelli, Vesperal, Vol(ume), Work, Year, Zephadiah

Bookbinder, Bookbinding Fanfare, Grolier, Mutton-thumper, Organdie

Book-case Credenza, Press, Satchel

Bookie(s), Bookmaker John, Layer, Librettist, Luke, Mark, Matthew, Printer, Ringman, To-bit

Booking Reservation

Bookkeeper, Bookkeeping Clerk, Double entry, Librarian, Posting, Recorder, Satchel, Single-entry

Booklet B, Brochure, Folder

Book-like Solander

Book-lover Incunabulist

Bookmark Tassel

Book-scorpion Chelifer

Bookseller(s) Bibliopole, Colporteur, Conger, Sibyl

Bookworm Sap, Scholar

Boom(ing) Baby, Beam, Boost, Bowsprit, Bump, Increase, Jib, Orotund, Prosper, Roar, Sonic, Spar, Thrive, Wishbone

Boomer Bittern, Bull-of the-bog, Kangaroo, Mire-drum

Boomerang Backfire, Kiley, Kyley, Kylie, Recoil, Ricochet, Throwstick, Woomera

Boon Bene, Benefit, Blessing, Bounty, Cumshaw, Gift, Godsend, Mills, Mitzvah, Prayer, Windfall

Boor(ish) Bosthoon, Chuffy, Churl, Clodhopper, Crass, Goth, Grobian, Hog, Ill-bred, Jack, Keelie, Kern(e), Kernish, Kill-courtesy, Lob, Lout, Lumpen, Ocker, Peasant, Philistine, Trog, Uncouth, Yahoo, Yob

Boost(er) Afterburner, Bolster, Encourage, Fillip, Help, Hoist, Impetus, Increase, Injection, Lift, Promote, Raise, Reheat, Reinforce, Reinvigorate, Spike, Supercharge, Tonic

Boot(s) Addition, Adelaide, Avail, Balmoral, Beetle-crushers, Benefit, Blucher, Bottine, Bovver, Brogan, Brogue, Buskin, Cerne, Chukka, Cockers, Cold, Combat, Concern, Cothurn(us), Cowboy, Cracowe, Crowboot, Denver, Derby, Desert, Dismiss, Field, Finn(e)sko, Finsko, Fire, Galage, Galosh, Gambado, Go-go, Granny, Gum, Hessian, Hip, Jack, Jemima, Kamik, Kletterschuh, Lace-up, Larrigan, Last, Mitten, Muchie, Muc(k)luc(k), Mukluk, Pac, Para, Profit, Sabot, ➤ SACK, ➤ SHOE, Surgical, Toe, Tonneau, Tops, Trunk, Ugh, Vibram®, Vibs, Wader, Warm, Weller, Wellie, Wellington, Welly

Booth Assassin, Crame, Kiosk, Polling, Stall, Stand, Voting

Bootlegger Cooper, Coper, Runner

Bootless Futile, Idle, Vain

Booty Creach, Creagh, Haul, Loot, Prey, Prize, Spoil(s), Spolia optima, Swag

Booze ➤ DRINK, Liquor, Spree, Tipple

Borage Bugloss, Comfrey, Gromwell

Borax Tincal

Border(land), Borderline Abut, Adjoin, Apron, Bed, Bind, Bound, Checkpoint, Coast, Cot(t)ise, Dado, Dentelle, ➤ EDGE, Engrail, Fimbria, Frieze, Fringe, Frontier, Furbelow, Guilloche, Head-rig, Hedgerow, Hem, Herbaceous, Impale, Kerb, Lambrequin, Limb, Limbo, Limen, Limes, Limit, Limitrophe, Lip, List, March, Marchland, ➤ MARGIN, Mat, Mattoid, Meith, Mete, Mount, Neighbour, Orle, Pand, Pelmet, Perimeter, Purfle, Purlieu, Rand, Rim, Roadside, Roon, Royne, Rund, Rymme, Selvage, Selvedge, Side, Skirt, Strand, Strip, Surround, Swage, The Marches, Trench, Tressure, Valance, Valence, ➤ VERGE

▷ **Borders** may indicate first and last letters

Bore(d), Boredom, Borer, Boring Aiguille, Anobium, Anorak, Apathy, Aspergillum, Aspergillus, Aspersoir, Auger, Awl, Beetle, Bind, Bit, Broach, Brog, Bromide, Calibre, Chokebore, Deadly, Drag, ➤ DRILL, Dry, Dweeb, Eagre, Eat, Eger, Elshin, Elsin, Endured, Ennui, Ennuye, Foozle, Gim(b)let, Gouge, Gribble, Grind, Had, Heigh-ho, Ho-hum, Irk, Listless, Longicorn, Longueur, Miser, Mole, Nerd, Noyance, Nudni(c)k, Nuisance, Nyaff, Oporose, Pall, Penetrate, Perforate, Pest, Pholas, Pierce, Pill, Probe, Prosaic, Prosy, Punch, Ream(ingbit), Rime, Sat, Schmoe, Scolytus, Screw, Severn, Snooze, Snore, Sondage, Spleen, Sting, Stob, Tediosity, Tedious, Tedisome, Tedium, Tedy, Terebra, Teredo, Termes, Termite, Thirl, Tire, Trocar, Tunnel, ➤ WEARY, Well, Wimble, Windbag, Wonk, Woodworm, Worldweary, Xylophoga, Yawn

Borgia Cesare, Lucretia

Boric Sassolin, Sassolite

Born B, Free, Great, Nascent, Nat(us), Né(e)

Boron B

Borough Borgo, Pocket, Port, Quarter, Rotten, Township, Wick

Borrow(ed), Borrowing Adopt, Appropriate, Cadge, Copy, Eclectic, George, Hum, Scunge, Straunge, ➤ TAKE, Touch

Bosh Humbug, Nonsense, Rot

Bosom Abraham's, Breast, Close, Gremial, Inarm, Intimate

Boss(ed), Bossy Blooper, Burr, Cacique, Director, Dominate, Gadroon, Headman, Honcho, Hump, Inian, Inion, Jewel, Knob, Knop, Knot, ➤ MISTAKE, Maestro, ➤ MANAGER, Massa, Mistress, Netsuke, Noop, Nose-led, Omphalos, Overlord, Overseer, Owner, Pellet, Protuberance, Ruler, Run, Stud, Superintendent, Taskmaster, Umbo(nate)

Boston Hub

Bot Oestrus

Botanist, Botany Banks, Bryology, Candolle, Carpology, Cockayne, Dendrologist, Frees, Garden, Godet, Herbist, Linnaeus, Weigel

Botch Bungle, Clamper, Cock-up, Flub, Fudge, Mismanage, Spoil, Tink

Both Together, Two

Bother Ado, Aggro, Care, Deave, Deeve, Disturb, Drat, Fash, Fluster, Fuss, Get, Hector, Incommode, Irritate, Moither, Nuisance, Perturb, Pest(er), Pickle, Reke, Todo, ➤ TROUBLE

Bottle(s) Ampul(la), Bacbuc, Balthasar, Balthazar, Belshazzar, Borachio, Bundle, Carafe, Carboy, Cock, Cork, Costrel, Courage, Cruet, Cruse, Cucurbital, Cutter, Dead-men, Decanter, Demijohn, Fearlessness, Feeding, Fiasco, Flacket, Flacon, Flagon, Flask, Goatskin, Gourd, Hen, Imperial, Jeroboam, Klein, Lachrymal, Lagena, Magnum, Marie-Jeanne, Matrass, Medicine, Methuselah, Mettle, Nebuchadnezzar, Phial, Pitcher, Pooter, Rehoboam, Resource, Retort, Salmanaser, Salmanazar, Siphon, Split, Vial, Vinaigret(te), Wad, Water, Winchester, Woulfe

▷ **Bottle(d)** may indicate an anagram or a hidden word

Bottom(ness) Anus, Aris, Arse, Ass, Base, Beauty, Bed, Benthos, Bilge, Breech, Bum, Butt, Buttocks, Croup(e), Croupon, Demersal, Derrière, Doup, Fanny, Floor, Foot, Foundation, Fud, Fundus, Haunches, Hunkers, Hurdies, Keel(son), Kick, Nadir, Podex, Posterior, Pottle-deep, Prat, Pyramus, Rear, Rock, Root, Rump, Seat, Sill, Ship, Sole, Staddle, Tail, Tush, Weaver

Bottom drawer Glory box

Botulism Limberneck

Boudoir Bower, Room

Bouffant Pouf

Bough Branch, Limb

Bought Coft

Boulder Gibber, Rock, ➤ STONE

Boule Senate

Bounce(r), Bouncy Bang, Blague, Bound, Caper, Dap, Dead-cat, Doorman, Dop, Dud, Eject, Evict, Jounce, Kite, Lie, Lilt, Resilient, Ricochet, Spiccato, Spring, Stot, Tale, Tamp, Verve, Vitality, Yorker, Yump

▷ **Bouncing** may indicate an anagram

Bound(er), Boundary Adipose, Apprenticed, Articled, Bad, Barrier, Beholden, Border, Bourn(e), Bubalis, Cad, Cavort, Certain, Circumference, Curvet, Decreed, Demarcation, Demarkation, Dool, Duty, End, Engirt, Entrechat, Erub, Eruv, Event horizon, Exciton, Fence, Four, Galumph, Gambado, Gambol, Girt, Harestane, Hedge, Heel, Held, Hoarstone, Hops, Hourstone, Interface, Jump, Kangaroo, ➤ LEAP, Limes, Limit, Linch, Lollop, Lope, Meare, Meer, Meith, Mere, Merestone, Mete, Moho, Muscle, Obliged, Outward, Pale, Parameter, Perimeter, Periphery, Plate, Prance, Precinct, Prometheus, Purlieu, Redound, Ring-fence, Roller, Roo, Roped, Rubicon, Scoup, Scowp, Side, Sideline, Six(er), Skip, Spang, Spring, Sten(d), Stoit, Stylolite, T(h)alweg, Tied, Touchline, Upstart, Vault, Verge, Wallaby

▷ **Bounds** may indicate outside letters

Bountiful, Bounty Aid, Bligh, Boon, Christian, Generosity, ➤ GIFT, Goodness, Grant, Head money, Honorarium, Largess(e), Lavish

Bouquet Aroma, Attar, Aura, Compliment, Corsage, Fragrancy, Garni, Nose, Nosegay, Plaudit, Posy, Spiritual, Spray

Bourbon Alfonso

Bourgeois Common, Pleb(ian)

Bout Bender, Bust, Contest, Dose, Go, Jag, Match, Spell, Spree, Turn, Venery, Venewe, Venue

Boutique Shop

Bow(er), Bowing, Bowman Alcove, Arbour, Arc, Arch, ➤ ARCHER, Arco, Arson, Beck, Bend, Boudoir, Clara, Congé(e), Crescent, Crook, Cupid, ➤ CURVE, Defer, Dicky, Drail, Droop, Duck, Echelles, Eros, Eugh, Eye, Fiddle(r), Fiddlestick, Foredeck, Halse, Hawse, Jook, Jouk, Kneel, Kotow, Laval(l)ière, Lean, Lout, Moulinet, Namaste, Nameste, Nod, Nutate, Obeisance, Obtemper, Paganini, Pergola, Quarrel, Reverence, Salaam, Seamer, Shelter, Slope, Spiccato, Stick, ➤ SUBMIT, Tie, Yew, Yield

Bowdler(ize) Edit(or), Water

Bowels Entrails, Guts, Innards, Viscera

▷ **Bower** may indicate using a bow

Bowl(er), Bowling, Bowl over, Bowls B, Basin, Begging, Bicker, Bocce, Bocci(a), Boccie, Bodyline, Bool, Bosey, Bouncer, Cage-cup, Calabash, Candlepins, Cap, Carpet, Caup, Chalice, Cheese, Chinaman, Christie, Christy, Cog(g)ie, Coolamon, Crater, Cup, Derby, ➤ DISH, Dismiss, Dome, Drake, Dumbfound, Dust, Ecuelle, End, Finger, Goldfish, Googly, Grub, Hog, Hoop, Jack, Jeroboam, Jorum, Kegler, Krater, Lavabo, Laver, Leg-spin, Lightweight, Lob, Locke, Monteith, Night, Offbreak, Old, Over-arm, Pace, Pan, Pétanque, Piggin, Porringer, Pot-hat, Pottinger, Punch, Raku, Rink, Roll, Roundarm, Seam(er), Skip, Skittle(s), Spare, Spinner, Spofforth, Stadium, Stagger, Stummel, Sucrier, Super, Ten-pin, Tom, Underarm, Underhand, Underwood, Voce, Wassail, Wood, York(er)

Box(ing) Baignoire, Bandbox, Bareknuckle, Bijou, Binnacle, Black, Bonk, Buist, Bunk, Bush, Caddy, Call, Camera, Canister, Case, Cash, Cassolette, Chest, Chinese, Christmas, Ciborium, Coach, Coffer, Coffret, Confessional, Cool, Crate, Cuff, Deed, Dialogue, Dispatch, Drawer, Enclose, ➤ FIGHT, File, Fist, Fund, Fuse, Glory, Go-kart, Hedge, Honesty, Humidor, Hutch, Inro, Journal, Junction, Jury, Kiosk, Kite, Knevell, Ladle, Locker, Lodge, Loge, Mill, Mocock, Mocuck, Musical, Package, Pandora's, Papeterie, Peepshow, Penalty, Pew, Phylactery, Pillar, Pix, Pouncet, Press, Prompt, Protector, Pyxis, Register, Ring, Saggar(d), Sagger, Savate, Scrap, Seggar, Sentry, Shoe, Signal, Skinner, Skip(pet), Slipcase, Solander, ➤ SPAR, Swell, Tabernacle, Tefillin, Telephone, Telly, Thai, Tube, Tuck, TV, Vasculum, Voice, Witness, Yakhdan

Boxer Ali, Amycus, Bantamweight, Bruiser, Bruno, Canine, Carnera, Carpentier, Carthorse, Chinaman, Cooper, Crater, Cruiserweight, Dog, Eryx, Farr, Featherweight, Flyweight, Ham, Heavyweight, McCoy, Middleweight, Pandora, Pollux, Pug, Pugil(ist), Rebellion, Rocky, Shadow, Welterweight, Wilde

Boxing-glove Hurlbat, Muffle, Whirlbat, Whorlbat

Boy(s) Apprentice, Ball, Bevin, Blue-eyed, Breeches, Bub(by), Cabin, Chiel(d), ➤ CHILD, Chokra, Chummy, Cub, Callant, Catamite, Champagne, Galopin, Garçon, Gorsoon, Gossoon, Groom, Ha, Jack, Kid, Klonkie, Knave, Lackbeard, ➤ LAD, Loblolly's, Loon(ie), Minstrel, Nibs, Nipper, Page, Prentice, Principal, Putto, Rent, Roaring, Shaver, Son, Spalpeen, Sprig, Stripling, Tad, Ted(dy), Tiger, Toy, Urchin, Whipping, ➤ YOUTH

▷ **Boy** may indicate an abbreviated name

Boycott Avoid, Bat, Black, Blacklist, Exclude, Hartal, Isolate, Ostracise, Shun

Boyfriend Beau, Date, Steady

Boyle Juno

Bp Bishop, DD, RR

Brace(s), Bracing Accolade, Couple, Crosstree, Gallace, Gallows, Gallus(es), Gird, Hound, Invigorate, Pair, Pr, Rear-arch, Rere-arch, Skeg, Splint, Steady, Stiffener, Strut, ➤ SUPPORT, Suspenders, Tauten, Tone, Tonic, Two

Bracelet Armil(la), Armlet, Bangle, Cuff, Darbies, Handcuff, Manacle, Manilla

Brachiopod Ecardines, Spirifer

Bracken Brake, Fern, Pteridium, Tara

Bracket(s) Angle-iron, Bibb, Brace, Cantilever, Console, Corbel, Couple, Cripple, Misericord(e), Modillion, Mutule, Parenthesis, Potence, Pylon, Rigger, Sconce, Straddle, Strata, ➤ STRUT, Trivet, Truss

Bract Glume(lla), Involucel, Involucre, Leaf, Lemma, Palea, Palet, Phyllary, Spathe

Brad Nail, Pin, Rivet, Sprig

Brag(gart), Bragging Basilisco, Birkie, Bluster, Boast, Bobadil, Braggadocio, Bull, Cockalorum, Crow, Falstaff, Fanfaronade, Gab, Gascon, Hot-air, Loudmouth, Parolles, Puckfist, Puff, Rodomontader, Skite, Slam, Swagger, Thrason, Thrasonic, Tongue-doubtie, Tongue-doughty, Vainglorious, Vaunt

Brahma(n) Sannyasi(n)

Braid A(i)glet, Aiguillette, Frog, Galloon, Lacet, Plait, Plat, Rickrack, Ricrac, Rick-rack, Seaming-lace, Sennet, Sennit, Sinnet, Soutache, Tress, Trim, Twist, Weave

▷ **Brain(s)** may indicate an anagram

Brain(y), Brain disease, Brain-power Amygdala, Appestat, Bean, Bright, Cerebellum, Cerebrum, Cortex, Diencephalon, Dura mater, Encephalon, Epencephalon, Fornix, Genius, Gyrus, Harn(s), Head, Hippocampus, Hypothalamus, Insula, Intelligence, IQ, Kuru, Limbic, Loaf, Lobe, Mater, Medulla, Medulla oblongata, Mind, Noddle, Noesis, Nous, Peduncle, Pericranium, Pia mater, Pons, Pontile, Sconce, Sense, Sensorium, Striatum, Subcortex, Tectum, Thalamus, Upper stor(e)y, Vermis, Wetware

Brainless Anencephaly, Bimbo, Stupid, Thick

Brain-washing Menticide, Propaganda

Brake Adiantum, Air, Bracken, Curb, Disc, Drag, Drum, Fern, Grove, Hydraulic, Nemoral, Overrun, Ratchet, Rein, Shoe, ➤ SLOW, Spinney, Sprag, Tara, Thicket, Vacuum

Bramble, Brambly Batology, Blackberry, Boysenberry, Brier, Cloudberry, Rubus, Thorn, Wait-a-bit

Bran Cereal, Chesil, Chisel, Oats, Pollard

Branch(ed), Branches, Branching, Branch Office Affiliate, Antler, Arm, BO, Bough, Cladode, Cow, Dendron, Dept, Diversify, Diverticulum, Divide, Filiate, Fork, Grain, Kow, Jump, Lateral, Limb, Lobe, Loop, Lye, Lylum, Offshoot, Olive, Patulous, Raguly, Ramate, Ramulus, Reis, Rice, Shroud, Special, Spray(ey), Sprig, Spur, Tributary, Turning, Turn-off, Twig, Wattle, Yard

Branch-rib Lierne

Brand Broadsword, Buist, Burn, Cauterise, Chop, Class, Denounce, Earmark, Ember, Excalibur, Falchion, Faulchin, Faulchion, Idiograph, Iron, Label, Line, ➤ MARK, Marque, Sear, Stigma, Sweard, Sword, Torch, Wipe

Brandish Bless, Flaunt, Flourish, Waffle, Wampish, Wave

Brandy Aguardiente, Applejack, Aqua vitae, Armagnac, Bingo, Calvados, Cape smoke, Cold without, Dop, Eau de vie, Fine, Framboise, Grappa, Marc, Mampoer, Nantes, Nantz, Napoleon, Quetsch, Slivovic(a), Slivovitz, Smoke

Bras Arms

Brash Impudent, Pushy, Rain, Rash

Brass(ware), Brassy Benares, Brazen, Cheek, Corinthian, Cornet, Dinanderie, Face, Front, Harsh, Horn, Horse, Latten, Lip, Loot, Lota(h), Loud, Matrix, ➤ MONEY, Moola(h), Oof, Oricalche, Orichalc, Pyrites, Sopranino, Sass, Snash, Talus, Top, Trombone

Brassard Armlet

Brass hat Brig

Brassica Brussels (sprout), ➤ CABBAGE, Colza

Brat Bairn, Gait(t), Gamin, Geit, Git, Gyte, Imp, Lad, Terror, Urchin

Brave(ry) Amerind, Apache, Bold, Conan, Corragio, Courage, Creek, Dare, ➤ DEFY, Doughty, Dress, Face, Gallant, Game, Gamy, Gutsy, Hardy, Heroism, Indian, Injun, Intrepid, Lion, Manful, Manly, Nannup, Plucky, Prow(ess), Sannup, Stout, Uncas, Valiant, Valour, Wight

Bravo Acclaim, Bandit, Bully, Desperado, Euge, Murderer, Olé, Spadassin, Villain

Brawl Affray, Bagarre, Bicker, Brabble, Donnybrook, Dust, Fight, Flite, Flyte, Fracas, Fratch, Fray, Melee, Prawl, Rammy, Roughhouse, Scuffle, Set-to, Shindig, Stoush, Tar, Wrangle

Brawn(y) Beef, Burliness, Headcheese, He-man, Muscle, Power, Rillettes, Sinew

Bray Cry, Heehaw, Stamp, Vicar, Whinny

Brazen Bold, Brassy, Flagrant, Impudent, Shameless, Unabashed

Brazier Brasero, Fire, Hibachi, Mangal, Scaldino

Brazil(ian) Caboclo, Carioca, Para

Breach Assault, Break, Chasm, Cleft, Gap(e), Infraction, Redan, Rupture, Saltus, Schism, Solution, Trespass, Violate

Bread Afrikomen, Azym(e), Bagel, Baguette, Bannock, Bap, Barmbrack, Batch, Brewis, Brioche, Brownie, Bun, Cash, Chal(l)ah, Chametz, Chapati, Cheat, Ciabatta, Cob, Coburg, Corn, Corsned, Croute, Crouton, Crumpet, Crust, Damper, Dibs, Dika, Doorstep, Elephant's-foot, Eulogia, Flatbread, Focaccia, French, Garlic, Gluten, Graham, Grissino, Guarana, Hametz, Hometz, Host, Indian, Injera, Jannock, Johnny-cake, Laver, Leavened, Loaf, Long tin, Manchet, ➤ MONEY, Na(a)n, Panada, Panary, Paneity, Paratha, Pikelet, Pit(t)a, Pone, Poultice, Pumpernickel, Puri, Ravel, Roll, Rooty, Roti, Rusk, Rye, Sally Lunn, Schnecken, Shive, Sippet, Smor(re)brod, Soda, Sourdough, Staff of life, Stollen, Sugar, Sweet, Tartine, Tommy, Tortoise-plant, Wastel, Zakuski, Zwieback

Breadfruit Ja(c)k

Breadwinner Earner, Pa

Break(ing), Break-down, Break-in, Break-up, Broken Adjourn, Aposiopesis, Bait, Breach, Caesura, Caesure, Cark, Cesure, Chinaman, Chip, Cleave, Comb, Comma, Commercial, Comminute, Compost, Crack, Crock, Crumble, Deave, Debacle, Deeve, Demob, Destroy, Diffract, Disintegrate, Disperse, Disrupt, Erupt, Exeat, Fast, Fault, Four, ➤ FRACT(URE), Fritter, Frush, Gaffe, Greenstick, Half-time, Half-term, Hernia, Holiday, Infringe, Interim, Interlude, Intermission, Interrupt, ➤ INTERVAL, Irrupt, Knap, Knickpoint, Lacuna, Lapse, Leave, Lysis, Moratorium, Nickpoint, Nooner, Outage, Pause, Phreak, Polarise, Recess, Recrudescent, Relief, Rend, Resorption, Respite, Rest, Rift, Ruin, Rupture, Saltus, Schism(a), Secede, Shatter, Shiver, Smash, Smokeho, Smoko, Snap, Stave, Stop, Stove, Sunder, Tame, Tea-ho, Tear, Time-out, Torn, Transgress, Truce, Vacation, Violate

Breakable Brittle, Delicate, Fissile, Frail, Friable

Breakdown Analyse, Autolysis, Cataclasm, Collapse, Conk, Glitch, Glycolosis, Histolysis, Lyse, Lysis, Ruin

Breaker Billow, Comber, Ice, Roller, Smasher, Surf

Breakfast B, Brunch, Chota-hazri, Continental, Disjune, Kipper, Wedding

Breakneck Headlong

Breakwater Groyne, Jetty, Mole, Pier, Tetrapod

Bream Fish, Porgy, Sar(gus), Tai

Breast(bone), Breasts, Breastwork Bazuma, Blob, Bosom, Brave, Brisket, Bristols, Bust, Counter, Diddy, Duddy, Dug, Garbonza, Gazunga, Heart-spoon, Jubbies, Jugs, Knockers, Norg, Nork, Rampart, Redan, Sangar, Sungar, Stem, Sternum, Supreme, Tit, Xiphisternum

Breastplate Armour, Byrnie, Curat, Curiet, Pectoral, Plastron, Rational, Rest, Shield, Thorax, Xiphiplastron

Breath(ing), Breathe(r) Aerobe, Aspirate, Branchia, Cheyne-Stokes, Cypress-knee, Eupnoea, Exhalation, Expiration, Flatus, Gasp, Gill, H, Halitosis, Hauriant, Haurient, Hobday, Hypernoea, Hyperventilation, Hypopnoea, Inhale, Inspiration, Lung, Nares, Nostril, Oxygenator, Pant,

Pneuma, Prana, Pulmo, Rale, Respire, Respite, Rest, Rhonchus, Scuba, Snorkel, Snortmast, Snuffle, Spiracle, Spirit, Spiritus, Vent, Wheeze, Whiff, Whisper, Whift, Whist, Wind, Windpipe

Breathless(ness) Anhelation, Apnoea, Asthma, Dyspnoea, Emphysema, Orthopnoea, Puffed-out, Tachypnoea, Wheezing

Breathtaking Amazing, Asphyxia

Breech(es) Bible, Buckskin, Chaps, Flog, Galligaskins, Hose, Jodhpurs, Kneecords, Knickerbockers, Plushes, Smallclothes, Smalls, Trews, Trouse(rs), Trusses

Breed(ing), Breeding-place Bear, Beget, Cleck, Endogamous, Engender, Engend(r)ure, Eugenics, Gentrice, Lineage, ➤ MANNERS, Origin, Panmixia, Procreate, Pullulate, Race, Rear, Seminary, Sire, Species, Stock, Strain, Stud, Telegony, Thremmatology, Tribe, Voltinism

Breeze, Breezy Air, Breath, Brisk, Catspaw, Chipper, Doctor, Gust, Mackerel, Slant, Sniffler, Tiff, Zephyr

Brethren Bohemian, Darbyite, Exclusive, Kin, Plymouth

Breton Armoric, Brezonek

Breve Minim, Note, O

Breviary Portesse, Portous

➤ **Brevity** see Brief

Brew(er), Brewery, Brewing Ale, Billycan, Brose, Browst, Bummock, ➤ CONCOCT, Contrive, Dictionary, Ferment, Infusion, Liquor, Malt, Potion, Steep, Yeast, Yill, Zymurgy

Briar Bramble, Canker, Lawyer

Bribe(ry) Backhander, Bonus, Boodle, Bung, Dash, Embracery, Get at, Graft, Grease, Hush-money, Insult, Kickback, Oil, Palm, Payola, Schmear, Slush, Soap, Sop, Square, Straightener, Suborn, Sweeten(er), Tempt, Tenderloin, Vail, Vales

Bric-a-brac Bibelot, Curio, Rattle-trap, Smytrie, Tatt, Virtu

Brick(s), Brickwork Adobe, Bat, Bath, Boob, Bullnose, Bur(r), Clanger, Clinker, Closer, Course, Fletton, Gaffe, Gault, Header, Ingot, Klinker, Lateritious, Lego®, Malm, Nogging, Red, Soldier, Sport, Stalwart, Stretcher, Terra-cotta, Testaceous, Tile, Trojan, Trump

Brickbat Missile

Bricklayer Churchill

Bride(s) Bartered, Danaides, Ellen, Spouse, War, Wife, Ximena

Bridesmaid Paranymph

Bridge(head), Bridge player Acol, Al Sirat, Aqueduct, Auction, Bailey, Balance, Barre, Bascule, Bestride, Bifrost, Biritch, Bridle-chord, Brooklyn, Cantilever, Capo, Capodastro, Capotasto, Catwalk, Chevalet, Chicago, Chicane, Clapper, Clifton, Contract, Counterpoise, Cross, Cut-throat, Deck, Declarer, Drawbridge, Duplicate, Gangplank, Gangway, Gantry, Hog's back, Humpback, Humpbacked, Jigger, Ligger, Link, London, Menai, Nasion, Overpass, Pivot, Plafond, Ponceau, Ponticello, Pontoon, Rialto, Rubber, Sighs, Sinvat, ➤ SPAN, Spanner, Stamford, Straddle,

Suspension, Swing, Tay, Tête-de-pont, Transporter, Trestle, Truss, Vertical lift, Viaduct, Vint, Waterloo, Wheatstone

Bridge pair EW, NS, SN, WE

Bridge protector Ice-apron

Bridge system Acol

Bridle Bit, Branks, Bridoon, Bristle, Browband, Curb, Hackamore, Halter, Headstall, Musrol, Noseband, Rein

Bridle path Orbit, Track

Brief(s), Briefing, Briefly, Brevity Awhile, Bluette, Brachyology, Breviate, Cape, Compact, ➤ CONCISE, Curt, Dossier, Fleeting, Instruct, Laconic, Nearly, Pants, Pennorth, Pithy, Prime, Scant, Short-term, Short-winded, ➤ SHORT(EN), Sitrep, Succinct, Summing, Tanga, Terse, Transient, Undies, Update, Watching

Brig Br, Jail, Nancy Bell, ➤ SHIP, Snow

Brigade Boys', Corps, Fire, International, Red, Troop

Brigand Bandit, Bandolero, Cateran, Haiduck, Heiduc, Heyduck, Klepht, Pillager, Pirate, Rob Roy, ➤ ROBBER, Trailbaston

Bright(en), Brightness Afterglow, Alert, Brainy, Breezy, Brilliant, Brisk, Cheery, Cla(i)re, Clear, Clever, Effulgent, Elaine, Fair, Floodlit, Florid, Garish, Gay, Glad, Glow, Hono(u)r, Light, Lit, Loud, Lucid, Luculent, Lustre, Net(t), Nit, Radiant, Rosy, Scintillating, Sematic, Sharp, Sheeny, Sheer, Shere, Skyre, Smart, Stilb, Sunlit, Sunny, Vive, Vivid, White

Bright spot Facula

Brilliance, Brilliant Ace, Blaze, Brainy, Def, Effulgent, Flashy, Galaxy, Gay, Gemmy, Glossy, Inspired, Lambent, Lustre, Mega-, Meteoric, Nitid, Pear, ➤ RADIANT, Refulgent, Resplendent, Shiny, Spangle, Splendour, Star, ➤ VIVID, Virtuoso, Water

Brim Edge, Lip, Rim, Ugly

Brimstone Hellfire, S, Sulphur

Brindisi Skolion, Toast

Brindled Piebald, Tabby, Tawny

Brine Muriatic, Ozone, Pickle, Saline, Salt

Bring(ing) Afferent, Bear, Carry, Cause, Conduct, Convey, Earn, Evoke, Fet, Fetch, Hatch, Induce, Land, Produce, Wreak

Bring up Breed, Educate, Exhume, Foster, Nurture, Raise, ➤ REAR

Brink ➤ EDGE, Lip, Rim, Shore, ➤ VERGE

Brisk(ness) Active, Alacrity, Alert, Allegro, Breezy, Busy, Chipper, Crank, Crisp, Crouse, Fresh, Gaillard, Galliard, Jaunty, Kedge, Kedgy, Kidge, Lively, Perk, Pert, Rattling, Roaring, Scherzo, Sharp, Smart, Snappy, Spanking, Spirited, Sprightly, Vivace, Yare, Zippy

Bristle(d), Bristling, Bristly Aciculum, Arista, Awn, Barb, Birse, Bridle, Campodeiform, Chaeta, Flurry, Fraught, Frenulum, Glochidium, Gooseflesh, Hackles, Hair, Herissé, Hispid, Horrent, Horripilation, Nereid, Polychaete, Seta, Setose, Striga, Strigose, Stubble, Whisker, Vibraculum, Villus

Bristle-tail Campodea

Britain Alban(y), Albion

Britannia, Britannia metal Tutania

Brit(ish), Briton(s) Anglo, Herring, Iceni, Insular, Isles, Limey, Pict, Pom, Rooinek, Saxon, Silurian, UK

Brittany Armorica

Brittle Bruckle, Crackly, Crimp, Crisp, Delicate, ➤ FRAGILE, Frush, Redsear, Red-share, Red-shire, Redshort, Shivery, Spall, Spalt

▷ **Brittle** may indicate an anagram

Broach Approach, Open, Raise, Spit, Suggest, Tap, Widen

Broad(ly) Crumpet, Dame, Doll, Doxy, Drab, General, Generic, Largo, Latitudinous, Loose, Outspoken, Ovate, Pro, Roomy, Spatulate, Thick, Tolerant, Wide, Woman

Broad-beaked Latirostrate

Broadcast(er), Broadcasting Ad(vertise), Air, Announce, Beam, Breaker, CB, Disperse, Disseminate, Emission, Ham, IBA, OB, On, Outside, Pirate, Programme, Promulgate, Radiate, Radio, Relay, ➤ SCATTER, Scattershot, Screen(ed), SECAM, Seed, Sky, Sow, Sperse, Spread, Sprinkle, Transmission, Ventilate, Wavelength

Broad-nosed Platyrrhine

Broadside Barrage, Criticism, Salvo, Tire

Broadway Boulevard, Esplanade, Motorway

Brocade Arrasene, Baldachin, Baldaquin, Baudekin, Bawdkin, Kincob, Zari

Brochure Leaflet, Pamphlet, Tract

Brogue Accent, ➤ SHOE

Broke(n) Bankrupt, Bust(ed), Duff, Evans, Fritz, Insolvent, Kaput, Puckeroo, Shattered, Skint, Stony, Stove, Strapped

▷ **Broken** may indicate an anagram

Broken off Prerupt

Broker Agent, Banian, Banyan, Jobber, Go-between, Mediator, ➤ MERCHANT, Shadchan, Uncle

Bromide Halide, Haloid

Bromine Br

Bronchitic Chesty

Bronte(s) Bell, Cyclops

Brontosaurus Apatosaurus

Bronze, Bronze age Bell, Bras(s), Brown, Gunmetal, Hallstatt(ian), Helladic, Minoan, Mycenean, Ormolu, Phosphor, Schillerspar, Sextans, Talos, Tan, Third

Brooch Cameo, Clasp, Fibula, Luckenbooth, Ouch, Owche, Pin, Preen, Prop, Spang, Sunburst

Brood Clock, Clutch, Cogitate, Covey, Eye, Eyrie, Hatch, Hover, Incubate, Introspect, Kindle, Litter, Meditate, Mill, Mull, Nest, Nid, Perch, Pet, ➤ PONDER, Repine, Roost, Sit, Sulk, Team

Brook Babbling, Beck, Branch, Burn, Countenance, Creek, Endure, Ghyll, Gill, Kerith, Kill, Pirl, Purl, Rill(et), River, Rivulet, Runlet, Runnel, Stand, Stomach, Stream, Suffer, Tolerate

Broom Besom, Brush, Cow, Genista, Gorse, Greenweed, Knee-holly, Kow, Orobranche, Retama, Spart, Sweeper, Whisk

Broth Bouillon, Brew(is), Cullis, Dashi, Kail, Kale, Muslin-kale, Pottage, Scotch, Skilly, ➤ SOUP, Stock

Brothel Bagnio, Bordel(lo), Cathouse, Corinth, Crib, Den, Honkytonk, Hothouse, Kip, Knocking shop, Seraglio, Stew

Brother Ally, Bhai, Billie, Billy, Blood, Brethren, Bro, Bud, Comrade, Fellow, Fra, Freemason, Lay, ➤ MONK, Moose, Sib(ling), Theatine, Trappist, Worker

Brow Crest, Forehead, Glabella, Ridge, Sinciput, Tump-line

Browbeat Badger, Bully, Hector

Brown Abram, Adust, Amber, Auburn, Bay, Biscuit, Bisque, Bister, Bistre, Bole, Br, Braise, Brindle, Bronzed, Brunette, Burnet, Capability, Caramel, Caromel, Cinnamon, Cook, Coromandel, Dun, Fallow, Filemot, Fulvous, Fusc(ous), Grill, Hazel, Ivor, John, Khaki, Liver, Meadow, Mocha, Mousy, Philamot, Rufous, Rugbeian, Russet, Rust, Scorch, Sepia, Sienna, Soare, Sore, Sorrel, Tan, Tawny, Tenné, Testaceous, Toast, Tom, Umber, Vandyke, Wholemeal, Windsor

Browne Sam

Brownie Dobbie, Dobby, Goblin, Hob, Kobold, Leprechaun, Nis(se), Rosebud, Sprite

Browse Graze, Pasture, Read, Scan, Stall-read, Surf

Bruce Robert

Bruise Contund, Contuse, Crush, Damage, Ding, Ecchymosis, Frush, Golp(e), Hurt, Intuse, Livedo, Lividity, Mark, Mouse, Pound, Purpure, Rainbow, Shiner, Ston(n), Stun, Surbate

Brummagen Tatty

Brunette Dark, Latin

Brush (off), Brushwood Bavin, Brake, Broom, Carbon, Chaparral, Clash, Dandy, Dismiss, Dust, Encounter, Fan, Filbert, Filecard, Firth, Fitch, Frith, Grainer, Hag, Hog, Kiss, Liner, Loofah, Mop, Paint, Pig, Pope's head, Putois, Rebuff, Rice, Rigger, Sable, Scrub, Scuff, Skim, Striper, Thicket, Touch

Brusque Abrupt, Blunt, Curt, Downright, Pithy, Short

Brussels Carpet, Lace

Brutal, Brute Animal, Beast, Bête, Caesar, Caliban, Cruel, Hun, Iguanodon, Inhuman, Nazi, Nero, Ostrogoth, Pitiless, Quagga, Roughshod, Ruffian, Thresher-whale, Yahoo

Brutus Wig

Bryophyte Moss, Tree-moss

Bubble(s), Bubbly Air-bell, Air-lock, Barmy, Bead(ed), Bell, Bleb, Blister, Boil, Buller, Cavitate, Champagne, Cissing, Ebullition, Effervesce, Embolus, Enthuse, Espumoso, Foam, ➤ FROTH, Gassy, Globule, Gurgle,

Head, Mantle, Mississippi, Popple, Rale, Reputation, Roundel, Rowndell, Seed, Seethe, Simmer, South Sea, Vesicle, Widow

Bubble and squeak Colcannon

Buccaneer Corsair, Dampier, Drake, Freebooter, Morgan, Picaroon, Pirate

Buck (up) Bongo, Brace, Cheer, Dandy, Deer, Dollar, Elate, Encheer, Hart, Jerk, Leash, Male, Ourebi, Pitch, Pricket, Ram, Rusa, Sore, Sorel(l), Sorrel, Spade, Spay(a)d, ➤ STAG, Staggard, Stud, Wheel

Buckaroo Cowboy, Cowpoke

Bucket(s) Bail, Bale, Clamshell, Ice, Kibble, Noria, Pail, Piggin, Scuttle, Situla, Stoop(e), Stope, Stoup, Tub

Buckeye Ohio

Buckle Artois, Clasp, Contort, Crumple, Deform, Dent, Fasten, Warp

▷ **Buckle** may indicate an anagram

Buckle-beggar Patrico

Buckler Ancile, Rondache, ➤ SHIELD, Targe

▷ **Bucks** may indicate an anagram

Buckshee Free

Buckthorn Cascara, Wahoo

Buckwheat Brank, Sarrasin, Sarrazin

Bucolic Aeglogue, Eglogue, Idyllic, Pastoral, Rural, Rustic

Bud(ding), Buddy Botoné, Bottony, Bulbil, Burgeon, Clove, Cobber, Deb, Eye, Gem(ma), Germinate, Knosp, Knot, Nascent, Pal, Scion, Serial, Shoot, Sprout, Taste, Turion

Buddha, Buddhism, Buddhist Abhidhamma, Ahimsa, Amitabha, Anata, Anicca, Arhat, Asoka, Bodhisattva, Dalai Lama, Gautama, Hinayana, Jain, Jataka, Jodo, Mahatma, Mahayana, Maya, Pali, Pitaka, Pure Land, Sakya-muni, Sila, Soka Gakkai, Theravada, Tripitaka, Triratna, Zen(o)

Budge Jee, Move, Stir, Submit

Budget Estimate, Plan, Programme, Shoestring

Buff Beige, Birthday suit, Eatanswill, Fan, Fawn, Nankeen, Nude, Nut, Polish, ➤ RUB, Streak

Buffalo African, Anoa, Arna, Asiatic, Bison, Bonasus, Bugle, Cap, Cape, Carabao, Ox, Perplex, Takin, Tamarao, Tamarau, Timarau, Water, Zamouse

Buffer Bootblack, Cofferdam, Cutwater, Fender

Buffet Bang, Blow, Box, Counter, Cuff, Hit, Lam, Maltreat, Perpendicular, Shove, Sideboard, Smorgasborg, Strike, Strook(e)

Buffoon(ery) Antic, Clown, Droll, Goliard, Harlequin, Horseplay, Jester, Mime(r), Mome, Mummer, Nutter, Pantagruel, Pantaloon(ery), Pickle-herring, Pierrot, Scaramouch, Scogan, Scoggin, Scurrile, Slouch, Tomfool, Vice, Wag, Zany

Bug(s) Anoplura, Arthropod, Assassin, Bacteria, Beetle, Capsid, Chinch, Cimex, Coccidae, Cockchafer, Corixid, Croton, Damsel, Debris, Dictograph®, Eavesdrop, Harlequin, Hassle, Hemiptera, ➤ INSECT, Jitter, June, Kissing, Lace, May, Mealy, Micrococcus, Mike, Milkweed, Millennium, Mite, Squash, Tap, Vex, Wheel, Wiretap

Bugbear Anathema, Bogey, Bogle, Bogy, Eten, Ettin, Poker, Rawhead
Buggy Beach, Car, Cart, Shay, Tipcart, Trap
Bughouse Fleapit, Loco
Bugle, Bugle call Chamade, Clarion, Cornet, Hallali, Last post, Ox, Reveille, Taps, ➤ TRUMPET, Urus
Build(ing), Building site Anabolism, Ar(a)eostyle, Accrue, Assemble, Bhavan, Big, Capitol, Colosseum, Commons, Cot, ➤ CREATE, Cruck, Curia, Develop, Dipteros, Drystone, Duplex, Edifice, Edify, Erect, Fabric, Hut, Infill, Insula, Kaaba, Ken, Linhay, Listed, Low-rise, Lyceum, Minaret, Monopteron, Mould, Observatory, Outhouse, Palazzo, Phalanstery, Phalanx, Pile, Portakabin®, Premises, Prytaneum, Quonset®, Raise, Rotunda, Skyscraper, Stance, Structure, Synthesis, Tectonic, Telecottage, Temple, Tenement, Tholos, Tower, Triplex®
Builder Brick, Constructor, Engineer, Millwright
▷ **Building** may indicate an anagram
Bulb Camas(h), Chive, Cive, Corm, Globe, Lamp, Light, Pearl, Scallion, Set, Shallot, Squill
Bulge, Bulging Astrut, Bag, Bias, Biconvex, Bug, Bulbous, Bunchy, Cockle, Entasis, Expand, Exsert, Inion, Protrude, Relievo, Rotund, Strout, Strut, ➤ SWELL, Tumid
Bulk(y) Aggregate, Ample, Big, Body, Corpulent, Extent, Gross, Hull, Massive, Preponderance, Roughage, Scalar, ➤ SIZE, Stout, Vol(ume), Weight
Bull(ock), Bully Anoa, Apis, Bakha, Beef, Blarney, Bluster, Bovine, Brag, Brave, Browbeat, Buchis, Bucko, Despot, Dragoon, Drawcansir, Encierro, Englishman, Eretrian, Fancyman, Farnese, Flashman, Flatter, Gold, Gosh, Hapi, Harass, Hawcubite, Haze(r), Hector, Hoodlum, Huff, Intimidate, Investor, Iricism, Irish(ism), John, Killcow, Lambast, Maltreat, Merwer, Mick(e)(y), Mistake, Mithraism, Mohock, Nandi, Neat, Papal, Piker, Pistol, Placet, Poler, Rhodian, Roarer, Rot, Ruffian, Sitting, Souteneur, Stag, Strong-arm, Swash-buckler, Taurine, Taurus, Toitoi, Tommy-rot, Tosh, Trash, Twaddle, Tyran(ne), Tyrannise, Tyrant, Unigenitus, Zo(bo)
Bulldog Marshal, Tenacious
Bulldoze(r) Coerce, Earthmover, Leveller, Overturn
Bullet Balata, Ball, Biscayan, Dumdum, Fusillade, Minié, Minié ball, Missile, Pellet, Plastic, Round, Rubber, Shot, Slug, Tracer
Bulletin Memo, Newsletter, Report, Summary
Bull-fight(er) Banderillero, Banderillo, Corrida, Cuadrilla, Escamillo, Matador, Picador, Rejoneador, Tauromachy, Toreador, Torero
Bull-head Cottoid, Father-lasher, Pogge, Sea-poacher
Bull-rider Europa
Bull-roarer Rhombos, Tu(r)ndun
Bull's eye Carton, God, Humbug, Target
Bulrush Pandanaceous, Reed, Reed-mace, Tule
Bulwark Bastion, Defence, Rampart, Resistor
Bum Ass, Beg, Prat, Sponge, Thumb, Tramp, Vagabond

Bumble Beadle, Bedel(l)

▷ **Bumble** may indicate an anagram

Bumboat woman Buttercup

Bump(er), Bumps Big, Blow, Bradyseism, Bucket, Clour, Collide, Dunch, Encephalocele, Fender, Hillock, Immense, Inian, Inion, Joll, Jo(u)le, Jowl, Keltie, Kelty, Knar, Knock, Mamilla, Mogul, Organ, Phrenology, Reveille, Rouse, Speed, Thump

Bumpkin Bucolic, Bushwhacker, Clodhopper, Hawbuck, Hayseed, Hick, Jock, Lout, Oaf, Put(t), Rube, Rustic, Yokel, Zany

Bumptious Arrogant, Brash, Randie, Randy, Uppity

Bun Barmbrack, Bath, Chelsea, Chignon, Chou, Hot-cross, Huffkin, Mosbolletjie, Roll, Teacake, Toorie, Wad

Bunch Acinus, Anthology, Bob, Botryoid, Cluster, Fascicle, Finial, Flock, ➤ GROUP, Hand, Handful, Lot, Lump, Panicle, Raceme, Spray, Staphyline, Tassel, Tee, Truss, Tuft

Bundle Axoneme, Bale, Bavin, Bluey, Bottle, Byssus, Desmoid, Dorlach, Drum, Fag(g)ot, Fascicle, Fascine, Fibre, Fibrovascular, Kemple, Knitch, Lemniscus, Matilda, ➤ PACK(AGE), Parcel, Sack, Sheaf, Shiralee, Shock, Shook, Stook, Swag, Tie, Top, Trousseau, Truss, Vascular, Wad, Wadge, Wap

Bung Cork, Dook, Obturate, Plug, Stopgap, Stopper

Bungalow Dak

Bungle(r) Blunder, Blunk, Bodge, Boob, Botch, Bumble, Bummle, Duff, Fluff, Foozle, Foul, Goof, Mess, Mis(h)guggle, Muddle, Muff, Mull, Prat, Screw, Spoil

Bunk(er), Bunkum Abscond, Absquatulate, Balderdash, Baloney, Berth, Blah, Bolt, Casemate, Claptrap, Clio, Entrap, Guy, Hazard, History, Hokum, Humbug, Malarky, Rot, Scuttle, Tosh, Trap, Tripe

Bunter Billy, Owl

Bunthorne Aesthete, Poet

Bunting Bird, Cirl, Flag, Fringilline, Ortolan, Snow, Streamer, Yellow-hammer, Yowley

Buoy Bell, Breeches, Can, Dan, Daymark, Dolphin, Float, Marker, Nun, Raft, Ring, Seamark, Sonar, Sustain

Buoyant Blithe, Floaty, Resilient

Burble Blat, Gibber

Burden(ed) Albatross, Beare, Bob, Cargo, Cark, Chant, Chorus, Cross, Cumber, Drone, Droore, Encumber, Encumbrance, Fa-la, Fardel, Folderol, Fraught, Freight, Gist, Handicap, Hum, Lade, ➤ LOAD, Lumber, Millstone, Monkey, Oercome, Onus, Oppress, Put-upon, Refrain, Rumbelow, Saddle, Servitude, Shanty, Substance, Tax, Tenor, Torch, Trouble, Weight, Woe, Yoke

Burdensome Irksome, Onerous, Oppressive, Weighty

Burdock Clote(-bar), Clothur, Cockle-bar, Weed

Bureau Agency, Agitprop, Cominform, Davenport, Desk, Interpol, Kominform, Marriage, ➤ OFFICE

Bureaucracy, Bureaucrat(ic) CS, Impersonal, Jack-in-office, Mandarin, Red tape, Tapist, Wallah

Burgeon(ing) Asprout, Bud, Grow, Sprout

Burgess, Burgher Citizen, Freeman

Burglar, Burgle Area-sneak, Cat, Crack(sman), Intruder, Peterman, Picklock, Raffles, Robber, Screw, Thief, Yegg

Burgundy Macon, Vin

Burial, Burial place Catacomb, Charnel, Committal, Crypt, Darga, Funeral, Golgotha, Grave, Interment, Kurgan, Lair, Last rites, Sepulture, Tomb, Vault, Zoothapsis

Burin Graver

Burlesque Caricatura, Caricature, Comedy, Farce, Heroicomical, Hudibrastic(s), Hurlo-thrumbo, Lampoon, Macaronic, Parody, Satire, Skimmington, Skit, Spoof, Travesty

Burlington RA

Burly Bluff, Stout

Burmese Karen(ni), Naga, Shan

Burn(er), Burning, Burnt Adust, Afire, Alow(e), Ardent, Argand, Arson, Ash, Auto-da-fé, Bats-wing, Beck, Bishop, Blaze, Blister, Brand, Bren(ne), Brent, Brook, Bunsen, Caustic, Cauterise, Char, Chark, Chinese, Cinder, Coal, Coke, Combust, Conflagration, Cremate, Crucial, Deflagrate, Destruct, Eilding, Ember, Emboil, Empyreuma, Fervid, Fircone, ➤ FIRE, Fishtail, Flagrant, Flare, Flash, Fresh(et), Gleed, Gut, Holocaust, Ignite, In, Incendiary, Incinerate, Inure, Inust(ion), Kill, Live, Lunt, Offering, On, Oxidise, Plo(a)t, Pyric, Rill, Sati, Scald, Scorch, Scouther, Scowder, Scowther, Sear, Sienna, Sike, Singe, Smart, Smoulder, Suttee, Swale, Thurible, Torch, Umber, Urent, Ustion, Weeke, Welsbach, Wick

Burp Belch

Burr(ing) Clote, Croup, Dialect, Knob, Rhotacism

Burrow(er), Burrowing Dig, Earth, Fossorial, Gopher, Groundhog, Hole, How, Howk, Mole, Nuzzle, Sett, Tunnel, Viscacha, Warren, Wombat, Worm

Bursar(y) Camerlengo, Camerlingo, Coffers, Grant, Purser, Scholarship, Treasurer

Bursitis Beat

Burst(ing) Blowout, Brast, Break, Dehisce, Disrupt, Dissilient, Ebullient, Erumpent, Erupt, ➤ EXPLODE, Fly, Implode, Pop, Sforzato, Shatter, Spasm, Spirt, Split, Sprint, Spurt, Stave, Tetterous

Bury Cover, Eard, Earth, Embowel, Engrave, Enhearse, Graff, Graft, Imbed, Inhearse, Inhume, Inter, Inurn, Landfill, Repress, Sepulture, Sink, Ye(a)rd, Yird

Bus Aero, Bandwagon, Car, Charabanc, Coach, Double-decker, Hondey, Hopper, ISA, Jitney, Mammy-wagon, Rattletrap, Single-decker, Tramcar, Trolley

Bus conductor Cad, Clippy

Bush(y) Bramble, Brier, Bullace, Busket, Clump, Dumose, Firethorn, Hawthorn, Hibiscus, Kapok, Mallee, Matagouri, Mulberry, Outback, Poinsettia, Poly-poly, Sallee, Shepherd, Shrub, Thicket, Tire, Tod(de)

Bush-baby Durukuli, Galago, Nagapie, Night-ape

Bushel Bu, Co(o)mb, Cor, Ephah, Fou, Homer, Peck, Weight, Wey

Business Affair, Agency, Biz, Bus, Cartel, Cerne, Co, Commerce, Company, Concern, Conglomerate, Craft, Duty, Enterprise, Ergon, Establishment, Exchange, Fasti, Firm, Funny, Game, Gear, Hong, Industry, Line, Métier, Monkey, Office, Palaver, Pi(d)geon, Pidgin, Practice, Professional, Shebang, Shop, To-do, Trade, Traffic, Transaction, Tread, Turnover, Vocation, Zaikai

Businessman Babbitt, City, Realtor, Taipan, Trader, Tycoon

Busk(er) Bodice, Corset, Entertainer, German-band

Buskin(s) Brod(e)kin, Cothurn(us), Shoe

Buss Kiss, Osculate, Smack

Bussu Troelie, Troely, Troolie

Bust Beano, Brast, Boob, Break, Chest, Falsies, Herm(a), Sculp, Shatter(ed), Spree, Statue, Term(inus), To-tear, To-torne, Ups(e)y

▷ **Bust** may indicate an anagram

Bustard Bird, Otis, Turkey

Buster Keaton

Bustle Ado, Do, Flap, Pad, Scurry, ➤ STIR, Swarm, Tournure, Whew

Busy Active, At (it), ➤ DETECTIVE, Deedy, Detective, Dick, Eident, Employ, Ergate, Eye, Goer, Hectic, Hive, Humming, Occupied, Ornate, Prodnose, Stir, Tec, Throng, Worksome

Busybody Bustler, Meddler, Noser, Pragmatic, Snooper, Trout, Yenta

But Aber, Bar, Except, However, Merely, Nay, Only, Save, Sed, Simply, Tun

Butch He-man, Macho

Butcher(y) Cumberland, Decko, Dekko, Flesher, Kill, Killcow, Look, Massacre, Ovicide, Sever, Shambles, Shochet, Shufti, Slaughter, Slay

Butler Bedivere, Bread-chipper, Jeeves, RAB, Rhett, Samuel, Servant, Sewer, Sommelier, Steward

Butt (in) Aris, Barrel, Bunt, Clara, Enter, Geck, Glasgow kiss, Goat, Header, Horn, Jesting-stock, Laughing-stock, Mark, Outspeckle, Pantaloon, Pipe, Push, Ram, Roach, Scapegoat, Snipe, ➤ STOOGE, Straight man, Stump, Target, Tun, Ups

Butter Adulation, Billy, Brandy, Butyric, Cocoa, Coconut, Drawn, Flatter, Galam, Garcinia, Ghee, Ghi, Goat, Illipi, Illupi, Kokum, Mahua, Mahwa, Mow(r)a, Nutter, Pat, Peanut, Print, Ram, Scrape, Shea, Spread

▷ **Butter** may indicate a goat or such

Buttercup Crow-foot, Crow-toe, Goldilocks, Ranunculus, Reate, Thalictrum

Butterfingers Muff

Butterfish Nine-eyes

Butterfly Apollo, Argus, Blue, Brimstone, Brown, Cabbage white, Camberwell beauty, Cardinal, Cleopatra, Clouded yellow, Comma,

Common blue, Dilettante, Eclosion, Emperor, Fritillary, Gate-keeper, Grayling, Hair-streak, Heath, Hesperid, Imaginal, Kallima, Large copper, Large white, Leaf, Lycaena, Meadow brown, Monarch, Morpho, Mourning-cloak, Nerves, Nymphalid, Nymphean, Orange-tip, Owl, Painted lady, Papilionidae, Peacock, Pieris, Psyche, Red admiral, Rhopalocera, Ringlet, Satyr(idae), Satyrinae, Silverspot, Skipper, Stamper, Sulphur, Swallow-tail, Thecla, Thistle, Tiger swallowtail, Two-tailed pasha, Vanessa, White admiral

Buttermilk Bland, Lassi

Butternut Souari

Butter-tree Mahua, Mahwa, Mow(r)a

Buttock(s) Arse, Ass, Bahookie, Bottom, Coit, Derrière, Doup, Duff, Fundament, Gluteus maximus, Hinderlan(d)s, Hurdies, Jacksie, Jacksy, Keester, Keister, Nates, Prat, Quoit, Seat

Button(s) Barrel, Bellboy, Fastener, Frog, Hot, Knob, Netsuke, Olivet, Page(boy), Panic, Snooze, Stud, Switch, Toggle

Buttonhole Accost, Detain, Eye, Flower

Buttress Brace, Counterfort, Pier, Prop, Stay, Support

Buxom Bonnie, Busty, Plump, Sonsy

Buy(er), Buying Believe, Bribe, Coff, Corner, Customer, Emption, Engross, Monopsonist, Purchase, Shop, Shout, Spend, Take, Trade, Vendee

▷ **Buyer** may indicate money

Buzz(er) Bee, Bombilate, Bombinate, Button, Fly, Hum, Rumour, Scram, Whirr, Whisper, Zed, Zing, Zoom

Buzzard Bee-kite, Bird, Buteo, Hawk, Pern, Puttock, Vulture

By Alongside, At, Gin, Gone, In, Near, Neighbouring, Nigh, Of, Past, Per, Through, With, X

Bye Extra

Bye-bye Adieu, Farewell, Tata

Bygone Dead, Departed, Past, Yore

By Jove Egad

Bypass Avoid, Circuit, Coronary, ➤ DETOUR, Evade, Ignore, Omit, Shunt, Skirt

By-product Epiphenomenon, Spin-off

Byre Cowshed, Manger, Stable, Trough

By so much The

By the way Incidentally, Obiter

Byway Alley, Lane, Path

Byword Ayword, Phrase, Proverb, Slogan

Byzantine Catapan, Complicated, Intricate, Intrince, Theme

C c

C Around, Caught, Celsius, Cent, Centigrade, Charlie, Conservative, San

Cab Boneshaker, Crawler, Drosky, Fiacre, Growler, Hackney, Hansom, Mini, Noddy, Taxi, Vettura

Cabal(ler) Arlington, Ashley, Buckingham, Clifford, Clique, Conspiracy, Coterie, Faction, Junto, Lauderdale, Party, Plot

Cab(b)alistic Abraxis, Mystic, Notarikon, Occult

Cabaret Burlesque, Floorshow

Cabbage(-head), Cabbage soup Book choy, Borecole, Castock, Cauliflower, Chinese, Choucroute, Cole, Collard, Crout, Custock, Kohlrabi, Kraut, Loaf, Loave, Pak-choi, Pamphrey, Pe-tsai, Sauerkraut, Savoy, Shchi, Shtchi, Thieve, Turnip, Wort

Caber Fir, Janker, Log, Sting

Cabin Berth, Bibby, Bothy, Box, Cabana, Caboose, Camboose, Coach, Cottage, Crannog, Crib, Cuddy, Den, Gondola, Hovel, Hut, Izba, Lodge, Log, Long-house, Room, Roundhouse, Saloon, Shanty, Stateroom

Cabin-boy Grummet

Cabinet Bahut, Cabale, Case, Closet, Commode, Console, Cupboard, Kitchen, Ministry, Secretaire, Shadow, Shrinal, Vitrine

Cabinet maker Ebeniste, Joiner, PM

Cable(way) Coax(ial), Extension, Flex, Halser, Hawser, Jump leads, Junk, Landline, Lead, Lead-in, Lifeline, Outhaul, Rope, Slatch, Téléférique, ➤ TELEGRAM, Telpher(age), Wire

Cache Deposit, Hidlin(g)s, ➤ HOARD, Inter, Stash, Store, Treasure

Cackle Cluck, Gaggle, Gas, Haw, Snicker, Titter

Cacography Scrawl

Cacophony Babel, Caterwaul, Charivari, Discord, Jangle

Cactus, Cactus-like Alhagi, Barel, Cereus, Cholla, Christmas, Dildo, Easter, Echino-, Hedgehog, Jojoba, Maguey, Mescal, Nopal, Ocotillo, Opuntia, Organ-pipe, Peyote, Prickly pear, Retama, Saguaro, Star, Torch-thistle, Tuna, Xerophytic

Cad Base, Boor, Bounder, Churl, Cocoa, Heel, Oik, Rascal, Rotter, Skunk

Cadaver(ous) Body, Corpse, Ghastly, Haggard, Stiff

Caddy Porter, Teapoy

Cadence Beat, Close, Fa-do, Flow, Lilt, Meter, Plagal, Rhythm

Cadenza Fireworks

Cadet(s) Junior, OTC, Scion, Syen, Trainee

Cadge(r) Bludge, Bot, Bum, Impose, ➤ SCROUNGE, Sponge

Cadmium Cd

Caesar Nero

Caesium Cs

Cafe(teria) Automat, Brasserie, Bistro, Buvette, Canteen, Commissary, Diner, Dinette, Donko, Estaminet, Filtré, Greasy spoon, Juke joint, Pizzeria, Pull-in, Tearoom, Transport

Cage Bar, Battery, Box, Cavie, Confine, Coop, Corf, Dray, Drey, Enmew, Faraday, Fold, Frame, Grate, Hutch, Mew, Pen, ➤ PRISON, Trave

Cahoots Hugger-mugger

Cairn Barp, Dog, Man, Mound, Raise

Caisson Bends

Caitiff Meanie

Cajole(ry) Beflum, Beguile, Blandish, Blarney, Carn(e)y, ➤ COAX, Cuittle, Inveigle, Jolly, Persuade, Wheedle

Cake Agnus dei, Angel, Baba, Babka, Baklava, Banbury, Bannock, Bara brith, Barmbrack, Battenberg, Birthday, Brioche, Brownie, Buckwheat bun, Carcake, Chapat(t)i, Chillada, Chupati, Chupattie, Chupatty, Clapbread, Clot, Coburg, Cotton, Croquette, Cruller, Crumpet, Dainty, Devil's food, Dundee, Eccles, Eclair, Farl(e), Filter, Flapjack, Frangipane, Frangipani, Fritter, Galette, Genoa, Gingerbread, Girdle, ➤ HARDEN, Hockey, Idli, Jannock, Jumbal, Jumbles, Koeksister, Kruller, Kush, Lamington, Lardy, Latke, Layer, Linseed, Macaroon, Madeira, Madeleine, Maid of honour, Marble, Meringue, Millefeuille, Mud, Muffin, Napoleon, Nut, Oatmeal, Oil, Pan, Panettone, Paratha, Parkin, Pat, Patty, Pavlova, Pikelet, ➤ PLASTER, Pomfret, Pone, Pontefract, Poori, Pound, Profiterole, Puff, Puftaloon(a), Puri, Queencake, Ratafia, Religieuse, Rock, Rosti, Roti, Rout, Rusk, Sachertorte, Sally Lunn, Sandwich, Savarin, Scone, Set, Simnel, Singing-hinny, Slab, Soul, Sponge, Stollen, Sushi, Swiss roll, Tablet, Tansy, Tipsy, Torte, Tortilla, Upside down, Vetkoek, Wad, Wafer, Waffle, Wedding, Wonder

▷ **Cake** may indicate an anagram

Cake-shaped Placentiform

Cakestand Curate

Cakewalk Doddle

Calaboose Jail, Loghouse

Calamitous, Calamity Blow, Catastrophe, Dire, ➤ DISASTER, Distress, Fatal, Ill, Jane, Ruth, Storm, Tragic, Unlucky, Visitation, Woe

Calcareous Lithite

Calcium Ca, Dogger, Dripstone, Quicklime, Scawtite, Whewellite

Calculate(d), Calculation, Calculator Abacus, Actuary, Compute(r), Cost, Design, Estimate, Extrapolate, Log, Prorate, Quip(p)u, Rate, ➤ RECKON, Slide-rule, Sofar, Soroban, Tactical, Tell

Calculus Cholelith, Differential, Integral, Lith, Science, Sentential, Sialolith, Stone, Urolith

Caledonian Kanak

Calendar Advent, Agenda, Almanac, Chinese, Diary, Fasti, Gregorian, Intercalary, Jewish, Journal, Julian, Luach, Menology, Newgate, New Style, Ordo, Perpetual, Revolutionary, Roman, Sothic

Calender(ing) Dervish, Mangle, Swissing

Calf Ass, Bobby, Box, Cf, Deacon, Dogie, Dogy, Freemartin, Golden, Leg, Poddy, Stirk, Sural, Tollie, Tolly, Veal, Vitular

Caliban Moon-calf

Calibrate, Calibre Bore, Capacity, Graduate, Mark, ➤ QUALITY, Text

Californium Cf

Caliph Abbasid(e), Vathek

Call(ed), Calling, Call on, Call up Adhan, Appeal, Arraign, Art, Awaken, Azan, Banco, Bawl, Beck, Behote, Bevy, Bid, Business, Buzz, Career, Chamade, Cite, Claim, Clang, Clarion, Cleep, Clepe, Close, Cold, Conference, Conscript, Convene, Convoke, Cooee, Cry, Curtain, Dial, Drift, Dub, Evoke, Gam, Go, Hallali, Haro, Heads, Hech, Hete, Hey, Hight, Ho, Hot(e), Howzat, Huddup, Hurra(h), Job, Junk, Last (post), Line, Local, Métier, Misère, Mobilise, Mot, Name, Nap, Need, Nempt, Nominate, Olé, Page, Phone, Photo, Post, Proo, Pruh, Pursuit, Rechate, Recheat, Retreat, Reveille, Ring, Roll, Rort, Route, SOS, Sa-sa, Sennet, ➤ SHOUT, Shut-out, Slam, Slander, Slogan, Soho, Sola, STD, Style, Subpoena, Summon(s), Tails, Tantivy, Taps, Telephone, Term, Toho, Toll, Trumpet, Trunk, Visit, Vocation, Wake-up, Waken, Whoa-ho-ho, Wo ha ho, Yell, Yo, Yodel, Yodle, Yo-ho(-ho), Yoicks, Yoo-hoo

Calla(s) Aroid, Lily, Maria

Caller Fresh, Guest, Herring, Inspector, Muezzin, Rep, Traveller, ➤ VISITOR

Calligraphy Kakemono

Callosity, Call(o)us Bunion, Cold, Corn, Hard, Horny, Obtuse, Ringbone, Seg, Thylose, Tough, Tylosis, Unfeeling

Callow Crude, Green, Immature, Jejune

Calm Abate, Alegge, Allay, Allege, Aleye, Appease, Ataraxy, Composed, Cool, Doldrums, Easy, Easy-osy, Eevn, Equable, Equanimity, Even, Eye, Flat, Glassy, Halcyon, Loun(d), Lown(d), Lull, Mellow, Mild, Milden, Millpond, Nonchalant, Pacify, Peaceful, Philosophical, Phlegmatic, Placate, Placid, Quell, Quiet, Relax(ed), Repose, Seraphic, Serene, Settle, Sleek, ➤ SOOTHE, Sopite, Still, Stilly, Subside, Tranquil(lise), Unturbid, Windless

Calumniate, Calumny Aspersion, Backbite, Defame, Libel, Malign, Slander, Slur

Calvary Golgotha

Calvin(ist) Accusative, Coolidge, Genevan, Hopkins, Huguenot, Infralapsarian, Predestination, Sublapsarian, Supralapsarian

Calydonian Boar

Calypso Ogygia, Siren, ➤ SONG

Cam Cog, River, Snail, Tappet

Camaraderie Fellowship, Rapport

Camber Slope

Cambium Phellogen

Cambodian Khmer (Rouge)

Cambria Wales

Cambridge Cantab, Squat

Came Arrived

Camel, Camel train Arabian, Artiodactyla, Bactrian, Caisson, Colt, Dromedary, Kafila, Llama, Oont, Sopwith, Tulu

Cameo Anaglyph, Camaieu, Carving

Camera Box, Brownie®, Camcorder, Candid, Chambers, Cine, Compact, Disc, Flash, Gamma, Iconoscope, Kodak®, Obscura, Orthicon, Palmcorder, Panoramic, Pantoscope, Pinhole, Polaroid®, Reflex, Schmidt, SLR, Somascope, Speed, Steadican®, Video

Camouflage Conceal, ➤ DISGUISE, Mark, Maskirovka, War-dress

▷ **Camouflaged** may indicate an anagram

Camp(er) Affectation, Aldershot, Banal, Belsen, Bivouac, Boma, Boot, Caerleon, Castral, Colditz, Concentration, David, Depot, D(o)uar, Dumdum, Faction, Flaunt, Gulag, Holiday, L(a)ager, Lashkar, Leaguer, Manyat(t)a, Oflag, Outlie, Peace, Side, Stagey, Stalag, Stative, Swagman, Tent, Theatrical, Transit, Work, Zare(e)ba, Zariba, Zereba, Zeriba

Campaign(er) Barnstorm, Battle, Blitz, Blitzkreig, Canvass, Crusade, Drive, Field, Jihad, Lobby, Mission, Promotion, Run, Satyagraha, Smear, Stint, Strategist, Venture, Veteran, War, Warray, Warrey, Whistle-stop

Campanula Rampion

Campeador Chief, Cid

Camp-follower Lascar, Sutler

Camphor Menthol

Campion Knap-bottle, Lychnis, Silene

▷ **Camptown** may indicate de-

Can(s) Able, Billy, Bog, Capable, Churn, Cooler, Dow, Gaol, Gents, Headphones, Is able, Jug, Karsy, Loo, May, Nick, Pail, Pot, Preserve, ➤ PRISON, Privy, Stir, Tin

Canada, Canadian Abenaki, Acadian, Canuck, Dene, Herring choker, Inuit, Johnny Canuck, Quebeccer, Quebecker, Québecois

Canal Alimentary, Ampul, Birth, Caledonian, Channel, Conduit, Corinth, Duct, Duodenum, Ea, Erie, Foss(e), Gota, Grand (Trunk), Grand Union, Groove, Gut, Haversian, Kiel, Klong, Lode, Meatus, Midi, Navigation, Panama, Pipe, Pound, Resin, Root, Scala, Schlemm's, Semi-circular, Ship, Soo, Spinal, Suez, Urethra, Waterway, Welland, Zanja

Canal-boat Barge, Fly-boat, Gondola, Vaporetto

Canapé Cate, Snack, Titbit

Canary Bird, Grass, Roller, Serin, Singer, Yellow

Cancel Abrogate, Adeem, Annul, Counteract, Countermand, Cross, Delete, Destroy, Erase, Kill, Negate, Nullify, Obliterate, Override, Remit, Repeal, Rescind, Retrait, Revoke, Scrub, Undo, Unmake, Void, Wipe

Cancer(ous) Big C, Carcinoma, Crab, Curse, Kaposi's Sarcoma, Leukaemia, Oat-cell, Tropic, Tumour, Wolf

Candela Cd

▶ **Candelabra** see CANDLE(STICK)

Candid, Candour Albedo, Blunt, Camera, Franchise, Frank, Honesty, Open, Round, Upfront

Candidate(s) Applicant, Aspirant, Contestant, Entrant, Field, Nominee, Ordinand, Postulant, Testee

Candied, Candy Caramel, Eryngo, Glace, Snow, Succade, Sweet

Candle(stick), Candelabra Amandine, Bougie, C(i)erge, Dip, Fetch, Girandole, Hanukiah, Jesse, Lampadary, Light, Menorah, Padella, Paschal, Pricket, Roman, Rushlight, Sconce, Serge, Shammash, Shammes, Slut, Sperm, Tace, Tallow, Tallow-dip, Taper, Torchère, Tricerion, Wax

Candlefish Eulachon, Oolakon, Oulachon, Oulakon, Ulic(h)an, Ulic(h)on, Ulikon

Cane Arrow, Baculine, Bamboo, Baste, Beat, Birk, Dari, Dhurra, Doura, Dur(r)a, Ferula, Ferule, Goor, Gur, Jambee, Malacca, Narthex, Penang-lawyer, Pointer, Rat(t)an, Rod, Stick, Sugar, Swagger-stick, Swish, Switch, Swordstick, Tan, Tickler, Vare, Wand, Whangee, Wicker(-work)

Canine Biter, C, Dog, Eye-tooth

Canker Corrosion, Curse, Lesion, Ulcer

Cannabis Benj, Bhang, Boneset, Ganja, Ganny, Grass, Hash, Hemp, Henry, Louie, Pot, Zol

Cannibal Anthropophagus, Heathen, Long pig, Ogre, Thyestean

Cannon Amusette, Barrage, Basilisk, Bombard, Breechloader, Carom, Carronade, Chaser, Collide, Criterion, Culverin, Drake, Falcon, Gun, Howitzer, Kiss, Long-tom, Monkey, Nursery, Saker, Stern-chaser, Water, Zamboorak, Zomboruk, Zumbooru(c)k

Cannot Canna, Cant, Downa(e), Downay

Canny Careful, Frugal, Prudent, Scot, Shrewd, Slee, Sly, Thrifty, Wice, Wily, Wise

Canoe(ist) Bidarka, Bidarkee, Canader, Dugout, Faltboat, Kayak, Monoxylon, Montaria, Oomiack, Paddler, Piragua, Pirogue, Rob Roy, Woodskin

Canon Austin, Brocard, Camera, Chapter, Chasuble, Code, Crab, Isodorian, ➤ LAW, Line, Mathurin(e), Nocturn, Nursery, Pitaka, Polyphony, Prebendary, Premonstratensian, Rota, Round, Rule, Square, Squier, Squire, Standard, Tenet, Unity

Canopy Awning, Baldachin, Baldaquin, Chuppah, Ciborium, Dais, He(a)rse, Huppah, Majesty, Marquee, Marquise, Pavilion, Shamiana(h), State, Tabernacle, Tent, Tester

Cant Argot, Bevel, Heel, Incline, Jargon, Mummery, Patois, Patter, Rogue's Latin, Shelta, Slang, Slope, Snivel, Snuffle, Tip

Cantankerous Cussed, Fire-eater, Ornery

Cantata Kinderspiel, Motet, Tobacco

Canteen Chuck-wagon, Mess, Munga, Naafi

Canter Amble, Hypocrite, Jog, Lope, Tit(t)up, Tripple

Canto Air, Fit(te), Fitt, Fytte, Melody, Verse

Canton Appenzell, Basle, District, Jura, Quarter, Uri, Vaud

Cantred Commot(e)

Canvas Awning, Burlap, Dra(b)bler, Lug-sail, Mainsail, Marquee, Oil-cloth, Paint, Raven's-duck, Reef, ➤ SAIL, Staysail, Stunsail, Tent, Trysail, Wigan

Canvass(er) Agent, Doorstep, Drum, Poll, Solicit

▷ **Canvasser** may indicate a painter or a camper

Canyon Box, Canada, Defile, Grand, Nal(l)a, Nallah

Cap(ped) Abacot, Amorce, Balaclava, Balmoral, Barret, Baseball, Bathing, Bellhop, Bendigo, Ber(r)et, Biggin, Biretta, Blakey, Blue, Bonnet-rouge, Bycoket, Call, Calotte, Calpac(k), Calyptrate, Capeline, Caul, Chaco, Chape, Chapeau, Chaperon, Chapka, Chechia, Cheese-cutter, Cloth, Cockernony, Coif, Cope, Cornet, Cowl, Cradle, ➤ CROWN, Czapka, Davy Crockett, Deerstalker, Dunce's, Dutch, Fatigue, Ferrule, Flat, Forage, Gandhi, Garrison, Glengarry, Grannie, Granny, Havelock, ➤ HAT, Iceberg, International, Jockey, Juliet, Kalpak, Kepi, Kilmarnock, Kippa, Kippoth, Kipput, Kiss-me(-quick), Knee, Liberty, Lid, Mob, Monmouth, Monteer, Montero, Mor(r)ion, Mortar-board, Mutch, Newsboy, Outdo, Pagri, Patellar, Percussion, Perplex, Phrygian, Pileus, Pinner, Polar, Puggaree, Quoif, Schapska, Shako, Skullcap, Square, Stocking, Summit, ➤ SURPASS, Taj, Tam(-o'-shanter), Thinking, Toe, Toorie, Top, Toque, Toy, Trenchard, Trencher, Tuque, Turk's, Yarmulka, Yarmulke, Zuchetto

Capable, Capability Able, Brown, Capacity, Competent, Deft, Effectual, Efficient, Firepower, Qualified, Skilled, Susceptible, Up to

Capacitance, Capacity Ability, Aptitude, C, Cab, Competence, Content, Cor, Cubic, Endowment, Function, Limit, Log, Power, Qua, Receipt, Scope, Size, Tonnage, Valence, Vital, Volume

Caparison Trap(pings)

Cape Agulhas, Almuce, Burnouse, Byron, Canaveral, Canso, Cloak, Cod, Comorin, Delgado, Domino, Dungeness, Fairweather, Faldetta, Fanion, Fanon, Farewell, Fear, Fichu, Finisterre, Flattery, Guardafui, Good Hope, Hatteras, Head(land), Helles, Hoe, Hogh, Horn, Inverness, Leeuwin, Lindisnes, Lizard, Mant(e)let, Mantilla, Mantle, Matapan, May, Mo(z)zetta, Muleta, Naze, Ness, North, Palatine, Parry, Pelerine, Peninsula, Point, Poncho, Race, Ras, Reinga, Roca, Ruana, Runaway, Sable, Sandy, Scaw, Skaw, Sontag, St Vincent, Southwest, Talma, Tippet, Trafalgar, Ushant, Verde, Waterproof, Western, Wrath

Caper(ing) Antic, Boer, Capparis, Capriole, Cavort, Dance, Dido, Flisk, Frisk, Frolic, Gambado, Gambol, Harmala, Harmalin(e), Harmel, Harmin(e), Prance, Prank, Saltant, Scoup, Scowp, Skip, Tit(t)up

Capet Marie Antoinette

Cape Town SA

Capital(s) A1, Assets, Block, Boodle, Bravo, Cap, ➤ CAPITALS, Chapiter, Chaptrel, Doric, Euge, Excellent, Float, Floating, Fonds, Great, Helix, Initial, Ionic, Lethal, Lulu, Metropolis, Principal, Rustic, Seat, Splendid, Sport, Stock, Super, Topping, UC, Upper case, Working

Capitalist Financier, Moneyer

▷ **Capitalist** may indicate one living in a capital

Capitulate Acquiesce, Comply, ➤ SURRENDER

CAPITALS

3 letters:
Jos
Rio
Ufa
4 letters:
Acra
Apia
Bonn
Brno
Caen
Cali
Doha
Faro
Ipoh
Kiel
Kiev
Kobe
Laos
Lima
Male
Nuuk
Oslo
Riga
Rome
Susa
Suva
Xian
5 letters:
Abiya
Abuja
Accra
Agana
Amman
Bully
Cairo
Dacca
Dakar
Delhi
Enugu
Hanoi
Kabul
Lagos
Lassa
Lhasa
Minsk
Paris
Quito
Rabat
Seoul
Sofia

Sucré
Vaduz
6 letters:
Albany
Ankara
Asmara
Astana
Athens
Austin
Bamako
Bangui
Banjul
Bastia
Beirut
Berlin
Bogota
Bruges
Darwin
Dodoma
Dublin
Harare
Havana
Hobart
Ibadan
Lisbon
London
Lusaka
Madrid
Maputo
Moscow
Muscat
Nassau
Ottawa
Peking
Riyadh
Sendai
Skopje
Sokoto
Taipei
Tallin
Tehran
Thebes
Thimbu
Tirana
Topeka
Vienna
Warsaw
Zagreb
7 letters:
Abidjan

Antioch
Atlanta
Baghdad
Barnaul
Beijing
Caracas
Colombo
Cordoba
Douglas
Funchal
Jakarta
Kampala
Karachi
Mathura
Memphis
Nairobi
Nicosia
Nineveh
Palermo
Rangoon
Tallinn
Tbilisi
Teheran
Thimphu
Venture
Xanthus
Yerevan
8 letters:
Abu Dhabi
Adelaide
Asuncion
Belgrade
Belmopan
Brasilia
Brisbane
Brussels
Budapest
Cagliari
Calcutta
Canberra
Djibouti
Eraklion
Freetown
Gabarone
Helsinki
Honolulu
Istanbul
Katmandu
Kingston

Kinshasa
Kirkwall
Pretoria
Santiago
Sarajevo
Shanghai
Tashkent
Valletta
Windhoek
Winnipeg
9 letters:
Annapolis
Bangalore
Bucharest
Bujumbura
Cartagena
Fongafale
Heraklion
Khatmandu
Leningrad
Mogadishu
Nashville
Reykjavik
Samarkand
Stockholm
Stuttgart
Trebizond
10 letters:
Addis Ababa
Baton Rouge
Bratislava
Bridgetown
Charleston
Copenhagen
Georgetown
Little Rock
Montevideo
Persepolis
Providence
Valladolid
Washington
Wellington
11 letters:
Buenos Aires
Pandemonium
12 letters:
Pandaemonium
14 letters:
Constantinople

Capless Bare

▷ **Capless** may indicate first letter missing

Capone Al, Scarface

▷ **Capriccioso** may indicate an anagram

Caprice, Capricious Arbitrary, Boutade, Capernoitie, Conceit, Desultory, Erratic, Fancy, Fitful, Freak, Humoresk, Humoresque, Irony, Mood, Perverse, Quirk, Vagary, Wayward, Whim(sy)

Capsize Overbalance, Purl, Tip, Turn turtle, Upset, Whemmle, Whomble

▷ **Capsized** may indicate a word upside down

Capstan Sprocket, Windlass

Capsule Amp(o)ule, Bowman's, Cachet, Habitat, Ootheca, Orbiter, Ovisac, Pill, Spacecraft, Spermatophore, Time, Urn

Captain Ahab, Bligh, Bobadil, Bones, Brassbound, Capt, Chief, Cid, Commander, Condottiere, Cook, Copper, Cuttle, Flint, Group, Hornblower, Kettle, Kidd, Leader, Macheath, Master, Nemo, Old man, Owner, Patroon, Post, Privateer, Protospatharius, Skip(per), Standish, Subah(dar), Subedar, Swing, Trierarch

Caption Heading, Headline, Inscription, Masthead, Sub-title, Title

Captious Critical, Peevish

Captivate(d), Captivating Beguile, Bewitch, Charm, Enamour, Enthrall, Epris(e), Take, Winsome

Captive, Captivity Bonds, Duress, POW, Prisoner, Slave

Capture Abduct, Annex, Bag, Catch, Collar, Cop, Grab, Land, Net, Prize, Rush, Seize, Snabble, Snaffle, Snare, ➤ TAKE

Capuchin Cebus, Monkey, Sajou

Car Astra, Audi, Auto, Banger, Beetle, Biza, BL, Bomb, Brake, Bubble, Buffet, Bugatti, Buick, Bumper, Bus, Cab(riolet), Cadillac, Catafalco, Catafalque, Chariot, Coach, Company, Convertible, Cortina, Coupé, Crate, Daimler, Diner, Dodgem®, Drag(ster), Drophead, Elf, Estate, Fastback, Fiat, Flivver, Ford, Formula, Freight, Gondola, GT, Hardtop, Hatchback, Heap, Hearse, Hillman, Hot-rod, Jalop(p)y, Jamjar, Jammy, Jaunting, Kart, Lada, Lagonda, Lancia, Landaulet, Landrover, Limo, Limousine, Merc(edes), MG, Mini, Morris, Nacelle, Notchback, Observation, Opel, Panda, Patrol, Prowl, Racer, Ragtop, Rattletrap, Restaurant, Roadster, Roller, Rolls, RR, Runabout, Rust bucket, Sedan, Skoda, Sleeper, Sports, Squad, Station wagon, Stock, Stretch-limo, Subcompact, Sunbeam, Tank, Telepherique, Telpher, Three-wheeler, Tin Lizzie, Tonneau, Tourer, Tram, Trolley, Turbo, Two-seater, Vehicle, Veteran, Vintage, VW, Wheeler, Wheels

Caramel Brûlé

Carat Point

Caravan Caf(f)ila, Convoy, Fleet, Kafila, Safari, Trailer

Caravanserai Choltry, Choutry, Inn, Khan

Caraway Aj(o)wan, Carvy, Seed

Car-back Boot, Dick(e)y, Tonneau

Carbamide Urea

Carbine Gun, Musket

Carbohydrate Agarose, Carrageenan, Cellulose, Chitin, Dextran, Disaccharide, Glycogen, Heptose, Hexose, Inulin, Ketose, Laminarin, Mannan, Pectin, Pentosane, Pentose, Saccharide, Sorbitol, Starch, Sucrose, Sugar

Carbolic Orcin

Carbon(ate) Ankerite, Austenite, Buckminsterfullerene, Buckyball, C, Charcoal, Coke, Dialogite, Diamond, Flame, Flimsy, Fullerene, Graphite, Lampblack, Natron, Scawtite, Soot, Spode, Spodium, Urao, Witherite, Zaratite

Carbon deficiency Acapnia

Carboy Demijohn

Carbuncle Anthrax, Ruby

Carcase, Carcass Body, Cadaver, Carrion, Corpse, Cutter, Krang, Kreng, Morkin, Mor(t)ling

Card(s), Cardboard Ace, Affinity, Amex®, Baccarat, Basto, Bill, Birthday, Bower, Business, Calling, Canasta, Cartes, Cash, Caution, Charge, Chicane, Club, Comb, Compass, Court(esy), Credit, Cue, Dance, Debit, Deck, Deuce, Diamond, Donor, Ecarté, Eccentric, Euchre, Expansion, Flaught, Flush, ➤ GAME, Green, Hand, Heart, Honour, Identity, Jack, Jambone, Joker, Kanban, Key, King, Loo, Loyalty, Manille, Matador, Meishi, Mise, Mistigris, Mogul, Mournival, Oddity, Ombre, Pack, Pasteboard, PC, Picture, Placard, Plastic, Playing, Proximity, Quatorze, Queen, Quiz, Red, Rippler, Rove, Scribble, Singleton, Smart, Soda, Solo, Sound, Spade, Spadille, Squeezer, Store, Strawboard, Swab, Swipe, Swish, Switch, Swob, Swot, Talon, Tarok, Tarot, Tease(r), Tenace, Test, Thaumatrope, Ticket, Tose, Toze, Trading, Trey, Trump, Valentine, Visiting, Wag, Weirdie, Wild, Yellow, Zener

Cardigan Jacket, Wam(m)us, Wampus, Woolly

Cardinal Camerlingo, Chief, College, Eight, Eminence, Eminent, Grosbeak, Hat, HE, Hume, Legate, Manning, Mazarin, Newman, Number, Pivotal, Polar, Prelate, Radical, Red, Red-hat, Richelieu, Sacred college, Sin, Spellman, Virtue, Vital, Ximenes

Card-player Dealer, Pone

Care(r), Caring Attention, Burden, Cark, Caution, Cerne, Cherish, ➤ CONCERN, Cosset, Grief, Heed, Intensive, Kaugh, Keep, Kiaugh, Maternal, Mind, Pains, Palliative, Parabolanus, Reck(e), Reke, Respite, Retch, Solicitude, ➤ TEND, Tenty, Worry

Career Course, Hurtle, Life, Line, Run, Rush, Speed, Start, Tear, Vocation

▷ **Career** may indicate an anagram

▶ **Carefree** see CARELESS

Careful(ly) Canny, Chary, Discreet, Gentle, Hooly, Meticulous, Mindful, Pernickety, Provident, Prudent, Scrimp, Studious, Tentie, Tenty, Thorough, Vigilant, Ware, Wary

Careless(ly) Casual, Cheery, Debonair, Easy, Free-minded, Gallio, Improvident, Imprudent, Inadvertent, Insouciance, Lax, Lighthearted, Négligé, ➤ NEGLIGENT, Nonchalant, Oversight, Raffish, Rash, Remiss, Resigned, Riley, Slam-bang, Slapdash, Slaphappy, Slipshod, Sloven(ly), Slubber, Taupie, Tawpie, Unguarded, Unmindful, Untenty, Unwary

▷ **Carelessly** may indicate an anagram

Caress Bill, Coy, Embrace, Fondle, Kiss, Lallygag, Lollygag, Noursle, Nursle, Pet, Touch

Caretaker Concierge, Curator, Custodian, Guardian, Janitor, Nightwatchman, Sexton, Shammash, Shammes, Superintendent, Verger, Warden

Careworn Haggard, Lined, Tired, Weary

Cargo Bulk, Burden, Fraught, Freight, Lading, Last, ➤ LOAD, Payload, Shipment

Caribbean Belonger, Puerto Rican, Soca, Sokah, Taino, WI

Caricature, Caricaturist Ape, Beerbohm, Burlesque, Caron d'Ache, Cartoon, Cruikshank, Doyle, Farce, Gillray, Rowlandson, Skit, Spy, Travesty

Carlin Pug

Carmelite Barefoot

Carmen AA, BL, Chai, RAC

Carnage Butchery, Massacre, Slaughter

Carnal Bestial, Lewd, Sensual, Sexual, Worldly

Carnation Dianthus, Malmaison, Picotee, Pink

Carnival Fair, Festival, Fete, Moomba, Revelry

Carnivore Cacomistle, Cacomixl, Creodont, Fo(u)ssa, Genet, Glutton, Meerkat, Ratel, Suricate, Vivervidae, Wolverine

Carob Algarroba, Locust, St John's bread

Carol Noel, Sing, Song, Wassail, Yodel

Carousal, Carouse Bend, Birl(e), Bouse, Bride-ale, Compotation, Drink, Mallemaroking, Mollie, Orge, Orgy, ➤ REVEL, Roist, Screed, Spree, Upsee, Upsey, Upsy, Wassail

Carp(er) Beef, Censure, Complain, Crab, Critic, Crucian, Crusian, Gibel, Goldfish, Id(e), Kvetch, Mirror, Mome, Nag, Nibble, Roach, Roundfish, Scold, Twitch, Yerk, Yirk

Carpenter Cabinet-maker, Carfindo, Chips, Fitter, Joiner, Joseph, Menuisier, Quince, Tenoner, Wright

▷ **Carpenter** may indicate an anagram

Carpet Aubusson, Axminster, Beetle, Berate, Bessarabian, Broadloom, Brussels, Castigate, Chide, Drugget, Durrie, Kali, Kelim, Khilim, Kidderminster, Kilim, Kirman, Lecture, Lino, Mat, Moquette, Persian, Rate, Red, Reprimand, Reproach, Rug, Runner, Shagpile, Shark, Turkey, Wall-to-wall, Wig, Wilton

Carriage Air, Bandy, Barouche, Bearing, Berlin(e), Bier, Brake, Brit(sch)ka, Britska, Britzka, Brougham, Buckboard, Buggy, Cab, Calash, Calèche, Car, Cariole, Caroche, Carriole, Carryall, Cartage, Chaise, Charet, Chariot, Chassis, Chay, Clarence, Coach, Coch, Conveyance, Coupé, Curricle, Demeanour, Dennet, Deportment, Désobligeante, Diner, Dos-a-dos, Do-si-do, Drag, Dros(h)ky, Ekka, Equipage, Fiacre, Fly, Four-in-hand, Gait, Gig, Gladstone, Go-cart, Growler, Haulage, Herdic, Horseless, Hurly-hacket, Landau(let), Limber, Non-smoker, Norimon, Phaeton, Pick-a-back, Pochaise, Pochay, Poise, Port(age), Portance, Postchaise, Posture, Poyse, Pram, Pullman, Railcar, Random, Ratha, Remise, Rickshaw, Rockaway, Shay, Sled, Sleeper, Smoker, Sociable, Spider, Stanhope, Sulky, Surrey, Tarantas(s), Taxi, Tender, Tenue, Tilbury, Tim-whiskey, Tonga,

Trail, Trap, Vetture, Victoria, Voiture, Wagonette, Waterage, Whirligig, Whisk(e)y

Carrier Airline, Arm, Baldric, Barkis, Barrow, Bomb-ketch, Caddy, Cadge, Camel, Coaster, Conveyor, Fomes, Fomites, Frog, Grid, Hamper, Haversack, Hod, Janker, Jill, Nosebag, Noyade, Packhorse, Pigeon, Porter, Rucksack, Satchel, Schistosoma, Semantide, Sling, Stretcher, ➤ TRAY, Vector

Carrion Cadaver, Carcase, Carcass, Flesh, Ket, Stapelia

Carrots Seseli, Titian

Carry(ing) Bear, Chair, Convey, Enlevé, Ferry, Frogmarch, Hawk, Hent, Hump, Land, Pack, Pickaback, Port, Stock, Sustain, Tote, ➤ TRANSPORT, Trant, Wage, With, Yank

Carry on Continue, Create, Wage

Carry out Execute, Pursue

Cart Bandy, Barrow, Bogey, Buck, Car(r)iole, Chapel, Dog, Dolly, Dray, Furphy, Gambo, Gill, Governess, Gurney, Hackery, Jag, Jill, Lead, Mail, Rickshaw, Shandry, T, Telega, Trolley, Tumbrel, Tumbril, Wag(g)on, Wain, Whitechapel

Cartel Duopoly, Ring, Syndicate

Carthaginian Punic

Carthorse Shire

Carthusian Bruno

Cartilage Antitragus, Arytenoid, Chondrus, Cricoid, Disc, Epiglottis, Gristle, Hyaline, Lytta, Meniscus, Semilunar, Tendron, Thyroid, Tragus

Cartload Seam

Cartographer Cabot, Chartist, Mercator, Speed

Carton Box, Case, Crate, Sydney, Tub

Cartoon(ist) Animated, Bairnsfather, Caricature, Comic, Disney, Drawn, Emmet, Fougasse, Fumetto, Garland, Leech, Low, Manga, Mel, Partridge, Popeye, Short, Spy, Strip, Tenniel, Tintin, Trog

Cartridge Blank, Bullet, Cartouche, Doppie, Shell

Cart-track Rut

Cartwheel Handspring

Caruncle Aril, Carnosity

Carve(d), Carver, Carving Alcimedon, Armchair, Bas relief, Cameo, Chisel, Cilery, Crocket, Cut, Dismember, Doone, Enchase, Engrave, Entail, Entayle, Fiddlehead, Gibbons, Glyptic, Hew, Incise, Inscribe, Insculp, Intaglio, Netsuke, Nick, Petroglyph, Scrimshaw, Sculp(t), Slice, Tondo, Truncheon, Whittle

Caryatid Column, Telamon

Casanova Leman

Cascade Cataract, Fall, Lin(n), Stream, Waterfall

Cascara Buckthorn, Rhamnus, Wahoo

Case(s), Casing Abessive, Ablative, Accusative, Action, Adessive, Allative, Altered, Appeal, Aril, Ascus, Assumpsit, Attaché, Basket, Beer, Bere, Blimp,

Box, Brief, Bundwall, Burse, C, Ca, Cabinet, Calyx, Canister, Canterbury, Capsule, Cartouch(e), Cartridge, Cellaret, Chase, Chitin, Chrysalis, Cocoon, Compact, Crate, Croustade, Crust, Dative, Declension, Detinue, Dispatch, Dossier, Elative, Elytron, Enallage, Essive, Etui, Etwee, Example, Flan, Flapjack, Frame, Genitive, Grip, Hanaper, Hard, Hold-all, Housewife, Hull, Humidor, Husk, ➤ IN CASE, Indusium, Inessive, Instance, Keister, Locative, Locket, Lorica, Manche, Matter, Nacelle, Nominative, Non-suit, Nutshell, Objective, Ochrea, Ocrea, Papeterie, Patient, Penner, Phylactery, Plight, Plummer-block, Pod, Port, Possessive, Prima facie, Quiver, Recce, Reconnoitre, Sabretache, Scabbard, Sheath(e), Situation, Six-pack, Sporran, Stead, Sted, Subjunctive, Suit, Tantalus, Tea-chest, Telium, Test, Theca, Tichborne, Trunk, Valise, Vasculum, Vocative, Volva, Walise, Wallet, Wardian

Case-harden Nitrode
Casein Curd
Casement Frame, Roger, Sash, Window
Cash Blunt, Bonus, Bounty, Change, Coin, Dosh, Dot, Float, Imprest, Lolly, ➤ MONEY, Needful, Ochre, Pence, Petty, Ready, Realise, Rhino, Spondulicks, Stumpy, Tender, Tin, Wampum, Wherewithal
Cashier Annul, Break, Depose, Disbar, Dismiss, Teller, Treasurer
Cashmere Circassienne
Cask(et) Armet, Barrel, Barrico, Bas(i)net, Box, Breaker, Butt, Cade, Casque, Cassette, Drum, Firkin, Galeate, Harness, Heaume, Hogshead, Keg, Leaguer, Octave, Pin, Pipe, Puncheon, Pyxis, Run(d)let, Salade, Sallet, Sarcophagus, Shrine, Solera, Tierce, Tun
Cask-stand Stillion
Cassava Manioc, Tapioca, Yucca
Casserole Diable, Osso bucco, Pot, Salmi, Terrine, Tzimmes
Cassette Cartridge, Tape, Video
Cassia Cleanser, Senna
Cassio Lieutenant
Cassiterite Needle-tin, Tinstone
Cassock Gown, Soutane
Cast (down, off, out), Casting Abattu, Actors, Add, Appearance, Bung, Die, Discard, Ecdysis, Eject, Exorcise, Exuviae, Exuvial, Fling, Found, Fusil, Heave, Hob, Hue, Hurl, Impression, Ingo(w)es, Keb, Look, Lose, Mew, Molt, Moulage, Mould, Plaster(stone), Players, Put, Reject, Shed, Shoot, Sling, Slive, Slough, Spoil, Stookie, Tailstock, ➤ THROW, Toss, Tot, Warp, Wax, Ytost
▷ **Cast** may indicate an anagram or a piece of a word missing
Castanet Crotal(um), Knackers
Castaway Adrift, Crusoe, Gunn, Left, Outcast, Selkirk, Stranded
▷ **Cast by** may indicate surrounded by
Caste Class, Dalit, Group, Harijan, Hova, Kshatriya, Rank, Sect, Sudra, Varna
Caster Truckle
Castigate Berate, Chastise, Criticise, Keelhaul, Lash, Punish

Cast-iron Spiegeleisen

Castle(d) Adamant, Arundel, Balmoral, Bamburgh, Bastille, Belvoir, Bouncy, Broch, C, Calzean, Carbonek, Carisbrooke, Casbah, Chateau, Chillon, Citadel, Corfe, Dangerous, Despair, Doubting, Dunsinane, Egremont, Elephant, Elsinore, Fastness, Fort, Fotheringhay, Glamis, Gormenghast, Harlech, Hever, Kasba(h), Leeds, Malperdy, Man, More, Mot(t)e, Otranto, Perilous, Rackrent, Raglan, Rook, Schloss, Spain, Stokesay, Stronghold, Tintagel, Villa, Windsor

Castor-oil Ricinus

Castrate(d) Cut, Doctor, Emasculate, Eunuch, Evirate, Geld, Glib, Lib, Mutilate, Spado, Spay, Swig

Castro Fidel

Casual Accidental, Adventitious, Airy, Blasé, Chance, Flippant, Grass, Haphazard, Idle, Incidental, Informal, Jaunty, Lackadaisical, Odd(ment), Offhand, Orra, Passing, Promiscuous, Random, Sporadic, Stray, Temp, Throwaway

Casualty Caduac, Chance-medley, ➤ VICTIM

Casuist Jesuit

Cat Abyssinian, Alley, Angora, Asparagus, Balinese, Baudrons, Binturong, Bluepoint, Bobcat, Burmese, Cacomistle, Cacomixl, Caracal, Cheetah, Cheshire, Civet, Clowder, Colourpoint, Cop, Cougar, Dandy, Dasyure, Delundung, Eyra, Fat, Felid, Feline, Felix, Foss(a), Foumart, Foussa, Genet(te), Gib, Gossip, Grimalkin, Gus, Himalayan, Hipster, Hodge, Jaguar(ondi), Jaguarundi, Jazzer, Kilkenny, Kit, Korat, Lair, Lash, Leopard, Linsang, Lion, Long-hair, Lynx, Maine coon, Malkin, Maltese, Manul, Manx, Margay, Marmalade, Mehitabel, Mewer, Mog, Mouser, Musang, Nandine, Neuter, Nib, Ocelot, Ounce, Painter, Pallas's, Panther, Pard, Pardal, Persian, Pharaoh, Polecat, Practical, Puma, Puss, Rasse, Rex, Ringtail, Rumpy, Russian blue, Scourge, Sealpoint, Serval, Shorthair, Siamese, Sick, Spew, Spue, Swinger, Tabby, Tibert, Tiger, Tigon, Tigress, Tobermory, Tom, Tortoise-shell, Tybalt, Viverra, Weasel, Zibet(h)

Catacomb Cemetery, Crypt, Hypogeum, Vault

Catalepsy Catatony, Trance

Catalogue Dewey, Index, Inventory, List, Litany, Magalog, Messier, Ragman, Ragment, Raisonné, Record, Register, Table, Tabulate

Catalyst Accelerator, Agent, Influence, Unicase, Ziegler

Catamite Ingle

Catapult Ballista, Ging, Launch, Mangon(el), Perrier, Petrary, Propel, Scorpion, Shanghai, Sling, Slingshot, Stone-bow, Tormentum, Trebuchet, Wye, Y

Cataract Cascade, Film, Pearl, Torrent, Waterfall, Web and pin

Catarrh Coryza, Rheum

Catastrophe Calamity, ➤ DISASTER, Doom, Epitasis, Fiasco, Meltdown

Cat-call Boo, Mew, Miaow, Miaul, Razz, Wawl, Wrawl

Catch(y), Caught Air, Apprehend, Attract, Bag, Benet, Bone, C, Capture, Chape, Clasp, Cog, Collar, Contract, Cop, Corner, Ct, Deprehend, Detent,

Dolly, Engage, Enmesh, Ensnare, Entoil, Entrap, Fang, Field, Fumble, Gaper, Get, Glee(some), Grasp, Had, Hank, Haud, Haul, Hear, Hold, Hook, Inmesh, Keddah, Keight, Kep(pit), Kheda, Kill, Land, Lapse, Lasso, Latch, Lime, Lock, Morse, Nab, Nail, Net, Nick, Nim, Nobble, Noose, Overhear, Overhent, Overtake, Parti, Pawl, Rap, Release, Rope, Round, Rub, Safety, Sean, Sear, See(n), Seize, ➤ SNAG, Snap, Snare, Snig, ➤ SONG, Surprise, Swindle, Tack, Take, Trammel, Trap, Trawl, Trick, Tripwire, Troll, Twig, Understand, Wrestle

Catchword Motto, Shibboleth, Slogan, Tag

Catechism Carritch, Test

Categorise, Category ➤ CLASS, Etic, Genus, Label, Order, Pigeonhole, Range, Taxon

Cater(er) Acatour, Cellarer, Feed, Manciple, ➤ PROVIDE, Serve, Steward, Supply, Victualler, Vivandière

Caterpillar Aweto, Boll worm, Cotton-worm, Cutworm, Eruciform, Geometer, Hop-dog, Hornworm, Inchworm, Larva, Looper, Osmeterium, Palmer, Tent, Webworm, Woolly-bear

Catfish Hassar, Woof

Cathartic Turbeth

Cathedral Basilica, Chartres, Chester, Cologne, Dome, Duomo, Ely, Lateran, Minster, Notre Dame, Rheims, Sens, St Paul's, Wells, Westminster, Winchester

Catherine Braganza, Parr

Catherine-wheel Girandole

Cathode Electrode, Filament, Ray

Catholic Broad, Defenders, Doolan, Ecumenical, Fenian, General, Irvingism, Jebusite, Latin, Left-footer, Liberal, Marian, Ostiary, Papalist, Papaprelatist, Papist, Recusant, Redemptionist, Roman, Salesian, Spike, Taig, Te(a)gue, Teigue, Thomist, Tory, Tridentine, Universal, Ursuline, Wide

Catkin Amentum, Chat, Lamb's tail, Pussy-willow, Salicaceous

Cat-lover Ailurophile

Catmint Nep, Nepeta

Cato Porcian, Uticensis

Cats-eye Chatoyant, Cymophane

Catsmeat Lights

Catspaw Pawn, Tool

Cat's tail Reed-mace, Typha

Cat's whiskers Vibrissa

Cattle(pen) Aberdeen Angus, Africander, Ankole, Aver, Ayrshire, Beefalo, Brahman, Buffalo, Carabao, Charbray, Charol(l)ais, Chillingham, Dexter, Drove, Durham, Fee, Friesland, Galloway, Gaur, Gayal, Guernsey, Gyal, Heard, Herd, Hereford, Highland, Holstein (Friesian), Jersey, Kerry, Kine, Kouprey, Kraal, Ky(e), Kyloe, Lairage, Limousin, Lincoln, Longhorn, Luing, Neat, Nout, Nowt, Owsen, Oxen, Piemontese, Rabble, Redpoll, Rother,

Shorthorn, Simment(h)al, Soum, Sowm, Steer, Stock, Store, Stot, Sussex, Teeswater, Welsh black

Cattle disease Anthrax, Black water, Hoove, Johne's, Listeriosis, Mange, Mastitis, Moorill, Quarter-ill, Red-water, Rinderpest, Scours, Scrapie, Texas fever, Wire-heel, Woody-tongue

Cattle food Fodder

Cattleman Cowboy, Herder, Maverick, Rancher, Ringer, Stock-rider

Catty Kin, Spiteful

Caucasian Aryan, Azabaijani, European, Melanochroi, Paleface, Semite, Shemite, White, Yezdi, Yezidee, Zezidee

Caucus Assembly, Cell, Gathering, Race

▶ **Caught** see CATCH

Caul Baby-hood, Kell, Membrane, Sillyhow

Cauldron Kettle, Pot

Cauliflower Curd, Ear, Floret

Caulk Fill, Pitch, Snooze

Causation, Cause(d), Causes Aetiology, Agent, Beget, Breed, Bring, Compel, Create, Crusade, Determinant, Due, Effect, Efficient, Factor, Flag-day, Formal, Gar(re), Generate, Ideal, Induce, Lead, Lost, Make, Material, Motive, ▶ OCCASION, Parent, Provoke, Reason, Root, Sake, Source, Teleology, Topic, Ultimate, Wreak

Caustic Acid, Acrimonious, Alkaline, Burning, Erodent, Escharotic, Moxa, Pungent, Sarcastic, Scathing, Seare, Tart, Vitriol, Waspish, Withering

Cauterise Brand, Burn, Disinfect, Inustion

Caution, Cautious (person) Achitophel, Admonish, Ahithophel, Alert, Amber, Awarn, Beware, Cagey, Care, Cave, Caveat, Chary, Circumspect, Credence, Cure, Deliberate, Defensive, Discretion, Fabian, Gingerly, Guard(ed), Heedful, Leery, Prudent, Rum, Skite, Tentative, Vigilant, Ware, ▶ WARN, Wary, (Yellow) card

Cavalcade Pageant, Parade, Procession, Sowarree, Sowarry

Cavalier Brusque, Cicisbeo, Gallant, Lively, Malignant, Offhand, Peart, Rider, Royalist

Cavalry(man) Blues, Car(a)bineer, Car(a)binier, Cornet, Cossack, Dragoon, Equites, Horse, Hussar, Ironsides, Lancers, Plunger, Ressaldar, Risaldar, Rutter, Sabres, Silladar, Sillidar, Spahi, Uhlan, Yeomanry

Cave(rn), Caves, Cave-dwelling Acherusia, Altamira, Antar, Antre, Beware, Cellar, Collapse, Corycian, Den, Domdaniel, Erebus, Fingal's, Fore, Grot(to), Hollow, Jenolan, Lascaux, Look-out, Lupercal, Mammoth, Nix, Pot-hole, Proteus, Sepulchre, Spel(a)ean, Speleology, Spelunker, Speos, Tassili, Vault, Waitomo, Ware, Weem

Caveman Adullam, Aladdin, Fingal, Neanderthal, Primitive, Troglodyte, Troll

Caviare Beluga, Roe, Sevruga, Sturgeon

Cavil Carp, Haggle, Quibble

Cavity Acetabulum, Amygdale, Atrial, Camera, Celom, Chamber, Coelom(e), Concepticle, Concha, Countermark, Crater, Crypt, Dent, Druse,

Enteron, Follicle, Foss, Gap, Geode, Glenoid, Hold, Hole, Lacuna, Locule, Orbita, Mediastinum, Orifice, Pocket, Sinus, Tear, Tympanum, Vacuole, Vein, Ventricle, Vesicle, Vitta, Vomica, Vug, Well

Cavort(ing) Jag

Cavy Agouti, Capybara, Hograt, Paca

Cease(fire) Abate, Blin, Cut, Desist, Die, Disappear, Halt, Intermit, Lin, Lose, Pass, Refrain, Sessa, ➤ STOP, Truce

Ceaseless Eternal, Incessant

Cecil Rhodes

Cedar(wood) Arolla, Atlas, Deodar, Incense, Toon

Cede Grant, Yield

Ceiling Absolute, Barrel, Coffered, Cove, Cupola, Dome, Glass, Lacunar, Laquearia, Limit, Plafond, Roof, Soffit

Celebrate(d), Celebration, Celebrity Ale, Beanfeast, Besung, Bigwig, Binge, Carnival, Chant, Commemorate, Distinguished, Do, Emblazon, Encaenia, Epithalamion, Epithalamium, Fame, Feast, Fest, Festivity, Fete, Fiesta, Gala, Gaudeamus, Gaudy, Glorify, Grog-up, Harvest home, Hold, Holiday, Honour, Jamboree, Jollifications, Jollities, Jubilee, Keep, Laud, Legend, Lion, Loosing, Lowsening, Maffick, Mardi gras, Mawlid al-Nabi, Monstre sacre, Name, Noted, Nuptials, Observe, Occasion, Orgy, Panathenaea, Praise, Randan, Rejoice, Renown, Repute, Revel, Roister, Saturnalia, Sing, Spree, Star, Storied, Sung, Triumph, Wassail, Wet

Celerity Dispatch, Haste, Speed, Velocity

Celery Alexanders, Smallage, Stick

Celestial Chinese, Divine, Ethereal, Heavenly, Supernal, Uranic

Celibate, Celibacy Bachelor, Chaste, Paterin(e), Rappist, Rappite, Shakers, Single, Spinster

Cell(s), Cellular Adipocyte, Akaryote, Aplanogamete, Aplanospore, Arthrospore, Astrocyte, Athrocyte, Ascus, Basal, Basidium, Basophil(e), Battery, Blasteme, Blastoderm, Blastula, Bullpen, Button, Cadre, Cambium, Cathode, Censor, Centrosome, Chamber, Chapel, Chromaffin, Chromatophore, Chromosome, Clark, Cnidoblast, Coenocyte, Comb, Companion, Cone, Congenic, Corpuscle, Crypt, Cubicle, Cybrid, Cyte, Cytoid, Cytology, Daniell, Daughter, Death, Defensin, Diaxon, Dry, Dungeon, Ectomere, Ectoplasm, Electrolytic, Embryo-sac, Endoderm, Endosarc, Endothelium, Eosinophil, Epiblast, Epithelium, Erythrocyte, Eukaryon, Fibroblast, Fibroma, Flame, Fuel, Gad, Gamete, Gemmule, Gland, Goblet, Gonidium, Granulocyte, Group, Guard, H(a)emocyte, Haematoblast, Hair, Hapteron, HeLa, Helper T, Histiocyte, Hybridoma, Idioblast, Interneuron, Internode, Iridocyte, Karyology, Killer, Kinetoplast, Laticifer, Laura, Leclanché, Leucoblast, Leucocyte, Leukoblast, Linin, Lithite, Lymphocyte, Macromere, Macrophage, Mast, Megaloblast, Melanoblast, Melanocyte, Meristem, Merozoite, Mesenchyme, Microcyte, Microgamete, Microvillus, Mitochondroin, Monocyte, Morula, Motor neuron, Myeloblast, Myelocyte, Myoblast, Myotome, Myotube, Neoblast, Neurite, Neuroblast, Neuron, Neurone, Neutron, Neutrophil, Normoblast,

Odontoblast, Oocyte, Organelle, Osteoblast, Osteoclast, Oxum, Padded, Palisade, Parietal, Pec, Perikaryon, Periplasm, Periplast, Peter, Phagocyte, Phelloderm, Photoelectric, Photoreceptor, Photovoltaic, Plasma, Plastid, Poikilocyte, Primary, ➤ PRISON, Proembryo, Propoceptor, Protoplast, Purkinje, Receptor, Reticulocyte, Retinula, Schistocyte, Schizont, Schwann, Secondary, Selenium, Sensor, Seredium, Sertoli, Sickle, Solar, Soma(tic), Somite, Spermatocyte, Spermatogonium, Spermat(ozo)id, Spherocyte, Spheroplast, Spongioblast, Spore, Sporocyte, Sporule, Squamous, Standard, Stem, Stone, Storage, Suspensor, Swarm, Sweatbox, Symplast, Syncytium, Synergid, Synkaryon, T, Tapetum, Thymocyte, Totipotent, Trabecula, Unipolar, Unit, Vesicle, Voltaic, Wet, X-body, Zeta, Zoosperm, Zoospore, Zygote

Cellar Basement, Bodega, Coalhole, Dunny, Hypogeum, Storm, Vault, Vaut

Cell division Amitosis

Cellist, Cello Hermit, Prisoner

Celluloid, Cellulose Acetate, Cel, Viscose

Celt(ic) Breton, Brython, Druid, Gadhel, Gael, Goidel, Helvetii, Kelt, Taffy, Welsh

Cement Araldite®, Compo, Concrete, Fix, Flaunch, Glue, Grout, Lute, Maltha, Mastic, Mortar, Paste, Pointing, Portland, Putty, Rubber, ➤ STICK, Trass

Cemetery Aceldama, Arenarium, Arlington, Boneyard, Boot Hill, Campo santo, Catacomb, God's Acre, Golgotha, Graveyard, Musall, Necropolis, Père Lachaise, Saqqara, Urnfield

Censer Cassolette, Navicula, Thurible

Censor(ious), Censure Accuse, Admonition, Animadvert, Appeach, Ban, Banner, Berate, Blame, Blue-pencil, Bowdler, Braid, Cato, Comstockery, ➤ CONDEMN, Critical, Criticise, Damn, Dang, Decry, Dispraise, Edit, Excommunicate, Excoriate, Expurgate, Gag, Obloquy, Rap, Reprimand, Repress, Reproach, Reprobate, Reprove, Satirise, Slam, Slate, Suppress, Tax, Tirade, Traduce, Wig

Census Count, Poll

Cent Bean, Coin, Ct, Penny, Red

Centaur Ch(e)iron, Horseman, Nessus, Sagittary, Therianthropic

Centenary, Centennial Anniversary, Colorado

Centipede Chilopoda, Earwig, Polypod, Scolopendra, Scutiger

Central, Centre Amid, Attendance, Axis, Bunt, Cardinal, Chakra, Civic, Core, Day, Dead, Detention, Deuteron, Deuton, Downtown, Epergne, Eye, Focus, Frontal, Garden, Health, Heart, Hotbed, Hothouse, Hub, Inmost, Internal, Kernel, Kingpin, Leisure, Lincoln, Main, Mecca, Medulla, Mid(st), Nave, Nucleus, Pompidou, Reception, Rehabilitation, Remand, Storm, Waist, Weather

Central heating Cen, CH

▷ **Centre** may indicate middle letters

Centrepiece Epergne

Century Age, C, Era, Magdeburg, Period, Ton

Cephalopod Ammonite, Calamary, Cuttle, Loligo, Nautilus, Octopus, Sepia, Squid

Ceramic(s) Arcanist, China, Earthen, Ferrite, Porcelain, Pottery, Sialon, Tiles

Cereal Amelcorn, Barley, Blé, Bran, Buckwheat, Bulgar, Bulg(h)ur, Cassava, Corn, Couscous, Emmer, Farina, Gnocchi, Grain, Granola, Hominy, Maize, Mandioc(a), Mandiocca, Mani(h)oc, Manihot, Mealie, Millet, Muesli, Oats, Paddy, Popcorn, Rye(corn), Sago, Samp, Seed, Semolina, Sorghum, Spelt, Tapioca, Tef(f), Triticale, Wheat, Zea

Cerebrate, Cerebration Pore, Thought

Ceremonial, Ceremony Amrit, Barmitzvah, Chanoyu, Common Riding, Coronation, Doseh, Durbar, Encaenia, Enthronement, Eucharist, Flypast, Form(al), Habdalah, Havdalah, Havdoloh, Heraldry, Investiture, Matsuri, Maundy, Mummery, Observance, Ordination, Pageantry, Parade, Pomp, Powwow, Protocol, Rite, Ritual, Sacrament, Seder, Service, State, Tea, Usage

Cerium Ce

Cert(ain), Certainty Absolute, Actual, Assured, Banker, Bound, Cast-iron, Cinch, Cocksure, Confident, Convinced, Decided, Exact, Fact, Fate, Indubitable, Inevitable, Infallible, Monte, Nap, One, Positive, Poz, Precise, Shoo-in, Siccar, Sicker, Some, Snip, ➤ SURE, Sure-fire, Truth, Yes

Certainly Agreed, Ay, Certes, Fegs, Forsooth, Indeed, Iwis, Jokol, OK, Oke, Pardi(e), Pardy, Perdie, Siccar, Sicker, ➤ SURE, Truly, Verily, Yea, Yes, Yokul, Ywis

Certificate, Certified, Certify Affirm, Attest, Bond, Chit, Cocket, Confirm, Credential, Debenture, Depose, Diploma, Docket, Document, Enseal, Guarantee, Licence, Lines, MOT, Paper, Patent, Proven, Scrip, Sworn, Testamur, Testimonial, U, Voucher, Warrant

Cesspit Bog, Dungmere, Sinkhole, Slurry

Cetacean Dolphin, Porpoise, Whale

Ceylon(ese) Serendip, Vedda(h)

Chafe, Chafing Chunter, Fray, Fret, Harass, Intertrigo, Irritate, ➤ RUB, Seethe, Worry

Chaff(y) Badinage, Banter, Bran, Chip, Dross, Hay, Husk, Rag, Raillery, Rally, Ramentum, Refuse, Roast, Rot, Tease, Twit

Chaffer(ing) Bandy, Bargain, Haggle, Higgle, Hucksterage, Traffic

Chaffinch Whitewing

Chagrin Envy, Mortify, Spite, Vexation

Chain(ed) Acre's-breadth, Albert, Anklet, Bind, Bond, Bracelet, Bucket, Cable, Catena, Choke, Cistron, Daisy, Decca, Drive, Dynasty, Engineer's, Esses, Fanfarona, Fetter, Fob, Food, Furlong, Gleipnir, Gunter's, Gyve, Markov, Mayor, Micella(r), Micelle, Noria, Pennine, Pitch, Range, Roller, Seal, ➤ SERIES, Shackle, Slang, Sprocket, String, Strobila, Team, Tug, Watch

Chain-gang Coffle

Chair Basket, Bath, Bench, Berbice, Bergère, Birthing, Bosun's, Butterfly, Captain's, Carver, Club, Curule, Deck, Easy, Electric, Estate, Fauteuil,

Fiddle-back, Gestatorial, Guérite, Jampan, Jampanee, Jampani, Ladder-back, Lounger, Morris, Pew, Preside, Recliner, Rocker, ➤ SEAT, Sedan, Stool, Swivel, Throne, Wainscot, Windsor, Wing

Chair-back Ladder, Splat

Chairman Convener, Emeritus, Mao, MC, Pr(a)eses, Prof, Prolocutor, Sheraton, Speaker

Chalaza Albumen, Treadle, Treddle

Chaldean Babylonian, Ur

Chalet Cabana, Cot, Skio

Chalk(y) Calcareous, Cauk, Cawk, Crayon, Credit, Cretaceous, French, Senonian, Soapstone, Steatite, Tailor's, White(n), Whit(en)ing

Challenge(r), Challenging Acock, Assay, Call, Cartel, Champion, Confront, Contest, Dare, Defy, Gage, Gauntlet, Glove, Hazard, Hen(ner), Iconoclasm, Impugn, Oppugn, Provoke, Query, Question, Recuse, Sconce, Shuttle, Tackle, Taker, Tall order, Tank, Threat, Vie, Whynot

Chamber(s) Atrium, Auricle, Camarilla, Camera, Casemate, Cavern, Cavitation, Cavity, Cell(a), Chanty, Cloud, Cofferdam, Combustion, Cubicle, Decompression, Dene-hole, Dolmen, Echo, Float, Gas, Gazunder, Hall, Horrors, Hypogea, Ionization, Jerry, Jordan, Kiva, Lethal, Locule, Mattamore, Po(t), Privy, Roum, Serdab, Silo, Spark, Star, Swell-box, Synod, Thalamus, Undercroft, Upper, Utricle, Vault, Ventricle, Zeta

Chamberlain Camerlengo, Camerlingo, Censor

Chameleon Ethiopian, Lizard, Tarand

Chamfer Bevel, Groove

Chamois Ibex, Izard, Shammy

Champ Bite, Chafe, Chew, Chomp, Eat, Gnash, Gnaw, Mash, Morsure, Munch

Champagne Boy, Bubbly, Charlie, Fizz, Gigglewater, Pop, Sillery, Simkin, Simpkin, Stillery, Troyes, Widow

Champion Ace, Adopt, Ali, Apostle, Belt, Campeador, Cid, Cock, Defend, Don Quixote, Doucepere, Douzeper, Dymoke, Enoch, Espouse, Gladiator, Harry, ➤ HERO, Horse, Kemp, Kemper(yman), King, Knight, Maintain, Matchless, Messiah, Messias, Neil, Paladin, Palmerin, Peerless, Perseus, Promachos, Proponent, Protagonist, Roland, St Anthony, St David, St Denis, St George, St James, St Patrick, Spiffing, Spokesman, Star, Support, Tribune, Upholder, Victor, Wardog, ➤ WINNER, Yokozuna

Championship Open, Title

Chance, Chancy Accident, Aleatory, Aunter, Bet, Break, Buckley's, Cast, Casual, Cavel, Contingent, Dice, Earthly, Even, ➤ FATE, Fluke, Fortuity, Fortuitous, Fortune, ➤ GAMBLE, Game, Hap, Happenstance, Hobnob, Iffy, Kevel, Light, Look-in, Lot, ➤ LOTTERY, Luck, Meet, Mercy, Occur, Odds, Opening, Opportunity, Posse, Potluck, Probability, Prospect, Random, Rise, Risk, Serendipity, Slant, Spec, Stake, Stochastic, Sweep, Toss-up, Treble, Turn, Tychism, Ventre, Venture, Wager

Chancel Adytum, Bema, Nave

Chancellor Adolf, Bismarck, Dollfuss, Kohl, Logothete, Minister, More

Chancery Court, Hanaper

Chandelier Candlestick, Corona, Drop, Electrolier, Gasolier, Girandole, Lustre, Pendant

Chandler Acater, Raymond

Chaney Lon

Change(able), Changing Adapt, Adjust, Agio, ➤ ALTER, Amendment, Attorn, Backtrack, Barter, Become, Bob-major, Capricious, Cash, Catalysis, Chop, Cline, Commute, Convert, Coppers, Denature, Departure, Dichrony, Edit, Enallage, Esterify, Eustatic, Exchange, Find, Flighty, Fluctuate, Float, Flux, Guard, Gybe, Inflect, Innovate, Killcrop, Labile, Make-over, Metabolic, Metabolise, Metamorphose, Metamorphosis, Mobile, Modify, Mutable, Mutalis mutandis, Mutanda, Mutation, Parallax, Peal, Peripet(e)ia, Permute, Prophase, Protean, Realise, Recant, Rectify, Reform, Refraction, Rejig, Rest, Revise, Rework, Sandhi, Scourse, Sd, Seesaw, Shake-out, Shake-up, Shift, Silver, Small, Substitute, Swap, Swing, Switch, Tolsel, Tolsey, Tolzey, Transfer, Transfiguration, Transform, Transition, Transmogrify, Transmute, Transpose, Transubstantial, Turn, Uncertain, Upheaval, U-turn, Vagary, Variant, Variation, Vary, Veer, Vicissitude, Volatile, Volte-face, Wankle, Washers, Wheel, Wow

▷ **Change(d)** may indicate an anagram

Changeling Auf, Killcrop, Oaf, Turncoat

Channel Access, Aflaj, Aqueduct, Artery, Beagle, Bed, Billabong, Bristol, Canal, Canaliculus, Chimb, Chime, Chine, Chute, Conduit, Culvert, Cut, Ditch, Drain, Duct, Dyke, Ea, Euripus, Fairway, Falaj, Flume, Foss, Funnel, Furrow, Gat, Geo, Gio, Glyph, Grough, Gully, Gut, Gutter, Head-race, Ingate, Katabothron, Katavothron, Khor, Kill, Lane, Leat, Leet, Limber, Major, Meatus, Medium, Minch, Moat, Narrows, North, Penstock, Pipeline, Qanat, Race, Rebate, Rigol(l), Rivulet, Sea-gate, Seaway, Sewer, Sinus, Sloot, Sluice, Sluit, Sny(e), Solent, Solway Firth, Sound, Sow, Spillway, Sprue, St George's, Strait, Suez, Sure, Swash, Tailrace, Tideway, Tracheole, Trough, Ureter, Vallecula, Wireway

Chant Anthem, Antiphon, Cantillate, Cantus, Chaunt, Decantate, Euouae, Evovae, Gregorian, Haka, Harambee, Hymn, Intone, Introit, Motet, Pennillion-singing, Psalm, Sing, Slogan, Te deum, Yell

Chantilly Cream, Lace

Chaos, Chaotic Abyss, Anarchy, Confusion, Disorder, Fractal, Hun-tun, Jumble, Mess, Muss, Shambles, Snafu, Tohu bohu

▷ **Chaotic** may indicate an anagram

Chap(s) Beezer, Bloke, Bo, Bod, Bor, Chafe, Cheek, Chilblain, Chop, Cleft, Cod, Codger, Cove, Crack, Customer, Dog, Fella, Fellow, Flews, Genal, Gent, Gink, Guy, Hack, Joll, Jowl, Kibe, Lad, ➤ MAN, Mouth, Mum, Ocker, Rent, Rime, Spray, Spreathe, Spreethe, Spreaze, Spreeze, Wang

▷ **Chaps** may indicate an anagram

Chapel Bethel, Bethesda, Beulah, Cha(u)ntry, Ebenezer, Feretory, Galilee, Lady, Oratory, Parabema, Prothesis, Sacellum, Sistine

Chaperon(e) Beard, Cap, Duenna, Escort, Gooseberry, Griffin, Griffon, Gryphon, Muffin

Chaplain CF, Ordinary, Padre, Priest, Skypilot, Slope

Chaplet Anadem, Coronet, Fillet, Garland, Wreath

Chapter Accidents, C, Canon, Cap, Capitular, Ch, Chap, Cr, Division, Episode, Lodge, Phase, Section, Social, Sura(h), Verse

Char(woman) Adust, Burn, Cleaner, Coal, Daily, Duster, Mop(p), Scorch, Sear, Singe, Smoulder, Toast, Togue, Torgoch

Charabanc Bus, Chara, Coach

Character(s) Aesc, Alphabet, Ampersand, Ampussyand, Aura, Backslash, Brand, Calibre, Case, Cipher, Clef, Cliff, Climate, Complexion, Contour, Credit, Delimiter, Devanagari, Digamma, Dramatis personae, Eta, Ethos, ➤ FEATURE, Fish, Fist, Form, Grain, Grit, Hieroglyphic, Ideogram, Ideograph, Italic, Kanji, Kern, Kind, La(m)bda, Letter, Logogram, Make-up, Mark, Mu, Nagari, ➤ NATURE, Nu, Ogam, Ogham, Pahlavi, Pantaloon, Part, Pehlevi, Person(a), Personage, ➤ PERSONALITY, Phonogram, Physiognomy, Protagonist, Psi, Reference, Repute, Rho, Role, Rune, Runic, Sampi, San, Self, Sirvente, Slash, Sonancy, Stamp, Subscript, Superscript(ion), Swung dash, Syllabary, Symbol, Testimonial, Ton(e), Trait, Uncial, Vav, Vee, Waw, Wen, Wyn(n), Yogh, Zeta

Characterise(d), Characterism, Characteristic Attribute, Aura, Cast, Colour, Distinctive, Ethos, Facies, Feature, Hair, Hallmark, Has, Headmark, Idiomatic, Idiosyncrasy, Jizz, Lineament, Mien, Nature, Notate, Peculiar, Persona, Point, Property, Quality, Stigma, Strangeness, Streak, Style, ➤ TRAIT, Typical, Vein

Characterless Anon, Inane, Wet

Charade Enigma, Pretence, Riddle

Charcoal Carbon, Coke, Fusain

Charge(s), Charged, Charger Accuse, Agist, Allege, Annulet, Arraign, Ascribe, Baton, Bear, Behest, Blame, Brassage, Brush, Buckshot, Care, Cathexis, Commission, Complaint, Cost, Count, Cover, Criminate, Damage, Debit, Delate, Delf, Delph, Demurrage, Depth, Depute, Directive, Dittay, Due, Duty, Electron, Entrust, Expense, Fare, Fee, Fill, Flock, Freight, Fullage, Gazump, Gravamen, Heraldic, Hot, Hypothec, Impeach, Impute, Indict, Inescutcheon, Inform, Instinct, Ion, Isoelectric, Last, Lien, Lioncel(le), Lionel, Live, Load, Mandate, Mine, Mount, Objure, Obtest, Onrush, Onus, Ordinary, Orle, Overhead, Pervade, Plaint, Positive, Premium, Prime, Q, Rack-rent, Rap, Rate, Red-dog, Rent, Report, Reprise, Roundel, Run, ➤ RUSH, Saddle, Service, Specific, Steed, Tariff, Tax, Tear, Terms, Tilt, ➤ TRAY, Tressure, Trickle, Trust, Upfill, Verdoy, Vigorish, Ward, Wharfage

Chariot(eer) Auriga, Automedon, Biga, Cart, Curricle, Hur, Quadriga, Wagon, Wain

Charisma Oomph

Charitable, Charity Alms, Awmous, Benign, Caritas, Dole, Dorcas, Eleemosynary, Largesse, Leniency, Liberal, Lion, Love, Mercy, Oddfellow, Openhanded, Oxfam, Pelican, Zakat

Charivari Rough music, Uproar

Charlatan Cheat, Crocus, Escroc, Faker, Imposter, Katerfelto, Mountebank, Poseur, Quack(salver), Saltimbanco

Charlemagne Carlovingian

Charles, Charley, Charlie Beard, Car, Champagne, Chan, Chaplin, Checkpoint, Elia, Lamb, (Old) Rowley, Pretender, Rug-gown, Sap, Tail-end, Watchman

Charles de Gaulle Airport

Charlotte Bronte, Russe, Yonge

Charm(er), Charming Abracadabra, Abrasax, Abraxas, Allure, Amulet, Appeal, Aroma, Attraction, Beguile, Bewitch, Captivate, Charisma, Circe, Comether, Cute, Cutie, Emerods, Enamour, Enchant, Engaging, ➤ ENTRANCE, Fascinate, Fay, Fetish, Grace, Greegree, Gri(s)gris, Hand of glory, Houri, Juju, Magnetic, Mascot, Mojo, Obeah, Obi(a), Periapt, Phylactery, Porte-bonheur, Prince, Quaint, Quark, Ravish, Siren, Smoothie, Spellbind, Suave, Sweetness, Taking, Talisman, Telesm, Tiki, Trinket, Unction, Voodoo, Winsome

▷ **Charming** may indicate an anagram

Chart(ed), Charting Abac, Bar, Breakeven, Card, Diagram, Eye, Flip, Flow, Gantt, Graph, Histogram, Hydrography, Isogram, Isopleth, List, Magna Carta, ➤ MAP, Mappemond, Nomogram, Plot, Portolano, Ringelmann, Social, Table, Timetable, Waggoner, Weather

Charter Book, Covenant, Hire, Lease, Novodamus, Rent

Chary Cagey, Careful, Cautious, Frugal, Shy, Wary

Charybdis Maelstrom, Whirlpool

Chase(r), Chasing Cannock, Chace, Chevy, Chivy, Ciseleur, Ciselure, Course, Cranbome, Decorate, Drink, Game, Harass, Hound, ➤ HUNT, Jumper, Oxo, Pursuit, Race, Scorse, Sic(k), Steeple, Sue, Suit, Wild-goose

Chasm Abyss, Crevasse, Gap, Gorge, Fissure, Gulf, Schism, Yawn

Chaste, Chastity Agnes, Attic, Celibate, Classic, Clean, Florimell, Ines, Innocent, Modesty, Nessa, ➤ PURE, Vestal, Virginal, Virtue

Chasten, Chastise(d), Chastisement Beat, Correct, Discipline, Disple, Lash, Rib-roast, Rollicking, Scold, Scourge, Shame-faced, Spank, Strap, Whip

Chat, Chatter(box) Babble, Bavardage, Blab(ber), Blether, Campanero, Causerie, Chelp, Chinwag, Clack, Clishmaclaver, Confab(ulate), Converse, Cosher, Coze, Crack, Dialogue, Froth, Gab(ble), Gas, Gossip, Gup, Hobnob, Jabber, Jargon, Jaw, Kilfud, Madge, Mag(pie), Natter, Patter, Pie, Pourparler, Prate, Prattle, Rabbit, Rabble, Rap, Rattle, Scuttlebutt, Shmoose, Talk, Talkee-talkee, Tattle, Twattle, Waffle, Windbag, Witter, Wongi, Yacketyyak, Yak, Yarn, Yatter, Yoking

Chateau Castle, Cru, Malmaison, Schloss

Chateaubriand René

Chattel Asset, Chose, Deodand

Chaucer(ian) Dan, OE

Chauffeur Cabby, Coachy, Driver, Sice, Syce

Chauvinist Alf, Bigot, Jingo, MCP, Partisan, Sexist

Cheap Bargain, Base, Catchpenny, Cheesy, Chintzy, Cut-price, Downmarket, Giveaway, Knockdown, Low, Off-peak, Poor, Sacrifice, Shoddy, Stingy, Tatty, Tawdry, Ticky-tacky, Tinpot, Tinselly, Trivial, Undear, Vile

▷ **Cheap** may indicate a d- or p- start to a word

Cheapside Bow

Cheat(ers), Cheating Bam, Beguile, Bilk, Bite(r), Bob, Bonnet, Bullock, Bucket, Cardsharp(er), Chiaus, Chicane(ry), Chisel, Chouse, Clip, Cod, Cog(ger), Colt, Con, Cozen, Crib, Cross, Cross-bite(r), Cuckold, Cully, Defraud, Delude, Diddle, Dingo, Dish, Do, Doublecross, Duckshove, Dupe, Escroc, Faitor, Fiddle, Finagle, Flam, Fleece, Fob, Foister, Fox, Fraud, Gaff, Gip, Glasses, Gum, Gyp, Hoax, Hocus, Hoodwink, Hornswoggle, Horse, Intake, Jockey, Magsman, Mulct, Mump, Nick, Pasteboard, Picaro(on), Poop, Queer, Rib, Rig, Rogue, Rook, Rush, Scam, Screw, Shaft, Sharper, Short-change, Slur, Smouch, Snap, Stack, Stiff, Sting, Swindle, Thimble-rigging, Trepan, Trim, Two-time, Welsh, Wheedle

Check Arrest, Audit, Ba(u)lk, Bauk, Bill, Bridle, Collate, Compesce, Control, Count, Cramp, Curb, Dam, Damp, Detent, Dogs-tooth, Examine, Foil, Frustrate, Halt, Hamper, Hobble, Houndstooth, Inhibit, Jerk, Jerque, Let, Limit, Mate, Monitor, Observe, Overhaul, Prevent, Rebuff, Rebuke, Rein, Repress, Reprime, Repulse, Reread, ➤ RESTRAIN, Revoke, Saccade, Screen, Service, Setback, Shepherd's, Sit-upon, Sneap, Sneb, Snib, Snub, Spot, ➤ STEM, Stop, Stunt, Tab, Tally, Tartan, Tattersall, Test, Thwart, Tick, Trash, Verify, Vet

Checkers Chinese, Piece

Cheddar Cheese, Gorge

Cheek(y) Alforja, Audacity, Buccal, Chap, Chollers, Chutzpah, Crust, Flippant, Fresh, Gum, Hussy, Jowl, Lip, Malapert, Malar, Masseter, Neck, Nerve, Noma, Pert, Presumption, Quean, Sass, Sauce, Sideburns, Wang, Yankie, Zygoma

Cheep Chirp, Chirrup, Peep

Cheer(s), Cheerful(ness), Cheering Acclaim, Agrin, Applaud, Banzai, Barrack, Blithe, Bonnie, Bravo, Bright, Bronx, Bubbly, Buck, Buoy, Cadgy, Canty, Cherry, Chin-chin, Chipper, ➤ COMFORT, Crouse, Debonair, Drink, Ease, Elate, Elevate, Enliven, Exhilarate, Festive, Genial, Gladden, Happy-go-lucky, Hearten, Hilarity, Holiday, Hooch, Hoorah, Huzzah, Insouciance, Jocund, Jovial, Kia-ora, Lightsome, Lively, Ovate, Peart, Please, Praise, Prosit, Rah, Riant, Rivo, Root, Rumbustious, Shout, Sko(a)l, Slainte, Sonsie, Sunny, Ta, Tata, Tiger, Toodle-oo, Winsome, Yell

Cheerless Dismal, Drab, Drear, Gloomy, Glum

Cheese, Cheesy American, Amsterdam, Appenzell, Bel Paese, Blue, Boursin, Brie, Caboc, Caerphilly, Camembert, Cantal, Casein, Caseous,

Cheddar, Cheshire, Chessel, Chèvre, Cottage, Coulommiers, Cream, Crowdie, Curd, Damson, Derby, Dolcelatte, Dunlop, Edam, Emmental(er), Emmenthal(er), Ermite, Esrom, Ewe, Fet(a), Fontina, Fromage frais, Fynbo, Gloucester, Goat, Gouda, Grand Panjandrum, Gruyère, Haloumi, Hard, Havarti, Huntsman, Ilchester, Islay, Jarlsberg®, Junket, Kebbock, Kebbuck, Kenno, Killarney, Leicester, Limburg(er), Lymeswold, Mascarpone, Mousetrap, Mozzarella, Mu(e)nster, Mycella, Neuchatel, Orkney, Parmesan, Pecorino, Port Salut, Provolone, Quark, Raclette, Rarebit, Reblochon, Rennet, Ricotta, Romano, Roquefort, Sage Derby, Samso, Sapsago, Skyr, Stilton®, Stracchino, Tilsit, Tofu, Truckle, Vacherin, VIP, Wensleydale

Cheesecake Pin-up

Cheese-scoop Pale

Chef Commis, Escoffier

Chekhov Anton

Chemical Acanthin, Acid, Acrolein, Adrenalin®, Alar, Aldehyde, Alkali, Alum, Amide, Barilla, Bradykinin, Bute, Carbide, Carnallite, Caseose, Catalyst, Cephalin, Cerebroside, Depside, Developer, Dopamine, Encephalin, Enkephalin(e), Fixer, Fluoride, Formyl, Fungicide, Glutamine, Glycol, Halon, Harmin, Hecogenin, Heptane, Hexylene, Hexylresorcinol, Histamine, Hypo, ICI, Imine, Imipramine, Indican, Interleukin, Morphactin, Natron, Nitre, Oestregen, Olein, Olefin, Oxide, Oxysalt, Pentane, Pentene, Pentyl, Peptide, Phenol, Phenyl, Pheromone, Potash, Potassa, Psoralen, Ptomaine, Reagent, Resorcin, Serotonin, Soman, Soup, Strontia, Sulphide, Thio-salt, Trimer, Weedicide, Weedkiller

Chemise Cymar, Sark, Serk, Shift, Shirt, Simar(re), Smock, Symar

Chemist(ry) Alchemy, Alchymy, Analyst, Apothecary, Bunsen, Butenandt, Cavendish, Davy, Debye, Dispenser, Druggist, Drugstore, FCS, Gahn, Hevesy, Inorganic, Lavoisier, Liebig, LSA, MPS, Nernst, Newlands, Nobel, Organic, Paracelsus, Pasteur, Pothecary, Pharmacist, Physical, Pottingar, Proust, Prout, RIC, Sabatier, Sanger, Spageric, Spagiric, Spagyric, Spicer, Stinks, Stoich(e)iometry

Cheops Khufu

Cheque Blank, Giro, Gregory, Stumer, Tab, Traveller's

Chequer Dice

Cherish(ed) Dear, Dote, Enshrine, Entertain, Esteem, Foment, Foster, Harbour, Inshrine, Nestle, Nurse, Pamper, Pet, Precious, Treasure

Cheroot Cigar, Manil(l)a

Cherry (tree) Amarelle, Ball, Bigaroon, Bigarreau, Blackheart, Cerise, Cornelian, Gean, Ground, Heart, Jerusalem, Kearton, Kermes, Kermesite, Malpighia, Marasca, Maraschino, May-duke, Maz(z)ard, Merry, Morel(lo), Red, Whiteheart

Cherry-pie Heliotrope

Cherub Angel, Putto, Seraph

Chess (move), Chess player, Chess term Black, Blindfold, Euwe, Fianchetto, FIDE, J'adoube, Karpov, Lightning, Miranda, Patzer, Plank, Shogi, Speed, White, Zugzwang, Zwischenzug

Chessman Bishop, Black, Castle, Horse, King, Knight, Pawn, Pin, Queen, Rook, White

Chest(y) Ark, Bahut, Bosom, Box, Breast, Buist, Bunker, Bureau, Bust, Caisson, Cap-case, Case, Cassone, Chapel, Chiffonier, Coffer, Coffin, Coffret, Commode, Cub, Hope, Inro, Kist, Larnax, Locker, Lowboy, Medicine, Ottoman, Pectoral, Pereion, Pigeon, Pleural, Safe, Scrine, Scryne, Shrine, Sternum, Tallboy, Tea, Thorax, Toolbox, Trunk, Wangun, Wanigan, War

Chester Deva

Chestnut Auburn, Badious, Ch, Chincapin, Chinese, Chinkapin, Chinquapin, Cliché, Conker, Favel(l), Hoary, Marron, Marron glacé, Moreton Bay, Russet, Saligot, Soare, Sorrel, Spanish, Sweet, Water

Chest protector ➤ ARMOUR, Bib

Chevalier Bayard, Knight, Pretender

Chevron Dancette, Stripe

Chew Bite, Champ, Chaw, Cud, Gnaw, Gum, Manducate, Masticate, Maul, Meditate, Moop, Mou(p), Munch, Ruminate, Siri(h), Spearmint

Chiastolite Macle

Chic Dapper, Elegant, In, Kick, Modish, Posh, Smart, Soigné, Stylish, Swish, Tonish, Trim

Chicane(ry) Artifice, Deception, Fraud, Wile

Chichester Yachtsman

Chichi Precious

Chick(en) Battery, Biddy, Broiler, Cheeper, Chittagong, Chuckie, Clutch, Cochin, Coward, Cowherd, Eirack, Gutless, Hen, Howtowdie, Kiev, Layer, Marengo, Minorca, Niderling, Poltroon, Poot, Poult, Pout, Prairie, Precocial, Quitter, Roaster, Spatchcock, Spring, Squab, Supreme, Timorous, Unheroic, Windy, Wyandotte, Yellow

Chickenfeed Maize

Chickenpox Varicella

Chicory Endive, Succory, Witloof

Chide Admonish, Berate, Objurgate, Rate, Rebuke, Reprove, Row, Scold, Tick off, Twit, Upbraid

Chief(tain) Arch, Ardrigh, Boss, Caboceer, Cacique, Calif, Caliph, Capital, Capitan, Capitayn, Capo, Caradoc, Cazique, Ch, Chagan, Dat(t)o, Dominant, Emir, First, Foremost, Geronimo, Grand, Haggis, ➤ HEAD, Hereward, Jarl, Kaid, King, Leader, ➤ MAIN, Mass, Mugwump, Nizam, Oba, Overlord, Pendragon, Premier, Primal, Prime, Principal, Quanah, Raja(h), Rajpramukh, Rangatira, Ratoo, Ratu, Sachem, Sagamore, Sarpanch, Sudder, Supreme, Tanist, Tank, Top

Chiffonier Cabinet, Commode

Chilblain Kibe

Child(ish), Children Aerie, Alannah, Babe, Baby, Badger, Bairn, Bambino, Bantling, Boy, Brat, Brood, Butter-print, Ch, Changeling, Cherub, Chick, Chickabiddy, Chit, Collop, Cub, Dream, Elfin, Eyas, Foundling, Gangrel, Ge(i)t, Girl, Gyte, Heir, Hurcheon, Imp, Infant, Issue, It, Jailbait, Jejune, Juvenile, Kid(die), Kiddie(wink), Kiddy, Kinder, Lad, Limb, Litter, Littlie, Mamzer, Minion, Minor, Mite, Munchkin, Naive, Nipper, Nursling, Offspring, Papoose, Piccaninny, Pickin, Progeny, Puerile, Puss, Putto, Ragamuffin, Rip, Rug rat, Scion, Smout, Smowt, Sprog, Street arab, Subteen, Ted, Tike, Toddle(r), Tot(tie), Totty, Trot, Tyke, Urchin, Wean, Weanel, Weanling, Weeny-bopper, Whelp, Younker, Youth

Childbearing, Childbirth Couvade, Lamaze, Parity, Puerperal

Child-killer Herod

Childless Atocous, Atokous, Barren, Nullipara, Sp

Chill(er), Chilly Bleak, ➤ COLD, Frappé, Freeze, Freon®, Frigid, Frosty, Gelid, Ice, Iciness, Mimi, Oorie, Ourie, Owrie, Parky, Raw, Refrigerate, Rigor, Scare

Chime(s) Bell, Cymar, Jingle, Peal, Semantron, Tink, ➤ TOLL

Chimera Graft

Chimney (pot), Chimney corner Can, Cow(l), Femerall, Flare stack, Flue, Funnel, Lug, Lum, Smokestack, Stack, Stalk, Tallboy, Tunnel

Chimp Ape, Jocko

Chin, Chinwag Chitchat, Double, Genial, Jaw, Jowl, Mentum

China(man), Chinese Ami, Amoy, Boxer, Cameoware, Cantonese, Cathay, Celestial, Ch, Chelsea, Chink(y), Chow, Coalport, Cochin, Cock, Confucius, Crackle, Crockery, Delft, Derby, Dresden, Eggshell, Etrurian, Flowery land, Friend, Google, Googly, Goss, Hakka, Han, Hizen, Hmong, Imari, Kanji, Kaolin, Kuo-yu, Limoges, Manchu, Mandarin, Mangi, Maoist, Mate, Meissen, Ming, Minton, Oppo, Pal, Pareoean, Pekingese, Pe-tsai, Pinyin, Porcelain, ➤ POTTERY, Putonghua, Rockingham, Seric, Sèvres, Shanghai, Sinic, Spode®, Sun Yat-sen, Tai-ping, Taoist, Teng, Tocharian, Tungus, Uigur, Wal(l)y, Ware, Wedgwood®, Willowware, Worcester, Wu

Chine Chink, Chynd, Ridge

Chink Chinaman, Chop, Cleft, Clink, Cloff, Crack, Cranny, Crevice, Gap, Rent, Rift, Rima, Sinic, Window

Chintz Kalamkari

Chip(s) Bo(a)st, Carpenter, Counter, Cut, Deep-fried, Fish, Flake, Fragment, Hack, Knap, Nacho(s), Nick, Pin, Shaving, Silicon, Spale, Spall, Tortilla, Transputer

▷ **Chip** may indicate an anagram

Chipmunk Gopher, Hackee, Suslik, Zizel

Chipper Jaunty, Spry, Wedge

Chiron Centaur

Chiropody Podiatry

Chirp(y), Chirrup Cheep, Cherup, Chirm, Chirr, Cicada, Peep, Pip, Pipe, Pitter, Stridulate, Trill, Tweet, Twitter

Chisel(ler), Chisel-like Bam, Boaster, Bolster, Bur, Burin, Carve, Cheat, Clip, Drove, Firmer, Gad, ➤ GOUGE, Mason, Scalpriform, Scauper, Scorper, Sculpt, Sting

Chit Docket, Girl, Note, Voucher

Chivalry, Chivalrous Brave, Bushido, Courtly, Gallant, Quixotic

Chivvy Badger, Harass, Pursue

Chloride, Chlorine Calomel

Chock Trig

Chocolate Aero, Brown, Cacao, Carob, Cocoa, Dragee, Ganache, Neapolitan, Noisette, Pinole, Theobroma, Truffle, Vegelate

Choice, Choose, Choosy, Chosen Adopt, Anthology, Appoint, Aryan, Cherry-pick, Cull, Dainty, Decide, Druthers, Eclectic, Elect, Elite, Esnecy, Fine, Fork, Free will, Hobson's, Leet, Leve, Lief, List, Opt, Option, Or, Ossian, Peach, Peculiar, ➤ PICK, Picking, Plum(p), Precious, Predilect, Prefer, Proairesis, Rare, Recherché, ➤ SELECT, Superb, Try(e), Via media, Volition, Wale

Choiceless Beggar

Choir, Choral, Chorister, Chorus Antiphony, Antistrophe, Anvil, Apse, Burden, Dawn, Decani, Faburden, Fauxbourdon, Group, Hallelujah, Harmony, Hymeneal, Motet, Parabasis, Precentor, ➤ REFRAIN, Singing, Strophe, Treble, Triad, ➤ UNISON

Choir-master Precentor

Choke(r) Block, Clog, Gag, Silence, Smoor, Smore, Smother, Stifle, Stop, Strangle(hold), Strangulate, ➤ THROTTLE

Choky Can, Prison

Choliamb Scazon

➤ **Choose** see CHOICE

Chop(per), Chops, Chopper(s), Choppy Adze, Ax(e), Celt, Charge, Cheek, Chump, Cleave, Côtelette, Cuff, Cutlet, Dice, Fell(er), Flew, Hack, Helicopter, Hew, Ivory, Karate, Lop, Mince, Mouth, Rotaplane, Rough, Suey, Teeth, Wang

Chopin Pantoufle, Shoe

Chopstick(s) Waribishi

Chord Arpeggio, Barré, Common, Diameter, Harmony, Intonator, Nerve, Triad, Vocal

Chore Darg, Duty, Task

Choreographer Arranger, Ashton, Balanchine, Cecchetti, Cranko, Fokine, Laban, Massine

Chorus Antistrophe, Dawn

Chosen Korea

Chough Chewet

Chowder Bouillabaisse, Soup

Christ Ecce homo, Jesus, Messiah, Saviour, X

Christen(ing) Baptise, Launch, Name-day

Christian Adventist, Albigenses, Beghard, Believer, Cathar(ist), Coptic, D(o)ukhobor, Dior, Donatist, Ebionite, Galilean, Giaour, Gilbertine, Gnostic, Goy, Holy roller, Homo(i)ousian, Jehovah's Witness, Marrano, Melchite, Melkite, Moral, Mozarab, Mutineer, Nazarene, Nestorian, Phalange, Pilgrim, Protestant, RC, Quartodeciman, Sabotier, Scientist, SCM, Traditor, Uniat(e), Unitarian, Waldensian, Wesleyan, Xian, Zwinglian

Christian Scientist Eddy

Christmas(time) Dec, Island, Nativity, Noel, Yuletide

Christopher Kit, Robin, Sly, Wren

Chromium Cr

Chromosome Aneuploid, Autosome, Centromere, Cistron, Genome, Haploid, Id(ant), Karyotype, Operon, Ploid(y), X, Y

Chronicle(r) Anglo-Saxon, Annal, Brut, Calendar, Diary, Froissart, Hall, History, Holinshed, Logographer, Paralipomena, Parian, ➤ RECORD, Register, Stow

Chrysalis Nymph, Pupa

Chrysanthemum Corn-marigold, Feverfew

Chrysolite Olivine, Peridot

Chub Cheven, Chevin, Fish

Chubby Butterball, Plump

Chuck (out) Berry, Buzz, Chook(ie), Discard, Eject, Food, Grub, Pat, Pitch, Shy, Sling, Toss, Turf

Chuckle Chortle, Giggle, Gurgle

Chukka Polo

Chum(my) Buddy, Cobber, Cock, Companion, Mate, Pal, Sociable, Sodality

Chump Mug(gins), Noddle, Sap, Stupid

Chunk(y) Boxy, Chubby, Gob, Piece, Slab, Squat, Wad

Church Abbey, Armenian, Autocephalous, Basilica, Bethel, Bethesda, Brood, Byzantine, CE, Ch, Chapel, Chevet, Clergy, Collegiate, Congregational, Coptic, Delubrum, EC, Ecumenical, Episcopal, Episcopalian, Established, Faith, Fold, Free, High, Kirk, Lateran, Low, Lutheran, Maronite, Methodist, Minster, Moravian, Mormon, Orthodox, Prebendal, Presbyterian, RC, Reformed, Rome, Shrine, Smyrna, Stave, Steeple, Temple, Unification, Wee Free, Western

Churchgoer, Churchwarden Antiburgher, Baptist, Believer, Classis, Clay, Cleric, Clerk, Congregation, Deacon, Dom, Dopper, Elder, Evangelist, Hatto, Ignorantine, Incumbent, Invisible, Knox, Lector, Lutheran, Methodist, Militant, Moderator, Mormon, MU, Newman, Once, Parson, PE, Pipe, Pontiff, Prebendary, Precentor, Prelate, Presbyterian, Priest, Protestant, Puritan, Rector, Sacristan, Sidesman, Sim, Simeonite, Swedenborgian, Tantivy, Triumphant, Unitarian, Visible, Wesleyan, Worshipper, Wren

Churchill Tank, Winston

Church house Manse, Parsonage, Presbytery, Rectory, Vicarage

Churchyard God's acre

Churl(ish) Attercop, Boor, Crabby, Curmudgeonly, Cynical, Ethercap, Ettercap, Gruff, Nabal, Peasant, Rustic, Serf, Surly

Churn Bubble, Kirn, Seethe

Chute Flume, Runway

CIC Shogun, Sirdar

Cicada Greengrocer, Locust, Tettix

Cicatrix Scar

Cicely Myrrh, Sweet

Cicero Cic, Tully

Cid Campeador, Chief, Hero

Cider Drink, Perry, Scrumpy

Ci-devant Ex

Cigar(ette), Cigarette cards Beedi(e), Bumper, Cancer stick, Caporal, Cartophily, Cheroot, Claro, Coffin nail, Conch, Concha, Corona, Dog-end, Durry, Fag, Filter-tip, Gasper, Giggle(-stick), Havana, Joint, Locofoco, Long-nine, Maduro, Manilla, Panatella, Perfecto, Reefer, Regalia, Roach, Roll-up, Smoke, Snout, Splif(f), Stogie, Stog(e)y, Stompie, Weed, Whiff, Zol

Cinch Belt, Certainty, Girth

Cinchona Kina, Quina

Cinder(s) Ash, Breeze, Clinker, Dander, Embers, Slag

Cinderella Drudge, Stepdaughter

Cinema(s) Biograph, Bioscope, Circuit, Drive-in, Films, Fleapit, Flicks, Movies, Multiplex, Mutoscope, Nickelodeon, Nouvelle Vague, Odeon, Plaza, Theatre, Tivoli

Cinnabar Vermilion

Cinnamon, Cinnamon stone Canella, Cassia(bark), Essonite, Spice

Cipher Chi-rho, Code, Cryptogram, Nihil, Nobody, ➤ NOTHING, Number, O, Steganogram, Zero

Circle Almacantar, Almucantar, Annulet, Antarctic, Arctic, Circassian, Co, Colure, Company, Compass, Corolla, Coterie, Cromlech, Crop, Cycloid, Cyclolith, Dip, Disc, Dress, Eccentric, Embail, Enclose, Epicyclic, Equant, Equator, Equinoctal, Euler's, Family, Fraternity, Full, Galactic, Girdle, Gyre, Halo, Hoop, Horizon, Inner, Inorb, Lap, Longitude, Loop, Malebolge, Mandala, Meridian, O, Orbit, Parhelic, Penannular, Peristalith, Polar, Rigol, ➤ RING, Rotate, Roundure, Set, Setting, Sphere, Stemme, Surround, Tinchel, Tropic, Turning, Umbel, Upper, Vertical, Vicious, Vienna, Volt, Wheel

Circuit(ous) AND, Ambit, Autodyne, Bypass, Closed, Comparator, Daughterboard, Diocese, Dolby®, Eyre, IC, Integrated, Lap, Limiter, Logic, Loop, Motherboard, NAND, NOR, NOT, OR, Perimeter, Phase, Reactance, Ring, Round, Scaler, Series, Short, Tour, Windlass

Circular Annular, Court, Folder, Leaflet, Mailshot, Orby, Spiral, Unending, Wheely

Circulate, Circulation Astir, Bloodstream, Cyclosis, Disseminate, Flow, Gyre, Issue, Mix, Orbit, Pass, Publish, Revolve, Rotate, Scope, Spread, Stir, Troll, Utter

▷ **Circulating** may indicate an anagram

Circumcise(r), Circumcision Bris, Brit milah, Brith, Infibulate, Milah, Mohel

Circumference Boundary, Girth, Perimeter, Size

Circumlocution Periphrasis, Tautology

Circumnavigation Periplus

Circumscribe Define, Demarcate, Enclose, Restrain

Circumspect Chary, Guarded, Prudential, Wary

Circumstance, Circumstantial Case, Detail, Event, Fact, Formal,
➤ INCIDENT, Precise

Circumvent Bypass, Dish, Evade, Outflank, Outwit, Usurp

Circus, Circus boy Arena, Big top, Eros, Flying, Harrier, Hippodrome,
Marquee, Maximus, Media, Monty Python, Ring, Sanger, Slang, Three-ring

Cistercian Trappist

Cistern Sump, Tank, Tub, Vat

Citadel Acropolis, Alhambra, Castle, Fort(ress), Keep, Kremlin

Citation, Cite Adduce, Allegation, Mention, Name, Quote, Recall,
Reference, Repeat, Sist, Summon

Citizen(ship) Burgess, Burgher, Civism, Cleruch, Denizen, Dicast, Ephebe,
Franchise, Freeman, Jus sanguinis, Jus soli, Kane, National, Oppidan,
Patrial, People, Quirites, Resident, Roman, Senior, Snob, Subject,
Venireman, Voter

Citroen DS

Citrus Acid, Calamondin, Cedrate, Lemon, Lime, Mandarin, Min(n)eola,
Orange, Pomelo, Tangerine, Ugli

City Agra, Athens, Atlantis, Babylon, Burgh, Carthage, Cosmopolis,
Ctesiphon, EC, Empire, Eternal, Forbidden, Gath, Holy, Inner, LA, Leonine,
Medina, Megalopolis, Metropolis, Micropolis, Mycenae, NY, Petra,
Pompeii, Rhodes, Smoke, Sparta, Tech, Town, Ur, Vatican, Weldstadt

Civet Binturong, Cat, Fo(u)ssa, Genet(te), Herpestes, Linsang, Musang,
Nandine, Paradoxine, Paradoxure, Rasse, Suricate, Toddy-cat, Viverra,
Zibet

Civil(ian), Civilisation, Civilised, Civility Amenity, Christian, Citizen,
Civ(vy), Comity, Courtesy, Culture, Fertile crescent, Humane, Indus Valley,
Maya, Municipal, Nok, Polite, Politesse, Secular, Temporal, Urbane

Civil Service CS

Clad(ding) Weatherboard

Clag(gy) Stickjaw

Claim Appeal, Arrogate, Assert, Bag, Challenge, Charge, Darraign(e),
Darrain(e), Darrayn, Demand, Deraign, Droit, Encumbrance, Haro,
Harrow, Lien, List, Maintain, Nochel, Plea, Pose, Posit, Postulate, Pretence,
Pretend, Profess, Pulture, Purport, Puture, Revendicate, Right, Set-off,
Sue, Title

Claimant Irredentist, Petitioner, Pot-waller, Pretender, Prospector,
Tichborne, Usurper

Clairvoyance, Clairvoyancy ESP, Fey, Insight, Lucidity, Psiphenomena, Taisch, Taish

· **Clam** Bivalve, Cohog, Geoduck, Giant, Gweduc, Littleneck, Mollusc, Mya, Quahang, Quahog, Tridacna, Venus

Clamant Vociferous

Clamber Climb, Crawl, Scramble, Spra(i)ckle, Sprauchle

Clammy Algid, Damp, Dank, Moist, Sticky, Sweaty

Clamour(ing), Clamorous Blatant, Brouhaha, Din, Hubbub, Hue, Outcry, Racket, Raird, Reird, Rout, Shout, Strepitant, Uproar, Utis, Vociferate

Clamp Clinch, Denver boot, Fasten, Grip, Holdfast, Jumar, Pinchcock, Potato-pit, Stirrup, Tread, Vice, Wheel

Clan(sman) Cameron, Clique, Gens, Gentile, Group, Horde, Kiltie, Kindred, Name, Phratry, Phyle, Sect, Sept, Society, Stewart, Stuart, Tribe

Clandestine Covert, Furtive, Secret

Clang(er), Clanging, Clank Belleter, Boob, Boo-boo, Clash, Gong, Jangle, Plangent, Ring

Clap(per), Clapping Applaud, Blow, Castanet, Chop, Crotal, Dose, Jinglet, Peal, Thunder, Tonant

Claptrap Bilge, Blab, Bombast, Bunkum, Eyewash, Hokum, Rot, Tripe

Claque(ur) Fans, Hat, Laudator, Sycophant

Clara Bow, Butt

Claret Blood, Loll-shraub, Loll-shrub, Vin

Clarify, Clarifier Clear, Despumate, Dilucidate, Explain, Explicate, Finings, Purge, Refine, Render, Simplify

Clarinet Reed

Clarion Brassy, Clear, Trumpet

Clary Orval, Sage

Clash(ing) Bang, Clangour, Clank, Claver, Coincide, Collide, Conflict, Friction, Gossip, ➤ IMPACT, Incident, Jar, Loud, Missuit, Shock, Showdown, Strike, Swash

Clasp(ing) Adpress, Agraffe, Barrette, Brooch, Button, Catch, Chape, Clip, Embrace, Fibula, Grasp, Hasp, Hesp, Hook, Hug, Inarm, Interdigitate, Link, Morse, Ochreate, Ouch, Tach(e), Unite

Class(ify), Classification, Classy Acorn, Arrange, Assort, Bourgeois(ie), Bracket, Brand, Breed, Business, Cabin, Canaille, Caste, ➤ CATEGORY, Cheder, Cl, Clan, Clerisy, Clinic, Club, Course, Criminal, Dewey, Division, Economy, Estate, Evening, Faction, Form, Genera, Genus, Gentry, ➤ GRADE, Group, Heder, Hubble, Ilk, Keep-fit, League, Linn(a)ean, List, Lower, Mammal, Master, Middle, Number, Order, Phylum, Pigeon-hole, Race, Range, Rank, Rate, Rating, Remove, Salariat, Seminar, Shell, Siege, Sort(ation), Steerage, Stratum, Stream, Syntax, Taxonomy, Teach-in, Third, Tourist, Tribe, ➤ TYPE, U, Upper, Varna, Water, Working, World, Year

Classic(al), Classics, Classicist Ageless, Ancient, Basic, Derby, Elzevir, Grecian, Greek, Humane, Leger, Literature, Pliny, Purist, Roman, Standard, Traditional, Vintage

Clatch Blunk, Smear, Spoil

Clatter Bicker, Charivari, Clack, Din, Noise, Rattle

Clause Apodosis, Article, Condition, Escalator, Escape, Filioque, Four, Golden parachute, Grandfather, Member, Poison-pill, Protasis, Proviso, Reddendum, Reservation, Rider, Salvo, Sentence, Subordinate, Tenendum, Testatum

Claw Chela, Claut, Crab, Dewclaw, Edate, Falcula, Grapple, Griff(e), Hook, Nail, Nipper, Pounce, Scrab, Sere, Talent, ➤ TALON, Tear, Telson, Unguis

Clay Allophane, Argil, Barbotine, B(e)auxite, Bentonite, Blaes, Blaise, Blaize, Bole, Calm, Cam, Caum, Ceramic, China, Cimolite, Charoset(h), Cloam, Clunch, Cob, Earth, Engobe, Fango, Figuline, Fuller's earth, Gault, Glei, Gley, Gumbotil, Hardpan, Haroset(h), Illite, Kaolin, Laterite, Lithomarge, Loam, Lute, Malm, Marl, Meerschaum, Mire, Mortal, Mud, Papa, Pipeclay, Pipestone, Pise, Plastilina, Potter's, Pottery, Pug, Saggar(d), Sagger, Scroddle(d), Seggar, Sepiolite, Slip, Slurry, Smectite, Thill, Till(ite), Tumphy, Varve, Warrant, Warren, Wax

Clean(se), Cleansing, Cleaner Absterge, Besom, Bleach, Bream, Broom, Careen, Catharise, Catharsis, Chaste, Clear, Daily, Debride, Depurate, Deterge(nt), Dhobi, Dialysis, Douche, Dust(er), Eluant, Emunge, Enema, Erase, Ethnic, Evacuant, Evacuate, Expurgate, Fay, Fettle, Fey, Floss, Flush, Full, Grave, Groom, Gut, Heels, Hoover®, Hygienic, Immaculate, Innocent, Launder, Lave, Lustrum, Lye, Mouthwash, Mrs Mop(p), Mundify, Net, Overhaul, Porge, Pull-through, Pumice, Pure, Purgative, Purge, Ramrod, Rebite, Rub, Rump, Scaffie, Scavenge, Scour, Scrub, Shampoo, Snow-white, Soap, Soogee, Soogie, Soojey, Sponge, Spotless, Squeaky, Squeegee, Sterile, Sujee, Swab, Sweep, Vac(uum), Valet, ➤ WASH, Whistle, Wipe

Clear(ance), Clearly Absolve, Acquit, Aloof, Apparent, Bell, Berth, Bold, Bore, Brighten, Bus, Clarify, Crystal, Decode, Definite, Diaphanous, Dispel, Distinct, Downright, Eidetic, Evacuate, Evident, Exculpate, Exonerate, Explicit, Fair, Gain, Headroom, Hyaline, Intelligible, Iron, Laund, Leap, Legible, Limpid, Lucid, Luculent, Manifest, Mop, Neat, Negotiate, Net(t), ➤ NOT CLEAR, Observable, Obvious, Ope(n), Overleap, Palpable, Pellucid, Perspicuous, Plain, Play, Pratique, Predy, Pure, Quit, Rack, Realise, Remble, Rid, Ripple, Serene, Sheer, Shere, Slum, Sweep, Thro(ugh), Thwaite, Transire, Translucent, Transparent, Unblock, Vault, Vivid, Well, Windage, Wipe

Clearing Assart, Glade, Opening, Shire, Slash

Cleat Bitt, Wedge

Cleave, Cleavage, Cleft Adhere, Bisulcate, Chine, Cling, Cloff, Cohere, Cut, Divide, Division, Divorce(ment), Gap, Ghaut, Goose-grass, Grike, Gryke, Pharynx, Rift, Riva, Scissure, Severance, Slack, Space, Spathose

Clef Treble

Clematis Montana, Old man's beard, Virgin's-bower

Clemenceau Tiger

Clemency, Clement Ahimsa, Grace, Lenience, Lenity, Mercy, Mildness, Quarter, Temperate

Cleopatra Needle

Clergy(man), Cleric(al) Abbé, Canon, Cantor, Cardinal, Chaplain, Cleric, Clerk, Cloth, Curate, Curé, Deacon, Dean, Ecclesiast(ic), Goliard, Incumbent, Josser, Levite, Ministerial, Ministry, Non-juror, Non-usager, Notarial, Parson, Pastor, Pontifex, Pontiff, Preacher, Prebendary, Precentor, Prelate, Presbyter, Presenter, Priest, Primate, Prior, Proctor, Rabbi, Rector, Red-hat, Reverend, Rome-runner, Scribal, Secretarial, Shaveling, Shepherd, Slope, Spin-text, Squarson, Subdeacon, Theologian, Vartabed, Vicar

Clergy-hater Misoclere

Clerk(s) Actuary, Baboo, Babu, Basoche, Cleric, Cratchit, Cursitor, Limb, Notary, Penman, Penpusher, Poster, Protocolist, Prot(h)onotary, Recorder, Scribe, Secretariat, Tally, Vicar, Writer

Clever(ness) Able, Adroit, Astute, Brainy, Bright, Canny, Cute, Daedal(e), Deep-browed, Deft, Gleg, Ingenious, Jackeen, Natty, Sage(ness), Shrewd, Skilful, Smart(y), Smarty-pants, Souple, Subtle

Clevis Becket

Cliché Banality, Boilerplate, Commonplace, Corn, Platitude, Saying, Tag

Click(er), Clicking Castanet, Catch, Forge, Pawl, Ratch(et), Snick, Succeed, Tchick, Ticktack

Client Customer, Gonk, John, Patron, Trick

Cliff(s) Beachy Head, Bluff, Cleve, Crag, Craig, Escarp, Palisade, Precipice, Sca(u)r

Cliffhanger Samphire, Serial, Thriller

Climate Atmosphere, Attitude, Continental, Mood, Sun, Temperament, Temperature, Weather

Climax Apex, Apogee, Catastasis, Come, Crescendo, Crest, Crisis, Edaphic, End, Head, Heyday, Orgasm, Top, Zenith

Climb(er) Alpinist, Aralia, Aristolochia, Ascend, Breast, Briony, Bryony, Clamber, Clematis, Clusia, Cowage, Cowhage, Cowitch, Crampon, Creeper, Cucumber, Dodder, Heart-pea, Hedera, Ivy, Kie-kie, Kudzu, Lawyer, Layback, Liana, Liane, ➤ MOUNT, Pareira, Parvenu, Prusik, Rat(t)an, Rise, Scale, Scan, Scandent, Scansores, Sclim, Shin, Shinny, Sklim, Smilax, Social, Speel, Steeplejack, Sty(e), Swarm, Timbo, Tuft-hunter, Udo, Up(hill), Uprun, Vine, Wistaria, With(y)wind, Zoom

Clinch Attach, Carriwitchet, Ensure, Fix, Quibble, Rivet, Secure, Settle

Cling(er), Clinging Adhere, Bur(r), Cherish, Cleave, Embrace, Hold, Hug, Ring, Tendril

Clinic Dispensary, Hospital, Hospitium, Mayo

Clink Gingle, Jail, Jingle, Lock up, Prison, Stir, Ting, Tinkle

Clinker Ash, Slag

Clip(ped), Clipper, Clipping Barrette, Brash, Bulldog, Butterfly, Clasp, Crocodile, Crop-ear, Crutch, Curt, Curtail, Cut, Cutty Sark, Dag, Dock, Dod, Excerpt, Fleece, Jubilee, Jumar, Krab, Lop, Pace, Pare, Prerupt, Prune, Scissel, Secateur, Shear, Ship, Shore, Shorn, Snip, Staccato, Tie, Tie-tack, Tinsnips, Topiarist, Trim

Clippy Cad, Conductor

Clique Cabal, Clan, Club, Coterie, Faction, Gang, Ring, Set

Clive Arcot

Cloak(room), Cloaks Aba, Abaya, Abba, Abolla, Amice, Bathroom, Burnous, Capa, Cape, Capote, Caracalla, Cardinal, Cassock, Chasuble, Chimer(e), Chlamydes, Chlamys, Chuddah, Chuddar, Conceal, Cope, Cover, Disguise, Dissemble, Djellaba(h), Domino, Gabardine, Gaberdine, Gal(l)abea(h), Gal(l)abi(y)a(h), Gal(l)abi(y)eh, Gentlemen, Gents, Hall-robe, Heal, Hele, Himation, Hood, Inverness, Jelab, Jellaba, Joseph, Kaross, Manta, Manteel, Mant(e)let, Mantle, ➤ MASK, Mousquetaire, Mozetta, Paenula, Paletot, Pallium, Paludamentum, Pelisse, Pilch, Poncho, Rail, Revestry, Rocklay, Rokelay, Roquelaure, Sagum, Sarafan, Scapular, ➤ SCREEN, Shroud, Swathe, Talma, Toga, Vestiary, Vestry, Visite

Clobber Anoint, Dress, Garb, Habiliments, Lam, Tack

Clock Alarm, Ammonia, Analogue, Astronomical, Atomic, Beetle, Big Ben, Biological, Blowball, Body, Bracket, Bundy, Caesium, Carriage, Clepsydra, Cuckoo, Dandelion, Floral, Grandfather, Grandmother, Hit, Knock, Long case, Meter, Repeater, Solarium, Speaking, Speedo, Strike, Sundial, Tell-tale, Time(r), Wag at the wa', Water

Clockmaker Fromanteel, Graham, Harrison, Knibb, Mudge, Tompion

Clockwise Deasil, Deasiul, Deasoil, Deiseal, Deisheal

Clockwork Precision, Regular

Clod Clumsy, Divot, Glebe, Lump, Mool, Mould, Put(t), Scraw, Sod, Stupid, Turf

Clog Accloy, Ball, Block, Clam, Crowd, Dance, Fur, Galosh, Golosh, Hamper, Jam, Lump, Mire, Obstruct, Overshoe, Patten, Sabot

Cloisonné Shippo

Cloister Arcade, Confine, Cortile, Immure, Monastery, Mure, Refuge

Clone Ramet, Reproduce

Cloots Worricow

Close(d), Closing, Closure Airless, Atresia, Block, Boon, By, Cadence, Clammy, Clench, Complete, Dear, Debar, Dense, ➤ END, Epilogue, Ewest, Finale, Gare, Grapple, Handy, Hard, Imminent, Inbye, Infibulate, Intent, Intimate, Lock, Lucken, Mean, Miserly, Muggy, Mure, Narre, Narrow, Near, Neist, Nie, Nigh, Niggardly, Nip and tuck, Obturate, Occlusion, Oppressive, Parochial, Precinct, Reserved, Reticent, Seal, Secret, Serre, Serried, Serry, Shet, Shut(ter), Shutdown, Silly, Slam, Snug, Stap, Stuffy, Sultry, Tailgate, Temenos, Tight, Uproll, Warm, Yard

Close-cropped Crewcut, Not-pated

Close-fitting Skintight, Slinky, Tight

Closet Cabinet, Confine, Cubicle, Cupboard, Earth, Locker, Safe, Wardrobe, WC, Zeta

Close-up Detail, Fill, Shut, Stop, Zoom

Closing-time Eleven, End

Clot(ting) Agglutinate, Ass, Clag, Clump, Coagulate, Congeal, Crassamentum, Cruor, Curdle, Dag, Embolism, Embolus, Gel, Globule,

Gob, Gout, Grume, Incrassate, Incrust, Jell, Lapper, Lopper, ➤ LUMP, Mass, Prothrombin, Splatch, Stupid, Thicken, Thrombosis, Thrombus

Cloth Antependium, Carmelite, Clergy, Cloot, Clout, Draper, ➤ FABRIC, ➤ FELT, Frocking, Frontal, Gremial, Loin, Lungi, ➤ MATERIAL, Nap, Napery, Napje, Nappie, Needlework, Netting, Pall, Pane, Panel, Pilch, Priesthood, Print(er), Puke, Rag, Raiment, Roll, Sashing, Scarlet, Serviette, Sheet, Sheeting, Shoddy, Stripe, Sudarium, Tapestry, Tea, ➤ TEXTILE, Throw, Tissue, Vernicle, Veronica

TYPES OF CLOTH

1 letter:	Duroy	Tweed	Frieze
J®	Fanon	Tweel	Gloria
3 letters:	Foulé	Twill	Greige
Abb	Frisé	Union	Gurrah
Rep	Gauze	Voile	Haique
Say	Gunny	Wigan	Harden
Web	Haick	**6 letters:**	Herden
4 letters:	Honan	Aertex®	Hodden
Aida	Jaspe	Alpaca	Humhum
Baft	Kente	Angora	Hurden
Ciré	Kanga	Armure	Jersey
Doek	Khadi	Barège	Kersey
Drab	Khaki	Beaver	Khanga
Duck	Kikoi	Bouclé	Kincob
Fent	Linen	Broche	Lampas
Gair	Llama	Burlap	Madras
Haik	Loden	Burnet	Medley
Harn	Lurex®	Burrel	Melton
Hyke	Lycra®	Byssus	Merino
Ikat	Moiré	Caddis	Mohair
Kelt	Mongo	Calico	Mongoe
Knit	Monks	Camlet	Moreen
Lamé	Mungo	Camlot	Muslin
Lawn	Ninon	Canvas	Nankin
Leno	Orlon®	Chintz	Oxford
Line	Panne	Cilice	Pongee
Mull	Perse	Cloqué	Rateen
Nude	Piqué	Coburg	Ratine
Pina	Plaid	Coutil	Runner
Rund	Plush	Covert	Russel
Shag	Rayon	Crepon	Samite
Slop	Scrim	Cubica	Satara
Sulu	Serge	Cyprus	Sateen
Wool	Slops	Damask	Saxony
5 letters:	Stupe	Devoré	Sendal
Atlas	Surah	Dimity	Shalli
Baize	Surat	Domett	Sherpa
Beige	Surge	Dossal	Sindon
Binca	Tabby	Dossel	Soneri
Budge	Tamin	Dowlas	Stroud
Chino	Tammy	Duffel	Tamine
Crash	Tibet	Duffle	Tartan
Crepe	Terry	Dupion	Thibet
Denim	Toile	Durrie	Velour
Dobby	Towel	Faille	Velvet
Drill	Tulle	Fannel	Vicuna

Types of cloth

Wadmal
Wincey
Winsey
7 letters:
Abattre
Alepine
Baracan
Batiste
Brocade
Cabbage
Cambric
Camelot
Challie
Challis
Cheviot
Chiffon
Crombie
Cypress
Delaine
Dhurrie
Doeskin
Dornick
Drabbet
Drapery
Droguet
Drugget
Duvetyn
Etamine
Faconné
Fannell
Fishnet
Flannel
Foulard
Fustian
Galatea
Genappe
Gingham
Gore-tex®
Grogram
Hessian
Holland
Hopsack
Jaconet
Jamdani
Khaddar
Kitenge
Lockram
Mockado
Nankeen
Organza
Orleans
Ottoman
Paisley
Percale
Rabanna
Raploch
Raschel

Ratteen
Rattine
Sacking
Sagathy
Schappe
Silesia
Sinamay
Spandex
Stammel
Tabaret
Tabinet
Taffeta
Tiffany
Tussore
Viyella®
Wadmaal
Webbing
Woolsey
Worsted
Zanella
8 letters:
Algerine
American
Armozeen
Armozine
Arresine
Bagheera
Barathea
Barracan
Bayadere
Bobbinet
Brocatel
Cameline
Cashmere
Casimere
Celanese
Chambray
Chamelot
Chenille
Ciclaton
Corduroy
Corporal
Coteline
Coutille
Cretonne
Drabette
Duchesse
Dungaree
Duvetine
Duvetyne
Eolienne
Gambroon
Gossamer
Homespun
Jacquard
Jeanette
Lava-lava

Lustring
Mackinaw
Mantling
Marcella
Marocain
Mazarine
Moleskin
Moquette
Nainsook
Organdie
Osnaburg
Pashmina
Prunella
Rodevore
Sarsenet
Shabrack
Shalloon
Shantung
Sicilian
Swanskin
Tabbinet
Tarlatan
Toilinet
Whipcord
Wild silk
Zibeline
9 letters:
Balzarine
Bengaline
Bombasine
Calamanco
Cassimere
Cerecloth
Charmeuse®
Ciclatoun
Corporale
Crepoline
Crimplene®
Crinoline
Evenweave
Farandine
Filoselle
Folk-weave
Gaberdine
Georgette
Grenadine
Grosgrain
Haircloth
Horsehair
Indiennes
Levantine
Mandylion
Marseille
Matelassé
Messaline
Paramatta
Penistone

Percaline
Persienne
Polyester
Ravenduck
Sailcloth
Sharkskin
Silkaline
Stockinet
Swansdown
Tarpaulin
Tricotine
Velveteen
Wire gauze
Worcester
Zibelline
10 letters:
Balbriggan
Broadcloth
Brocatelle
Candlewick
Farrandine
Fearnought
Ferrandine
Florentine
Kerseymere
Lutestring
Mousseline
Parramatta
Polycotton
Ravensduck
Seersucker
Shabracque
Sicilienne
Tattersall
Toilinette
Tuftaffeta
Winceyette
11 letters:
Abercrombie
Cloth of gold
Dotted Swiss
Drap-de-berry
Dreadnought
Hammercloth
Interfacing
Kendal green
Marquisette
Sempiternum
Stockinette
Stretch knit
12 letters:
Brilliantine
Crepe de chine
Leather-cloth
13 letters:
Linsey-woolsey

Cloth-designing Batik

Clothe(s), Clothing, Clothed Apparel, Array, Attire, Baggies, Besee, Cape, Casuals, Choli, Cits, Clad, Clericals, Clobber, Combinations, Coordinates, Costume, Cour, Cover, Croptop, Dicht, Dight, Don, Drag, ➤ DRESS, Duds, Emboss, Endue, Finery, Frippery, Garb, Garments, Gear, Gere, Get-up, Glad rags, Habit, Haute couture, Innerwear, Judogi, Jumps, Layette, Outfit, Pannicle, Raiment, Rami, Rigout, Robes, Samfoo, Samfu, Schmutter, Scungies, Shroud, Slops, Swaddling, Swathe, Swothling, Tackle, Togs, Tracksuit, Trappings, Trousseau, Tweeds, Vernicle, Vestiary, Vestiture, Vestment, Wardrobe, Watteau, Weeds, Workwear, Yclad, Ycled

Cloud(ed), Cloudiness, Cloudy Altocumulus, Altostratus, Benight, Cirrocumulus, Cirrostratus, Cirrus, Coalsack, Coma, Crab Nebula, Cumulonimbus, Cumulus, Dim, Dull, Emission nebula, Fog, Fractostratus, Funnel, Goat's hair, Haze, Horsehead Nebula, Infuscate, Magellanic, Mare's tail, Milky, Mist, Mushroom, Nacreous, Nephele, Nephelometer, Nepho-, Nimbostratus, Nimbus, Nubecula, Nubilous, Nuée ardente, Obscure, Oort, Overcast, Pall, Pother, Rack, Stain, Storm, Stratocumulus, Stratus, Thunderhead, Turbid, Virga, War, Water-dog, Woolpack, Zero-zero

Cloudberry Mountain bramble

Cloudless Serene

Clough Dale, Gorge, Ravine

Clout Belt, Cloth, Hit, Influence, Lap(pie), Lapje, Pull, Raddle

Clove Chive, Eugenia, Rose-apple, Split

Clover Alfalfa, Alsike, Berseem, Calvary, Cinque, Cow-grass, Hare's foot, Japan, Ladino, Lespedeza, Medic(k), Melilot, Owl's, Rabbit-foot, Serradella, Serradilla, Shamrock, Souple, Suckling, Trefoil, Trilobe

Clown(ish) Antic, Antick, August(e), Boor, Bor(r)el, Buffoon, Carl, Chough, Chuff, Coco, Clout-shoe, ➤ COMEDIAN, Comic, Costard, Daff, Feste, Froth, Girner, Gobbo, Goon, Gracioso, Grimaldi, Harlequin, Hob, Jack-pudding, Jester, Joey, Joker, Joskin, Leno, Merry Andrew, Mountebank, Nedda, Nervo, Peasant, Pickle-herring, Pierrot, Put, Rustic, Slouch, Thalian, Touchstone, Trinculo, Wag, Zany

Cloy(ing) Choke, Clog, Glut, Pall, Satiate, Surfeit, Sweet

Club(s), Club-like Adelphi, Airn, Almack's, Alpeen, Artel, Association, Athen(a)eum, Baffy, Band(y), Basto, Bat, Beefsteak, Blackjack, Blaster, Bludgeon, Boodles, Bourdon, Brassie, Brook's, Bulger, C, Card, Carlton, Caterpillar, Cavalry, Cleek, Clip-joint, Combine, Cosh, Cotton, Country, Crockford's, Cudgel, Disco(theque), Driver, Driving iron, Drones, Fan, Fascio, Fustigate, Garrick, Glee, Golf, Guild, Hampden, Hell-fire, Honky-tonk, Indian, Iron, Jacobin, Jigger, Jockey, Kierie, Kiri, Kitcat, Kiwanis, Knobkerrie, League, Leander, Lofter, Mace, Mallet, Mashie, Maul, Mell, Mere, Meri, Mess, Midiron, Monday, Niblick, Night(stick), Nitery, Nulla(-nulla), Oddfellows, Patu, Polt, Priest, Pudding, Putter, RAC, Reform, Ring, Rota, Rotarian, Rotary, Savage's, Shillelagh, Slate, Society, Sorosis, Spoon, Spot, Spurs, Strike, Strip, Trefoil, Truncheon, Trunnion, Union, Variety, Waddy, Wedge, White's, Wood, Youth

Club-foot Kyllosis, Polt-foot, Talipes, Varus

Clubman Member

Club-rush Deer-hair, Scirpus, Sedge

Cluck Dent

Clue Across, Anagram, Ball, Charade, Clave, Dabs, Down, ➤ HINT, Inkling, Key, Lead, Light, Rebus, Scent, Signpost, Thread, Tip

Clueless Ignorant

Clump Cluster, Finial, Knot, Mass, Mot(te), Patch, Plump, Tread, Tuft, Tump, Tussock

▷ **Clumsily** may indicate an anagram

Clumsy Artless, Awkward, Bauchle, Bungling, Butterfingers, Cack-handed, Calf, Chuckle, Clatch, Clodhopper, Cumbersome, Dub, Dutch, Galoot, Gauche, Gimp, Ham(-fisted), Heavy-handed, Horse-godmother, Inapt, Inelegant, Klutz, Lob, Loutish, Lubbard, Lubber, Lummox, Lumpish, Maladroit, Mauther, Mawr, Mawther, Messy, Mor, Nerd, Nurd, Off-ox, Palooka, Rough, Schlemihl, S(c)hlemiel, Spastic, Spaz(zy), Squab, Stot, Swab, Swob, Taupie, Tawpie, Two-fisted, Ungain, Unwieldy

Cluster Assemble, Bunch, Clump, Collection, Constellate, Conurbation, Corymb, Cyme, Gather, Globular, Knot, Oakleaf, Packet, Plump, Raceme, Sheaf, Sorus, Strap, Thyrse, Truss, Tuffe, Tuft, Umbel, Verticillaster

Clutch Battery, Brood, Chickens, Clasp, Cling, Eggs, Glaum, Grab, ➤ GRASP, Gripe, Nest, Seize, Sitting, Squeeze

Clutter Confusion, Litter, Mess, Rummage

Coach Battlebus, Berlin, Bogie, Bus, Car, Carriage, Chara, Clerestory, Crammer, Diligence, Dilly, Double-decker, Drag, Edifier, Fly, Gig, Hackney, Landau(let), Microbus, Phaeton, Pullman, Railcar, Rattler, Repetiteur, Saloon, Shay, Sleeper, Stage, Surrey, Tally(-ho), Teach(er), Thoroughbrace, Train(er), Tutor, Voiture

Coach-horse Rove-beetle

Coachman Automedon, Bunene, Coachy, Dragsman, Jarvey, Jehu, John

Coagulant, Coagulate, Coagulation Cautery, Clot, Congeal, Curds, Jell, Rennet, Run, Runnet, Set, Solidify

Coal Anthracite, Bituminous, Burgee, Cannel, Cherry, Clinker, Coom, Crow, Culm, Eldin, Ember, Fusain, Gathering, Jud, Knob, Lignite, Open-cast, Purse, Sapropelite, Score, Slack, Splint, Vitrain, Wallsend

Coalesce(d) Amalgamate, Fuse, Merge, Sintery, Unite

Coalfish Saith

Coalition Alliance, Bloc, Janata, Merger, Tie

Coal-tar Cresol, Indene

Coal-tub Corf, Dan, Scuttle

Coarse(ness) Base, Blowzy, Bran, Broad, Common, Crude, Dowlas, Earthy, Fisherman, Foul, Grained, Grobian, Gross, Haggery, Ham, Illbred, Indelicate, Low-bred, Plebeian, Rank, Rappee, Raunchy, Ribald, Rough, Rudas, Rude, Sackcloth, Slob, Sotadic, Vulgar

Coast(al) Barbary, Beach, Causeway, Coromandel, Costa, Drift, Freewheel, Glide, Hard, Ivory, Littoral, Longshore, Maritime, Orarian, Riviera, Seaboard, Seafront, Seaside, ➤ SHORE, Sledge, Strand, Toboggan

Coaster Beermat, Drog(h)er, Mat, Ship

Coastguard Gobby

Coastline Watermark

Coast-road Corniche

Coat(ing) Ab(b)a, Abaya, Achkan, Acton, Admiral, Anarak, Anodise, Anorak, Balmacaan, Barathea, Bathrobe, Belton, Benjamin, Blazer, Box, Buff, Calcimine, Car, Chesterfield, Cladding, Claw-hammer, Clearcole, Cloak, Clutch, Cocoon, Coolie, Cover, Covert, Creosote, Crust(a), Cutaway, Dress, Duffel, Duster, Enamel, Encrust, Extine, Film, Fleece, Frock, Fur, Gabardine, Galvanise, Gambeson, Glaze, Grego, Ground, Ha(c)queton, Hair, Happi, Impasto, Integument, Inverness, Jack(et), Jemmy, Jerkin, Jodhpuri, Joseph, Jump, Jupon, Lacquer, Lammie, Lammy, Layer, Loden, Mac, Mackinaw, Matinee, Metallise, Morning, Newmarket, ➤ OVERCOAT, Paint, Paletot, Palla, Parka, Parkee, Passivate, Patinate, Pebbledash, Pelage, Pelisse, Perfuse, Peridium, Petersham, Plate, Polo, Pos(h)teen, Primer, Primine, Prince Albert, Raglan, Redingote, Resin, Resist, Riding, Sack, Saque, Sclera, Seal, Sheepskin, Shellac, Sherardise, Sherwani, Silver, Skinwork, Spencer, Stadium, Surtout, Swagger, Tabard, Taglioni, Tail, Tar, Teflon, Tent, Top, Trench, Truss, Trusty, Tunic, Tuxedo, Ulster(ette), Veneer, Verdigris, Warm, Wash, Windjammer, Wool, Wrap-rascal, Zamarra, Zamarro, Zinc

Coat of arms Crest, Hatchment

Coat-tail Flap

Coax Blandish, Blarney, Cajole, Carn(e)y, Cuittle, Flatter, Lure, Persuade, Wheedle, Whilly(wha), Whillywhaw

Cob Hazel(nut), Horse

Cobalt Co, Zaffer, Zaffre

Cobble(rs) Cosier, Cozier, Mend, Patch, Rot, Snob, Soutar, Souter, Sowter, Stone, Sutor, Twaddle, Vamp

Cobweb(by) Arachnoid, Araneous, Gossamer, Snare, Trap

Cocaine Basuco, C, Charlie, Coke, Freebase, Moonrock, Nose candy, Number, Ready-wash, Snow

Coccid Wax-insect

Cock(y) Alectryon, Ball, Capon, Chanticleer, Chaparral, Erect, Flip, Fowl, France, Fugie, Half, Hay, Jack-the-lad, Jaunty, Penis, Roadrunner, Robin, Rooster, Snook, Strut, Swaggering, Tilt, Turkey, Valve, Vain, Vane

Cock-a-hoop Crowing, Elated

Cockatoo Bird, Corella, Galah, Major Mitchell, Parrot

Cockboat Cog

Cockchafer Humbuzz, Maybug

Cocker Blenheim, Cuiter, Spaniel

Cockeyed Agee, Askew, Skewwhiff

Cockfight Main

Cockle Bulge, Crease, Wrinkle

▷ **Cockle(s)** may indicate an anagram

Cockney 'Arriet, 'Arry, Bow, Londoner, Londonese

▷ **Cockney** may indicate a missing h

Cockpit Greenhouse

Cockroach Archy, Beetle, German

▶ **Cockscomb** see COXCOMB

Cocktail Alexander, Aperitif, Atomic, Bloody Mary, Buck's fizz, Bumbo, Cold duck, Crusta, Daiquiri, Drink, Egg-flip, Fustian, Gibson, Gimlet, Manhattan, Margarita, Martini®, Mix, Molotov, Old-fashioned, Piña colada, Pink lady, Prawn, Rickey, Rusty nail, Sazerac®, Screwdriver, Side-car, Stengah, Stinger, Swizzle, Tom Collins, Twist, White-lady

Cocoa Criollo, Nib(s)

Coconut Coco-de-mer, Coir, Copra, Head, Toddy-palm

Cocoon Dupion, Swathe, Trehala

Cod Bag, Cape, Coalfish, Fish, Gade, Gadus, Haberdine, Keeling, Kid, Lob, Man, Morrhua, Saith, Stockfish, Torsk, Tusk, Whiting

Coda End(ing), Epilogue, Rondo, Tail

Coddle Cosset, Molly, Nancy, Pamper, Pet, Poach

Code Access, Alphanumeric, Amalfitan, Bar, Binary, Bushido, Canon, Cipher, City, Civil, Clarendon, Codex, Cryptogram, Disciplinary, Dogma, Dress, ▶ EBCDIC, Error, Escape, Ethics, Fuero, Genetic, Gray, Hammurabic, Highway, Hollerith, Iddy-umpty, Justinian, Morse, Napoleon, Object, Omerta, Penal, ▶ PGP, Postal, Rulebook, Scytale, Signal, Source, Talmud, Zip

Code-breaker Malpractitioner

Codger Buffer, Fellow

Codicil Addition, Label, PS

Coefficient Correlation, Young modulus

Coerce, Coercion Bully, Compel, Dragoon, Gherao, Pressure, Railroad, Restrain, Threaten

Coffee, Coffee beans, Coffee pot Arabica, Brazil, Cafetiere, Cappuccino, Decaff, Demi-tasse, Espresso, Expresso, Filter, Gaelic, Gloria, Granules, Instant, Irish, Java, Latte, Mocha, Peaberry, Robusta, Tan, Triage, Turkish

Coffee-house Lloyd's

Coffer Ark, Box, Casket, Cassone, Chest, Lacunar, Locker

Coffin Bier, Casket, Hearse, Kist, Larnax, Sarcophagus, Shell, Wooden overcoat

Cog(ged) Contrate, Mitre-wheel, Nog, Pinion, Tooth

Cogent Compelling, Forceful, Good, Sound, Telling

Cogitate Deliberate, Mull, Muse, Ponder

Cognate Paronym

Cohabit Bed, Indwell, Share

Co-heir Parcener

Cohere(nt) Agglutinate, Clear, Cleave, Cling, Logical, Stick

Cohort Colleague, Crony, Soldier

Coif Calotte, Cap, Hood

Coiffure Hairdo, Pompadour, Tête

Coil(ed) Bight, Bought, Choke, Clew, Clue, Curl, Fake, Fank, Furl, Hank, Helix, Induction, Mortal, Rouleau, Scorpioid, Solenoid, Spark, Spiral, Spiraster, Spire, Tesla, Tickler, Toroid, Twine, Twirl, ➤ WIND, Wound, Wreath, Writhe

Coin Base, Bean, Bit, Cash, Change, Copper, Create, Doctor, Dump(s), Fiver, Han(d)sel, Imperial, Invent, Make, Mint, Mite, ➤ MONEY, Neoterise, Numismatic, Nummary, Piece, Plate, Proof, Shiner, Slip, Smelt, Specie, Stamp, Strike, Tenner, Unite, Unity

---

COINS

1 letter:	**4 letters:**	Pula	Eagle
D	Anna	Punt	Eyrir
2 letters:	Baht	Rand	Franc
As	Bani	Real	Fugio
DM	Birr	Reis	Gerah
Kr	Buck	Rial	Groat
Rd	Cedi	Riel	Grosz
Xu	Cent	Rock	Haler
3 letters:	Chon	Ryal	Krona
Ban	Dibs	Sene	Krone
Bar	Dime	Slog	Kroon
Bob	Doit	Spur	Kurus
Cob	Dong	Tael	Laari
Dam	Dram	Taka	Laree
Ecu	Duro	Tala	Leone
Fen	Euro	Toea	Liard
Fil	Fiat	Vatu	Litas
Fin	Fils	Yuan	Livre
Flu	Inti	Zack	Louis
Hao	Jack	**5 letters:**	Lyart
Jun	Jane	Agora	Maile
Kip	Jiao	Angel	Manat
Lat	Kina	Asper	Maneh
Lei	Kobo	Aurar	Mohur
Lek	Kuna	Baiza	Mongo
Leu	Kyat	Bekah	Mopus
Lev	Lari	Belga	Naira
Lew	Lion	Bodle	Nakfa
Mil	Lira	Broad	Ngwee
Mna	Loti	Brown	Noble
Moy	Maik	Butat	Obang
Ore	Mark	Butut	Oscar
Pul	Merk	Chiao	Paisa
Pya	Mina	Colon	Paolo
Red	Obol	Conto	Pence
Sen	Para	Crore	Pengo
Sol	Paul	Crown	Penie
Som	Peag	Daric	Penni
Sou	Peni	Dibbs	Penny
Won	Peso	Dinar	Plack
Yen	Pice	Dobra	Pound
Zuz	Puli	Ducat	Razoo

Rider	Guinea	Cardecu	Louis d'or
Ruble	Gulden	Carolus	Maravedi
Royal	Halala	Centavo	Millieme
Rupee	Heller	Chetrum	Napoleon
Sceat	Hryvna	Cordoba	Ngultrum
Scudo	Jitney	Crusado	Picayune
Scute	Kobang	Drachma	Pistolet
Semis	Koruna	Ekpwele	Planchet
Sente	Kroner	Guilder	Portague
Shand	Kroona	Guarani	Portigue
Soldo	Kwacha	Hryvnya	Quadrans
Souon	Kwanza	Jacobus	Rigmarie
Sucre	Lepton	Joannes	Semuncia
Sycee	Likuta	Kreuzer	Sesterce
Tenge	Loonie	Lemoira	Shilling
Thebe	Makuta	Metical	Skilling
Tical	Mancus	Millime	Solidare
Ticky	Markka	Milreis	Stotinka
Tolar	Mawpus	Moidore	Xeraphim
Toman	Pa'anga	Ostmark	Zecchino
Tyiyn	Pagoda	Ouguiya	**9 letters:**
Zaire	Pataca	Patrick	Boliviano
Zimbi	Pennia	Piastre	Britannia
Zloty	Peseta	Piefort	Centesimo
6 letters:	Pesewa	Pistole	Dandiprat
Aureus	Qintar	Pollard	Dandyprat
Balboa	Rappen	Quarter	Didrachma
Bawbee	Rouble	Quetzal	Dupondius
Bender	Rupiah	Ringgit	Luckpenny
Bezant	Santum	Ruddock	Pistareen
Boddle	Satang	Rufiyaa	Rennminbi
Byzant	Sceatt	Sextans	Rix-dollar
Canary	Seniti	Solidus	Rose noble
Centas	Sequin	Spanker	Schilling
Copeck	Shekel	Tambala	Sovereign
Couter	Sickle	Testoon	Spur-royal
Dalasi	Siglos	Testril	Yellowboy
Danace	Stater	Thrimsa	Zwanziger
Deaner	Stiver	Thrymsa	**10 letters:**
Décime	Stotin	Tughrik	Broadpiece
Denier	Talent	Unicorn	Chervonets
Derham	Tanner	Xerafin	Krugerrand
Dirham	Tester	**8 letters:**	Portcullis
Dirhem	Teston	Brockage	Reichsmark
Dodkin	Thaler	Cardecue	**11 letters:**
Dollar	Tickey	Cruzeiro	Deutschmark
Double	Toonie	Denarius	Sword-dollar
Drachm	Tugrik	Doubloon	Tetradrachm
Ekuele	Turner	Ducatoon	**12 letters:**
Escudo	Vellon	Emalengi	Antoninianus
Filler	Wakiki	Farthing	**13 letters:**
Florin	**7 letters:**	Groschen	Rennminbi yuan
Forint	Afghani	Johannes	**18 letters:**
Gourde	Austral	Kreutzer	Maria Theresa
Gilder	Bolivar	Llangeni	dollar

Coinage Currency, Invention, Nonce-word

Coincide(nt), Coincidence Accident, Chance, Consilience, Fit, Fluke, Overlap, Rabat(to), Simultaneous, Synastry, Synchronise, Tally

Coke Chark, Coal, Cocaine, Kola

Col Pass, Poort, Saddle

Cold(-blooded) Ague, Algid, Arctic, Austere, Biting, Bitter, Bleak, C, Catarrh, Cauld(rife), Chill(y), Colubrine, Common, Coryza, Ectotherm, Frem(d), Fremit, Frigid, Frost(y), Gelid, Glacial, Hiemal, Icy, Impersonal, Jeel, Nippy, Nirlit, Parky, Passionless, Perishing, Poikilotherm(ic), Polar, Psychro-, Remote, Rheumy, Rigor, Rume, Snap, Snell, Sour, Streamer, Subzero, Taters, Weed, Wintry

Coldstream Borderer, Guard

Cole Colza, King, Nat, Porter

Colic Batts, Bots, Botts, Gripe, Upset

Collaborate, Collaborator, Collaboration Assist, Combine, ➤ COOPERATE, Quisling, Synergy, Vichy

Collapse Apoplexy, Cave, Conk, Crash, Crumble, Crumple, Debacle, Downfall, Fail(ure), Fall, Fold, Founder, Give, Implode, Inburst, Landslide, Meltdown, Phut, Purler, Rot, Ruin, Scat(ter), Sink, Slump, Stroke, Subside, Sunstroke, Swoon, Telescope, Tumble, Wilt, Zonk

▷ **Collapsing** may indicate an anagram

Collar(ed) Arrest, Astrakhan, Bermuda, Bertha, Berthe, Bib, Bishop, Brecham, Butterfly, Button-down, Buttonhole, Capture, Carcanet, Chevesaile, Choke(r), Clerical, Collet, Dog, Esses, Eton, Falling-band, Flea, Gorget, Grandad, Hame, Holderbat, Jabot, Jampot, Karenni, Mandarin, Moran, Mousquetaire, Nab, Nail, Neckband, Necklet, Ox-bow, Peter Pan, Piccadell, Piccadillo, Piccadilly, Pikadell, Polo, Puritan, Rabato, Rebater, Rebato, Revers, Rollneck, Roman, Ruff, Sailor, Seize, Tackle, Tappet, Tie-neck, Torque, Turndown, Turtleneck, Vandyke, Whisk, Wing, Yoke

Collation Comparison, Meal, Repast

Colleague Associate, Bedfellow, Confrère, Mate, Oppo, Partner

Collect(ed), Collection, Collector Accrue, Agglomerate, Aggregate, Album, Alms, Amass, Amildar, Ana, Anthology, Assemble, Aumil, Bank, Bow, Budget, Bundle, Burrell, Caboodle, Calm, Cap, Cete, Clowder, Compendium, Compile, Congeries, Conglomerate, Covey, Cull, Dossier, Dustman, Earn, Egger, Exaltation, Exordial, Fest, (Fest)schrift, Florilegium, Gaggle, Garner, Gather, Gilbert, Glean, Glossary, Grice, Heap, Herd, Hive, Idant, Jingbang, Kit, Kitty, Levy, Magpie, Meal, Meet, Menagerie, Miscellany, Mish-mash, Montem, Murmuration, Museum, Muster, Nide, Offertory, Omnibus, Omnium-gatherum, Paddling, Pile, Plate, Pod, Post, Prayer, Quest, Raft, Raise, Recheat, Sedge, Serene, Set, Shoe, Siege, Skein, Smytrie, Sord, Sottisier, Sounder, Spring, Stand, Tahsildar, Team, Troop, Unkindness, Watch, Whipround, Wisp

Collecting-box Brod

▷ **Collection** may indicate an anagram

Collectorate Taluk

College(s) Academy, Ampleforth, All Souls, Balliol, Brasenose, Business, C, Caius, Campus, CAT, Cheltenham, Clare, Classical, Commercial, Community, Corpus, Downing, Electoral, Emmanuel, Eton, Exeter, Foundation, Girton, Hall, Herald's, Jail, Keble, King's, Lancing, Linacre, Lincoln, LSE, Lycée, Lyceum, Madras(s)a(h), Madressah, Magdalen(e), Medresseh, Merton, Newnham, Nuffield, Oriel, Poly, Polytechnic, Protonotariat, Queen's, Ruskin, St. Johns, Saliens, Selwyn, Seminary, Sixth-form, Somerville, Sorbonne, Staff, Tech(nical), Tertiary, Theologate, Training, Trinity, Tug, UMIST, Up, Village, Wadham, Winchester, Yeshwa(h)

Collide, Collision Afoul, Barge, Bird-strike, Bump, Cannon, Carom(bole), Clash, Dash, Fender-bender, Foul, Head-on, Impact, Into, Kiss, Meet, Pile-up, Strike, Thwack

Collie Border, Dog, Kelpie, Kelpy, Sheepdog

Collier Geordie, Hoastman, Miner, Necklace, Patience, Ship

Colloid Gel, Lyophil(e)

Collude, Collusive Abet, Cahoots, Conspire, Deceive

Colon Aspinwall, Sigmoid, Spastic

Colonel Blimp, Bogey, Chinstrap, Col, Everard, Goldstick, Newcome, Nissen, Pride

Colonial, Colonist Ant, Antenatal, Boer, Creole, Emigré, Oecist, Oikist, Overseas, Phoenician, Pioneer, Polyp(e), Settler, Sicel(iot), Sikel(ian), Sikeliot, Stuyvesant, Swarm, Territorial

Colonnade Eustyle, File, Gallery, Porch, Portico, Stoa

Colony Aden, Cleruchy, Crown, Dependency, Hongkong, Nudist, Penal, Presidio, Proprietary, Rookery, Settlement, Swarm, Termitarium, Zambia

Colophony Rosin

Colossal ➤ ENORMOUS, Epochal, Gigantic, Huge, Vast

Colosseum Amphitheatre

Colour(ed), Colouring Alizarin(e), Anil, Anthocyan, An(n)atta, An(n)atto, Arnotto, Aquamarine, Auburn, Bay, Bedye, Bice, Bister, Bistre, Blee, Blue, Blush, Buff, C, Camel, Cap, Cappagh-brown, Cardinal, Cerise, Chica, Chromatic, Chrome, Complementary, Complexion, Coral, Crayon, Criant, Cyan, Day-Glo®, Distort, Dye, Ecru, Eosin, False, Filemot, Flag, Florid, Gamboge, Gouache, Gules, Haem, ➤ HUE, Ink, Isabel, Jet, Kalamkari, Lake, Leer, Lemon, Lilac, Lime, Local, Lovat, Lutein, Magenta, Maroon, Mauve, Metif, Nankeen, Oatmeal, Ochre, Olive, Or, Orange, Orpiment, Palette, Pastel, Peach, Philamot, Philomot, Pied, Pigment, Pochoir, Polychrome, Primary, Prism, Puke, Reddle, Reseda, Rince, Riot, Roucou, Rouge, Ruddle, Sand, Sepia, Shade, Sienna, Solferino, Spectrum, Startle, Tartrazine, Taupe, Tinc(ture), Tinge, Tint, Titian, Tone, Ultramarine, Umber, Umbrage, Uvea, Vert

▷ **Coloured** may indicate an anagram

Colour blindness Daltonism, Deuteranopia, Dichromism, Monochromatic, Protanopia, Protanopic, Tritanopia

Colourful Abloom, Brave, Flamboyant, Flowery, Iridescent, Kaleidoscope, Opalescent, Splashy, Vivid

Colourless Albino, Bleak, Drab, Dull, Hyalite, Pallid, Pallor, Wan, White

Colt Cade, Foal, Gun, Sta(i)g, Teenager

Columbine Aquilegia

Column(s), Column foot Agony, Anta, Atlantes, Commentary, Corinthian, Correspondence, Cylinder, Decastyle, Diastyle, Doric, Editorial, Eustyle, Fifth, File, Gossip, Hypostyle, Impost, Lat, Lonelyhearts, Monolith, Nelson's, Newel, Obelisk, Pericycle, Peristyle, Persian, Personal, Pilaster, ➤ PILLAR, Pilotus, Prostyle, Rouleau, Row, Spina, Spinal, Spine, Stalactite, Stalagmite, Steering, Stylobate, Systyle, Tabulate, Telamone, Third, Tige, Tore, Torus, Trajan's

Columnist Advertiser, Caryatid, Newsman, Stylite, Telamon, Writer

Coma Apoplexy, Crown, Sleep, Torpor, Trance

Comb(er), Combed, Combing Alveolate, Beehive, Breaker, Card, Copple, Crest, Curry, Dredge, Fine-tooth, Hackle, Heckle, Hot, Kaim, Kame, Kangha, Kemb, Noils, Pecten, Rake, Red(d), Ripple(r), Scribble, Search, Smooth, Tease(l), Toaze, Tose, Toze, Trawl, Wave

Combat(ant), Combative Argument, ➤ BATTLE, Competitor, Conflict, Contest, Dispute, Duel, ➤ FIGHT, Gladiator, Joust, Jujitsu, Just, Karate, Kendo, List, Mêlée, Militant, Oppose, Protagonist, Spear-running, Unarmed, War

Combination, Combine(d), Combining Accrete, Alligate, Ally, Amalgam, Associate, Axis, Bloc, Cartel, Cleave, Clique, Coalesce, Coalition, Concoction, Conflated, Conglomerate, Consortium, Coordinate, Crasis, Fuse, Group, Harvester, Integration, Join, Junta, Kartell, League, Meld, Merge(r), Mingle, Mixture, Perm(utation), Piece, Pool, Quill, Ring, Solvate, Splice, Syncretize, Synthesis, Terrace, Trona, Unite, Valency, Wed

Comb-like Ctenoid, Pecten

Combustible, Combustion Ardent, Fiery, Inflammable, Phlogistic, Phlogiston, Spontaneous, Wildfire

▷ **Combustible** may indicate an anagram

Come, Coming (back), Coming out Advent, Anear, Anon, Appear, Approach, Ar(r), Arise, Arrive, Attend, Debouch, Derive, Future, Happen, Iceman, Issue, Millenarian, Orgasm, Parousia, Pass, Pop, Respond, Second, Via

Comeback Bounce, Echo, Homer, Quip, Rally, Rearise, Rebound, Recovery, Repartee, Reply, Retort, Retour, Return, Reversion, Riposte

Comedian Benny, Buffoon, Chaplin, ➤ CLOWN, Comic, Durante, Emery, Goon, Groucho, Joker, Karno, Leno, Quipster, Robey, Scream, Screwball, Tate, Tati, Wag, Wise, Yell

Comedo Blackhead

Comedown Avale, Bathetic, Bathos, Disappointment, Drop, Letdown, Shower

Comedy Com, Drama, Errors, Farce, Humour, Keystone, Knockabout, Lazzo, Millamant, Situation, Slapstick, Thalia, Travesty

Comely Beseen, Bonny, Fair, Goodly, Graceful, Jolly, Pleasing, Pretty, Proper

Comestible(s) Cate, Eats, Fare

Comet Geminid, Halley's, Kohoutek, Meteor, Oort cloud, Xiphias

Come through Weather

Comfort(er), Comforting Amenity, Analeptic, Balm, Bildad, Calm, Cheer, Cherish, Cold, Consolation, Console, Creature, Crumb, Dummy, Ease, Eliphaz, Featherbed, Reassure, Relief, Relieve, Scarf, Solace, Soothe, Succour, Zophar

Comfortable, Comfy Bein, Canny, Cose, Cosh, Cosy, Couthie, Couthy, Cushy, Easy, Gemutlich, Heeled, Homely, Mumsy, Relaxed, Rug, Snug, Tosh, Trig, Warm, Well, Well-to-do

Comic(al) Beano, Buff, Buffo(on), Bumpkin, Buster, Chaplin, Clown, ➤ COMEDIAN, Dandy, Droll, Eagle, Facetious, Fields, ➤ FUNNY, Gagster, Hardy, Horror, Jester, Knock-about, Laurel, Leno, Mag, Manga, Quizzical, Robey, Strip, Tati, Trial, Zany

Command(ing), Commandeer, Commandment(s) Behest, Bid, Categorical imperative, Charge, Coerce, Control, Decalogue, Direction, Dominate, Easy, Edict, Fiat, Fighter, Firman, Haw, Hest, Imperious, Instruction, Jussive, Mandate, Mastery, Mitzvah, ➤ ORDER, Precept, Press, Requisition, Rule, Seize, Ukase, Warn, Warrant, Will, Wish, Writ

Commander Ag(h)a, Barleycorn, Bey, Bloke, Blucher, Boss, Brennus, Brig, Caliph, Centurion, Cid, Decurion, Emir, Emperor, Field cornet, Generalissimo, Hetman, Hipparch, Imperator, Killadar, Leader, Manager, Marshal, Master, Meer, Moore, Officer, Overlord, Pendragon, Raglan, Seraskier, Shogun, Sirdar, Taxiarch, Trierarch, Turcopolier, Vaivode, Voivode, Waivode, Warlord

Commando Chindit(s), Fedayee(n), Green Beret, Raider, Ranger, SAS

Commemorate, Commemoration Encaenia, Epitaph, Eulogy, Keep, Memorial, Monument, Plaque

Commence Begin, Initiate, Open, Start

Commend(ation) Belaud, Bestow, Encomium, Entrust, Laud, Panegyric, ➤ PRAISE, Roose, Tribute

Commensal Epizoon, Messmate

Commensurate Adequate, Enough, Equivalent, Relevant

Comment(ary), Commentator Analyst, Animadvert, Annotate, Comm, Coryphaeus, Critic, Descant, Discuss, Editorial, Essay, Explain, Exposition, Expound, Footnote, Gemara, Gloss(ographer), Glosser, Hakam, Kibitz, Margin, Midrashim, Note, Par, Platitude, Postil, Remark, Scholiast

Commerce, Commercial Ad, Barter, Cabotage, Jingle, Marketable, Mercantile, Mercenary, Merchant, Shoppy, Simony, Trade, Traffic

Commercial traveller Drummer, Rep

Commiserate, Commiseration Compassion, Pity, Sympathise

Commission(er), Commissioned Brevet, Brokerage, Charge, Charity, Countryside, Delegation, Depute, ECE, Employ, Engage, Envoy, Errand, Factor, High, Husbandage, Job, Kickback, Magistrate, Mandate, Office(r),

Official, Ombudsman, Order, Percentage, Perpetration, Place, Poundage, Rake-off, Roskill, Task, Task force, Trust

Commit(al), Commitment Consign, Contract, Decision, Dedication, Delegate, Devotion, Do, Engage, Entrust, Enure, Perpetrate, Pledge, Rubicon

Committee Board, Body, Commission, Council, Group, Joint, Junta, Politburo, Presidium, Propaganda, Review body, Samiti, Select, Standing, Steering, Syndicate, Table, Vigilance, Watch, Works

Commode, Commodious Ample, Closestool, Roomy, Spacious

Commodity Article, Item, Staple, Ware

Common(s), Commoner, Commonly Average, Cad, Conventional, Diet, Dirt, Ealing, Eatables, Enclosure, Epicene, Everyday, Familiar, Fare, Folk, General, Green, House, Law, Lay, Low, Mark, Mere, MP, Mutual, Naff, Non-U, Normal, People, Pleb, Prevalent, Prole, Public, Related, Rife, Roturier, Ryfe, Scran, Sense, Shared, Stray, Tie, Trite, Tritical, Tuft, Tye, Use, ➤ USUAL, Vile, Vul(gar), Vulgo, Vulgus, Widespread, Wimbledon

Commonplace Banal, Copybook, Hackneyed, Homely, Humdrum, Idée reçue, Mot, Ordinary, Philistine, Plain, Platitude, Prosaic, Quotidian, Trite, Workaday

Commonsense Gumption, Nous, Smeddum, Wit

Commotion Bluster, Bustle, Carfuffle, Clangour, Clatter, Curfuffle, Dirdam, Dirdum, Do, Dust, Ferment, Flap, Flurry, Fraise, Fuss, Hell, Hoo-ha(h), Pother, Racket, Romage, Rort, Ruckus, Ruction, Rumpus, Shemozzle, Shindy, Shivaree, Steery, Stir, Storm, Stushie, Tirrivee, Tirrivie, To-do, Toss, Tumult, Turmoil, Upheaval, Uproar, Whirl, Wroth

Communal, Commune Agapemone, Collective, Com, Meditate, Mir, Phalanstery, Public, Talk, Township

Communicate, Communication Ampex, Announce, Baud, Boyau, Cable, Channelling, Conversation, Convey, Cybernetic, E-mail, Expansive, Impart, Infobahn, Inform, Intelsat, Internet, Message, Note, Oracy, Prestel®, Proxemics, Reach, Road, Semiotics, Signal, Tannoy®, Telepathy, Telex, Telstar, Tieline, Transmit, Utraquist

Communion Creed, Fellowship, Host, Housel, Intinction, Lord's Supper, Species, Viaticum

Communiqué Announcement, Statement

Communism, Communist Apparat(chik), Aspheterism, Bolshevist, Com, Comecon, Cominform, Comintern, Commo, Comsomol, Deviationist, Essene, Fourier, Khmer Rouge, Komsomol, Leninite, Maoist, Nomenklatura, Perfectionist, Pinko, Politburo, Red, Revisionism, Soviet, Spartacist, Tanky, Titoist, Trot, Vietcong, Vietminh

Communities, Community Alterne, Ashram, Biome, Body, Brotherhood, Clachan, Climax, Coenobitism, Coenobium, Colonia, Colony, Consocies, Ecosystem, EEC, Enclave, European, Frat(e)ry, Kahal, Kibbutz, Mesarch, Neighbourhood, People, Phyle, Public, Pueblo, Seral, Sere, Shtetl, Sisterhood, Society, Street, Town, Tribe, Ujamaa, Village, Virtual, Zupa

Commute(r) Change, Convert, Reduce, Straphanger, Travel

Como Lake, Perry

Compact Agreement, Cement, Concise, Conglobe, Covenant, Covin, Coyne, Dense, Entente, Fast, Firm, Flapjack, Hard, Knit, League, Match, Neat, Pledge, Powder, Solid, Terse, Tight, Treaty, Well-knit

Companion(able) Achates, Arm candy, Associate, Attender, Barnacle, Bedfellow, Bonhomie, Bud(dy), Butty, CH, China, Comate, Comrade, Consort, Contubernal, Crony, Cupman, Duenna, Ephesian, Escort, Felibre, ➤ FELLOW, Fere, Handbook, Mate, Pal, Pard, Sidekick, Thane, Thegn, Vade-mecum

Company, Companies Actors, Artel, Ass, Assembly, Band, Bank, Battalion, Bevy, ➤ BUSINESS, Bv, Cahoot, Cartel, Cast, Cavalcade, CIA, Circle, Club, Co, Conger, Consort, Cordwainers, Core, Corporation, Corps, Coy, Crew, Crowd, Decury, East India, Enterprise, Faction, Financer, ➤ FIRM, Flock, Gang, Garrison, Ging, Guild, Haberdashers, Heap, Holding, Hudson's Bay, ICI, In-house, Inc, Indie, Intercourse, Investment, Jingbang, Joint-stock, Limited, Listed, Livery, Maniple, Muster, Order, Organisation, Plc, Private, Public, Rep(ertory), SA, Set, Shell, Siege, Sort, Syndicate, Team, Thiasus, Troop, Troupe, Twa, Two(some), SpA, Stock, Table, Touring, Trust, Visitor, White

Compare(d), Comparison Analogy, Beside, Bracket, Collate, Confront, Contrast, Correspond, Cp, Equate, Liken, Match, Odious, Parallel, Relation, Simile, Weigh

Compartment Bay, Booth, Box, Carriage, Casemate, Cell, Chamber, Cubbyhole, Cubicle, Dog box, Locellate, Loculament, Loculus, Panel, Partition, Pigeonhole, Pocket, Room, Room(ette), Severy, Stall, Till

Compass Ambit, Area, Beam, Bounds, Bow, Gamut, Goniometer, Gyro, Gyroscope, Infold, Magnetic, Needle, Orbit, Pelorus, Perimeter, ➤ RANGE, Reach, Rhumb, Room, Scale, Sweep, Tessitura

Compassion(ate) Aroha, Clemency, Empathy, Humane, Mercy, Pity, Samaritan, Sympathy

Compatible Consistent, Fit, Harmonious

Compatriot National

Compel(led), Compulsion, Compulsive, Compulsory Addiction, Coact, Coerce, Command, Constrain, Dragoon, Duress, Enforce, Extort, Fain, ➤ FORCE, Gar, Make, Mandatory, Oblige, Pathological, Steamroller, Strongarm, Tyrannise

Compendium Breviate

Compensate, Compensation Amend(s), Balance, Boot, Comp, Counterbalance, Counterpoise, Damages, Demurrage, Guerdon, Offset, Payment, Recoup, Redress, Reparation, Reprisal, Requital, Restitution, Restore, Retaliation, Salvage, Satisfaction, Solatium, Wergild, X-factor

Compère Emcee, Host, MC, Presenter

Compete Contend, Emulate, Enter, Match, Outvie, Play, Rival, Vie

Competence, Competent Ability, Able, Adequate, Can, Capacity, Dab, Efficient, Fit, Responsible, Sui juris, Worthy

Competition, Competitive, Competitor Agonist, Bee, Biathlon, Contest, Cup, Drive, Entrant, Event, Field, Gymkhana, Heptathlon, Match, Open, Opponent, Pairs, Panellist, Pentathlon, Player, Puissance, Race, Rally, Repechage, Rival(ise), Rodeo, Show-jumping, Tension, Test, Tiger, Tournament, Tourney, Trial, Triallist, Wap(p)enshaw

Compile(r), Compilation Anthology, Arrange, Collect, Edit, Prepare, Zadkiel

Complacent Babbitt, Fatuous, Joco, Pleasant, Smug

Complain(t), Complainer Adenoids, Affection, Affliction, Alas, Alastrim, Alopecia, Anaemia, Angashore, Angina, Asthma, BSE, Barrack, Beef, Bellyache, Bitch, Bleat, Carp, Charge, Chorea, Colic, Crab, Cramp, Criticise, Diatribe, Disorder, Dropsy, Epidemic, Ergot, Exanthema, Girn, Gout, Gravamen, Groan, Grouch, Grouse, Growl, Grudge, Grumble, Grutch, Harangue, Hives, Hone, Hypochondria, ➤ ILLNESS, Jeremiad, Kvetch, Lupus, Malady, Mange, Mean(e), Mein, Mene, Moan, Morphew, Mumps, Murmur, Nag, Natter, Neuralgia, Pertussis, Plica, Poor-mouth, Protest, Pyelitis, Querimony, Rail, Remonstrate, Repine, Rickets, Sapego, Sciatica, Scold, Sigh, Silicosis, Squawk, Staggers, Thrush, Tic, Tinea, Upset, Wheenge, Whimper, Whine, Whinge, Yammer, Yawp

Complaisant Agreeable, Flexible, Suave, Supple

Complement Alexin, Amount, Balance, Finish, Gang, Lot, Reciprocate

Complete(ly) Absolute, Accomplish, All, Arrant, Attain, Clean, Congenital, Consummate, Crown, Do, End, Entire, Finalise, Finish, Fruition, Fulfil, Full, Full-blown, Hollow, Incept, Integral, In toto, One, Out, Out and out, Perfect, Plenary, Quite, Sheer, Spang, Sum, Teetotal, Thorough, Total, Uncut, Unequivocal, Unmitigated, Whole (hog)

Complex(ity) Abstruse, Compound, Difficult, Electra, Hard, Inferiority, Intricate, Intrince, Involute, Knot, Manifold, Mixed, Multinucleate, Nest, Network, Obsession, Oedipus, Paranoid, Phaedra, Superiority, Syndrome, Web

Complexion Aspect, Blee, Hue, Leer, Temper, Tint, View

Compliance, Compliant, Complicit, Comply Agree, Assent, Conform, Deference, Hand-in-glove, Obey, Observe, Sequacious, Surrender, Wilco

Complicate(d), Complication Bewilder, Complex, Deep, Elaborate, Embroil, Implex, Intricate, Involve, Inweave, Node, Nodus, Perplex, Ramification, Rigmarole, Tangle, Tirlie-wirlie

▷ **Complicated** may indicate an anagram

Compliment(s) Baisemain, Bouquet, Congratulate, Devoirs, Douceur, Encomium, Flatter, Flummery, Praise, Soap, Tribute

Component Constituent, Contact, CRT, Element, Factor, Impedor, Ingredient, Longeron, ➤ PART, Subunit

Compose(d), Composure Aplomb, Arrange, Calm, Consist, Cool, ➤ CREATE, Equanimity, Even, Face, Improvise, Indite, Lull, Notate, Placid, Poise, Produce, Reconcile, Sangfroid, Sedate, Serenity, Settle, Soothe, Tranquil

Composer ➤ COMPOSERS, Contrapuntist, Inventor, Maker, Melodist, Musician, Serialist, Symphonist, Triadist, Tunesmith, Writer

▷ **Composing** may indicate an anagram

Composite Aster, Costmary, Foalfoot, Gerbera, Groundsel, Hybrid, Integral, Motley, Opinicus, Rag(weed), Sphinx, Synthesized, Thistle

Composition, Compositor Aleatory, Azione, Beaumontage, Beaumontague, Capriccio, Caprice, Cob, Concerto, Creation, Dite, Essay, Etude, Exaration, Fantasia, Ingredient, Inditement, Loam, Met, Montage, Morceau, Nonet(te), Opus, Oratorio, Pastiche, Piece, Poem, Polyphony, Printer, Quartette, Raga, Rhapsody, Ship, Sing, Smoot, Sonata, Sonatina, Structure, Symphony, Synthesis, Terracotta, Texture, Toccata, Treatise, Typesetter, Work

Compost Dressing, Fertilizer, Humus, Vraic

Compound Amalgam, Blend, ➤ CAMP, Composite, ➤ COMPOUNDS, Constitute, Cpd, Derivative, Mix, Multiply, Racemate, Type

▷ **Compound(ed)** may indicate an anagram

Comprehend, Comprehensive All-in, Catch-all, Catholic, Compass, Compendious, Contain, Exhaustive, Fathom, Follow, General, Global, Grasp, Include, Indepth, Ken, Large, Omnibus, Panoramic, Perceive, School, Sweeping, Thoroughgoing, ➤ UNDERSTAND, Wide

Compress(ed), Compression Astrict, Bale, Coarctate, Contract, Solidify, Squeeze, Stupe, Thlipsis

Comprise Contain, Embody, Embrace, Include

Compromise Avoision, Brule, Commit, Concession, Endanger, Involve, Settlement, Time-server, Trade off

▶ **Compulsion** see COMPEL

Compunction Hesitation, Regret, Remorse, Scruple, Sorrow

Computation, Computer (language), Computer term, Computer user ActiveX, Ada, Algol, Analog(ue), Antialising, Apple, ASCII, Authoring, Autosave, Basic, Boot, Brain, C, CADMAT, Calculate, Calculus, Cast(er), Checksum, Chiphead, Clickstream, COBOL, COL, CORAL, Counter, Cyber(netics), Cyberpunk, Cybersurfer, Desktop, Digerati, Digital, Earcon, Earom, Eniac, ERNIE, EPROM, Estimate, Extranet, FAT, Figure, Fileserver, Fortran, Freenet, GIGO, Groupware, Hacker, HAL, Hardware, Holmes, Hypermedia, ICL, IDE, Integrator, Interface, Internet, IT, JANET, Java®, Kludge, LISP, Laptop, Linker, Macro, Mainframe, Measure, Micro, MIDI, Modem, Number-cruncher, Numlock, OCCAM, OCR, On-line, Palmtop, PASCAL, Patch, Personal, Pixel, Processor, Program, PROM, Pushdown, RAM, README file, Read-out, Realtime, Reboot, Reckoner, ROM, Scratchpad, Shareware, SNOBOL, Software, Spreadsheet, Sprite, Stand-alone, Superserver, TALISMAN, TAURUS, Tally, Toggle, Tower, Track(er)ball, Unix, Vaccine, Voxel, WIMP, WORM, Wysiwyg

Comrade Achates, Ally, Buddy, Butty, China, Fellow, Friend, Kamerad, Mate, Pal, Pard, Tovarich, Tovaris(c)h

Con(man) Against, Anti, Bunco, Diddle, Dupe, Hornswoggle, Jacob, Learn, Peruse, Read, Scam, Scan, Steer, Sucker, Swindle, Tweedler

COMPOSERS

3 letters:
Bax
4 letters:
Adam
Arne
Bach
Berg
Blow
Brel
Bull
Byrd
Cage
Dima
Ives
Kern
Lalo
Monk
Nono
Orff
Peri
Raff
Wolf
5 letters:
Auric
Balfe
Berio
Bizet
Bliss
Bloch
Boito
Boyce
Brian
Bruch
Crumb
D'Indy
Dukas
Elgar
Fauré
Field
Finzi
Glass
Gluck
Grieg
Harty
Haydn
Henze
Holst
Ibert
Lasso
Lehar
Liszt
Loewe
Lully
Parry
Prout
Ravel

Reger
Rossi
Satie
Sousa
Suppe
Tosti
Verdi
Watts
Weber
Weill
6 letters:
Alfven
Arnold
Azione
Barber
Bartók
Berlin
Boulez
Brahms
Bridge
Burney
Busoni
Chopin
Coates
Delius
Dvořák
Flotow
Franck
German
Glière
Glinka
Gounod
Handel
Hummel
Joplin
Kodaly
Lassus
Ligeti
Mahler
Mingus
Morley
Mozart
Ogolon
Rameau
Rubbra
Schutz
Tallis
Varese
Wagner
Walton
7 letters:
Albeniz
Allegri
Bantock
Bellini

Berlioz
Berners
Borodin
Britten
Brubeck
Copland
Corelli
Debussy
De Falla
Delibes
Dowland
Ireland
Janáček
Lambert
Martinu
Nielsen
Novello
Poulenc
Puccini
Purcell
Purnell
Quilter
Rodgers
Rodrigo
Romberg
Rossini
Roussel
Salieri
Smetana
Stainer
Strauss
Tartini
Tippett
Vivaldi
Warlock
Youmans
8 letters:
Alaleona
Albinoni
Bruckner
Chabrier
Couperin
Gershwin
Gesualdo
Glazunov
Grainger
Granados
Honegger
Kreutzer
Marcello
Mascagni
Massenet
Messager
Messiaen
Paganini

Respighi
Schubert
Schumann
Scriabin
Sibelius
Sondheim
Sullivan
Taverner
Telemann
9 letters:
Bacharach
Beethoven
Bernstein
Boulanger
Broughton
Buxtehude
Chaminade
Cherubini
Donizetti
Dunstable
Hindemith
Offenbach
Pergolesi
Prokofiev
Scarlatti
Schnittke
10 letters:
Cole Porter
Monteverdi
Mussorgsky
Palestrina
Ponchielli
Rawsthorne
Saint-Saëns
Schoenberg
Stravinsky
Williamson
11 letters:
Birtwhistle
Charpentier
Humperdinck
Leoncavallo
Mendelssohn
Stockhausen
Tchaikovsky
Wolf Ferrari
12 letters:
Khachaturian
Shostakovich
13 letters:
Maxwell Davies
14 letters:
Rimsky-Korsakov
15 letters:
Vaughan Williams

COMPOUNDS

3 letters:
Azo
4 letters:
Alum
EDTA
Enol
Haem
Heme
TEPP
Urea
5 letters:
Allyl
Amide
Amino
Azide
Azine
Azole
Diazo
Diene
Dimer
Diode
Erbia
Ester
Furan
Halon
Imide
Imine
Lipid
Olein
Oxide
Oxime
Potin
Pyran
Sarin
Tabun
Thiol
Trona
Vinyl
6 letters:
Acetal
Alkane
Alkene
Arsine
Baryta
Borane
Calque
Cetane
Chrome
Cresol
Epimer
Fluate
Glycol
Halide
Haloid
Hexene
Isatin

Isomer
Ketone
Lithia
Niello
Phenol
Pinene
Potash
Purine
Pyrone
Retene
Silane
Speiss
Tartar
Tetryl
Thymol
Triene
Trimer
Uranyl
7 letters:
Acetone
Acridin
Aglycon
Ammonia
Benzene
Betaine
Bromide
Caliche
Calomel
Camphor
Carbide
Chelate
Choline
Cinerin
Cumarin
Creatin
Cyanide
Diamine
Diazine
Diazole
Dioxide
Dvandva
Epoxide
Erinite
Ethanol
Eugenol
Fenuron
Flavone
Hormone
Hydrate
Hydride
Indican
Indoxyl
Lactate
Menthol
Metamer
Monomer

Nitrite
Oxazine
Peptone
Polymer
Protein
Quassia
Quinoid
Quinone
Realgar
Skatole
Steroid
Sulfide
Syncarp
Taurine
Terpene
Toluene
Tritide
Uridine
Wolfram
8 letters:
Acridine
Aglycone
Aldehyde
Alizarin
Arginine
Butyrate
Catenane
Chloride
Chromene
Coenzyme
Coumarin
Creatine
Cyanogen
Datolite
Dieldrin
Dopamine
Farnesol
Fluoride
Glycogen
Hydroxyl
Indoform
Isologue
Ketoxime
Lecithin
Massicot
Melamine
Monoxide
Pentosan
Peroxide
Piperine
Ptomaine
Pyrazole
Rock-alum
Rotenone
Selenate
Silicide

Siloxane
Sodamide
Stilbene
Sulphide
Sulphone
Tautomer
Tetroxid
Thiazide
Thiazine
Thiazole
Thiotepa
Thiourea
Titanate
Triazine
Triazole
Trilling
Tyramine
Urethane
Xanthate
Xanthine
Zirconia
9 letters:
Aflatoxin
Alicyclic
Aliphatic
Anhydride
Bahuvrihi
Biguanide
Carbazole
Carnitine
Cellulose
Cementite
Cortisone
Deuteride
Dipeptide
Disulfram
Endorshin
Ferrocene
Flavanone
Glycoside
Guanosine
Haematein
Histamine
Hydrazide
Hydroxide
Imidazole
Impsonite
Ionophore
Monoamine
Pentoxide
Phenoxide
Pheromone
Phosphide
Piperonal
Polyamine
Porphyrin

Qinghaosu	Nucleoside	Electrolyte	
Quercetus	Phenocaine	Fluorescein	
Quinidine	Picrotoxin	Ghitathione	
Serotonin	Piperazine	Hydrocarbon	**13 letters:**
Tetroxide	Piperidine	Neostigmine	Catecholamine
Veratrine	Propionate	Sesquioxide	Cycloheximide
10 letters:	Putrescine	**12 letters:**	Isoproterenol
Amphoteric	Tatpurusha	Carbohydrate	Metronidazole
Argyrodite	Thimerosal	Formaldehyde	Nortriptyline
Dimethoate	Tocopherol	Haematoxylin	Trinucleotide
Disulphide	**11 letters:**	Hydroquinone	**14 letters:**
Enkephalin	Acetanilide	Permanganate	Oxyhaemoglobin
Isocyanate	Amphetamine	Polyurethane	Polycarboxylic
Lumisterol	Coprosterol	Triglyceride	Polyunsaturate
Mercaptide	Dimercaprol	Trimethadine	Trohalomethane

Concave Dished, Invexed

Conceal(ed), Concealment Blanket, Blind, Closet, Clothe, Cover, Curtain, Dissemble, Doggo, Feal, Heal, Heel, Hele, ➤ HIDE, Latent, Occult, Misprision, Palm, Perdu(e), Recondite, Screen, Scriene, Secrete, Shroud, Sleeve, Stash, Subreption, Ulterior, Wrap

Concede, Concession Acknowledge, Admit, Allow, Carta, Charter, Compromise, Confess, Favour, Forfeit, Franchise, Munich, Ou, Owe, Own, Privilege, Sop, Synchoresis

Conceit(ed) Bumptious, Caprice, Carriwitchet, Concetto, Crank, Crotchet, Device, Dicty, Egomania, Fancy, Fastuous, Fop, Fume, Hauteur, Idea, Notion, Podsnappery, Prig, Princock, Princox, Puppyism, Quiblin, Side, Snotty, Stuck-up, Swellhead, Toffee-nose, Vain(glory), Wind

Conceive, Conceivable Beget, Create, Credible, Imagine, Possible, Surmise

Concentrate(d), Concentration Aim, Bunch, Centre, Collect, Condense, Dephlegmate, Distil, Elliptical, Essence, Extract, Focalise, Focus, Intense, Listen, Major, Mantra, Mass, Molality, Molarity, Potted, Rivet, Samadhi, Titrate, Titre

Concept(ion) Brain, Hent, Ideal, Ideation, Image, Immaculate, Myth, Notion, Stereotype

Concern(ing) About, After, Ail, Altruism, Anent, As to, Business, Care, Cerne, Company, Disturb, Firm, In re, Intéressé, Interest, Into, Lookout, ➤ MATTER, Mell, Misease, Over, Pidgin, Part, Pigeon, Re, Reck, Regard, Reke, Respect, Retch, Solicitude, Touch, Trouble

▷ **Concerned** may indicate an anagram

Concert (place) Agreement, Benefit, Charivari, Cooperation, Device, Gig, Hootananny, Hootenanny, Hootnannie, Odeon, Odeum, Pop, Prom(enade), Recital, Singsong, Smoker, Symphony, Together, Unity, Wit

Concertina Bandoneon, Pleat, Squeezebox, Squiffer

Concerto Brandenburg, Emperor, Grosso

▶ **Concession** see Concede

Conch Shell, Strombus

Conchie CO

Conciliate Allay, Calm, Disarm, Ease, Mollify, Placate, Reconcile

Concise Compact, Curt, Laconic, Short, Succinct, Terse, Tight

Conclave Assembly, Caucus, Confab, Meeting

Conclude(d), Conclusion, Conclusive Achieve, A fortiori, Afterword, Amen, Binding, Cease, Clinch, Close, Complete, Dead, Decide, Deduce, ➤ END, Envoi, Explicit, Finding, Fine, Finis, ➤ FINISH, Foregone, Gather, Illation, Infer, Limit, Omega, Peroration, Point, Postlude, Punchline, Reason, Resolve, Settle, Summary, Upshot, Uptie

Conclusive Cogent, Convincing, Estoppel, Final

Concoct(ion) Brew, Compound, Creation, Plan, Trump

Concord Consonance, Harmony, Peace, Plane, Sympathy, Treaty, Unity

Concorde SST

Concourse Assembly, Confluence, Esplanade, Throng

Concrete, Concretion Actual, Aggregate, Beton, Bezoar, Cake, Calculus, Clot, Dogger, Gunite, Hard, Mass, Minkstone, No-fines, Pile-cap, Positive, Reify, Siporex, Solid, Tangible, Tremie

Concubine Apple-squire, Campaspe, Harem, Hetaria, Madam, Mistress, Odalisk

Concur Accord, Agree, Coincide, Comply, ➤ CONSENT, Gree

Concuss(ion) Clash, Shock, Stun

Condemn(ation) Blame, Blast, Cast, Censor, Censure, Convict, Damn, Decry, Denounce, Deprecate, Doom, Judge, Kest, Obelise, Proscribe, Sentence, Theta, Upbraid

Condense(r), Condensation Abbreviate, Abridge, Capacitator, Compress, Contract, Distil, Encapsulate, Epitomise, Liebig, Précis, Rectifier, Reduce, Shorten, Shrink, Summarise

Condescend Deign, Patronise, Stoop, Vouchsafe

Condiment Caraway, Cayenne, Chutney, Flavour, Kava, Relish, Sambal, Sambol, Sauce, Tracklement, Turmeric, Vinegar

Condition(al), Conditioning Circ(s), Connote, Fettle, Going, Hammertoe, Hood, If, ➤ IN GOOD CONDITION, Kelter, Kilter, Nick, Order, Pass, Pavlovian, Plight, Pliskie, Ply, Point, Position, Predicament, Prepare, Prerequisite, Presupposition, Protasis, Proviso, Provisory, Repair, Reservation, Reserve, Rider, Ropes, Sine qua non, Sis, Standing, State, Sted, Stipulation, String, Term, Tid, Tox(a)emia, Trim, Trisomy, Unless

Condom Cap, Gumboot, Johnny, Letter, Prophylactic, Rubber, Safe, Sheath

Condone Absolve, Excuse, Forgive, Overlook

Conduct(or), Conductress Accompany, Anode, Arm, Arrester, Bearing, Behaviour, Bulow, Bus-bar, Cad, Chobdar, Clippie, Coil, Comport, Demean(our), Deportment, Direct, Drive, Editor, Electrode, Escort, Feelthrough, Fetch, Haitink, Hallé, Ignitron, Jark, Karajan, Kempe, Klemperer, Lead, Liber, Lightning, Maestro, Mho, Microchip, Nerve, Officiate, Outer, Parts, Photodiode, ➤ PILOT, Previn, Prosecute, Psychopomp, Rattle, Safe, Sargent, Scudaller, Scudler, Skudler, Solicit, Solti, Tao, Thermistor, Toscanini, Transact, ➤ USHER, Varactor, Varistor, Wire, Wood

▷ **Conducting** may indicate an '-ic' ending

Conduit Aqueduct, Canal, Carrier, Duct, Main, Panstock, Pipe, Tube

Cone, Conical Cappie, Fir, Moxa, Pastille, Peeoy, Pineal, Pingo, Pioy(e), Puy, Pyramid, Spire, Storm, Strobilus, Taper, Tee, Traffic, Volcanic, Windsock

Coney Daman, Doe, Hyrax

Confection(er) Candy, Caramel, Chocolate, Concoction, Conserve, Countline, Ice, Kiss, Marzipan, Noisette, Nougat, Quiddery, Rock, Sweet, Sweetmeat

Confederal, Confederacy, Confederate, Confederation Accessory, Alliance, Ally, Association, Body, Bund, Bunkosteerer, Cover, Illinois, League, Partner, Union

Confer(ence) Bestow, Cf, Collogue, Colloqium, Colloquy, Congress, Council, Diet, Do, Dub, Fest, Forum, Grant, Huddle, Imparlance, Indaba, Intercommune, Lambeth, Meeting, Munich, Negotiate, Palaver, Parley, Pawaw, Pear, Potsdam, Pourparler, Powwow, Press, Pugwash, Quadrant, Seminar, Settle, Summit, Symposium, Synod, ➤ TALK, Vouchsafe, Yalta

Confess(or), Confession Acknowledge, Admit, Agnise, Avowal, Concede, Declare, Disclose, Edward, Own, Recant, Shrift, Shriver, Sing, Whittle

Confide(nce), Confident(ial), Confidant Aplomb, Aside, Assertive, Assured, Bedpost, Belief, Cocksure, Cred, Crouse, Entre nous, Entrust, Faith, Feisty, Gatepost, Hardy, Hope, Hush-hush, Intimate, Morale, Pack, Private, Privy, Sanguine, Secret, Self-possessed, Sub rosa, Sure, Tell, Trust, Unbosom, Under the rose, Vaulting

Confine(d), Confines, Confinement Ambit, Bail, Bale, Cage, CB, Chain, Constrain, Cramp, Crib, Detain, Emmew, Encase, Enclose, Endemic, Enmew, Ensheath, Gate, Immanacle, Immew, Immure, Impound, ➤ IMPRISON, Incommunicado, Inhoop, Intern, Local, March, Mail, Mew, Mure, Narrow, Pen, Pent, Pinion, Poky, Restrict, Rules, Solitary, Tether, Thirl, Trammel

Confirm(ed), Confirmation Addict, Assure, Attest, Bear, Certify, Chrisom, Christen, Chronic, Clinch, Corroborate, Endorse, Homologate, Obsign, OK, Ratify, Sacrament, Sanction, Seal, Strengthen, Ten-four, Tie, Validate, Vouch

Confiscate, Confiscation Attainder, Deprive, Dispossess, Distrain, Escheat, Garnishee, Impound, Infangenethef, Seize, Sequestrate

Conflagration Blaze, Holocaust, Inferno, Wildfire

Conflict(ing) Agon, Armageddon, Battle, Camp, Clash, Contend, Contravene, Controversy, Disharmony, Encounter, Feud, Fray, Inconsistent, Jar, Lists, Mêlée, Muss, Oppose, Rift, Strife, ➤ STRUGGLE, Tergiversate, War

Conform(ity) Accord, Adjust, Comply, Consistence, Correspond, Normalise, Obey, Observe, Propriety, Standardize, Stereotype(d), Suit, Trimmer, Yield

Confound(ed) Abash, Amaze, Astound, Awhape, Baffle, Bewilder, Blamed, Blasted, Blest, Bumbaze, Contradict, Darn, Drat, Dumbfound, Elude, Floor,

Jigger, Mate, Murrain, Nonplus, Perishing, Perplex, Rabbit, Spif(f)licate, Stump, Throw

▷ **Confound** may indicate an anagram

Confrère Ally

Confront(ation) Appose, Beard, Breast, Eyeball, Face, Mau-mau, Meet, Nose, Oppose, Showdown, Tackle

Confuse(d), Confusion Addle, Anarchy, Astonishment, Babel, Baffle, Bazodee, Bedevil, Befog, Befuddle, Bemuse, Bewilder, Blur, Burble, Bustle, Chaos, Cloud, Clutter, Complicate, Debacle, Didder, Disconcert, Disorient, Distract, Dither, Dizzy, Dudder, Dust, Egarement, Embrangle, Embroglio, Embroil, Farrago, Flap, Flummox, Flurry, Fluster, Fog, Fox, Fuddle, Galley-west, Hash, Havoc, Hazy, Hubble-bubble, Huddle, Hugger-mugger, Hurly-burly, Hurry-scurry, Hurry-skurry, Imbrangle, Imbroglio, ➤ IN CONFUSION, Indistinct, Litter, Lost, Lurry, Maelstrom, Maffled, Mayhem, Maze, Melange, Melee, Mess, Mingle, Mish-mash, Mixtie-maxtie, Mizzle, Moider, Moither, Moonstruck, ➤ MUDDLE, Mudge, Muzzy, Overset, Pellmell, Perplex, Pi(e), Pose, Ravel, Razzle-dazzle, Razzmatazz, Rout, Snafu, Spin, Stump, Stupefy, Synchysis, Tangle, Throw, Topsy-turvy, Tzimmes, Welter, Whemmle, Whomble, Whummle, Woolly, Woozy

▷ **Confuse(d)** may indicate an anagram

Confute Confound, Contradict, Deny, Disprove, Infringe, Redargue, Refel

Congeal Coagulate, Freeze, Gel, Gunge, Set, Solidify

Congenial Agreeable, Amiable, Compatible, Connate, Happy, Kindred, Simpatico, Sympathique

Congenital Inborn, Innate, Inveterate

Congest(ed), Congestion Coryza, Cram, Crowd, Engorge, Impact, Jam, Logjam, Turgid

Conglomerate, Conglomeration Aggregate, Banket, Gather, Heap, Mass

Congo(u) Tea

Congratulate, Congratulation Applaud, Felicitate, Laud, Mazeltov, Preen, Salute

Congregate, Congregation(alist) Assembly, Barnabite, Body, Brownist, Class, Community, Conclave, Ecclesia, Flock, Fold, Gathering, Host, Laity, Oratory, Propaganda, Synagogue

Congress(man) Assembly, Conclave, Council, Eisteddfod, Intercourse, Legislature, Rally, Senator, Solon, Synod, Vienna

Conifer(ous) Araucaria, Cedar, Cypress, Cyrus, Evergreen, Larch, Picea, Pine, Spruce, Taiga, Thuja, Yew

Conjecture Fancy, Goldbach's, Guess, Speculate, Surmise, View

Conjoin Alligate, Ally, Connect, Knit

Conjugate, Conjugation Couple, Join, Nuptial, Synopsis, Typto

Conjunction Alligation, Ampersand, And, Combination, Consort, Synod, Syzygy, Together, Union

Conjure, Conjuror Angekkok, Charm, Contrive, Heypass, Heypresto, Hocus-pocus, Illusionist, Imagine, Invoke, Mage, Magic, Palmer, Prestidigitator, Thaumaturgus

Connect(ed), Connection, Connector Accolade, Adaptor, Affinity, Agnate, Anastomosis, And, Associate, Attach, Band, Bind, Bridge, Bridle, Cable, Clientele, Coherent, Colligate, Conjugate, Couple, Cross-link, Delta, Dovetail, Drawbar, Fishplate, Fistula, ➤ IN CONNECTION WITH, Interlink, Interlock, Join, Jumper, Kinship, Liaison, Lifeline, Link, Marry, Merge, Nexus, On, Online, Pons, Raphe, Rapport, Relate, Relative, Respect, S-R, Shuttle, Splice, Tendon, Through, Tie, Tie-in, Union, Yoke, Zygon

Connecticut Ct

Connive, Connivance Abet, Cahoots, Collude, Condone, Conspire, Plot

Connoisseur Aesthete, Cognoscente, Epicure, Expert, Fancier, Gourmet, Judge, Oenophil

Connotate, Connotation Imply, Infer, Intent, Meaning

Conquer(or), Conquest Beat, Conquistador, Crush, Debel, Genghis Khan, Hereward, ➤ MASTER, Moor, Norman, Ostrogoth, Overcome, Overpower, Overrun, Pizarro, Subjugate, Tame, Tamerlane, Vanquish, Victor

Conquistador Cortes, Cortez

Conscience, Conscientious Casuistic, Heart, Inwit, Morals, Painstaking, Pang, Remorse, Scruple(s), Sense, Superego, Syneidesis, Synteresis, Thorough, Twinge

Conscious(ness) Awake, Aware, Limen, Sensible, Sentient

Conscript(ion) Blood-tax, Choco, Commandeer, Draft(ee), Impress, Landsturm, Levy, ➤ RECRUIT, Register

Consecrate, Consecration Bless, Hallow, Noint, Oint, Sacring, Sanctify, Venerate

Consecutive Sequential, Successive

Consensus Agreement, Harmony, Unanimity

Consent Accord, Affo(o)rd, Agree, Approbate, Comply, Concur, Grant, Informed, Permit, Ratify, Volens, Yes-but, Yield

Consequence, Consequent(ial) Aftermath, Consectaneous, Corollary, Effect, End, Importance, Issue, Karma, Knock-on, Moment, Outcome, Ramification, Repercussion, ➤ RESULT, Sequel

Conservative Blimpish, Blue, C, Cautious, Diehard, Disraeli, Fabian, Hard-hat, Hunker, Neanderthal, Old guard, Rearguard, Right(-wing), Square, Thrifty, Tory, True blue, Unionist, Verkramp

Conservatory Hothouse, Orangery, Solarium

Conserve, Conservation(ist) Comfiture, Husband(ry), Jam, Jelly, Maintain, Maintenance, Protect, NT, Save

Consider(able), Consideration Animadvert, Attention, Avizandum, By-end, Case, Cogitate, Contemplate, Count, Courtesy, Debate, Deem, Deliberate, Entertain, Envisage, Factor, Fair, Feel, Heed, Importance, Inasmuch, Judge, Many, Meditate, Muse, Pay, Perpend, Poise, Ponder, Pretty, Rate, Reckon, Reflect, Regard, Respect, See, Several, Solicitous,

Song, Speculate, Steem, Study, Substantial, Think, Tidy, Vast, View, Ween, Weigh

Consign(ment) Allot, Award, Batch, Bequeath, Delegate, Deliver, Entrust, Lading, Ship, Transfer

Consist(ent), Consistency Coherent, Comprise, Enduring, Liaison, Rely, Steady

Consolation, Console Ancon, Appease, Balm, Comfort, Relief, Solace

Consolidate Coalesce, Combine, Compact, Gel, Merge, Unify

Consommé Julienne, Soup

Consonant(s) Affricate, Agma, Agreeing, Cacuminal, Cerebral, Explosive, Fortis, Fricative, Harmonious, Labial, Lateral, Lenis, Media, Mouillé, Plosive, Sonorant, Spirant, Tenuis, Velar

Consort Ally, Associate, Maik, Mate, Moop, Moup, Partner, Spouse

Consortium Combine, Ring

Conspicuous Arresting, Blatant, Clear, Eminent, Glaring, Kenspeck(le), Landmark, Light, Manifest, Patent, Salient, Signal, Striking

Conspiracy, Conspirator, Conspire, Conspiring Cabal, Casca, Cassius, Catiline, Cato St, Cinna, Collaborate, Colleague, Collogue, Collude, Complot, Connive, Covin, Covyne, Guy, In cahoots, Intrigue, Oates, Omerta, ➤ PLOT, Ring, Scheme

Constable Beck, Catchpole, Cop, Dogberry, Dull, Elbow, Harman(-beck), Headborough, John, Officer, Painter, Pointsman, Posse, Special, Thirdborough, Tipstaff, Verges

Constancy, Constant Abiding, Boltzmann, C, Chronic, Coefficient, Devotion, Dirac, Eccentricity, Faith, G, H, Honesty, Hubble's, K, Lambert, Leal(ty), Logical, Loyal, Often, Parameter, ➤ PERPETUAL, Planck's, Pole star, Resolute, Sad, Staunch, Steadfast, Steady, True, Unfailing, Uniform, Usual

Constellation Andromeda, Antlia, Apus, Aquarius, Aquila, Ara, Argo, Aries, Auriga, Bootes, Caelum, Canis major, Canis minor, Carina, Cassiopeia, Centaurus, Cepheus, Cetus, Cham(a)eleon, Circinus, Columba, Coma Berenices, Corvus, Crater, Cygnus, Cynosure, Delphinus, Dorado, Draco, Equuleus, Eridanus, Fornax, Galaxy, Gemini, Gru(i)s, Hercules, Hydra, Hydrus, Indus, Lacerta, Leo, Lepus, Libra, Lupus, Lynx, Lyra, Mensa, Monoceros, Musca, Norma, Octans, Ophiuchus, Orion, Pavo, Pegasus, Perseus, Phoenix, Pictor, ➤ PLANET, Puppis, Pyxis, Reticulum, Sagitta, Sagittarius, Scorpius, Sculptor, Scutum, Serpens, Sextans, Southern Cross, ➤ STAR, Telescopium, Triangulum (Australe), Tucana, Twins, Unicorn, Vela, Virgo, Volans, Vulpecula, Whale

Consternation Alarm, Dismay, Doodah, Fear, Horror

Constipated, Constipation Astrict, Block, Costive, Stegnotic, Stenosis

Constituency, Constituent Borough, Component, Element, Part, Seat, Voter

▷ **Constituents** may indicate an anagram

Constitute, Constitution(al) Appoint, Charter, Compose, Comprise, Congenital, Creature, Establishment, Form, Fuero, Health, Physique, Policy, Polity, Seat, State, Synthesis, Upmake, Walk

Constrain(ed), Constraint Bind, Bondage, Coerce, Confine, Coop, Curb, Duress(e), Hard, Oblige, Pressure, Repress, Stenosis, Taboo

Constrict(ed), Constriction Bottleneck, Choke, Coarctate, Contract, Cramp, Hour-glass, Impede, Limit, Phimosis, Squeeze, Stegnosis, Stenosis, Thlipsis, Tighten, Venturi

Construct(ion), Constructor, Constructive Build, Compile, Engineer, Erect, Fabricate, Facture, Fashion, Form, Frame, Make, Manufacture, Seabee, Tectonic, Weave

Construe Deduce, Explain, Expound, Infer

Consul Ambassador, Attaché, Horse, Praetor

Consult(ant), Consultation Confer, Deliberate, Discuss, Imparl, Peritus, See, Surgery

Consume(r), Consumption, Consumptive Bolt, Burn, Caterpillar®, Decay, Devour, Diner, Eat, Engross, Exhaust, Expend, Feed, Glutton, Hectic, Mainline, Scoff, Spend, Swallow, TB, Use, Waste, Wear

Consummate, Consummation Keystone, Seal

Contact Abut, Adpress, Contingence, Hook-up, Lens, Liaise, Liaison, Meet, Reach, Shoe, ➤ TOUCH

Contagious, Contagion Infection, Noxious, Poison, Taint, Variola, Viral

Contain(er) Amphora, Ampulla, Aquafer, Aquifer, Bass, Bidon, Bin, Bottle, Box, Buddle, Cachepot, Can, Canakin, Canikin, Canister, Cannikin, Cantharus, Capsule, Carboy, Carry, Carton, Case, Cask, Cassette, Chase, Chest, Churn, Coffer, Comprise, Coolamon, Crate, Crater, Crucible, Cup, Cupel, Dracone, Dredger, Enclose, Encompass, Enseam, Esky®, Feretory, ➤ HOLD, House, Igloo, Include, Incubator, Jerrican, Jerrycan, Kirbeh, Leaguer, Lekythos, Monkey, Monstrance, Mould, Olpe, Pail, Piscina, Pithos, Pod, Pottle, Reliquary, Repository, Restrain, Saggar, Scyphus, Shaker, Skin, Skip, Spittoon, Stamnos, Tank, Terrarium, Tinaja, Tub, Tun, Tupperware®, Urn, Vessel, Vinaigrette, Woolpack

Contaminate(d) Corrupt, Defile, Flyblown, Impure, Infect, Soil, Stain, Tarnish

Contemplate, Contemplation Consider, Ecce, Envisage, Hesychasm, Meditate, Muse, Ponder, Reflect, Rue, Spell, Study, Think, Watch

Contemporary AD, Coetaneous, Current, Equal, Fellow, Modern, Present, Verism

Contempt(ible), Contemptuous Abject, Ageism, Aha, Arsehole, Bah, BEF, Cheap, Contumely, Crud, Crumb, Cullion, Cynical, Derision, Disparaging, Dog-bolt, Fig, Ignominious, Low, Mean, Measly, Misprision, Paltry, Phooey, Pish, Poxy, Pshaw, Rats, Razoo, Scabby, Scarab, ➤ SCORN, Scumbag, Sexism, Shabby, Shithead, Sneeze, Sniff, Snooty, Snot, Soldier, Sorry, Squirt, Squit, Supercilious, Toad, Toerag, Weed, Wretched

Contend(er) Candidate, Claim, Clash, Compete, Cope, Debate, Dispute, Fight, Grapple, Oppose, Stickle, ➤ STRIVE, Struggle, Submit, ➤ VIE, Wrestle

Content Apaid, Apay, Appay, Blissful, Happy, Inside, Please, Satisfy, Volume

▷ **Content** may indicate a hidden word

Contention, Contentious Argument, Bellicose, Case, Cantankerous, Combat, Competitive, Perverse, Polemical, Rivalry, Strife, Struggle, Sturt

Contest(ant) Agon, Battle, Bout, Catchweight, Challenge, Combat, Competition, Concours, Decathlon, Defend, Duel(lo), Entrant, Eurovision, Examinee, Fronde, Heptathlon, Kriegspiel, Lampadephoria, Match, Matchplay, Olympiad, Pentathlon, Pingle, Prizer, Race, Roadeo, Rodeo, Set-to, Skirmish, Slugfest, Strife, Struggle, Tenson, Tournament, Triathlon, Vie, War, With

Continent(al) Abstinent, Asia, Atlantis, Austere, Chaste, Epeirogeny, Euro, Gallic, Gondwanaland, Laurasia, Lemuria, Mainland, Moderate, Pang(a)ea, Shelf, Teetotal, Temperate, Walloon

Contingency, Contingent Accident, Arm, Casual, Chance, Conditional, Dependent, Event, Fluke, Group, Prospect

Continual(ly), Continuous Adjoining, Away, Chronic, Connected, Eer, Endlong, Eternal, Ever, Frequent, Incessant, On(going)

Continue, Continuation, Continuing, Continuity Abye, Duration, Dure, During, Enduring, Enjamb(e)ment, Hold, Keep, Last, Link, Onward, Persevere, Persist, Proceed, Prolong, Resume, Sequence, Stand, Subsist, Survive, Sustain, Tenor

▷ **Continuously** may indicate previous words to be linked

Contort(ion) Deform, Gnarl, Jib, Twist, Warp, Wry

Contour Curve, Graph, Isallobar, Isobase, Isocheim, Isochime, Isogeothermal, Line, Profile, Silhouette, Streamline, Tournure

Contraband Hot, Illicit, Prohibited, Smuggled

Contraception, Contraceptive Cap, Coil, Condom, Diaphragm, IU(C)D, Minipill, Oral, Pessary, Pill, Prophylactic, Loop, Sheath, Vimule®

Contract(ion), Contractor Abbreviate, Abridge, Agreement, Appalto, Astringency, Bargain, Biceps, Bottomry, Bridge, Builder, Catch, Champerty, Charter, Clonus, Condense, Constringe, Contrahent, Covenant, Cramp, Crasis, Curtail, Debt, Dwindle, Engage, Entrepreneur, Escrow, Fitzgerald-Lorentz, Gainsay, Gooseflesh, Guarantee, Hand-promise, Hire, Incur, Indenture, Jerk, Ketubah, Knit, Lease, Levator, Lorentz-Fitzgerald, Make, Miosis, Myosis, Narrow, Obligee, Party, Peristalsis, Promise, Pucker, Purse, Restriction, Shrink, Shrivel, Sign, Slam, Social, Spasm, Specialty, Steelbow, Stenosis, Stipulation, Supplier, Sweetheart, Systole, Tetanise, Tetanus, Tic, Tighten, Tonicity, Treaty, Triceps, Yellow-dog, Wrinkle, Z

Contradict(ion), Contradictory Ambivalent, Antilogy, Antinomy, Bull, Contrary, Counter, Dementi, Deny, Disaffirm, Disprove, Dissent, ➤ GAINSAY, Negate, Oxymoron, Paradox, Sot, Stultify, Sublate, Threap, Threep, Traverse

Contrarily, Contrary Adverse, A rebours, Arsy-versy, But, Captious, Converse, Counter, Crosscurrent, Froward, Hostile, Inverse, Mary, Opposite, Ornery, Perverse, Rebuttal, Retrograde, Wayward, Withershins

Contrast Chiaroscuro, Clash, Compare, Differ, Foil, Relief

Contravene Infringe, Oppose, Thwart, Violate

Contribute, Contribution Abet, Add, Assist, Conduce, Donate, Dub, Furnish, Go, Help, Input, Mite, Offering, Share, Sub, Subscribe, Whack

▷ **Contributing to** may indicate a hidden word

Contrite, Contrition Penance, Penitent, Remorse, Repentant, Rue, ➤ SORRY

Contrivance, Contrive Art, Contraption, Deckle, Deus ex machina, Device, Engine, Finesse, Gadget, Gin, Hokey, Invention, Plot

Contrive(r) Chicaner, Cook, Devise, Engineer, Frame, Hatch, Intrigue, Machinate, Manage, Manoeuvre, Plan, Procure, Scheme, Secure, Stage, Trump, Weave

Control(ler), Controllable Ada, Appestat, Big Brother, Birth, Boss, Bridle, Cabotage, Chair, Check, Christmas tree, Corner, Corset, Cybernetics, Dirigible, Dirigism(e), Dominion, Fet(ch), Finger, Gerent, Govern, Gubernation, Harness, Have, Heck, Helm, Influence, Influx, Joystick, Knee-swell, Lead, Lever, ➤ MANAGE, Martinet, Mastery, Moderate, Mouse, Nipple, Pilot, Police, Possess, Power, Preside, Puppeteer, Quality, Regulate, Regulo, Rein, Remote, Repress, Restrain, Rheostat, Ride, Rule, Run, School, Servo, Snail, Solion, Steady, Steer, Stop, Stranglehold, Stringent, Subdue, Subject, Subjugate, Supervise, Suzerain, Sway, Takeover, Thermostat, Throttle, Tiller, Valve, Weld, Wield, Zapper

Controversial, Controversy Argument, Contention, Debate, Dispute, Eristic(al), Furore, Hot potato, Polemic(al), Tendentious

Conundrum Acrostic, Egma, Enigma, Puzzle, Riddle

Convalesce(nt), Convalescence Anastatic, Mend, Rally, Recover, Recuperate, Rest-cure

▶ **Convene** see CONVOKE

Convenience, Convenient Behoof, Eft, Expedient, Facility, Gain, Gents, ➤ HANDY, Hend, Lav, Leisure, Near, Opportune, Pat, Privy, Public, Suitable, Toilet, Use, Well

Convent Cloister, Fratry, Friary, House, Motherhouse, Nunnery, Port-royal, Priory, Retreat

Convention(al) Academic, Accepted, Babbitt, Blackwood, Bourgeois, Caucus, Conclave, ➤ CUSTOMARY, Diet, Done, Formal, Geneva, Iconic, Meeting, More, Nomic, Orthodox, Pompier, Staid, Starchy, Stereotyped, Stock, Synod, Uptight, Usage, Warsaw

Converge Approach, Focus, Meet

Conversation(alist), Converse, Conversant Abreast, Antithesis, Board, Buck, Cackle, Causerie, Chat, Chitchat, Colloquy, Commune, Deipnosophist, Dialogue, Discourse, Eutrapelia, Eutrapely, Hobnob, Interlocution, Jaw-jaw, Natter, Opposite, Palaver, Parley, Rap, Rhubarb, Shop, Socialise, ➤ TALK, Transpose, Wongi, Word

Conversion, Converter, Convert(ible) Adapt, Alter, Assimilate, Azotobacter, Bessemer, Catalytic, Catechumen, Change, Commute, Cyanise, Diagenesis, Disciple, Encash, Etherify, Exchange, Expropriate, Fixation, Gummosis, Hodja, Kho(d)ja, Liquid, Marrano, Metanoia, Neophyte, Noviciate, Novitiate, Persuade, Proselyte, Put, Ragtop, Realise, Rebirth, Recycle, Revamp, Souper, Tablet, Transduce, Transmute, Try

▷ **Conversion, Converted** may indicate an anagram

Convex (surface) Arched, Bowed, Camber, Curved, Extrados, Gibbous, Lenticle, Nowy

Convey(ance) Assign, BS, Carousel, Carry, Charter, Coach, Conduct, Cycle, Deed, Eloi(g)n, Enfeoffment, Grant, Guide, Lease, Litter, Lorry, Mailcar(t), Re-lease, Sac and soc, Tip, Title deed, Tote, Tram, Transfer, Transit, Transmit, Transport, Vehicle

Convict(ion) Attaint, Belief, Bushranger, Certitude, Cockatoo, Cogence, Crawler, Credo, Creed, Criminal, Demon, Dogma, Faith, Felon, Forçat, Lag, Magwitch, ➤ PERSUASION, Plerophory, Ring, Trusty, Vehemence, Yardbird

Convince(d), Convincing Assure, Cogent, Doubtless, Luculent, Persuade, Satisfy, Sold, Sure

Convivial(ity) Boon, Bowl, Festive, Gay, Genial, Jovial, Social

Convoke Assemble, Call, Convene, Summon

Convolute(d), Convolution Coiled, Gyrus, Intricate, Spiral, Tortuous, Twisty, Whorl, Writhen

Convoy Caravan, Column, Conduct, Escort, Pilot, Train, Wagon-train

Convulsion(s), Convulsive Agitate, Clonic, Commotion, Disturb, DT, Eclampsia, ➤ FIT, Galvanic, Paroxysm, Spasm, Throe, Tic

Cook(s), Cooker, Cooking Aga®, Babbler, Bake, Balti, Beeton, Benghazi, Bhindi, Bouche, Braise, Broil, Cacciatore, Calabash, Captain, Charbroil, Chargrill, Chef, Coddle, Concoct, Cordon bleu, Cuisine, Devil, Do, Doctor, Dumple, Edit, Escoffier, Fake, Falsify, Fiddle, Flambé, Forge, Fricassee, Fry, Fudge, Greasy, Grill, Haute cuisine, Haybox, Marinière, Meunière, Microwave, Poach, Prepare, Pressure, Ring, Roast, Roger, Sous-chef, Spit, Steam, Stew, Stir-fry, Tandoori, Tire

▷ **Cook** may indicate an anagram

Cool(er), Coolness Aloof, Aplomb, Calm, Can, Chill, Collected, Composed, Cryogen, Cryostat, Defervescence, Dispassionate, Distant, Esky®, Fan, Frappé, Fridge, Frigid, Frosty, Gaol, Goglet, Ice(box), Jail, Jug, Keel, Phlegm, Prison, Quad, Quod, Refresh, Reserved, Sangfroid, Serene, Skeigh, Stir, Temperate, Thou(sand), Unruffled

Coop Cage, Cavie, Confine, Gaol, Hutch, Mew, Pen, Rip

Cooper Gary, Henry, Tubman

Cooperate, Cooperation, Cooperative Collaborate, Combine, Conspire, Contribute, Coop, Liaise, Teamwork, Together

Coordinate(d), Coordination Abscissa, Abscisse, Agile, Arrange, Cartesian, Ensemble, Harmony, Nabla, Orchestrate, Ordonnance, Peer, Polar, Synergy, X, Y, Z

Coot Stupid, Sultan

Cop(s) Bag, Bull, Catch, Dick, Keystone, Peeler, Peon, ➤ POLICEMAN

Copal Dammar, Resin

Cope Chlamys, Deal, Face, Handle, ➤ MANAGE, Mantle, Meet, Negotiate, Pallium, Poncho

Coping (stone) Balustrade, Capstone, Skew

Copious Abundant, Affluent, Ample, Fecund, Fluent, Fruitful, Fulsome, Plentiful, Profuse

Copper As, Atacamite, Blister, Bluebottle, Bobby, Bornite, Busy, Cash, Cent, Chessylite, ➤ COIN, Cu, D, Dam, Double, Erinite, Flatfoot, Lawman, Lota(h), Malachite, Mountain-blue, Ormolu, Pence, Penny, Pfennig, Pie, Pig, Plack, Policeman, Red, Rosser, Rozzer, S, Sen(s), Slop, Special, Traybit, Venus, Washer, Wire bar

Copse Thicket

Copulate Intercourse, Line, Mate, Roger, Tup

Copy(ing), Copier, Copyist Aemule, Ape, Apograph, Autotype, Calk, Calque, Carbon, Clerk, Clone, Counterpart, Crib, Cyclostyle, Diazo, Ditto, Dyeline, Echo, Echopraxia, Ectype, Edition, Eidograph, Electro, Emulate, Engross, Estreat, Example, Facsimile, Fair, Fax, Flimsy, Forge, ➤ IMITATE, Issue, Manifold, Manuscript, Match, Me-tooer, Milline, Mimeograph®, Mimic, Mirror, MS, Parrot, Photostat®, Plagiarism, Read-out, Replica, Repro, Reproduce, Roneo®, Scribe, Script, Scrivener, Sedulous, Simulate, Spit, Stencil, Stuff, Tenor, Tenure, Trace, Transcribe, Transume, Vidimus, Xerox®

Copyright C

Coquette Agacerie, Flirt, Rosina, Tease, Vamp

Coracle Currach, Curragh

Coral (reef) Alcyonaria, Aldabra, Atoll, Brain, Gorgonia(n), Laccadives, Madrepore, Millepore, Pink, Reef, Sea fan, Sea ginger, Sea whip, Sea-pen, Zoothome

Cord, Cord-like Aiguillette, Band, Bedford, Bind, Boondoggle, Cat-gut, Chenille, Communication, Creance, Drawstring, Flex, Fourragère, Funicle, Gasket, Heddle, Laniard, Lanyard, Ligature, Line, Moreen, Myelon, Net, Ocnus, Piping, Quipo, Quipu, Rep(s), Restiform, Rip, Rope, Sash, Sennit, Service, Spermatic, Spinal, ➤ STRING, Tendon, Tie, Twine, Umbilical, Vocal

Cordial Anise(ed), Anisette, Benedictine, Cassis, Drink, Gracious, Hearty, Hippocras, Kind, Neighbourly, Oporice, Orangeade, Persico(t), Pleasant, Ratafia, Rosa-solis, Roso(g)lio, Shrub, Tar-water, Warm

Cordon Picket, Ring, Surround

Corduroy Rep(p)

Cordyline Ti-tree

Core Barysphere, Calandria, Campana, Centre, Essence, Filament, Heart, Hub, Nife, Plerome, Quintessence

Co-religionist Brother

Corinthian(s) Casuals, Caulis, Epistolaters

Cork(ed), Corker Balsa, Bouché, Bung, Float(er), Humdinger, Oner, Phellem, Phellogen, Plug, Seal, Shive, Stopper, Suber(ate)

Corkscrew Bore, Opening, Spiral

Cormorant Duiker, Duyker, Scart(h), Skart(h)

Corn(y) Bajr(a), Banal, Blé, Cereal, Cob, Emmer, Epha, Flint, Gait, Graddan, Grain, Grist, Icker, Indian, Kaffir, Mabela, Maize, Mealie, Muid, Nubbin, Pickle, Pinole, Posho, Rabi, Shock, Stitch, Straw, Thrave, Trite, Zea

Corncrake Landrail

Cornel Dogberry, Tree

Corner Amen, Angle, Bend, Cantle, Canton, Cranny, Dangerous, Diêdre, Elbow, Entrap, Hole, Hospital, Lug, Monopoly, NE, Niche, Nook, NW, Predicament, Quoin, SE, Spot, Speaker's, SW, Tack, Trap, Tree, Vertex

Cornerstone Coi(g)n, Encoignure, Skew-corbel, Skew-put, Skew-table

Cornet Cone, Horn

Cornice Surbase

Cornish(man) Cousin Jack

Cornstalks Strammel, Straw, Strummel, Stubble

Cornucopia Amalthea, Horn

Cornwall SW

Corollary Conclusion, Dogma, Porism, Rider, Theory, Truism

Corona Aureole, Cigar, Larmier, Nimbus, Wreath

Coroner Procurator fiscal

Corporal Bardolph, Bodily, Bombardier, Brig(adier), Lance-pesade, Lance-prisade, Lance-prisado, Lance-speisade, NCO, Nym, Pall, Physical, Trim

Corporation Belly, Body, Commune, Company, Conglomerate, Guild, Kite, Kyte, Paunch, Stomach, Swag-belly, Tum, Wame, Wem

Corps Body, C, Crew, Diplomatic, Peace, RAC, REME, Unit

Corpse Blob, Body, Cadaver, Carcass, Carrion, Goner, Like, Mort, Relic, Remains, Stiff, Zombi(e)

Corpulence, Corpulent Adipose, Fat, Obese, Stout, Tubby

Corpuscle Cell, Erythrocyte, Malpighian, Meissner's, Microcyte, Neutrophil, Pacinian, Phagocyte

Correct(ing), Correctly, Correctness, Correction, Corrector Accurate, Alexander, Align, Amend, Aright, Bodkin, Castigate, Chasten, Chastise, Check, Decorous, Diorthortic, Emend, Exact, Fair, Grammatical, Legit, Mend, Preterition, Probity, Proofread, Proper, Propriety, Punctilious, Punish, Rebuke, Rectify, Redress, Remedial, Reprove, Revise, Right(en), Scold, Spot-on, Sumpsimus, Trew, True, U

▷ **Corrected** may indicate an anagram

Correspond(ence), Corresponding Accord, Agree, Analogy, Assonance, Coincident, Communicate, Congruence, Counterpart, Equate, Eye-rhyme, Fit, Homolog(ue), Identical, Match, On all fours, One to one, Par, Parallel, Relate, Symmetry, Tally, Veridical, Write

Corridor Air, Aisle, Gallery, Lobby, Passage

Corroborate Confirm, Support, Verify

Corrode(d), Corrosion, Corrosive Acid, Brinelling, Burn, Canker, Decay, Eat, Erode, Etch, Fret, Gnaw, Hydrazine, Mordant, ➤ ROT, Rubiginous, Rust, Waste

Corrugate Gimp

Corrupt(er), Corrupting, Corruption Adulterate, Bent, Bobol, Bribable, Canker, Debase, Debauch, Debosh, Decadent, Defile, Depravity, Dissolute, Dry rot, Emancipate, Embrace(o)r, Embrasor, Empoison, Etch, Fester, Gangrene, Graft(er), Immoral, Impure, Inquinate, Jobbery, Leprosy, Malversation, Nefarious, Obelus, Payola, Perverse, Poison, Pollute, Power, Ret(t), Rigged, Rot, Scrofulous, Seduce, Sepsis, Septic, Sleaze, Sodom, Sophisticate, Spoil, Suborn, Tammany, Twist, Venal, Vice, Vitiate

Corsage Buttonhole, Pompadour, Posy, Spray

Corsair Barbary, Picaroon, Pirate, Privateer, Robber, Rover

Corset, Corslet Belt, Bodice, Busk, Girdle, Lorica, Roll-on, Stays, Thorax, Waspie

Corsican Napoleon

Cortege Parade, Retinue, Train

Cortisone Hecogenin

Corundum Emery, Sapphire

Corvo Rolfe

Cosh Sap

Cosmetic Beautifier, Blusher, Eye-black, Eyeliner, Eye-shadow, Foundation, Fucus, Kohl, Lip gloss, Lip liner, Lipstick, Lotion, Maquillage, Mascara, Paint, Powder, Reface, Rouge, Talcum, Toner

➤ **Cosmic** see COSMOS

Cosmonaut Gagarin, Spaceman, Tereshkova

Cosmopolitan International, Urban

Cosmos, Cosmic Globe, Heaven, Infinite, Nature, Universe, World

Cossack Ataman, Hetman, Mazeppa, Russian, Tartar, Zaporogian

Cosset Caress, Coddle, Fondle, Pamper

Cost(ly) Bomb, Carriage, Charge, Damage, Earth, Escuage, Estimate, Exes, ➤ EXPENSE, Hire, Loss, Marginal, Outlay, Overhead, Precious, Price, Quotation, Rate, Sacrifice, Sumptuous, Toll, Unit, Upkeep, Usurious

Costa Rica(n) Tico

Costermonger Barrow-boy, Kerb-merchant, Pearly

Costume Apparel, Attire, Camagnole, Cossie, Dress, Ensemble, Get-up, Gi(e), Guise, Judogi, Livery, Maillot, Motley, Nebris, Polonaise, Rig, Surcoat, Tanga, Uniform

Cosy Cosh, Intime, Snug

Cot Moses basket

Coterie Cell, Cenacle, Circle, Clan, Clique, Club, Ring, Set, Society

Cottage(r) Bach, Bordar, Bothie, Bothy, Box, Bungalow, Cabin, Chalet, Cot, Crib, Dacha, Hut, Lodge, Mailer

Cotton Agree, AL, Alabama, Balbriggan, Batiste, Batting, Calico, Candlewick, Ceiba, Chambray, Chino, Chintz, Collodion, Coutil(le), Cretonne, Denim, Dho(o)ti, Dimity, Ducks, Fustian, Galatea, Gossypine, Gossypium, Humhum, Ihram, Jaconet, Lawn, Lea, Lille, Lint, Lisle, Manchester, Marcella, Muslin, Nainsook, Nankeen, Nankin, Pongee, Sea-island, Seersucker, Silesia, Stranded, Surat, T-cloth, Thread, Twig, Upland

Cotton soil Regar, Regur

Cotyledon Seed-leaf

Couch Bed, Davenport, Daybed, ➤ DIVAN, Express, Grass, Lurk, Palanquin, Palkee, Palki, Quick, Recamier, Sedan, Settee, Sofa, Studio, Triclinium, Word

Coué Auto-suggestion

Cougar Cat, Painter

Cough(ing) Bark, Croup, Expectorate, Hack, Hawk, Hem, Hoast, Kink, Pertussis, Phthisis, Rale, Tisick, Tussis, Ugh, Whooping

Could Couth

Council (meeting), Councillor, Counsel(lor) Achitophel, Admonish, Admonitor, Advice, Advocate, Ahithophel, Alfred, Amphictryon, Anziani, Aread, A(r)re(e)de, Assembly, Attorney, Aulic, Ayuntamiento, Board, Body, Boule, Bundesrat, Burgess, Cabinet, Casemate, Committee, Consistory, Corporation, County, Cr, Decurion, Dergue, Devil, Dietine, Divan, Douma, Duma, Egeria, Exhort, Greenbag, Hebdomadal, Indaba, Induna, Info, Jirga, Junta, Kabele, Kebele, Kite, Landst(h)ing, Lateran, Leader, Legislative, Majlis, Mentor, Nestor, Nicaean, Nicene, Panchayat, Paraclete, Parish, Powwow, Privy, Provincial, Rede, Reichsrat, Samaritan, Sanhedrim, Sanhedrin, Security, Senate, Shura, Sobranje, Sobranye, Soviet, Syndicate, Synedrion, Synod, Thing, Trent, Tridentine, Trullan, Volost, Whitley, Witan, Witenagemot, Works, Zila, Zillah

Count(ed), Counter, Counting Abacus, Add, Algoriam, Anti, Bar, Basie, Buck, Buffet, Calculate, Cavour, Census, Chip, Compute, Coost, Desk, Dracula, Dump, Earl, Enumerate, Fish, Geiger, Geiger-Muller, Graf(in), Grave, Itemise, Jet(t)on, Landgrave, Margrave, Matter, Merel(l), Meril, Number, Obviate, Olivia, Oppose, Palatine, Palsgrave, Paris, Pollen, Presume, Rebut, ➤ RECKON, Refute, Rejoinder, Rely, Retaliate, Retort, Rhinegrave, Scintillation, Score, Sperm, Squail, Statistician, Stop, Sum, Table, Tally, Tell, Tiddleywink, Ugolino, Weigh, Zeppelin

Countenance Approve, Endorse, Face, Favour, Mug, Sanction, Support, Visage

Counteract(ing) Ant-, Antidote, Cancel, Correct, Frustrate, Talion

Counterbalance Bascule, Offset, Undo, Weigh

Counter-charge Recrimination

Counterclockwise L(a)evorotatory

Counterfeit(er) Belie, Bogus, Boodle, Brum, Coiner, Duffer, Dummy, Fantasm, Flash, Forge, Imitant, Phantasm, Phoney, Pinchbeck, Postiche,

Pseudo, Queer, Rap, Sham, Schlenter, Shan(d), Simulate, Slang, Slip, Smasher, Snide, Spurious, Stumer

Counterglow Gegenschein

Counter-irritant Seton

Countermand Abrogate, Annul, Cancel, Override, Rescind, Retract, Revoke

Counterpart Copy, Double, Obverse, Oppo, Parallel, Similar, Spit(ting), Twin

Counterpoint Descant

Countersign Endorse, Password

Counterthrust Riposte

Countless Infinite, Innumerable, Myriad, Umpteen, Untold

Country Annam, Bangladesh, Boondocks, Bucolic, Champaign, Clime, Colchis, Edom, Enchorial, Fatherland, Karoo, Karroo, ➤ LAND, Lea, Lee, Mongolia, Motherland, Nation, Parish, Paysage, People, Province, Realm, Region, Republic, Rural, Satellite, Soil, State, Tundra, Weald, Wold, Yemen

Country girl Amaryllis

Country house Hall, Manor, Quinta

Countryman Arcadian, Bacon, Boor, Culchie, Hick, Hillbilly, Hodge, National, Native, Peasant, Un, Yokel

County Antrim, Armagh, Avon, Beds, Buteshire, Cavan, Champagne, Clare, Cleveland, Co, Comital, Cork, Cornwall, District, Donegal, Dorset, Down, Durham, Fife, Flint, Gwent, Gwynedd, Herts, Hunts, Kent, Kesteven, Kildare, Leitrim, Loamshire, Longford, Louth, Mayo, Meath, Midlothian, NI, Norfolk, Notts, Offaly, Omagh, Palatine, Parish, Powys, Roscommon, Ross, Seat, Shire, Som(erset), Suffolk, Sy, Tipperary, Tyrone, Waterford, Westmeath, Wexford, Wicklow, Wilts, Worcs

Coup Blow, Deal, KO, Move, Putsch, Scoop, Stroke

Coupé Cabriolet, Landaulet

Couple(r), Coupling Ally, Band, Brace, Bracket, Connect, Duet, Duo, Dyad, Fishplate, Gemini, Geminy, Hitch, Item, ➤ JOIN, Marry, Mate, Meng(e), Ment, Ming, Pair, Pr, Relate, Shackle, Tie, Tirasse, Turnbuckle, Tway, Union, Universal, Voltaic, Wed, Yoke

Couple of ducks Spectacles

Couplet Distich

Coupon(s) Ration, Ticket, Voucher

Courage(ous) Balls, Bottle, Bravado, Bravery, Bulldog, Dutch, Fortitude, Gallantry, Game, Gimp, Grit, Gumption, Guts, Heart, Heroism, Lion-heart, Macho, Mettle, Moxie, Nerve, Pluck, Rum, Spirit, Spunk, Stalwart, Steel, Valiant, Valour, Wight

Courgette Zucchini

Courier Estafette, Guide, Harbinger, Herald, ➤ MESSENGER, Postillion, Postman

Course(s) Afters, Aim, Aintree, Antipasto, Appetiser, Arroyo, Ascot, Assault, Atlantic, Bearing, Beat, Canal, Career, Chantilly, Chase, Circuit, Consommé, Correspondence, Crash, Current, Curriculum, Cursus, Dessert, Diadrom, Dish, Dromic, Entrée, Fish, Food, Foundation, Going,

Goodwood, Greats, Heat, Isodomon, Lane, Lap, Layer, Leat, Leet, Line, Lingfield, Links, Longchamp, Meal, Meat, Mess, Newbury, Newmarket, Nine-hole, Nulla, ➤ OF COURSE, Orbit, Period, Policy, PPE, Procedure, Process, Programme, Progress, Pursue, Quadrivium, Race, Raik, Refresher, Regimen, Rhumb, Ride, Ring, Rink, Road, Rota, Route, Routine, Run, Rut, Sandown, Sandwich, Semester, Series, Soup, Starter, Stearage, Steerage, Step(s), Stratum, Streak, Stretch, String, Syllabus, Tack, Tanride, Tenor, Track, Trade, Troon, Via media, Way

Court(ier) Address, Arches, Areopagus, Atrium, Attention, Audience, Audiencia, Aula, Banc, Bar, Basecourt, Bench, Beth Din, Boondock, Caravanserai, Cassation, Centre, Chancery, Chase, Clay, Consistory, County, Crown, CS, Ct, Curia, Curia Regis, Curtilage, Cutcher(r)y, Dale, Dedans, Dicastery, Diplock, District, Doctor's Commons, Duchy, Durbar, Dusty Feet, En tout cas, Evora, Eyre, Federal, Fehm(gericht), Fehmgerichte, Forensic, Forest, Forum, Fronton, Galleria, Garth, Grass, Guildenstern, Halimot(e), Hampton, Hard, High, Hof, Hustings, Hypaethron, Intermediate, Invite, Jack, Kachahri, Kacheri, Kangaroo, Keys, King, King's Bench, Kirk Session, Knave, Law, Leet, Lobby, Marshalsea, Moot, Old Bailey, Parvis, Patio, Peristyle, Philander, Piepowder, Porte, Praetorium, Presbytery, Probate, Provincial, Quad, Queen, Queen's Bench, Retinue, Royal, Sanhedrim, Sanhedrin, See, Session, Shire-moot, Spoon, Stannary, Star Chamber, Sue, Supreme, Swanimote, Sweetheart, Thane, Thegn, Tribunal, Vehm, Vehmgericht(e), Vestibulum, Ward, Wench, Woo, Wow, Yard

Courteous, Courtesy Affable, Agrement, Bow, Comity, Devoir, Etiquette, Genteel, Gracious, Hend, Polite, Refined, Urbanity

Courtesan Aspasia, Bona-roba, Delilah, Demi-monde, Demi-rep, Geisha, Hetaera, Lais, Lampadion, Lorette, Madam, Phryne, Plover, Pornocracy, Prostitute, Stallion, Thais

Courtly Chivalrous, Cringing, Dignified, Flattering, Refined

Court-martial Drumhead

Courtyard Area, Cortile, Marae, Patio, Quad

Cousin(s) Bette, Cater, Country, Coz, Cross, German, Kin, Kissing, Robin, Skater

Couturier Dior, Dressmaker

Cove Abraham's, Arm, Bay, Bight, Buffer, Creek, Cure, Gink, Grot, Guy, Hithe, Hythe, Inlet, Lulworth, Nook

Covenant(er) Abrahamic, Alliance, Bond, Contract, Hillmen, Pledge, Restrictive, Warranty, Whiggamore

Coventry Isolation

Cover(ed), Covering A l'abri, Adventitia, Amnion, Antependium, Antimacassar, Apron, Aril, Attire, Awning, Barb, Bard(s), Bark, Bedspread, Bestrew, Bind, Blanket, Bodice, Brood, Bubblewrap, Camouflage, Canopy, Cap, Caparison, Cape, Casing, Casque, Catch-all, Caul, Ceil, Ciborium, Cladding, Clapboard, Cleithral, Clithral, Coat, Cocoon, Coleorhiza, Conceal, Cope, Copyright, Cosy, Counterpane, Cour, Covert, Cowl, Curtain, Deck, Deputise, Dome, Drape(t), Dripstone, Dust-sheet, Duvet,

Eiderdown, Encase, Endue, Enguard, Enlace, Enshroud, Envelop(e), Exoderm(is), Exoskeleton, Extra, Face, Falx, Fanfare, Felting, Fielder, Figleaf, First-day, Flashing, Fother, Front, Gaiter, Gambado, Grolier, Ground, Hap, Harl, Hat, Hatch, Havelock, Heal, Heel, Hejab, Hele, Hell, Helmet, Hood, Housing, Hubcap, Immerse, Incase, Indusium, Insulate, Insurance, Insure, Jacket, Lag, Lay, Leap, Leep, Legging, Legwarmer, Lid, Manche, Mantle, Mount, Mulch, Notum, Numnah, OC, Obscure, Occlude, On, Operculum, Orillion, Orlop, Overlay, Palampore, Palempore, Pall, Pand, Parcel, Pasties, Patch, Pebbledash, Pelmet, Periderm, Plaster, Plate, Pleura, Point, Pseudonym, Pullover, Quilt, Radome, Regolith, Robe, Roof, Roughcast, Rug, Sally, Screen, Serviette, Setting, Sheath, Sheet, Shell, Shelter, Shield, Shrink-wrap, Shroud, Shuck, Skin, Smokescreen, Span, Spat, Stand-by, Stifle, Swathe, Tampian, Tampion, Tapis, Tarpaulin, Teacosy, Tectorial, Tegmen, Tegument, Tent, Test(a), Tester, Thatch, Thimble, Tick(ing), Tilt, Top, Trapper, Trench, Trip, Turtleback, Twill, Twilt, Umbrella, Upholster, Valance, Veil, Vele, Veneer, Ventail, Vesperal, Vest, Visor, Volva, Wainscot, Whelm, Whitewash, Wrap, Yapp

Covert(ly) Clandestine, Copse, Privy, ➤ SECRET, Shy, Sidelong, Sub rosa, Tectrix, Ulterior

Covet(ed), Covetous Avaricious, Crave, Desiderata, Desire, Eager, Envy, Greedy, Hanker, Yearn

Cow Adaw, Alderney, Amate, Appal, Awe, Bovine, Browbeat, Cash, Charolais, Colly, Crummy, Danton, Daunt, Dexter, Dsomo, Dun, Galloway, Gally, Goujal, Guernsey, Hawkey, Hawkie, Heifer, Hereford, Intimidate, Jersey, Kouprey, Kyloe, Mart, Milch, Mog(gie), Moggy, Mooly, Muley, Mulley, Overawe, Red Sindhi, Redpoll, Rother(-beast), Sacred, Santa Gertrudis, Scare, Simmental, Stirk, Subact, Teeswater, Threaten, Unnerve, Vaccine, Zebu, Z(h)o

Coward(ly) Bessus, Cat, Chicken, Cocoa, Craven, Cuthbert, Dastard, Dingo, Dunghill, Fraidy-cat, Fugie, Funk, Gutless, Hen, Hilding, Lily-livered, Meacock, Niddering, Nidderling, Nidering, Niderling, Niding, Nithing, Noel, Panty-waist, Poltroon, Pusillanimous, Recreant, Scaramouch, Sganarelle, Slag, Sook, Viliaco, Viliago, Villagio, Villiago, Yellow, Yellow-belly

Cowboy, Cowgirl Buckaroo, Gaucho, Inexpert, Io, Jerrybuilder, Leger, Llanero, Puncher, Ranchero, Ritter, Roper, Vaquero, Waddy, Wrangler

Cow-catcher Fender, Reata

Cower Croodle, Crouch, Fawn, Quail, Skulk, Wince

Cowl Bonnet, Capuchin, Granny, Hood, Kilmarnock

Cowshed, Cowstall Byre, Crib, Shippen, Shippon, Stable, Stall, Staw

Cowslip Culver-key, Pa(i)gle

Cox Steerer

Coxcomb Copple, Crest, Dandy, Dude, Fop, Jackanapes, Popinjay, Yellow-rattle

Coy Arch, Coquettish, Laithfu', Mim, Shamefast, ➤ SHY, Skeigh, Skittish

Coyote SD

CPRS Think tank

Crab(by), Crablike Apple, Attercop, Cancer, Cancroid, Cantankerous, Capernoity, Cock, Coconut, Daddy, Decapoda, Diogenes, Ethercap, Ettercap, Fiddler, Ghost, Grouch, Hard-shell, Hermit, Horseman, Horseshoe, King, Land, Limulus, Mantis, Mitten, Nebula, Ochidore, Oyster, Pagurian, Partan, Perverse, Podite, Roast, Robber, Rock, Saucepan-fish, Scrawl, Sentinel, Sidle, Soft-shell, Soldier, Spider, Xiphosura, Zoea

▷ **Crab** may indicate an anagram

Crab-apple Scrog-bush, Scrog-buss

Crab-eater Urva

Crabs-eye Abrus

Crack(ed), Cracker(s), Cracking Ad-lib, Admirable, Bananas, Biscuit, Bonbon, Break, Cat, Catalytic, Chap, Chasm, Chat, Chink, Chip, Chop, Clap, Cleave, Cleft, Cloff, Confab, Cranny, Craquelure, Craqueture, Craze, Cream, Crepitate, Crevasse, Crevice, Crispbread, Dawn, Decode, Doom, Dunt, Elite, Fatiscent, Fent, Firework, First-rate, Fisgig, Fissure, Fizgig, Flaw, Flip-flop, Fracture, Go, Graham, Grike, Gryke, Gully, Hairline, Hit, Jibe, Joint, Leak, Liar, Little-endian, Matzo, Moulin, Oner, Peterman, Pore, Praise, Prawn, Quip, Rap, Report, Rhagades, Rictus, Rift, Rille, Rima, Rime, Rimous, Rive, Rock, Saltine, Seam, Snap, Soda, Solve, Split, Squib, Sulcus, Top, Try, Waterloo, Yegg

Crackerjack Ace, Nailer, Trump

Crackle, Crackling Craze, Crepitation, Crepitus, Crinkle, Decrepitate, Fizz, Glaze, Skin

Crackpot Nutter

Cracksman Burglar, Peterman, Raffles

Cradle Bassinet, Berceau, Cat's, Cot, Crib, Cunabula, Hammock, Knife, Nestle, Rocker

Craft(y) Arch, Art, Aviette, Barbola, Boat, Canal boat, Cautel, Cunning, Disingenuous, Finesse, Fly, Guile, Hydroplane, Ice-breaker, Insidious, Kontiki, Landing, Machiavellian, Mister, Mystery, Oomiack, Reynard, Saic, Shallop, Ship, Shuttle, ➤ SKILL, Slee, Sleeveen, Slim, Slippy, Sly, Slyboots, State, Subdolous, Subtil(e), Subtle, Suttle, Triphibian, Umiak, Underhand, Versute, ➤ VESSEL, Wile, Workmanship

Craftsman AB, Artificer, Artisan, Artist, Chippy, Cutler, Ebonist, Fabergé, Finisher, Gondolier, Guild, Hand, Joiner, Journeyman, Mason, Mechanic, Morris, Opificer, Wainwright, Wright

Crag(gy) Eyrie, Height, Heuch, Heugh, Krantz, Noup

Cram(mer) Bag, Candle-waster, Cluster, Craig, Fill, Gag, Gavage, Neck, Pang, Prime, Rugged, Scar(p), Spur, Stap, Stodge, Stow, Swat, Tuck

Cramp(ed) Agraffe, Charleyhorse, Confine, Constrict, Crick, Hamper, Hamstring, Incommodious, Myalgia, Pinch, Poky, Potbound, Restrict, Rigor, Squeeze, Stunt, Tetany, Writer's

Crane Brolga, Cherry picker, Davit, Demoiselle, Derrick, Gantry, Herd, Heron, Hooper, Ichabod, Jib, Jigger, Luffing-jib, Rail, Sarus, Sedge, Shears, Sheer, Siege, Stork, Stretch, Whooper, Winch

Crane-fly Leatherjacket, Tipulidae

Crank(y) Eccentric, Grouch, Handle, Lever, Mot, Perverse, Whim, Wince, Winch, Wind

Crash Bingle, Collapse, Dush, Fail, Fall, Fragor, Intrude, Linen, Nosedive, Prang, Rack, Ram, Rote, Shunt, Slam, Smash, Thunderclap, Topple

▷ **Crashes** may indicate an anagram

Crass Coarse, Crude, Rough, Rude

Crate Biplane, Box, Case, Ceroon, Crib, Hamper, Sero(o)n, Tube

Crater Alphonsus, Aristarchus, Aristotle, Autolycus, Bailly, Caldera, Cavity, Clavius, Copernicus, Fra Mauro, Grimaldo, Hipparchus, Hollow, Hole, Maar, Plato, Sinus iridium, Theophilus, Tycho

Cravat Ascot, Neckatee, Neck-cloth, Oerlay, Overlay, Scarf, Soubise, Steenkirk, Tie

Crave, Craving Appetite, Aspire, Beg, Beseech, Covet, Desire, Entreat, Hanker, Hunger, Itch, Libido, Long, Lust, Malacia, Methomania, Orexis, Pica, Polyphagia, Sitomania, The munchies, Thirst, Yearn, Yen

Craven Abject, Coward, Dastard, Recreant

Crawl(er) All fours, Clamber, Creep, Cringe, Drag, Grovel, Lag, Lickspittle, Pub, Reptile, Scramble, Skulk, Snail, Swim, Sycophant, Tantony, Trail, Trudgen, Yes-man

Crayfish Astacology, Gilgie, Jilgie, Yabbie, Yabby

Crayon Chalk, Colour, Conté, Pastel, Pencil

Craze(d), Crazy Absurd, Ape, Barmy, Bats, Batty, Berserk, Bonkers, Break, Cornflake, Crack(ers), Crackpot, Cult, Daffy, Dement, Derange, Dingbats, Dippy, Distraught, Doiled, Doilt, Doolally, Dottle, Dotty, Fad, Flake, Flaw, Folie, Frantic, Furious, Furore, Gaga, Geld, Gonzo, Gyte, Haywire, Headbanger, Insane, Loco, Loony, Lunatic, Madden, Maenad(ic), Mania, Manic, Mattoid, Meshug(g)a, Nuts, Porangi, Potty, Psycho(path), Rage, Rave, Scatty, Screwball, Skivie, Stunt, Unhinge, Wacko, Wacky, Wet, W(h)acky, Whim, Wowf, Zany

Creak(y) Cry, Grate, Grind, Rheumatic, Scraich, Scraigh, Scroop, Seam, Squeak

Cream(y) Barrier, Bavarian, Best, Chantilly, Cold, Crème fraiche, Devonshire, Double, Elite, Foundation, Glacier, Lanolin, Liniment, Lotion, Mousse, Off-white, Ointment, Opal, Paragon, Pick, Ream, Rich, Salad, Sillabub, Single, Skim, Syllabub, Vanishing

Crease Crumple, ➤ FOLD, Lirk, Pitch, Pleat, Popping, Ridge, Ruck(le), Ruga, Rugose, Wrinkle

Create, Creation Build, Coin, Compose, Devise, Dreamtime, Engender, Establish, Fabricate, Forgetive, Form, Found, Generate, Genesis, Godhead, Ideate, ➤ INVENT, Oratorio, Originate, Produce, Shape, Universe

Creator Ahura Mazda, Author, Demiurge, God, Inventor, Maker, Ormazd, Ormuzd

Creature Animal, Ankole, Basilisk, Beast, Being, Chevrotain, Cratur, Critter, Crittur, Man, Nekton, Sasquatch, Sphinx, Whiskey, Wight

Credence, Credential(s) Certificate, Document, Papers, Qualifications, Shelf, Testimonial

Credibility Street

Credible, Credit(or) Ascribe, Attribute, Belief, Byline, Esteem, Honour, HP, Kite, Kudos, LC, Lender, Mense, Probable, Reliable, Renown, Shylock, Strap, Tally, Tick, Title, Trust, Weight

Credulous Charlie, Gullible, Naive, Simple, Trusting

Creed Apostle's, Athanasian, Belief, Doctrine, Faith, Ism, Nicene, Ophism, Outworn, Sect, Tenet

Creek Bay, Breaches, Cove, Estuary, Fleet, Goe, Indian, Inlet, Pow, Slough, Vae, Voe, Wick

Creel Basket, Hask, Scull, Skull

Creep(er), Creeping, Creeps Ai, Ampelopsis, Arbutus, Aseismic, Cleavers, Crawl, Grew, Grovel, Grue, Heebie-jeebies, Heeby-jeebies, Herpetic, Inch, Insect, Ivy, Nerd, Nuthatch, Pussyfoot, Repent, Reptant, Sarmentous, Sittine, Skulk, Slink, Snake, Sobole(s), Toad, Tropaeolum, Truckle, Vine, Virginia, Willies

Creeping Jenny Moneywort

Cremate, Cremation, Crematorium Burn, Char, Cinerarium, Ghaut, Incinerate, Pyre, Sati, Suttee, Ustrinium

Creole Gullah, Haitian, Kriol, Papiamento, Tok Pisin

Crepe Blini, Blintz(e), Canton, Pancake

Crescent Barchan(e), Bark(h)an, Fertile, Lune(tte), Lunulate, Lunule, Meniscus, Moon, Red, Sickle, Waxing

Cress Cardamine, Isatis

Crest(ed) Acme, Chine, Cimier, Cockscomb, Comb, Copple, Crista, Height, Kirimon, Knap, Mon, Peak, Pileate, Pinnacle, Plume, Ridge, Summit, Tappit, Tee, ➤ TOP

Cretaceous Chalky, Senonian

Cretan Minoan

Crevasse Bergschrund, Chasm, Gorge, Rimaye

Crew Boasted, Company, Core, Eight, Equipage, Four, Lot, Manners, Men, Oars, Sailors, Salts, Seamen, Team, Teme, Torpid

Crew-cut Not(t)

Crib Cheat, Cot, Cowhouse, Cratch, Filch, Horse, ➤ KEY, Manger, Pony, Purloin, Putz, Shack, Stall, Steal, Trot

Crick Cramp, Kink, Spasm

Cricket(er) Balm, Bat, Botham, Bowler, Bradman, CC, Cicada, Dry-bob, French, Grasshopper, Grig, Hopper, Jerusalem, Katydid, Keeper, Knott, Leg, Long-leg, Long-off, Long-on, Longstop, March, May, Mid-on, Mole, Muggleton, Nightwatchman, Opener, Packer, Point, Slip, Stridulate, Tate, Test, Tettix, Tip and run, Warner, Windball, Wisden, XI(gent)

Crier Bellman, Herald, Muezzin, Niobe, Outrooper

Crime Attentat, Barratry, Caper, Chantage, Chaud-mellé, Computer, Corpus delicti, Ecocide, Fact, Felony, Fraud, Graft, Heist, Iniquity,

Malefaction, Mayhem, Misdeed, Misdemeanour, ➤ OFFENCE, Organised, Ovicide, Peccadillo, Perjury, Pilferage, Rap, Rape, Rebellion, ➤ SIN, Tort, Transgression, Treason, Wrong

Criminal Bent, Bushranger, Con, Cosa Nostra, Counterfeiter, Crack-rope, ➤ CROOK, Culpable, Culprit, Delinquent, Escroc, Felon, Flagitious, Forensic, Gangster, Heavy, Heinous, Highbinder, Hood(lum), Jailbird, Ladrone, Lag, Larcener, Looter, Lowlife, Maf(f)ia, Malefactor, Maleficent, Mob(ster), Mobster, Ndrangheta, Nefarious, Nefast, Outlaw, Perp(etrator), Racketeer, Receiver, Recidivist, Rustler, Triad, Underworld, Villain, Wicked, Wire, Yakuza, Yardie, Yegg

▷ **Criminal** may indicate an anagram

Crimp Pleat

Crimson Carmine, Incarnadine, Modena, Red, Scarlet

Cringe, Cringing Cower, Creep, Crouch, Fawn, Grovel, Shrink, Sneaksby, Truckle

Crinkle, Crinkly Rugate, Rugose

Crinoline Farthingale, Hoop

Cripple(d) Damage, Disable, Game, Hamstring, Handicap, Injure, ➤ LAME, Lameter, Lamiter, Maim, Paralyse, Polio, Scotch, Spoil

Crisis Acme, Crunch, Drama, Emergency, Exigency, Fastigium, Fit, Flap, Head, Identity, Make or break, Mid-life, Panic, Pass, Shake-out, Solution, Test

Crisp Brisk, Clear, Crimp, Crunchy, Fresh, Sharp, Short, Succinct, Terse

Crispin Sutor(ial)

Criss-cross Alternate, Fret, Interchange, Vein

Criterion Benchmark, Gauge, Measure, Precedent, Proof, Rule, Shibboleth, ➤ STANDARD, Test, Touchstone

Critic(al), Criticism, Criticize Acute, Agate, Animadversion, Archer, Aristarch, Armchair, Arnold, Attack, Badmouth, Bagehot, Barrack, Bellettrist, Bird, Blame, Boileau, Captious, Carp, Castigate, Cavil, Censor(ious), ➤ CENSURE, Climacteric, Clobber, Comment, Condemn, Connoisseur, Crab, Criticaster, ➤ CRUCIAL, Crunch, Dangle, Decisive, Denigrate, Denounce, Deprecate, Desperate, Diatribe, Dutch uncle, Etain, Exacting, Excoriate, Fastidious, Fateful, Feuilleton, Flak, Flay, Gosse, Harrumph, Important, Impugn, Inge, Inveigh, Judge, Knock(er), Lash, Leavis, Masora(h), Mas(s)orete, Mordacious, Nag, Nasute, Nibble, Nice, Niggle, Pan, Pater, Puff, Pundit, Quibble, Rap, Rebuke, Reprehend, Review(er), Rip, Roast, Ruskin, Scalp, Scarify, Scathe, Scorn, Serious, Severe, Shaw, Sideswipe, Slag, Slam, Slashing, Slate, Sneer, Snipe, Stick, Stricture, Strop, Tense, Textual, Threap, Touch and go, Ultracrepidate, Urgent, Vet, Vituperation, Zoilism

Croak Creak, Crow, Die, Grumble, Gutturalise

Croatian Cravates, Glagolitic, Serb

Crochet Lace, Weave

Crock Crate, Jar, Mug, Pig, Pitcher, Pot, Potshard, Potshare, Potsherd, Stean(e)

Crockery Ceramics, China, Dishes, Earthenware, Oddment, Ware

▷ **Crocks** may indicate an anagram

Crocodile Cayman, File, Garial, Gavial, Gharial, Line, Mugger, River-dragon, Saltwater, Sebek, Teleosaur(ian)

Crocus Autumn, Saffron

Croesus Lydia

Cromwell(ian) Ironside, Noll, Oliver, Protector, Richard, Roundhead

Crone(s) Beldam(e), Ewe, Graeae, Hag, Mawkin, Ribibe, Rudas, Sibyl, Sybil, Trot, Trout, ➤ WITCH

Crony Anile, Chum, Intimate, Mate, Pal, Sidekick

Crook(ed) Adunc, Ajee, Awry, Bad, Bend, Bow, Cam, Camsho(ch), Camsheugh, Criminal, Cromb, Crome, Crosier, Crummack, Crummock, Crump, Curve, Elbow, Fraud, Heister, Hook, Indirect, Kam(me), Kebbie, Lituus, Malpractitioner, Shyster, Sick, Skew(whiff), Slick(er), Staff, Swindler, Thraward, Thrawart, Thrawn, Twister, Wonky, Yeggman

▷ **Crooked** may indicate an anagram

Croon(er), Crooning Bing, Como, Lament, Lull, Monody, Murmur, Sing

Crop(s), Cropped Basset, Browse, Cash, Catch, Clip, Craw, Cut, Distress, Dock, Emblements, Epilate, Eton, Foison, Forage, Harvest, Hog, Ingluvies, Kharif, Milo, Not(t), Plant, Poll, Produce, Riding, Rod, Root, Shingle, Stow, Succession, Top, Truncate

Cropper Downfall, Header, Purler

Croquet (Croquet term) Peel

Croquette Kromesky, Rissole

Cross(ing), Crossbred Angry, Ankh, Ansate, Archiepiscopal, Basta(a)rd, Beefalo, Boton(n)e, Burden, Calvary, Cantankerous, Capital, Cattalo, Celtic, Channel, Chi, Chiasm(a), Cleche, Clover-leaf, Compital, Constantine, Crosslet, Crotchety, Crucifix, Crux, Decussate, Demi-wolf, Dihybrid, Dso(mo), Dzobo, Eleanor, Encolpion, Faun, Fiery, Fitché, Fleury, Foil, Footbridge, Ford, Frabbit, Fractious, Frampold, Franzy, Funnel, Fylfot, Geneva, George, Grade, Greek, Holy rood, Humette, Hybrid, Ill, Imp, Indignant, Interbreed, Intersect, Intervein, Iracund, Irate, Irked, Iron, Jerusalem, Jomo, Jumart, Krest, Ladino, Latin, Level, Liger, Lorraine, Lurcher, Maltese, Mameluco, Mermaid, Military, Mix, Moline, Mongrel, Mule, Narky, Nattery, Node, Northern, Nuisance, Ordinary, Orthodox, Overpass, Overthwart, Papal, Patonce, Patriarchal, Patté, Pectoral, Pelican, Plumcot, Plus, Pommé, Potence, Potent, Quadrate, Ratty, Red, Rood, Rouen, Rouge, Rubicon, Ruthwell, Sain, St Andrew's, St Anthony's, St George's, Saltier, Saltire, Satyr, Shirty, Sign, Snappy, Southern, Strid, Svastika, Swastika, Tangelo, Tau, Ten, Testy, Thraw, Thwart, Tiglon, Tigon, Times, Transit, Transom, Transverse, Traverse, Tree, Urdé, Vexed, Vext, Victoria, ➤ VOTE, Weeping, Whippet, Wry, X, Yakow, Zambo, Zebra(ss), Zebrinny, Zebroid, Zebrula, Zebrule, Z(h)o, Zedonk, Zobu

▷ **Cross** may indicate an anagram

▶ **Cross-bar** see CROSSPIECE

Cross-bearer Crucifer

Cross-bill Metagnathous
Cross-bow Arbalest, Bal(l)ista
Cross-country Langlauf, Overland
Cross-dressing Eonism
Cross-examine Grill, Interrogate, Question, Targe
Cross-fertilisation Allogamy, Heterosis, Xenogamy
Cross-grained Ill-haired, Mashlam, Mashlim, Mas(h)lin, Mashlock, Mashlum, Stubborn
Crosspiece, Cross-bar, Cross-timber Bar, Cancelli, Footrail, Inter-tie, Lierne, Phillipsite, Putlock, Putlog, Serif, Seriph, Stempel, Stemple, Stretcher, Stull, Swingle-tree, Toggle, Transom, Whiffle-tree, Whipple-tree, Yoke
Crossroads Carfax, Carfox, Compital, Soap
Crossword Cryptic, Grid, Puzzle, Quickie
Crotchet(y) Eccentric, Fad, Fancy, Grouch, Kink, Toy
Crouch Bend, Cringe, Falcade, Fancy, Lordosis, Ruck, Set, Squat, Squinch
Croup Angina, Cough, Kink, Rump
Crow Boast, Brag, Carrion, Chewet, Chough, Corbie, Corvus, Crake, Currawong, Daw, Gorcrow, Hooded, Hoodie, Huia, Jackdaw, Jim(my), Murder, Raven, Rook, Skite, Squawk, Swagger, Vaunt
Crowbar Gavelock, James, Jemmy, Lever
Crowd(ed) Abound, Army, Bike, Boodle, Bumper, Bunch, Byke, Caboodle, Clutter, Concourse, Cram, Crush, Crwth, Dedans, Doughnut, Drove, Fill, Flock, Galere, Gate, Gathering, Herd, Horde, ➤ HOST, Huddle, Jam, Lot, Meinie, Mein(e)y, Menyie, Mob, Mong, Ochlo-, Pack, Pang, Press, Rabble, Raft, Ram, Ratpack, Ring, Ruck, Scrooge, Scrouge, Scrowdge, Scrum, Serr(é), Shoal, Shove, Slew, Slue, Squeeze, Stuff, Swarm, Swell, Three, Throng, Trinity, Varletry
Crowfoot Gilcup, Reate
Crown Acme, Bays, Bull, Camp, Cantle, Cap, Capernoity, Cidaris, Civic, Coma, Corona, Cr, Diadem, Ecu, Engarland, Enthrone, Fillet, Garland, Gloria, Haku, Head, Headdress, Instal, Iron, Ivy, Krantz, Laurel, Monarch, Mural, Naval, Nole, Noll, Noul(e), Nowl, Olive, Ore, Ovation, Pate, Peak, Pschent, Sconce, Taj, Tiara, ➤ TOP, Triple, Triumphal, Trophy, Vallary, Vertex
Crucial Acute, Critical, Essential, Key, Pivotal, Vital, Watershed
Crucible Cruset, Melting-pot, Vessel
Crucifix, Crucify Cross, Mortify, Rood, Torment, Torture
Crude Bald, Brash, Brute, Earthy, Halfbaked, Immature, Incondite, Primitive, Raw, Rough, Rough and ready, Rough-hewn, Rough-wrought, Tutty, Uncouth, Vulgar, Yahoo
Cruel Barbarous, Bloody, Brutal, Dastardly, De Sade, Draconian, Fell, Fiendish, Flinty, Hard, Heartless, Immane, Inhuman, Machiavellian, Neronic, Pitiless, Raw, Remorseless, Sadist(ic), Stern, Tormentor, Vicious
▷ **Cruel** may indicate an anagram

Cruet Ampulla, Condiments, Decanter

Cruise(r) Busk, Cabin, Nuke, Prowl, Sail, Ship, Tom, Travel, Trip, Voyager

Crumb(le), Crumbly, Crumbs Coo, Decay, Disintegrate, Ee, Fragment, Friable, Law, Leavings, Moulder, Mull, Murl, Nesh, Nirl, Ort, Particle, Ped, Raspings, Rot

Crumpet Dish, Girl, Muffin, Nooky, Pash, Pikelet

Crumple Collapse, Crunkle, Crush, Raffle, Scrunch, Wrinkle

Crunch(y) Chew, Craunch, Crisp, Gnash, Grind, Munch, Occlude, Scranch

Crusade(r) Baldwin, Campaign, Cause, Pilgrim, Tancred

Crush(ed), Crusher Acis, Anaconda, Annihilate, Bow, Champ, Comminute, Conquer, Contuse, Cranch, Crunch, Destroy, Graunch, Grind, Hug, Jam, Knapper, Levigate, Mangle, Mash, Molar, Oppress, Overcome, Overwhelm, Pash, Policeman, Pound, Press, Pulp, Pulverise, Quash, Ruin, Schwarmerei, Scotch, Scrum, Smash, Squabash, Squash, Squeeze, Squelch, Squish, Stamp, Stave, Steam-roll, Stove, Suppress, Telescope, Trample

Crust(y) Argol, Beeswing, Cake, Coating, Coffin, Continental, Cover, Crabby, Craton, Fur, Gratin, Heel, Horst, Kissing, Kraton, Lithosphere, Osteocolla, Pie, Reh, Rind, Rine, Sal, Salband, Scab, Shell, Sial, Sima, Sinter, Surly, Tartar, Teachie, Terrane, Tetchy, Upper, Wine-stone

Crustacea(n) Amphipod, Barnacle, Brachyuran, Branchiopoda, Camaron, Cirriped, Cirripede, Cirripid, Cladoceran, Copepod, Crab, Crayfish, Cumacean, Cyclops, Cyprid, Cypris, Decapod(a), Entomostraca, Euphausia, Fishlouse, Foot-jaw, Gribble, Isopod, Krill, Lobster, Macrura, Malacostracan, Maron, Nauplius, Ostracoda, Pagurian, Phylliopod, Prawn, Rhizocephalan, Sand-hopper, Scampi, Scampo, Schizopod, Shrimp, Slater, Squilla, Stomatopod, Woodlouse

Crux Essence, Nub

Cry(ing) Aha, Alalagmus, Alew, Banzai, Bark, Battle, Bawl, Bell, Blat, Bleat, Bleb, Blub(ber), Boo, Boohoo, Bray, Bump, Caramba, Caw, Cheer, Chevy, Chirm, Chivy, Clang, Crake, Croak, Crow, Dire, Euoi, Eureka, Evoe, Exclaim, Fall, Field-holler, Gardyloo, Geronimo, Gowl, Greet, Halloo, Harambee, Haro, Harrow, Havoc, Heigh, Hemitrope, Herald, Hinny, Holler, Hoo, Hoop, Hosanna, Hout(s)-tout(s), Howl, Humph, Io, Kaw, Low, Mewl, Miaou, Miau(l), Miserere, Mourn, Night-shriek, O(c)hone, Oi, Olé, Ow, Pugh, Rivo, Sab, Scape, Scream, Screech, Sell, Sese(y), Sessa, ➤ SHOUT, Shriek, Slogan, Snivel, Snotter, Sob, Soho, Sola, Squall, Squawk, Tantivy, Umph, Vagitus, Vivat, Vociferate, Wail, War, Watchword, Waul, Wawl, Weep, Westward ho, Whee(ple), Whimper, Whine, Whinny, Whoa, Whoop, Winge, Wolf, Yammer, Yelp, Yikker, Yippee, Yodel, Yoick, Yoop, Yowl

Crypt(ic) Catacomb, Cavern, Chamber, Crowde, Encoded, Favissa, Grotto, Hidden, Obscure, Occult, Secret, Sepulchre, Short, Steganographic, Tomb, Unclear, Undercroft, Vault

Cryptogam Acotyledon, Acrogen, Fern(-ally), Moss, Pteridophyte

Crystal(s), Crystal-gazer, Crystalline, Crystallise Allotriomorphic, Axinite, Baccara(t), Beryl, Candy, Clathrate, Clear, Copperas, Coumarin,

Cumarin, Dendrite, Druse, Enantiomorph, Epitaxy, Erionite, Geode, Glass, Hemihedron, Hemimorphic, Hemitrope, Ice-stone, Imazadole, Jarosite, Lead, Liquid, Lithium, Love-arrow, Macle, Macro-axis, Melamine, Nicol, Orthogonal, Orthorhombic, Pellucid, Phenocryst, Piezo, Piezoelectric, Pinacoid, Pinakoid, Prism, Pseudomorph, Purin(e), Quartz, R(h)aphide, R(h)aphis, Rhinestone, Rock, Rotenone, Rubicelle, Scryer, Shoot, Skryer, Smectic, Snowflake, Sorbitol, Spar, Spicule, Table, Trichite, Trilling, Watch-glass, Xanthene, Xenocryst

Cub Baby, Kit, Novice, Pup, Whelp

Cube, Cubic, Cubist Bath, Braque, Cu, Die, Nosean, Quadrate, Rubik's®, Serac, Smalto, Solid, Stere, Stock

Cubicle Alcove, Booth, Carrel(l), Stall

Cuckold Actaeon, Cornute, Homer, Lenocinium, Wittol

Cuckoo Ament, Ani, April fool, Bird, Gouk, Gowk, Inquiline, Insane, Koel, ➤ MAD, Mental, Piet-my-vrou, Stupid

▷ **Cuckoo** may indicate an anagram

Cuckoopint Arum

Cucumber Choko, Colocynth, Coloquintida, Dill, Elaterium, Gherkin, Pickle, Sea-slug, Squirting, Trepang, Wolly

Cuddle Canoodle, Caress, Clinch, Embrace, Fondle, Hug, Nooky, Smooch, Smuggle, Snuggle

Cudgel Alpeen, Ballow, Bludgeon, Brain, Club, Cosh, Drub, Fustigate, Plant, Shillelagh, Souple, Stick, Tan, Towel, Truncheon

Cue Cannonade, Catchword, Feed, Half-butt, Hint, Mace, ➤ PROMPT, Reminder, Rod, Sign, Signal, Wink

Cuff Box, Buffet, Clout, Iron, Strike, Swat

Cuirass Armour, Corselet, Lorica

Cuisine Cookery, Food, Menu, Nouvelle

Cul-de-sac Blind, Dead-end, Impasse, Loke

Cull Gather, Pick, Select, Thin, Weed

Culminate, Culmination Apogean, Apogee, Climax, Conclusion, Crest, End

Culpable Blameworthy

Cult Cabiri, Cargo, Creed, Rastafarian, Sect, Shinto, Wicca, Worship

Cultivate(d), Cultivation Agronomy, Arty, Civilise, Dig, Dress, Farm, Genteel, Grow, Hoe, Hydroponics, Improve, Labour, Pursue, Raise, Refine, Sative, Sophisticated, Tame, Tasteful, Till, Tilth

Culture(d), Cultural Acheulean, Acheulian, Agar, Art(y), Aurignacian, Azilian, Bel esprit, Brahmin, Capsian, Civil(isation), Ethnic, Experiment, Explant, Gel, Grecian, Hallstatt, Hip-hop, Humanism, Kultur(kreis), La Tène, Learning, Mousterian, Polish, Refinement, Solutrean, Sophisticated, Strepyan, Tissue

Cumbersome Clumsy, Heavy, Lumbering, ➤ UNWIELDY

Cunctator Dilatory

Cuneiform Wedge(d)

Cunning Arch, Art, Artifice, Cautel, Craft(y), Deceit, Deep, Devious, Down, Finesse, Foxy, Insidious, Leery, Machiavellian, Quaint, Skill, Slee(kit), Sleight, Slim, Sly(boots), Smart, Sneaky, Subtle, Vulpine, Wile

Cup(s), Cupped Aecidium, America's, Beaker, Calcutta, Calix, Calyculus, Cantharus, Chalice, Claret, Cotyle, Cruse, Cupule, Cyathus, Cylix, Davis, Demitasse, Deoch-an-doruis, Deuch-an-doris, Dish, Doch-an-dorach, Dop, Final, Fingan, Finjan, Glenoid, Goblet, Grace, Hanap, Horn, Kylix, Loving, Melbourne, Merry, Monstrance, Moustache, Mug, Noggin, Nut, Pannikin, Planchet, Plate, Pot, Procoelus, Quaich, Quaigh, Rhyton, Rider, Ryder, Sangrado, Scyphus, Stirrup, Tantalus, Tass(ie), Tastevin, Tazza, Tea-dish, Tig, Tot, ➤ TROPHY, Tyg, Volva, World

Cup-bearer Ganymede, Hebe

Cupboard Almery, Almirah, A(u)mbry, Beauf(f)et, Cabinet, Chiffonier, Chiff(o)robe, Closet, Court, Credenza, Dresser, Locker, Press

Cup-holder Hanaper, Hebe, Plinth, Saucer, Zarf, Zurf

Cupid Amoretto, Amorino, Archer, Blind, Cherub, Dan, Eros, Love, Putto

Cupola Belfry, Dome, Tholos

Cup-shaped Poculiform

Cur Dog, Messan, Mongrel, Mutt, Pi-dog, Scab, Scoundrel, Wretch, Yap

Curare, Curari Ourali, Wourali

Curassow Crax

Curate Minister, Nathaniel, Padré, Priest

Curb Bit, Brake, Bridle, Check, Clamp, Coaming, Dam, Edge, Puteal, Rein, Restrain, Rim, Snub

Curd(s) Cheese, Junket, Lapper(ed)-milk, Skyr, Tofu

Curdle Congeal, Clot, Earn, Erne, Lopper, Posset, Rennet, Run, Set, Sour, ➤ TURN, Whig, Yearn

Cure(d), Curative Amend, Antidote, Antirachitic, Bloater, Cold turkey, Dry-salt, Euphrasy, Ginseng, Hobday, Heal, Jadeite, Jerk, Kipper, Medicinal, Nostrum, Panacea, Park-leaves, ➤ PRESERVE, Recover, Recower, Reest, Remede, Remedy, Restore, Salt, Salve, Serum, Smoke, Smoke-dry, Tan, ➤ TREATMENT, Tutsan

▷ **Cure** may indicate an anagram

Curfew Gate, Prohibit, Proscribe

Curie Ci

Curio, Curiosity, Curious Agog, Bibelot, Freak, Inquisitive, Meddlesome, Nos(e)y, Objet d'art, Objet de vertu, Odd, Peculiar, Prurience, Rarity, Rum, ➤ STRANGE

▷ **Curious(ly)** may indicate an anagram

Curium Cm

Curl(er), Curling, Curly Bonspiel, Cirrus, Coil, Crimp, Crimple, Crinkle, Crisp, Crocket, Dildo, Earlock, Friz(z), Frizzle, Heart-breaker, Hog, Inwick, Kiss, Leaf, Loop, Love-lock, Outwick, Perm, Pin, Quiff, Repenter, Ringlet, Roll, Roulette, Shaving, Spiral, Spit, Twiddle, ➤ TWIST, Ulotrichous, Wave, Wind

Curlew Bird, Whaup, Whimbrel

Curmudgeon Boor, Churl, Grouch, Route, Runt

Currant Berry, Raisin, Rizard, Rizzar(t), Rizzer

Currency Cash, Circulation, ➤ COIN, Coinage, Decimal, Euro, Finance, Jiao, Kip, Koruna, Monetary, ➤ MONEY, Prevalence

▷ **Currency** may indicate a river

Current Abroad, AC, Actual, Alternating, Amperage, Amp(ere), California, Canary, Contemporaneous, Cromwell, DC, Direct, Draught, Drift, Dynamo, Ebbtide, Electric, El Nino, Equatorial, Euripus, Existent, Flow, Foucault, Going, Humboldt, I, Immediate, Inst, Intermittent, Japan, Kuroshio, Labrador, Millrace, Modern, Newsy, Now, Ongoing, Present, Prevalent, Race, Rapid, Rife, Rip, Roost, Running, Stream, Thames, Thermal, Thermionic, Tide, Topical, Torrent, Turbidity, Underset, Undertow

Curriculum Cursal, Programme

Curry Bhuna, Brush, Comb, Cuittle, Dhansak, Fawn, Groom, Ingratiate, Korma, Spice, Tan, Turmeric, Vindaloo

Curse Abuse, Anathema, Badmouth, Ban, Bane, Beshrew, ➤ BLASPHEME, Blast, Chide, Dam(me), Damn, Dee, Drat, Excommunicate, Execrate, Heck, Hex, Imprecate, Jinx, Malison, Maranatha, Mau(l)gré, Mockers, Moz(z), Mozzle, Oath, Pize, Plague, Rant, Rats, Scourge, Spell, Swear, Upbraid, Weary, Winze, Wo(e)

Cursive Run

Cursor Mouse, Turtle

Cursorily, Cursory Casual, Hasty, Lax, Obiter, Passing, Sketchy, Speedy, Superficial

Curt Abrupt, Blunt, Crusty, Laconic, Offhand, Short, Snappy

Curtail(ment) Apocope, Crop, Cut, Reduce, Shorten

Curtain(s), Curtain-rod Arras, Backdrop, Bamboo, Canopy, Caudle, Cloth, Death, Demise, Drape, Drop, Dropcloth, Dropscene, Fatal, Hanging, Iron, Louvre, Net, Pall, Portière, Purdah, Safety, Scene, Screen, Scrim, Tab, Tormentor, Tringle, Vail, Valance, Veil, Vitrage

Curtsey Bob, Bow, Dip, Dop

Curve(d), Curvy, Curvature, Curvaceous Adiabatic, Aduncate, Apophyge, Arc, Arch, Archivolt, Axoid, Bend, Bow, Camber, Cardioid, Catacaustic, Catenary, Caustic, Cissoid, Conchoid, Contrapposto, Crescent, Cycloid, Diacaustic, Entasis, Epicycloid, Epinastic, Epitrochoid, Ess, Evolute, Exponental, Extrados, Felloe, Felly, Gaussian, Geodesic, Gooseneck, Growth, Hance, Helix, Hodograph, Hyperbola, Hypocycloid, Inswing, Intrados, Isochor, J, Jordan, Kyphosis, Laffer, Learning, Lemniscate, Limacon, Liquidus, Lituus, Lordosis, Loxodrome, Nowy, Ogee, Parabola, Pothook, Rhumb, Roach, Rotundate, Scoliosis, Sheer, Sinuate, Spiral, Spiric, Strophoid, Swayback, Tautochrone, Tie, Tractrix, Trajectory, Trochoid, Tumble-home, Twist, Undulose, Witch

Cushion Air, Allege, Bolster, Buffer, Hassock, ➤ PAD, Pillow, Pouf(fe), Pulvillus, Soften, Squab, Upholster, Whoopee

Cusp Horn, Tine, Spinode

Custard (apple) Flam(m), Flan, Flaune, Flawn, Flummery, Pa(w)paw, Zabaglione

Custodian, Custody Care, Claviger, Guard, Hold, Janitor, Keeping, Sacrist, Steward, Trust, Ward

Custom(ary), Customs Agriology, Coast-waiters, Consuetude, Conventional, Couvade, De règle, Douane, Exciseman, Familiar, Fashion, Folklore, ➤ HABIT, Lore, Manner, Montem, Mores, Nomic, Octroi, Ordinary, Practice, Praxis, Relic, Rite, Routine, Rule, Sororate, Sunna, Tax, Thew, Tidesman, Tradition, Unwritten, Usance, Used, Usual, Won, Wont, Woon, Zollverein

Customer Client, Cove, Patron, Prospect, Purchaser, Shillaber, Shopper, Smooth, Trade, Trick

Cut(ter), Cutting Abate, Abjoint, Abridge, Abscission, Abscond, Acute, Adeem, Adze, Aftermath, Ali Baba, Amputate, Apocope, Axe, Bang, Bisect, Bit, Bite, Bowdlerise, Boycott, Brilliant, Broach, Caesarean, Caique, Canal, Cantle, Caper, Carve, Castrate, Caustic, Censor, Chap, Chisel, Chop, Chynd, Circumscribe, Clinker-built, Clip, Colter, Commission, Concise, Coulter, Coupé, Crew, Crop, Cruel, Culebra, Curtail, Deadhead, Decrease, Dice, Die, Discide, Disengage, Dismember, Dissect, Division, Divorce, Dock, Dod, Edge, Edit, Emarginate, Embankment, Engrave, Entail, Entayle, Epistolary, Epitomise, Eschew, Estrepe, Excalibur, Excide, Excise, Exscind, Exsect, Exude, Fashion, Fell, Fillet, Flench, Flense, Flinch, Form, Froe, Frow, Gaillard, Garb, Gash, Grate, Graven, Gride, Gryde, Hack, Handsaw, Hew(er), Ignore, Incision, Incisor, Indent, Intersect, Jigsaw, Joint, Junk, Kerf, Kern, Kirn, Lacerate, Lance, Leat, Lesion, Lin, Lop, Math, Medallion, Microtome, Milling, Mohel, Mortice, Mortise, Mow, Nache, Nick, Not, Notch, Nott, Occlude, Omit, Open, Operate, Osteotome, Oxyacetylene, Padsaw, Pare, Pink, Plant, Pliers, Ploughshare, Pollard, Pone, Power, Precisive, Proin, Quota, Race, Rake off, Rase, Razor, Re-enter, Reap, Rebate, Reduction, Resect, Retrench, Revenue, Ring, Ripsaw, Roach, Rose, Rout, Saddle, Sarcastic, Saw(n), Scarf, Scathing, Scion, Scission, Scissor, Score, Sculpt, Scye, Scythe, Secant, Secateurs, Sect, Sever, Sey, Share(out), Shave, Shear, Shingle, Ship, Shorn, Short, Shred, Shun, Sickle, Sirloin, Skip, Slane, Slash, Slice, Slip, Slit, Sloop, Sned, Snee, Snib, Snick, Snip, Snub, Spade, Spin, Spud, Steak, Stencil, Stereotomy, Stir, Stramac, Stramazon, Style, Surgeon, Tailor(ess), Tart, Tenderloin, Tenotomy, Tomial, Tomium, Tonsure, Tooth, Topside, Transect, Trash, Trench, Trenchant, Trepan, Trim, Truant, Truncate, Urchin, Whang, Whittle, Winey

▷ **Cut** may indicate an anagram

▷ **Cutback** may indicate a reversed word

Cute Ankle, Pert, Pretty, Taking

Cuticle Eponychium, Periplast, Skin

Cut in Interpose, Interrupt

Cutlass Machete, Sword

Cutlery Canteen, Flatware, Fork, Knife, Setting, Silver, Spoon, Tableware, Trifid

Cutlet Schnitzel

Cut off Elide, Enisle, Inisle, Insulate, Intercept, ➤ ISOLATE, Lop, Prune

Cut-throat Razor, Ruinous

Cuttlebone, Cuttlefish Octopus, Pen, Polyp(e)s, Polypus, Sea-sleeve, Sepia, Sepiost(aire), Sepium, Squid

CV Biodata

Cyanide Acrylonitrile, Nitrile

Cycad Coontie, Coonty

Cyclamen Sow-bread

Cycle, Cyclist Anicca, Arthurian, Bike, Biorhythm, Cal(l)ippic, Calvin, Carbon, Carnot, Cell, Circadian, Daisy, Eon, Era, Fairy, Frequency, Heterogony, Indiction, Ko, Krebs, Life, Metonic, Oestrus, Orb, Otto, Pedal, Peloton, Period, Repulp, Revolution, Ride, Roadster, Rota, Round, Samsara, Saros, Scorch, Series, Sheng, Solar, Song, Sonnet, Sothic, Spin, TCA, Trike, Turn, UCI, Water, Wheeler, Wheelman, Wu

Cyclone Storm, Tornado, Typhoon, Willy-willy

Cyclops Arges, Arimasp(i), Brontes, Polyphemus, Steropes

Cylinder, Cylindrical Clave, Column, Drum, Pipe, Roll, Rotor, Slave, Spool, Steal, Stele, Terete, Torose, Treadmill, Tube

Cymbal(s) High-hat, Hi-hat, Zel

Cynic(al) Crab, Diogenes, Doubter, Hard-boiled, Menippus, Pessimist, Sardonic, Sceptic, Timon

Cynosure Centre, Focus

Cynthia Artemis, Moon

Cypress Bald, Retinospora, Tree

Cypriot Enosis, Eoka

Cyst Atheroma, Bag, Blister, Chalazion, Dermoid, Hydatid, Impost(h)ume, Meibomian, Ranula, Sac, Vesicle, Wen

Czechoslovakia CZ, Sudetenland

D d

D Daughter, Delta, Died, Edh, Eth, Penny

Dab(s) Bit, Daub, Fish, Flounder, Pat, Print, Ringer, Smear, Spot, Stupe, Whorl

Dabble(r) Dally, Dilettante, Plouter, Plowter, Potter, Smatter, Splash, Stipple, Trifle

Dachshund Teckel

Dactyl Anapaest

Dad(dy) Blow, Dev(v)el, Father, Generator, Hit, Male, Pa(pa), Pater, Polt, Pop, Slam, Sugar, Thump

Daddy-longlegs Crane-fly, Jennyspinner, Leather-jacket, Spinning-jenny, Tipula

Daffodil Asphodel, Jonquil, Lent-lily, Narcissus

Daft Absurd, Crazy, Potty, Ridiculous, Silly, Simple, Stupid

Dag Jag, Pierce, Pistol, Prick, Stab, Tag, Wool

Dagger(s) An(e)lace, Ataghan, Baselard, Bayonet, Bodkin, Crease, Creese, Da(h), Diesis, Dirk, Double, Dudgeon, Han(d)jar, Hanger, Jambiya(h), Katar, Kindjahl, Kirpan, Kreese, Kris, Lath, Misericord(e), Obelisk, Obelus, Poi(g)nado, Poniard, Puncheon, Sgian-dubh, Skean, Skene(-occle), Stiletto, Whiniard, Whinyard, W(h)inger, Yatag(h)an

Dahlia Cosmea

Daily Adays, Char, Circadian, Diurnal, Domestic, Guardian, Help, Journal, Mail, Mirror, Paper, Per diem, Quotidian, Rag, Regular, Scotsman, Sun, Tabloid

Dainty Cate(s), Cute, Delicacy, Elegant, Elfin, Entremesse, Entremets, Exquisite, Junket, Lickerish, Liquorish, Mignon(ne), ➤ MORSEL, Neat, Nice, Particular, Petite, Pussy, Sunket, Twee

Dairy Creamery, Loan, Parlour

Dairymaid Dey, Patience

Dais Estate, Machan, Platform, Podium, Pulpit, Stage

Daisy African, Bell, Felicia, Gowan, Hen and chickens, Livingstone, Michaelmas, Ox-eye, Shasta, Transvaal, Vegetable sheep

Dale Dell, Dene, Dingle, Glen, Vale, Valley

Dally Coquet(te), Dawdle, Finger, Flirt, Play, Spoon, Sport, Toy, Trifle, Wait

Dam An(n)icut, Aswan, Bar, Barrage, Barrier, Block, Boulder, Bund, Cauld, Check, Hoover, Kariba, Kielder, Ma, Mater, Obstacle, Obstruct, Pen, ➤ STEM, Sudd, Weir

Damage(d), Damages Bane, Banjax, Bruise, Buckle, Charge, Contuse, Cost, Cripple, Dent, Desecrate, Detriment, Devastate, Devastavit, Estrepe, Fault, Flea-bite, Harm, Havoc, Hit, Hole, Hurt, Impair, Injury, Loss, Mar, Mayhem, Moth-eaten, Nobble, Prang, Price, Retree, Sabotage, Scaith, Scath(e),

Scotch, Scratch, Skaith, Smirch, Solatium, ➤ SPOIL, Tangle, Toll, Value, Vandalise, Violate, Wear and tear, Wing, Wound, Wreak, Wreck

Dambuster Ondatra

Dame Crone, Dowager, Edna, Gammer, Lady, Matron, Nature, Naunt, Partlet, Peacherino, Sis, Title(d), Trot, Woman

Damn(ed), Damnation Accurst, Attack, Blame, Condemn, Curse, Cuss, Darn, Dee, Execrate, Faust, Hell, Hoot, Jigger, Malgre, Perdition, Predoom, Sink, Swear, Very

Damp(ness) Aslake, Black, Check, Clam(my), Dank, Dewy, Fousty, Humid, Moist, Muggy, Raw, Rheumy, Rising, Roric, Soggy, Sordo, Sultry, Unaired, ➤ WET

Damper Barrier, Check, Dashpot, Killjoy, Mute

Damsel Girl, Lass, Maiden, Wench

Damson Plumdamas

Dan Box, Cupid, Leno, Scuttle, Tribe

Dance(r), Dancing Allemande, Alma(in), Antimasque, Antistrophe, Apache, Astaire, Baladin(e), Ball, Ballabile, Ballant, Ballerina, Ballet, Barn, Bayadère, Beguine, Belly, Bergamask, Bergomask, Bharat Natyam, Black bottom, Bogle, Bolero, Boogie, Bop, Bossanova, Boston, Bourrée, Bran(s)le, Brantle, Brawl, Breakdance, Buck and wing, Bunnyhug, Caballero, Cachucha, Cakewalk, Canary, Can-can, Cantico(y), Caper, Capoeira, Capuera, Carioca, Carmagnole, Carol, Ceroc®, Cha-cha(-cha), Chaconne, Charleston, Chorus-girl, Cinque-pace, Clog, Comprimario, Conga, Coranto, Corroboree, Corybant, Coryphee, Cotill(i)on, Country, Courant(e), Cracovienne, Csardas, Dervish, Diaghilev, Disco, Divertissement, Dolin, Do-si-do, Dump, Ecossaise, Egg-dance, Eightsome, Excuse-me, Fading, Fado, Fan, Fandango, Farandole, Farruca, Figurant, Flamenco, Fling, Flip-flop, Floral, Folk, Foot, Forlana, Formation, Frug, Foxtrot, Furlana, Furry, Galliard, Gallopade, Galop, Gavotte, German, Ghost, Gig, Giga, Gigolo, Gigue, Glide, Go-go, Gopak, Habanera, Haka, Hailing, Hay, Hay-de-guise, Hay-de-guy(es), Haymaker, Headbang, Hetaera, Hetaira, Hey, Hey-de-guise, Hey-de-guy(es), Heythrop, Hoe-down, Hokey-cokey, Hoofer, Hoolachan, Hoolican, Hop, Hora(h), Hornpipe, Hula(-hula), Hustle, Ice, Irish jig, Jack-in-the-green, Jitterbug, Jive, Joncanoe, Jota, Juba, Juke, Jump-up, Junkanoo, Kantikoy, Kathak(ali), Kazachok, Kazatzka, Kick-up, Knees-up, Kolo, Labanotation, Lambada, Lambeth walk, Lancers, Landler, Lap, Lavolt(a), Leap, Limbo, Lindy hop, Lion, Loup, Loure, Macaber, Macabre, Maenad, Malaguena, Mambo, Marinera, Matachin, Maxixe, Mazurka, Measure, Medicine, Merengue, Minuet, Mooch, Moresco, Morisco, Morrice, Morris, Moshing, Murciana, Na(t)ch, Nautch-girl, Nureyev, Nijinsky, Oberek, Orchesis, Palais glide, Partner, Pas (de deux), Paso doble, Paspy, Passacaglia, Passamezzo, Passemeasure, Passepied, Passy-measure, Pastourelle, Paul Jones, Pavan(e), Paven, Pavin, Pavlova, Pericon, Petipa, Petronella, Pierette, Planxty, Pogo, Poi, Polacca, Polka, Polo, Polonaise, Poussette, Progressive, Pyrrhic, Quadrille, Quickstep, Raver, Redowa, Reel, Ridotto, Rigadoon, Robotics, Romaika, Ronggeng, Round, Roundelay, Roundle, Routine,

Rug-cutting, Sir Roger de Coverley, Slam, Smooch, Snake, Square, St Vitus, Salome, Salsa, Saltarello, Saltatorious, Samba, Saraband, Sardana, Sashaya, Schottische, Seguidilla, Shag, Shimmy(-shake), Shuffle, Siciliano, Sicilienne, Sink(e)-a-pace, Skank, Snowball, Soft-shoe, Spin, Spring, Stag, Step, Stomp, Strathspey, Strut, Sun, Sword, Taglioni, Tambourin, Tanagra, Tango, Tap, Tarantella, Taxi, Terpsichore, Thé dansant, Toe, Tordion, Toy(i)-toy(i), Tread, Trenchmore, Trenise, Trip(pant), Tripudiate, Tripudium, Trophe, Trucking, Turkey trot, Twist, Two-step, Tyrolienne, Valeta, Valse, Variation, Varsovienne, Veleta, Vogue(ing), Volta, Waltz, War, Whirl, Zapateado, Ziganka

Dance movement Brisé, Chassé, Entrechat, Glissade, Jeté, Lassu, Pantalon, Pirouette, Poule, Poussette, Routine, Step

Dance tune Toy

▷ **Dancing** may indicate an anagram

Dancing party Ball, Ridotto

Dandelion Kok-sagyz, Piss-a-bed, Scorzonera, Taraxacum

Dander Anger, Gee, Passion, Saunter, Temper

Dandle Dance, Doodle, Fondle, Pet

Dandruff Furfur, Scurf

Dandy Adonis, Beau, Blood, Boulevardier, Buck(een), Cat, Coxcomb, Dapper, ➤ DUDE, Exquisite, Fantastico, Fop, Gem, Jay, Jessamy, Johnny, Kiddy, Knut, Lair, Macaroni, Masher, Modist, Monarcho, Muscadin, Nash, Nut, Posh, Roy, Smart, Spark, Spiff, Swell, Ted, U, Yankee-doodle

Dandy-horse Draisene, Draisine

Dane(s) Clemence, Dansker, Ogier, Ostmen

Danger(ous) Apperil, Breakneck, Crisis, Dic(e)y, Dire, Emprise, Fear, Hairy, Hazard, Hearie, Hot, Insecure, Jeopardy, Lethal, Menace, Mine, Nettle, Nocuous, Parlous, ➤ PERIL, Pitfall, Precarious, Quicksand, Risk, Serious, Severe, Snag, Tight, Trap

Dangle A(i)glet, Aiguillette, Critic, Flourish, Hang, Loll, Swing

Daniel Dan, Defoe, Deronda, Lion-tamer, Portia, Quilp

Dank Clammy, Damp, Humid, Moist, Wet, Wormy

Daphne Agalloch, Agila, Eaglewood, Lace-bark, Laura, Laurel, Mezereon

Dapper Dressy, Natty, Neat, Smart, Spiff, Spruce, Sprush, Spry, ➤ TRIM

Darbies Cuffs, Irons, Snaps

Dare, Daring Adventure, Bold, Brave, Challenge, Courage, Da(u)nton, Defy, Durst, Emprise, Face, Gallant, Gallus, Hardihood, Hazard, Hen, Prowess, Racy, Taunt, Venture

Dark(en), Darkie, Darkness Aphelia, Aphotic, Apophis, Black, Blind, Cimmerian, Cloud, Depth, Dim, Dingy, Dirk(e), Dusky, Eclipse, Erebus, Evil, Gloom, Glum, Inumbrate, Mare, Maria, Melanous, Mulatto, Murk(y), Negro, Night, Obfuscate, Obscure, Ominous, Ousel, Ouzel, Pall, Phaeic, Pitch-black, Pit-mirk, Rooky, Sable, Sad, Secret, Shady, Shuttered, Sinister, Solein, Sombre, Sooty, Sphacelate, Sullen, Swarthy, Tar, Tenebr(i)ous, Tenebrose, Unfair, Unlit, Wog, Woosel, Yellowboy, Yellowgirl

Darling Acushla, Alannah, Asthore, Beloved, Charlie, Cher, Chéri(e), Chick-a-biddy, Chick-a-diddle, Chuck-a-diddle, Dear, Dilling, Do(a)ting-piece, Duck(s), Favourite, Grace, Honey, Idol, Jarta, Jo(e), Lal, Love, Luv, Mavourneen, Mavournin, Minikin, Minion, Oarswoman, Own, Peat, Pet, Poppet, Precious, Sugar, Sweetheart, Yarta, Yarto

Darn Begorra, Blow, Doggone, Hang, Mend, Repair, Sew

Dart(er) Abaris, Arrow, Banderilla, Dace, Dash, Deadener, Dodge, Fleat, Fléchette, Flit, Harpoon, Javelin, Launch, Leap, Scoot, Skrim, Speck, Spiculum, Strike, Thrust, Wheech

Dash(ed), Dashing Backhander, Bally, Blade, Blight, Blow, Buck, Charge, Collide, Cut, Dad, Dah, Damn, Dapper, Dart(le), Daud, Debonair, Ding, Elan, Fa(s)cia, Flair, Fly, Go-ahead, Hang, Hurl, ➤ HURRY, Hustle, Hyphen, Impetuous, Jabble, Jaw, Jigger, Lace, Line, Minus, Natty, Nip, Panache, Pebble, Ramp, Rash, Rule, Rush, Run, Sally, Scamp(er), Scart, Scoot, Scrattle, Scurry, Scuttle, Shatter, Showy, Soupçon, Souse, Spang, Speed, Splash, Splatter, Sprint, Strack, Streak, Stroke, ➤ STYLE, Throw, Touch, Viretot

Dashboard Fascia

Dashwood Hell-fire club

Dastard(ly) Base, Coward, Craven, Nid(d)erling, Poltroon

Data, Database Archie, Evidence, Facts, Fiche, File, Floating-point, Gen, Info, Input, Material, Matrix, News, Soft copy

Date(d), Dates, Dating AD, Age, AH, Almanac, Appointment, Blind, Boyfriend, Calendar, Carbon, Carbon-14, Computer, Court, Deadline, Engagement, Epoch, Equinox, Era, Escort, Exergue, Expiry, Fixture, Girlfriend, Ides, Julian, Meet, Outmoded, ➤ OUT OF DATE, Passé, Past, Radio-carbon, Rubidium-strontium, See, System, ➤ TRYST, Ult(imo)

Daub Begrime, Blob, Dab, Gaum, Mess, Moil, Noint, Plaister, Plaster, ➤ SMEAR, Smudge, Splodge, Teer, Wattle

Daughter (in law) Child, D, Elect, Girl, Jephthah's, Niece, Offspring

Daunt Adaw, Amate, Awe, Deter, Dishearten, Intimidate, Overawe, Quail, Stun, Stupefy, Subdue

Dauphin Delphin

David Dai, Psalmist

Davit Crane, Derrick, Hoist

Davy Crockett, Jones

Daw Bird, Magpie, Margery

Dawdle(r) Dally, Draggle, Drawl, Idle, ➤ LOITER, Potter, Shirk, Slowcoach, Troke, Truck

Dawn Aurora, Cockcrow, Daw, Daybreak, Day-peep, Dayspring, Eoan, Eos, False, Light, Morrow, Occur, Prime, Start, Sunrise

Day(s) All Fools', All Hallows', All Saints', All Souls', Anniversary, Annunciation, Anzac, April Fool's, Armistice, Ascension, Australia, Bad hair, Banian, Bastille, Boxing, Calends, Calpa, Canada, Columbus, Commonwealth, D, Date, Distaff, Dog, Ember, Empire, Fasti, Father's, Feast, Ferial, Field, Flag, Fri, Groundhog, Guy Fawkes', Halcyon,

Hogmanay, Holy Innocents', Hundred, Ides, Inauguration, Independence, Intercalary, Judgment, Kalends, Kalpa, Labo(u)r, Lady, Lammas, Laetare, Lay, Mardi, May, Memorial, Midsummer, Mon, Morrow, Mother's, Mufti, New year's, Nones, Nychthemeron, Oak-apple, Octave, Open, Pancake, Poppy, Present, Primrose, Quarter, Remembrance, Robin, Rock, Rogation, Rood, Rosh Chodesh, Salad, Sat, Shick-shack, Solstice, St Swithin's, St Valentine's, Settling, Sidereal, Solar, Speech, Sun, Tag, Thanksgiving, Thurs, Ticket, Time, Tues, Twelfth, Utas, VE, Veterans', Victoria, VJ, Waitangi, Wed

Daybreak Cockcrow

Daydream(er) Brown study, Dwam, Fancy, Imagine, Mitty, Muse, Reverie, Rêveur

Daylight Dawn, Space, Sun

Daze(d) Amaze, Bemuse, Confuse, Dwaal, Gally, Muddle, Muzzy, Reeling, ➤ STUN, Stupefy, Stupor, Trance

Dazzle(d), Dazzling Bewilder, Blend, Blind, Eclipse, Foudroyant, Glare, Meteoric, Outshine, Radiance, Resplendent, Splendour, Yblent

Deacon Cleric, Doctor, Minister

Deactivate Unarm

Dead(en) Abrupt, Accurate, Alamort, Asgard, Asleep, Blunt, Bung, Cert, Cold, Complete, D, Deceased, Defunct, Doggo, Expired, Extinct, Gone(r), Inert, Infarct, Late, Lifeless, Muffle, Mute, Napoo, Numb, Obsolete, Obtund, Ringer, She'ol, Smother, Stillborn, True, Utter, Waned

Dead end, Deadlock Cut-off, Dilemma, Impasse, Logjam, Stalemate, Stoppage

Dead-leaf colour Filemot, Philamot, Philomot

Deadline Date, Epitaph, Limit

Deadlock Stand-off, Sticking-point

Deadly Baleful, Dull, Fell, Funest, Internecine, ➤ LETHAL, Malign, Mortal, Pestilent, Unerring, Venomous

Deadly Nightshade Dwale, Belladonna

Deadpan Expressionless

Dead reckoning Dr

Dead tree Rampick, Rampike

Deaf(en), Deafness Adder, Asonia, Deave, Deeve, Dunny, Heedless, Paracusis, Presbyc(o)usis, Surd(ity)

Deal(er), Dealings Agent, Agreement, Allot(ment), Arb, Arbitrageur, Bargain, Brinjarry, Broker, Business, Cambist, Chandler, Chapman, Commerce, Cope, Coup, Cover, Croupier, Dispense, Distributor, Do, Dole, Eggler, Exchange, Fripper, Goulash, Hand(le), Help, Inflict, Insider, Jiggery-pokery, Jobber, Lashing, Let, Manage, Mercer, Merchant, Mickle, Middleman, Monger, Mort, Negotiate, New, Operator, Package, Pine, Raft, Raw, Sale, Serve, Sort, Spicer, Square, Stockjobber, Takeover, Tape, Timber, Tout(er), ➤ TRADE, Traffic, Transaction, Treat, Truck, Wheeler, Wield, Woolstapler, Yardie

Dean Acheson, Arabin, Colet, Decani, Doyen, Forest, Head, Inge, Nellie, Provost, RD, Rural, Rusk, Slade, Spooner, Swift, Vale, Vicar-forane

Dear(er), Dearest, Dear me Ay, Bach, Beloved, Cara, Caro, Cher(e), Cherie, Chuckie, Darling, Duck(s), Expensive, High, Honey(bun), Lamb, Leve, Lief, Lieve, Loor, Love, Machree, Mouse, My, Pet, Pigsney, Pigsnie, Pigsny, Steep, Sweet, Toots(ie), Up

Dearth Famine, Lack, Paucity, Scantity, Scarcity, ➤ SHORTAGE

Deaspiration Psilosis

Death(ly) Auto-da-fe, Bane, Bargaist, Barg(h)est, Black, Cataplexis, Charnel, Curtains, Cypress, Demise, Departure, Dormition, End, Eschatology, Euthanasia, Exit, Extinction, Fatality, Funeral, Gangrene, Grim Reaper, Hallal, Infarction, Jordan, Lethee, Leveller, Mors, Napoo, Necrosis, Nemesis, Night, Obit, Quietus, Reaper, Sati, Sergeant, SIDS, Small-back, Strae, Sudden, Suttee, Terminal, Thanatism, Thanatopsis, Thanatos

Death-flood Styx

Deathless(ness) Athanasy, Eternal, Eterne, Immortal, Struldberg, Timeless, Undying

Debacle Cataclysm, Collapse, Disaster, Fiasco

Debar Deny, Exclude, Forbid, ➤ PREVENT, Prohibit

Debase(d) Adulterate, Allay, Bemean, Corrupt, Demean, Depreciate, Dialectician, Dirty, Grotesque, Hedge, Lower, Pervert, Traduce, Vitiate

Debate(r) Argue, Combat, Contention, Contest, Deliberate, Dialectic, Discept, Discuss(ion), ➤ DISPUTE, Flyte, Forensics, Moot, Polemics, Reason, Teach-in, Warsle, Wrangle, Wrestle

Debauch(ee), Debauchery Corrupt, Defile, Degenerate, Dissipate, Heliogabalus, Libertine, Licence, Orgy, Profligate, Rake-hell, Riot, Roist, Royst, Seduce, Spree, Stuprate, Wet, Whore

Debenture Bond, Security

Debilitate(d), Debility Asthenia, Atonic, Cachexia, Feeble, Languid, Weak

Debit Charge, Debt

Debonair Cavalier, Gay, Gracious, Jaunty

Debris Bahada, Bajada, Detritus, Eluvium, Moraine, Moslings, Refuse, ➤ RUBBLE, Ruins, Tephra, Waste

▷ **Debris** may indicate an anagram

Debt(or) Alsatia, Arrears, Arrestee, Dr, Due, Insolvent, IOU, Liability, Moratoria, National, Obligation, Score, Tie

Debt-collector Bailiff, Forfaiter, Remembrancer

Debut Launch, Opening

Debutante Bud, Deb

Decade Rosary, Ten

Decadence, Decadent Babylonian, Decaying, Degeneration, Dissolute, Effete, Fin-de-siècle, Libertine

Decamp Abscond, Absquatulate, Bolt, Bunk, Depart, Flee, Guy, Levant, Mizzle, Slide, Slope, Vamoose

Decant Pour, Unload

Decapitate, Decapitation Aphesis, ➤ BEHEAD, Guillotine
▷ **Decapitated** may indicate first letter removed
Decay(ed), Decaying Alpha, Appair, Beta, Biodegrade, Blet, Canker, Caries, Caseation, Crumble, Decadent, Declension, Decline, Decrepit, Dieback, Disintegrate, Doat, Doddard, Doddered, Dote, Dricksie, Druxy, Dry rot, F(o)etid, Fail, Forfair, Gangrene, Heart-rot, Impair, Moulder, Pair(e), Plaque, Putrefy, Ret, Rot, Saprogenic, Sap-rot, Seedy, Sepsis, Spoil, Tabes, Wet-rot
Decease(d) Death, Decedent, Demise, Die, Stiff
Deceit(ful), Deceive(r) Abuse, Artifice, Bamboozle, Barrat, Befool, Bitten, Blind, Bluff, Braide, ➤ CHEAT, Chicane, Chouse, Cozen, Cuckold, Defraud, Delude, Diddle, Dissemble, Do brown, Double-cross, Double-tongued, Dupe, Duplicity, False(r), Fast-talk, Fiddle, Flam, Fox, Fraud, Gag, Gloze, Guile, Gull, Hoax, Hoodwink, Hornswoggle, Humbug, Hype, Imposition, Inveigle, Invention, Jiggery-pokery, Kid, Malengine, Mata Hari, Mislead, Mislippen, Phenakism, Poop, Poupe, Pretence, Punic, Rig, Ruse, Sell, Sham, Sinon, Spruce, Stratagem, Subreption, Swindle, Swizzle, Tregetour, Trick, Trump, Two-time, Wile
Decency, Decent Chaste, Decorum, Fitting, Healsome, Honest, Kind, Modest, Seemly, Sporting, Wholesome
Decentralise Disperse
Deception, Deceptive Artifice, Catchpenny, Catchy, Cheat, ➤ DECEIT, Disguise, Dupe, Duplicity, Eyewash, Fallacious, False, Flam, Fraud, Gag, Gammon, Guile, Have-on, Hocus-pocus, Hokey-pokey, Hum, Hunt-the-gowks, Ignes-fatui, Ignis-fatuus, Illusion, Insidious, Lie, Moodies, Ruse, Sell, Specious, ➤ TRICK, Trompe l'oeil, Two-timing
Decide(d), Decider Addeem, Agree, Ballot, Barrage, Cast, Clinch, Conclude, ➤ DECISION, Deem, Definite, Determine, Distinct, Firm, Fix, Jump-off, Mediate, Opt, Parti, Predestination, Pronounced, Rescript, ➤ RESOLVE, Rule, Run-off, See, Settle, Tiebreaker, Try
Decimal Mantissa, Terminating
Decimate Destroy, Lessen, Weaken
Decipher(ing) Cryptanalysis, Decode, Decrypt, Descramble, Discover, Interpret
▷ **Decipher(ed)** may indicate an 'o' removed
Decision Arbitrium, Arrêt, Crossroads, Crunch, Decree, Fatwa, Fetwa, Firman, Judg(e)ment, Placit(um), Referendum, Resolution, Resolve, Responsa, Ruling, Sentence, Verdict
Decisive Climactic, Clincher, Critical, Crux, Definite, Final, Pivotal
Deck Adorn, Array, Attrap, Bejewel, Boat, Cards, Clad, Daiker, Daub, Decorate, Dizen, Embellish, Equip, Flight, Focsle, Forecastle, Garland, Hang, Helideck, Hurricane, Lower, Orlop, Pack, Platform, Poop, Prim, Promenade, Quarter, Sun, Tape, Upper, Void
Declaim, Declare, Declaration, Decree Absolute, Affidavit, Affirm, Air, Allege, Announce, Assert, Asseverate, Aver, Avow, Balfour, Bann(s), Breda, Dictum, Diktat, Doom, Edict, Enact, Fatwa(h), Fiat, Firman, Go, Grace,

Harangue, Hatti-sherif, Insist, Interlocutory, Irade, Law, Mandate, Manifesto, Mecklenburg, Meld, Motu proprio, Mou(th), Nisi, Noncupate, Novel(la), Nullity, Orate, Ordain, Order, Ordinance, Parlando, Pontificate, Proclaim, Profess, Promulgate, Pronounce, Protest, Psephism, Publish, Rant, Recite, Resolve, Rescript, Rights, Rule, Ruling, SC, Sed, Senecan, Signify, Speak, Spout, State, Testimony, Testify, UDI, Ultimatum, Unilateral, Vie, Voice, Vouch, Word

▷ **Declaring** may indicate a word beginning 'Im'

Decline, Declining Age, Comedown, Decadent, Degringoler, Deny, Descend, Deteriorate, Devall, Die, Dip, Dissent, Downtrend, Downturn, Droop, Dwindle, Ebb, Fade, Fall, Flag, Forbear, Paracme, Quail, Recede, Recession, Refuse, Retrogression, Rot, Rust, Sag, Senile, Set, Sink, Slump, Stoop, Wane, Welke, ➤ WILT, Withdraw, Wither

Decoct(ion) Apozem, Cook, Devise, Ptisan, Tisane

Decode(d) En clair

Decolleté Low, Neckline

Decompose, Decomposition Biodegradable, Crumble, Decay, Disintegrate, Hydrolysis, Mor, Pyrolysis, Rot, Wither

Decompression Bends

Decor Background, Scenery

Decorate(d), Decoration, Decorative Adorn, Angelica, Aogai, Arpillera, Attrap, Award, Baroque, Beaux-arts, Biedermeier, Bordure, Braid, Brooch, Cartouche, Champlevé, Centrepiece, Chambranle, Chinoiserie, Christingle, Cinquefoil, Cloissoné, Crocket, Cul-de-lampe, Dentelle, Diamante, Doodad, Dragée, Emblazon, Emboss, Embrave, Enrich, Epergne, Etch, Fancy, Festoon, Filigree, Finial, Fleuret(te), Fleuron, Floriated, Fourragère, Frieze, Frill, Frog, Furbish, Garniture, Gaud, Goffer, Gradino, Guilloche, Historiated, Ice, Illuminate, Impearl, Inlay, Intarsia, Intarsio, Interior, Knotwork, Linen-fold, Marquetry, MC, Medal(lion), Mola, Moulding, Oath, OBE, Order, ➤ ORNAMENT, Ornate, Orphrey, Ovolo, Paint, Paper, Parament, Pokerwork, Prettify, Prink, Purfle, Rag-rolling, Rangoli, Repoussé, Rich, Rosemaling, Ruche, Scallop, Schwarzlot, Scrimshander, Scrimshaw, Set-off, Sgraffito, Skeuomorph, Soutache, Spangle, Staffage, Stomacher, Storiated, Strapwork, Tailpiece, Tattoo, TD, Titivate, Tool, Topiary, Trim, Wallpaper

Decorous, Decorum Becoming, Demure, Etiquette, Fitness, Parliamentary, Prim, ➤ PROPER, Propriety, Seemlihe(a)d, ➤ SEEMLY, Staid

Decoy Allure, Bait, Bonnet, Button, Call-bird, Coach, Crimp, Entice, Lure, Piper, Roper, Ruse, Shill, Stale, Stalking-horse, Stool-pigeon, Tole, Toll, Trap, Trepan

Decrease Decrew, Diminish, Dwindle, Iron, Lessen, Press, Reduce, Rollback, Step-down, Subside, Wane, Wanze

▶ **Decree** see DECLAIM

Decrepit Dilapidated, Doddery, Failing, Feeble, Frail, Moth-eaten, Tumbledown, Warby, Weak

Decry Condemn, Crab, Denounce, Derogate, Detract, Downgrade

Dedicate(d), Dedication Corban, Devote, Endoss, Hallow, Inscribe, Oblate, Pious, Sacred, Votive

Deduce, Deduction, Deductive A priori, Assume, Conclude, Consectary, Corollary, Derive, Discount, Gather, Illation, Infer(ence), Reason, Rebate, Recoup, Reprise, Stoppage, Surmise, Syllogism

Deed(s) Achievement, Act(ion), Atweel, Backbond, Charta, Charter, Derring-do, Escrol(l), Escrow, Exploit, Fact(um), Indeed, Indenture, Manoeuvre, Mitzvah, Muniments, Specialty, Starr, ➤ TITLE

Deem Consider, Opine, Ordain, Proclaim, Repute, Think

Deep(en), Deeply Abstruse, Bass(o), Brine, Briny, Enhance, Excavate, Grum, Gulf, Hadal, Intense, Low, Mindanao, Mysterious, ➤ OCEAN, Profound, Re-enter, Rich, Sea, Sonorous, Throaty, Upsee, Ups(e)y

Deep-rooted Inveterate

Deer(-like) Axis, Bambi, Barasing(h)a, Barking, Brocket, Buck, Cariacou, Carjacou, Cervine, Chevrotain, Chital, Doe, Elaphine, Elk, Fallow, Gazelle, Hart, Moose, Mouse, Mule, Muntjac, Muntjak, Musk, Père David's, Pricket, Pudu, Red, Rein, Roe, Rusa, Sambar, Sambur, Selenodont, Sika, Sorel(l), Spade, Spay(d), Spayad, Spitter, Spottie, Stag(gard), Tragule, Ungulate, Virginia, Wapiti

Deer-hunter Tinchel

Deface Disfigure, Spoil

▷ **Defaced** may indicate first letter missing

Defame, Defamatory, Defamation Abase, Blacken, Calumny, Cloud, Denigrate, Detract, Dishonour, Impugn, Libel, Mud, Mudslinging, Scurrilous, Slander, Smear, Stigmatise, Traduce, Vilify

Default(er) Absentee, Bilk, Dando, Delinquent, Flit, Levant, Neglect, Omission, Waddle, Welsh

Defeat(ed), Defeatist Beat, Best, Caning, Capot, Codille, Conquer, Counteract, Debel, Defeasance, Demolish, Discomfit, Dish, Ditch, Fatalist, Floor, Foil, Foyle, Hammer, Hiding, Lick, Loss, Lurch, Marmelize, Master, Mate, Negative, Out, Outclass, Outdo, Outplay, ➤ OVERCOME, Overpower, Overreach, Overthrow, Pip, Reverse, Rout, Rubicon, Scupper, Set, Shellacking, Sisera, Stump, Tank, Thrash, Thwart, Tonk, Trounce, Vanquish, War, Waterloo, Whap, Whip, Whitewash, Whop, Whup, Wipe-out, Worst

Defecate Horse, Mute, Poop, Shit

Defect(ion), Defective, Defector Abandon, Amateur, Apostasy, Bug, Coma, Faulty, Flaw, ➤ FORSAKE, Frenkel, Halt, Hamartia, Kink, Manky, Mote, Natural, Psellism, Rachischisis, Renegade, Renegate, Ridgel, Ridgil, Rig, Rogue, Runagate, Shortcoming, Spina bifida, Terrace, Treason, Trick, Want, Weakness

Defence, Defend(er) Abat(t)is, Alibi, Antibody, Antidote, Antihistamine, Apologia, Back, Bailey, Barbican, Barmkin, Barricade, Bastion, Battery, Battlement, Berm, Bridgehead, Bulwark, Calt(h)rop, Catenaccio, CD, Champion, Civil, Curtain, Demibastion, Ditch, Embrasure, Hedgehog, Herisson, Hold, J(i)u-jitsu, Justify, Kaim, Keeper, Laager, Laer, Linebacker,

Maintain, Martello Tower, Miniment, Moat, Muniment, Outwork, Palisade, Parapet, Rampart, Redan, Redoubt, Resist, Ringwall, ➤ SHELTER, Shield, Stonewall, Support, Tenail(le), Testudo, Tower, Trench, Trou-de-loup, Uphold, Vallation, Vallum, Vindicate, Wall, Warran(t)

Defenceless Helpless, Inerm, Naked, Sitting duck, Vulnerable

Defendant Accused, Apologist, Respondent, Richard Roe

Defer(ence), Deferential Bow, Delay, Dutiful, Homage, Morigerous, Obeisant, Pace, Polite, Postpone, Procrastinate, Protocol, Respect, Shelve, Submit, Suspend, Waive, Yield

Defiance, Defiant, Defy Acock, Bold, Brave, Dare, Daring, Disregard, Do or die, Outbrave, Outdare, Recusant, Stubborn, Titanism, Truculent, Unruly

Deficiency, Deficient Absence, Acapnia, Anaemia, Beriberi, Defect, Inadequate, Incomplete, Kwashiorkor, Lack, Osteomalacia, SCID, Scant, Scarcity, Shortage, Spanaemia, Want

▷ **Deficient** may indicate an anagram

Deficit Anaplerotic, Arrears, Defective, Ischemia, Loss, Poor, Shortfall

Defile(ment) Abuse, Array, Barranca, Barranco, Besmear, Col, Conspurcation, Desecrate, Dishonour, Donga, Enseam, ➤ FOUL, Gate, Gorge, Gully, Inquinate, Inseem, Kloof, Moil, Pass, Pollute, Poort, Ravine, Ray, Roncesvalles, Smear, Spoil, ➤ SULLY

Define(d), Definition, Definitive Decide, Demarcate, Determine, Diorism, Distinct, Explain, Fix, Limit, Parameter, Set, Tangible, Term

Definite(ly) Classic, Clear, Emphatic, Firm, Hard, Positive, Precise, Specific, Sure, Yes

Deflate Burst, Collapse, Flatten, Lower, Prick

Deflect(or), Deflection Avert, Bend, Detour, Diverge, Divert, Glance, Otter, Paravane, Refract, Snick, Swerve, Throw, Trochotron, Veer, Windage

Deform(ed), Deformity Anamorphosis, Blemish, Crooked, Disfigure, Distort, Gammy, Hammer-toe, Harelip, Mishapt, Mutilate, Polt-foot, Stenosed, Talipes, Valgus, Warp

▷ **Deformed** may indicate an anagram

Defraud Bilk, Cheat, Cozen, Gyp, Mulct, Sting, Swindle, Trick

Defray Bear, Cover, Meet

Defrost Thaw

Deft Adept, Agile, Dab, Dexterous, Handy, Nimble

Defunct Deceased, Extinct, Obsolete

▶ **Defy** see DEFIANCE

Degenerate, Degeneration Acorn-shell, Ascidian, Atrophy, Balanus, Base, Cirrhipedea, Cirrhipedia, Cirrhopod(a), Cirripedea, Cirripedia, Decadent, Deprave, Descend, Deteriorate, Fatty, Kaliyuga, Necrobiosis, Pejorate, Pervert, Rakehell, Relapse, Retrogress, Salp, Tunicate

Degrade, Degradation Abase, Cheapen, Culvertage, Debase, Demote, Diminish, Disennoble, Humble, Imbase, Lessen, Lower, ➤ SHAME, Waterloo

Degree(s) Aegrotat, As, Azimuthal, B es S, BA, Baccalaureate, BCom, BD, C, Class, D, Desmond, Doctoral, Engler, Extent, External, F, First, German,

Gradation, Grade, Grece, Gree(s), Greece, Gre(e)se, Grice, Griece, Grize, ➤ IN A HIGH DEGREE, K, Lambeth, Latitude, Letters, Level, Licentiate, MA, Measure, Mediant, Nuance, Peg, PhD, Pin, Poll, Rate, Remove, Second, Stage, Status, Step, Third, Water

Dehiscence Suture

Dehydrate Exsiccate

Deification, Deify Apotheosis

Deign Condescend, Stoop

Deity Avatar, Demogorgon, Faun, Divine, ➤ GOD, ➤ GODDESS, Idolise, Immortalise, Numen, Pan, Satyr

Dejected, Dejection Abase, Abattu, Alamort, Amort, Chap-fallen, Crab, Crestfallen, Despondent, Dismay, Dispirited, Downcast, Gloomy, Hangdog, Humble, Melancholy

Delay(ed) Ambage, Avizandum, Behindhand, Check, Cunctator, Defer, Demurrage, Detention, Fabian, Filibuster, For(e)slow, Forsloe, Frist, Hesitate, Hinder, Hitch, Hold up, Hysteresis, Impede, Laches, Lag, Late, Laten, Let, Linger, Mora(torium), Obstruct, Procrastinate, Prolong, Prorogue, Remanet, Reprieve, Respite, Retard, Setback, Slippage, Sloth, Slow, ➤ STALL, Stand-over, Stay, Stonewall, Temporise, Wait

Delectable Delicious, Luscious, Tasty

Delegate, Delegation Agent, Amphictyon, Appoint, Assign, Decentralise, Depute, Devolution, Mission, Nuncio, Representative, Transfer, Vicarial

Delete Cancel, Cut, Erase, Expunge, Purge, Rase, Scratch, Scrub

Deliberate(ly) Adagio, Consider, Debate, Intentional, Meditate, Moderate, Prepensely, Ponder, Studied, Voulu, Weigh, Witting

Delicacy, Delicate Airy-fairy, Beccafico, Canape, Cate, Caviare, Dainty, Difficult, Discreet, Ectomorph, Eggshell, Elfin, Ethereal, Fastidious, Finespun, Flimsy, Fine, Finesse, Fragile, ➤ FRAIL, Friand, Gossamer, Guga, Hothouse, Inconie, Incony, Kickshaw, Kidglove, Ladylike, Light, Lobster, Morbidezza, Nesh, Nicety, Nimby-piminy, Oyster, Reedy, Roe, Sensitive, Soft, Subtle(ty), Sunket, Taste, Tender, Tenuous, Ticklish, Tidbit, Titbit, Truffle

Delicious Ambrosia, Delectable, Exquisite, Fragrant, Goloptious, Goluptious, Gorgeous, Lekker, Lip-smacking, Mor(e)ish, Mouthwatering, Scrummy, Scrumptious, Tasty, Toothsome, Yummy, Yum-yum

▷ **Delight** may indicate 'darken'

Delight(ed), Delightful Bliss, Chuff, Delice, Dreamy, Elated, Enamour, Enjoyable, Enrapture, Exuberant, Felicity, Fetching, Frabjous, Gas, Glad, Glee, Gratify, Honey, Joy, Overjoy, Please, Pleasure, ➤ RAPTURE, Regale, Scrummy, Super, Taking, Turkish, Whacko, Whee, Whoopee, Yippee, Yum-yum

Delineate Draft, Sketch, Trace

Delinquent Bodgie, Criminal, Halbstarker, Negligent, Offender, Ted

Delirious, Delirium Deranged, DT, Frenetic, Frenzy, Insanity, Mania, Phrenetic, Spazz, Wild

Deliver(ance), Deliverer, Delivery Accouchement, Ball, Birth, Bowl, Caesarean, Consign, Convey, Deal, Escape, Give, Lead, Liberate, Orate, Over, Pronounce, Recorded, Redeem, Release, Relieve, Render, Rendition, ➤ RESCUE, Rid, Round(sman), Salvation, Save, Say, Seamer, Sell, Shipment, Speak, Special, Tice, Transfer, Underarm, Underhand, Utter, Wide, Yorker

Dell Dale, Dargle, Dene, Dimble, Dingle, Dingl(e)y, Glen, Valley

Delphic Pythian

Delta Camargue, D, Del, Kronecker, Nabla, Nile, Triangle

Delude, Delusion Bilk, Cheat, Deceive, Fallacy, Fool, Hoax, ➤ MISLEAD, Trick

Deluge Avalanche, Flood, Ogygian, Saturate, Submerge, ➤ SWAMP

De luxe Extra, Plush, Special

Delve Burrow, Dig, Excavate, Exhume, Explore, Probe, Search

Demagogue Agitator, Fanariot, Leader, Mobsman, Phanariot, Speaker, Tribune

Demand(ing) Appetite, Call, Claim, Cry, Dun, Exact, Exigent, Fastidious, Final, Hest, ➤ INSIST, Market, Need, Order, Postulate, Pressure, Request, Requisition, Rush, Sale, Stern, Stipulate, Stringent, Summon, Ultimatum, Want

Demean(ing) Comport, Debase, Degrade, Infra dig, Lower, Maltreat

Demeanour Air, Bearing, Conduct, Expression, Front, Gravitas, Mien, Port

Demented Crazy, Hysterical, Insane, Mad

Demi-god Aitu, Daemon, Garuda, Hero

Demi-mondaine Cocotte, ➤ LOOSE WOMAN, Prostitute

Demise Death, Decease, Finish

Demo March, Parade, Protest, Rally, Sit-in

Democracy, Democrat D, Locofoco, Montagnard, Popular, Republic, Sansculotte, Social, Tammany

Demoiselle Crane, Damselfish

Demolish, Demolition Bulldoze, Devastate, Devour, Floor, KO, Level, Rack, ➤ RAZE, Smash, Wreck

▶ **Demon** see DEVIL

Demoness Lilith

Demonstrate, Demonstration, Demonstrator Agitate, Barrack, Display, Endeictic, Evènement, Explain, Evince, Maffick, Manifest, March, Morcha, Ostensive, Portray, Protest, Prove, Provo, ➤ SHOW, Sit-in, Touchy-feely

Demoralize Bewilder, Corrupt, Destroy, Shatter, Unman, Weaken

Demote, Demotion Comedown, Degrade, Disbench, Embace, Embase, Reduce, Relegate, Stellenbosch

Demur Hesitate, Jib, Object

Demure Coy, Mim, Modest, Prenzie, Primsie, Sedate, Shy

Den Dive, Domdaniel, Earth, Hide-away, Hell, Holt, Home, Lair, Lie, Room, Shebeen, Study, Sty, Wurley

▶ **Denial** see DENY

Denigrate Besmirch, Blacken, Defame, Tar

Denim Jeans

Denizen Diehard, Inhabitant, Resident

Denomination Category, Cult, Sect, Variety

Denote Import, Indicate, Mean, Signify

Denouement Anagnorisis, Climax, Coda, Exposure, Outcome, Showdown

Denounce, Denunciation Ban, Commination, Condemn, Criticise, Decry, Diatribe, Hatchet job, Hereticate, Proclaim, Proscribe, Shop, Stigmatise, Upbraid

Denry Card

Density Compact, D, Firm, Opaque, Relative, Solid, Spissitude, Tesla, Thick, Woofy

Dent Batter, Dancette, Depress, Dimple, Dinge, Dint, Nock, V

Dental, Dentist DDS, Extractor, Kindhart, LDS, Odontic, Periodontic, Toothy

Dentures Biteplate, Bridge, Bridgework, Plate, Wallies

Deny, Denial, Denier Abnegate, Antinomian, Aspheterism, Bar, Contradict, Démenti, Disavow, Disenfranchise, Disown, Forswear, ➤ GAINSAY, Nay, Negate, Nick, Protest, Refuse, Refute, Renague, Renay, Reneg(e), Renegue, Reney, Renig, Renounce, Reny, Repudiate, Sublate, Withhold

Deoxidise Outgas, Reduce

Depart(ed), Departing, Departure Abscond, Absquatulate, Bunk, D, Dead, Decession, Defunct, Die, Digress, Divergence, Exit, Exodus, Flight, ➤ GO, Leave, Lucky, Outbound, Remue, Vade, Vamoose, Walkout

Department Achaea, Ain, Aisne, Allier, Alpes Maritimes, Angers, Arcadia, Ardeche, Ardennes, Argo, Ariege, Arrondissement, Arta, Attica, Aube, Aude, Bas-Rhin, Belfort, Beziers, Branch, Bureau, Calvados, Cantal, Charente, Cher, Commissariat, Correze, Cote d'Or, Cotes d'Armor, Cotes du Nord, Creuse, Deme, Deux-Sevres, Division, Dordogne, Doubs, Essonne, Eure, Faculty, Finistere, FO, Gard, Gironde, Greencloth, Guadeloupe, Gulag, Hanaper, Heraud, Indre, Isere, Jura, Loire, Lot, Lot-et-Garonne, Lozere, Ministry, Nome, Nomos, Office, Oise, Orne, Province, Region, Sanjak, Savoie, Secretariat(e), Section, Somme, Sphere, State, Treasury, Tuscany, Var, Vienne, Wardrobe, Yonne

Depend(ant), Dependency, Dependent Addicted, Child, Client, Colony, Conditional, Contingent, Count, Dangle, Fief, Habit, Hang, Hinge, Icicle, Lean, Minion, Pensioner, Relier, Rely, Retainer, Sponge, Subject, Trust, Turn on, Vassal

Dependable Reliable, Reliant, Secure, Solid, Sound, Staunch, Sure, ➤ TRUSTWORTHY

Depict Delineate, Display, Draw, Limn, Paint, Portray, Present, Represent

Depilate, Depilatory Grain, Rusma, Slate

Deplete Diminish, Drain, Exhaust, Reduce

Deplorable, Deplore Base, Bemoan, Chronic, Complain, Deprecate, Dolorous, Grieve, Lament, Mourn, Piteous, Rue

Deploy(ment) Extend, Herse, Unfold, Use

▷ **Deploy(ment)** may indicate an anagram

Depopulate Deracinate

Deport(ment) Address, Air, Banish, ➤ BEARING, Carriage, Demeanour, Mien, Renvoi, Renvoy

Depose, Deposition Affirm, Banish, Dethrone, Displace, Dispossess, Overthrow, Pieta, Testify

Deposit Alluvial, Alluvium, Arcus, Argol, Atheroma, Bank, Bathybius, Bergmehl, Calc-sinter, Calc-tuff, Caliche, Cave-earth, Coral, Crag, Delta, Depone, Diluvium, Evaporite, Fan, File, Firn, Fur, Gyttja, Kieselguhr, Land, Lay, Lodge(ment), Loess, Löss, Measure, Natron, Outwatch, Park, Placer, Plank, Plaque, Put, Repose, Residuum, Saburra, Saprolite, ➤ SEDIMENT, Silt, Sinter, Sludge, Stockwork, Stratum, Surety, Tartar, Terramara, Terramare, Tophus, Turbidite

Depot Barracoon, Base, Camp, Depository, Station, Terminus, Treasure-city, Warehouse

Depraved, Depravity Bestial, Cachexia, Cachexy, ➤ CORRUPT, Dissolute, Evil, Immoral, Low, Rotten, Sodom, Turpitude, Ugly, Vice, Vicious, Vile

Deprecate Censure, Deplore, Expostulate, Reproach

Depreciate Abase, Belittle, Derogate, Detract, Discount

Depredate, Depredation Pillage, Plunder, Rob

Depress(ed), Depressing, Depression Accablé, Alamort, Alveolus, Amort, Astrobleme, Attrist, Black dog, Blight, Blues, Cafard, Canada, Canyon, Chill, Col, Combe, Couch, Crab, Crush, Cyclone, Dampen, Deject, Despair, Dell, Dene, Dent, ➤ DIMPLE, Dip, Dismal, Dispirit, Dolina, Doline, Drear, Drere, Dumpish, Endogenous, Exanimate, Flatten, Fonticulus, Foss(ula), Fossa, Fovea, Frog, Geosyncline, Ghilgai, Gilgai, Gilgie, Glen, Gloom, Graben, Ha-ha, Hammer, Hilar, Hilum, Hilus, Hollow, Howe, Hyp, Joes, Kettle, Kick(-up), Lacuna, Leaden, Low-spirited, Low(ness), Moping, Neck, Pit, Postnatal, Prostrate, Qattara, Recession, Re-entrant, Sad, Saddle, Salt-cellar, Salt-pan, Sink, Sinkhole, Sinus, Sitzmark, Slot, ➤ SLUMP, Slumpflation, Soakaway, Spiritless, Stomodaeum, Sump, Swag, Swale, Trench, Trough, Vale, Valley, Wallow

Deprive(d), Deprivation Bereft, Deny, Disenfranchise, Disfrock, Disseise, Disseize, Expropriate, Geld, Have-not, Hunger, Reduce, Remove, Rob, Withhold

Depth F, Fathom, Gravity, Intensity, Isobath, Pit, Profundity

Deputise, Deputy Act, Agent, Aide, Assistant, Commis(sary), Delegate, Legate, Lieutenant, Locum, Loot, Number two, Proxy, Represent, Secondary, Standby, Sub, Substitute, Succentor, Surrogate, Vicar, Vice, Viceregent, Vidame

Derange(d) Craze, Détraqué, Disturb, Insane, Manic, Troppo, Unhinge, Unsettle

Derby Donkey, Eponym, Hat, Kentucky, Kiplingcotes, Race

Derek Bo

Derelict Abandoned, ➤ DECREPIT, Deserted, Negligent, Outcast, Ramshackle

Deride, Derision, Derisive Contempt, Gup, Guy, Hoot, Jeer, Mock, Nominal, Raspberry, ➤ RIDICULE, Sardonic, Scoff, Scorn, Snifty, Snort, Yah, Ya(h)boo

Derive, Derivation, Derivative Ancestry, Creosote, Deduce, Descend, Extract, Get, Kinone, Of, Offshoot, Origin, Pedigree, Secondary

▶ **Dermatitis** see SKIN DISEASE

Derogate, Derogatory Belittle, Decry, Defamatory, Demeaning, Detract, Discredit, Pejorative, Personal, Slighting, Snide

Deronda Daniel

Derrick Crane, Davit, Hoist, Jib, Spar, Steeve

Dervish Calender, Doseh, Mawlawi, Mevlevi, Revolver, Santon, Whirling

Descant Comment, Discourse, Faburden, Melody, Song

Descartes René

Descend(ant), Descent Ancestry, Avail, Avale, Bathos, Blood, Chute, Cion, Decline, Degenerate, Derive, Dismount, Dive, Drop, Epigon, Extraction, Heir, Heraclid, ➤ LINEAGE, Offspring, Pedigree, Prone, Rappel, Said, Say(y)id, Scarp, Scion, Seed, Shelve, Sien(t), Sink, Stock, Syen, Vest, Volplane

Describe, Description Blurb, Define, Delineate, Depict, Designate, Epithet, Exposition, Expound, Narrate, Outline, Paint, Portray, Recount, Relate, Report, Sea-letter, Sketch, Specification, Term, Trace

▷ **Describing** may indicate 'around'

Descry Behold, Discern, Get, Notice, Perceive

Desecrate, Desecration Abuse, Defile, Dishallow, Profane, Sacrilege, Unhallow

▷ **Desecrated** may indicate an anagram

Desert(s), Deserted, Deserter, Dissident Abandon, Apostasy, Arabian, Arid, Arunta, Atacama, AWOL, Badland, Barren, Bug, Bunk, Come-uppance, D, Defect, Desolate, Dissident, Due, Empty, Eremic, Etosha Pan, Factious, Fail, Fezzan, Foresay, Forhoo, Forhow, Forlorn, Forsake, Forsay, Frondeur, Garagum, Gibson, Gila, Gobi, Great Basin, Great Sandy, Great Victoria, Heterodox, Kalahari, Kara Kum, Kavir, Kyzyl Kum, Libyan, Lurch, Merit, Mojave, Nafud, Namib, Negev, Nubia, Ogaden, Painted, Pategonian, Pindan, Rat, Refus(e)nik, Reg, ➤ RENEGADE, Reward, Rub'al-Khah, Run, Sahara, Sahel, Sands, Secede, Simpson, Sinai, Sonoran, Sturt, Syrian, Tergiversate, Thar, Turncoat, Ust(y)urt, Void, Wadi, Waste, Worthiness

Deserve(d) Condign, Earn, ➤ MERIT, Well-earned, Worthy

Desiccate(d) Dry, Sere

Design(er) Adam, Aim, Architect, Ashley, Batik, Broider, Cardin, Cartoon, Castrametation, Chop, Cloisonné, Create, Cul de lampe, Damascene, Decal(comania), Decor, Depict, Devise, Dévoré, Dior, Draft, Embroidery, End, Engine(r), Engineer, Erté, Etch, Fashion, Former, Hepplewhite, Hitech, Iconic, Impresa, Imprese, Intend(ment), Intent(ion), Interior,

Layout, Linocut, Logo, Marquetry, Mascle, Mean, Meander, Modiste, Monogram, Morris, Mosaic, Motif, ➤ PLAN, Plot, Propose, Pyrography, Quant, Ruse, Schema, Scheme, Seal, Sheraton, Sketch, Specification, Stencil, Stubble, Tatow, Tattoo, Tattow, Tatu, Think, Tooling, Trigram, Vignette, Watermark, Whittle

Designate Earmark, Style, Title

Desirable, Desire, Desirous Ambition, Appetite, Aspire, Avid, Best, Cama, Conation, Concupiscence, Covet, Crave, Cupidity, Dreamboat, Earn, Epithymetic, Fancy, Gasp, Hanker, Hope, Hunger, Itch, Kama(deva), Le(t)ch, Libido, Long, Luscious, Lust, Mania, Owlcar, Reck, Request, Residence, Salt, Streetcar, Thirst, Velleity, Vote, Wanderlust, Want, Whim, Will, Wish, Yearn, Yen

Desist Abandon, Cease, Curb, Quit, Stop

Desk Almemar, Ambo, Bureau, Carrel(l), Cash, Check-in, Cheveret, City, Desse, Davenport, Devonport, E(s)critoire, Faldstool, Lectern, Lettern, Pedestal, Prie-dieu, Pulpit, Roll-top, Vargueno

Desolate, Desolation Bare, Barren, Desert, Devastate, Disconsolate, Forlorn, Gaunt, Gousty, Moonscape, Waste, Woebegone

Despair, Desperate Acharne, De profundis, Despond, Dire, Extreme, Frantic, Gagging, Giant, Gloom, Hairless, Headlong, Reckless, Unhopeful, Urgent, Wanhope

▶ **Despatch** see DISPATCH

Desperado Bandit, Bravo, Ruffian, Terrorist

Despicable Abject, Base, Caitiff, Cheap, Churl, Contemptible, Heinous, Ignoble, Ignominious, Mean, Ratfink, Shabby, Toerag, Wretched

Despise Condemn, Contemn, Forhow, Hate, Ignore, Scorn, Spurn, Vilify, Vilipend

Despite For, Malgré, Notwithstanding, Pace, Though, Venom

Despoil Mar, Ravage, Vandalise

Despondent Dejected, Downcast, Forlorn, Gloomy, Sad

Despot(ism) Autarchy, Autocrat, Caesar, Darius, Dictator, Napoleon, Nero, Satrap, Stratocrat, Tsar, Tyrant, Tzar

Dessert Afters, Baked Alaska, Baklava, Bavarois, Bombe, Charlotte, Charlotte russe, Cobbler, Compote, Coupe, Crème brulée, Crème caramel, Entremets, Flummery, Fool, Junket, Kissel, Knickerbocker glory, Kulfi, Marquise, Mousse, Nesselrode, Parfait, Pashka, Pavlova, Pud(ding) Sawine, Pudding, Strudel, Sundae, Syllabub, Tiramisu, Trifle, Vacherin, Zabaglione

Destination, Destine Design, End, Fate, Foredoom, Goal, Home, Intend, Joss, Port, Purpose, Weird

Destiny Doom, ➤ FATE, Karma, Kismet, Lot, Manifest, Moira, Yang, Yin

Destitute Bankrupt, Bare, Broke, Devoid, Helpless, Indigent, Needy, Poor, Sterile

Destroy(er) Annihilate, Antineutrino, Antineutron, Antiparticle, Apollyon, Atomise, Blight, D, Decimate, Deface, Delete, Demolish, Denature, Destruct, Dish, Dismember, Dissolve, Eat, Efface, End, Eradicate, Erase,

Estrepe, Exterminate, Extirpate, Flivver, Fordo, Harry, Iconoclast, ➤ KILL, Murder, Obliterate, Overkill, Perish, Predator, Ravage, Raze, Ruin, Saboteur, Scuttle, Slash, Smash, Spiflicate, Sterilize, Stew-can, Stonker, Subvert, Undo, Uproot, Vandal, Vitiate, Whelm, Wreck, Zap

Destruction, Destructive Adverse, Bane, Can, Collapse, Deathblow, Deleterious, Devastation, Doom, Downfall, End, Götterdämmerung, Grave, Havoc, Holocaust, Insidious, Internecine, Kali, Lethal, Loss, Pernicious, Rack, Ragnarok, Ravage, Sabotage, Stroy, Wrack

Desultory Aimless, Cursory, Fitful, Idle

Detach(ed), Detachment Abstract, Alienate, Aloof, Body, Calve, Clinical, Cut, Detail, Discrete, Isolate, Loose, Outlying, Outpost, Patrol, Separate, Sever, Staccato, Stoic, Unfasten, Unhinge

Detached work Ravelin

Detail(s), Detailed Dock, Elaborate, Embroider, Expatiate, Explicit, Expound, Instance, ➤ ITEM, Minutiae, Nicety, Particular(ise), Pedantry, Point, Recite, Relate, Respect, Send, Spec, Special, Specification, Technicality

▷ **Detailed** may indicate last letter missing

Detain(ee), Detention Arrest, Buttonhole, Collar, Custody, Delay, Detinue, Gate, Glasshouse, Hinder, Intern, Keep, POW, Retard, Stay, ➤ WITHHOLD

Detect(ive), Detector Agent, Arsène, Asdic, Bloodhound, Brown, Bucket, Busy, Catch, Chan, CID, Cuff, Dick, Discover, Divine, Doodlebug, Dupin, Espy, Eye, Fed, Find, Flambeau, Flic, Fortune, French, Geigercounter, Geophone, Gumshoe, Hanaud, Hercule, Holmes, Interpol, Investigator, Jack, Lecoq, Lupin, Maigret, Minitrack®, Nose, Peeper, PI, Pinkerton, Plant, Poirot, Private eye, Prodnose, Radar, Reagent, Rumble, Scent, Scerne, Sense, Sensor, Shadow, Shamus, Sherlock, ➤ SLEUTH, Sofar, Sonar, Sonobuoy, Spot, Tabaret, Take, Tec, Thorndyke, Toff, Trace, Trent, Vance, Wimsey, Yard

Detent Pawl, Trigger

Deter(rent) Block, Check, Daunt, Dehort, Delay, Dissuade, Prevent, Restrain, Turn-off

Detergent Cleaner, Solvent, Surfactant, Syndet, Tepol, Whitener

Deteriorate, Deterioration Decadence, Degenerate, Derogate, Pejoration, Rust, Worsen

▷ **Deterioration** may indicate an anagram

Determination, Determine(d) Arbitrament, Ascertain, Assign, Assoil, Bent, Condition, Dead-set, ➤ DECIDE, Define, Doctrinaire, Dogged, Dour, Drive, Earnest, Fix, Govern, Grit(ty), Headstrong, Hell-bent, Indomitable, Influence, Intent, Judgement, Law, Out, Point, Purpose, Quantify, ➤ RESOLUTE, Resolve, Rigwiddie, Rigwoodie, Self-will, Set, Settle, Shape, Stalwart, Type, Weigh

▷ **Determination** may indicate 'last letter'

Detest(able) Abhor, Despise, Execrable, Execrate, Hate, Loathsome, Pestful, Vile

Detonate, Detonator Blast, Explode, Fire, Fuse, Fuze, Ignite, Kindle, Plunger, Primer, Saucisse, Saucisson, Tetryl, Trip-wire

Detour Bypass, Deviate, Divert

Detract Belittle, Decry, Diminish, Discount, Disparage

Detriment(al) Adverse, Damage, Harm, Injury, Loss, Mischief

Deuce Dickens, Old Harry, Twoer

Deuteron Diplon

Devalue Debase, Reduce, Undermine

Devastate Demolish, Destroy, Overwhelm, Ravage, Sack, Waste

Develop(ed), Developer, Development Advance, Amidol®, Aplasia, Breed, Build, Catechol, Educe, Elaborate, Enlarge, Epigenetic, Escalate, Evolve, Expand, Expatriate, Fulminant, Germinate, Gestate, Grow, Hatch, Hydroquinone, Hypo, Imago, Improve, Incubate, Lamarckism, Larva, Mature, Metamorphose, Metol, Morphogenesis, Oidium, Ontogenesis, Pathogeny, Pullulate, Pupa, Pyro, Pyrogallol, Quinol, Ribbon, Ripe(n), Shape, Soup, Sprawl, Unfold, Upgrow

▷ **Develop** may indicate an anagram

Deviant, Deviate, Deviation Aberrance, Abnormal, Anomaly, Brisure, Deflect, Depart, Derogate, Digress, Diverge, Divert, Error, Kurtosis, Pervert, Quartile, Sheer, Solecism, Sport, Stray, Swerve, ➤ TURN, Valgus, Varus, Veer, Wander, Wend

Device Afterburner, Appliance, Applicator, Artifice, Aspirator, Atlatl, Atomiser, Audio, Autodial, Autowinder, Baffle-plate, Balun, Baton-sinister, Bearing, Betatron, Biodot, Bootjack, Bug, Bungee, Buzzer, Capacitor, Capo, Carburettor, Centrifuge, Chaff, Charge, Cleat, Cleaver, Clicker, Commutator, Comparator, Compass, Compasses, Concentrator, Contraption, Contrivance, Converter, Conveyor, Counter, Coupler, Cramp, Dasher, Deckle, Delayline, Derailleur, Descendeur, Detector, Detent, Detonator, Diode, Divider, Dodge, Dongle, Doubler, Dynamotor, Ecraseur, Elevon, Emblem, Engine, Enlarger, Episcope, Episemon, Etalon, Excelsior, Expedient, FET, Frame, Fret, Fuse, Fuzzbox, Gadget, Generator, Geophone, Gimbals, Gimmick, Gizmo, Gland, Gobo, Grapnel, Gubbins, Hendiadys, Imprese, Inhaler, Instrument, Interferometer, Intervalometer, Jaws of Life, Jetpack, LED, Lighter, Lithotripter, Logo, Machine, Maser, Metronome, Microphone, Microscope, Mnemonic, Modem, Monogram, Mouse, Multiplexer, Mux, Nebuliser, Octophone, Optic®, Orle, Pacemaker, Pager, Paravane, Pattern, Petar(d), Phonoscope, Pickoff, Plan, Polygraph, Possum, Prism, Ratchet, Rectifier, Relay, Resister, Resonator, Responsor, Rest, Roller, Satellite, Scanner, Scart, Scrambler, Selsyn, Sensitometer, Sensor, Servo, Shoehorn, Shut-off, Siderostat, Smokejack, Snooperscope, Snow-eyes, Snowplough, Snuffer, Solenoid, Sonde, Sonograph, Spectograph, Spectroscope, Spirograph, Sprag, Spreader, Squeegee, Stabiliser, ➤ STRATAGEM, Subterfuge, Swellbox, Swingometer, Switch, Synchro, Tachograph, Tachometer, Tactic, Tag, Temple, Thermistor, Thermocouple, Thermopile, Thermostat, Timer, Tipple, Tokamak, Tonepad, Tourniquet, Trademark, Transducer, Transformer, Transistor, Transponder, Tremie, Trick, Triode, Tromp(e), Turnbuckle, Tympan, Valve,

Varactor, Ventilator, Vernier, Vibrator, Videophone, Viewer, Viewfinder, Vocorder, Waldo, Widget

Devil(ish) Abaddon, Afree, Afrit, Ahriman, Amaimon, Apollyon, Asmodeus, Atua, Auld Hornie, Azazel, Barbason, Beelzebub, Belial, Buckra, Clootie, Cloots, Dasyure, Davy Jones, Deev, Deil, Demogorgon, Demon, Deuce, Devling, Diable, Diabolic, Dickens, Div, Drudge, Eblis, Familiar, Fend, Fiend, Ghoul, Goodman, Goodyear, Grill, Hangie, Hornie, Iblis, Imp, Incubus, Infernal, Lamia, Legion, Lilith, Lord of the Flies, Lori, Lucifer, Mahoun(d), Manta, Mara, Mazikeen, Mephisto(pheles), Mischief, Nick, Old Bendy, Old Nick, Old One, Old Pandemonium, Old Poker, Old Roger, Old Split-foot, Old Toast, Ragamuffin, Rahu, Ralph, Satan, Sathanas, Satyr, Scour, Scratch, Screwtape, Season, Setebos, Shaitan, Shedeem, Sorra, Succubine, Succubus, Tailard, Tasmanian, Tempter, Titivil, Tutivillus, Wendigo, Wicked, Wirricow, Worricow, Worrycow, Zernebock

Devious Braide, Cunning, Deep, Eel(y), Erroneous, Implex, Indirect, Scheming, Shifty, Subtle, Tortuous, Tricky

Devise(d) Arrange, Contrive, Decoct, Hit-on, Imagine, Invenit, Invent, Plot

Devitrified Ambitty

Devoid Barren, Destitute, Empty, Vacant, Wanting

Devolve Occur, Result, Transmit

Devote(e), Devotion(al), Devoted Addiction, Aficionado, Angelus, Attached, Bhakti, Consecrate, Corban, Dedicate, Employ, Fan, Fervid, Fiend, Holy, Hound, Loyalty, Novena, Ophism, Passion, Pious, Puja, Religioso, S(h)akta, Solemn, True, Zealous

Devour Consume, Eat, Engorge, Engulf, Manducate, Moth-eat, Scarf, Scoff, ➤ SWALLOW

▷ **Devour** may indicate one word inside another

Devout Holy, Pious, Reverent, Sant, Sincere

Dew(y) Bloom, Moist, Mountain, Rime, Roral, Roric, Rorid, Roscid, Serene, Tranter

Dexterity, Dexterous Adept, Adroit, Aptitude, Cleverness, Craft, Feat(e)ous, Featuous, ➤ HANDY, Knack, Shrewd, Sleight, Slick

Diabolic Cruel, ➤ DEVILISH, Infernal

Diacritic (mark) Acute, Angstrom, Cedilla, Circumflex, Diaresis, Eth, Grave, Háček, Thorn, Tilde, Umlaut

Diadem Coronet, Fillet, Garland, Tiara

Diagnose, Diagnosis Findings, Identify, Scan, Scintigraphy

Diagonal Bias, Cater(-corner), Counter, Oblique, Slant, Solidus, Twill

Diagram Argand, Butterfly, Chart, Compass rose, Decision tree, Drawing, Feynman, Figure, Graph, Graphics, Grid, Map, Plan, Plat, Scatter, Schema, Stemma, Stereogram, Venn

Dial(ling) Card, Face, Mug, Phiz, Phone, STD, Visage

Dialect Accent, Aeolic, Alemannic, Burr, Doric, Eldin, Eolic, Erse, Eye, Franconian, Friulian, Gallo-Romance, Gascon, Geechee, Geordie, Idiom, Ionic, Isogloss, Jargon, Jockney, Joual, Khalka, Koine, Konkani, Ladin, Lallans, Landsmaal, Langobardic, Langue d'oc, Langue d'oil, Langue d'oui, Lingo, Low German, Norman, Norn, Parsee, Patois, Prakrit, Riffian, Romansch, Scouse, Syriac, Taal, Talkee-talkee, Tongue, Tshi, Wu, Yealdon, Yenglish, Yinglish

Dialogue Colloquy, Conversation, Critias, Discussion, Exchange, Lazzo, Pastourelle, Speech, Stichomythia, Talk, Upspeak

Diameter Breadth, Calibre, Gauge, Width

Diamond(s), Diamond-shaped Adamant, Black, Boart, Brilliant, Bristol, Carbonado, Cullinan, D, DE, Delaware, Eustace, Florentine, Hope, Ice, Isomer, Jim, Koh-i-noor, Lasque, Lattice, Lozenge, Paragon, Pick, Pitch, Pitt, Rhinestone, Rhomb, Rock, Rose-cut, Rosser, Rough, Sancy, Solitaire, Spark, Sparklers, Squarial, Suit

Diana Artemis, Di

Diapason Ottava

Diaphanous Clear, Sheer, Translucent

Diaphoretic Sweater

Diaphragm Cap, Iris, Mid-riff, Phrenic

Diaresis Trema

▶ **Diarist** see DIARY

Diarrhoea Collywobbles, Gippy tummy, Lientery, Montezuma's revenge, Runs, Scours, Squitters, The shits, Trots, Verbal

Diary, Diarist Chronicle, Dale, Day-book, Evelyn, Hickey, Journal, Kilvert, Log, Nobody, Pepys, Pooter, Record

Diaspora Exodus, Galuth

Diatribe Harangue, Invective, Philippic, Tirade

Dice(y) Aleatory, Astragals, Bale, Bones, Chop, Craps, Cube, Dodgy, Fulham, Fullams, Fullans, Gourd(s), Highman, Jeff, Shoot, Snake-eyes, Tallmen

Dichotomy Split

Dick(y), Dickey Clever, Deadeye, Front, Moby, OED, Policeman, Rumble, Shaky, Shirt, Spotted, Tec, Tonneau, Tucker, Unstable, Wankle, Weak, Whittington

▷ **Dick** may indicate a dictionary

Dickens Boz, Deuce, Devil, Mephistopheles

Dicker Bargain, Barter, Haggle, Trade

▷ **Dicky** may indicate an anagram

Dictate, Dictator(ial) Amin, Autocrat, Caesar, Castro, Cham, Command, Czar, Decree, Demagogue, Despot, Duce, Franco, Fu(e)hrer, Gauleiter, Hitler, Impose, Lenin, Ordain, Peremptory, Peron, Salazar, Shogun, Stalin, Tell, Tito, Totalitarian, Tsar, Tyrant, Tzar

Diction Language, Lexis, Speech, Style

Dictionary Alveary, Calepin, Chambers, Etymologicon, Fowler, Gazetteer, Glossary, Gradus, Hobson-Jobson, Johnson's, Idioticon, Larousse, Lexicon, Lexis, OED, Onomasticon, Thesaurus, Webster, Wordbook

Did Began, Couth, Fec(it), Gan

Didactic Sermonical   .

Diddle Cheat, Con, Hoax

Dido Antic, Caper, Elissa

Die(d), Dying Ache, Cark, Choke, Crater, Croak, Cube, D, Decadent, Desire, End, Evanish, Exit, Expire, Fade, Fail, Forfair, Fulham, Fulhan, Fullam, Go, Highman, Hop, Kark, Long, Morendo, Moribund, Ob(iit), Orb, Pass, Perdendosi, Perish, Peter, Snuff, Solidum, Sphacelation, Stamp, Sterve, Succumb, Suffer, Swage, Swelt, Tine, Wane

Diehard Blimp, Fanatic, Intransigent, Standpatter, Zealot

Diet(er) Assembly, Bant(ing), Cacatrophy, Council, Dail, Eat, Fare, Hay, Intake, Kashrut(h), Landtag, Lent, Macrobiotic, Parliament, Reduce, Regimen, Reichstag, Slim, Solid, Sprat, Staple, Strict, Tynwald, Vegan, Vegetarian, Weightwatcher, Worms

Dietetics Sit(i)ology

Differ(ence), Differing, Different(ly) Allo, Barney, Change, Cline, Contrast, Deviant, Diesis, Disagree, Discord, Discrepant, Disparate, Dispute, Dissent, Distinct, Diverge, Diverse, Else, Elsewise, Nuance, Omnifarious, Other, Othergates, Otherguess, Otherness, Otherwise, Separate, Several, Tiff, Unlike, Variform, Various, Vary

Differential, Differentiate Calculus, Distinguish, Taxeme

Difficult(y) Abstruseness, Ado, Aporia, Arduous, Augean, Badass, Balky, Ballbuster, Block, Bolshie, Bother, Catch, Choosy, Complication, Corner, Deep, Depth, Dysphagia, Fiddly, Formidable, Gordian, ➤ HARD, Hassle, Hazard, Hiccup, Hobble, Hole, Ill, Impasse, Indocile, Kink, Knot, Lurch, Mulish, Net, Nodus, Obstacle, Pig, Plight, Quandary, Recalcitrant, Rough, Rub, Scrape, Scrub, Setaceous, Shlep, Snag, Soup, Steep, Stick, Sticky, Stiff, Strait, Stubborn, Ticklish, Trial, Tricky, Troublous, Une(a)th, Uphill, Via dolorosa

Diffident Bashful, Meek, Modest, Reserved, Shy

Diffuse, Diffusion Disperse, Disseminate, Endosmosis, Exude, Osmosis, Pervade, Radiate, Spread

Dig(ger), Digging, Digs, Dig up Antipodean, Australian, Backhoe, Beadle, Bed(e)ral, Billet, Bot, Burrow, Costean, Delve, Enjoy, Excavate, Flea-bag, Fossorial, Gaulter, Gibe, Gird, Graip, Grub, Howk, Jab, Kip, Lair, Like, Lodgings, Mine, Navvy, Nervy, Nudge, Pad, Pioneer, Probe, Prod, Raddleman, Resurrect, Root, Ruddleman, Sap, See, Spade, Spit, Spud, Star-nose, Taunt, Tonnell, Trench, Tunnel, Undermine, Unearth

Digest(ible), Digestion, Digestive Abridgement, Absorb, Abstract, Aperçu, Archenteron, Assimilate, Codify, Concoct, Endue, Epitome, Eupepsia, Eupepsy, Gastric, Indew, Indue, Light, Pandect, Pem(m)ican, Pepsin(e), Peptic, Précis, Salt-cat, ➤ SUMMARY

Digit Bit, Byte, Dactyl, Finger, Hallux, Number, Pollex, Prehallux, Thumb, Toe

Dignified, Dignify August, Elevate, Exalt, Handsome, Honour, Lordly, Majestic, Manly, Proud, Stately

Dignitary Dean, Name, Personage, Provost, ➤ VIP

Dignity Aplomb, Bearing, Cathedra, Decorum, Face, Glory, Grandeur, Maestoso, Majesty, Nobility, Poise, Presence, Scarf, Tiara

Digress(ion) Deviate, Diverge, Ecbole, Episode, Excurse, Excursus, Maunder, Veer, Wander

Dike Bank, Channel, Cludgie, Dam, Ditch, ➤ DYKE, Embank(ment), Estacade, Lav(atory), Levee, Wall

Dilapidate(d), Dilapidation Decrepit, Desolate, Disrepair, Eroded, Ruined, Tumbledown

Dilate(d), Dilation, Dilatation Amplify, Develop, Diastole, Ecstasis, Enlarge, Expand, Increase, Mydriasis, Sinus, Tent, Varix

Dilatory Protracting, Slow, Sluggish, Tardy

Dilemma Casuistry, Choice, Cleft, Dulcarnon, Fix, Horn, Predicament, Quandary, Why-not

Dilettante Aesthete, Amateur, Butterfly, Dabbler, Playboy

Diligence, Diligent Active, Application, Assiduous, Coach, Conscience, Eident, Industry, Intent, Painstaking, Sedulous, Studious

Dill Anise, Pickle

Dilute, Dilution Adulterate, Delay, Diluent, Lavage, Simpson, Thin, Water, Weaken

Dim(ness), Dimming, Dimwit Becloud, Blear, Blur, Brownout, Caligo, Clueless, Crepuscular, Dense, Dusk, Eclipse, Fade, Faint, Feint, Gormless, Ill-lit, Indistinct, Mist, Nebulous, Ninny, Obscure, Overcast, Owl, Pale, Shadow, Unsmart

Dimension Area, Breadth, Extent, Height, Length, Measure, Size, Volume, Width

Diminish(ed), Diminuendo, Diminution, Diminutive Abatement, Assuage, Baby, Calando, Contract, Cot(t)ise, Deactivate, Decrease, Détente, Detract, Disparage, Dissipate, Dwarf, Dwindle, Erode, Fourth, Hypocorism(a), Lessen, Lilliputian, Minify, Minus, Mitigate, Petite, Pigmy, Scarp, Small, Stultify, Subside, Toy, Trangle, Wane, Whittle

Dimple(d) Dent, Depression, Hollow, Orange-peel

Din Babel, Charivary, Chirm, Commotion, Deen, Discord, Gunga, Hubbub, ➤ NOISE, Rackct, Racket, Raird, Randan, Reel, Reird, Uproar, Utis

Dine, Dining Aristology, Eat, Feast, Refect, Sup

Dingbat Doodad

Dinghy Shallop, Ship, Skiff

Dingo Warrigal

Dingy Crummy, Dark, Dirty, Drear, Dun, Fusc(ous), Grimy, Isabel(la), Isabelline, Lurid, Oorie, Ourie, Owrie, Shabby, Smoky

Dining-room Cafeteria, Cenacle, Commons, Frater, Hall, Langar, Refectory, Restaurant, Triclinium

Dinner Banquet, Collation, Feast, Hall, Kail, Kale, Meal, Prandial, Repast

Dinosaur Allosaurus, Ankylosaur, Apatosaurus, Brachiosaurus, Brontosaurus, Ceratopsian, Coelurosaur, Cotylosaur, Diplodocus, Dolichosaurus, Elasmosaur, Hadrosaur, Ichthyosaur(us), Iguanodon, Megalosaur, Ornithiscian, Ornithopod, Pelycosaur, Placoderm,

Plesiosaur, Prehistoric, Pteranodon, Pterodactyl, Pterosaur, Saurischian, Sauropod, Smilodon, Stegosaur, Teleosaurus, Theropod, Titanosaurus, Triceratops, Tyrannosaurus, Velociraptor

Dint Brunt, Dent, Depression, Force, Means, Power

Diocese Bishopric, District, Eparchate, See

Diogenes Cynic

Dioxide Cassiterite, Needle-tin

Dip(per) Baptise, Basin, Bathe, Bob, Brantub, Dabble, Dap, Dean, Dib, Diver, Dop, Duck, Dunk, Foveola, Geosyncline, Guacomole, Houmous, H(o)ummus, Hum(m)us, Immerse, Intinction, Ladle, Lucky, Ouzel, Paddle, Rinse, Rollercoaster, Salute, Star, Submerge, Tzatziki, Ursa

Diphthong Synaeresis, Synizesis

Diploma Charter, Parchment, Qualification, Scroll, Sheepskin

Diplomacy, Diplomat(ic) Altemat, Ambassador, Attaché, CD, Chargé d'affaires, Consul, DA, Dean, Doyen, El(t)chi, Envoy, Fanariot, Finesse, Gunboat, Legation, Lei(d)ger, Phanariot, Suave, ➤ TACT

▷ **Dippy** may indicate a bather

Dipsomania Oenomania

Dire Dreadful, Fatal, Fell, Hateful, Ominous, Urgent

Direct(ly), Director Administer, Advert, Aim, Airt, Auteur, Board, Boss, Cann, Channel, Charge, Command, Compere, Con(n), Conduct, Control, Cox, Dead, Due, Enjoin, Explicit, Fellini, First-hand, Forthright, Frontal, Guide, Helm, Hitchcock, Immediate, Impresario, Instruct, Kappelmeister, Lead, Lean, Manager, Navigate, Outright, Pilot, Play, Point-blank, Ready, Refer, Régisseur, Rudder, Set, Signpost, Stear, ➤ STEER, Straight, Teach, Tell, Truffaut, Vector

Direction Aim, Airt, Arrow, Astern, Bearings, Course, Cross-reference, E, End-on, Guidance, Guide, Heading, Keblah, L, Line, N, Orders, Passim, R, Route, Rubric, S, Sanction, Send, Sense, Side, Slap, Tack, Tenor, Thataway, Trend, W, Way

Direction-finder Asdic, Compass, Decca, Quadrant, Radar, Sextant, Sonar

Directory Crockford, Debrett, Encyclop(a)edia, Kelly, List, Red book, Register

Dirge Ballant, Coronach, Dirige, Epicedium, Knell, Monody, Requiem, Song, Threnody

Dirigible Airship, Balloon, Blimp, Zeppelin

Dirk Dagger, Skean, Whinger, Whiniard, Whinyard

Dirt(y) Begrime, Bemoil, Chatty, Clag, Clarty, Colly, Contaminate, Coom, Crock, Crud, Draggle, Dung, Dust, Earth, Filth, Foul, Gore, Grime, Grufted, Grungy, Impure, Manky, Moit, Mote, Muck, Obscene, Ordure, Pay, Ray, Sculdudd(e)ry, Scum, Scuzzy, Skulduddery, Smirch, Smut(ch), Sordor, Squalid, Soil, Stain, Trash, Unclean, Yucky, Yukky

Dis Hades, Hell

Disable, Disability Cripple, Lame, Maim, Paralyse, Scotch, Wreck

Disadvantage Detriment, Drawback, Handicap, Mischief, Out, Penalise, Penalty, Supercherie, Upstage, Wrongfoot, Zugswang

Disagree(ing), Disagreeable, Disagreement Argue, Argy-bargy, Bad, Clash, Conflict, Contest, Debate, Differ, Discrepant, Dispute, Dissent, Dissonant, Evil, Fiddlesticks, Friction, Heterodoxy, Pace, Rift

Disallow Forbid, Overrule

Disappear(ing) Cook, Dispel, Evanesce, Evanish, Evaporate, Fade, Kook, Latescent, Melt, Occult, Pass, Skedaddle, Slope, ➤ VANISH

Disappoint(ed), Disappointment Anticlimax, Balk, Chagrin, Crestfallen, Delude, Disgruntle, Frustrate, Gutted, Heartsick, Lemon, Letdown, Regret, Sell, Shucks, Sick, Suck-in, Sucks, Swiz(zle), Thwart

Disapproval, Disapprove Ach, Animadvert, Boo, Catcall, Censure, Deplore, Deprecate, Expostulate, Frown, Harrumph, Hiss, Napoo, Object, Pejorative, Po-faced, Raspberry, Reject, Reproach, Reprobate, Squint, Tush, Tut, Umph, Veto, Whiss

Disarm(ament), Disarming Bluff, Defuse, Demobilise, Nuclear, Winsome

Disarrange Disturb, Muddle, Ruffle, Tousle, Unsettle

Disarray Disorder, Mess, Rifle, Tash, Undress

Disaster, Disastrous Adversity, Apocalypse, Bale, Calamity, Cataclysm(ic), Catastrophe, Debacle, Dire, Doom, Evil, Fatal, Fiasco, Flop, Impostor, Meltdown, Mishap, Pitfall, Rout, Ruin, Shipwreck, Titanic, Tragedy, Wipeout

Disavow Abjure, Deny, Disclaim, Recant, Retract

Disbelief, Disbelieve(r) Acosmism, Anythingarian, Atheism, Incredulity, Mistrust, Nothingarianism, Occamist, Phew, Phooey, Puh-lease, Puh-leeze, Question, Sceptic, Voetsak

Disburse Distribute, Expend, Outlay, Spend

Disc, Disk Bursting, Button, Compact, Coulter, Counter, Diaphragm, Dogtag, EP, Epiphragm, Floppy, Frisbee®, Gold, Gong, Hard, Harrow, Intervertebral, Laser, LP, Magnetic, Mono, O, Optical, Paten, Patin, Planchet, Plate, Platinum, Puck, Rayleigh, Record, Rosette, Roundel, Roundlet, Rowel, Slipped, Slug, Stereo, Stylopodium, Tax, Token, Video, Wafer, Whorl, Wink

Discard(ed) Abandon, Crib, Dele, Jettison, Kill, Leave, Obsolete, Off, Offload, Oust, ➤ REJECT, Scrap, Shuck, Slough, Sluff, Supersede

Discern(ing), Discernment Acumen, Acute, Descry, Discrimination, Flair, Insight, Perceive, Percipient, Perspicacity, Realise, Sapient, Scry, See, Skry, ➤ TASTE, Tell, Wate

Discharge Acquit, Arc, Assoil, Blennorrhoea, Brush, Cashier, Catamenia, Catarrh, Conditional, Corona, Dejecta, Demob, Disembogue, Disgorge, Dismiss, Dump, Efflux, Egest, Ejaculate, Eject, Embogue, Emission, Emit, Encopresis, Effusion, Enfilade, Evacuate, Excrete, Execute, Exemption, Expulsion, Exude, Fire, Flower, Flux, Frass, Free, Gleet, Glow, Lava, Lay off, Leak, Leucorrhoea, Lochia, Loose, Maturate, Menses, Mitimus, Mute, Offload, Otorrhoea, Oust, Ozaena, Pay, Perform, Period, Planuria, Purulence, Pus, Pyorrhoea, Quietus, Rheum, Rhinorrhoeal, Sack, Salvo, Sanies, Secretion, Show, Shrive, Snarler, Spark, Suppurate, Teem, Unload, Vent, Void, Whites

Disciple Adherent, Apostle, Catechumen, Follower, John, Judas, Luke, Mark, Matthew, Peter, Simon, Son, Student, Thomist, Votary

Discipline, Disciplinarian Apollonian, Ascesis, Chasten, Chastise, Correct, Despot, Drill, Exercise, Feng Shui, Inure, Martinet, Mathesis, Punish, Regimentation, Regulate, School, Science, Spartan, Stickler, Subject, Train, Tutor

Disc jockey Deejay, DJ, Shock jock

Disclaim(er) Deny, Disown, No(t)chel, Recant, Renounce, ➤ REPUDIATE, Voetstoots

Disclose, Disclosure Apocalypse, Confess, Divulge, Expose, Impart, Leak, Manifest, Propale, ➤ PUBLISH, Report, Reveal, Spill, Tell, Unheal, Unhele, Unrip, Unveil

Discolour, Discolo(u)ration Bruise, Dyschroa, Ecchymosis, Livor, Stain, Streak, Tarnish, Tinge, Weather

Discomfit(ure) Abash, Confuse, Disconcert, Disturb, Frustrate, Lurch

Discomfort Ache, Angst, Dysphoria, Gyp, Heartburn, Pain, Unease

Disconcert Abash, Confuse, Disturb, Embarrass, Faze, Feeze, Flurry, Nonplus, Phase, Pheese, Pheeze, Phese, ➤ RATTLE, Shatter, Throw, Upset, Wrong-foot

▷ **Disconcert(ed)** may indicate an anagram

Disconnect(ed) Asynartete, Detach, Disjointed, Off-line, Sever, Staccato, Uncouple, Undo, Unplug

Disconsolate Desolate, Doleful, Downcast, ➤ GLOOMY

Discontent(ed) Disquiet, Dissatisfied, Humph, Repined, Sour, Umph

Discontinue Abandon, Desist, Drop, Prorogue, Stop, Terminate

Discord(ant) Absonant, Ajar, Conflict, Din, Dispute, Eris, Faction, Hoarse, Jangle, Jar, Raucous, Ruction, Strife

▷ **Discord(ant)** may indicate an anagram

Discount Agio, Cashback, Deduct, Disregard, Forfaiting, Invalidate, ➤ REBATE, Trade

Discountenance Disfavour, Efface, Embarrass

Discourage(ment) Caution, Chill, Dampen, Dash, Daunt, Demoralise, Deter, Dishearten, Disincentive, Dismay, Dissuade, Enervate, Frustrate, Opposition, Stifle

Discourse Address, Argument, Conversation, Descant, Diatribe, Dissertate, Eulogy, Expound, Homily, Lecture, Lucubrate, Orate, Preach, Relate, Rigmarole, Sermon

Discourteous, Discourtesy Impolite, Insult, Rude, Slight, Uncivil, Unmannerly

Discover(er), Discovery Amundsen, Anagnorisis, Ascertain, Betray, Breakthrough, Columbus, Cook, Descry, Detect, Discern, Discure, Eureka, ➤ FIND, Heureka, Heuristic, Learn, Locate, Manifest, Moresby, Protege, Rumble, Serendip, Serendipity, Spy, Tasman, Trace, Unearth, Unhale, Unmask, Unveil

▷ **Discovered in** may indicate an anagram or a hidden word

Discredit(able) Debunk, Decry, Disgrace, Explode, Infamy, Scandal, Unworthy

Discreet, Discretion Cautious, Circumspect, Freedom, Option, Polite, Politic, Prudence, Prudent, Trait, Wise

Discrepancy Difference, Gap, Lack, Shortfall, Variance

Discrete Distinct, Separate, Unrelated

Discriminate, Discriminating, Discrimination Ag(e)ism, Colour bar, Diacritic, Differentiate, Discern, Distinguish, Elitism, Invidious, Nasute, Racism, Secern, Segregate, Select, Sexism, Siz(e)ism, Speciesism, Subtle, Taste

Discuss(ing), Discussion Agitate, Air, Canvass, Commune, Conf(erence), Debate, Dialectic, Dialogue, Dicker, Disquisition, Examine, Handle, Hob and nob, Interlocution, Korero, Moot, Over, Palaver, Parley, Pourparler, Prolegomenon, Quodlibet, Rap, Re, Symposium, Talk, Tapis, Treatment

Disdain(ful) Belittle, Contempt, Coy, Deride, Despise, Geck, Poof, Pooh-pooh, Puh, Sassy, ➤ SCORN, Scout, Sniffy, Spurn, Supercilious

Disease(d) Acromegaly, Addison's, Affection, Aids, Ailment, Alastrim, Alzheimer's, Amoebiasis, Anbury, Anthracosis, Asbestosis, Ascites, Autoimmune, Babesiasis, Bagassosis, Bang's, Beri-beri, Blight, Blotch, Boba, Bornholm, Brand, Bright's, British, Brittle-bone, Brown lung, BSE, Bunt, Byssinosis, Caisson, Canker, Cardiopathy, CD, Chagas', Chancroid, Chickenpox, Cholera, Chorea, Christmas, Cirrhosis, Clap, Clubroot, Coeliac, Conk, Consumption, Contagion, Cowpox, Crewels, Crohn's, Cruels, Cushing's, Cynanche, Cystic fibrosis, Dandy-fever, Dartre, Deficiency, Dengue, Diabetes, Diathesis, Diphtheria, Distemper, Dourine, Dread, Dutch elm, Dysentery, Ebola, Economo's, Eczema, Edema, Elephantiasis, Endemic, English, Epidemic, Ergot, Erysipelas, Exanthema, Farcin, Fascioliasis, Favus, Fever, Filariasis, Finger and toe, Fishskin, Flu, Framboesia, Frounce, Gaucher's, Glaucoma, Gonorrh(o)ea, Gout, Graves', Gummosis, H(a)emophilia, Hansen's, Haw, Heartwater, Hebephrenia, Histoplasmosis, Hodgkin's, Hookworm, Huntington's, Hydatid, Iatrogenic, Ichthyosis, Icterus, Ideopathy, Impaludism, Impetigo, Income, Infection, Ixodiasis, Jaundice, Johne's, Kala-azar, Kawasaki's, Kuru, Kwashiorkor, Lathyrism, Legionnaires', Leichmaniasis, Leprosy, Leptospirosis, Leuc(h)aemia, Leucodystrophy, Leukaemia, Limber-neck, Listeriosis, Loco, Loose smut, Loose-cut, Lou Gehrig's, Louping ill, Lues, Lupus, Lurgi, Lurgy, Lyme, Maidism, Malady, Malaria, Marburg, Meazel, Menières, Mesel, Mildew, Minamata, Molybdenosis, Moniliasis, Moor-ill, Morbus, Motor neurone, MS, Murrain, Muscardine, Myiasis, Myx(o)edema, Myxomatosis, N(a)gana, Nephritis, Nephrosis, Newcastle, Nosography, Nosology, Oedema, Onchocerciasis, Ornithosis, Osteomyelitis, Osteoporosis, Paget's, Palsy, Pandemic, Parasitosis, Parkinson's, Pathogen, Pébrine, Pellagra, Pellagrin, Pemphigus, Phthisis, Phytosis, Pinta, Pip, Pneumo(no)coniosis, Polio, Poliomyelitis, Porphyria, Porrigo, Pott's, Pox, Progeria, Psittacosis, Pullorum, Purples, Rabid, Rabies, Rachitis, Reynaud's, Rickets, Rose-rash, Rosette, Rot, Roup, Sapego, Scabies, Scarlatina, Schistosomiasis, Scourge, Scrofula, Scurvy,

Septicaemia, Sequela, Serpigo, Shaking palsy, Shingles, Sickness, Siderosis, Silicosis, Sleeping sickness, Smallpox, Social, Sporotrichosis, ➤ STD, Sprue, Still's, Suppeago, Surra, Swayback, Swinepox, Syphilis, Syringomyelia, Tay-Sachs, TB, Tetanus, Tetters, Tinea, Toxoplasmosis, Trichinosis, Trichomoniasis, Trichophytosis, Trichosis, Trypanosomiasis, TSE, Tsutsugamushi, Tuberculosis, Tular(a)emia, Typhoid, Typhus, Ulitis, Urosis, Variola, VD, Venereal, Weil's, Wilson's, Wog, Yaws, Yellow-fever, Zoonosis, Zoster, Zymosis

▷ **Diseased** may indicate an anagram

Disembark Alight, Detrain, Land

Disembarrass Extricate, Rid, Unthread

Disembowel Exenterate, Eviscerate, Gralloch, Gut

Disenchant Disabuse, Dismay, Embitter

Disencumber Free, Rid, Unburden

Disengage(d), Disengagement Clear, Divorce, Liberate, Loosen, Release, Untie

Disentangle Debarrass, Extricate, Red(d), Solve, Unravel, Unsnarl

Disestablishmentarian Cosmist

Disfavour Maugre

Disfigure(d) Agrise, Agryze, Camsho, Deface, Deform, Mutilate, Scar, Spoil, Tash, Ugly

▷ **Disfigured** may indicate an anagram

Disgorge Discharge, Spew, Spill, Vent, Void

Disgrace Atimy, Attaint, Baffle, Blot, Contempt, Contumely, Degrade, Discredit, Dishonour, Dog-house, Ignominy, Indignity, Infamy, Obloquy, Opprobrium, Scandal, Shame, Shend, Slur, Soil, Stain, Stigma, Yshend

Disgraceful Ignoble, Ignominious, Indign, Infamous, Mean, Notorious, Shameful, Turpitude

▷ **Disgruntled** may indicate an anagram

Disguise(d) Alias, Blessing, Camouflage, Cloak, Colour, Conceal, Cover, Covert, Dissemble, Hide, Hood, Incog(nito), Mantle, Mask, Masquerade, Obscure, Peruke, Pretence, Pseudonym, Ring, Travesty, Veil, Vele, Veneer, Visagiste, Vizard

▷ **Disguised** may indicate an anagram

Disgust(ing) Ach-y-fi, Ad nauseam, Aversion, Aw, Bah, Cloy, Discomfort, Execrable, Faugh, Fie, Foh, Fulsome, Grody, Irk, Loathsome, Manky, Nauseous, Noisome, Obscene, Odium, Oughly, Ouglie, Pah, Pho(h), Pish, Repel, Repugnant, ➤ REVOLT, Revulsion, Scomfish, Scumfish, Scunner, Scuzz, ➤ SICKEN, Squalid, Tush, Ugsome, Vile, Yech, Yu(c)k

Dish(es) Adobo, Allot, Apollo, Ashet, Balti, Basin, Belle, Bharta, Biriani, Bitok, Blanquette, Bobotie, Bowl, Brandade, Brose, Buck-rarebit, Burrito, Cacciatore, Calzone, Caponata, Carbonara, Ceviche, Chafing, Champ, Charger, Chilli con carne, Chop suey, Chow mein, Cocotte, Comport, Compote, Compotier, Cook-up, Coolamon, Coq au vin, Coquille, Couscous(ou), Crostini, Crowdie, Crubeen, Crumble, Curry, Cuscus, Custard, Cutie, Cuvette, Dariole, Dent, Dhansak, Diable, Dog's-body, Dole,

Dolma, Doner kebab, Dopiaza, Dreamboat, Egg-fo-yang, Egg-foo-yung, Egg roll, Enchilada, Entrée, Entremes, Entremets, Epergne, Fajitas, Fal-a-fel, Feijoada, Fel-a-fel, Flasket, Fool, Foo Yung, Fricassee, Fritto misto, Friture, Gado-gado, Galantine, Gomer, Grail, Grav(ad) lax, Guacamole, Haggis, Halloumi, Howtowdie, Jambalaya, Jugged hare, Kasha, Keftedes, Kibbe, Kickshaw, Kimchu, Kishke, Kitchen, Kofta, Korma, Koulibiaca, Kouskous, Kreplach, Laggen, Laggin, Lanx, Luggie, Manicotti, Maror, Mazarine, Mess, Mous(s)aka, Mousse, Muesli, Nachos, Nasi goreng, Olla, Padella, Paella, Pakora, Pan, Panada, Pandowdy, Pannikin, Parmigiana, Pastitsio, Pastrami, Paten, Patera, Patin(e), Pepper-pot, Petri, Pilau, Pilow, Plate, Platter, Poi, Poori, Porridge, Porringer, Pot-au-feu, Pot-roast, Poutine, Provencale, Puri, Quesadilla, Quiche, Raclette, Ragout, Raita, Ramekin, Ramen, Ramequin, Rarebit, Receptacle, Regale, Reistafel, Rijst(t)afel, Rumbledethump(s), Salmagundi, Salmi(s), Saltimbocca, Sangraal, Sangreal, Sangrail, Sashimi, Satay, Satellite, Saucer, Sauerbraten, Sauerkraut, Scallop, Serve, Service, Seviche, Shashli(c)k, Side, Sillabub, Smasher, Soss, Soufflé, Souvlaki(a), Sowans, Sowens, Spanakopita, Special, Spitchcock, Squarial, Steak tartare, Stovies, Stroganoff, Subgum, Succotash, Sukiyaki, Sushi, Syllabub, Tamal(e), Taramasalata, Tempura, Teriyaki, Terrine, Tikka, Timbale, Toad-in-the-hole, Tostada, Tsamba, Tzatziki, Watchglass, Welsh rarebit, White-pot, Yakimono, Yakitori

Dishabille Disarray, Négligé, Undress

Dishearten Appal, Core(r), Cow, Daunt, Depress, Discourage, Dispirit

Dishevel(led) Blowsy, Blowzy, Daggy, Mess, Rumpled, Touse, Tousle, Touzle, Tumble, Uncombed, Unkempt, Windswept

Dishonest(y) Bent, Crooked, Cross, Dodgy, False, Fraud, Graft, Hooky, Hot, Knavery, Malpractice, Malversation, Shonky, Stink, Twister, Underhand, Venal

Dishonour Defile, Disgrace, Disparage, Ignominy, Seduce, ➤ SHAME, Violate, Wrong

Disillusion Disenchant, Sour

Disinclined Loth, Off, Reluctant

Disinfect(ant) Acriflavin(e), Carbolic, Cineol(e), Cleanse, Eucalyptole, Formalin, Fumigate, Fuchsine, Lysol®, Phenol, Purify, Sheep-dip, Terebene

Disingenuous Insincere, Mask, Oblique, Two-faced

Disinherit Deprive, Dispossess

Disintegrate, Disintegration Break, Collapse, Crumble, Decay, Erode, Fragment, Lyse, Lysis, Osteoclasis, Rd, Rutherford

Disinter Exhume, Unearth

Disinterested Apathetic, Impartial, Incurious, Mugwump, Unbiased

Disjointed Bitty, Incoherent, Rambling, Scrappy

▶ **Disk** see DISC

Dislike(d) Allergy, Animosity, Animus, Antipathy, Aversion, Derry, Disesteem, Displeasure, Distaste, Lump, Mind, Scunner, Warling

Dislocate, Dislocation Break, Diastasis, Displace, Fault, Luxate, Slip

Dislodge Budge, Displace, Expel, Oust, Rear, Tuft, Unship, Uproot

Disloyal(ty) False, Treason, Unfaithful, Untrue

Dismal Black, Bleak, Dark, Dowie, Drack, Dreary, Funereal, ➤ GLOOMY, Grey, Morne, Obital, Sepulchral, Sombre, Sullen, Trist(e), Wae

Dismantle(d), Dismantling Derig, Divest, Get-out, Sheer-hulk, Strike, Strip, Unrig

Dismast Unstep

Dismay Amate, Appal, Confound, Consternation, Coo, Daunt, Ha, Horrify, Lumme, Qualms

Dismiss(al) Annul, Ax, Boot, Bounce, Bowl(er), Bum's rush, Cancel, Cashier, Catch, Chuck, Congé, Daff, Discard, Discharge, Expulsion, Fire, Heave-ho, Lay off, Marching orders, Mitten, Och, Prorogue, Push, Recall, Reform, Remove, Road, Sack, Scout, Send, Shoo, Spit, Stump, Via, Walking papers, York

Dismount Alight

Disobedience, Disobedient, Disobey Contumacy, Defy, Flout, Insubordination, Rebel, Wayward

Disorder(ed), Disorderly Ague, Ailment, Anarchy, Ariot, Asthma, Ataxia, Catatonia, Chaos, Clutter, Confuse, Contracture, Defuse, Derange, Deray, Diabetes, Dishevel, Dystrophy, Echolalia, Entropy, Farrago, Grippe, Haemophilia, Huntingdon's chorea, Hypallage, Inordinate, Irregular, ME, Mess, Mistemper, ➤ MUDDLE, Muss(y), Neurosis, Oncus, Onkus, Pandemonium, Para-, Psychomatic, Psychosis, Rile, SAD, Seborrh(o)ea, Shell-shock, Slovenly, Thalass(a)emia, Tousle, Unhinge, Unruly, Upset, Virilism

▷ **Disorder(ed)** may indicate an anagram

Disorganised Deranged, Scatterbrain, Shambolic

Disown Deny, Disclaim, Disinherit, Renounce, Repudiate, Unget

Disparage, Disparaging Abuse, Belittle, Decry, Defame, Denigrate, Depreciate, Detract, Discredit, Lessen, ➤ SLANDER, Slur, Snide, Traduce, Vilify

Dispassionate Calm, Clinical, Composed, Cool, Impartial, Objective, Serene

Dispatch Bowl, Celerity, Consign, Destroy, Dismiss, Expede, Expedite, Express, Gazette, Kibosh, Kill, Missive, Post, Pronto, Remit, Report, ➤ SEND, Ship, Slaughter, Slay

Dispel Disperse, Scatter

Dispensation, Dispense(r), Dispense with Absolve, Administer, Apothecary, Automat, Ax(e), Cashpoint, Chemist, Container, Distribute, Dose, Dropper, Exempt, Handout, Indult, Scrap

Dispersable, Disperse, Dispersion Diaspora, Diffract, Diffuse, Disband, Dissolve, Lyophil(e), Scail, Scale, ➤ SCATTER, Skail, Strew

Dispirit(ed) Dampen, Dash, Daunt, Discourage, Dishearten, Exorcism, Listless, Sackless

Displace(ment), Displaced Antevert, Blueshift, Depose, Disturb, Ectopia, Ectopy, Fault, Heterotopia, Luxate, Move, Oust, Proptosis, Ptosis, Reffo, Stir, Subluxation, Unsettle, Uproot, Valgus, Varus

Display, Display ground Air, Array, Blaze, Blazon, Brandish, Bravura, Depict, Eclat, Epideictic, Etalage, Evidence, Evince, Exhibition, Exposition, Express, Extend, Exude, Fireworks, Flaunt, Float, Gondola, Hang, LED, Lek, Liquid crystal, Manifest, Mount, Muster, Ostentation, Outlay, Overdress, Pageant, Parade, Paraf(f)le, Peepshow, Pixel, Pomp, Propale, Pyrotechnics, Rodeo, Scene, Shaw, ➤ SHOW, Sight, Spectacle, Splash, Splurge, Sport, Spree, State, Stunt, Tableau, Tattoo, Tournament, Up, Vaunt, Wear

Displease(d), Displeasure Anger, Dischuffed, Humph, Irritate, Provoke, Umbrage

Disport Amuse, Divert, Play

Dispose(d), Disposal Arrange, Bestow, Cast, Despatch, Dump, Eighty-six, Lay(-out), Prone, Sale, Sell, Service, Settle, Stagger

▷ **Disposed, Disposition** may indicate an anagram

Disposition Affectation, Attitude, Bent, Bias, Humour, Inclination, Kidney, Lie, Nature, Penchant, Talent, Temper(ament), Trim

Dispossess(ed) Abate, Attaint, Bereft, Depose, Deprive, Evict, Oust

Disproportion(ate) Asymmetric, Extreme, Imbalance, Unequal

Disprove Debunk, Discredit, Negate, Rebut, Redargue, Refel, Refute

Dispute(d), Disputant Argue, Barney, Brangle, Cangle, Case, Chaffer, Chorizont(ist), Contend, Contest, Contretemps, Controversy, Debate, Deny, Differ, Discept, Discuss, Eristic, Fray, Haggle, Kilfud-yoking, Lock-out, Militate, Ob and soller, Odds, Oppugn, Plea, Polemic, Pro-and-con, ➤ QUESTION, Resist, Rag, Spar, Stickle, Threap(it), Threep(it), Tiff, Tissue, Variance, Wrangle

Disqualify Debar, Incapacitate, Recuse, Reject, Unfit

Disquiet(ed) Agitate, Discomboberate, Discombobulate, ➤ DISTURB, Pain, Perturb(ation), Solicit, Turmoil, Uneasy, Unnerve, Vex

Disraeli Dizzy, Tancred

Disregard(ed) Anomie, Anomy, Contempt, Disfavour, Flout, Forget, Ignore, Oblivion, Omit, Overlook, Oversee, Pass, Pretermit, Slight, Spare, Violate, Waive

Disrepair Dilapidation, Ruin

Disreputable, Disrepute Base, Disgrace, Louche, Low, Lowlife, Raffish, Ragamuffin, Rip, Seamy, Shameful, Shy, Sleazy

Disrespect(ful) Contempt, Discourtesy, Impiety, Impolite, Irreverent, Profane, Slight, Uncivil

Disrupt(ion) Breach, Cataclasm, Disorder, Distract, Hamper, Interrupt, Jetlag, Mayhem, Perturb, Quonk, Screw, Upheaval

▷ **Disruption** may indicate an anagram

Dissatisfaction Displeasure, Distaste, Humph, Umph

Dissemble(r) Conceal, Feign, Fox, Hypocrite, Impostor

Dissension, Dissent(er), Dissenting Contend, Differ, Disagree, Discord, Dissident, Faction, Heretic, Jain, Lollard, Noes, Non-CE, Non-con(formist), Pantile, Protest, Raskolnik, Recusant, Splinter group, ➤ STRIFE, Vary

Dissertation Essay, Excursus, Lecture, Thesis, Treatise

▶ **Dissident** see DESERTER

Dissimilar Different, Diverse, Heterogeneous, Unlike

Dissipate(d) Debauch, Diffuse, Disperse, Dissolute, Gay, Revel, Scatter, Shatter, Squander, Waste

▷ **Dissipated** may indicate an anagram

Dissociate Separate, Sever, Withdraw

Dissolute Degenerate, Hell, Lax, Libertine, Licentious, Loose, Rake-helly, Rakish, Rip, Roué

▷ **Dissolute** may indicate an anagram

Dissolution Dismissal, Divorce, End, Separation

Dissolve Deliquesce, Digest, Disband, Disunite, Liquesce, Melt, Terminate, Thaw

Dissonance Wolf

Dissuade Dehort, Deter, Discourage

Distaff Clotho, Female, Lady, Rock, Stick

Distance Absciss(a), Afield, Apothem, Breadth, Coss, Declination, Eloi(g)n, Farness, Foot, Headreach, Height, Interval, Klick, Kos(s), Latitude, League, Length, Mean, Mileage, Parasang, Parsec, Range, Reserve, Rod, Span, Spitting, Stade, Striking, Way, Yojan

Distant Aloof, Far, Frosty, Icy, Long, Offish, Remote, Tele-, Timbuctoo, Yonder

Distaste(ful) Repugnant, Ropy, Scunner, Unpalatable, Unpleasant, Unsavoury

Distemper Ailment, Colourwash, Hard-pad, Paint, Panleucopenia, Tempera

Distend(ed), Distension Bloat, Dilate, Ectasia, Emphysema, Expand, Inflate, ➤ STRETCH, Swell, Turgid, Tympanites, Varicose

Distil(late), Distillation, Distiller, Distilling Alcohol, Alembic, Anthracine, Azeotrope, Brew, Condense, Drip, Pelican, Pyrene, Pyroligneous, Rosin, Turps, Vapour

▷ **Distillation** may indicate an anagram

Distinct(ive) Apparent, Characteristic, Clear, Different, Evident, Grand, Individual, Peculiar, Plain, Separate, Several, Signal, ➤ SPECIAL, Stylistic, Vivid

Distinction Beaut(y), Blue, Cachet, Credit, Diacritic, Difference, Dignity, Diorism, Disparity, Division, Eclat, Eminence, Honour, Lustre, Mark, Mystique, Note, Nuance, OM, Prominence, Quiddity, Rank, Renown, Speciality, Style, Title

Distinguish(ed), Distinguishing Classify, Demarcate, Denote, Diacritic, Different(iate), Discern, Discriminate, Divide, Elevate, Mark, Notable, Perceive, Prestigious, Prominent, Signal, Stamp

Distort(ed), Distortion Anamorphosis, Bend, Colour, Contort, Deface, Deform, Dent, Fudge, Helium speech, Jaundiced, Mangle, Misshapen, Pervert, Rubato, Thraw, Twist, ➤ WARP, Wow, Wrest, Wring, Wry

▷ **Distort(ed)** may indicate an anagram

Distract(ed), Distraction Absent, Agitate, Amuse, Avocation, Bewilder, Divert, Nepenthe, Éperdu, Forhaile, Frenetic, Lost, Madden, Mental, Perplex, Upstage

▷ **Distract(ed)** may indicate an anagram

Distrain(t) Na(a)m, Poind, Sequestrate, Stress

Distraught Deranged, Elfish, Elvan, Frantic, Mad, Troubled

Distress(ed), Distressing Afflict, Ail, Alack, Anger, Anguish, Antique, Distraint, Dolour, Exigence, Extremity, Grieve, Harass, Harrow, Hurt, Ill, ➤ IN DISTRESS, Irk, Misease, Misfortune, Need, Oppress, Pain, Poignant, Prey, Sad, Shorn, Sore, SOS, Straits, Traumatic, ➤ TROUBLE, Une(a)th

Distribute(d), Distribution Allocate, Allot, Binomial, Busbar, Carve, Chi-square, Colportage, Deal, Deliver(y), Deploy, Dish, Dispense, Dispose, Issue, Lie, Lot, Mete, Out, Pattern, Poisson's, Prorate, Repartition, Serve, Share

▷ **Distributed** may indicate an anagram

District Alsatia, Amhara, Arcadia, Ards, Area, Bail(l)iwick, Banat, Barrio, Belt, Canton, Cantred, Classis, Community, Diocese, End, Exurb, Federal, Gau, Ghetto, Hundred, Lathe, Liberty, Locality, Loin, Manor, Metropolitan, ➤ NEIGHBOURHOOD, Oblast, Pachalic, Pale, Parish(en), Paroch, Pashalik, Patch, Province, Quarter, Quartier, Rape, ➤ REGION, Ride, Riding, Ruhr, Sanjak, Section, Sheading, Sircar, Soc, Soke(n), Stannary, Suburb, Sucken, Talooka, Taluk, Tender, Township, Venue, Vicinage, Walk, Wapentake, Way, Zila, Zillah, Zone

Distrust Caution, Doubt, Suspect

Disturb(ance), Disturbed Ado, Aerate, Affray, Agitate, Atmospherics, Autism, Betoss, Brabble, Brainstorm, Brash, Brawl, Broil, Carfuffle, Collieshangie, Concuss, Delirium, Dementia, Derange, Desecrate, Disquiet, Dust, Feeze, Firestorm, Fray, Fret, Harass, Hoopla, Incommode, Infest, Interrupt, Jee, Kerfuffle, Kick-up, Kurfuffle, Muss, Outbreak, Prabble, Ramp, Ripple, Romage, Rook, Roughhouse, Rouse, Ruckus, Ruction, Ruffle, Rumpus, Shake, Shindy, Shook-up, Stashie, Static, Steer, Stir, Sturt, Tremor, Trouble, Turbulent, Unquiet, Unrest, Unsettle, Upheaval, Uproot, ➤ UPSET, Vex

▷ **Disturb(ed)** may indicate an anagram

Disunite Alienate, Dissever, Divide, Divorce, Split

Disuse Abandon, Abeyance, Desuetude, Discard

Ditch Barathron, Barathrum, Channel, Cunette, Delf, Delph, Dike, Discard, Donga, Drainage, Drop, Dyke, Euripus, Foss(e), Graft, Grip, Gully, Ha(w)-ha(w), Haw-haw, Jettison, Khor, Level, Lode, Moat, Na(l)la(h), Nulla(h), Rean, Reen, Rhine, Rid, Sea, Sheuch, Sheugh, Sike, Sloot, Sluit, Spruit, Stank, Syke, Trench

Dither Agitato, Bother, Faff, Hesitate, Pussyfoot, Twitter

Dittany Gas-plant

Ditty, Ditties Air, Arietta, Canzonet, Departmental, Jingle, Lay, Song

Diva Callas, Patti, Singer

Divan Compilement, Congress, Couch, Council, Settee, Sofa

Dive(s), Diving Belly-flop, Duck, Half-gainer, Header, Honkytonk, Jackknife, Joint, Ken, Nitery, Nose, Plummet, Plunge, Plutocrat, Power, Scoter, Skin, Sound, Stoop, Submerge, Swallow, Swoop, Urinant

Diver(s) Didapper, Duck, Embergoose, Flop, Frogman, Gainer, Grebe, Guillemot, Loom, Loon, Lungie, Many, Merganser, Pearl, Pike, Plong(e), Pochard, Poker, Puffin, Sawbill, Scuba, Snake-bird, Speakeasy, Sundry, Urinator, Various, Zoom

Diverge(nce) Branch, Deviate, Spread, Swerve, Variant, Veer

Divers Miscellaneous, Some

Diverse, Diversify Alter, Dapple, Different, Interlard, Intersperse, Manifold, Motley, Multifarious, Separate, Variegate, Various, Vary

Diversion, Divert(ing) Amuse, Avocation, Beguile, Deflect, Disport, Dissuade, Distract, Entertain, Game, Hare, Hobby, Interlude, Pastime, Pleasure, Prolepsis, Ramp, Red-herring, Refract, Reroute, Ruse, Shunt, Sideshow, Sidetrack, Sport, Stalking-horse, Stratagem, Sway, Switch, Upstage, Yaw

▷ **Diverting** may indicate an anagram

Divest Denude, Rid, Strip, Undeck, Undress

Divide(d) Apportion, Band, Bipartite, Bisect, Branch, Cantle, Cleft, Comminute, Commot(e), Continental, Counter-pale, Cut, Deal, Demerge, Dimidiate, Estrange, Fork, Great, Indent, Parcel, Part, Polarise, Rend, Rift, Separate, Sever, Share, ➤ SPLIT, Sunder, Watershed, Zone

Dividend Bonus, Div, Interim, Into, Share

Divine, Divine presence, Divinity Acoemeti, Atman, Avatar, Beatific, Clergyman, Conjecture, Curate, DD, Deduce, Deity, Douse, Dowse, Ecclesiastic, Forecast, Foretell, Fuller, ➤ GOD, ➤ GODDESS, Godhead, Guess, Hariolate, Heavenly, Holy, Immortal, Inge, Isiac, Mantic, Numen, Olympian, Pontiff, Predestinate, Predict, Presage, Priest, RE, RI, Rector, Rimmon, Scry, Sense, Seraphic, Shechinah, Shekinah, Spae, Supernal, Theanthropic, Theologise, Theology, Triune

Diviner, Divination Augury, Auspices, Axinomancy, Belomancy, Botanomancy, Capnomancy, Cartomancy, Ceromancy, Chiromancy, Cleromancy, Coscinomancy, Crithomancy, Crystallomancy, Doodlebug, Dowser, Empyromancy, Geomancy, Gyromancy, Hariolation, Haruspex, Hepatoscopy, Hieromancy, Hieroscopy, Hydromancy, I Ching, Intuition, Lampadomancy, Magic, Myomancy, Omphalomancy, Oneiromancy, Palmistry, Pyromancy, Rhabdomancy, Scapulimancy, Sciomancy, Seer, Sibyl, Sortes, Sortilege, Spae(man), Spodomancy, Taghairm, Tais(c)h, Tripudiary, Vaticanator, Xylomancy

Divisible, Division Amitosis, Arcana, Arm, Arrondissement, Bajocian, Banat(e), Bannet, Bar, Bizone, Branch, Brome, Caesura, Canton, Cantred, Cantref, Cassini's, Caste, Category, Champart, Chapter, Classification,

Cleft, Cloison, Clove, Comitatus, Commot(e), Commune, Compartment, Corps, County, Crevasse, Curia, Department, Dichotomy, Disagreement, Disunity, Duan, Eyalet, Farren, Fissile, Fork, Grisons, Guberniya, Gulf, Gulph, Hedge, Hide, Hundred, Inning, Isogloss, Keuper, Kim(m)eridgian, Lathe, Leet, Legion, Lindsey, List, Lobe, M(e)iosis, Mitosis, Mofussil, Nome, Pachytene, Pargana, Part, Partition, Passus, Pergunnah, Period, Phratry, Phyle, Phylum, Pipe, Pitaka, Platoon, Polarisation, Presidency, Quotition, Rape, Region, Reservation, Riding, Sanjak, Schism, Section, Sector, Segment, Semeion, Sept(ate), Sever, Share, Sheading, Shed, Shire, Stage, Subheading, Tahsil, Taxis, Telophase, Tepal, Thanet, Trichotomy, Trio, Troop, Tuath, Unit, Vilayet, Volost, Wapentake, Ward

Divisor Aliquant, Aliquot

Divorce(d) Diffarreation, Dissolve, Disunion, Div, Estrange, Get(t), Part, Separate, Sequester, ➤ SUNDER, Talak, Talaq

Divot Clod, Sod, Turf

Divulge Confess, Disclose, Expose, Publish, Reveal, Split, Tell, Unveil, Utter

Dizziness, Dizzy Beaconsfield, Ben, Capricious, Dinic, Disraeli, Giddy, Giglot, Lightheaded, Mirligoes, Swimming, Vertiginous, ➤ VERTIGO, Woozy

DJ Tuxedo

DNA Antisense, Centromere, Cistron, Complementary, Cytosine, Exon, Gene, Intron, Muton, Plasmid, Procaryote, Prokaryote, Purine, Recombinant, Replicon, Satellite, Selfish, Telomere, Thymidine, Transposon, Watson-Crick model

Do(es), Doing Accomplish, Achieve, Act, Anent, Beano, Char, Cheat, Chisel, Cod, Con, Cozen, Deed, Dich, Dish, Div, Doth, Dupe, Effectuate, Enact, Execute, Function, Gull, Handiwork, Hoax, Mill, Perform, Same, Serve, Settle, Shindig, Spif(f)licate, Suffice, Thrash, Ut

▷ **Do** may indicate an anagram

Do away Abolish, Banish, Demolish, Kill

Docile Agreeable, Amenable, Biddable, Dutiful, Facile, Meek, Submissive, Tractable, Yielding

Dock(er), Docked, Docks Abridge, Barber, Basin, Bistort, Bob, Camber, Canaigre, Clip, Curta(i)l, Cut, Deduct, De-tail, Dry, Floating, Grapetree, Knotweed, Lop, Marina, Moor, Off-end, Pare, Patience, Pen, Pier, Quay, Rhubarb, Rumex, Rump, Seagull, Shorten, Snakeweed, Sorrel, Sourock, Stevedore, Tilbury, Watersider, Wet, Wharf, Yard

Docket Invoice, Label, Tag

Dockyard Arsenal, Rosyth

Doctor(s) Allopath, Arnold, Asclepiad, Barefoot, Bleeder, BMA, Bones, Breeze, Bright, Brighton, Brown, Caius, Castrate, Chapitalize, Clinician, Cook, Cup(per), Cure(r), Dale, Diagnose, Dr, Dryasdust, Erasmus, Extern(e), Fake, Falsify, Faustus, Feldsher, Fell, Finlay, Flying, Foster, Fundholder, Galen, Geriatrician, Geropiga, GP, Hakeem, Hakim, Healer, Homeopath, Houseman, Hyde, Imhotep, Intern, Internist, Jekyll, Jenner, Johnson, Kildare, Lace, Leach, Leech, Load, Locum, Luke, Manette, Massage, MB,

MD, Medicate, Medico, Middleton, Mindererus, Minister, Misrepresent, MO, MOH, Molla(h), Moreau, Mulla(h), Neuter, No, Ollamh, Ollav, Paean, Panel, Pangloss, Paracelsus, Pedro, PhD, Physician, Pill(s), Practitioner, Quack, Quacksalver, Rabbi, RAMC, Registrar, Resident, Rig, Salk, Sangrado, Sawbones, Shaman, Slop, Spin, Stum, Surgeon, Syn, Syntax, Thorne, Treat, Vaidya, Vet, Watson, Who, Witch

▷ **Doctor(ed)** may indicate an anagram

Doctrine Adoptianism, Adoptionism, Antinomian, Apollinarian, Archology, Averr(h)oism, Bonism, Cab(b)ala, Calvanism, Chiliasm, Consubstantiation, Creed, Credo, Determinism, Ditheletism, Docetism, Dogma, Doxie, Doxy, Esotery, Federalism, Fideism, Gnosticism, Gospel, Holism, Infralapsarianism, Islam, Ism, Jansenism, Krypsis, Lore, Malthusian, Metempsychosis, Molinism, Monergism, Monism, Monroe, Pragmatism, Reformism, Satyagrahi, Sharia, Sheria, Shibboleth, Strong meat, Subjectivism, Sublapsarianism, Subpanation, Substantialism, Syndicalism, Synergism, System, Teleology, ➤ TENET, Terminism, Theory, Theravada, Thomism, Transubstantiation, Tutiorism, Voluntarism, Weismannism, Whiteboyism, Zoism, Zwinglian

Document(s), Documentary Bumph, Carta, Certificate, Charter, Contract, Conveyance, Covenant, Daftar, Deed, Diploma, Doco, Docket, Dompass, Dossier, Form, Holograph, Latitat, Logbook, Mandamus, Papers, Production, Ragman, Ragment, Roll, Roul(e), Screed, Waybill, Writ

Dod Pet, Poll

Dodder(y) Shake, Stagger, Strangleweed, Totter, Tremble

Doddle Easy

Dodge(r) Artful, Avoid, Column, Elude, Evade, Evasion, Jink, Jook, Jouk, Racket, Ruse, Shirk, Sidestep, Skip, Slalom, Slinter, Tip, Trick, Twist, Urchin, Weave, Welsh, Wheeze, Wire, Wrinkle

Doe(s) Deer, Faun, Hind

Doff Avail(e), Avale, Remove, Rouse, Shed, Tip

Dog(s) Aardwolf, Aberdeen, Affenpinscher, Afghan, Airedale, Alans, Akita Alsatian, Andiron, Apsos, Argos, Bandog, Barbet, Barker, Basenji, Beagle, Bedlington, Bichon frise, Bird, Bitser, Blanch, Blenheim, Bloodhound, Blueheeler, Bobbery, Boerbul, Boots, Border collie, Borzoi, Bowler, Bowwow, Bounce, Bouvier, Boxer, Brach(et), Brak, Bratchet, Briard, Buckhound, Bulldog, Bush, Caesar, Cairn, Canes, Canidae, Canine, Cant, Carriage, Cerberus, Chenet, Chihuahua, Chow(-chow), Coach, Cocker, Collie, Courser, Cur, Dachshund, Dalmatian, Dandie Dinmont, Dane, Dangle, Deerhound, Dhole, Dingo, Doberman(n)(-pinscher), Elkhound, Eskimo, Eye, Feet, Fido, Fox terrier, Gazehound, Gelert, Goorie, Great Dane, Greyhound, Griffon, Guard, Guide, Gun, Harlequin, Harrier, Haunt, Hearing, Heel(er), Hot, Hound, Huntaway, Husky, Hyena, Iron, Jackal, Jack Russell, Katmir, Keeshond, Kelpie, Kennel, Kennet, Kerry blue, Ketmir, Komondor, Kratim, Kuri, Kurre, Labrador, Laika, Landseer, Lassie, Lhasa apso, Lorel, Luath, Lurcher, Malamute, Malemute, Maremma, Mastiff, Mauthe, Messan, Mexican hairless, Moera, Mongrel, Montmorency, Moppet, Mutt, Newfoundland, Oath, Orthrus, Otterhound, Papillon,

Pariah, Peke, Pekinese, Pembroke, Pinscher, Pluto, Pointer, Pom(eranian), Pooch, Poodle, Prairie, Pug, Puli, Pursue, Pye-dog, Pyrenean mountain, Queue, Rab, Raccoon, Rach(e), Ranger, Retriever, Reynard, Rhodesian ridgeback, Rottweiler, Rover, Saint Bernard, Saluki, Samoyed(e), Sapling, Schipperke, Schnauzer, Scotch terrier, Sealyham, Setter, Shadow, Shaggy, Shar-Pei, Sheltie, Shih tzu, Shin-barker, Shock, Shough, Showghe, Sirius, Sled, Sniffer, Sothic, Spaniel, Spitz, Spoor, Springer, Stag, Staghound, Stalk, Starter, Sussex spaniel, Tag, Tail, Talbot, Teckel, ➤ TERRIER, Tike, Toby, Top, Tosa, Touser, Towser, Tracker, Trail, Tray, Trendle-tail, Trindle-tail, Tripehound, Trundle-tail, Turnspit, Tyke, Vizsla, Volpino, Warragal, Warrigal, Weimaraner, West Highland, Westie, Whelp, Whiffet, Whippet, Wishtonwish, Wolf, Wolfhound, Yap(per), Yapster, Yorkie, Zorro

Dog-bane Apocynum

Doge Dandolo

Dogfish Huss, Rigg

Dogged Determined, Die-hard, Dour, Indefatigable, Pertinacious, Stubborn, Sullen

Doggerel Crambo, Jingle, Laisse, Rat-rhyme

Dog Letter R

Dogma(tic) Assertive, Belief, Conviction, Creed, Doctrinal, Opinionative, Ideology, Pedagogic, Peremptory, Pontifical, Positive, ➤ TENET

Do-Gooder Piarist, Reformer, Salvationist, Samaritan, Scout

Dogsbody Bottle-washer, Gofer, Skivvy

Dog star Canicula, Lassie, Sirius, Sothic

Do it Dich

Dolce Stop, Sweet

Dole Alms, Batta, B(u)roo, Give, Grief, Maundy, Payment, Pittance, Ration, ➤ SHARE, Tichborne, Vail, Vales

Doll(y) Barbie®, Bimbo, Common, Corn, Crumpet, Dress, Dutch, Golliwog, Kachina, Kewpie®, Maiden, Marionette, Matryoshka, Maumet, Mommet, Mummet, Ookpik®, Ornament, Parton, Poppet, Puppet, Ragdoll, Russian, Sis(ter), Sitter, Toy, Tearsheet, Trolley, Varden, Washboard

Dollar(s) Balboa, Boliviano, Buck, Cob, Euro, Fin, Greenback, Iron man, Peso, Piastre, Pink, S, Sand, Sawbuck, Sawhorse, Scrip, Smacker, Spin, Wheel

Dollop Glob, Helping, Share

▷ **Dolly** may indicate an anagram

Dolly-bird Dish

Dolour Grief, Pain, Sorrow

Dolphin Amazon, Arion, Beluga, Bottlenose, Cetacean, Coryphene, Delphinus, Grampus, Lampuka, Lampuki, Meer-swine, Porpess(e), Risso's, River, Sea-pig

Dolt Ass, Blockhead, Clodhopper, Noodle, Oaf, Owl, ➤ STUPID

Domain Bourn(e), Demain, Demesne, Emirate, Empire, Estate, Manor, Public, Rain, Realm, Region, Reign

Dome(-shaped) Cap, Cupola, Dagoba, Geodesic, Head, Imperial, Louvre, Millennium, Onion, Periclinal, Rotunda, Stupa, Tee, Tholos, Tholus, Tope, Vault

Domestic(ate) Char, Cleaner, Dom, Esne, Familiar, Home-keeping, Homely, House, Housetrain, Humanise, Interior, Internal, Intestine, Maid, Menial, ➤ SERVANT, Tame, Woman

Domicile Abode, Dwelling, Hearth, Home, Ménage

Dominate, Dominance, Dominant Ascendancy, Baasskap, Bethrall, Clou, Coerce, Control, Henpeck, Maisterdome, Mesmerise, Monopolise, O(v)ergang, Override, Overshadow, Power, Preponderant, Preside, Rule, Soh, ➤ SUBDUE, Subjugate, Tower

Domineer Boss, Henpeck, Lord, Ride, Swagger, Tyrannize

Dominica(n) Jacobite, Monk, OP, Savonarola, WD

Dominie Maister, Master, Pastor, Sampson, Schoolmaster

Dominion Dom, Empire, Khanate, NZ, Realm, Reame, Reign, ➤ RULE, Supremacy, Sway, Territory

Domino(es) Card, Fats, Mask, Matador

Don Academic, Address, Assume, Caballero, Endue, Fellow, Garb, Giovanni, Indew, Juan, Lecturer, Prof, Quixote, Reader, Senor, Spaniard, Tutor, Wear

Dona(h) Duckie, Love

Donate, Donation Aid, Bestow, Contribution, Gift, Give, Peter's pence, Present, Wakf, Waqf

Done Achieved, Complete, Crisp, Ended, Executed, Had, Over, Spitcher, Tired, Weary

Donjon Dungeon, Keep

Donkey Ass, Burro, Cardophagus, Cuddie, Cuddy, Dapple, Dick(e)y, Eeyore, Fussock, Genet(te), Jennet, Jerusalem pony, Kulan, Modestine, Moke, Mule, Neddy, Onager, Stupid, Years

Donor Benefactor, Bestower, Settlor

Doo Dove

Doodle(r) Scribble, Yankee

Doodlebug Antlion, Larva, V1

Doom(ed) Condemned, Date, Destine, Destiny, ➤ FATE, Fay, Fey, Fie, Goner, Ill-starred, Lot, Predestine, Preordain, Ragnarok, Ruined, Sentence, Spitcher, Star-crossed, Weird

Doone Carver, Lorna

Door(way) Aperture, Dutch, Entry, Exit, French, Haik, Hake, Hatch, Heck, Ingress, Jib, Lintel, Oak, Portal, Postern, Revolving, Rory, Sliding, Stable, Stage, Storm, Swing, Up and over, Vomitory, Wicket, Yett

Doorkeeper, Doorman Bouncer, Commissionaire, Guardian, Janitor, Ostiary, Porter, Tiler, Tyler, Usher

Doorpost Architrave, Dern, Durn, Jamb, Yate, Yett

Dope Acid, Amulet, Bang, Coke, Crack, ➤ DRUG, Gen, Goose, Info, Narcotic, Nobble, Rutin, ➤ STUPID PERSON, Sedate, Soup, Tea

Dorcas Gazelle, Needle

Dorian, Doric Metope, Mutule
Doris Day, Lessing, Mollusc
Dormant Abed, Comatose, Hibernating, Inactive, Inert, Joist, Latent, Resting, ➤ SLEEPING, Torpescent
Dormitory Barrack, Dorter, Dortour, Hall, Hostel, Quarters
Dormouse Loir
Dorothy Bag, Dot, Sayers
Dorsal Back, Neural, Notal
Dory Fish, John
Dose(age) Administer, Cascara, Draught, Drug, Kilogray, ➤ MEASURE, Physic, Posology, Potion, Powder
Doss (house) Dharmsala, Dharmshala, Kip, Padding-ken
Dossier File, Record
Dot(s), Dotted, Dotty Absurd, Bullet, Criblé, Dit, Dower, Dowry, Engrailed, Leader, Lentiginose, Limp, Micro, Occult, Or, Particle, Pixel, ➤ POINT, Polka, Precise, Punctuate, Punctulate, Punctum, Schwa, Semé(e), Set, Speck, Spot, Sprinkle, Stigme, Stipple, Stud, Tap, Tittle, Trema, Umlaut
Dote, Dotage, Doting, Dotard Adore, Anile, Anility, Cocker, Dobbie, Idolise, Imbecile, Pet, Prize, Senile, Tendre, Twichild
Double(s) Amphibious, Ancipital, Bi-, Bifold, Binate, Counterpart, Crease, Dimeric, Doppel-ganger, Dual, Duo, Duple(x), Duplicate, Equivocal, Fetch, Fold, Foursome, Geminate, Gimp, Image, Ingeminate, Ka, Look-alike, Loop, Martingale, Pair, Parlay, Polyseme, Reflex, Replica, Ringer, Run, Similitude, Spit, Trot, Turnback, Twae, ➤ TWIN, Two(fold)
Double-barrelled Tautonym
Double-cross Two-time
Double-entendre Polyseme, Polysemy
Doublet Peascod, Pourpoint, TT
Doubt(ful), Doubter Ambiguous, Aporia, Askance, But, Debatable, Distrust, Dubiety, Dubitate, Hesitate, Hum, Iffy, Incertitude, Misgiving, Mistrust, ➤ NO DOUBT, Precarious, Qualm, Query, ➤ QUESTION, Rack, Scepsis, Sceptic, Scruple, Shady, Shy, Sic, Skepsis, Sus, Suspect, Suss, Thomas, Thos, Umph, Uncertain, Unsure, Waver
Doubtless Probably, Sure, Truly
Douceur Bonus, Sop, Sweetener
Douche Bath, Gush, Rinse, Shower, Wash
Dough(y) Boodle, Cake, Calzone, Cash, Duff, Hush-puppy, Knish, Loot, Magma, Masa, Money, Paste, Pop(p)adum, Ready, Sad, Spondulicks
Doughboy Dumpling, Soldier
Doughnut Cruller, Knish, Koeksister, Olycook, Olykoek, Sinker, Torus
Doughty Brave, Intrepid, Resolute, Stalwart, Valiant
Dour Glum, Hard, Mirthless, Morose, Reest, Reist, Sinister, Sullen, Taciturn
Douse Dip, Drench, Extinguish, Snuff, Splash
Dove Collared, Columbine, Culver, Cushat, Diamond, Doo, Ice-bird, Mourning, Pacifist, ➤ PIGEON, Ring, Rock, Stock, Turtle

Dove-cot(e) Columbarium, Columbary, Louver, Louvre, Lover
Dovetail Fit, Lewis(son), Mortise, Tally, Tenon
Dowager Elder, Widow
Dowdy Frumpish, Mums(e)y, Shabby, Sloppy, Slovenly
Dowel Peg, Pin
Down(beat), Downs, Downward, Downy A bas, Abase, Abattu, Alow, Amort, Bank, Below, Blue, Cast, Catabasis, Chapfallen, Comous, Cottony, Crouch, Darling, Dejected, Dowl(e), Drink, Epsom, Feather, Fledge, Flue, Floccus, Fluff, Fly, Fuzz, Goonhilly, Ground, Hair, Hill, Humble, Humiliate, Lanugo, Losing, Low, Lower, Nap, Oose, Ooze, Owing, Pappus, Pennae, Pile, Plumage, Quash, Repress, Sebum, Thesis, Thistle, Tomentum, Vail, Wretched
Downcast Abject, Chapfallen, Despondent, Disconsolate, Dumpish, Hopeless, Melancholy, Woebegone
Downfall, Downpour Cataract, Collapse, Deluge, Fate, Flood, Hail, Onding, Overthrow, Rain, Ruin, Thunder-plump, Torrent, Undoing, Waterspout
Downgraded Déclassé
Downright Absolute, Arrant, Bluff, Candid, Clear, Complete, Flat, Plumb, Plump, Pure, Rank, Sheer, Stark, Utter
Downstairs Below
Dowry Dot, Dower, Lobola, Lobolo, Merchet, Portion, Settlement, Tocher
Dowse(r), Dowsing Divine, Enew, Fireman, Rhabdomancy, Water-witch
Doxology Gloria, Glory
Doxy Harlot, Loose woman, Wench
Doyen Dean, Senior
Doze Ca(u)lk, Dove(r), Nap, Nod, Semi-coma, Sleep, Slip, Slumber
Dozen(s) Thr(e)ave, Twal, Twelve
Dr Debtor, Doctor, Dram
Drab Cloth, Dell, Dingy, Dull, Dun, Isabel(line), Lifeless, Livor, Prosaic, Pussel, Quaker-colour, Rig, Road, Slattern, Sloven, Subfusc, Tart, Trull, Wanton, Whore
Drabble Bemoil, Draggle
Dracula Bat, Count, Vampire
Draft Cheque, Draw, Ebauche, Essay, Landsturm, Minute, MS, Outline, Plan, Press, Rough, Scheme, Scroll, Scrowle, ➤ SKETCH
Drag Car, Drail, Dredge, Drogue, Elicit, Eonism, Epicene, Extort, Hale, Harl, ➤ HAUL, Keelhaul, La Rue, Lug, Puff, Pull, Rash, Sag, Schlep, Shoe, Skidpan, Sled, Snig, Sweep, Toke, Tote, Trail, Train, Travail, Travois, Trawl, Treck, Trek, Tump
Draggle Drail, Lag, Straggle
Dragon Basilisk, Bel, Bellemère, Chaperon(e), Chindit, Draco, Drake, Fire-drake, Gargouille, Komodo, Kung-kung, Ladon, Lindworm, Opinicus, Python, Rouge, Wantley, Wivern, Worm, Wyvern
Dragonfly Aeschna, Demoiselle, Nymph, Odonata
Dragon's teeth Cadmus, Spartae, Sparti

Dragoon Coerce, Force, Press, Trooper

Drain(age), Draining, Drainpipe Bleed, Brain, Buzz, Catchment, Catchwater, Channel, Cloaca, Cundy, Delf, Delph, Dewater, Ditch, Dry, Ea(u), ➤ EMPTY, Emulge(nt), Exhaust, Fleet, Grating, Grip, Gully, Gutter, Kotabothron, Ketavothron, Lade, Leach, Leech, Limber, Lose, Milk, Pump, Rack, Rone, Sap, Scupper, Seton, Sew(er), Sheuch, Sheugh, Sink, Silver, Siver, Sluice, Sluse, Soakaway, Sough, Spend, Stank, Sump, Sure, Syver, Tile, Trench, Trocar, Unwater, Ureter, U-trap

Dram Drink, Drop, Nipperkin, Portion, Snifter, Tickler, Tiff, Tot, Wet

Drama(tic), Drama school Auto, Catastasis, Charade, Comedy, Farce, Heroic, Histrionic, Kabuki, Kathakali, Kitchen sink, Legit, Mask, Masque, Mime, Moralities, No, Nogaku, Noh, Piece, Play, RADA, Scenic, Sensational, Singspiel, Stagy, Striking, Tetralogy, Theatric, Thespian, Tragedy, Unities, Wagnerian, Wild

Dramatist Adamov, Aeschylus, Albee, Aristophanes, Beaumarchais, Beaumont, Brecht, Bridie, Calderon, Congreve, Corneille, Coward, Drinkwater, Euripides, Fletcher, Fry, Gay, Genet, Goldoni, Havel, Ibsen, Ionesco, Kyd, Lyly, Massinger, Menander, Middleton, Molière, Odets, O'Neill, Osborne, Otway, Pinero, Pirandello, Plautus, ➤ PLAYWRIGHT, Racine, Rostand, Seneca, Schiller, Shadwell, Sophocles, Stoppard, Strindberg, Synge, Terence, Udall, Vanbrugh, ➤ WRITER, Webster, Wedekind, Wilde, Wilder, Will, Yeats

Dram-shop Bar, Boozingken, Bousingken

Drape Adorn, Coverlet, Coverlid, Curtain, Festoon, Fold, Hang, Swathe, Valance, Veil, Vest

Draper Gilpin, Hosier, Mercer, Ruth

Drastic Dire, Dramatic, Extreme, Harsh, Purge, Senna, ➤ SEVERE, Violent

Drat Bother, Dang, Darn

Draught(s), Draughtsman Aloetic, Breeze, Dam, Design, Drench, Drink, Fish, Gulp, Gust, Haal, Hippocrene, King, Men, Nightcap, Outline, Plan, Potation, Potion, Pull, Quaff, Sketch, Sleeping, Slug, Swig, Tracer, Veronal, Waucht, Waught, Williewaught

▷ **Draught** may refer to fishing

Draught-board Dam-board, Dambrod

Dravidian Tamil

Draw(er), Drawing, Drawn, Drawers, Draw off Adduct, Allure, Attract, Bottom, Cock, Crayon, Dead-heat, Delineate, Derivation, Describe, Doodle, Dr, Draft, Drag, Dress, Educe, Entice, Equalise, Evaginate, Extract, Fetch, Gather, Gaunt, Glorybox, Gut, Haggard, Hale, Halve, Haul, Induce, Indue, Inhale, Lengthen, Limn, Longbow, Lottery, Pantalet(te)s, Panty, Perpetual check, Petroglyph, Protract, Pull, Rack, Raffle, Remark, Scent, Sesquipedalian, Shottle, Shuttle, Siphon, Sketch, Slub, Stalemate, Snig, Spin, Stumps, Sweepstake, Syphon, Tap, Taut, Technical, Tempt, Tenniel, Tie, Till, Toke, Tole, Tombola, Top, Tose, Tow(age), Toze, Trice, Troll, Tug, Unsheathe, Uplift

▷ **Draw** may indicate something to smoke

Drawback Catch, Downside, Ebb, Impediment, ➤ OBSTACLE, Rebate, Retraction, Shrink, Snag

Drawbridge Bascule, Pontlevis

Drawing Cartoon, Charcoal, Crayon, Dentistry, Elevation, Freehand, Fusain, Graphics, Indraft, Monotint, Orthograph, Pastel, Profile, Seductive, Sepia, Silver-point, Study, Traction

Drawl Dra(u)nt, Haw, Slur, Twang

▷ **Drawn** may indicate an anagram

Drawn up Atrip, Drafted

Dray Cart, Lorry, Wagon

Dread Angst, Anxiety, Awe, Fear, ➤ HORROR, Redoubt, Thing

Dreadful Awful, Chronic, Dearn, Dire, Formidable, Ghastly, Horrendous, Penny, Sorry, Terrible

Dream(er), Dreamy, Dream state Alchera, Alcheringa, Aspire, Desire, Drowsy, Dwa(u)m, Fantast, Fantasy, Faraway, Idealise, Illusion, Imagine, Languor, Mare, Mirth, Moon, Morpheus, Muse, Nightmare, On(e)iric, Pensive, Pipe, ➤ REVERIE, Rêveur, Romantic, Somniate, Stargazer, Surreal, Sweven, Trance, Trauma, Vague, Vision, Walter Mitty, Wet

Dreary Bleak, Desolate, Dismal, Doleful, Dreich, Dull, Gloom, Gray, Grey, Oorie, Ourie, Owrie, Sad

Dredger Caster

Dregs Bottom, Draff, Dunder, F(a)eces, Fecula, Gr(e)aves, Grounds, Lees, Legge, Mother, Mud, Riffraff, Scaff, Sediment, Silt, Snuff, Ullage

Dreikanter Ventifact

Drench Dowse, Soak, Souse, Steep, Submerge

Dress(ed), Dressing Accoutre, Adorn, Align, Array, Attire, Attrap, Bandage, Bandoline, Bedizen, Black-tie, Bloomer, Blouson, Boast, Bodice, Boun, Bowne, Brilliantine, Busk, Caftan, Cataplasm, Charpie, Cheongsam, Chimer, Cimar, Clad, ➤ CLOTHING, Coat, Cocktail, Comb, Compost, Compress, Corsage, Corset, Costume, Court, Curry, Cymar, Dandify, Dashiki, Deck, Deshabille, Dight, Dirndl, Dizen, Doll, Dolly Varden, Dolman, Don, Drag, Dirndl, Dub, Dubbin, Elastoplast®, Empire, Endue, Enrobe, Evening, Fancy, Far(r)andine, Farthingale, Fatigues, Ferrandine, Fertiliser, Fig, Finery, Flamenco, French, Frock, Gamgee tissue, Garb, Garnish, Gauze, Girt, Gown, Graith, Granny, Gymslip, ➤ HABIT, Ihram, Italian, Jaconet, Kabuki, Ketchup, K(h)anga, Kimono, Kirtle, Line, Lint, Lounger, Mayonnaise, Merveilleuse, Mob, Morning, Mother Hubbard, Mufti, Mulch, Muu-muu, Oil, Patch, Peplos, Pinafore, Plaster, Pledget, Plumage, Polonaise, Pomade, Poultice, Prank, Preen, Prepare, Rag, Raiment, Ranch, Ray, Rehearsal, Rémoulade, Rig, Robe, Russet, Russian, Rybat, Sack, Salad, Samfo, Sari, Sarong, Sartorial, Sauce, Scutch, Seloso, Separates, Sheath, Shift, Shirt, Shirtwaister, Simar(re), Smock, Sterile, Stole, Stupe, Subfusc, Subfusk, Suit, Sundress, Symar, Tasar, Taw, Tent, Tenue, Tew, Thousand Island, Tiff, Tire, Tog, Toga, Toilet, Tonic, Top, Treat, Trick, Trim, Trollopee, Tunic, Tusser, Tussore, Tuxedo, Uniform, Vest, Vinaigrette, Wear, Wedding, White-tie, Wig, Yclad, Ycled

Dressage Demivolt(e), Manège, Passade, Passage, Pesade, Piaffe

▷ **Dressed up, Dressing** may indicate an anagram

Dresser Adze, Almery, Bureau, Chest, Couturier, Deuddarn, Dior, Lair, Lowboy, Sideboard, Transvestite, Tridarn, Welsh

Dressing-gown Bathrobe, Negligee, Peignoir

Dressing-room Apodyterium, Vestiary, Vestry

Dressmaker Costumier, Dorcas, Modiste, Seamstress, Tailor

Drew Steeld, Stelled

Dribble Drip, Drivel, Drop, Slaver, Slop, Trickle

Dried Fish Bum(m)alo, Bummaloti, Haberdine, Speld(r)in(g), Stockfish

▶ **Dried Fruit** see DRY FRUIT

Drift(er), Drifting Becalmed, Continental, Cruise, Current, Digress, Float, Heap, Impulse, Maunder, North Atlantic, Plankton, Purport, Rorke, Slide, Tendence, Tendency, ▶ TENOR, Waft, Wander

Drill Auger, Bore, Burr, Close order, Educate, Exercise, Form, Hammer, Jackhammer, Jerks, Monkey, Pack, PE, Pierce, Pneumatic, PT, Reamer, Ridge, Seeder, Sow, Square-bashing, Teach, Train, Twill, Twist, Usage, Wildcat

Drink(er), Drunk(enness) AA, Absorb, Alkie, Alky, Babalas, Bacchian, Bender, Beverage, Bev(v)y, Bezzle, Bib(ite), Binge, Birl(e), Blind, Blitzed, Bloat, Blotto, Bombed, Boose, Booze, Bosky, Bottled, Bouse, Bracer, Bumper, Carafe, Carousal, Cat-lap, Chaser, Corked, Crapulous, Crocked, Cuppa, Cut, Demitasse, Digestif, Dipsomaniac, Double, Down, Drain, Draught, ▶ DRINKS, Drop, Ebriate, Ebriose, Elixir, Entire, Eye-opener, Finger, Fou, Fuddle-cap, Fuddled, Full, Glug, Half-seas-over, High, Hogshead, Honkers, Hoo(t)ch, Hophead, Imbibe, Indulge, Inhaust, Intemperate, Irrigate, Ivresse, Jag, Jar, Jimmy Woodser, Juicehead, Lap, Legless, Lethean, Lit, Loaded, Lord, Lower, Lush(y), Maggoty, Maudlin, Merry, Methomania, Methysis, Mortal, Mug, Nightcap, Nog(gin), Obfuscated, Oenomania, Oiled, One, Oppignorate, Overshot, Paid, Paint, Partake, Particular, Pickled, Pick-me-up, Pie-eyed, Pint(a), Piss-artist, Pissed, Pisshead, Pisspot, Pixil(l)ated, Plonk(o), Potion, Primed, Quaff, Rat-arsed, Ratted, Refresher, Reviver, Rolling, Rotgut, Rotten, Rummer, Screwed, Sea, Shebeen, Shicker, Short, Shotover, Silenus, Sip(ple), Skinned, Slake, Slewed, Sloshed, Slued, Slug, Slurp, Smashed, Snifter, Snort, Soak, Soused, Sponge, Spongy, Spunge, Squiffy, Stewed, Stimulant, Stinko, Stocious, Stoned, Stonkered, Stotious, Sup, Swacked, Swallow, Swig, Swill, Tank, Temulence, Tiddl(e)y, Tiff, Tift, Tight, Tipple, Tipsy, Tope, Toss, Tossicated, Tost, Usual, Wash, Wassail, Wat, Wauch, Waught, Well-oiled, Wet, Whiffled, Williewaught, Winebag, Wino, Wrecked, Zonked

Drink store Cellar

Drip Bore, Dribble, Drop, Gutter, IV, Leak, Seep, Splatter, Stillicide, Trickle, Wimp

Dripstone Larmier

DRINKS

2 letters:
It

3 letters:
Ale
Ava
Bub
Cha
Cup
Dop
Fap
Gin
Hom
Kir
Mum
Pop
Rum
Rye
Tea
Tot
Vin

4 letters:
Asti
Bock
Bull
Coke®
Flip
Grog
Homa
Kava
Kola
Malt
Mead
Neck
Nipa
Port
Purl
Raki
Sack
Sake
Saki
Soda
Soft
Soma
Sour
Sura
Tape
Tass
Tent
Yill

5 letters:
Assai
Bingo
Bombo
Bumbo
Cider
Cocoa

Copus
Crush
Doris
Float
Glogg
Haoma
Hogan
Joram
Jorum
Julep
Kefir
Kelty
Kvass
Lassi
Mauby
Meths
Mâcon
Meath
Medoc
Mobby
Morat
Mulse
Nappy
Negus
Pekoe
Pepsi®
Perry
Polly
Pombe
Punch
Rakee
Rummy
Salop
Sarsa
Sarza
Shake
Shrub
Skink
Sling
Smile
Stout
Toddy
Tonic
Totty
Vodka
Xeres

6 letters:
Amrita
Apozem
Arrack
Bishop
Burton
Busera
Cassis
Caudle
Cauker

Chasse
Cooler
Cooper
Doctor
Eggnog
Enzian
Gimlet
Grappa
Hobnob
Kalied
Keltie
Kephir
Kirsch
Kumiss
Kümmel
Maotai
Meathe
Mickey
Mobbie
Nectar
Obarni
Oolong
Orgeat
Oulong
Pastis
Pernod®
Plotty
Posset
Pulque
Rickey
Saloop
Samshu
Shandy
Sherry
Smiler
Squash
Stingo
Strega
Strunt
Waragi
Yaqona
Zythum

7 letters:
Absinth
Akvavit
Alcopop
Amoroso
Aquavit
Bacardi®
Campari®
Chablis
Chianti
Cobbler
Cordial
Curaçao
Curaçoa

Daquiri
Eggflip
Fairish
Fustian
Guarana
Italian
Koumiss
Malmsey
Mineral
Nobbler
Oenomel
Oloroso
Persico
Philter
Philtre
Pilsner
Pink gin
Ratafia
Rosiner
Rosolio
Sangria
Screech
Scrumpy
Sherbet
Sherris
Sloe gin
Stengah
Swizzle
Tequila
Tio Pepe®

8 letters:
Absinthe
Aleberry
Ambrosia
Anisette
Aperitif
Borachio
Bordeaux
Burgundy
Calvados
Champers
Charneco
Ciderkin
Coca-cola®
Cold duck
Daiquiri
Dog's nose
Dubonnet®
Geropiga
Ginsling
Gluhwein
Highball
Homebrew
Hydromel
Lemonade
Mahogany

Nepenthe	Aqua-vitae	Whisky mac	
Persicot	Ayahuasco	**10 letters:**	
Pilsener	Badminton	Blackstone	
Ragmaker	Buck's fizz	Bloody Mary	
Red biddy	Champagne	Buttermilk	
Regmaker	Chocolate	Chartreuse®	
Resinata	Cuba libre	Maraschino	
Resinate	Eccoccino	Piña colada	
Riesling	Febrifuge	Pousse-café	
Rice beer	Gingerade	Shandygaff	**12 letters:**
Rosoglio	Grenadine	Tom Collins	Doch-an-dorach
Sangaree	Hippocras	**11 letters:**	Humpty-dumpty
Schnapps	Lambswool	Aguardiente	Jimmy Woodser
Skokiaan	Mint julep	Benedictine	Marcobrunner
Snowball	Manhattan	Black and tan	Old-fashioned
Spritzer	Metheglin	Black velvet	Sarsaparilla
Switchel	Milkshake	Boiler-maker	**13 letters:**
Tequilla	Nipperkin	Doch-an-doris	Deoch-an-doruis
Tincture	Sauternes	Half-and-half	Mops and
Vermouth	Slivovica	Niersteiner	brooms
Witblits	Slivovitz	Screwdriver	Prairie oyster
9 letters:	Snakebite	Soapolallie	**14 letters:**
Applejack	Sundowner	Tom and Jerry	John Barleycorn

Drive(r), Driving, Drive out AA, Actuate, Ambition, Backseat, Banish, Beetle, Bullocky, Ca', Cabby, Campaign, Carman, Charioteer, Chauffeur, Coachee, Coact, Crankshaft, Crew, Crowd, Disk, Dislodge, Dr, Drover, Drum, Economy, Eject, Emboss, Energy, Enew, Enforce, Engine, Expatriate, Faze, Feeze, Ferret, Fire, Firk, Fluid, Force, Four-wheel, Front-wheel, Fuel, Gadsman, Goad, Hack, Hammer, Haste, Heard, Helmsman, Herd, Hie, Hoon, Hoosh, Hot-rod, Hoy, Hunt, Hurl, Impel, Impetus, Impinge, Impulse, Jarvey, Jehu, Jockey, Juggernaut, Lash, Libido, Lunge, Mahout, Make, Mall, Miz(z)en, Motor, Motorman, Offensive, Overland, Peg, Penetrate, Piston, Power, Propel, Put, RAC, Rack, Ram, Rebut, Ride, Road, Roadhog, Run, Scorch, Screw, Scud, Shepherd, Shoo, Spank, Spin, Spur, Start, Stroke, Sumpter-horse, Sunday, Sweep, Task-master, Teamster, Tee, Test, Thrust, Toad, Tool, Torrential, Trot, Truckie, Tup, Two-stroke, Urge, Urgence, Wagoner, Whist, Wood, Wreak

Drivel Blether(skate), Drip, Drool, Humbug, Nonsense, Pap, Rot, Salivate, Slaver

Driving club AA, Iron, RAC

Drizzle Drow, Haze, Mist, Mizzle, Roke, Scouther, Scowther, Serein, Skiffle, Smir(r), Smur, Spit

Droll Bizarre, Comic, Funny, Jocular, Queer, Waggish

Drone Bee, Buzz, Dog-bee, Doodle, Dor(r), Drant, Draunt, Hanger-on, Hum, Idler, Parasite, Thrum, Windbag

Drool Drivel, Gibber, Salivate, Slaver

Droop(ing) Cernuous, Decline, Flag, Languish, Lill, Limp, Lob, Loll, Lop, Nutate, Oorie, Ourie, Owrie, Peak, Ptosis, ➤ SAG, Slink, Slouch, Weeping, Welk(e), Wilt, Wither

Drop(s), Dropping Acid, Airlift, Apraxia, Bag, Bead, Beres, Blob, Cadence, Calve, Cascade, Cast, Chocolate, Cowpat, Dap, Descent, Deselect, Dink,

Drappie, Drib(let), Ease, Ebb, Escarp(ment), Fall, Floor, Flop, Fumet, Gallows, Globule, Gout(te), Guano, Gutta, Guttate, Instil, Knockout, Land, Minim, Modicum, Muff, Mute, Omit, Pilot, Plonk, Plummet, Plump, Plunge, Plunk, Precepit, Precipice, (Prince) Rupert's, Rain, Scat, Scrap, Shed, Sip, Skat, Spraint, Stilliform, Tass, Taste, Tear, Virga

Drop-out Hippie, Hippy

Drop-shot Dink

Dropsy Anasarca, Ascites, Edema, Oedema

Dross Chaff, Dregs, Recrement, Scoria, Scorious, Scum, Sinter, Slack, Slag, Waste

Drought Dearth, Drouth, Lack, Thirst

Drove(r) Band, Crowd, Flock, Herd, Host, Masses, Overlander, Puncher

Drown(ing) Drook, Drouk, Engulf, Inundate, Noyade, Overcome, Sorrows, Submerge

Drowse, Drowsiness, Drowsy Blet, Comatose, Doze, Hypnagogic, Hypnopompic, Lethargic, Nap, Narcolepsy, Narcosis, Nod, Snooze

Drub Anoint, Thrash

Drudge(ry) Devil, Dogsbody, Fag, Grind, Hack, Jackal, Johnson, Plod, Scrub, Slave(y), Snake, Sweat, Thraldom, Toil, Trauchle, Treadmill

Drug(ged) Anti-depressant, Bag, Base, Blow, Bolus, Bomber, Boo, Deck, Designer, Dope, Downer, Elixir, Fantasy, Fertility, Fig, Gateway, Hallucinogen, Hard, High, Immunosuppressant, Lifestyle, Line, Load, Mainline, Medicine, Miracle, Nervine, Nobble, Opiate, Painkiller, Paregoric, Parenteral, Pharmaceutics, Pharmacopoeia, Poison, Prophylactic, Psychedelic, Psychodelic, Sedate, Snort, Soft, Spike, Stimulant, Stupefy, Substance, Truth, Upper, Weed, White stuff, Wonder

DRUGS

1 letter:	Bhang	Dragée	Ecstasy
Q	Candy	Heroin	Eucaine
3 letters:	Crank	Inulin	Guarana
Eve	Dagga	Joypop	Hashish
Hop	Ganja	Mescla	Henbane
Ice	Grass	Mummia	Hypnone
INH	Hocus	Peyote	Insulin
LSD	Intal®	Pituri	Jellies
Tab	L-dopa	Prozac®	Librium®
Tea	Mummy	Saloop	Metopon
4 letters:	Opium	Sulpha	Miltown®
Acid	Quina	Valium®	Mogadon®
Adam	Rutin	Viagra®	Morphia
Bang	Salep	**7 letters:**	Patulin
Bute	Salop	Atabrin	Quinine
Dopa	Speed	Atebrin®	Seconal®
Hemp	Sugar	Botanic	Steroid
Junk	Sulfa	Cascara	Suramin
Sida	Taxol	Charlie	Trional
Soma	**6 letters:**	Churrus	Turpeth
Toot	Amulet	Codeine	Veronal®
5 letters:	Ativan®	Damiana	**8 letters:**
Aloes	Charas	Dapsone	Adjuvant
Benny	Curare	Ecbolic	Ataraxic

Banthine
Curarine
Diazepam
Fentanyl
Goofball
Hyoscine
Katamine
Laetrile
Laudanum
Mersalyl
Mescalin
Methadon
Moonrock
Naloxone
Narcotic
Nepenthe
Nystatin
Oxytocic
Psilocin
Roborant
Scopolia
Serevent®
Snowball
Tetronal
Thiazide
Viricide
Zerumbet
9 letters:
Acyclovir
Analeptic
Angel-dust
Anovulant
Antrycide
Augmentin
Barbitone
Biguanide
Busulphan
Captopril
Carbachol
Cisplatin
Clozapine
Corticoid
Cyclizine
Dramamine®
Electuary
Ephedrine

Foscarnet
Frusemide
Ibuprofen
Iprindole
Isoniazid
Jaborandi
Lorazepan
Mepacrine
Methadone
Mydriasis
Novocaine
Nux vomica
Paludrine®
Pethidine
Phenytoin
Practolol
Quinidine
Quinquina
Reserpine
Sudorific
Synergist
Tamoxifen
Temazepam
Totaquine
Trinitrum
Verapamil
Vermifuge
10 letters:
Amantadine
Ampicillin
Antagonist
Anxiolytic
Atracurium
Belladonna
Benzedrine
Bufotenine
Cimetidine
Clofibrate
Clomiphene
Colestipol
Disulfiram
Ergotamine
Ethambutol
Formestane
Imipramine
Indapamide

Isoniazide
Mefloquine
Nalbuphine
Nifedipine
Nitrazepam
Papaverine
Pentaquine
Phenacetin
Prednisone
Primaquine
Probenecid
Propanolol
Psilocybin
Salbutamol
Selegiline
Sialogogue
Stramonium
Sucralfate
11 letters:
Aminobutene
Amphetamine
Beta-blocker
Chloroquine
Cinnarizine
Clenbuterol
Clindamycin
Deserpidine
Distalgesic
Fluconazole
Gemfibrozil
Haloperidol
Ipratropium
Isoxsuprine
Magic bullet
Meprobamate
Nikethamide
Paracetamol
Pentamidine
Pentazocine
Pravastatin
Purple heart
Succedaneum
Thalidomide
Theobromine
Tolbutamide
Tous-les-mois

Tropomyosin
Vinblastine
Vincristine
12 letters:
Alpha-blocker
Anthelmintic
Antiperiodic
Azathioprine
Chlorambucil
Fluphenazine
Gonadotropin
Guanethidine
Indomethacin
Methaqualone
Methotrexate
Mifepristone
Perphenazine
Physotigmine
Promethazine
Streptomycin
Trimethoprim
13 letters:
Amitriptyline
Anthelminthic
Antihistamine
Materia medica
Penicillamine
Pyrimethamine
Sulphadiazine
Thiabendazole
Triamcinolone
14 letters:
Bendrofluozide
Butyrhophenone
Flucloxacillin
Norethisterone
Pentobarbitone
Phenacyclidine
Phenobarbitone
Sulphanilamide

Druid Gorsedd

Drum(mer), Drumming, Drumbeat Arête, Atabal, Barrel, Beatbox, Bodhran, Bongo, Brake, Carousel, Chamade, Conga, Dash-wheel, Devil's tattoo, Dhol, Dr, Drub, Ear, Flam, Kettle, Lambeg, Mridamgam, Mridang(a), Mridangam, Myringa, Naker, Pan, Percussion, Rappel, Rataplan, Reel, Rep, Ridge, Rigger, Roll, Ruff, Ruffle, Salesman, Side, Snare, Steel, Tabla, Tabour, Tabret, Tambourine, Tam-tam, Tap, Tattoo, Thrum, Timbal, Timp(ano), Tom-tom, Touk, Traps, Traveller, Tuck, Tymbal, Tympanist, Tympano, Whim, Work

Drum-belly Hoven

Drumstick Attorney, Leg, Rute

▶ **Drunk(ard)** see DRINK

▷ **Drunken** may indicate an anagram

Druse Crystal

Dry(ing), Drier Air, Anhydrous, Arefaction, Arefy, Arid, Blot, Bone, Brut, Corpse, Crine, Dehydrate, Desiccate, Detox, Drain, Dull, Evaporate, Exsiccator, Firlot, Fork, Harmattan, Hasky, Hi(r)stie, Humidor, Jejune, Jerk, Khor, Kiln, Mummify, Oast, ▶ PARCH, Prosaic, Reast, Reist, Rizzar, Rizzer, Rizzor, Sciroc, Scorch, Sear, Sec(co), Seco, Sere, Shrivel, Siccative, Siroc(co), Sober, Sponge, Steme, Stove, Ted, Thirsty, Thristy, Toasted, Torrefy, Torrid, Towel, Tribble, Trocken, TT, Unwatery, Watertight, Welt, Wilt, Win(n), Wipe, Wither, Wizened, Xeransis, Xerasia, Xero(sis), Xerostomia

Dryad Nymph

Dry fruit Achene, Akene, Currant, Mebos, Prune, Raisin, Samara, Silicula, Siliqua, Silique, Sultana

Dry mouth Xerostoma

DT's Dingbats, Hallucinations, Zooscopic

Dual Double, Twin, Twofold

Dub Array, ▶ CALL, Entitle, Hete, Knight, Name

Dubious Doubtful, Equivocal, Fishy, Fly-by-night, Hesitant, Iffy, Improbable, Questionable, Scepsis, Sceptical, Sesey, Sessa, ▶ SHADY, Suspect, Unlikely

▷ **Dubious** may indicate an anagram

Dubliner Jackeen

Duce Leader, Musso(lini)

Duchess Anastasia, Malfi, Peeress, Titled

Duchy Brabant, Cornwall, Dukedom, Luxembourg, Omnium, Realm, Swabia, Westphalian

Duck(ed) Amphibian, Avoid, Aylesbury, Bald-pate, Bargander, Bergander, Blob, Blue, Bob, Bufflehead, Bum(m)alo, Canard, Canvasback, ▶ COUPLE OF DUCKS, Dead, Dearie, Decoy, Dip, Dodge, Dodo, Douse, Drook, Drouk, Dunk(er), Eider, Enew, Escape, Evade, Ferruginous, Flapper, Gadwall, Garganey, Garrot, Golden-eye, Goosander, Greenhead, Hareld, Harlequin, Heads, Herald, Immerse, Jook, Jouk, Long-tailed, Mallard, Mandarin, Muscovy, Musk, Nil, O, Oldsquaw, Paddling, Palmated, Paradise, Pekin(g), Pintail, Plunge, Pochard, Poker, Ruddy, Runner, Rush, Scaup, Scoter, Sheld(d)uck, Shieldrake, Shovel(l)er, Shun, Sitting, Smeath, Smee(th), Smew, Sord, Spatula, Sprigtail, Surf(scoter), Teal, Team, Tufted, Tunker, Velvet scoter, Whistling, Widgeon, Wigeon, Wood, Zero

Duckbill Ornithorhynchus, Platypus

Duckwalk Waddle

Duckweed Lemna

Ducky Sweet, Twee

Duct Bile, Canal(iculus), Channel, Conduit, Epididymus, Fistula, Gland, Lachrymal, Laticifer, Pipe, Tear, Thoracic, Tube, Ureter, Vas deferens

Dud Bouncer, Failure, Flop, Shan(d), Stumer

Dude Cat, Coxcomb, Dandy, Fop, Lair, Macaroni, Popinjay, Roy

Dudgeon Anger, Hilt, Huff, Pique

Due(s) Adequate, Arrearage, Claim, Debt, Deserts, Forinsec, Geld, Heriot, Just, Lot, Mature, Owing, Reddendo, Rent, Right, ➤ SUITABLE, Thereanent, Toll, Tribute, Worthy

Duel(list) Mensur, Monomachy, Principal, Tilt

Duenna Chaperone, Dragon

Duff Bungle, Dough, Nelly, NG, Plum, Pudding, Rustle

Duffer Bungler, Rabbit, Useless

Dug Ploughed, Teat, Titty, Udder

Dugong Halicore, Sea-cow, Sea-pig, Sirenian

Dug-out Abri, Canoe, Piragua, Pirogue, Shelter, Trench, Trough

Duke(dom) Alva, Clarence, D, Ellington, Fist, Iron, Milan, Orsino, Peer, Prospero, Rohan, Wellington

Dulcimer Cembalo, Citole, Cymbalo, Santir, Sant(o)ur

Dull(ard), Dullness Anorak, Banal, Besot, Bland, Blear, Blunt, Boeotian, Cloudy, Deadhead, Dense, Dim, Dinge, Dingy, Doldrums, Dowf, Dowie, Drab, Drear, Dreich, Dry, Dunce, Fozy, Grey, Heavy, Hebetate, Ho-hum, Insipid, Jejune, Lacklustre, Lifeless, Log(y), Lowlight, Mat(t), Matte, Monotonous, Mopish, Mull, Obtuse, Opacity, Opiate, Ordinary, Overcast, Owlish, Pall, Pedestrian, Perstringe, Podunk, Prosaic, Prose, Prosy, Rebate, Rust, Slow, Sopite, Staid, Stodger, Stodgy, Stolid, Stuffy, Stultify, ➤ STUPID, Sunless, Tame, Tarnish, Tedious, Ticky-tacky, Toneless, Torpor, Treadmill, Tubby, Vapid, Wonk, Wooden, Zoid

Dumb(ness) Alalia, Aphonic, Crambo, Hobbididance, Inarticulate, Mute, Stupid

Dumbfound(ed) Amaze, Astound, Flabbergast, Stun, Stupefy, Stupent

Dumb ox Aquinas

Dummy Comforter, Copy, Effigy, Fathead, Flathead, Mannequin, Mock-up, Model, Pacifier, Quintain, Table, Waxwork

Dump(s) Abandon, Blue, Core, Dispirited, Doldrums, Empty, Hole, Jettison, Junk, Scrap, Shoot, Store(house), Tip, Unlade, Unload

Dumpling Dim sum, Dough(boy), Gnocchi, Knaidel, Knaidloch, Kneidlach, Knish, Kreplach, Norfolk, Quenelle, Suet, Won ton

Dumpy Pudgy, Squat

Dun Annoy, Cow, Importune, Pester, ➤ SUE, Tan

Duncan Isadora

Dunce Analphabet, Booby, Dolt, Donkey, Dullard, Fathead, Schmo, Schmuck, Schnook, Stupid

Dune Areg, Bar, Barchan(e), Bark(h)an, Erg, Sandbank, Seif, Star, Whaleback

Dung(hill) Argol, Buttons, Chip, Coprolite, Cowpat, Droppings, Fewmet, Fumet, Guano, Hing, Manure, Midden, Mixen, Mute, Ordure, Puer, Pure, Scat, Scumber, Shard, Sharn, Siege, Skat, Skummer, Sombrerite, Sombrero, Spraint, Stercoraceous, Tath

Dungarees Overalls

Dungeon Bastille, Cell, Confine, Donjon, Durance, Oubliette, Souterrain

Dunk Immerse, Sop, Steep

Dunnock Accentor

Duo Couple, Pair, Twosome

Dupe Catspaw, Chiaus, Chouse, Cony, Cully, Delude, Geck, Gull, Hoax, Hoodwink, Mug, Pawn, Pigeon, Plover, Sitter, Sucker, Swindle, ➤ TRICK, Victim

Duplex Twofold

Duplicate, Duplicator Clone, Copy, Cyclostyle, Double, Facsimile, Match, Replica, Reproduce, Roneo®, Spare

Durable Enduring, Eternal, Eterne, Hardy, Lasting, Permanent, Stout, Tough

Duralumin® Y-alloy

Duration Extent, Period, Span

Duress Coercion, Pressure, Restraint

Durham Palatine

During Amid, Dia-, For, In, Over, Throughout, While, Whilst

Dusk(y) Dark, Dewfall, Dun, Eve, Gloaming, Gloom, Owl-light, Phaeic, Twilight, Umbrose

Dust(y) Arid, Ash, Bo(a)rt, Calima, Clean, Coom, Cosmic, Derris, Devil, Duff, Earth, Fuss, Khaki, Lemel, Limail, Lo(e)ss, Miller, Nebula, Pollen, Pother, Pouder, Poudre, Powder, Pozz(u)olana, Pudder, Rouge, Seed, Shaitan, Slack, Stour, Talc, Volcanic, Wipe

▷ **Dusted** may indicate an anagram

Duster Cloth, Feather, Talcum, Torchon

Dustman Garbo(logist), Scaffie

Dust measure Konimeter, Koniscope

Dutch(man), Dutchwoman Batavian, Boor, Cape, Courage, D(u), Double, Elm, Erasmus, Frow, Kitchen, Knickerbocker, Mynheer, Patron, Sooterkin, Taal, Wife

Dutiful, Duty Active, Ahimsa, Average, Blench, Bond, Charge, Customs, Death, Debt, Devoir, Docile, Drow, Due, Duplicand, End, Excise, Fatigue, Feu, Function, Heriot, Homage, Imposition, Impost, Incumbent, Lastage, Likin, Mission, Mistery, Mystery, Obedient, Obligation, Octroi, Office, Onus, Pia, Point, Pious, Prisage, Rota, Sentry-go, Shift, Stamp, Stint, Tariff, ➤ TASK, Tax, Toll, Trow, Watch, Zabeta

Duvet Doona, Quilt

Dwarf(ism) Achondroplasia, Agate, Alberich, Andvari, Ateleiosis, Bashful, Belittle, Bes, Black, Bonsai, Brown, Doc, Dopey, Droich, Drow, Durgan, Elf, Gnome, Grumpy, Happy, Hobbit, Homuncule, Hop o' my thumb, Knurl, Laurin, Little man, Man(n)ikin, ➤ MIDGET, Mime, Minikin, Minim, Nanism, Nectabanus, Ni(e)belung, Nurl, Overshadow, Pacolet, Pigmy, Pygmy, Red, Regin, Ront, Rumpelstiltskin, Runt, Skrimp, Sleepy, Sneezy, ➤ STUNT, Tiddler, Titch, Tokoloshe, Tom Thumb, Toy, Troll, Trow, White

Dwell(er), Dwelling Abide, Be, Bungalow, Cabin, Cell, Cot(tage), Descant, Discourse, Domicile, Harp, Heteroscian, Hogan, House, Hut, Laura, Lavra, Live, Lodge, Longhouse, Maison(n)ette, Mansion, Messuage, Palafitte, Pueblo, Reside, Roof, Tenement, Tepee, Terramara, Tipi, Won(ing), Woon

Dwindle Decline, Diminish, Fade, Lessen, Peter, Shrink, Wane

Dye(ing), Dyestuff Alkanet, Anil, Anthracene, Anthraquinone, Archil, Azo(benzine), Bat(t)ik, Camwood, Canthaxanthin, Carthamine, Catechin, Chay(a), Chica, Choy, Cinnabar, Cobalt, Cochineal, Colour, Congo, Corkir, Crocein, Crotal, Crottle, Cudbear, Dinitrobenzene, Direct, Embrue, Engrain, Envermeil, Eosin, Flavin(e), Fuchsin(e), Fustic, Fustoc, Gambi(e)r, Grain, Henna, Hue, Ikat, Imbrue, Imbue, Incardine, Indamine, Indican, Indigo, Indirubin, Indoxyl, Indulin(e), Ingrain, Kalamkari, Kamala, Kermes, Kohl, Korkir, Madder, Magenta, Mauveine, Myrobalan, Nigrosin(e), Orcein, Orchel(la), Orchil, Para-red, Phenolphthalein, Phthalein, ➤ PIGMENT, Primuline, Puccoon, Purpurin, Pyronine, Quercitron, Quinoline, Raddle, Resorcinol, Rhodamine, Rosanilin(e), Safranin(e), Shaya, ➤ STAIN, Stone-rag, Stone-raw, Sumac(h), Sunfast, Tannin, Tartrazine, Tie-dye, Tinct, Tint, Tropaelin, Turnsole, Valonia, Vat, Wald, Weld, Woad, Woald, Wold, Xanthium, Xylidine

➤ **Dying** see DIE

Dyke Aboideau, Aboiteau, Bund, Devil's, ➤ DIKE, Gall, Offa's

Dynamic Ballistics, Energetic, Forceful, High-powered, Potent

Dynamite Blast, Explode, Gelignite, TNT, Trotyl

Dynamo Alternator, Armature

Dynasty Angevin, Bourbon, Capetian, Carolingian, Ch'ing, Chin(g), Chou, Era, Habsburg, Han, Hapsburg, Honan, House(hold), Hyksos, Khan, Manchu, Maurya, Merovingian, Ming, Pahlavi, Ptolemy, Qajar, Qi'ng, Rameses, Romanov, Rule, Safavid, Saga, Sassanid, Seleucid, Seljuk, Shang, Sui, Song, Sung, Tai-ping, Tang, Tudor, Wei, Yi, Yuan, Zhou

Dysentery Slugellosis

Dyslexia Strephosymbolia

Dyspeptic Cacogastric

Dysprosium Dy

Dystrophy Duchenne's, Muscular

E e

E Boat, East, Echo, Energy, English, Spain

Each All, Apiece, Ea, ➤ EVERY, Ilka, Per, Severally

Eager(ly) Agog, Antsy, Ardent, Avid, Beaver, Bore, Earnest, Enthusiastic, Fain, Fervent, Fervid, Frack, Gung-ho, Hot, Intent, ➤ KEEN, Perfervid, Race, Raring, Rath(e), Ready, Roost, Sharp-set, Sore, Spoiling, Thirsty, Toey, Wishing, Yare

Eagle Al(l)erion, American, Aquila, Bald, Bateleur, Berghaan, Bird, Erne, Ethon, Gier, Golden, Harpy, Hawk, Legal, Lettern, Ossifrage

Ear(drum), Ear trouble Ant(i)helix, Attention, Audience, Auricle, Barotitis, Cauliflower, Cochlea, Concha, Conchitis, Deafness, Dionysius, Dolichotus, External, Glue, Hearing, Icker, Inner, Jenkins, Kieselguhr, Labyrinthitis, Listen, Locusta, Lug, Modiolus, Myringa, Myringitis, Nubbin, Otalgia, Otalgy, Otic, Paracusis, Paramastoid, Parotic, Pavilion, Periotic, Pinna, Prootic, Spike, Tin, Tragus, Tympanitis, Utricle

Earl(dom) Belted, Mar, Peer, Sandwich

Earlier, Early Above, Ago, Ahead, Alsoon, AM, Antelucan, Auld, Betimes, Cockcrow, Daybreak, Ere-now, Ex, Germinal, Incipient, Or, Precocious, Precursor, Prehistoric, Premature, Prevernal, Previous, Primeval, Primordial, Prior, Rath(e), Rath(e)ripe, Rear, Rudimentary, Soon, Timely, Tim(e)ous

▷ **Early** may indicate belonging to an earl

Early man Eoanthropus

▷ **Early stages of** may indicate first one or two letters of the word(s) following

Earmark Allocate, Bag, Book, Characteristic, ➤ RESERVE, Tag, Target

Earn(er) Achieve, Addle, Breadwinner, Deserve, Gain, Make, Merit, Win

Earnest Ardent, Arle(s)(-penny), Deposit, Fervent, Imprest, Intent, Promise, Serious, Token, Zealous

Earring Drop, Hoop, Keeper, Pendant, Sleeper, Snap, Stud

Earshot Hail, Hearing

Earth(y) Antichthon, Art, Asthenosphere, Capricorn, Clay, Cloam, Cologne, Diatomite, Dirt, Drey, Dust, Eard, Edaphic, Epigene, Foxhole, Friable, Fuller's, Gaea, Gaia, Gault, Ge, Globe, Ground, Horst, Kadi, Lair, Lemnian, Lithosphere, Loam, Malm, Mankind, Mantle, Mools, Mould, Mouls, Papa, Pise, Planet, Racy, Rare, Red, Seat, Sett, Sod, ➤ SOIL, Taurus, Telluric, Tellus, Terra, Terrain, Terramara, Terrene, Topsoil, Virgo, Ye(a)rd, Yird

Earth-bound Chthonian

Earthenware Biscuit, Ceramic, Creamware, Crock(ery), Delf(t), Della-robbia, Delph, Faience, Figuline, Maiolica, Majolica, Pig, Pot, Raku, Terracotta

Earthquake Aftershock, Bradyseism, Mercalli, Richter, Seism, Shake, Shock, Temblor

Earth's surface Sal, Sial

Earthworks Agger, Bank, Cursus, Gazon, Parados, Rampart, Remblai

Earthworm Annelid, Bait, Night-crawler

Earwig Clipshear(s)

Ease, Easing, Easygoing Alleviate, Carefree, Clear, Clover, Comfort, Content, Defuse, Deregulate, Détente, Facility, Hands down, Informal, Lax, Mellow, Mid(dy), Mitigate, Palliate, Peace, Pococurante, Quiet, Relieve, Reposal, Repose, Soothe

East(erly), Eastward Anglia, Asia, Chevet, E, Eassel, Eassil, Eothen, Eurus, Levant, Orient, Ost, Sunrise

Easter Festival, Island, Pace, Pasch, Pasque

Eastern(er), Eastern language Asian, Kolarian, Oriental, Virginian

East European Lettic, Slovene

Easy, Easily ABC, Cakewalk, Carefree, Cinch, Cushy, Doddle, Eath(e), Ethe, Facile, Free, Gift, Glib, Jammy, Lax, Light, Midshipman, Natural, Picnic, Pie, Pushover, Simple, Sitter, Snotty, Soft, Tolerant, Walk-over, Well, Yare

▷ **Easy** may indicate an anagram

Eat(able), Eater, Eating Bite, Bolt, Chop, Consume, Corrode, Edible, Edite, Endew, Endue, Erode, Esculent, Etch, Fare, Feast, ➤ FEED, Fret, Gnaw, Go, Gobble, Graze, Grub, Hog, Hyperphagia, Manducate, Munch, Nosh, Nutritive, Omnivore, Partake, Phagophobia, Refect, Scoff, Stuff, Sup, Swallow, Syssitia, Take, Taste, Trencherman, Trophesy, Whale

Eavesdrop(per) Cowan, Earwig, Icicle, Listen, Overhear, Snoop, Stillicide, Tap

Ebb Abate, Decline, Recede, Sink, ➤ WANE

Ebony Black, Cocus-wood, Coromandel, Hebenon

Ebullient Brash, Effervescent, Fervid

Eccentric(ity) Abnormal, Cam, Card, Character, Crank, Curious, Dag, Deviant, Dingbat, Ditsy, Ditzy, E, Farouche, Fey, Fie, Freak, Geek, Gonzo, Iffish, Irregular, Kinky, Kook(y), Mattoid, Nutcase, Odd(ball), Offbeat, Off-centre, Original, Outré, ➤ PECULIAR, Phantasime, Pixil(l)ated, Queer, Quirky, Quiz, Rake, Raky, Recondite, Rum, Scatty, Screwball, Screwy, Squirrelly, Wack(y), Way-out, Weird(o), W(h)acko

▷ **Eccentric** may indicate an anagram

Ecclesiastic Abbé, Clergyman, Clerical, Lector, Secular, Theologian

Echelon Formation

Echinoderm Asteroidea, Basket-star, Brittle-star, Comatulid, Crinoid, Sea-lily, Sea-egg, Sea-urchin, Starfish

Echo Angel, Answer, Ditto, E, Imitate, Iterate, Rebound, Repeat, Repercussion, Reply, Resonant, ➤ RESOUND, Respeak, Reverb(erate), Ring, Rote

Eclat Flourish, Glory, Prestige, Renown

Eclectic Babist, Broad, Complex, Liberal

Eclipse Annular, Block, Cloud, Deliquium, Hide, Lunar, Obscure, Occultation, Outmatch, Outweigh, Overshadow, Penumbra, Solar, Total, Transcend

Eclogue Bucolic, Idyll, Pastoral

Economic(s), Economise Budget, Conserve, Eke, Entrench, Husband, Intrench, Pinch, Retrench, Scrimp, Skimp, Spare, Sparing, Stagflation, ➤ STINT

Economist Angell, Bentham, Chrematist, Cole, Friedman, Keynes, Malthus, Marginalist, Meade, Mill, Pareto, Physiocrat, Ricardo, Webb

Economy, Economic(al), Economics Agronomy, Black, Careful, Cliometrics, Conversation, Frugal, Market, Neat, Parsimony, Retrenchment, Shoestring, Thrift

Ecstasy, Ecstatic Bliss, Delight, Dove, E, Exultant, Joy, Lyrical, Rapture, Sent, Trance, Transport

Ecumenical Catholic, Lateran

Eczema Pompholyx

Eddy Backset, Curl, Gurge, Maelstrom, Nelson, Pirl, Purl, Rotor, Swelchie, Swirl, Vortex, Weel, Well, Whirlpool, Wiel

Eden Bliss, Fall, Heaven, Paradise, PM, Utopia

Edentate Armadillo, Sloth, Tatou, Xenarthra

Edge, Edging Advantage, Arris, Border, Brim, Brink, Brittle, Brown, Burr, Chamfer, Coaming, Cutting, Dag, Deckle, End, Flange, Flounce, Frill, Fringe, Furbelow, Gunnel, Gunwale, Hem, Hone, Inch, Kerb, Leading, Leech, Limb(ate), Limbus, Limit, Lip, List, Lute, Marge(nt), Margin, Nosing, Orle, Parapet, Periphery, Picot, Pikadell, Piping, Rand, Rim, Rund, Rymme, Selvage, Selvedge, Sidle, Skirt, Strand, Trim, Tyre, Verge, Wear

▶ **Edible** see EAT(ABLE)

Edict Ban, Bull, Decree, Decretal, Extravagantes, Fatwa, Firman, Interim, Irade, Nantes, Notice, Pragmatic, Proclamation, Rescript, Ukase

Edifice Booth, Building, Structure

Edify Instruct, Teach

Edinburgh Auld Reekie

Edit(or), Editorial Abridge, Article, City, Cut, Emend, Dele, Expurgate, Garble, Leader, Prepare, Recense, Redact, Revise, Seaman

▷ **Edited** may indicate an anagram

Edition Aldine, Ed, Extra, Hexapla(r), Issue, Limited, Number, Omnibus, Variorium, Version

Edmond, Edmund Burke, Gosse, Ironside(s), Rostand, Spenser

Educate(d) Baboo, Babu, Enlighten, Evolué, Informed, Instruct, Learned, Noursle, Nousell, Nousle, Nurture, Nuzzle, Polymath, Preppy, Scholarly, School, ➤ TEACH, Train, Yuppie

Education(alist) Adult, B.Ed, Classical, Didactics, Heurism, Learning, Mainstream, Montessori, Paedotrophy, Pedagogue, Pestalozzi, Piarist, Primary, Schooling, Teacher, Tertiary, Upbringing

Educe Elicit, Evoke, Extract, Infer

Edward Confessor, Ed, Elder, Lear, Martyr, Ned, Ted

Eel Conger, Congo, Electric, Elver, Glass, Grig, Gulper, Gunnel, Hagfish, Lamper, Lamprey, Lant, Launce, Leptocephalus, Moray, Murray, Murr(e)y, Olm, Sand(ling), Snig, Spitchcock, Tuna, Vinegar, Wolf

Eerie Spooky, Uncanny, Unked, Weird

Efface Cancel, Delete, Dislimn, ➤ ERASE, Expunge, Obliterate

Effect(s), Effective(ness), Effectual Achieve, Acting, Auger, Babinski, Bags, Belongings, Bit, Bohr, Bricolage, Butterfly, C(h)erenkov, Causal, Chromakey, Competent, Compton, Consequence, Coriolis, Domino, Doppler, Efficacious, Enact, End, Estate, Functional, Fungibles, Gear, Goods, Greenhouse, Gunn, Hall, Hawthorne, Home, Impact, Implement(al), Impression, Josephson, Joule(-Thomson), Kerr, Knock-on, Meissner, Moire, Neat, Nisi, Operant, Outcome, Ovshinsky, Peltier, Perficient, Personal, Phi, Photovoltaic, Piezoelectric, Position, Potent, Promulgate, Raman, Repercussion, ➤ RESULT, Ripple, Scholtky, Seebeck, Side, Sound, Sovereign, Special, Spectrum, Spin-off, Striking, Stroop, Tableau, Teeth, Telling, Thomson's, Tyndall, Upshot, Valid, Viable, Virtual, Win, Work, Zeeman

Effeminate Camp, Carpet-knight, Carpet-monger, Cissy, Cookie-pusher, Dildo, Epicene, Female, Gussie, Jessie, Milksop, Panty-waist, Poovy, Prissy, Punce, Sissy, Tender, Unman

Effervescence, Effervescent Bubbling, Ebullient, Fizz, Pétillant, Soda

▷ **Effervescent** may indicate an anagram

Effete Camp, Epigon(e)

Efficacious Effective, Operative, Potent

Efficiency, Efficient Able, Capable, Competent, Despatch, Ergonomics, Productivity, Smart, Streamlined, Strong

Effigy Figure, Guy, Idol, Image, Statua, Statue

Efflorescence Bloom, Blossom, Reh

Effluence, Effluent, Effluvia Air, Aura, Billabong, Discharge, Fume, Gas, Halitus, Miasma, Odour, Outflow, Outrush

Effort Achievement, Attempt, Best, Conatus, Drive, Essay, Exertion, Fit, Herculean, Labour, Molimen, Nisus, Rally, Spurt, Stab, Strain, Struggle, ➤ TRY, Work, Yo

Effrontery Audacity, Brass, Cheek, Face, Gall, Neck, Nerve, Temerity

Effulgent Bright, Radiant, Shining

Effuse, Effusion, Effusive Emanate, Exuberant, Exude, Gush, Lyric, Ode, Outburst, Prattle, Rhapsody, Sanies, Screed, Spill

Eft After

Eg As, Example

Egest Eliminate, Evacuate, Excrete, Void

Egg(s) Abet, Benedict, Berry, Bomb, Caviar(e), Chalaza, Cleidode, Clutch, Cockney, Collop, Coral, Curate's, Darning, Easter, Edge, Fabergé, Fetus, Flyblow, Foetus, Free-range, Glair(e), Goad, Goog, Graine, Hoy, Incite, Instigate, Layings, Mine, Nit, Oocyte, Oophoron, Ova, Ovum, Prairie oyster, Press, Raun, Roe, Scotch, Seed, Spat, Spawn, Spur(ne), Tar(re), Tooth, Treadle, Urge, Yelk, Yolk

Egghead Don, Highbrow, Intellectual, Mensa, Pedant

Egg-plant Aubergine, Brinjal

Egg-producer Gametophyte, Hen, Ovipositor

Egg-shaped Obovate, Oval, Ovate

Egg-white Albumen, Glair

Ego(ism) Che, Conceit, I, Narcissism, Not-I, Pride, Self, Solipsism, Vanity

Egocentric Solipsistic

Egregious Eminent, Flagrant, Glaring, Shocking

Egypt(ian), Egyptologist Arab, Cairene, Carter, Cheops, Chephren, Copt(ic), ET, Gippo, Goshen, Gyppo, Imhetop, Nasser, Nefertiti, Nilote, Nitrian, Osiris, Ptolemy, Rameses, Syene, UAR, Wafd, Wog

Eiderdown Bedspread, Duvet, Quilt

Eight(h), Eighth day Acht, Byte, Crew, Cube, Nundine, Octa, Octad, Octal, Octastrophic, Octave, Octet, Ogdoad, Okta, Ottava, Ure

Eighteen Majority

Eighty R

Einsteinium Es

Either Also, Both, O(u)ther, Such

Ejaculate Blurt, Discharge, Emit, Exclaim

Eject Bounce, Disgorge, Dismiss, Emit, Erupt, Expel, Oust, Propel, Spew, Spit, Spue, Vent

Eke Augment, Eche, Enlarge, Husband, Supplement

Elaborate Detail, Develop, Enlarge, Evolve, Florid, Improve, Intricate, Ornate, Stretch

Elan Dash, Drive, Esprit, ➤ FLAIR, Gusto, Lotus, Spirit, Vigour

Elapse Glide, Intervene, Pass

Elastic(ity) Adaptable, Buoyant, Dopplerite, Elater, Flexible, Give, Resilient, Rubber, Spandex®, Springy, Stretchy, Tone, Tonus

Elate(d), Elation Cheer, Euphoric, Exalt, Exhilarate, Gladden, Hault, Ruff(e), Uplift

Elbow, Elbow tip Akimbo, Ancon, Angle, Bender, Cubital, Hustle, Joint, Jostle, Justle, Kimbo, Noop, Nudge, Olecranon, Tennis

Elder(ly), Eldest Ancestor, Ancient, Bourtree, Chief, Classis, Eigne, Geriatric, Guru, Kaumatua, OAP, Presbyter, ➤ SENIOR, Sire, Susanna, Wallwort

Eldorado Ophir

Eleanor(a) Bron, Duse, Nora(h)

Elect(ed), Election(eer), Electoral Choice, Choose, Chosen, Eatanswill, Elite, Gerrymander, Hustings, In, Israelite, Khaki, Opt, Pick, PR, Primary, Psephology, Rectorial, Return, Select, Stump

Electrical discharge Corposant, Ion, Zwitterion

Electrical instrument Battery, Charger, Galvaniser, Mains, Rheostat, Shoe

Electrical unit Amp(ere), Coulomb, Farad, Kilowatt, Ohm, Volt, Watt

Electric eye Pec

Electrician Gaffer, Lineman, Ohm, Siemens, Sparks, Tesla

Electricity Galvanism, HT, Juice, Power, Static

Electrify Astonish, Galvanise, Startle, Stir, Thrill

Electrode Anode, Cathode, Element, Photocathode

Electrolyte Ampholyte

Electromagnet(ic) Abampere, Armature, Oersted, Solenoid, Weber

Electronic, Electronic device Exciton, FET, Linac, Martenot, Valance

Elegance, Elegant Artistic, Bijou, Chic, Classy, Debonair, Fancy, Feat, Finesse, Gainly, Galant, Grace, Jimp, Luxurious, Polished, Refined, Ritzy, ➤ SMART, Soigné(e), Swish, Tall, Urbane

Elegy Dirge, Lament, Poem

Element(s), Elementary Abcee, Abecedarian, Absey, Actinide, Actinium (Ac), Air, Alabamine, Alloy, Aluminium (Al), Americium (Am), Antimony (Sb), Argon (Ar), Arsenic (As), Astatine (At), Atom, Barebones, Barium (Ba), Berkelium (Bk), Beryllium (Be), Bismuth (Bi), Boron (B), Brimstone, Bromine (Br), Cadmium (Cd), Caesium (Cs), Calcium (Ca), Californium (Cf), Carbon (C), Cerium (Ce), Cesium, Chlorine (Cl), Chromium (Cr), Cobalt (Co), Columbium, ➤ COMPONENT, Copper (Cu), Curium (Cm), Detail, Didymium, Dubnium (Db), Dysprosium (D), Earth, Einsteinium (Es), Erbium (Er), ➤ ESSENCE, Europium (Eu), Factor, Feature, Fermium (Fm), Fire, Fluorine (F), Francium (Fr), Gadolinium (Gd), Gallium (Ga), Germanium (Ge), Gold (Au), Hafnium (Hf), Hahnium (Hn), Halogen, Hassium (Hs), Helium (He), Holmium (Ho), Hydrogen (H), Illinium, Inchoate, Indium (In), Iodine (I), Iridium (Ir), Iron (Fe), Isotope, Juliotium, Krypton (Kr), Kurchatovium, Lanthanide, Lanthanum (La), Lawrencium (Lr), Lead (Pb), Lithium (Li), Lutetium (Lu), Magnesium (Mg), Manganese (Mn), Masurium, Meitnerium (Mt), Mendelevium (Md), Mercury (Hg), Metalloid, Milieu, Molybdenum (Mo), Morph(eme), Nebulium, Neodymium (Nd), Neon (Ne), Neptunium (Np), Nickel (Ni), Nielsbohrium, Niobium (Nb), Niton, Nitrogen (N), Nobelium (No), Osmium (Os), Oxygen (O), Palladium (Pd), Phitonium, Phlogiston, Phosphorus (P), Platinum (Pt), Plutonium (Pu), Polonium (Po), Potassium (K), Praseodymium (Pr), Primary, Principle, Promethium (Pm), Protactinium (Pa), Radium (Ra), Radon (Rn), Rare Earth, Rhenium (Re), Rhodium (Rh), Rubidium (Rb), Rudimental, Ruthenium (Ru), Rutherfordium, Samarium (Sm), Scandium (Sc), Seaborgium (Sg), Selenium (Se), Silicon (Si), Silver (Ag), Simple, Sodium (Na), Strontium (Sr), Sulphur (S), Tantalum (Ta), Technetium (Tc), Tellurium (Te), Terbium (Tb), Terra, Thallium (Tl), Thorium (Th), Thulium (Tm), Tin (Sn), Titanium (Ti), Trace, Transactinide, Transition, Transuranic, Tungsten (W), Unnilennium (Une), Unnilhexium (Unh), Unniliquadium (Unq), Unniloctium (Uno), Unnilpentium (Unp), Unnilseptium (Uns), Ununquadium (Uuq), Uranide, Uranium (U), Vanadium (V), Virginium, Water, Weather, Wolfram, Xenon (Xe), Ylem, Ytterbium (Yb), Yttrium (Y), Zinc (Zn), Zirconium (Zr)

Elephant African, Babar, Hathi, Indian, Jumbo, Kheda, Mammoth, Mastodon, Oliphant, Pachyderm, Rogue, Subungulata, Trumpeter, Tusker, White

Elephant-headed Ganesa

Elephant's ears Begonia

Elevate(d), Elevation, Elevator Agger, Attitude, Cheer, Colliculus, El, Eminence, Ennoble, Heighten, Hoist, Jack, Lift, Machan, Montic(u)le, Monticulus, Promote, ➤ RAISE, Random, Relievo, Ridge, Rise, Steeve, Sublimate, Up(lift), Uplying, Upraise, Wallclimber

Eleven Elf, Hendeca-, Legs, Side, Team, XI

Elf, Elves Alfar, Chiricaune, Fairy, Goblin, Imp, Kobold, Ouph, Pigwiggen, Pixie, Ribhus

Elicit Evoke, Extract, Toase, Toaze, Tose, Toze

Eligible Available, Catch, Fit, Nubile, Parti, Qualified, Worthy

Eliminate, Elimination Cull, Delete, Discard, Exclude, Execute, Extirpate, Heat, Liquidate, Omit, Preclude, Purge, Rid, Separate, Void, Zap

Elision Syncope

Elite Best, Choice, Crack, ➤ CREAM, Elect, Flower, Meritocracy, Ton, U, Zaibatsu

Elixir Amrita, Arcanum, Bufo, Cordial, Daffy, Essence, Medicine, Panacea, Quintessence, Tinct

Elizabeth Bess(ie), Gloriana, Oriano

Elk Deer, Gang, Moose

Elkoshite Nahum

Ellipse, Elliptic Conic, Oblong, Oval

Elm Slippery, Wich, Wych

Elmer Gantry

Elongate Extend, Lengthen, Protract, Stretch

Elope Abscond, Decamp

Eloquence, Eloquent Articulate, Demosthenic, Facundity, Fluent, Honey-tongued, Oracy, Rhetoric, Vocal

Else(where) Absent, Alibi, Aliunde, Other

Elucidate Explain, Expose

Elude, Elusive Avoid, Dodge, Escape, ➤ EVADE, Evasive, Foil, Intangible, Jink, Slippy, Subt(i)le, Will o' the wisp

➤ **Elves** see ELF

Em Mut(ton), Pica

Emaciated, Emaciation Atrophy, Erasmus, Gaunt, Haggard, Lean, Skinny, Sweeny, Tabid, Thin, Wanthriven, Wasted

Emanate, Emanation Arise, Aura, Discharge, Exude, Issue, Miasma, Radiate, Spring

Emancipate, Emancipation Deliver, Forisfamiliate, Free, ➤ LIBERATE, Manumission, Uhuru

Emasculate Castrate, Debilitate, Evirate, Geld, Unsex

Embalm Anoint, Mummify, Preserve

Embankment Bund, Causeway, Dam, Dyke, Earthwork, Levee, Mattress, Mound, Rampart, Remblai, Sconce, Staith(e), Stopbank

Embargo ➤ BAN, Blockade, Edict, Restraint

Embark Begin, Board, Enter, Inship, Launch, Sail

Embarrass(ed), Embarrassment Abash, Ablush, Cheap, Disconcert, Gêne, Mess, Pose, Predicament, Shame, Sheepish, Squirming, Straitened, Upset

▷ **Embarrassed** may indicate an anagram

Embassy Consulate, Embassade, Legation, Mission

Embed(ded) Fix, Immerse, Inlaid, Set

Embellish(ed), Embellishment Adorn, Beautify, Bedeck, Deck, Decorate, Dress, Embroider, Enrich, Garnish, Garniture, Mordent, ➤ ORNAMENT, Ornate, Rel(l)ish, Roulade

Ember(s) Ash, Cinder, Clinker, Gleed

Embezzle Defalcate, Peculate, Purloin, ➤ STEAL

Embitter(ed) Acerbate, Aggravate, Enfested, Rankle, Sour

Emblem(atic) Badge, Bear, Colophon, Daffodil, Ichthys, Impresa, Insignia, Kikumon, Leek, Lis, Maple leaf, Oak, Rose, Roundel, Shamrock, Sign, Spear-thistle, ➤ SYMBOL, Tau-cross, Thistle, Token, Totem(ic), Triskelion, Wheel

Embody, Embodied, Embodiment Epitome, Fuse, Incarnation, Incorporate, Personify, Quintessence

Embolism Clot, Infarct

Emboss(ed) Adorn, Chase, Cloqué, Engrave, Pounce, Raise, Repoussé, Toreutic

Embrace(d) Abrazo, Accolade, Arm, Canoodle, Clasp, Clinch, Clip, Coll, Complect, Comprise, Cuddle, Embosom, Encircle, Enclasp, Enclose, Enfold, Enlacement, Envelop, Espouse, Fold, Grab, Halse, Haulst, Hause, Hesp, Hug, Imbrast, Inarm, Inclip, Include, Kiss, Lasso, Neck, Press, Stemme, Twine, Welcome, Wrap

▷ **Embraces, Embracing** may indicate a hidden word

Embrocate, Embrocation Anoint, Arnica, Liniment

Embroider(y) Appliqué, Arrasene, Assisi, Battalia-pie, Braid, Brede, Couching, Crewel-work, Cross-stitch, Cutwork, Drawn threadwork, Embellish, Exaggerate, Fag(g)oting, Fancywork, Featherstitch, Filet, Framework, Gros point, Handiwork, Lace(t), Mola, Needlepoint, Needlework, Open Anglicanum, Orfray, Ornament, Orphrey, Orris, Petit point, Pinwork, Pulled threadwork, Purl, Sampler, Sew, Smocking, Stitch, Stumpwork, Tambour, Tent, Wrap

Embroideress Mimi

Embroil Confuse, Entangle, Involve, Trouble

Embryo(nic) Blastocyst, Blastula, Conceptus, Epicotyl, Fo(e)tus, Gastrula, Germ, Mesoblast, Morula, Nepionic, Neurula, Origin, Rudiment, Undeveloped

Emend Adjust, Alter, Edit, Reform

Emerald Beryl, Gem, Green, Smaragd

Emerge(ncy), Emerging Anadyomene, Arise, Craunch, Crise, Crisis, Crunch, Debouch, Eclose, Emanate, Enation, Erupt, Exigency, Issue, Lash-up, Last-ditch, Loom, Need, Outcrop, Pinch, Spring, Stand-by, Strait, Surface
▷ **Emerge from** may indicate an anagram or a hidden word
Emerson Waldo
Emetic Apomorphine, Cacoon, Epicac, Evacuant, Ipecacuanha, Puke, Sanguinaria, Stavesacre, Tartar
Emigrant, Emigration Chozrim, Colonist, Italiot, Jordim, Redemptioner, Settler, When-we, Yordim
Emile Zola
Emily Ellis
Eminence, Eminent Alp, Altitude, Cardinal, Distinguished, Eximious, Grand, Height, Hill, Inselberg, Light, Lion, Lofty, Luminary, Noble, ➤ NOTABLE, Palatine, Prominence, Renown, Repute, Stature, Tor, Trochanter, ➤ VIP
Emissary Agent, Envoy, Legate, Marco Polo
Emission, Emit Discharge, Emanate, Give, Issue, Utter, Spallation
Emmer Amelcorn, Wheat
Emollient Paregoric
Emolument Income, Perk, Remuneration, Salary, Stipend, Tip, Wages
Emotion(al) Anger, Anoesis, Breast, Chord, Ecstasy, Excitable, Feeling, Freak-out, Hysteria, Joy, Limbic, Passion, Reins, Roar, Sensibility, Sensitive, Sentiment, Spirit, Transport, Weepy
Empathy Identifying, Rapport, Rapprochement, Sympathy
Emperor Agramant(e), Akbar, Akihito, Antoninus, Augustus, Babur, Barbarossa, Bonaparte, Caligula, Caracalla, Charlemagne, Claudius, Commodus, Concerto, Constantine, Diocletian, Domitian, Ferdinand, Gaius, Genghis Khan, Gratian, Hadrian, Heraclius, Hirohito, Imp, Inca, Jimmu, Justinian, Kaiser, Keasar, Kesar, King, Maximilian, Menelik, Mikado, Ming, Mogul, Montezuma, Mpret, Napoleon, Negus, Nero, Nerva, Otho, Otto, Penguin, Peter the Great, Purple, Pu-yi, Rex, Rosco, Ruler, Severus, Shah Jahan, Shang, Sovereign, Sultan, Tenno, Theodore, Theodosius, Tiberius, Titus, Trajan, Tsar, Valens, Valentinian, Valerian, Vespasian, Vitellius
Emphasize, Emphatic Accent, Bold, Dramatise, Forcible, Forzando, Hendiadys, Italic, Marcato, Positive, Sforzando, ➤ STRESS, Underscore, Vehement
Empire Assyria, British, Byzantine, Celestial, Chain, Domain, Empery, Georgia, Kingdom, NY, Ottoman, Realm, Reich, Roman, Second
Emplacement Battery, Platform
Employ(ment) Business, Calling, Engage, Exercitation, Hire, Occupy, Pay, Place, Practice, Pursuit, Shiftwork, Trade, Use, Using, Utilise, Vocation
Employee(s) Factotum, Hand, Help, Intrapreneur, Minion, Munchkin, Payroll, Personnel, Rainmaker, Servant, Staff, Staffer, Valet, Walla(h), Worker

Employer Baas, Boss, Master, Padrone, User

▷ **Employs** may indicate an anagram

Emporium Bazaar, Shop, Store

Empower Authorise, Enable, Entitle, Permit

Empress Eugenie, Josephine, Messalina, Queen, Sultana, Tsarina

Empty Addle, Bare, Barren, Blank, Boss, Buzz, Claptrap, Clear, Deplete,
  Devoid, Disembowel, Drain, Exhaust, Expel, Futile, Gousty, Gut, Inane,
  Jejune, Lade, Lave, Null, Phrasy, Pump, Shallow, Teem, Toom, Tume,
  Unoccupied, Unpeople, Vacant, Vacate, Vacuous, Vain, Viduous, ➤ VOID

▷ **Empty** may indicate an 'o' in the word or an anagram

Emulate Ape, Copy, Envy, Equal, Imitate, Match

Emulsion Pseudosolution, Tempera

Enable Authorise, Empower, Potentiate, Qualify, Sanction

Enact Adopt, Effect, Ordain, Personate, Portray

Enamel(led), Enamel work Aumail, Champlevé, Cloisonné, Della-robbia,
  Dentine, Fabergé, Ganion, Lacquer, Polish, Porcelain, Schwarzlot, Shippo,
  Smalto, Stoved, Vitreous

Encampment Bivouac, Douar, Dowar, Duar, Laager, Laer, Settlement

Encase(d), Encasement Box, Crate, Emboîtement, Encapsulate, Enclose,
  Obtect

Enchant(ed), Enchantment Captivate, Charm, Delight, Gramary(e),
  Incantation, Magic, Necromancy, Rapt, Sorcery, Spellbind, Thrill

Enchanter, Enchantress Archimage, Archimago, Armida, Comus, Circe,
  Fairy, Lorelei, Magician, Medea, Mermaid, Prospero, Reim-kennar,
  Sorcerer, Vivien, Witch

Encircle(d) Enclose, Encompass, Enlace, Entrold, Gird, Inorb, Introld, Orbit,
  Pale, Ring, ➤ SURROUND

Enclave Cabinda, Ceuta, ➤ ENCLOSURE, Melilla, Pocket

Enclose(d), Enclosing, Enclosure Bawn, Beset, Boma, Box, Cage, Carol,
  Carrel, Case, Common, Compound, Corral, Court, Embale, Embowel,
  Embower, Enceinte, Encircle, Enclave, Enshrine, Fence, Fold, Forecourt,
  Garth, Haggard, Haw, Hem, Henge, Hope, Impound, In, Incapsulate,
  Insert, Interclude, Lairage, Pale, Peel, Pele, Pen(t), Petavius, Pightle, Pin,
  Pinfold, Playpen, Plenum, Rail, Rath, Recluse, Ree(d), Ring, Run, Saddling,
  Seal, Sekos, Sept, Seraglio, Serail, Several, Sin bin, Steeld, Stell, Stockade,
  Sty, ➤ SURROUND, Tine, Vibarium, Ward, Wrap, Yard

Encomium Eulogy, Praise, Sanction, Tribute

Encompass Bathe, Begird, Beset, Environ, Include, Surround

Encore Again, Agen, Ancora, Bis, Ditto, Do, Iterum, Leitmotiv, Recall,
  Repeat

Encounter Battle, Brush, Combat, Contend, Cope, Face, Hit, Incur,
  Interview, ➤ MEET, One-one, Rencontre, Ruffle, Skirmish, Tilt

Encourage(ment), Encouraging Abet, Acco(u)rage, Alley-oop, Animate,
  Attaboy, Bolster, Boost, Brighten, Cheer, Cohortative, Comfort,
  Commend, Dangle, Egg, Elate, Embolden, Empatron, Exhort, Fillip, Fire,
  Fortify, Foster, Fuel, Gee, Hearten, Heigh, Help, Hope, Hortatory, Incite,

Inspirit, Nourish, Pat, Patronise, Proceleusmatic, Prod, Protreptic, Push, Reassure, Root, Support, Tally-ho, Train, Upcheer, Uplift, Urge, Wean, Yo

Encroach(ment) Impinge, Infringe, Intrude, Invade, Overlap, Overstep, Poach, Purpresture, Trespass, Usurp

Encrypt(ion) CODING, Public key

Encumber, Encumbrance Burden, Charge, Clog, Deadwood, Dependent, ➤ HANDICAP, Impede, Load, Obstruct, Saddle

Encyclopaedic Comprehensive, Diderot, Extensive, Universal, Vast

End(ing) Abolish, Abut, Aim, Ambition, Amen, Anus, Arse, Big, Bitter, Bourn(e), Butt, Cease, Climax, Close, Closure, Cloture, Coda, Conclude, Crust, Curtain, Cut off, Death, Decease, Denouement, Desinence, Desistance, Destroy, Determine, Dissolve, Domino, Effect, Envoi, Envoy, Epilogue, Exigent, Expire, Extremity, Fatal, Fattrels, Final(e), Fine, Finis, ➤ FINISH, Finite, Grave, Heel, Ish, Izzard, Izzet, Kill, Kybosh, Last, Loose, Mill, Nirvana, No side, Ort, Period, Peter, Point, Purpose, Quench, Receiving, Remnant, Rescind, Result, Roach, Scotch, Scrag, Shank, Slaughter, Sopite, Split, Sticky, Stub, Supernaculum, Surcease, Swansong, Tag, Tail, Tailpiece, Telesis, Telic, Telos, Term, Terminal, Terminate, Terminus, Thrum, Tip, Toe, Ultimate, Up, Upshot, Z

Endanger Hazard, Imperil, Risk

Endear(ing), Endearment Adorable, Affection, Asthore, Caress, Cariad, Ducky, Enamour, Ingratiate, Jarta, Luv, Machree, Mavourneen, Peat

Endeavour Aim, Effort, Enterprise, Morse, Strive, Struggle, Try, Venture

Endemic Local, Prevalent

Endless Continuous, Ecaudate, Eternal, Eterne, Infinite, Interminable, Perpetual, Undated

▷ **Endlessly** may indicate a last letter missing

End of the world Ragnarok

Endorse(ment) Adopt, Affirm, Allonge, Approve, Assurance, Back, Confirmation, Initial, Okay, Oke, Ratify, Rubber stamp, Sanction, Second, Sign, Subscript, ➤ SUPPORT, Underwrite, Visa

Endow(ment) Assign, Bequeath, Bestow, Bless, Cha(u)ntry, Dot, Dotation, Enrich, Foundation, Gift, Leave, Patrimony, State, Vest

Endure(d), Endurance, Enduring Abought, Aby(e), Bear, Brook, Dree, Have, Hold, ➤ LAST, Livelong, Lump, Patience, Perseverance, Pluck, Ride, Stamina, Stand, Stay, Stout, Support, Sustain, Tether, Thole, Tolerance, Undergo, Wear

Endymion Bluebell

Enema Catharsis, Clyster, Purge

Enemy Adversary, Antagonist, Boer, Devil, Fifth column, Foe(n), Fone, Opponent, Public, Time

Energetic, Energise, Energy Active, Amp, Animation, Arduous, Cathexis, Chakra, Chi, Dash, Drive, Dynamic, Dynamo, E, Enthalpy, Entropy, EV, Fermi, Fireball, Force, Fructan, Gism, Go, Hartree, Input, Instress, Internal, Horme, ➤ JET, Jism, Jissom, Joie de vivre, Joule, Kinetic, Kundalini, Libido, Luminous, Magnon, Moxie, Nuclear, Orgone, Pep, Phonon, Potency,

Potential, ➤ POWER, Powerhouse, QI, Quantum, Rad, Radiant, Radiatory, Rydberg, Sappy, Solar, Steam, Trans-uranic, Verve, Vigour, Vim, Vital, Wave, Zing, Zip

Enfold Clasp, Envelop, Stemme, Swathe, Wrap

Enforce(ment) Administer, Coerce, Control, Exact, Implement, Impose

Eng Agma

Engage(d), Engagement, Engaging Absorb, Accept, Appointment, At, Attach, Bespoken, Betrothal, Bind, Book, Busy, Contract, Date, Embark, Employ, Engross, Enlist, Enmesh, Enter, Gear, Gig, Hire, Hold, Interest, Interlock, Lock, Mesh, Met, Occupy, Pledge, Promise, Prosecute, Reserve, Residency, Skirmish, Sponsal, Sponsion, Spousal, Sprocket, Trip, Wage, Winsome

▷ **Engagement** may indicate a battle

Engender Beget, Breed, Cause, Occasion, Produce

Engine, Engine part Athodyd, Beam, Booster, Bricole, Bypass, Carburettor, Catapult, Diesel, Donkey, Dynamo, Fan-jet, Fire, Four, Gin, Heat, Ion, Jet, Lean-burn, Locomotive, Machine, Mangonel, ➤ MOTOR, Nacelle, Onager, Outboard, Petard, Petrary, Petter, Plasma, Pulsejet, Put-put, Radial, Ramjet, Reaction, Rocket, Rotary, Scorpion, Scramjet, Search, Steam, Stirling, Tank, Terebra, Testudo, Traction, Trompe, Turbine, Turbofan, Turbojet, Turbo-prop, Turboprop, Two-handed, Two-stroke, V, Vernier, Wankel, Warwolf, Winch

Engineer(ing), Engineers AEU, Arrange, BE, Brindley, Brunel, CE, De Lessops, Greaser, Heinkel, Junkers, Manoeuvre, Marconi, Marine, McAdam, Mastermind, Mechatronics, Mime, Operator, Organise, Otto, Planner, RE, Repairman, Rig, Sapper, Scheme, Siemens, Smeaton, Stage, Stephenson, Telford, Wangle, Wankel, Watt, Whittle, Whitworth

England Albany, Albion, Blighty, Demi-paradise, Eden, John Bull, Merrie

English(man) Anglican, Anglice, Baboo, Babu, Basic, Brit, Choom, E, Eng, Estuary, Hawaiian, Hong Kong, Indian, Irish, Jackeroo, John Bull, King's, Kipper, Limey, Mister, New Speak, Oxford, Philippine, Pidgin, Pom(my), Pommie, Pongo, Pork-pudding, Queen's, Qui-hi, Qui-hye, Rock, Rooinek, Sassenach, Saxon, Shopkeeper, Side, Singapore, Standard, South African, South Asian, Southron, Strine, Woodbine, Yanqui, Yinglish

Engorge Devour, Glut, Swallow

Engraft Inset

Engrave(r), Engraving Aquatint, Blake, Carve, Cerotype, Chalcography, Character, Chase, Cut, Die-sinker, Dry-point, Durer, Enchase, Eng, Etch, Glyptic, Glyptograph, Hogarth, Impress, Inciser, Inscribe, Insculp, Intagliate, Inter, Lapidary, Line, Mezzotint, Niello, Photoglyphic, Plate, Scalp, Scrimshander, Scrimshandy, Scrimshaw, Steel, Stillet, Stipple, Stylet, Stylography, Turn, Xylographer

Engross(ed) Absorb, Engage, Enwrap, Immerse, Monopolise, ➤ OCCUPY, Preoccupy, Prepossess, Rapt, Sink, Writ large

Enhance Augment, Elevate, Embellish, Exalt, Heighten, Intensify

Enigma(tic) Charade, Conundrum, Dilemma, Gioconda, Mystery, Oracle, Poser, Problem, ➤ PUZZLE, Quandary, Question, Rebus, Riddle, Secret, Sphinxlike, Teaser

Enjoin Command, Direct, Impose, Prohibit, Require

Enjoy(able), Enjoyment Apolaustic, Appreciate, Ball, Brook, Delectation, Fruition, Glee, Groove, Gusto, Have, Lekker, Like, Own, Possess, Relish, Ripping, Savour, Taste, Wallow

Enlarge(ment), Enlarger Accrue, Acromegaly, Add, Aneurism, Aneurysm, Augment, Blow-up, Diagraph, Dilate, Exostosis, Expand, Expatiate, Explain, Increase, ➤ MAGNIFY, Piece, Ream, Rebore, Sensationalize, Swell, Telescope, Tumefy, Varicosity

Enlighten(ment) Awareness, Bodhisattva, Dewali, Divali, Edify, Educate, Explain, Haskalah, Illumine, Instruct, Nirvana, Revelation, Satori

Enlist Attest, Conscript, Draft, Engage, Enrol, Induct, Join, Levy, Prest, Recruit, Roster, Volunteer

Enliven(ed) Animate, Arouse, Brighten, Cheer, Comfort, Exhilarate, Ginger, Invigorate, Merry, Pep, Refresh, Warm

Enmity Animosity, Aversion, Hatred, Malice, Nee(d)le, Rancour, Spite

Ennoble Dub, Elevate, Exalt, Honour, Raise

Ennui Boredom, Tedium

Enormous Colossal, Exorbitant, Googol, Huge, Humongous, Humungous, ➤ IMMENSE, Jumbo, Mammoth, Mega, Vast

Enough Adequate, ➤ AMPLE, Anow, Basta, Belay, Enow, Fill, Geyan, Nuff, Pax, Plenty, Qs, Sate, Satis, Suffice, Sufficient, Via

Enounce Affirm, Declare, State

Enquire, Enquiring, Enquiry Ask, Check, Curious, Eh, Inquire, Organon, Request, Scan, See, Trial

Enrage(d) Emboss, Enfelon, Imboss, ➤ INCENSE, Inflame, Infuriate, Livid, Madden, Wild

Enrapture(d) Enchant, Ravish, Sent, Transport

Enrich Adorn, Endow, Enhance, Fortify, Fructify, Oxygenate

Enrol(ment) Attest, Empanel, Enlist, Enter, Incept, ➤ JOIN, List, Matriculate, Muster, Register

Ensconce(d) Establish, Settle, Shelter, Snug

Ensemble Band, Orchestra, Octet(te), Outfit, Ripieno, Set, Tout, Whole

Enshrine Cherish, Sanctify

Ensign Ancient, Badge, Banner, Duster, ➤ FLAG, Gonfalon, Officer, Pennon, Red, White

Enslave(ment) Addiction, Bondage, Captivate, Chain, Enthral, Thrall, Yoke

Ensue Follow, Result, Succeed, Transpire

Entail Involve, Necessitate, Require

Entangle(ment) Ball, Elf, Embroil, Encumber, Ensnarl, Entrail, Fankle, Implicate, ➤ KNOT, Mat, Ravel, Retiarius, Trammel

Enter Admit, Board, Broach, Come, Enrol, Infiltrate, Ingo, Inscribe, Insert, Invade, Lodge, Log, Penetrate, Pierce, Record, Run, Submit, Table

Enterprise, Enterprising Adventure, Ambition, Aunter, Dash, Emprise, Free, Goey, Go-getter, Gumption, Industry, Plan, Private, Public, Push, Spirit, Stunt, Venture

Entertain(er), Entertaining, Entertainment Accourt, Acrobat, Afterpiece, Amphitryon, Amuse, Balladeer, Beguile, Busk, Cater, Cheer, Chout, Circus, Comedian, Comic, Conjure, Consider, Cottabus, Cuddy, Diseur, Diseuse, Divert, Divertissement, ENSA, Extravaganza, Fete, Fleshpots, Floorshow, Foy, Fun, Gaff, Gala, Gaudy, Harbour, Have, Hospitality, Host(ess), Interest, Interlude, Intermezzo, Karaoke, Lauder, Light, Masque, Minstrel, Olio, Panto, Pap, Peepshow, Piece, Pierrot, Raree-show, Regale, Review, Revue, Rodeo, Serenade, Showbiz, Snake-charmer, Striptease, Table, Tamasha, Tattoo, Treat, Variety, Vaudeville, Wattle

Enthral(l) Charm, Enchant, Enslave, Spellbind

Enthuse, Enthusiasm, Enthusiast(ic) Acclamatory, Amateur, Ardour, Buff, Bug, Cat, Cheerleader, Crusader, Demon, Devotee, Ebullience, Ecstatic, Estro, Fandom, Fiend, Fire, Flame, Freak, Furor(e), Get-up-and-go, Gung-ho, Gusto, Hacker, Hearty, Hype, Into, Keen, Lyrical, Mad, Mania, Muso, Nympholept, Oomph, Outpour, Overboard, Passion, Perfervid, Rah-rah, Raring, Rave, Rhapsodise, Schwärmerei, Sold, Spirit, Verve, Warmth, Whole-hearted, Zealot, Zest

Entice(ment), Enticing Allure, Angle, Cajole, Carrot, Decoy, Lure, Persuade, Seductive, ➤ TEMPT, Tole, Toll

Entire(ly), Entirety Absolute, All, Clean, Complete, Inly, Intact, Integral, In toto, Lot, Purely, Systemic, Thorough, Total, Tout, ➤ WHOLE

Entitle(ment) Empower, Enable, Legitim, Name, Right

Entity Being, Body, Existence, Holon, Tao, Tensor, Thing

Entomologist Fabré

Entourage Cortège

Entrail(s) Bowels, Chawdron, Giblets, Gralloch, Guts, Ha(r)slet, Humbles, Lights, Numbles, Offal, Quarry, Tripe, Umbles, Viscera

Entrance(d), Entrant, Entry Access, Adit, Anteroom, Arch, Atrium, Avernus, Bewitch, Charm, Contestant, Door, Dromos, Eye, Fascinate, Foyer, Gate, Ghat, Hypnotise, Ingress, Inlet, Introitus, Jawhole, Jaws, Jib-door, Mesmerise, Narthex, Pend, Porch, Portal, Porte-cochère, Postern, Propylaeum, Propylon, Ravish, Reception, Record, Regest, Registration, Starter, Stem, Spellbound, Stoa, Stoma, Stulm, Torii

Entreat(y) Appeal, Ask, Beg, Beseech, Flagitate, Impetrate, ➤ IMPLORE, Orison, Petition, Plead, Pray, Precatory, Prevail, Prig, Rogation, Solicit, Sue, Supplicate

Entrée Access, Dish, Entry, Ingate

Entrench(ment) Coupure, Encroach, Fortify, Trespass

Entrepreneur Businessman, Executor, Impresario, Wheeler-dealer

Entrust Aret(t), Confide, Consign, Delegate, Give

▶ **Entry** see ENTRANCE

Entwine Complect, Impleach, Intervolve, Lace, Twist, Weave

Enumerate, Enumeration Catalogue, Count, Detail, Fansi, List, Tell

Enunciate Articulate, Declare, Deliver, Proclaim

Envelop(e) Arachnoid, Bangtail, Chorion, Corolla, Cuma, Corona, Cover(ing), Enclose, Entire, Invest, Involucre, Jiffy(bag)®, Muffle, Mulready, Perianth, Sachet, Serosa, Smother, Surround, Swathe

Environment, Environmental(ist) Ambience, Ecofreak, Econut, Entourage, Green, Habitat, Milieu, Realo, Setting, Sphere, Surroundings

Envisage Contemplate, Imagine, Suppose

Envoi Farewell, RIP

Envoy Agent, Diplomat, Elchee, El(t)chi, Hermes, Legate, Plenipotentiary

Envy Begrudge, Covet, Jealousy

Enzyme ACE, Aldolase, Allosteric, Amylase, Amylopsin, Apyrase, Arginase, Asparaginase, Autolysin, Bromel(a)in, Carbohydrase, Carboxylase, Casease, Catalase, Cathepsin, Cellulase, Cholinesterase, Chymopapain, Chimotrypsin, Collagenase, Cyclase, Cytase, Deaminase, Decarboxylase, Diastase, Dipeptidase, Elastase, Enolase, Enterokinase, Erepsin, Esterase, Fibrinolysin, Flavoprotein, Guanase, Histaminase, Hydrase, Hydrolase, Inulase, Invertase, Isomerase, Kallikrein, Kinase, Lactase, Ligase, Lipase, Luciferase, Lyase, Lysin, Lysozyme, Maltase, Mutase, Nuclease, Oxdoreductase, Oxidase, Oxygenase, Papain, Pectase, Pectinesterase, Pepsin(e), Permease, Peroxidase, Phosphatase, Plasmin, Polymerase, Protease, Proteinase, Ptyalin, Reductase, Ren(n)in, Restriction, Ribonuclease, Saccharase, Steapsin, Streptodornase, Streptokinase, Subtilisin, Sulfatase, Sulphatase, Thrombin, Thromboplastin, Transaminase, Transcriptase, Transferase, Trehalase, Trypsin, Tyrosinase, Urease, Urokinase, Zymase

Eon Arch(a)ean

Epaminondas Theban

Ephemera(l) Brief, Day, Drake, Fungous, Mayfly, Passing, Transitory, Trappings

Epic Aeneid, Ben Hur, Beowulf, Calliope, Colossal, Dunciad, Edda, Epopee, Gilgamesh, Heroic, Homeric, Iliad, Kalevala, Lusiad(s), Mahabharata, Nibelungenlied, Odyssey, Ramayana, Rhapsody, Saga

Epicene Hermaphrodite

Epicure(an) Apicius, Apolaustic, Connoisseur, Friand, Gastronome, Gastrosopher, Glutton, ➤ GOURMAND, Gourmet, Hedonist, Sybarite

Epidemic Pandemic, Pestilence, Plague, Prevalent, Rampant, Rash

Epigram Adage, Apophthegm, Gnomic, Mot, Proverb

Epigraph Citation, Inscription, RIP

Epilepsy, Epileptic Clonic, Eclampsia, Fit, Grand mal, Petit mal, Turn

Epilogue Appendix, Coda, Postscript

Epiphenomenon ESP

Epiphyte Air-plant

Episcopalian PE, Prelatic

Episode, Episodic Chapter, Incident, Page, Picaresque, Scene

Epistle(s) Lesson, Letter, Missive, Pastoral

Epitaph Ci-git, Hic jacet, Inscription, RIP

Epithet Adj(ective), Antonomasia, Apathaton, Byword, Curse, Expletive, Panomphaean, ➤ TERM, Title

Epitome, Epitomise Abridge, Abstract, Digest, Image, Model, Summary, Typify

Epoch Age, Era, Holocene, Miocene, Ogilocene, Palaeocene, Period, Pleistocene, Pl(e)iocene

Epsom salts Kieserite

Equable, Equably Calm, Just, Pari passu, Smooth, Tranquil

Equal(ly), Equality Alike, Ana, As, Balanced, Commensurate, Compeer, Egal(ity), Emulate, Equinox, Equiparate, Equity, Even, Even-steven, Fifty-fifty, For, Identical, Identity, Is, Iso-, Isocracy, Level, Level-pegging, Maik, Make, Match, Mate, Owelty, Par, Pari passu, ➤ PEER, Peregal, Pheer(e), Rise, Rival, ➤ SO, Square, Upsides, Wyoming, Ylike

Equanimity Aplomb, Balance, Poise, Serenity

Equate, Equation Balance, Differential, Diophantine, Dirac, Identity, Parametric, Quadratic, Reduce, Relate, Rhizic, Simultaneous, Van der Waals'

Equator(ial) Celestial, Line, Tropical

Equerry Courtier, Officer, Page

Equilibrium Balance, Composure, Homeostasis, Isostasy, Poise, Stasis, Tautomerism

Equinox Autumnal, Vernal

Equip(age), Equipment Accoutrement, Adorn, Aguise, Aguize, Apparatus, Apparel, Appliance, Array, Attire, Carriage, Deadstock, Deck, Dight, Expertise, ➤ FURNISH, Gear, Gere, Get-up, Graith, Habilitate, Kit, Material, Matériel, Muniments, Outfit, Retinue, Rig, Sonar, Stock, Stuff, Tack(le), Tool, Trampet(te), Trampoline, Turn-out

Equity Actors, Equality, Justice, Law, Negative, Union

Equivalent Correspondent, Equal, Equipollent, In-kind, Same, Tantamount

Equivocal Ambiguous, Dubious, Evasive, Fishy, Oracular, Vague

Equivocate Flannel, Lie, Palter, Prevaricate, Quibble, Tergiversate, Weasel

Er Um

Era Age, Archaean, C(a)enozoic, Christian, Common, Cretaceous, Decade, Dynasty, Epoch, Hadean, Hegira, Hej(i)ra, Hijra, Jurassic, Lias, Mesozoic, Period, Precambrian, Proterozoic

Eradicate, Erase Abolish, Delete, Demolish, Destroy, Efface, Expunge, Extirp, Obliterate, Purge, Root, Scratch, Stamp-out, Uproot, Uptear

Erasmus Humanist

Erbium Er

Erect(ing), Erection Attolent, Build, Construct(ion), Elevate, Hard-on, Perpendicular, Priapism, Prick, Rear, Tentigo, Upright, Vertical

Ergo Argal, Hence, Therefore

Erica Heather, Ling

Ermine Fur, Minever, Miniver, Stoat

Ernie Bondsman

Erode, Erosion Corrasion, Denude, Destroy, Deteriorate, Etch, Fret, Wash, Wear, Yardang

Eros, Erotic(a) Amatory, Amorino, Amorous, Aphrodisiac, Carnal, Cupid, Curiosa, Lascivious, Philtre, Prurient, Salacious, Steamy

Err(or) Aliasing, Anachronism, Bish, Blip, Blooper, Blunder, Boner, Bug, Clanger, Comedy, Corrigendum, EE, Fault, Glaring, Human, Jeofail, Lapse, Lapsus, Literal, Mackle, Mesprise, Mesprize, Misgo, Misprint, Misprise, Misprize, ➤ MISTAKE, Mumpsimus, Out, Rove, Sin, Slip, Solecism, Stray, Trip, Typo, Typographical, Wander

Errand Chore, Commission, Message, Mission, Sleeveless, Task

Errand-boy Cad, Galopin, Page

Erratic Haywire, Temperamental, Unstable, Vagary, Vagrant, Wayward

Erroneous False, Inaccurate, Mistaken, Non-sequitur

Ersatz Artificial, Synthetic

Erudite, Erudition Academic, Didactic, Learned, Savant, Scholar, Wisdom

Erupt(ion), Erupture Belch, Brash, Burst, Ecthyma, Eject, Emit, Emphlysis, Exanthem(a), Exanthemata, ➤ EXPLODE, Fumarole, Hives, Hornito, Lichen, Mal(l)ander, Mallender, Morphew, Outbreak, Outburst, Papilla, Pompholyx, Pustule, Rash, Scissure

Escalate, Escalator Accrescence, Expand, Granary, Grow, Lift, Travolator

Escape(e), Escapade Abscond, Atride, Avoid, Bolt, Bolthole, Breakout, Caper, Eject, Elope, Elude, Elusion, Esc, Evade, Exit, Flee, Flight, Frolic, Gaolbreak, Hole, Hoot, Houdini, Hout, Lam, Leakage, Leg-it, Levant, Loop(-hole), Meuse, Mews, Muse, Outlet, Prank, Refuge, Runaway, Sauve qui peut, Scapa, Scarper, Seep(age), Shave, Slip, Vent, Wilding, Wriggle

Escapement Foliot

Eschew Abandon, Avoid, For(e)go, Ignore, ➤ SHUN

Escort Accompany, Attend, Bodyguard, Chaperone, Comitatus, Conduct, Convoy, Cortege, Corvette, Date, Destroyer, Entourage, Frigate, Gallant, Gigolo, Guide, Lead, Outrider, Protector, Retinue, See, Squire, Take, Tend, Usher, Walker

Escutcheon Crest, Shield

Eskimo Aleut, Caribou, Husky, In(n)uit, Inukitut, Thule, Yupik

Esoteric Abstruse, Acroamatic, Inner, Mystic, Occult, Orphic, Private, Rarefied, Recondite, Secret

Especial(ly) Chiefly, Esp, Espec, Outstanding, Particular

Espionage Industrial, Spying, Surveillance

Esplanade Promenade, Walk

Esprit Insight, Spirit, Understanding, Wit

Esquire Armiger(o), Esq, Gent

Essay Article, Attempt, Causerie, Critique, Dabble, Disquisition, Dissertation, Endeavour, Go, Paper, Prolusion, Stab, Theme, Thesis, Tractate, Treatise, Try

Essayist Addison, Bacon, Columnist, Elia, Ellis, Emerson, Hazlitt, Holmes, Hunt, Huxley, Lamb, Locke, Montaigne, Pater, Prolusion, Ruskin, Scribe, Steele, ➤ WRITER

Essence Alma, Atman, Attar, Aura, Being, Core, Element, Entia, Esse, Extract, Fizzen, Flavouring, Foison, Gist, Heart, Hom(e)ousian, Inbeing, Inscape, Kernel, Marrow, Mirbane, Myrbane, Nub, Nutshell, Ottar, Otto, Perfume, Per-se, Pith, Quiddity, Ratafia, Soul, Ylang-ylang

Essential(ly) Basic, Central, Crucial, Entia, Fundamental, Imperative, Indispensable, Inherent, Integral, Intrinsic, Key, Lifeblood, Linch-pin, Marrow, Material, Must, Necessary, Need, Nitty-gritty, Nuts and bolts, Per-se, Prana, Prerequisite, Quintessence, Radical, Requisite, Vital, Whatness

Establish(ed) Abide, Anchor, Ascertain, Base, Build, Create, Enact, Endemic, Ensconce, Fix, ➤ FOUND, Haft, Instal(l), Instate, Institute, Inveterate, Ordain, Pitch, Pre-set, Prove, Raise, Root(ed), Set, Stable, Standing, Trad, Trite, Valorise, Verify

Establishment Building, Business, CE, Church, Co, Concern, Engrain, Evince, Hacienda, Institution, Lodge, Salon, School, Seat, System

Estate Allod(ium), Alod, Assets, Commons, Demesne, Domain, Dominant, Dowry, Fazenda, Fee-simple, Fee-tail, Fen, First, Fourth, General, Hacienda, Hagh, Haugh, Having, Hay, Housing, Industrial, Land-living, Latifundium, Legitim, Life, Manor, Messuage, Odal, Personality, Plantation, Press, ➤ PROPERTY, Real, Runrig, Situation, Spiritual, Standing, Talooka, Taluk(a), Temporal, Thanage, Trading, Udal

Estate agent Realtor

Esteem(ed), Estimable Account, Admiration, Appreciation, Count, Have, Honour, Izzat, Los, Precious, Prestige, Price, Pride, Prize, Rate, ➤ REGARD, Respect, Store, Value, Venerate, Wonder, Worthy

Ester Depside, Glyceride, Olein, Palmitin, Phthalate, Urethan(e)

▶ **Estimable** see ESTEEM

Estimate, Estimation Appraise, Assess, Calculate, Carat, Conceit, Cost, Esteem, Extrapolation, Forecast, Gauge, Guess, Guess(timate), Opinion, Projection, Quotation, Rate, Rating, Reckon, Regard, Sight, Value, Weigh

Estrange Alienate, Disunite, Wean

Estuary Bay, Creek, Delta, Firth, Gironde, Humber, Inlet, Mouth, Ostial, Para

Esurient Arid, Insatiable

Etc(etera) Et al(ia), So on

Etch(ing) Aquafortis, Aquatint(a), Bite, ➤ ENGRAVE, Incise, Inscribe

Eternal, Eternity Ageless, Endless, Eviternal, Ewigkeit, Forever, Immortal, Infinity, Never-ending, Perdurable, Perpetual, Tarnal, Timeless

Ether Atmosphere, Ch'i, Gas, Sky, Yang, Yin

Ethereal Airy, Delicate, Fragile, Heavenly, Nymph

Ethic(al), Ethics Deontics, Marcionite, Moral, Principles

Ethiopia(n) African, Amharic, Asmara, Cushitic, Geez, Kabele, Kebele

Ethnic Racial, Roots

Etiquette Code, Conduct, ➤ MANNERS, Propriety, Protocol, Ps and Qs, Punctilio

Etna Empedocles, Vessel, Volcano

Etonian Oppidan, Victim

Etymologist Isodore

Eucalyptus Bloodwood, Coolabah, Gum-tree, Ironbark, Mallee, Marri, Morrell, Sallee, Stringybark, Tewart, Tooart, Tuart, Wandoo

Eucharist Communion, Housel, Mass, Supper, Viaticum

Eugene Aram, Onegin

Eulogy Encomium, Panegyric, Praise, Tribute

Euphausia Krill, Shrimp

Euphemism Fib, Gosh, Gracious, Heck, Hypocorism

Euphoria, Euphoric Cock-a-hoop, Elation, High, Jubilation, Rapture, Rush

Euphrasia Eyebright

Eurasian Chee-chee, Chi-chi

Europe(an) Balt, Bohunk, Catalan, Community, Continent, Croat, E, Faringee, Faringhi, Feringhee, Fleming, Hungarian, Hunky, Japhetic, Lapp, Lithuanian, Palagi, Polack, Ruthene, Ruthenian, Serb, Slavonian, Slovene, Topi-Wallah, Transleithan, Tyrolean, Vlach, Yugoslav

Europium Eu

Eustace Diamonds

Evacuate, Evacuation Excrete, Expel, Getter, Planuria, Planury, Scramble, Stercorate, Stool, Vent, Void, Withdraw

Evade, Evasion, Evasive Ambages, Avoid, Cop-out, Coy, Dodge, Duck, Elude, Escape, Fence, Fudge, Hedge, Loophole, Parry, Prevaricate, Quibble, Quillet, Scrimshank, Shifty, Shirk, Shuffling, Sidestep, Skive, Skrimshank, Stall, Subterfuge, Tergiversate, Waive, Weasel, Whiffler

Evaluate, Evaluation Appraise, Assess, Estimate, Gauge, Rate, Review, Waid(e), Weigh

Evanescent Cursory, Fleeting, Fugacious

Evangelical, Evangelist Converter, Crusader, Fisher, Gospeller, Happy-clappy, Jesus freak, John, Luke, Marist, Mark, Matthew, Moody, Morisonian, Peculiar, Preacher, Revivalist, Sim(eonite), Stundist, Wild

Evaporate, Evaporation Condense, Dehydrate, Desorb, Exhale, Steam, Steme, Ullage, Vaporise

Evelyn Diarist, Hope

Eve(n), Evening Albe(e), Albeit, All, Average, Balanced, Clean, Drawn, Dusk, Een, Ene, Equable, Equal, Erev, Fair, Flush, Iron, Level, Meet, Nightfall, Pair, Par, Plain, Plane, Plateau, Quits, Rib, Smooth, Soirée, Subfusc, Subfusk, Sunset, Tib(b)s, Toss-up, Twilight, Vesperal, Vespertinal, Vigil, Yester, Yet

Evening flight Ro(a)ding

Evensong Vespers

Event Case, Circumstance, Discus, Encaenia, Episode, Fest, Field, Gymkhana, Happening, Heat, Incident, Landmark, Leg, Media, Milestone,

Occasion, Occurrence, Ongoing, Outcome, Pass, Regatta, Result, Three-ring circus, Track

Even-toed Artiodactyl

Eventual(ly), Eventuality Case, Contingent, Finally, Future, In time, Nd

Ever Always, Ay(e), Constantly, Eternal, Eviternity

Everglade Vlei

Evergreen Abies, Ageless, Arbutus, Cembra, Cypress, Gaultheria, Ivy, Myrtle, Olearia, Periwinkle, Pinaster, Privet, Thuja, Thuya, Washington, Winterberry

Everlasting Cat's ear, Enduring, Eternal, Immortal, Immortelle, Perdurable, Recurrent, Tarnal

Every(one), Everything All, Complete, Each, Ilk(a), Sum, The works, Tout, Tout le monde, Universal, Varsal

Everyday Informal, Mundane, Natural, Ordinary, Plain

Everywhere Omnipresent, Passim, Rife, Throughout, Ubiquity

Evict Disnest, Eject, Expel, Oust

Evidence, Evident Adminicle, Apparent, Argument, Axiomatic, Circumstantial, Clear, Confessed, Distinct, Document, Flagrant, Indicate, Internal, Manifest, Obvious, Overt, ➤ PATENT, Plain, Premise, Proof, Record, Sign, Surrebuttal, Testimony, Understandable

Evil Ahriman, Alastor, Amiss, Badmash, Bale, Beelzebub, Budmash, Corrupt, Depraved, Eale, Guilty, Harm, Hydra, Ill, Iniquity, Malefic, Mara, Mischief, Necessary, Night, Perfidious, Rakshas(a), Shrewd, Sin, ➤ SINISTER, Turpitude, Vice, Wicked

Evil eye Jettatura

Evince Disclose, Exhibit, Indicate, ➤ MANIFEST, Show

Eviscerate(d) Debilitate, Disembowel, Drawn, Gralloch

Evoke Arouse, Awaken, Elicit, Move, Stir

Evolution Countermarch, Development, Growth, Holism, Lamarck, Moner(on), Phylogeny, Turning

▷ **Evolution** may indicate an anagram

Ewe Crone, Gimmer, Keb, Sheep, Teg, Theave

Ewer Aquamanale, Aquamanile

Ex Former, Late, Quondam, Ten

Exacerbate Aggravate, Embitter, Exasperate, Irritate, Needle

Exact(ing), Exactitude, Exactly Accurate, Authentic, Careful, Dead, Definite, Due, Elicit, Estreat, Even, Exigent, Extort, Fine, Formal, It, Jump, Literal, Literatim, Mathematical, Meticulous, Nice(ty), Pat, Point-device, ➤ PRECISE, Require, Slap-bang, Spang, Specific, Spot-on, Strict, T, Verbatim

Exaction Blackmail, Extortion, Impost, Montem, Sorelion, Tax

Exaggerate(d), Exaggeration Agonistic, Amplify, Boast, Brag, Camp, Colour, Distend, Dramatise, ➤ EMBROIDER, Goliathise, Hoke, Hyperbole, Inflate, Line-shoot, Magnify, Munch(h)ausen, Overdo, Overdraw,

Overpaint, Overplay, Overrate, Over-the-top, Overstate, Romance, Stretch, Tall, Theatrical

Exalt(ed), Exaltation Attitudes, Deify, Dignify, Elation, Enhance, Ennoble, Erect, Extol, Glorify, High, Jubilance, Larks, Lofty, ➤ PRAISE, Raise, Rapture, Ruff(e), Sama, Sublime, Supernal, Throne

Exam(ine), Examinee, Examiner, Examination Agrégé, A-level, Analyse, Analyst, Appose, Audit, Auscultation, Autopsy, Baccalauréat, Biopsy, Case, Check-up, Cognosce, Collate, Comb, Consideration, Cross-question, CSE, Deposal, Depose, Dissect, Docimasy, Endoscopy, Entrance, Expiscate, Explore, Eyeball, GCE, GCSE, Grade(s), Greats, Gulf, Haruspex, Hearing, Inspect, Inter, Interrogate, Introspection, Jerque, Jury, Little-go, Local, Mark, Matriculation, Medical, Mocks, Moderator, Mods, Mug, O-level, Once-over, Oral, Ordalian, Ordeal, Overhaul, Palp(ate), Paper, Peruse, Physical, Post-mortem, Prelim, Probe, Pry, Psychoanalyse, Pump, ➤ QUESTION, Quiz, Ransack, Recce, Reconnaissance, Responsions, Review, Sayer, Scan, Schools, Scrutator, Scrutineer, Scrutinise, Search, Seek, Shroff, Sift, Sit, Smalls, Sus(s), Test, Trial, Tripos, Try, Unseen, Vet, Viva, Voir dire

Example Apotheosis, Assay-piece, Byword, Epitome, ➤ FOR EXAMPLE, Foretaste, Illustration, Instance, Lead, Lesson, Model, Paradigm, Paragon, ➤ PATTERN, Praxis, Precedent, Prototype, Say, Shining, Showpiece, Specimen, Standard, Touchstone, Type, Typify

Exasperate, Exasperating, Exasperation Anger, Galling, Irk, Irritate, Nettle, Provoke

Excavate, Excavation, Excavator Armadillo, Burrow, Catacomb, Crater, Delf, Delph, ➤ DIG, Dike, Ditch, Dragline, Dredge, Drive, Gaulter, Hollow, JCB, Mine, Pichiciago, Pioneer, Pioner, Pyoner, Quarry, Shaft, Sink, Sondage, Stope, Well

Exceed, Exceeding(ly) Amain, Outdo, Overstep, Surpass, Transcend, Very

Excel(lence), Excellency, Excellent A1, Admirable, A-per-se, Assay-piece, Beat, Beaut, Better, Bitchin, Blinder, Boffo, Bonzer, Boss, Bottler, Bravo, Brill, Bully, Capital, Castor, Champion, Cheese, Choice, Class(y), Copacetic, Copesettic, Copybook, Corking, Crack, Crackerjack, Crucial, Daisy, Def, Dic(k)ty, Dilly, Dominate, Elegant, Exemplary, Extraordinaire, Fab, Fantastic, Five-star, Great, Grit, Grouse, HE, High, Humdinger, Inimitable, Jake, Jammy, Jim-dandy, Lalapalooza, Lollapalooza, Lummy, Matchless, Mean, Mega-, Merit, Noble, Outbrag, Outdo, Outtop, Overdo, Overtop, Paragon, Phat, Prime, Pure, Rad, Rare, Rattling, Ring, Ripping, Say-piece, ➤ SHINE, Shit-hot, Spanking, Spiffing, Stellar, Stonking, Stupendous, Sublime, Superb, Super-duper, Superior, Supreme, Swell, Terrific, Tip-top, Top flight, Top-hole, Topnotch, Topping, Transcend, Transcendant, Triff, Virtue, Wal(l)y, War, Way-out, Wicked, Worth

Except(ion) Bar, But, Else, Exc, Nobbut, Omit, Save, Unless

Exceptional Abnormal, Anomaly, Egregious, Especial, Extraordinary, Rare, Ripsnorter, Singular, Special, Uncommon, Zinger

Excerpt Extract, Passage, Scrap

Excess(ive), Excessively All-fired, Basinful, Exorbitant, Extortionate, Extravagant, Flood, Fulsome, Glut, Hard, Inordinate, ➤ LAVISH, Mountain, Nimiety, OD, Old, OTT, Outrage, Over, Overage, Overblown, Overcome, Overdose, Overkill, Overmuch, Overspill, Owercome, Plethora, Preponderance, Profuse, Salt, Satiety, Spate, Spilth, Steep, Superabundant, Superfluity, Surfeit, Surplus, Troppo, Ultra, Undue, Unequal, Woundily

Exchange Baltic, Bandy, Barter, Bourse, Cambist, Catallactic, Change, Chop, Commute, Contango, Convert, Cope, Corn, Enallage, Excambion, Foreign, Inosculate, Interplay, Ion, Labour, Logroll, ➤ MARKET, Mart, ➤ PBX, Paraphrase, Post, Rally, Recourse, Rialto, Royal, Scorse, Scourse, Stock, Swap, Switch, Swop, Tolsel, Tolsey, Tolzey, ➤ TRADE, Traffic, Trophallaxis, Truck

Exchequer Remembrancer

Excise(man), Excise district Ablate, Bobbitt, Crop, Expunge, Gauger, Resect, Ride, Tax

Excite(d), Excitable, Excitement, Exciting Ablaze, Abuzz, Aerate, Agog, Amove, Animate, Aphrodisiac, Arouse, Athrill, Atwitter, Awaken, Brouhaha, Buck-fever, Climatic, Combustible, Commotion, Delirium, Electrify, Emove, Enthuse, Erethism, Feisty, Fever, Fire, Flap, Frantic, Frenzy, Frisson, Furore, Fuss, Galvanise, Gas, Headiness, Heat, Hectic, Het, Hey-go-mad, Hilarity, Hobson-Jobson, Hoopla, Hothead, Hyped, Hyper, Hysterical, Impel, Incite, Inebriate, Inflame, Intoxicate, Jimjams, Kick, Kindle, Metastable, Must, Neurotic, Oestrus, Orgasm, Overheat, Overwrought, Panic, Passion, Pride, Provoke, Racy, Radge, Red-hot, Rile, Roil, ➤ ROUSE, Ruff(e), Rut, Send, Spin, Spur, Startle, Stimulate, Stir(e), Suscitate, Tetany, Tew, Thrill, Titillate, Trickle, Turn-on, Twitter, Upraise, Waken, Whee, Whoopee, Yahoo, Yerk, Yippee, Yoicks

▷ **Excite(d)** may indicate an anagram

Exclaim, Exclamation Ahem, Begorra, Blurt, Bo, Ceas(e), Crikey, Criv(v)ens, Dammit, Ecphonesis, Eina, Ejaculate, Epiphonema, Eureka, Expletive, Fen(s), Good-now, Haith, Heigh-ho, Hem, Hosanna, Inshallah, Interjection, Oops, Pling, Protest, Pshaw, Sasa, Sese(y), Sessa, Walker, Whau, Whoops, Yippee, Zounds

Exclude, Excluding, Exclusion Ban, Bar, Block, Debar, Deforcement, Disbar, Eliminate, Ex, Except, Excommunicate, Omit, Ostracise, Outbar, Outwith

Exclusive Closed-shop, Complete, Debarment, Elect, Monopoly, Particular, Pure, Rare, Scoop, Select, Single, Sole

Excommunicate Curse

Excoriate Flay, Slam

Excrement, Excretion Dirt, Doo-doo, Dung, Faeces, Frass, Jobbie, Keech, Meconium, Ordure, Poo(p), Poo-poo, Refuse, Puer, Pure, Scatology, Sir-reverence, Shit(e), Turd, Urea, Waste

Excrescence Aril, Carnosity, Caruncle, Enate, Gall, Growth, Knob, Lump, Pimple, Pin, Spavin(e), Strophiole, Talpa, Twitter(-bone), Wart

Excruciate, Excruciating Agonising, Rack, Torment, Torture

Exculpate Acquit, Clear, Forgive

Excursion Airing, Cruise, Dart, Digression, Jaunt, Outing, Road, Sally, Sashay, Sortie, Tour, Trip

Excusable, Excuse Absolve, Alibi, Amnesty, Bunbury, Condone, Essoin, Essoyne, Evasion, Exempt, Exonerate, Faik, Forgive, Mitigate, Occasion, Off come, Out, Overlook, Palliate, ➤ PARDON, Pretext, Release, Salvo, Venial, Viable, Whitewash

Execrate Abhor, Ban, Boo, Curse

Execute(d), Executioner, Executive, Executor Abhorson, Accomplish, Administrate, Behead, Carnifex, Discharge, Exor, Finish, Fry, Gan, Gar(r)otte, Gin, Guardian, Hang, Headsman, Implement, Ketch, Kill, Koko, Lynch, Management, Noyade, Official, Perform, Pierrepoint, Politburo, Scamp, Top, Trustee, Tyburn

Exemplar(y) Byword, Impeccable, Laudable, Model, Paragon, St, Warning

Exemplify Cite, Epitomise, Illustrate, Instantiate, Satisfy

Exempt(ion) Dispensation, Exclude, Exeem, Fainites, Fains, Free, Immune, Impunity, Indemnity, Overslaugh, Quarter, Spare, Vains

Exercise(s) Aerobics, Air, Antic, Apply, Cal(l)isthenics, Callanetics®, Chi kung, Cloze, Constitutional, Drill, Employ, Enure, Eurhythmics, Exert, Floor, Gradus, Inure, Isometrics, Kata, Lesson, Limber, Medan, Op, Operation, PE, Ply, Popmobility, Practice, Practise, Press-up, PT, Push-up, Qigong, Shintaido, Sit-up, Solfeggi(o), Step (aerobics), Tai chi (ch'uan), Thema, Theme, Thesis, Train, Use, Warm-up, Wield, Work, Work-out, Xyst(us), Yomp

▷ **Exercise(d)** may indicate an anagram

Exert(ion) Conatus, ➤ EFFORT, Exercise, Labour, Operate, Strain, Strive, Struggle, Trouble, Wield

Ex-European Japhetic

Exhalation, Exhale Breath, Fume, Miasma, Reek, Vapour, Transpire

Exhaust(ed), Exhausting, Exhaustion, Exhaustive All-in, Beaten, Bugger(ed), Burn, Burn-out, Bushed, Consume, Deadbeat, Debility, Deplete, Detailed, Do, Done, Drain, Eduction, Effete, Emission, Empty, End, Fatigue, Forfachen, Forfeuchen, Forfoughen, Forfoughten, Forjaskit, Forjeskit, Forspent, Forswink, Frazzle, Gruelling, Heat, Inanition, Jet-lagged, Jet-stream, Jiggered, Mate, Milk, Out, Outwear, Poop, Puggled, Rag, Rundown, Shatter, Shot, Spend, Spent, Stonkered, Tire, Trauchled, Use, Wabbit, Wappend, Warby, Washed-up, Wasted, Waygone, ➤ WEARY, Wind, Worn, Zonked

Exhibit(ion), Exhibitioner Circus, Concours, Demo, Demonstrate, Demy, Diorama, Discover, Display, Evince, Expo, Expose, Fair, Hang, Indicate, ➤ MANIFEST, Olympia, Pageant, Panopticon, Parade, Present, Retrospective, Salon, Scene, Show(piece), Viewing

Exhilarate(d) Bubble, Cheer, Elate, Enliven

Exhort(ation) Admonish, Allocution, Caution, Counsel, Incite, Lecture, Para(e)nesis, Persuade, Urge

Exhume Delve, Disinter, Resurrect, Unearth

Exigency, Exigent Emergency, Pressing, Taxing, Urgent, Vital

Exile Adam, Babylon, Banish, Deport, Emigré, Eve, Expatriate, Exul, Galut(h), Ostracise, Outlaw, Relegate, Tax, Wretch

Exist(ence), Existing Be(ing), Corporeity, Dwell, Enhypostasia, Entelechy, Esse, Extant, Identity, Life, Live, Ontology, Perseity, Solipsism, Substantial, Ubiety

Existentialist Camus, Sartre

Exit Débouché, Door, Egress, Gate, Leave, Outlet

Exodus Book, Departure, Flight, Hegira, Hejira

Ex-official Outler

Exonerate(d) Absolve, Acquit, Clear, Excuse, Exempt, Shriven

Exorbitant Excessive, Expensive, Steep, Tall, Undue

Exorcise, Exorcist Benet, Lay

Exordium Opening, Preface, Prelude

Exotic Alien, Ethnic, Foreign, Strange, Outlandish

Expand, Expanse, Expansion Amplify, Boom, Develop, Diastole, Dilate, Distend, Ectasis, Elaborate, ➤ ENLARGE, Escalate, Grow, Increase, Magnify, Ocean, Snowball, Spread, Stretch, Swell, Wax, Wire-draw

Expatiate Amplify, Descant, Dwell, Enlarge, Perorate

Expatriate Banish, Colonial, Emigrate, Émigré, Exile, Outcast

Expect(ant), Expectation, Expected, Expecting Agog, Anticipate, Ask, Await, Due, Foresee, Gravid, Hope, Lippen, Look, Natural, Par, Pip, Pregnant, Presume, Prospect, Require, ➤ SUPPOSE, Tendance, Think, Thought, Usual, Ween

Expectorate Expel, Hawk, Spit

Expedient Advisable, Artifice, Contrivance, Fend, Make-do, Makeshift, Measure, Politic, Resort, Resource, Shift, Stopgap, Suitable, Wise

Expedite, Expedition Advance, Alacrity, Anabasis, Celerity, Crusade, Dispatch, Excursion, Fastness, Field trip, Hasten, Hurry, Kon-tiki, Pilgrimage, Post-haste, Safari, Speed, Trek, Trip, Voyage

Expel Amove, Dispossess, Egest, Evacuate, Evict, Exile, Exorcize, Hoof, Oust, Out(cast), Void

Expend(iture) Budget, Consume, Cost, Dues, Gavel, Mise, Occupy, Oncost, Outgo(ing), Outlay, Poll, Squander, Tithe, Toll, Use, Waste

Expendable Cannon-fodder

Expense(s) Charge, Cost, Exes, Fee, Law, Oncost, Outgoing, Outlay, Overhead, Price, Sumptuary

Expensive Chargeful, Costly, Dear, Executive, Salt, Steep, Upmarket, Valuable

Experience(d) Accomplished, A posteriori, Assay, Blasé, Discovery, Empiric, Encounter, Expert, ➤ FEEL, Felt, Freak-out, Gust, Hands-on, Have, Incur, Know, Learn, Live, Mature, Meet, Mneme, Old hand, Pass, Plumb, Seasoned, See, Senior, Sense, Sensory, Stager, Stand, Street-smart,

Streetwise, Taste, Transference, Trial, Trip, Trocinium, Try, Undergo, Versed, Work

Experiment(al) Attempt, Avant-garde, Empirical, Essay, Peirastic, Pilot, Sample, Taste, Tentative, ➤ TRIAL, Try, Venture

Expert(ise) Accomplished, Ace, Adept, Adroit, Arch, Authority, Boffin, Buff, Cambist, Cocker, Cognoscente, Connoisseur, Crack, Dab(ster), Dan, Deft, Don, Egghead, Fundi, Gourmet, Gun, Hotshot, Karateka, Know-all, Know-how, Luminary, Maestro, Masterly, Maven, Mavin, Meister, Nark, Oner, Oneyer, Oneyre, Peritus, Practised, Pro, Proficient, Pundit, Ringer, Savvy, Science, Skill(y), Sly, Specialist, Technique, Technocrat, Ulema, Used, Whiz

Expiate, Expiation, Expiatory Amends, Atone, Penance, Piacular

Expire(d), Expiry Blow, Collapse, Croak, ➤ DIE, End, Exhale, Invalid, Ish, Lapse, Neese, Pant, Sneeze, Terminate

Explain Account, Annotate, Aread, Arede, Arreede, Clarify, Conster, Construe, Decline, Define, Describe, Elucidate, Expose, Expound, Extenuate, Gloss, Gloze, Justify, Parabolize, Salve, Solve, Upknit

Explanation, Explanatory Apology, Commentary, Exegesis, Exegetic, Exposition, Farse, Gloss, Gloze, Hypothesis, Key, Note, Preface, Reading, Rigmarole, Solution, Theory

Expletive Arrah, Darn, Exclamation, Oath, Ruddy, Sapperment

Explicit Clean-cut, Clear, Definite, Express, Frank, Outspoken, ➤ PRECISE, Specific

Explode Backfire, Burst, Cramp, Debunk, Detonate, Erupt, ➤ EXPLOSION, Pop, Snake

Exploit(er), Exploitation Act, Adventure, Deed, Develop, Escapade, Gest, Harness, Ill-use, Impose, Kulak, Manoeuvre, Milk, Mission, Parlay, Rachmanism, Ramp, Stunt, Sweat, Use

Explore(r), Exploration Amerigo, Amundsen, Baffin, Balboa, Bandeirante, Banks, Barents, Bering, Boone, Burton, Cabot, Cartier, Chart, Columbus, Cook, Cortes, Da Gama, Dampier, Darwin, De Soto, Dias, Diaz, Discover, Dredge, Eric, Eriksson, Examine, Feel, Frobisher, Fuchs, Humboldt, Investigate, Livingstone, Magellan, Map, Marco Polo, Mungo Park, Nansen, Navigator, Pathfinder, Peary, Pioneer, Potholer, Probe, Przewalski, Rale(i)gh, Research, Rhodes, Ross, Scott, Scout, Search, Shackleton, Spaceship, Speke, Stanley, Sturt, Tasman, Vancouver, Vasco da Gama, Vespucci

Explosion, Explosive Agene, Amatol, Ammonal, ANFO, Antimatter, Aquafortis, Backfire, Bang, Bangalore torpedo, Blast, Cap, Cheddite, Chug, Cordite, Crump, Dualin, Dunnite, Egg, Euchloric, Euchlorine, Fireball, Firecracker, Firedamp, Firework, Fulminant, Gasohol, Gelatine, Gelignite, Grenade, Guncotton, Gunpowder, HE, High, Iracund, Jelly, Landmine, Lyddite, Megaton, Melinite, Mine, Nitroglycerine, Outburst, Ozonide, Paravane, Payload, Petar(d), Petre, Phut, Plastic, Plastique, Pluff, Population, Pow, Priming, Propellant, Ptarmic, Pustular, Report, Roburite, SAM, Semtex®, Sneeze, Soup, Supernova, Tetryl, Thunderflash, Tonite, TNT, Trinitrobenzene, Trotyl, Volcanic, Warhead, Xyloidin(e)

▷ **Explosive** may indicate an anagram
Exponent Advocate, Example, Index, Interpreter, Logarithm
Export(s) Despatch, Klondike, Klondyke, Ship, Visible
Expose(d), Exposure Air, Anagogic, Bare, Blot, Debag, Debunk, Denude, Desert, Disclose, Endanger, En prisé, Exhibit, Flashing, Indecent, Insolate, Moon, Nude, Object, Open, Out, Over, Propale, Reveal, Snapshot, Streak, Strip, Subject, Sun, Time, Unmask, Windswept
Exposition Aperçu
Expostulate, Expostulation Argue, Arrah, Protest, Remonstrate
Expound(er) Discourse, Discuss, Exegete, Explain, Open, Prelict, Red, Scribe, Ulema
Express(ed), Expression Air, APT, Aspect, Breathe, Cacophemism, Cliché, Conceive, Concetto, Couch, Countenance, Declare, Denote, Embodiment, Epithet, Explicit, Face, Fargo, Formulate, Good-luck, Gup, Hang-dog, Idiom, Locution, Manifest, Metonym, Mien, Mot (juste), Neologism, Non-stop, Orient, Paraphrase, Phrase, Pleonasm, Pony, Precise, Pronto, Put, Quep, Register, Say(ne), Show, Soulful, ➤ SPEAK, State, Strain, Succus, Term, Token, Tone, Topos, Utterance, Vent, ➤ VOICE
Expressionless Blank, Deadpan, Impassive, Inscrutable, Po(ker)-faced, Vacant, Wooden
Expressman Fargo
Expropriate Dispossess, Pirate, Seize
Expulsion Discharge, Eccrisis, Ejection, Eviction, Exile, Sacking, Synaeresis
Expunge Cancel, Delete, Erase, Obliterate
Expurgate Bowdlerize, Castrate, Censor, Purge
Exquisite Beautiful, Choice, Ethereal, Fine, Intense, Macaroni, Pink, Princox, Refined, Soigné(e), Too-too
Ex-serviceman Vet
Extemporise Ad lib, Improvise, Pong
Extend(ed), Extension Aspread, Augment, Cremaster, Draw, Eke, Elapse, Elongate, Enlarge, Escalate, Expand, Exsert, Fermata, Grow, Increase, Length, Long, Long-range, Long-stay, Long-term, Offer, Outgrowth, Overbite, Overlap, Porrect, Proffer, Prolong, Propagate, Protract, Reach, Retrochoir, Span, Spread, Steso, ➤ STRETCH, Substantial, Widen
Extensive, Extent Ambit, Area, Capacious, Catch-all, Compass, Comprehensive, Distance, Large, Length, Limit, ➤ MAGNITUDE, Panoramic, Range, Reach, Scale, Size, Spacious, Sweeping, Wide, Widespread
Extenuate Diminish, Lessen, Mitigate, Palliate
Exterior Aspect, Crust, Derm, Facade, Outer, ➤ OUTSIDE, Shell, Surface, Veneer
Exterminate, Extermination Abolish, Annihilate, Destroy, Holocaust, Uproot
External Exoteric, Exterior, Extraneous, Foreign, Outer
Extinct(ion) Archaeopteryx, Bygone, Chalicothere, Creodont, Dead, Death, Defunct, D(e)inothere, Dodo, Obsolete, Rasure, Saururae

Extinguish Douse, Dout, Dowse, Extirpate, Obscure, Quash, Quell, Quench, Slake, Snuff, Stifle, Suppress

Extirpate End, Erase, Excise, Obliterate, Root, Uproot

Extol Commend, Enhance, Eulogise, Exalt, Laud, Puff

Extort(ion), Extortioner Barathrum, Blackmail, Bleed, Bloodsucker, Chantage, Chout, Churn, Compel, Exact, Force, Gombeen, Rachman, Rack, Racketeer, Ransom, Screw, Shank, Squeeze, Sweat, Urge, Vampire, Wrest, Wring

Extra Accessory, Additament, Addition(al), Additive, Adjunct, And, Annexe, Attachment, Bisque, Bonus, By(e), Debauchery, Encore, Etcetera, Further, Gash, Lagniappe, Left-over, Leg bye, Make-weight, More, Nimiety, Odd, Optional, Out, Over, Perk, Plus, Plusage, Reserve, Ripieno, ➤ SPARE, Spilth, Staffage, Sundry, Super, Supernumerary, Supplementary, Suppletive, Surplus, Trop, Undue, Walking-gentleman, Walking-lady, Wide, Woundy

Extract(ion), Extractor Apozem, Bleed, Breeding, Catechu, Clip, Corkscrew, Decoction, Descent, Distil, Draw, Educe, Elicit, Emulsin, Enucleate, Essence, Estreat, Excerpt, Exodontics, Extort, Gist, Gobbet, Insulin, Kino, Milk, Mine, Parentage, Passage, Pericope, Pick, Piece, Pry, Pyrene, Quintessence, Retour, Smelt, Suck, Summary, Tap, Trie, Try, Vanilla, Winkle, Worm, Wring, Yohimbine

Extradition Renvoi

Extraneous Foreign, Irrelevant, Outlying, Spurious

Extraordinary Amazing, By-ordinar, Case, Curious, Humdinger, Important, Phenomenal, Preternatural, Rare, Singular, Startling, Strange, Unusual

Extravagance, Extravagant, Extravaganza Excessive, Fancy, Feerie, Heroic, High-flown, Hyperbole, Lavish, Luxury, Outré, Prodigal, Profuse, Rampant, Reckless, Riotise, Splash, Splurge, Squander, Sumptious, Superfluous, Waste

Extreme(ly), Extremist Acute, Almighty, Butt, Desperate, Die-hard, Drastic, Edge, Exceptional, Farthermost, Gross, In spades, ➤ INTENSE, Jacobin, Mega-, Mondo, Nazi, Opposite, Parlous, Pretty, Radical, Root and branch, Steep, Thule, Too, Tremendous, Ultima thule, Ultimate, Ultra, Utmost, Utter, ➤ VERY, Vitally, Wing

▷ **Extreme** may indicate a first or last letter

Extremity Bourn(e), Crisis, Digit, Ending, Finger(-tip), Limb, Limit, Outrance, Pole, Tip, Toe, Utterance

Extricate Liberate, Loose, Rescue, Untangle

Extrinsic Aliunde, External, Irrelevant, Outward

Extrovert Outgoing

Extrude Debar, Eject, Project

Exuberance, Exuberant Brio, Copious, Ebullient, Effusive, Gusto, Hearty, Lavish, Mad, Profuse, Rambustious, Skippy, Streamered

Exudation, Exude Bleed, Ectoplasm, Emit, Guttate, Ooze, Secrete, Still, Sweat, Ulmin, Weep

Exult(ant) Crow, Elated, ➤ GLOAT, Glorify, Jubilant, Paeonic, Rejoice, Triumphant, Whoop

Eye(s), Eye-ball, Eye-piece Canthus, Compound, Cringle, Eagle, Ee, Eine, Emmetropia, Evil, Glass, Glim, Glom, Goggles, Hurricane, Huygen's, Iris, Jack, Keek, Klieg, Lamp, Lazy, Lens, Magic, Mincepie, Mind's, Naked, ➤ OBSERVE, Ocellar, Ogle, Ommateum, Optic, Orb, Pedicel, Peeper, PI, Pigsn(e)y, Pigsnie, Pineal, Pupil, Regard, Retina, Rhabdom, Roving, Sclera, Sight, Spy, Storm-centre, Tec, Uvea, Watch, Water-pump, Weather, Whally, Windows, Winker

Eyebright Euphrasy

Eyebrow Bree, Brent-hill, Glib, Penthouse, Superciliary

Eyeglass Loupe

Eyelash Cilium

Eyelet Cringle, Grommet, Hole

Eyelid Canthus, Ectropion, Haw, Palpebral

Eye-rod Rhabdom

Eye-shadow Kohl

Eyesore Blot, Disfigurement, Sty(e)

Eye-stalk Ommatophore, Stipes

Eye trouble Amblyopia, Ametropia, Aniseikonia, Anisomatropia, Asthenopia, Astigmatism, Cataract, Ceratitis, Coloboma, Diplopia, Entropion, Exophthalmus, Glaucoma, Hemeralopia, Hemi(an)op(s)ia, Hypermetropia, Iritis, Keratitis, Leucoma, Lippitude, Micropsia, Miosis, Myosis, Nebula, Nyctalopia, Nystagmus, Ommateum, Presbyopia, Retinitis, Scotoma(ta), Shiner, Stigmatism, Strabismus, Synechia, Teichopsia, Thylose, Thylosis, Trachoma, Tritanopia, Tylosis, Wall-eye, Xeroma, Xerophthalmia

Eye-wash Collyrium

Eyrie Nest

Ezra Pound

F f

F Fahrenheit, Fellow, Feminine, Fluorine, Following, Force, Foxtrot

Fab Super

Fabian, Fabius Dilatory, Washington

Fable(s) Aesop, Allegory, Apologue, Exemplum, Fiction, Hitopadesa, La Fontaine, Legend, Marchen, Milesian, Myth, Panchatantra, Parable, Romance, Tale

Fabric ➤ CLOTH, Framework

Fabricate, Fabrication Artefact, Concoct, Construct, Contrive, Cook, Fake, Figment, Forge, ➤ INVENT, Lie, Porky, Trump, Weave, Web

Fabulous, Fabulous beast Apocryphal, Apologue, Chichevache, Chimera, Cockatrice, Eldorado, Fictitious, Fung, Gear, Griffin, Hippogriff, Hippogryph, Huma, Incredible, Jabberwock(y), Kylin, Legendary, Magic, Manticora, Manticore, Merman, Monoceros, Mythical, Opinicus, Orc, Phoenix, Roc, Romantic, Simorg, Simurg(h), Sphinx, Tarand, Tragelaph, Unicorn, Unreal, Wivern, Wyvern, Yale

Facade Front(age), Frontal, Mask, Pretence

Face, Facing Abide, Affront, Ashlar, Ashler, Aspect, Audacity, Brave, Brazen, Caboched, Caboshed, Cheek, Chiv(v)y, Coal, Countenance, Culet, Dalle, Dare, Dartle, Deadpan, Dial, Eek, Elevation, Encounter, Facade, Fat, Favour, Features, Fineer, Fortune, ➤ FRONT, Girn, Gonium, Groof, Grouf, Groue, Gurn, Hatchet, Head-on, Jib, Kisser, Lining, Look, Lore, Mascaron, Meet, Metope, Moe, Mug, Mush, Opposite, Outstare, Outward, Pan, Paper tiger, Phisnomy, Phiz(og), Physiognomy, Poker, Puss, Revet, Revetment, Roughcast, Rud, Rybat, Side, Snoot, Socle, Stucco, Type, Veneer, Vis(age), Visnomy, Withstand, Zocco(lo)

Face-ache Noli-me-tangere

Face-lift Rhytidectomy

Face-saving Redeeming, Salvo

Facet(ed) Angle, Aspect, Bezel, Culet, Face, Polyhedron

Facetious Frivolous, Jocular, Waggish, Witty

Facile Able, Adept, Complaisant, Ductile, Easy, Fluent, Glib

Facilitate, Facility Amenity, Assist, Benefit, Capability, ➤ EASE, Expedite, Fluency, Gift, ISO, Knack, Skill

Facsimile Copy, Replica, Repro

Fact(s), Factual Actual, Case, Correct, Data, Datum, Detail, Info, Literal, Mainor, Nay, Really, Truism, Truth, Veridical, Yes

Faction Bloc, Cabal, Camp, Caucus, Clique, Contingent, Junto, Schism, Sect, Tendency, Wing

Factor Agent, Aliquot, Broker, Cause, Co-efficient, Common, ➤ COMPONENT, Divisor, Edaphic, Element, Feel-good, Intrinsic, Load, Modulus, Representative, Rh, Rhesus, Risk, Steward, Wind chill

Factory Cannery, Gasworks, Glassworks, Hacienda, Maquiladora, Mill, Plant, Refinery, Sawmill, Steelworks, Sweatshop, Tinworks, Works, Workshop

Factotum Circar, Handyman, Servant, Sircar, Sirkar

Faculty Aptitude, Arts, Capacity, Department, Ear, Ease, Indult, Knack, Power, School, Sense, Speech, ➤ TALENT, Teachers, Wits

Fad(dish) Crank, Craze, Cult, Fashion, Foible, Ismy, Thing, Vogue, Whim

Fade(d), Fading Blanch, Die, Diminuendo, Dinge, Elapsion, Etiolate, Evanescent, Fall, Filemot, Lessen, Mancando, Pale, Passé, Perdendo(si), Peter, Smorzando, Smorzato, Stonewashed, Vade, Vanish, Wallow, Wilt, Wither

Faeces Dingleberry, Dung, Kak, Meconium, Scybalum, Skatole, Stercoraceous, Stools

Fag Chore, Cigarette, Drag, Drudge, Fatigue, Gasper, Homosexual, Menial, Quean, Reefer, Snout, Tire, Toil, Weary

Fag-end Ash, Lag, Stub

Fag(g)ot(s) Bavin, Bundle, Fascine, Firewood, Homosexual, Kid, Knitch, Twigs

Fail(ing), Failure Anile, Blemish, Blow, Bomb, Bummer, Cark, ➤ COLLAPSE, Conk, Crash, Cropper, Debacle, Decline, Default, Defect, Demerit, Die, Dog, Dry, Dud, Fault, Feal, Fiasco, Flivver, Flop, Flow, Flunk, Fold, Founder, Frost, Glitch, Gutser, Infraction, Lapse, Lose, Malfunction, Manqué, Mis-, Miscarry, Miss, Muff, Nerd, No-no, Omit, Oversight, Pip, Plough, Pluck, Refer, Refusal, Shambles, Short circuit, Short(coming), Slippage, Smash, Spin, Stumer, Turkey, Vice, Wash-out, Weakness, White elephant, Wipeout

Fain Lief

Faineant Gallio

Faint(ness) Black-out, Conk, Darkle, Dim, Dizzy, Dwalm, Fade, Lassitude, Pale, Stanck, Swarf, Swarve, Swelt, Swerf, Swerve, Swoon, Swound, Syncope, Unclear, Wan, Whitish

Faint-heart Coward, Craven, Timid, Wet

Fair A(e)fald, Aefauld, Aefwld, Barnet, Bartholomew, Bazaar, Beauteous, Belle, Blond, Bon(n)ie, Bonny, Brigg, Decent, Donnybrook, Equal, Equitable, Evenhanded, Exhibition, ➤ FESTIVAL, Feeing-market, Fine, Funfair, Gaff, Gey, Goose, Gwyn, Hiring, Honest, Hopping, Isle, ➤ JUST, Kermess, Kermis, Kirmess, Market, Mart, Mediocre, Mela, Mop, Nundinal, Objective, OK, Paddington, Passable, Play, Pro rata, Rosamond, Sabrina, Square, Statute, Straight, Tavistock, Tidy, Tolerable, Tow-headed, Trade, Tryst, Unbias(s)ed, Vanity, Wake, Widdicombe

Fair-buttocked Callipygean

Fairing Ornament, Spat

Fairly Clearly, Enough, Evenly, Midway, Moderately, Pari passu, Pretty, Properly, Quite, Ratherish

Fairway Dog-leg, Pretty

Fairy Banshee, Befana, Cobweb, Dobbie, Dobby, Elf(in), Fay, Gloriana, Hob, Hop o' my thumb, Leprechaun, Lilian, Mab, Morgan le Fay, Morgane(tta), Moth, Nis, Peri, Pigwidgin, Pigwiggen, Pisky, Pixie, Pouf, Puck, Punce, Sandman, Spirit, Sprite, Sugar-plum, Tink(erbell), Titania, Tooth, Urchin-shows

Faith(ful) Accurate, Achates, Belief, Constant, Creed, Devoted, Doctrine, Faix, Fay, Feal, Fegs, Fideism, Fiducial, Haith, Implicit, Islam, Lay, Loyal, Plerophory, Puritanism, Quaker, Religion, Shema, Solifidian, Staunch, Strict, Troth, ➤ TRUE, True-blue, Trust, Truth, Umma(h)

Faithless Atheist, Disloyal, False, Hollow, Nullifidian, Perfidious, Punic

Fake(r), Faking Bodgie, Bogus, Copy, Counterfeit, Duffer, Ersatz, False, Fold, Fraud, Fudge, Imitation, Imposter, Impostor, Paste, Phoney, Postiche, Pretend, Sham, Spurious, Trucage, Truquage, Truqueur, Unreal

Falcon Gentle, Hawk, Hobby, Kestrel, Lanner(et), Merlin, Nyas, Peregrine, Prairie, Saker, Sakeret, Sparrow-hawk, Stallion, Staniel, Stannel, Stanyel, Tassel-gentle, Tassell-gent, Tercel-gentle

Falklander Kelper

Fall(s), Fallen, Falling Abate, Accrue, Angel, Arches, Astart, Autumn, Boyorna, Cadence, Cascade, Cataract, Chute, Collapse, Crash, Cropper, Cross press, Declension, Decrease, Degenerate, Descent, Dip, Domino effect, Douse, Downswing, Dowse, ➤ DROP, Ebb, Firn, Flop, Flump, Folding press, Free, Grabble, Gutser, Gutzer, Horseshoe, Idaho, Incidence, Iguacu, Kabalega, Kaieteur, Lag, Landslide, Lapse, Lin(n), Niagara, Oct(ober), Owen, Perish, Plonk, Plummet, Plump, Plunge, Prolapse, Purl(er), Rain, Reaction, Relapse, Ruin, Sheet, Sin, Sleet, Snow, Spill, Sutherland, Tailor, Takakkau, Topple, Toss, Trip, Tugela, Tumble, Victoria, Voluntary, Wipeout, Yosemite

Fallacious, Fallacy Elench(us), Error, Idolum, Illogical, Illusion, Pathetic, Sophism, Unsound

Fallible Human, Imperfect

▷ **Falling** may indicate an anagram or a word backwards

Fallow Barren, Lea, Tan, Uncared, Uncultivated, Untilled

False, Falsify Adulterate, Bastard, Bodgie, Bogus, Braide, Canard, Cavil, Charlatan, Cook, Deceitful, Disloyal, Dissemble, Doctor, Fake, Feigned, Fiddle, Forge, Illusory, Knave, Lying, Meretricious, Mock, Perjury, Pinchbeck, Postiche, Pretence, Pseudo, Roorback, Sham, Specious, Spoof, Spurious, Treacherous, Two-faced, Untrue

False notions Idola

Falter Hesitate, Limp, Totter, Waver

Fame, Famous Bruit, Eminent, Glitterati, Gloire, Glory, History, Humour, Kudos, Legendary, Luminous, Name, Noted, Notorious, Prestige, Reclamé, Renown, Repute, Rumour, Spur, Stardom, Word

Familiar(ise), Familiarity Accustom, Acquaint, Assuefaction, Au fait, Auld, Chummy, Comrade, Conversant, Crony, Dear, Demon, Easy, Free, Friend, Habitual, Homely, Homey, Incubus, Intimate, Known, Liberty, Maty, Old, Old-hat, Privy, Python, Used, Versed, Warhorse

Family Ancestry, Bairn-team, Blood, Breed, Clan, Class, Cognate, Consanguine, Descent, Dynasty, Extended, House(hold), Issue, Kin, Kind, Line, Mafia, Medici, Name, Nuclear, Orange, People, Phratry, Progeny, Quiverful, Race, Sept, Sib(b), Sibship, Stem, Stirps, Strain, Taffy, Talbot, Tribe

Family tree Pedigree, Stemma

Famine Dearth, Lack, Scarcity

Famish(ed) Esurient, Hungry, Ravenous, Starving

▷ **Famished** may indicate an 'o' in the middle of a word

Fan(s), Fan-like Alligator, Admirer, Aficionado, Alluvial, Arouse, Bajada, Blow, Cat, Clapper, Claque, Colmar, Cone, Cool, Cuscus, Devotee, Diadrom, Dryer, Enthusiast, Extractor, Fiend, Flabellum, Following, Groupie, Hepcat, Khuskhus, Outspread, Partisan, Punka(h), Rhipidate, Ringsider, Sail, Spread, Supporter, Tail, Tifosi, Ventilate, Votary, Voteen, Washingtonia, Wing, Winnow, Zealot, Zelant

▷ **Fan** may indicate an anagram

Fanatic(al) Bigot, Devotee, Energumen, Enthusiastic, Extremist, Fiend, Frenetic, Glutton, Mad, Maniac, Nut, Partisan, Phrenetic, Picard, Rabid, Santon, Ultra, Wowser, Zealot

Fancy, Fanciful Caprice, Chim(a)era, Conceit, Concetto, Crotchet, Daydream, Dream, Dudish, Elaborate, Fangle, Fantasy, Fit, Flam, Florid, Frothy, Guess, Hallo, Idea(te), Idolon, ➤ IMAGINE, Inclination, Lacy, Liking, Maya, Mind, My, Nap, Notion, Ornamental, Ornate, Picture, Predilection, Rococo, Suppose, Thought, Vagary, Visionary, Ween, Whigmaleerie, Whigmaleery, Whim(sy)

▷ **Fancy** may indicate an anagram

Fane Banner, Pronaos

Fanfare Flourish, Sennet, Show, Tantara, Trump, Tucket

Fang Tooth, Tusk

Fanny Adams, Bottom, Gas-lit, Price

Fantastic, Fantasy Absurd, Antic, Bizarre, Caprice, Chimera, Cockaigne, Cockayne, Escapism, Fab, Fanciful, Grotesque, Hallucination, Kickshaw(s), Lucio, Myth, Outré, Phantasmagoria, Queer, Romance, Unreal, Untrue, ➤ WHIM, Whimsical, Wild

Far Apogean, Away, Distal, Distant, Extreme, Outlying, Remote, Thether, Thither

Farce(ur) Burletta, Charade, Comedy, Exode, Feydeau, Lazzo, Mime, Mockery, Pantomime, Rex, Sham

Fare Apex, Charge, Cheer, Commons, Do, Eat, ➤ FOOD, Go, Passage, Passenger, Rate, Table, Traveller

Farewell Adieu, Adios, Aloha, Apopemptic, Bye, Cheerio, Departure, Godspeed, ➤ GOODBYE, Leave, Prosper, Sayonara, Send off, So long, Toodle-oo, Toodle-pip, Totsiens, Vale, Valediction

Far-fetched Fanciful, Improbable, Recherché

Farm(ing), Farmhouse Agronomy, Arable, Bowery, Cold Comfort, Collective, Croft, Cultivate, Dairy, Deep-litter, Emmerdale, Estancia,

Extensive, Factory, Fat, Fish(ery), Funny, Geoponical, Grange, Hacienda, Health, Home, Homestead, Husbandry, Intensive, Kibbutz, Kolkhoz, Land, Ley, Loaf, Location, Mains, Mas, No-tillage, Onstead, Orley, Pen, Poultry, Ranch, Rent, Sewage, Shamba, Smallholding, Sovkhoz, Station, Stead(ing), Sted(d), Stedde, Steed, Stock, Subsistence, Tank, Till, Toon, Toun, Town, Wick, Wind

Farmer Boer, Campesino, Carl, Cockatoo, Cocky, Collins Street, Colon, Crofter, Estanciero, Gebur, George, Giles, Hick, Macdonald, Metayer, Nester, NFU, Peasant, Pitt Street, Ryot, Share-cropper, Sodbuster, Squatter, Tenant, Tiller, Whiteboy, Yeoman, Zeminda(r)

Farmhand Cadet, Cottar, Cotter, Cottier, Ditcher, Hand, He(a)rdsman, Hind, Ploughman, Redneck, Rouseabout, Roustabout, Shearer

▶ **Farmhouse** see FARM

Farmyard Barton, Villatic

Farouche Awkward, Shy, Sullen

Farrago Hotch-potch, Jumble, Medley, Mélange

Farrier Marshal, Smith

Farrow Litter, Mia, Sow

Farthing Brass, F, Fadge, Har(r)ington, Mite, Q, Quadragesimal, Rag

Fascia Band, Fillet, Platband

Fascinate, Fascinating Allure, Attract, Bewitch, ▶ CHARM, Dare, Enchant, Engross, Enthral(l), Fetching, Inthral, Intrigue, Kill, Mesmeric, Rivet, Siren, Witch

Fascist Blackshirt, Blue shirt, Brownshirt, Dictator, Falange, Falangist, Iron Guard, Lictor, Nazi, Neo-nazi, NF, Rexist, Sinarchist, Sinarquist

Fashion(able), Fashioned Aguise, A la (mode), Bristol, Build, Chic, Construct, Convention, Corinthian, Craze, Create, Cult, Custom, Cut, Design, Directoire, Elegant, Entail, Fad, Feat, Feign, Forge, Form, Genteel, Go, Hew, Hip, In, Invent, Kitsch, Look, ▶ MAKE, Manière, Manners, Mode, Mondain(e), Mould, Newgate, Pink, Preppy, Rage, Rate, Sc, Shape, Smart, Smith, Snappy, Snazzy, Stile, Stylar, Style, Swish, Tailor, Ton, Ton(e)y, ▶ TREND(Y), Turn, Twig, Vogue, Way, Wear, With-it, Work, Wrought

Fast(er) Abstain, Apace, Ashura, Breakneck, Citigrade, Clem, Daring, Double-quick, Elaphine, Express, Fizzer, Fleet, Immobile, Lent, Lightning, Loyal, Maigre, Meteoric, Moharram, Muharram, Muharrem, Pac(e)y, Posthaste, Presto, Pronto, Quadragesimal, Quick, Raffish, Raking, Ramadan, Ramadhan, Rash, Spanking, Speedy, Stretta, Stretto, Stuck, Supersonic, Swift, Tachyon, Thick, Tisha b'Av, Whistle-stop, Yarer, Yom Kippur

Fast and loose Fickle, Pick-the-garter, Strap-game

Fasten(er), Fastening Anchor, Attach, Bar, Belay, Bind, Bolt, Buckle, Button, Chain, Clamp, Clasp, Clinch, Clip, Cramp, Dead-eye, Diamond-hitch, Espagnolette, Eye-bolt, Frog, Gammon, Hasp, Hesp, Hook, Lace, Latch, Lock, Moor, Morse, Nail, Netsuke, Padlock, Parral, Pectoral, Pin, Preen, Reeve, Rivet, Rope, Rove, Seal, ▶ SECURE, Shut, Spar,

Sprig, Staple, Tach(e), Tag, Tassel, Tether, Tintack, Toggle, Velcro®, Wedge, Zip

Fastidious Chary, Critical, Dainty, Fussy, Neat, Nice, Particular, Squeamish

Fat(s), Fatten, Fatty Adipic, Adipocere, Adipose, Aldermanly, Aliphatic, Arcus, Atheroma, Bard, Batten, Battle, Blubber, Brown, Butter, Calipash, Calipee, Cellulite, Chubbed, Chubby, Corpulent, Creesh, Degras, Dika-oil, Dosh, Dripping, Embonpoint, Enarm, Endomorph, Flab, Flesh, Flick, Fozy, Fubsy, Galam-butter, Grease, Gross, Keech, Lanolin, Lard, Lipaemia, Lipoma, Love handles, Margarine, Marge, Obese, Oil, OS, Palmitin, Pinguid, Plump, Poddy, Podgy, Polyunsaturated, Portly, Puppy, Pursy, Rich, Rolypoly, Rotund, Saginate, Saim, Saturated, Schmal(t)z, Seam(e), Sebacic, Sebum, Shortening, Soil, Spe(c)k, Squab, Stearic, Steatopygia, Steatorrhea, Suberin, Suet, Tallow, Tin, Tomalley, Triglyceride, Tub, Unsaturated, Vanaspati, Waller, Wool

Fatal(ism), Fate(ful), Fated Apnoea, Atropos, Cavel, Chance, Clotho, Deadly, Death, Decuma, Destiny, Doom, End, Fay, Fell, Joss, Karma, Kismet, Lachesis, Lethal, Lot, Meant, Moira, Mortal, Mortiferous, Nemesis, Norn(a), Parca, Pernicious, Predestination, Portion, Skuld, Urd, Verdande, Waterloo, Weird

Father(ly) Abba, Abbot, Abuna, Adopt, Apostolic, Bapu, Begetter, Breadwinner, Brown, City, Curé, Dad, Engender, Founding, Fr, Generator, Genitor, Getter, Governor, Male, Pa, Padre, Papa, Pappy, Parent, Paterfamilias, Pater(nal), Patriarch, Père, Pop(pa), Popper, Priest, Rev, Sire, Stud, Thames, Tiber, William

Father-lasher Sea-scorpion

Fathom Depth, Delve, Dig, F, Plumb, Plummet, Understand

Fatigue Battle, Exhaust, Fag, Jade, Jet lag, ME, Neurosthenia, Overdo, Tire, Weariness, Weary

Fatuous Gaga, Idiotic, Silly, Stupid

Faucet Cock, Spigot, Tap

Fault(y) Arraign, Bad, Beam, Blame(worthy), Blunder, Bug, Cacology, Carp, Culpable, Defect, Demerit, Dip, Drop-out, Duff, ➤ ERROR, Failing, Flaw, Frailty, Gall, Glitch, Henpeck, Imperfect, Literal, Massif, ➤ MISTAKE, Nag, Nibble, Niggle, Nit-pick, Out, Outcrop, Overthrust, Peccadillo, Rate, Reprehend, Rift, Rupes Recta, San Andreas, Sclaff, Short, Slip, Strike, Trap, Vice

Faultless Impeccable, Lily-white, Perfect

Fauvist Matisse

Faux pas Blunder, Boner, Gaffe, Leglen-girth, Solecism

Favour(able), Favoured, Favourite Advance, Advantage(ous), Aggrace, Agraste, Alder-liefest, Approval, Back, Befriend, Behalf, Benign, Bless, Boon, Bribe, Cert, Chosen, Cockade, Curry, Darling, Ex gratia, Fancy, Favodian, Grace, Gratify, Graste, Gree, Hackle, Hot, In, Indulge, Kickback, Minion, Odour, Particular, Peat, Persona grata, Pet, Pettle, Popular, ➤ PREFER, Promising, Propitious, Resemble, Rib(b)and, Roseate, Rose-knot, Rosette, Smile, Toast, Token

Fawn(er), Fawning Adulate, Bambi, Beige, Blandish, Brown-nose, Crawl, Creep, Cringe, Deer, Ecru, Flatter, Fleech, Grovel, Ko(w)tow, Lickspittle, Obsequious, Servile, Smarm, Smoo(d)ge, Subservient, Sycophant, Tasar, Toady, Truckle, Tussah, Tusseh, Tusser, Tussore

Fay Fairy, Korrigan, Peri

FBI G-men

Fear Angst, Apprehension, Awe, Bugbear, Claustrophobia, Cold sweat, Crap, Cyberphobia, Dismay, Doubt, Drad, Dread, Foreboding, ➤ FOR FEAR, Fright, Funk, Hang-up, Horror, Kenophobia, Mysophobia, Nyctophobia, Ochlophobia, ➤ PHOBIA, Redoubt, Revere, Taphephobia, Taphophobia, Terror, Trepidation, Willies

Fearful Afraid, Cowardly, Dire, Horrific, Nervous, Pavid, Rad, Redoubtable, Timorous, Tremulous, Windy

Fearless Bold, Brave, Courageous, Gallant, Impavid, Intrepid

Fearsome Dire, Formidable

Feasible Goer, Likely, On, Possible, Practical, Probable, Viable

Feast Adonia, Agape, Assumption, Banquet, Barmecide, Beano, Belshazzar's, Blow-out, Candlemas, Carousal, Celebration, Dine, Do, Double, Eat, Encaenia, Epiphany, Epulation, Festival, Fleshpots, Fool's, Gaudeamus, Gaudy, Hallowmas, Hockey, Hogmanay, Holy Innocents, Id-al-Adha, Id-al-Fitr, Immaculate Conception, Isodia, Junket, Kai-kai, Lady Day, Lamb-ale, Lammas, Luau, Martinmas, Michaelmas, Movable, Noel, Passover, Pentecost, Pig, Potlatch, Purim, Regale, Revel, Roodmas, Seder, Shindig, Spread, Succoth, Sukkot(h), Tabernacles, Tuck-in, Wayzgoose, Weeks, Yule, Zagmuk

Feast-day Mass

Feat Achievement, Deed, Effort, Exploit, Gambado, Stunt, Trick

Feather(ed), Feathers Alula, Barbicel, Boa, Braccate, Cock, Contour, Covert, Crissum, Down, Duster, Filoplume, Fledged, Fletch, Flight, Gemmule, Hackle, Harl, Hatchel, Herl, Lure, Macaroni, Oar, Ostrich, Pen(na), Pin, Pinna, Pith, Plumage, Plume, Plumule, Pteryla, Ptilosis, ➤ QUILL, Rectrix, Remex, Remiges, Rocket-tail, Saddle-hackle, Scapula, Scapus, Semiplume, Sickle, Standard, Stipa, Swansdown, Tectrix, Tertial, Vibrissa, White, Wing covert

Feather-worker Plumassier

Feature(s) Amenity, Appurtenance, Article, Aspect, Attribute, Brow, Character, Chin, Depict, Eye, Eyebrow, Face, Figure, Hallmark, Highlight, Item, Jizz, Landmark, Lineament, Neotery, Nose, Nucleus, Overfold, Phiz(og), Physiognomy, Spandrel, Star, Temple, Trait, Underlip

Featureless Flat

Febrifuge Atabrin, Atebrin®, Mepacrine, Quina

February Fill-dyke

Fecund(ity) Fertile, Fruitful, Prolific, Uberty

Federal, Federation Alliance, Axis, Bund, Commonwealth, Interstate, League, Statal, Union

Fee Charge, Corkage, Dues, Duty, Faldage, Fine, Hire, Honorarium, Mortuary, Mouter, Multure, Obvention, Pay, Premium, Refresher, Retainer, Sub, Transfer, Tribute

Feeble Banal, Characterless, Daidling, Debile, Decrepit, Droob, Effete, Feckless, Flaccid, Footling, Fragile, Geld, Ineffective, Infirm, Jessie, Namby-pamby, Pale, Puny, Sickly, Slender, Slight, Tailor, Tame, Thin, Tootle, Wallydrag, Wallydraigle, Washy, Wastrel, Weak, Weak-kneed, Weak-minded, Weed, Weedy, Wersh, Wet, Wimpish, Worn

Feed(er), Feeding Battle, Bib, Browse, Cake, Cater, Cibation, Clover, Dine, Drip, ➤ EAT, ➤ EMPLOYED, Fatten, Fire, Fishmeal, Fodder, Food, Gavage, Graze, Hay, Lunch, Meal, Nourish, Paid, Pecten, Provender, Refect, Repast, Sate, Soil, Stoke, Stooge, Stover, Sustain, Tire, Tractor, Wean

Feel, Feeling(s) Aesthesia, Affetuoso, Atmosphere, Compassion, Darshan, ➤ EMOTION, Empathy, Empfindung, Euphoria, ➤ EXPERIENCE, Fellow, Finger, Flaw, Frisk, Grope, Groundswell, Handle, Heart, Heartstrings, Hunch, Intuit, Knock, Know, Palp, Passible, Passion, Pity, Premonition, Presentiment, Probe, Realise, Sensate, Sensation, ➤ SENSE, Sensitive, Sentiment, Spirit, Tactual, Touch, Turn, Undercurrent, Vehemence, Vibes, Zeal

Feeler Antenna, Barbel, Exploratory, Overture, Palp, Sensillum, Tentacle

▶ **Feet** see FOOT

Feign Act, Affect, Colour, Fake, Malinger, Mime, Mock, ➤ PRETEND, Sham, Simulate

Feint Deke, Disguise, Dodge, Faint, Fake, Spoof, Trick

Fel(d)spar Adularia, Albite, Anorthite, Gneiss, Hyalophane, Moonstone, Orthoclase, Petuntse, Petuntze, Plagioclase, Sun-stone

Felicity Bliss, Happiness, Joy, Relevance

▶ **Feline** see CAT

Fell Axe, Chop, Cruel, Deadly, Dire, Dread, Fierce, Hew, Hide, Hill, Inhuman, Knock-down, KO, Lit, Log, Moor, Pelt, Poleaxe, Ruthless, Sca, Shap, Skittle

Fellow(ship) Academic, Associate, Bawcock, Birkie, Bloke, Bo, Bro, Buffer, Carlot, Cat, Chal, Chap, Chi, China, Cock, Cod(ger), Collaborator, Co-mate, Communion, Companion, Comrade, Confrère, Cove, Cully, Cuss, Dandy, Dean, Dog, Don, Dude, Equal, F, Fogey, Fop, Gadgie, Gadje, Gaudgie, Gauje, Gink, Guy, Joe, Joker, Josser, Lad, Like, M, Mall, Man, Mate, Member, Mister, Mun, Partner, Peer, Professor, Rival, Sister, Sociate, Sodality, Swab, Twin, Waghalter, Wallah

Felon(y) Bandit, Convict, Crime, Gangster, Offence, Villain

Felt Bat(t), Drugget, Knew, Met, Numdah, Numnah, Pannose, Roofing, Sensed, Tactile, Underlay, Velour

Female (bodies), Feminine, Feminist Anima, Bint, Bit, Dame, Distaff, Doe, F, Filly, Girl, Harem, Hen, Her, Kermes, Lady, Libber, Maiden, Pen, Petticoated, Riot girl, Sakti, Shakti, She, Sheila, Shidder, Soft, Spindle, Thelytoky, -trix, ➤ WOMAN, Yin

▷ **Female, Feminine** may indicate an -ess ending

Fen Bog, Carr, Ea, Jiao, Marsh, Morass

Fence(r), Fencing (position) Bar, Barrier, Botte, Carte, Dogleg, Enclose, Epee, Flanconade, Foils, Fraise, Haha, Hay, Hedge, Hurdle, Iaido, Imbrocate, Kendo, Link, Mensur, Netting, Obstacle, Oxer, Pale, Paling, Palisade, Passado, Pen, Picket, Quart(e), Quinte, Raddle, Rail, Rasper, Receiver, Reset, Ring, Scrimure, Seconde, Sept(um), Septime, Singlestick, Sixte, Stacket, Stockade, Stramac, Stramazon, Sunk, Swordplay, Tac-au-tac, Trellis, Virginia, Wattle, Wear, Weir, Wire

Fend(er) Buffer, Bumper, Cowcatcher, Curb, Mudguard, Parry, Provide, Resist, Skid, Ward, Wing

Fennel Finoc(c)hio, Finnochio, Herb, Love-in-a-mist, Narthex, Ragged lady

Fent Offcut, Remnant, Slit

Feral Brutal, Fierce, Savage, Wild

Ferdinand Archduke, Bull

Ferment(ation) Barm, Enzym(e), Leaven, Mowburn, Protease, Ptyalin, Seethe, Solera, Stum, Trypsin, Turn, Vinify, Working, Ye(a)st, Zyme, Zymosis, Zymurgy

Fermium Fm

Fern Acrogenous, Adder's-tongue, Adiantum, Archegonial, Asparagus, Aspidium, Asplenium, Azolla, Barometz, Bird's nest, Bladder, Bracken, Brake, Buckler, Ceterach, Cinnamon, Cryptogram, Cyathea, Cycad, Dicksonia, Elkhorn, Filicales, Filices, Filmy, Grape, Hard, Hart's-tongue, Isoetes, Maidenhair, Marsh, Marsilea, Marsilia, Meadow, Moonwort, Mosquito, Mulewort, Nardoo, Nephrolepsis, Ophioglossum, Osmunda, Parsley, Pepperwort, Pillwort, Polypod, Ponga, Pteridology, Pteris, Punga, Rachilla, Rockbrake, Royal, Schizaea, Scolopendrium, Silver, Spleenwort, Staghorn, Sword, Tara, Tree, Venus's hair, Woodsia

Ferocious Brutal, Cruel, Fell, Predatory, Rambunctious

Ferret Business, Fesnyng, Gill, Hob, Jill, Nose, Polecat, Ribbon, Rootle, Snoop, Trace, Unearth

Ferry(man) Charon, Convey, Hovercraft, Passage, Plier, Roll-on, RORO, Sealink, Shuttle, Traject, Tranect

Fertile, Fertility (symbol) Battle, Fat, Fecund, Fruitful, Linga, Priapus, Productive, Prolific, Rhiannon, Rich, Uberous

Fertilise(r), Fertilisation Ammonia, Auxin, Bee, Bone-ash, Bone-earth, Bone-meal, Caliche, Caprify, Compost, Fishmeal, Guano, Heterosis, Humogen, Humus, In-vitro, IVF, Kainite, Manure, Marl, Nitrate, Nitre, Pearl-ash, Phosphate, Pollen, Potash, Self, Sham, Stamen, Superphosphate, Top dressing

Fervent, Fervid, Fervour Ardent, Burning, Earnest, Heat, Hwyl, Intense, Keen, Passionate, White-hot, Zeal, Zeloso

Fester Beal, Putrefy, Rankle, Rot, Suppurate

Festival, Festive, Festivity Adonia, Al Hijra(h), Aldeburgh, Ale, All Saints' Day, Ambarvalia, Anniversary, Anthesteria, Ashora, Bairam, Baisak(h)i, Bayreuth, Beano, Beltane, Biennale, Candlemas, Carnival, Celebration, Cerealia, Chanuk(k)ah, Childermas, Church-ale, Circumcision, Commemoration, Convivial, Corpus Christi, Corroboree, Crouchmas,

Dassehra, Dewali, Dionysia, Divali, Diwali, Doseh, Druid, Easter,
Eisteddfod, Encaenia, En fête, Epiphany, ➤ FAIR, Feast, Feis, Fete, Fiesta,
Fringe, Gaff, ➤ GALA, Gaudy, Gregory, Hallowmas, Hanukkah, Harvest,
Hock-tide, Hogmanay, Holi, ➤ HOLIDAY, Holy-ale, Hosay, Hosein, Id-al-fitr,
Kermess, Kermiss, Kirmess, Lady-day, Lailat-ul-Qadr, Lammas,
Laylat-al-Miraj, Lemural, Lemuria, Lesser Bairam, Lupercalia, Matsuri,
Mela, Merry-night, Michaelmas, Miraj, Mod, Navaratra, Navaratri, Noel,
Obon, Palilia, Panathenaean, Panegyry, Pardon, Pasch, Passover,
Pentecost, Pesa(c)h, Play, Pongal, Pooja(h), Potlach, Puja, Purim,
Quirinalia, Revel, Rosh Hashanah, Samhain, Saturnalia, Seder,
Semi-double, Shabuath, Shavuath, Shrove(tide), Simchat Torah, Slugfest,
Terminalia, Tet, Thargelia, Thesmophoria, Tide, Transfiguration,
Up-Helly-Aa, Utas, Vesak, Vinalia, Visitation, Vulcanalia, Wake, Wesak,
Yomtov, Yule(tide)

Festoon Deck, Decorate, Encarpus, Garland, Swag, Wreathe

Fetch(ing) Arrive, Attract, Bring, Charming, Fet(t), Get, Gofer, Realise

Fete Bazaar, Champetre, Entertain, ➤ FESTIVITY, Gala, Honour, Tattoo

Fetish Charm, Compulsion, Idol, Ju-ju, Obeah, Obi(a), Talisman, Totem,
Voodoo

Fetter Basil, Bilboes, Chain, Gyve, Hamshackle, Hopple, Iron, Leg-iron,
Manacle, Shackle

Fettle Arrange, Condition, Frig, Potter, Repair

Feud Affray, Clash, Feoff, Fief, Quarrel, Strife, ➤ VENDETTA

Feudal (service) Arriage, Auld-farrant, Forinsec, Old

Fever(ish) Ague, Blackwater, Brain, Breakbone, Buck, Cabin, Calenture,
Childbed, Dengue, Enteric, Ferment, Frenetic, Glandular, Hay, Heatstroke,
Hectic, Hyperpyretic, Insolation, Intense, Intermittent, Jungle, Kala-azar,
Lassa, Malaria, Malta, Marsh, Mediterranean, Miliary, Milk, Parrot,
Paratyphoid, Passion, Puerperal, Pyretic, Pyrexia, Pyrogenic, Q, Quartan,
Quintan, Quotidian, Rheumatic, Rock, Sandfly, Scarlatina, Scarlet, Spring,
Sunstroke, Swamp, Swine, Tap, Temperature, Tertian, Tick, Trench,
Typhoid, Typhus, Undulant, Verruga, Vomito, Whot, Yellow(jack)

Few(er) Handful, Infrequent, ➤ LESS, Limited, Scarce, Some, Wheen

Fey Clairvoyant, Eccentric, Elfin, Weird

Fez Tarboosh, Tarboush, Tarbush

Fiancé(e) Betrothed, Intended, Promised

Fiasco Bomb, Debacle, Disaster, Failure, Flask, Flop, Lash-up, Wash-out

Fiat Command, Decree, Edict, Order, Ukase

Fib Gag, ➤ LIE, Prevaricate, Story, Taradiddle

Fibre, Fibrous Abaca, Acrilan®, Acrylic, Aramid, Arghan, Backbone, Bass,
Bast, Buaze, Bwazi, Cantala, Carbon, Coir, Constitution, Courtelle®,
Cuscus, Dralon®, Elastane, Filament, Filasse, Flax, Funicle, Hair, Hemp,
Henequen, Henequin, Herl, Hypha, Istle, Ixtle, Jute, Kapok, Kenaf, Kevlar®,
Kittul, Lemniscus, Monkey-grass, Monofil, Monomode, Mungo, Myotube,
Natural, Noil(s), Oakum, Olefin(e), Optic(al), Orlon®, Peduncle, Piassaba,
Piassava, Pita, Polyarch, Pons, Pontine, Pulu, Raffia, Ramee, Rami, Rhea,

Roughage, Rove, Sida, Silk, Sisal, Sleave, Slub(b), Spandex, Staple, Splenium, Strand, Strick, Sunn-hemp, Tampico, Toquilla, Tow, Uralite, Viver, Watap, Whisker, Wood pulp

Fibula Bone, Brooch, Perone

Fickle(ness) Capricious, Change, False, Inconstant, Light, Mutable, Protean, Shifty, Varying, Volatile

Fiction(al), Fictitious Bogus, Cyberpunk, Fable, Fabrication, Pap, Phoney, Romance, Science, Splatterpunk, ➤ STORY

Fiddle(r), Fiddling Amati, Bow, Calling-crab, Cello, Cheat, Crab, Cremona, Croud, Crouth, Crowd, Crwth, Fidget, Fix, Gju, Ground, Gu(e), Jerrymander, Kit, Launder, Nero, Peculate, Petty, Potter, Racket, Rebec(k), Rig, Rote, Sarangi, Saw, Sawah, Scam, Scrape, Second, Scrapegut, Spiel, Strad, Sultana, ➤ TAMPER, Tinker, Trifle, Tweedle(-dee), Twiddle, Viola, ➤ VIOLIN, Wangle

Fidelity Accuracy, Faith, Fealty, Loyalty, Troth

Fidget(y) Fantad, Fanteeg, Fantigue, Fantod, Fike, Fuss, Fyke, Hirsle, Hotch, Jimjams, Jittery, Niggle, Trifle, Twiddle, Twitch, Uneasy

Fiduciary Trustee

Fief Benefice, Fee

Field(er), Fields(man) Aalu, Aaru, Abroad, Aceldama, Aerodrome, Area, Arena, Arish, Arpent, Arrish, Campestral, Campestrian, Catch, Champ(s), Close, Cover, Domain, Electromagnetic, Elysian, Entry, Fid, Flodden, Flying, Forte, Fylde, Glebe, Grid(iron), Gully, Hop-yard, Killing, Land, Lare, Lay, Lea(-rig), Ley, Line, Long-off, Long-on, Longstop, Lords, Magnetic, Mead(ow), Mid-on, Mid-off, Mine, Oil, Padang, Paddock, Paddy, Parrock, Pasture, Pitch, Playing, Point, Province, Runners, Salting, Sawah, Scarecrow, Scope, Scout, Shamba, Shortstop, Silly, Slip, Sphere, Stage, Territory, Tract, Unified, World

▷ **Field** may indicate cricket

Field marshal Allenby, Bulow, French, Haig, Ironside, Kesselring, Kitchener, Montgomery, Roberts, Robertson, Rommel, Slim, Wavell

Fieldwork Lunette, Ravelin, Redan, Redoubt

Fiend Barbason, Demon, ➤ DEVIL, Enthusiast, Flibbertigibbet, Frateretto, Hellhound, Hobbididance, Mahn, Modo, Obidicut, Smulkin, Succubus

Fierce(ly) Billyo, Breem, Breme, Cruel, Draconic, Dragon, Grim, Hard-fought, Ogreish, Rampant, Renfierst, ➤ SAVAGE, Severe, Tigrish, Violent, Wild, Wood, Wud

Fiery Ardent, Argand, Aries, Con fuoco, Dry, Fervent, Hot, Igneous, Leo, Mettlesome, Phlogiston, Sagittarius, Salamander, Zealous

Fiesta Festival, Fete, Gala, Holiday

Fife Piffero

Fifth Column, Diapente, Hemiol(i)a, Nones, Quint, Sesquialtera

Fifty Demi-c, Jubilee, L

Fig Bania, Benjamin-tree, Caprifig, Fico, Figo, Footra, Fouter, Foutra, Foutre, Hottentot, Moreton Bay, Sycamore, Sycomore, Syncomium, Trifle

Fight(er), Fighting Affray, Agonistics, Alpino, Altercate, Barney, ➤ BATTLE, Bicker, Bout, Box, Brave, Brawl, Bruiser, Bundeswehr, Bush-whack, Campaign, Chaud-mellé, Chindit, Combat, Conflict, Contest, Crusader, Cuirassier, Defender, Dog, Donnybrook, Duel, Encounter, Fecht, Fence, Fisticuffs, Flyting, Fray, Freedom, Free-for-all, Ghazi, Gladiator, Grap(p)le, Gunslinger, Gurkha, Hurricane, Kumite, Lapith, Marine, Med(d)le, Medley, Mêlée, Mercenary, MIG, Militate, Mill, Mujahed(d)in, Mujahidin, Naumachy, Partisan, Pellmell, PLO, Prawle, Press, Pugilist, Pugnacity, Rammy, Repugn, Resist, Ring, Ruck, Ruction, Rumble, Savate, Sciamachy, Scrap, Scrimmage, Scuffle, Shine, Skiamachy, Skirmish, Slam, Soldier, Spar, Spitfire, Squabble, Stoush, Strife, Struggle, Sumo, Swordsman, Tar, Thersites, Toreador, Tuilyie, Tuilzie, Tussle, Umbrella, War(-dog), War-horse, War-man, Warrior, Wraxle, Wrestle, Yike, Zero

Figment Delusion, Fiction, Invention

Figure(s), Figurine Arabic, Aumail, Bas-relief, Body, Build, Canephorus, Caryatid, Cast, Chladni, Cinque, Cipher, Cone, Cube, Cypher, Decahedron, Digit, Ecorché, Effigy, Eight, Ellipse, Enneagon, Enneahedron, Epanadiplosis, Eschar, ➤ FORM, Fusil, Girth, Gnomon, Graph, Heptagon, Hexagon, Hour-glass, Icon, Icosahedron, Idol, Ikon, Image, Insect, Intaglio, Integer, Lay, Lissajous, Magot, Motif, Nonagon, Number, Numeral, Numeric, Octagon, Octahedron, Orant, Outline, Parallelogram, Pentacle, Pentalpha, Polygon, Poussette, Prism, Puppet, Pyramid, Reckon, Repetend, See, ➤ SHAPE, Sheela-na-gig, Simplex, Statistics, Statue(tte), Tanagra, Telamon, Tetragon, Torus, Triangle, Trihedron, Triskele, Triskelion, Ushabti, Waxwork

Figure of speech Allegory, Analogy, Antimask, Antimasque, Antimetabole, Antithesis, Asyndeton, Catachresis, Chiasmus, Deixis, Diallage, Ellipsis, Euphemism, Hypallage, Hyperbaton, Hyperbole, Hysteron proteron, Irony, Litotes, Meiosis, Metalepsis, Metaphor, Metonymy, Oxymoron, Paral(e)ipsis, Prosopoea, Simile, Syllepsis, Synecdoche, Taxeme, Tmesis, Trope, Zeugma

Figure study Arithmetic, Mathematics, Numeration

Figure-weaver Draw-boy

Filament Barbule, Byssus, Cirrus, Fibre, Fimbria, Floss, Gossamer, Hair, Hypha, Mycor(r)hiza, Myofibril, Paraphysis, Protonema, ➤ THREAD

Filch Appropriate, Drib, Pilfer, Pinch, Prig, Purloin, Smouch, ➤ STEAL

File, Filing(s) Abrade, Archive, Batch, Binary, Box, Burr, Clyfaker, Coffle, Croc(odile), Crosscut, Data set, Disc, Disk, Dossier, Enter, Floatcut, Generation, Index, Indian, Line, Nail, Pigeon-hole, Pollute, Quannet, ➤ README, Rank, Rasp, Rat-tail, Riffler, Risp, Row, Scalprum, Scratch, Single, String, Swarf, Text, Tickler, TIF(F)

Filial generation F1

Filibuster Freebooter, Hinder, Obstruct, Run on, Stonewall

Filigree Delicate, Fretwork, Sheer

Filipino Igorot, Moro, ➤ PHILLIPINE(S)

Fill(er), Filling Anaplerosis, Balaam, Banoffee, Banoffi, Beaumontag(u)e, Beaumontique, Billow, Bloat, Brick-nog, Brim, Bump, Centre, Charge, Cram, Gather, Gorge, Heart, Imbue, Impregnate, Inlay, Jampack, Line, Mastic, Occupy, Pabulous, Packing, Permeate, Plug, Repletive, Salpicon, Sate, Satisfy, Shim, Stack, Stock, Stocking, Stopping, ➤ STUFF, Tales, Teem, Ullage

Fillet(s) Anadem, Annulet, Band, Bandeau, Bandelet, Bone, Cloisonné, Flaunching, Fret, Goujons, Grenadine, Headband, Infula, Label, Lemniscus, List(el), Mitre, Moulding, Reglet, Regula, Ribbon, Rollmop, Slice, Snood, Sphendone, Stria, Striga, Taeniate, Tape, Teniate, Tournedos, Vitta

Fillip Boost, Kick, Snap, Stimulus

Filly Colt, Foal, She

Film(s), Filmy, Filming Acetate, Actioner, Amnion, Biopic, Blockbuster, Bollywood, Buddy, Caul, Cel, Cine, Cinema vérité, Cinerama®, Circlorama®, Cliffhanger, Cling, Clip, Deepie, Dew, Diorama, Docudrama, Documentary, Dust, Epic, ET, Exposure, Feature, Fiche, Flick, Floaty, Footage, Gigi, Gossamer, Hammer, Haze, Hollywood, Horror, Infomercial, Kell, Lacquer, Layer, Loid, Mask, Membrane, Microfiche, Mist, Montage, Newsreel, Noddy, Noir, Oater, Omnimax®, Outtake, Panchromatic, Patina, Pellicle, Photo, Plaque, Prequel, Psycho, Quickie, Reel, Release, Rush, Scale, Scent-scale, Screen, Scum, Shoot-'em-up, Short, Shot, Silent, Skin, Skin flick, Slick, Slo-mo, Snuff, Spaghetti western, Splatter, Studio, Talkie, Tear-jerker, Trailer, Trippy, Two-shot, Ultrafiche, Varnish, Video, Video-nasty, Web, Weepie, Weepy, Weft, Western

Film star Extra, Vedette

Filter(ing) Clarify, Dialysis, Leach, Percolate, Perk, Seep, Sieve, ➤ SIFT, Skylight, Strain

Filth(y) Addle, Augean, Bilge, Colluvies, Crock, Crud, Defile, Dirt, Dung, Foul, Grime, Lucre, Mire, Muck, Obscene, Pythogenic, Refuse, Slime, Smut(ch), Soil, Squalor, Stercoral, Yuck

Fin Caudal, Ctene, Dollars, Dorsal, Fluke, Pectoral, Pinna, Pinnule, Rib, Skeg, Stabiliser, Ventral

Final(e), Finalise Absolute, Closing, Coda, Conclusive, Decider, End, Eventual, Extreme, Last, Net(t), Peremptory, Sew up, Swansong, Ultimate, Utter

Finance, Financial, Financier Ad crumenan, Angel, Back, Banian, Banker, Bankroll, Banyan, Cambism, Chrematistic, Exchequer, Fiscal, Gnome, Grubstake, Monetary, Revenue, Sponsor, Subsidise, Treasurer, Underwrite

Finch Bird, Brambling, Bunting, Canary, Charm, Chewink, Crossbill, Darwin's, Fringillid, Linnet, Marsh-robin, Peter, Serin, Siskin, Spink, Twite

Find(ing) Ascertain, Detect, Discover(y), Get, Hit, Inquest, ➤ LOCATE, Meet, Provide, Rumble, Trace, Trouvaille, Verdict

Fine, Fine words Amende, Amerce, Amerciament, Arts, Assess, Beau(t), Bender, Boshta, Boshter, Boss, Brandy, Brave, Braw, Champion, Dainty,

Dandy, Dick, End, Eriach, Eric(k), Estreat, F, Fair, Famous, Forfeit, Godly, Good(ly), Gossamer, Gradely, Grand, Grassum, Hair, Hairline, Handsome, Heriot, Hunkydory, Immense, Impalpable, Inconie, Incony, Infangthief, Issue, Keen, Leirwite, Log, Maritage, Merchet, Mooi, Mulct, Nifty, Niminy-piminy, Noble, OK, Oke, Outfangthief, ➤ PENALTY, Precise, Pure, Relief, Sconce, Safe, Sheer, Sicker, Slender, Spanking, Subtle, Summery, Super, Tax, Ticket(t)y-boo, Tiptop, Topping, Unlaw, Waly, Wally, Wer(e)gild

Fine-collector Cheater

Finery Braws, Fallal, Frills, Frippery, Gaudery, Ornament, Trinket, Wally, Warpaint

Finesse Artifice, Artistry, Delicacy, Skill, Strategy

Fine-weather All-hallond, All-hallow(e)n, All-hollown

Finger, Fingernail Dactyl, Digit, Fork, Handle, Index, Lunula, Medius, Name, Nip, Piggy, Pinky, Pointer, Prepollex, Pusher, Ring(man), Shop, Talaunt, Talon, Tot, Trigger, White

Finger-hole Lill, Ring

Fingerprint Dabs, Dactylogram, Genetic, Loop, Whorl

Fingerstall Hutkin

Finial Bunch, Knob, Ornament, Tee

Finicky Fastidious, Fussy, Particular, Precise

Finis, Finish(ed), Finishing touch Arch, Close, Coating, Coda, Complete, ➤ CONCLUDE, Crown, Die, Dish, Do, Dope, Dress, ➤ END, Epiphenomena, Exact, Full, Kibosh, Lacquer, Neat, Outgo, Outwork, Pebbledash, Perfect, Photo, Refine, Ripe, Round, Settle, Shot, Spitcher, Surface, Terminate, Through, Up (tie), Veneer, Wind-up

Finite Bounded, Limited

Finn(ish) Esth, Huck(leberry), Karelian, Mickey, Mordvin, Suomic, Udmurt, Votyak

Fiord Bay, Hardanger, Inlet, Trondheim

Fir Abies, Balsam, Douglas, Larch

Fire(side) Accend, Agni, Animate, Ardour, Arson, Arouse, Atar, Axe, Bake, Bale, Barbecue, Barrage, Beacon, Behram, Blaze, Boot, Brand, Brazier, Brush, Burn, Bush, Chassé, Corposant, Delope, Discharge, Dismiss, Elan, Element, Embolden, Ena, Energy, Enfilade, Enkindle, Enthuse, Flak, Flame, Furnace, Greek, Gun, Hearth, Hob, Ignite, Inferno, Ingle, Inspire, Kentish, Kiln, Kindle, Launch, Light, Lowe, Pop, Prime, Prometheus, Pull, Rapid, Red cock, Sack, St Anthony's, St Elmo's, Scorch, Shell, Shoot, Smudge, Spark, Spunk, Stoke, Stove, Strafe, Tracer, Wake, Wisp, Zeal

▶ **Firearm** see GUN

Fireback Reredos

Fireball Bolide

Fire-break Epaulement, Greenstrip

Fire-dog Andiron

Fire-extinguisher Halon, Hell-bender, Salamander

Firefly Glow-worm, Luciferin, Pyrophorus

Fire-guard Fender

Fireman Abednego, Brigade, Deputy, Prometheus, Stoker

Fire-opal Girasol

Fireplace Chimney, Grate, Hearth, Hob, Ingle, Loop-hole, Range

Fireplug H, Hydrant

Fireproof Abednego, Asbestos, Incombustible, Inflammable, Meshach, Salamander, Shadrach, Uralite

Firewalker Salamander

Firewood Billet, Faggot, Knitch, Tinder

Firework(s) Banger, Bengal-light, Bunger, Cherry bomb, Cracker, Devil, Fisgig, Fizgig, Fountain, Gerbe, Girandole, Iron sand, Jumping Jack, Maroon, Pastille, Peeoy, Petard, Pinwheel, Pioy(e), Pyrotechnics, Realgar, Rocket, Roman candle, Serpent, Skyrocket, Sparkler, Squib, Tantrum, Throwdown, Tourbill(i)on, Volcano, Wheel, Whizzbang

Fire-worshipper Parsee

Firing Baking, Fusillade, Mitten, Salvo

Firm Adamant, Agency, Binding, Business, Collected, Compact, Company, Concern, Concrete, Constant, Crisp, Decided, Determined, Duro, Faithful, Fast, Fixed, Hard, Inc, Oaky, Obdurate, Obstinate, ➤ RESOLUTE, Sclerotal, Secure, Set, Siccar, Sicker, ➤ SOLID, Stable, Stalwart, Staunch, Ste(a)dfast, Steady, Steely, Steeve, Stern, Stieve, Stiff, Strict, Sturdy, Tight, Tough, Well-knit

Firmament Canopy, Empyrean, Heaven, Sky

First Ab initio, Alpha, Arch, Archetype, Best, Calends, Champion, Chief, Earliest, E(a)rst, Foremost, Former, Front, Head, I, Ideal, Imprimis, Initial, 1st, Kalends, Led, Maiden, No 1, One, Opener, Or, Original, Pioneer, Pole, Premier, Prima, Primal, Prime, Primo, Principal, Prototype, Rudimentary, Senior, Starters, Top, Victor, Yama

First-aid(ers) Zambu(c)k

First born Ariki, Eigne, Eldest, Heir, Major, Senior

First class, First rate A1, Crack, Prime, Supreme, Tiptop, Top(notch)

First day Calends

First fruits Annat, Arles, Primitiae, Windfalls

First man Adam, Ask, Premier, President, Yama

First offender Eve, Probationer

➤ **First rate** see FIRST CLASS

First woman Embla, Eve, Pandora, Premier

Firth Estuary, Forth, Inlet, Moray, Tay

Fish(ing) Angle, Angler, Bob, Cast, Catch, Chowder, Coarse, Cran, Creel, Dredge, Dry-fly, Episcate, ➤ FISH, Fly, Flying, Fry, Gefilte, Goujons, Guddle, Halieutics, Haul, Ledger, Mess, Net, Otterboard, Overnet, Pilot, Piscine, Roe, Sashimi, Shoal, Snigger, Sniggle, Spin, Spot, Trawl, Troll, Tub, White

Fish-basket Creel, Hask, Kipe

Fish disease Argulus

FISH

2 letters:
Ai
Id

3 letters:
Ayu
Bar
Bib
But
Cat
Cod
Cow
Dab
Dib
Dog
Eel
Gar
Ged
Hag
Ide
Koi
Lax
Lob
Par
Pod
Ray
Rig
Sar
Tai
Top

4 letters:
Bass
Blay
Bley
Brit
Butt
Carp
Cero
Chad
Char
Chub
Chum
Coho
Cray
Cusk
Dace
Dare
Dart
Dory
Fugu
Gade
Goby
Gump
Hake
Harl
Hoki
Huso

Huss
Jack
Kelt
Keta
Lant
Leaf
Ling
Luce
Lump
Maid
Maze
Moki
Mort
Opah
Orfe
Parr
Peal
Peel
Pike
Pope
Pout
Raun
Rawn
Rigg
Rudd
Ruff
Scad
Scar
Scat
Scup
Seer
Seir
Shad
Sild
Slip
Snig
Sole
Star
Tope
Trot
Tuna
Tusk
Woof

5 letters:
Ablet
Allis
Angel
Apode
Basse
Bleak
Bream
Brill
Bully
Capon
Charr
Cisco

Clown
Cobia
Cohoe
Coley
Cuddy
Danio
Dorad
Doras
Doree
Dorse
Elops
Elver
Fluke
Gadus
Gibel
Grunt
Jurel
Laker
Lance
Loach
Lythe
Maise
Maize
Manta
Masus
Mease
Molly
Murre
Murry
Nerka
Padle
Perai
Perca
Perch
Piper
Pirai
Platy
Pogge
Powan
Prawn
Roach
Roker
Ruffe
Saith
Sargo
Saury
Scrod
Sewen
Sewin
Shark
Sheat
Skate
Slope
Smelt
Snoek
Snook

Solen
Speck
Sprat
Sprod
Tench
Tetra
Togue
Torsk
Trout
Tunny
Umber
Wahoo
Whiff
Wirra
Witch
Yabby
Zebra

6 letters:
Alevin
Allice
Anabas
Angler
Archer
Ballan
Barbel
Belone
Beluga
Big-eye
Blenny
Bonito
Bounce
Bowfin
Braise
Braize
Bumalo
Burbot
Callop
Caplin
Caranx
Caribe
Cheven
Clupea
Cockle
Comber
Conger
Conner
Cottus
Cudden
Cuddie
Cuddin
Cunner
Cuttle
Dentex
Diodon
Dipnoi
Discus

Doctor
Dorado
Dun-cow
Finnac
Finnan
Fogash
Fumado
Gadoid
Garvie
Gilgie
Goramy
Grilse
Groper
Gulper
Gunnel
Gurami
Gurnet
Haddie
Hapuka
Hassar
Inanga
Jerker
Jilgie
Kipper
Labrus
Lancet
Launce
Lizard
Louvar
Lunker
Mad Tom
Mahsir
Marlin
Meagre
Medaka
Medusa
Megrim
Milter
Minnow
Morgay
Mudcat
Mullet
Murena
Nerite
Oyster
Paddle
Paidle
Pakoko
Parrot
Pholas
Piraya
Plaice
Podley
Pollan
Porgie
Puffer
Redfin
Remora

Robalo
Roughy
Saithe
Salmon
Samlet
Sander
Sardel
Sargus
Sauger
Saurel
Scampi
Sea-bat
Sea-owl
Seeder
Serran
Shanny
Sheath
Shiner
Skelly
Sparid
Sucker
Tailor
Tarpon
Tautog
Toitoi
Tomcod
Trygon
Twaite
Ulicon
Ulikon
Vendis
Weever
Wrasse
Yabbie
Zander
Zingel

7 letters:
Ale-wife
Anchovy
Anemone
Asterid
Azurine
Batfish
Bellows
Bergylt
Bloater
Bluecap
Boxfish
Brassie
Buffalo
Cabezon
Capelin
Cavalla
Cavally
Ceviche
Cichlid
Codfish
Copepod

Crappie
Croaker
Crucian
Crusian
Cutlass
Dogfish
Eel-pout
Eelfare
Escolar
Findram
Finnack
Finnock
Garfish
Garvock
Geelbek
Gemfish
Goldeye
Gourami
Grouper
Growler
Grunion
Gudgeon
Gurnard
Gwiniad
Gwyniad
Haddock
Hagdown
Hagfish
Halibut
Herling
Herring
Hirling
Hogfish
Homelyn
Houting
Ichthys
Inconnu
Jewfish
Kahawai
Keeling
Koi carp
Lampern
Lamprey
Lampuki
Lantern
Lingcod
Lobster
Lyomeri
Mahseer
Medacca
Merling
Mojarra
Moon-eye
Morwong
Muraena
Oarfish
Old-wife
Oolakan

Opaleye
Osseter
Oulakan
Oulicon
Panchax
Pandora
Pegasus
Pigfish
Pinfish
Piranha
Pollack
Pomfret
Pompano
Ragfish
Rasbora
Ratfish
Rat-tail
Redfish
Rorqual
Sand dab
Sardine
Scalare
Scallop
Sculpin
Sea-bass
Sea-cock
Sea-dace
Sea-moth
Sea-pike
Sea-star
Sea-wife
Sillock
Skegger
Skitter
Snapper
Sock-eye
Sparoid
Speldin
Sterlet
Sunfish
Surgeon
Teleost
Tiddler
Tilapia
Titling
Torgoch
Torpedo
Ulichon
Vendace
Wall-eye
Whipray
Whiting
Wide-gab

8 letters:
Albacore
Anableps
Arapaima
Asteroid

267

Fish

Atherine
Billfish
Bloodfin
Blowfish
Blueback
Bluefish
Bluegill
Brisling
Bullhead
Bullhorn
Cabezone
Cabrilla
Cardinal
Cavefish
Characid
Characin
Chimaera
Coalfish
Corkwing
Cucumber
Cyprinid
Dealfish
Dragonet
Drumfish
Eagle-ray
Escallop
Eulachon
Fallfish
Filefish
Flathead
Flounder
Four-eyes
Ganoidei
Gillaroo
Gilthead
Goatfish
Gobiidae
Graining
Grayling
Hackbolt
Hair-tail
Half-beak
Hard-head
Holostei
Hornbeak
Hornpout
Kabeljou
Killfish
Kingfish
Kingklip
Kukukuma
Lionfish
Luderick
Lumpfish
Lungfish
Mackerel
Mahi-mahi
Mata Hari

Menhaden
Milkfish
Monkfish
Mulloway
Nannygai
Nennigai
Nine-eyes
Oulachon
Paradise
Pickerel
Pilchard
Pirarucu
Redbelly
Rock-cook
Rockfish
Rockling
Roncador
Rosefish
Saibling
Sailfish
Saltfish
Sardelle
Scabbard
Sciaenid
Scorpion
Scuppaug
Sea-devil
Seahorse
Sea-raven
Sea-lemon
Sea-robin
Sergeant
Serranus
Skipjack
Smear-dab
Snake-eel
Sparling
Stenlock
Sting-ray
Stonecat
Sturgeon
Tarakihi
Tarwhine
Teraglin
Terakihi
Tile-fish
Toadfish
Trevally
Tropical
Tubenose
Tullibee
Weakfish
Whitling
Wolffish
9 letters:
Amberjack
Barracuda
Blackfish

Butterfly
Cascadura
Ceratodus
Chaetodon
Chavender
Clingfish
Clupeidae
Coregonus
Coryphene
Devilfish
Gaspereau
Glassfish
Globefish
Goldfinny
Goldsinny
Golomynka
Greenling
Grenadier
Haberdine
Hornyhead
Hottentot
Houndfish
Ichthyoid
Jacksmelt
Jewelfish
Kabeljouw
Killifish
Labyrinth
Latimeria
Menominee
Mudhopper
Neon tetra
Pikeperch
Porbeagle
Porcupine
Quillback
Roussette
Scaldfish
Schnapper
Scorpaena
Selachian
Shubunkin
Siluridae
Slickhead
Snailfish
Snakehead
Spadefish
Spearfish
Speldring
Stargazer
Steenbras
Stingaree
Stockfish
Stonefish
Surfperch
Surmullet
Swellfish
Swordfish

Sword-tail
Thornback
Threadfin
Tittlebat
Topminnow
Trachinus
Troutfish
Trunkfish
Whitebait
White-bass
Wreckfish
10 letters:
Barracoota
Barracouta
Barramunda
Bitterling
Bombay duck
Bottlehead
Butterfish
Candlefish
Cockabully
Cornetfish
Cyclostome
Damselfish
Demoiselle
Etheostoma
Fingerling
Flutemouth
Groundling
Lumpsucker
Maskalonge
Maskanonge
Maskinonge
Midshipman
Mossbunker
Mudskipper
Needlefish
Nurse-hound
Red-snapper
Ribbonfish
Rudderfish
Scopelidae
Sea-poacher
Sea-surgeon
Serrasalmo
Shovelnose
Silverside
Springfish
Squeteague
Teleostome
Titarakura
Tripletail
Yellowtail
11 letters:
Chondrostei
Dolly Varden
Istiophorus
Lepidosiren

Maskallonge	Soldierfish	Father-lasher	
Moorish idol	Stickleback	Heterosomata	
Muskellunge	Triggerfish	Histiophorus	Squirrelfish
Oxyrhynchus	Trumpetfish	Miller's thumb	**13 letters:**
Plagiostome	**12 letters:**	Mouthbreeder	Leatherjacket
Scolopendra	Ballan-wrasse	Plectognathi	**15 letters:**
Seventy-four	Elasmobranch	Rainbow-trout	Crossopterygian

Fisher(man) Ahab, Andrew, Angler, Black cat, Caper, High-liner, Liner, Pedro, Peter, Piscator, Rodster, Sharesman, Walton

▶ **Fisherwoman** see FISHSELLER

Fish-hawk Osprey

Fishing-ground Haaf

Fishing-line G(u)imp, Gymp, Paternoster

Fishpond Ocean, Stew, Vivarium

Fishseller, Fisherwoman Fishwife, Molly Malone, Ripp(i)er, Shawley, Shawlie

Fishy Botargo, Suspicious, Vacant

Fissure Chasm, Cleft, Crack, Crevasse, Crevice, Gap, Grike, Gryke, Lode, Rent, Sand-crack, Scam, Vallecula, Vein, Zygon

Fist Clench, Dukes, Hand, Join-hand, Neaf(fe), Neif, Neive, Nief, Nieve, Pud, Punch, Thump

Fit(s), Fitting(s), Fitness Able, Access, Adapt, Ague, Appointment, Appropriate, Apropos, Apt, Babbitt, Bout, Canto, Capable, Cataleptic, Cataplexy, Concinnous, Condign, Congruous, Conniption, Convulsion, Culver-tail, Decent, Decorous, Dod, Dove-tail, Due, Eclampsia, Eligible, Ensconce, Epilepsy, Equip, Exies, Expedient, Fairing, Fay, Fiddle, Furniment, Furnishing, Fytte, Gee, Germane, Habile, Hale, Hang, Health, Huff, Hysterics, In-form, Just, Kashrut(h), Lune, Mate, Meet, Mood, Nest, Paroxysm, Passus, Pertinent, Prepared, ▶ PROPER, Queme, Ready, Rig, Rind, Ripe, Rynd, Seemly, Seizure, Set, Sit, Sort, Sound, Spasm, Spell, Start, Suit(able), Syncope, Tantrum, Throe, To prepon, Turn, Up to, Well, Worthy, Wrath

▷ **Fit(ting)** may indicate a 't'

Fitful Intermittent

Fitment Adaptor, Unit

Fitzgerald Edward, Ella, Scott

Five(s) Cinque, Mashie, Pallone, Pedro, Pentad, Quinary, Quintet, Sextan, Towns, V

Five years Lustre, Lustrum

Fix(ed), Fixer, Fixative Affeer, Anchor, Appoint, Appraise, ▶ ARRANGE, Assess, Assign, Attach, Bind, Brand, Cement, Clamp, Clew, Clue, Constant, Corking-pin, Cure, Decide, Destine, Destinate, Determine, Do, Embed, Empight, Encastré, Engrain, Establish, Fast, Firm, Fit, Freeze, Gammon, Hold, Hypo(sulphite), Immutable, Impaction, Imprint, Inculcate, Ingrain, Jag, Jam, Locate, Lodge, Nail, Name, Narcotic, Nobble, Orientate, Peg, Persistent, Pin, Point, Quantify, Repair, Resolute, Rig, Rigid, Rivet, Rove,

Rut, Scrape, Screw, Seat, Seize, Set, Settle, Ship, Shoo, Skatole, Skewer, Splice, Staple, Static, Stell, Step, Stew, Tie, Valorize, Weld

Fixture Attachment, Event, Match, Permanence, Unit

Fizz(ed), Fizzy Buck's, Effervesce, Gas, Hiss, Pop, Sherbet, Sod, Soda

Fizzle Failure, Flop, Hiss, Washout

▶ **Fjord** see Fiord

Flabbergast(ed) Amaze, Astound, Floor, Thunderstruck

Flabby Flaccid, Lank, Lax, Limp, Pendulous, Saggy

Flaccid Flabby, Limp, Soft

Flag(gy), Flags Acorus, Ancient, Ashlar, Banderol, Banner, Black, Blackjack, Blue Peter, Bunting, Burgee, Calamus, Chequered, Colour(s), Dan(n)ebrog, Decline, Droop, Duster, Ensign, Fail, Falter, Fane, Fanion, Gladdon, Gonfalon, Guidon, Hail, Hoist, Irideal, Iris, Jack, Jade, Jolly Roger, Kerbstone, Languish, Lis, Old Glory, Orris, Pave(ment), Pavilion, Pencel, Pennant, Pennon, Penoncel(le), Pensel, Pensil, Peter, Pin, Rag, Red, Red Duster, Red Ensign, Sag, Sedge, Semaphore, Sink, Slab(stone), Slack, Standard, Stars and bars, Stars and stripes, Streamer, Tire, Tricolour, Union (Jack), Vane, Vexillology, Waif, Whift, White (ensign), Wilt, Wither

Flagday Tagday

Flagellate Beat, Mastigophora, Scourge, Trypanosome, Whip

Flagon Bottle, Carafe, Jug, Stoop, Stoup, Vessel

Flagpole Pin, Staff

Flagrant Egregious, Glaring, Heinous, Patent, Wanton

Flagship Admiral, Victory

Flail Beat, Drub, Swingle, Threshel

Flair Art, Bent, Elan, Gift, Knack, Panache, Style, ➤ TALENT

Flak AA, Attack, Criticism

Flake Chip, Flame, Flaught, Flaw, Floccule, Flocculus, Fragment, Peel, Scale, Smut, Snow

Flam Impose

Flamboyant Baroque, Brilliant, Florid, Garish, Grandiose, Ornate, Ostentatious, Paz(z)azz, Piz(z)azz, Swash-buckler

Flame, Flaming Ardent, Blaze, Fire, Flake, Flambé, Flammule, Glow, Kindle, Leman, Lover, Lowe, Oxyacetylene, Sweetheart

Flan Pastry, Quiche, Tart

Flanders Mare, Moll

Flange Border, Collar, Collet, Lip, Rim

Flank(s) Accompany, Anta, Flange, Flitch, Ilia, Lisk, Loin, Side, Spur

Flannel Blather, Canton, Cloth, Soft-soap, Waffle, Zephyr

Flap(ped), Flapper, Flapping Agnail, Aileron, Alar, Alarm(ist), Aventail(e), Bate, Beat, Bird, Bobbysoxer, Bustle, Chit, Dither, Elevon, Epiglottis, Fipple, Flacker, Flaff, Flag, Flaught, Flutter, Fly, Fuss, Giglet, Giglot, Hover, ➤ IN A FLAP, Labium, Labrum, Lapel, Loma, Lug, Operculum, Panic, Spin, Spoiler, Tab, Tag, Tailboard, Tailgate, Tiswas, To-do, Tongue, Volucrine, Wave, Whisk

Flare(d), Flare up Bell, Fishtail, Flame, Flanch, Flaunch, Godet, Magnesium, Scene, Signal, Spread, Spunk, Ver(e)y, Widen

Flash(y), Flasher Coruscate, Cursor, Fire-flag, Flare, Flaught, Fulgid, Fulgural, Garish, Gaudy, Glaik, Gleam, Glisten, Glitzy, Green ray, Instant, Jay, Lairy, Levin, Lightning, Loud, Magnesium, Meretricious, Mo, Photopsy, Raffish, Ribbon, Roary, Scintillation, Second, Sequin, Showy, Sluice, Snazzy, Spark, Streak, Strobe, Swank(e)y, Tick, Tigrish, Trice, Twinkle, Vivid, Wire

▷ **Flashing** may indicate an anagram

Flask Ampulla, Aryballos, Bottle, Canteen, Carafe, Costrel, Cucurbit, Dewar, Erlenmeyer, Fiasco, Flacket, Flacon, Florence, Goatskin, Hip, Lekythos, Matrass, Mick(e)(y), Reform, Retort, Thermos®, Vacuum, Vial

Flat(s), Flatten(ed), Flattener Apartment, Bachelor, Bald, Banal, Beat, Blow-out, Bulldoze, Callow, Complanate, Compress, Condominium, Corymb(ose), Coulisse, Dead, Demolish, Dorsiventral, Dress, Dull, Even, Feeble, Flew, Floor, Flue, Fool, Granny, Guyot, Haugh, Homaloid, Horizontal, Insipid, Ironed, Jacent, Key, KO, Law, Level, Lifeless, Llano, Marsh, Monotonous, Nitwit, Norfolk, Oblate, Pad, Pancake, Pedestrian, Peneplain, Peneplane, Penthouse, Pentice, Pied-à-terre, Plain, Planar, Plane, Planish, Plat, Plateau, Prone, Prostrate, Recumbent, Rooms, Scenery, Smooth, Splayfoot, Spread-edged, Squash, Studio, Tableland, Tabular, Tame, Tasteless, Tenement, True, Vapid

Flat-chested Cithara

Flat-faced Socle

Flat-foot(ed) Policeman, Splay

Flat-nosed Camus

Flatter(ing), Flatterer, Flattery Adulate, Beslaver, Blandish, Blarney, Bootlick, Butter, Cajole, Candied, Carn(e)y, Claw(back), Complimentary, Earwiggy, En beau, Fawn, Fillibrush, Flannel, Flannen, Fleech, Flummery, Fulsome, Gloze, Gnathonic(al), Honey, Imitation, Lip-salve, Moody, Palp, Phrase, Poodle-faker, Puffery, Sawder, Smarm, Snow job, Soap, Soother, Souk, Spaniel, Stroke, Sugar, Sweet talk, Sycophant, Taffy, Toady, Treacle, Unction, Wheedle, Word

Flatulence Belch, Borborygmus, Burp, Carminative, Colic, Gas, Wind

Flaunt Brandish, Flourish, Gibe, Parade, Skyre, Strout, Strut, Wave

Flavour(ed), Flavouring Absinth(e), Alecost, Anethole, Angostura, Anise, Aniseed, Aroma, Bold, Borage, Bouquet garni, Clove, Coriander, Cumin, Dill, Essence, Fenugreek, Flor, Garni, Marinate, Mint, Orgeat, Quark, Race, Ratafia, Relish, Sair, Sassafras, Tack, Tang, Tarragon, ➤ TASTE, Tincture, Twang, Vanilla

Flaw Blemish, Brack, Bug, Chip, Crack, Defect, Fallacy, ➤ FAULT, Gall, Hamartia, Imperfection, Kink, Lophole, Rima, Spot, Taint, Tear, Thief, Windshake

Flawless Impeccable

Flax(en) Aleseed, Blonde, Codilla, Harden, Hards, Herden, Herl, Hurden, Line, Linseed, Lint, Linum, Mill-mountain, Poi, Tow

Flay Excoriate, Fleece, Scourge, Skin, Strip, Uncase, Whip

Flea Aphaniptera, Chigger, Chigoe, Chigre, Daphnid, Hopper, Itch-mite, Lop, Pulex, Sand, Water

Fleabite Denier

Fleck Dash, Freak, Spot, Streak

Fledgling Aerie, Eyas, Sorage

Flee Abscond, Bolt, Decamp, Escape, Eschew, Fly, Lam, Loup, Run, Scapa, Scarper, Scram

Fleece, Fleecy Bleed, Coat, Despoil, Flocculent, Golden, Lambskin, Lanose, Pash(i)m, Pashmina, Plot, Pluck, Rifte, Ring, Rob, Rook, Shave, Shear, Sheepskin, Skin, ➤ SWINDLE, Toison

Fleer Ogle

Fleet(ing) Armada, Brief, Camilla, Ephemeral, Evanescent, Fast, Flit, Flota, Flotilla, Fugacious, Fugitive, Hasty, Hollow, Lightfoot, Navy, Pacy, Passing, Prison, Spry, Street, Transient, Velocipede

Flesh(y) Beefy, Body, Carneous, Carrion, Corporeal, Corpulent, Creatic, Digastric, Finish, Gum, Hypersarcoma, Joint, Longpig, Lush, Meat, Mons, Muscle, Pulp, Sarcous, Spare tyre, Tissue

Flesh-eating Cannibalism, Carnassial, Creophagus, Omophagic

Fleshless Dry, Maigre, Pem(m)ican

Flex(ible), Flexibility Adaptable, Bend(y), Elastic, Genu, Limber, Lissom(e), Lithe, Pliant, ➤ RESILIENT, Rubbery, Squeezy, Tensile, Tonus, Wieldy, Willing, Wiry

▷ **Flexible, Flexuous** may indicate an anagram

Flick(er), Flicks Bioscope, Cinema, Fillip, Film, Flip, Flirt, Flutter, Glimmer, Gutter, Movie, Movy, Snap, Snow, Switch, Talkie, Twinkle, Waver

Flickertail ND

Flier Airman, Alcock, Amy, Aviator, Blimp, Brown, Crow, Daedalus, Erk, Fur, George, Gotha, Handout, Icarus, Leaflet, Lindbergh, Pilot, ➤ RAF, Scotsman, Spec, Speedy

▷ **Flier** may indicate a bird

Flight(y) Backfisch, Birdbrain, Bolt, Bubble-headed, Capricious, Charter, Dart, Departure, Escalier, Escape, Exaltation, Exodus, Fast, Fickle, Flaught, Flibbertigibbet, Flip, Flock, Flyby, Fugue, Giddy, Grese, Grise, Guy, Hegira, Hejira, Hejra, Hellicat, Hijra, Lam, Milk-run, Open-jaw, Pair, R(a)iser, Redeye, Ro(a)ding, Rode, Rout, Skein, Sortie, Stairs, ➤ STAMPEDE, Steps, Swarm, Tower, Trap, Vol(age), Volatile, Volley, Whisky-frisky, Wing

Flightless Kakapo, Ostrich, Rhea, Struthious

▷ **Flighty** may indicate an anagram

Flimsy Finespun, Gimcrack, Gossamer, Jimcrack, Sleazy, Sleezy, Tenuous, Thin, Weak, Wispy

Flinch Blench, Cringe, Funk, Quail, Recoil, Shrink, Shudder, Start, Wince

Fling Dance, Flounce, Highland, Hurl, Pitch, Shy, Slat, Slug, Slump, Spanghew, Spree, Throw, ➤ TOSS

Flint Chert, Firestone, Granite, Hag-stone, Hornstone, Pirate, Rock, Silex, Microlith, Mischmetal, Silica, Stone, Touchstone

Flip(pant), Flipping Airy, Bally, Brash, Cocky, Flick, Frivolous, Impudent, Jerk, Nog, Pert, Purl, Sassy, Saucy, Toss, Turn

Flipper(s) Fin-toed

Flirt(ing), Flirtatious Bill, Buaya, Carve, Chippy, Cockteaser, Come-hither, Come-on, Coquet(te), Dalliance, Demivierge, Footsie, Gallivant, Heart-breaker, Mash, Minx, Neck, Philander(er), Prick-teaser, Rig, Toy, Trifle, Vamp, Wow

Flit Dart, Decamp, Flicker, Flutter, Scoot

Float(er), Floating Balsa, Bob, Buoy, Caisson, Carley, Clanger, Drift, Fleet, Flutterboard, Levitate, Lifebuoy, Milk, Neuston, Oropesa, Outrigger, Planula, Pontoon, Pram, Quill, Raft, Ride, Sail, Skim, Sponson, Trimmer, Vacillate, Waft, Waggler, Waterwings

Floating garden Chinampa

Flock(s) Assemble, Bevy, Charm, Chirm, Company, Congregation, Drove, Flight, Fold, Forgather, Gaggle, Gather, Gregatim, Herd, Mob, Rally, Sedge, Sord, Spring, Trip, Tuft, Vulgar, Wing, Wisp, Wool

Flog(ger), Flogging Beat, Birch, Breech, Cane, Cat, Exert, Flay, Hawk, Hide, Knout, Lace, Lambast, Larrup, Lash, Lather, Lick, Orbilius, Rope's end, Scourge, Sell, Strap, Tat, ➤ THRASH, Thwack, Tout, Vapulate, Welt, Whip

Flood Bore, Cataclysm, Deluge, Deucalion, Diluvium, Dump, Eger, Flash, Freshet, Gush, Inundate, Irrigate, Noachic, Overflow, Overwhelm, Pour, Rage, Smurf, Spate, Speat, Swamp, Tide, ➤ TORRENT, Undam

Floodgate St(a)unch

Floodlight Blond(e)

Floor(ing) Area, Astound, Baffle, Chess, Deck, Dev(v)el, Down, Entresol, Etage, Fell, Flags(tone), Flatten, Flight, Gravel, Kayo, KO, Parquet, Piano nobile, Planch, Platform, Puncheon, Screed, Stage, Story, Stump, Tessella, Tessera, Thill, Woodblock

Flop Belly-landing, Bomb, Collapse, Dud, Failure, Fizzer, Fosbury, Lollop, Mare's-nest, Misgo, Phut, Plump, Purler, Washout, Whap, Whitewash

Flora Benthos, Biota, Cybele, Flowers

Florence, Florentine Tuscan

Florid Coloratura, Cultism, Flamboyant, Fresh, Gongorism, High, Red, Rococo, Rubicund, Ruddy, Taffeta

Florida Fa

Floss(y) Flashy, Florence, Ornate, Silk

Flotilla Armada, Escadrille

Flotsam Detritus, Driftwood, Flotage, Waift, Waveson, Weft

Flounce Falbala, Frill, Furbelow, Huff, Prance, Ruffle, Sashay, Toss

Flounder Blunder, Fluke, Reel, Slosh, Struggle, Stumble, Tolter, Toss, Wallow

Flour Cassava, Couscous(ou), Cribble, Crible, Farina, Graham, Gram, Kouskous, Meal, Middlings, Pinole, Powder, Red-dog, Wheatmeal, Wholegrain, Wholemeal, Wholewheat

Flourish(ed), Flourishing Blague, Bless, Bloom, Blossom, Boast, Brandish, Bravura, Burgeon, Cadenza, Epiphonema, Fanfare, Fiorita, Fl, Flare, Grow, Kicking, Melisma, Mort, Palmy, Paraph, Prosper, Rubric, Scroll, Swash, Tantara, Thrive, Tucket, Veronica, Vigorous, Wampish, Wave, Welfare

Flout Disdain, Disobey, Insult, Malign, Mock, Profane, Scorn, Scout

Flow(ing) Abound, Afflux, Cantabile, Cash, Current, Cursive, Cusec, Distil, Ebb, Emanate, Estrang(h)elo, Fleet, Fluent, Fluid, Flush, Flux, Freeform, Gush, Knickpoint, Laminar, Liquid, Loose-bodied, Nappe, Nickpoint, Obsequent, Onrush, Ooze, Popple, Pour, Purl, Rail(e), Rayle, Rill, Rin, Run, Scapa, Seamless, Setter, Slur, Spate, Stream, Streamline, Teem, Tidal, Torrent

Flower (part), Flowering, Flowers, Flower bed Abutilon, Aconite, Adonis, Agave, Alyssum, Amaranth, Anemone, Arabis, Argemone, Arum, Asphodel, Aster, Astilbe, Bald-money, Bel(l)amoure, Best, Bindi-eye, Bloom, Bloosme, Blossom, Bluebell, Boutonniere, Brook, Bugle, Bugloss, Bur-marigold, Buttercup, Buttonhole, Camas(s), Camash, Campion, Carolina, Clematis, Columbine, Coronation, Corymb, Crants, Cream, Cyclamen, Cyme, Daffodil, Dahlia, Daisy, Develop, Disa, Edelweiss, Efflorescence, Eglantine, Elite, Enemy, Flag, Floscule, Foxglove, Freesia, Fumaria, Gardenia, Gentian, Gessamine, Gillyflower, Gillyvor, Gilt-cup, Glacier, Glory-pea, Godetia, Gold, Gollan(d), Gool, Gowland, Gule, Heliotrope, Hellebore, Henbit, Hepatica, Hibiscus, Hortus siccus, Hosta, Hydrangea, Immortelle, Inflorescence, Ipomoea, Irid, Iris, Jessamine, Kikumon, Knot, Kok-sagyz, Larkspur, Lily, Loose-strife, Madder, Magnolia, Maguey, Marigold, Meadow-sweet, Melampode, Melilot, Myosotis, None-so-pretty, Nosegay, Nuphar, Oleander, Onagra, Orchid, Padma, Paeony, Parterre, Pentstemon, Petunia, Phlox, Picotee, Pimpernel, Pink, Plant, Poinsettia, Pompom, Pompon, Poppy, Pre-vernal, Prime, Primrose, Protea, Quamash, Rampion, ➤ RIVER, Rose, Rudbeckia, Safety, Santonica, Saxifrage, Scabious, Scilla, Sesame, Silene, Smilax, Snapdragon, Spadix, Speedwell, Spray, Stalked, Stapelia, Stavesacre, Stream, Strobilus, Sulphur, Tansy, Tassel, Tibouchine, Toran(a), Touch-me-not, Tradescantia, Trollius, Tuberose, Tulip, Turnsole, Umbel, Valerian, Verbena, Vernal, Wreath, Yulan

▷ **Flower** may indicate a river

Flower arrangement, Flower work Barbola, Ikebana, Lei

Flowery Anthemia, Damassin, Orchideous, ➤ ORNATE, Pseudocarp, Verbose

Flu Asian, Grippe, Lurgi, Yuppie

Fluctuate(r), Fluctuation Ambivalence, Balance, Seiche, Trimmer, Unsteady, Vacillate, Vary, Waver

Flue Chimney, Duct, Funnel, Pipe, Tewel, Uptake, Vent

Fluent(ly) Eloquent, Facile, Flowing, Glib, Liquid, Oracy, Verbose, Voluble

Fluff(y) Bungle, Dowl(e), Down, Dust, Feathery, Flocculent, Floss, Flue, Fug, Fuzz, Girl, Lint, Muff, Noil, Oose, Ooze, Thistledown

Fluid Amniotic, Anasarca, Ascites, Broo, Chyle, Cisterna, Colostrum, Condy's, Enema, Fixative, Fl, Humour, Juice, ➤ LIQUID, Lymph, Mucus,

Oedema, Perilymph, Plasma, Sap, Serum, Shifting, Succus, Synovia, Vitreum, Vril, Water

▷ **Fluid** may indicate an anagram

Fluke Accident, Anchor, Chance, Fan, Flounder, Ga(u)nch, Grapnel, Killock, Liver, Lobe, Redia, Scratch

Flummox Baffle, Bamboozle, Floor

Flunk Fail

Flunkey Chasseur, Clawback, Haiduck, Heyduck, Jeames, Lackey, Servant, Toady

Fluorescence Bloom, Epipolism, Glow

Fluorine F

Flurry Bustle, Fluster, Haste, Hoo-ha, Shower

Flush(ed) Affluent, Beat, Even, Ferret, Florid, Flow, Gild, Hectic, Hot, Level, Red, Rolling, Rose, Royal, Rud, Scour, Sluice, Spaniel, Start, Straight, Sypher, Thrill, Tierce, Vigour, Wash

Fluster Befuddle, Confuse, Disconcert, Faze, Flap, Rattle, Shake

Flute (player) Bellows-maker, Bohm, Channel, Claribel(la), Crimp, Fife, Fipple, Flageolet, Glass, Glyph, Groove, Marsyas, Nose, Ocarina, Piccolo, Pipe, Poogye(e), Quena, Shakuhachi, Sulcus, Thisbe, Tibia, Toot, Transverse, Whistle

Flutter Bat, Bet, Fan, Fibrillate, Flacker, Flaffer, Flaught, Flichter, Flicker, Flitter, Fly, ➤ GAMBLE, Hover, Palpitate, Play, Pulse, Sensation, Twitter, Waft, Winnow

Flux D, Flow, Fusion, Luminous, Maxwell, Melt, Tesla, Weber

Fly(ing), Flies Abscond, Agaric, Airborne, Alder, Alert, Assassin, Astute, Aviation, Awake, A-wing, Baker, Bedstead, Bee, Blowfly, Bluebottle, Bolt, Bot, Breese, Breeze, Brize, Brommer, Bulb, Bush, Cab, Caddis, Carriage, Carrot, Cecidomyia, Cheesehopper, Cheese skipper, Cleg, Cluster, Cock-a-bondy, Crane, ➤ CUNNING, Decamp, Deer, Diptera, Doctor, Dragon, Drake, Drone, Drosophila, Dry, Dung, Dutchman, Escape, Fiacre, Flee, Flesh, Flit, Fox, Frit, Fruit, Glide, Glossina, Gnat, Grannom, Greenbottle, Greenhead, Hackle, Harvest, Hedge-hop, Hessian, Homoptera, Hop, Horn, Hurtle, Ichneumon, Jenny-spinner, Jock Scott, Lace-wing, Lantern, Laputan, March brown, Mosquito, Moth, Motuca, Murragh, Musca, Mutuca, Nymph, Opening, Ox-warble, Palmer, Para, Pilot, Pium, Plecopteran, Pomace, Rapid, Robber, Saucer, Sciaridae, Scorpion, Scotsman, Screwworm, Scud, Sedge, Simulium, Smart, Snake, Snipe, Soar, Spanish, Speed, Spinner, Stable, Syrphidae, Tabanid, Tachina, Tear, Thrips, Tipula, Trichopteran, Tsetse, Vinegar, Volatic, Volitate, Warble, Watchet, Welshman's button, Wide-awake, Wily, Wing, Yogic, Zebub, Zimb, Zipper

Fly-catcher Attercop, Cobweb, Darlingtonia, Dionaea, King-bird, Phoebe, Spider, Tanrec, Tyrant

Flying-fox Fruit-bat, Kalong

Flying saucer UFO

Fly-killer Chowri, Chowry, DDT, Swat

Foam(ing) Barm, Bubble, Froth, Lather, Mousse, Oasis®, Polystyrene, Ream, Scum, Seethe, Spindrift, Spooming, Spume, Sud(s), Surf, Yeast, Yest

Fob Chain, Defer, Fub, Pocket, Slang

Focal, Focus Centre, Converge, Fix, Hinge, Hub, Narrow, Pinpoint, Point, Spotlight, Train

Fodder Alfalfa, Browsing, Buckwheat, Cannon, Clover, Eatage, Ensilage, Foon, Forage, Gama-grass, Grama, Guar, Hay, Lucerne, Oats, Pasture, Provender, Rye-grass, Sainfoin, Silage, Stover

Foe Contender, ➤ ENEMY, Opponent, Rival

Foetus Embryo

Fog Aerosol, Brume, Cloud, Damp, Fret, Haar, Miasm(a), Mist, Murk, Obscure, Pea-soup(er), Roke, Sea-fret, Sea-haar, Smog, Smoke, Soup, Thick, Vapour, Yorkshire

Fogey Die-hard

Fogg Phileas, Solicitor

Foible Failing, Flaw, Idiosyncrasy, Quirk, Weakness

Foil(ed) Ba(u)lk, Chaff, Cross, Dupe, Epée, Fleurette, Frustrate, Lametta, Leaf, Offset, Paillon, Pip, Scotch, Silver, Stooge, Stump, Thwart, Touché

Foist Fob, Insert, Suborn, Wish

Fold(ed), Folder, Folding Anticline, Bend, Binder, Close, Collapse, Concertina, Corrugate, Cote, Crash, Crease, Crimp, Crinkle, Crunkle, Diapir, Diptych, Double, Epicanthus, Epiploon, Fake, Fan, File, Fr(a)enum, Frill, Furl, Gather, Groin, Gyrus, Jack-knife, Lap, Lap(p)et, Lapel, Lirk, Mesentery, Monocline, Nappe, Nympha, Obvolute, Octuple, Omentum, Pastigium, Pen, Pericline, Pintuck, ➤ PLEAT, Plica, Ply, Pran(c)k, Prancke, Ptyxis, Ruck(le), Ruga, Sheep-pen, Syncline, Triptych, Tuck, Wrap

Foliage Coma, Finial, Frond, Greenery, Leafage

Folio(s) Elephant, F(f), File, Percy

Folk(sy) Beaker, Homespun, Kin, People, Public

Follicle Graafian

Follow(er), Following Adhere, After, Agree, Anthony, Attend(ant), Believer, Clientele, Consequence, Copy, Dangle, Disciple, Dog, Echo, Ensew, Ensue, Entourage, Epigon(e), Equipage, F, Fan, Groupie, Heel(er), Henchman, Hereon, Hunt, Man, Merry men, Muggletonian, Myrmidon, Neist, Next, Obey, Pan, Post, Pursue, Rake, Road, Run, Satellite, School, Secundum, Seewing, Segue, Sequel, Seriation, Shadow, Sheep, Sidekick, Stag, Stalk, Stear, Steer, Subsequent, Succeed, Sue, Suivez, Supervene, Tag, Tail, Tantony, Trace, Track, Trail, Train, Use, Vocation, Votary

▷ **Follower** 'a follower' may indicate B

Folly Antic, Bêtise, Idiocy, Idiotcy, Imprudence, Lunacy, Mistake, Moria, Unwisdom, Vanity

Foment(ation) Arouse, Brew, Embrocation, Excite, Poultice, Stupe

Fond(ness) Amatory, Ardour, Dote, Keen, Loving, Partial, Tender, Tendre

Fondant Ice, Sweet

Fondle Canoodle, Caress, Dandle, Grope, Hug, Nurse, Pet, Snuggle

Font Aspersorium, Bénitier, Delubrum, Ennage, Source

Food Aliment, Ambrosia, Bakemeat, Batten, Battill, Battle, Bellytimber, Board, Bord, Broth, Browse, Bully, Burger, Cate, Cheer, Cheese, Chop, Chow, Chuck, Chyme, Collation, Comestible, Comfort, Commons, Convenience, Course, Curd, Deutoplasm, Dietetics, ➤ DISH, Dodger, Dog's body, Dunderfunk, Eats, Esculents, Eutrophy, Falafel, Fare, Fast, Felafel, Fodder, Forage, Fuel, Grub, Hangi, Incaparina, Ingesta, Jootha, Jorts, Junk, Kai, Keep, Leben, Lerp, Long-pig, Manna, Mato(o)ke, Matzoon, Meat, Nacho, Nardoo, Nosebag, Nosh, Nourishment, Nourriture, Pabulum, Pannage, Pap, Pasta, Peck, Pemmican, Provender, Provision, Sambal, Sap, Sashimi, Scaff, Scoff, Sizings, Snack, Soil, Soul, Staple, Stodge, Sushi, Table, Tack, Takeaway, Tamale, Taro, Tempura, Tofu, Trimmings, Trophallaxis, Tuck(er), Viand, Victuals, Vivers, Waffle, Yittles

Food-plant Laser, Silphium

Foodstore Delicatessen, Grocery, Larder, Pantry, Silo

Fool(hardy), Foolish(ness) Air-head, Anserine, April, Assot, Berk, BF, Bob, Brash, Buffoon, Cake, Capocchia, Chump, Clot, Clown, Cockeyed, Coxcomb, Cully, Dagonet, Daw, Delude, Dummy, Dunce, Empty, Etourdi, Feste, Flannel(led), Folly, Fon, Fond, Fox, Gaby, Gaga, Galah, Git, Glaikit, Goat, Gobbo, Goon, Goose, Gooseberry, Groserts, Gubbins, Gull, Gullible, Halfwit, Hare-brained, Highland, Huntiegowk, Hunt-the-gowk, Idiotic, Imbecile, Inane, Ineptitude, Injudicious, Jest, Joke, Kid, Kissel, Lark, Loon, Mamba, Mislead, Mome, Moron, Muggins, Niaiserie, Nignog, Ni(n)compoop, Ninny, Nong, Omadhaun, Patch, Poop, Poupe, Punk, Rash, Sawney, Scogan, Scoggin, Senseless, Shallow, Snipe, Soft, Sot, Spoony, ➤ STUPID, Tom (noddy), Trifle, Unwitty, Vice, Wantwit, Yorick, Yoyo, Zany

Foolproof Fail-safe

Foot(ing), Footwork, Feet Amphibrach, Amphimace, Anap(a)est, Antibacchius, Antispast, Athlete's, Bacchius, Ball, Base, Choliamb, Choree, Choriamb, Club, Cretic, Dactyl, Dance, Dochmii, Dochmius, Epitrite, F, Hephthemimer, Hoof, Hoppus, Iamb(us), Infantry, Ionic, Molossus, Pad, Paeon, Palama, Pastern, Paw, Pay, Pedate, Pedicure, Plates, Podium, Procleusmatic, Pyrrhic, Roothold, Scazon, Semeia, Serif, Shanks's mare, Shanks's pony, Spondee, Standing, Syzygy, Tarsus, Terms, Tootsie, Tootsy, Tootsy-wootsy, Tread, Trench, Tribrach, Trilbies, Triseme, Trochee, Trotter, Tube, Verse

Football(er) Back, Barbarian, Ba'spiel, Camp, Centre, Fantasy, FIFA, Flanker(back), Gaelic, Goalie, Gridder, Keeper, Kicker, Libero, Lineman, Lock, Midfield, Pack, Pele, Pigskin, RU, Rugby, Rugger, Rules, Safety, Soccer(oos), Sport, Striker, Sweeper, Table, Total, Touch(back), Wing

Foot-fault Bunion, Corn, Hammer-toe, Verruca

Foothold Lodgement, Purchase, Stirrup

Footloose Peripatetic

Footman Attendant, Flunkey, Lackey, Pedestrian, Pompey, Yellowplush

Footnote Addendum, PS

Footpad Land-rat, Mugger, Robber

Footplate Horseshoe

Footprint Ichnite, Ichnolite, Pad, Prick, Pug, Seal, Slot, Trace, Track, Vestige

Footrest, Footstool Coaster, Cricket, Hassock, Stirrup, Stool, Tramp

Footrot, Footsore Blister, Bunion, Corn, Halt, Surbate, Surbet, Weary, Wire-heel

Footwashing Maundy, Nipter

Footway Banquette

Footwear Gumboot, Shoe, Slipper, Sock, Spats, Stocking

Fop(pish) Apery, Barbermonger, Beau, Buck, Cat, Coxcomb, Dandy, Dude, Exquisite, Fallal, Fantastico, Finical, La-di-da, Macaroni, Monarcho, Muscadin, Popinjay, Skipjack, Toff

For Ayes, Because, Concerning, Cos, Pro, Since, To

Forage Alfalfa, Fodder, Graze, Greenfeed, Lucern(e), Pickeer, Prog, Raid, Rummage, Sainfoin, Search

Foray Attack, Creach, Creagh, Raid, Sortie, Spreagh

Forbear(ance), Forbearing Abstain, Clement, Endure, Indulgent, Lenience, Lineage, Longanimity, Mercy, Pardon, Parent, Patient, Quarter, ➤ REFRAIN, Suffer, Tolerant, Withhold

Forbid(den), Forbidding Ban, Bar, City, Denied, Don't, Dour, Enjoin, For(e)speak, Gaunt, Grim, Haram, Hostile, Loury, NL, Prohibit, Stern, Taboo, Tabu, Tapu, Tref(a), Verboten, Veto

Force(d), Forceful, Forces, Forcible Activist, Agency, Air-arm, Army, Bathmism, Bind, Birr, Bludgeon, Body, Bounce, Brigade, Bring, Brunt, Bulldoze, Cadre, Cascade, Centrifugal, Centripetal, Chi, Coerce, Cogency, Commando, Compel, Constrain, Coriolis, Cram, Delta, Detachment, Dint, Domineer, Downflow, Dragoon, Drive, Duress(e), Dynamic, Dyne, E, Emphatic, Energetic, Equilibrant, Erdgeist, Erg, Expeditionary, Extort, Extrude, F, Farci, Fire brigade, Frogmarch, G, Gar, Gendarmerie, Gilbert, Gism, Gouge, Hale, Host, Hurricane, Impetus, Impress, Inertial, Instress, Intense, Irgun, Irrupt, Jism, Juggernaut, Kinetic, Labour, Lashkar, Legion, Life, Linn, Lorentz, Magnus, Make, Mana, Manpower, Militia, Moment, Momentum, Muscle, Navy, Newton, Numen, Oblige, Od, Odyl(e), OGPU, Orgone, Personnel, Phrenism, Pigs, Pion, Pithy, Police, Posse, Potent, Poundal, Prana, Press(gang), Pressure, Prise, Procrustean, Pull, Put, Qi, Railroad, Rape, Ravish, Reave, Regular, Require, Restem, Route, Rush, SAS, Sforzando, Shear, Snorting, Spetsnaz, Squirt, Steam(roller), Strained, ➤ STRESS, Strong-arm, Subject, TA, Task, Telergy, Telling, Thrust, Torque, Troops, Van den Waals', Vehement, Vigorous, Violence, Vim, Vires, Vis, Vital, Vively, Vociferous, Vril, Wrench, Wrest, Wring, Zap

▷ **Force(d)** may indicate an anagram

Forced labour Begar

Force-feeding Gavage

Forceps Crow(s)bill, Pedicellaria, Pincers, Tenaculum, Vulsella

Ford Anglia, Car, Crossing, Drift, Escort, Strid, Tin Lizzy, Wade

Forearm Radius, Ulna

▶ **Forebear** see FORBEAR

Foreboding Anxiety, Augury, Cloudage, Croak, Feeling, Freet, ➤ OMEN, Ominous, Presage, Presentiment, Sinister, Zoomantic

Forecast(er), Forecasting Augury, Auspice, Divine, Extrapolation, Horoscope, Metcast, Perm, Precurse, Predict, Presage, Prescience, Prognosis, Prognosticate, Prophesy, Rainbird, Shipping, Soothsay, Spae, Tip, Weather

Foreclose Bar, Block, Obstruct, Preclude

Forefather(s) Ancestor, Elder, Forebear, Parent, Rude

Forefront Van

Forehead Brow, Front(let), Glabella(r), Sincipitum, Temple

Foreign(er) Alien, Arab, Auslander, Barbarian, Easterling, Eleanor, Ethnic, Exclave, Exotic, External, Extraneous, Extrinsic, Forane, Forinsecal, Forren, Fraim, Fremit, Gaijin, German, Gringo, Gweilo, Malihini, Metic, Moit, Mote, Outlander, Outside, Oversea, Peregrine, Remote, ➤ STRANGE, Stranger, Taipan, Tramontane, Uitlander, Unfamiliar, Wog

Foreman Baas, Boss, Bosun, Chancellor, Gaffer, Ganger, Manager, Overseer, Steward, Superintendent, Topsman

Foremost First, Front, Leading, Prime, Primary, Supreme, Van

▷ **Foremost** may indicate first letters of words following

Forenoon Undern

Forepart Cutwater, Front

Forerunner Augury, Harbinger, Herald, Messenger, Omen, Pioneer, Precursor, Trailer, Vaunt-courier

Foresee Anticipate, Divine, Preview, Prophesy, Scry

Foreshadow Adumbrate, Augur, Bode, Forebode, Hint, Portend, Prefigure, Presage, Type

Foreshow Betoken, Bode, Signify

Foresight Ganesa, Prescience, Prophecy, Prospect, Providence, Prudence, Taish, Vision

Foreskin Prepuce

Forest Arden, Ashdown, Black, Bush, Caatinga, Charnwood, Chase, Cloud, Dean, Epping, Gallery, Gapo, Glade, Greenwood, Igapo, Jungle, Monte, Nandi, Nemoral, New, Savernake, Selva, Sherwood, Taiga, Urman, Virgin, ➤ WOOD

Forestall Anticipate, Obviate, Pip, Prevent, Queer

Forester Foster, Lumberjack, Verderer, Walker, Woodman, Woodward

Forestry Woodcraft

Foretaste Antepast, Antipasto, Appetiser, Pregustation, Prelibation, Sample, Trailer

Foretell(ing), Forewarn Augur, Bode, Caution, Divine, Fatidic, Forecast, Portend, Predict, Premonish, Presage, Prognosticate, Prophecy, Soothsay, Spae

Forethought Anticipation, Caution, Prometheus, Provision, Prudence

Forever Always, Amber, Ay(e), Eternal, Evermore, Keeps

▶ **Forewarn** see FORETELL

Foreword Introduction, Preamble, Preface, Proem, Prologue

For example Eg, Say, Vg, ZB

For fear Lest

Forfeit Deodand, Fine, Forgo, ➤ PENALTY, Relinquish, Rue-bargain, Sconce

Forge(d), Forger(y) Blacksmith, Copy, Counterfeit, Drop, Dud, Fabricate, Fashion, Foundry, Hammer, Heater, Horseshoe, Ireland, Lauder, Mint, Paper-hanger, Pigott, Progress, Smith(y), Smithery, Spurious, Stiff, Stithy, Stumer, Tilt, Trucage, Truquage, Utter, Valley, Vermeer, Vulcan

Forget(ful), Forget-me-not Amnesia, Dry, Fluff, Lethe, Myosotis, Neglect, Oblivious, Omit, Overlook

Forgive(ness), Forgiving Absolution, Amnesty, Clement, Condone, Merciful, Overlook, Pardon, Placable, Remission, Remittal

Forgo(ne) Abstain, Expected, Refrain, Renounce, Waive

Forgotten Bygone, Missed, Sad

Forjeskit Overscutched

Fork(ed) Bifurcate, Biramous, Branch, Caudine, Cleft, Crotch, Divaricate, Forficate, Fourchette, Grain, Graip, Morton's, Osmeterium, Prong, Runcible, Tine, Toaster, Tormenter, Tormentor, Trident, Trifid, Tuner, Tuning, Y

Forlorn(ness) Abject, Aidless, Desolate, Destitute, Drearisome, Miserable, Nightingale, Sad

Form(s) Alumni, Bench, Bumf, Cast, Ceremonial, Class, Constitute, Coupon, Create, Document, Experience, Fashion, Feature, Fig, ➤ FIGURE, Formula, Game, Gestalt, Hare, Image, Keto, Mode, Mood, Mould, Order, Originate, ➤ OUT OF FORM, Protocol, Questionnaire, Redia, Remove, Rite, Ritual, Schedule, Shape, Shell, Stage, Stamp, State, Structure, Style, Symmetry, Version

Formal Conventional, Dry, Exact, Fit, Literal, Methodic, Official, Pedantic, Precise, Prim, Routine, Set, Starched, Stiff, Stodgy, Tails

Formality Ceremony, Ice, Pedantry, Protocol, Punctilio, Starch

Formation Battalion, Configuration, Diapyesis, Echelon, Eocene, Fours, Growth, Line, Manufacture, Origin, Pattern, Phalanx, Prophase, Riss, Wedge

▷ **Former** may indicate something that forms

Former(ly) Ance, Auld, Before, Ci-devant, Earlier, Ere-now, Erst(while), Ex, Late, Maker, Matrix, Old, Once, One-time, Past, Previous, Prior, Pristine, Quondam, Sometime, Then, Umquhile, Whilom

Formidable Alarming, Armipotent, Battleaxe, Fearful, Forbidding, Gorgon, Powerful, Shrewd, Stoor, Stour, Stowre, Sture, Tiger

Formless Amorphous, Invertebrate, Nebulous, Shapeless

▷ **Form of, Forming** may indicate an anagram

Formosan Tai

Formula(te) Define, Devise, Doctrine, Equation, Frame, Invent, Lurry, Paternoster, Protocol, Prescription, ➤ RECIPE, Rite, Ritual

Forsake Abandon, Desert, Quit, Renounce

Forsooth Certes, Certy, Even, Marry

Forswear Abandon, Abjure, Disavow, Renounce, Reny

Forsyte Fleur, Saga

Fort(ification), Fortress Acropolis, Alamo, Alhambra, Balclutha, Bastille, Bastion, Battlement, Bawn, Blockhouse, Bonnet, Breastwork, Burg, Casbah, Castellated, Castellum, Castle, Citadel, Contravallation, Crémaillère, Deva, Dun, Earthwork, Edinburgh, Enceinte, Epaule, Escarpment, Fastness, Fieldwork, Flèche, Fortalice, Fortilage, Fortlet, Fraise, Ft, Gabion(ade), Garrison, Golconda, Haven, Hedgehog, Kaim, Kame, Kasba(h), Keep, Knox, La(a)ger, Malakoff, Martello tower, Masada, Merlon, Mile-castle, Moineau, Motte and bailey, Orillion, Pa(h), Peel, Pele, Pentagon, Place, Rampart, Rath, Ravelin, Redoubt, Reduit, Ring, Salient, Sangar, Sconce, Stronghold, Sumter, Tenaille, Terreplein, Tower, Vitrified, William, Worth

Forte F, Metier, Specialty, Strength

Forth Away, From, Hence, Out

Forthright Candid, Direct, Frank, Prompt

Forthwith Anon, Directly, Eft(soons), Immediately

Fortify Arm, Augment, Brace, Casemate, Embattle, Lace, Munify, Steel, ➤ STRENGTHEN

Fortitude Endurance, Grit, Mettle, Patience, Pluck, ➤ STAMINA

Fortunate Auspicious, Blessed, Blest, Happy, ➤ LUCKY, Providential, Well

Fortune (teller), Fortune-telling Auspicious, Bonanza, Bumby, Cartomancy, Chaldee, Cha(u)nce, Destiny, Dukkeripen, Fame, Fate, Felicity, Genethliac, Geomancy, Hap, Hydromancy, I Ching, Lot, Luck, Mint, Motser, Motza, Oracle, Packet, Palmist, Peripety, Pile, Prescience, Pyromancy, Sibyl, Soothsayer, Sortilege, Spaewife, Success, Taroc, Tarok, Tarot, Tyche, Wealth, Windfall

Forty, Forties Capot, F, Hungry, Kemple, Roaring

Forty-ninth Parallel

Forum Arena, Assembly, Debate, Platform, Tribunal

Forward(s) Accede, Advanced, Ahead, Along, Arch, Assertive, Assuming, Bright, Early, Flanker, Forrad, Forrit, Forth, Fresh, Future, Hasten, Hooker, Immodest, Impudent, Insolent, Lock, Malapert, On(wards), Pack, Pert, Petulant, Porrect, Precocious, ➤ PROGRESS, Promote, Prop, Readdress, Redirect, Scrum, Send, Stem, To(ward), Van, Wing

Fossil(ise), Fossils Amber, Ammonite, Baculite, Belemnite, Blastoid(ea), Calamite, Ceratodus, Chondrite, Conodont, Cordaites, Derived, Enerinite, Eohippus, Eozoon, Eurypterus, Exuviae, Fogy, Goniatite, Graptolite, Ichnite, Ichnolite, Ichthyodurolite, Ichthyolite, Index, Lingulella, Mosasauros, Nummulite, Olenus, Orthoceras, Osteolepis, Ostracoderm, Petrifaction, Phytolite, Plesiosaur, Pliohippus, Pliosaur, Pterygotus, Pythonomorph, Relics, Reliquiae, Remanié, Sigillaria, Sinanthropus, Snakestone, Stigmaria, Stromatolite, Taphonomy, Titanotherium, Trace, Trilobite, Uintatherium, Wood-opal, Zinganthropus, Zoolite

Foster (child, mother), Fostering Adopt, Cherish, Da(u)lt, Develop, Feed, Fornent, Further, Harbour, Incubation, Metapelet, Metaplot, Nourish, Nourse(l), Noursle, Nousell, Nurse, Nurture, Nuzzle, ➤ REAR

Foul, Foul-smelling Base, Beray, Besmirch, Besmutch, Bewray, Bungle, ➤ DEFILE, Dreggy, Drevill, Enseam, Evil, Feculent, Gross, Hassle, Hing, Mephitic, Mud, Noisome, Olid, Osmeterium, Professional, Putid, Putrid, ➤ RANK, Reekie, Rotten, Sewage, Soiled, Squalid, Stagnant, Stain, Stapelia, Technical, Unclean, Unfair, Vile, Violation, Virose

▷ **Foul** may indicate an anagram

Found (in) Among, Base, Bed, Bottom, Build, Cast, Emong, Endow, ➤ ESTABLISH, Eureka, Institute, Introduce, Met, Occur, Plant, Recovered, Rest, Start, Table

Foundation(s) Base, Bedrock, Cribwork, Establishment, Footing, Girdle, Grillage, Ground, Groundwork, Hard-core, Infrastructure, Institution, Matrix, Pile, Roadbed, Rockefeller, Scholarship, Stays, Substrata, Substructure, Trackbed, Underlie, Underlinen

▷ **Foundations** may indicate last letters

Founder Author, Crumple, Fail, Inventor, Iron-master, Miscarry, Oecist, Oekist, Patriarch, Perish, Settle, Sink, Stumble

Fount Aonian, Source, Springlet

Fountain Acadine, Aganippe, Bubbler, Castalian, Cause, Conduit, Drinking, Fauwara, Forts, Gerbe, Head, Hippocrene, Jet, Pant, Pirene, Salmacis, Scuttlebutt, Soda, Spring, Trevi, Youth

Fountain basin Laver

Four(some) Cater, Georges, Horsemen, IV, Mess, Quartet, Quaternary, Quaternion, Reel, Tessara, Tessera, Tetrad, Tetralogy, Tiddy, Warp

Fourpence Groat

Fourteenth Bastille, Trecento, Valentine

Fourth Deltaic, Estate, Fardel, Forpet, Forpit, July, Quartet, Quaternary, Quintan, Sesquitertia, Tritone

Fowl Barnyard, Biddy, Boiler, Brahma, Brissle-cock, Burrow-duck, Capon, Chicken, Chittagong, Cob, Cock, Coot, Duck, Ember, Gallinaceous, Gallinule, Game, Guinea, Hamburg(h), ➤ HEN, Houdan, Jungle, Kora, Leghorn, Moorhen, Partridge, Pheasant, Pintado, Poultry, Quail, Rooster, Rumkin, Rumpy, Solan, Spatchcock, Spitchcock, Sultan, Sussex, Teal, Turkey, Wyandotte

Fox(y) Alopecoid, Arctic, Baffle, Blue, Charley, Charlie, Corsac, Cunning, Desert, Fennec, Fool, Friend, Fur, Grey, Kit, Lowrie(-tod), Outwit, Pug, Puzzle, Quaker, Red, Reynard, Rommel, Russel, Silver, Skulk, ➤ SLY (BOOTS), Swift, Tod, Uffa, Uneatable, Vixen, White, Zerda, Zoril(le), Zorro

Foxglove Digitalis, Witches-thimble

Foxhole Earth

Foyer Hall, Lobby

Fracas Brawl, Dispute, Mêlée, Prawle, Riot, Rumpus, Shindig, Uproar

Fraction Complex, Improper, Ligroin, Mantissa, Part, Piece, Proper, Scrap, Simple, Some, Vulgar

Fracture Break, Colles, Comminuted, Compound, Crack, Fault, Fissure, Greenstick, Hairline, Impacted, Pott's, Rupture, Split, Stress

Fragile Brittle, Crisp, Delicate, Frail, Frangible, Nesh, Slender, Tender, Vulnerable, Weak

Fragment(s) Atom, Bit, Bla(u)d, Brash, Breccia, Brockram, Cantlet, Clastic, Crumb, End, Flinder, Fritter, Frust, Graile, Lapilli, Mammock, Morceau, Morsel, Ort, ➤ PARTICLE, Piece, Potshard, Potsherd, Relic, Rubble, Scrap, Segment, Shard, Shatter, Sheave, Shiver, Shrapnel, Skerrick, Sliver, Smithereens, Smithers, Snatch, Splinter

▷ **Fragment of** may indicate a hidden word

Fragrance, Fragrant Aromatic, Attar, Bouquet, Conima, Nosy, Odour, Olent, ➤ PERFUME, Pot-pourri, Redolent, ➤ SCENT, Sent, Spicy, Suaveolent

Frail Brittle, Creaky, Delicate, Feeble, Flimsy, ➤ FRAGILE, Puny, Slight, Slimsy, Weak

Framboesia Morula, Yaws

Frame(work) Adjust, Airer, Angle, Armature, Bail, Bayle, Body, Brickbat, Build, Cadre, Cadge, Cage, Case, Casement, Casing, Cent(e)ring, Centreing, Chase, Chassis, Cold, Compages, Companion, Cowcatcher, Cradle, Cratch, Deckel, Deckle, Entablature, Fabric, Fiddley, Flake, Form, Frisket, Gambrel, Gantry, Gate, Grid-iron, Heck, Horse, Hull, Jungle gym, Lattice, Limit, Louvre, Mantel, Mixter, Mood, Mount, Mullion, Muntin(g), Newsreel, Ossature, Pannier, Pantograph, Parameter, Partner, Passe-partout, Pergola, Pillory, Plant, Plot, Poppet head, Puncheon, Rack, Rave, Redact, Retable, Rim, Sash, Scaffold, Scuncheon, Sect(ion), Set, Setting, Skeleton, Spring-box, Stanchion, Still(age), Stocks, Stroma, ➤ STRUCTURE, Surround, Tambour, Tent(er), Tepee, Trave, Trellis, Tress, Tressel, Trestle, Tribble, Trussing, Victimize, Wattle, Ways, Yoke, Zarf, Zimmer®

Framley Parsonage

Franc Fr, Leu, Lev, Lew

France Anatole, Marianne, RF, Thibault

Franchise Charter, Contract, Liberty, Privilege, Right, Suffrage, Vote, Warrant

Franciscan Observant, Salesian, Scotist, Tertiaries

Francium Fr

Franck Cesar

Frank(ish) Blunt, ➤ CANDID, Direct, Easy, Free, Free-spoken, Honest, Ingenuous, Man-to-man, Merovingian, Natural, Open, Outspoken, Postage, Postmark, Ripuarian, Salian, Sincere, Stamp, Straight, Sty, Upfront

Frankincense Laser, Olibanum, Thus

Frans, Franz Hals, Lehar

Frantic Demoniac, Deranged, Distraught, Frenzied, Hectic, Mad, Overwrought, Phrenetic, Rabid, Violent, Whirl(ing)

▷ **Frantic** may indicate an anagram

Frappé Iced

Fraternise, Fraternity Affiliate, Brotherhood, Burschenschaft, Consort, Elk, Fellowship, Lodge, Mingle, Moose, Order

Fratricide Cain

Fraud(ulent) Barratry, Bobol, Bubble, Charlatan, Cheat, Chisel, Collusion, Covin, Cronk, Deceit, Diddle, Do, Fineer, Gyp, Humbug, Hypocrite, ► IMPOSTOR, Imposture, Jiggery-pokery, Jobbery, Liar, Peculator, Piltdown, Pious, Pseud(o), Put-up, Ringer, Rip-off, Roguery, Rort, Scam, South Sea Bubble, Stellionate, Supercherie, Swindle, Swiz(z), Swizzle, Tartuffe, Trick

Fraught Perilous

Fray(ed) Bagarre, Brawl, Contest, Feaze, Frazzle, Fret, Fridge, Ravel, Riot, Scrimmage

Freak Cantrip, Caprice, Chimera, Control, Deviant, Geek, Sport, Teras, Whim, Whimsy

Freckle Ephelis, Fern(i)tickle, Fern(i)ticle, Heatspot, Lentigines, Lentigo, Spot, Sunspot

Frederick Barbarossa, Carno, Great

Free(d), Freely Acquit, Assoil, Buckshee, Candid, Canny, Church, Clear, Cuffo, Dead-head, Deregulate, Devoid, Disburden, Disburthen, Disengage, Eleutherian, Emancipate, Enfranchise, Enlarge, Excuse, Exeem, Exeme, Exempt, Exonerate, Extricate, Familiar, Footloose, Frank, French, Gratis, House, Idle, Immune, Independent, Kick, Large, Lavish, Lax, Leisure, Let, Liberate, Loose, Manumit, Open, Parole, Pro bono, Quit(e), Range, Ransom, Redeem, ► RELEASE, Relieve, Rescue, Reskew, Rick, Rid, Sciolto, Solute, Spring, Stald, Stall, Trade, Unlock, Unmew, Unmuzzle, Unshackle, Unsnarl, Untie, Vacant, Verse, Voluntary

▷ **Free** may indicate an anagram

Freebooter Cateran, Corsair, Franklin, Marauder, Pad, Pindaree, Pindari, Pirate, Rapparee, Snapha(u)nce, Snaphaunch, Thief, Viking

Freedom Abandon, Autonomy, Breadth, Carte blanche, Eleutherian, Exemption, Fear, Fling, Four, Immunity, Impunity, Latitude, Liberty, Licence, Play, Releasement, Speech, Uhuru, UNITA, Want, Worship

Free gift Bonus, Charism, Perk

Freehold(er) Enfeoff, Franklin, Frank tenement, Seisin, Udal(ler), Yeoman

Freelance Eclectic, Independent, Mercenary

Freeloader Sponge

▷ **Freely** may indicate an anagram

Freeman Burgess, Ceorl, Churl, Franklin, Liveryman, Thegn, Thete, Villein

Freemason(ry), Freemason's son Craft, Lewis, Lodge, Moose, Templar

Free-range Eggs, Outler

Free State Orange

Freethinker Agnostic, Bradlaugh, Cynic, Libertine, Sceptic

Free-trade(r) Cobdenism, Wright

Free-wheel Coast

Freeze(r), Freezing Alcarrazo, Benumb, Congeal, Cool, Cryogenic, Eutectic, Freon®, Frost, Harden, Ice, Lyophilize, Nip, Numb, Paralyse, Regelate, Riss, Stiffen

Freight Cargo, Carriage, Fraught, Goods, Load

French(man), Frenchwoman Alsatian, Basque, Breton, Crapaud, Creole, Dawn, Frog, Gallic(e), Gaston, Gaul, Gombo, Grisette, Gumbo, Huguenot, Joual, M, Mamselle, Marianne, Midi, Mounseer, Neo-Latin, Norman, Parleyvoo, René, Rhemish, Savoyard

Frenetic Deranged, Frantic, Overwrought

Frenzied, Frenzy Amok, Berserk, Corybantic, Deliration, Delirium, Demoniac, Enrage, Enrapt, Euhoe, Euoi, Evoe, Fit, Fury, Hectic, Hysteric, Lune, Maenad, Mania, Must, Nympholepsy, Oestrus, Phrenetic, Rage

Frequency, Frequent(er), Frequently Attend, Audio, Channel, Common, Constant, Familiar, Formant, FR, Fresnel, Habitué, Hang-out, Haunt, Hertz, High, Incidence, Megahertz, Often, Penetrance, Pulsatance, Radio, Recurrent, Spectrum, Superhigh, Thick

Fresco Intonaco, Sinopia, Tempera

Fresh(en), Freshness Aurorean, Brash, Caller, Chilly, Clean, Crisp, Dewy, Entire, Forward, Green, Hot, Insolent, Lively, Maiden, New, Novel, Quick, Rebite, Recent, Roral, Roric, Rorid, Smart, Span-new, Spick, Sweet, Tangy, Uncured, Verdure, Vernal, Virent

Freshman Bajan, Bejan(t), Fresher, Pennal, Recruit, Student

Fret(ful) Chafe, Filigree, Fray, Grate, Grecque, Haze, Impatient, Irritate, Ornament, Peevish, Repine, Rile, Ripple, Roil, Rub, Tetchy, Tracery, Whittle, Worry

Friable Crisp, Crumbling, Powdery

Friar(s) Augustinian, Austin, Bacon, Barefoot, Black, Brother, Bungay, Capuchin, Carmelite, Conventual, Cordelier, Crutched, Curtal, Dervish, Dominican, Fra(ter), Franciscan, Frate, Jacobin, Laurence, Limiter, Lymiter, Minim, Minorite, ➤ MONK, Observant, Observantine, Predicant, Recollect, Recollet, Rush, Tuck, White

Friction Attrition, Conflict, Dissent, Drag, Rift, Rub, Stridulation, Tribology, Tripsis, Wear, Xerotripsis

Friday Black, Good, Man, Savage

Fridge Esky®, Freezer, Icebox, Rub

Fried cake Croquette, Cruller

Friend(ly), Friends Achates, Affable, Ally, Alter ego, Ami(cable), Amigo, Approachable, Avuncular, Belamy, Benign, Boet(ie), Bosom, Bud(dy), Buster, Butty, Cater-cousin, China, Chum, Circle, Cobber, Cock, Cohort, Companion, Companionable, Confidant, Comrade, Cordial, Couthie, Crony, Cully, Damon, Downhome, Edwin, Familiar, Feare, Feathered, Feer, Fere, Fiere, Gemütlich, Gossib, Gossip, Gregarious, Hail-fellow-well-met, Ingle, Intimate, Inward, Kith, Marrow, Mate, Mentor, Mucker, Near, Outgoing, Paisano, Pal, Paranymph, Pen, Penn, Pheere, Privado, Prochain ami, Prochein ami, Quaker, Sidekick, Sociable, Societal, Sport, Steady, Tonga, Tosh, Wack(er), Well-wisher, Wus(s)

Friendliness, Friendship Amity, Bonhomie, Camaraderie, Contesseration, Entente, Platonic, Sodality

Frieze Dado, Metope

Fright(en), Frightened, Frightful Afear, Affear(e), Agrise, Agrize, Agryze, Alarm, Aroint, Aroynt, Ashake, Chilling, Cow, Dare, Daunt, Deter, Eek, Eerie, Faceache, Fear(some), Flay, Fleg, Fleme, Fley, Flush, Gallow, Gally, Ghast, Gliff, Glift, Grim, Grisly, Hairy, Horrid, Horrific, Intimidate, Ordeal, Panic, Scar, ➤ SCARE, Scarre, Scaur, Schrecklich, Sight, Skear, Skeer, Skrik, Spook, Stage, Startle, Terrible, Terrify, Terror, Tirrit, Unco, Windy

Frigid Bleak, Cold, Dry, Frosty, Ice, Indifferent, Serac, Stiff

Frill Armil, Armilla, Bavolet, Falbala, Furbelow, Jabot, Ornament, Papillote, Ruche, Ruff(le), Tucker, Valance

▷ **Frilly** may indicate an anagram

Fringe(d) Bang, Border, Bullion, Ciliated, Ciliolate, Edge, Fall, Fimbria, Frisette, Laciniate, Loma, Lunatic, Macramé, Macrami, Pelmet, Peripheral, Robin, Ruff, Run, Thrum, Toupee, Toupit, Tzitzith, Valance, Verge, Zizith

Frisk(y) Caper, Cavort, Curvet, Fisk, Flimp, Frolic, Gambol, Search, Skip, Wanton

Fritillary Snake's-head

Fritter Batter, Beignet, Dribble, Dwindle, Fragment, Fribble, Pakora, Potter, Puf(f)taloon, Squander, Waste

Frivolous Butterfly, Empty(-headed), Featherbrain, Flighty, Flippant, Frothy, Futile, Giddy, Idle, Inane, Light, Lightweight, Playboy, Skittish, Trifling, Trivial

Frizz(le), Frizzly Afro, Crape, Crimp, Crinkle, Curly, Fry, Fuzz, Hiss

Frock Dress, Gown, Ordain, Robe, Smock

Frog Anoura, Anura, Batrachia(n), Braid, Bullfrog, Depression, Fourchette, Frenchman, Frush, Goliath, Hairy, Hyla, Marsupial, Mounseer, Nic, Nototrema, Paddock, Paradoxical, Peeper, Pelobatid, Platanna, Puddock, Puttock, Rana, Ranidae, Tree, Wood, Xenopus

Frogman Diver

Frogmouth Mo(re)poke, Podargus

Frog spawn Redd, Tadpole

Frolic(some) Bender, Bust(er), Cabriole, Caper, Disport, Escapade, ➤ FRISK(Y), Fun, Galravage, Galravitch, Gambol, Gammock, Gil(l)ravage, Jink, Kittenish, Lark, Play, Prank, Rag, Rand, Rig, Romp, Scamper, Skylark, Splore, Sport, Spree, Tittup, Wanton

From A, Against, Ex, For, Frae, Off, Thrae

Frond Fern, Leaf, Tendril

Front(al), Frontman Antependium, Anterior, Bow, Brass, Brow, Cold, Cover, Dead, Dickey, Dicky, Facade, Face, Fore(head), Foreground, Groof, Grouf, Head, Home, Metope, National, Newscaster, Occluded, Paravant, People's, Plastron, Polar, Popular, Pose, Pro, Prom, Prow, Sector, Sinciput, Stationary, Tabula, Van, Vaward, Warm, Western

Frontier(sman) Afghan, Barrier, Border, Boundary, Checkpoint, Limit, Limitrophe, List, March, North-west, Pathan

Front page P1

Front-ranker Pawn

Frost(ing), Frosty Alcorza, Chill, Cranreuch, Cryo-, Freon®, Frigid, Frore(n), Frorne, Glacé, Ground, Hoar, Hore, Ice, Icing, Jack, Mat, Rime, White

Froth(y) Barm, Bubble, Cuckoospit, Despumate, Foam, Frogspit, Gas, Head, Lather, Off-scum, Ream, Saponin, Scum, Seethe, Shallow, Spoom, Spoon, Spume, Sud, Yeasty, Yest

Frown Glower, Lour, Lower, Scowl

Frozen Froren, Gelid, Glacé, Graupel, Ice-bound

Fructification, Fructify Aecidium, Basidium, Fertilise, Flower, Fruit

Frugal Meagre, Parsimonious, Provident, Prudent, Scant, Skimpy, Spare, Spartan, Thrifty

Fruit(ing), Fruit tree, Fruity Abricock, Achene, Acinus, Ackee, Akee, Akene, Algarroba, Allocarpy, Almond, Anana(s), Anona, Apothecium, Apple(-john), Apricock, Apricot, Assai, Aubergine, Autocarp, Avocado, Babaco, Bacciform, Bael, Banana, Banian, Banyan, Bergamot, Berry, Bilberry, Bito, Blackberry, Blackcurrant, Blimbing, Blueberry, Boysenberry, Bread, Bullace, Calabash, Canteloup(e), Carambola, Carica, Caryopsis, Cedrate, Chayote, Cherimoya, Cherimoyer, Cherry, Chocho, Choko, Citron, Citrus, Clementine, Clingstone, Coccus, Compot(e), Confect, Conserve, Crab-nut, Cranberry, Cremocarp, Crop, Custard-apple, Cypsela, Date, Dessert, Dewberry, Drupe, Durian, Durion, Eater, Elderberry, Emblic, Encarpus, Etaerio, Feijoa, Fig, Follicle, Forbidden, Fraughan, Freestone, Fritter, Gage, Gean, Geebung, Genipap, Goosegog, Gourd, Granadilla, Grenadilla, Guava, Haanepoot, Hackberry, Hagberry, Harvest, Hastings, Haw, Hedgehog, Hep, Hesperidium, Hip, Hop, Huckleberry, Issue, Ja(c)k, Jaffa, Jargonelle, Kaki, Kalumpit, Key, Leechee, Lime, Li(t)chee, Litchi, Longan, Lotus, Lychee, Mammee, Mango(steen), Manjack, Marionberry, Medlar, Minneola, Mirabelle, Morello, Mulberry, Myrobalan, Nancy, Nar(r)as, Naseberry, Nashi, Nectarine, Neesberry, Neli(e)s, Nut, Olive, Orchard, Ortanique, Pampelmoose, Pampelmouse, Papaya, Passion, Pa(w)paw, Pepino, Pepo, Persimmon, Pick-cheese, Pimento, Pinguin, Plantain, Plumdamas, Pomace, Pomegranate, Pome(lo), Pompelmoose, Pompelmouse, Poof, Poperin, Poppering, Product(ion), Pruine, Prune, Pseudocarp, Punicaceae, Pupunha, Quince, Raisin, Rambutan, Rath(e)ripe, Regma(ta), Rennet, Replum, Result, Return, Rich, Rowan, Ruddock, Russet, Samara, Sapota, Saskatoon, Satsuma, Scaldberry, Schizocarp, Sebesten, Seed, Service-berry, Shadberry, Shaddock, Sharon, Sloe, Soft, Sorb, Sorosis, Soursop, Squash, Star(-apple), Stoneless, Succade, Sunberry, Sweetie, Sweety, Syconium, Syncarp, Tamarind, Tangelo, Tayberry, Tomatillo, Tomato, Tuna, Ugli, Utricle, Valve, Victorine, Wampee, Watermelon, Whimberry, Whort, Whortleberry, Winesap, Worcesterberry, Xylocarp, Yield, Youngberry

Fruitful(ness) Calathus, Ephraim, Fat, Fecund, Feracious, Fertile, Productive, Prolific, Uberty, Worthwhile

Fruitless Bare, Futile, Sisyphean, Sterile, Useless, Vain

Frump(ish) Dowdy, Judy, Shabby, Unkempt

287 **Frustrate → Function(al)**

Frustrate Baffle, Ba(u)lk, Beat, Blight, Bugger, Check, Confound, Dash, Discomfit, Dish, Foil, Hogtie, Outwit, Scotch, Stymie, Thwart

Fry, Fried Blot, Brit, Fricassee, Fritter, Frizzle, Parr, Sauté, Small, Spawn, Whippersnapper, Whitebait

Fuddle(d) Drunk, Fluster, Fuzzle, Maudlin, Ta(i)vert, Tosticated, Woozy

▷ **Fuddle(d)** may indicate an anagram

Fudge Cook, Doctor, Dodge, Drivel, Evade, Fiddlesticks, Nonsense, Rot, Stop-press

Fuel Anthracite, Argol, Astatki, Avgas, Biodiesel, Biogas, Briquet(te), Bunker, Butane, Candle-coal, Cannel, Coal, Coke, Derv, Diesel, Eilding, Eldin(g), Faggot, Fire(wood), Fossil, Gasohol, Gasoline, Haxamine, Hydrazine, Hydyne, Kerosene, Kerosine, Kindling, Knitch, Lignite, Mox, Napalm, Naphtha, Nuclear, Paraffin, Peat, Propane, Propellant, Stoke, Triptane, Yealdon

Fug Frowst

Fugitive Absconder, Ephemeral, Escapee, Fleeting, Hideaway, Lot, Outlaw, Refugee, Runaway, Runner, Transient

Fugue Ricercar(e), Ricercata

Fulcrum Key-pin, Pivot

Fulfil(ment) Accomplish, Complete, Fruition, Honour, Meet, Pass, Realise, ➤ SATISFY, Steed

Fulgent Bright, Shining

Full(ness), Fully Abrim, Ample, Arrant, Bouffant, Capacity, Chock-a-block, Chocker, Complete, Copious, Embonpoint, Engorged, Entire, Fat, Fed, Fou, Frontal, German, High, Hoatching, Hotch, Mill, Plein, Plenary, Plenitude, Pleroma, Plethora, Replete, Rich, Sated, Satiated, Thorough, Toss, Turgid, Turgor, Ullage, Up, Wau(l)k, Wholly

Full-faced Caboched, Caboshed

Full-throated Goitred

Fulminate, Fulmination Detonate, Explode, Levin, Lightning, Rail, Renounce, Thunder

Fumarole Mofette

Fumble Blunder, Faff, Grope, Misfield, Muff

Fume(s) Bluster, Gas, Halitus, Nidor, Rage, Reech, Reek, Settle, Smoke, Stum, Vapours

Fumigate Disinfect, Smoke

Fun(ny), Funny bone Amusing, Antic, Boat, Buffo, Caper, Clownery, Comedy, Comic(al), Delight, Droll, Frolic, Gammock, Giocoso, Gig, Glaik, Guy, Hilarity, Humerus, Humorous, Hysterical, Jest, Jouisance, Jouysaunce, Killing, Lark, Pleasure, Priceless, Rag, Rich, Rummy, Scream, Sidesplitting, Skylark, Sport, Weird(o), Yell

Funambulist Blondin, Equilibrist, Tight-rope

Function(al) Act, Antilog, Arccos, Arcsine, Arctan, Ceremony, Cosec, Cosh, Cotangent, Coth, Discriminant, Dynamic, Exponential, Gibbs, Hamilton(ian), Helmholtz, Hyperbolic, Integrand, Inverse, Job, Logarithm,

➤ OPERATE, Periodic, Quadric, Quantical, Role, Run, Sech, Service, Sine, Sinh, Ste(a)d, Step, Surjection, Tan(h), Tick, Use, Wave, ➤ WORK

Functionless Otiose

Fund(s) Bank, Bankroll, Barrel, Capital, Consolidated, Emendals, Endow, Evergreen, Fisc, Fisk, Gild, Index, Jackpot, Kitty, Pool, Pork-barrel, Prebend, Purse, Sinking, Slush, Sou-sou, Stabilisation, Stock, Subsidise, Treasury, Trust, War chest

Fundamental(ist) Basic(s), Bedrock, Cardinal, Essence, Grass-roots, Hamas, Nitty-gritty, Organic, Prime, Principle, Radical, Rudimentary, Ultimate

Fund-holder Rentier

Funeral, Funereal Charnel, Cortege, Dismal, Exequy, Feral, Obit, Obsequy, Sad-coloured, Solemn, Tangi

Fungicide Biphenyl, Bordeaux mixture, Captan, Diphenyl, Ferbam, Menadione, Thiram, Zineb

Fungoid, Fungus Agaric, Amadou, Aminata, Ambrosia, Anthracnose, Apothecium, Asci(us), Asomycete, Aspergillus, Barm, Basidium, Beefsteak, Black, Blackknot, Blewits, Boletus, Bootlace, Bracket, Bunt, Candida, Chantarelle, Chanterelle, Cladosporum, Clubroot, Craterellus, Cryptococcus, Cup, Death-cap, Death-cup, Dermatophytosis, Destroying angel, Discomycetes, Earth-star, Elf-cup, Empusa, Ergot, Eumycetes, Favus, Fuss-ball, Fuzz-ball, Gall, Gibberella, Gill, Honey, Horsehair, Hypersarcoma, Hypha, Imperfect, Ink-cap, Ithyphallus, Jelly, Jew's ear, Liberty cap, Lichen, Magic mushroom, Merulius, Mildew, Milk cap, Monilia, Morel, Mould, Mucor(ales), Mushroom, Mycelium, Mycetes, Mycology, Noble rot, Oak-leather, Oidium, Orange-peel, Penicillium, Pest, Peziza, Phallus, Phycomycete, Pileum, Pore, Prototroph, Puccinia, Puckfist, Puffball, Pythium, Rhizopus, Rhytisma, Russula, Rust, Saccharomyces, Saprolegnia, Saprophyte, Sariodes, Scab, Shoestring, Smut, Sooty mould, Spunk, Stinkhorn, Stipe, Sulphur tuft, Tarspot, Thalline, Thallophyte, Toadstool, Torula, Tremella, Trichophyton, Truffle, Tuckahoe, Uredine, Ustilago, Witches' butter, Wood hedgehog, Yeast, Yellow rust, Zygospore

Fungus-eater Mycophagist

Funicular Cable-car

Funk(y) Dodge, Dread, Fear, Scared, Stylish

Funnel Buchner, Chimney, Choana, Flue, Hopper, Infundibulum, Smokestack, Stack, Stovepipe, Tun-dish

Fur Astrakhan, Beaver(skin), Boa, Broadtail, Budge, Calabre, Caracul, Castor, Chinchilla, Crimmer, Ermelin, Ermine, Fitchew, Flix, Flue, Galyac, Galyak, Genet, Kolinsky, Krimmer, Lettice, Minever, Miniver, Mink, Mouton, Musquash, Ocelot, Otter, Pashm, Pean, Pekan, Roskyn, Sable, Sealskin, Sea-otter, Stole, Tincture, Tippet, Vair(e), Victorine, Wolverine, Zorino

Furbish Polish, Renovate, Spruce, Vamp

Furl Fold, Roll, Stow, Wrap

Furlough Congé, Leave

Furnace Arc, Athanor, Blast, Bloomery, Bosh, Calcar, Cockle, Cremator, Cupola, Destructor, Devil, Finery, Firebox, Forge, Glory-hole, Kiln, Lear, Lehr, Lime-kiln, Oast, Oon, Oven, Producer, Reverberatory, Scaldino

Furnish(ing) Appoint, Array, Deck, Decorate, Endow, Endue, Equip, Feed, Fledge, Gird, Lend, Produce, Provision, Soft, Stock, Supply, Tabaret, Upholster

Furniture Biedermeier, Chattels, Chippendale, Encoignure, Escritoire, Flatpack, Hepplewhite, Insight, Lumber, Moveable, Sheraton, Sideboard, Sticks, Stoutherie, Tire, Unit, Whatnot

Furore Brouhaha, Commotion, Outburst, Storm, Uproar

Furrier Trapper

Furrow(ed) Crease, Feer, Feerin(g), Furr, Groove, Gutter, Plough, Pucker, Rill(e), Rugose, Rut, Stria, Sulcus, Vallecula, Wrinkle

Fur-seal Seecatch(ie)

Further(more), Furthest Additional, Advance, Again, Aid, Also, Besides, Deeper, Else, Expedite, Extra, Extend, Extreme, Fresh, Infra, Longer, Mo(e), Mow, Other, Promote, Serve, Speed, Then

Furtive(ly) Clandestine, Cunning, Secret, Sly, Sneaky, Stealthy, Stowlins, Stownlins

Fury, Furies, Furious Acharné, Agitato, Alecto, ➤ ANGER, Apoplexy, Atropos, Avenger, Eriny(e)s, Eumenides, Exasperation, Frantic, Frenzied, Furor, Incensed, ➤ IRE, Livid, Maenad, Megaera, Rabid, Rage, Savage, Tisiphone, Virago, Wood, Wrath, Yond

Furze Gorse, Whin

Fuse(d), Fusion Anchylosis, Ankylosis, Blend, Coalesce, Cohere, Colliquate, Conflate, Encaustic, Endosmosis, Flow, Flux, Match, Merge, Merit, Nuclear, Portfire, Proximity, Rigelation, Run, Saucisson, Slow-match, Syncretism, Syngamy, Tokamak, Unite

Fuselage Body, Monocoque, Structure

Fuss(y) Ado, Agitation, Anile, Ballyho, Bobsie-die, Bother, Br(o)uhaha, Bustle, Carfuffle, Chichi, Coil, Commotion, Complain, Cosset, Create, Cu(r)fuffle, Dust, Faff, Fantad, Fantod, Fiddle-faddle, Finical, Finikin, Hairsplitter, Hoohah, Hoopla, Mither, Niggle, Nit-pick, Old-womanish, Overnice, Palaver, Particular, Perjink, Pernickety, Picky, Pother, Precise, Prejink, Primp, Prissy, Racket, Razzmatazz, Rout, Song, Song and dance, Spoffish, Spoffy, Spruce, Stashie, Stickler, ➤ STIR, Stishie, Stooshie, Stushie, Tamasha, To-do, Tracasserie

Fustian Bombast, Gas, Pompous, Rant

Futile Empty, Feckless, Idle, Inept, No-go, Nugatory, Null, Otiose, Pointless, Sleeveless, Stultified, Trivial, ➤ VAIN

Future, Futurist Again, Be-all, Coming, Demain, Hence, Horoscope, Later, Long-range, Offing, Ovist, Prospect, To-be, Tomorrow

Fuzz(y) Crepe, Fluff, Foggy, Lint, Pig, Policeman

G g

G George, Golf, Gravity

Gab(ble), Gabbler Chatter, Dovercourt, Jabber, Pie, Prattle, Talkative, Yabber

Gable Clark, Corbie, Jerkinhead, Pediment

Gabriel Angel, Walter

Gad(about), Gadzooks Gallivant, Lud, Rover, Sbuddikins, Sdeath, Traipse, Trape(s), Viretot

Gadfly Breese, Breeze, Brize

Gadget Appliance, Artifice, Device, Dingbat, Dingus, Doodad, Doodah, Doofer, Doohickey, Gismo, Gizmo, Gubbins, Hickey, Jimjam, Notion, Possum, Utility, Widget

Gadolinium Gd

Gadzooks Odsbobs

Gaekwar Baroda

Gael(ic) Celt, Erse, Goidel, Teague

Gaff(e), Gaffer Bêtise, Blague, Bloomer, Error, Floater, Foreman, Gamble, Game, Solecism, Spar, Throat, Trysail, Yokel

Gag Brank, Choke, Estoppel, Joke, Pong, Prank, Silence(r), Smother, Wheeze

Gage Challenge, Pawn, Pledge, Plum

▶ **Gaiety** see GAY

Gain(s), Gained Acquire, Appreciate, Attain, Avail, Boot, Bunce, Carry, Catch, Chevisance, Clean-up, Derive, Earn, Edge, Fruit, ➤ GET, Good, Gravy, Land, Lucre, Obtain, Plus, Profit, Purchase, Rake-off, Reap, Thrift, Use, Velvet, Wan, Win, Windfall, Winnings

Gainsay Contradict, Deny

Gait Bearing, Canter, Pace, Piaffer, Rack, Trot

Gaiter(s) Cootikin, Cu(i)tikin, Gambado, Hogger, Legging(s), Puttee, Spat(s), Spattee, Spatterdash, Vamp

Gala Banquet, Festival

Galaxy Heaven, Magellanic cloud, Milky Way, Radio, Seyfert, Spiral, Stars

Galbanum Ferula

Gale Backfielder, Peal, Ripsnorter, Sea turn, Snorter, Squall, Storm, Tempest, Winder

Gall Aleppo, Bedeguar, Bitterness, Canker, Ellagic, Enrage, Fell, Irritate, Mad-apple, Maugre, Maulgre, Oaknut, Sage-apple, Sandiver, ➤ SAUCE, Tacahout

Gallant(ry) Admirer, Amorist, Beau, Blade, Buck, Cavalier, Chevalier, Cicisbeo, Courtliness, Lover, Prow, Romeo, Sigisbeo, Spark, Valiance

Galleon Galloon, Ghostly, Ship

Gallery Accademia, Alure, Amphitheatre, Arcade, Assommoir, Belvedere, Brattice, Bretasche, Bretesse, Brettice, Brow, Catacomb, Celestials, Cupola, Dedans, Fly, Gods, Hayward, Hermitage, Jube, Loft, Loggia, Louvre, Machicolation, Mine, Minstrel, National, Pawn, Pinacotheca, Pinakothek, Pitti, Prado, Press, Rogues', Serpentine, Shooting, Stranger's, Tate, Terrace, Triforium, Uffizi, Veranda(h), Whispering, Whitechapel

Galley Bireme, Bucentaur, Caboose, Drake, Galliot, Kitchen, Lymphad, Penteconter, Proof

Gallimaufry Macedoine, Mishmash, Stew

Gallium Ga

Gallon(s) Bushel, Cong(ius), Cran, Hin, Imperial

Gallop(er) Aide, Canter, Career, Lope, Trot, Wallop

Gallows Bough, Cheat, Drop, Dule-tree, Forks, Gibbet, Nub, Nubbing-cheat, Patibulary, Tree, Tyburn, Tyburn-tree, Widow, Woodie

Gallows-bird Crack-halter, Crack-hemp, Crack-rope

Gall-stone Cholelith

Galore Abundance, A gogo, Plenty, Whisky

Galosh Overshoe, Rubber

Galvanise Ginger, Rouse, Zinc

Gam Pod

Gambit Manoeuvre, Ploy, Stratagem

Gamble(r), Gambling (place) Adventure, Back, Bet, Casino, Chance, Dice(-play), Flutter, Gaff, Hold, Jeff, Martingale, Mise, Pari-mutuel, Parlay, Partingale, Piker, Plunge, Policy, Punter, Raffle, Reno, Risk, Roulette, School, Spec, Speculate, Speculator, Sweep(stake), Throw(ster), Tinhorn, Tombola, Tontine, Two-up, ➤ WAGER

Gambol Frisk, Frolic

Game(s) All-fours, Angel-beast, Baccarat, Badminton, Bagatelle, Barley-brake, Base, Ba'spiel, Basketball, Basset, Battledore, Bezique, Billiards, Bingo, Black-cock, Black-jack, Bocce, Boston, Bouillotte, Boules, Bowls, Braemar, Brag, Broomball, Bull, Bumble-puppy, Bumpball, Camogie, Canasta, Candlepins, Canfield, Cards, Cas(s)ino, Cat, Catch, Catch-the-ten, Cat's cradle, Charade, Chemin de fer, Chemmy, Chess, Chouette, Cinch, Clumps, Codille, Commonwealth, Computer, Conkers, Consequences, Coon-can, Cottabus, Crambo, Crap(s), Cribbage, Croquet, Curling, Darts, Decider, Deck tennis, Diabolo, Dibs, Doubles, Ducks and drakes, Dumb Crambo, Duplicate, Ecarté, Eo, Euchre, Fa-fi, Fair, Fantan, Faro, Fillipeen, Fivepins, Five-stones, Fives, Football, Footer, Forfeits, Foursome, Frame, Gallant, Gammon, Gammy, Gerrymander, Gleek, Go, Gobang, Goff, Golf, Gomoku, Goose, Grab, Gutsy, Halma, Handball, Handicap, Handy-dandy, Hangman, Highland, Hob, Hockey, Hoopla, Hopscotch, Horseshoes, House, Hurley, Hurling, In-and-In, Intrepid, I-spy, Isthmian, Jacks(tones), Jackstraws, Jai Alai, Jeu, Jingo-ring, Jukskei, Kabaddi, Keeno, Keno, Kill, Kino, Kitcat, Klondike, Klondyke, Knurr-spell, Korfball, Laik, ➤ LAME, Lansquenet, Lanterloo, Leapfrog, Level-coil, Loo, Loto, Lottery, Lotto, Ludo, Lurch, Mahjong(g), Main, Mancala, Marbles, Matador, Match, Matrimony, Maw, Merel(l), Meril, Mistigris, Monopoly®,

Monte, Mor(r)a, Muggins, Mumchance, Nap, Nemean, Netball, Newmarket, Nim, Ninepins, Nintendo®, Noddy, Novum, Octopush, Old Maid, Olympic, Omber, Ombre, On, One-and-thirty, Pachinko, Pachisi, Paddleball, Paintball, Pall-mall, Pallone, Palm, Pam, Paralympic, Parcheesi®, Parlour, Pastance, Patience, PE, Peekabo(o), Pelmanism, Pelota, Penneech, Penneeck, Penuchle, Petanque, Pharaoh, Phillipina, Phillipine, Philopoena, Pinball, Ping-pong, Pinochle, Pintable, Piquet, Pit, Pitch and toss, Plafond, Play, Plaything, Poker, Polo, Pool, Pope Joan, Postman's knock, Preference, Primero, Prisoner's base, Punchball, Put(t), Pythian, Quadrille, Quidditch®, Quino, Quinze, Quoits, Rackets, Racquetball, Raffle, Reversi(s), Ring-taw, Rolypoly, Roque, Rouge et noir, RU, Roulette, Rounders, Rubber, Ruff, Rummy, Sancho-pedro, Scat, Scrabble®, Seven-up, Shinny, Shinty, Shogi, Shove-halfpenny, Shovelboard, Shuffleboard, Singles, Skat, Skittles, Slam, Slapjack, Snap, Snip-snap-snorum, Snooker, Soccer, Socker, Softball, Solitaire, Solo, Span-farthing, Speculation, Sphairee, Spillikins, Spoilfive, Spoof, Sport, Squail, Square, Squash, Stoolball, Subbuteo®, Swy, Tablanette, Tag, Tarok, Tarot, Taws, Tchoukball, Teetotum, Thimblerig, Tick-tack-toe, Three-card monte, Tiddlywinks, Tie-break, Tig, Tip-and-run, Tipcat, Tray-trip, Tred(r)ille, Trente-et-quarante, Tric(k)-trac(k), Troll-madam, Troll-my-dame(s), Trou-madame, Trugo, Twenty-one, Two-up, Uckers, Verquere, Verquire, Video, Vie, Vigoro, Vingt(-et)-un, Vint, Volley-ball, Wall, War, Whisk, Whist, Willing, Word

Game, Game birds Bag, Fowl, Grouse, Guan, Hare, Meat, Partridge, Pheasant, Prairie chicken, Ptarmigan, Quail, ➤ QUARRY, Rype(r), Snipe, Spatchcock, Woodcock

Gamekeeper Velveteen, Venerer, Warrener

Gaming place Bucket-shop, Casino, Saloon, Table

Gammerstang Taupie, Tawpie

Gammon Baloney, Bilge, Tosh

Gamut Compass, Range

Gander Airport, Look-see

Gandhi Mahatma

Gang Band(itti), Bing, Canaille, Chain, Coffle, Core, Crew, Crue, Elk, Go, Horde, Mob, Nest, Outfit, Pack, Posse, Press, Push, Ratpack, Tribulation, Troop, Yardie

Gangrene Canker, Phaged(a)ena, Sphacelate, Thanatosis

Gangster Bandit, Capone, Crook, Hatchet-man, Highbinder, Hood, Mafioso, Ochlocrat, Skollie, Skolly, Yakuza, Yardie

Gangway Brow, Catwalk, Road

Gannet Booby, Guga, Solan(d)

Gantry Elmer

Ganymede Cupper

▶ **Gaol(er)** see JAIL(ER)

Gap Belfort, Breach, Chasm, Chink, Credibility, Day, Diastema, Embrasure, F-hole, Flaw, Fontanel(le), Gender, Generation, Hair-space, Hiatus, Hole, Interlude, Interstice, Kirkwood, Lacunae, Lin(n), Loophole, M(e)use, Mews,

Muset, Musit, Opening, Ostiole, Pass, Rest, Shard, Sherd, Slap, ➤ SPACE, Spark, Street, Synapse, Trade

Gape(r), Gaping Comber, Dehisce, Fatiscent, Gant, Ga(u)p, Gerne, Hiant, Mya, Rictal, Rictus, Ringent, Rubberneck, Stare, Yawn, Yawp

Garage Carport, Chopshop, Hangar, Lock-up

Garb Apparel, Costume, Gear, Gere, Guise, Ihram, Invest, Leotard, Raiment, Toilet

Garbage Bunkum, Junk, Refuse, Rubbish, Trash

Garble Edit, Jumble, Muddle

▷ **Garble** may indicate an anagram

Garden(ing), Gardens Arbour, Area, Babylon(ian), Bagh, Bear, Beer, Botanic, Chinampa, Colegarth, Cottage, Covent, Cremorne, Dig, Eden, Erf, Floriculture, Garth, Gethsemane, Hanging, Hesperides, Hoe, Kailyard, Kew, Kitchen, Knot, Lyceum, Monastery, NJ, Olitory, Paradise, Pleasance, Plot, Ranelagh, Rockery, Roji, Roof, Rosary, Rosery, Tea, Tilth, Topiary, Tuileries, Vauxhall, Welwyn, Yard, Zoological

Gardener Adam, Capability Brown, Jekyll, Landscape, Mali, Mallee, Mary, Nurseryman, Tradescant

Gargantuan Enormous, Huge, Pantagruel, Vast

Gargle Gargarism, Mouthwash

Gargoyle Waterspout

Garish Criant, Flashy, Gaudy, Glitzy, Jazzy, Painty, Roary, Rorie, Rory

Garland Anadem, Anthology, Chaplet, Coronal, Crants, Festoon, Lei, Stemma, Toran(a), Vallar(y), Wreath

Garlic Clove, Elephant, Rams(on), Rocambole

Garment Aba(ya), Abba, Alb, Ao dai, Barrow, Blouse, Blouson, Bodice, Bolero, B(o)ub(o)u, B(o)urk(h)a, Burnous, Burqa, Busuuti, Caftan, Catsuit, Cerements, Chador, Chasuble, Chimer, Cilice, Cimar, Clout, Cote-hardie, Cotta, Cover-slut, Dalmatic, Dashiki, Dirndl, Djibbah, Doublet, Dreadnought, Ephod, Exomion, Exomis, Fanon, Foundation, Gambeson, Habiliment, Habit, Hand-me-down, Himation, Ihram, Izar, Jeistiecor, Jibbah, Jubbah, Jumpsuit, Kaftan, Kanzu, Kaross, K(h)anga, Kittel, Levis, Lingerie, Mandilion, Mandylion, Mantle, Negligee, Pallium, Pantihose, Pantyhose, Partlet, Pelerine, Pelisse, Peplos, Pilch, Rail, Ramée, Rami(e), Rochet, Rompers, Ruana, Salopettes, Sanbenito, Sari, Sarong, Scapular, Singlet, Slop, Soutane, Step-in, Stola, Stole, Surcoat, Surplice, Swimsuit, Tabard, Tank-top, Thong, Togs, Tunic(le), Unitard, Vestment, Vesture, Waistcoat, Weed, Woolly, Zephyr

Garnet Alabandine, Almandine, Andradite, Carbuncle, Demantoid, Essonite, Grossular(ite), Melanite, Pyrenite, Pyrope, Rhodolite, Spessartite, Topazolite, Uvarovite

Garnish Adorn, Attach, Crouton, Decorate, Gremolata, Lard, Parsley, Sippet, Staffage

Garret Attic, Loft, Sol(l)ar, Sol(l)er

Garrison Fort, Man, Presidial

Garrulity, Garrulous Babbling, Gas, Gushy, Windbag

Garter Bowyang, Crewel, Flash, G(r)amash, Gramosh, Nicky-tam

Gary Glitter, Player

Gas(sy) Acetylene, Afterdamp, Air, Ammonia, Argon, Argonon, Arsine, Blah(-blah), Blather, Blether, Bottle(d), Butadiene, Butane, Butene, BZ, Calor®, Chat, Chlorine, Chokedamp, Chrom(at)osphere, CN, Coal(-oil), Crypton, CS, Cyanogen, Damp, Diphosgene, Emanation, Ethane, Ethene, Ether(ion), Ethine, Ethylene, Firedamp, Flatulence, Flatus, Flocculus, Flue, Fluorin(e), Formaldehyde, Gabnash, Greenhouse, H, Halitus, He, Helium, Hot-air, Hydrogen, Ideal, Inert, Jaw, Ketene, Kr(ypton), Laughing, Lewisite, Lurgi, Mace®, Marsh, Methane, Mofette, Mustard, Natural, Ne, Neon, Nerve, Nitrogen, Noble, Nox, O, Olefin(e), Orotund, Oxyacetylene, Oxygen, Perfect, Petrol, Phosgene, Phosphene, Plasma, Poison, Prate, Propane, Propellant, Propylene, Propene, Protostar, Radon, Rare, RN, Sarin, Silane, Solfatara, Stibine, Sulphur dioxide, Synthesis, Tabun, ➤ TALK, Tear, Therm, Thoron, Town, V-agent, Vapour, Waffle, Water, Whitedamp, ➤ WIND, Xenon, Yackety-yak

Gasbag Blimp, Envelope, Prattler

Gas-mask Inhaler

Gascon(ade) Boast, Braggart, Skite

Gash Incise, Rift, Score, Scotch, ➤ SLASH

Gasp(ing) Anhelation, Apn(o)ea, Chink, Exhale, Kink, Oh, Pant, Puff, Singult, Sob

Gast(e)ropod Cowrie, Cowry, Dorididae, Euthyneura, Fusus, Glaucus, Harp-shell, Limpet, Mollusc, Murex, Nerita, Nerite, Nudibranch, Opisthobranch, Ormer, Periwinkle, Purpura, Sea-ear, Sea-hare, Slug, Snail, Spindle-shell, Stromb, Top, Turbo, Whelk

Gate(s), Gateway Alley, Brandenburg, Caisson, Crowd, Decuman, Entry, Erpingham, Golden, Head, Kissing, Lych, Menin, Nor, Pearly, Portal, Portcullis, Postern, Propylaeum, Propylon, Pylon, Starting, Toran(a), Torii, Traitor's, Turnstile, Wicket, Yate, Yet(t)

Gatecrash(er) Interloper, Intrude, Ligger, Sorn, Unasked

Gatepost Sconcheon, Scontion, Scuncheon

▷ **Gateshead** may indicate 'g'

Gather(ed), Gathering Amass, Assemble, Bee, Braemar, Cluster, Collate, ➤ COLLECT, Colloquium, Concourse, Conglomerate, Congregate, Conventicle, Corral, Corroboree, Crop, Crowd, Cull, Eve, Fest, Function, Gabfest, Galaxy, Glean, Glomerate, Harvest, Hootenanny, Hotchpot, Hui, Husking, In, Infer, Jamboree, Kommers, Lek, Lirk, Love-in, Pleat, Plica, Plissé, Pucker, Raft, Rake, Reef, Reunion, Round-up, Rout, Ruche, Ruff(le), Salon, Shindig, Shir(r), Shoal, Shovel, Singsong, Social, Spree, Take, Tuck, Vindemiate, Vintage, Wappensc(h)aw

Gauche Awkward, Clumsy, Farouche, Graceless

Gaudy Criant, Fantoosh, Flash, Garish, Glitz(y), Meretricious, Tacky, Tinsel

Gauge Alidad(e), Anemometer, ➤ ASSESS, Bourdon, Broad, Calibre, Denier, Etalon, Estimate, Evaluate, Feeler, Judge, Loading, Manometer, Marigraph, Measure, Meter, Narrow, Ombrometer, Oncometer, Pressure,

Rate, Scantle, Size, Standard, Strain, Tape, Tonometer, Tram, Tread, Udometer

Gauguin Paul

Gaul Cisalpine

Gaunt Haggard, Lancaster, Lean, Randletree, Ranneltree, Rannletree, Rantletree, Rawbone, ➤ THIN, Wasted

Gauntlet C(a)estus, Gantlope

Gauss G

Gautama Buddha

Gauze, Gauzy Gas mantle, Gossamer, Muslin, Sheer, Tiffany

Gawky Clumsy, Cow, Gammerstang

Gay, Gaiety Blithe, Bonny, Boon, Buxom, Camp, Canty, Daffing, Debonair, Festal, Frolic, Gallant, Gladsome, Glee, Gordon, Grisette, Inverted, Jolly, Lightsome, May, Merry, Nitid, Rackety, Riant, Rorty, Tit(t)upy, Volatile

Gaze Moon, Pore, Stare

Gazelle Ariel, Gerenuk, Goa, Mhorr, Mohr, Tabitha, Thomson's

Gazette London, Paper

Gear(ing) Attire, Bags, Bevel, Clobber, Dérailleur, Differential, Draw, Duds, Engrenage, Fab, Finery, Granny, Harness, Helical, Hypoid, Involute, Kit, Lay-shaft, Mesh, Neutral, Overdrive, Ratio, Rig, Rudder, Sun and planet, Synchromesh, ➤ TACKLE, Top, Trim, Worm(-wheel)

Gecko Tokay

Gee Horse, Hump, My, Reist, Sulk, Tout, Towt, Urge

Geiger-counter Scintillator

Geisha Maiko

Gel Pectin, Silica

Gelatine, Gelatinous Calipash, Collagen, Glutinous, Isinglass, Tunicin

Geld(ing) Castrate, Lib, Neuter, Spado

Geller Uri

Gem Agate, Alexandrite, Almandine, Amazonite, Andradite, Asteria, Baguette, Bloodstone, Boule, Brilliant, Briolette, Cabochon, Cachalong, Cairngorm, Carnelian, Cat's eye, Chrysolite, Chrysoprase, Cornelian, Cymophane, Demantoid, Diamante, Diamond, Dumortierite, Emerald, Hawk's eye, Heliodor, Hessonite, Hiddenite, Hyacinth, ID, Idaho, Indicolite, Iolite, Jacinth, Jargo(o)n, Jasper, Jaspis, ➤ JEWEL, Kunzite, Lapis lazuli, Ligure, Marquise, Melanite, Menilite, Moonstone, Morganite, Pearl, Peridot(e), Prase, Pyrope, Rhinestone, Rhodolite, Rubellite, Ruby, Sapphire, Sard, Sardonyx, Scarab, Scarabaeoid, Smaragd, Solitaire, Sparkler, Starstone, Stone, Tiger's eye, Tourmaline, Turquoise, Verd antique

Gemination, Gemini Diplogenesis, Twins

Gen Info

Gendarme Flic

Gender Form, Sex

Gene(tics) Allele, Allelomorph, Anticodon, Codon, Creation, Designer, Disomic, Episome, Exon, Factor, Genome, Hereditary, Heterogamy,

Holandric, Hologynic, Intron, Jumping, Lysenkoism, Mendel, Michurinism, Muton, Operon, Selfish, Terminator, Weismannism

Genealogist, Genealogy Armory, Family, Heraldry, Line, Pedigree, Seannachie, Seannachy, Sennachie, Whakapapa

General Agamemnon, Agricola, Agrippa, Alcibiades, Allenby, Antigonus, Antipater, Ataman, Booth, Broad, Boulanger, C in C, Common, Communal, Conde, Cornwallis, Crassus, Current, Custer, De Gaulle, De Wet, Diadochi, Eclectic, Ecumenical, Election, Franco, Gamelin, Gen, GOC, Gordon, Grant, Hadrian, Hannibal, Holofernes, Ike, Inspector, Joshua, Kitchener, Lafayette, Lee, Leslie, Macarthur, Main, Marian, Marshall, Montcalm, Napier, Napoleon, Omnify, Overall, Overhead, Patton, Pershing, Prevailing, Pompey, Raglan, Regulus, Rife, Rommel, Scipio, Sherman, Shrapnel, Smuts, Stilwell, Strategist, Tom Thumb, Turenne, ➤ UNIVERSAL, Vague, Wide, Wolfe

Generate, Generation, Generator Abiogenetic, Age, Beat, Beget, Breeder, Charger, Create, Dynamo, Epigon, Father, Fuel-cell, House, Kipp, Lost, Magneto, Olds, Sire, Spawn, Stallion, Van de Graaff, Yield

Generosity, Generous Bounty, Charitable, Free-handed, Handsome, Kind, Largess(e), ➤ LAVISH, Liberal, Magnanimous, Munificent, Noble(-minded), Open, Open-handed, Open-hearted, Philanthropic, Plump, Profuse, Sporting

➤ **Genetic** see GENE

Geneva(n) Calvinist, Gin, Hollands

Genial(ity) Affable, Amiable, Benign, Bluff, Bonhomie, Human, Mellow

Genie Mazikeen, Shedeem

Genipap Lana

Genital(s) Ballocks, Bol(l)ix, Bollocks, Box, Crack, Cunt, Fanny, Minge, Muff, Naff, Private parts, Privates, Pubes, Pudendum, Pussy, Quim, Secrets, Tail, Twat, Vagina, Vulva, Yoni

Genius Agathodaimon, Daemon, Einstein, Engine, Flash, Inspiration, Ka, Michaelangelo, Numen, Prodigy

Genteel Conish, Polite, Proper, Refined

Gentian Felwort, Violet

Gentile Aryan, Ethnic, Goy, Shi(c)ksa

Gentle Amenable, Amenage, Bland, Clement, Delicate, Gradual, Grub, Light, Maggot, Mansuete, Mild, Tame, Tender

Gentleman(ly), Gentlemen Amateur, Baboo, Babu, Caballero, Cavalier, Duni(e)wassal, Dunniewassal, Esq(uire), Gemman, Gemmen, Ja(u)nty, Knight, Messrs, Milord, Mister, Mr, Nob, Proteus, Ritter, Runner, Rye, Sahib, Senor, Signor, Sir, Sirra(h), Smuggler, Squire, Sri, Stalko, Stir(rah), Tea, Toff, Von, Yeoman

Gentry County, Landed, Quality, Squir(e)age

Gents Bog, John, Lav, Loo

Genuflexion Bend, Curts(e)y, Kowtow, Salaam

Genuine Authentic, Bona-fide, Dinkum, Dinky-di, Echt, Frank, Heartfelt, Intrinsic, Jonnock, Kosher, Legit(imate), Nain, Pucka, Pukka, Pure, Pusser,

➤ REAL, Real McCoy, Right, Simon-Pure, Sincere, Square, Sterling, True, Veritable

Genus Class, -ia, Mustela

Geode Druse

Geographer, Geography Chorography, Hakluyt, Mercator, Pausanias, Strabo

Geology Self-rock, Tectonics

Geometer, Geometrician, Geometry Conics, Euclid(ean), Moth, Riemannian, Solid, Topologist

George(s) Autopilot, Best, Borrow, Eliot, Farmer, Lloyd, Orwell, Pilot, Sand

Georgia(n) Ga, Hanover, Iberian

Geraint Knight

Geranium Dove's foot, Stork's bill

Gerbil Jird

Germ Bacteria, Bug, Klebsiella, Seed, Spirilla, Strep, Virus, Zyme

German(y) Al(e)main(e), Alemannic, Angle, Bavarian, Blood-brother, Boche, Cimbri, Composer, Cousin, Frank, Fritz, G, Goth, Habsburg, Hans, Hapsburg, Herr, Hessian, High, Hun, Jerry, Jute, Kaiser, Kraut, Landgrave, Low, Lusation, Neanderthal, Ossi, Ostrogoth, Otto, Palsgrave, Plattdeutsch, Pruce, Prussian, Salic, Saxon, Tedesco, Teuton(ic), Vandal, Visigoth, Wessi

Germane Apt, ➤ PERTINENT, Relevant

Germanium Ge

Germ-free Aseptic

Germinate Grow, Pullulate, Sprout

Gesticulate, Gesticulation, Gesture(s) Ameslan, Beck(on), Ch(e)ironomy, Fico, Gest(e), Mime, Motion, Mudra, Salute, ➤ SIGN, Signal, Spook, Token

Get, Get by, Get On Acquire, Advance, Aggravate, Annoy, Attain, Become, Brat, Bring, Capture, Cop, Cope, Derive, Fet(ch), Fette, Gain, Gee, Learn, Make, Manage, Milk, Net, Noy, ➤ OBTAIN, Peeve, Procure, Progress, Reach, Realise, Rile, Roil, Secure, See, Sire, Twig, Understand, Win

Getaway Escape, Vamoose

▷ **Getting** may indicate an anagram

Getting better Convalescing, Improving, Lysis

Get-up Tog(s)

Geum Avens

Gewgaw Bagatelle, Bauble, Doit, Tat, Trifle

Geyser Soffioni, Therm

Ghanaian Ashanti, Fantee, Fanti, Tshi, Twi

Ghastly Gash, Grim, Hideous, Lurid, Macabre, Pallid, Welladay, White

Ghetto Barrio, Slum

Ghost(ly) Acheri, Apparition, Apport, Caddy, Chthonic, Duende, Duppy, Eerie, Eery, Fantasm, Fetch, Gytrash, Haunt, Hint, Jumbie, Jumby, Larva(e), Lemur, Malmag, No'canny, Paraclete, Pepper's, Phantasm(agoria),

Phantom, Revenant, Sampford, Shade, Shadow, Spectre, ➤ SPIRIT, Spook, Trace, Truepenny, Umbra, Vision, Visitant, Waff, Wraith

Ghoul Fiend

GI Joe, Yankee

Giant(ess) Alcyoneus, Alifanfaron, Anak, Antaeus, Archiloro, Argus, Ascapart, Balan, Balor, Bellerus, Blunderbore, Bran, Briareus, Brobdingnagian, Cacus, Colbrand, Colbronde, Colossus, Coltys, Cormoran, Cottus, Cyclop(e)s, Despair, Enceladus, Ephialtes, Eten, Ettin, Ferragus, Gabbara, Galligantus, Gargantua, Géant, Gefion, Geirred, Gigantic, Gog, Goliath, Grim, Harapha, Hrungnir, Hymir, Idris, Jotun(n), Jumbo, Krasir, Lestrigon, Leviathan, Magog, Mammoth, Mimir, Monster, Oak, Og, Ogre, Otus, Pallas, Pantagruel, Patagonian, Polyphemus, Pope, Red, Rounceval, Skrymir, Slaygood, Talos, Talus, Thrym, Titan, Tityus, Tregeagle, Triton, Troll, Tryphoeus, Typhon, Urizen, Utgard, Ymir, Yowie

Gibberish Claptrap, Double Dutch, Greek, Jargon

Gibbet Gallows, Patibulary, Potence, Ravenstone, Tree

Gibbon(s) Hoolock, Hylobate, Orlando, Siamang, Stanley, Wou-wou, Wow-wow

Gibe Barb, Brocard, Chaff, Fleer, Glike, Jeer, Jibe, Shy, Slant

Gibraltar Calpe

Giddy (girl), Giddiness Dizzy, Fisgig, Fishgig, Fizgig, Giglot, Glaikit, Glaky, Haverel, Hellicat, Hoity-toity, Jillet, Light, Light-headed, Staggers, Sturdy, Turn, Volage(ous), Wheel, Woozy

Gift(s), Gifted Ability, Alms, Aptitude, Bef(f)ana, Bequest, Blessing, Blest, Bonbon, Bonsel(l)a, Boon, Bounty, Charism(a), Congiary, Corban, Covermount, Cumshaw, Dash, Deodate, ➤ DONATION, Etrenne, Fairing, Flair, Foy, Freebie, Gab, Garnish, Godsend, Grant, Han(d)sel, Handout, Hogmanay, Indian, Knack, Koha, Kula, Lagniappe, Largesse, Legacy, Manna, Ne'erday, Nuzzer, Offering, Parting, Potlatch, ➤ PRESENT, Presentation, Prezzie, Propine, Reward, Sop, Talent, Tongues, Windfall

Gig Cart, Dennet, Moze, Whisk(e)y

Gigantic Atlantean, Briarean, Colossal, Goliath, ➤ HUGE, Immense, Mammoth, Rounceval, Titan

Giggle Cackle, Ha, Keckle, Simper, Snigger, Snicker, Tehee, Titter

Gigolo Gallant, Ladykiller, Pimp

Gilbert Bab, Gb, White, WS

Gild(ed), Gilding Checklaton, Embellish, Enhance, Inaurate, Ormolu, S(c)hecklaton, Vermeil

Gill(s) Beard, Branchia, Cart, Ctenidium, Jill, Noggin, Spiracle

Gillman's Aqualung

Gilpin Draper, John, Renowned

Gilt Sow

Gimcrack Gewgaw, Tawdry, Trangam

Gimmick Doodad, Doodah, Hype, Ploy, Ruse, Stunt

Gin Bathtub, Geneva, Genever, Hollands, Juniper, Lubra, Max, Noose, Old Tom, Ruin, Schiedam, Schnapp(s), Sloe, Snare, Springe, Toil, Trap, Trepan, Twankay

Ginger Activist, Amomum, Asarum, Cassumunar, Costus, Curcuma, Galanga(l), Galengale, Galingale, Malaguetta, Nut, Pachak, Pep, Pop, Putchock, Putchuk, Race, Rase, Red(head), Spice, Stem, Turmeric, Zedoary, Zingiber

Gingerbread D(o)um-palm, Lebkuchen, Parkin, Parliament(-cake)

Gingivitis Ulitis

▶ **Gipsy** see GYPSY

Giraffe Camelopard, Okapi

Gird Accinge, Belt, Equip, Quip

Girder Beam, Binder, I-beam, Loincloth, Spar

Girdle Baldric, Center, Cestus, Chastity, Cincture, Cingulum, Corset, Enzone, Hippolyte, Hoop, Mitre, Sash, Surcingle, Surround, Zona, Zone, Zonulet

Girl(s) Backfisch, Ball, Bimbo, Bint, Bird, Bit, Bobby-dazzler, Bohemian, Broad, Burd, Call, Charlie, Chit, Chorus, Coed, Colleen, Crumpet, Cummer, Cutey, Cutie, Cutty, Dam(o)sel, Deb, Dell, Demoiselle, Dish, Doll, Dollybird, Essex, Filly, Fisgig, Fizgig, Flapper, Fluff, Fraulein, Frippet, Gaiety, Gal, Gammerstang, Geisha, Gibson, Gill(et), Gouge, Grisette, Hen, Hoiden, Hoyden, Hussy, Italian, Judy, Kimmer, Kinchinmort, Land, Lass(ock), Lorette, Maid(en), Mauther, Mawr, Mawther, May, Miss(y), Moppet, Mor, Mot, Mousmé, Mousmee, Mystery, Nautch, Number, Nymph(et), Peach, Petticoat, Piece, Pigeon, Popsy, Puss, Quean, Queyn, Quin(i)e, Randy, Senorita, Sheila, Shi(c)ksa, Sis(s), Smock, Tabby, Taupie, Tawpie, Tit, Trull, Wench, Widgie, Wimp

▷ **Girl** may indicate a female name

Girl friend Baby, Chérie, Confidante, Date, Flame, Hinny, Leman, Moll, Peat

Girth Cinch, Compass, Size, Surcingle

Gist Essence, Kernel, ▶ NUB, Pith, Substance

Give, Give up, Giving Abandon, Abstain, Accord, Administer, Afford, Award, Bend, Bestow, Buckle, Cede, Confiscate, Dative, Dispense, Dole, ▶ DONATE, Duck, Elasticity, Enable, Forswear, Gie, Impart, Jack, Largition, Render, Resign, Sacrifice, Sag, Spring, Stop, Tip, Vacate, Yeve

Give-away Freebie, Gift-horse

Given If

Give out Bestow, Dispense, Emit, Exude, Peter

Give over Cease, Lin

Glacial, Glaciation Gunz, Mindel, Riss, Wurm

Glacier Aletsch, Crevasse, Drumline, Fox, Franz-Josef, Iceberg, Ice-cap, Icefall, Moraine, Muir, Riss, Serac, Tasman

Glad(ly), Gladden Cheer, Fain, ▶ HAPPY, Lief, Willing

Glade La(u)nd

Gladiator Retiarius, Spartacus

Glamour(ise), Glamorous Charm, Glitter(ati), Glitz, Halo, It, Prestige, SA, Spell

Glamour girl Cheesecake, Odalisk, Odalisque, Pin-up

Glance Amoret, Argentite, Blink, Browse, Carom(bole), Coup d'oeil, Dekko, Draw, Eld, Eliad, Eye-beam, Galena, Glimpse, Illiad, Inwick, Oeillade, Once-over, Peek, ➤ PEEP, Ray, Redruthite, Ricochet, Scan, Shufti, Shufty, Skellie, Skelly, Snick, Squint, Twire, Vision

Gland Adenoid, Adrenal, Apocrine, Bartholin's, Bulbourethral, Colleterial, Conarium, Cowper's, Crypt, Digestive, Eccrine, Endocrine, Epiphysis, Exocrine, Goitre, Green, Helocrine, Hypophysis, Ink-sac, Lachrymal, Lacrimal, Liver, Lymph, Mammary, Melbomian, Musk-sac, Nectary, Oil, Osmeterium, Ovary, Pancreas, Paranephros, Parathyroid, Parotid, Parotis, Pineal, Pituitary, Pope's eye, Prostate, Prothoracic, Salivary, Scent, Sebaceous, Silk, Suprarenal, Sweat, Tarsel, Testicle, Testis, Thymus, Thyroid, Tonsil, Uropygial, Vesicle

Glanders Farcy

Glandular (trouble) Adenitis

Glare, Glaring Astare, Blare, Dazzle, Flagrant, Garish, Gleam, Glower, Holophotal, Iceblink, Lour, Low(e), Shine, Vivid, Whally

Glass(es), Glassware, Glassy Amen, Ampul(la), Aneroid, Avanturine, Aventurine, Baccara(t), Barometer, Bifocals, Bottle, Brimmer, Bumper, Burning, Calcedonio, Cheval, Cloche, Copita, Coupe, Crookes, Crown, Crystal, Cullet, Cupping, Cut, Dark, Eden, Euphon, Favrile, Field, Flint, Float, Flute, Frigger, Frit, Fulgurite, Glare, Goblet, Goggles, Granny, Ground, Horn-rims, Humpen, Hyaline, Jar, Jena, Jigger, Lalique, Lanthanum, Latticinio, Lead, Lens, Liqueur, Liquid, Lorgnette, Loupe, Lozen(ge), Magma, Magnifying, Metal, Mica, Middy, Milk, Millefiori, Mirror, Monocle, Mousseline, Murr(h)ine, Obsidian, Opaline, Opera, Optical, Pane, Parison, Paste, Pearlite, Pebble, Peeper, Pele, Pele's hair, Perlite, Pince-nez, Pitchstone, Plate, Pon(e)y, Prunt, Psyche, Pyrex®, Quarrel-pane, Quarry, Quartz, Roemer, Rummer, Schmelz, Schooner, Seam, Seidel, Silex, Sleever, Slide, Smalt(o), Snifter, Specs, Spun, Stained, Stein, Stemware, Stone, Strass, Supernaculum, Tachilite, Tachylite, Tachylyte, Tektite, Telescope, Tiffany, Trifocals, Triplex®, Tumbler, Varifocals, Venetian, Vernal, Vita, Vitrail, Vitreous, Vitro-di-trina, Volcanic, Waterford, Wire

Glass-gall Sandiver

Glass-house Conservatory, Orangery

Glassite Sandemania

Glass-maker Annealer, Blower, Glazier, Pontie, Pontil, Ponty, Puntee, Punty

Glaze(d), Glazing Aspic, Ciré, Coat, Eggwash, Film, Flambé, Frit, Glost, Ice, Majolica, Sancai, Slip, Tammy, Temmoku, Velatura

Gleam(ing) Blink, Flash, Glint, Glitter, Gloss, Leme, Light, Ray, Relucent, Sheen, Shimmer, ➤ SHINE

Glean(er) Gather, Harvest, Lease, Stibbler

Glee Exuberance, Joy, Mirth, Song

Glen Affric, Ghyll, Gill, Rushy, Vale

Glib Flip, Slick, Smooth

Glide(away), Glider, Gliding Aquaplane, Coast, Elapse, Float, Illapse, Lapse, Luge, Microlight, Portamento, Sail, Sailplane, Sashay, Scorrendo, Scrieve, Skate, Ski, Skim, Sleek, Slide, Slip, Swim, Volplane

Glimmer Gleam, Glent, Glint, Glow, Inkling, Stime, Styme, Twinkle, Wink

Glimpse Aperçu, Flash, Glance, Glisk, Stime, Styme, Waff, Whiff

Glint Flash, Shimmer, ➤ SPARKLE, Trace, Twinkle

Glisten(ing) Ganoid, Glint, Sheen, Shimmer, ➤ SHINE, Sparkle

Glitter(ing) Clinquant, Garish, Gemmeous, Paillon, Sequin, Spang(le), Sparkle, Tinsel

Gloat(ing) Crow, Drool, Enjoy, Exult, Schadenfreude

Globe, Globule Ball, Bead, Celestial, Drop, Earth, Orb, Shot, Sphear, Sphere

Globulin Legumin, Protein

Gloom(y) Atrabilious, Benight, Blues, Cheerless, Cimmerian, Cloud, Crepuscular, Damp, Dark, ➤ DESPAIR, Dingy, Disconsolate, Dismal, Dool(e), Drab, Drear, Drumly, Dump(s), Dyspeptic, Funereal, Glum, Grey, Louring, Mirk, Misery, Mopish, Morne, Morose, Murk, Obscurity, Overcast, Sable, Sad, Saturnine, Sepulchral, Solein, Solemn, ➤ SOMBRE, Stygian, Tenebrous

Glorification, Glorify Aggrandise, Apotheosis, Avatar, Bless, ➤ EXALT, Halo, Laud, Lionise, Praise, Radiance, Splendour

Glorious, Gloria, Glory Chorale, Grand, Halo, Hosanna, Ichabod, Kudos, Lustre, Magnificent, Nimbus, Strut, Sublime, Twelfth

Glory-pea Kaka-beak, Kaka-bill, Kowhai

Gloss(y) Enamel, Gild, Glacé, Japan, Lustre, Patina, ➤ POLISH, Postillate, Sheen, Sleek, Slick, Slide, Slur, Veneer, Whitewash

Glossary Catalogue, Clavis, Index, K'thibh

Glove Boxing, Cestus, Dannock, Gage, Gauntlet, Kid, Mitten, Oven, Velvet

Glow(ing) Aflame, Ashine, Aura, Bloom, Burn, Calescence, Candent, Candescence, Flush, Foxfire, Gegenschein, Gleam, Halation, Iceblink, Incandescence, Lambent, Leam, Leme, Luculent, Luminesce, Lustre, Phosphorescence, Radiant, Reflet, Rushlight, Shine, Snowblink, Translucent, ➤ WARMTH

Glucin(i)um Gl

Glucose, Glucoside Aesculin, Amygdalin, Dextrose, Digitalin, Indican, Saponin, Solanine

Glue(y) Araldite®, Bee, Cement, Colloidal, Gelatin(e), Ichthyocolla, Isinglass, Paste, Propolis, Size, Spetch

Glum Dour, Livery, Lugubrious, Moody, Morose, Ron, Sombre

Glut Choke, Gorge, Sate, Satiate, Saturate, Surfeit

Gluten, Glutinous Goo, Ropy, Seiten, Sticky, Tar, Viscid, Zymome

Glutton(ous), Gluttony Bellygod, Carcajou, Cormorant, Edacity, Gannet, Gorb, Gourmand, Gulosity, Gutsy, Lurcher, Pig, Ratel, Scoffer, Sin, Trencherman, Trimalchio, Wolverine

Glyceride, Glycerine Ester, Olein

Gnarl(ed) Knot, Knuckly, Knur, Nob

Gnash(ing) Bruxism, Champ, Grate

Gnat Culex, Culicidae, Midge, Mosquito

Gnaw(ing) Corrode, Erode, Fret, Lagomorph, Rodent

Gnome Adage, Bank-man, Chad, Cobalt, Financier, Kobold, Motto, Proverb, Saw, Sprite

Gnostic Archontic, Cainite, Mand(a)ean, Ophite, Sabian, Tsabian, Zabian

Gnu Wildebeest

Go, Going (after, for, off, on, up, etc) Advance, Afoot, Anabasis, Animation, Assail, Attempt, Bash, Bing, Brio, Choof, Clamber, Continuance, Depart, Die, Do, Energy, Fare, Gae, Gang, Gee, Green, Hamba, Hark, Hence, Hie, Imshi, Imshy, Ish, ➤ LEAVE, March, Match, Off, Path, Pep, Perpetual, Ply, Quit, Raik, Repair, Resort, Resume, Run, Scat, Scram, Segue, Shoo, Skedaddle, Snick-up, Sour, Spank, Stab, Success, Transitory, Trine, Try, Turn, Vam(o)ose, Verve, Via, Viable, Wend, Work, Yead, Yede, Yeed, Zap, Zing, Zip

Goad Ankus, Brod, Gad, Incite, ➤ NEEDLE, Prod, Spur, Stimulate, Stimulus, Taunt

Goal Ambition, Basket, Bourn(e), Destination, Dool, Dream, Drop, Dule, End, Ettle, Field, Grail, Hail, Home, Horme, Hunk, Limit, Mission, Moksha, Own, Score, Target, Tip-in, Ultima Thule

Goat(-like) Alpine, Amalthea, Angora, Antelope, Antilope, Billy, Bok, Buck, Caprine, Cashmere, Gate, Goral, Hircine, Ibex, Izard, Kashmir, Kid, Libido, Markhor, Nan(ny), Nubian, Saanen, Sassaby, Serow, Serpent-eater, Steenbok, Steinbock, Tahr, Takin, Tehr, Thar, Toggenburg

Goatsucker Fern-owl, Nightjar

Gob Clot, Mouth, Yap

Gobble Bolt, Devour, Gorge, Gulp, Slubber, Wolf

Gobelin Tapestry

Go-between Broker, Factor, Intermediate, Link, Mediate, Middleman, Pandarus, Pander, Shuttle

Goblet Chalice, Hanap

Goblin Bargaist, Barg(h)est, Bodach, Bogey, Bogle, Bogy, Bucca, Croquemitaine, Empusa, Erl-king, Genie, Gnome, Gremlin, Knocker, Kobold, Lutin, Nis(se), Phooka, Phynnodderree, Pooka, Pouke, Puca, Pug, Red-cap, Red-cowl, Shellycoat, ➤ SPRITE, Troll, Trow

Goby Dragonet

God(s) Abba, Achelous, Adonai, Adrammelech, Aeolus, Aesculapius, Aesir, Agni, Aitu, Alastor, All-father, Alpheus, Amen-ra, Ammon, Amon-ra, Amun, An(u), Anubis, Apis, Apollo, Ares, As, Asclepius, Ashtar, Asshur, Asur, Aten, Atum, Avatar, Baal, Bacchus, Balder, Bel, Bes, Bodhisattva, Boreas, Brag(i), Brahma, Bran, Cabiri, Cama, Chemos(h), Comus, Cupid, D, Dagan, Dagon, Daikoku, Delian, Demogorgon, Deva, Dieu, Dionysus, Dis, Divine, Donar, Elegabalus, Elohim, Eros, Fabulinus, Faun(us), Frey(r), Gad, Gallery, Ganes(h)a, Garuda, Geb, Gracious, Haoma, HaShem, Heimdal, Heimdall(r), Helios, Hephaistos, Hermes, Horus, Hughie, Hymen, Hyperion, Hypnos, Indra, Jagganath, Jah, Janus, Jehovah, Joss,

Juggernaut, Jupiter, Kama, Kami, Karttikaya, Krishna, Kronos, Lar, Liber, Light, Lir, Lludd, Llyr, Loki, Lug(h), Mahadeva, Maker, Mammon, Marduk, Mars, Mercury, Mexitl, Mextli, Mimir, Mithra(s), Moloch, Momus, Morpheus, Mors, Mot, Mulciber, Mumbo-jumbo, Nataraja, Nebo, Neptune, Nereus, Nisroch, Numen, Oannes, Oceanus, Od(d), Odin, Orcus, Ormazd, Ormuzd, Osiris, Pales, Pan, Panisc, Panisk, Pantheon, Penates, Picus, Pluto, Plutus, Poseidon, Priapus, Principle, Promachos, Prometheus, Proteus, Ptah, Quetzalcoati, Quirinus, Ra, Rama, Rameses, Re, Rimmon, Rudra, Sarapis, Sat guru, Saturn, Satyr, Serapis, Set, Setebos, Shamash, Silenus, Silvanus, Siva, Sol, Soma, Somnus, Supreme Being, Surya, Tammuz, Terminus, Teshup, Tetragrammaton, Thamiz, Thammuz, Thor, Thoth, Thunderer, Tin, Titan, Tiu, Tiw, Trimurti, Trinity, Triton, Truth, Tum, Tyr, Unknown, Uranus, Vanir, Varuna, Vertumnus, Vishnu, Vulcan, Wahiguru, Woden, Yahve, Yahwe(h), Zagreus, Zephyrus, Zernebock, Zeus, Zombie

God-bearing Deiparous

Goddess(es) Amphitrite, Aphrodite, Artemis, Aruru, Ashnan, Ashtaroth, Ashtoreth, Astarte, Ate, Athene, Aurora, Bastet, Bellona, Ceres, Cloacina, Cotytto, Cybele, Cynthia, Cyrene, Demeter, Dian(a), Dione, Divine, Durga, Eastre, Eos, Erato, Eris, Eumenides, Flora, Fortuna, Frey(j)a, Frigga, Gaea, Gaia, Ge, Grace, Graeae, Graiae, Hathor, Hecate, Hel, Hera, Hertha, Hestia, Horae, Houri, Hulda(r), Hyaeia, Idalia, Idun(a), Irene, Iris, Ishtar, Isis, Juno, Kali, Kotys, Kotytto, Lakshmi, Leda, Leto, Libitina, Lucina, Luna, Maat, Maut, Minerva, Mnemosyne, Muse, Mut, Nemesis, Nike, Norn, Nox, Nyx, Ops, Pales, Pallas, Parcae, Parvati, Pele, Phoebe, Pomona, Proserpina, Proserpine, Rhea, Sabrina, Satyra, Selene, Semele, Strenia, Tanit, Tellus, Tethys, Thea, Themis, Thetis, Tyche, Valkyrie, Venus, Vesta, Walkyrie

Godfather, Godmother Capo, Cummer, Gossip, Kimmer, Rama, Sponsor, Woden

Godless Agnostic, Atheistic, Atheous, Impious, Profane

Godly Deist, Devout, Holy, Pious

Godown Hong

God-willing Deo volente, DV

Go-getter Arriviste, Hustler

Goggle(s) Snow-eyes, Stare

Going wrong Aglee, Agley, Misfiring

▷ **Going wrong** may indicate an anagram

Goitre Exophthalmic, Graves' disease, Struma

Gold(en) Age, Amber, Apple, Ass, Au, Auriferous, Bough, Bull, Bullion, California, Doubloon, Dutch, Eagle, Electron, Electrum, Emerods, Filigree, Fleece, Fool's, Gate, Handshake, Hind, Horde, Horn, Ingot, Leaf, Lingot, Moidore, Mosaic, Muck, Nugget, Oaker, Obang, Ochre, Ophir, Or, Oreide, Ormolu, Oroide, Pistole, Placer, Pyrites, Red, Reef, Rolled, Silence, Sol, Standard, Stubborn, Talmi, Tolosa, Treasury, White, Yellow

Gold-digger Forty-niner, Prospector

Goldfield Rand

Goldfinch Charm, Chirm, Redcap

Goldsmith Cellini, Fabergé, Oliver

Golf (ball) Clock, Gutta, Matchplay, Repaint

Golfer Alliss, Braid, Cotton, Faldo, Hogan, Pivoter, Rees, Roundsman, Seve, Snead, Teer, Trevino, Wolstenholme, Yipper

Golly Crumbs, Gosh

Gondolier Balloonist, Bargee

Gone Ago, Defunct, Napoo, Out, Past, Ygo(e), Yod

▷ **Gone off** may indicate an anagram

Gone west Had it

Gong Bell, DSO, Medal, Tam-tam, VC

Goo Gleet, Gunge, Poise, Ulmin

Good(ness), Goody-goody Agathodaimon, Angelic, Bad, Bein, Benefit, Bon, Bonzer, Bosker, Blesses, Bounty, Brod, Budgeree, Canny, Castor, Coo, Cool, Dab, Dow, Enid, Estimable, Fantabulous, First-class, G, Gear, Gosh, Guid, Humdinger, Lois, Lor, Nobility, ➤ NO GOOD, Pi, Plum, Proper, Purler, Rectitude, Riddance, Right, Rum, Salutary, Samaritan, Sanctity, Slap-up, Smashing, Spiffing, St, Suitable, Tollol, Topping, Valid, Virtue, Virtuous, Weal, Welfare, Whacko, Wholesome, Worthy

Goodbye Addio, Adieu, Adios, Aloha, Apopemptic, Arrivederci, Cheerio, Ciao, Congé, Farewell, Hooray, Hooroo, Sayonara, Tata, Toodle-oo, Toodle-pip, Vale

Good evening Den

Goodfellow Brick, Puck, Robin, Samaritan, Worthy

Good-for-nothing Bum, Donnat, Donnot, Dud, Idler, Layabout, Lorel, Lorrell, Losel, Napoo, Sca(l)lawag, Scallywag, Scant o'grace, Sculpin, Shot-clog, Useless, Vaurien, Waff, Waster, Wastrel

Good Friday Parasceve

Good-looking Bon(n)ie, Bonny, Bonwie, Comely, Fair, Handsome, Personable, Pretty, Wally

Good-nature(d) Amiable, Bonhomie, Kind

Good news Evangel

Good number Thr(e)ave

Good order Eutaxy, Shipshape

Goods Bona, Brown, Cargo, Durables, Fancy, Flotsam, Freight, Futures, Gear, Insight, Ironware, Lagan, Lay-away, Line, Property, Sparterie, Truck, Wares, White

Goodwill Amity, Bonhom(m)ie, Favour, Gree

Goon Secombe, Sellers

Goose Anserine, Barnacle, Brent, Canada, Daftie, Ember, Gander, Gannet, Greylag, Grope, Hawaiian, Idiot, Juggins, Magpie, Nene, Quink, Roger, Silly, Simpleton, Skein, Snow, Solan, Strasbourg, Stubble, Team, Wav(e)y, Wawa, Whitehead

Gooseberry Cape, Chaperon(e), Chinese, Detrop, Fool, Gog, Groser(t), Groset, Grossart, Grozer, Kiwi, Physalis, Tomato

Gooseflesh Horripilation

Goosefoot Allgood, Amarantaceae, Beet, Blite, Fat-hen, Mercury, Orache, Saltbush

Gooseherd Quill-driver

Gopher Camass-rat, Minnesota

Gordian Knot

Gordon Chinese, Flash, Rioter

Gore Blood, Cloy, Gair, Horn

Gorge(s) Abyss, Barranca, Barranco, Canyon, Chasm, Cheddar, Cleft, Couloir, Cram, Defile, Donga, Flume, Gap, Ghyll, Glut, Grand Canyon, Grand Coulee, Gulch, Khor, Kloof, Lin(n), Nala, Nalla(h), Nulla(h), Olduvai, Overeat, Pass, Ravine, Staw, ➤ STUFF, Throat, Tire, Tums, Valley, Yosemite

Gorgeous Grand, Splendid, Superb

Gorgon Euryale, Medusa, Ogress, Stheno

➤ **Gorilla** see MONKEY

Gorse Broom, Furze, Gosse, Ulex, Whin

Gosh Begad, Begorra, Blimey, Cor, Gadzooks, Gee, Gum, Lor, My, Odsbobs, Odso

Gospel(ler) Creed, Diatessaron, Evangel, Fact, John, Kerygma, Luke, Mark, Matthew, Nicodemus, Synoptic, Truth, Waldensian

Gossamer(y) Araneous, Byssoid, Cobwebby, Gauzy

Gossip Ana(s), Aunt, Backbite, Cackle, Cat, Causerie, Chat, Chin, Chitchat, Clash, Claver, Cleck, Clish-clash, Clishmaclaver, Confab, Coze, Crack, Cummer, Dirt, Flibbertigibbet, Gab(nash), Gabfest, Gas, Gup, Hen, Jaw, Loose-tongued, Maundrel, Nashgab, Natter, Noise, On dit, Pal, Personalist, Prattle, Quidnunc, Rumour, Scandal(monger), Schmooze, Scuttlebutt, Shmoose, Shmooze, Tabby(cat), Talk(er), Tattle, Tibby, Tittle(-tattle), Twattle, Yatter, Yenta

Got Gat, Obtained

Goth(ic) Alaric, Moesia

Gothamite Abderian, New Yorker

Gouge Chisel, Groove, Scoop

Gourd Bottle, Calabash, Courgette, Guiro, Loofa, Melon, Monkeybread, Pumpkin, Squash, Zucchini

Gourmand, Gourmet Apicius, ➤ EPICURE, Gastronome, Gastrosopher, Lickerish, Table, Trencherman, Ventripotent

Gout Chiragra, Hamarthritis, Podagra, Taste, Tophus

Govern(or), Government Adelantado, Administer, Ag(h)a, Agricola, Alderman, Amban, Amman, Amtman, Autarchy, Autocrat, Autonomy, Bahram, Ban, Beehive, Beg, Beglerbeg, Bencher, Bey, Bridler, Bureaucracy, Burgrave, Cabinet, Caretaker, Castellan, Catapan, Cham, Circar, Classics, Coalition, Command, Commonweal, Condiminium, Congress, Constable, Constitution, Consulate, Cybernetic, Darogha, Dey, Diarchy, Dinarchy, Dominate, Duarchy, Dulocracy, Duumvirate, Dyarchy, Dynast, Earl, Empery, Eparch, Escapement, Ethnarch, Exarch, Federal, G, Gauleiter, Gerontocracy, Gov, Grieve, Gubernator, Hagiocracy, Hague, Hajjaz, Hakim, Harmost, HE, Helm, Hierocracy, Honcho, Hospodar, Ins, Inspector, Isocracy, Junta, Kaimakam, Kakistocracy, Kebele, Khalifate, Khan, Kremlin,

Legate, Majlis, Majorism, Monarchy, Monocracy, Mudir, Nabob, Naik, Nomarch, Nomocracy, Ochlocracy, Oireachtas, Oligarchy, Optic®, Pa, Pacha, Padishah, Pasha, Pater, Polity, Polyarchy, Propraetor, Père, Pentarch, Petticoat, Pilate, Placemen, Plutocracy, Podesta, Porte, Power, Priest-king, Proconsul, Proveditor, Provedor(e), Providor, Quadrumvirate, Quirinal, Raj, Realpolitik, Rection, Rector, Rectrix, Regency, Regime(n), Reign, Rein, Ride, ➤ RULE, Satrap, Senate, Serkali, Shogun, Signoria, Sircar, Sirkar, Stad(t)holder, Statecraft, Steer, Stratocracy, Subadar, Sway, Technocracy, Thatcherism, Thearchy, Timocracy, Totalitarianism, Triumvirate, Tuchun, Vali, Viceregal, Viceroy, Wali, Warden, Wealsman, White House, Whitehall, Witan

Governess Duenna, Eyre, Fraulein, Griffin, Mademoiselle, Prism, Vicereine

Government revenue Jaghir(e), Jagir

Gown Banian, Banyan, Dressing, Empire, Geneva, Green, Johnny, Kirtle, Manteau, Manto, Mantua, Mother Hubbard, Peignoir, Polonaise, Robe, Silk, Slammakin, Slammerkin, Slop, Stola, Tea, Wrap(per)

Grab Annexe, Bag, Clutch, Cly, Collar, Glaum, Grapnel, Hold, Holt, Rap, Seise, Seize, ➤ SNATCH, Swipe

Gracchi Jewels

Grace(s), Graceful Aglaia, Amnesty, Anna, Beauty, Become, Benediction, Bethankit, Blessing, Charis(ma), Charites, Charity, Darling, Dr, Elegance, Euphrosyne, Fluent, Gainly, Genteel, Genty, Godliness, Grazioso, Mense, Mercy, Molinism, Mordent, Omnium, Ornament, Pralltriller, Sacrament, Streamlined, Style, Thalia, Thanks, WG, Willowy

Gracious Benign, By George, Charismatic, Generous, Good, Handsome, Hend, Merciful, Polite

Gradation Cline, Degree, Nuance, Stage

Grade, Gradient Analyse, Angle, Assort, Class(ify), Dan, Degree, Echelon, Gon, Hierarchy, Inclination, Kyu, Lapse, Measure, Order, Rank, Score, Seed, Slope, Standard, Status

Gradual Gentle, Grail, Imperceptible, Inchmeal, Slow

Graduate, Graduation Alumnus, BA, Bachelor, Calibrate, Capping, Incept, Laureateship, Licentiate, LlB, MA, Master, Nuance, Optime, Ovate

Graffiti Bomb, Doodle, Tag, Tagger

Graft Anaplasty, Autoplasty, Boodle, Bribery, Bud, Dub, Enarch, Enrace, Heteroplasty, Imp, Implant, Inarch, Inoculate, Payola, Pomato, Racket, Scion, Shoot, Slip, Transplant, Ympe

Grail Chalice, Cup, Sangraal, Sangrail, Sangreal

Grain(y) Bajra, Bajree, Bajri, Bear, Bere, Boll, Bran, Cereal, Corn, Couscous, Crop, Curn, Curn(e)y, Cuscus, D(o)urra, Extine, Frumentation, Gr, Graddan, Granule, Groats, Grumose, Intine, Kaoliang, Knaveship, Malt, Mashlam, Mashlin, Mashloch, Mashlum, Maslin, Mealie, Millet, Milo, Minim, Mongcorn, Oats, Pickle, Pinole, Pollen, Polynology, Popcorn, Puckle, Rabi, Raggee, Ragi, Raggy, Rhy, Rye, Sand, Scruple, Seed, Semsem, Sorghum, Tola, Touch, Wheat, Wholemeal

Gram Chich, Chick-pea, Teen, Tene, Urd

Grammar(ian), Grammatical Accidence, Amphibology, Anacoluthia, Anacoluthon, Anastrophe, Case, Categorical, Donat, Donet, Gr, Linguistics, Paradigm, Primer, Priscianist, Scholiast, Stratificational, Syndetic, Syndeton, Syntax, Tagmeme, Trivium, Typto, Universal

Grampus Orc, Whale

Granary Barn, Girnal, Silo

Grand Canyon, Epical, Flugel, G, Gorgeous, Guignol, High-faluting, Hotel, Imposing, La(h)-di-da(h), Lordly, Magnificent, Majestic, Palatial, Piano(forte), Pompous, Regal, Splendid, Stately, Stoor, Stour, Stowre, Sture, Sublime, Swell, Tour

Grandchild Niece, Oe, Oy(e)

Grandee Adelantado, Don, Magnifico

Grandfather Ancient, Avital, Clock, Goodsire, Gramps, Gutcher, Oldster, Old-timer, Oupa

Grandmother Babushka, Gran(nie), Granny, Moses, Nan(a), Ouma

Grandparent(al) Aval, Avital

Grand Prix Race(-cup)

Grandsire Peal

Grange Moated

Granite Aberdeen, Chinastone, Greisen, Luxul(l)ianite, Luxulyanite, NH, Pegmatite, Protogine

Grannie Forebear, Knot, Nan(a)

Grant(ed) Accord, Aid, Award, Bestow, Beteem(e), Bounty, Bursary, Carta, Cary, Charta, Charter, Concession, ➤ CONFER, Cy, Datum, Endow, Exhibition, Feoff, Lend, Let, Munich, Patent, President, Send, Sop, Subsidy, Subvention, Teene, Vouchsafe, Yeven, Yield

Granule, Granulate(d) Kern, Otolith, Plastid, Pound, Prill

Grape(s) Aligoté, Botros, Botryoid, Cabernet, Cabernet Sauvignon, Catawba, Chardonnay, Chenin blanc, Concord, Delaware, Fox, Gamay, Gewurztraminer, Haanepoot, Hamburg(h), Hanepoot, Honeypot, Hyacinth, Lambrusco, Malmsey, Malvasia, Malvesie, Malvoisie, Merlot, Muscadel, Muscadine, Muscat(el), Noble rot, Pinot, Racemose, Raisin, Rape, Riesling, Sauvignon, Scuppernong, Sémillon, Sercial, Shiraz, Sour, Staphyline, Sultana, Sweet-water, Sylvaner, Syrah, Tokay, Uva, Verdelho, Véronique, Vino, Wineberry, Zinfandel

Grapefruit Pampelmoose, Pomelo, Pompelmouse, Pompelo, Pumple-nose, Ugli

Grapeshot Mitraille

Grape-sugar Glucose

Grapevine Hearsay

Graph(ic) Bar, Chart, Contour, Diagram, Histogram, Ogive, Picturesque, Pie (chart), Profile, Sonogram, Table, Vivid

Graphite Kish, Plumbago

Grapple Clinch, Close, Hook, Lock, Struggle, Wrestle

Grasp(ing) Apprehend, Catch, Clat, Claut, ➤ CLUTCH, Compass, Comprehend, Fathom, Get, Grab, Grapple, Greedy, Grip(e), Hent, Hug, Prehend, Prehensile, Raptorial, Realise, Rumble, Sense, Snap, Snatch, Twig, Uptak(e)

Grass(land), Grass roots, Grassy Agrostology, Alang, Alfa(lfa), Avena, Bahia, Bamboo, Bang, Barley, Barnyard, Bennet, Bent, Bermuda, Bhang, Blade, Bristle, Brome-grass, Bromus, Buffalo, Bush, Canary, Cane, Canna, Cannach, Carpet, Cat's tail, Chess, Citronella, Cleavers, Clivers, Clover, Cochlearia, Cocksfoot, Cogon, Cord, Cortaderia, Cotton, Couch, Crab, Culm, Cuscus, Cutty, Dactylis, Danthonia, Dari, Darnel, Deergrass, Dhur(r)a, Diss, Divot, Dogstail, Doob, Doura, Dura, Durra, Eddish, Eel, Eelwrack, Elephant, Emmer, Esparto, Feather, Fescue, Fiorin, Flinders, Flote, Fog, Foggage, Foxtail, Gama-grass, Ganja, Glume, Glumella, Goose, Grama, Green(sward), Hair, Halfa, Harestail, Hassock, Hay, Haycock, Heath(er), Hemp, High veld, ➤ INFORM, Jawar(i), Job's tears, Johnson, Jowar(i), Kangaroo, Kans, Kentucky blue, Khuskhus, Kikuyu, Knoll, Knot, Lalang, Laund, Lawn, Lemon, Locusta, Lolium, Lop, Lucern(e), Lyme, Machair, Manna, Marram, Marrum, Mary Jane, Materass, Matweed, Mead, Melic, Melick, Millet, Milo, Miscanthus, Moor, Nark, Oat, Oryza, Palet, Pamir, Pampas, Panic, Paspalum, Pasturage, Peach, Pennisetum, Persicaria, Phleum, Plume, Poa, Porcupine, Pot, Puszta, Quack, Quaking, Quick, Quitch, Ramee, Rami(e), Rat, Rat on, Reed, Redtop, Ribbon, Rice, Rips, Roosa, Rough, Rumble(r), Rusa, Rye, Sacaton, Salt, Savanna(h), Saw, Scorpion, Scraw, Scurvy, Scutch, Sea-reed, Sedge, Seg, Sesame, Shop, Sing, Sinsemilla, Sisal, Sneak(er), Snitch, Snout, Snow, Sorghum, Sour-gourd, Sourveld, Spelt, Spinifex, Split, Squeal, Squitch, Squirrel-tail, Stag, Star(r), Stipa, Stool-pigeon, Storm, Sward, Swath(e), Sword, Tape, Tath, Tea, Tef(f), Tell, Teosinte, Timothy, Toetoe, Toitoi, Triticale, Tuffet, Turf, Tussac, Tussock, Twitch, Veld(t), Vetiver, Whangee, Wheat, Whitlow, Windlestraw, Wire, Witch, Worm, Yard, Yorkshire fog, Zizania, Zostera, Zoysia

Grasshopper Cicada, Cricket, Grig, Katydid, Locust, Long-horned, Meadow, Tettix, Wart-biter, Weta

Grate(r), Grating Abrade, Burr, Cancelli, Chirk, Crepitus, ➤ FRET, Graticule, Grid, Grill, Guichet, Guttural, Hack, Hearth, Heck, Hoarse, Ingle, Jar, Portcullis, Rasp, Risp, Rub, Ruling, Scrannel, ➤ SCRAPE, Scrat, Shred, Siver, Strident, Syver

Grateful Beholden, Cinders, Indebted, Obliged

Gratification, Gratify Aggrate, Indulge, Kick, Oblige, Pleasure, Regale, Reward

Gratitude God 'a mercy, Ta, Thanks

Gratuitous, Gratuity Baksheesh, Beer-money, Bonsella, Bonus, Bounty, Cumshaw, Free, Glove-money, Gratis, Tip

Grave(yard) Accent, Arlington, Bass, Bier, Burial, Charnel, Chase, Darga, Demure, Dust, God's acre, Heavy, Heinous, Important, Ingroove, Kistvaen, Kurgan, Mound, Passage, Pit, Sad, Saturnine, Serious, Sober, Sombre, Speos, Staid, Stern, Tomb, Watery

Grave-digger Bederal, Fossor, Sexton

Gravel(ly) Calculus, Channel, Chesil, Chisel, Eskar, Esker, Glareous, Grail(e), Grit, Hoggin(g), Murram, Nonplus, Pingo, Shingle

Gravity Barycentric, G, Geotaxis, Geotropism, Magnitude, Mascon, Specific, Weight

Gravy Baster, Browning, Coin, Jus

Gravy-boat Argyle, Argyll

▶ **Gray** see GREY

Grayling Umber

Graze, Grazing Abrade, Agist, Bark, Brush, Crop, Feed, Herdwick, Leasow(e), Pasture, Rake, Rangeland, Scrape, Scrawn, Shave, Shieling

Grease, Greasy Bribe, Creesh, Dope, Dubbing, Elaeolite, Elbow, Enseam, Glit, Lanolin, Lard, Seam(e), Shearer, Sheep-shearer, Smarm, Suint, Unctuous

Great(er), Greatest Ali, Astronomical, Bully, Extreme, Gay, Gey, Gran(d), Grit, Gt, Guns, Helluva, Immortal, Important, Lion, Macro, Main, Major, Mickle, Mochell, Much, Muchel(l), Muckle, OS, Stoor, Stour, Sture, Super, Superb, Swingeing, Synergy, Tall, Titan(ic), Tremendous, Unco, Utmost, Vast, Zenith

Great deal Mort

Grebe Cargoose

Grecian Bend, Nose

Greed(y) Avarice, Avid, Bulimia, Bulimy, Cupidity, Edacious, Esurient, Gannet, Gare, Gulosity, Killcrop, Lickerish, Mercenary, Piggery, Pleonexia, Rapacity, Selfish, Solan, Voracity, Wolfish

Greek(s) Achaean, Achaian, Achilles, Aeolic, Agamemnon, Ajax, Aonian, Arcadia, Archimedes, Argive, Aristides, Athenian, Attic, Cadmean, Cleruch, Corinthian, Cretan, Delphian, Demotic, Ding, Diomedes, Dorian, Doric, Eoka, Eolic, Epaminondas, Ephebe, Epirus, Euclid, Evzone, Fanariot, Gr, Helladic, Hellene, Hellenic, Homer, Hoplite, Ionian, Isocrates, Italiot(e), Javan, Katharevousa, Klepht, Koine, Lapith, Leonidas, Linear B, Locrian, Lucian, Macedonia, Momus, Nestor, Nike, Nostos, Orestes, Paestum, Patroclus, Pelasgic, Pelopid, Perseus, Phanariot, Pythagoras, Romaic, Samiot, Seminole, Spartacus, Spartan, Stagirite, Strabo, Sybarite, Tean, Teian, Theban, Thersites, Theseus, Thessal(on)ian, Thracian, Timon, Typto, Uniat, Xenophon, Zorba

Green(ery) Apple, Bice, Biliverdin, Bottle, Bowling, Caesious, Callow, Celadon, Cerulein, Chard, Chartreuse, Chlorophyll, Chrome, Cole, Collard, Common, Copper, Corbeau, Crown, Dioptase, Eau de nil, Eco-, Ecofriendly, Emerald, Emerande, Envious, Erin, Fingers, Foliage, Forest, Fundie, Fundy, Gaudy, Glaucous, Go, Goddess, Gretna, Gull, Immature, Inexpert, Jade, Jungle, Kendal, Kensal, Lawn, Leafage, Lime, Lincoln, Loden, Lovat, Mead, Moss, Moulding, Naive, New, Nile, Oasis, Olive, Paris, Pea, Peridot, Pistachio, Porraceous, Putting, Raw, Realo, Reseda, Rifle, Rink, Sage, Scheele's, Sludge, Smaragdine, Sward, Teal, Tender, Turacoverdin, Tyro, Unfledged, Uninitiated, Unripe, Uranite, Verdant, Verdigris, Verdure, Vert, Vir(id)escent, Virent, Virid

Greenheart Bebeern

Greenhorn Baby, Dupe, Put(t), Rookie, Sucker

Greenhouse Conservatory, Orangery, Phytotron

Greens Broccoli, Cabbage, Calabrese, Cash, Money, Sprout, Vegetable(s)

Greet(ing) Abrazo, Accost, Arvo, Banzai, Benedicite, Blubber, Chimo, Ciao, Hail, Hallo, Halse, Handclasp, Handshake, Haway, Heil, Heita, Hello, Herald, Hi, High-five, Hiya, Hongi, How, Howsit, Jambo, Kia ora, Kiss, Namaskar, Namaste, Respects, Salaam, Salute, Salve, Sd, Shalom, Shalom aleichem, Sorry, Strippagram, Strippergram, Tena Koe, Wave, ➤ WELCOME, Wotcher, Yo

Gregarious Social

Gregorian Chant, NS

▶ **Gremlin** see GOBLIN

Grenade Bomb, Egg, Pineapple

Greta Garbo

Grey, Gray Age, Agnes, Argent, Ashen, Ashy, Battleship, Beige, Bloncket, Charcoal, Cinereous, Dapple, Dorian, Dove, Drab, Glaucous, Gloomy, Gr, Gridelin, Griesie, Gries(l)y, Grise, Grisy, Grizzled, Gunmetal, Gy, Hoary, Hore, Inn, Iron, Leaden, Liard, Livid, Lucia, Lyart, Mouse-coloured, Pearl, Putty, Slaty, Steel, Taupe, Zane

Greyfriars Bunter, Magnet

Greyhound Grew, Longtail, Ocean, Saluki, Sapling, Whippet

Grey matter Cinerea

Grid(dle), Gridiron Bar, Barbecue, Brandreth, Cattle, Dot matrix, Grate, Graticule, Grating, Network, Reseau, Reticle, Roo-bar, Tava(h), Tawa, Windscale

Gride Creak, Grate

Grief, Grievance, Grieve, Grievous Axe, Bemoan, Bitter, Complaint, Condole, Cry, Dear(e), Deere, Distress, Dole, Dolour, Gram(e), Gravamen, Heartbreak, Hone, Illy, Io, ➤ MISERY, Monody, O(c)hone, Pain, Pathetic, Plaint, Rue, Sorrow, Teen, Tene, Tragic, Wayment, Weeping, Woe, Wrong

Griffin Gripe, Grype, Novice, Pony

Grill(ing), Grille Braai, Brander, Broil, Carbonado, Crisp, Devil, Gridiron, Inquisition, Interrogate, Kebab, Mixed, Pump, Question, Rack, Reja, Yakimona

Grim Dire, Dour, Gaunt, Glum, Gurly, Hard, Stern

▷ **Grim** may indicate an anagram

Grimace Face, Girn, Moe, Mop, Moue, Mouth, Mow, Murgeon, Pout

Grime(s), Grimy Colly, Dirt, Peter, Reechie, Reechy, Soil, Sweep

Grin Fleer, Girn, Risus, Simper, Smirk, Sneer

Grind(ing), Grinder Bray, Bruxism, Chew, Crunch, ➤ CRUSH, Droil, Gnash, Grate, Graunch, Grit, Kern, Kibble, Levigate, Mano, Mill, Mince, Molar, Muller, Pug, Pulverise, Slog, Stamp, Triturate

Grip(ping), Gripper Ascendeur, Bite, Chuck, Clam, Clamp, Clip, Clutch, Craple, Embrace, Enthral, Get, Grapple, ➤ GRASP, Haft, Hairpin, Handhold,

Hend, Hold, Hug, Kirby®, Lewis, Obsess, Pincer, Pinion, Prehensile, Purchase, Raven, Rhine, Sally, Sipe, Strain, Streigne, Valise, Vice, Walise, Wrestle

Gripe(s) Colic, Complain, Ditch, Grasp, Griffin, Ileus, Pain, Tormina

Grist Burden

Gristle, Gristly Cartilage, Chondroid, Lytta

Grit(ty) Blinding, Clench, Gnash, Granular, Grate, Guts, Pluck, Resolution, Sabulose, Sand, Shingle, Swarf

Grizzle(d) Grey

Groan(er) Bewail, Bing, Moan

Grocer Grasshopper, Jorrocks, Pepperer

Groggy Dazed, Shaky

Groin Gnarr, Inguinal, Lisk

Groom(ed) Coistrel, Coistril, Curry, Dress, Fettler, Kempt, Ostler, Palfrenier, Paranymph, Preen, Prink, S(a)ice, Smarten, Strapper, Syce, Tiger, Tracer, Train, Wrangler

▷ **Groom** may indicate an anagram

Groove(d), Groovy Bezel, Canal, Cannelure, Chamfer, Channel, Chase, Clevis, Coulisse, Croze, Dièdre, Exarate, Fissure, Flute, Fuller, Furr, Furrow, Glyph, Gouge, Kerf, Key-seat, Keyway, Oche, Pod, Rabbet, Race(way), Raggle, Rebate, Rif(f)le, Rigol(l), Rout, ➤ RUT, Scrobe, Sipe, Slot, Sulcus, Throat, Track, Trough, Vallecula

Grope(r) Feel, Fumble, Grabble, Hapuka, Ripe, Scrabble

Gross All-up, Coarse, Complete, Crass, Dense, Earthy, Flagrant, Frankish, Gr, Material, Obese, Outsize, Overweight, Pre-tax, Rank, Ribald, Rough, Stupid, Whole

▷ **Gross** may indicate an anagram

Grotesque Antic, Bizarre, Fantastic, Fright, Gargoyle, Magot, Outlandish, Rabelaisian, Rococo

Grotto Cave, Lupercal

Ground(s) Arena, Astroturf, Basis, Bottom, Breeding, Campus, Cause, Common, Criterion, Crushed, Deck, Dregs, Eard, Earth, Epig(a)eal, Epig(a)ean, Epig(a)eous, Footing, Grated, Grist, Grouts, Lees, Leeway, Lek, Lords, Lot, Marl, Mealed, Occasion, Oval, Parade, Pitch, Plat, Plot, Policy, Proving, Quad, ➤ REASON, Recreation, Réseau, Ring, Sediment, Slade, Soil, Solum, Stadium, Terra, Terrain, Tract, Turf, Udal, Venue, Waste(land), Yard, Yird

▷ **Ground** may indicate an anagram

Groundbait Chum

Ground-crew Erk

Ground-rent Crevasse

Groundsheet Hutchie

Groundsman Greenkeeper

Group Abelian, Acyl, Band, Batch, Beatles, Bee, Bevy, Bloc(k), Blood, Bloomsbury, Body, Bracket, Bratpack, Caboodle, Cadre, Camarilla, Camp, Cartel, Category, Caucus, Cave, Cell, Chain, Chordata, Circle, Clade,

Class(is), Clique, Cluster, Cohort, Colony, Combo, Commune, Community, Concertina, Congregation, Consort(ium), Contact, Contingent, Coterie, Covey, Crew, Deme, Denomination, Detail, Enclave, Encounter, Ensemble, Faction, Fascio, Focus, Fold, Front, Galère, Gemeinschaft, Genus, Gesellschaft, Ginger, Globe, Guild, Hapu, Heading, Hexad, Hirsel, House, In-crowd, Ketone, Kit, Knot, League, Marshal, Nexus, Order, Outfit, Oxford, Pack(et), Panel, Parti, Party, Peer, Phalange, Phratry, Phylum, Platoon, Pleiad, Pocket, Pool, Push, Raceme, Racemose, Ring, Rush, School, Sector, Seminar, Series, Set, Several, Sex, Shower, Society, Sort, Sorus, Splinter, Strain, Stream, String, Sub-order, Syndicate, Tales, Taxon, Tetrad, Tithing, Trainband, T-Rex, Tribe, Tribune, Trilogy, Trio, TU, Umbrella, Unit, User, Zupa

Grouse Blackcock, Bleat, Caper(caillie), Capercailzie, Covey, Gorcock, Greyhen, Gripe, Growl, Grumble, Hazel-hen, Heath-cock, Heath-hen, Jeremiad, Moan, Moorcock, Moorfowl, Moor-pout, Muir-poot, Muir-pout, Mutter, Natter, Peeve, Pintail, Prairie-hen, Ptarmigan, Resent, Rype(r), Snarl, Spruce, Twelfth, Wheenge, W(h)inge, Willow

Grove Academy, Arboretum, Bosk, Bosquet, Copse, Glade, Hurst, Lyceum, Nemoral, Orchard, Orchat, Silva, Tope

Grovel Cheese, Crawl, Creep, Fawn, Ko(w)tow

Grow(ing), Grow out, Growth Accrete, Accrue, Acromegaly, Adenoma, Aggrandisement, Angioma, Apophysis, Arborescence, Auxesis, Bedeguar, Boom, Braird, Breer, Burgeon, Car(b)uncle, Cholelith, Chondroma, Compensatory, Condyloma, Crescendo, Crop, Culture, Cyst, Ectopia, Edema, Ellagic, Enate, Enchondroma, Enlarge, Epinasty, Epitaxy, Excrescence, Exostosis, Expansion, Fibroid, Flor, Flourish, Flush, Gain, Gall, Germinate, Get, Goitre, Hepatocele, Hummie, Hyponasty, Increase, Knur(r), Lichen, Lipoma, Mushroom, Myoma, Nur(r), Oedema, Oncology, Osselet, Osteoma, Polyp, Proleg, Proliferate, Rampant, Scirrhus, Septal, Snowball, Spavin, ➤ SPROUT, Stipule, Sympodial, Tariff, Thrive, Tylosis, Vegetable, Wart, Wax, Wox

▷ **Grow(n)** may indicate an anagram

Growl(ing) Fremescent, Gnar, Groin, Grr, Gurl, Roar(e), Roin, Royne, Snar(l)

Grown up Adult, Mature, Risen

Grub(by) Assart, Bardy, Caddis, Caterpillar, Cheer, Chow, Chrysalis, Dig, Eats, Fare, Fodder, ➤ FOOD, Gentle, Groo-groo, Gru-gru, Larva, Leatherjacket, Mawk, Mess, Nosh, Palmerworm, Peck, Pupa, Root(le), Rout, Rowt, Sap, Slave, Stub, Tired, Wireworm, Witchetty, Worm

Grudge, Grudging Chip, Derry, Envy, Grutch, Resent, Score, Sparse, Spite, Spleen

Gruel Brochan, Bross, Loblolly, Skilligalee, Skilligolee, Skilly

Gruesome Ghastly, Grisly, Grooly, Horror, Macaberesque, Macabre, ➤ MORBID, Sick

Gruff Guttural, Hoarse, Surly

Grumble Beef, Bellyache, Bitch, Bleat, Chunter, Croak, Girn, Gripe, Grizzle, Groin, Growl, Moan, Murmur, Mutter, Nark, Natter, Repine, Rumble, Whinge, Yammer

Grump(y) Attercop, Bearish, Cross, Ettercap, Grouchy, Moody, Sore-headed, Surly

Grunt Groin, Grumph, Humph, Oink, Pigfish, Ugh, Wheugh

Guano Dung, Sombrerite

Guanoco Llama

Guarantee Assure, Avouch, Certify, Ensure, Gage, Hallmark, Insure, Mainprise, Money-back, Pignerate, Pignorate, ➤ PLEDGE, Plight, Seal, Secure, Sponsion, Surety, ➤ VOUCH(SAFE), Warrandice, Warrant(y)

Guard(ed), Guards Acolouthos, Beefeaters, Blues, Bostangi, Bouncer, Bracer, Cabiri, Cag(e)y, Cage, Cerberus, Chaperon(e), Chary, Cheesemongers, Cherry-pickers, Coast, Coldstream, Cordon, Curator, Custodian, Custos, Diehards, Dragoons, Duenna, Equerry, Escort, Eunuch, Excubant, Exon, Fence, Fender, Grenadiers, Greys, Hedge, Home, INS, Jaga, Jailer, Keep, Lancers, Lilywhites, Look out, Mort-safe, Nutcrackers, Out-rider, Out-sentry, Pad, Patrol, Picket, Praetorian, ➤ PROTECT, Quillon, Rail, Red, Secure, Sentinel, Sentry, Shield, SS, Strelitz, Streltzi, Swiss, Tapadera, Tapadero, Tile, Toecap, Tsuba, Vamplate, Varangian, Vigilante, Visor, Wage, Wait(e), Ward, Wary, Watch (and ward), Watchdog, Watchman, Wear, Weir, Yeoman

Guardian Altair, Argus, Curator, Custodian, Custos, Dragon, Gemini, Granthi, Hafiz, Janus, Julius, Miminger, Templar, Trustee, Tutelar(y), Warder, Watchdog, Xerxes

Gudgeon Fish, Pin, Trunnion

Guenon Grivet, Vervet

Guer(r)illa Bushwhacker, Chetnik, Contra, ETA, Fedayee, Gook, Khmer Rouge, Komitaji, Maquis, Mujahadeen, Mujaheddin, Mujahedeen, Mujahed(d)in, Mujahideen, Partisan, Terrorist, Tupamaro, Urban, Viet cong, Zapata

Guess Aim, Aread, Arede, Arreede, Conjecture, Divine, Estimate, Harp, Hazard, Imagine, Infer, Level, Mor(r)a, Mull, Shot, Speculate, Suppose, Surmise, Theorise

Guessing game Handy-dandy, Mor(r)a, Quiz

Guest(s) Caller, Company, Parasite, Paying, PG, Symbion(t), Symphile, Synoecete, Visitant, ➤ VISITOR, Xenial

Guesthouse Minshuku, Xenodochium

Guff Bosh, Gas

Guianian S(a)ouari

Guidance, Guide(line) Advice, Antibarbus, Auspice, Baedeker, Bradshaw, Cicerone, Clue, Concordance, Conduct, Counsel, Courier, Curb, Cursor, Director(y), Docent, Dragoman, Drive, ➤ ESCORT, Field, Gillie, Helm, Index, Inertial, Inspire, Itinerary, Jig, Key, Lad, Landmark, Lead, Mark, Map, Mentor, Model, Navaid, Navigate, Nose, Pelorus, Pilot, Pointer, Postil(l)ion, Principle, Range, Ranger, Reference, Rein, Relate, Rudder, Sabot, Shepherd, Sherpa, Shikaree, Shikari, Sign, Sixer, Stear, Steer, Stire, Template, Templet, Tiller, Train, Travelogue, Tutelage, Vocational, Voyageur, Waymark, Weise, Weize, Wise

Guild Artel, Basoche, Company, Gyeld, Hanse, Hoastman, League, Society, Tong, Union

Guile Art, Cunning, Deceit, Dole, Malengine

Guillotine Closure, Louisiette, Maiden, Marianne

Guilt(y) Angst, Blame, Cognovit, Flagitious, Nocent, Peccavi, Remorse, Wicked

Guinea(s) Geordie, Gns, Job, Ls, Meg, Spade

Guinea-fowl Pintado

Guinea-pig Agoute, Agouti, Cavie, Cavy

Guinea-worm Dracunculus

Guise Form, Manner, Shape

Guitar(ist) Acoustic, Axe(man), Bottleneck, Cithern, Cittern, Dobro®, Fender®, Gittern, Hawaiian, Humbucker, Lute, Plankspanker, Samisen, Sancho, Sanko, Shamisen, Sitar, Spanish, Steel, Uke, Ukulele

Gulf Aden, Aqaba, Bay, Bothnia, California, Cambay, Carpentaria, Chasm, Chihli, Darien, Exmouth, Fonseca, Hauraki, Honduras, Lepanto, Lingayen, Lion, Mannar, Martaban, Maw, Mexico, Persian, Queen Maud, Saronic, Sidra, Spencer, Tonkin, Trieste, Tunis

Gull(s) Bonxie, Cheat, Cob(b), Cod, Cozen, Dupe, Fool, Geck, Graucous, Hoodwink, Laridae, Larus, Maw, Mew, Pickmaw, Pigeon, Queer, Rook, Scaury, Scourie, Scowrie, Sea-cob, Sea-mew, Sell, Simp, Skua, Sucker, Tern, Tystie, Xema

Gullet Crop, Enterate, Maw, Throat, Weasand-pipe

Gullible Green, Naive, Sucker

Gulliver Lemuel

Gully Couloir, Donga, Geo, Gio, Goe, Grough, Gulch, Pit, Rake, Ravine, Sloot, Sluit, Wadi

Gulp Bolt, Draught, Gollop, Quaff, Slug, Sob, ➤ SWALLOW, Swipe, Wolf

Gum (tree) Acacia, Acajou, Acaroid, Agar, Algin, Angico, Arabic, Arabin, Arar, Arctic, Asafoetida, Bablah, Balata, Balm, Bandoline, Bdellium, Benjamin, Benzoin, Bloodwood, Boot, Bubble, Cerasin, Chicle, Chuddy, Chutty, Coolabah, Courbaril, Dextrin(e), Dragon's-blood, Ee-by, Eucalyptus, Frankincense, Galbanum, Gamboge, Gingival, ➤ GLUE, Goat's-thorn, Gosh, Guar, Ironbark, Karri, Kauri, La(b)danum, Lac, Lentisk, Mastic(h), Mucilage, Myrrh, Nicotine, Olibanum, Opopanax, Oshac, Sagapenum, Sarcocolla, Scribbly, Size, Sleep, Spearmint, Spirit, Sterculia, Stringybark, Sugar, Tacamahac, Tragacanth, Tupelo, Xanthan

Gumbo Okra

Gumboil Parulis

Gumption Nous, Spirit

Gun(fire), Guns Amusette, Archibald, Archie, Arquebus, Automatic, Barker, Bazooka, Big Bertha, Biscayan, Bofors, Bombard, Breech(-loader), Bren, Broadside, Brown Bess, Bulldog, Bundook, Burp, Caliver, Cannonade, Carbine, Carronade, Chokebore, Coehorn, Colt®, Dag, Derringer, Electron, Elephant, Escopette, Falcon(et), Fieldpiece, Flame, Flintlock, Fowler, Fowlingpiece, Garand, Gat(ling), Gingal(l), HA, Hackbut, Harquebus, Heater, Hired, Howitzer, Jezail, Jingal, Kalashnikov, Lewis,

Long Tom, Luger®, Machine, Magnum, Martini-Henry®, Matchlock, Mauser®, Maxim, Metal, Minnie, Minute, Mitrailleuse, Morris Meg, Mortar, Musket(oon), Muzzle-loader, Noonday, Oerlikon, Ordnance, Paderero, Paterero, Ped(e)rero, Pelican, Perrier, Petronal, Piece, Pistol(et), Pompom, Quaker, Radar, Ray, Repeater, Rev, Riot, Rod, Roscoe, Saker, Sarbacane, Self-cocker, Shooter, Siege, Smoothbore, Snapha(u)nce, Spear, Spray, Squirt, Staple, Starting, Sten, Sterculia, Sterling, Stern-cannon, Stern-chaser, Stun, Swivel, Taser®, Tea, Thirty eight, Thompson, Tier, Tommy, Tool, Tupelo, Uzi, Zip

Gunman Ace, Assassin, Bandit, Earp, Greaser, Pistoleer, Sniper, Starter

Gunner, Gunner's assistant Arquebusier, Arsenal, Artillerist, Cannoneer, Cannonier, Culverineer, Gr, Matross, RA

Gunpowder Charcoal, Saucisse, Saucisson

Gunwale Gunnel, Portland, Portlast, Portoise

Guppy Million

Gurgle Clunk, Gollar, Goller, Guggle, Ruckle, Squelch

Gurnard Tubfish

Guru Sadhu, Teacher

Gush(ing) Blether, Effusive, ➤ FLOOD, Flow, Jet, Outpour, Rail, Regurgitate, Scaturient, Spirt, Spout, Spurt, Too-too

Gusset Godet, Gore, Insert, Inset, Mitre

Gust Blast, Blore, Flaught, Flaw, Flurry, Puff, Sar, Waff

Gusto Elan, Relish, Verve, Zest

Gut(s), Gutty Archenteron, Balls, Beer, Bowel(s), Chitterlings, Cloaca, Disembowel, Duodenum, Draw, Enteral, Enteron, Entrails, Gill, Ileum, Insides, Kyle, Mesenteron, Omental, Omentum, Remake, Sack, Sand, Snell, Stamina, Staying-power, Strip, Thairm, Tripe, Ventriculus, Viscera

Gutta-percha Jelutong, Pontianac, Pontianak

Gutter(ing) Channel, Conduit, Cullis, Grip, Kennel, Rhone, Rigol(l), Roan, Rone, Sough, Spout, Strand, Sweal, Sweel

Guttersnipe Arab, Gamin, Thief

Guttural Throaty

Guy Backstay, Bo, Burgess, Chaff, Clewline, Decamp, Deride, Effigy, Fall, Fawkes, Fellow, Gink, Josh, Mannering, Parody, Rib, Rope, Scarecrow, Stay, Tease, Vang, Wise

Guzzle(d) Gannet, Gorge, Go(u)rmandize, Overeat

Gwyn Nell

Gym(nasium), Gymnast(ic) Acrobat, Akhara, Arena, Dojo, Jungle, Lyceum, Palaestra, PE, PT, Rhythmic, Sokol, Tumbler

Gymnosophist Yogi

Gypsum Alabaster, Gesso, Plaster, Satin-stone, Selenite

Gypsy Bohemian, Cagot, Caird, Caqueux, Chai, Chal, Chi, Collibert, Esmeralda, Faw, Gipsen, Gitano, Hayraddin, Lavengro, Meg, Rom(any), Rye, Scholar, Tinker, Tsigane, Vagabond, Wanderer, Zigan, Zigeuner, Zincala, Zincalo, Zingaro

Gyrate Revolve, Rotate, ➤ SPIN, Twirl

Hh

H Ache, Aitch, Aspirate, Height, Hospital, Hotel, Hydrant, Hydrogen

Haberdasher(y) Clothier, Ferret, Hosier, Notions

Habit(s), Habitual, Habituate, Habitué Accustom, Addiction, Apparel, Assuefaction, Assuetude, Bent, Cacoethes, Chronic, Clothes, Coat, Consuetude, Custom, Diathesis, Dress, Ephod, Frequenter, Garb, Inure, Inveterate, Motley, Mufti, Nature, Outfit, Practice, Raiment, Regular, Riding, Robe, Rochet, Routine, Scapular, Schema, Season, Set, Soutane, Suit, Surplice, Toge, Trait, Tway, Usual, Way, Won, Wont, Xerotes

Habitat Element, Environment, Haunt, Home, Locality, Station

Hack Chip, Chop, Cough, Cut, Drudge, Garble, Gash, Ghost, Grub-street, Hag, Hash, Hedge-writer, Heel, Hew, Horse, Mangle, Mutilate, Nag, Notch, Pad, Paper-strainer, Penny-a-liner, Pot-boiler, Rosinante, Spurn, Tadpole, Taper, Tussis, Unseam

Hackle(s) Comb, Rough

Hackneyed Banal, Cab, Cliché, Corny, Percoct, Stale, Threadbare, Tired, Trite

Haddock Arbroath smokie, Findram, Finnan, Fish, Speldin(g), Speldrin(g), Whitefish

Hades Dis, Hell, Orcus, Pit, Tartarus

Had to Moten, Must, Obliged

Haematite Oligist

Haemorrhoid Pile

Hafnium Hf

Hag(-like) Anile, Beldame, Besom, Carlin(e), Crone, Harpy, Harridan, Hell-cat, Hex, Nickneven, Occasion, Rudas, Runnion, Trot, Underwood, Witch

Haggard Drawn, ➤ GAUNT, Pale, Rider

Haggis Kishke

Haggle Argue, Badger, ➤ BARGAIN, Barter, Chaffer, Dicker, Horse-trade, Niffer, Palter, Prig

Ha-ha Dike, Sunk-fence

Hahnium Hn

Hail(er) Acclaim, Ahoy, Ave, Bull-horn, Cheer, Fusillade, Graupel, Greet, Hi, Ho, Megaphone, Salue, Salute, Shower, Signal, Skoal, Skol, Sola, Stentor, Storm, Whoa-ho-ho

Hair(like), Hairy, Hair condition/cut/style Afro, Ainu, Alopecia, Bang, Barnet, Beard, Bezoar, Bingle, Bob, Bouffant, Braid, Brede, Bristle, Brutus, Bun, Bunches, Butch, Cadogan, Capillary, Catogan, Chignon, Cilia, Coat, Cockernony, Coiffure, Comal, Comate, Comb-over, Cornrow, Corymbus, Cowlick, Crew-cut, Crinal, Cronet, Crop, Cue, DA, Dangerous, Dreadlocks, Elf locks, Esau, Feather, Fetlock, Filament, Floccus, Frenulum, Fringe, Fur,

Glib(s), Heard, Heer(i)e, Hispid, Hog, Indumentum, Kemp, Kesh, Lanugo, Lash, List, Lock, Lovelock, Lowlights, Madarosis, Mane, Marcel, Mohican, Mop, Muttonchops, Not(t), Pageboy, Pappus, Pele(s), Pelt, Perm(anent), Pigtail, Pika, Pile, Pilus, Plait, Plica, Pompadour, Ponytail, Pouf(fe), Puberulent, Pubescent, Pudding basin, Queue, Quiff, Radicle, Rat-tail, Rhizoid, Roach, Scalp lock, Scopate, Scopula, Set, Shag, Shingle, Shock, Sideburns, Snell, Strammel, Strand, Strigose, Strummel, Switch, Tête, Thatch, Tomentose, Tonsure, Topknot, Tragus, Tress, Trichoid, Trichology, Trichome, Trim, Velutinous, Vibrissi, Villi, Villosity, Villus, Wig, Wisp, ➤ WOOL, Xerasia

Hair-cream, Hair-oil Conditioner, Pomade

Hairdresser Barber, Coiffeur, Comb, Crimper, Friseur, Marcel, Salon, Stylist, Trichologist

Hairless Bald, Callow, Glabrate, Glabrous, Irate

Hairnet Kell, Snood

Hairpiece Merkin, Strand, Toupee, Wig

Hairpin Bodkin, Slide, U, U-turn

Hair-shirt Ab(b)a, Cilice

Haiti RH

Hal Prince

Halberd Spontoon

Halcyon Calm, Kingfisher, Mild

Hale(r) Drag, Healthy, Koruna, Robust, Well

Half, Halved Bifid, Demi, Dimidiate, Divide, Hemi, Moiety, Semi, Share, Split, Stand-off, Term

Half-a-dozen Six, VI

Half-asleep, Half-conscious Dove, Dozy

Half-baked Mediocre, Samel, Slack-bake

Half-breed, Half-caste Bastard, Baster, Creole, Eurasian, Mameluco, Mestee, Mestiza, Mestizo, Metif, Métis(se), Mongrel, Mulatto, Mustee, Octaroon, Quadroon, Quarteroon, Quintero, Quintroon, Sambo, Yellow-boy, Yellow-girl, Zambo

Half-guinea Smelt

Half-hearted Reluctant, Tepid

Half-hour Bell

Half-pence, Half-penny Mag, Maik, Mail(e), Make, Obolus, Patrick, Portcullis, Posh, Rap, Wood's

Half-turn Caracol(e), Demivolt

Half-wit Changeling, Mome, Simpleton, ➤ STUPID

Hall Anteroom, Apadana, Atrium, Auditorium, Aula, Basilica, Carnegie, Casino, Chamber, Citadel, City, Concourse, Corridor, Dance, Dojo, Domdaniel, Dome, Dotheboys, Ex(h)edra, Festival, Foyer, Gallen, Holkham, Kedleston, Liberty, Lobby, Locksley, Megaron, Music, Narthex, Odeon, Palais, Passage, Rathaus, Salle, Saloon, Tammany, Tara, Tolsel, Town, Valhalla, Vestibule, Wildfell

Hallmark(ed) Brand, Contrôlé, Logo, Seal, Stamp

▶ **Hallo** see HELLO

Hallucinate, Hallucination, Hallucinogen Autoscopy, Fantasy, Formication, Freak, Illusion, Image, Mirage, Psilocin, Psilocybin, Psychedelic

Halo Antheolion, Areola, Aura, Aureola, Corona, Gloria, Gloriole, Mandorla, Nimbus, Rim, Vesica

Halogen Iodine

Halt(er) Arrest, Block, Brake, Bridle, Cavesson, Cease, Check, Game, Hackamore, Heave-to, Hilch, Lame(d), Limp, Noose, Prorogue, Rope, Stall, Standstill, Staw, ➤ STOP, Stopover, Toho, Tyburn-tippet, Whoa

Ham(s) Amateur, Barnstormer, Flitch, Gammon, Haunch, Hock, Hoke, Hough, Hunker, Jambon, Jay, Nates, Overact, Overplay, Parma, Prat, Prosciutto, Tiro, Westphalian, York

Hamfisted Maladroit, Unheppen

Hamite Berber, Nilot(e)

Hamlet Aldea, Auburn, Cigar, Dane, Dorp, Hero, Kraal, Stead, Thorp(e), Vill(age), Wick

Hammer(ed), Hammerhead About-sledge, Ballpeen, Ballpein, Beetle, Bully, Bush, Celt, Claw, Excudit, Flatten, Fuller, Gavel, Hack, Incuse, Kevel, Knap, Knapping, Madge, Mall(et), Malleate, Martel, Maul, Mjol(l)nir, Nevel, Oliver, Pane, Pean, Peen, Pein, Pene, Percussion, Piledriver, Planish, Plessor, Plexor, Rawhide, Repoussé, Sheep's-foot, Shingle, Sledge, Strike, Tenderizer, Tendon, Tilt, Trip, Umbre, Water, Wippen

▷ **Hammered** may indicate an anagram

Hammerthrower Thor

Hammock Cott

▷ **Hammy** may indicate an anagram

Hamper Basket, Cabin, Ceroon, Cramp, Cumber, Delay, Encumber, Entrammel, Hamstring, Handicap, Hobble, Hog-tie, Obstruct, Pad, Pannier, Ped, Pinch, Restrict, Rub, Sero(o)n, Shackle, Tangle, Trammel, Tuck

Hamster Cricetus

Hamstring Cramp, Hock, Hox, Lame, Popliteal, Thwart

Hand(s), Hand down, Hand-like, Handwriting Assist(ance), Bananas, Bequeath, Cacography, Calligraphy, Charge, Chicane, Chirography, Clap(ping), Claque, Club, Clutch, Copperplate, Court, Crew, Cursive, Daddle, Danny, Deal, Deck, Deliver, Devolve, Donny, Dukes, Dummy, Famble, Fin, Fist, Flipper, Flush, Free, Glad, Graphology, Help, Helping, Hond, Impart, Israel, Italian, Jambone, Jamboree, Kana, L, Man, Manual, Manus, Maulers, Medieval, Mitt(en), Nes(h)ki, Niggle, Operative, Pad, Palm(atifid), Part, Pass, Paw, Podium, Post, Pud, R, Rein (arm), Script, Signature, Span, Spencerian, Station, Straight, Sweep, Text, Tiger, Upper, Whip, Widow, Worker, Yarborough

Handbag Caba(s), Grip, Indispensable, Pochette, Purse, Reticule, Valise

Handbook Baedeker, Companion, Enchiridion, Guide, Manual, Vade-mecum

Handcuff(s) Bracelet, Darbies, Irons, Manacle, Mittens, Nippers, Snaps

Handful Few, Gowpen, Grip, Problem, Pugil, Rip(p), V

Handicap Bisque, Burden, Ebor, Encumber, Hamper, Impede, Impost, Lame, Liability, Lincolnshire, ➤ OBSTACLE, Off, Restrict, Weigh(t), Welter-race

Handicraft Marquetry

Handkerchief, Hanky Bandan(n)a, Belcher, Billy, Buffon, Clout, Fogle, Foulard, Kleenex®, Madam, Madras, Monteith, Muckender, Napkin, Nose-rag, Orarium, Romal, Rumal, Sudary, Tissue, Wipe(r)

Handle(d) Ansate, Bail, Bale, Bitstock, Brake, Broomstick, Cope, Crank, Dead man's, Deal, Doorknob, Dudgeon, Ear, Feel, Finger, Forename, Gaum, Gorm, Grip, Haft, Helve, Hilt, Hold, Knob, Knub, Lug, ➤ MANAGE, Manipulate, Manubrium, Maul, Name, Nib, Palp, Paw, Pommel, Process, Rounce, Shaft, Snath, Snead, Sneath, Sned, Staff, Staghorn, Stale, Steal(e), Steel, Steil, Stele, Stilt, Stock, Tiller, Title, To-name, Touch, Treat, Use, Whipstock, Wield, Withe

Handmaid(en) Iras, Manicurist, Valkyrie

Hand-out Alms, Charity, Dole, Gift, Release, Sample

Hand-signal Beck(on), Point, Wave

Handsome Adonis, Apollo, Bonny, Brave, Comely, Dishy, Featuous, Gracious, Liberal

Handspring Cartwheel

Hand-warmer Muff, Pome

Hand-washer Pilate

▶ **Handwriting** see HAND

Handy(man) Accessible, Close, Convenient, Deft, Dext(e)rous, Digit, Factotum, Jack(-of-all-trades), Near, Nigh, Palmate, Palmist, Ready, Skilful, Spartan, Useful

Hang, Hanger, Hanging(s) Append, Arras, Aweigh, Chick, Chik, Dangle, Darn, Depend, Dewitt, Dossal, Dossel, Dosser, Drape, Droop, Execute, Frontal, Gobelin, Hinge, Hoove, Hove(r), Kakemono, Kilt, Lobed, Loll, Lop, Lynch, Mooch, Noose, Nub, Pend(ant), Sag, Scenery, Scrag, Set, Sit, Sling, Suspend, Suspercollate, Swing, Tapestry, Tapet, Tapis, Toran(a)

Hanger-on Bur, Lackey, Leech, Limpet, Liripoop, Parasite, Satellite, Sycophant, Toady

Hangman, Hangmen Bull, Calcraft, Dennis, Derrick, Gregory, Ketch, Marwood, Nubbing-cove, Pierrepoint

Hangnail Agnail

Hangover Canopy, Cornice, Crapulence, Drape, DT's, Head, Hot coppers, Katzenjammer, Mistletoe, Tester

Hank Bobbin, Coil, Fake, Skein

Hanker(ing) Desire, Envy, Hunger, Itch, Long, Yearn, Yen

Hannibal Punic

Hansard Minutes

Haphazard Casual, Chance, Helter-skelter, Higgledy-piggledy, Hitty-missy, Promiscuous, ➤ RANDOM, Rough and tumble, Slapdash, Willy-nilly

Happen(ing), Happen to Afoot, Be, Befall, Befortune, Betide, Come, Event(uate), Fall-out, ➤ OCCUR, Pan, Pass, Prove, Thing, Tide, Transpire, Worth

Happiness, Happy Apposite, Ave, Beatific, Beatitude, Blessed, Bliss, Bonny, Carefree, Cheery, Chuffed, Cock-a-hoop, Dwarf, Ecstatic, Elated, Eud(a)emony, Felicity, Felix, Fortunate, Glad(some), Gleeful, Golden, Goshen, Gruntled, Halcyon, Half-cut, Hedonism, Jovial, Joy, Larry, Light-hearted, Merry, Opportune, Radiant, Rapture, Sandboy, Seal, Seel, Sele, Serene, Sunny, Tipsy, Trigger, Warrior

Hara-kiri Eventration, Seppuku, Suicide

Harangue Declaim, Diatribe, Lecture, Oration, Perorate, Philippic, Sermon, Speech, Spruik, Tirade

Harass(ed) Afflict, Annoy, Badger, Bait, Beleaguer, Bother, Chivvy, Distract, Dun, Gall, Grill, Grind, Grounden, Hassle, Haze, Heckle, Hector, Hound, Irritate, Persecute, Pester, Plague, Press, Thwart, Trash, Vex

Harbinger Herald, Omen, Precursor, Usher

Harbour Anchorage, Basin, Brest, Cherish, Dock, Entertain, Herd, Hide, Marina, Mulberry, Pearl, PLA, Port, Quay, Reset, ➤ SHELTER, Watemata

Hard(en), Hardness Abstruse, Adamant(ine), Adularia, Augean, Bony, Brinell, Brittle, Bronze, Cake, Calcify, Callous, Caramel, Cast-iron, Chitin, Cornute, Crusty, Difficult, Dour, Draconian, Ebonite, Endure, Enure, Firm, Flint(y), Geal, Granite, Gruelling, H, Hellish, Herculean, HH, Horny, Indurate, Inure, Iron(y), Knotty, Liparite, Lithoid, Metallic, Metally, Moh, Moh's scale, Nails, Obdurate, Obdure, Osseous, Ossify, Permafrost, Petrify, Picrite, Raw, Rugged, Ruthless, Schist, Scleral, Set, Severe, Solid, Sore, Steel(y), Steep, Stereo, Stern, Stoic, Stony, Teak, Temper, Tough, Wooden

Hard-core Riprap, Scalpins

Hard-headed Stegochepalian

Harding Warden

Hardliner Hawk

Hardly Borderline, Ill, Just, Scarcely, Uneath(es), Unnethes

Hard-pressed Strait, Taxed

Hardship Affliction, Grief, Mill, Mishap, Penance, Privation, Rigour, Trial, Trouble

Hardware Gear, Ironmongery

Hardy Brave, Dour, Durable, Manful, Oliver, Ollie, Rugged, Spartan, Sturdy, Thomas

Hare Arctic, Baud(rons), Bawd, Belgian, Doe, Dolicholis, Down, Electric, Husk, Jugged, Lam, Leporine, Malkin, Mara, Mawkin, Ochotona, Pika, Puss, Scut, Snowshoe, Wat

Hare-brained Giddy, Madcap, Scatty

Harem Gynaeceum, Gynoecium, Seraglio, Serai(l), Zenana

Hark(en) Ear, Hear, List(en)

Harlequin Chequered, Columbine, Pantaloon

Harlot Blue gown, Drab, Hussy, Loose, Paramour, Plover, Pusle, Pussel, Quail, Rahab, Slut, Strumpet, Whore

Harm(ed), Harmful Aggrieve, Bane, Blight, Deleterious, Detriment, Evil, Hurt, Inimical, Injury, Insidious, Maleficent, Malignant, Maltreat, Mischief, Noxious, Pernicious, Sinister, Spoil, Wroken, Wrong

Harmless Benign, Canny, Drudge, Informidable, Innocent, Innocuous, Innoxious, Inoffensive

Harmonica Harpoon

Harmonious, Harmonise, Harmony Agree(ment), Alan, Assort, Atone, Attune, Balanced, Blend, Chord, Concent, Concentus, Concert, Concinnity, Concord, Congruous, Consonant, Consort, Correspondence, Counterpoint, Descant, Diapason, Diatessaron, Doo-wop, Euphony, Eur(h)ythmy, Faburden, Feng-shui, Jibe, Melody, Musical, Solidarity, Symmetry, Sympathy, Sync, Thorough-bass, Tone, Tune, Unanimity, Unison

Harmotome Cross-stone

Harness(maker) Breeching, Bridle, Cinch, Equipage, Frenum, Gear, Girth, Hitch, Inspan, Lorimer, Loriner, Pad-tree, Partnership, Tack(le), Throat-stop, Trace, Yoke

Harp(sichord) Aeolian, Clairschach, Clarsach, Clavier, Drone, Dwell, Irish, Lyre, Nebel, Trigon, Virginal, Welsh, Zither

Harpagon Miser

Harpoon(er) Bart, Fis(h)gig, Fizgig, Grain, Iron, Lily iron, Peg, Spear, Specktioneer, Toggler, Tow-iron, Trident

Harpy Aello, Celeno, Eagle, Ocypete

Harridan Hag, Harpy, Shrew, Xantippe, Zantippe, Zentippe

Harrier Montagu's

Harriet Hetty, Martineau

Harrow Alas, Appal, Brake, Disc, Frighten, Herse, Plough, Rake, Rend, Shock

Harry Aggravate, Badger, Bother, Champion, Chase, Chivvy, Coppernose, Dragoon, Flash, Fret, Hal, Harass, Hassle, Hector, Herry, Houdini, Hound, Lauder, Lime, Maraud, Molest, Nag, Pester, Plague, Rag, Reave, Reive, Rieve, Rile, Tate, Tchick, Torment

▷ **Harry** may indicate an anagram

Harsh(ness) Acerbic, Austere, Barbaric, Brassy, Cruel, Desolate, Discordant, Draconian, Glary, Grating, Gravelly, Grim, Gruff, Guttural, Hard, Inclement, Raucle, Raucous, Raw, Rigour, Rude, Scabrid, Screechy, ➤ SEVERE, Sharp, Spartan, Stark, Stern, Stoor, Stour, Stowre, Strict, Strident

Hart Deer, Spade, Spay, Spay(a)d, Venison

Harte Bret

Hartebeest Bubal, Kaama, Kongoni

Harum-scarum Bayard, Chaotic, Madcap, Rantipole

Harvest(er), Harvest home Combine, Crop, Cull, Fruit, ➤ GATHER, Hairst, Hawkey, Hay(sel), Hockey, Horkey, In(ning), Ingather, Kirn, Lease, Nutting,

Pick, Produce, Rabi, Random, Reap, Shock, Spatlese, Tattie-howking, Thresh, Vendage, Vendange

Has Habet, Hath, 's, Owns

Has-been Effete, Ex, Outmoded

Hash(ish) Bungle, Charas, Discuss, Garble, Garboil, Hachis, Lobscouse, Mince, Pi(e), Ragout

▷ **Hashed** may indicate an anagram

Hasn't Hant, Nas

Hassle Aggro, Bother

Hassock Kneeler, Pouf(fe), Stool, Tuffet

Haste(n), Hastening, Hastily, Hasty Cursory, Despatch, Express, Festinately, Fly, Hare, Headlong, Hie, Hotfoot, ➤ HURRY, Impetuous, Precipitant, Race, Ramstam, Rash, Rush, Scuttle, Speed, Spur, Stringendo, Subitaneous, Sudden, Tear, Tilt

Hastings Banda, Bustles, Senlac, Warren

Hat Akuba, Ascot, Astrakhan, Balibuntal, Balmoral, Basher, Beanie, Beany, Bearskin, Beaver, Beret, Billycock, Biretta, Boater, Bollinger, Bowler, Boxer, Brass, Breton, Broad-brim, Busby, Cap, Capotain, Cartwheel, Castor, Chapeau, Cheese-cutter, Chimneypot, Christie, Christy, Claque, Cloche, Cocked, Cockle-hat, Coolie, Cowboy, Crusher, Curch, Deerstalker, Derby, Dolly Varden, Dunstable, Envoy, Fedora, Fez, Flat-cap, Fore-and-after, Gaucho, Gibus, Glengarry, Hard, Hattock, Headdress, Head-rig, Hennin, Homburg, Kamelaukion, Leghorn, Lid, Lum, Matador, Mitre, Mob-cap, Mountie's, Mushroom, Nab, Opera, Pagri, Panama, Petasus, Picture, Pilion, Pill-box, Pilleus, Pilos, Planter's, Plateau, Poke(-bonnet), Pork-pie, Profile, Puggaree, Puritan, Ramil(l)ies, Red, Runcible, Safari, Sailor, Shako, Shovel, Silk, Skimmer, Skull-cap, Slouch, Snap-brim, Snood, Sola(-helmet), Solah, Sola-topi, Sombrero, Souwester, Steeple-crown, Stetson®, Stovepipe, Straw, Sugarloaf, Sunbonnet, Sundown, Sunhat, Tam(o'shanter), Tarboosh, Tarb(o)ush, Tarpaulin, Ten-gallon, Terai, Tile, Tin, Tit(fer), Toorie, Top(per), Topee, Topi, Toque, Tricorn(e), Trilby, Turban, Tyrolean, Ugly, Wide-awake

Hat-band Weeper

Hatch(ment), Hatching Achievement, Altricial, Booby, Breed, Brood, Cleck, Clutch, Companion, Concoct, Cover, Devise, Eclosion, Emerge, Escape, Incubate, Set, Trap-door

Hatchet(-shaped) Axe, Bill, Chopper, Cleaver, Dolabriform, Tomahawk

▷ **Hatching** may indicate an anagram

Hatchway (surround) Fiddley, Porthole, Scuttle

Hate(ful), Hatred Abhor, Abominable, Abominate, Anims, Aversion, Bugbear, Detest, Enmity, Haterent, Loathe, Misogyny, Odium, Phobia, Racism, Resent, Spite, Ug(h), Vitriol

Hat-plant S(h)ola

Hatty Etta

Haughty Aloof, Aristocratic, Arrogant, Bashaw, Disdainful, Fastuous, High, Hogen-mogen, Hoity-toity, Hye, Imperious, Lofty, Orgillous, Orgulous, Paughty, ➤ PROUD, Scornful, Sdeignful, Sniffy, Upstage

Haul(ier) Bag, Bouse, Bowse, Brail, Carry, Cart, Catch, Drag, Heave, Hove, Kedge, Loot, Plunder, Pull, Rug, Sally, Scoop, Snig, Touse, Touze, Tow(se), Towze, Transporter, Trice, Winch, Yank

Haunch Hance, Hip, Huckle, Hunkers, Quarter

Haunt(s) Catchy, Den, Dive, Frequent, Ghost, Hang-out, Honky-tonk, Houf(f), Howf(f), Infest, Obsess, Purlieu, Resort, Spot, Spright

Hauteur Bashawism, Height, Morgue, Vanity

Have, Having Bear, Ha(e), Han, Hoax, Hold, Of, ➤ OWN, Possess, Sell

Haven Asylum, Harbour, Hithe, Hythe, Oasis, Port, Refuge, Refugium, Retreat, Shelter, Tax

Haver(s) Blether, Clanjamfray, Dither, Gibber, Nigel

▶ **Haversack** see RUCKSACK

Havoc Desolation, Devastation, Hell, Ravage, Waste

▷ **Havoc** may indicate an anagram

Haw Hip, Sloe

Hawaiian Kanaka

Hawk(er), Hawkish Accipitrine, Auceps, Badger, Bastard, Buzzard, Cadger, Camelot, Caracara, Cast, Cheapjack, Cooper's, Cry, Eagle, Elanet, Eyas, Falcon, Gerfalcon, Goshawk, Haggard, Hardliner, Harrier, Hobby, Keelie, Kestrel, Kite, Lammergeier, Lanner(et), Marsh, Merlin, Molla(h), Monger, Moolah, Mullah, Musket, Nyas, Osprey, Ossifrage, Passage, Pearlie, Pearly, Pedlar, Peddle, Peregrine, Ringtail, Sacre(t), Sell, Slab, Soar(e), Sorage, Sore(-eagle), Sparrow, Spiv, Staniel, Sutler, Tallyman, Tarsal, Tarsel(l), Tassel, Tercel(et), Tiersel, Trant(er), Warlike

Hawkeye IA, Iowa

Hawk-keeper Austringer, Ostreger

Hawser Line, Rope

Hawthorn Albespine, Albespyne, May(flower), Quickset

Hay, Hey Antic, Cock, Contra-dance, Fodder, Goaf, Hi, Kemple, Math, Mow, Pleach, Salt, Stack, Straw, Windrow

Hayfever Pollenosis

Haymaker Blow, Slog

Hayseed Chaw-bacon, Hodge, Rustic

Hazard(ous) Breakneck, Bunker, Chance, Danger, Dare, Die, Dye, Game, Gremlin, Guess, Imperil, In-off, Jeopardy, Main, Nice, Occupational, Peril, Play, Pothole, Queasy, ➤ RISK, Stake, Trap, Venture, Vigia, Wage

Haze, Hazy Blear, Cloud, Filmy, Fog, ➤ MIST, Mock, Muzzy, Nebulous, Smog, Tease

▷ **Haze** may indicate an anagram

Hazel(wort) Amenta, Asarabacca, Catkin, Cob, Corylus, Filbert

HC Encomia, Encomium

He, HE A, Helium, Tag, Tig, ➤ TNT, Tom

Head(s), Heading, Headman, Heady Aim, Apex, Ard-ri(gh), Beachy, Bean, Behead, Bill, Block, Bonce, Boss, Brain, Brainpan, Bregma, Brow, But(t), Caboceer, Cape, Capitani, Capitulum, Capo, Captain, Caption, Caput, Caudillo, Cephalic, Chaton, Chief, Coarb, Coconut, Coma, Commander, Conk, Cop, Coppin, Costard, Crest, Crisis, Crown, Crumpet, Director, Dome, Each, Ear, Exarch, Figure, Flamborough, Foam, Froth, Glomerate, Grand Mufti, Herm(a), Hoe, Hogh, Jowl, Knob, Knowledge-box, Lead(er), Lid, Lizard, Loaf, Loave, Loo, Lore, Malik, Manager, Mayor, Maz(z)ard, Melik, Mocuddum, Mokaddam, Mull, Muqaddam, Nab, Nana, Napper, Nappy, Ness, Nob, Noddle, Noggin, Noll, Noup, Nowl, Nut, Obverse, Occiput, Onion, Panicle, Parietal, Pash, Pate, Pater(familias), Patriarch, Point, Poll, Pow, Prefect, President, Principal, Promontory, Provost, Ras, Read-write, Ream, Rubric, Sarpanch, Scalp, Scaup, Scaw, Scholarch, Scolex, Sconce, Short, Sinciput, Skaw, Skull, Source, Spume, Squeers, Starosta, Superior, Tanadar, Tete, Thanadar, Throne, Tight, Title, Toilet, Top, Topic, Twopenny, Vaivode, Voivode, Yorick, Zupan

▷ **Head** may indicate the first letter of a word

Headache Hangover, Megrim, Migraine, Neuralgia, Red out, Scotodinia, Splitter

Headband Fillet, Garland, Infula, Sphendone

Headdress, Head cover Ampyx, Balaclava, Bandeau, Bas(i)net, Bonnet, Burnous(e), Busby, Calotte, Caul, Chaplet, Circlet, Comb, Cor(o)net, Cowl, Coxcomb, Crownet, Curch, Doek, Dopatta, Dupatta, Fascinator, Fontange, Hat(tock), Helm(et), Juliet cap, Kaffiyeh, Kuffiyeh, Kufiah, Kufiya(h), Kell, Kerchief, Mantilla, Mitre, Mobcap, Modius, Mortarboard, Nubia, Periwig, Pill-box, Plug-hat, Porrenger, Porringer, Romal, Sakkos, Ship-tire, Silly-how, Skullcap, Sphendome, Stephane, Taj, Tarbush, Tiara, Tower, Tulban, Turban, War bonnet, Wig, Wimple

Header Bonder, Dive, Fall, Rowlock

Headhunter Naga

Headland Bill, Cape, Head-rig, Hoe, Hogh, Morro, Naze, Ness, Noup, Promontory, Ras, Ross, Scaw, Skaw

Headless Acephalous

Headlight Beam, Dip, Halo

Headline Banner, Caption, Frown, Scare-head, Screamer, Streamer, Title

Headlock Chancery

Headlong Breakneck, Pell-mell, Precipitate, Ramstam, Reckless, Steep, Sudden, Tantivy, Tearaway

▶ **Headman** see HEAD

Headmaster Principal, Squeers

Headphone(s) Cans, Earpiece, Walkman®

Headquarters Base, Command, Depot, Guildhall, Pentagon, SHAPE, Station

▷ **Heads** may indicate a lavatory

Headstrong Obstinate, Rash, Stubborn, Unruly, Wayward

Head-to-tail Tête-bêche

Headway Advancement, Headroom, Progress

Head-word Lemma

Heal(ing) Aesculapian, Balsam, Chiropractic, Cicatrise, Cleanse, Cure, Esculapian, G(u)arish, Hele, Hippocratise, Intention, Knit, Mend, Olosis, Osteopathy, Restore, Sain, Salve, Sanitory, Therapeutic, Vulnerary

Healer Asa, Doctor, Homeopath, Naturopath, Osteopath, Sangoma, Shaman, Time

Health(y) Bracing, Chin-chin, Doer, Fit, Flourishing, Gesundheit, Hail, Hale, Hartie-hale, Heart, Holism, Kia-ora, L'chaim, Lustique, Lusty, Medicaid, Medicare, Pink, Prosit, Robust, Salubrious, Sane, Slainte, Sound, Toast, Tope, Valetudinarian, Vigour, Well, WHO, Wholesome

Heap(ed) Acervate, Agglomerate, Amass, Bing, Bulk, Car, Clamp, Cock, Concervate, Congeries, Cumulus, Drift, Hog, Jalopy, Lot, Pile, Rick(le), Ruck, Scrap, Slag, Stash, Tass, Toorie, Up-piled

Hear(ing) Acoustic, Attend, Audience, Audile, Avizandum, Captain's mast, Catch, Clairaudience, Dirdum, Ear, Harken, Learn, List(en), Oyer, Oyez, Panel

▷ **Hear(say)** may indicate a word sounding like one given

Hearsay Account, Gossip, Report, Rumour, Surmise

Hearse Bier, Catafalco, Catafalque

Heart(en), Heartily, Hearty, Heart-shaped AB, Agood, Auricle, Backslapping, Beater, Bluff, Bosom, Bradycardia, Cant, Cardiac, Centre, Cheer, Cockles, Columella, Cordate, Cordial, Core, Crossed, Courage, Daddock, Embolden, Essence, Gist, H, Hale, Herz, Inmost, Jarta, Kernel, Lepid, Memoriter, Mesial, Mid(st), Nub, Nucleus, Obcordate, Purple, Robust, Root, Sacred, Sailor, Seafarer, Seaman, Sinoatrial, Staunch, Tachycardia, Tar, Ticker, Yarta, Yarto

Heart-break Crève-coeur, Grief, Sorrow

Heartburn Brash, Cardialgia, Pyrosis

Heartfelt Deep, Genuine, Real, Sincere

Hearth Cupel, Fireside, Home, Ingle

Heartless Callous, Cored, Cruel, Three-suited

Heart's ease Pansy

Heart trouble Bradycardia, Fibrillation

Heat(ed), Heater, Heating Anneal, Ardour, Atomic, Barrage, Beath, Brazier, Calcine, Califont, Caloric, Calorifier, Central, Chafe, Convector, Dudgeon, Eccaleobion, Element, Eliminator, Endothermic, Enthalpy, Etna, Excite, Exothermic, Ferment, Fever, Fire, Fluster, Fug, Furnace, Het, Hibachi, Hyperthermia, Hypocaust, Immersion, Incalescence, J, Kindle, Latent, Liquate, Lust, Moxibustion, Normalise, Oestrus, Prelim, Prickly, Q, Radiant, Radiator, Rankine, Recalescence, Render, Repechage, Rut, Salt, Scald, Sinter, Sizzle, Space, Specific, Spice, Stew, Storage, Stove, Teend, Tind, Tine, Torrefy, Tynd(e), Underfloor, Warming-pan, Warmth, White

Heath Bearberry, Bent, Briar, Brier, Egdon, Epacrid, Erica, Lande, Manoao, Manzanita, Moor, Muir, Stead, Ted

Heathen Ethnic, Gentile, Infidel, Litholatrous, Pagan, Pa(i)nim, Paynim, Philistine, Primitive, Profane

Heather Bell, Broom, Calluna, Epacrid, Erica, Ling, Sprig

▷ **Heating** may indicate an anagram

Heave(d) Cast, Fling, Heeze, Hoist, Hump, Hurl, Popple, Retch, Shy, Sigh, Vomit

▷ **Heave** may indicate 'discard'

Heaven(s), Heavenly Air, Aloft, Ama, Ambrosial, Asgard, Bliss, Celestial, Celia, Divine, Ecstasy, Elysian, Elysium, Empyrean, Ethereal, Fiddler's Green, Firmament, Hereafter, Himmel, Holy, Leal, Lift, Mackerel, Olympus, Paradise, Pole, Seventh, Shangri-la, Sion, Sky, Supernal, Svarga, Swarga, Swerga, Tur-na-n'og, Uranian, Welkin, Zion

Heavy(weight), Heavily, Heaviness Ali, Dutch, Elephantine, Embonpoint, Endomorph, Grave, Hefty, Last, Leaden, Onerous, Osmium, Pesante, Ponderous, Sad, Scelerate, Stout, Upsee, Ups(e)y, Weighty, Wicked

Hebe Barmaid

Hebrew Aramaic, Eli, Heb, Jesse, Levi, Mishnayoth, Yid

Hebridean Harris

Heckle Badger, Gibe, Harass, Needle, Spruik

Hectic Ding-dong, Feverish, Frenetic

Hector Badger, Bluster, Browbeat, Bully, ➤ HARASS, Nag

Hedge, Hedging Box, Bullfinch, Enclosure, Equivocate, Haw, Hay, Lay off, Meuse, Mews, Muse, Pleach, Privet, Quickset, Raddle, Sepiment, Shield, Stonewall, Thicket

Hedgehog Gymnure, Hérisson, Tenrec, Tiggywinkle, Urchin

Hedge-parson Bucklebeggar, Patercove

Hedge-sparrow Accentor

Hedonist Cyreniac, Epicurean, Playboy

Heed(ed), Heedful Attend, Listen, ➤ MIND, Notice, Observe, Rear, Reck, Regard(ant), Respect, Rought, Tent

Heedless Careless, Incautious, Rash, Scapegrace, Scatterbrain

Heel Cad, Calcaneum, Cant, Careen, Cuban, Dogbolt, Foot, French, Kitten, List, Louse, Rogue, Seel, Spike, Stacked, Stiletto, Tilt, Wedge

Heel-tap Snuff

Hefty Brawny, Heavy, Weighty

Heifer Io, Quey, Stirk

Height(en), Heights Abraham, Altitude, Cairngorm, Ceiling, Dimension, Elevation, Embroider, Eminence, Enhance, Golan, H, Hill, Hypsometry, Level, Might, Peak, Procerity, Stature, Stud, Sum, ➤ SUMMIT, Tor

Heinous Abominable, Atrocious, Flagrant

Heir Alienee, Claimant, Coparcener, Dauphin, Devisee, Eigne, Institute, Intitule, Legatee, Parcener, Scion, Sprig, Tanist

Heirless Escheat, Intestate

Held Captive, Hostage, Sostenuto

▷ **Held by** may indicate a hidden word

Helen Elaine, Nell(y)

Helicopter, Heliport Airstop, Chopper, Egg-beater, Gunship, Hover, Rotodyne, Sikorsky, Sky-hook, Whirlybird

Helios Hyperion

Heliotrope Cherry-pie

Helium He

Hell(ish) Abaddon, Ades, Agony, Amenthes, Annw(yf)n, Avernus, Below, Chthonic, Dis, Erebus, Furnace, Gehenna, Hades, Heck, Inferno, Malebolge, Naraka, Orcus, Pandemonium, Perditious, Pit, Sheol, Stygian, Tartar(ean), Tartarus, Tophet, Torment

Hellbender Menopome, Mud-puppy

Hellebore Itchweed, Setterwort

Hellespont Dardanelles

Hello, Hallo, Hullo Aloha, Chin-chin, Ciao, Dumela, Hi, Ho(a), Howdy, Howzit, Yoo-hoo

Helm(sman) Cox, Pilot, Steer, Tiller, Timon(eer)

Helmet Armet, Balaclava, Basinet, Beaver, Burganet, Burgonet, Cask, Casque, Comb, Crash, Galea, Heaume, Knapscal, Knapscull, Knapskull, Montero, Mor(r)ion, Nasal, Pickelhaube, Pith, Plumed, Pot, Salade, Sal(l)et, Shako, Skid-lid, Topee, Topi

Helot Esne, Slave

Help(er), Helping, Helpful Abet, Accomplice, Adjuvant, Advantage, Aid(ance), Aidant, Aide, Alleviate, Ally, ➤ ASSIST, Avail, Back, Benefit, Befriend, Bestead, Boon, Brownie, Char(woman), Coadjutor, Complice, Daily, Dollop, Dose, Forward, Further(some), Go, Hand, Hint, Instrumental, Leg-up, Maid, Mayday, Obliging, Order, Patronage, Ration, Recourse, Relieve, Servant, Serve, Slice, SOS, Stead, Sted, Subserve, Subvention, Succour, Taste, Therapeutic, Use

Helpless(ness) Adynamia, Anomie, Feeble, Impotent, Paralytic, Useless

Hem Border, Fringe, Hoop, List

He-man Adonis, Hunk, Jock, Macho

Hemisphere, Hemispherical Magdeburg, Rose-cut

Hemlock Conia, Cowbane, Insane root, Tsuga

Hemp Abaca, Bhang, Bowstring, Choke-weed, Codilla, Dagga, Fimble, Ganja, Hards, Indian, K(a)if, Kef, Love-drug, Manil(l)a, Moorva, Murva, Neckweed, Pita, Sida, Sunn, Tat, Tow

Hen Ancona, Andalusian, Australorp, Biddy, Buff Orpington, Chock, Cochin, Dorking, Eirack, Fowl, Houdan, Langshan, Layer, Leghorn, Orpington, Partlet, Pertelote, Plymouth Rock, Poulard, Pullet, Ree(ve), Rhode Island Red, Sitter, Sultan, Tappit, Welsummer, Wyandotte

Hence Apage, Avaunt, Ergo, Go, Hinc, So, Therefore, Thus

Henchman Attendant, Follower, Satellite

Hen-house Battery, Eggery

Hen-pecked Spineless, Woman-tired

Henna Camphire

Hennery Run

Henry Eighth, H, Hal, Hooray, Hy, James, Navigator, O

Hep Bacca, Berry, Hip

Hepatic Scale-moss

Hepatitis Favism, Jaundice

Herald(ic), Heraldry Abatement, Argent, Armory, Azure, Bars, Bend, Bendwise, Blazonry, Bloody Hand, Bluemantle, Bordure, Caboched, Chevron, Chief, Cicerone, Cinquefoil, Clarenc(i)eux, Compone, Compony, Couchant, Counter-passant, Coue, Couped, Coward, Crier, Difference, Displayed, Dormant, Endorse, Erased, Fecial, Fess(e), Fetial, File, Flory, Forerunner, Gardant, Garter, Golp(e), Gules, Hauriant, Hermes, Issuant, Lionel, Lodged, Lyon, Martlet, Messenger, Mullet, Naiant, Naissant, Nascent, Nombril, Norroy, Opinicus, Or, Ordinary, Pale, Pallet, Paly, Passant, Pile, Portcullis, Potent, Precursor, Proclaim, Purpure, Pursuivant, Quartering, Rampant, Red Hand, Regardant, Roundel, Roundle, Sable, Salient, Scarp, Sea lion, Segreant, Sejant, Statant, Stentor, Subordinary, Trangle, Tressure, Trick, Trippant, Trundle, Umbrated, Urinant, Usher, Verdoy, Vert, Vol(ant), Vorant, Yale

Herb(s) Aconite, Angelica, Anise, Aristolochia, Arugula, Avens, Basil, Bay, Bennet, Bergamot, Borage, Centaury, Chamomile, Chervil, C(h)ive, Cilanto, Comfrey, Coriander, Costmary, Cum(m)in, Dill, Dittany, Echinacea, Eruca, Exacum, Eyebright, Felicia, Fennel, Fenugreek, Ferula, Feverfew, Fireweed, Fluellin, Forb, Garlic, Garnish, Gentian, Germander, Good-King-Henry, Gunnera, Haworthia, Hyssop, Inula, Kalanchoe, Knapweed, Lamb's ears, Laserpicium, Laserwort, Lovage, Madder, Madwort, Mandrake, Marjoram, Maror, Medic, Mint, Moly, Mustard, Oca, Oleraceous, Oregano, Origan(e), Origanum, Ornithogalum, Orval, Parsley, Paterson's curse, Pia, Pipsissewa, Plantain, Purpie, Purslane, Pussytoes, Rest-harrow, Rhizocarp, Rodgersia, Rosemary, Rue, Sage, Salsify, Savory, Senna, Sesame, Soapwort, Sorrel, Southernwood, Spearmint, Staragen, Sweet cicely, Tacca, Tansy, Tarragon, Thyme, Tormentil, Typha, Valerian, Vervain, Weed, Willow, Wormwood, Wort, Yarrow, Yerba

Herbert Alan, AP(H), Lom, Spencer

Herbicide Agent Orange, Atrazine, Defoliant, Picloram

Herbivore Iguanodon, Sauropod

Hercules Alcides, Huge, Rustam, Rustem

Herd(er), Herdsman Band, Corral, Drive, Drover, Flock, Gang, Mob, Pod, Raggle-taggle, Round-up, Shepherd, Tinchel, Vaquero

Here Adsum, Hi, Hic, Hither, Local, Now, Present

Hereditary, Heredity Ancestry, Blood, Breeding, Codon, Eugenics, Genetics, Id(ant), Idioplasm, Mendelism

▷ **Herein** may indicate a hidden word

Here is laid HS

Heresiarch Nestor

Heresy, Heretic(al) Agnoitae, Albi, Albigensian, Apostasy, Arian, Bogomil, Bugger, Cathar, Docete, Dulcinist, Eudoxian, Giaour, Heresearch,

Heterodoxy, Lollard, Montanism, Nestorian, Nonconformist, Origen, Patarin(e), Pelagius, Phrygian, Racovian, Rebel, Unitarian, Zendik

Heritage Birthright, Due, Ottilie, Patrimony

Hermaphrodite Androgenous, Gynandromorph, Monochinous, Monoecious

Hermes (rod) Caduceus, Mercury

Hermetic Alchemist, Sealed

Hermit(age) Anchoret, Anchorite, Ascetic, Ashram(a), Augustinian, Austin, Cell, Cloister, Crab, Eremite, Grandmontine, Marabout, Monk, Museum, Nitrian, Peter, Recluse, Retreat, Robber-crab, Sannyasi, Soldier-crab, Solitary, Troglodyte

Hernia Bubonocele, Cystocoele, Diverticulum, Enterocele, Hiatus, Rupture

Hero(ic) Achilles, Agamemnon, Aitu, Ajax, Alcides, Amadis, Bellerophon, Beowulf, Brave, Champ(ion), Cid, Couplet, Crockett, Cuchulain, Cuchullain, Cyrano, Demigod, Epic, Eponym, Eric, Everyman, Faust, Fingal, Finn, Finn MacCool, Folk, Garibaldi, God, Goody, Great, Hector, Heracles, Hercules, Hiawatha, Howleglass, Hudibrastic, Ideal, Idol, Jason, Kaleva, Kami, Leonidas, Lion, Lochinvar, Lothair, Marmion, Meleager, Nestor, Noble, Oliver, Onegin, Owl(e)glass, Ow(l)spiegle, Paladin, Parsifal, Pericles, Perseus, Priestess, Principal, Resolute, Revere, Rinaldo, Roderick, Roderego, Roland, Rustem, Rustum, Saladin, Sheik, Siegfried, Sigurd, Superman, Tam o'Shanter, Tancred, Tell, Theseus, Tragic, Triptolemus, Tristan, Trist(r)am, Ulysses, Valiant, Vercingetorix, Volsung, White knight

Herod Agrippa

Heroin Dogfood, Doojie, Dynamite, Gumball, H, Harry, Henry, Horse, Jack, Junk, Scag, Shit, Skag, Smack, Snow, Snowball, Sugar

Heroine Andromeda, Ariadne, Candida, Darling, Hedda, Imogen, Isolde, Juliet, Leda, Leonora, Manon, Mimi, Nana, Norma, Pamela, Star, Tess, Una

Heron(s) Ardea, Bird, Bittern, Butter-bump, Egret, Handsaw, Kotuko, Screamer, Sedge, Siege, Squacco

Herpes Cold sore, Dartre, Shingles, Shiver

Herring Bismarck, Bloater, Brisling, Brit, Buckling, Caller, Cisco, Clupea, Gaspereau, Kipper, Lake, Maise, Maize, Ma(a)tjes, Mattie, Maze, Mease, Menhaden, Red, Rollmop, Sea-stick, Shotten, Sild, Silt, Teleost

Herringbone Sloping

Hesitate, Hesitation Balance, Boggle, Cunctation, Delay, Demur, Dicker, Dither, Doubtful, Falter, Halting, Haver, Haw, Mammer, ➤ PAUSE, Qualm, Scruple, Shillyshally, Shrink, Stagger, Stammer, Swither, Tarrow, Teeter, Tentative, Um, Ur, Vacillate, Wait, Waver

Hesperus Vesper

Hessian Burlap, Hireling

Heterodoxy Heresy

Heterogeneous Diverse, Motley, Piebald

Heterosexual Straight

Hew Ax, Chop, Cut, Hack, Sever

Hex Jinx, Voodoo

▶ **Hey** see HAY

Heyday Prime, Summer

Hi Cooee, Hello

Hiatus Caesura, Gap, Hernia, Interregnum, Lacuna, Lull

Hibernate, Hibernating Estivate, Latitant, Sleep, Winter

Hibernian Irish

Hibiscus Okra, Roselle, Rozelle

Hiccup Glitch, Singultus, Snag, Spasm, Yex

Hick Jake, Oaf, Podunk, Rube, Yokel

Hickory Jackson, Pecan, Shagbark

Hidden Buried, Covert, De(a)rn, Doggo, Hooded, Latent, Obscure, Occult, Pentimento, Recondite, Screened, Shuttered, Sly, Ulterior, Unseen, Veiled, Wrapped

▷ **Hidden** may indicate a concealed word

Hide, Hiding Abscond, Befog, Bield(y), Box-calf, Burrow, Cache, Camouflage, Ceroon, Coat, ➤ CONCEAL, Cordwain, Couch, Cour, Crop, Curtain, Doggo, Earth, Eclipse, Encave, Ensconce, Enshroud, Envelop, Epidermis, Fell, Flaught, Flay, Harbour, Heal, Heel, Hele, Hell, Incave, Inter, Kip, Kipskin, Lair, Leather, Mask, Nebris, ➤ OBSCURE, Parfleche, Pell, Pelt, Plank, Plant, Robe, Saffian, Screen, Secrete, Shadow, Shellac(k), Skin, Spetch, Stash, Strap-oil, Tappice, Thong, Thrashing, Trove, Veil, Wallop, Whang, Wrap

Hideous(ness) Deform(ed), Enormity, Gash, Grotesque, Horrible, Odious, Ugly, Ugsome

Hierarchic, Hierarchy Byzantine, Elite, Theocracy

Hieroglyph Cipher, Pictogram

Higgledy-piggledy Mixtie-maxtie

High(er), Highly, Highness Alt(a), Altesse, Altissimo, Apogee, Atop, Brent, Climax, Doped, Drugged, E-la, Elation, Elevated, Eminent, Exalted, Excelsior, Frequency, Gamy, Haut(e), Intoxicated, Lofty, Maggotty, Mind-blowing, Orthian, Prime, Rancid, Ripe, School, Senior, Sent, Shrill, So, Steep, Stenchy, Stoned, String-out, Strong, Superior, Swollen, Tall, Tension, Tipsy, Top-lofty, Topmost, Treble, Up(per), Very, Wired

▷ **High** may indicate an anagram

High and mighty Haughty, Hogen-mogen

Highball Drink, Lob, Loft

Highbrow Brain, Egghead, Intelligentsia, Long-hair

High-class Best, Superior, U

High-crowned Copataine

Highest Best, Climax, Mostwhat, Ne plus ultra, Progressive, Supreme

Highest note E-la

High-flown Bombastic, Euphuism

Highland(er), Highlands Blue-bonnet, Blue-cap, Cameron, Cat(h)eran, Down, Dun(n)iewassal, Duniwassal, Gael, Kiltie, Nainsel(l), Plaid(man), Redshank, Riff, Scot, Seaforth, Shire, Teuchter

Highlight Feature, Focus, Heighten, Stress

▶ **High-pitched** see HIGH

High tension HT

Highway Alaska, Alcan, Autobahn, Autopista, Autostrada, Flyover, Freeway, Interstate, Motorway, Overpass, Pass, Thoroughfare, Tightrope

Highwayman, Highway robber(y) Bandit, Bandolero, Duval, Footpad, Fraternity, Gilderoy, Jack Sheppard, Land-pirate, Land-rat, Latrocinium, MacHeath, Motorist, Rank-rider, Scamp, Skyjacker, Toby, Turpin, Twitcher, Wheel

Hijack(er) Abduct, Pirate

Hike(r) Backpack, Bushbash, Bushwalk, Raise, Rambler, Ramp, Rise, Traipse, Tramp, Trape(s), Upraise

Hilarious, Hilarity Hysterical, Jollity, Mirth

Hilary Term

Hill(ock), Hills, Hillside Arafat, Areopagus, Aventine, Barrow, Beacon, Ben, Bent, Berg, Beverly, Black, Bluff, Brae, Broken, Bunker, Butte, Caelian, Calvan, Capitol(ine), Cheviots, Chiltern, Chin, Cleve, Cone, Coteau, Crag-and-tail, Crest, Djebel, Drumlin, Dun(e), Eminence, Esquiline, Fell, Gebel, Golan Heights, Golgotha, Gradient, Grampians, Hammock, Height, Helvellyn, Highgate, Horst, How, Hummock, Incline, Inselberg, Janiculum, Jebel, Kip(p), Knap, Knoll, Knot, Kop(je), Koppie, Lammermuir, Lavender, Law, Loma, Low, Ludgate, Mamelon, Man, Mendip, Merrick, Mesa, Monadnock, Monticule, Morro, Mound, Mount Lofty Ranges, Nab, Nanatak, North Downs, Otway Ranges, Palatine, Pennines, Pike, Pingo, Pnyx, Quantocks, Quirinal, Rand, Range, Saddleback, Scaur, Silbury, Sion, Stoss, Tara, Tel(l), Toft, Toot, Tump, Tweedsmuir, Viminal, Wolds, Wrekin, Zion

Hillbilly Yap

Hill-dweller Ant

Hillman Areopagite, Nepalese

Hilltop Crest, Knoll, Nab

Hilt Basket, Coquille, Haft, Handle, Hasp, Shaft

Him(self) He, Ipse, Un

Himalaya(n) Nepali, Panda, Sherpa, Tibetan

Hind(most) Back, Deer, Lag, Rear

Hinder, Hindrance Back, Bar, Block, Check, Counteract, Cumber, Debar, ➤ DELAY, Deter, Estop, Hamper, Harass, Holdback, Impeach, Impede, Obstacle, Overslaugh, Posterior, Rear, Rein, Remora, Rump, Shackle, Slow, Stop, Stunt, Taigle, Thwart, Trammel

Hindquarters Backside, Crupper, Haunches

Hindu Arya Samaj, Babu, Bania(n), Banyan, Brahman, Brahmin, Dalit, Gentoo, Gurkha, Harijan, Jaina, Kshatriya, Maharishi, Pundit, Rajpoot, Rajput, Rama, Sad(d)hu, Saiva, S(h)akta, Sankhya, Shaiva, Sheik(h), Shudra, Sudra, Swami, Trimurti, Untouchable, Urdu, Vais(h)ya, Varna, Vedanta

Hinge Butt, Cardinal, Cross-garnet, Garnet, Gemel, Gimmer, Joint, Knee, Pivot

▷ **Hinge(s)** may indicate a word reversal

Hingeless Ecardinate

Hinny Ass, Donkey, Joe

Hint Allude, Clew, Clue, Cue, Element, Gleam, Hunch, Imply, Inkle, Inkling, Innuendo, Insinuate, Intimate, Key, Mint, Nuance, Office, Overtone, Pointer, Preview, Scintilla, Shadow, Soupçon, ➤ SUGGEST, Tang, Tip, Touch, Trace, Trick, Wind, Wink, Wisp, Word, Wrinkle

▷ **Hint** may indicate a first letter

Hip(pie), Hippy, Hips Cafard, Cheer, Coxa(l), Drop-out, Huck(le), Hucklebone, Hunkers, Informed, Ischium, Sciatic, Tonish

Hippopotamus Behemoth, River-horse, Sea-cow

Hire(d), Hiring Affreightment, Charter, Engage, Fee, Freightage, Job, Lease, Merc(enary), Never-never, Rent, Shape-up, Ticca, Wage

Hirsute Hairy, Pilose, Shaggy

▷ **His** may indicate greetings

Hiss Boo, Fizzle, Goose, Hish, Sibilant, Siffle, Sizzle, Swish

Historian Acton, Adams, Antiquary, Archivist, Arrian, Asellio, Bede, Biographer, Bryant, Buckle, Camden, Carlyle, Centuriator, Chronicler, Etain, Froude, Gibbon, Gildas, Green, Griot, Herodotus, Knickerbocker, Livy, Macaulay, Oman, Pliny, Plutarch, Ponsonby, Renan, Roper, Sallust, Strachey, Suetonius, Tacitus, Thiers, Thucydides, Toynbee, Trevelyan, Wells, Xenophon

History, Historical Account, Anamnesis, Annal, Bunk, Case, Chronicle, Clio, Epoch(a), Ere-now, Ever, Heritage, Legend, Life, Mesolithic, Natural, Ontogency, Past, Record

Histrionic Operatic, Theatrical

Hit Bang, Bash, Baste, Bat, Bean, Belt, Blip, Blockbuster, Bloop, Blow, Bludgeon, Bolo, Bonk, Bunt, Clobber, Clock, Clout, Club, Collide, Cuff, Dot, Flail, Flick, Flip, Foul, Fourpenny-one, Fungo, Get, Hay, Head-butt, Home(-thrust), Impact, Knock, Lam, Magpie, Mug, Pandy, Pepper, Polt, Prang, Ram, Score, Sensation, Six, Skier, Sky, Slam, Slap, Slosh, Smash(eroo), Smit(e), Sock, Spank, Stoush, Straik, Stricken, Strike, Strook, Struck, ➤ SUCCESS, Swat, Switch, Thwack, Tip, Tonk, Touché, Venewe, Venue, Wallop, Wing, Ythundered, Zap, Zonk

Hitch Catch, Contretemps, Edge, Espouse, Hike, Hirsle, Hoi(c)k, Hotch, Jerk, Lorry-hop, Rub, Sheepshank, Sheet bend, Shrug, Snag, Technical, Thumb

Hitherto Before, Yet

Hittite Uriah

Hive(s) Nettlerash, Skep, Spread, Swarm

Hoar(y) Ashen(-grey), Canescent, Froren, Frost, Gaudy-day, Grizzled, Rime

Hoard(ing) Accumulate, Amass, Bill, Cache, Coffer, Eke, Heap, Hoord, Husband, Hutch, Mucker, Plant, Pose, Save, Sciurine, Snudge, Squirrel, Stash, Stock, Store, Treasure

Hoarse(ness) Croupy, Frog, Grating, Gruff, Husky, Raucous, Roar(er), Roopit, Roopy, Throaty

Hoax Bam, Canard, Cod, Do, Doff, Fub, Fun, Gag, Gammon, Gull, Hum, Huntie-gowk, Kid, Leg-pull, Piltdown, Sell, Skit, Spoof, String, Stuff, ➤ TRICK

Hobble, Hobbling Game, Hamshackle, Hilch, Hitch, Lame, Limp, Pastern, Picket, Spancel, Stagger, Tether

Hobby Avocation, Fad, Falcon, Interest, Pastance, ➤ PASTIME, Predator, Pursuit, Recreation, Scrimshaw

Hobby-horse Dada, Obsession, Play-mare

Hobgoblin Bog(e)y, Puck

Hobnail Clinker, Tacket

Hobnob Chat, Mingle

Hobo Bum, ➤ TRAMP, Vagrant

Hock Cambrel, Dip, Gambrel, Gambril, Gammon, Ham, Heel, Hough, Hypothecate, Pawn, Pledge, Rhenish, Wine

Hockey Hurling, Shinny, Shinty

Hod Carrier, Tray

Hodge Peasant, Rustic, Yokel

Hoe Claut, Dutch, Grub, Jembe, Nab, Pecker, Rake, Scuffle, Weed

Hog Babiroussa, Babirussa, Boar, Glutton, Guttle, Peccary, Pig, Porker, Shoat, Shott

Hogmanay Ne'erday

Hog-rat Hutia

Hogshead Butt, Cask, Muid

Hogwash Bull, Nonsense, Swill, Twaddle

Hoi-polloi Prole(tariat), Rabble

Hoist Boom, Bouse, Crane, Davit, Derrick, Gin, Heft, Hills, Jack, Lewis, Lift, Raise, Shearlegs, Shears, Sheerlegs, Sheers, Sway, Teagle, Trice, Whip-and-derry, Wince, Winch, Windas, Windlass

Hold(er), Holding, Hold back, up, etc Absorb, Anchor, Backbreaker, Belay, Believe, Boston crab, Canister, Cease, Cement, Cinch, Clamp, Clasp, Cling, Clutch, Contain, Cotland, Delay, Detain, Display, Dog, Embrace, Engross, Er, Fast, Fief, Fistful, Frog, Full nelson, Garter, ➤ GRASP, Grip, Grovet, Half-nelson, Hammerlock, Handle, Haud, Have, Headlock, Heft, Heist, Hiccup, Hinder, Hitch, Ho(a), Hoy, Hug, Impedance, Impede, Impediment, Impound, Incumbent, Intern, Japanese stranglehold, Keep, Keepnet, Lease, Maintain, Nelson, Own, Port, Proffer, Rack, Reluct, Reserve, Rivet, Rob, Rundale, Runrig, Save, Scissors, Shelve, Shore, Sleeve, Sostenuto, Stand, Suplex, Suspend, Tenancy, Tenement, Tenure, Toehold, Toft, Tripod, Wristlock, Zarf

Hole(d), Holey Agloo, Aglu, Albatross, Antrum, Aubrey, Beam, Birdie, Black, Cave, Cavity, Cenote, Coalsack, Crater, Cubby, Dell, Den, Dene, Dog-leg, Dolina, Doline, Dreamhole, Dugout, Eagle, Earth, Ethmoid, Eye(let), Faveolate, Finger, Foramen, Funk, Gap, Geat, Gnamma, Gutta, Hag(g), Hideout, Lenticel, Lill, Loop, Loup, Lubber's, Lumina, Maar,

Mortise, Moulin, Namma, Nineteenth, Oillet, ➤ OPENING, Orifex, Orifice, Perforate, Pierce, Pigeon, Pinprick, Pit, Pocket, Pore, Port, Pot, Priest's, Punctuate, Punctum, Puncture, Rowport, Sallyport, Scupper, Scuttle, Scye, Slot, Snag, Soakaway, Socket, Spandrel, Spiraculum, Stead, Stew, Stop, Stove, Swallow, Tear, Thirl, Trema, Vent, Ventage, Ventige, Voided, Vug, Watering, Wookey

Holiday(s) Bank, Benjo, Break, Childermas, ➤ FESTIVAL, Ferial, Festa, Fete, Fiesta, Furlough, Gala, Half(term), High, Laik, Leasure, Leave, Leisure, Long, Minibreak, Outing, Packaged, Pink-eye, Playtime, Recess, Repose, Rest, Roman, Seaside, Shabuoth, Shavuot, Stay, Sunday, Trip, ➤ VAC(ATION), Villegiatura, Wake(s), Whitsun

Holinshed Chronicler

Holland(s) Genevese, Gin, Hogen-mogen, Netherlands, NL

Hollow Acetabulum, Alveary, Antar, Antre, Antrum, Armpit, Blastula, Boss, Bowl, Cave(rn), Cavity, Chasm, Cirque, Cleché, Comb(e), Concave, Coomb, Corrie, Crater, Cup(mark), Cwm, Deaf, Dean, Dell, Delve, Den(e), Dent, Dimple, Dingle, Dip, Dish(ing), Dolina, Doline, Empty, Fossette, Gilgai, Glenoid, Gnamma-hole, Grot(to), Hole, How, Igloo, Incavo, Insincere, Keck(sy), Kex, Khud, Lip-deep, Mortise, Namma-hole, Niche, Omphaloid, Orbita, Pan, Pit, Punt, Redd, Rout, Rut, Scoop, Sinus, Slade, Sleepy, Slot, Slough, Socket, Swire, Thank-you-ma'am, Trematic, Trough, Vlei, Vola, Wame, Wem

Holly Aquifoliaceae, Eryngo, Ilex, Mate, Yaupon

Hollyhock Althaea

Hollywood Bowl, Tinseltown

Holm Isle

Holmes Sherlock, Wendell

Holmium Ho

Holocaust Shoah

Hologram, Holograph Laser, MS

Holothurian Trepang

Holster Sheath

Holy(man), Holiness Adytum, Alliance, Blessed, ➤ DIVINE, Godly, Grail, Halidom, Helga, Hery, Khalif, Loch, Mountain, Orders, Pious, Sacred, Sacrosanct, Sad(d)hu, Saintly, Sanctitude, Sannayasi(n), Santon, Sekos, Sepulchre, Shrine, Starets, Staretz, SV, Tirthankara, War

Holy Books, Holy writing Adigranth, Atharvaveda, Bible, Gemara, Granth, Hadith, Koran, Mishnah, NT, OT, Pia, Purana, Rigveda, Sama-Veda, ➤ SCRIPTURE, Shaster, Shastra, Smriti, Sura(h), Tanach, Writ

Holy building, Holy place Chapel, Church, Kaaba, Penetralia, Synagogue, Temenos, Temple

Holy water Amrit

Homage Bow, Cense, Honour, Kneel, Manred, Obeisance, Tribute, Vail

Home Abode, Base, Blighty, Burrow, Cheshire, Chez, Clinic, Domal, Domicile, Earth, Eventide, Fireside, Gaff, Goal, Habitat, Harvest, Heame,

Hearth, Heme, Hospice, House, Lair, Libken, Mobile, Montacute, Nest, Pad, Plas Newydd, Remand, Rest, Stately, Villa

Homecoming Nostos

Home counties SE

Homeless Rootless, Skell

Homer(ic) Comatose, Cor, Nod, Pigeon, Somnolent

Home-rule Parnellism, Swaraj

Homesick(ness) Heimweh

Homespun Plain, Raploch, Russet, Simple

Homestead Ranch, Toft

Homework Prep

Homicide Chance-medley, Killing, Manslaughter

Homily Lecture, Pi, Postil, Prone, Sermon

▷ **Homing** may indicate coming back

Hominid Oreopitheous

Homogeneous Indiscrete

Homosexual(ity) Bardash, Bender, Bent, Camp, Cat, Closet queen, Cocksucker, Dike, Dyke, Fag(got), Fairy, Fruit, Gay, Ginger, Invert, Lesbian, Muscle Mary, Poof(tah), Poofter, Poove, Pouf(fe), Poufter, Puff, Quean, Queer, Quiff, Rough trade, Tonk, Tribade, Uranism, Urning, Woofter

Hone Grind, ➤ SHARPEN, Whet

Honest(y) Aboveboard, Afauld, Afawld, Candour, Clean, Genuine, Incorruptible, Injun, Jake, Legitimate, Lunaria, Lunary, Open-faced, Penny, Probity, Rectitude, Reputable, Righteous, Round, Sincere, Square, Squareshooter, Straight, Trojan, ➤ TRUE(PENNY), Upright, Upstanding

Honey Comb, Flattery, Hybla, Hymettus, Mel, Melliferous, Nectar, Oenomel, Oxymel, Peach, Popsy-wopsy, Sis, Sugar, Sweetheart, Sweetie

Honeycomb(ed) Cellular, Faveolate, Favose, Waxwork

Honey-eater Bear, Blue-eye

Honeypot Haanepoot

Honeysuckle Abelia, Anthemion, Caprifoil, Caprifole, Lonicera, Woodbind, Woodbine

Honorary, Honour(able), Honours, Honorific Accolade, Ace, Birthday, Blue, CBE, Commemorate, Credit, Dan, Elate, Emeritus, Ennoble, ➤ ESTEEM, Ethic, Face-card, Fame, Fete, Grace, Greats, Glory, Homage, Insignia, Invest, King, Knave, Knight, Kudos, Laudation, Laurels, MBE, Mention, OBE, Pundonor, Queen, Remember, Repute, Respect, Revere, Reward, Ten, Tenace, Titular, Tripos, Venerate, Worship

Honourable companion CH

Honourless Yarborough

Hooch Moonshine

Hood(ed) Almuce, Amaut, Amice, Amowt, Apache, Balaclava, Bashlik, Biggin, Blindfold, Calash, Calèche, Calyptra, Capeline, Capuccio, Capuche, Chaperon(e), Coif, Cope, Cowl, Cucullate(d), Gangster, Jacobin, Kennel,

Liripipe, Liripoop, Mantle, Mazarine, Pixie, Robin, Rowdy, Trot-cosey, Trot-cozy

Hoodlum Gangster, Roughneck, Thug

Hoodwink(ed) Blear, Bluff, Cheat, ➤ DECEIVE, Gull, Nose-led, Seel

Hoof(ed) Artiodactyla, Cloot, Coffin, Frog, Trotter, Ungula

Hoohah Humdudgeon

Hook(ed), Hooker Addict, Adunc, Aduncous, Barb(icel), Becket, Butcher's, Cant(dog), Catch, Chape, Claw, Cleek, Clip, Corvus, Crampon, Cromb, Crome, Crook, Crotchet, Cup, Drail, Fish, Gaff, Grapnel, Hamate, Hamose, Hamulus, Heel, Hitch, Inveigle, Kype, Meat, Pot, Prostitute, Snell, Sniggle, Tala(u)nt, Tenaculum, Tenter, Tie, Trip, Uncus, Wanton

Hookah Chillum, Hubble-bubble, Pipe

Hooligan Apache, Casual, Desperado, Droog, Hobbledehoy, Keelie, Larrikin, Lout, Ned, Rough(neck), Ruffian, Skollie, Skolly, Tearaway, Ted, Tough, Tsotsi, Yahoo, Yob(bo)

Hoop Bail, Band, Circle, Farthingale, Garth, Gird, Girr, Hula®, O, ➤ RING, Tire, Trochus

Hooray Whoopee, Yippee

Hoot(er) Deride, Honk, Madge, Nose, Owl, Riot, Screech-owl, Siren, Ululate

Hoover Dam

Hop(per) An(o)ura, Ball, Bin, Cuscus, Dance, Flight, Jeté, Jump, Kangaroo, Leap, Lilt, Opium, Pogo, Saltate, Scotch, Skip, Tremié, Vine

Hope(ful) Anticipate, Aspirant, Contender, Daydream, Desire, Dream, Esperance, Evelyn, Expectancy, Forlorn, Gleam, Pipe-dream, Promising, Roseate, Rosy, Sanguine, Trust, Valley, White, Wish

Hopeless(ness), Hopeless quest Abattu, Anomie, Anomy, Black, Buckley's chance, Despair, Despondent, Forlorn, Goner, Perdu, Pessimist

Hopscotch Peever

Horace Flaccus, Ode, Satirist

Horatio Nelson

Horatius Cocles

Horde Golden, Many, Mass, Swarm

Horizon Artificial, Event, Scope, Sea-line, Skyline

Horizontal Advection, Flat, Level, Prone, Supine

Hormone Adrenalin®, Adrenaline, Aldosterone, Androgen, Androsterone, Angiotensin, Autacoid, Auxin, Biosynthesis, Bursicon, Calcitonin, Corticoid, Corticosteroid, Cortisone, Cytokinin, Ecdysone, Endocrine, Erythropoietin, Estrogen, Florigen, Gastrin, Gibberellin, Glucagon, Gonadotrop(h)in, Gonadotrophic, Growth, Hydrocortisone, Inhibin, Insulin, Intermedin, Juvenile, Kinin, Lipotropin, Melatonin, Noradrenalin(e), Oestradiol, Oestriol, Oestrogen, Oestrone, Oxytocin, Parathyroid, Progesterone, Progestogen, Prolactin, Prostaglandin, Relaxin, Secretagogue, Secretin, Secretion, Somatomedin, Somatostatin, Somatotrop(h)in, Serotonin, Steroid, Stilboestrol, Testosterone, Thymosin, Thyroid, Thyrotrop(h)in, Thyroxine, Vasopressin

Horn(y) Advancer, Amalthea, Antenna(e), Baleen, Basset, Brass, Bez, Bugle, Cape, Ceratoid, Cor, Cornet, Cornett, Cornopean, Cornu(a), Cornucopia, Cromorna, Cromorne, Cusp, Dilemma, Flugel-horn, French, Frog, Golden, Gore, Hooter, ➤ HORNBLOWER, Hunting, Ivory, Keratin, Klaxon, Lur, Morsing, Mot, Oliphant, Periostracum, Plenty, Post, Powder, Pryse, Shofar, Shophor, Spongin, Tenderling, Trey, Trez, Trumpet, Waldhorn

Hornblower Brain, Horatio, Peel, Triton, Trumpeter

Hornbook Battledoor, Battledore

Horned (sheep) Cabrié, Cabrit, Cornute, Hamate, Lunate, Mouflon, Muflon

Hornless Doddy, Humbel, Humlie, Hummel, Mooly, Mul(l)ey, Poley, Polled

Hornpipe Matelote

Horoscope Figure, Future, Prophecy, Star-map

Horrible, Horror Aw(e)some, Brat, Dire, Dread(ful), Execrable, Ghastly, Grisly, Gruesome, Hideous, Odious, Shock, Terror, Ugh

Horrid, Horrific, Horrify(ing) Dire, Dismay, Dreadful, Frightful, Ghastly, Gothic, Grim, Grisly, H, Loathy, Odious, Spiteful, Ugly

Hors d'oeuvres Antipasto, Canapé, Carpaccio, Ceviche, Hoummos, Houmus, Hummus, Mez(z)e, Pâté, Smorgasbord, Zak(o)uski

Horse Airer, Ambler, Andalusian, Appaloosa, Aquiline, Arab, Arion, Arkle, Ass, Aver, Bangtail, Barb, Bathorse, Bay, Bayard, Bevis, Bidet, Black Bess, Bloodstock, Bobtail, Boerperd, Borer, Breaker, Bronco, Brumby, Bucephalus, Buck(jumper), Buttermilk, Caballine, Calico, Camargue, Canuck, Caple, Capul, Cavalry, Cayuse, Centaur, Cert, Charger, Chaser, Chestnut, Clavileno, Clay-bank, Clipper, Clydesdale, Coacher, Cob, Cocktail, Coldblood, Colt, Connemara, Cooser, Copenhagen, Courser, Crib, Crollo, Cu(i)sser, Curtal, Cut, Cutting, Daisy-cutter, Dale, Dappled, Dark, Dartmoor, Destrier, Dobbin, Doer, Draught, Drier, Dun, Eclipse, Entire, Equine, Eventer, Exmoor, Favel(l), Fell, Filly, Foal, Friesian, Galloway, Ganger, Garran, Garron, Gee, Gelding, Genet, Gennet, GG, Gringolet, H, Hack(ney), Hambletonian, ➤ HEROIN, High, Highland, High-stepper, Hobbler, Hobby, Hogget, Holstein, Houyhnhnm, Hunter, Hyperion, Icelandic, Incitatus, Jade, Jennet, Kanuck, Keffel, Knabstrup, Knight, Kochlani, Kt, Lampos, Liberty, Lipizzaner, Lippizaner, Livery, Lusitano, Mare, Marengo, Marocco, Morel, Morgan, Morocco, Mount, Mudder, Mustang, Nag, Neddy, Novice, Outsider, Pacer, Pad, Pad-nag, Palomino, Palfrey, Pantomime, Pegasus, Percheron, Perissodactyl, Piebald, Pinto, Plater, Pliohippus, Plug, Pole(r), Pommel, Pony, Post(er), Pot, Prad, Przewalski(s), Punch, Quagga, Quarter, Random, Remount, Remuda, Ride, Rip, Roan, Roarer, Rocking, Rogue, Rosinante, Rouncy, Rozinante, Runner, Sabino, Saddle(r), Scag, Schimmel, Screw, Seian, Sense, Sheltie, Shetland, Shire, Shoo-in, Skewbald, Sleipnir, Snow, Sorrel, Span, Spanker, Springer, Stallion, Starter, Stayer, Steed, Stibbler, String, Stud, Stumer, Suffolk punch, Stalking, Summer, Sumpter, Svadilfari, Swallow, Swinger, Tacky, Tak(h)i, Tandem, Tarpan, Thoroughbred, Tit, Tracer, Trestle, Trigger, Trojan, Troop, Trot(ter), Vanner, Vaulting, Waler, Warmblood, Warragal, Warragle, Warragul, Warrigal, Welsh cob,

Wheel(er), Whistler, White, Wooden, Xanthos, Xanthus, Yale, Yarraman, Yaud, Yearling

Horseback Croup

Horse-box Stable, Stall

Horse-chestnut Aesculus, Conker

Horse collar Brecham, Hame

Horse complaint, Horse disease Bogspavin, Curb, Dourine, Equinia, Eweneck, Farcy, Fives, Frush, Glanders, Gourdy, Head staggers, Heaves, Hippiatric, Malander, Megrims, Mooneye, N(a)gana, Poll-evil, Quitter, Quittor, Ringbone, Sallenders, Scratches, Seedy-toe, Spavie, Spavin, Strangles, Stringhalt, Surra, Sween(e)y, Thorough-pin, Thrush, Vives, Windgall, Wire-heel, Yellows

Horse-dealer Buster, Coper

Horse-lover Philip

Horseman Ataman, Caballero, Cavalry, Centaur, Conquest, Cossack, Cowboy, Death, Dragman, Famine, Farrier, Hobbler, Hussar, Knight, Lancer, Nessus, Ostler, Parthian, Picador, Pricker, Quadrille, Revere, ► RIDER, Slaughter, Spahi, Stradiot, Tracer

Horsemanship Manège

Horseplay Caper, Polo, Rag, Rant, Romp

Horsepower Hp, Ps

Horseradish Ben, Moringa

Horseshoe(-shaped) Henge, Hippocrepian, King-crab, Lunette, Manilla, Oxbow, Plate

Horsetail Equisetum

Horse thief Blanco, Rustler

Horticulturist Grower, RHS

Hose Chausses, Fishnet, Galligaskins, Gaskins, Lisle, Netherstock(ing), Nylons, Panty, Sock, Stockings, Tights, Trunk, Tube

Hospitable, Hospitality Convivial, Entertainment, Euxine, Lucullan, Open house, Philoxenia, Social, Xenial

Hospital Ambulance, Asylum, Barts, Base, Bedlam, Clinic, Cottage, Day, ENT, Field, Guys, H, Home, Hospice, Imaret, Karitane, Lazaretto, Leprosarium, Leprosery, Lock, Loony bin, MASH, Mental, Nosocomial, Pest-house, Polyclinic, San, Scutari, Sick bay, Spital, Spittle, Teaching, UCH

Host(ess) Amphitryon, Army, Barmecide, Chatelaine, Crowd, Definitive, Emcee, Entertainer, Hirsel, Hotelier, Innkeeper, Laban, Landlady, Landlord, Legend, Legion, Lion-hunter, Lot, Mass, Mavin, MC, Publican, Quickly, Swarm, Taverner, Throng, Trimalchio

Hostage Gherao, Pawn, Pledge, POW

Hostel Dharms(h)ala, Dorm, Entry, Inn, YHA, Youth

Hostile, Hostility Adverse, Aggressive, Alien, Animus, Bitter, Currish, Diatribe, Feud, Hating, Icy, Ill, Ill-will, Inimical, Inveterate, Oppugnant, Unfriendly, Vitriolic, War

Hot (tempered) Ardent, Breem, Breme, Cajun, Calid, Candent, Dog days, Enthusiastic, Facula, Fervid, Feverish, Fuggy, Gospeller, In, Incandescent, Irascible, Lewd, Mustard, Pepper, Piping, Potato, Randy, Red, Roaster, Scorcher, Sizzling, Spicy, Stewy, Stifling, Stolen, Sweltering, Sweltry, Tabasco®, Thermidor, Torrid, Toustie, Tropical, Zealful

Hotchpotch Bricolage, Farrago, Mish-mash, Powsowdy, Welter

Hotel Bo(a)tel, Flophouse, Gasthaus, Gasthof, H, Hilton, Hydro, Inn, Motel, Parador, Posada, Ritz, Roadhouse, Savoy, Tavern

Hothead(ed) Impetuous, Rash, Spitfire, Volcano

Hot-house Conservatory, Nursery, Orangery, Vinery

Hot plate Salamander

Hot rod Dragster

Hotspur Harry, Hothead, Rantipole

Hottentot Griqua, Khoikhoi, Strandloper

Hot water Soup, Therm

Hound(s) Afghan, Basset, Beagle, Bellman, Brach, Cad, Canine, Cry, ➤ DOG, Entry, Harass, Harrier, Hen-harrier, Javel, Kennet, Lyam, Lym(e), Mute, Otter, Pack, Pursue, Rache, Ranter, Reporter, Saluki, Talbot, True, Tufter

Hound's bane Palay

Hour(s) Canonical, H, Holy, Hr, Complin(e), Elder's, Happy, None(s), Orthros, Peak, Prime, Rush, Sext, Small, Terce, Tide, Time, Undern, Vespers, Visiting, Witching, Zero

House(s), Household(er) Abode, Admiralty, Althing, Astrology, Audience, Auditorium, B, Bach, Bastide, Beehive, Beth, Bhavan, Bhawan, Biggin, Bingo, Block, Boarding, Bondage, Bourbon, Brownstone, Bundestag, Burghley, Bush, Casa, Chalet, Chamber, Chapter, Charnel, Chateau, Chatsworth, Chez, Clapboard, Clearing, Commons, Concern, Convent, Cote, Council, Crib, Custom(s), Dacha, Dail, Demain, Demesne, Derry, Des res, Discount, Disorderly, Domal, Domicile, Donga, Door, Dower, Drum, Duplex, Dwelling, Dynasty, Edifice, Entertain, Establishment, Este, Familial, Fashion, Fibro(cement), Firm, Frame, Full, Gaff, Garage, Habitat, Hacienda, Halfway, Hanover, Harbour, Heartbreak, Hearth, HK, Ho, Home, Igloo, Inn, Insula, Ken, Keys, Knesset, Lagthing, Lancaster, Leo, Longleat, Lords, Lot(t)o, Maison(ette), Manor, Manse, Mansion, Mas, Meeting, Meinie, Meiny, Ménage, Messuage, Montagne, Odelst(h)ing, Opera, Orange, Osborne, Pad, Parliament, Pent, Plantagenet, Pondokkie, Prefab, Quinta, Ranch, Ratepayer, Residence, Rough, Safe, Satis, Scala, Schloss, Seat, Semi, Shanty, Sign, Somerset, Stable, Stuart, Tavern, Terrace, Theatre, Tied, Toft, Tombola, Tower, Town, Tract, Trinity, Tudor, Upper, Usher, Vicarage, Villa, Weatherboard, Wendy, Whare, Windsor, York, Zero

House-boat Wan(i)gan, Wangun

House-builder Jack

House-keeper Chatelaine, Matron, Publican

House-leek Sengreen

Housemaid's knee Bursa

Houseman Betty, Doctor, Intern, Peer

House-warming Infare
Housewife Etui, Needlecase
Housework Chore, Diy
Housing Case, Crankcase, Shabrack, Shelter, Slum, Tenement
Hova Malagash
Hove Plim, Swell
Hovel Cru(i)ve, Den, Pigsty, Shack, Shanty
Hover Hang, Lurk, Poise
How Hill, Hollow
How'dyedo, How d'ye do Hallo, Pass, Salve
However As, But, Leastwise, Sed, Still, Though, Yet
Howitzer Gun
Howl(er) Banshee, Bawl, Bay, Bloop, Clanger, Hue, Mycetes, Ululate, Wow, Yawl, Yowl
How much The
Hoy Bilander, Ship
HQ Centre, Headquarters, SHAPE
Hub Boss, Centre, Focus, Hob, Nave, Pivot, Tee
Hubbub Charivari, Chirm, Coil, Din, Level-coil, Palaver, Racket, Row, Stir
Hubris Pride
Huckster Hawker, Kidd(i)er, Pedlar
Huddle Cringe, Gather, Hunch, Ruck, Shrink
Hue Colour, Dye, Outcry, Proscription, Steven, Tincture, Tinge, Utis
Huff Dudgeon, Hector, Pant, Pet, Pique, Strunt, Umbrage, Vex
Hug Cuddle, ➤ EMBRACE, Squeeze
Huge (number) Astronomical, Brobdingnag, Colossal, Enorm(ous), Gargantuan, Giant, ➤ GIGANTIC, Gillion, Ginormous, Humongous, Humungous, Immane, Immense, Leviathan, Lulu, Mega-, Milliard, Octillion, Socking, Titanian, Tremendous, Whacking
Hugo Victor
Huguenot Canisard
Hulk Lout, Ruin, Shale, Shell, Ship
Hull Bottom, Framework, Husk, Inboard, Monocoque, Pod, Sheal, Sheel, Shell, Shiel, Shill
Hullabaloo Outcry, Raz(z)mataz(z), Razzamatazz
▶ **Hullo** see HELLO
Hum(ming) Bombilate, Bombinate, Bum, Chirm, Drone, Lilt, Moan, Murmur, Nos(e)y, Pong, Rank, Reek, Sowf(f), Sowth, Stink, Stir, Whir(r), Zing
Human(e), Humanist, Humanity Anthropoid, Bang, Colet, Earthling, Erasmus, Incarnate, Kindness, Mandom, Merciful, Mortal, Philanthropic, Species, Sympathy, Ubuntu
Humble Abase, Abash, Afflict, Baseborn, Degrade, Demean, Demiss(ly), Lower, Lowly, Mean, ➤ MEEK, Modest, Obscure, Poor, Rude, Small, Truckle

Humbug Berley, Blarney, Blague, Burley, Claptrap, Con, Delude, Flam, Flummery, Fraud, Fudge, Gaff, Gammon, Gas, Guff, Gum, Hoax, Hoodwink, Hookey-walker, Kibosh, Liar, Maw-worm, Nonsense, Shenanigan, Wind

Humdinger Lulu

Humdrum Banal, Bourgeois, Monotonous, Mundane, Ordinary, Prosaic, Tedious

Humid Clammy, Damp, Dank, Muggy, Steam, Sticky

Humiliate, Humiliation, Humility Abase, Abash, Baseness, Degrade, Disbench, Eating crow, Fast, Indignity, Mortify, Put-down, ➤ SHAME, Skeleton, Take-down, Wither

Humming-bird Colibri, Hermit, Rainbow, Sappho, Sylph, Thornbill, Topaz, Trochilus

Hummock Tump

Humorist Cartoonist, Comedian, Jester, Leacock, Lear, Punster, Twain, Wodehouse

Humour, Humorous Aqueous, Bile, Caprice, Cardinal, Chaff, Coax, Cocker, Coddle, Cosher, Cuiter, Cuittle, Daut, Dawt, Dry, Facetious, Fun, Gallows, Ichor, Indulge, Irony, Jocose, Jocular, Juice, Kidney, Levity, Light, ➤ MOOD, Observe, Pamper, Phlegm, Pun, Pythonesque, Ribaldry, Serum, Temper, Trim, Vein, Vitreum, Wetness, Whim, Wit

Humourless Dry, Po(-faced)

Hump(ed) Boy, Bulge, Dorts, Dowager's, Gibbose, Gibbous, Hog, Huff, Hummock, Hunch, Pip, Ramp, Tussock

▶ **Humpback** see HUNCHBACK

Humphrey Bogart

Humus Compost, Leafmould, Moder, Mor, Mull

Hun Alaric, Atli, Attila, Fritz, German

Hunch, Hunchback Camel, Chum, Crookback, Intuition, Kyphosis, Premonition, Quasimodo, Roundback, Urchin

Hundred(s) Burnham, C, Cantred, Cantref, Cent, Centum, Century, Chiltern, Commot, Desborough, Host, ➤ IN A HUNDRED, Northstead, Shire, Stoke, Ton, Wapentake

Hundred and fifty CL, Y

Hundredweight Centner, Quintal

Hung Displayed, Executed, Framed, High

Hungarian, Hungary Bohunk, Csardas, Magyar, Nagy, Szekely, Tzigane, Ugric, Vogul

Hunger, Hungry Appestat, Appetite, Bulimia, Bulimy, Clem, ➤ CRAVE, Desire, Edacity, Empty, Esurient, Famine, Famish, Fast, Hanker, Hunter, Pant, Peckish, Rapacious, Raven, Ravin, Sharp-set, Unfed, Yaup

▷ **Hungry** may indicate an 'o' in another word

Hunk(s) Chunk, Dry-fist, Miser(ly), Slab

Hunt(er), Hunting, Huntress, Huntsman Actaeon, Alew, Archer, Atalanta, Battue, Beagle, Bellman, Calydon, Chace, Chase(r), Chasseur, Chevy,

Coursing, (Drag)net, Crockett, Cynegetic, Dog, Drag, Esau, Ferret, Free-shot, Gun, Halloo, Herne, Hound, Jager, Lamping, Leigh, Lurcher, Montero, Nimrod, Orion, Peel, Poot, Pout, Predator, Pursue, Quest, Quorn, Rabbit, Rach(e), Ran, Rancel, Ranzel, Ride, Rummage, Run, Scavenge(r), Scorse, ➤ SEARCH, Seek, Shikar(ee), Shikari, Skirter, Slipper, Stalk, Sticker, Terrier, Thimble, Tinchel, Tower, Trail, Trap, Treasure, Venatic, Venator, Venerer, Venery, ➤ WATCH, Whip, Whipper-in, Wolfer, Woodman, Yager

Hunting-call Rechate, Recheat, Tally-ho, View-halloo

Hunting-ground Forestation, Walk

Hurdle(r) Barrier, Doll, Fence, Flake, Gate, Hemery, Raddle, Sticks, Wattle

Hurdy (gurdy) Barrel-organ, Hainch, Haunch, Vielle

Hurl(ing) Camogie, Cast, Dash, ➤ FLING, Heave, Put(t), Throw, ➤ TOSS

Hurly-burly Furore, Noise

Hurrah Cheers, Huzza, Io, Whee

Hurricane Baguio, Tornade, Tornado, Typhoon, ➤ WIND

Hurry Belt, Bustle, Chivvy, Chop-chop, Dart, Dash, Drive, Festinate, Fisk, Frisk, Gad, Giddap, Giddup, Hadaway, Hare, Haste, Hie, Hightail, Mosey, Post-haste, Press, Push, Race, ➤ RUSH, Scamper, Scoot, Scramble, Scur(ry), Scutter, Scuttle, Skelter, Skurry, Spank, Speed, Streak, Tear

Hurt(ful) Abuse, Ache, Ake, Bruise, Damage, De(a)re, Disservice, Harrow, Hit, ➤ INJURE, Lesion, Maim, Nocent, Nocuous, Noxious, Noyous, Pain, Pang, Prick(le), Scaith, Wring

Hurtle Rush, Spin, Streak, Streek

Husband(ry), Husbands Add, Baron, Darby, Ear, Eche, Economy, Eke, Ere, Farm, Georgic, Goodman, Groom, H, Hubby, Ideal, Man, Mate, Partner, Polyandry, Retrench, Save, Scrape, Scrimp, Spouse, Squirrel, ➤ STORE, Tillage

Hush(-hush) Bestill, Gag, Sh, Silent, Smug, St, Tace, Wheesh(t), Whisht

Husk(s), Husky Acerose, Bran, Draff, Eskimo, Hoarse, Hull, Malemute, Seed, Sheal, Shuck

Hussar Cherry-picker, Cherubim

Hussite Calixtin(e)

Hussy Besom, Hen, Loose, Minx, Vamp

Hustle(r) Frogmarch, Jostle, Pro, Push, Railroad, Shoulder, Shove, Skelp

Hut(s) Banda, Booth, Bothie, Bothy, Bustee, Cabin, Chalet, Choltry, Gunyah, Hogan, Humpy, Igloo, Mia-mia, Nissen, Pondok(kie), Quonset, Rancheria, Rancho, Rondavel, Shack, Shanty, Sheal(ing), Shebang, Shed, Shiel(ing), Skeo, Skio, Succah, Sukkah, Tilt, Tolsel, Tolsey, Tolzey, Wan(n)igan, Wi(c)kiup, Wigwam, Wil(t)ja, Wurley

Hutch Buddle, Crate, Pen

Hybrid Bigener, Bois-brûlé, Catalo, Centaur, Chamois, Chichi, Citrange, Cross, Dso, Funnel, Geep, Graft, Interbred, Jomo, Jumart, Lurcher, Mameluco, Mermaid, Merman, Metis, Mongrel, Mule, Mutation, Ox(s)lip, Percolin, Plumcot, Pomato, Ringed, Tangelo, Tiglon, Tigon, Topaz, Ugli, Zho(mo)

▷ **Hybrid** may indicate an anagram

Hydra Polyp

Hydrant Fireplug, H

Hydrocarbon Acetylene, Aldrin, Alkane, Alkene, Alkyl, Alkyne, Amylene, Arene, Asphaltite, Benzene, Butadiene, Butane, Butene, Camphane, Camphene, Carotene, Cetane, Cubane, Cyclohexane, Cyclopropane, Decane, Diene, Dioxin, Diphenyl, Ethane, Gutta, Halon, Hatchettite, Heptane, Hexane, Hexene, Hexyl(ene), Indene, Isobutane, Isoprene, Ligroin, Limonene, Mesitylene, Naphtha, Naphthalene, Nonane, Octane, Olefine, Paraffin, Pentane, Pentene, Pentylene, Phenanthrene, Phene, Picene, Polyene, Propane, Pyrene, Retene, Squalene, Stilbene, Styrene, Terpene, Toluene, Triptane, Wax, Xylene, Xylol

Hydrogen Deut(er)on, Diplon, Ethene, H, Protium, Tritium

Hydrophobic Rabid

Hydroponic Soil

Hydrozoa(n) Campanularia, Millepore, Siphonophore

Hyena Aard-wolf, Earthwolf, Strand-wolf, Tiger-wolf

Hygiene, Hygienic Aseptic, Sanitary, Sepsis

Hymn(s) Anthem, Benedictine, Bhajan, Canticle, Carol, Cathisma, Choral(e), Coronach, Dies Irae, Dithyramb, Doxology, Gloria, Hallel, Introit(us), Ithyphallic, Lay, Magnificat, Mantra, Marseillaise, Nunc dimittis, Ode, P(a)ean, Psalm, Recessional, Rigveda, Sanctus, Sequence, Stabat mater, Sticheron, Tantum ergo, Te deum, Trisagion, Troparion, Veda

Hymnographer, Hymnologist David, Faber, Heber, Moody, Neale, Parry, Sankey, Watts

Hyperbole, Hyperbolic Auxesis, Exaggeration, Sech

Hypercritical Captious

Hyperion Titan

Hypersensitive Allergic, Idiosyncratic

Hypha(e) Conidiophore, Stroma

Hyphen(ated) Dash, Parasyntheton, Soft

Hypnosis, Hypnotise, Hypnotic, Hypnotism Braidism, Chloral, Codeine, Entrance, Magnetic, Mesmerism, Svengali

Hypochondria(c) Hyp, Nosophobia, Phrenesiac, Valetudinarian

Hypocrisy, Hypocrite, Hypocritical Archimago, Bigot, Byends, Cant, Carper, Chadband, Deceit, Dissembler, Heep, Holy Willie, Humbug, Mucker, Nitouche, Pecksniff, Pharisaic, Pharisee, Prig, Sepulchre, Tartuf(f)e, Two-faced, Whited sepulchre

Hypothetical Biophor, Gluon, Graviton, Suppositious, Virtual

Hyrax Cony, Daman, Dassie, Klipdas

Hysteria, Hysteric(al) Conniption, Delirium, Frenzy, Meemie, Mother

I i

I A, Ch, Cham, Che, Dotted, Ego, Ich, Indeed, India, Iodine, Italy, J, Je, Me, Self

Ian Scot

Ibex Izard

Ibis Sacred, Waldrapp

Ice(d), Ice cream, Icing, Icy Alcorza, Arctic, Berg, Black, Camphor, Cassata, Cone, Cool, Cornet, Coupe, Cream, Crystal, Diamonds, Drift, Dry, Floe, Frappé, Frazil, Freeze, Frigid, Frore, Frosting, Frosty, Gelato, Gelid, Gems, Glacé, Glacial, Glacier, Glare, Granita, Graupel, Growler, Hailstone, Hok(e)y-pok(e)y, Hommock, Hummock, Knickerbocker glory, Kulfi, Lolly, Macallum, Marzipan, Neapolitan, Pack, Pancake, Pingo, Polar, Rime, Rink, Royal, Serac, Sconce, Shelf, Sherbet, Slider, Slob, Sludge, Sorbet, Spumone, Spumoni, Sugar, Topping, Tortoni, Tutti-frutti, Verglas, Virga, Wafer, Water, Wintry

Ice-axe Piolet

Iceberg Calf, Floe, Growler

Ice-box Cooler, Freezer, Fridge, Frig, Yakhdan

▶ **Ice-cream** see ICE

Iceland IS

Ice-skating Choctaw, Figure, Glide

Icicle Tangle

Icon Idol, Image, Madonna, Sprite

Icterus Jaundice

Id(e) Ego, Fish, Orfe

Idea(s) Archetype, Brainwave, Clou, Clue, Conceit, Concept, Fancy, Germ, Hunch, Idolum, Idée fixe, Image, Inkling, Inspiration, Interpretation, Light, ▶ NOTION, Obsession, Plan, Plank, Rationale, Recept, Theory, Thought, Zeitgeist

Ideal(ise) Abstract, A1, Dream, Eden, Goal, Halo, Hero, Model, Monist, Nirvana, Notional, Paragon, Pattern, ▶ PERFECT, Siddhi, Sidha, Sublimate, Utopian, Vision

Idealist(ic) More, Perfectionist, Quixotic, Visionary

Identical Alike, Clone, Congruent, Equal, Menechmian, Same, Selfsame, Verbatim, Very

Identification, Identify Bertillonage, Credentials, Diagnosis, Differentiate, Discern, Document, Dog-tag, Earmark, Empathy, Espy, Finger(print), ID, Label, Mark, Password, Pin, Place, Recognise, Reg(g)o, Secern, Spot, Swan-hopping, Swan-upping, Verify

Identikit® E-fit

Identity Appearance, Corporate, Credentials, Equalness, Likeness, Oneness, Seity, Self

Ideologue Hard-liner

Idiom Americanism, Argot, Britishism, Cant, Expression, Idioticon, Jargon, Language, Pahlavi, Parlance, Pehlevi, Syri(a)cism, Syrism

Idiosyncrasy Foible, Mannerism, Nature, Quirk, Way

Idiot(ic), Idiocy Congenital, Dingbat, Fool, Goose, Imbecile, Inane, Moron, Natural, Nerk, Nidget, Oaf, Ouph(e), ➤ STUPID (PERSON), Tony, Twit, Zany

Idle(ness), Idler Bludger, Boondoggle, Bum, Bumble, Bummle, Cockaigne, Dally, Deadbeat, Diddle, Dilly-dally, Dole-bludger, Donnat, Donnot, Do-nothingism, Drone, Fainéant, Fallow, Fester, Flaneur, Flim-flam, Footle, Frivolous, Groundless, Hawm, Inaction, Indolent, Inert, Lackadaisical, Laesie, Lallygag, Layabout, Laze, Lazy, Lead-swinger, Lie, Light, Limer, Loaf, Lollop, Lollygag, Lotophagus, Lounge, Lusk, Micawber, Mike, Mollusc, Mooch, Mouch, Otiose, Otium, Patagonian, Piddle, Ride, Shiftless, Sloth, Sluggard, Spiv, Stalko, Stock-still, Stooge, Stroam, Tarry, Transcendental, Trock, Troke, Truant, Truck, Unbusy, Vain, Vegetate, Veg out, Waste

Idol(ise) Adore, Adulate, Baal(im), Baphomet, Bel, Crush, Fetich(e), Fetish, God, Hero, Icon, Image, Joss, Juggernaut, Lion, Mammet, Manito, Manitou, Matinee, Maumet, Mawmet, Molech, Moloch, Mommet, Mumbo-jumbo, Swami, Teraph(im), Termagant, Vision, Wood, Worship

Idyll(ic) Arcady, Eclogue, Pastoral, Peneian

Ie Sc

If, If it All-be, An('t), Condition, Gif, Gin, In case, Pot, Provided, Sobeit, Whether

Igloo Snowden

Ignis-fatuus Elf-fire, Fire-dragon, Fire-drake, Friar's lanthorn, Wildfire

Ignite, Ignition Coil, Flare, Kindle, Lightning, Spark, Starter

Ignoble Base, Inferior, Mean, Vile

Ignominious, Ignominy Base, Dishonour, Fiasco, Infamous, Scandal, ➤ SHAME

Ignorance, Ignorant Analphabet, Anan, Artless, Clueless, Darkness, Green, Hick, Illiterate, Inerudite, Ingram, Ingrum, Inscient, Lewd, Lumpen, Misken, Nescience, Night, Oik, Philistine, Purblind, Red-neck, Unaware, Uneducated, Unlettered, Unread, Unschooled, Untold, Unversed, Unwist

Ignore Ba(u)lk, Blink, Bypass, Connive, Cut, Discount, Disregard, Forget, Neglect, Omit, Overlook, Override, Pass, Rump, Snub

Igor Prince

I Know Iwis, Ywis

Ill Adverse, All-overish, Bad, Bilious, Cronk, Evil, Income, Off-colour, Poorly, Queer, Sea-sick, ➤ SICK, Unweal, Unwell, Valetudinarian, Wog, Wrong

▷ **Ill** may indicate an anagram

Ill-balanced Lop-sided

Ill-bred Churlish, Plebeian, Uncouth, Unmannerly

▷ **Ill-composed** may indicate an anagram

Ill-defined Diagnosis, Hazy, Unclear, Vague

Ill-dressed Frumpish

Illegal, Illicit Adulterine, Black, Breach, Bootleg, Furtive, Ill-gotten, Misbegotten, Shonky, Unlawful

Illegitimate Bastard, By-blow, Come-o'-will, Fitz, Irregular, Lucky-piece, Mamzer, Misborn, Momzer, Natural, Scarp, Spurious, Unlineal

Ill-favoured Offensive, Lean, Thin, Ugly

Ill-feeling, Ill-humour Bad blood, Bile, Curt, Dudgeon, Glum, Hate, Miff, Peevish, Pique, Rheumatic

Illiberal Insular

▶ **Illicit** see ILLEGAL

Illiterate Ignoramus, Unlettered, Unread

Ill-looking Peaky, Poorly

Ill-luck Ambs-ace, Ames-ace, Deuce-ace, Misfortune

Ill-mannered, Ill-natured Attercop, Crabby, Ethercap, Ettercap, Guttersnipe, Huffy, Stingy, Sullen, Ugly, Unkind

Illness Aids, Ailment, Attack, Autism, Brucellosis, Complaint, Croup, Diabetes, Disease, DS, Dwalm, Dwaum, Dyscrasia, Eclampsia, Grippe, Hangover, Hypochondria, ME, Malady, Scarlatina, Sickness, Toxaemia, Urosis, Weed, Weid, Wog

Ill-nourished Emaciated

Illogical Non-sequitur

Ill-smelling F(o)etid, High, Hing, Miasmic, Stinking

▶ **Ill-tempered** see ILL-MANNERED

Ill-timed Inopportune, Unseasonable

Illuminate(d), Illumination Brighten, Clarify, Cul-de-lampe, Decorate, Enlighten, Floodlit, Lamplight, Langley, Light, Limn, Miniate, Nernst, Pixel, Radiate, Rushlight

Illusion, Illusory Air, Apparition, Barmecide, Deception, Fallacy, Fancy, Fantasy, Hallucination, Ignis-fatuus, Mare's-nest, Maya, Mirage, Muller-Lyer, Optical, Phantom, Specious, Will o'the wisp

Illustrate, Illustration, Illustrator Case, Centrefold, Collotype, Demonstrate, Drawing, Eg, Elucidate, Epitomise, Exemplify, Explain, Figure, Frontispiece, Grangerize, Graphic, Half-tone, Illume, Illumin(at)e, Instance, Instantiate, Limner, Plate, Show, Sidelight, Spotlight, Tenniel, Vignette

Illustrious Bright, Celebrated, Famous, Legendary, Renowned

Ill-will Animosity, Enmity, Grudge, Hostility, Malice, Spite

I'm I'se

Image(s) Blip, Discus, Effigy, Eidetic, Eidolon, Eikon, Eiluned, Enantiomorph, Graven, Hologram, Hypnagogic, Icon, Iconograph, Idol, Invultuation, Joss, Latent, Likeness, Matte, Mirror, Paranthelium, Pentimento, Phantasmagoria, Photogram, Photograph, Pic(ture), Pixel(l)ated, Pixil(l)ated, Poetic, Profile, Recept, Scintigram, Shadowgraph, Simulacrum, Spectrum, Spitting, Stereotype, Symbol, Teraph(im), Tiki, Tomogram, Totem, Virtual, Xoanon

Imaginary, Imaginative, Imagine(d) Assume, Believe, Cloud-cuckoo-land, Conceive, Conjure, Cyborg, Dystopia, Envisage,

Esemplasy, Faery, Faine, Fancy, Feign, Fictional, Fictitious, Fictor, Figment, Figure, Hallucinate, Hobbit, Ideate, Invent, Oz, Picture, Poetical, Prefigure, Recapture, Replicant, Scotch mist, Straw, ➤ SUPPOSE, Surmise, Think, Vicarious, Visualise, Whangam

Imbecile Anile, Fool, Idiot, ➤ STUPID

▷ **Imbecile** may indicate an anagram

Imbibe Absorb, Drink, Lap, Quaff, Suck, Swallow

Imbricate Overlie

Imbroglio Complication, Maze

Imbrue, Imbue Colour, Impregnate, Infuse, Indoctrinate, Inoculate, Permeate, Soak, Steep

Imitate, Imitation, Imitator Act, Ape, Copy(cat), Counterfeit, Dud, Echo, Echopraxia, Emulate, Epigon(e), Ersatz, Fake, False, Faux, Marinist, Me-too, Mime, Mimetic, Mimic(ry), Mockery, Monkey, Parody, Parrot, Paste, Pastiche, Pinchbeck, Potichomania, Rip-off, Sham, Simulate, Stumer, Take-off, Travesty

Immaculate Conception, Flawless, Lily-white, Perfect, Pristine, Spotless, Virgin

Immaterial Insignificant, Spiritual, Trifling

Immature(ly), Immaturity Callow, Crude, Embryo, Ergate(s), Green, Inchoate, Larval, Neotenic, Non-age, Puberal, Puberulent, Pupa, Raw, Sophomoric, Tender, Unbaked, Unripe, Young

▷ **Immature** may indicate a word incompleted

Immediate(ly) Alsoon, At once, Direct, Eftsoons, Ekdum, First-time, Forthwith, Imminent, Incontinent, Instantaneous, Instanter, Near, ➤ NOW, Outright, Present, Pronto, Right-off, Short-term, Slapbang, Spontaneous, Stat, Straight, Straight off, Sudden, Then

Immense Brobdingnag, Cosmic, Enormous, ➤ GIGANTIC, Huge, Vast

Immerse Baptise, Demerge, Demerse, Drench, Emplonge, Enew, Engage, Plunge, Soak, Steep

Immigrant, Immigration Aliya(h), Aussiedler, Carpet-bagger, Chalutz, Greener, Greenhorn, Halutz, Illegal, Incomer, Issei, Merino, Metic, Nisei, Olim, Outsider, Pilgrim, Pommy, Redemption(er), Reffo, Sanei, Sansei, Settler, Wetback

Imminent Approaching, Close, Immediate, Pending

Immobility, Immobilize Cataplexy, Catatonia, Hog-tie, Inertia, Pinion, Rigidity, Tether

Immoderate Excessive, Extreme, Inordinate, Lavish, Undue

Immodest Brash, Brazen, Forward, Indelicate, Unchaste

Immolation Sacrifice, Sati, Suttee

Immoral(ity) Corrupt, Dissolute, Evil, Lax, Libertine, Licentious, Nefarious, Peccable, Reprobate, Turpitude, Unsavoury, Wanton

Immortal(ity) Agelong, Amarant(h), Amritattva, Athanasy, ➤ DIVINE, Enoch, Eternal, Famous, Godlike, Memory, Sin, Struldbrug, Timeless, Undying

Immovable Fast, Firm, Obdurate, Rigid, Stable, Stubborn

Immune, Immunisation, Immunise(r), Immunity Anamnestic, Anergy, Cree, Diplomatic, Free, Inoculate, Klendusic, Properdin, Serum, Vaccine

Immure Confine, Encloister, Imprison

Imp(ish) Devilet, Elf, Flibbertigibbet, Gamin(e), Hobgoblin, Limb, Lincoln, Litherly, Nickum, Nis(se), Puck, Rascal, Sprite

Impact Bearing, Bump, Clash, Collision, Feeze, Impinge, Jar, Jolt, Pack, Percuss, Pow, Slam, Souse, Wham

Impair(ed), Impairment Cripple, Damage, Disease, Enfeeble, ➤ HARM, Injure, Lame, Mar, Odd, Paralogia, Stale, Vitiate

Impale Elance, Ga(u)nch, Skewer, Spike, Transfix

Impart Bestow, Convey, Divulge, Impute, Infect, Shed, Tell

Impartial Candid, Detached, Equitable, Even-handed, Fair, Just, Neutral, Unbiased

Impassable, Impasse Deadlock, Dilemma, Invious, Jam, Snooker, Stalemate, Zugzwang

Impassioned Emotional, Fervid, Fiery, Heated, Zealous

Impassive Apathetic, Deadpan, Stoical, Stolid

Impatience, Impatient Chafing, Chut, Dysphoria, Fiddle-de-dee, Fiddlesticks, Fidgety, Fretful, Hasty, Irritable, Och, Peevish, Peremptory, Petulant, Pish, Tilly-fally, Till(e)y-vall(e)y, Tut

Impeach Accuse, Challenge, Charge, Indict

Impeccable Faultless, Novice

Impecunious Penniless, Poor, Short

Impedance, Impede, Impediment Burr, Clog, Dam, Encumber, Halt, Hamstring, Handicap, ➤ HINDER, Hog-tie, Let, Log, Obstacle, Obstruct, Reactance, Rub, Shackle, Snag, Stammer, Tongue-tie, Trammel, Veto, Z

Impel(led) Actuate, Coerce, Drave, Drive, Drove, Goad, Inspire, ➤ URGE

Impend(ing) Imminent, Looming, Toward

Impenetrable Adamantine, Air-tight, Dense, Hard, Impervious, Proof

Imperative Dire, Jussive, Mood, Need-be, Pressing, Vital

Imperceptible Invisible, Latent, Subtle

Imperfect(ion) Aplasia, Aplastic, Blotch, Defect, Deficient, Faculty, Flawed, Half-pie, Kink, Lame, Poor, Rough, Second

Imperial(ist), Imperious Beard, Commanding, Haughty, Majestic, Masterful, Mint, Peremptory, Regal, Rhodes, Royal, Tuft

Imperil Endanger, Risk

Imperishable Eternal, Immortal, Indestructible

Impermeable Athermanous, Proof, Resistant

Impersonal Abstract, Cold, Detached, Inhuman

Impersonate, Impersonation Amphitryon, Ape, As, Imitate, Impression, Mimic, Pose

Impertinence, Impertinent Crust, Flip(pant), Fresh, Impudent, Irrelevant, Rude, Sass, Sauce

Imperturbable Cool, Placid, Stoic, Tranquil

Impervious(ness) Athermancy, Callous, Hardened, Obdurate, Proof, Tight

Impetigo Scrumpox

Impetuous, Impetuosity Birr, Brash, Bullheaded, Elan, ➤ HASTY, Headstrong, Heady, Hothead, Impulsive, Rash, Tearaway, Vehement, Violent

Impetus Birr, Drift, Incentive, Momentum, Propulsion, Slancio

Impious Blasphemous, Godless, Irreverent, Unholy

Implant(ation) AID, Embed, Engraft, Enroot, Graft, Inset, Instil, Sow

Implausible Lame

Implement Agent, Celt, Eolith, Flail, Fork, Fulfil, Hacksaw, Harrow, Hayfork, Muller, Pin, Pitchfork, Plectrum, Plough, Rest, Ripple, Seed drill, Spatula, Squeegee, Strickle, Tongs, ➤ TOOL, Toothpick, Utensil

Implicate, Implication Accuse, Concern, Connotation, Embroil, Incriminate, Innuendo, ➤ INVOLVE, Overtone

Implore Beg, Beseech, Crave, ➤ ENTREAT, Obsecrate, Petition, Plead, Pray

Imply, Implied Hint, Insinuate, Involve, Predicate, Signify, ➤ SUGGEST, Tacit

Impolite Ill-bred, Rude, Uncivil

Import Convey, Denote, Drift, Mean, Sense, Signify, Spell

Importance, Important (person) Big, Big cheese, Calibre, Cardinal, Central, Cheese, Cob, Core, Cornerstone, Critical, Crucial, Crux, Eminent, Epochal, Grave, Gravitas, Greatness, Heavy, High-muck-a-muck, Honcho, Hotshot, Huzoor, Key, Macher, Magnitude, Main, Major, Material, Matters, Mighty, Milestone, Moment(ous), Nabob, Nib, Note, Numero uno, Personage, Pivotal, Pot, Prime, Principal, Salient, Seminal, Serious, Something, Special, Status, Stress, Substantive, Urgent, VIP, Weight, Weighty

Importune, Importunate Beg, Coax, Flagitate, Press(ing), Prig, Solicit, Urgent

Impose, Imposing, Imposition Allocate, Assess, August, Burden, Charge, Diktat, Dread, Enforce, Enjoin, Epic, Fine, Flam, Foist, Fraud, Grand(iose), Hidage, Homeric, Hum, Impot, Inflict, Kid, Levy, Lumber, Majestic, Obtrude, Pensum, Pole, Scot, Sponge, Statuesque, Sublime, Whillywhaw

Impossible Hopeless, Incorrigible, Insoluble, Insurmountable, No-no, Unacceptable

Impost Excise, Levy, Tax, Toll

Imposter, Impostor Bunyup, Charlatan, Disaster, Faitor, Faitour, ➤ FAKE, Fraud, Idol, Pretender, Sham, Triumph, Warbeck

Impotent Barren, Helpless, Spado, Sterile, Weak

Impound(er) Appropriate, Bond, Confiscate, Intern, Pen, Pinder, Poind

Impoverish(ed) Bankrupt, Bare, Beggar, Exhaust, Straiten

Impractical Absurd, Academic, Chim(a)era, Idealist, Laputan, Not on, Other-worldly, Quixotic, Useless

Imprecation Oath, Pize

Imprecise Approximate, Inaccurate, Indeterminate, Loose, Nebulous, Rough, Sloppy, Vague

Impregnate Conceive, Imbue, Inseminate, Milt, Permeate, Resinate

Impresario Maestro, Manager, Producer, Showman

Impress(ive), Impression(able), Impressionist Air, Astonish, Awe, Blur, Blurb, Brand, Cliché, Conscript, Crimp, Deboss, Dent, Dramatic, Edition, Effect, Engram(ma), Engrave, Enstamp, Epic, Feel(ing), Fingerprint, Frank, Gas, Grab, Grandiose, Homeric, Idée, Imprint, Incuse, Knock, Let, Matisse, Niello, Noble, Note, Palimpsest, Plastic, Plate, Pliable, Powerful, Prent, Press(gang), Print, Proof, Recruit, Repute, Responsive, Ripsnorter, Rotund, Seal, Seize, Sense, Shanghai, Slay, Smite, Soft, Spectacular, Stamp, Stereotype, Strike, Susceptible, Sway, Tableau, Touch, Watermark, Weal, Weighty, Wow

Impressionist Liebermann, Lumin(ar)ist, Manet, Monet, Morisot, Renoir

Imprint Edition, Engrave, Etch, Stamp

Imprison(ment) Cape, Confine, Constrain, Custody, Durance, Immure, Incarcerate, Intern, Jail, Quad, Quod, Time

Improbable Buckley's chance, Buckley's hope, Dubious, Unlikely

Impromptu Ad lib, Extempore, Improvised, Offhand, Spontaneous, Sudden, Unrehearsed

Improper, Impropriety Abnormal, Blue, Demirep, False, Indecent, Indecorum, Outré, Prurient, Solecism, Undue, Unmeet, Unseemly, Untoward

▷ **Improperly** may indicate an anagram

Improve(ment), Improver, Improving Advance, Ameliorate, Beet, Benefit, Bete, Break, Buck, Cap, Chasten, Conditioner, Détente, Didactic, Ease, Edify, Embellish, Emend, Enhance, Enrich, Eugenic, Euthenics, File, Gentrify, Kaizen, Meliorate, Mend, Potentiate, Promote, Rally, Refine, Reform, Resipiscence, Retouch, Slim, Surpass, Tart, Tatt, Titivate, Top, Touch-up, Turn round, Uptrend, Upturn

Improvident Feckless

Improvise(d), Improvisation Adlib, Break, Devise, Extemporise, Invent, Knock-up, Lash-up, Noodle, Ride, Scratch, Sudden, Vamp, Wing

Imprudent Foolhardy, Foolish, Impetuous, Impolitic, Indiscreet, Injudicious, Rash, Reckless, Unwary

Impudence, Impudent Audacious, Backchat, Bardy, Bold, Brash, Brassy, Brazen, Cheeky, Cool, Crust, Effrontery, Forward, Gall, Gallus, Impertinent, Insolent, Jackanapes, Lip, Neck, ➤ NERVE, Pert, Sass(y), Sauce, Saucy, Temerity, Whippersnapper, Yankie

Impugn Censure, Challenge, Defame, Impeach, Malign

Impulse, Impulsive Compelling, Conatus, Dictate, Drive, Efferent, Headlong, Horme, Ideopraxist, Impetus, Instigation, ➤ INSTINCT, Madcap, Nisus, Premature, Premotion, Send, Signal, Snap, Spontaneous, Tendency, Thrust, Tic, Urge, Whim

Impure, Impurity Adulterated, Donor, Faints, Feints, Indecent, Lees, Lewd, Regulus, Scum, Unclean

Imputation, Impute Ascribe, Attribute, Charge, Scandal, Slander, Slur

In A, Amid, Chic, Home, Hostel, I', Inn, Intil, Occupying, Pop(ular), Pub, Trendy, Within

Inability Anosmia, Aphagia, Aphasia, Apraxia

Inaccessible Abaton, Impervious, Remote, Unattainable

Inaccurate Distorted, Erroneous, Faulty, Imprecise, Inexact, Out, Rough, Slipshod

Inactive, Inaction, Inactivity Acedia, Cabbage, Comatose, Dead, Dormant, Extinct, Fallow, Hibernate, Idle, Inert, Moratorium, Passive, Quiescent, Rusty, Sluggish, Torpid, Veg(etate)

In addition Else, Further, Moreover, Plus, Too

Inadequate Derisory, Feeble, Inapt, Inferior, Pathetic, Poor, Ropy, Thin

Inadvertent(ly) Accidental, Careless, Chance, Unwitting

▷ **In a flap** may indicate an anagram

In a high degree So

In a hundred Percent

Inane Empty, Fatuous, Foolish, Imbecile, Silly, Vacant

Inanimate Abiotic

Inappropriate Amiss, Infelicitous, Malapropos, Off-key, Unapt, Unbecoming, Undue, Unsuitable, Untoward

Inapt Maladroit, Unsuitable

Inarticulate(ness) Indistinct, Mumbling, Psellism

Inartistic Artless, Crude

Inattentive, Inattention Deaf, Distrait, Dwaal, Dwa(l)m, Dwaum, Heedless, Loose, Slack, Unheeding

Inaudible Silent, Superhet

Inaugurate Han(d)sel, Initiate, Install, Introduce

Inauspicious Adverse, Ominous, Sinister

▷ **In a whirl** may indicate an anagram

▷ **In a word** may indicate two clue words linked to form one

Inborn, Inbred Inherent, Innate, Native, Selfed, Sib

Incalculable Endless, Unpredictable, Untold

Incandescent Alight, Bright, Brilliant, Excited

Incantation Charm, Magic, Mantra, Spell

Incapable Can't, Powerless, Unable, Useless

Incarnation Advent, Avatar, Embodiment, Fleshing, Krishna, Rama

In case Lest, So

Incautious Foolhardy, Rash, Reckless, Unwary

Incendiary Arsonist, Combustible, Firebug, Fire-lighter, Napalm

Incense(d), Incenser Anger, Aroma, Elemi, Enfelon, Enrage, Homage, Hot, ► INFLAME, Joss-stick, Navicula, Onycha, Outrage, Pastil(le), Provoke, Thurible, Thus, Vex, Wrathful

Incentive Carrot, Fillip, Impetus, Motive, Premium, Spur, Stimulus

Incessant Constant, Endless

Inch Ait, Edge, Isle, Sidle, Uncial

Inchoate Formless, Immature, Incipient

Incident(al) Affair, Baur, Bawr, Carry-on, Chance, Circumstance, Episode, Event, Facultative, Negligible, Occasion, Occurrent, Page, Scene

Incinerate, Incinerator Burn, Combust, Cremate, Destructor

Incipient Beginning, Germinal, Inchoate

Incise, Incision, Incisive(ness) Bite, Cut, Engrave, Incavo, Mordant, Phlebotomy, Scribe, Slit, Surgical, Tracheotomy, Trenchant

Incite(ment) Abet, Drive, Egg, Fillip, Hortative, Hoy, Inflame, Instigate, Kindle, Motivate, Prod, Prompt, Provoke, Put, Rouse, Sa sa, Set, Sic(k), Sool, ➤ SPUR, Sting, Tar, Urge

Incline(d), Inclination Acclivity, Angle, Aslope, Atilt, Bank, Batter, Bent, Bias, Bow, Clinamen, Declivity, Dip, Disposed, Drift, Enclitic, Glacis, ➤ GRADIENT, Grain, Hade, Heel, Hill, Kant, Kip, Lean, Liking, List, Maw, Minded, Nod, On, Partial, Peck, Penchant, Prone, Propensity, Rake, Ramp, Ready, Rollway, Set, Shelve, Slant, ➤ SLOPE, Steep, Steeve, Stomach, Supine, Tend, Tilt, Tip, Trend, Upgrade, Velleity, Verge, Weathering, Will

Include(d) Add, Bracket, Compass, Comprise, Connotate, Contain, Cover, Embody, Embrace, Enclose, Involve, Subsume, Therein

Incognito Anonymous, Disguised, Faceless, Secret, Unnamed

Incoherent Confused, Disconnected, Disjointed, Rambling, Spluttering

Income Annuity, Disposable, Dividend, Earned, Entry, Living, Meal-ticket, Milch cow, Penny-rent, Prebend, Primitiae, Proceeds, Rent, Rent-roll, Returns, Revenue, Salary, Stipend, Unearned, Wages

Incommunicado Isolated, Silent

Incomparable Supreme, Unequalled, Unmatched

Incompatible, Incompatibility Contradictory, Dyspathy, Inconsistent, Mismatched, Unsuited

Incompetent Bungler, Deadhead, Helpless, Ill, Inefficient, Inept, Palooka, Unable, Unfit

Incomplete Cagmag, Catalectic, Deficient, Inchoate, Lacking, Partial, Pendent, Rough, Unfinished

Incomprehensible Hard, Unbelievable

Inconceivable Impossible, Incredible

▷ **In confusion** may indicate an anagram

Incongruous, Incongruity Absurd, Discordant, Irish, Ironic, Sharawadgi, Sharawaggi

In connection with Re

Inconsiderable Light, Slight

Inconsiderate High-handed, Petty, Presumptuous, Roughshod, Thoughtless, Unkind

Inconsistency, Inconsistent Alien, Anacoluthon, Anomaly, Contradictory, Discrepant, Oxymoronic, Paradoxical, Unequal, Variance

Inconsolable Heartbroken, Niobe

Inconstant Chameleon, Desultory, Fickle, Light, Mutable, ➤ VARIABLE

Inconvenience, Inconvenient Awkward, Bother, Discommode, Fleabite, Incommodious, ➤ TROUBLE, Unseemly, Untoward

Incorporate(d), Incorporation Absorb, Embody, Inc, Integrate, Introgression, Join, Merge, Subsume

Incorporeal Aery, Airy, Spiritual

Incorrect Catachresis, False, Improper, Naughty

Incorrigible Hopeless, Obstinate

Incorruptible Copper-bottomed, Honest, Immortal, Pure, Robespierre, Sea-green

Increase, Increasing Accelerando, Accelerate, Accession, Accrue, Add, Aggrandise, Amplify, Appreciate, Approve, Augment, Auxetic, Bolster, Bulge, Crescendo, Crescent, Crescive, Deepen, Dilate, Double, Ech(e), Eech, Eik, Eke, Enhance, Enlarge, Escalate, ➤ EXPAND, Explosion, Greaten, ➤ GROW, Heighten, Ich, Increment, Interbreed, Jack, Jack up, Magnify, Mark up, Mount, Multiply, Plus, Proliferate, Propagate, Redshift, Reflation, Regrate, Rise, Snowball, Swell, Up, Upswing, Wax

Incredible Amazing, Cockamamie, Extraordinary, Fantastic, Steep, Stey, Tall

Incredulity, Incredulous Distrust, Infidel, Suspicion, Thunderstruck, Unbelief

Increment Accrual, Augment, Growth, Increase

Incriminate Accuse, Implicate, Inculpate

Incubate, Incubator Brooder, Develop, Eccaleobion, Hatch

Incubus Demon, Load, Nightmare

Inculcate Infuse

Incumbent Lying, Obligatory, Occupier, Official

Incur Assume, Earn, Involve

Incursion Foray, Inroad, Invasion, Raid, Razzia

Indecent Bare, Blue, Fescennine, Free, Immodest, Immoral, Improper, Lewd, Obscene, Racy, Scurril(e), Sotadic, Unproper, Unseem(ly)

Indecision, Indecisive Demur, Dithery, Doubt, Hamlet, Hung jury, Suspense, Swither, Weakkneed

Indeclinable Aptote

Indecorous Graceless, Immodest, Outré, Unbecoming

Indeed Atweel, Ay, Da, Een, Even, Faith, Haith, Insooth, La, Marry, Quotha, Verily, Yah, Yea

Indefensible Implausible, Inexcusable, Vincible

Indefinite(ly) A, An, Any, Evermore, Hazy, Nth, Some, Undecided, Vague

Indelible Fast, Permanent

Indelicate Broad, Coarse, Improper, Vulgar, Warm

Indemnify, Indemnification, Indemnity Assythement, Compensation, Insurance

Indent(ed), Indentation Apprentice, Contract, Crenellate, Dancetty, Dimple, Impress, Niche, Notch, Order, Subentire

Independence, Independent Autocephalous, Autogenous, Autonomy, Crossbencher, Detached, Extraneous, Free(dom), Free-lance, I, Liberty, Maverick, Mugwump, Perseity, Self-sufficient, Separate, Separatist, Swaraj, UDI, Udal, Uhuru

Indescribable Incredible, Ineffable

Indestructible Enduring, Impenetrable, Inextirpable

Indeterminate Borderline, Formless, Incalculable, Open-ended, Unknown

Index Alidad(e), Catalogue, Dial, Dow Jones, Exponent, Finger, Fist, Footsie, Forefinger, Gazetteer, Hang Seng, Kwic, Librorum Prohibitorum, Nikkei, Opsonic, Price, Refractive, ➤ REGISTER, Table, Thumb, UV

Indiaman Clive

India(n) Adivisi, Ayah, Baboo, Babu, Bharat(i), Canarese, Chin, Dard, Dravidian, File, Gond(wanaland), Gujarati, Harijan, Harsha, Hindu, Ink, Jain, Jat, Jemadar, Kanarese, Kannada, Khalsa, Kisan, Kolarian, Kshatriyas, Lepcha, Ma(h)ratta, Maratha, Mazhbi, ➤ MEXICAN, Mofussil, Mogul, Munda, Munshi, Nagari, Nair, Nasik, Nation, Nayar, ➤ NORTH AMERICAN, Ocean, Oriya, Pali, Parsee, Parsi, Peshwa, Prakrit, Punjabi, Sanskrit, Sepoy, Shri, Sikh, Sind(h), ➤ SOUTH AMERICAN, Sowar, Summer, Swadeshi, Tamil, Telegu, Vakeel, Vakil

Indicate, Indication, Indicative, Indicator Adumbrate, Allude, Argue, Cite, Clue, Cursor, ➤ DENOTE, Design, Desine, Dial, Endeixis, Evidence, Evince, Gesture, Gnomon, Litmus, Manifest, Mean, Mood, Nod, Notation, Pinpoint, Point, Portend, Proof, Ray, Register, Remarque, Representative, Reveal, ➤ SIGN, Signify, Specify, Symptom, Tip, Token, Trace, Trait, Winker

Indictment Accusation, Caption, Charge, Dittay, Reproach

Indifference, Indifferent Adiaphoron, Aloof, Apathetic, Apathy, Blasé, Blithe, Callous, Cold, Cool(th), Dead, Detached, Disdain, Incurious, Insouciant, Jack easy, Mediocre, Neutral, Nonchalant, Perfunctory, Phlegm, Pococurante, So-so, Stoical, Supine, Tepid, Unconcerned

Indigence, Indigent Need, Pauper, Penury, Poverty, Want

Indigenous Aboriginal, Endemic, Native

▷ **Indi-gent** may indicate Baboo or Babu

Indigestion Apepsia, Apepsy, Dyspepsia, Heartburn

Indignant, Indignation Anger, Annoyed, Incensed, Irate, Resentful, Wrathful

Indignity Affront, Outrage

Indigo Anil, Blue, Bunting, Carmine, Indole, Isatin(e)

Indirect Back-handed, By(e), Devious, Implicit, Mediate, Oblique, Remote, Roundabout, Sidelong, Zig-zag

Indiscreet, Indiscretion Folly, Gaffe, Imprudence, Indelicate, Injudicious, Loose cannon, Rash, Unguarded

Indiscriminate Haphazard, Random, Scattershot, Sweeping

Indispensable Basic, Essential, King-pin, Necessary, Vital

Indispose(d), Indisposition Adverse, Disincline, Ill, Incapacitate, Sick, Unwell

Indistinct Ambiguous, Bleary, Blur, Bumble, Bummle, Faint, Fuzzy, Hazy, Pale, Sfumato, ➤ VAGUE

▷ **In distress** may indicate an anagram

Indite Compose, Pen, Write

Indium In

Individual(ist), Individuality Being, Discrete, Free spirit, Haecceity, Gemma, Identity, Ka, Libertarian, Loner, Man, Man-jack, One-to-one, Particular, Person, Poll, Respective, Separate, Single, Singular, Solo, Soul, Special, Unit, Zoon

Indoctrinate Brainwash, Discipline, Instruct

Indo-European Aryan

Indolence, Indolent Fainéance, Inactive, Languid, Lazy, Sloth, Sluggish, Supine

Indomitable Brave, Dauntless, Invincible

Indonesia(n) Batavian, Nesiot, RI

Indoor(s) Within

Indubitably Certainly, Certes, Manifestly, Surely

Induce Bribe, Cause, Coax, Draw, Encourage, Get, Inveigle, Lead, Motivate, ➤ PERSUADE, Prevail, Suborn, Tempt

Induct(ion), Inductance Epagoge, Henry, Inaugurate, Initiate, Install, L, Logic, Prelude, Remanence

Indulge(nce), Indulgent Absolution, Binge, Coddle, Drink, Favour, Gratify, Humour, Luxuriate, Oblige, Pamper, Pander, Pardon, Pet, Pettle, Please, ➤ SATISFY, Splurge, Spoil, Spoonfeed, Surfeit, Tolerant, Venery, Voluptuous, Wallow

Industrial, Industrious, Industry Appliance, Application, Business, Busy, Cottage, Deedy, Diligence, Eident, Energetic, Labour, Ocnus, Operose, Ruhr, Service, Technical, Tourism, Zaibatsu

▶ **Inebriate** see INTOXICATE

Inedible Inesculent, Noisome, Rotten

Ineffective, Ineffectual Clumsy, Deadhead, Drippy, Droob, Dud, Empty, Fainéant, Fruitless, Futile, Idle, Ill, Impotent, Mickey Mouse, Neutralised, Powerless, Resty, Sterile, Toothless, ➤ USELESS, Void, Weak, Wet

Inefficient Clumsy, Incompetent, Lame, Shiftless, Slack

Inelegant Awkward, Inconcinnity, Stiff, Turgid, Unneat

Ineligible Unqualified

Inept Absurd, Anorak, Farouche, Nerd, Otaku, Sad sack, Schlimazel, Unskilled, Wet

Inequality Anomaly, Disparity, Injustice, Odds

Inert(ia) Catatonia, Comatose, Dead, Dull, Excipient, Inactive, Leaden, Mollusc, Neon, Oblomovism, Potato, Sluggish, Stagnant, Stagnation, Thowless, Torpid

Inestimable Incalculable, Invaluable, Priceless

Inevitable, Inevitably Automatic, Certain, Fateful, Inexorable, Needs, Perforce, TINA, Unavoidable

Inexact(itude) Cretism, Incorrect, Terminological, Wrong

Inexorable Relentless

Inexpedient Impolitic, Imprudent, Unwise

Inexpensive Bargain, Cheap, Dirt-cheap

Inexperience(d), Inexpert Amateur, Callow, Colt, Crude, Fresh, ➤ GREEN, Ham, Ingénue, Jejune, Raw, Rookie, Rude, Tender, Unconversant, Unseasoned, Unseen, Unversed, Youthful

Inexplicable Magical, Mysterious, Paranormal, Unaccountable

Infallible Foolproof, Right, Unerring

Infamous, Infamy Base, Ignominious, Notorious, Opprobrium, Shameful, Villainy

Infant Babe, Baby, Innocent, Lamb, Minor, Oral, Rug rat

Infantry(man) Buff, Foot, Grunt, Jaeger, Phalanx, Pultan, Pulto(o)n, Pultun, ➤ SOLDIER, Tercio, Turco

▷ **Infantry** may refer to babies

Infatuate(d), Infatuation Assot, Besot, Crush, Enamoured, Engou(e)ment, Entêté, Fanatic, Foolish, Lovesick, ➤ OBSESSION, Rave, Turn

Infect(ed), Infecting, Infection, Infectious Angina, Anthrax, Candidiasis, Catching, Catchy, Cholera, Communicable, Contagious, Contaminate, Corrupt, Cowpox, Diseased, Fascioliasis, Fester, Fomes, Giardiasis, Gonorrhoea, Herpes, Leishmaniasis, Listeria, Lockjaw, NSU, Orf, Overrun, Poison, Polio(myelitis), ➤ POLLUTE, Py(a)emia, Ringworm, Roup, Salmonella, Sarcoid, Septic, Shingles, Smit(tle), Strongylosis, Taint, Tetanus, Thrush, Tinea, Trichuriasis, Typhoid, Typhus, Virion, Virulent, Whitlow, Wog, Yersiniosis, Zymosis

Infeftment Sasine, Seisin

Infer(ence) Conclude, Deduce, Divine, Educe, Extrapolate, Generalise, Guess, Illation, Imply, Judge, Surmise

▷ **Infer** may indicate 'fer' around another word

Inferior Base, Cheap-jack, Cheesy, Degenerate, Dog, Gimcrack, Grody, Grub-street, Indifferent, Infra, Jerkwater, Less, Lo-fi, Low-grade, Lower, Minor, Naff, Nether, One-horse, Ornery, Paravail, Petty, Poor, Rop(e)y, Schlock, Second, Second-best, Shlock, Shoddy, Sprew, Sprue, Subjacent, Subordinate, Substandard, Surat, Tatty, Tinpot, Trashy, Under(man), Underneath, Understrapper, Untermensch, Waste, Worse

Infernal Demogorgon, Diabolic, Hellish, Unholy

Infest(ed), Infestation Acariasis, Acrawl, Beset, Blight, Dog, Hoatching, Overrun, Pediculosis, Phthiriasis, ➤ PLAGUE, Stylopised, Swarm, Torment, Trombiculiasis, Trombidiasis, Uncinariasis

Infidel Atheist, Caffre, Giaour, Heathen, Heretic, Kafir, Pagan, Paynim, Saracen

Infield Intown

Infiltrate Encroach, Enter, Instil, Intrude, Pervade

Infinite, Infinity Cosmic, Endless, Eternal, N

Infirm Decrepit, Doddery, Feeble, Lame, Shaky

▷ **Infirm** may indicate 'co' around another word

Inflame(d), Inflammable, Inflammation Acne, Adenitis, Afire, Ancome, Anger, Angina, Aortisis, Appendicitis, ➤ AROUSE, Arteritis, Arthritis, Asbestosis, Balanitis, Blepharitis, Bloodshot, Bronchitis, Bronchopneumonia, Bubonic, Bunion, Bursitis, Carditis, Catarrh, Cellulitis, Cervicitis, Cheilitis, Colitis, Conjunctivitis, Coryza, Croup, Cystisis, Dermatitis, Diverticulitis, Ecthyma, Eczema, Enamoured, Encephalitis, Encephalomyelitis, Enchafe, Endocarditis, Enfire, Enkindle, Enteritis, Enterocolitis, Erysipelas, Farmer's lung, Felon, Fever, Fibrosis, Fibrositis, Fire, Folliculitis, Founder, Garget, Gastritis, Gastroenteritis, Gingivitis, Gleet, Glossitis, Hepatitis A, Hepatitis B, Hyalitis, Ignatis, Ignite, Incense, Infection, Intertrigo, Ire, Iritis, Keratitis, Labyrinthitis, Laminitis, Laryngitis, Mastitis, Mastoiditis, Meningitis, Meningocephalitis, Metritis, Misenteritis, Mycetoma, Myelitis, Myocarditis, Myositis, Napalm, Naphtha, Nephritis, Neuritis, Noma, Onychia, Oophoritis, Ophthalmia, Orchitis, Osteitis, Osteoarthritis, Osteomyelitis, Osteoporosis, Otitis, Ovaritis, Pancreatitis, Paronychia, Parotitis, Pericarditis, Perihepatitis, Perinephritis, Periodontisis, Peritonitis, Perityphlitis, Pharyngitis, Phlebitis, Phlegmasia, Phlegmon, Phlogistic, Phrenitis, Pinkeye, Pleurisy, Pneumonia, Polyneuritis, Proctitis, Prostatitis, Prurigo, Pyelitis, Pyorrhoea, Quinsy, Rachitis, ➤ RED, Retinitis, Rhinitis, Salpingitis, Scleritis, Shin splints, Sinusitis, Splenitis, Spondylitis, Stimulate, Stomatitis, Strumitis, Sty(e), Sunburn, Swelling, Swimmer's itch, Sycosis, Synovitis, Tendinitis, Tenosynovitis, Thoroughpin, Thrombosis, Thrush, Thyroiditis, Tonsillitis, Touchwood, Tracheitis, Tylosis, Typhlitis, Ulitis, Urethritis, Uvulitis, Vaginitis, Valvulitis, Vasculitis, Vincent's angina, Whitlow, Windburn

Inflate(d), Inflation Aerate, Aggrandise, Bloat, Bombastic, Dilate, Distend, Distent, Increase, Pneumatic, Pump, Remonetise, RPI, Spiral, Stagnation, Swell

Inflect(ion) Accidence, Conjugation

Inflexible, Inflexibility Adamant(ine), Byzantine, Doctrinaire, Hard-ass, Hard-liner, Iron, Obstinate, Ossified, Relentless, Resolute, Rigid, Rigour, Set, Stubborn

Inflict(ion) Deal, Force, Give, Impose, Subject, Trouble, Visit, Wreak

Inflorescence Bostryx, Catkin, Ci(n)cinnus, Drepanium, Glomerule, Panicle, Pleiochasium, Raceme, Umbel

Inflow Affluence, Influx

Influence(d), Influential Act, Affect, After, Backstairs, Charm, Clout, Credit, Determine, Drag, Earwig, Embracery, Eminence grise, Factor, Force, Govern, Hold, Impact, Impress, Incubus, Inspire, Interfere, Lead, Leverage, Lobby, Mastery, Militate, Mogul, Octopus, Operation, Power, Pressure, Prestige, ➤ PULL, Push, Reach, Rust, Say, Seminal, Significant, Star, Star-blasting, Stimulus, Suggest, Svengali, Sway, Swing, Telegony, Undue, Will, Work, Wull

Influenza Flu, Grippe, Wog

Inform(ation), Informed, Informer Acquaint, Advise, Agitprop, Apprise, Au fait, Aware, Beagle, Bit, Burst, Canary, Ceefax®, Clype, Contact, Datum,

Delate, Dob(ber), Dope, Education, Facts, Feedback, Fink, Fisgig, Fiz(z)gig, Gen, Genome, Grapevine, Grass, Griff, Gunsel, Hep, Input, Inside, Instruct, Izvesti(y)a, Light, Lowdown, Media, Moiser, Nark, Nepit, Nit, Nose, Occasion, Peach, Pem(m)ican, Poop, Prestel®, Prime, Propaganda, Prospectus, Rat, Read-out, Revelation, Rheme, Rumble, Shelf, Shop, Sidelight, Sing, Sneak, Snitch, Squeak, Squeal, Stag, Stoolie, Stool-pigeon, Supergrass, Sycophant, Tell, Tidings, Tip-off, Up, Whistle(-blower), Wire

Informal Casual, Intimate, Irregular, Outgoing, Unofficial

Infra Under

Infrequent Casual, Occasional, Rare, Scant, Seldom, Sparse

Infringe Contravene, Violate

Infuriate Anger, Bemad, Bepester, Enrage, Exasperate, Incense, Madden, Pester, Provoke

Infuse(r), Infusion Brew, Distill, Gallise, Instil, Mash, Saloop, Saturate, Steep, Tea, Tea-ball, Tea-egg, Tisane, Uva-ursi

Ingenious, Ingenuity Adept, Adroit, Art, Artificial, Clever, Cunning, Cute, Inventive, Natty, Neat, Resourceful, Smart, Subtle, Wit

Ingenuous Artless, Candid, Green, Innocent, Naive, Open

Ingest Eat, Endue, Incept, Indue, Swallow

In good condition Fit, Shipshape, Taut, Trim

Ingot Bar, Billet, Bullion, Lingot, Sycee

Ingrain Fix, Impregnate, Train

Ingrate Thankless, Viper

Ingratiate, Ingratiating Butter, Court, Flatter, Greasy, Smarm(y)

Ingredient(s) Additive, Admixture, Basis, Content, Element, Factor, Formula, Makings, Staple

Ingrowing, Ingrowth Onychocryptosis, T(h)ylosis

Inhabit(ants) Affect, Children, Denizen, Dweller, Inholder, Inmate, Live, Native, Occupant, People, Resident

Inhale, Inhalation Aspirate, Breath(e), Draw, Gas, Inspire, Sniff, Snort, Snuff, Take

Inharmonious Out, Patchy

Inherent Characteristic, Essential, Immanent, Inbred, Innate, Native

Inherit(ance), Inherited, Inheritor Accede, Birthright, Borough-English, Congenital, Gene, Genom, Heirloom, Inborn, Legacy, Legitim, Meek, Mendelism, Particulate, Patrimony, Portion, Reversion, Succeed, Tichborne

Inhibit(ing), Inhibition Captopril, Chalone, Chalonic, Deter, Enalapril, Forbid, Hang-up, Restrain, Suppress

Inhuman Barbarous, Brutal, Merciless

Inimical Adverse, Harmful, Hostile

Iniquity, Iniquitous Diabolical, Evil, Offence, Sin, Vice

Initial Acronym, First, Letter, Monogram, Paraph, Prelim(inary), Primary, Rubric

▷ **Initially** may indicate first letters

Initiate(d), Initiation, Initiative Begin, Bejesuit, Blood, Bora, Bring, Ceremony, Debut, Enter, Enterprise, Epopt, Esoteric, Gumption, Induct, Instigate, Instruct, ➤ LAUNCH, Nous, Spark, ➤ START

Inject(or), Injection Booster, Enema, Epidural, Hypo, Implant, Innerve, Inoculation, Instil, Introduce, Jab, Mainline, Pop, Reheat, Serum, Shoot, Skin-pop, Syringe, Venipuncture

Injunction Command, Embargo, Mandate, Mareva, Swear, Writ

Injure(d), Injury, Injurious, Injustice ABH, Abuse, Aggrieve, Bale, Bled, Bruise, Contrecoup, Damage, De(a)re, Forslack, Frostbite, Gash, GBH, Harm, ➤ HURT, Ill-turn, Impair, Iniquity, Lesion, Malign, Mar, Mayhem, Mistreat, Mutilate, NAI, Nobble, Nocuous, Noxal, Nuisance, Oppression, Outrage, Packet, Paire, Prejudice, Rifle, RSI, Scaith, Scath(e), Scotch, Sore, Sprain, Teen(e), Tene, Tort, Trauma, Umbrage, Whiplash, Wound, Wrong

▶ **Injury** see AFTER INJURY

Ink(y) Atramental, Black, Bray, Cyan, Indian, Invisible, Marking, Sepia, Stained, Tusche

Inkling Clue, Glimpse, Hint, Idea

Inkpot Standish

Inlaid, Inlay(er) Boulle, Buhl, Damascene, Emblemata, Empaestic, Enamel, Enchase, Incrust, Intarsia, Intarsio, Koftgar(i), Marquetrie, Marquetry, Pietra-dura, Piqué, Set, Tarsia, Veneer

Inland Hinterland, Interior, Up

Inlet Arm, Bay, Cove, Creek, Entry, Fiord, Firth, Fjord, Fleet, Geo, Gio, Gusset, Infall, McMurdo Sound, Sullom Voe, Table Bay, Wash

▷ **Inlet** may indicate 'let' around another word

Inmate Intern(e), Lodger, Patient, Prisoner, Resident

Inn(keeper) Albergo, Alehouse, Auberge, Barnard's, Boniface, Caravanserai, Coaching, Gray's, Halfway-house, Host, Hostelry, House, Hotel, Imaret, In, Inner Temple, Khan, Ladin(ity), Law, Licensee, Lincoln's, Lodging, Luckie, Lucky, Middle Temple, Padrone, Parador, Patron, Porterhouse, Posada, Posthouse, Pothouse, Publican, Roadhouse, Ryokan, Serai, Tabard, Tavern(er), Victualler

▷ **Inn** may refer to the law

Innards Entrails, Giblets, Gizzard, Guts, Harigals, Harslet, Haslet, Rein, Viscera

Innate Congenital, Essential, Inbred, Inbuilt, Natural, Inborn, Instinctive

Inner(most) Bencher, Esoteric, Internal, Intima, Lining, Medulla, Private

Innings Chance, Turn

▶ **Innkeeper** see INN

Innocent Absolved, Angelic, Arcadian, Babe, Blameless, Canny, Chaste, Cherub, Childlike, Clean, Doddypoll, Dodipoll, Dove, Encyclical, Green, Idyllic, Ingenue, Lamb, Lily-white, Maiden, Naive, Opsimath, Pope, ➤ PURE, Sackless, Seely, Simple, St, White

Innocuous Harmless, Innocent

Innovation, Innovator Alteration, Newell, Novelty, Pioneer

Inn-sign Bush

Innumerable Countless, Infinite, N

Inoculate, Inoculation Engraft, Immunise, Jab, Protect, Vaccine, Variolate

Inoffensive Mild, Pleasant

Inoperative Futile, Nugatory, Silent, Void

Inopportune Inconvenient, Intempestive, Untimely

Inordinate Excessive, Irregular, Undue

▷ **Inordinately** may indicate an anagram

In place of For, Qua, Vice, With

Inquest Debriefing, Hearing, Inquiry, Investigation

Inquire, Inquiring, Inquiry Ask, Demand, Investigation, Maieutic, Nose, Organon, Probe, Query, Question, See, Speer, Speir

Inquisition, Inquisitive, Iniquisitor Curious, Interrogation, Meddlesome, Nosy, Prying, Rubberneck, Snooper, Stickybeak, Torquemada

▷ **In revolt, In revolution** may indicate an anagram

Inroad(s) Breach, Encroachment, Honeycomb, Invasion

Insane, Insanity Absurd, Batty, Crazy, Deranged, Hebephrenia, Loco, Lune, Mad, Manic, Mattoid, Paranoia, Pellagra, Psycho, Schizo, Yarra

Insatiable Greedy, Ravenous, Voracious

Insatiate child Killcrop

Inscribe(d), Inscription Chisel, Chronogram, Colophon, Dedicate, Emblazon, Engrave, Enter, Epigraph, Epitaph, Exergue, Graffiti, Hic jacet, Hierograph, Lapidary, Legend, Lettering, Posy, Writ

Inscrutable Deadpan, Esoteric, Mysterious, Sphinx

Insect(s) Acarid, Alderfly, Ametabola, Ant, Antlion, Aphis, Apterygota, Bark mantis, Bee, Bishop's mitre, Bluebottle, Booklouse, Bookworm, Borer, Bot, Breeze, Bristletail, Bug, Buzzard, Caddis-fly, Capsid, Casebearer, Centipede, Chalcid, Chigger, Chigoe, Chironomid, Cicada, Cicala, Cimex, Circutio, Coccidae, Cochineal, Cockchafer, Cockroach, Coleoptera, Collembola, Compodeid, Cornfly, Crane-fly, Creepy-crawly, Cricket, Daddy-long-legs, Damselfly, Daphnid, Day-fly, Dermopteran, Dictyopteran, Dipteras, Dobsonfly, Dragonfly, Emmet, Entomic, Ephemeron, Ergates, Fan-cricket, Fen-cricket, Firebrat, Firefly, Flea, Fly, Froghopper, Gadfly, Gallfly, Gall-wasp, Girdler, Glossina, Gnat, Gogga, Grasshopper, Grayfly, Greenbottle, Grig, Harvestman, Hemiptera, Heteropteran, Hexapod, Hive-bee, Homoptera, Hopper, Hornet, Horntail, Horsefly, Humbuzz, Hymenoptera, Instar, Itchmite, Jenny-longlegs, Katydid, Lac, Lacewing, Ladybird, Ladybug, Leaf-cutter, Leafhopper, Leatherjacket, Lice, Locust, Louse, Lygus bug, Mallophaga, Mantid, Mantis, Mayfly, Mealybug, Mecoptera, Metabola, Midge, Millepede, Milliped(e), Mite, Mosquito, Moth, Myriapod, Neuropteran, Nit, Nonentity, Non-person, Nymph, Odonata, Oestrus, Oniscus, Orthoptera, Ox-bot, Phasmid, Phylloxera, Pill-bug, Pium, Plant-louse, Pond-skater, Praying mantis, Psocid, Psocoptera, Psylla, Punkie, Pupa, Puss-moth, Pyralis, Rearhorse, Redbug, Reduviid, Rhipidoptera, Rhipiptera, Ruby-tail, Sandfly, Sawfly, Scale, Scarab(ee), Silverfish, Slater, Snowflea, Spectre, Spider, Springtail, Staphylinidae, Stick, Stinkbug, Stonefly, Strepsiptera,

Stylops, Tabanidae, Termite, Tettix, Thousand-legs, Thrips, Thysanoptera, Thysanuran, Tick, Tiger-beetle, Tiger-moth, Treehopper, Trichoptera, Walker, Wasp, Waterbug, Weevil, Weta, Whitefly, Wog, Woodlouse, Xylophage, Zebub, Zimb

Insecticide Allethrin, Aphicide, Carbaryl, Chromene, DDT, Deet, Derris, Dieldrin, Endosulfan, Endrin, Flycatcher, Gammexane®, Ivermectin, Lindane®, Malathion®, Menazon, Methoxychlor, Miticide, Naphthalene, Parathion, Paris green, Pyrethrin, Pyrethrum, Rotenone, Spray, Timbo, Toxaphene, Zineb

Insectivore Agoura, Desman, Donaea, Drosera, Hedgehog, Jacamar, Nepenthaceae, Tanrec, Tenrec(idae), Venus flytrap, Zalambdodont

Insecure Infirm, ➤ LOOSE, Precarious, Shaky, Unsafe, Unstable, Unsteady, Vulnerable

Insensitive, Insensitivity Analgesia, Blunt, Callous, Dead, Log, Numb, Obtuse, Pachyderm, Stolid, Tactless, Thick-skinned

Inseparable Indiscrete, One, United

Insert(ion), Inset Cue, Empiecement, Enchase, Enter, Entry, Foist, Fudge, Godet, Gore, Graft, Gusset, Immit, Imp, Implant, Inject, Inlay, Input, Interject, Interpolate, Interpose, Intersperse, Introduce, Intromit, Mitre, Pin, Sandwich

Inside(r) Content, Core, Entrails, Gaol, Heart, Indoors, Interior, Internal, Interne, Inward, Inwith, Mole, Tum, ➤ WITHIN

Insidious Artful, Crafty, Sly

Insight Acumen, Anagoge, Aperçu, Hunch, Inkling, Intuition, ➤ PERCEPTION, Tais(c)h

Insignia Armour, Arms, Badger, Charge, Chevron, Mark, Regalia, Ribbon, Roundel, Tab

Insignificant (person) Dandiprat, Fico, Flea-bite, Fractional, Gnat, Inconsiderable, Insect, Minimus, Miniscule, Minnow, Nebbich, Nobody, Nominal, Nonentity, One-eyed, Petit, Petty, Pipsqueak, Quat, Scoot, Scout, Scrub, Shrimp, Slight, Small-time, Squirt, Squit, Trifling, Trivial, Two-bit, Unimportant, Venial, Whippersnapper

Insincere Affected, Artificial, Barmecide, Cant, Double, Empty, Factitious, Faithless, False, Glib, Hollow, Janus-faced, Mealy-mouthed, Pseudo, Shallow, Synthetic

Insinuate, Insinuating, Insinuation Allude, Hint, Imply, Innuendo, Intimate, Sleek, Sneck-draw

Insipid Banal, Blab, Bland, Fade, Flat, Insulse, Jejune, Lash, Mawkish, Shilpit, Tame, Tasteless, Vapid, Weak, Wearish

Insist(ent) Assert, Demand, Dogmatic, Exact, ➤ STIPULATE, Stress, Swear, Threap, Threep, Urge

Insolence, Insolent Audacity, Bardy, Brassy, Cheek, Contumely, Effrontery, Gum, Hubris, Hybris, Impudence, Lip, Rude, Snash, Stroppy, Wanton

Insoluble Cerasin, Hard, Irresolvable, Mysterious

Insolvent Bankrupt, Broke, Destitute, Penniless

Insomnia Agrypnotic, Sleeplessness, Wakefulness

Insouciant Carefree, Careless, Cavalier

Inspect(ion), Inspector Alnage(r), Auditor, Comb, Conner, Examine, Government, Investigator, Jerque, Keeker, Muster, Once-over, Peep, Perlustrate, Proveditor, Rag-fair, Recce, Review, Scrutinise, Survey, Test, Vet, Vidimus, Visitation

Inspiration, Inspire(d), Inspiring Actuate, Afflatus, Aerate, Aganippe, Animate, Brainstorm, Brainwave, Breath(e), Castalian, Elate, Exalt, Flash, Draw, Fire, Hearten, Hunch, Idea, Illuminate, Impulse, Induce, Inflatus, Infuse, Move, Muse, Pegasus, Prompt, Prophetic, Satori, Sniff(le), Stimulus, Taghairm, Theopneust(y), Uplift, Vatic

In spite of Augre

Instability Anomie, Anomy

Install(ation) Enchase, Enthrone, Inaugurate, Induction, Infrastructure, Invest, Put (in)

Instalment Episode, Fascicle, Heft, Livraison, Never-never, Part, Serial, Tranche

Instance, Instant As, Case, Chronon, Example, Flash, Jiffy, Moment, Present, Say, Shake, Spur, Tick, Trice, Twinkling, Urgent

Instead (of) Deputy, For, Lieu, Locum, Vice

Instigate Arouse, Foment, Impel, Incite, Prompt, Spur

Instil(l) Implant, Inculcate, Infuse, Teach, Transfuse

Instinct(ive) Automatic, Flair, Herd, Id, Impulse, Inbred, Innate, Intuition, Nature, Nose, Pleasure principle, Talent, Tendency, Visceral

Institute, Institution Academy, Activate, Asylum, Bank, Begin, Bring, Charity, College, Erect, Found(ation), I, Inaugurate, MORI, Orphanage, Poorhouse, Raise, Redbrick, Retraict, Retrait(e), Retreat, Smithsonian, Start, University, Women's, Workhouse

Instruct(ed), Instruction, Instructor Advice, Apprenticeship, Brief, Catechism, Clinic, Coach, Course, Didactic, Direct(ive), Document, Edify, Educate, Ground(ing), Inform, Lesson, Manual, Mystagogue, Mystagogus, Notify, Order, Percept, Recipe, Rubric, Swami, ➤ TEACH, Train, Tutelage, Tutorial, Up

Instrument(al) Ablative, Act, Aethrioscope, Agent, Alidade, Almacantar, Almucantar, Alphonsin, Altazimuth, Anemometer, Astrolabe, Atmometer, Aux(an)ometer, Barnacle, Barometer, Baryscope, Bolometer, Bougie, Brake, Broach, Bronchoscope, Cadrans, Caltrop, Ceilometer, Celt, Cephalometer, Chronograph, Chronometer, Chronoscope, Clam, Clinometer, Coelostat, Colposcope, Crows-bill, Cryophorus, Curette, Cymograph, Cystoscope, Dermatome, Diagraph, Dip-circle, Dividers, Dropsonde, Dupe, Ecraseur, Eriometer, Etalon, Fan, Fibrescope, Fleam, Float, Forceps, Fork, Gadge, Groma, Haemostat, Helicograph, Heliostat, Helpful, Hodometer, Hydrometer, Hydroscope, Hygrometer, Hypsometer, Interferometer, Jacob's staff, Keraunograph, Konimeter, Laparascope, Machmeter, Manometer, Marigraph, Mean(s), Megascope, Meter, Metronome, Micrometer, Microphone, Mike, Miser, ➤ MUSICAL INSTRUMENT, Myringoscope, Nocturnal, Odometer, Ophthalmoscope,

Organ(ic), Otoscope, Oximeter, Pelican, Penetrometer, Pilliwinks, Pinniewinkle, Pinnywinkle, Pointel, Polarimeter, Potometer, Probang, Probe, Prog, Protractor, Quadrant, Radiosonde, Rasp(atory), Respirometer, ➤ RESPONSIBLE, Retractor, Rheometer, Rocketsonde, Rote, Scarificator, Scissors, Scriber, Scythe, Seismograph, Sensitometer, Sextant, Solarimeter, Sonde, Spatula, Spectroscope, Sphygmomanometer, Spirograph, Spirometer, Stauroscope, Stethoscope, Strickle, Strigil, Strobe, Stroboscope, Swazzle, Swingle, Swozzle, Synchroscope, Synthesizer, Syringe, Tacheometer, Tachigraph, Tachistoscope, Tachometer, Tasimeter, Telemeter, Telescope, Tellurian, Tellurion, Tenaculum, Tens(i)ometer, Theodolite, Thermometer, Tonometer, ➤ TOOL, Tram(mel), Trephine, Tribometer, Tripmeter, Trocar, Turbidimeter, ➤ UTENSIL, Volt(a)meter, Wavemeter, Waywiser, Wecht, Zenith-sector

Insubordinate Contumacious, Faction, Mutinous, Rebel, Refractory

Insubstantial Airy, Brief, Flimsy, Frothy, Illusory, Jackstraw, Slight, Thin, Wispy, Ye(a)sty

Insufficient Exiguous, Inadequate, Poor, Scant, Shortfall

Insular Isolated, Moated, Narrow, Xenophobe

Insulate, Insulation, Insulator Biotite, Dielectric, Electret, Enwind, Grommet, Inwind, Lagging, Mica, Non-conductor, Padding, Pugging, Sleeving, Tog

Insult(ing) Abuse, Affront, Aspersion, Barb, Contumely, Cut, Dyslogistic, Embarrass, Facer, Fig, Lese-majesty, Mud, Mud-pie, Offend, Opprobrious, Skit, Slagging, Slight, Slur, Snub, Trauma, Uncomplimentary, Verbal, Yenta, Yente

Insurance, Insure(r) Abandonee, Cover, Fire, Guarantee, Hedge, Indemnity, Knock-for-knock, Life, Lloyds, Medicare, Mutual, National, Policy, Reversion, Security, Underwrite

Insurgent, Insurrection Cade, Mutiny, Outbreak, Rebel, Revolt, Sedition

Intact Complete, Entire, Inviolate, Unused, Whole

Intaglio Diaglyph

Intake Absorption, Entry, Fuel

Integer, Integral Component, Entire, Inbuilt, Needful, Number, Organic, Unitary

Integrate(d) Amalgamate, Assimilate, Combine, Fuse, Harmonious, Mainstream, Merge

Integrity Honesty, Principle, Rectitude, Strength, Uprightness, Whole

Integument Coat, Sheath, Skin, Velum

Intellect(ual) Academic, Aptitude, Brain, Cerebral, Dianoetic, Egghead, Far-out, Genius, Intelligent, Intelligentsia, Luminary, Mastermind, Titan, -ist, Learned, Mental(ity), Mind, Noesis, Noetic, Noology, Nous, Profound, Reason

Intelligence, Intelligent Advice, Boss, Brains, Bright, CIA, Discerning, Dope, Eggmass, Esprit, G, Grey matter, GRU, Info, Ingenious, IQ, Knowledgeable, Machiavellian, MI, Mossad, Mother wit, News, Pate,

Pointy-headed, Rational, Sconce, Sense, Shrewd, Spetsnaz, Spetznaz, Tidings, Wit

Intemperance Acrasia, Crapulent, Excess, Gluttony, Immoderation

Intend(ed), Intending Allot, Contemplate, Design, Destine, Ettle, Fiancé(e), Going, ➤ MEAN, Meditate, Propose, Purpose

Intense, Intensify, Intensity Acute, Aggravate, Ardent, Depth, Earnest, Enhance, Emotional, Escalate, Estro, Excess, Extreme, Fervent, Keen, Might, Profound, Redouble, Sharpen, Vehement, Vivid

Intent, Intention(al) A dessein, Animus, Deliberate, Dole, Earnest, Hellbent, Manifesto, Mens rea, Mind, Purpose, Rapt, Resolute, Set, Studious, Systematic, Thought, Witting, Yrapt

Inter Bury, Entomb

Interaction Enantiodromia, Solvation

Interbreed(ing) Miscegenation

Intercalation Embolism

Intercede, Intercession Mediate, Negotiate, Plead, Prayer

Intercept Absciss(a), Abscisse, Check, Hack, Meet

Interchange(d) Altercation, Alternate, Clover-leaf, Crossing, Mutual, Permute, Reciprocate, Substitute

Intercourse Ball, Bang, Bed, Boff, Bonk, Coition, Coitus, Commerce, Commixture, Congress, Consummation, Converse, Copulation, Cottaging, Cunnilingus, Deflowering, Enjoy, Fluff, Fornication, Gamahuche, Gamaruche, Greens, Jass, Jazz, Jump, Knee-trembler, Laying, Leg-over, Make, Naughty, Nookie, Nooky, Poontang, Pussy, Quickie, Ride, Rim, Roger, Root, Rumpy(-pumpy), Screw, Shaft, Shag, Shtup, Sixty-nine, Sociality, Sodomy, Stuff, Swive, Tail, Tie, Trade, Trock, Troilism, Truck, Whoredom

Interdict Ban, Forbid, Prohibit, Taboo

Interest(ed), Interesting Amusive, APR, Attention, Behalf, Benefit, Clou, Compound, Concern, Contango, Coupon, Dividend, Engage, Engross, Fad, Fee-simple, Fee-tail, Grab, Hot, Import, Income, Int(o), Intrigue, Line, Part, Partisan, Percentage, Readable, Respect, Revenue, Scene, Share, Side, Simple, Spice, Stake, Topical, Usage, Usance, Usure, Usury, Vested, Vigorish, Warm

Interfere(r), Interference Busybody, Clutter, Disrupt, Hamper, Hinder, Intrude, Mar, ➤ MEDDLE, Molest, Officious, Pry, Shash, Static, Tamper, Teratogen

Interferometer Etalon

Intergrowth Perthite

Interim Break, Meanwhile, Temporary

Interior Backblocks, Cyclorama, Domestic, Innards, Innate, Inner, Inside, Outback, Plain, Up-country, Vitals

Interject(ion) Ahem, Begorra(h), Haith, Hoo-oo, Interpolate, Lumme, Nation, Sese(y), Sessa, 'Sheart, 'Slid, Tarnation, Tush

Interlace Mingle, Weave, Wreathe

Interlock Dovetail, Knit, Tangle

Interlocutor Elihu, MC, Questioner

Interloper Gate-crasher, Intruder, Trespasser

Interlude Antimask, Antimasque, Divertimento, Entr'acte, Interruption, Kyogen, Lunch-hour, Meantime, Pause, Verset

Intermediary, Intermediate Agent, Bardo, Comprador(e), Go-between, Instar, Mean, Medial, Mesne, Mezzanine, Middle-of-the-road, Middleman

Interminable Endless, Infinite

Intermission Apyrexia, Break, Interval, Pause, Recess

Intermittent Broken, Fitful, Periodic, Random, Spasmic, Spasmodic, Sporadic

Intern(e) Confine, Doctor, Impound, Restrict, Trainee

Internal Domestic, Inner, Internecine, Inward, Within

International Cap, Cosmopolitan, Lion, UN, Universal

Interpolate(r) Diaskeuast, Insert, Intercalate, Interrupt

Interpose Interject, Interlay, Interprone, Intervene, Spatchcock, Stickle

Interpret(er) Conster, Construe, Decipher, Decode, Dobhash, Dragoman, Exegete, Explain, Exponent, Expositor, Expound, Hermeneutist, Hierophant, Jehovist, Latiner, Lingster, Moonshee, Moonshi, Munshi, Oneirocritic, Origenist, Prophet, Read, Rede, Render, Represent, Spokesman, ➤ TRANSLATE, Truchman, Ulema

Interpretation Anagoge, Anagogy, Construction, Copenhagen, Eisegesis, Exegesis, Exegete, Gematria, Gloss(ary), Gospel, Halacha(h), Halakah, Hermeneutics, Midrash, Portray, Reading, Rede, Rendition, Targum, Translation

Interrogate, Interrogation Catechism, Debrief(ing), Enquire, Examine, Grill, Pump, ➤ QUESTION, Quiz

Interrupt(ion), Interrupter Ahem, Aposcopesis, Blip, Break, Butt, Chequer, Chip in, Disturb, Entr'acte, Heckle, Hiatus, Intercept, Interfere, Interpellate, Interpolate, Interpose, Interregnum, Intrusion, Overtalk, Pause, Portage, Rheotome, Stop, Suspend

Intersect(ion) Carfax, Carfox, Chiasm(a), Cross, Crunode, Cut, Decussate, Divide, Groin, Metacentre, Orthocentre, Trace

Intersperse Dot, Interpose, Scatter, Sprinkle

Interstice Areole, Interlude, Pore, Space

Intertwine Braid, Impleach, Knit, Lace, Plait, Splice, Twist, Writhe

Interval Between, Break, Breather, Class, Closed, Comma, Diapente, Diastaltic, Diatesseron, Diesis, Distance, Ditone, Duodecimo, Entr'acte, Fifth, Gap, Half-time, Hiatus, Hourly, Interim, Interlude, Interregnum, Interspace, Interstice, Meantime, Meantone, Meanwhile, Microtone, Ninth, Octave, Ottava, Pycnon, Respite, Rest, Schisma, Semitone, Sixth, Space, Span, Spell, Tritone, Unison, Wait

Intervene, Intervention Agency, Arbitrate, Interfere, Interjacent, Interrupt, Mediate, Mesne, Theurgy, Up

Interview Audience, Audition, Conference, Examine, Hearing, Oral, Press conference, See, Vox pop

Interweave, Interwoven Entwine, Interlace, Monogram, Plait, Plash, Pleach, Raddle, Wreathed

Intestate Heirless, Unwilling

Intestine(s) Bowel, Chit(ter)lings, Duodenum, Entrails, Guts, Harigals, Innards, Jejunum, Mesenteron, Omenta, Rectum, Splanchnic, Thairm, Viscera

Intimacy, Intimate(ly) Achates, Boon, Bosom, Communion, Connote, Familiar, Friend, Inmost, Innuendo, Intrigue, Nearness, Opine, Pack, Private, Signal, Special, Thick, Throng, Warm, Well

Intimation Clue, Hint, Implication, Inkling, Si quis

Intimidate, Intimidating Browbeat, Bulldoze, Bully, Cow, Daunt, Dragon, Hector, Niramiai, Psych, Threaten, Tyrannise, Unnerve

Into Intil, Within

Intolerable, Intolerant Allergic, Bigotry, Excessive, Illiberal, Impossible, Ombrophobe, Self-righteous

Intone, Intonation Cadence

In touch Au fait

Intoxicant, Intoxicate(d), Intoxicating, Intoxication Alcoholic, Areca-nut, Benj, Coca, Corn, Cup, Disguise, Fuddle, Ganja, Heady, ➤ HIGH, Hocus, Hou high, Inebriate, Jag, Merry, Mescal, Peyote, Pixil(l)ated, Rumbullion, Slewed, Soma, Sozzle, Spirituous, Temulent, Whiskeyfied, Whiskified

Intractable Disobedient, Kittle, Mulish, Obdurate, Perverse, Surly, Unruly, Wilful

Intransigent Adamant, Inflexible, Rigid, Uncompromising

Intransitive Neuter, Objectless

Intrepid Aweless, Bold, Brave, Dauntless, Doughty, Firm, ➤ RESOLUTE, Valiant

Intricate Complex, Daedal(ian), Daedale, Dedal, Gordian, Intrince, Involute, Knotty, Pernickety, Tirlie-wirlie, Tricky, Vitruvian

Intrigue(r), Intriguing Affaire, Artifice, Brigue, Cabal, Camarilla, Cloak and dagger, Collogue, Conspiracy, Fascinate, Hotbed, Ignatian, Jesuit, Jobbery, Liaison, Machinate, Plot, Politic, Rat, ➤ SCHEME, Strategy, Traffic, Trinketer

Intrinsic(ally) Basically, Genuine, Inherent, Innate, Inner, Per se

▷ **Intrinsically** may indicate something within a word

Introduce(r), Introduction, Introductory Acquaint, Anacrusis, Curtain-raiser, Emcee, Enseam, Exordial, Foreword, Immit, Import, Induct, Initiate, Inject, Insert, Instil(l), Intercalate, Interpolate, Introit, Isagogic, Lead-in, Opening, Plant, Preamble, Preface, Preliminary, Prelude, Prelusory, Preparatory, Present, Proem, Prolegomena, Prolegomenon, Prologue, Proponent, Referral, Start, Usher

▷ **Introduction** may indicate a first letter

Introspective Musing, Reflex, Ruminant

▷ **In trouble** may indicate an anagram

Introvert(ed) Cerebrotonic, Ingrow, In-toed, Reserved, Shy

Intrude(r), Intrusion, Intrusive Abate, Aggress, Annoy, Bother, Burglar, ➤ ENCROACH, Gatecrash, Interloper, Invade, Meddle, Nosey, Porlocking, Presume, Raid, Sorn, Trespass

Intuition Belief, ESP, Hunch, Insight, Instinct, Inwit, Noumenon, Premonition, Seat-of-the-pants, Telepathy, Theosophy

▷ **In two words** may indicate a word to be split

Inuit Eskimo, Yupik

Inundate, Inundation Flood, Overflow, Overwhelm, Submerge, Swamp

Inure Acclimatise, Accustom, Harden, Season, Steel

Invade(r), Invasion Angle, Attack, Attila, Dane, Descent, Encroach, Hacker, Hengist, Horsa, Hun, Infest, Inroad, Intruder, Jute, Lombard, Martian, Norman, Norsemen, Ostrogoth, Overrun, Permeate, Raid, Trespass, Vandal

Invalid(ate), Invalidation Bad, Bogus, Bunbury, Cancel, Chronic, Clinic, Defunct, Diriment, Erroneous, Expired, False, Inauthentic, Inform, Inoperative, Irritate, Lapsed, Nugatory, Null, Nullify, Refute, Shut-in, Terminate, Vitiate, Void

Invaluable Essential, Excellent, Precious, Useful

Invariable, Invariably Always, Constant, Eternal, Habitual, Perpetual, Steady, Uniform

Invective Abuse, Billingsgate, Diatribe, Philippic, Reproach, Ribaldry, Tirade

Inveigh Declaim, Denounce, Protest, Rail

Invent(ion), Inventive Adroit, Babe, Baby, Brainchild, Chimera, Coin, Contrive, ➤ CREATE, Daedal, Design, Device, Fabricate, Fain, Feign, Figment, Imaginary, Improvise, Ingenuity, Mint, Originate, Patent, Resourceful, Synectics, Wit

Inventor Archimedes, Arkwright, Artificer, Author, Babbage, Baird, Bell, Biro, Boys, Bramah, Cartwright, Celsius, Coiner, Creator, Crompton, Daedalus, Edison, Engineer, Galileo, Geiger, Hansom, Marconi, Maxim, Minié, Mint-master, Morse, Nernst, Newcomen, Nobel, Patentee, Savery, Tesla, Torricelli, Tull, Watt, Wheatstone

Inventory Account, Index, Itemise, List, Register, Steelbow, Stock

Inversion, Invert(ed) Anastrophe, Antimetabole, Antimetathesis, Capsize, Chiasmus, Entropion, Entropium, Opposite, Overset, Resupinate, Reverse, Turn, Upset

Invertebrate Annelida, Anthozoan, Arthropod, Brachiopod, Crinoid, Ctenophore, Decapod, Echinoderm, Echinoid, Euripterid, Feather star, Gast(e)ropod, Globigerina, Hydrozoan, Mollusc, Onychophoran, Parazoan, Pauropod, Peritrich, Polyp, Poriferan, Protostome, Rotifer, Roundworm, Scyphozoan, Sea-cucumber, Sea-lily, Spineless, Starfish, Tardigrade, Trepang, Trochelminth, Water bear, Worm, Zoophyte

Invest(or), Investment Agamemnon, Ambient, Angel, Bate, Beleaguer, Besiege, Bet, Blockade, Blue-chip, Capitalist, Collins Street farmer, Dignify, Embark, Empanoply, Enclothe, Endow, Enrobe, Flutter, Gilt, Girt, Holding, Infeft, Install, On, Pannicle, Panniculus, Parlay, Place, Portfolio, Put, Ring,

Robe, Share, Siege, Sink, Spec, Stake, Stock, Surround, Tessa, Trust, Venture, Zaitech

▷ **Invest** may indicate one word surrounding another

Investigate, Investigator, Investigation Canvass, Case, CID, Delve, Examine, Explore, Fed, Fieldwork, Hunt, Inquest, Inquirendo, Inquiry, Inquisition, McCarthyism, Nose, Organon, Organum, Probe, Pry, Quester, Rapporteur, Research, Scan, Scrutinise, Search, Sleuth, Snoop, Study, Suss, T-man, Tec, Test, Track, Try, Zetetic

Investiture Award, Inauguration

Inveterate Chronic, Dyed-in-the-wool, Engrained, Habitual, Hardened

Invidious Harmful, Hostile, Malign

Invigilator Proctor

Invigorate, Invigorating, Invigoration Analeptic, Brace, Brisk, Cheer, Elixir, Energise, Enliven, Fortify, Insinew, Pep, Refresh, Renew, Stimulate, Tonic, Vital

Invincible Almighty, Brave, Stalwart, Valiant

Inviolable Sacred, Sacrosanct

Invisible Hidden, Imageless, Infra-red, Secret, Tusche, Unseen

Invite, Invitation Ask, Attract, Bid, Call, Card, Overture, ➤ REQUEST, Solicit, Stiffie, Summons, Tempt, Woo

Invocation, Invoke Appeal, Call, Conjure, Curse, Entreat, Epiclesis, Solicit

Invoice Account, Bill, Itemise, Manifest, Pro forma

Involuntary Automatic, Instinctive, Unwitting

Involve(d), Involvement Commitment, Complicate, Complicit, Concern, Embroil, Engage, Entail, Envelop, Imbroglio, Immerse, ➤ IMPLICATE, Include, Intricate, Meet, Necessitate, Tangle

▷ **Involved** may indicate an anagram

Inward(s) Afferent, Homefelt, Introrse, Mental, Private, Varus, Within

Iodine I, Kelp

Ion Anion, Carbanion, Carborium, Hydroxyl, Isomer, Onium, Zwitterion

Ionian Iastic

Iota Atom, Jot, Subscript, Whit

IOU Cedula, Market, PN, Vowels

IOW Vectis

IRA Provisional, Provo

Iranian Babist, Kurd, Mede, Parsee

Irascible Choleric, Crusty, Fiery, Peevish, Snappy, Tetchy, Toustie

Irate Angry, Cross, Infuriated, Wrathful

Ire Anger, Cholera, Fury, Rage, Wrath

Ireland Composer, Deirdre, Gaeltacht, Hibernia, Innisfail, Irena, IRL, Iverna

Iridescence, Iridescent Chatoyant, Opaline, Reflet, Shimmering, Shot, Water-gall

Iridium Ir

Iris Areola, Eye, Flag, Fleur-de-lis, Gladden, Ixia, Lily, Lis, Orris, Rainbow, Sedge, Seg, Sunbow

Irish(man) Bark, Boy, Bog-trotter, Celt(ic), Clan-na-gael, Defender, Dermot, Dubliner, Eamon(n), Eirann, Erse, Fenian, Gaeltacht, Goidel, Greek, Keltic, Kern(e), Mick(e)(y), Milesian, Mulligan, Ogamic, Orange(man), Ostmen, Paddy(-whack), Partholon, Pat(rick), Rapparee, Redshank, Reilly, Riley, Rory, Sean, Shoneen, Teague, Temper, Ultonian, Whiteboy, Wildgeese

Irk(some) Annoy, Bother, Irritate, Tedious

Iron(s), Ironwork(s) Airn, Angle, Carron, Cautery, Chains, Chalybeate, Chancellor, Channel, Climbing, Coquimbite, Cramp(on), Crampon, Crimp, Cross, Curling, Curtain, Delta, Derringer, Dogs, Fayalite, Fe, Ferredoxin, Fetter, Fiddley, Flip-dog, Gem, Golfclub, Goose, Grappling, Grim, Grozing, ➤ GUN, Gyve, Horse, Ingot, Kamacite, Laterite, Maiden, Marcasite, Mars, Martensite, Mashie, Mashy, Pig, ➤ PRESS, Pro-metal, Rabble, Rations, Rod, Sad, Smoother, Soft, Soldering, Spiegeleisen, Steam, Stirrup, Strong, Taconite, Taggers, Terne, Tin terne, Waffle, Wedge, Wrought

Iron age Latene, Villanovan

Ironic, Irony Antiphrasis, Asteism, Dramatic, Meiosis, Metal, Ridicule, Sarcasm, Satire, Socratic, Tongue-in-cheek, Tragic, Trope, Wry

Ironside Edmund

Ironwood Pyengadu

▶ **Ironwork(s)** see IRON

Irrational Absurd, Brute, Delirious, Foolish, Illogical, Superstitious, Surd, Wild

Irrefutable Evident, Positive, Undeniable

Irregular(ity) Abnormal, Alloiostrophus, Anomaly, Aperiodic, A salti, Asymmetric, Bashi-bazouk, Blotchy, Crazy, Erratic, Evection, Fitful, Flawed, Formless, Guerilla, Heteroclitic, Incondite, Inordinate, Kink, Occasional, Orthotone, Para-military, Partisan, Patchy, Random, Scalene, Sebundy, Scrawl, Sharawadgi, Sharawaggi, Snatchy, Solecism, Sporadic, TA, Uneven, Unsteady, Unwonted, Variable, Wayward, Zigzag

▷ **Irregular** may indicate an anagram

Irrelevant Digression, Extraneous, Gratuitous, Immaterial, Inept

Irreligious Heathen, Impious, Pagan, Profane

Irremedial Hopeless, Incurable, Laches

Irreproachable Blameless, Spotless, Stainless

Irresistible Almighty, Endearing, Inevitable, Mesmeric, Overwhelming

Irresolute, Irresolution Aboulia, Doubtful, Hesitant, Timid, Unsure

Irresponsible Capricious, Feckless, Flighty, Slap-happy, Strawen, Trigger-happy, Wanton, Wildcat

Irreverent Disrespectful, Impious, Profane

Irrigate, Irrigation Canalise, Colonic, Douche, Enema, Flood, Get, Water

Irritable, Irritability, Irritant, Irritate(d), Irritation Acerbate, Anger, Annoy, Blister, Bug, Chafe, Chauff, Chippy, Crabby, Cross-grained, Crosspatch, Crotchety, Crusty, Dod, Dyspeptic, Eat, Edgy, Enchafe, Erethism, Ewk, Exasperate, Fantod, Feverish, Fiery, Fleabite, Frabbit, Fractious, Fraught, Gall, Get, Goad, Grate, Gravel, Heck, Intertrigo, Irk, Itch, Jangle, Livery, Mardy, Narky, Needle, Nettle, Niggly, Ornery, Peevish,

Pesky, Pet, Petulance, Pinprick, Pique, Provoke, Rag'd, Ragde, Rankle, Rasp, Rattle, Ratty, Rile, Roil, Rub, Ruffle, Savin(e), Scratchy, Shirty, Snappy, Snit, Splenetic, Sting, Tease, Techy, Testy, Tetchy, Thorn, Tickle, Toey, Touchy, Uptight, ➤ VEX, Yuke

▷ **Irritated** may indicate an anagram

Irving Actor, Berlin

Is Est, Ist

Isaiah Is

Isinglass Carlock, Fish-glue, Mica, Sturgeon

Islam(ic) Crescent, Druse, Druz(e), Kurd(ish), Senus(si), Sheriat, Shia(h), Shiite, Wah(h)abi

Island, Isle(t) Ait, Archipelago, Atoll, Cay, Desert, Eyot, Floating, I, Inch, Is, Key, Lagoon, Mainland, Refuge, Traffic

ISLANDS			
2 letters:	Idse	Clare	Samos
TT	Iona	Cocos	Saria
3 letters:	Java	Coney	Spice
Aru	Jolo	Coral	Sunda
Cos	Jura	Corfu	Thera
Diu	King	Crete	Thule
Fyn	Line	Delos	Timor
Hoy	Long	Disko	Tiree
Kos	Mahe	Ellis	Tonga
Man	Maui	Faial	Upolu
May	Mazu	Farne	Whale
Rat	Mona	Faroe	White
Rum	Motu	Fayal	Wight
Yap	Muck	Funen	Zante
4 letters:	Mull	Haiti	**6 letters:**
Amoy	Niue	Ibiza	Achill
Aran	Oahu	Islay	Aegean
Arru	Sark	Isola	Amager
Attu	Skye	Jerba	Andros
Bali	Uist	Kiska	Avalon
Bute	Unst	Kuril	Azores
Calf	Wake	Lewis	Baffin
Cebu	Yell	Lundy	Bangka
Char	**5 letters:**	Luzon	Banaba
Coll	Aland	Malta	Barrow
Cook	Apple	Matsu	Bikini
Cuba	Arran	Melos	Borneo
Dogs	Aruba	Nauru	Bounty
Eigg	Banka	Naxos	Caicos
Elba	Banks	Nevis	Canvey
Erin	Barra	North	Cayman
Fair	Batan	Oland	Ceylon
Fiji	Belle	Ormuz	Chiloe
Guam	Bioko	Pemba	Cyprus
Heat	Bohol	Reil's	Devil's
Herm	Bonin	Rhode	Diomed
Holm	Canna	South	Djerba
Holy	Capri	Samar	Easter
Hova	Chios	Samoa	Ellice

Euboea	Aldabra	Socotra	Mustique
Flores	Andaman	Solomon	Pitcairn
Fraser	Antigua	Stewart	Portland
Harris	Austral	Sumatra	Pribilof
Hawaii	Bahamas	Surtsey	Principe
Hobart	Baranof	Tenedos	St Martin
Honshu	Barbuda	Tortuga	Somerset
Hormuz	Battery	Waihake	St Helena
Imbros	Bedloe's	Wrangel	Sardinia
Indies	Bermuda	Zealand	Sporades
Insula	Cartier	Zetland	Sverdrup
Ionian	Celebes	**8 letters:**	Tasmania
Ischia	Channel	Alderney	Tenerife
Ithaca	Chatham	Aleutian	Terceira
Jersey	Cipango	Anglesey	Thursday
Kodiak	Corsica	Anguilla	Trinidad
Kurile	Crannog	Antilles	Tsushima
Kyushu	Curacao	Atlantis	Unalaska
Labuan	Cythera	Auckland	Venetian
Laputa	Diomede	Balearic	Windward
Lemnos	Emerald	Barbados	Zanzibar
Lesbos	Eriskay	Bathurst	**9 letters:**
Lipari	Falster	Billiton	Admiralty
Lizard	Frisian	Blefuscu	Anticosti
Lombok	Fur Seal	Bora-Bora	Antipodes
Madura	Gambier	Canaries	Ascension
Majuro	Gilbert	Caroline	Barataria
Marajo	Gotland	Catalina	Benbecula
Mercer	Grenada	Choiseul	Christmas
Midway	Hawaiki	Colonsay	Elephanta
Negros	Jamaica	Cyclades	Ellesmere
Ogygia	Laaland	Dominica	Falklands
Paphos	Leeward	Farquhar	Fortunate
Patmos	Liberty	Flinders	Galapagos
Penang	Lofoten	Foulness	Governors
Pharos	Lolland	Friendly	Halmahera
Pladdy	Madeira	Gothland	Innisfree
Ramsey	Majorca	Gottland	Jamestown
Rhodes	Mayotte	Guernsey	Kerguelen
Rjukyu	Mindoro	Hamilton	Lampedusa
Skyros	Minorca	Hebrides	Lanzarote
Snares	Moreton	Hokkaido	Macquarie
Scilly	Nicobar	Jan Mayen	Manhattan
Sicily	Norfolk	Kangaroo	Mascarene
Skerry	Oceania	Kermadec	Melanesia
Staffa	Okinawa	Ladrones	Nantucket
Staten	Orcades	Lilliput	Polynesia
Tahiti	Orkneys	Lord Howe	Rangitoto
Thanet	Palawan	Luggnagg	Runnymede
Thasos	Rathlin	Maldives	Sjaelland
Tobago	Reunion	Mallorca	Shetlands
Tresco	Rockall	Marianas	Stromboli
Tuvalu	St Kilda	Marquesa	Teneriffe
Ushant	St Kitts	Marshall	Trobriand
Veneti	St Lucia	Melville	Vancouver
Virgin	Salamis	Mindanao	**10 letters:**
7 letters:	Sheppey	Miquelon	Basse-Terre
Aeolian	Shikoku	Moluccas	Bermoothes

Campobello	Micronesia	Philippines	
Cephalonia	Pescadores	**12 letters:**	
Corregidor	Poor Knight	Bougainville	
Dodecanese	Seychelles	Cassiterides	
Formentera	Samothrace	Glubbdubdrib	
Grand Terre	Three Kings	Newfoundland	
Heligoland	West Indies	Prince Edward	**14 letters:**
Hispaniola	Whitsunday	San Cristobal	D'Entrecasteaux
Kiritimati	**11 letters:**	Santa Barbara	Queen Charlotte
Langerhans	Dry Tortugas	Torres Strait	Queen Elizabeth
Madagascar	Glubdubdrib	**13 letters:**	Tristan da Cunha
Manitoulin	Guadalcanal	Forneaux Group	Turks and Caicos
Marinduque	Lakshadweep	Fuerteventura	**15 letters:**
Martinique	Lindisfarne	Prince of Wales	Wallis and Futuna

Islander Chian, Cretan, D(a)yak, Filipino, Kanaka, Kelper, Laputan, Madeiran, Maltese, Mauritian, Native, Nesiot, Newfie, Orcadian, Parian, Rhodian, Samiot, Sican, Singalese, Taiwanese

Isle of Wight Vectis

Isn't Aint, Nis, Nys

Isolate(d) Ancress, Backwater, Cut off, Enclave, Enisle, In vacuo, Incommunicado, Inisle, Island, Lone, Maroon, Pocket, Quarantine, Sea-girt, Seclude, Secret, Segregate, Separate, Sequester, Solitary, Sporadic, Stray

Isomer Carvacrol

Isosceles Triangle

Isotope Actinon, Deuterium, Muonium, Protium, Strontium-90, Thoron, Tritium

Israel(i) IL, Meir, Sabra

Issue(s) Come, Crux, Debouch, Denouement, Derive, Disclose, Dispense, Edition, Effluence, Egress, ➤ EMANATE, Emerge, Emit, Exit, Exodus, Family, Fiduciary, Flotation, Gush, Ish, Litter, Number, Offspring, Outflow, Part, Proof, Publish, Result, Rights, Sally, Seed, Son, Spawn, Spring, Stream, Subject, Topic, Turn, Utter

Isthmus Darien, Karelian, Kra, Neck, Panama

It A, Chic, Hep, Id, Italian, Oomph, SA, 't, Vermouth

Italian, Italy Alpini, Ausonia, Bolognese, Calabrian, Chian, Dago, Ding, Este, Etnean, Etrurian, Etruscan, Eyeti(e), Eytie, Faliscan, Florentine, Genoese, Ghibelline, Guelf, Guelph, Hesperia, Irredentist, It, Latian, Latin, Lombard, Medici, Moro, Oscan, Paduan, Patarin(e), Roman, Sabine, Samnite, Sicel, Sikel, Sienese, Signor(i), Spag, Tuscan, Umbrian, Venetian, Vermouth, Volscian, Wop

Italic Swash

Itch(ing), Itchiness Acariasis, Annoy, Cacoethes, Dhobi, Euk, Ewk, Hanker, Jock, Miliaria, Photopsy, Prickle, Prurience, Prurigo, Pruritis, Psora, Scabies, Scrapie, Seven-year, Tickle, ➤ URGE, Yeuk, Youk, Yuck, Yuke

Item(ise) Also, Article, Bulletin, Detail, Entry, Flash, List, Number, Piece, Point, Spot, Too, Topic

Iterate Repeat

Itinerant, Itinerary Ambulant, Didakai, Didakei, Did(d)icoy, Gipsy, Gypsy, Journey, Log, Pedlar, Peripatetic, Pie-powder, Roadman, Roamer, Romany, Rootless, Route, Stroller, Traveller

Itself Per se

Ivan Russian, Terrible

Ivory (tower) Bone, Dentine, Distant, Eburnean, Impractical, Incisor, Key, Solitude, Teeth, Tusk, Vegetable

Ivy Angelica-tree, Aralia, Boston, Bush, Cat's-foot, Creeper, Evergreen, Gill, Grape, Ground, Hedera, Helix, Panax, Poison, Udo

J j

J Curve, Juliet, Pen

Jab(ber) Chatter, Foin, Gabble, Immunologist, Inject, Jaw, Jook, Nudge, Poke, Prattle, Prod, Proke, Punch, Puncture, Sook, Sputter, Stab, Venepuncture, Yak

Jack(s) AB, Apple, Artocarpus, Ass, Ball, Boot, Bower, Bowl(s), Boy, Card, Cheap, Deckhand, Dibs(tones), Flag, Frost, Hoist, Honour, Hopper, Horner, Idle, J, Jock, Ketch, Kitty, Knave, Knucklebones, London, Mark, Matlow, Mistress, Nob, Noddy, Pilot, Point, Pot, Pur, Rabbit, Raise, Ripper, Robinson, Russell, Sailor, Salt, Shaun, Sprat, Steeple, Sticker, Straw, Tar, Tee, Tradesman, Turnspit, Union, Wood

Jackal Anubis, Dieb, Hack, Stooge

Jackass Aliboron, Goburra, Kookaburra, Stupid

Jackdaw Bird, Chough, Daw, Kae, Raven, Rheims, Thief

Jacket Acton, Afghanistan, Amauti(k), Anorak, Bainin, Baju, Bania(n), Banyan, Basque, Bawneen, Barbour®, Battle, Bed, Bellhop, Blazer, Blouson, Bolero, Bomber, Brigandine, Bumfreezer, Bush, Cagoul(e), Camisole, Can, Caraco, Cardigan, Carmagnole, Casing, ➤ COAT, Dinner, Dolman, Donkey, Dust-cover, Dustwrapper, Fearnought, Flak, Gambeson, Gendarme, Grego, Habergeon, Hacking, Ha(c)queton, Hug-me-tight, Jerkin, Jupon, Kagool, Kaross, Life, Lumber, Mackinaw, Mae West, Mandarin, Mandilion, Mao, Matinée, Mess, Monkey, Nehru, Newmarket, Norfolk, Parka, Pea, Petenlair, Pierrot, Pilot, Polka, Potato, Railly, Reefer, Safari, Sayon, Shearling, Shell, Shortgown, Simar(re), Sleeve, Slip-cover, Smoking, Spencer, Sports, Strait, Tabard, Tailcoat, Toreador, Tunic, Tux(edo), Tweed, Vareuse, Waistcoat, Wam(m)us, Wampus, Water, Windbreaker®, Windcheater, Windjammer, Wrapper, Zouave

Jackknife Dive, Fold, Jockteleg, Pike

Jackpot Cornucopia, Kitty, Pool

Jackson Stonewall

Jackstraw Spellican, Spil(l)ikin

Jacobite(s) Non-compounder, Non juror, Wild Geese

Jacquard Matelasse

Ja(c)ques Melancholy, Tati

Jade(d) Axe-stone, Bidet, Cloy, Crock, Disjaskit, Exhaust, Fatigue, Greenstone, Hack, Hag, Horse, Hussy, Limmer, Minx, Nag, Nephrite, Pounamu, Rosinante, Sate, Screw, Slut, Stale, Tired, Trite, Weary, Yaud, Yu(-stone)

Jag(ged) Barbed, Cart, Drinking, Erose, Gimp, Injection, Laciniate, Ragde, Ragged, Serrate, Snag, Spree, Spur, Tooth

Jagger Mick, Pedlar

Jaguar Car, Caracal, Cat, E-type, Ounce, Tiger

Jail(er) Adam, Alcaide, Alcatraz, Bedford, Bin, Bridewell, Can, Clink, Commit, Cooler, Gaol, Hoosegow, Imprison, Incarcerate, Jug, Keeper, Kitty, Lockup, Marshalsea, Newgate, Nick, Pen, Pokey, ➤ PRISON, Screw, Shop, Strangeways, Turnkey, Warder

Jailbird Con, Lag, Lifer, Trusty

Jain(ism) Mahavira

Jakarta Batavia

Jake Honest, Hunkydory, OK, Rube

Jalopy Banger, Boneshaker, Buggy, Car, Crate, Heap, Shandry(dan), Stock-car

Jam(my) Block, Choke, Clog, Confiture, Crush, Cushy, Dilemma, Gridlock, Hold-up, Jeelie, Jeely, Lock, Log, Plight, ➤ PREDICAMENT, Preserve, Press, Quince, Seize, Snarl-up, Spot, Squeeze, Stick, Tailback, Traffic, Vice, Vise, Wedge

Jamaica(n) Rasta(farian), Rastaman, Yardie

Jamb Doorpost, Durn, Sconcheon, Scontion, Scuncheon, Upright

James Agee, Bond, Bothwell, Henry, Jacobite, Jemmy, Jesse, Jim, Joyce, Screw, Seamus, Seumas, Watt

Jane Austen, Calamity, Eyre, Seymour, Shore, Sian

Jangle Clank, Clapperclaw, Clash, Rattle, Wrangle

Janitor Servitor, Tiler

Jankers KP

Jansky Jy

Janus Two-faced

Japan(ese), Japanese drama Ainu, Burakumin, Daimio, Eta, Geisha, Genro, Gloss, Haiku, Heian, Hondo, Honshu, Issei, Kabuki, Kami, Kana, Kirimon, Lacquer, Mandarin, Mikado, Mousmé, Mousmee, Nippon, Nisei, No(h), Resin, Sansei, Satsuma, Shinto, Shogun, Togo, Tycoon, Yamato

Jape Jeer, Joke, Prank, Trick

Jar(ring) Albarello, Amphora, Bell, Canopus, Churr, Clash, Crock, Cruet, Din, Dolium, Enrough, Gallipot, Grate, Greybeard, Gride, Grind, Gryde, Humidor, Hydria, ➤ JOLT, Kalpis, Kang, Kilner, Leyden, Mason, Off-key, Olla, Pint, Pithos, Pot(iche), Rasp, Shelta, Shock, Stamnos, Start, Stean, Steen, Stein, Tankard, Tinaja, Turn, Vessel, Water-monkey

Jargon Argot, Baragouin, Beach-la-mar, Buzzword, Cant, Chinook, Eurobabble, Eurospeak, Gobbledegook, Gobbledygook, Jive, Kennick, Legalese, Lingo, Lingoa geral, Lingua franca, Mumbo-jumbo, Newspeak, Parlance, Patois, Patter, Shelta, Shoptalk, ➤ SLANG, Technospeak, Vernacular

Jasmine Cape, Frangipani, Gelsemine, Gessamine, Jessamy

Jasper Basanite, Bloodstone, Egyptian

Jaundice(d) Cynical, Icterus, Prejudiced, Sallow, Yellow

Jaunt Journey, Outing, Sally, Stroll, Swan, Trip

Jaunty Airy, Akimbo, Chipper, Debonair, Perky, Rakish

▷ **Jaunty** may indicate an anagram

Java man Pithecanthropus

Javelin Dart, Gavelock, Harpoon, Jereed, Jerid, Pile, Pilum, Spear

Jaw(s), Jawbone Blab, Chaft, Chap, Chat, Chaw, Cheek, Chide, Chin, Entry, Glass, Gnathite, Gonion, Jobe, Lantern, Mandible, Maxilla, Mesial, Muzzle, Mylohyoid, Natter, Opisthognathous, Overshot, Phossy, Pi, Premaxillary, Prognathous, Ramus, Shark, Stylet, Underhung, Undershot, Wapper-jaw, Ya(c)kety-Ya(c)k

Jay Bird, J, Sirgang, Whisky-jack, Whisky-john

Jazz(er), Jazzman Acid, Barber, Barrelhouse, Bebop, Blues, Boogie, Boogie-woogie, Bop, Cat, Cool, Dixieland, Enliven, Gig, Gutbucket, Hipster, Jive, Latin, Lick, Mainstream, Modern, Progressive, Ragtime, Riff, Scat, Skiffle, Stomp, Swinger, Trad, Traditional

Jealous(y) Envious, Green(-eyed), Grudging, Zelotypia

Jean(s) Chinos, Denims, Levis®, Pants, Trousers, Wranglers®

Jeer(ing) Ballyrag, Barrack, Belittle, Birl, Boo, Burl, Digs, Fleer, Flout, Gird, Hoot, Jape, Jibe, ➤ MOCK, Rail, Razz, Ridicule, Scoff, Sneer, Taunt, Twit, Yah

Jeeves Valet

Jehovah God, Lord, Yahve(h), Yahwe(h)

Jehu Charioteer, Driver

Jejune Arid, Barren, Dry, Insipid, Juvenile

Jelly Acaleph(a), Acalephe, Agar(-agar), Aspic, Brawn, Calf's foot, Chaudfroid, Comb, Cow-heel, ➤ EXPLOSIVE, Flummery, Gel, Isinglass, Jam, Kanten, Macedoine, Medusa, Mineral, Mould, Napalm, Neat's foot, Petroleum, Quiddany, Royal, Shape, Tunicin, Vaseline®

▷ **Jelly** may indicate an anagram

Jellyfish Acaleph(a), Acalephe, Aurelia, Blubber, Box, Cnidaria, Discomedusae, Discophora, Hydromedusa, Irukandji, Medusa, Mesogloea, Planoblast, Portuguese man-of-war, Quarl, Scyphistoma, Sea-wasp, Sea-blubber, Sea-nettle, Strobila

Jemmy Betty, Crowbar, Lever

Jenkins Ear, Roy, Up

Jenny Ass, Lind, Mule, Spinner, Spinster, Wren

Jeopardise, Jeopardy Danger, Expose, Hazard, Peril, Risk

Jerboa Desert rat

Jeremiad Lament, Tragedy, Woe

Jeremy Fisher, Jerry

Jerk(ily), Jerking, Jerks Aerobics, A salti, Bob, Braid, Cant, Diddle, Ebrillade, Flirt, Flounce, Gym(nastics), Hike, Hitch, Hoi(c)k, Jut, Kant, PE, Peck, Physical, Saccade, Shove, Spasm, Start, Surge, Sydenham's chorea, Tic, Toss(en), Tweak, ➤ TWITCH, Wrench, Yank

Jerkin Jacket

Jerome Kern, Vulgate

Jerry, Jerry-built Boche, Flimsy, Fritz, Hun, Kraut, Mouse, Po(t)

Jersey(s) Cow, Frock, Gansey, Guernsey, Kine, Lily, Maillot, Polo, Roll-neck, Singlet, ➤ SWEATER, Sweatshirt, Yellow, Zephyr

Jerusalem Ariel, Hierosolymitan, Zion

Jess(e) James, Strap

Jest(er), Jesting Badinage, Barm, Baur, Bawr, Bourd(er), Buffoon, Clown, Cod, Comic, Droll, Goliard, Inficete, Jape, Joker, Josh, Miller, Motley, Patch, Quip, Raillery, Ribaldry, Rigoletto, Scogan, Scoggin, Sport, Toy, Trinculo, Wag, Wit, Yorick

Jesuit Bollandist, Ignatius, Loyola, SJ

Jesus Christ, Emmanuel, IHS, INRI, Jabers, Lord

Jet Airbus®, Aircraft, Beadblast, Black, Burner, Chirt, Douche, Fountain, Geat, Harrier, Jumbo, Plane, Pump, Soffione, Spirt, Spout, Spray, Spurt, Squirt, Stream, Turbine, Turbo, Vapour

Jettison Discard, Dump, Flotsam, Jetsam, Lagan, Ligan

Jetty Groin, Mole, Pier, Wharf

Jew(ish), Jews Ashkenazi, Chas(s)id, Diaspora, Essene, Falasha, Grecian, Greek, Has(s)id, Hebrew, Kahal, Karaite, Landsman, Levite, Lubavitch, Maccabee, Marrano, Mitnag(g)ed, Nazarite, Pharisee, Refusenik, Sabra, Sadducee, Semite, Sephardim, Sheeny, Shemite, Shtetl, Smouch, Smouse, Tobit, Wandering, Yid(dish), Zealot

Jewel(ler), Jewellery Agate, Almandine, Artwear, Beryl, Bijouterie, Brilliant, Chrysoprase, Cloisonné, Cornelian, Costume, Diamond, Earbob, Ear-drop, Emerald, Ewe-lamb, Fabergé, Ferron(n)ière, Finery, Garnet, ➤ GEM, Girandole, Gracchi, Jade, Lherzolite, Marcasite, Navette, Olivine, Opal, Parure, Paste, Pavé, Pearl, Pendant, Peridot, Rivière, Rubin(e), Ruby, Sapphire, Sard, Scarab, Smaragd, Solitaire, Stone, Sunburst, Tom, Tomfoolery, Topaz, Torc, Treasure

Jezebel Harlot, Loose, Whore

Jib Ba(u)lk, Boggle, ➤ DEMUR, Face, Foresail, Genoa, Milk, Reest, Reist, Stay-sail

Jibe Bob, Correspond, Fling, ➤ JEER, Mock, Sarcasm, Slant, Taunt

Jiffy Mo, Pronto, Twinkling

Jig(gle) Bob, Bounce, Dance, Fling, Frisk, Hornpipe, Jog, Juggle

Jigger(ed) Beat, Chigoe, Jolley, Ruin

Jilt Discard, Reject, Shed, Throw-over

Jim(my) Diamond, Dismal, Jas, Lucky, Pee, Piddle, Riddle

Jingle(r) Clerihew, Clink, Ditty, Doggerel, Rhyme, Tambourine, Tinkle

Jingo(ism) Odzooks, Patriot, War-rant

Jinn(i) Afreet, Eblis, Genie, Marid, Spirit

Jinx Curse, Hex, Jonah, Kibosh, Spoil, Voodoo, Whammy

Jitter(s), Jittery Coggly, DT, Fidgets, Funk, Jumpy, Nervous, Willies

▷ **Jitter(s)** may indicate an anagram

Jo ➤ LOVER, Sweetheart

Job Appointment, Berth, Career, Chore, Comforter, Crib, Darg, Errand, Gig, Homer, Inside, Metier, Oratorio, Patient, Pensum, Plum, Position, Post,

Problem, Put-up, Sinecure, Spot, Steady, ➤ TASK, Ticket, Trotter, Undertaking, Work

▷ **Job** may indicate the biblical character

Jock Deejay, DJ, Mac, Sawn(e)y, Scot

Jockey Carr, Cheat, Diddle, Jostle, Jump, Lester, Manoeuvre, Rider, Steve, Swindle, Trick, Video, Winter

▷ **Jockey** may indicate an anagram

Jocose, Jocular, Jocund Cheerful, Debonair, Facete, Facetious, Jesting, Lepid, Scurril(e), Waggish

Joe(y), Joseph Addison, Dogsbody, GI, Kangaroo, Pal, Roo, Sloppy, Stalin, Surface, Trey

Jog(gle), Jog-trot Arouse, Dunch, Dunsh, Heich-how, Heigh-ho, Hod, Jiggle, Jolt, Jostle, Mosey, Nudge, Prompt, Ranke, Remind, Run, Shake, Shog, Tickle, Trot, Whig

John(ny) Ajax, Augustus, Barleycorn, Bog, Bright, Brown, Bull, Bunyan, Cloaca, Collins, Doree, Dory, Elton, Evan, Gaunt, Gents, Gilpin, Groats, Halifax, Ivan, Lackland, Latecomer, Lav, Little, Loo, Peel, Prester, Stage-door, Throne, WC

Johnson Cham, Doctor, Idler

Join(er), Joined Abut, Accede, Accompany, Add, Ally, And, Annex, Associate, Attach, Braze, Butt-end, Cement, Cleave, Combine, Conflate, Conjugate, Connect, ➤ COUPLE, Dovetail, Engraft, Enlist, Enrol, Enter, Federate, Fuse, Glue, Graft, Hasp, Hitch, Hyphen, Include, Jugate, Knit, Link, Marry, Meet, Menuisier, Merge, Mix, Mortar, Mortise, Oop, Oup, Overlaunch, Piece, Piecen, Rebate, Rivet, Scarf, Seam, Se-tenant, Siamize, Snug, Solder, Splice, Spot-weld, Squirrel, Staple, Stylolite, Tenon, Unite, Wed, Weld, Yoke

Joint(ed) Ancon, Ankle, Arthrosis, Articular, Ball and socket, Bar, Baron, Butt, Cardan, Carpus, Chine, Clip, Co, Commissure, Cuit, Cut, Dive, Dovetail, Elbow, Enarthrosis, Entrecôte, Expansion, Fish, Gambrel, Gimmal, Gimmer, Ginglymus, Hainch, Haunch, Heel, Hinge, Hip, Hough, Huck, Hunker, J, Joggle, Jolly, Junction, Knee, Knuckle, Lap(ped), Lith, Loin, Marijuana, Meat, Mitre, Mortise, Mouse (buttuck), Mouse-piece, Mutton, Mutual, Phalange, Phalanx, Popliteal, Psoas, Rack, Raphe, Reducer, Reefer, Rhaphe, Ribroast, Roast, Saddle, Scarf, Schindylesis, Seam, Shoulder, Silverside, Sirloin, Splice, Spliff, Stifle, Strip, Symphysis, T, Tarsus, T-bone, Tenon, Together, Toggle, Tongue and groove, Topside, Trochanter, Undercut, Universal, Vertebra, Weld, Wrist

Joist Bar, Beam, Dormant, Groundsill, I-beam, Rib, Sleeper, Solive, String

Joke(r), Joke-book Banter, Bar, Booby-trap, Card, Chaff, Chestnut, ➤ CLOWN, Cod, Comedian, Comic, Crack, Cut-up, Farceur, Farceuse, Fool, Fun, Funster, Gab, Gag, Glike, Guy, Have-on, Hazer, Hoax, Hum, Humorist, Jape, Jest, Jig, Lark, Legpull, Merry-andrew, Merryman, Mistigris, One, One-liner, Pleasantry, Practical, Prank(ster), Pun, Punchline, Pundigrion, Quip, Sally, Scherzo, Scogan, Scoggin, Sick, Skylark, Sottisier, Squib, Standing, Wag, Wheeze, Wisecrack, Wild, Wit

Jollity, Jolly 'Arryish, Bally, Convivial, Cordial, Do, Festive, Galoot, Gaucie, Gaucy, Gawcy, Gawsy, Gay, Hilarious, Jocose, Jovial, Marine, Mirth, Rag, RM, Roger, Sandboy, Tar, Very

Jolt Bump, Jar, Jig-a jig, Jostle, Jounce, Shake, Shog, Start

Jonah Hoodoo, Jinx, Moz(z)

Jones Davy, Emperor, Inigo

Jordan Pot, Urinal

Joris Horseman

▶ **Joseph** see JOE

Josh Chaff, Kid, Rib, Tease

Josiah Stamp, Wedgewood

Joss Incense, Luck, Stick

Jostle Barge, Bump, Compete, Elbow, Hustle, Push, Shoulder, ➤ SHOVE

Jot(ter), Jotting(s) Ace, Fig, Iota, Memo, Mite, Note, Pad, Stime, Styme, Tittle, Whit

Journal Daily, Daybook, Diary, Ephemeris, Gazette, Hansard, Lancet, Log, Noctuary, Organ, Paper, Periodical, Pictorial, Punch, Rag, Record, TES, TLS, Trade

Journalism, Journalist Columnist, Contributor, Diarist, Diurnalist, Ed, Fleet St, (GA) Sala, Freelance, Hack, Hackette, Hatchetman, Inkslinger, Lobby, Northcliffe, NUJ, Pepys, Press(man), Reporter, Reviewer, Scribe, Stead, Stringer, Wireman, ➤ WRITER

Journey Circuit, Cruise, Errand, Expedition, Eyre, Foray, Hadj, Jaunce, Jaunse, Jaunt, Mush, Odyssey, Passage, Periegesis, Ply, Raik, Rake, Red-eye, Ride, Run, Sentimental, Tour, Travel, Trek, Walkabout

Journeyman Artisan, Commuter, Craftsman, Sterne, Yeoman

Joust Tilt, Tournament, Tourney

Jove Egad, Gad, Igad, Jupiter, Thunderer

Jovial Bacchic, Festive, Genial, Jolly

Jowl Cheek, Chops, Jaw

Joy(ful), Joyous Blithe, ➤ DELIGHT, Dream, Ecstasy, Elation, Exulting, Fain, Felicity, Festal, Frabjous, Glad, Glee, Gloat, Hah, Hey, Jubilant, Nirvana, Rapture, Schadenfreude, Sele, Tra-la, Transport, Treat, Yippee

JP Beak, Quorum

Jubilant, Jubilation, Jubilee Celebration, Cock-a-hoop, Diamond, Ecstatic, Elated, Holiday, Joy, Triumphant

Judaism Semitism

Judas Double-crosser, Traitor, Tree

Judder Put-put, Shake, Vibrate

Jude Obscure

Judge(ment), Judges Addoom, Adjudicator, Agonothetes, Alacus, Alcalde, Arbiter, Areopagite, Aret(t), Arrêt, Assess, Assize, Auto-da-fé, Avizandum, Banc, Brehon, Cadi, Calculate, Censure, Centumvirus, Circuit(eer), Connoisseur, Consider, Coroner, Court, Critic(ise), Daniel, Daysman, Deborah, Decern(e), Decide, Decision, Decreet, Deem(ster),

Dempster, Dicast, Differential, Dikast, Discern(ment), Ephor, Ermined, Estimate, Evaluate, Gauge, Gesse, Gideon, Good-sense, Guess, Hakeem, Hakim, Hearing, Hold, Honour, Interlocutor, J, Jeffreys, Jephthah, Justice, Justicier, Lud, Lynch, Minos, Mufti, Non prosequitur, Nonsuit, Old Fury, Opine, Opinion, Ordinary, Outfangthief, Panel, Paris, Podesta, Providence, Puisne, Puny, Reckon(ing), Recorder, Ref(eree), Regard, Rhadamanthus, Ruler, Sapience, Scan, See, Sentence, Sentiment, Shallow, Sheriff, Sober, Solomon, Sound, Suppose, Surrogate, Syndic, Tact, Think, Touch, Trior, Try, Umpire, Verdict, Wig, Wik, Wisdom, Worship

Judicious Critical, Discreet, Politic, Rational, Sage, Sensible, Shrewd, Sound

Judo, Judo costume Dojo, Gi(e)

Jug Amphora, Bellarmine, Bird, Blackjack, Bombard, Can, Cooler, Cream(er), Crock, Enghalskrug, Ewer, Gaol, Gotch, Greybeard, Growler, Malling, Olpe, Pitcher, Pound, Pourer, Pourie, ➤ PRISON, Quad, Quod, Shop, Stir, Toby, Urceolus

Juggle(r) Conjuror, Cook, Escamotage, Fake

Juice, Juicy Bacca, Cassareep, Cassaripe, Cremor, Current, Fluid, Fruity, Gastric, Hypocist, Ichor, La(b)danum, Laser, Latex, Lush, Must, Oil, Pancreatic, Perry, Rare, Sap, Soma, Spanish, Succulent, Succ(o)us, Thridace, Vril, Zest

Juju Charm, Fetish

Jujube Lotus, Padma, Sweet

Jukebox Nickelodeon

Julian Apostate

Jumble Chaos, Conglomeration, Farrago, Garble, Huddle, Jabble, Lumber, Mass, Medley, Mingle-mangle, Mish-mash, Mixter-maxter, Mixtie-maxtie, Mixture, Mix(t)y-max(t)y, Pastiche, Raffle, Ragbag, Scramble, Shuffle, Wuzzle

▷ **Jumbled** may indicate an anagram

Jumbo Aircraft, Elephant, Jet, Large-scale, Mammoth, OS

Jump(er), Jumping, Jumpy Assemble, Axel, Bate, Batterie, Boomer, Bound, Bungee, Bungy, Caper, Capriole, Cicada, Cicata, Crew-neck, Cricket, Croupade, Desultory, Entrechat, Euro, Eventer, Flea, Fosbury flop, Gansey, Gazump, Gelande (sprung), Guernsey, Halma, Hurdle, Impala, Itchy, Jersey, Joey, Kangaroo, Katydid, Knight, Lammie, Lammy, Leap(frog), Lep, Lope, Lutz, Nervous, Nervy, Parachute, Pogo, Polo-neck, Pounce, Prance, Prank, Pronking, Quantum, Quersprung, Salchow, Saltatory, Saltigrade, Saltus, Scissors, Scoup, Scowp, Skipjack, ➤ SPRING, Start, Sweater, Trampoline, Triple, Turtle-neck, Vau(l)t, Water, Western roll

Jumping jack Pantine

Junction Abutment, Alloyed, Box, Bregma, Carfax, Clover-leaf, Connection, Crewe, Crossroads, Intersection, Joint, Josephson, Knitting, Meeting, Point, Raphe, Spaghetti, Suture, T, Union

Juneberry Saskatoon, Shadbush

Jungle Asphalt, Blackboard, Boondocks, Bush, Concrete, Forest, Shola, Tangle

Junior Cadet, Chota, Cion, Dogsbody, Fils, Name-son, Petty, Puisne, Scion, Sub(ordinate), Underling, Understrapper, Younger
Juniper Red-cedar, Savin(e)
Junk Bric-a-brac, Jettison, Litter, Lorcha, Lumber, Refuse, Ship, Tatt, Trash
▷ **Junk** may indicate an anagram
Junker Prussian
Junket(ing) Beano, Creel, Custard, Feast, Picnic, Rennet, Spree
Junta Cabal, Council
Jupiter Jove, Newspaper
Jurassic Lias, Rhaetic
Jurisdiction Authority, Bailiwick, Domain, Province, Soke(n)
Juror(s), Jury Assize, Dicast, Grand, Hung, Inquest, Judges, Mickleton, Old Fury, Pais, Panel, Petit, Petty, Sail, Tales, Tribunal, Venire, Venue
Just(ice) Alcalde, All, Aristides, Astraea, Balanced, Condign, Cupar, Deserved, Equity, Fair, Honest, Impartial, J, Jasper, Jeddart, Jethart, Jurat, Mere, Nemesis, Newly, Nice, Only, Piso, Poetic, Provost, Puisne, Recent, Right(ful), Rightness, Shallow, Silence, Sommer, Themis, Tilt, Upright
Justifiable, Justification, Justify Apology, Autotelic, Avenge, Aver, Avowry, Clear, Darraign(e), Darrain(e), Darrayn, Defend, Deraign, Excusable, Explain, Grounds, Rationale, Vindicate, Warrant
Just so Exactly, Sic, Stories
Jut Beetle, Bulge, Overhang, Project, Protrude, Sail
Jute Burlap, Corchorus, Gunny, Hengist, Hessian, Horsa, Urena
Juvenile Childish, Teenage(r), Yonkers, Young, Younkers

K k

K Kelvin, Kilo, King, Kirkpatrick
K2 Dapsang, Godwin Austen
Kaffir Shares, Xosa
Kail, Kale Cabbage, Cole, Ninepins
Kaiser Doorn
Kaleidoscope Dappled, Motley, Myrioscope, Various
Kangaroo Bettong, Bongary, Boomer, Bounder, Cus-cus, Diprotodont, Euro, Forester, Joey, Macropodidae, Nototherium, Old man, Potoroo, Rat, Steamer, Tree, Troop, Wallaby, Wallaroo
Karate Kung Fu, Wushu
Karma Destiny, Fate, Predestination
Kate Greenaway, Shrew
Kayak Bidarka
Kebab Cevapcici, Gyro, Satay, Sate, Shashli(c)k, Souvlakia
Keel Bottom, Carina, Centreboard, Faint, Fin, List, Overturn, Skeg(g)
Keen(ness), Keener Acid, Acute, Agog, Aspiring, Argute, Astute, Athirst, Avid, Aygre, Bemoan, Bewail, Breem, Breme, Cheap, Coronach, Dash, Devotee, Dirge, Eager, Elegy, Enthusiastic, Fanatical, Fell, Greet, Grieve, Hone, Howl, Into, Lament, Mourn, Mustard, Mute, Narrow, Ochone, Ohone, Peachy, Perceant, Persant, Raring, Razor, Red-hot, Rhapsodic, Sharp, Shrewd, Shrill, Snell, Thirsting, Threnodic, Thrillant, Trenchant, Ululate, Wail, Whet, Zeal(ous)
Keep(er), Keeping Ames, Armature, Austringer, Castellan, Castle, Celebrate, Chatelain(e), Citadel, Conceal, Conserve, Curator, Custodian, Custody, Depositary, Depository, Detain, Donjon, Finder, Fort, Gaoler, Goalie, Guardian, Have, Hoard, ➤ HOLD, Maintain, Nab, Net, Observe, Ostreger, Pickle, Preserve, Retain, Stet, Stock, Store, Stow, Support, Sustain, Tower, Withhold
Keep back Detain, Recoup, Reserve, Retard, Stave
Keepsake Memento, Token
Keep under Cow, Subdue, Submerge
Keg Barrel, Cask, Tub, Tun, Vat
Kelly('s) Eye, Gene
Kelvin K
Ken Eyeshot, Know(ledge), Range
Kennel(s) Guard, Home, House, Shelter
Kent Lathe, SE, Superman
Kentuckian, Kentucky Chicken, Corn-cracker, Derby, KY
Kenya(n) Masai, Mau Mau
Kerala Nair, Nayar
Kerb Edge, Gutter, Roadside

Kerchief Babushka, Bandan(n)a, Headcloth, Romal, Scarf

Kernel Copra, Core, Grain, Nucleus, Praline, Prawlin

Kestrel Bird, Hawk, Keelie, Stallion, Staniel, Stannel, Stanyel, Windhover

Ket Carrion, Wool

Ketch Jack

Ketchup Relish, Sauce, Tomato

Kettle Boiler, Cauldron, Dixie, Dixy, Drum, Fanny, Pot, Turpin

Key(hole) A, Ait, Allen, Alt, Ash, B, Basic, C, Cay, Central, Chip, Cipher, Clavis, Clew, Clink, Clue, Crib, D, Digital, Dital, E, Essential, F, Flat, Fruit, Function, G, Greek, Holm, Hot, Ignition, Important, Inch, Index, Instrumental, Islet, Ivory, Kaie, King-pin, Latch, Legend, Linchpin, Locker, Main, Major, Minor, Note, Octachord, Opener, Oustiti, Outsiders, Passe-partout, Pivot, Pony, Reef, Semibreve, Shift, Signature, Skeleton, Spanner, Spline, Stimulate, Tab, Table, Tonal, Vital, Wedge, Woodruff, Yale®

Keyboard Azerty, Console, Digitorium, DVORAK, Manual, Martenot, Piano, Pianola®, Qwerty, Spinet

Keyholder Occupant, Resident, Tenant, Warder

Key man Islander, Kingpin

Keynote Line, Mese, Theme, Tonic

Keystone Cops, Crux, PA, Pennsylvania, Quoin, Sagitta, Voussoir

Keyword Kwic, Sesame

Khan Aga, Chagan, Cham, Serai, Shere

Kick(ing) Back-heel, Boot, Buzz, Corner, Dribble, Drop, Fling, Fly, Frog, Garryowen, Goal, Hack, Hoof, Lash, Penalty, Pause, Pile, Punt, Recalcitrate, Recoil, Recoyle, Savate, Scissors, Sixpence, Speculator, Spur, Spurn, Squib, Tanner, Thrill, Toe, Vigour, Wince, Yerk, Zip

Kid(s) Arab, Befool, Billy, Brood, Cheverel, Chevrette, Child, Chit, Con, Delude, Goat, Hoax, Hocus, Hoodwink, Hum, Joke, Leather, Misguide, Nipper, Offspring, Pretend, Rag, Rib, Spoof, Suede, Sundance, ➤ TEASE, Tot, Trick, Whiz(z), Wiz

Kidnap Abduct, Hijack, Plagium, Snatch, Spirit, Steal

Kidney(-shaped) Character, Mettle, Nature, Reins, Renal, Reniform, Sort

Kill(er), Killing Assassin, Attrit, Battue, Behead, Biocidal, Boojum, Butcher, Carnage, Carnifex, Chance-medley, Comical, Croak, Crucify, Cull, Despatch, Destroy, Euthanasia, Execute, Exterminate, Extirpate, For(e)do, Frag, Garotte, Germicide, Gun, Hatchet man, Hilarious, Homicide, Ice, Immolate, K, Knacker, Liquidate, Lynch, Matador(e), Misadventure, Mortify, Murder, Napoo, Ninja, NK, Off, Orc(a), Serial, Settle, Vaticide, Waste, -phage, Pip, Predator, Prolicide, Quell, Quietus, Regrate, Sacrifice, Shochet, Slaughter, Slay(er), Slew, Smite, Snuff, Stifle, Stonker, Swat, Tailor, Thagi, Thug(gee), Top, Toreador, Veto, Zap

Killjoy Crab, Puritan, Sourpuss, Spoilsport, Wowser

Kiln Oast, Oven

Kilometre Km, Verst

Kilt Drape, Filabeg, Fil(l)ibeg, Fustanella, Phil(l)abeg, Phil(l)ibeg, Plaid, Tartan

Kin(sman) Ally, Family, Kith, Like, Nearest, Relation, Sib(b), Sybbe

Kind(ly) Akin, Amiable, Avuncular, Benefic, Benevolent, Benign, Boon, Breed, Brood, Brotherly, Category, Class, Clement, Considerate, Favourable, Gender, Generic, Generous, Genre, Gentle, Genus, Good, Humane, Ilk, Kidney, Kin, Lenient, Manner, Modal, Nature, Sisterly, ➤ SORT, Species, Strain, Strene, Trine, Type, Understanding, Variety, Well-disposed, Ylke

Kindle, Kindling Accend, Fire, Ignite, Incense, Incite, Inflame, ➤ LIGHT, Litter, Lunt, Stimulate, Teend, Tind, Tine, Touchwood, Tynd(e)

Kindness Aloha, Benevolence, Clemency, Favour, Humanity

Kindred Allied, Blood, Like, Related

King(s), Kingly Acestes, Aegeus, Agag, Agamemnon, Agis, Ahab, Ahasuerus, Alexander, Alfred, Alonso, Amasis, Apple, Ard-ri(gh), Arthur, Asa, Athelstan, Attila, Bal(l)iol, Balak, Baldwin, Belshazzar, Beowulf, Bretwalda, Brian Boru, Brut(e), Brutus, Busiris, Butcher, Cadwaladar, Cambyses, Canute, Caractacus, Caradoc, Cecrops, Ceyx, Charlemagne, Cheops, Clovis, Cnut, Cobra, Cole, Conchobar, Cophetua, Cotton, Creon, Croesus, Cunobelin, Cymbeline, Cyrus, Darius, David, Duncan, Edgar, Edmund, Edwin, Edwy, Egbert, Elidure, Endymion, English, ER, Erl, Ethelbert, Ethelred, Evander, Evil, Fahd, Farouk, Fergus, Frederick, Florestan, Gargantua, GR, Gyges, Hardicanute, Harold, Hellen, Herod, Hezekeah, Highness, Hiram, Hyksos, Idris, Inca, Ine, Ixion, James, Jehoshaphat, Jehu, Jereboam, Jonathan, Kenneth, Kong, Laius, Lear, Leonidas, Lionheart, Lir, Lludd, Log, Louis, Lucomo, Lud, Ludwig, Macbeth, Majesty, Malcolm, Memnon, Menander, Menelaus, Midas, Milesian, Minos, Monarch, Mpret, Nebuchadnezzar, Negus, Nestor, Ninus, Nudd, Numa, Oberon, Odysseus, Oedipus, Offa, Og, Ogyges, Olaf, Ozymandias, Paphos, Pearly, Peleus, Penda, Penguin, Peishwa(h), Peshwa, Pharaoh, Philip, Potentate, Priam, Ptolemy, Pygmalion, Pyrrhus, R, Ram(e)ses, Ransom, Ras Tafari, Re, Rehoboam, Reigner, Rex, Rhesus, Rial, Roi, Royalet, Rufus, Ruler, Ryal, Sailor, Saul, Sennacherib, Servian, Seven, Shah, Shilling, Sigismund, Sisyphus, Solomon, Sovereign, Stephen, Stork, Sweyn Forkbeard, Tantalus, Tarquin(us), Thyestes, Tigranes, Umberto, Uther (Pendragon), Vortigern, Wayland Smith, Wenceslas, Wenceslaus, Xerxes, Zedekiah, Zog

Kingdom, Kingship Animal, Aragon, Barataria, Bhutan, Bohemia, Brunel, Dominion, Edom, Elam, Fife, Heptarchy, Jordan, Lydia, Mercia, Meroe, Mineral, Moab, Navarre, Nepal, Noricum, Parthia, Pontic, Realm, Reign, Royalty, Sphere, Throne, Tonga, Vegetable, Wessex, World

Kingfisher Alcyone, Halcyon

Kingmaker Neville, Warwick

King-of-arms Clarenc(i)eux, Garter, Lyon, Norroy (and Ulster)

King's evil Crewels, Cruels, Scrofula

King's son Dauphin, Delphin, P, Prince

Kink(y) Bent, Buckle, Crapy, Enmeshed, Flaw, Gasp, Knurl, Null, Nurl, Odd, Perm, Perverted, Quirk, Twist, Wavy

▷ **Kink(y)** may indicate an anagram

Kinkajou Honey-bear, Potto

385 Kip(per) → Knight

Kip(per) Cure, Dosser, Doze, Limey, Nap, ➤ SLEEPER, Smoke
Kipling Beetle
Kirkpatrick K
Kismet Destiny, Fate, Karma, Predestination
Kiss(er), Kissing Buss, Butterfly, Caress, Contrecoup, Cross, French, Lip, Neck, Osculate, Pax(-board), Pax-brede, Peck, Pet, Plonker, Pree, Salue, Salute, Smack(er), Smooch, Smouch, Snog, Spoon, Thimble, X, Yap
Kit Christopher, Clobber, Housewife, Layette, Marlowe, Mess, ➤ OUTFIT, Rig, Set, Slops, Sportswear, Tackle, Uniform
Kitchen Caboose, Cookhouse, Cuisine, Galley, Scullery, Soup
Kite Belly, Bird, Box, Chil, Crate, Dragon, Elanet, Forktail, Gled(e), Hawk, Milvus, Paunch, Puttock, Rokkaku
Kitten(ish) Cute, Kindle, Sexy
Kittiwake Bird, Gull, Hacklet, Haglet
Kitty Ante, Cat, Fisher, Float, Fund, Jackpot, Pool, Pot, Tronc
Kiwi Apteryx, NZ, Ratitae
Klu-Klux-Klan Nightrider
Knack Art, Flair, Forte, Gift, Hang, Instinct, ➤ TALENT, Trick
Knacker Castanet, Exhaust
Knapsack Musette
Knapweed Matfelon
Knave(ry) Bezonian, Bower, Boy, Card, Coistril, Coystril, Custrel, Dog, Drôle, Fripon, Jack(-a-napes), Jock, Loon, Makar, Maker, Nob, Noddy, Pam, Pur, Rapscallion, ➤ RASCAL, Recreant, Ropery, Scoundrel, Taroc, Tarot, Tom, Treachery, Varlet, Villain
Knead Conch, Malax(ate), Massage, Mould, Pug, Pummel, Work
Knee(-cap), Knee-pan Genu, Hock, Housemaid's, Lap, Patella, Poleyn, Popliteal, Punch, Rotula, Whirl bone
Kneel(er) Defer, Genuflect, Hassock, Kowtow, Truckle
Knell Bell, Curfew, Dirge, Peal, Ring, Toll
Knicker(bocker), Knickers Bloomers, Culottes, Directoire, Irving, Panties, Plus-fours, Shorts, Trousers
Knick-knack Bagatelle, Bibelot, Bric-a-brac, Gewgaw, Pretty(-pretty), Quip, Smytrie, Toy, Trangam, Trifle, Victoriana
Knife Anelace, Barlow, Barong, Bistoury, Blade, Bolo, Bolster, Bowie, Carver, Catling, Chakra, Clasp, Cleaver, Couteau, Cradle, Cuttle, Cutto(e), Da(h), Dagger, Fleam, Flick, Gull(e)y, Hunting, Jockteleg, Kard, Kukri, Lance(t), Machete, Matchet, Palette, Panga, Parang, Pocket, Scalpel, Sheath, Shiv, Simi, Slash, Snee, Snickersnee, Spade, Stab, Stanley, Steak, Switchblade, Tranchet
Knight Accolon, Aguecheek, Alphagus, Artegal, Banneret, Bayard, Bedivere, Black, Bliant, Bors, Britomart, Caballero, Calidore, Cambel, Caradoc, Carpet, Cavalier, Chevalier, Companion, Crusader, Douceper, Douzeper, Dub, Equites, Errant, Galahad, Gallant, Gareth, Garter, Gawain, Guyon, Hospitaller, Kay, KB, KBE, KG, La(u)ncelot, Launfal, Lionel, Lochinvar, Lohengrin, Maecenas, Malta, Medjidie, Melius, Modred, N, Noble, Orlando, Paladin, Palmerin, Parsifal, Perceforest, Perceval, Percival,

Pharamond, Pinel, Ritter, Samurai, Sir, Tannhauser, Templar, Teutonic, Trencher, Tristan, Tristram, Vavasour, Valvassor, White

Knit(ting), Knitwear Contract, Crochet, Entwine, Hosiery, Interlock, K, Mesh, Porosis, Purl, Seam, Set, Stockinet, Weave, Wrinkle

Knob(by) Berry, Boll, Boss, Botoné, Bottony, Bouton, Bur(r), Cam, Caput, Cascabel, Croche, Handle, Hill, Inion, Knur(r), Node, Noop, Pellet, Pommel, Protuberance, Pulvinar, Snib, Snub, Snuff, Stud, Torose, Tuber, Tuner

Knobless Enodal

Knock (down, off, out) Bang, Beaut, Biff, Blow, Bonk, Bump, Ca(a), Chap, Clash, Clour, Collide, Con, Criticise, Daud, Dawd, Degrade, Denigrate, Deride, Dev(v)el, Ding, Dinnyhauser, Etherise, Eyeful, Floor, Grace-stroke, ➤ HIT, Innings, KO, Lowse, Lowsit, Mickey Finn, Pan, Pink, Quietus, Rap, Rat-tat, Skittle, Spat, Steal, Stop, Strike, Stun(ner), Tap, Technical, Thump, Tonk, Wow

Knock-kneed Valgus

Knot(ted), Knotty Apollo, Baff, Bend, Blackwell hitch, Bow, Bowline, Burl, Bur(r), Carrick-bend, Cat's paw, Clinch, Clove hitch, Cluster, Crochet, Englishman's, Entangle, Figure of eight, Fisherman's (bend), French, Gnar, ➤ GNARL, Gordian, Granny, Half-hitch, Harness hitch, Hawser-bend, Herculean, Hitch, Interlace, Knag, Knap, Knar, Knur(r), Loop, Love(r's), Macramé, Macrami, Magnus hitch, Matthew Walker, Mouse, Nirl, Node, Nowed, Nub, Nur(r), Overhand, Picot, Problem, Prusik, Quipu, Reef, Rosette, Seizing, Sheepshank, Sheetbend, Sleave, Slip, Slub, Spurr(e)y, Stevedore's, Surgeon's, Sword, Tangle, Tat, Thumb, Tie, Timberhitch, Truelove, Tubercle, Turk's head, Wale, Wall, Windsor

Know(how), Knowing, Knowledge(able), Known Acquaintance, Autodidactic, Aware, Cognition, Compleat, Comprehend, Cred, Epistemics, Erudite, Expertise, Famous, Fly, Gnosis, Gnostic, Have, Hep, Hip, Info, Information, Insight, Intentional, Intuition, Jnana, Ken, Kith, Kydst, Lare, Light, Lore, Mindful, Omniscience, On, Pansophy, Party, Polymath, Positivism, Privity, Recherché, ➤ RECOGNISE, Sapient, Savvy, Science, Scilicet, Sciolism, Shrewd, Smattering, Understand(ing), Up, Versed, Wat(e), Weet(e), Well-informed, Well-read, Wise, Wist, Wit, Wot

Know-all Arrogant, Besserwisser, Bumptious, Cognoscenti, Pansophist, Polymath, Poseur, Smart alec(k), Smart-arse, Smart-ass, Wiseacre

Knuckle Apply, Fist, Joint, Ossein, Submit

Koko List

Kop Spion

Koran Scripture, Sura(h)

Korean ROK

Kosher Approved, Genuine, Legitimate, Real

Kremlin Fortress

Kri Masora

Krypton Kr

Kudos Credit, Glory, Praise

Kurd Yezidi

Kyanite Disthene

L l

L Latitude, League, Learner, Left, Length, Liberal, Lima, Litre, Long, Luxembourg, Pound

La Indeed, My

Label Band, Book-plate, Brand, Designer, Docket, File, Mark, Own, Seal, Sticker, Style, Tab, Tag, Tally, Ticket, Trace

Labiate Catmint, Hoarhound, Horehound

Laboratory Lab, Language, Skylab, Space-lab, Studio, Workshop

Labour(er), Laboured, Laborious Arduous, Begar, Birth, Carl, Casual, Chirl, Chore, Coolie, Corvée, Cottager, Cottar, Culchie, Dataller, Dwell, Gandy-dancer, Ganger, Gibeonite, Grecian, Grind, Hard, Hercules, Hodge, Ida, Job, Journeyman, Kanaka, Katorga, Leaden, Manpower, Moil, Navvy, Okie, Operose, Pain, Peon, Pioneer, Prole, Redneck, Roll, Roustabout, Rouster, Sisyphean, Slave, Stint, Strive, Sudra, Sweated, Task, ➤ TOIL(SOME), Toss, Travail, Uphill, Vineyard, ➤ WORK(ER), Workmen

Labrador Retriever, Tea

Labyrinth Daedalus, Maze, Mizmaze, Warren, Web

▷ **Labyrinthine** may indicate an anagram

Lac Lacquer, Lakh, Resin, Shellac, Tomans

Lace, Lacy Alençon, Babiche, Beat, Bobbin, Bourdon, Brussels, Chantilly, Cluny, Colbertine, Dash, Dentelle, Duchesse, Filet, Galloon, Guipure, Honiton, Inweave, Irish, Jabot, Lash, Macramé, Malines, Mechlin, Mignonette, Mode, Net, Orris, Pearlin, Picot, Pillow, Point, Reseau, Reticella, Ricrac, Rosaline, Shoestring, Shoe-tie, Spike, Tat(ting), Thrash, Torchon, Trim, Trol(le)y, Valenciennes, Venise, Weave, Welt, Window-bar

Lacerate(d) Ganch, Gash, Gaunch, Maul, Rent, Rip, Slash, Tear

Lachrymose Maudlin, Niobe, Tearful, Water-standing, ➤ WEEPY

Lack(ing), Lacks Absence, Aplasia, Bereft, Dearth, Famine, Ha'n't, Manqué, Minus, ➤ NEED, Poverty, Privation, Remiss, Sans, Shortfall, Shy, Void, Want

Lackadaisical Languid, Listless, Torpid

Lackaday Haro

Lackey Boots, Flunkey, Moth, Page, Poodle, Satellite, Skip-kennel

Lacklustre Dull, Insipid, Matt

Lack of confidence Doubt, Scepsis

Laconic Blunt, Close-mouthed, Curt, Spartan, Succinct, Terse

Lacquer Coromandel, Enamel, Japan, Shellac, ➤ VARNISH

Lad Boy(o), Bucko, Callan(t), Chield, Geit, Gyte, Knight, Loonie, Nipper, Shaver, Stableman, Tad, Whipper-snapper

Ladder(y) Accommodation, Bucket, Companion, Companionway, Etrier, Jack, Jacob's, Pompier, Potence, Rope, Run, Salmon, Scalado, Scalar, Scaling, Stie, Sty, Trap, Turntable

Ladle Bail, Dipper, Scoop

Lady Baroness, Bevy, Bountiful, Burd, Dame, Dark, Don(n)a, Duenna, Female, Frau, Frow, Gemma, Godiva, Hen, Khanum, Luck, Maam, Madam(e), Memsahib, Nicotine, Peeress, Senora, Signora, Tea, Windermere

▷ **Lady** may indicate an '-ess' ending

Ladybird Cushcow, Hen, Vedalia

▷ **Ladybird** may indicate a female of a bird family

Ladykiller Bluebeard, Wolf

Lady of the lake Vivian

Lady's Fingers Gumbo, Okra

Lady's maid Abigail

Lag Culture, Dawdle, Delay, Drag, Flag, Hysteresis, Inmate, Jailbird, Leng, ► LINGER, Loiter, Prisoner, Retard, Time, Tortoise, Trail

Lager Pils(e)ner

Lagoon Haff, Pool, Salina, Saline

► **Laic, Laid** see LAY

Lair Couch, Den, Earth, Haunt, Hideaway, Kennel, Lodge, Warren

Lake(s) Alkali, Basin, Bayou, Carmine, Chott, Crater, Crimson, Finger, L, Lacustrine, Lagoon, Lagune, ► LAKES, ► LOCH, Lochan, Lough, Madder, Mead, Mere, Ox-bow, Poets, Pool, Red, Reservoir, Salt, Shott, Tarn, Vlei

Lake-dwelling Crannog

Lakeland Cumbria

Lam Flee, Scram

Lamb(skin) Baa, Barometz, Budge, Bummer, Cade, Canterbury, Caracul, Cosset, Ean(ling), Elia, Innocent, Keb, Larry, Noisette, Paschal, Persian, Rack, Shearling, Target, Yean(ling)

Lambent Flickering, Glowing, Licking

Lambert Constant

Lame(ness) Accloy, Claude, Cripple, Crock, Game, Gammy, Gimp(y), Halt, Hamstring, Hirple, Hors de combat, Maim, Main, Spavined, Springhalt, Stringhalt, Weak

Lament(able), Lamentation, Lamenter Bemoan, Bewail, Beweep, Complain, Croon, Cry, Dirge, Dumka, Elegy, Funest, Jeremiad, Jeremiah, Keen, Meane, Mein, Mene, Moon, Mourn, Ochone, Paltry, Piteous, Plain, Repine, Sorry, Threne, Threnody, Ululate, ► WAIL, Welladay, Wel(l)away, Yammer

Lamia Deadnettle

Lamina(te) Film, Flake, Folium, Formica®, Lamella, Layer, Plate, Scale, Table

Lamp(s) Aldis, Anglepoise, Arc, Argand, Bowat, Bowet, Buat, Cru(i)sie, Crusy, Davy, Eye, Eyne, Fluorescent, Geordie, Hurricane, Incandescent, Lantern, Lava, Lucigen, Mercury vapour, Neon, Nernst, Nightlight, Padella, Quartz, Scamper, Signal, Sodium, Spirit, Standard, Stride, Stroboscope, Tilley, Torchier(e), Tungsten, Uplight(er), Veilleuse, Xenon

Lamplighter Leerie, Spill

Lampoon Caricature, Parody, Pasquil, Pasquin(ade), Satire, Skit, Squib

LAKES

2 letters:	Taupo	Lucerne	Great Salt
No	Tsana	Manapua	Innisfree
3 letters:	Urmia	Nipigon	Killarney
Ewe	**6 letters:**	Ontario	Macquarie
Van	Albert	Rotonia	Manapouri
4 letters:	Argyle	Toronto	Maracaibo
Bala	Baikal	Torrens	Naumachia
Bled	Barlee	Turkana	Nipissing
Chad	Bitter	**8 letters:**	Serbonian
Como	Broads	Balkhash	Trasimene
Erie	Cayuga	Bodensee	Trasimono
Erne	Corrib	Carnegie	Ullswater
Eyre	Edward	Gairdner	Wairarapa
Kivu	Geneva	Maggiore	Wastwater
Nyos	Kariba	Manitoba	Winnebago
Tana	Ladoga	Menindee	**10 letters:**
Thun	Lugano	Michigan	Buttermere
5 letters:	Malawi	Naumachy	Clearwater
Atlin	Miveru	Okanagan	Great Slave
Cowal	Mobutu	Onondaga	Haweswater
Cowan	Nakura	Regillus	Ijsselmeer
Frome	Nyanza	Reindeer	Mistassini
Garda	Oneida	Superior	Okefenokee
Gatun	Rudolf	Titicaca	Serpentine
Huron	Saimaa	Veronica	Tanganyika
Ilmen	Te Anau	Victoria	Windermere
Leven	Tekapo	Wakatipu	**11 letters:**
Lower	Vanern	Wanawaka	Lesser Slave
Malar	Zurich	Winnipeg	**12 letters:**
Morar	**7 letters:**	**9 letters:**	Derwentwater
Mungo	Amadeus	Athabasca	Memphremagog
Myall	Aral Sea	Bangweulu	**13 letters:**
Nyasa	Avernus	Champlain	Coniston Water
Onega	Axolotl	Constance	Crummock Water
Playa	Balaton	Ennerdale	**14 letters:**
Sevan	Iliamna	Everglade	Disappointment
Tahoe	Koko Nor	Great Bear	Ennerdale Water

Lamprey Hag, Lampern

Lancaster Burt, Osbert

Lance Dart, Harpoon, Morne, Pesade, Pike, Prisade, Prisado, Rejon, Spear, Speisade, Thermic

Lancelet Amphious

Lancer Bengal, Picador, Uhlan

Lancet Fleem

Land(ed) Acreage, Aina, Alight, Alluvion, Arpent, Bag, Beach, Bigha, Bovate, Carse, Carucate, Cavel, Conacre, Country, Croft, Demain, Demesne, Disbark, Disembark, Ditch, Doab, Dock, Earth, Edom, Estate, Fallow, Farren, Fee, Feod, Feoff, Feud, Fief, Freeboard, Gair, Glebe, Gondwanaland, Ground, Hide, Holding, Holm, Horst, Innings, Isthmus, Kingdom, Laurasia, Lea, Leal, Ley, Light, Machair, Maidan, Manor, Métairie, Morgen, Mortmain, Nation, Never-never, Nod, No man's, Odal, Onshore, Oxgang, Oxgate, Pangaea, Panhandle, Parcel, Pasture,

Peninsula, Piste, Plot, Ploughgate, Polder, Pr(a)edial, Promised, Property, Purlieu, Realm, Realty, Reservation, Roman candle, Rundale, Savanna(h), Settle, Spit, Swidden, Taluk, Terra(e), Terrain, Territory, Thwaite, Tie, Tir na n'Og, Touchdown, Turbary, Tye, Udal, Unship, Ure, Van Diemen's, Veld(t), Wainage, Whenua, Yird

▶ **Landfall** see LANDSLIDE

Landing (craft, stair, system) Autoflare, Forced, Gha(u)t, Halfpace, LEM, Module, Pancake, Pier, Quay, Soft, Solar, Splashdown, Three-point, Touchdown, Undercarriage

Landlock Embay

Landlord, Land owner Absentee, Balt, Boniface, Copyholder, Fiar, Franklin, Herself, Host, Innkeeper, Junker, Laird, Lessor, Letter, Patron, Proprietor, Publican, Rachman, Rentier, Squattocracy, Squire, Squirearchy, Squireen, Thane, Zamindar(i), Zemindar

Landmark Meith, Watershed

Landmass Laurasia

Land right Emphyteusis

Landscape Karst, Paysage, Picture, Saikei, Scene

Landslide, Landfall Avalanche, Earthfall, Eboulement, Lahar, Scree

Landsman Lubber

Land-tenure Frankalmoign, Raiyatwari, Ryotwari

Lane Boreen, Bus, Corridor, Crawler, Drury, Express, Fast, Fetter, Gut, Loan, Lois, Loke, Memory, Mincing, Passage, Petticoat, Pudding, Ruelle, Sea-road, Twitten, Twitting, Vennel, Wynd

Langerhans Insulin, Islets

Language(s) Argot, Artificial, Assembly, Auxiliary, Basic, Body, Cant, Dialect, Georgian, Hobson-Jobson, Humanities, Idioglossia, Idiolect, Idiom, Inclusive, Jargon, Langue, Ledden, Lingo, Lingua franca, Macaroni, Machine code, Mellowspeak, Neo, Newspeak, Novelese, Object, Parlance, Philology, Pidgin, Polysynthetic, Pragmatics, Procedural, Programming, Prose, Rhetoric, Sea-speak, Semitic, Sign, Sociolect, ▶ SPEECH, Style, Symbolic, Target, Technobabble, Telegraphese, Tone, ▶ TONGUE, Vedic, Venetic, Verbiage, Vernacular, Vocabulary, Words

LANGUAGES

3 letters:	Twi	Motu	Zulu
Ada	**4 letters:**	Nupe	Zuni
Bat	Ainu	Pali	**5 letters:**
Fur	Avar	Pedi	Aleut
Giz	Erse	Pict	Aryan
Gur	Geez	Shan	Azeri
Ibo	Igbo	Taal	Balti
Ido	Inca	Thai	Bantu
Kwa	Komi	Tshi	Batak
Mon	Krio	Tupi	Cajun
Tai	Lozi	Urdu	Carib
Tiv	Maya	Xosa	Chewa

Cobol	Centum	Bislama	Chichewa
Dogon	Chadic	Catalan	Croatian
Doric	Coptic	Chaldee	Dzongkha
Fanti	Creole	Chinook	Etruscan
Farsi	Cymric	Chuvash	Fanagalo
Ganda	Dardic	Cushite	Filipino
Gondi	Fantee	Dzongka	Gujarati
Hausa	Fijian	Frisian	Gujerati
Hindi	Fulani	Hin Motu	Gurkhali
Hokan	Gaelic	Hittite	Illyrian
Indic	Gaguaz	Janlish	Japhetic
Joual	Gullah	Japlish	Kingwana
Kafri	Hebrew	Kannada	Kolarian
Koine	Herero	Khoisan	Kwakiuti
Kuo-yu	Ladino	Kurdish	Landsmal
Ladin	Lahnda	Kushite	Mandarin
Lamba	Lu wian	Lallans	Mon-Khmer
Lamut	Lydian	Lingala	Pilipino
Latin	Manchu	Marathi	Polabian
Lubon	Micmac	Miao-Yao	Romansch
Lunda	Mishmi	Mingrel	Rumansch
Lyele	Na-Dene	Nahuatl	Rumonsch
Malay	Nepali	Nilotic	Sanscrit
Maori	Novial	Nyungar	Sanskrit
Mayan	Ostyak	Oceanic	Setswana
Munda	Pahari	Ossetic	Sumerian
Norse	Paiute	Prakrit	Tahitian
Oriya	Pakhti	Pushtoo	Teutonic
Oscan	Papuan	Quechua	Tigrinya
P-Celt	Pashto	Romance	Turanian
Sakai	Pashtu	Romansh	Turkoman
Satem	Pushto	Samoyed	Ugaritic
Sotho	Pushtu	Sesotho	Wakashan
Suomi	Romany	Sinhala	**9 letters:**
Swazi	Rwanda	Sinitic	Algonkian
Taino	Salish	Slovene	Algonquin
Tajik	Shelta	Sudanic	Anatolian
Tamil	Sindhi	Swahili	Cantonese
Tonga	Siouan	Tagalog	Chari-Nile
Turki	Strine	Tibetan	Diglossia
Wolof	Tanoan	Tlingit	Dravidian
World	Tartar	Turkish	Esperanto
Xhosa	Telugu	Turkmen	Euskarian
Yakut	Tuareg	Umbrian	Franglais
Yuman	Tungus	Uralian	Gujarathi
Yupik	Turkic	Volapuk	Gujerathi
6 letters:	Udmurt	Voltaic	Hottentot
Adyahe	Ugrian	Walloon	Inuktitut
Adygei	Uralic	Wendish	Kamilaroi
Altaic	Yoruba	Yerkish	Landsmaal
Arabic	Zyrian	Yiddish	Leizghian
Aranda	**7 letters:**	**8 letters:**	Malayalam
Aymara	Adamawa	Akkadian	Messapian
Basque	Amerind	Albanian	Muskogean
Basutu	Amharic	Arawakan	Nostratic
Brahui	Aramaic	Assamese	Provencal
Breton	Austric	Bulgaric	Putonghua
Celtic	Bengali	Chibchan	Roumansch

Sinhalese	Himyaritic	Uto-Aztecan	
Tocharian	Hindustani	**11 letters:**	
Tokharian	Malayalaam	Dagestanian	
Tokharish	Melanesian	Interglossa	
Ukrainian	Mingrelian	Interlingua	
10 letters:	Papiamento	Kordofanian	
Algonquian	Rajasthani	Osso-Umbrian	**12 letters:**
Azerbayani	Serbo-croat	Pama-Nyungan	Billingsgate
Circassian	Singhalese	Sino-Tibetan	Platt-deutsch
Diachronic	Synchronic	Sranantongo	Tibeto-Burman
Eteocretan	Ural-Altaic	Tessaraglot	Volga-Baltaic

Languid, Languish Die, Divine, Droop, Feeble, Flagging, Listless, Lukewarm, Lydia, Melancholy, Quail, Torpid, Wilt

Languor Lassitude

Lanky Beanpole, Gangly, Gawky, Spindleshanks, Windlestraw

Lanolin Yolk

Lantern Aristotle's, Bowat, Bowet, Buat, Bull's eye, Chinese, Dark(e)y, Epidiascope, Episcope, Glim, Jaw, Lanthorn, Magic, Sconce, Stereopticon, Storm

Lanthanum La

Laodicean Lukewarm

Lap Gremial, Leg, Lick, Lip, Luxury, Override, Pace, Sypher

Lapdog Messan, Shough, Showghe

Lapel Revers

Laplander, Lapp Saam(e), Sabme, Sabmi, Sami

Lapse Drop, Error, Expire, Fa', Fall, Nod, Sliding, Trip

Larch Hackmatack, Tamarack

Lard Enarm, Leaf, Saim, Seam(e)

Larder Buttery, Pantry, Spence, Springhouse

Large(ness), Largest Ample, Astronomical, Big, Boomer, Buster, Colossus, Commodious, Decuman, Enormous, Epical, Gargantuan, ➤ GIGANTIC, Ginormous, Great, Grit, Gross, Hefty, Helluva, Huge, Hulking, Humdinger, Humongous, Humungous, Kingsize, L, Lunker, Macrocephaly, Massive, Maximin, Maximum, Plethora, Prodigious, Rounceval, Rouncival, Skookum, Slew, Slue, Sollicker, Spanking, Stonker, Stout, Swingeing, Tidy, Titanic, Vast, Voluminous, Whopping

Large number Centillion, Fermi, Giga, Gillion, Googol, Googolplex, Infinitude, Jillion, Legion, Nation, Nonillion, Quadrillion, Quintillion, Raft, Ruck, Scads, Sea, Septillion, Sextillion, Slew, Slue, Squillion, Toman, Trillion, Zillion

Largess Alms, Charity, Frumentation

Lariat Lasso, Reata, Riata

Lark Adventure, Aunter, Caper, Dido, Dunstable, Exaltation, Fool, Giggle, Guy, Laverock, Mud, Pipit, Prank

Larkspur Stavesacre

Larva Aphid lion, Army-worm, Axolotl, Bagworm, Bloodworm, Bot(t), Budworm, Caddice, Caddis, Cankerworm, Caterpillar, Cercaria, Chigger,

Chigoe, Doodlebug, Grub, Hellgram(m)ite, Hydatid, Indusium, Jigger, Jointworm, Leather-jacket, Leptocephalus, Maggot, Mealworm, Measle, Miracidium, Muckworm, Naiad, Nauplius, Ox-bot, Planula, Pluteus, Porina, Redia, Shade, Silkworm, Tadpole, Trochosphere, Veliger, Water penny, Wireworm, Witchetty, Woodworm, Zoea

Laryngitis Croup, Hives

Lascar Seacunny, Tindal

Lascivious(ness) Crude, Goaty, Horny, Lewd, Lubric, Paphian, Satyric, Sotadic, Tentigo

Lash(ed), Lashings Cat, Cilium, Firk, Flagellum, Frap, Gammon, Knout, Mastigophora, Oodles, Oup, Quirt, Riem, Rope's end, Scourge, Secure, Sjambok, Stripe, Swinge, Tether, Thong, Trice, Whang, ➤ WHIP

Lass(ie) Damsel, Maid, Quean, Queyn, Quin(i)e

Lassitude Accidie, Acedie, Languor, Lethargy

Lasso Lariat, Reata, Rope

Last(ing) Abide, Abye, Aftermost, ➤ AT LAST, Boot-tree, Bottom, Chronic, Dernier, Dure, Endurance, Endure, Extend, Extreme, ➤ FINAL, Hinder, Latest, Linger, Live, Long-life, Model, Nightcap, Outstay, Perdure, Permanent, Perpetuate, Persist, Spin, Stable, Stay, Supper, Survive, Swan-song, Thiller, Thule, Tree, Trump, Ult(imate), Ultimo, Utmost, Wear, Weight, Whipper-in, Z

Last drop Supernaculum

Last resort Pis aller

Last syllable Ultima

Last word(s) Amen, Envoi, Farewell, Ultimatum, Zythum

Latch Bar, Clicket, Clink, Espagnolette, Lock, Sneck

Late(r), Latest After(wards), Afterthought, Behindhand, Chit-chat, Dead, Ex, Former, Gen, Infra, Lag, Lamented, New(s), Overdue, Past, Recent, Sine, Slow, Stop-press, Syne, Tardive, Tardy, Trendy, Umquhile

Late-learner Opsimath

Latent Concealed, Delitescent, Dormant, Maieutic, Potential

Lateral Askant, Edgeways, Sideways

Latex Antiar, Gutta-percha, Jelutong, Ule

Lath Lag, Splat

Lathe Capstan, Mandrel, Mandril, Turret

Lather Flap, Foam, Froth, Sapples, Suds, Tan

Latin(ist) Criollo, Dago, Dog, Erasmus, Eyeti, Greaseball, Humanity, Italiot, L, Low, Neapolitan, Pig, Romanic, Romish, Scattermouch, Spic, Vulgar, Wop

Latin-American Criollo, Tico

Latitude Breadth, Celestial, Free hand, Horse, L, Leeway, Liberty, Licence, Meridian, Parallel, Play, Roaring forties, Scope, Tropic, Width

Latrine Ablutions, Bog, Cloaca, Furphy, Garderobe, Loo, Privy, Rear

Latter Last, Previous

Latter-day Recent, Saints, Young

Lattice Bravais, Clathrate, Espalier, Grille, Treillage, Trellis
Lattice-leaf Ouvirandra
Latvian Lett
Laud(er) Commend, Eulogist, Extol, Harry, Praise
Lauderdale Caballer
Laugh(ing), Laughable, Laughter Belly, Cachinnate, Cackle, Chortle, Chuckle, Cod, Corpse, Democritus, Deride, Derision, Fit, Fou rire, Gelastic, Giggle, Goster, Guffaw, Ha, He-he, Ho-ho, Homeric, Hoot, Horse, Hout, Howl, Irrision, Lauch, Leuch, Levity, ➤ MIRTH, Mock, Nicker, Peal, Present, Riancy, Riant, Rich, Rident, Ridicule, Risus, Scream, Snigger, Snirt(le), Snort, Tehee, Titter, Yo(c)k
Laughing-stock Outspeckle, Sport
Launcelot Gobbo
Launch(ing) Begin, Blast-off, Catapult, Chuck, Fire, Float, Hurl, Initiate, Lift-off, Pioneer, Presentation, Release, Shipway, Slipway, Unstock, Upsend, VTO
Launder, Laundry Bagwash, Clean, Lav, Steamie, Tramp, Transfer, Wash, Washhouse, Whites
Laurel(s) Aucuba, Bay, Camphor, Daphne, Kalmia, Kudos, Pichurim, Sassafras, Spicebush, Spurge, Stan, Sweet-bay
Laurence Sterne
Lava Aa, Bomb, Coulee, Cysticercus, Dacite, Lahar, Lapilli, Magma, Nuée ardente, Pahoehoe, Palagonite, Pitchstone, Pumice, Pyroclast, Scoria, Tephra, Toadstone
Lavatory Ajax, Can, Carsey, Carzey, Cludgie, Comfort station, Convenience, Cottage, Dike, Dunnakin, Dunny, Dyke, Elsan®, Facilities, Forica, Furphey, Gents, Jakes, Jane, John, Kars(e)y, Karzy, K(h)azi, Kleinhuisie, Ladies, Lat(rine), Loo, Necessary, Netty, Office, Outhouse, Privy, Rear(s), Reredorter, Shithouse, Shouse, Siege, Throne, Thunderbox, Toot, Tout, Urinal, Washroom, WC
Lave Lip, Wash
Lavender Aspic, Spike
Lavengro Borrow
Laver Moabite, Nori, Ore-weed
Lavish Barmecidal, Copious, Excessive, Exuberant, Flush, Free, Fulsome, Generous, Lucullan, Lush, Prodigal, Shower, Sumptuous, Wanton, Waste
Law Abingdon, Act, Agrarian, Anti-trust, Ass, Avogadro's, Babo's, Bar, Barratry, Bernoulli's, ➤ BILL, Bode's, Bonar, Boyle's, Bragg's, Brehon, Brewster's, Brocard, Buys Ballot's, Byelaw, Cain, Canon, Capitulary, Case, Chancery, Charles's, Civil, Code, Common, Constitution, Corn, Coulomb's, Cupar, Curie's, Curie-Weiss, Cy pres, Dalton's, Dead-letter, Decree, Decretals, De Morgan's, Deodand, Dharma, Dictate, Digest, Din, Edict, Einstein's, Enact, Fuero, Fundamental, Fuzz, Gay-Lussac's, Gresham's, Grimm's, Haeckel's, Halifax, Hardy-Weinberg, Henry's, Homestead, Hooke's, Hubble's, Hume's, International, Irade, Joule's, Jura, Jure, Jus, Kain, Kashrut(h), Kepler's, Lay, Lien, Lor(d), Losh, Lydford, Lynch, Martial,

Mendel's, Military, Mishna(h), Mishnic, Mosaic, Murphy's, Natural, Newton's, Noahide, Nomothetic, Ohm's, Oral, Ordinance, Pandect, Parkinson's, Pass, Periodic, Planck's, Plebiscite, Poor, Principle, Public, Roman, Rubric, Rule, Salic, Salique, Sharia(h), Sheria(t), Snell's, Sod's, ➤ STATUTE, Sunna, Table, Talmud, Tenet, Thorah, Torah, Tort, Tradition, Ulema, Unwritten, Use, Verner's, Vigilante

Lawlessness Anarchy, Anomie, Anomy, Antinomian, Piratical

Lawmaker, Lawman, Lawyer Alfaqui, Attorney, AV, Barrack room, Barrister, Bencher, BL, Bluebottle, Bramble, Bush, Coke, Counsel, DA, Defence, Doge, Draco, Enactor, Fiscal, Greenbag, Grotius, Hammurabi, Jurisconsult, Jurist, Legist, Mooktar, Moses, MP, Mufti, Mukhtar, Nomothete, Notary, Penang, Pettifoggers, Rabbi, Shirra, Shyster, Silk, Solicitor, Spenlow, Stratopause, Talmudist, Templar, Thesmothete, Vakil, WS

Lawn Cloth, Grass, Green, Linen, Sward, Turf

Lawrence DH, Ross, Shaw, TE

Lawrencium Lr

Lawsuit Case, Cause, Plea, Trover

▶ **Lawyer(s), Lawman** see LAWMAKER

▷ **Lax** may indicate an anagram

Lax(ity) Freedom, Inexact, Laissez-aller, Latitude, Loose, Remiss, ➤ SLACK, Wide

Laxative Aloin, Aperitive, Cascara, Cathartic, Eccoprotic, Elaterin, Elaterium, Glauber's salt, Gregory (powder), ➤ PURGE, Saline, Senna-pod, Taraxacum

Lay(ing), Layman, Laic, Laid Air, Aria, Ballad, Bed, Bet, Blow, Chant, Ditty, Drop, Earthly, Egg, Embed, Fit, Impose, Lied, Lodge, Man, Minstrel, Oat, Oblate, Ode, Outsider, Oviparous, Oviposit, Parabolanus, Secular, Set, Sirvente, ➤ SONG, Sypher, Tertiary, Tribal, Wager, Warp

Layabout Loafer, Lotophagus

Layer(s) Ancona, Appleton, Battery, Cake, Caliche, Cladding, Coating, Crust, D, Depletion, E, Ectoplasm, Ectosarc, Epiblast, Epilimnion, Epithelium, Erathem, Exine, Exocarp, Film, Flake, Ganoin, Gossan, Gozzan, Granum, Heaviside, ➤ HEN, Kennelly(-Heaviside), Kerf, Lamella, Lamina, Lap, Leghorn, Lie, Malpighian, Media, Miocene, Ozone, Pan, Patina, Paviour, Photosphere, Ply, Retina, Scale, Sclerite, Screed, Skin, Sliver, Spathic, Stratify, Stratum, Substratum, Tabular, Tapetum, Tier, Tremie, Trophoblast, Trophoderm, Varve, Vein, Velamen

Lay-off Dismiss, Hedge, Redundance

Lay-out Ante, Design, Fell, Format, Map, Mise, Pattern, Spend, Straucht, Straught, Streak, Streek, Stretch

Laze, Laziness, Lazy (person) Bed-presser, Bummer, Cabbage, Faineant, Hallian, Hallion, Hallyon, Indolent, Inert, Lackadaisical, Languid, Layabout, Lie-abed, Lig(ger), Lime, Lither, Loaf, Lotus-eater, Lusk, Mollusc, Oblomovism, Resty, Sloth, Slouch, Slug(-a-bed), Sluggard, Susan, Sweer, Sweir, Workshy

▷ **Lazily** may indicate an anagram

Lea Grass, Meadow

Leaching Lixivial, Ooze

Lead(er), Leading, Leadership Ag(h)a, Ahead, Akela, Anglesite, Article, Atabeg, Atabek, Ayatollah, Bab, Bluey, Cable, Cade, Calif, Caliph, Capitano, Capo, Captain, Castro, Caudillo, Causal, Centre, Ceruse, Cheer, Chieftain, Chiliarch, Chin, Choragus, Choregus, CO, Condottiere, Conducive, Conduct, Coryphaeus, Demagogue, Dictator, Duce, Dux, Editorial, Escort, Ethnarch, Extension, Figurehead, Floor, Frontrunner, Fugleman, Fu(e)hrer, Gaffer, Garibaldi, Gerent, Graphite, Guide(r), Halter, Hand, Headman, Headmost, Headnote, Hegemony, Heresiarch, Hero, Hetman, Honcho, Idi, Imam, Imaum, Jason, Jefe, Jump, Kabir, Kame, King, Ksar, Leam, Litharge, Livid, Loss, Lost, Lyam, Mahatma, Mahdi, Main, Market, Marshal, Massicot, Masticot, Mayor, Nanak, No 1, Nomarch, Nose, Numero uno, Omrah, Pacemaker, Pacesetter, Padishah, Pb, Pilot, Pioneer, Pit, Plumb(um), Plummet, PM, Precentor, Premier(e), President, Rebbe, Rebecca, Red, Role, Ruler, Sachem, Sagamore, Saturn, Scuddaler, Scudler, Sharif, Sheik(h), Sixer, Skipper, Skudler, Soul, Spearhead, Staple, Star, Sultan, Taoiseach, Tecumseh, Tribune, Tsaddik, Tsaddiq, Tzaddik, Up, Usher, Vaivode, Van(guard), Vanadinite, Va(u)nt, Vaunt-courier, Voivode, Vozhd, Waivode, Warlord, White, Whitechapel, Wulfenite, Zaddik, Zia

▷ **Lead(s), Leaders** may indicate first letters of words

Leaden Flat, Plumbeous, Saturnine

Lead-glance Galena

Leading to Pre

Leaf(y), Leaves Acanthus, Acrospire, Amphigastrium, Amplexicaul, Betel, Blade, Bract, Carpel, Cataphyll, Cladode, Consent, Corolla, Costate, Cotyledon, Drop, Duff, Fig, Finial, Foil, Foliage, Foliar, Folio(se), Folium, Frond, Glume, Gold, Holiday, Induviae, Jugum, K(h)at, Megaphyll, Needle, Nervate, Out, P, Pad, Page, Phyllid, Phyllome, Qat, Repair, Riffle, Rosula, Scale, Sclerophyll, Secede, Sepal, Siri(h), Skip, Spathe, Stipule, Tea, TTL, Valve, Vert, Withdraw

Leafhopper Thrip

Leafless Ebracteate, Scape

Leaflet At(t)ap, Bill, Bracteole, Circular, Dodger, Fly-sheet, Foliolose, Handbill, Pinna, Pinnula, Prophyll, Stipel, ➤ TRACT

League Alliance, Band, Bund, Compact, Delian, Entente, Federation, Gueux, Guild, Hanse(atic), Holy, Ivy, Land, Major, Parasang, Primrose, Redheaded, Rugby, Super, Union, Zollverein, Zupa

Leak(y) Bilge, Drip, Escape, Extravasate, Gizzen, Holed, Holey, Ooze, Pee, Porous, Seepage, Sype, Trickle, Wee, Weep

Leamington Spa

Lean(ing) Abut, Barren, Batter, Bend, Careen, Carneous, Carnose, Griskin, Heel, ➤ INCLINE, Lie, Lig(ge), Minceur, Propend, Rake, Rely, Rest, Scraggy, Scrawny, Skinny, Spare, Stoop, Taste, Tend, Tilt, Tip, Walty

Leander Abydos

Lean-to Skillion

Leap(ing), Leapt Assemblé, Bound, Brise, Cabriole, Caper, Capriole, Cavort, Clear, Croupade, Curvet, Echappé, Entrechat, Falcade, Fishdive, Frisk, Gambado, Gambol, Jeté, Jump, Loup, Luppen, Over, Pronk, Quantum, Sally, Salto, Somersa(u)lt, Somerset, ➤ SPRING, Transilient, Vault, Volte

Leap year Bissextile, Penteteric

Lear Edward, King, Nonsense

Learn(ed), Learner, Learning Beginner, Blue, Bluestocking, Chela, Con, Discover, Distance, Doctor, Don, Erudite, Gather, Get, Glean, Hear, Instrumental, Kond, L, Lear(e), Leir, Lere, Literate, Literati, Literato, Lucubrate, Master, Memorise, Mirza, Mug up, ➤ NOVICE, Pandit, Programmed, Pundit, Pupil, Rookie, Savant, Scan, Scholar, See, Starter, Student, ➤ STUDY, Tiro, Trainee, Tutee, Tyro, Wise

Learning Culture, Discipline, Erudition, Insight, Lore, Opsimathy, Rep, Wit

Lease(-holder) Charter, Farm, Feu, Gavel, Hire, Let, ➤ RENT, Set(t), Tack, Tacksman

Leash Lead, Lyam, Lym(e), Slip, Three, Trash, Triplet

Least Minimum

Leather(y) Bouilli, Bouilly, Box-calf, Buckskin, Buff, Cabretta, Calf, Capeskin, Chamois, Checklaton, Cheverel, Chevrette, Cordovan, Cordwain, Corium, Cowhide, Crispin, Cuir(-bouilli), Deacon, Deerskin, Diphthera, Dogskin, Durant, Hide, Hog-skin, Horsehide, Kid, Kip(-skin), Lamp, Levant, Marocain, Maroquin, Mocha, Morocco, Nap(p)a, Ooze, Oxhide, Patent, Pigskin, Rand, Rawhide, Rexine®, Riem(pie), Roan, Rough-out, Russia, Saffian, Shagreen, Shammy, Sharkskin, Shecklaton, Sheepskin, Skiver, Spetch, Split, Strand, Strap, Suede, Tan, Upper, Wallop, Whitleather, Yuft

Leatherneck Marine, RM

Leave(r), Leavings Abandon, Abiturient, Abscond, Absit, Absquatulate, Acquittal, Adieu, Bequeath, Blessing, Bug, Compassionate, Congé, Congee, Decamp, Depart, Desert, Devisal, Devise, Ditch, Exeat, Exit, Exodus, Forego, Forgo, Forsake, French, Furlough, Garlandage, ➤ GO, Inspan, Ish, Legate, Licence, Maroon, Mizzle, Omit, Orts, Pace, Park, Part, ➤ PERMISSION, Permit, ➤ QUIT, Residue, Resign, Sabbatical, Scapa, Scat, Scram, Shore, Sick, Skedaddle, Skidoo®, Strand, Vacate, Vade, Vamo(o)se

Leaven Barm, Ferment, Yeast

Lebanese, Lebanon Druse, RL

Lecher(ous), Lechery Gate, Goaty, Lascivious, Libertine, Lickerish, Lustful, Profligate, Rake, Roué, Salaciousness, Satirisk, Satyr, Silen, Wolf

Lectern Ambo, Desk, Eagle, Oratory

Lecture(r), Lectures, Lecturing Address, Aristotelian, Creed, Curtain, Dissert(ator), Don, Earful, Erasmus, Expound, Homily, Hulsean, Jaw, Jawbation, Jobe, L, Lector, Prelect, Prone, Rate, Read(er), Rede, Reith, Sententious, ➤ SERMON, Spout, Talk, Teacher, Teach-in, Wigging, Yaff

Ledge Altar, Berm, Channel, Fillet, Linch, Misericord(e), Scarcement, Settle, ➤ SHELF

Ledger Book, Purchase, Register

Lee(s) Dregs, Dunder, Heeltaps, Sediment, Shelter, Ullage

Leech Bleeder, Horse, Medicinal, Parasite, Rhynchobdellida

Leek Allium, Fouat, Fouet, Porraceous, Rocambole

Leer Eliad, Fleer, Oeillade, Ogle

Leeway Drift

Left(-handed), Left-hander, Left-winger Balance, Bolshy, Corrie-fisted, Hie, High, L, Laeotropic, Laevorotation, Larboard, Links, Lorn, Near, Other, Over, Pink, Port, Quit, Rad, Red, Relic, Residuum, Resigned, Sinister, Soc(ialist), Southpaw, Thin, Titoism, Trot, Verso, Vo, Went, West, Wind, Yet

Left-over End, Lave, Oddment, Orra, Remanet, ➤ REMNANT, Waste

Leg(s), Leggings, Leggy, Leg-wear Antigropelo(e)s, Bandy, Breeches, Cabriole, Cannon, Chaparajos, Chaparejos, Chaps, Crural, Crus, Dib, Drumstick, Fine, Gaiter, Galligaskins, Gam(b), Gamash, Gambado, Garter, Gaskin, Gigot, Gramash, Gramosh, Haunch, Jamb, Limb, Long, Member, Myriapod, Oleo, On(side), Peg, Peraeopod, Periopod, Pestle, Pin, Podite, Proleg, Puttees, Pylon, Relay, Section, Shanks, Shanks's pony, Shaps, Shin, Short, Spats, Spatterdash, Spindleshanks, Square, Stage, Stump, Thigh, Tights

Legacy Bequest, Dowry, Entail, Heirloom

Legal(ism), Legally, Legitimate Bencher, Forensic, Halacha, Halaka(h), Halakha, Lawful, Licit, Nomism, Scienter

Legal book Halacha, Halaka(h), Halakha, Talmud

Leg-armour, Leg-covering Cootikin, Cu(i)tikin, Gambado, Jamb(e), Pad

Legate, Legator Ambassador, Consul, Devisor, Emissary, Envoy, Nuncio

Legend Arthurian, Caption, Edda, Fable, Folklore, Motto, Myth, Saga, Story

▷ **Legend** may indicate leg-end, (e.g. foot, talus)

Leger Swindler

Leghorn Livorno

Legible Clear, Lucid, Plain

Legion(ary), Legionnaire Alauda, Army, British, Cohort, Countless, Deserter, Foreign, Geste, Honour, ➤ HOST, Maniple, Many, Throng, Zillions

Legislate, Legislator, Legislature Assemblyman, Decemvir, Decree, MP, Nomothete, Oireachtas, Persian, Solon, Zemstvo

Legitimate Loyal

Legless Amelia, Blotto, Caecilia, Psyche

Leg-pull Chaff, Joke, Rise, Rot

Legume Bean, Guar, Lentil, Pea, Pod, Pulse

Leibniz Monadism

Leigh Amyas

Leisure(ly) Adagio, Ease, Liberty, Moderato, Otium, Respite, Rest, Vacation

Lemon Answer, Cedrate, Citron, Citrus, Smear-dab, Sole, Yellow

Lemur Angwantibo, Aye-aye, Babacoote, Bush-baby, Colugo, Galago, Half-ape, Indri(s), Loris, Macaco, Malmag, Mongoose, ➤ MONKEY, Potto, Ringtail, Sifaka, Tana, Tarsier

Lend Advance, Loan, Prest, Vaunce

Length(y), Lengthen(ing), Lengthwise Archine, Arsheen, Arshin(e), Aune, Barleycorn, Braccio, Cable, Chain, Cubit, Distance, Eke, Ell, ➤ ELONGATE, Endways, Epenthetic, Expand, Extensive, Foot, Furlong, Inch, Ley, Mile, Nail, Passus, Perch, Piece, Plethron, Pole, Prolix, Prolong, Protract, Reach, Remen, Rod, Rope, Slow, Span, Stadium, Toise, Vara, Verbose, Yard

Lenient Clement, Exurable, Lax, Mild, Permissive, Tolerant

Lens Achromatic, Anamorphic, Anastigmat, Aplanatic, Apochromat(ic), Bifocal, Contact, Cornea, Crookes, Crown, Crystalline, Dielectric, Diopter, Dioptre, Diverging, Electron, Eye, Eyeglass, Eye-piece, Fish-eye, Fresnel, Gravitational, Hard, Lentil, Macro, Magnetic, Metallic, Mirror, Optic, Pantoscope, Phacoid, Piano-concave, Piano-convex, Soft, Stanhope, Sunglass, Telephoto, Toric, Trifocal, Wide-angle, Zoom

Lent Careme, Fast, Laetare, Out, Quadragesimal, Term

Lentil(s) D(h)al, Dholl, Ervalenta, Lens, Phacoid, Pulse, Revalenta

Leonora Overture

Leopard Clouded, Leap, Libbard, Ounce, Panther, Pard, Snow, Spots

Leopold Bloom

Leotard Maillot

Leper, Leprosy, Leprous Gehazi, Lazar, Leontiasis, Lionism, Meazel, Mesel, Outcast, Pariah

Lepidopterist Aurelian, Moth-er, Pendleton, Treacler

Leprechaun Elf, Gremlin, Imp

Lesbian Bull dyke, Crunchie, Diesel, Dike, Dyke, Homophile, Lipstick, Sapphist, Tribade

Lesion Cut, Gash, Scar, Serpiginous, Sore

Less(en), Lesser, Lessening Abate, Alaiment, Bate, Contract, Decline, Deplete, Derogate, Dilute, ➤ DWINDLE, Extenuate, Fewer, Junior, Littler, Minus, Reduce, Relax, Remission, Under

Lesson Example, Lear(e), Lection, Leir, Lere, Moral, Object, Period, Sermon, Tutorial

Let (go, off, out), Letting Allow, Cap, Charter, Conacre, Displode, Divulge, Enable, Entitle, Explode, Hire, Impediment, Indulge, Lease, Litten, Loot(en), Luit(en), Lutten, Obstacle, Obstruct, ➤ PERMIT, Rent, Reprieve, Sett, Unhand, Warrant

Let down Abseil, Betray, Lower, Sell, Vail

Lethal Deadly, Fatal, Fell, Mortal

Lethargic, Lethargy Accidie, Apathy, Coma, Drowsy, Hebetude, Inertia, Passive, Sleepy, Sluggish, Stupor, Supine, Torpid

Letter(s) Ache, Aerogam, Aesc, A(y)in, Airgraph, Aleph, Alif, Alpha, Ascender, Bayer, Begging, Beta, Beth, Block, Breve, Cadmean, Caph, Capital, Capon, Casket, Chain, Cheth, Chi, Circular, Col, Collins, Consonant, Cue, Cuneiform, Daled, Daleth, Dead, Delta, Digamma, Digraph, Dominical, Edh, Ef(f), Emma, Encyclical, Ep(isemon), Epistle, Epsilon, Eta, Eth, Fan, Favour, Fraktur, French, Gamma, Gimel, Grapheme,

He, Heth, Initial, Iota, Izzard, Kaph, Kappa, Koppa, Kufic, Labda, Lambda, Lamed(h), Landlady, Landlord, Lessee, Lessor, Literal, Mail, Mail-shot, Majuscule, Mem, Memo, Miniscule, Minuscule, Missive, Monogram, Mu, Note, Notelet, Nu, Nun, Og(h)am, Omega, Omicron, Pahlavi, Paston, Pastoral, Patent, Pehlevi, Phi, Pi, Plosive, Poison-pen, Polyphone, Postbag, Psi, Qoph, Resh, Rho, Rom, Runestave, Sad(h)e, Samekh, Samian, Sampi, San, Scarlet, Screed, Screwtape, Script, See, Shin, Siglum, Sigma, Sign, Sin, Sort, Swash, Tau, Tav, Taw, Teth, Theta, Thorn, Toc, Tsade, Typo, Uncial, Upsilon, Vau, Vav, Versal, Vowel, Waw, Wen, Wyn, Wynn, Xi, Yod(h), Yogh, Ypsilon, Zayin, Zed, Zeta

Lettering Cufic, Kufic

Lettuce Chicon, Corn-salad, Cos, Iceberg, Lactuca, Lamb's, Lollo rosso, Romaine, Salad, Thridace

Leucoma Albugo

Levant(ine) Coptic, Go, Israelite, Jew, Ottamite, Ottomite

Levee Bank, Dyke, Embankment, Party

Level(ler) A, Abney, Abreast, Aclinic, Aim, Base, Break even, Champaign, Countersink, Degree, Dumpy, Echelon, Equal, ➤ EVEN, Extent, Flat, Flush, Grade, O, Par, Plane, Plat(eau), Point, Race, Rank, Rase, Raze, Savanna, Spirit, Split, ➤ SQUARE, Stratum, Strew, Strickle, Tier, Trophic, Water

Lever(age) Backfall, Bell-crank, Crampon, Crowbar, Dues, Gear, Handspike, Jemmy, Joystick, Key, Landsturm, Peav(e)y, Prise, Prize, Pry, Purchase, Tappet, Tiller, Treadle, Tremolo arm, Trigger, Typebar

Leviathan Whale

Levitate Float, Hover, Rise

Levity Flippancy, Glee, Humour, Jollity

Levy Impose, Imposition, Leave, Militia, Octroi, Raise, Scutage, Talliate, Tax, Tithe

Lewd(ness) Bawdy, Blue, Impure, Libidinous, Lubricity, Obscene, Priapism, Prurient, Silen(us), Unclean

Lewis Carroll, Tenon

Lexicographer, Lexicon Compiler, Craigie, Drudge, Etymologist, Florio, Fowler, Grove, Johnson(ian), Larousse, Liddell, Murray, OED, Thesaurus, Vocabulist, Webster, Words-man

Liability, Liable Anme, Apt, Debt, Incur, Limited, Open, Prone, Subject, Susceptible

Liaison Affair, Contact, Link

Liana Guarana

Libel(lous) Defamatory, Malign, Slander, Smear, Sully, Vilify

Liberal(ity) Abundant, Adullamites, Ample, Besant, Bounteous, Bountiful, Breadth, Bright, Broad, Free(hander), Free-hearted, ➤ GENEROUS, Giver, Grey, Grimond, Handsome, Indulgent, L, Largesse, Lavish, Octobrist, Open, ➤ PROFUSE, Rad(ical), Samuelite, Simonite, Steel, Tolerant, Trivium, Unstinted, Verlig, Verligte, Whig

Liberate(d), Liberation, Liberator Bolivar, Deliver, Emancipate, Fatah, ➤ FREE, Inkatha, Intolerant, Messiah, PLO, Release, Save, Sucre, Unfetter, UNITA, Women's

Liberian Kroo, Kru

Libertarian, Libertine Chartered, Corinthian, Debauchee, Laxist, Lecher, Lothario, Lovelace, Rake, Rip, Roué, Wencher, Wolf

Liberty Bail, Discretion, Franchise, Freedom, Hall, Mill, Sauce

Library Bibliothecary, BL, Bodleian, Bookmobile, Cottonian, Harleian, Laurentian, Lending, Mazarin, Public, Radcliffe, Reference, Tauchnitz

Librettist Boito, Gilbert, Lyricist

▶ **Lice** see LOUSE

Licence, License Abandon, Allow, Authorisation, Carnet, Charter, Dispensation, Driving, Enable, Exequatur, Fling, Franchise, Free(dom), Gale, Imprimatur, Indult, ➤ LATITUDE, Let, Passport, ➤ PERMIT, Poetic, Pratique, Provisional, Rope, Slang, Special

Licentious Artistic, Corinthian, Debauchee, Hot, Immoral, Large, Lax, Liberal, Loose, Prurient, Ribald, Sensual, Wanton

Lichen Apothecia, Archil, Corkir, Crotal, Crottle, Epiphyte, Epiphytic, Graphis, Korkir, Lecanora, Litmus, Orchel, Orchil(la), Orcine, Orseille, Parella, Parelle, Roccella, Rock tripe, Stone-rag, Stone-raw, Tree-moss, Usnea, Wartwort

Lick(ing) Bat, Beat, Deer, Lambent, Lap, Leather, Salt, Slake, Speed, Whip

▶ **Licorice** see LIQUORICE

Lid Cover, Hat, Kid, Maximum, Opercula, Screwtop, Twist-off

Liddell Alice

Lido Beach, Pool

Lie(s), Liar, Lying Abed, Accubation, Accumbent, Ananias, Bam, Bare-faced, Bask, Billy, Bounce(r), Braide, Cau(l)ker, Cellier, Clipe, Clype, Contour, Couchant, Cracker, Cram(mer), Cretism, Cumbent, Deception, Decubitous, Decumbent, Direct, Doggo, Fable, False(r), Falsehood, Falsify, Falsity, Fib, Figment, Flam, Gag, Gonk, Incumbent, Invention, Inveracity, Kip, Lair, Leasing, Lee(ar), Lig(ge), Lurk, Mythomania, Obreption, Oner, Perjury, Plumper, Porky, Porky (pie), Procumbent, Prone, Prostrate, Pseudologia, Recline, Recumbent, Repent, Reptant, Ride, Romance(r), Sham, Sleep, Strapper, Stretcher, Supine, Tale, Tappice, Tar(r)adiddle, Thumper, Tissue, Try, Untruth, Whid, White, Whopper, Yanker

Lien Mortgage, Title

Lieu Locus, Place

Lieutenant Flag, Loot, Lt, No 1, Sub(altern)

Life Age, Animation, Being, Bio, Biog(raphy), Brio, Clerihew, Esse, Existence, Good, Heart, Plasma, Span, Spirit, Still, Subsistence, Time, Vita, Zoe

Life-blood Essence, Lethee

Lifeboat Ark

Life-cell Energid

Life-cycle Redia

Life-force Ch'i, Chi, Qi

Lifeguard Cheesemonger

Lifeless(ness) Abiosis, Algidity, Amort, Arid, Azoic, Barren, Cauldrife, ➤ DEAD, Dull, Flat, Inanimate, Inert, Log, Mineral, Possum, Sterile, Stonen, Wooden

Lifelike Breathing, Speaking

Lifeline Umbilicus

Life-rent Usufruct

Life-saver Preserver, Raft

Lift(ed), Lifter, Lifting Arayse, Arsis, Attollent, Bone, Cable-car, Camel, Chair, Cly, Copy, Crane, Davit, Dead, Dumb waiter, Elate, Elevator, Enhance, Extol, Filch, Fillip, Heave, Heeze, Heezie, Heft, Heist, Hitch, Hoise, Hoist, Hove, Jack, Jigger, Kleptomania, Leaven, Lefte, Lever, Lewis, Nab, Nap, Paternoster, Pilfer, Pulley, ➤ RAISE, Ride, Scoop, Ski, Sky, Snatch, Steal, T-bar, Thumb, Up, Winch, Windlass

Ligament Fr(a)enum, Suspensory, Tendon, Urachus

Ligature Aesc, Bandage, Bind

Light(en), Lighting, Lights Aerate, Airy, Albedo, Ale, Alow, Amber, Ancient, Ans(wer), Arc, Aurora, Batswing, Beacon, Beam, Bengal, Bezel, Bleach, Brake, Bude, Bulb, Candle, Cannel, Casement, Chiaroscuro, Cierge, Clue, Courtesy, Day, Dewali, Direct, Diwali, Dream-hole, Drummond, Earth-shine, Eddystone, Electrolier, Ethereal, Fairy, Fall, Fan, Fantastic, Fastnet, Fidibus, Fill, Fire, Flambeau, Flame, Flare, Flax(y), Flicker, Flippant, Flit(t), Flood, Fog (lamp), Frothy, Fuffy, Gegenschein, Gleam, Glim(mer), Glow, Gossamer, Green, Guiding, Gurney, Haggis, Hazard, Head, Ignite, Illum(in)e, Incandescence, Indirect, Inner, Irradiate, Junior, Kindle, Klieg, Lamp, Land, Lantern, Lanthorn, Laser, Leading, Leerie, Leggiero, Lime, Link, Loadstar, Lobuli, Lodestar, Lozen, Lucarne, Lucigen, Luminaire, Lumine, Luminescence, Luminous, Lustre, Lux, Match, Mercurial, Merry-dancers, Mithra(s), Moon, Naphtha, Neon, Nit, Northern, Od(yl), Offal, Optics, Pale, Pane, Phosphene, Phosphorescence, Phot, Photon, Pilot, Portable, Producer-gas, Red, Relume, Riding, Rocket, Rush, Satori, Sea-dog, Search, Shy, Spill, Spot, Spry, Strip, Strobe, Subtle, Sun, Suttle, Svelte, Tail, Taper, Taps, Tind, Tine, Torch, Torchère, Touchpaper, Traffic, Trivial, Ultraviolet, Unchaste, Unoppressive, UV, Ver(e)y, Vesta, Windock, Window, Winnock, Zodiacal

▷ **Light** may indicate an anagram

Lighter Barge, Birlinn, Casco, Gas-poker, Keel, Linstock, Lunt, Match, Pontoon, Pra(a)m, Spill, Taper

Lighthouse Beacon, Caisson, Eddystone, Fanal, Fastnet, Phare, Pharos, Signal

Lightless Aphotic, Dark, Obscure, Unlit

Lightness Buoyancy, Galant, Levity, Pallor

Lightning Ball, Catequil, Eclair, Enfouldered, Forked, Fulmination, Levin, Sheet, Thunderbolt, Wildfire, Zigzag

Lightship Nore

Lightweight Oz, Trivial

Lignite Jet, Surtarbrand, Surturbrand

Like(ness), Liking As, Broo, Care, Corpse, Dig, Duplicate, Effigy, Eg, Egal, Enjoy, Equal, Fancy, Fellow, Lich, Palate, Parallel, Peas, Penchant, Please, Predilection, Semblant, Shine, Similar, Simile, Sort, Speaking, Tiki

Likely Apt, Fair, Odds-on, On, Plausible, Possible, Probable, Probit, Prone

Likewise Also, Do, Eke, Item, So, Too

Lilac Laylock, Mauve, Pipe-tree, Syringa

Lilliputian Minute

Lilt Swing

Lily African, Agapanthus, Aloe, Amaryllis, Annunciation, Arum, Asphodel, Aspidistra, Belladonna, Calla, Camas(h), Camass, Canada, Candock, Chincherinchee, Colchicum, Colocasia, Convallaria, Corn, Crinum, Dale, Day, Easter, Elaine, Fawn, Fleur de lys, Fritillary, Galtonia, Haemanthus, Hemerocallis, Herb-paris, Jacob's, Kniphofia, Laguna, Lent, Leopard, Lote, Lotus, Madonna, Mariposa, Martagon, Moorva, Mount Cook, Nelumbo, Nenuphar, Nerine, Nuphar, Padma, Phormium, Plantain, Quamash, Regal, Richardia, Sarsa, Scilla, Sego, Skunk cabbage, Smilax, Solomon's seal, Spider, Star of Bethlehem, Stone, Sword, Tiger, Trillium, Tritoma, Turk's cap, Victoria, Water, Yucca, Zephyr

Lily-maid Elaine

Lima Sugar bean

Limb Arm, Bough, Branch, Crural, Exapod, Flipper, Hindleg, Imp, Leg, Leg-end, Member, Proleg, Ramus, Scion, Shin, Spald, Spall, Spaul(d), Wing

Limbless Amelia

Limbo Bardo, Isolation

Lime Bass(wood), Beton, Calc, Lind(en), Malm, Mortar, Slaked, Soda, Teil, Tilia, Trap, Viscum, Whitewash

Limerick Doggerel, Twiner, Verse

Limestone Calp, Ca(u)m, Clint, Coquina, Cornbrash, Karst, Kentish rag, Kunkar, Kunkur, Oolite, Pisolite, Rottenstone, Scaglia, Travertine

Limey Rooinek

Limit(ation), Limited, Limiting Ambit, Bind, Border, Borné, Bound, Bourn(e), Brink, Cap, Ceiling, Chandrasekhar, Circumscribe, Climax, Compass, Confine, Deadline, Define, Demark, Determine, Earshot, Edge, End, Entail, Esoteric, ➤ EXTENT, Extreme, Finite, Frontier, Gate, Goal, Gole, Impound, Induciae, Insular, Limes, Lynchet, March, Meare, Mete, Nth, Outedge, Pale, Parameter, Perimeter, Periphery, Predetermine, Qualify, Range, Rate-cap, Ration, Reservation, Restrict, Rim, Roche, Roof, Scant, Shoestring, Sky, Speed, Stint, String, Sumptuary, Tail(lie), Tailye, Tailzie, Term(inus), Tether, Three-mile, Threshold, Thule, Tie, Time, Tropic, Utmost, Utter, Verge

▷ **Limit** may indicate 'surrounding'

Limner RA

Limousine Daimler, Rolls, Zil

Limp Claudication, Dot, Droopy, Flabby, Flaccid, Flimsy, Floppy, Hilch, Hirple, Hitch, Hobble, Hop, Lifeless, Spancel, Tangle
Limpet Patella, Slipper, Streptoneura
Limpid Clear, Lucid, Pure
Linch Terrace
Lincoln(shire) Abe, Poacher
Linden Baucis, Lime, Tilia
Line(d), Lines, Lining Abreast, Aclinic, Agate, Agonic, Allan, Anacreontic, ➤ ANCESTRY, Anent, Angle, Apothem, Arew, Asclepiadean, Assembly, Asymptote, Axis, Babbitt, Bar, Battle, Baulk, Becket, Bikini, Bluebell, Bombast, Bottom, Boundary, BR, Brail, Branch, Bread, Bush, Canal, Carolingian, Casing, Ceil, Ceriph, Chord, Ciel, Coffle, Column, Contour, Cord(on), Coseismal, Course, Crease, Crowsfoot, Curve, Cushion, Dancette, Date, Datum, Delay, Descent, Diagonal, Diameter, Directrix, Distaff, Dotted, Doublure, Downrigger, Dress, Dynasty, Earing, E-la-mi, Encase, Equator, Faint, Fall(s), Fault, Feint, Fess(e), Fettle, File, Finishing, Firing, Firn, Flex, Fraunhofer, Frontier, Frost, Furr(ow), Geodesic, Gimp, Giron, Graph, Gridiron, Gymp, Gyron, Hachure, Hard, Hatching, Hawser, Heptameter, Hexameter, Hexapody, Hindenburg, Hockey, Hogscore, Hot, House, Impot, Inbounds, Incase, Interfluve, Intima, Isallobar, Isentrope, Isobar, Isobath, Isobront, Isocheim, Isochime, Isoclude, Isocryme, Isogloss, Isogonal, Isohel, Isohyet, Isolex, Isopach(yte), Isophone, Isopleth, Isotach, Isothere, Isotherm, Knittle, L, Lane, Lap, Lariat, Latitude, Lead, Leash, Le(d)ger, Ley, Lie, Ling, LMS, Load, Log, Longitude, Lubber, Lye, Macron, Maginot, Main, Mark, Marriage, Mason-Dixon, Median, Meridian, Mesal, Miurus, Monorail, Multiplet, Nazca, Nidation, Noose, Norsel, Northern, Oche, Octastichon, Ode, Og(h)am, Omentum, Onedin, Ordinate, Painter, Parallel, Parameter, Party, Paternoster, Path, Pencil, Phalanx, Picket, Pinstripe, Plimsoll, Plumb, Poetastery, Police, Popping-crease, Poverty, Product(ion), Profession, Queue, Race, Radial, Radius, Rail, Rank, Raster, Ratlin(e), Ratling, Rattlin, Ray, Retinue, Rew, Rhumb, Ripcord, Rope, Route, Row, Rugose, Rugous, Rule, Ry, Sarking, Score, Script, Secant, Serif, Seriph, Siding, Siegfried, Sield, Slur, Snood, Soft, Solidus, Spectral, Spunyarn, SR, Staff, Stance, Stanza, Starting, Static, Stave, Stean, Steen, Stein, Stem, Stich(os), Stock, Streak, Striate, String, Subtense, Swifter, Syzygy, T(h)alweg, Tangent, Teagle, Terminator, Thread, Throwaway, Timber, Trade, Transoceanic, Transversal, Trimeter, Tropic, Trunk, Tudor, Variety, Verse, Vinculum, Virgule, Wad, Wallace's, Washing, Water(shed), Widow, Wire, Wrinkle, Yellow, Zollner's
Lineage Ancestry, Descent, Extraction, Pedigree
Linen Amice, Amis, Barb, Bed, Byssus, Cambric, Crash, Damask, Dornick, Dowlas, Ecru, Harn, Huckaback, Inkle, Lawn, Lint, Lockram, Moygashel, Napery, Percale, Seersucker, Sendal, Silesia, Toile
Liner Artist, Bin-bag, RMS, Ship, Sleeve, Steamer, Steen, Titanic
Linesman Parodist, ➤ POET, Touch-judge
Linger Dawdle, Dwell, Hang, Hove(r), Lag, ➤ LOITER, Straggle, Tarry, Tie
Lingerie Bra, Drawers, Undies

Lingo Argot, Cant, Jargon, Speech

Linguist(ics) Glottic, Philological, Phonemics, Polyglot, Semantics, Stylistics, Taxeme

Liniment Balm, Carron-oil, Embrocation, Ointment, Opodeldoc, Salve

Link(ing), Links Associate, Between, Bond, Bridge, Chain, Cleek, Colligate, Concatenation, Copula, Couple, Desmid, Drag, Ess, Flambeau, Hookup, Hotline, Incatenation, Interface, Internet, Intertwine, Karabiner, Krab, Liaise, Machair, Missing, Nexus, Pons, Preposition, Relate, Tead(e), ➤ TIE, Tie-in, Tie-line, Torch, Unite, Yoke

Linkman Lamplighter, Mediator

Linnet Finch, Twite

Lint Charpie

Lintel Summer, Transom

Lion(ess) Androcles, Aphid, Chindit, Elsa, Glitterati, Hero, Leo, Maned, Nemean, Opinicus, Personage, Pride, Simba

Lionel Trilling

Lion-tamer Dan(iel)

Lip(py), Lips Cheek, Fat, Fipple, Flews, Helmet, Jib, Labellum, Labiate, Labret, Labrum, Ligula, Muffle, ➤ RIM, Rubies, Sass, Sauce, Slack-jaw, Submentum

Liquefy Dissolve, Fuse, Melt

Liqueur, Liquor Ale, Amaretto, Anise, Anisette, Bree, Brew, Broo, Broth, Calvados, Chartreuse, Chasse, Chicha, Cointreau®, Creature, Crème, Crème de menthe, Curaçao, Drambuie®, Eau des creoles, Elixir, Enzian, Feni, Fenny, Fustian, Geropiga, Hogan, Hogan-mogen, Hooch, Jungle juice, Kaoliang, Kir, Kirschwasser, Kirsh(wasser), Kummel, Lager, Lap, Malt, Maraschino, Mastic, Metheglin, Mickey Finn, Mirabelle, Mobbie, Mobby, Noyau, Oedema, Ooze, Ouzo, Pastis, Persico, Potation, Pousse-café, Prunelle, Rakee, Raki, Ratafia, Rotgut, Rum, Sambuca, Samshoo, Schnapps, Shypoo, Skink, Stingo, Stock, Stout, Strega®, Strunt, Stuff, Supermaculum, Tape, Taplash, Tequila, Tiff, Van der Hum, White lightning, Wine, Witblits, Wort

Liquid(ate), Liquidity, Liquids, Liquefaction Acetal, Amortise, Annihilate, Apprize, Azeotrope, Bittern, Bouillon, Bromine, Butanal, Butanol, Butyraldehide, Butyrin, Cacodyl, Cadaverine, Cash, Chloramine, Cinerin, Clyster, Court-bouillon, Creosol, Decoction, Dope, Eluate, Erase, Ethanol, Ether, Eucalyptol, Eugenol, Fluid, Fural, Furfural, Furol, Jaw, Lewisite, Lye, Massacre, Mess, Minim, Mouillé, Picamar, Pipe, Potion, Protoplasm, Ptisan, Serum, Solution, Solvent, Syrup, Terebene, Thixotropy, Titer, Titre, Tuberculin, Tusche, Ullage, Verjuice, Whey, Wort

Liquorice Indian, Jequirity, Nail, Nail-rod, Pomfret, Pontefract-cake, Sugarallie, Sugarally

Lis Iris, Lily

Lisa Mona

Lisp(er) Ephraimite, Sibilance

Lissom(e) Agile, Lithe, Nimble, Svelte

▷ **List** may indicate 'listen'

List(s), Listing Active, Agenda, Antibarbarus, Appendix, Army, Atilt, Barocco, Barrace, Bead-roll, Canon, Cant, Catalog(ue), Categorise, Catelog, Civil, Class, Entry, Enumerate, Glossary, Hark, Hearken, Heel, Honours, Index, Inventory, Itemise, Lean, Leet, Line-up, Mailing, Navy, Notitia, Panel, Register, Repertoire, Roll, Roon, Roster, Rota, Rund, Schedule, Short, Sick, Slate, Slope, Strip, Syllabus (of Errors), Table, Tariff, Ticket, Tilt, Timetable, Tip, Transfer, Waiting, Waybill

Listen(er) Attend, Auditor, Auscultate, Ear, Eavesdropper, Gobemouche, Hark, ➤ HEED, Lithe, Lug, Monitor, Oyez, Wire-tap

▷ **Listen to** may indicate a word sounding like another

Listless(ness) Abulia, Accidie, Acedia, Apathetic, Atony, Dawney, Indolent, Lackadaisical, Languor, Mooning, Mope, Mopus, Sloth, Thowless, Torpor, Waff

Lit Alight, Landed

▷ **Lit** may indicate an anagram

Litany Eirenicon

Literal(ly), Literal sense Etymon, Misprint, Simply, Verbatim

Literary Academic, Bas bleu, Booksie, Erudite, Lettered

Literary girls Althea, Jenny, Maud, Pippa

Literature Belles lettres, Corpus, Fiction, Gongorism, Midrash, Page, Picaresque, Prose, Responsa, Wisdom

Lithe Flexible, Limber, Pliant, Souple, ➤ SUPPLE, Svelte, Willowy

Lithium Li

Litigant Barrator, John-a-Nokes, John-a-Stiles, John Doe, Party, Richard Roe, Suer, Suitor

Litmus Indicator, Lacmus

Litre L

Litter Bed, Brancard, Brood, Cacolet, Cubs, Debris, Doolie, Emu-bob, Farrow, Jampan, Kago, Kajawah, Kindle, Mahmal, Nest, Norimon, Palankeen, Palanquin, Palkee, Palki, Pup, ➤ REFUSE, Scrap, Sedan, Stretcher, Team

Little Bagatelle, Billee, Brief, Chota, Curn, Dorrit, Drib, Drop, Fewtrils, Insect, Iota, John, Jot, Leet, Lilliputian, Limited, Lite, Lyte, Mini, Miniscule, Minnow, Minuscule, ➤ MINUTE, Modicum, Morceau, Nell, Paltry, Paucity, Petite, Pink, Scant, Scut, Shade, Shoestring, Shred, Shrimp, Slight, Sma', ➤ SMALL, Smattering, Smidge(o)n, Smidgin, Some, Soupçon, Spot, Tad, Tich, Tine, Titch, Touch, Tyne, Vestige, Wee, Weedy, Whit, Women

Liturgical, Liturgy Doxology, Rite, Versicle

Live(d), Liveliness, Lively, Lives Active, Alert, Allegretto, Allegro, Animated, Animation, Animato, AV, Awake, Be, Birkie, Breezy, Brio, Brisk, Cant(y), Capriccio(so), Cheery, Chipper, Chirpy, Cohabit, Con moto, Crouse, Durante vita, ➤ DWELL, Ebullient, Entrain, Exist, Feisty, Frisky, Galliard, Gay, Giocoso, Grig, Hang-out, Hard, Is, Jazz, Kedge, Lad, Lead, Mercurial, Merry, Outgo, Pacey, Peart, Pep, Piert, Quicksilver, Rackety, Racy, Reside, Rousing, Saut, Scherzo, Skittish, Spiritoso, Sprack, Spry,

Spunky, Vibrant, Vigoroso, Vital, Vitality, Vivace, Vivo, ➤ VOLATILE, Vyvyan, Zappy, Zoe

➤ **Livelihood** see LIVING

Liver(ish) Foie gras, Hepar, Hepatic(al), Porta, Puce, Resident, Tomalley

Liverpool, Liverpudlian Scouse

Liverwort Gemma-cup, Hepatica, Riccia

Livery(man) Ermine, Flunkeydom, Goldsmith, Skinner, Tiger, Uniform

Livid Blae, Bruised, ➤ FURIOUS, Pale

Living Advowson, Benefice, Biont, Bread, Canonry, Crust, Glebe, Inquiline, Lodging, Quick, Resident, Simony, Subsistence, Symbiotic, Vicarage, Vital

Livingstone Doctor, Ken

Liza, Lizzie Bess, Betty, Flivver, Hexam, Tin

Lizard Abas, Agama, Amphisboena, Anguis, Anole, Basilisk, Bearded, Blindworm, Blue-tongued, Brontosaurus, Chameleon, Chuckwalla, Dinosaur, Draco, Eft, Evet, Frilled, Galliwasp, Gecko(ne), Gila, Gila monster, Glass snake, Goanna, Guana, Hatteria, Hellbender, Horned, Iguana, Jew, Kabaragoya, Komodo (dragon), Lacerta, Legua(a)n, Lounge, Mastigure, Menopome, Moloch, Monitor, Mosasaur(us), Newt, Perentie, Perenty, Reptile, Sand, Sauria, Scincoid, Seps, Skink, Slow-worm, Snake, Stellio(n), Sungazer, Tegu(exin), Tokay, Tuatara, Tuatera, Varan, Wall, Whiptail, Worm, Worral, Worrel, Zandoli

Llama Alpaca, Alpaco, Guanaco, Paco, Vicuna

Load(ed), Loader Accommodation, Affluent, Ballast, Boot-strap, Burden, Cargo, Charge, Cobblers, Dead weight, Dope, Drunk, Fardel, Fother, Freight, Fulham, Full, Gestant, Heap, Input, Jag, Lade, Lard, Last, Live, Onus, Pack, Pay, Prime, Rich, Seam, Shipment, Some, Surcharge, ➤ TIGHT, Tod, Weight, Wharfinger

Loaf(er), Loaves Baguette, Baton, Bloomer, Bludge, Brick, Bum, Bu(r)ster, Cad, Cob, Coburg, Cottage, Farmhouse, Hawm, Hoe-cake, Idle, ➤ LAZE, Long tin, Lusk, Manchet, Miche, Mouch, Pan(h)agia, Roll, Roti, Shewbread, Showbread, Slosh, Split tin, Sugar, Tin, Vantage, Yob

Loam Clay, Loess, Loss, Malm

Loan(s) Advance, Balloon, Benevolence, Bottomry, Bridging, Debenture, Imprest, Lane, Mutuum, Omnium, Out, Prest, Respondentia, Roll-over, Start-up, Sub

Loathe, Loathing, Loathsome Abhor(rent), Abominate, Carrion, Detest, Hate, Nauseate, Scunner, Ug(h)

Lob Loft, Sky, Underarm

Lobby Demo, Entry, Foyer, Gun, Hall, Press, Urge

Lobe(d) Anisocercal, Fluke, Frontal, Jugum, Lacinia, Lap, Occipital, Palmate, Parietal, Pinnule, Runcinate, Uvula, Vermis

Lobster Cock, Crawfish, Crayfish, Crustacean, Decapoda, Langouste, Norway, Pot, Scampo, Spiny, Thermidor, Tomalley

Local(ity) Area, Endemic, Home, Inn, Landlord, Native, Near, Nearby, Neighbourhood, Number, Parochial, Pub, Regional, Resident, Tavern, Topical, Vicinal

▷ **Local** may indicate a dialect word

Locale Scene, Site

Locate Connect, Find, Fix, Lay, Pinpoint, Plant, Site, Spot

Location Address, Milieu, Place, Recess, Site, Situation, Sofar, Ubiety, Website, Zone

Loch, Lough Ashie, Awe, Derg, Earn, Eil, Erne, Etive, Fine, Gare, Garten, Holy, Hourn, Katrine, ➤ LAKE, Larne, Leven, Linnhe, Lomond, Long, Moidart, Morar, More, Nakeel, Neagh, Ness, Rannoch, Ryan, Shiel, Strangford, Tay, Torridon

Lock(er), Locks, Lock up Bar, Bolt, Canal, Chubb®, Clinch, Combination, Cowlick, Curlicue, Davy Jones, Deadbolt, Detent, Drop, Fastener, Foretop, Gate, Haffet, Haffit, Handcuff, Hasp, Intern, Key, Latch, Lazaretto, Mortise, Percussion, Quiff, Ragbolt, Ringlet, Sasse, Scalp, Scissors, ➤ SECURE, Sluice, Snap, Spring, Strand, Tag, Talon, Time, Trap, Tress, Tuft, Villus, Ward, Wheel, Wrestle, Yale®

Locket Lucy

Lockjaw Tetanus, Trismus

Locksmith Garret-master, Hairdresser

Locomotive Banker, Bogie, Bul(l)gine, Engine, Iron horse, Mobile, Rocket, Steamer, Train

Locum Deputy, Relief, Stopgap

Locus Centrode, Horopter, Lemniscate, Place, Spot

Locust, Locust tree Anime, Carob, Cicada, Hopper, Nymph, Robinia, Seventeen-year, Voetganger

Lode Comstock, Lodge, Reef, Vein

Lodestone Magnes, Magnet

Lodge(r) Billet, Board(er), Box, Cosher, Deposit, Dig, Doss, Entertain, Freemason, Grange, Guest, Harbour, Host, Inmate, Layer, Lie, Masonic, Nest, Orange, Parasite, PG, Quarter, Rancho, Room(er), Stay, Storehouse, Stow, Tenant, Tepee, Wigwam

Lodging(s) Abode, B and B, Chummage, Dharms(h)ala, Digs, Dosshouse, Ferm, Grange, Grove, Hostel, Inquiline, Kip, Minshuku, Pad, Pension, Pied-à-terre, Quarters, Resiant, Rooms, Singleen, YHA

Loft(iness), Lofty Aerial, Airy, Arrogant, Attic, Celsitude, Chip, Garret, Grand, Haymow, High, Jube, Lordly, Magniloquent, Noble, Rarefied, Rigging, Rood, Roost, Tallat, Tallet, Tallot

Log Billet, Black box, Cabin, Chock, Diarise, Diary, Hack, Mantissa, Nap(i)erian, Neper, Patent, ➤ RECORD, Stock, Yule

Logarithm Nap(i)erian, Natural

Logic(al) Alethic, Aristotelian, Chop, Dialectic(s), Doxastic, Epistemics, Modal, Organon, Ramism, Rational(e), Reason, Sequacious, Sorites, Symbolic, Trivium

Loin(s) Flank, Inguinal, Lungie, Lunyie, Reins

Loincloth Dhoti, Lungi, Waist-cloth

Loiter(ing) Dally, Dare, Dawdle, Dilatory, Dilly-dally, Idle, Lag, Lallygag, Leng, Lime, ➤ LINGER, Mooch, Mouch, Potter, Saunter, Scamp, Suss, Tarry

Lola Dolores

Loll Hawm, Lounge, Sprawl

Lollipop Lulibub

Lolly Money, Sweetmeat

London(er) 'Arry, Big Smoke, Cockaigne, Cockney, Co(c)kayne, East-ender, Flat-cap, Jack, Roseland, Smoke, Town, Troynovant, Wen

London pride None-so-pretty

Lone(r), Lonely Remote, Rogue, Secluded, Sole, Solitary, Unked, Unket, Unkid

Long(er), Longing, Longs Ache, Aitch, Ake, Appetent, Aspire, Brame, Covet, Desire, Die, Earn, Erne, Far, Greed, Green, Grein, ➤ HANKER, Huey, Hunger, Island, Itch, L, Lanky, Large, Lengthy, Longa, Lust, Macron, Miss, More, ➤ NO LONGER, Nostalgia, Option, Pant, Parsec, ➤ PINE, Prolix, Side, Sigh, Tall, Thirst, Trews, Weary, Wish, Wist, Yearn, Yen

Long-eared Spicate

Longitude Celestial, Meridian

Long-lashed Mastigophora(n)

Long live(d) Banzai, Macrobian, Viva, Zindabad

Longshoreman Hobbler, Hoveller, Wharfinger

Long-suffering Job, Patient, Stoical

Long-tailed Macrural

Long-winded Prolix, Verbose

Loo Ajax, Bog, Can, Chapel, Dike, Game, Gents, Jakes, John, Privy, Toilet

Look Air, Aspect, Behold, Belgard, Bonne-mine, Busk, Butcher's, Clock, Close-up, Crane, Daggers, Decko, Deek, Dekko, Ecce, Ecco, Expression, Eye, Face, Facies, Gander, Gawp, Gaze, Geek, Glance, Glare, Gledge, Glimpse, Goggle, Grin, Hallo, Hangdog, Hey, Iliad, Inspect, La, Lo, Mien, New, Ogle, Peek, Peep, Prospect, Ray, Recce, Refer, ➤ REGARD, Scan, Scrutinise, Search, See, Seek, Shade, Shufti, Shufty, Spy, Squint, Squiz, Toot, V, Vista

Look-out (man) Cockatoo, Crow's nest, Huer, Mirador, Sangar, Sentry, Sungar, Toot(er), Watch, Watchtower

▷ **Look silly** may indicate an anagram

Loom Beamer, Dobby, Emerge, Impend, Jacquard, Lathe, Menace, Picker, Temple, Threaten, Tower

Loon Diver

Loop(ed), Loophole, Loopy Becket, Bight, Billabong, Bouclé, Carriage, Chink, Closed, Coil, Eyelet, Eyesplice, Fake, Frog, Frontlet, Grom(m)et, Grummet, Hank, Henie's, Hysteresis, Infinite, Kink, Knop, Lasket, Lug, Noose, Oillet, Parral, Parrel, Pearl(-edge), Picot, Purl, Staple, Stirrup, Terry, Toe, Twist

Loos Anita

Loose(n), Loose woman Absolve, Abstrict, Afloat, Anonyma, Baggage, Bail, Besom, Bike, Chippie, Chippy, Cocotte, Demi-mondaine, Demirep, Desultory, Dissolute, Dissolve, Doxy, Draggletail, Dratchell, Drazel, Emit,

Flirt-gill, Floosie, Floozie, Floozy, Floppy, Franion, Free, Gangling, Gay, Hussy, Insecure, Jade, Jezebel, Lax, Loast, Mob, Mort, Pinnace, Profligate, Quail, Ramp, ➤ RELAX, Sandy, Scrubber, Slag, Slapper, Streel, Tart, Tramp, Trull, Unhasp, Unhitch, Unlace, Unpin, Unreined, Unscrew, Untie, Vague, Wappend, Whore

Loot Boodle, Booty, Cragh, Creach, Foray, Haul, Mainour, Peel, Pluck, ➤ PLUNDER, Ransack, Rape, Reave, Rieve, Rob, Sack, Smug, Spoils, Spoliate, Swag, Treasure, Waif

Lop Behead, Clop, Curtail, Detruncate, Droop, Shroud, Sned, Trash

Lope Stride

Loquacious Chatty, Gabby, Rambling

Lord(s), Lordship Adonai, Arrogant, Boss, Byron, Dieu, Domineer, Dominical, Duc, Earl, Elgin, Gad, God, Haw-haw, Herr, Imperious, Jim, Justice, Kami, Kitchener, Landgrave, Law, Ld, Liege, Lonsdale, Losh, Lud, Misrule, Mynheer, Naik, Oda Nobunaga, Omrah, Ordinary, Ormazd, Ormuzd, Peer, Seigneur, Seignior, Shaftesbury, Sire, Spiritual, Taverner, Temporal, Tuan, Ullin

Lords and ladies Wake-robin

Lore Cab(b)ala, Edda, Lair, Lare, Riem, Upanis(h)ad

Lorelei Siren

Lorgnette Starers

Lorry Artic(ulated), Camion, Crummy, Drag, Flatbed, Juggernaut, Low-loader, Rig, Tipper, Tonner, ➤ TRUCK, Wagon

Lose(r) Also-ran, Decrease, Drop, Elude, Forfeit, Leese, Misère, Mislay, Misplace, Nowhere, Tank, Throw, Tine(r), Tyne, Underdog, Unsuccessful, Waste, Weeper

Loss, Lost Anosmia, Aphesis, Aphonia, Apocope, Apraxia, Astray, Attainder, Boohai, Chord, Cost, Dead, Decrease, Depreciation, Detriment, Disadvantage, Elision, Extinction, Foredamned, Forfeited, Forgotten, Forlorn, Gone, Lore, Lorn, Lurch, Missing, Omission, Outage, Pentimento, Perdition, Perdu, Perished, Preoccupied, Privation, Psilosis, Tine, Tinsel, Tint, Toll, Traik, Tribes, Tyne(d), Ullage, Unredeemed, Wastage, Wasted, Will, Wull

Loss of memory Amnesia, Black-out, Fugue, Infonesia, Paramnesia

▷ **Lost** may indicate an anagram or an obsolete word

Lot(s) Abundant, Amount, Aret(t), Badly, Batch, Boatload, Caboodle, Cavel, Chance, Deal, Dole, Doom, Due, ➤ FATE, Fortune, Hantle, Hap, Heaps, Horde, Host, Item, Job, Kevel, Kismet, Lashings, Legion, Luck, Manifold, Many, Mass, Moh, Moira, Mony, Mort, Myriad, Oceans, Omnibus, Oodles, Pack, Parcel, Plenitude, Plenty, Portion, Power, Purim, Raft, Scads, Set, Sight, Slather, Slew, Slue, Sortilege, Stack, Sum, Tall order, Tons, Vole, Wagonload, Weird

Loth Averse, Circumspect, Sweer(t), Sweir(t)

Lothario Lady-killer, Libertine, Rake, Womaniser

Lotion After-shave, Blackwash, Calamine, Collyrium, Cream, Humectant, Suntan, Unguent, Wash

Lottery, Lotto Bingo, Cavel, Draw, Gamble, Pakapoo, Pools, Punchboard, Raffle, Rollover, Scratchcard, Sweepstake, Tombola

Lotus (eater), Lotus land Asana, Djerba, Lotophagus, Padmasana

Loud(ness), Loudly Bel, Big, Blaring, Booming, Brassy, Decibel, F, FF, Flashy, Forte, Fracas, Garish, Gaudy, Glaring, Hammerklavier, High, Lumpkin, Noisy, Orotund, Raucous, Roarie, Siren, Sone, Stentor(ian), Strident, Tarty, Vociferous, Vulgar

Loudspeaker Action, Boanerges, Bullhorn, Hailer, Megaphone, Stentor, Subwoofer, Tannoy®, Tweeter, Woofer

▶ **Lough** see LOCH

Louis Baker, Roi

Louisianian Cajun

Lounge Daiker, Da(c)ker, Departure, Hawm, Idle, Laze, Lizard, Loll, Lollop, Parlour, Slouch, Sun, Transit

Louse (up), Lousy, Lice Acrawl, Argulus, Bolix, Bollocks, Chat, Cootie, Crab, Crummy, Head, Isopod(a), Kutu, Nit, Oniscus, Pedicular, Phthiriasis, Psocoptera, Psylla, Slater, Snot, Sowbug, Sucking, Vermin

Lout Clod(hopper), Coof, Cuif, Hallian, Hallion, Hallyon, Hick, Hob, Hobbledehoy, Hooligan, Hoon, Jack, Jake, Keelie, Lager, Larrikin, Lob(lolly), Loord, Lubber, Lumpkin, Oaf, Oik, Rube, Swad, Tout, Yahoo, Yob(bo)

Love(r) Abelard, Adore, Adulator, Affection, Agape, Aloha, Amant, Amateur, Ami(e), Amoret, Amoroso, Amour, Antony, Ardour, Ariadne, Aucassin, Beau, Bidie-in, Blob, Calf, Care, Casanova, Chamberer, Cicisbeo, Concubine, Coquet, Court, Courtly, Cupboard, Cupid, Dotard, Dote, Doxy, Duck(s), Ducky, Dulcinea, Eloise, Eloper, Emotion, Enamorado, Eros, Fan, Flame, Frauendienst, Free, Goose-egg, Idolise, Inamorata, Inamorato, Isolde, Jo, Lad, Leman, Like, Lochinvar, Loe, Loo, Lurve, Nihility, Nil, Nothing, Nought, O, Pairs, Paramour, Pash, Passion, Philander, Platonic, Protestant, Psychodelic, Puppy, Revere, Romance, Romeo, Spooner, Stale, Storge, Suitor, Swain, Thisbe, Toyboy, Troilus, True, Turtle(-dove), Valentine, Venus, Virtu, Zeal, Zero

Love-apple Tomato, Wolf's-peach

Love-child Come-by-chance

Love-in-a-mist Nigella

Lovely Adorable, Belle, Dishy, Dreamy, Nasty

Love-making ➤ INTERCOURSE, Kama Sutra, Sex, Snog

Love-sick Smit(ten), Strephon

Loving(ly) Amoroso, Amorous, Fond, Tender

Low(est), Low-cut, Lower(ing) Abase, Abate, Abysmal, Amort, Area, Avail(e), Avale, B, Basal, Base(-born), Bass(o), Beneath, Cartoonist, Cheap, Church, Condescend, Contralto, Cow, Croon, Crude, Darken, Debase, Décolleté, Degrade, Demean, Demit, Demote, Depress, Devalue, Dim, Dip, Dispirited, Doldrums, Drawdown, Drop, Early, Embase, Flat, Foot, Frown, Gazunder, Glare, Guernsey, Gurly, Hedge, Humble, Ignoble, Imbase, Inferior, Jersey, Laigh, Lallan, Law, Mass, Mean, Menial, Moo,

Mopus, Morose, Nadir, Net, Nether, Nett, Ostinato, Paravail, Plebeianise, Profound, Prole, Relegate, Ribald, Rock-bottom, Sad, Scoundrel, Scowl, Shabby, Short, Soft, Stoop, Subordinate, Sudra, Undermost, Vail, Vulgar, Weak, Wretched

Lowbrow Philistine

Lowdown Gen, Info

▷ **Lower** may refer to cattle

Lowland(er) Carse, Gallovidian, Glen, Laigh, Lallans, Merse, Mudflat, Plain, Polder, Sassenach, Vlei

Low-lying Callow, Epigeous, Fens, Inferior, Sump

Low person Boor, Bunter, Cad, Caitiff, Cocktail, Demirep, Ratfink, Snot

Loyal(ty) Adherence, Allegiant, Brick, Dependable, Faithful, Fast, Fidelity, Gungho, Leal, Patriotic, Stalwart, Staunch, ➤ TRUE, Trusty

Loyalist Hard core, Paisley, Patriot, Tory

Lozenge Cachou, Catechu, Fusil, Jujube, Mascle, Pastille, Pill, Rhomb, Rustre, Tablet, Troche

LSD Acid, Money

Lubber(ly), Lubbers Booby, Clod, Clumsy, Gawky, Hulk, Lob, Looby, Oaf, Slowback, Swab, Swads

Lubricant, Lubricate Carap-oil, Coolant, Derv, Grease, Oil, Unguent, Wool-oil

Luce Ged

Lucerne Alfalfa, Medick, Nonsuch

Lucia Mimi

Lucid Bright, Clear, Perspicuous, Sane

Lucifer Devil, Match, Proud

Luck(y) Amulet, Auspicious, Beginner's, Bonanza, Break, Caduac, Cess, Chance, Charmed, Chaunce, Daikoku, Dip, Fate, Fluke, ➤ FORTUNE, Godsend, Hap, Heather, Hit, Jam(my), Joss, Lady, Lot, Mascot, Mozzle, Prosit, Providential, Pudding-bag, Purple patch, Seal, Seel, Sele, Serendipity, Sess, Sonsie, Sonsy, Star(s), Streak, Success, Talisman, Tinny, Tough, Turn-up, Windfall

Luckless Hapless, Wight

Lucre Money, Pelf, Tin

Lucy Locket

Lud Gad

Luddite Saboteur, Wrecker

Ludicrous Absurd, Bathetic, Bathos, Farcical, Inane, Irish, Jest, Laughable, Risible

Ludo Uckers

Luff Derrick

Lug Ear, Sea-worm, Sowle, Tote, Tow

Luggage Bags, Carryon, Cases, Dunnage, Hand, Kit, Petara, Traps, Trunk

Luggage-carrier Grid

Lugubrious Dismal, Drear

Luke-warm Laodicean, Lew, Tepid

Lull, Lullaby Berceuse, Calm, Cradlesong, Hushaby, Respite, Rock, Sitzkreig, Soothe, Sopite

Lulu Stunner

Lumber(ing) Clump, Galumph, Jumble, Pawn, Ponderous, Raffle, Saddle, Scamble, Timber

Lumberjack Bushwhacker, Feller, Logger

Luminance, Luminous, Luminosity Aglow, Arc, Glow, Ignis-fatuus, L, Light, Nit, Phosphorescent, Sea-dog, Wildfire, Will o' the wisp

Lumme Coo, Lor

Lump(y) Aggregate, Bubo, Bud, Bulge, Bur(r), Caruncle, Chuck, Clat, Claut, Clod, Clot, Cob, Combine, Da(u)d, Dallop, Dollop, Enhydros, Epulis, Flocculate, Ganglion, Geode, Gnarl, Gob(bet), Goiter, Goitre, Grape, Hunch, Hunk, Inium, Knarl, Knob, Knub, Knur(r), Knurl, Lob, Lunch, Malleolus, Mote, Mott, Myxoma, Neuroma, Nibble, Nirl, Node, Nodule, Nodulus, Nub, Nubble, Nugget, Nur(r), Nurl, Osteophyte, Plook, Plouk, Quinsy, Raguly, Sarcoma, Scybalum, Sitfast, Slub, Strophiole, Tragus, Tuber(cle), Wart, Wodge

Lumpsucker Sea-owl

Lunacy, Lunatic Bedlam, Dementia, Demonomania, Folly, Insanity, Mad(ness), Psychosis

Lunar Evection

▷ **Lunatic** may indicate an anagram

Lunch(time) Dejeune, Déjeuner, L, Nacket, Nuncheon, Packed, Piece, Ploughman, Pm, Tiffin, Working

Lung(s) Bellows, Coalminer's, Farmer's, Iron, Lights, Pulmo, Pulmonary, Soul

Lung disease Anthracosis, Emphysema, Pneumoconiosis, Siderosis, Silicosis

Lunge Breenge, Breinge, Dive, Stab, Thrust, Venue

Lungfish Dipnoi(an)

Lupin Arsene

Lurch Reel, Stoit, Stumble, Swee

Lure Bait, Bribe, Carrot, Decoy, Entice, Horn, Inveigle, Jig, Judas, Roper, Spinner, Stale, Temptation, Tice, Tole, Toll, Train, Trepan

Lurid Gruesome, Purple

Lurk(ing) Dare, Latitant, Skulk, Slink, Snoke, Snook, Snowk

Lusatia(n) Wend(ic), Wendish

Luscious Succulent

Lush Drunk, Fertile, Green, Juicy, Lydian, Sot, Tosspot, Verdant

Lust(ful), Lusty Cama, Concupiscence, Corflambo, Desire, Eros, Frack, Greed, Kama, Lech(ery), Lewd, Megalomania, Obidicut, Randy, Rank, Raunchy, Salacious, Venereous

Lustre, Lustrous Brilliance, Census, Galena, Gaum, Gilt, Gloss, Gorm, Inaurate, Lead-glance, Pentad, Reflet, Satiny, Schiller, ➤ SHEEN, Water

Lute, Lutist Amphion, Chitarrone, Cither, Dichord, Orpharion, Pandora, Theorbo, Vielle

Lutetium Lu

Lutheran Adiaphorist, Calixtin(e), Pietist

Lux Lx

Luxemburg L

Luxuriant, Luxuriate, Luxurious, Luxury (lover) Bask, Clover, Cockaigne, Cockayne, Copious, Deluxe, Dolce vita, Extravagant, Fleshpots, Lavish, Lucullan, Lush, Mollitious, Ornate, Pie, Plush, Posh, Rank, ➤ RICH, Ritzy, Sumptuous, Sybarite, Wallow

Lycanthropist Werewolf

Lydia Languish

▶ **Lying** see LIE

Lymph Chyle

Lynch Dewitt, Hang

Lynx Bobcat, Caracal, Rooicat

Lyre Cithern, Harp, Psaltery, Testudo

Lyric(al), Lyricist, Lyrist Cavalier, Dit(t), Epode, Gilbert, Melic, Ode, Orphean, Paean, Pean, Poem, Rhapsodic, Song

M m

M Married, Member, Metre, Mike, Mile, Thousand

Mac Mino, Scot, Waterproof

Macabre Gothic, Grotesque, Sick

Macaroni Beau, Blood, Cat, Dandy, Exquisite, Fop, Jack-a-dandy, Pasta, Petitmaitre

Macaroon Biscuit, Signal

Macaulay Layman

Mace Club, Nutmeg, Sceptre, Spice

Mace-bearer Beadle, Bedel, Poker

Macedonian Philip

Machine(ry) Apparat(us), Appliance, Automaton, Bathing, Calender, Centrifuge, ➤ DEVICE, Engine, Fax, Fruit, Gin, Heck, Instrument, Jawbreaker, Lathe, Life-support, Loom, Moulinet, Mule, Nintendo®, Plant, Press, Processor, Robot, Slot, Spinning jenny, Throstle, Turbine, Turing, Vending, Virtual, Washing

Macho Jock

Mackerel Albacore, Brack, Dory, Fish, Horse, Pimp, Scad, Scumber, Sky, Trevally

Mackintosh Burberry®, Mac, Mino, Oilskin, Slicker, Waterproof

Macropus Euro, Wallaroo

Mad(den), Madman, Madness Angry, Balmy, Bananas, Barking, Barmy, Bedlam, Besotted, Bonkers, Crackbrained, Crackpot, Crazy, Cuckoo, Cupcake, Delirious, Dement, Distract, Dotty, Enrage, Fay, Fey, Folie, Folly, Frantic, Frenetic(al), Fruitcake, Furioso, Fury, Gelt, Gyte, Harpic, Hatter, Idiotic, Insane, Insanie, Insanity, Into, Irritate, Kook, Loco, Lunatic, Lycanthropy, Madbrained, Maenad, Mania, Mental, Meshug(g)a, Midsummer, Mullah, Psycho, Rabid, Raving, Redwood, Redwud, Scatty, Screwy, Short-witted, Starkers, Tonto, Touched, Troppo, Unhinged, Wood, Wowf, Wrath, Wud, Xenomania, Yond, Zany

▷ **Mad(den)** may indicate an anagram

Madagascan Aye-aye, Hova, Indri, Malagasy

Madam(e) Baggage, Lady, Proprietress

Madcap Impulsive, Tearaway

Madder Alizari, Chay(a), Gardenia, Genipap, Rose, Rubia, Shaya

Made (it) Built, Did, Fec(it), Ff, Gart, Invented

Madge Pie

▷ **Madly** may indicate an anagram

Madonna Lady, Lily, Mary, Pietà, Virgin

Madrigal Ballet, Fala, Song

Maelstrom Voraginous, Vortex, Whirlpool

Maenad Devotee, Fan

Maestro Artist, Toscanini

Mafia Camorra, Capo, Cosa nostra, Godfather, Mob, Ndrangheta, Omerta

Mag Mail

Magazine Arsenal, Clip, Colliers, Cornhill, Cosmopolitan, Digizine, Economist, Field, Girlie, Glossy, Granta, Lady, Lancet, Listener, Magnet, Organ, Periodical, Pictorial, Playboy, Pulp, Punch, She, Slick, Spectator, Store, Strand, Tatler, Time, Vogue, Warehouse, Weekly, Yoof

Magdalene St. Mary

Maggie Rita

Maggot Bot, Flyblow, Gentiles, Gentle, Grub, Larva, Mawk, Myiasis, Whim, Worm

Magi Balthazar, Gaspar, Melchior

Magic(al), Magician Archimage, Art, Baetyl, Black, Charm, Conjury, Diablerie, Diablery, Enchanting, Faust, Genie, Goetic, Goety, Gramary(e), Grimoire, Hermetic, Houdini, Illusionist, Incantation, Math, Medea, Merlin, Mojo, Moly, Morgan le Fay, Myal, Necromancer, Pawaw, Powwow, Prospero, Reim-kenner, Rhombus, Sorcery, Spell, Speller, Supernatural, Talisman, Thaumaturgics, Theurgy, Voodoo, White, Wizard, Zendik

Magistracy, Magistrate Aedile, Amman, Amtman, Archon, Avoyer, Bailie, Bailiff, Bailli(e), Burgess, Burgomaster, Cadi, Censor, Consul, Corregidor, Demiurge, Doge(ate), Edile, Effendi, Ephor, Field cornet, Finer, Foud, Gonfalonier, JP, Judiciary, Jurat, Kotwal, Landamman(n), Landdrost, Maire, Mayor, Mittimus, Novus homo, Podesta, Portreeve, Pr(a)efect, Pr(a)etor, Prior, Proconsul, Propraetor, Provost, Qadi, Quaestor, Recorder, Reeve, Shereef, Sherif, Stad(t)holder, Stipendiary, Syndic, Tribune, Worship

Magnanimity, Magnanimous Big, Charitable, ➤ GENEROUS, Largeness, Lofty, Noble

Magnate Baron, Bigwig, Industrialist, Mogul, Onassis, Tycoon, Vanderbilt, VIP

Magnesia, Magnesium Humite, Kainite, Mg, Periclase

Magnet(ic), Magnetism Attraction, Charisma, Field, Gauss, Horseshoe, It, Loadstone, Lodestone, Maxwell, Od, Oersted, Permanent, Polar, Pole, Pole piece, Poloidal, Pull, Solenoid, Terrella, Tesla, Tole

Magnificence, Magnificent Gorgeous, Grandeur, Imperial, Laurentian, Lordly, Noble, Pride, Regal, Royal, Splendid, State, Superb

Magnifier, Magnify(ing) Aggrandise, Augment, Binocle, ➤ ENLARGE, Exaggerate, Increase, Loupe, Microscope, Teinoscope, Telescope

Magniloquent Bombastic, Orotund

Magnitude Abundance, Extent, Muchness, Size

Magnolia An(n)ona, Beaver-tree, Champac, Champak, Mississippi, Sweet bay, Umbrella-tree, Yulan

Magpie Bell, Bird, Chatterer, Madge, Mag, Margaret, Outer, Pica, Piet, Pyat, Pyet, Pyot

Magus Artist

Magyar Hungarian, Szekel(y), Szekler, Ugrian, Ugric

Mahogany Acajou, Carapa, Cedrela, Wood

Mahommedan Dervish, Shiah

Maid(en) Abigail, Aia, Amah, Biddy, Bonibell, Bonne, Bonnibell, Chamber, Chloe, Clothes-horse, Damosel, Dell, Dey, First, Girl, Guillotine, Ignis-fatuus, Imago, Inaugural, Io, Iras, Iron, Lorelei, M, Marian, May, Miss, Nymph, Opening, Over, Pucelle, Rhine, Skivvy, Soubrette, Suivante, Thestylis, Tirewoman, Tweeny, Valkyrie, Virgin, Wench

Maidenhair Fern, Ginkgo

Mail Air, ➤ ARMOUR, Byrnie, Cataphract, Chain, Da(w)k, E(lectronic), Express, Fan, Habergeon, Hate, Hauberk, Helm, Junk, Letter, Panoply, Pony express, Post, Ring, Send, Snail, Spam, Surface, Tuille(tte), Voice

Mailboat Packet

Maim Cripple, Impair, Lame, Main, Mayhem, Mutilate, Vuln

Main(s) Brine, Briny, ➤ CENTRAL, Chief, Cockfight, Conduit, Essential, Foremost, Generally, Grid, Gross, Head, ➤ KEY, Lead(ing), Palmary, Predominant, Prime, Principal, Ring, ➤ SEA, Sheer, Spanish, Staple, Water

Mainland Continent, Pomona

Mainstay Backbone, Bastion, Pillar, Support

Maintain, Maintenance Alimony, Allege, Ap(p)anage, Argue, Assert, Aver, Avouch, Avow, Claim, Contend, Continue, Defend, Escot, Insist, Preserve, Run, Sustain, Upbear, Uphold, Upkeep

Maize Corn, Hominy, Indian, Mealie, Popcorn, Samp, Silk, Stamp, Zea

Majestic, Majesty August, Britannic, Dignity, Eagle, Grandeur, Imperial, Maestoso, Olympian, Regal, SM, Sovereign, Stately, Sublime, Tuanku

Major (domo) Drum, ➤ IMPORTANT, PM, Seneschal, Senior, Sergeant, Star, Trumpet, Wig

Majority Absolute, Age, Body, Eighteen, Latchkey, Maturity, Most, Preponderance, Silent, Working

Make(r), Make do, Making Amass, Brand, Coerce, Coin, Compel, Compulse, Concoct, Creant, Create, Devise, Earn, Execute, Fabricate, Factive, Fashion, Faute de mieux, Fet(t), Forge, Form, Gar(re), God, Halfpenny, Mail(e), Manage, Prepare, Production, Reach, Render, Shape, Sort, Temporise, Wright

▷ **Make** may indicate an anagram

Make believe Fantasy, Fictitious, Pretend, Pseudo

Make good Abet, Compensate, Remedy, Succeed, Ulling

Make hay Ted

Make off Bolt, Leg it, Mosey, Run, Scarper

Makeshift Bandaid, Crude, Cutcha, Expedient, Jury-rigged, Kacha, Kludge, Kutcha, Pis-aller, Rude, Stopgap, Timenoguy

Make up Ad lib, Compose, Concealer, Constitution, Cosmetics, Gaud, Gawd, Gene, Identikit®, Kohl, Liner, Lipstick, Maquillage, Mascara, Metabolism, Paint, Pancake, Powder, Reconcile, Rouge, Slap, Tidivate, Titivate, Toiletry, White-face

Maladroit Awkward, Clumsy, Graceless, Inelegant, Unperfect
Malady Disease, Illness
Malagas(e)y Hova, RM
Malaise Affluenza
Malapropism Catachresis, Slipslop
Malaria Ague, Paludism, Tap, Vivax
Malawi Nyasa
Malay(an), Malaysian Austronesian, Datuk, D(a)yak, Jawi, Madurese, Moro, Sakai, Tokay
Male Arrhenotoky, Buck, Bull, Dog, Ephebe, Ephebus, Gent, Hob, John Doe, Macho, Mansize, Masculine, Ram, Rogue, Spear(side), Stag, Stamened, Telamon, Tom
Malediction Curse, Cuss, Oath, Slander
Malefactor Criminal, Felon, Villain
Malevolent, Malevolence Evil, Fell, Malign
Malformation Teratogenesis
Malfunction Glitch, Hiccup
Mali RMM
Malice, Malicious Bitchy, Catty, Cruel, Despiteous, Envy, Malevolent, Malign, Narquois, Schadenfreude, Serpent, Snide, Spite, Spleen, Venom, Virulent
Malign(ant), Malignity Asperse, Backbite, Baleful, Defame, Denigrate, Gall, Harm, Hate-rent, Hatred, Libel, Sinister, Slander, Spiteful, Swart(h)y, Toxin, Vicious, Vilify, Vilipend, Viperous, Virulent
Malinger(er) Dodge, Leadswinger, Scrimshank, Shirk, Skrimshank, Truant
Mallard Duck, Sord
Malleable Clay, Ductile, Fictile, Pliable
▷ **Malleable** may indicate an anagram
Mallet Beetle, Club, Hammer, Mace, Maul, Stick
Mallow Abutilon, Sida
Malodorous Mephitic
Malpractice(s) Sculduggery, Skulduggery
Malt Diastase, Grains, Grist, Wort
Maltese (cross) Falcon, GC
Maltreat Abuse, Harm, Maul, Mishandle, Misuse
Mammal Animal, Artiodactyl, Binturong, Bobcat, Cacomistle, Cacomixle, Caracal, Charronia, Chiropteran, Ciscus, Colugo, Creodont, Dhole, Dinothere, Dugong, Eutheria, Fisher, Glires, Grison, Guanaco, Hydrax, Hyrax, Indri, Kinkajou, Lagomorph, Linsang, Loris, Manatee, Margay, Marten, Mongoose, Monotreme, Musteline, Numbat, Olungo, Pachyderm, Pangolin, Peccary, Pekan, Perissodactyl, Pika, Pine marten, Pinniped, Platypus, Polecat, Porpoise, Primate, Pudu, Raccoon, Rasse, Rhytina, Sable, Shrew, Sirenian, Skunk, Sloth, Solenodon, Springhaas, Taguan, Tahr, Takin, Tanrec, Tapir, Tayra, Teledu, Tenrec, Titanothere, Tylopod, Vicuna, Viverrid, Weasel, Whale, Zorilla

Mammon Money, Riches, Wealth
Mammoth Epic, Gigantic, Huge, Jumbo, Mastodon, Whopping, Woolly
Man(kind) Ask(r), Best, Betty, Bimana(l), Biped, Bloke, Bo, Boy, Cad, Cairn, Calf, Castle, Cat, Chal, Chap, Checker, Chequer, Chiel, Cockey, Cod, Crew, Cro-Magnon, Cuffin, Cully, Dog, Don, Draught, Dude, Essex, Everyman, Family, Fella, Feller, Fellow, Folsom, Friday, G, Gayomart, Gent, Grimaldi, Guy, He, Heidelberg, Himbo, Hombre, Hominid, Homme, Homo, Inner, IOM, Isle, Jack, Java, Joe (Bloggs), Joe Blow, John(nie), John Doe, Josser, Lollipop, M, Male, Microcosm, Mister, Mon, Mr, Mun, Neanderthal, Oreopithecus, Ou, Paleolithic, Party, Pawn, Peking, Person, Piece, Piltdown, Pin, Pithecanthropus, Raff, Remittance, Renaissance, Rhodesian, Rook, Servant, Servitor, Ship, Sinanthropus, Sodor, Soldier, Solo, Staff, Stag, Straw, Third, Thursday, Twelfth, Tyke, Type, Valet, Vir, Wight
Manacle Fetter, Handcuff, Iron, Shackle
Manage(r), Manageable, Management, Managing Administer, Amildar, Attain, Aumil, Behave, Boss, Chief, Conduct, Contrive, Control, Cope, Darogha, Direct, Docile, Exec(utive), Fare, Find, Govern, Grieve, Handle, Honcho, IC, Impresario, Intendant, Logistical, MacReady, Maitre d('hotel), Manipulate, Manoeuvre, Proctor, Procurator, Regisseur, Rig, Roadie, ➤ RUN, Scrape, Shift, Steward, Succeed, Suit, Superintend, Tawie, Tractable, Treatment, Trustee, Wangle, Wield(y), Yare
Manatee Lamantum, Mermaid, Sea-ape
Manchu Fu
Mandarin Bureaucrat, Chinaman, Kuo-Yu, Nodding, Satsuma, Yamen
Mandate Authority, Decree, Fiat, Order
Mandrake Springwort
Mandrel Triblet
Mane(d), Manes Crest, Encolure, Jubate, Larva(e), Shades
Manege Horseplay, Train
Manganese Mn, Synadelphite, Wadd
Manger Cratch, Crib, Hack, Stall
Mangle Agrise, Butcher, Distort, Garble, Hack, Hackle, Haggle, Wring(er)
▷ **Mangle** may indicate an anagram
Mango Dika
Manhandle Frogmarch, Maul, Rough
Manhater Misanthrope
Manhattan Bowery
Mania Cacoethes, Craze, Frenzy, Passion, Rage
Manichaean Albi
Manifest(ation), Manifestly Attest, Avatar, Epiphany, Evident, Evince, Exhibit, Extravert, Extrovert, Feat, List, Marked, Mode, Notably, Obvious, Open, Show
Manifesto Plank, Platform, Policy, Pronunciamento
Manifold(ness) Many, Multeity, Multiple

Manila Abaca, Cheroot

Manioc Cassava

Maniple Fannel, Fanon

Manipulate, Manipulative, Manipulator Chiropractor, Control, Cook, Demagogic, Diddle, Fashion, Gerrymander, Handle, Jerrymander, Juggle, Logodaedalus, Osteopath, Ply, Rig, Tweeze, Use, Wangle, ➤ WIELD

▷ **Manipulate** may indicate an anagram

Manna Alhagi, Food, Trehala

Manner(ism), Mannerly, Manners Accent, A la, Appearance, Attitude, Bedside, Behaved, Behaviour, Bon ton, Breeding, Carriage, Conduct, Couth, Crew, Custom, Deportment, Ethos, Etiquette, Farand, Farrand, Farrant, Habit, How, Mien, Mode, Morality, Mores, Of, Ostent, Panache, Politesse, Presentation, P's & Q's, Quirk, Rate, Sort, Style, Thew(s), Thewe(s), Trick, Upsee, Upsey, Upsy, Urbanity, Way, Wise

Manoeuvre(s) Campaign, Castle, Engineer, Exercise, Faena, Fianchetto, Fork, Gambit, Heimlich, Hot-dog, Jink(s), Jockey, Manipulate, Op(eration), Pesade, Ploy, Ruse, Skewer, Use, U-turn, Valsalva, Wheelie, Whipstall, Wile, Zigzag

▷ **Manoeuvre** may indicate an anagram

Man-of-war Armada, Destroyer, Ironclad

Manor (house) Area, Demain, Demesne, Estate, Hall, Vill(a)

Mansion Casa, Seat

Mantle Asthenosphere, Authority, Burnous(e), Capote, Caracalla, Dolman, Elijah, Gas, Pall, Pallium, Paludament, Pelisse, Rochet, Sima, Toga, Tunic, Veil

Mantuan Maro, Virgil

Manual Blue collar, Bradshaw, Cambist, Console, Enchiridion, Guide, Hand, Handbook, How-to, Portolan(o), Positif

Manufacture Fabricate, Make, Produce

Manure Compost, Dressing, Dung, Fertiliser, Guano, Hen-pen, Lime, Muck, Sha(i)rn, Tath

Manuscript(s) Codex, Codicology, Folio, Hand, Holograph, Longhand, MS, Opisthograph, Palimpsest, Papyrus, Parchment, Script, Scroll, Scrowl(e), Vellum

Manx(man) Cat, IOM, Kelly, Kelt

▷ **Manx** may indicate a last letter missing

Many C, CD, Countless, D, Hantle, Herd, Horde, Host, L, Lot, M, Manifold, Mony, Multi(tude), Myriad, Scad, Sight, Stacks, Tons, Umpteen

▷ **Many** may indicate the use of a Roman numeral letter

Maori (house) Hauhau, Tangata whenua, Wahine, Whare

Map(ping) Atlas, Card, Cartogram, Chart, Chorography, Cognitive, Contour, Face, Genetic, Inset, Key, Loxodromic, Mappemond, OS, Plan, Plot, Relief, Sea-card, Sea-chart, Topography, Weather

Maple Acer, Mazer, Norway, Plane, Sugar, Sycamore, Syrup

Map-maker Cartographer, OS, Speed

Maquis Queach, Underground
Mar Blight, Denature, Impair, Soil, Spoil
Marabout Sofi, Sufi
Marathon Comrades, Huge, Race
Marauder Attacker, Bandit, Pillager, Pirate, Predator, Prowler
Marble(s), Marbling Aeginetan, Agate, All(e)y, Arch, Arundelian, Bonce,
    Bonduc, Bool, Boondoggle, Bowl, Carrara, Chequer, Cipollino,
    Commoney, Devil's, Dump, Elgin, Humite, Hymettus, Knicker, Languedoc,
    Lucullite, Marl, Marmarosis, Marmoreal, Mottle, Nero-antico, Nickar,
    Nicker, Onychite, Paragon, Parian, Pavonazzo, Petworth, Phigalian,
    Plonker, Plunker, Purbeck, Rance, Ringer, Ring-taw, Sanity, Scagliola,
    Spangcockle, Taw, Variegate, Xanthian
Marcel Proust
March(ing) Abut, Adjoin, Advance, Anabasis, Border(er), Borderland, Dead,
    Defile, Demo, Etape, File, Footslog, Forced, Freedom, Fringe, Galumph,
    Go, Goosestep, Hunger, Ides, Jarrow, Lide, Limes, Lockstep, Meare, Music,
    ➤ PARADE, Progress, Protest, Quick, Route, Slow time, Step, Strunt, Strut,
    Trio, Tromp, Wedding, Yomp
Marco Il Milione, Polo
Mare Dam, Flanders, Horse, M, Shanks's, Yaud
Margaret Anjou, Meg, Peg, Rita
Margarine Oleo
Marge, Margin(al) Annotate, Border, Brim, Brink, Curb, Edge, Hair's
    breadth, Lean, Limit, Littoral, Neck, Nose, Peristome, Profit, Rand, Repand,
    ➤ RIM, Selvedge, Sideline, Tail, Term
Marginal note Apostil(le), K'ri
Margosa Melia, Nim
Maria(nne) France, Tia
Marie Dressler, Tempest
Marigold Calendula, Kingcup, Tagetes
Marijuana Alfalfa, Dagga, Gage, Ganja, Grass, Greens, Gungeon, Ha-ha,
    Hay, Herb, Jive, Kaif, Kef, Kif, Leaf, Locoweed, Mary-Jane, Pot, Roach, Rope,
    Shit, Sinsemilla, Splay, Spliff, Tea, Toke
Marina Wharf
Marine (creature) Bootie, Bootneck, Cephalopod, Chaetognath,
    Cnidarian, Coelenterate, Comatulid, Ctenophora, Cunjevoi,
    Enteropneusta, Flustra, Foram(inifer), Galoot, Graptolite, Harumfrodite,
    Hemichorda, Holothurian, Hydrocoral, Hydroid, Hydromedusa, Jolly,
    Leatherneck, Lobster, Mercantile, Mere-swine, Mistress Roper, Oceanic,
    Physalia, Sea-soldier, Thalassian, Ultra
Mariner AB, Ancient, MN, RM, Sailor, Salt, Seafarer, Spacecraft, Tar
Marionette(s) Fantoccini, Puppet
Marjoram Amaracus, Sweet, Winter-sweet
Mark(ed) Accent, Antony, Apostrophe, Asterisk, Badge, Bethumb, Birth,
    Blaze, Blot, Brand, Bruise, Bull, Butt, Cachet, Caract, Caret, Caste, Cedilla,

Chatter, Chequer, Cicatrix, Clout, Colon, Comma, Coronis, Crease, Dash, Denote, Dent, Diacritic, Diaeresis, Dieresis, Distinction, DM, Ensign, Enstamp, Exclamation, Expression, Feer, Fleck, Glyph, Gospel, Hacek, Hash, Hatch, Heed, High water, Hyphen, Impress(ion), Indicium, Ink, Inscribe, Insignia, Kite, Kumkum, Lentigo, Line, Ling, Logo, Low water, M, Macron, MB, Merk, Mottle, NB, Notal, Note, Notice, Obelisk, Observe, Oche, Paraph, Period, Pilcrow, Pit, Plage, Pling, Point, Popinjay, Port wine, Presa, Punctuation, Record, Reference, Roundel, Scar, Score, See, Sigil, Sign, Smit, Smut, Speck, Splodge, Splotch, Stain, Stencil, Stigma(ta), Strawberry, Stress, Stretch, Sucker, Symbol, Target, Tatow, Tattoo, Tee, Theta, Thread, Tick, Tika, Tittle, Token, Touchmark, Trace, Track, Trout, Tug(h)ra, Twain, Umlaut, Ure, Victim, Wand, Watch, Weal, Welt

Marker Buck, Cairn, Fanion, Flag, Ink, Inukshuk, Label, Scorer, Tie

Market (day), Market place Agora, Alcaiceria, Baltic, Bazaar, Bear, Billingsgate, Borgo, Bull, Buyer's, Capital, Change, Common, Denet, Dragon, EC, Emporium, Errand, Exchange, Fair, Flea, Forum, Grey, Kerb, Lloyds, Mandi, Mart, Mercat, Nundine, Outlet, Piazza, Sale, Seller's, Shop, Sook, Souk, Stance, Staple, Stock, Tattersall's, Test, Third, Trade, Tron, Tryst, Vent, Wall Street

Marksman Sharpshooter, Shootist, Shot, Sniper, Tell

Marlborough Blenheim

Marlene Lilli

Marmalade Cat, Mammee-sapota, Preserve, Squish

Marmoset Jacchus, Mico, Midas, Monkey, Wistiti

Marmot Bobac, Bobak, Dassie, Hoary, Hyrax, Rodent, Whistler, Woodchuck

Maroon Brown, Castaway, Enisle, Firework, Inisle, Isolate, Strand

Marquee Pavilion, Tent, Top

Marquess, Marquis Granby, Lorne, Sade

Marquetry Boul(l)e, Buhl, Inlay

Marriage ➤ ALLIANCE, Bed, Beenah, Bigamy, Bridal, Coemption, Confarreation, Conjugal, Connubial, Digamy, Endogamy, Espousal, Exogamy, Gandharva, Genial, Hetaerism, Hetairism, Hymeneal, Jugal, Ketubah, Knot, Levirate, Match, Mating, Matrilocal, Matrimony, Mésalliance, Monandry, Monogamy, Morganatic, Noose, Nuptial, Pantagamy, Punalua, Sacrament, Shidduch, Tie, ➤ UNION, Wedding, Wedlock

Marriageable Marrow, Nubile, Parti

Marrow Courgette, Friend, Gist, Medulla, Myeloid, Pith, Pumpkin, Squash, Vegetable

Marry, Married Ally, Amate, Buckle, Cleek(it), Confarreate, Couple, Coverture, Espouse, Feme covert, Forsooth, Hitch, Join, Knit, M, Mate, Matron, Memsahib, Pair, Pardie, Quotha, Splice, Tie, Troggs, Troth, Unite, W, Wed, Wive

Mars Areography, Ares, Red (planet)

Marsh(y) Bayou, Bog, Chott, Corcass, Emys, Everglade, Fen, Hackney, Maremma, Merse, Mire, Morass, Ngaio, Paludal, Plashy, Pontine, Pripet,

Quagmire, Romney, Salina, Salt, Shott, Slade, Slough, Sog, Spew, Spue, Swale, Swamp, Taiga, Terai, Vlei, Wetlands

Marshal Arrange, Array, Commander, Earp, Foch, French, Hickok, MacMahon, Muster, Neil, Ney, Order, Pétain, Provost, Shepherd, Tedder, Usher

Marshmallow Althaea

Marsupial Bandicoot, Bilby, Cuscus, Dasyure, Dibbler, Didelphia, Diprotodont, Dunnart, Kangaroo, Koala, Macropod, Metatheria, Notoryctes, Nototherium, Numbat, Opossum, Petaurist, Phalanger, Possum, Potoroo, Quokka, Quoll, Roo, Tasmanian devil, Theria, Thylacine, Tuan, Wallaby, Wambenger, Wombat, Yapo(c)k

Marten Mustela, Pekan, Sable, Woodshock

Martha Vineyard

Martial (arts) Bellicose, Budo, Capoeira, Capuera, Chopsocky, Dojo, Iai-do, Judo, Ju-jitsu, Karate, Kung Fu, Militant, Ninjutsu, Shintaido, Tae kwon do, T'ai chi (chuan), Warlike, Wushu

Martin Bird, Luther, Swallow

Martinet Captious, Ramrod, Stickler

Martini® Cocktail, Henry

Martyr(dom), Martyrs Alban, Alphege, Colosseum, Donatist, Justin, Latimer, MM, Passional, Persecute, Sebastian, Stephen, Suffer, Tolpuddle, Wishart

Marvel(lous) Bodacious, Bully, Epatant, Fab, Marl, Miracle, Mirific, Phenomenon, Prodigious, Superb, Super-duper, Terrific, Wonder

Marx(ism), Marxist Aspheterism, Chico, Comintern, Commie, Groucho, Gummo, Harpo, Karl, Menshevik, Tanky, Zeppo

Mary Bloody, Celeste, Madonna, Moll, Morison, Tum(my), Typhoid, Virgin

Marylebone Station

Marzipan Marchpane

Masculine, Masculinity He, He-man, Linga(m), M, Machismo, Macho, Male, Manly, Virile

Maser Laser

Mash(er) Beau, Beetle, Brew, Lady-killer, Pap, Pestle, Pound, Sour, Squash

Mask(ed) Camouflage, Cloak, Cokuloris, Death, Disguise, Dissemble, Domino, Larvated, Life, Loo, Loup, Mascaron, Matte, Persona, Respirator, Screen, Semblance, Stalking-horse, Stocking, Template, Visor, Vizard

Mason(ry) Ashlar, Ashler, Brother, Builder, Cowan, Emplecton, Isodoma, Isodomon, Lodge, Moellon, Nogging, Opus, Perry, Random, Squinch

Masque(rade), Masquerader Comus, Domino, Guisard, Mum(m), Pose, Pretend

Mass(es) Aggregate, Agnus dei, Anniversary, Banket, Bezoar, Bike, Body, Bulk, Cake, Chaos, Clot, Congeries, Conglomeration, Consecration, Core, Crith, Critical, Crowd, Demos, Density, Flake, Flysch, Folk, Geepound, Great, Herd, High, Horde, Hulk, Jud, Kermesse, Kermis, Kilo(gram), Kirmess, Low, Lump, M, Majority, Missa, Mop, Nest, Phalanx, Pile, Plumb, Pontifical, Populace, Raft, Requiem, Ruck, Salamon, Salmon, Scrum, Sea,

Serac, Service, Shock, Sicilian, Size, Slub, Slug, Stack, Stroma, Sursum corda, Te lgitur, Tektite, Trental, Vesper, Volume, Wad, Weight, Welter

Massacre Amritsar, Blood-bath, Butcher, Carnage, Glencoe, Havock, Manchester, Peterloo, Pogrom, Purge, Scullabogue, Scupper, September, Sicilian vespers, Slaughter, Slay, Wounded Knee

Massage, Masseur Anmo, Chafer, Do-in, Effleurage, ➤ KNEAD, Malax, Palp, Petrissage, Physio, Rolf(ing), Rubber, Shampoo, Shiatsu, Swedish, Tapotement, Thai, Tripsis, Tui na

Massive Big, Bull, Colossal, Heavy, Herculean, Huge, Monumental, Strong, Titan

Mast(ed) Acorn, Crosstree, Hounds, Jigger, Jury, Mizzen, Pannage, Pole, Racahout, Royal, Ship-rigged, Spar, Top-gallant

Master(ly) Artful, Baalebos, Baas, Beak, Beat, Boss, Buddha, Bwana, Careers, Checkmate, Conquer, Control, Dan, Dominate, Dominie, Employer, Enslave, Exarch, Expert, Gov, Herr, Himself, Learn, Lord, MA, Maestro, Mas(s), Massa, Mes(s), Nkosi, Ollamh, Ollav, Oner, Oppress, Original, Overcome, Overpower, Overseer, Pedant, Rabboni, Seigneur, Seignior, Sir(e), Skipper, ➤ SUBDUE, Subjugate, Superate, Surmount, Swami, Tame, Thakin, Towkay, Tuan, Usher, Vanquish, Virtuoso

Mastermind Brain, Conceive, Direct

Masterpiece Chef d'oeuvre, Creation

Master-stroke Coup, Triumph

Masthead Banner, Flag, M, Truck

Masturbate, Masturbation Abuse, Frig, Gratify, Jock, Onanism, Wank

Mat(ted), Matting Bast, Coaster, Doily, Dojo, Doyley, Felt, Inlace, Pad, Paunch, Plat, Rug, ➤ TANGLE, Tat(ami), Tatty, Taut, Tawt, Tomentose, Welcome, Zarf

Matador Card, Espada, Ordonez, Theseus, Torero

Match(ed) Agree, Alliance, Amate, Balance, Besort, Bonspiel, Bout, Carousel, Compare, Congreve, Contest, Cope, Correspond, Counterpane, Doubles, Emulate, Engagement, Equal(ise), Equate, Even, Exhibition, Fellow, Fit, Fixture, Four-ball, Friction, Friendly, Fusee, Fuzee, Game, Go, International, Joust, Light, Locofoco, Lucifer, Main, Marrow, Marry, Meet, Mouse, Needle, Pair(s), Paragon, Parti, Pit, Promethean, Reproduce, Return, Rival, Roland, Rubber, Safety, Singles, Slanging, Slow, Spunk, Striker, Suit, Sync, ➤ TALLY, Team, Test, Tie, Twin, Union, Vesta, Vesuvian, Wedding

Matchbox label (collecting) Phillumeny

Match girl Bride

Match-holder Lin(t)stock

Matchless Non(e)such, Orinda

Matchmaker Blackfoot, Broker, Pairer, Promoter, Shadchan

Mate, Mating Achates, Adam, Amigo, Amplexus, Bedfellow, Bo, Breed, Buddy, Buffer, Butty, Chess, China, Chum, Cobber, Comrade, Consort, Crony, Cully, Digger, Eve, Feare, Feer, Fellow, Fere, Fiere, Fool's, Husband, Maik, Make, Marrow, Marry, Match, Mister, Oldster, Oppo, ➤ PAIR, Pal,

Paragon, Partner, Pheer(e), Pirrauru, Scholar's, Serve, Sex, Skaines, Smothered, Soul, ➤ SPOUSE, Tea, Wack, Wife, Wus(s)

Material Agalmatolite, Aggregate, Agitprop, Apt, Armure, Batiste, Blastema, Bole, Byssus, Calamanco, Cambric, Canvas, Cellulose, Ceramic, Cermet, Charmeuse®, Chiffon, Ciré, ➤ CLOTH, Cob, Coburg, Compo, Copy, Corporeal, Crash, Cretonne, Data, Dimity, Documentation, Earthy, ➤ FABRIC, Factual, Fettling, Fibrefill, Fibreglass, Fines, Fuel, Gaberdine, Galatea, Genappe, Germane, Gossamer, Hessian, Homespun, Hylic, Illusion, Jeanette, Lamé, Lawn, Macintosh, Marocain, Metal, Moquette, Oilskin, Papier-maché, Pertinent, Physical, Pina-cloth, Plasterboard, Polyester, Positive, Prunella, Relevant, Russel, Sackcloth, Sagathy, Say, Skirting, Soneri, Stockingette, Stuff, Substance, Swansdown, Tangible, Tape, Tarpaulin, Textile, Thingy, Toile, Toilinet(te), Towelling, Tusser, Twill, Wattle and daub, Winceyette, Wool, Worcester

Materialise Appear, Apport, Click, Reify

Materialist(ic) Banausian, Hylist, Hyloist, Philistine, Somatist

Mathematician Apollonius, Archimedes, Archytas, Bernoulli, Bessel, Boole, Briggs, Cantor, Cocker, Descartes, Diophantus, Dunstable, Eratosthenes, Euclid, Euler, Fermat, Fibonacci, Fourier, Gauss, Godel, Goldbach, Gunter, Hawking, Laplace, Leibniz, Lie, Mercator, Napier, Newton, Optime, Pascal, Penrose, Playfair, Poisson, Ptolemy, Pythagoras, Pytheas, Riemann, Torricelli, Turing, Wrangler, Zeno

Mathematics, Maths Algebra, Arithmetic, Arsmetrick, Calculus, Geometry, Logarithms, Mechanics, Numbers, Trig

Matilda Liar, Swag, Untruthful, Waltzing

Matinee Coat, Idol, Show

Mating Pangamy

Matins Nocturn

Matricide Orestes

Matrimony Bed, Conjugal, Marriage, Sacrament, Spousal, Wedlock

Matrix Array, Hermitian, Jacobian, Mould, Pattern, Uterus

Matron Dame, Hausfrau, Lucretia, Nurse, Warden

Matt(e) Dense, Dingy, Dull

Matter Alluvium, Bioblast, Biogen, Body, Concern, Consequence, Dark, Empyema, Epithelium, Gear, Gluon, Go, Grey, Hyle, Impost(h)ume, Issue, Mass, Material, Molecule, Phlegm, Pith, Point, Positron, Protoplasm, Pulp, Pus, Quark, Reck, Reke, Scum, Shebang, Signify, Subject, ➤ SUBSTANCE, Thing, Topic, Tousle, Touzle, Ylem

Matthew Arnold

Mattress Bed(ding), Biscuit, Foam, Futon, Lilo®, Pallet, Palliasse, Tick

Mature, Maturity Adult, Age, Blossom, Bold, Concoct, Develop, Mellow, Metaplasis, Puberty, Ripe(n), Rounded, Seasoned, Upgrow(n)

Maudlin Fuddled, Mawkish, Sentimental, Sloppy, Too-too

Maul Hammer, Manhandle, Paw, Rough

Maundy Money, Nipter, Thursday

Mauretanian, Mauritania(n) Moor, RIM

Mausoleum Mole, Sepulchre, Taj Mahal, Tomb

Mauve Lilac, Mallow

Maverick Misfit, Nonconformist, Rogue

Mavis Throstle

Maw Crop, Gorge, Gull(et), Oesophagus

Mawkish Sickly

Maxim Adage, Apo(ph)thegm, Byword, Gnome, Gorki, Gun, Hiram, Moral, Motto, Proverb, Restaurateur, ➤ RULE, Saw, Saying, Sentence, Sentiment, Watchword

Maximum All-out, Full, Highest, Most, Peak, Utmost

May Blossom, Can, Hawthorn, Merry, Might, Month, Mote, Quickthorn, Shall, Whitethorn

Maybe Happen, Mebbe, Peradventure, Percase, Perchance, Perhaps, Possibly

▷ **May become** may indicate an anagram

May day Beltane, SOS

Mayfair WI

Mayfly Ephemera, Ephemeroptera, Green-drake, Sedge

Mayhem Chaos, Crime, Damage

Mayonnaise Aioli, Rémoulade

Mayor Alcaide, Burgomaster, Casterbridge, Councilman, Porteeve, Provost, Whittington

Maze Labyrinth, Meander, Warren, Wilderness

MC Compere, Host, Ringmaster

MD Doctor, Healer

Me I, Mi

Mead(ow) Flood, Grass, Haugh, Hydromel, Inch, Lea(se), Ley, Meath(e), Metheglin, ➤ PASTURE, Runnymede, Saeter, Salting, Water

Meadowsweet Dropwort

Meagre Bare, Exiguous, Measly, Paltry, Pittance, Scant, Scrannel, Scranny, Skimpy, Skinny, Spare, Stingy, Thin

Meal(s) Barium, Board, Breakfast, Brunch, Buffet, Cassava, Cereal, Cholent, Chota-hazri, Collation, Cornflour, Cottoncake, Cou-cou, Cribble, Dejeune(r), Dinner, Drammock, Ervalenta, Fare, Farina, Flour, Food, Grits, Grout, Hangi, Lock, Lunch, Mandioc, Mandioc(c)a, Mani(h)oc, Melder, Meltith, Mensal, Mess, Mush, No-cake, Nosh, Nuncheon, Obento, Piece, Plate, Poi, Polenta, Porridge, Prandial, Prix fixe, Rac(c)ahout, Refection, Repast, Revalenta, Rijst(t)afel, Salep, Scambling, Scoff, Seder, Smorgasborg, Snack, Spread, Square, Supper, Takeaway, Tea, Tiffin, Tightener, Twalhours, Undern

Meal-ticket LV

Mean, Meaning, Meant Aim, Average, Base, Betoken, Caitiff, Connotation, Curmudgeon, Denotate, Denote, Design, Dirty, Drift, Essence, Ettle, Feck, Footy, Foul, Gist, Golden, Hang, Harmonic, Humble, Hunks, Ignoble, Illiberal, Imply, Import, Inferior, Intend, Intermediate, Low, Mang(e)y,

Marrow, Medium, Mesquin, Method, Mid, Miserly, Narrow, Near, Nothing, One-horse, Ornery, Paltry, Petty, Pinch-penny, Pith, Point, Purport, ➤ PURPOSE, Ratfink, Revenue, Roinish, Roynish, Scall, Scrub, Scurvy, Semanteme, Semantic(s), Sememe, Sense, Shabby, Signify, Slight, Small, Sneaky, Snot, Sordid, Sparing, Spell, Stingy, Stink(ard), Stinty, Substance, Symbol, Thin, Threepenny, Tightwad, Two-bit, Value, Whoreson

Meander Fret, Sinuate, Stray, Wander, Weave, Wind

Meaningless Ducdame, Empty, Hollow, Hot air, Nonny, Rumbelow

Means Agency, Dint, Income, Media, Method, Mode, Opulence, Organ, Resources, Staple, Substance, Tactics, Ways, Wherewithal

Meantime, Meanwhile Among, Emong, Greenwich, Interim

Measles Morbilli, Roseola, Rose-rash, Rubella, Rubeola

Measure(d), Measuring, Measurement Acre, Actinometer, Alnage, Amphimacer, Anemometer, Aneroid, Angstrom, Anker, Ardeb, Are, Arpent, Arshin(e), As, Astrolabe, Aune, Barleycorn, Barrel, Barren, Barye, Bath, Bathometer, Beegha, Bekah, Bel, Bigha, Boll, Bolometer, Bovate, Breadth, Burette, Bushel, By(e)law, Cab, Calibre, Cal(l)iper, Candela, Caneh, Carat, Carucate, Cathetometer, Centimetre, Chain, Chalder, Chaldron, Ch(o)enix, Chopin, Clove, Colorimeter, Comb(e), Coomb, Cor, Cord, Coss, Coulomb, Crackdown, Cran, Crannock, Crore, Cryometer, Cubage, Cubit, Cumec, Cusec, Cyathus, Cyclometer, ➤ DANCE, Decalitre, Decastere, Decibel, Demarche, Denier, Densi(to)meter, Depth, Dessiatine, Dessyatine, Desyatin, Diameter, ➤ DIMENSION, Distance, Dose, Dosimeter, Double, Dram, Drastic, Drosometer, Dynamometer, Electrometer, Ell, Em, En, Entropy, Epha(h), Erg, Ergometer, Eriometer, Etalon, Eudiometer, Extensimeter, Extensometer, Fat, Fathom, Fermi, Firkin, Firlot, Fistmele, Foot, Furlong, Ga(u)ge, Gallon, Gavotte, Geodesy, Gill, Goniometer, Grain, Gravimeter, Groma, Hanap, Height, Hemina, Hide, Hin, Hogshead, Homer, Humidistat, Hydrometer, Hygrometer, Inch, Intoximeter, Jigger, Joule, Kaneh, Kelvin, Kilerg, Kilogray, Kilometre, Koss, Lambert, Last, Lay, Lea, League(r), Lento, Ley, Liang, Ligne, Limit, Line, Lippie, Lippy, Liquid, Log, Loure, Lug, Lysimeter, Manometer, Maze, Mease, Mekometer, Metage, Mete(r), Metre, Micrometer, Mil, Mile, Millimetre, Modius, Mole, Morgan, Mott, Mu, Muid, Mutchkin, Nail, Nephelometer, Nipperkin, Noggin, Odometer, Oenometer, Of, Omer, Opisometer, Optic®, Oxgang, Oximeter, Pace, Parasang, Parsec, Pascal, Peck, Pelorus, Perch, Photometer, Piezometer, Pint, Plumb, Pole, Pood, Potometer, Pottle, Precaution, Prophylactic, Puncheon, Quart(er), Quickstep, Radius, Ream, Reau, Resistance, Riddle, Rod, Romer, Rood, Rope, Ruler, Run(d)let, Sazhen, Scale, Share, Shot, ➤ SIZE, Sleever, Sound, Span, Spondee, Stade, Stadia, Standard, Statute, Step, Steradian, Stere(ometer), Strike, Survey, Tape(-line), Tappet-hen, Telemeter, Tellurometer, Tesla, Therm, Thou, Tierce, Titration, Toise, Token, Tot, Tromometer, Unit, Vara, Venturi (tube), Verst, Virgate, Volt, Warp, Waywiser, Wecht, Weighbridge, Wey, Winchester, Yard, Yardstick, Yojan(a)

Meat(s) Aitchbone, Bacon, Bard, Beef, Biltong, Brawn, Burger, Cabob, Carbonado, Carrion, Charcuterie, Chop, Collop, Confit, Croquette, Cut, Devon, Edgebone, Entrecote, Escalope, Essence, Fanny Adams, Fleishig, Fleishik, Flesh, Flitch, Force, Galantine, Gigot, Gobbet, Gosht, Griskin, Ham, Haslet, Jerky, Joint, Junk, Kabab, Kabob, Kebab, Kebob, Lamb, Loin, Luncheon, Mart, Mince, Mutton, Noisette, Offal, Olive, Pastrami, Piccata, Pith, Pork, Rillettes, Roast, Saddle, Sasatie, Satay, Schnitzel, Scran, Scrapple, Sey, Shashlik, Shishkebab, Sirloin, Spam®, Spare rib, Spatchcock, Steak, Tenderloin, Tongue, Veal, Venison, Vifda, Virgate, Vivda, Weiner schnitzel, Wurst

Meatball(s) Cecils, Croquette, Faggot, Falafel, Felafel, Fricadel, Knish, Kofta, Kromesky, Quenelle, Rissole

Meat extract Brawn, Gravy, Juice, Stock

Meatless Banian, Lent, Maigre, Vegetarian

Mecca Centre, Kaaba, Keblah, Kibla(h), Qibla

Mechanic(s) Apron-man, Artificer, Artisan, Banausic, Engineer, Fitter, Fundi, Hand, Journeyman, Kinematics, Kinetics, Operative, Statics, Technician

Mechanical, Mechanism Action, Apparatus, Auto, Banausic, Derailleur, Escapement, Gimmal, Instrument, Machinery, Movement, Organical, Pulley, Pushback, Servo, Trippet, Works

Medal(lion)(s) Award, Bar, Bronze, Decoration, Dickin, DSM, GC, George, Gold, Gong, Gorget, MM, Numismatic, Pan(h)agia, Purple Heart, Putty, Roundel, Silver, Touchpiece, VC, Vernicle

Meddle(r), Meddlesome Busybody, Dabble, Finger, Hen-hussy, ➤ INTERFERE, Interloper, Marplot, Mell, Monkey, Officious, Potter, Pragmatic, Pry, Snooper, Spoilsport, Tamper, Tinker, Trifle

Media PR

Mediate, Mediator ACAS, Arbitrate, Inercede, Interpose, Intervene, Liaison, Muti, Referee, Thirdsman, Trouble-shooter

Medical, Medicament, Medication, Medicine (chest) Allopathy, Alternative, Andrology, Anodyne, Antacid, Antibiotic, Antidote, Antisepsis, Antiseptic, Arnica, Asafetida, Ayurveda, Bi, Bismuth, Brunonian, Buchu, Bucku, Calumba, Carminative, Charm, Chiropody, Chrysarobin, Clinician, Complementary, Cordial, Corpsman, Cubeb, Curative, Defensive, Diapente, Diascordium, Diatessaron, Dose, Drops, ➤ DRUG, Electuary, Elixir, Emmenagogue, Empirics, Enema, Epulotic, Excipient, Fall-trank, Febrifuge, Feldsher, Forensic, Galen, Galenism, Gutta, Herb, Herbal, Hesperidin, Holistic, Hom(o)eopathy, Horse-drench, Iatric(al), Imhotep, Industrial, Inro, Iodine, Ipecac(uanha), Iron, Laxative, Leechcraft, Lotion, Magnesia, Menthol, Mishmi, Mixture, Muti, Nephritic, Nervine, Nostrum, Nux vomica, Officinal, Oporice, Orthopoedics, Osteopath, Panacea, Paregoric, Patent, Pharmacy, Physic, Physical, Pill, Placebo, Polychrest, Posology, Potion, Poultice, Preparation, Preventive, Proctology, Psionic, Psychiatry, Quinacrine, Quinine, Radiology, Relaxative, ➤ REMEDY, Salve, Sanative, Sanguinaria, Senna, Serology, Simple, Specific, Steel, Stomachic, Stramonium, Stupe, Suppository,

Syrup, Tabasheer, Tabashir, Tablet, Tar-water, Tetracycline, Tisane, Tonic, Trade, Treatment, Traumatology, Troche, Valerian, Veronal

Medicine man Koradji

Medick Snail

Medieval Archaic, Feudal, Gothic, Med, Old, Trecento

Mediocre Fair, Indifferent, Middling, Ordinary, Pap, So-So, Undistinguished

Meditate, Meditation, Meditator Brood, Chew, Cogitate, Gymnosophy, Hesychast, Muse, Mystic, Ponder, Reflect, Reverie, Revery, Ruminate, Transcendental, Vipassana, Weigh, Zazen

Mediterranean Levant, Midi

Medium Agency, Average, Clairvoyant, Element, Ether, Even, Happy, Home, Intermediary, M, Magilp, Mean, Megilp, Midway, Milieu, Oils, Organ, Ouija, Press, Radio, Regular, Shaman, Spiritist, Spiritualist, Television, Telly, TV, Vehicle

Medley Charivari, Collection, Gallimaufry, Jumble, Macedoine, Melange, Mix, Pastiche, Patchwork, Pi(e), Pot-pourri, Quodlibet, Ragbag, Salad, Salmagundi, Series

▷ **Medley** may indicate an anagram

Meek Docile, Griselda, Humble, Milquetoast, Patient, Tame

Meerschaum Sepiolite

Meet(ing), Meeting place Abide, Abutment, AGM, Appointment, Apropos, Assemble, Assembly, Assignation, Audience, Baraza, Bosberaad, Camporee, Caucus, Chapterhouse, Chautauqua, Clash, Conclave, Concourse, Concur, Confluence, Confrontation, Congress, Connivance, Contact, Conterminous, Convene, Convent(icle), Convention, Converge, Conversazione, Convocation, Correspond, Cybercafé, Defray, Demo, EGM, Encounter, Ends, Face, Find, Fit, For(e)gather, Forum, Fulfil, Gemot, Giron, Gorsedd, Guild, Gyeld, Gymkhana, Gyron, Howf(f), Hunt, Hustings, Indaba, Infall, Interface, Interview, Join, Junction, Korero, Liaise, Marae, Moot, Obviate, Occlusion, Occur, Oppose, Pay, Plenary, Plenum, Pnyx, Pow-wow, Prosper, Quadrivial, Quorate, Quorum, Races, Rally, Rencontre, Rencounter, Rendezvous, Reunion, Sabbat(h), Satisfy, Seance, See, Seminar, Session, Sit, Social, Suitable, Summit, Symposium, Synastry, Synaxis, Synod, Tackle, Tryst, Venue, Vestry, Wapinshaw, Wardmote, Workshop

Megalith(ic) Sarsen, Skara Brae, Stonehenge

Megalomaniac Monarcho

Megaphone Bull-horn

Megapode Mound-bird, Talegalla

Meiosis Understatement

Melancholy, Melancholic Adust, Allicholy, Allycholly, Anatomy, Atrabilious, Cafard, Despond(ency), Dreary, Dump(s), Gloom, Heart-sore, Hipped, Hump, Hyp, Hypochondria, Jaques, Lienal, Pensieroso, Pensive, Saturnine, Sombre, Spleen, Splenetic, Triste, Tristesse

Melanesian Kanak

Melia Margosa, Neem, Nim

Mêlée Brawl, Commotion, Fracas, Rally, Salmagundi, Scrum

Mellifluent Melodic

Mellow Genial, Mature, Ripe, Smooth

Melodrama(tic) Bathos, Histrionic, Sensation, Transpontine

Melody, Melodious Air, Arioso, Cabaletta, Cantabile, Cantilena, Cantus, Conductus, Counterpoint, Descant, Dulcet, Euphonic, Fading, Musical, Orphean, Plainsong, Ranz-des-vaches, Strain, Theme, Tunable, ➤ TUNE(FUL)

Melon(like) Cantaloup(e), Cas(s)aba, Gourd, Honeydew, Mango, Musk, Nar(r)as, Ogen, Pepo, Persian, Rock, Spanspek, Winter

Melt(ed), Melting Ablate, Colliquate, ➤ DISSOLVE, Eutectic, Eutexia, Flux, Found, Fuse, Fusil(e), Liquescent, Liquid, Run, Smectic, Syntexis, Thaw, Touch

Member Adherent, Arm, Branch, Bro(ther), Chin, Confrère, Cornice, Crossbeam, Crypto, Direction, Felibre, Fellow, Forearm, Forelimb, Gremial, Insider, Leg, Limb, Longeron, M, MBE, Montant, MP, Organ, Part, Partisan, Private, Rood-beam, Soroptomist, Stringer, Strut, Syndic, Toe

Membrane, Membranous Amnion, Arachnoid, Axilemma, Caul, Chorioallantois, Chorion, Choroid (plexus), Chromoplast, Conjunctiva, Cornea, Decidua, Dissepiment, Dura (mater), Endocardium, Endometrium, Endostium, Ependyma, Exine, Extine, Film, Frenulum, Haw, Hyaloid, Hymen, Indusium, Intima, Intine, Involucre, Mater, Mediastinum, Meninx, Mesentery, Mucosa, Mucous, Nictitating, Patagium, Pellicle, Pericardium, Pericarp, Perichondrium, Pericranium, Periost(eum), Periton(a)eum, Pia mater, Pleura, Putamen, Rim, Sarcolemma, Scarious, Schneiderian, Sclera, Serosa, Serous, Synovial, Tela, Third eyelid, Tissue, Tonoplast, Trophoblast, Tympan(ic), Vacuolar, Velum, Vitelline, Web

Memento, Memoir Keepsake, Locket, Relic, Remembrancer, Souvenir, Token, Trophy

Memo(randum) Bordereau, Cahier, Chit, IOU, Jot, Jurat, Minute, Note, Notepad, ➤ REMINDER

Memorable, Memorise, Memory Bubble, Con, Core, Echoic, Engram(ma), Flash (bulb), Get, Iconic, Immortal, Learn, Memoriter, Mind, Mneme, Mnemonic, Mnemosyne, Notable, Photographic, RAM, Recall, ➤ REMEMBER, Retention, Retrospection, ROM, Ro(a)te, Samskara, Short-term, Souvenir, Sovenance, Virtual

Memorial Cenotaph, Cromlech, Ebenezer, Gravestone, Hatchment, Marker, Monument, Mount Rushmore, Obelisk, Plaque, Relic, Statue, Tomb, Trophy

▶ **Memory loss** see LOSS OF MEMORY

Men(folk) Chaps, Chess, Cuffins, Male, Mortals, OR, Race, Troops

Menace, Menacing Danger, Endanger, Foreboding, Minatory, Peril, Pest, Threat(en)

Menagerie Ark, Circus, Zoo

Mend Beet, Bete, Bushel, Cobble, Correct, Darn, Fix, Heal, Improved, Patch, Piece, Recover, Remedy, ➤ REPAIR, Set, Sew, Solder, Trouble-shoot

Mendelevium Md

Mendicant Beggar, Franciscan, Servite

Menial Drudge, Drug, Eta, Fag, Flunkey, Lowly, Scullion, Servile, Toady, Underling

Meninx (D)jerba

Menstruation Menarche, Menses

Mental (condition) Alienism, Doolally, Eject, Insane, Noetic, Paranoia, Psychic

▷ **Mental** may indicate the chin

Mention(ed) Allusion, Bename, Benempt, Broach, Bynempt, Citation, Hint, Name, Notice, Quote, Refer, Speech, State, Suggest, Touch

Menu Card, Carte, Carte du jour, Cascading, Fare, List, Table d'hôte, Tariff

Mercantile Commercial, Trade

Mercator Cartographer

Mercenary Arnaout, Condottiere, Freelance, Greedy, Hack, Hessian, Hireling, Landsknecht, Legionnaire, Pindaree, Pindari, Rutter, Sordid, Spoilsman, Venal, Wildgeese

Merchandise Cargo, Goods, Line, Produce, Ware(s)

Merchant(man) Abudah, Antonio, Broker, Bun(n)ia, Burgher, Chandler, Chap, Crare, Crayer, Dealer, Factor, Flota, Hoastman, Importer, Jobber, Magnate, Marcantant, Mercer, Monger, Négociant, Pedlar, Polo, Retailer, Shipper, Speed, Stapler, Trader, Vintner, Wholesaler

Mercia Offa

Merciful, Mercy Amnesty, Charity, Clement, Compassionate, Grace, Humane, Kind, Kyrie, Lenient, Miserere, Misericord(e), Pacable, Pity, Quarter, Ruth, Sparing

Merciless Cruel, Hard, Hard-hearted, Inclement, Pitiless

Mercurial, Mercuric sulphide, Mercury Azoth, Cyllenius, Herald, Hermes, Hg, Hydrargyrum, Messenger, Quicksilver, Red-man, Spurge, Tiemannite, Volatile

Mere(ly) Allenarly, Bare, Common, Lake, Pond, Pool, Pure, Sheer, Tarn, Very

Merge(r), Merging Amalgamate, Blend, Coalesce, Consolidate, Die, Fusion, Incorporate, Interflow, Meld, Melt, Mingle, Syncretism, Unify, Unite

Meridian Magnetic, Noonday, Prime

Merit(ed) CL, Condign, Deserve, Due, Earn, Found, Rate, Virtue, Worth(iness)

Mermaid Dugong, Halicore, Merrow, Siren, Tavern, Undine

Merriment, Merry Andrew, Bonny, Boon, Cherry, Chirpy, Crank, Full, Gaudy, Gay, Gean, Gleesome, Greek, Jocose, Jocular, Jocund, Jolly, Joyous, L'allegro, Lively, On, Page, Riant, Sportive, Sunny, Vogie, Waggery, Wassail

Merry Andrew Clown, Jack-pudding, Pickle-herring

Merry-go-round Carousel, Whirligig

Merry-making Carnival, Festivity, Gaiety, Gaud, Gawd, Revel

Merrythought Clavicle, Collarbone, Wishbone

Mesh Cancellate, Chain, Entangle, Net, Reseau

Mess(y) Balls-up, Bedraggled, Boss, Botch, Canteen, Caudle, Chaos, Clutter, Cock-up, Failure, Farrago, Fiasco, Flub, Garboil, Glop, G(l)oop, Guddle, Gunge, Gunk, Gun-room, Hash, Horlicks, Hotch-potch, Hugger-mugger, Imbroglio, Lash-up, Louse, Mash, Meal, Mismanage, Mix, Mixter-maxter, Modge, Muck, Muff, Muss, Mux, Pi(e), Piss-up, Plight, Pollute, Pottage, Screw-up, Scungy, Shambles, Shambolic, Shemozzle, Sight, Slaister, Smudge, Snafu, Soss, Sty, Sully, Untidy, Whoopsie

Message(s) Aerogram, Bull, Bulletin, Cable, Contraplex, Dépêche, Despatch, Dispatch, Errand, Flame, Missive, News, Note, Pager, Posting, Postscript, Radiogram, Rumour, Signal, Slogan, SOS, Subtext, Telegram, Telephone, Telex, Tidings, Wire, ➤ WORD

Messenger Angel, Apostle, Azrael, Caddie, Caddy, Chaprassi, Chuprassy, Courier, Culver, Despatch-rider, Emissary, Envoy, Gaga, Gillie Whitefoot, Hatta, Herald, Hermes, Internuncio, Iris, Ladas, Mercury, Nuncio, Peon, Post, Pursuivant, Runner, Send, Shellycoat, Valkyrie

Messiah Christ, Emmanuel, Immanuel, Mahdi, Mashiach, Saviour, Son of man

Met Old Bill, Weather

Metal(lic) Ag, Aglet, Aiglet, Aiguillette, Al, Aluminium, Babbitt, Base, Bell, Billon, Brassy, Britannia, Cadmium, Chrome, Cobalt, Copper, Death, Dysprosium, Er(bium), Europium, Filler, Foil, Gallium, Germanium, Gib, Heavy, Hot, Ingot, Invar®, Iridium, Iron, Jangling, Magnolia, Manganese, Mineral, Misch, Mitis, Monel(l), Muntz, Nickel, Noble, Ore, Osmium, Platinum, Precious, Prince's, Protore, Regulus, Rhenium, Ruthenium, Samarium, Sheet(-iron), Sm, Sn, Sodium, Speculum, Speiss, Sprue, Steel, Strontium, Taggers, Terbic, Terbium, Terne, Thallium, Thorium, Tin, Tole, Tutania, Tutenag, Type, Wolfram, Zinc

Metal-worker Founder, Lorimer, Smith, Spurrier, Tubal Cain

Metamorphose Transmogrify

▷ **Metamorphosing** may indicate an anagram

Metaphor Conceit, Figure, Image, Kenning, Mixed, Symbol, Trope, Tropical

Metaphysics Ontology

Mete Inflict

Meteor(ite) Achondrite, Aerolite, Aerosiderite, Bolide, Chondrite, Comet, Drake, Fireball, Germinid, Leonid, Perseid, Siderite, Siderolite, Star(dust), Stony

Meter Alidad(e), Electric, Exposure, Gas, Parking, Water

Methane Alkane

Methedrine Speed

Method(ical) Art, Billings, Formula, Gram's, Line, Manner, Mode, Modus, Modus operandi, Monte Carlo, Montessori, Neat, Orderly, Painstaking, Ploy, Procedure, Process, Stanislavski, ➤ SYSTEM, Tactics, Technique, Way

Methodism, Methodist Huntingdonian, Jumper, Methody, Primitive, Ranter, Scientism, Southcottian, Swaddler, Wesley

Methuselah Bottle, Macrobiote

Meticulous Careful, ➤ EXACT, Finicky, Minute, Precise, Punctilious, Quiddler, Scrupulous, Thorough

Metier Line, Trade, Vocation

Metre Alexandrine, Amphibrach, Amphimacer, Anapaest, Antispast, Arsis, Cadence, Choliamb, Choree, Choriamb, Common, Galliambic, Iambic, M, Prosody, Rhythm, Scansion, Scazon, Spondee, Strophe, Trochee

Metric (system) MKS

Metroland Subtopia

Metropolitan Eparch

Mettle Ardour, Bravery, Courage, Ginger, Guts, Pith, ➤ PLUCK, Pride, Smeddum, Spirit, Spunk, Steel

Mew Caterwaul, Miaou, Miaow, Pen, Purr, Seagull, Waul, Wrawl

Mews Meuse, Muse(t), Musit, Stables

Mexican (Indian) Atlalt, Aztec, Carib, Chicano, Chichibec, Diaz, Greaser, Hairless, Hispanic, Maya, Mixtec, Montezuma, Nahuatl, Otomi, Spic, Spik, Taino, Toltec, Wetback, Zapotec, Zuni

Mezzo-soprano Tessa

Mica Biotite, Daze, Fuchsite, Glimmer, Lepidolite, Lepidomelane, Muscovite, Paragonite, Phlogopite, Rubellan, Talc, Verdite, Vermiculite

Mick(ey) Greek, Mouse

Micro Mu

Microbe Germ, Organism

Microphone Bug, Crystal, Mike, Radio, Throat

Microscope Electron, Engyscope, Lens, SEM

Mid Amongst

Midas Goldinger, Tamarin

Midday Meridian, N, Noon

Middle, Middling Active, Basion, Centre, Core, Crown, Enteron, Eye, Girth, Heart, Loins, Median, Mediocre, Meridian, Meseraic, Mesial, Mesne, Meso, Midriff, Moderate, Noon, Passive, Turn, Twixt, Wa(i)st

Middle age Menopause

Middle-cambrian Menevian

Middle class Bourgeois, Hova

Middle Eastern Arab, Iraqi, Omani

Middleman Broker, Comprador(e), Diaphragm, Interlocutor, Intermediary, Jobber, Median, Navel, Regrater, Regrator

Middlesex Hermaphrodite

Midget Dwarf, Homunculus, Lilliputian, Pygmy, Shrimp

Midianite Prowler

Midlands Mercia

Midnight G, O am

Midriff Phrenic, Skirt, Waist

Midshipman Brass-bounder, Easy, Middy, Oldster, Reefer, Snottie, Snotty

Midwife Accoucheur, Doula, Gran(nie), Granny, Howdie, Howdy, Lucina, Mab, Obstetric

Mien Air, Bearing, Demean, Manner

Might(iness), Mighty Force, Main, Mote, Nibs, Potence, ➤ POWER, Prowess, Puissant, Should, Strength

Mignon(ette) Dyer's rocket, Fillet, Reseda, Weld

Migraine Megrim, Scotodinia, Teichopsia

Migrant Externe, Gastarbeiter, Lemming, Traveller

Migrate, Migration, Migratory Colonise, Diapedesis, Diaspora, Drift, Eelfare, Exodus, Fleet, Run, Tre(c)k

Mikado Kami

Mike Bug, Stentorphone

Milanese Patarine

Mild(ly) Balmy, Benign, Bland, Clement, Euphemism, Genial, Gentle, Lenient, Litotes, Mansuete, Meek, ➤ MODERATE, Pacific, Patient, Sarcenet, Sars(e)net, Temperate

Mildew Downy, Foxing, Fungus, Mould, Oidium

Mile(s) Coverdale, Geographical, Li, Milliary, Nautical, Roman, Royal, Soldier, Square, Standish

Milesian Teague

Milestone Milliary, MS

Milfoil Yarrow

Militant Activist, Aggressive, Hezbollah, Hizbollah, Hizbullah, Hostile, Ireton, Martial

Military Battailous, Commando, Hawkish, Landwehr, Mameluke, Martial, Presidio, Soldatesque, West Point

Militia Fyrd, Guard, Haganah, Minuteman, Reserve, Trainband, Yeomanry

Milk(er), Milky Acidophilus, Beestings, Bland, Bleed, Bonny-clabber, Bristol, Casein, Colostrum, Condensed, Creamer, Crud, Curd, Emulge, Evaporated, Exploit, Galactic, Glacier, Goat's, Jib, Kefir, Kephir, K(o)umiss, Lactation, Lacteal, Latex, Madzoon, Magnesia, Matzoon, Mess, Opaline, Pinta, Posset, Sap, Shedder, Skim(med), Soya, Squeeze, Strippings, Stroke, Suckle, UHT, Whig, Yaourt, Yogh(o)urt

Milking-machine, Milking parlour Loan, Tapper

Milking-pail Leglan, Leglen, Leglin

Milkless Agalactic, Dry, Eild

Milkmaid, Milkman Chalker, Dey, Emulge, Kefir, Kephir, Radha, Rounder, Roundsman, Skimmed

Milksop Coward, Meacock, Namby-pamby, Nance, Pance, Weakling

Milk-vetch Loco

Milkweed Asclepias

Milkwort Senega

Mill(ing), Mills Aswarm, Barker's, Economist, Grind(er), Hayley, Kibble, Knurl, Melder, Molar, Nurl, Post, Press, Pug, Quern, Reave, Rob, Rolling, Satanic, Scutcher, Smock, Stamp, Strip, Surge, Thou, Tower, Water, Works

Miller Dusty, Glen, Grinder, Jester, Joe, Molendinar, Multurer

Millet Bajra, Bajree, Bajrii, Couscous, Dari, Doura, Dur(r)a, Grain, Negro-corn, Pearl, Proso, Ragee, Raggee, Ragi, Whisk

Millionaire Astor, Carnegie, Rockefeller, Rothschild, Vanderbilt

Millions, Millionth Crore, Femto-, Milliard, Muckle, Pico-

Millipede Songololo

Millstone Ligger, Rind, Rynd

Mim Perjink

Mime, Mimic(ry) Ape, Batesian, Copycat, Farce, Imitate, Impersonate, Mina, Mullerian, Mummer, Sturnine

Mimosa Cacoon, Saman

Mince Cecils, Chop, Dice, Grate, Grind, Prance, Rice

Mind(er) Aide, Beware, Brain, Genius, Handler, ➤ HEED, Herd, Id, Intellect, Noology, Noosphere, Phrenic, Psyche, Psychogenic, Resent, Sensorium, Tabula rasa, Tend, Thinker, Wit, Woundwort

Mine Acoustic, Bomb, Bonanza, Burrow, Camouflet, Claymore, Colliery, Dane-hole, Dig(gings), Egg, Eldorado, Excavate, Explosive, Fougade, Fougasse, Gallery, Gob, Golconda, Gopher, Grass, Land, Limpet, Magnetic, Nostromo, Open-cast, Ophir, Pit, Placer, Prospect, Sap, Set(t), Show, Sonic, Stannary, Stope, Strike, Undercut, Wheal, Win, Workings

Mine-deflector Otter, Paravane

Mine-owner Operator

Miner, Mine-worker, Mine-working Butty-gang, Collier, Cutter, Digger, Forty-niner, Geordie, Leaf, Molly Maguire, NUM, Oncost(man), Pitman, Shot-firer, Stall, Tributer, UDM

Mineral Acmite, Actinolite, Adularia, Alabandine, Alabandite, Alabaster, Albite, Alexandrite, Allanite, Allophane, Alunite, Amazonite, Amphibole, Analcime, Analcite, Anatase, Andalusite, Andesine, Anglesite, Anhydrite, Ankerite, Annabergite, Anorthite, Antimony, Apatite, Aphanite, Apophyllite, Aragonite, Arfvedsonite, Argentite, Arsenopyrite, Asbestos, Atacamite, Augite, Autunite, Axinite, Azurite, Babingtonite, Baddeleyite, Balas, Barytes, Bastna(e)site, Biotite, Blackjack, Blacklead, Blende, Blue john, Boehmite, Boracite, Borax, Bornite, Brookite, Brucite, Calamine, Calaverite, Calcite, Calomel, Carnallite, Carnelian, Carnotite, Cassiterite, Catseye, Celestine, Celestite, Cerus(s)ite, Chabazite, Chalcopyrite, Cheralite, Chert, Chessylite, Chiastolite, Chlorite, Chondrule, Chromite, Chrysoberyl, Chrysolite, Cinnabar, Cleveite, Clinochlore, Cobaltite, Coccolite, Colemanite, Columbate, Columbite, Cordierite, Corundum, Covellite, Cristobalite, Crocidolite, Crocoite, Cryolite, Cummingtonite, Cuprite, Cyanite, Cystolith, Dendrachate, Dendrite, Diallage, Diamond, Diaspore, Disthene, Dolomite, Dolomitic, Dumortierite, Dyscrasite, Dysodil(e), Dysodyle, Elaeolite, Emery, Endomorph, Enhydrite, Enstatite, Epidote, Epsomite, Erionite, Erythrite, Euclase, Eucrite, Euxenite, Fahlore, Fayalite, Feldspar, Feldspathoid, Felspar, Fibrolite®, Flinkite, Flint, Fluor(ite), Fluorapatite, Fluorspar, Forsterite, Franklinite, Gadolinite, Gahnite, Galena, Galinite, Gang(ue), Garnet, Garnierite, Gehlenite,

Germanite, Geyserite, Gibbsite, Glance, Glauconite, Gmelinite, Goethite, Goslarite, Göthite, Greenockite, Gummite, Gypsum, Gyrolite, Halloysite, Harmotome, Hauyne, H(a)ematite, Hercynite, Hessite, Heulandite, Honey-stone, Hornblende, Hypersthene, Ice spar, Idiomorphic, Idocrase, Illite, Ilmenite, Indicolite, Indigolite, Iodyrite, Jadeite, Jamesonite, Jargon, Jargoon, Jarosite, Josephinite, Kainite, Kermesite, Kernite, Kieserite, Kyanite, Laurdalite, Lazulite, Lazurite, Leucite, Lewisite, Lithia, Macle, Mafic, Magnetite, Malachite, Manganite, Marcasite, Margarite, Marialite, Massicot, Meerschaum, Melilite, Mellite, Mica, Microcline, Microlite, Microlith, Mimetite, Mispickel, Mizzonite, Molybdenite, Monazite, Montmorillonite, Moonstone, Mullite, Muscovite, Nacrite, Nepheline, Nephrite, Niccolite, Nitratine, Nitre, Nosean, Noselite, Oligoclase, Olivenite, Olivine, Orpiment, Orthoclase, Ottrelite, Paramorph, Parnasite, Pectolite, Pennine, Pentlandite, Periclase, Pericline, Peridot, Perimorph, Perovskite, Petuntse, Phenacite, Phosgenite, Phosphorite, Piedmontite, Pinite, Pitchblende, Pleonaste, Polianite, Pollucite, Polybasite, Polyhalite, Powellite, Prase, Prehnite, Proustite, Pseudomorph, Pyragyrite, Pyrite(s), Pyrolusite, Pyroxene, Quartz, Realgar, Redruthite, Resalgar, Rhodochrosite, Rhodonite, Riebeckite, Ripidolite, Rock-salt, Rosaker, Rubellite, Rutile, Samarskite, Sanidine, Saponite, Sard, Scapolite, Scheelite, Schorl, Scolecite, Serpentine, Siderite, Silica, Sillimanite, Skutterudite, Smaragdite, Smectite, Smithsonite, Sodalite, Spar, Sperrylite, Sphalerite, Sphene, Spinel, Spodumene, Stannite, Staurolite, Stibnite, Stilbite, Sylvanite, Sylvite, Synadelphite, Taconite, Talc, Tantalite, Tennantite, Tenorite, Thaumasite, Thorianite, Thorite, Thulite, Tincal, Titanite, Topaz, Torbernite, Tourmaline, Trap, Tremolite, Tripoli, Troilite, Trona, Troostite, Turgite, Ulexite, Umber, Uran(in)ite, Uranium, Urao, Uvarovite, Variscite, Vermiculite, Vesuvianite, Vulpinite, Wavellite, Wernerite, Willemite, Witherite, Wolframite, Wollastonite, Wulfenite, Xenotime, YAG, Ythro-cerite, Zaratite, Zeolite, Zincite, Zinkenite, Zircon, Zoisite, Zorgite
Mineral water Apollinaris, Tonic
Minesweeper Oropesa, Unity
Mingle Blend, Consort, Interfuse, Mell, ➤ MIX, Participate, Socialise, Unite
Mini Car, Skirt, Teen(s)y
Miniature, Miniaturist Cosway, Microcosm, Midget, Model, Toy, Young
Minimise, Minimum (range) Bare, Downplay, Fewest, Least, Neap, Shoestring, Stime, Styme, Threshold, Undervalue
▷ **Minimum of** may indicate the first letter
Minion Flunkey, Lackey, Pet, Subordinate, Tool, Vassal
Minister Ambassador, Attend, Buckle-beggar, Chancellor, Chaplain, Cleric, Coarb, Commissar, Deacon, Dewan, Diplomat, Divine, Dominee, Dominie, D(i)wan, Envoy, Mas(s)john, Mes(s)john, Moderator, Nurse, Officiant, Padre, Parson, Peshwa, Preacher, Predikant, Presbyter, Rector, Secretary, Seraskier, ➤ SERVE, Stickit, Tend, Visier, Vizier, Wazir, Wizier
Ministry Defence, Department, Dept, DoE, MOD, MOT, Orders, Service
Mink Kolinsky, Mutation, Vison

Minnow Penk, Pink, Tiddler

Minor(ity) Child, Comprimario, Ethnic, Faction, Few, Infant, Junior, Less, Minutia, Nonage, One-horse, Petty, Pupillage, Slight, Trivial, Ward

Minotaur Bull-headed

Minstrel Allan-a-dale, Bard, Blondel, Bones, Busker, Cantabank, Christy, Cornerman, Gleeman, Hamfatter, Joculator, Jongleur, Minnesinger, Nigger, Pierrot, Scop, Singer, Taillefer

Mint Aim, Bugle-weed, Catnip, Coin, Ettle, Fortune, Herb, Horse, Humbug, Labiate, Monarda, Monetise, Nep, New, Penny-royal, Polo®, Poly, Selfheal, Stamp, Strike, Unused, Utter

Minute(s), Minutiae Acta, Alto, Degree, Detailed, Diatom, Entry, Infinitesimal, Little, Micron, Mo, Mu, Nano-, Resume, Small, Teen(t)sy, Teeny, Tine, Tiny, Trivia, Tyne, Wee

Minx Hellion

Miracle Cana, Marvel, Merel(l), Meril, Morris, Mystery, Phenomenon, Thaumaturgic, Theurgy, Wonder

Mirage Fata morgana, Illusion, Loom, Northern lights

Mire Bog, Glaur, Lair(y), Latch, Lerna, Lerne, Loblolly, Marsh, Mud, Quag, Sludge, Soil

Mirky Dark, Dirk(e)

Mirror(ed) Alasnam, Busybody, Cambuscan, Catoptric, Cheval, Coelostat, Conde, Enantiomorph, Glass, Image, Imitate, Lao, Merlin, Pierglass, Psyche, Rearview, ➤ REFLECT, Reynard, Shisha, Siderostat, Sign, Specular, Speculum, Stone, Vulcan, Wing

Mirror-image Perversion

Mirth(ful) Cheer, Dream, Festive, Hilarity, Joy, Laughter, Spleen

▷ **Misalliance** may indicate an anagram

Misanthrope Cynic, Timon

Misapplication Catachresis, Misuse

Misappropriate Asport, Purloin, Steal

Miscarry Abort, Backfire, Fail, Slink

Miscegenation Allocarpy

Miscellaneous, Miscellany Assortment, Chow, Collectanea, Diverse, Misc, Olio, Omnium-gatherum, Potpourri, Raft, Ragbag, Sundry, Various

Mischief(-maker), Mischievous Ate, Bale, Bane, Cantrip, Cloots, Devilment, Diablerie, Dido, Disservice, Gremlin, Harm, Hellery, Hellion, Hob, Imp, Injury, Jinks, Larrikin, Malicho, Mallecho, Nickum, Owl-spiegle, Pestilent, Pickle, Prank, Puckish, Rascal, Scally(wag), Scamp, Scapegrace, Shenanigans, Spriteful, Tricksy, Wag, Wicked

Misconception Delusion, Idol(on), Idolum, Misunderstanding

Misconduct Impropriety, Malfeasance, Malversation

Miscreant Reprobate, Sinner

Misdeed Offence, Peccadillo, Trespass, Wrong

▷ **Misdelivered** may indicate an anagram

Misdemeanour Delict, Peccadillo, Tort

Miser(ly) Carl, Cheapskate, Cheese-parer, Close, Curmudgeon, Gare, Grasping, Harpagon, Hunks, Marner, Meanie, Mingy, Niggard, Nipcheese, Nipfarthing, Pennyfather, Pinch-commons, Puckfist, Runt, Scrape-good, Scrape-penny, Screw, Scrimping, Scrooge, Skinflint, Snudge, Storer, Tightwad, Timon

Miserable, Misery Abject, Bale, Cat-lap, Crummy, Distress, Dole, Forlorn, Gloom, Grief, Hell, Joyless, Lousy, Perdition, Sorry, Sourpuss, Tragic, Triste, ➤ UNHAPPY, Woe(begone), Wretched

Misfire Dud

Misfit Drop-out, Geek, Loner, Maverick

Misfortune Accident, Affliction, Bale, Calamity, Curse, Disaster, Distress, Dole, Hex, Ill, Reverse, Rewth, Ruth, Wroath

Misgiving(s) Anxiety, Doubt, Dubiety, Qualms, Scruples

Misguide(d) Impolitic

▷ **Misguided** may indicate an anagram

Mishandle Abuse

Mishap Accident, Contretemps, Misaunter, Misfortune, Wroath

Mishit, Misstroke Crab, Draw, Edge, Fluff, Muff, Sclaff, Shank, Slice, Thin, Top

Misinterpret Wrest

Mislay Leese, Lose

Mislead(ing) Blind, Cover-up, Deceive, Delude, Dupe, Equivocate, Fallacious, False, Gag, Red herring, Runaround

▷ **Misled** may indicate an anagram

Mismanage Blunder, Bungle, Muddle

Mismatch Kludge

Misplace(ment) Ectopia

Misplay Fluff, Whitechapel

Misprint Error, Literal, Slip, Typo

Mispronunciation Cacoepy, Lallation, Lambdacism

Misrepresent(ation) Abuse, Belie, Calumny, Caricature, Colour, Distort, Falsify, Garble, Lie, Slander, Traduce

Miss(ing) Abord, Avoid, Colleen, Desiderate, Dodge, Drib, Err(or), Fail, Forego, Gal, ➤ GIRL, Kumari, Lack, Lass, Link, Lose, Mademoiselle, Maid, Maiden, Mile, Muff(et), Neglect, Negligence, Omit, Otis, Overlook, Senorita, Skip, Spinster, Unmeet, Wanting

▷ **Miss** may refer to Missouri

Missal Breviary, Te igitur, Triodion

Misshapen Crooked, Deformed, Dysmelia, Gnarled

Missile Air-to-air, Ammo, Anti-ballistic, Arrow, Artillery, Atlas, Ball, Ballistic, Blue streak, Bolas, Bomb, Boomerang, Brickbat, Bullet, Cruise, Dart, Dingbat, Doodlebug, Dum-dum, Exocet®, Fléchette, Grenade, Harpoon, ICBM, Interceptor, Jired, Kiley, Kyley, Kylie, Maverick, Minuteman, MIRV, Missive, Onion, Patriot, Pellet, Pershing, Polaris, Poseidon, Quarrel, Rocket, SAM, Scud, Shell, Shot, Side-winder, Smart bomb, Snowball,

Spear, SSM, Standoff, Styx, Surface to air, Surface to surface, Thor, Titan, Torpedo, Tracer, Trident, UAM, Warhead

Mission(ary) Aidan, Alamo, Antioch, Apostle, Assignment, Bethel, Caravan, Charge, Delegation, Embassage, Embassy, Errand, Evangelist, Iona, Legation, Livingstone, LMS, Message, NASA, Ninian, Op, Paul, Quest, Reclaimer, Task, Vocation, Xavier

Missis, Missus, Mrs Devi, Maam, Mrs, Wife

Missive Letter, Message, Note

Missouri Mo

▶ **Misstroke** see MISHIT

Mist(y) Blur, Brume, Cloud, Dew, Drow, Fog, Haar, Haze, Hoar, Miasma, Moch, Nebular, Niflheim, Rack, Roke, Scotch, Sfumato, Smir(r), Smog, Smur, Vapour

Mistake(n) Bish, Bloomer, Blooper, Blunder, Boner, Booboo, Boss, Botch, Clanger, Clinker, Confound, Deluded, Erratum, Error, Fault, Floater, Flub, Fluff, Gaffe, Goof, Howler, Incorrect, Lapse, Malapropism, Miss, Muff, Nod, Oversight, Plonker, Pratfall, ➤ SLIP, Slip-up, Solecism, Stumer, Trip, Typo

▷ **Mistake(n)** may indicate an anagram

Mister Babu, Effendi, Mr, Sahib, Senor, Shri, Sir, Sri

Mistletoe Album, Missel, Parasite, Viscum

Mistreat Abuse, Attrite, Violate

Mistress Amie, Aspasia, Canary-bird, Chatelaine, Concubine, Courtesan, Demimondaine, Devi, Doxy, Goodwife, Herself, Hussif, Inamorata, Instructress, Lady, Leman, Maintenon, Montespan, Mrs, Natural, Paramour, Stepney, Teacher, Wardrobe, Wife

Mistrust Doubt, Gaingiving, Suspect, Suspicion

Misunderstand(ing) Disagreement, Discord, Mistake

Misuse Abuse, Defalcate, Malappropriate, Malapropism, Maltreat, Perversion, Torment

Mite Acaridian, Acarus, Bit, Child, Fowl, Lepton, Little, Rust, Sarcoptes, Speck, (Red) spider, Tyroglyphid, Varroa, Widow's

Mitigate, Mitigating Abate, Allay, Allieve, Ameliorate, Extenuating, Lenitive, Lessen, Palliate, Quell, Relief, Relieve

Mitosis Anaphase

Mitre Hat, Tiar(a)

Mitt(en) Fist, Glove, Hand, Paw

Mix(ed), Mixture, Mix-up Alloy, Amalgam, Associate, Assortment, Attemper, Balderdash, Bigener, Bland, Blend, Blunge, Brew, Card, Caudle, Chow, Cocktail, Co-meddle, Compo, Compound, Conglomerate, Consort, Cross, Disperse, Dolly, Drammock, Embroil, Emulsion, Farrago, Garble, Grill, Griqua, Heather, Hobnob, Hotchpotch, Hybrid, Imbroglio, Interlace, Intermingle, Jumble, Lace, Lard, Linctus, Load, Macedoine, Matissé, Meddle, Medley, Melange, Mell, Meng(e), Ment, Mess, Mestizo, Ming(le), Miscellaneous, Miscellany, Mishmash, Mong, Motley, Muddle, Muss(e), Neapolitan, Octaroon, Octoroon, Olio, Olla, Pi(e), Potin, Pousowdie,

Powsowdy, Praiseach, Promiscuous, Raggle-taggle, Ragtag, Salad, Scramble, Stew, Stir, Temper, Through-other, Yblent

▷ **Mixed** may indicate an anagram

Mizzle Scapa, Scarper

Mnemonic Quipo, Quipu, Reminder

Moab(ite) Balak, Ruth, Wash-pot

Moan(ing) Beef, Bleat, Groan, Hone, Keen, ➤ LAMENT, Meane, Plangent, Sough, Wail, W(h)inge

Moat Dike, Ditch, Fuss

Mob(ster) Army, Assail, Canaille, Crew, Crowd, Gang, Herd, Hoi-polloi, Hoodlum, Lynch, Ochlocrat, Press, Rabble, Raft, Ragtag, Riff-raff, Rout, Scar-face

Mobile, Mobilise, Mobility Donna, Fluid, Movable, Plastic, Rally, Thin, Upward(ly), Vagile, Vertical

Mob-rule Ochlocracy

Mocassin Larrigan, Shoe, Snake

Mock(ery), Mocking Ape, Banter, Chaff, Chyack, Cod, Cynical, Deride, Derisory, Dor, Ersatz, False, Farce, Fleer, Flout, Gab, Geck, Gibe, Guy, Imitation, Irony, Irrisory, ➤ JEER, Jibe, Lampoon, Mimic, Narquois, Paste, Pillorise, Rail(lery), Ridicule, Sacrilege, Sardonic, Satirise, Scout, Sham, Simulate, Slag, Travesty, Wry

Mocking-bird Mimus, Sage-thrasher

Mode Aeolian, Convention, Dorian, Fashion, Form, Iastic, Lydian, Manner, Phrygian, Plagal, Rate, Step, Style, Ton

Model(ler) Archetype, Bozzeto, Cast, Copy, Diorama, Doll, Dummy, Ecorché, Effigy, Epitome, Example, Exemplar, Fictor, Figure, Figurine, Icon, Ideal, Image, Instar, Jig, Last, Layman, Manakin, Manikin, Mannequin, Maquette, Mock-up, ➤ MOULD, Norm, Original, Orrery, Parade, Paragon, Pattern, Pilot, Pose(r), Posture-maker, Prototype, Replica, Sedulous, Sitter, Specimen, Standard, Superwaif, T, Template, Templet, Terrella, Toy, Trilby, Twiggy, Type, Typify, Waif, Waxwork, Working

▷ **Model(s)** may indicate an anagram

Modem Subset

Moderate(ly), Moderation Abate, Allay, Alleviate, Average, Centre, Chasten, Continent, Diminish, Discretion, Ease, Gentle, Girondist, Ho, Lessen, Lukewarm, Measure, Medium, Menshevik, Mezzo, Middling, Mild, Mitigate, OK, Politique, Reason(able), Slake, So-so, Temper(ate), Tolerant, Tone, Via media, Wet

Modern(ise) AD, Aggiornamento, Contemporary, Fresh, Latter(-day), Neonomian, Neoterical, ➤ NEW, Present-day, Progressive, Recent, Swinger, Update

Modest(y) Aidos, Blaise, Chaste, Decent, Demure, Humble, Ladylike, Maidenly, Mim, Mussorgsky, Propriety, Prudish, Pudency, Pure, Reserved, Shame, Shy, Unpretending, Unpretentious, Verecund

Modifiable, Modification, Modify Adapt, Alter, Backpedal, Change, Enhance, Extenuate, H, Leaven, Plastic, Qualify, Retrofit, Sandhi, Scumble, Soup, Streamline, Temper, Vary

Modulation, Module, Modulus Accent, Cadence, Command, Inflexion, Lem, Mitigate, Tune, Unit, Vary, Young

Mogul Bigwig, Magnate, Padishah, Plutocrat, Taipan, VIP

Mohair Moire

Mohammed, Mohammedan (era) Hegira, Hejira, Hejra, Hijra, Islamite, Mahdi, Mahoun(d), Moslem, Muezzin, Mussulman, Prophet, Said, Shiite, Sunna(h)

Moist(en), Moisture Baste, Bedew, Damp, Dank, De(a)w, Humect, Latch, Love-in-a-mist, Madefy, Mesarch, Nigella, Sponge, Wet

▷ **Moither** may indicate an anagram

Molar Grinder, Mill-tooth, Secodont, Tooth, Wang

Molasses Blackstrap, Sorghum, Treacle

Mole(hill) Breakwater, Fen-cricket, Jetty, Miner, Mo(u)diewart, Moudi(e)wart, Mouldiwarp, Naeve, Notoryctes, Orology, Pier, Sea-wall, Sleeper, Spot, Spy, Star-nose, Talpa, Want(hill), Warp

Molecular, Molecule Acceptor, Atom, Buckyball, Carbene, Cavitand, Chiral, Chromophore, Closed chain, Cobalamin, Codon, Coenzyme, Cofactor, Dimer, DNA, Enantiomorph, Footballene, Fullerene, Gram, Hapten, Iota, Isomer, Kinin, Ligand, Long-chain, Metabolite, Metameric, Monomer, Peptide, Polymer, Polysaccharide, Quark, Replicon, Semantide, Stereoisomer, Trimer, Uridine

Molendinar Mill

Molest(er) Annoy, Bother, Harass, Nonce, Scour

Moll(y) Bloom, Bonnie, Cutpurse, Flanders, Girl, Maguire, Malone, May, Sissy

Mollify Appease, Fob, Mease, Mitigate, Pacify, Relax, Soften, Temper

Mollusc(s) Ammonite, Amphineura, Arca, Argonaut, Ark-shell, Belemnite, Bulla, Capiz, Chiton, Clam, Cockle, Conch, Cone-shell, Cowrie, Cowry, Cuttle(fish), Dentalium, Doris, Gaper, Gast(e)ropod, Helix, Lamellibranch, Limpet, Malacology, Murex, Mussels, Mya, Nautilus, Neopilina, Octopod, Octopus, Olive, Opisthobranch, Oyster, Paper nautilus, Paper-sailor, Pearly nautilus, Pecten, Pelican's-foot, Pholas, Piddock, Pinna, Polyp, Poulpe, Pteropod, Quahaug, Quahog, Razorshell, Saxicava, Scallop, Scaphopoda, Sea-hare, Sea-lemon, Sea-slug, Sepia, ➤ SHELLFISH, Shipworm, Slug, Snail, Solen, Spat, Spoot, Squid, Strombus, Tectibranch, Tellen, Tellin, Teredo, Toheroa, Triton, Trochophore, Trochus, Turbo, Tusk-shell, Unio, Univalve, Veliger, Venus, Vitrina, Wentletrap, Whelk, Wing-shell, Winkle

Mollycoddle Indulge, Pamper

Moloch Thorn-devil

Molten Dissolved, Fusil, Melted

Molybdenum Mo

Moment(s), Momentous Bit, Flash, Import, Instant, Jiffy, ➤ MINUTE, Mo, Nonce, Pun(c)to, Sands, Sec, Shake, Stound, Stownd, Tick, Time, Trice, Twinkling, Weighty, Wink

Momentum Impetus, L, Speed, Thrust

Mona(s) I, IOM

Monaco Grimaldi

Monarch(y) Autocrat, Butterfly, Crown, Emperor, HM, Karling, King, Potentate, Queen, Raine, Reign, Ruler, Tsar

Monastery Abbey, Abthane, Charterhouse, Chartreuse, Cloister, Community, Gompa, Hospice, Lamaserai, Lamasery, Laura, Priory, Vihara, Wat

Monastic Abthane, Celibate, Holy, Monkish, Oblate, Secluded

Monday Collop, J'ouvert, Meal, Oatmeal, Plough, Whit

Mondrian Piet

Monetary, Money Ackers, Akkas, Allowance, Annat, Ante, Assignat, Banco, Batta, Blood, Blunt, Boodle, Bottle, Brass, Bread, Cabbage, Capital, Cash, Change, Chink, ➤ COIN, Collateral, Conscience, Currency, Danger, Dib(s), Dingbat, Dosh, Dust, Easy, Even, Fat, Fee, Float, Folding, Fonds, Fund, Funny, Gelt, Gilt, Gold, Grant, Gravy, Greens, Hoot, Hot, Hush, Ingots, Investment, Kale, Key, L, Lolly, Loot, Lucre, M, Mammon, Maundy, Mazuma, Means, Mint, Moola(h), Needful, Nest-egg, Note, Numismatic, Nummary, Oaker, Ochre, Offertory, Oof, Outlay, P, Packet, Peanuts, Pecuniary, Pelf, Pin, Plastic, Plum, Pocket, Posh, Prize, Proceeds, Profit, Protection, Purse, Ready, Rebate, Resources, Revenue, Rhino, Rowdy, Salt(s), Scratch, Scrip, Seed, Shin-plaster, Ship, Siller, Silver, Smart, Soap, Spondulicks, Stake, Sterling, Stuff, Sugar, Sum, Table, Takings, Tin, Tranche, Viaticum, Wad, Wealth, Wonga

Money-box Penny-pig, Piggy bank

Moneylender Gombeen, Shylock, Usurer

Moneymaking Earner, Profitable, Quaestuary

Mongol(ian) Bashkir, Buriat, Buryat, Calmuck, Chuvash, Evenski, Golden Horde, Kalmuck, Kara-Kalpak, Kazak(h), Kublai Khan, Kyrgyz, Lapp, Lepcha, Manchoo, Manchu, Mishmi, Mogul, Samoyed, Shan, Tamerlane, Tatar, Tungus(ic), Ural-altaic

Mongoose Ichneumon, Mangouste, Meerkat, Suricate, Urva

Mongrel Bitser, Cross(bred), ➤ DOG, Hybrid, Kuri, Lurcher, Mutt, Quadroon, Tyke, Underbred

Monitor Detect, Goanna, Iguana, Lizard, Observe, Prefect, Record, Track, Warship, Watchdog, Worral, Worrel

Monk(s) Abbey-lubber, Abbot, Acoemeti, Archimandrite, Arhat, Asser, Augustinian, Austin, Basilian, Bede, Beghard, Benedictine, Bernardine, Bethlehemite, Bhikhu, Black, Bonaventura, Bonze, Brother, Bruno, Caedmon, Caloyer, Carthusian, Celestine, Cellarist, Cenobite, Cistercian, Cluniac, Coenobite, Cowl, Culdee, Dan, Dervish, Dom, Dominican, Félibre, Feuillant, Fraticelli, Friar, General, Gyrovague, Hegumen, Hermit, Hesychast, Hildebrand, Ignorantine, Jacobin, Jacobite, Jerome, Lama,

Maurist, Mechitharist, Mekhitarist, Mendel, Norbertine, Obedientiary, Oblate, Olivetan, Order, Pelagian, Prior, Rakehell, Rasputin, Recluse, Recollect, Roshi, Salesian, Sangha, Savonarola, Silverback, Sub-prior, Talapoin, Theatine, Thelemite, Thelonius, Thomas à Kempis, Tironensian, Trappist, Votary

Monkey Anger, Ape, Baboon, Bandar, Bonnet, Bushbaby, Capuchin, Catar(r)hine, Cebidae, Cebus, Chacma, Coaita, Colobus, Cynomolgus, Diana, Douc, Douroucouli, Drill, Durukuli, Entellus, Galago, Gelada, Gibbon, Grease, Green, Grison, Grivet, Guenon, Guereza, Hanuman, Hoolock, Howler, Hylobates, Indri, Jacchus, Jackey, Jocko, Kippage, Langur, Leaf, Lemur, Macaque, Magot, Malmag, Mandrill, Mangabey, Marmoset, Meddle, Meerkat, Mico, Midas, Mona, Mycetes, Nala, Nasalis, Ouakari, Ouistiti, Phalanger, Platyrrhine, Powder, Proboscis, Pug, Rage, Ram, Rhesus, Sago(u)in, Saguin, Sai(miri), Sajou, Saki, Sapajou, Siamang, Silen(us), Silverback, Simian, Simpai, Slender loris, Spider, Squirrel, Talapoin, Tamarin, Tamper, Tarsier, Tee-tee, Titi, Toque, Trip-hammer, Troop, Tup, Uakari, Vervet, Wanderoo, Wistiti, Wou-wou, Wow-wow, Wrath, Zati

Monkey-nut Earth-pea

Monkey-puzzle Araucaria, Bunya-bunya

Monkshood Aconite

Monocle Eye-glass, Gig-lamp, Lorgnon, Quiz(zing-glass)

Monocot(yledon) Araceae, Endogen, Tradescantia

Monodon Narwhal

Monogram, Monograph Chi-rho, Cipher, Study, Treatise, Tug(h)ra

Monolith Ayers Rock, Cenotaph, Chambers Pillar

Monologue Patter, Rap, Recitation, Soliloquy, Speech

Monopolise, Monoply Appalto, Bloc, Cartel, Corner, Engross, Octroi, Régie, Trust

Monotonous, Monotony Boring, Dull, ➤ FLAT, Grey, Humdrum, Same(y), Sing-song, Tedious

Monsoon Hurricane, Typhoon, ➤ WIND

▷ **Monsoon** may indicate weekend (Mon soon)

Monster, Monstrous Alecto, Asmodeus, Bandersnatch, Behemoth, Bunyip, Caliban, Cerberus, Cete, Chichevache, Chim(a)era, Cockatrice, Colossal, Cyclops, Dabbat, Deform, Dinoceras, Dismayd, Div, Dragon, Echidna, Enormous, Erebus, Erinys, Erl-king, Eten, Ettin, Evil-one, Fiend, Fire-drake, Frankenstein, Freak, Geryon, Ghost, Giant, Gila, Golem, Gorgon, Green-eyed, Grendel, Harpy, Hippocampus, Hippogriff, Huge, Hydra, Jabberwock, Kraken, Lamia, Leviathan, Lilith, Mastodon, Medusa, Minotaur, Misbegotten, Moloch, Mylodont, Nessie, Nicker, Nightmare, Ogre, Ogr(e)ish, Opinicus, Orc, Outrageous, Pongo, Sarsquatch, Satyral, Scylla, Shadow, Simorg, Simurg(h), Siren, Skull, Snark, Spectre, Sphinx, Spook, Stegodon, Stegosaur, Succubus, Taniwha, Teras, Teratoid, Triceratops, Troll, Typhoeus, Typhon, Unnatural, Vampire, Vast,

Wasserman, Wendego, Wendigo, Wer(e)wolf, Wyvern, Xiphopagus, Yowie, Ziffius

Month(ly) Ab, Abib, Adar, April, Asadha, Asvina, August, Bhadrapada, Brumaire, Bul, Cheshvan, Chislev, December, Dhu-al-Hijjah, Dhu-al-Qadah, Elul, February, Floreal, Frimaire, Fructidor, Germinal, Hes(h)van, Iy(y)ar, January, July, Jumada, June, Jysaitha, Kartuka, Kisleu, Kislev, Lide, Lunar, Magha, March, Margasirsa, May, Messidor, Mo, Moharram, Moon, Muharram, Muharrem, Nisan, Nivose, November, October, Periodical, Phalguna, Pluviose, Prairial, Rabia, Rajab, Ramadan, Safar, Saphar, September, S(h)ebat, Sha(a)ban, Shawwal, Sivan, Solar, Tammuz, Tebeth, Thermidor, Tisri, Vaisakha, Veadar, Vendemiaire, Ventose

Monument Ancient, Arch, Archive, Cenotaph, Column, Cromlech, Dolmen, Henge, Megalith, Memorial, Menhir, National, Pantheon, Pyramid, Stele(ne), Stone, Stonehenge, Stupa, Talayot, Tombstone, Trilith, Trilithon, Urn

Mood(y) Active, Anger, Atmosphere, Attitude, Capricious, Dudgeon, Enallage, Fit, Glum, Grammar, Humour, Hump, Imperative, Morale, Optative, Passive, Peat, Pet, Revivalist, Sankey, Spleen, Subjunctive, Temper, Tid, Tone, Tune, Vein, Vinegar, Whim

Moon(light), Moony Aah, Alignak, Aningan, Apogee, Artemis, Astarte, Callisto, Calypso, Cheese, Cynthia, Diana, Epact, Eye, Flit, Full, Ganymede, Gibbous, Glimmer, Grimaldi, Harvest, Hecate, Hunter's, Hyperion, Inconstant, Juliet, Leda, Lucina, Luna(r), Mani, Mascon, McFarlane's Buat, Month, Mope, Nocturne, Octant, Paddy's lantern, Paraselene, Pasiphaë, Phoebe, Proteus, Raker, Satellite, Selene, Set, Shot, Sickle, Sideline, Silvery, Sonata, Stargaze, Stone, Syzygy, Thebe, Thoth, Titan, Triton, Umbriel, Wander

Moonraker Astrogeologist, Gothamite

Moonshine(r) Hootch, Poteen, Rot, Shebeener

Moor(ing), Moorish Berth, Culloden, Dock, Fen, Heath, Iago, Ilkley, Makefast, Moresque, Moroccan, Mudéjar, Othello, Palustrine, Roadstead, Ryepeck, Saracen, Tether, ➤ TIE, Wold

Mop(ping) Dwile, Flibbertigibbet, Girn, Glib, Shag, Squeegee, Squilgee, Swab, Swob, Thatch, ➤ WIPE

Mope Boody, Brood, Peak, Sulk

Moral(ity), Morals Apologue, Deontic, Ethic(al), Ethos, Everyman, Fable, High-minded, Integrity, Precept, Principled, Puritanic, Righteous, Sittlichkeit, Tag, Upright, Virtuous, Well-thewed

Morale Ego, Mood, Spirit, Zeal

Moralise, Moralising Preach, Sententious

Moralist Prig, Prude, Puritan, Whitecap

Morass Bog, Fen, Flow, Marsh, Moss, Quagmire, Slough

Morbid(ity) Anasarca, Ascites, Cachaemia, Dropsy, Ectopia, Ghoul(ish), Gruesome, Pathological, Plethora, Prurient, Religiose, Sick, Sombre

Mordant Biting, Caustic, Critic(al), Sarcastic, Tooth

More Additional, Else, Extra, Increase, Less, Mae, Merrier, Mo(e), ➤ NO MORE, Over, Piu, Plus, Stump, Utopia

Moreover Also, Besides, Eft, Either, Further, Too, Yet

Morgan Buccaneer, Pirate

Moribund Dying, Stagnant, Withered

Mormon Danite, Utah, Young

Morning Ack-emma, Am, Antemeridian, Dawn, Daybreak, Early, Matin(al), Morrow

Morning-glory Bindweed, Ipomoea, Turbith, Turpeth

Morning-star Morgenstern, Phosphor(us), Threshel, Venus

Moroccan, Morocco Agadir, Leather, MA, Mo(o)r, Riff, Tangerine, Venus

Moron Fool, Idiot, Schmuck, ➤ STUPID

Morose Acid, Boody, Churlish, Cynical, Gloomy, Glum, Grum, Moody, Sour-eyed, Sullen, Surly

Morph Phase

Morris Car, Dance, Merel(l), Meril

Morrow Future

Morse Code, Iddy-umpty, Walrus

Morsel Bit, Bite, Bouche, Canape, Crumb, Dainty, Morceau, Ort, Scrap, Sippet, Sop, Tidbit, Titbit

Mortal(ity) Averr(h)oism, Being, Deathly, ➤ FATAL, Grave, Human, Lethal, Yama

Mortar, Mortar-board Bowl, Cannon, Cement, Co(e)horn, Compo, Grout, Gunite, Hawk, Minnie, Parget, Plaster, Screed, Square, Squid, Toc emma, Trench(er)

Mortgage(e) Balloon, Bond, Cedula, Debt, Dip, Encumbrance, Endowment, Hypothecator, Loan, Pledge, Wadset(t)

Mortification, Mortified, Mortify Abash, Chagrin, Crucify, Crush, Gangrene, Humble, Humiliate, Infarct, Necrose, Penance, Sick, Wormwood

Mosaic Buhl, Cosmati, Inlay, Intarsia, Musive, Piltra dura, Screen, Terrazzo, Tessella(te), Tessera

Moscow Dynamo

Moses Grandma

▶ **Moslem** see MUSLIM

Mosque Dome of the Rock, El Aqsa, Jami, Masjid, Medina

Mosquito Aedes, Anopheles, Culex, Culicine, Gnat, Parasite, Stegomyia

Moss(y) Acrogen, Agate, Bryology, Carrag(h)een, Ceylon, Club, Fog, Fontinalis, Hag(g), Hypnum, Iceland, Irish, Lecanoram, Lichen, Litmus, Long, Lycopod, Marsh, Musci, Muscoid, Parella, Peat, Polytrichum, Reindeer, Rose, Scale, Selaginella, Spanish, Sphagnum, Staghorn, Usnea, Wolf's claw

Most Largest, Major, Maxi(mum), Optimum

Mot Quip, Saying

Mote Atom, Particle, Speck

Moth(s) Abraxas, Antler, Arch, Arctiidae, Atlas, Bag, Bee, Bell, Bobowler, Bogong, Bombycid, Brown-tail, Buff-tip, Bugong, Burnet, Cabbage, Carpenter, Carpet, Cecropia, Cinnabar, Clearwing, Clothes, Codlin(g), Dagger, Dart-moth, Death's head, Diamondback, Drinker, Eggar, Egger, Emperor, Ermine, Flour, Fox, Geometer, Geometrid, Ghost, Goat, Goldtail, Grass, Gypsy, Hawk, Herald, Hook-tip, House, Hummingbird, Imago, Io, Kentish glory, Kitten, Lackey, Lappet, Leafroller, Leopard, Lepidoptera, Lichen, Lobster, Luna, Lymantriidae, Magpie, Meal, Mother of pearl, Mother Shipton, Muslin, Noctua, Noctuid, Notodonta, Nun, Oak-Egger, Owlet, Peppered, Polyphemus, Psyche, Pug-moth, Puss, Pyralidae, Sallow-kitten, Saturnia, Saturniid, Scavenger, Silkworm, Sphingid, Sphinx, Tapestry, Tiger, Tinea, Tineidae, Tortrix, Turnip, Tussock, Umber, Underwing, Unicorn, Vapourer, Veneer, Wainscot, Wax, Winter, Woodborer, Y-moth, Zygaena

Mothball(s) Abeyance, Camphor, Naphtha, Preserver

Mother Bearer, Church, Cognate, Cosset, Courage, Dam(e), Dregs, Ean, Earth, Eve, Generatrix, Genetrix, Goose, Hubbard, Lees, Ma, Machree, Mam(a), Mamma, Mater, Maya, Minnie, Mom, Multipara, Mum, Native, Nature, Nourish, Parity, Pourer, Reverend, Shipton, Superior, Surrogate, Wit

▷ **Mother** may indicate a lepidopterist (moth-er)

Motherless Adam, Orphan

Motif Anthemion, Design, Gist, Idée, Theme

Motion Early day, Gesture, Harmonic, Impulse, Kinetic, Move, Offer, Perpetual, PL, Proper, Proposal, Rack and pinion, Rider, Slow, Spasm

Motionless Doggo, Frozen, Immobile, Quiescent, Stagnant, Stasis, Still, Stock-still

Motive, Motivate, Motivation Actuate, Cause, Ideal, Impel, Incentive, Intention, Mainspring, Mobile, Object, ➤ PURPOSE, Spur, Ulterior

Motley Jaspé, Medley, Piebald, Pied

Motor(boat) Auto, Car, Dynamo, Engine, Hot rod, Inboard, Induction, Jato, Linear, Outboard, Scooter, Thruster, Turbine, Universal

Motor-cycle Moped, Pipsqueak, Scooter, Scramble

Motorist(s) AA, Driver, RAC

Motorman Austin, Benz, Ford, Morris

Motor race Rally, Scramble, TT

Motorway Autobahn, Autopista, Autoput, Autoroute, Autostrada, Expressway, M(1)

Mottle(d) Brindled, Chiné, Jaspé, Marbled, Marly, Mirly, Pinto, Poikilitic, Tabby

Motto Device, Epigraph, Gnome, Impresa, Imprese, Impress(e), Legend, Maxim, Mot, Poesy, Posy, Saw

Mou(e) Grimace, Mim

Mould(ed), Moulding, Mouldy Accolade, Architrave, Archivolt, Astragal, Baguette, Balection, Beading, Bend, Black, Bolection, Bread, Briquet(te), Cabling, Casement, Cast(ing), Cavetto, Chessel, Chill, Cornice, Coving,

Cyma, Cymatium, Dariole, Die, Doucine, Dripstone, Echinus, Egg and dart, Flong, ➤ FORM, Foughty, Fousty, Fungose, Fungus, Fusarol(e), Fust, Gadroon, Godroon, Hood-mould, Hore, Humus, Injection, Matrix, Mildew, Model, Mool, Moulage, Mucid, Mucor, Must, Myxomycete, Nebule, Noble rot, Ogee, Ovolo, Palmette, Papier-mâché, Phycomycete, Pig, Plasm(a), Plastic, Plat, Platband, Prototype, Prunt, Reeding, Reglet, Rhizopus, Rot, Rust, Sandbox, Scotia, Shape, Smut, Soil, Storiated, Stringcourse, Surbase, Tailor, Talon, Template, Templet, Timbale, Tondino, Torus, Trochilus, Vinew, Water table

Moult(ing) Cast, Metecdysis, Mew, Shed

Mound Agger, Bank, Barp, Barrow, Berm, Cone, Dike, Dun, Embankment, Heap, Hog, Kurgan, Mogul, Monticule, Mote, Motte, Orb, Pile, Pingo, Pome, Rampart, Rampire, Tel(l), Teocalli, Teopan, Tuffet, Tumulus

Mound-bird Megapode

Mount(ed), Mounting, Mountain (peak) ➤ ALP(INE), Aspiring, Back, Barp, Ben, Berg, Board, Breast, Butter, Chain, Charger, ➤ CLIMB, Colt, Cordillera, Cradle, Dew, Display, Djebel, Dolly, Escalade, Frame, Hinge, Horse, Jebel, Massif, Monture, Mt, Nunatak, Orography, Orology, Passe-partout, Pike, Pile, Pin, Pownie, Quad, Ride, Saddlehorse, Scalado, Scale, Set, Soar, Stage, ➤ STEED, Stie, Strideways, Tel, Tier, Tor, Turret, Upgo, Volcano

MOUNTAINS

2 letters:	Andes	Welsh	Sorata
K2	Aneto	**6 letters:**	Steele
3 letters:	Athos	Amhara	Tasman
Apo	Atlas	Anadyr	Taunus
Ida	Badon	Arafat	Taurus
Kaf	Black	Ararat	Vernon
Ore	Blanc	Averno	Vosges
Pin	Coast	Balkan	Zagros
4 letters:	Djaja	Bogong	**7 letters:**
Alai	Eiger	Carmel	Aorangi
Blue	Ellis	Cho Oyu	Arcadia
Bona	Ghats	Dragon	Bernina
Cook	Green	Egmont	Brocken
Etna	Guyot	Elberz	Buffalo
Fuji	Hekla	Elbrus	Calvary
Harz	Horeb	Erebus	Cariboo
Hoss	Idris	Gilead	Cascade
Jaya	Kamet	Hermon	Chianti
Jura	Kenya	Hoggar	Corbett
Meru	Logan	Hoosac	Dapsang
Nebo	Munro	Kunlin	Everest
Oeta	Ozark	Lhotse	Helicon
Ossa	Rocky	Makalu	Kennedy
Rigi	Rydal	Mourne	Khingan
Zeil	Sinai	Ortles	Lebanon
5 letters:	Snowy	Pamirs	Lucania
Abora	Table	Pelion	Manaslu
Adams	Tabor	Pisgah	Markham
Aldan	Tatra	Pocono	Nan Shan
Altai	Tyree	Robson	Olympus
Amara	Urals	Scopus	Palomar

Pilatus	Blue Ridge	Matterhorn	
Rainier	Cairngorm	Montserrat	
Rhodope	Catskills	Monte Corno	
Scafell	Caucasian	Pentelikon	**13 letters:**
Selkirk	Connemara	Puncak Jaya	Carrantuohill
Skiddaw	Demavrand	Puy de Sancy	Flinders Range
Snowdon	Dolomites	St Michael's	Grossglockner
Sperrin	Grampians	Wellington	Humphrey's Peak
Sudeten	Guadalupe	**11 letters:**	Kangchenjunga
Travers	Helvellyn	Adirondacks	Massif Central
Wicklow	Highlands	Alaska Range	San Bernardino
8 letters:	Himalayas	Appalachian	**14 letters:**
Ben Nevis	Hindu Kush	Bartle Frere	Bohemian Forest
Cambrian	Inselberg	Bimberi Peak	Carnarvon Range
Cevennes	Jebel Musa	Brooks Range	Hamersley Range
Demavend	Karakoram	Drakensberg	Kaikoura Ranges
Grampian	Lenin Peak	Fairweather	Kommunizma
Hymettus	Longs Peak	Kilimanjaro	Peak
Illimani	Marmolada	Kolyma Range	Liverpool Range
Jungfrau	Mont Blanc	Nanga Parbat	Musgrove Ranges
Kinabalu	Nanda Devi	Salmon River	Ruwenzori Range
King Peak	Parnassus	Scafell Pike	Stirling Ranges
Leibnitz	Sugarloaf	Sierra Madre	**16 letters:**
McKinley	Vancouver	**12 letters:**	Macdonnell
Pennines	Venusberg	Albert Edward	Ranges
Pyrenees	Woodroffe	Cascade Range	**17 letters:**
Rushmore	**10 letters:**	Godwin Austen	Continental
St Helen's	Arakan Yoma	Gran Paradiso	Divide
Taraniki	Cantabrian	Kanchenjunga	Transylvanian
Tien Shan	Carpathian	Ruahine Range	Alps
Vesuvius	Delectable	Sierra Nevada	**19 letters:**
Wrangell	Dhaulagiri	Slieve Donard	Macgillicuddy's
9 letters:	Erymanthus	Tararua Range	Reeks
Aconcagua	Erzgebirge	Victoria Peak	**20 letters:**
Allegheny	Great Gable	Vinson Massif	Salmon River
Annapurna	Horselberg	Western Ghats	Mountains
Apennines	Laurentian		

Mountain-building Orogenesis

Mountaineer(ing) Abseil, Alpinist, Arnaut, Climber, Hunt, Sherpa, Smythe, Upleader

Mountebank Antic(ke), Baladin(e), Charlatan, Jongleur, Quack, Saltimbanco

Mourn(er), Mournful, Mourning Adonia, Black, Dirge, Dole, Elegiac, Grieve, Grone, Hatchment, Keen, Lament, Niobe, Omer, Ovel, Plangent, Saulie, Shivah, Shloshim, Sorrow, Tangi, Threnetic, Threnodial, Weeds, Weep, Willow

Mouse(like), Mousy Black eye, Deer, Dun(nart), Flitter, Harvest, Honey, Icon, Jumping, Meadow, Muridae, Murine, Pocket, Rodent, Shiner, Shrew, Vermin, Waltzer

Moustache Charley, Charlie, Excrement, Fu Manchu, Handlebar, Pencil, Walrus, Zapata

Mouth(piece) Aboral, Bazoo, Brag, Buccal, Cakehole, Chapper, Check, Crater, Debouchure, Delta, Embouchure, Estuary, Fipple, Gab, Gam, Gills,

Gob, Gum, Hard, Kisser, Labret, Lawyer, Lip, Manubrium, Maw, Neb, Orifex, Orifice, Os, Oscule, Ostium, Outfall, Port, Potato trap, Speaker, Spokesman, Spout, Stoma, Swazzle, Swozzle, Teat, Trap, Uvula

Mouthful Bite, Gob, Morceau, Morsel, Sip, Sup, Taste

Mouthless Astomatous

Mouth-organ Harmonica, Harp, Palp, Sang

Move(d), Mover, Movable, Moving Act, Actuate, Affect, Andante, Astir, Budge, Carry, Catapult, Chattel, Coast, Counter-measure, Coup, Decant, Démarche, Displace, Disturb, Ease, Eddy, Edge, Evoke, False, Flit, Fluctuate, Forge, Frogmarch, Gambit, Gee, Go, Gravitate, Haulier, Hustle, Inch, Instigate, Jee, Jink, Kedge, Kinetic, Link, Mill, Mobile, Mosey, Motivate, Nip, Opening, Overcome, Pan, Poignant, Proceed, Progress, Prompt, Propel, Qui(t)ch, Quicken, Rearrange, Redeploy, Relocate, Remuage, Retrocede, Roll, Rouse, Roust, Scoot, Scramble, Scuttle, Sell, Shift, Shog, Shoo, Shunt, Sidle, Skelp, Slide, Soulful, Spank, Steal, Steer, Step, Stir, Styre, Tack, Tactic, Taxi, Transfer, Translate, Translocate, Transplant, Transport, Troll, Trundle, Turn, Unstep, Up, Upsticks, Vacillate, Vagile, Veronica, Volt(e), Wag, Wapper, Whirry, Whish, Whisk, Whiz, Wuther, Yank, Zoom, Zwischenzug

Movement Action, Advection, Aerotaxis, Al Fatah, Allegro, Allemande, Almain, Andantino, Antic, Azapo, Badinerie, Bandwagon, Brownian, Cadence, Cell, Chartism, Chemonasty, Constructivism, Course, Crusade, Dadaism, Diaspora, Diastole, Ecumenical, Enlightenment, Eoka, Eurhythmics, Expressionism, Feint, Fianchetto, Fris(ka), Gait, Gallicanism, Geneva, Gesture, Groundswell, Indraught, Inkatha, Intermezzo, Jhala, Jor, Kata, Keplarian, Kinesis, Kin(a)esthetic, Kinetic, Larghetto, Largo, Lassu, Ligne, Manoeuvre, Nastic, Naziism, New Wave, Nihilism, Operation, Orchesis, Oxford, Parallax, Pase, Passade, Pedesis, Piaffer, Pincer, Play, Poule, Poulette, Procession, Progress, Punk, REM, Romantic, Rondo, Saccade, Scherzo, Seiche, Sinn Fein, Solifluction, Solifluxion, Stir(e), Sturm und Drang, Swadeshi, Tachism, Taxis, Telekinesis, Tide, Tractarianism, Transhumance, Trend, Trenise, ➤ UNITA, Verismo, Veronica, Wheel, Zionism

Movie Bioscope, Cine(ma), Film, Flick, Nudie, Road, Slasher

Mow(er), Mowing Aftermath, Cut, Grimace, Lattermath, Math, Rawing, Rawn, Rowan, Rowen, Rowing, Scytheman, Shear, Sickle, Tass, Trim

MP Backbencher, Commoner, Gendarme, Member, Provost, Redcap, Retread, Snowdrop, Stannator, Statist, TD

➤ **Mrs** see MISSIS

Mrs Copperfield Agnes, Dora

Mrs Siddons Tragic muse

Much Abundant, Far, Glut, Great, Lots, Mickle, Scad, Sore, Viel

Mucilage Gum, ➤ MUCUS, Putty, Resin

Muck (up), Mucky Bungle, Dirt, Dung, Island, Leep, Manure, Midden, Mire, Rot, Soil, Sordid, Spoil, Stercoral

Mucker Fall, Pal, Purler

Mucus Phlegm, Snivel, Snot, Sputum

Mud(dy) Adobe, Clabber, Clart, Clay, Cutcha, Dirt, Dubs, Fango, Glaur, Gutter, Kacha, Lahar, Lairy, Limous, ➤ MIRE, Moya, Ooze, Peloid, Pise, Riley, Roily, Salse, Slab, Slake, Sleech, Slime, Slob, Slough, Sludge, Slur(ry), Slush, Turbid

Muddle Befog, Bemuse, Botch, Cock up, Confuse, Disorder, Embrangle, Fluster, Gump, Mash, Mêlée, Mess, Mix, Mull, Pickle, Puddle, Shemozzle, Stupefy, Tangle

▷ **Muddled** may indicate an anagram

Mudfish Lepidosiren

Mudguard Splashboard, Wing

Mudlark Ragamuffin, Urchin

Muesli Granola

Muff Boob, Botch, Bungle, Drop, Snoskyn

Muffin Bun, Mule, Popover

Muffle(d), Muffler Damp, Envelop, Hollow, Mob(b)le, Mute, Scarf, Silencer, Sourdine, Stifle

Mug(ger), Muggy Assault, Attack, Bash, Beaker, Bock, Can, Club, Con, Croc(odile), Cup, Dial, Dupe, Enghalskrug, Face, Fool, Footpad, Gob, Humid, Idiot, Latron, Learn, Mou, Noggin, Pan, Pot, Puss, Rob, Roll, Sandbag, Sap, Sconce, Simpleton, Steamer, Stein, Sucker, Swot, Tankard, Tax, Thief, Thug(gee), Tinnie, Tinny, Toby, Trap, Ugly, Visage, Yap

Mulatto Griff(e)

Mulberry Artocarpus, Breadfruit, Cecropia, Contrayerva, Cow-tree, Jack, Morat, Morus, Murrey, Overlord, Sycamine

Mulch Compost

Mule Ass, Bab(o)uche, Barren, Donkey, Funnel, Hybrid, Mocassin, Moccasin, Moyl(e), Muffin, Muil, Rake, Shoe, Slipper, Sumpter

Muleteer Arriero

Mull Brood, Chew, Kintyre, Ponder, Promontory, Study

Mullein Aaron's rod

Mullet Goatfish

Mullion Monial

Multi-coloured Scroddled

Multiform Allotropic, Diverse, Manifold

Multiple, Multiplied, Multiplier, Multiply Augment, Breed, Double, ➤ INCREASE, Modulus, Populate, Product, Proliferate, Propagate, Severalfold

Multi-purpose Polychrest

Multitude Army, Crowd, Hirsel, Horde, Host, Legion, Populace, Shoal, Sight, Throng, Zillion

Mum(my) Boutonné, Carton(n)age, Corpse, Egyptian, Embalm, Mamma, Mute, Quiet, Sh, Silent, Tacit, Whisht, Wordless

Mumble Grumble, Moop, Moup, Mouth, Mump, Mushmouth, Mutter, Royne, Slur

Mumbo jumbo Hocus pocus, Mammet, Maumet, Mawmet, Mommet

Mummer Actor, Mime, Scuddaler, Scudler, Skudler

Mumps Parotitis

Munch Champ, Chew, Chomp, Scranch

Mundane Banal, Common, Earthly, Nondescript, Ordinary, Prosaic, Quotidian, Secular, Trite, Workaday, Worldly

Munificent Bounteous, Generous, Liberal, Profuse

Munition(s) Arms, Artillery, Matériel, Ordnance

Munro Saki

Mural(s) Fresco, Graffiti

Murder(er), Murderess, Murderous Aram, Assassin, Blue, Bluebeard, Bravo, Burke, Butcher, Butler, Cain, Cathedral, Crackhalter, Crippen, Cutthroat, Do in, Eliminate, Filicide, First degree, Fratricide, Genocide, Hare, Hitman, Homicide, Internecine, ➤ KILL, Liquidate, Locusta, Made man, Massacre, Matricide, Modo, Parricide, Patricide, Poison, Red, Regicide, Ripper, Ritual, Ritz, Second degree, Sikes, Slaughter, Slay, Strangle(r), Take out, Thagi, Throttle, Thug(gee), Whodun(n)it

Murk(y) Black, Dirk(e), Gloom, Obscure, Rookish, Stygian

Murmur(ing) Brool, Bur(r), Burble, Coo, Croodle, Croon, Grudge, Hum, ➤ MUTTER, Purr, Repine, Rhubarb, Rumble, Rumour, Souffle, Sowf(f), Sowth, Sturnoid, Undertone, Whisper

Murphy Chat, Potato, Pratie, Spud, Tater

Muscle, Muscular Abductor, Abs, Athletic, Attollens, Beef(y), Biceps, Bowr, Brawn, Buccinator, Ciliary, Clout, Corrugator, Creature, Cremaster, Deltoid, Depressor, Diaphragm, Digastric, Effector, Elevator, Erecter, Erector, Evertor, Extensor, Flexor, Force, Gastrocnemius, Glut(a)eus, Gluteus maximus, Hamstring, Iliacus, Intrinsic, Involuntary, Kreatine, Lat, Latissimus dorsi, Laxator, Levator, Lumbricalis, Masseter, Mesomorph, Might, Motor, Mouse, Myalgia, Occlusor, Omohyoid, Pathos, Pec(s), Pectoral, Perforans, Perforatus, Peroneus, Platysma, ➤ POWER, Pronator, Protractor, Psoas, Pylorus, Quad(riceps), Quadratus, Rectus, Retractor, Risorius, Rotator, Sarcolemma, Sarcous, Sartorius, Scalene, Scalenus, Serratus, Sinew, Smooth, Soleus, Sphincter, Splenial, Sthenic, Striated, Supinator, Tenaculum, Tendon, Tensor, Teres, Thenar, Thew, Tonus, Trapezius, Triceps, Voluntary

Muscovite Mica, Talc

Muse(s), Muse's home, Musing Aglaia, Aonia(n), Attic, Calliope, Clio, Cogitate, Consider, Erato, Euphrosyne, Euterpe, Helicon, Inspiration, IX, Melpomene, Nine, Nonet, Pensée, Pierides, Poly(hy)mnia, Ponder, ➤ REFLECT, Ruminate, Study, Teian, Terpsichore, Thalia, Tragic, Urania, Wonder

Museum Ashmolean, BM, British, Fitzwilliam, Gallery, Guggenheim, Hermitage, Louvre, Metropolitan, Parnassus, Prado, Repository, Smithsonian, Tate, Uffizi, VA, V and A

Mush Cree, Goo, Mess, Porridge, Puree, Schmaltz, Slop

Mushroom Agaric, Blewits, Burgeon, Button, Cep, Champignon, Darning, Enoki, Expand, Fly agaric, Fungus, Gyromitra, Horse, Hypha(l), Ink-cap, Magic, Matsutake, Meadow, Morel, Oyster, Parasol, Penny-bun, Porcino, Russula, Sacred, Scotch bonnet, Shaggymane, Shiitake, Sickener, Spread, Start-up, Straw, Truffle, Upstart, Velvet shank, Waxcap

Music Acid-house, Acid rock, Air, Ala(a)p, Alapa, Albumblatt, Aleatory, Allegro, Allemande, Anacrustic, Andante, Antiphony, AOR, Arabesque, Art, Bagatelle, Ballade, Bebop, Bebung, Berceuse, Bhangra, Bluegrass, Bluette, Boogie-woogie, Bour(r)ee, Britpop, Cadenza, Canon, Cantata, Cantilena, Ceilidh, Chamber, Chant, Chopsticks, Chorale, Cliff, Coloratura, Concerto, Concertstuck, Concrete, Contrapuntal, Coranoch, Coronach, Country, Cu-bop, Detroit techno, Disco, Divertimento, Dixieland, Dream, Dub, Duet, Early, Enigma, Entracte, Euterpe, Facade, Fanfare, Fantasia, Fioritura, Flamenco, Folk, Fugato, Fugue, Funk(y), Gagaku, Galant, Gangsta, Gangsta rap, Garage, Gat, Glam rock, Go-go, Gospel, Gothic, Gothic rock, Grandioso, Grunge, Handbag, Hard core, Hard rock, Heavy metal, High life, Hillbilly, Hindustani, Hip-hop, Honky-tonk, House, Humoresque, Incidental, Indie, Intermezzo, Introit, Jam session, Jazz, Jhala, Jor, Jungle, Karnatak, Khayal, Klezmer, Kwela, Landler, Largo, Loco, Lollipop, Lydian, Madrigal, Maggiore, Mantra, Marabi, Marcato, March, Mariachi, Martellato, Mbaqanga, Melisma, Melody, Meno, Modality, Morceau, Motet, Motor rhythm, Motown®, ➤ MUSICAL INSTRUMENTS, Musique concrete, Muzak®, Neume, New Age, New Wave, Nocturne, Nonet, Notation, Note, Numbers, Obbligato, Opus, Oratorio, Organum, Orphean, Parlando, Partita, Passacaglia, Passion, Pastiche, Pastorale, Pecking, Phase, Pibroch, Piece, Piped, Plainsong, Polyhymnia, Polyphony, Pop, Postlude, Pralltriller, Prelude, Progressional, Progressive rock, Prom, Psalmody, Punk rock, Pycnon, Qawwali, Quartet, Quintet, Quodlibet, Rag, Raga, Ragga(muffin), Ragini, Ragtime, Rai, Rastrum, Redowa, Requiem, Rhapsody, Rhythm, Ricercar(e), Riff, Ritornello, Rock, Rockabilly, Rock'n'roll, Rocksteady, Romanza, Romo, Rondeau, Rondino, Rondo, Roots(y), Rosalia, Roulade, Salon, Salsa, Sanctus, Saraband, Scherzo, Score, Seguidilla, Septimole, Serenade, Serenata, Setting, Sextet, Sheet, Sinfonietta, Ska, Skiffle, Soca, Sokah, Solmisation, Son, Sonata, Soukous, Soul, Spiritual, Stadium rock, Staff, Strain, Suite, Swing, Swingbeat, Symphony, Tala, Tambourin, Techno, Technopop, Thema, Third stream, Thrash, Thrash metal, Toccata, Toccatella, Toccatina, Tonal, Trad, Trance, Trio, Trip hop, Truth, Tune, Twelve-tone, Urban blues, Verset, Voluntary, Warehouse, Ziganka, Zouk, Zydeco

Musical Arcadian, Azione, Brigadoon, Cats, Chess, Euphonic, Evergreen, Evita, Gigi, Grease, Hair, Harmonious, Kabuki, Kismet, Lyric, Mame, Melodic, Oliver, Opera, Operetta, Orphean, Revue, Showboat

Musical box Juke-box, Polyphon(e)

Musical chairs Level-coil

Music-hall Alhambra, Disco, Empire, Odeon

MUSICAL INSTRUMENTS

2 letters:
Ax
Gu
3 letters:
Axe
Gue
Kit
Oud
Saz
Uke
Zel
4 letters:
Crwd
Drum
Fife
Gong
Harp
Horn
Kora
Koto
Lure
Lute
Lyre
Moog®
Oboe
Pipa
Rate
Reed
Rote
Sang
Tuba
Vina
Viol
Zeze
5 letters:
Aulos
Banjo
Cello
Clave
Cobza
Corno
Crowd
Crwth
Flute
Guiro
Gusla
Gusle
Gusli
Kazoo
Mbira
Naker
Nebel
Organ
Piano
Quena
Rebec

Regal
Sanko
Sansa
Sarod
Shalm
Shawm
Sitar
Tabla
Tabor
Tibia
Veena
Viola
Zanze
Zinke
6 letters:
Antara
Citole
Cornet
Cymbal
Euphon
Flugel
Guitar
Kanoon
Maraca
Poogye
Racket
Rebeck
Ribibe
Sancho
Santir
Santur
Shalme
Sittar
Spinet
Syrinx
Trigon
Vielle
Violin
Zither
Zufolo
7 letters:
Bagpipe
Bandore
Bandura
Baryton
Bassoon
Bazooka
Celesta
Celeste
Cembalo
Chikara
Cithara
Cittern
Clarion
Clavier
Console

Cornett
Dichord
Dulcian
Fagotto
Flutina
Gamelan
Gittern
Hautboy
Helicon
High-hat
Kalimba
Kantela
Kantele
Kithara
Klavier
Lyricon
Mandola
Marimba
Ocarina
Pandora
Pandore
Pandura
Piccolo
Poogyee
Posaune
Rackett
Sackbut
Sambuca
Samisen
Santour
Sarangi
Saxhorn
Saxtuba
Serpent
Tambour
Tambura
Theorbo
Timbrel
Trumpet
Tympany
Ukelele
Vihuela
Zuffolo
8 letters:
Angklung
Archlute
Autoharp®
Barytone
Bouzouki
Calliope
Canorous
Charango
Cimbalom
Clarinet
Clarsach
Clavecin

Cornetto
Cornpipe
Cromorna
Cromorne
Crumhorn
Dulcimer
Gemshorn
Guarneri
Guimbard
Hautbois
Humstrum
Jew's harp
Key-bugle
Langspel
Lyra-viol
Mandolin
Manzello
Martenot
Melodeon
Melodica
Mirliton
Ottavino
Pan pipes
Phorminx
Polyphon
Psaltery
Recorder
Slughorn
Spinette
Sticcado
Sticcato
Surbahar
Tamboura
Tamburin
Tenoroon
Theremin
Triangle
Trombone
Virginal
Vocalion
Zambomba
Zampogna
9 letters:
Accordion
Alpenhorn
Balalaika
Bandoneon
Baryulele
Bombardon
Chalumeau
Cornemuse
Decachord
Euphonium
Flageolet
Flexatone
Gutbucket

Harmonica	Washboard	Sousaphone	
Harmonium	Xylophone	Squeeze-box	
Idiophone	Xylorimba	Stylophone®	**12 letters:**
Kent-bugle	**10 letters:**	Symphonium	Clavicembalo
Krummhorn	Bullroarer	Tambourine	Glockenspiel
Langspiel	Chitarrone	Thumb piano	Harmoniphone
Mandoline	Clavichord	Vibraphone	Metallophone
Monochord	Concertina	**11 letters:**	Penny-whistle
Mouth-harp	Cor anglais	Chordophone	Sarrusophone
Orpharion	Didgeridoo	Clairschach	Stock and horn
Pantaleon	Flugelhorn	Contrabasso	Stradivarius
Pastorale	French horn	Harmoniphon	Tromba-marina
Polyphone	Gramophone	Harpsichord	**13 letters:**
Saxophone	Hurdy-gurdy	Heckelphone	Contrabassoon
Seraphine	Kettledrum	Nickelodeon	Contrafagotto
Slughorne	Mellophone	Orchestrion	Ondes Martenot
Snare-drum	Ophicleide	Phonofiddle	Panharmonicon
Sopranino	Orpheoreon	Straduarius	Physharmonica
Stockhorn	Pantachord	Trump-marine	**14 letters:**
Trompette	Shakuhachi	Violincello	Glass harmonica

Musician(s), Musicologist Accompanist, Arion, Arist, Brain, Chanter, Combo, ➤ COMPOSER, Conductor, Crowder, Ensemble, Executant, Flautist, Gate, Grove, Guslar, Handel, Jazzer, Jazzman, Joplin, Mahler, Mariachi, Menuhin, Minstrel, Muso, Orphean, Pianist, Rapper, Reed(s)man, Répétiteur, Rubinstein, Sideman, Spohr, String, Tortelier, Trouvère, Violinist, Wait

Musk Civet, Mimulus, Must

Musket Brown Bess, Caliver, Carabine, Eyas, Flintlock, Fusil, Hawk, Nyas, Queen's-arm, Weapon

Musketeer Aramis, Athos, D'Artagnan, Fusilier, Ja(e)gar, Porthos, Rifleman, Sam

Muslim (ritual), Moslem Alaouite, Ali, Almohad(e), Balochi, Baluchi, Berber, Caliph, Dato, Dervish, Fatimid, Ghazi, Hadji, Hafiz, Hajji, Iranian, Islamic, Ismaili, Karmathian, Khotbah, Khotbeh, Khutbah, Mahometan, Mogul, Moor, Morisco, Moro, Mufti, Mus(s)ulman, Mutazilite, Nawab, Paynim, Pomak, Said, Saracen, Say(y)id, Senussi, Shafiite, Shia(h), Shiite, Sofi, Sonnite, Sufi, Sulu, Sunna, Sunni(te), Turk, Wahabee, Wahabi(te)

Muslin Butter, Cloth, Coteline, Gurrah, Jamdani, Leno, Mousseline, Mull, Nainsook, Organdie, Tarlatan, Tiffany

Musquash Ondatra

Mussel(s) Bearded, Bivalve, Clabby-doo, Clam, Clappy-doo, Deerhorn, Moules marinières, Mytilus, Niggerhead, Unio, Zebra

Mussorgsky Modest

Must(y) Amok, Essential, Foughty, Froughy, Frowsty, Frowy, Funky, Fust, Man, Maun(na), Mote, Mould, Mucid, Mun, Need(s)-be, Shall, Should, Stum, Wine

▷ **Must** may indicate an anagram

Mustard Charlock, Cress, English, Erysimum, French, Nitrogen, Praiseach, Runch, Sauce-alone, Senvy

Mustard plaster Sinapism
Muster Assemble, Call up, Mass, Raise, Rally, Really, Recruit, Round-up, Wappenshaw
Mutant, Mutation Auxotroph(ic), Change, Sport, Terata, Transform
▷ **Mutation** may indicate an anagram
Mute(d) Deaden, Dumb, Noiseless, Silent, Sordino, Sordo, Sourdine, Stifle
Mutilate(d), Mutilation Castrate, Concise, Deface, Dismember, Distort, Garble, Hamble, Injure, Maim, Mangle, Mayhem, Obtruncate, Riglin, Tear
▷ **Mutilate(d)** may indicate an anagram
Mutineer, Mutiny Bounty, Caine, Curragh, Indian, Insurrection, Nore, Pandy, ➤ REVOLT, Rising, Sepoy
Mutter(ing) Chunter, Fremescent, Mumble, Mump, Murmur, Mussitate, Rhubarb, Roin, Royne, Rumble, Whittie-whattie, Witter
Mutton Colonial goose, Em, Ewes, Fanny Adams, Gigot, Macon, Saddle, Sheep, Theave, Traik
Mutual (aid) Common, Log-roll, Reciprocal, Symbiosis
Muzzle Decorticate, Gag, Jaw, Mouth, Restrain, Snout
My Coo, Gemini, Golly, Ha, Odso, Oh, Our, Tush
Mynah Stare, Starling
Mynheer Stadholder
Myopia, Myopic Hidebound, Mouse-sight, Narrow, Short-sighted, Thick-eyed
Myriad Host, Zillion
Myristic Nutmeg
Myrrh Stacte
Myrtle Callistemon, Eucalyptus, Gale, Jambolana, Tooart, Tuart
Mysterious, Mystery Abdabs, Abdals, Acroamatic, Arcane, Arcanum, Cabbala, Craft, Cryptic, Dark, Deep, Eleusinian, Enigma, Esoteric, Grocer, Incarnation, Miracle, Numinous, Occult, Original sin, Orphic, Riddle, ➤ SECRET, Telestic, Trinity, UFO, Uncanny
▷ **Mysterious(ly)** may indicate an anagram
Mystic (word), Mystical Abraxas, Agnostic, Cab(e)iri, Epopt, Fakir, Familist, Hesychast, Mahatma, Occultist, Rasputin, Secret, Seer, Sofi, Sufi, Swami, Theosophy, Transcendental
Mystify Baffle, Bamboozle, Bewilder, Metagrabolise, Metagrobolise, Puzzle
Myth(ology), Mythical (beast) Allegory, Centaur, Cockatrice, Euhemerism, Fable, Fantasy, Fictitious, Folklore, Garuda, Geryon, Griffin, Impundulu, Kylin, Legend, Lore, Otnit, Pantheon, Pegasus, Selkie, Speewah, Sphinx, Unicorn, Urban, Wivern, Wyvern, Yale

Nn

N Name, Nitrogen, Noon, North, November

Nab Arrest, Capture, Collar, Grab, Seize

Nabob Deputy, Nawab, Wealthy

Nadir Bottom, Depths, Dregs, Minimum

Nag(ging) Badger, Bidet, Brimstone, Callet, Cap, Captious, Complain, Fret, Fuss, Harangue, Harp, Henpeck, Horse, Jade, Jaw, Keffel, Peck, Pester, Plague, Rosinante, Rouncy, ➤ SCOLD, Tit, Yaff

Nail(ed) Brad, Brod, Catch, Clinker, Clout, Fasten, Hob, Keratin, Onyx, Pin, Rivet, Sisera, Sparable, Sparrow-bill, Spick, Spike, Sprig, Staple, Stub, Stud, Tack(et), Talon, Tenterhook, Thumb, Tingle, Toe, Unguis

Naive(té) Artless, Green, Guileless, Ingenuous, Innocence, Open, Pollyanna, Simpliste, Simplistic, Unsophisticated, Wide-eyed

Naked Adamical, Artless, Bare, Blunt, Buff, Clear, Cuerpo, Defenceless, Encuerpo, Exposed, Gymno-, Nuddy, Nude, Querpo, Raw, Scud, Simple, Stark(ers), Uncovered

Namby-pamby Sissy, Weak, White-shoe

Name(d), Names Agnomen, Alias, Allonym, Appellation, Appoint, Baptise, Behight, Byline, Call, Celeb(rity), Cite, Cleep, Clepe, Cognomen, Designate, Dinges, Dingus, Dit, Dub, Epithet, Eponym, Exonym, Handle, Hete, Hight, Hypocorism, Identify, Identity, Label, Marque, Mention, Metronymic, Moni(c)ker, N, Nemn, Nom, Nomen(clature), Noun, Onomastics, Onymous, Patronymic, Pennant, Personage, Proprietary, Pseudonym, Quote, Red(d), Repute, Scilicet, Sign, Signature, Sir, Specify, Street, Substantive, Tag, Teknonymy, Term, ➤ TITLE, Titular, Titule, Toponymy, Trade, Trivial

Name-dropper Eponym

Nameless Anon, Unchrisom

Namely Ie, Scilicet, To-wit, Videlicet, Viz

Namesake Homonym

Name unknown Anon, A N Other, NU

Nancy Coddle, Effeminate, Milksop

Nanny Ayah, Foster, Goat, Nurse

Naos Cell(a)

Nap(py) Bonaparte, Diaper, Doze, Drowse, Fluff, Frieze(d), Fuzz, Kip, Moze, Oose, Ooze, Oozy, Put(t), Shag, Siesta, ➤ SLEEP, Slumber, Snooze, Tease, Teasel, Teaze, Tipsy, Tuft

Nape Noddle, Nucha, Scrag, Scruff, Scuft

Napier Logarithm

Napkin Cloth, Diaper, Doily, Doyley, Muckender, Sanitary, Serviette

Napless Threadbare

Napoleon Badinguet, Bonaparte, Boustrapa, Cognac, Coin, Corporal Violet, Corsican, December, Little Corporal, Nantz, Nap, Pig, Rantipole

Napper Bonce, Shearman

Narcissus Echo, Egocentric, Jonquil

Narcotic Ava, B(h)ang, Benj, Charas, Churrus, Coca, Codeine, Datura, Dope, ➤ DRUG, Heroin, Hop, Laudanum, Mandrake, Marijuana, Meconium, Morphia, Opiate, Pituri, Sedative, Tea, Trional

Nark Grass, Inform, Irritate, Nose, Pique, Roil, Squealer, Stag

Narrate, Narration, Narrative, Narrator Allegory, Anecdote, Cantata, Describe, Diegesis, Fable, History, Periplus, Plot, Raconteur, Récit, Recite, Recount, Saga, Scheherazade, Splatterpunk, Story, Tell

Narrow(ing), Narrow-minded Alf, Bigoted, Borné, Constringe, Cramp, Ensiform, Grundy(ism), Hidebound, Illiberal, Insular, Kyle, Limited, Meagre, Nary, One-idead, Parochial, Phimosis, Pinch, Prudish, Puritan, Scant, Shrink, Slender, Slit, Specialise, Squeak, Stenosed, Strait, Suburban, Verkramp, Waist

Narwhal Monodon

Nasal Adenoidal, Twang

Nash Beau

Nashville Bath

Nastiness, Nasty Disagreeable, Drevill, Filth, Fink, Ghastly, Lemon, Lo(a)th, Malign(ant), Noxious, Obscene, Odious, Offensive, Ribby, Sordid, Vile

Nat(haniel) Hawthorne, Winkle

Natal Inborn, Native, Patrial

Natant Afloat, Swimming

Nation, National(ist) Anthem, Baathist, Casement, Chetnik, Country, Cuban, Debt, Eta, Federal, Folk, Grand, Indian, IRA, Jingoist, Land, Mexican, Pamyat, Patriot, ➤ PEOPLE, Polonia, Race, Risorgimento, Scottish, Subject, Swadeshi, United, Wafd, Yemini, Young Ireland, Zionist

Native(s) Abo(rigin), Aborigine, African, Amerind, Annamese, Arab, Ascian, Australian, Autochthon, Aztec, Basuto, Belonging, Bengali, Boy, Cairene, Carib, Carioca, Chaldean, Citizen, Colchester, Conch, Creole, Criollo, Domestic, Dyak, Edo, Enchorial, Eskimo, Fleming, Genuine, Habitual, Inborn, Indigene, Indigenous, Inhabitant, Intuitive, Kaffir, Libyan, Local, Malay, Maori, Micronesian, Moroccan, Norwegian, Oyster, Polack, Portuguese, Son, Spaniard, Te(i)an, Thai, Tibetan, Uzbeg, Uzbek, Whitstable, Yugoslav

Nativity Birth, Jataka, Putz

Natron Urao

Natter Chat, Gossip, Jack, Prate

Natty Bumppo, Chic, Dapper, Leatherstocking, Smart, Spruce

Natural(ly) Artless, Ass, Easy, Genuine, Homely, Idiot, Illegitimate, Inborn, Inbred, Indigenous, Ingenerate, Inherent, Innate, Moron, Native, Nidget, Nitwit, Nude, Ordinary, Organic, Prat, Real, Simpleton, Simpliciter, Sincere, True, Untaught

Naturalist Buffon, Darwin, Wallace, White

Nature Adam, Character, Disposition, Esse(nce), Ethos, Inscape, Mould, Quintessence, Second, SN, Temperament

Naught Cypher, Failure, Nil, Nothing, Zero

Naughty Bad, Girly, Improper, Light, Marietta, Rascal, Remiss, Spright, Sprite, Wayward

Nausea, Nauseous Disgust, Fulsome, Malaise, Queasy, Sickness, Squeamish, Wamble, Wambly

Nave Aisle, Apse, Centre, Hub, Nef

Navel Naff, Nave, Omphalos, Umbilicus

Navigate, Navigator Albuquerque, Bougainville, Cabot, Cartier, Columbus, Control, Da Gama, Dias, Direct, Franklin, Frobisher, Gilbert, Hartog, Haul, Henry, Hudson, Keel, Magellan, Navvy, Orienteer, Pilot, Sail, Star-read, ➤ STEER, Tasman, Traverse, Vespucci

Navigation (aid, system) Asdic, Cabotage, Decca, Dectra, Fido, Gee, Loran, Navarho, Portolan(o), Portulan, Radar, Satnav, Shoran, Tacan, Teleran®, Vor

Navvy Workhorse

Navy, Naval AB, Armada, Blue, Fleet, French, Maritime, Merchant, N, Red, RN, Wren

Nawab Huzoor, Nabob, Viceroy

Nazi Brownshirt, Gauleiter, Hess, Hitler, Jackboot, SS, Stormtrooper, Wer(e)wolf

NCO Bombardier, Corp(oral), Havildar, Noncom, Sergeant, SM

Neanderthal Mousterian

Neap Low, Tide

Neapolitan Ice

Near(est), Nearby, Nearly, Nearness About, Adjacent, All-but, Almost, Anigh, Approach, Approximate, Beside, By, Close, Cy pres, Degree, Even, Ewest, Forby, Gain, Handy, Hither, Imminent, Inby(e), Mean, Miserly, Neist, Next, Nie, Niggardly, Nigh, Outby, Propinquity, Proximity, Short-range, Stingy, To, Warm, Well-nigh

Neat(ly) Bandbox, Cattle, Clean-cut, Clever, Dainty, Dapper, Deft, Dink(y), Doddy, Donsie, Elegant, Feat(e)ous, Featuous, Gayal, Genty, Gyal, Intact, Jemmy, Jimpy, Nett, Ninepence, Orderly, Ox(en), Preppy, Pretty, Rother, Shipshape, Short, Smug, Snod, Spruce, Straight, ➤ TIDY, Trig, Trim, Unwatered

Neb Beak, Bill, Nose, Snout

Nebula, Nebulous Aeriform, Celestial, Cloudy, Hazy, Horsehead, Obscure, Planetary, Shadowy, Vague

Necessary, Necessarily Bog, Cash, De rigueur, ➤ ESSENTIAL, Estovers, Important, Indispensable, Intrinsic, Money, Needful, Ought, Perforce, Requisite, Vital, Wherewithal

Necessitate, Necessity Ananke, Compel, Constrain, Emergency, Entail, Exigent, Fate, Indigence, Must, Need, Need-be, Oblige, Perforce, Require, Requisite

Neck(ed) Bottle, Brass, Canoodle, Cervical, Cervix, Channel, Col, Crag, Craig, Crop, Embrace, Gall, Gorgerin, Halse, Hawse, Inarm, Inclip, Isthmus, Kiss, Mash, Nape, Pet, Polo, Rubber, Scrag, Scruff, Smooch, Snog, Strait, Swan, Swire, Theorbo, Torticollis, Trachelate, Vee

▷ **Necking** may indicate one word around another

Necklace Anodyne, Brisingamen, Chain, Choker, Collar, Corals, Lava(l)lière, Lunula, Mangalsutra, Negligee, Pearls, Rope, Sautoir, String, Torc, Torque

Neckline Boat, Collar, Cowl, Crew, Décolletage, Plunging, Sweetheart, Turtle, Vee

Neckwear Ascot, Barcelona, Boa, Bow, Collar, Cravat, Fur, Steenkirk, Stock, Tie

Necromancer Goetic, Magician, Ormandine, Osmand, Witch, Wizard

Necrosis Infarct, Sphacelus

Nectar Ambrosia, Amrita, Honey, Mead

Ned(dy) Donkey, Kelly, Ludd

Need(ed), Needy Call, Demand, Desiderata, Egence, Egency, Exigency, Gap, Gerundive, Impecunious, Indigent, ➤ LACK, Mister, Pressing, PRN, Require, Strait, Strapped, Want

Needle Acerose, Acicular, Aciform, Between, Bodkin, Darning, Dip, Goad, Hype, Hypodermic, Icicle, Inoculate, Leucotome, Magnetic, Miff, Monolith, Neeld, Neele, Obelisk, Pinnacle, Pointer, Prick, R(h)aphis, Sew, Sharp, Spicule, Spike, Spine, Stylus, Tattoo, Tease, Thorn, Wire

Needlewoman Cleopatra, Seamstress

Needlework Baste, Crewel, Embroidery, Mola, Patchwork, Rivière, Sampler, Tapestry, Tattoo

Ne'er-do-well Badmash, Budmash, Bum, Good-for-nothing, Shiftless, Skellum, Wastrel

Negation, Negative Anion, Apophatic, Cathode, Denial, Enantiosis, Ne, No, Non, Nope, Nullify, Photograph, Refusal, Resinous, Unresponsive, Veto, Yin

Neglect(ed), Neglectful, Negligence, Negligent Careless, Casual, Cinderella, Cuff, Default, Dereliction, Disregard, Disuse, Failure, Forget, Forlorn, Heedless, Inattention, Incivism, Laches, Malpractice, Misprision, Omission, Oversight, Pass, Pass-up, ➤ REMISS, Shirk, Slight, Slipshod, Undone

▷ **Neglected** may indicate an anagram

Negligee Déshabillé, Manteau, Mob, Nightgown, Peignoir, Robe

Negligible Fig

Negotiate, Negotiator Arbitrate, Arrange, Bargain, Clear, Confer, Deal, Diplomat, Intermediary, Liaise, Manoeuvre, Mediator, Parley, Trade, Transact, Treat(y), Weather

Negro(id) ➤ AFRICAN, Barotse, Black, Buck, Chewa, Creole, Cuffee, Cuffy, Damara, Dinge, Duala, Dyula, Ebon(y), Edo, Efik, Ethiop, Ewe, Fang, Gullah, Hausa, Hottentot, Ibo, Igorot, Jim Crow, Kikuyu, Kongo, Luba, Malinke, Maninke, Mestee, Moke, Moor, Mustee, Nilote, Nupe, Nyanja, Pondo,

Quashee, Quashie, Sambo, Snowball, Spade, Susu, Thick-lips, Tiv, Tonga, Tswana, Uncle Tom, Watu(t)si, Zambo, Zulu

Negus Emperor, Rumfruction, Selassie

Nehru Pandit

Neigh Bray, Hinny, Nicker, Whicker, Whinny

Neighbour(ly), Neighbouring, Neighbours Abut(ter), Alongside, Amicable, Bor, Border, But, Friendly, Joneses, Nearby, Next-door

Neighbourhood Area, Community, District, Environs, Locality, Precinct, Vicinage, Vicinity

Neither Nor

Nell(ie), Nelly Bly, Dean, Trent

Neolithic Avebury, Stonehenge

Nelson Columnist, Eddy, Horatio

Nemesis Alastor, Avenger, Deserts, Downfall, Fate, Retribution, Revenge

Neodymium Nd

Neon Ne

Nepalese Gurkha

Neper N

Nephrite Yu

Nepotism Kin, Partisan, Patronage

Neptune God, Planet, Poseidon

Neptunium Np

Nerd Anorak, Otaku

Nereid Cymodoce, Nymph, Panope

Nerve(s), Nervous (centre), Nervure, Nervy Abdabs, Abducens, Accessory, Acoustic, Afferent, Aflutter, Afraid, Appestat, Axon, Baroreceptor, Bottle, Bouton, Chord, Chutzpah, Collywobbles, Column, Commissure, Courage, Cranial, Cyton, Depressor, Edgy, Electrotonus, Epicritic, Excitor, Facial, Gall, Ganglion, Grit, Guts, Habdabs, High, Highly-strung, Hyp, Hypoglossal, Impudence, Jitters, Jittery, Mid-rib, Motor, Myelon, Neck, Nidus, Octulomotor, Optic, Pavid, Perikaryon, Proprioceptor, Rad, Radial, Restless, Sangfroid, Sauce, Sciatic, Screaming abdabs, Screaming meemies, Sensory, Shaky, Shpilkes, Solar plexus, Spunk, Squirrel(l)y, Steel, Strung-up, Synapse, Tense, Tizzy, Toey, Tongue-tied, Trembler, Tremulous, Trigeminal, Trochlear, Twitchy, Ulnar, Vagus, Vapours, Windy, Yips

Nervous disease Chorea, Epilepsy, Neuritis

▷ **Nervously** may indicate an anagram

Ness Cape, Headland, Ras

Nessus Centaur

Nest Aerie, Aery, Aiery, Ayrie, Bike, Bink, Brood, Byke, Cabinet, Cage, Caliology, Clutch, Dray, Drey, Eyrie, Eyry, Lodge, Nid, Nide, Nidify, Nidus, Sett, Termitarium, Wurley

Nestle Burrow, Cose, Cuddle, Nuzzle, Snug(gle)

Nestor Counsellor, Kea, Sage

Net(ting), Nets, Network Anastomosis, BR, Bunt, Cast, Catch, Caul, Clathrate, Clear, Cobweb, Crinoline, Drift, Earn, Eel-set, Enmesh, Filet, Final, Fish, Flew, Flue, Fyke, Gill, ➤ GRID, Hammock, Heliscoop, JANET, Kiddle, Lace, LAN, Land, Lattice, Leap, Line, Linin, Mains, Malines, Maze, ➤ MESH, Mosquito, Old boys', Plexus, Portal system, Pout, Purse-seine, Reseau, Rete, Retiary, Reticle, Reticulate, Reticulum, Safety, Sagene, Screen, Sean, Seine, Set(t), Snood, Sweep-seine, System, Tela, Telex, Toil, Trammel, Trap, Trawl, Tulle, Tunnel, Usenet, WAN, Web, Wire

Netball Let

Nether Below, Inferior, Infernal, Lower, Under

Nettle(rash) Anger, Annoy, Day, Dead, Hemp, Hives, Horse, Irritate, Labiate, Nark, Pellitory, Pique, Ramee, Rami, Ramie, Rile, Ruffle, Sting, Urtica(ceae), Urticaria

Neuralgia, Neuritis Migraine, Sciatica, Tic

Neuter Castrate, Gib, Impartial, Neutral, Sexless, Spay

Neutral(ise) Alkalify, Buffer zone, Counteract, Grey, Impartial, Inactive, Schwa, Sheva, Shiva, Unbiased

Neutron Nucleon

Never(more) Nary, Nathemo(re), No more, Nowise, St Tibb's Eve

Nevertheless Algate, Anyhow, But, However, Still, Yet

▷ **New** may indicate an anagram

New(s), News agency Bulletin, Copy, Coranto, Dope, Euphobia, Evangel, Flash, Forest, Fresh, Fudge, Gen, Green, Griff, Info, Innovation, Intelligence, Item, Kerygma, Latest, Mint, Modern, N, Novel, Oil(s), Original, PA, Paragraph, Pastures, Pristine, Propaganda, Recent, Report, Reuter, Scoop, Span, Tass, Teletext®, Tidings, Ultramodern, Unco, Word

New boy Gyte

Newcomer Dog, Freshman, Griffin, Immigrant, Jackaroo, Jackeroo, Jillaroo, Johnny-come-lately, Novice, Parvenu, Pilgrim, Settler, Tenderfoot, Upstart

Newfoundland Dog, Nana, Vinland

Newgate Calendar

Newly wed Benedick, Benedict, Bride, Groom, Honeymooner, Neogamist

Newman Cardinal, Noggs

Newsman, News-reader Announcer, Editor, Journalist, Press, Reporter, Sub, Sysop

Newsmonger, News-vendor Butcher, Gossip, Quidnunc

Newspaper Blat(t), Broadsheet, Courier, Daily, Express, Fanzine, Feuilleton, Freesheet, Gazette, Guardian, Herald, Journal, Jupiter, Le Monde, Mercury, National, Organ, Patent inside, Patent outside, Post, Pravda, Press, Print, Rag, Red-top, Sheet, Spoiler, Squeak, Sun, Tabloid, Today

Newsreel Actualities

Newt(s) Ask(er), Eft, Evet, Swift, Triton, Urodela

Newton N

New world USA

New year Hogmanay, Neer-day, Tet

New York(er) Big apple, Gotham, Knickerbocker

New Zealand(ers) Aotearoa, Enzed, Kiwis, Maori, Moriori, Pakeha, Pig Island, Shagroon

Next Adjacent, Adjoining, After, Alongside, Beside, Following, Immediate, Later, Nearest, Neist, Proximate, Proximo, Sine, Subsequent, Syne

Nib J, Pen, Point, Tip

Nibble Bite, Brouse, Browse, Byte, Crop, Eat, Gnaw, Knap(ple), Moop, Moup, Munch, Nag, Nepit, Nosh, Peck, Pick, Snack

Nice(ty) Accurate, Amene, Appealing, Dainty, Fastidious, Fine, Finical, Genteel, Lepid, Ninepence, Pat, Pleasant, Precise, Quaint, Rare, Refined, Subtil(e), Subtle, Sweet, T

Niche Alcove, Almehrahb, Almery, Ambry, Apse, Aumbry, Awmrie, Awmry, Columbarium, Cranny, Exedra, Fenestella, Mihrab, Recess, Slot

Nicholas Santa

Nick(ed) Appropriate, Arrest, Bin, Blag, Can, Chip, Cly, Colin, Copshop, Cut, Denay, Dent, Deny, ➤ DEVIL, Erose, Groove, Hoosegow, Kitty, Knock, Nab, Nap, Nim, Nock, Notch, Pinch, Pook, Pouk, Prison, Scratch, ➤ STEAL, Steek, Swan-upping, Swipe, Thieve, Wirricow, Worricow, Worrycow

Nickel (silver) Coin, Garnierite, Millerite, Ni, Packfong, Paktong, Zaratite

Nicker Bonduc, Neigh, Whinny

Nickname Alias, Byname, Byword, Cognomen, So(u)briquet, To-name

Nicotine Tobacco, Weed

Nifty Smart, Stylish

Nigeria(n) Efik, Hausa, Ibo, Igbo, Nupe, WAN, Yoruba

Niggard(ly) Illiberal, Mean, Miser, Near-(be)gaun, Nippy, Nirlit, Parsimonious, Pinchcommons, Pinchgut, Pinchpenny, Scrunt, Tightwad

Niggle Carp, Gripe, Nag, Trifle

Night(s), Nightfall Acronychal, Arabian, Darkmans, Guest, Guy Fawkes, Leila, Nacht, Nicka-nan, Nutcrack, Nyx, Stag, Twelfth, Twilight, Walpurgis, Watch

Night-blindness Day-sight, Nyctalopia

Night-cap Biggin, Cocoa, Nip, Pirnie, Sundowner

Nightclub Dive, Honkytonk

Night-dew Serein, Serene

Nightingale Bulbul, Florence, Jugger, Lind, Philomel, Scutari, Swedish, Watch

Nightjar Evejar, Fern-owl, Goatsucker, Poorwill, Potoo

Night-light Moonbeam

Nightmare, Nightmarish Cacod(a)emon, Ephialtes, Incubus, Kafkaesque, Oneirodynia, Phantasmagoria

Nightshade Belladonna, Bittersweet, Circaea, Dwale, Henbane, Morel, Solanum

Nightwatchman Charley, Charlie, Rug-gown

Nightwork Lucubrate

Nihilist Anarchist, Red, Sceptic

Nil Nothing, Nought, Zero

Nimble Active, ➤ AGILE, Alert, Deft, Deliver, Fleet, Light, Lissom(e), Lithe, Quiver, Springe, Spry, Supple, Swack, Wan(d)le, Wannel, Wight, Ya(u)ld

Nimbus Aura, Aureole, Cloud, Gloriole, Halo

Nimrod Hunter

Nincompoop Ass, Imbecile, Ninny, Stupid

Nine, Ninth Choral, Ennead, Muses, Nonary, Nonet, Novenary, Pins, Sancho, Skittles, Tailors, Worthies

Nine hundred Sampi

Nineteen(th) Bar, Decennoval

Ninety N

Ninevite Assyrian

Ninny (hammer) Fool, Goose, Idiot, Stupid, Tony

Ninon Nan

Niobium Nb

Nip(per) Bite, Check, Chela, Chill, Claw, Dram, Gook, Jap, Lad, Lop, Nep, Nirl, Peck, Pincers, Pinch, Pook, Scotch, Sneap, Susan, Taste, Tot, Tweak, Urchin, Vice, Vise

Nipa At(t)ap, Palm

Nipple Dug, Mastoid, Pap, Teat

Nis Brownie, Goblin, Kobold, Sprite

Nit Egg, Insect, Louse

Nitre Saltpetre

Nitric, Nitrogen Azote, Azotic, Gas, N, Quinoline

Nitroglycerine Glonoin

Nitwit Ass, Flat, Fool, Simpleton, ➤ STUPID

No Aikona, Denial, Na(e), Nah, Negative, Nix, Nope, Nyet, O, Refusal

Noah Arkite, Beery, Utnapishtim

Nob(by) Grandee, Parage, Prince, Swell, Toff

Nobble Dope, Hilch, Injure, Interfere

▷ **Nobbled** may indicate an anagram

Nobelium No

Noble(man), Noblility Adeline, Aristocrat, Atheling, Baron(et), Bart, Boyar, Bt, Childe, Count, County, Daimio, Dom, Don, Doucepere, Douzeper(s), Duc, Duke, Earl, Eorl, Ethel, Eupatrid, Fine, Gent, Glorious, Graf, Grandee, Grandeur, Great, Heroic, Hidalgo, Highborn, Jarl, Junker, King, Landgrave, Lord, Manly, Margrave, Marquis, Palatine, Patrician, Peer, Rank, Seigneur, Seignior, Sheik(h), Stately, Thane, Thegn, Titled, Toiseach, Toisech, Vavasour, Vicomte, Vidame, Viscount

Nobody Gnatling, Jack-straw, Nebbish, Nemo, None, Nonentity, Nyaff, Pooter, Quat, Schlepp, Scoot, Shlep

Nocturnal (creature) Bat, Galago, Moth, Night, Owl

Nod(ding) Agree, Assent, Beck(on), Bob, Browse, Catnap, Cernuous, Doze, Mandarin, Nutant, Somnolent

Node, Nodular, Nodule Boss, Enhydros, Geode, Knot, Lump, Lymph, Milium, Pea-iron, Ranvier, Swelling, Thorn, Tubercle

No doubt Iwis, Ywis

Noel Christmas, Coward, Yule

Nog(gin) Ale, Cup, ➤ DRINK, Peg

No good Dud, NG, Ropy

No-hoper Gone goose

Noise, Noisy Babel, Bedlam, Blare, Blip, Bobbery, Boing, Boink, Bruit, Cangle, Charm, Clamant, Clamour, Clangour, Clash, Clatter, Clitter, Clutter, Coil, Creak, Deen, Din, Dirdum, Euphonia, Euphony, F, Fuss, Hewgh, Hubbub, Hue, Hum, Hurly-burly, Knocking, Loud, Obstreperous, Ping, Plangent, Quonk, Racket, Report, Roar, Robustious, Rorie, Rort, Row(dow-dow), Rowdedow, Rowdy(dow)(dy), Scream, Screech, Shindig, Shindy, Shreek, Shreik, Shriech, Shriek, Sone, Sonorous, Sound, Strepent, Strepitation, Strepitoso, Stridor, Surface, Tinnitus, Tumult, ➤ UPROAR, VIP, Vociferous, White, Zoom

Noisome Fetid, Invidious, Noxious, Offensive, Rank

No longer Ex, Past

Nomad(ic) Bedawin, Bedu, Bed(o)uin, Berber, Chal, Edom(ite), Fula(h), Gypsy, Hottentot, Kurd, Kyrgyz, Rom, Rootless, Rover, Saracen, Sarmatian, Strayer, Tsigane, Tsigany, Tuareg, Vagabond, Vagrant, Zigan

Noman Ta(r)tar

Nome Province

Nominal Formal, Onomastic, Titular, Trifling

Nominate, Nomination Appoint, Baptism, Designate, Elect, Present, ➤ PROPOSE, Slate, Specify, Term

Nomogram Abac

No more Gone, Napoo

Nomothete Enactor, Legislator

Non-attender Absentee, Recusant

Non-believer Atheist, Cynic, Infidel, Sceptic

Nonchalance, Nonchalant Blasé, Casual, Cool, Debonair, Jaunty

Noncommittal Trimmer

Non-communist West

Non-conformist, Non-conformity Beatnik, Bohemian, Chapel, Deviant, Dissent(er), Dissident, Ebenezer, Heresiarch, Heretic, Maverick, Odd-ball, Outlaw, Pantile, Patarine, Rebel, Recusant, Renegade, Renegate, Sectarian, Wesleyan

Nondescript Dull, Grey, Insipid, Nyaff

None Nada, Nary, Nil, Nought, Zero

Nonentity Cipher, Nebbich, Nebbish(er), Nebish, Nobody, Pipsqueak, Quat

Non-essential Adiaphoron, Extrinsic

Nonesuch Model, Nonpareil, Paradigm, Paragon, Rarity

Nonetheless Mind you

▷ **Nonetheless** may indicate an 'o' to be omitted

Non-finite Verbid

Non-gypsy Gajo, Gorgio
Non-interference Laissez faire
Non-Jewish Goy, Shi(c)ksa, Shkitzim, Sho(y)getz
Non-juror Usager
Non-Muslim Rayah
Nonpareil Nonesuch, Pearl, Peerless, Type, Unequal, Unique
Nonplus(sed) Baffle, Bewilder, Blank, Perplex, Stump
Non-professional Amateur, Laic
Non-radiative Auger
Non-resident Outlier
Non-runner Scratched, Solid
Nonsense Absurdity, Amphigon, Amphigory, Balderdash, Baloney, Bilge, Blague, Blah, Blarney, Blat(her), Blether, Bollocks, Boloney, Bora(c)k, Borax, Bosh, Bull, Bulldust, Bullshit, Buncombe, Bunkum, Claptrap, Cobblers, Cock, Cod, Codswallop, Crap, Drivel, Dust, Eyewash, Faddle, Falderal, Fandangle, Fiddlededee, Fiddle-faddle, Fiddlesticks, Flapdoodle, Flim-flam, Folderol, Footling, Fudge, Gaff, Galimatias, Gammon, Get away, Gibberish, Guff, Gum, Hanky-panky, Haver, Hogwash, Hokum, Hooey, Horsefeathers, Humbug, Jabberwocky, Kibosh, Kidstakes, Malark(e)y, Moonshine, My eye, Niaiserie, Piffle, Pishogue, Pshaw, Pulp, Rats, Rhubarb, Rigmarole, Rot, Rubbish, Scat, Shenanigans, Shit(e), Squit, Stuff, Tom(foolery), Tommy-rot, Tosh, Trash, Tripe, Tush, Twaddle, Unreason, Waffle
Non-sequitur Anacoluthia, Irrelevant
Non-stick Tusche
Non-stop Through
Non-U Naff
Non-violence Ahimsa, Pacificism, Satyagraha
Non-white Coloured, Yolk
Noodle(s) Capellini, Crispy, Daw, Fool, Head, Laksa, Lokshen, Manicotti, Mee, Moony, Pasta, Sammy, Simpleton
Nook Alcove, Angle, Corner, Cranny, Niche, Recess, Rookery
Noon Am end, M, Midday, N, Narrowdale
No one Nemo, None
Noose Fank, Halter, Lanyard, Loop, Necktie, Rope, Rope's end, Snare, Twitch
▶ **Nor** see NOT
Nordic Icelander, Scandinavian
Norm Canon, Criterion, Rule, Standard
Normal Average, Everyday, Natural, Norm, Ordinary, Par, Perpendicular, Regular, Standard, Usu(al)
Normal eyes Emmetropia
Norman French, Rufus
North(ern), Northerner Arctic, Boreal, Cispontine, Copperhead, Doughface, Eskimo, Hyperborean, Magnetic, N, Norland, Runic, Septentrion, True, Up

North American (Indian) Abenaki, Algonki(a)n, Algonqui(a)n, Apache, Arapaho, Assiniboine, Blackfoot, Brave, Caddoan, Cajun, Cayuga, Cherokee, Cheyenne, Chibcha, Chickasaw, Chinook, Chipewyan, Choctaw, Comanche, Copperskin, Creek, Crow, Delaware, Geronimo, Haida, Hiawatha, Hopi, Huron, Injun, Iroquois, Kiowa Apache, Kootenai, Kootenay, Kutenai, Kwakiutl, Lakota, Mahican, Malecite, Mandan, Manhattan, Massachuset, Melungeon, Menominee, Mescalero, Micmac, Mikasuki, Miniconjou, Minneconjou, Mogollon, Mohave, Mohawk, Mohegan, Mohican, Montagnais, Mound Builder, Mugwump, Muskogee, Narraganset, Natchez, Navaho, Nez Percé, Nootka, Northern P(a)iute, Oglala, Ojibwa(y), Okanagon, Omaha, Oneida, Onondaga, Osage, Palouse, Papago, Papoose, Pawnee, Pequot, Pima, Plains, Pocahontas, Pomo, Ponca, Pontiac, Potawatom, Pueblo, Quapaw, Red(skin), Sachem, Sagamore, Salish, Sannup, Sauk, Scalper, Seminole, Senecan, Serrano, Shawnee, Shoshone, Sioux, Sitting Bull, Siwash, Southern P(a)iute, Suquamash, Susquehannock, Tarahumara, Teton, Tewa, Tiwa, Tlingit, Tribe, Tsimshian, Tuscarora, Ute, Wampanoag, Wichita, Winnebago, Wyandot(te), Yalkama, Yaqui, Yuman

Northwestern Aeolis

Norway, Norwegian Bokmal, Fortinbras, Landsma(a)l, N, Nordic, Norweyan, Nynorsk, Rollo

Nose, Nosy A(d)jutage, Aquiline, Beak, Bergerac, Boko, Bouquet, Conk, Cromwell, Curious, Desman, Droop, Fink, Gnomon, Grass, Grecian, Honker, Hooter, Index, Informer, Meddle, Muffle, Muzzle, Nark, Neb, Nozzle, Nuzzle, Proboscis, Prying, Pug, Rhinal, Roman, Schnozzle, Shove, Smelly, Sneb, Sniff, Snoot, Snout, Snub, Squeal, Stag, Stickybeak, Toffee

Noseband Barnacle, Cavesson, Musrol

Nose-bleed Epistaxis

Nosh Eat, Food, Nibble, Snack

Nostalgia Longing, Retrophilia, Yearning

Nostril(s) Blowhole, Cere, Choana, Nare

Nostrum Elixir, Medicine, Remede, Remedy

Not, Nor Dis-, Na(e), Ne, Neither, Never, No, Pas, Polled, Taint

Notable, Notability Conspicuous, Distinguished, Eminent, Especial, Landmark, Large, Lion, Memorable, Signal, Striking, Unco, VIP, Worthy

Not allowed NL

▷ **Not allowed** may indicate a word to be omitted

Notary Escribano, Scrivener

Notation Benesh, Entry, Memo, Polish, Positional, Romic, Tablature

Notch(ed) Crena(l), Crenel, Cut, Dent, Erode, Erose, Gain, Gap, Gimp, Indent, Jag, Kerf, Nick, Nock, Raffle, Sinus, Snick, Tally, Vandyke

Not clear Blocked, NL, Obscure, Opaque, Pearl

Note(s) A, Acciaccatura, Accidental, Adversaria, Agogic, Apostil(le), Apparatus, Appoggiatura, Arpeggio, Auxiliary, B, Bill(et), Bradbury, Breve, C, Cedula, Chit(ty), Cob, Comment, Conceit, Continental, Cover, Credit, Crotchet, D, Demand, Dig, Dominant, E, E-la, F, Fa(h), Fame, Fiver, Flat, G,

Gamut, Gloss(ary), Grace, Greenback, Hemiole, IOU, Item(ise), Jot(tings), Jug(-jug), Key, Kudos, La, Large, Lichanos, Line, Log, Long, Longa, Marginalia, Masora(h), Me, Melisma, Melody, Memo(randum), Mese, Mi, Minim, Minute, ➤ MONEY, Mordent, Nachschlag, Natural, NB, Nete, Neum(e), Oblong, Observe, Octave, Oncer, Ostmark, Outline, Parhypate, Pound, Promissory, Proslambanomenos, Protocol, PS, Quaver, Rag-money, Re, Record, Remark, Renown, Root, Scholion, Scholium, Semibreve, Semiquaver, Semitone, Sextolet, Sharp, Shinplaster, Si, Sick, Sol, Stem, Subdominant, Submediant, Subtonic, Supertonic, Te, Ten(ner), Third, Tierce, Tonic, Treasury, Treble, Undecimole, Ut, Variorum, Wad, Warison

Note-case Pochette, Purse, Wallet

▷ **Notes** may indicate the use of letters A-G

Noteworthy Eminent, Extraordinary, Memorable, Particular, Signal, Special

Nothing, Nought Cipher, Devoid, Diddlysquat, Emptiness, FA, Gratis, Nada, Naught, Nihil, Niks-nie, Nil, Nix(-nie), Noumenon, Nowt, Nuffin, O, Rap, Rien, Sweet FA, Void, Zero, Zilch, Zip(po)

Notice(able) Ad(vertisement), Advice, Affiche, Apprise, Attention, Avis(o), Banns, Bill, Blurb, Caveat, Circular, Cognisance, Crit, D, Descry, Discern, Dismissal, Gaum, Get, Gorm, ➤ HEED, Intimation, Marked, Mensh, Mention, NB, No(t)chel, Obit, Observe, Oyez, Placard, Plaque, Playbill, Poster, Press, Proclamation, Prominent, ➤ REMARK, Review, See, Si quis, Spot, Sticker, Tent, Whip

Notify Acquaint, Advise, Apprise, Awarn, Inform, ➤ TELL

Notion Conceit, ➤ CONCEPT, Crotchet, Fancy, Hunch, Idea, Idolum, Inkling, Opinion, Reverie, Vapour, Whim

Notoriety, Notorious Arrant, Byword, Crying, Egregious, Esclandre, Fame, Flagrant, Infamous, Infamy, Proverbial, Reclame, ➤ RENOWN, Repute

No trump Laical, Lay, NT

Notwithstanding Although, Despite, Even, Howbeit, However, Natheless(e), Nath(e)less, Naythles, Nevertheless, Spite

Nougat Sundae

▶ **Nought** see NOTHING

Noughts and crosses Tic(k)-tac(k)-to(e)

Noun Agent, Aptote, Collective, Common, Count, Gerund, Mass, N, Proper, Substantive, Tetraptote, Verbal

Nourish(ing), Nourishment Aliment, Cherish, Cultivate, Feed, Ingesta, Meat, Nurse, Nurture, Nutrient, Promote, Replenish, Sustenance, Trophic

Nous Intellect, Intelligence, Reason

Nova Scotia(n) Acadia, Blue-nose

Novel(ty) Aga-saga, Bildungsroman, Book, Campus, Change, Different, Dime, Dissimilar, Emma, Epistolary, Fad, Fiction, Fresh, Gimmick, Gothic, Innovation, Ivanhoe, Kenilworth, Kidnapped, Kim, Middlemarch, ➤ NEW, Newfangled, Original, Pamela, Paperback, Pendennis, Persuasion, Picaresque, Pot-boiler, Primeur, Rebecca, Romance, Roman-à-clef, Roman fleuve, Unusual, Whodun(n)it, Yellowback

▷ **Novel** may indicate an anagram
▶ **Novelist** see WRITER
Novice Acolyte, Apprentice, Beginner, Chela, Colt, Cub, Greenhorn, Griffin, Jackaroo, Jillaroo, Kyu, L, Learner, Neophyte, Patzer, Postulant, Prentice, Rookie, Tenderfoot, Tyro(ne), Unweaned
Now(adays) AD, Alate, Anymore, Current, Here, Immediate, Instanter, Interim, Nonce, Nunc, Present, Pro tem, This
Nowhere Limbo
Nowt Cattle, Cows, Ky(e), Neat, Nothing
Noxious Harmful, Offensive, Poisonous, Venomous
Nozzle A(d)jutage, Fishtail, Nose, Nose-piece, Rose, Spout, Stroup, Syringe, Tewel, Tuyere, Tweer, Twier, Twire, Twyer(e)
Nuance Gradation, Nicety, Overtone, Shade
Nub Crux, Gist, Knob, Lump, Point
Nubile Beddable, Marriageable, Parti
Nuclear, Nucl(e)ide, Nucleus Cadre, Calandria, Centre, Core, Crux, Daughter, Deuteron, Eukaryon, Euratom, Heartlet, Hub, Isomer, Isotone, Karyon, Kernel, Linin, Mushroom, Nuke, Pith, Prokaryon, Triton
▷ **Nucleus** may indicate the heart of a word
Nude, Nudism, Nudist, Nudity Adamite, Altogether, Aphylly, Bare, Buff, Eve, Exposed, Gymnosophy, ▶ NAKED, Nuddy, Scud, Stark, Stripped, Undress
Nudge Dunch, Dunsh, Elbow, Jostle, Poke, Prod
Nudibranch Sea-slug
Nugget Chunk, Cob, Gold, Lump
Nuisance Bore, Bot, Bugbear, Chiz(z), Drag, Impediment, Inconvenience, Mischief, Pest, Plague, Public, Terror, Trial
Null(ification), Nullify Abate, Cancel, Counteract, Defeasance, Destroy, Diriment, Disarm, Invalid(ate), Negate, Neutralise, Recant, Terminate, Undo, Veto, Void
Numb(ness) Asleep, Blunt, Dead(en), Stun, Stupor, Torpefy, Torpescent, Torpid
Number(s) Abscissa, Abundant, Air, Aleph-null, Aleph-zero, Algebraic, Algorithm, Aliquant, Aliquot, Amiable, Anaesthetic, Antilog, Apocalyptic, Apostrophus, Army, Atomic, Augend, Avogadro, Babylonian, Binary, Box, Brinell, Calculate, Cardinal, Cetane, Chromosome, Class, Cocaine, Coefficient, Complex, Concrete, Constant, Coordination, Count, Cyclic, Decillion, Deficient, Deficit, Diapason, Digit, Drove, E, Epidural, Ether, Feck, Frost(bite), Froude, Gas, Gobar, Googol, Handful, Hantle, Hemlock, Host, Imaginary, Include, Index, Infimum, Irrational, Isospin, Lac, Lakh, Legion(s), Lepton, Local, Mach, Magazine, Magic, Melodic, Milliard, Minuend, Minyan, Mixed, Mort, Muckle, Multiple, Multiplex, Multiplicity, Multitude, Myriadth, Nasik, No(s), Nonillion, Nth, Nucleon, Num, Numerator, Numerical, Octillion, Opiate, Opium, Opposite, Opus, Ordinal, OT, Paginate, Par, Peck, Perfect, Pile, PIN, Plural, Prime, Quantum, Quarternion, Quorum, Quotient, Radix, Raft, Random, Rational, Reckon,

Registration, Regulo, Repunit, Reynolds, Sampi, Scads, Serial, Sight, Slew,
Slue, Some, Square, Strangeness, Strength, Subtrahend, Surd, Tale, Tell,
Totient, Totitive, Transcendental, Transfinite, Troop, Turn-out, Umpteen,
Umpty, Urethane, Verse, Wave, Whole, Zeroth
▷ **Number** may indicate a drug
Numeral(s) Arabic, Chapter, Figure, Ghubar, Gobar, Integer, Number,
Roman
Numerous Divers, Galore, Legion, Lots, Many, Myriad
Numskull Blockhead, Booby, Dunce, Stupid
Nun Beguine, Bhikkhuni, Clare, Cluniac, Conceptionist, Dame, Minim,
Minoress, Mother Superior, Pigeon, Poor Clare, Religeuse, Sister, Top,
Vestal, Vowess, Zelator, Zelatrice, Zelatrix
▷ **Nun** a biblical character, father of Joshua
Nuptial (chamber) Bridal, Marital, Marriage, Thalamus
Nurse(ry) Aia, Alice, Amah, Ayah, Bonne, Caledonia, Care(r), Cavell, Charge,
Cherish, Crèche, Day, Deborah, District, EN, Flo(rence), Foster, Gamp,
Glumdalclitch, Harbour, Karitane, Mammy, Minister, Mother, Mrs Gamp,
Nan(n)a, Nanny, Nightingale, Nourice, Nourish, Parabolanus, Probationer,
RN, Seminary, SEN, Sister, Staff, Suckle, Tend, VAD, Wet
Nursery(man) Conservatory, Crèche, Garden, Hothouse, Rhyme,
Seedsman, Slope
▷ **Nursing** may indicate one word within another
Nurture Cultivate, Educate, Feed, Foster, Suckle, Tend
Nut(s), Nutcase, Nutshell, Nut tree, Nutty Acajou, Acorn, Amygdalus,
Anacardium, Aphorism, Arachis, Areca, Arnut, Babassu, Barcelona, Barmy,
Bats, Beech-mast, Bertholletia, Betel, Briefly, Butterfly, Butternut, Cashew,
Cob, Cola, Coquina, Core, Cranium, Cuckoo, En, Filberd, Filbert, Gelt,
Gilbert, Gland, Glans, Godser, Gum, Hazel, Head, Hickory, Illipe, Ivory,
Kernel, Kola, Lichee, Li(t)chi, Litchi, Loaf, Lug, Lunatic, Lychee, Macadamia,
Manic, Mast, Mockernut, Monkey, Noodle, Nucule, Palmyra. Pine, Para,
Pate, Pecan, Philippina, Philippine, Philopoena, Pili, Pistachio, Praline,
Prawlin, Queensland, Rhus, Sapucaia, Sassafras, Shell, Skull, Slack, Sleeve,
Supari, Wing, Zany, Zealot
▷ **Nut** may indicate Egyptian god, father of Osiris
▶ **Nutcase, Nutshell** see NUT
Nutmeg Connecticut, CT, Mace
Nutrient, Nutriment, Nutrition Eutrophy, Food, Ingesta, Protein,
Sustenance, Trace element, Trophic
▷ **Nuts** may indicate an anagram
Nuzzle Snoozle
Nymph(et) Aegina, Aegle, Amalthea, Arethusa, Callisto, Calypso, Camenae,
Carme, Clytie, Constant, Cymodoce, Daphne, Doris, Dryad, Echo, Egeria,
Eurydice, Galatea, Hamadryad, Hesperides, Houri, Hyades, Ida, Insect,
Larva, Liberty, Lolita, Maelid, Maia, Maiden, Mermaid, Naiad, Nereid,
Oceanid, Oenone, Oread, Pupa, Rusalka, Sabrina, Scylla, Siren, Sylph,
Syrinx, Tessa, Tethys, Thetis

O o

O Blob, Duck, Nought, Omega, Omicron, Oscar, Oxygen, Spangle, Tan, Zero

Oaf Auf, Changeling, Dolt, Fool, Ocker, Stupid

Oak Bur, Cerris, Cork, Dumbarton, Durmast, Flittern, Fumed, Gabriel, Herne, Holly, Holm, Honour, Ilex, Jerusalem, Kermes, Live, Major, Parliament, Philemon, Poison, Quercus, Roble, Royal, Sessile, Silky, Swilcar, ➤ TREE, Watch

Oakley Annie

Oar(s), Oarsmen Blade, Ctene, Eight, Leander, Organ, Paddle, Propel, Rower, Scull, Spoon, Sweep

Oasis Buraimi, Haven, Hotan, Refuge, Spring

Oat(meal), Oats Ait, Athole brose, Avena, Brome-grass, Fodder, Grain, Grits, Groats, Gruel, Haver, Loblolly, Parritch, Pilcorn, Pipe, Porridge, Quaker®, Rolled, Wild

Oatcake Bannock, Clapbread, Farle, Flapjack, Jannock

Oath Affidavit, Begorrah, Curse, Dang, Demme, Doggone, Drat, Ecod, Egad, Expletive, God-so, Halidom, Hippocratic, Igad, Imprecation, Jabers, Lumme, Lummy, Nouns, Oons, Promise, Sacrament, Sal(a)mon, Sapperment, Sdeath, Sfoot, Sheart, Strewth, Stygian, Swear, Tarnation, Tennis-court, Voir dire, Vow, Zbud

Obdurate Adamant, Cruel, Hard, Intransigent, Stony, Stubborn, Tenacious

Obedient, Obedience, Obey Bridlewise, Comply, Dutiful, Follow, Hear, Mindful, Obsequious, Observe, Obtemper, Perform, Pliant, Servant, Yielding

Obeisance ➤ BOW, Salaam

Obelisk, Obelus Aguilla, Column, Dagger, Monument, Needle, Pillar

Oberon King, Merle

Obese, Obesity Bariatrics, Corpulent, Fat, Stout

Object(s), Objection(able), Objective(ness), Objector Ah, Aim, Ambition, Argue, Article, Bar, Beef, Case, Cavil, Challenge, Clinical, Complain(t), Conchy, Conscientious, Cow, Demur, Direct, End, Exception, Fuss, ➤ GOAL, Her, Him, Impersonal, Improper, Indifferent, Indirect, Intention, It, Item, Jib, Loathe, Mind, Moral, Niggle, Non-ego, Noumenon, Obnoxious, Offensive, Oppose, Outness, Point, Protest, Question, Quibble, Quiddity, Rebarbative, Recuse, Refuse, Resist, Sake, Scruple, Subject, Sublime, Target, Thing, Tut, Ultimate, Unbiased, Virtu, Wart

▷ **Object** may indicate a grammatical variant

Objectless Intransitive

Oblate, Oblation Gift, Monk, Offering, Sacrifice

Oblige, Obliging, Obligation, Obligatory Accommodate, Affable, Behold, Binding, Burden, Charge, Compel, Complaisant, Compliant, Contract, Corvée, Debt, De rigueur, Duty, Easy, Encumbent, Force, Giri,

Gratify, Impel, Incumbent, IOU, Mandatory, Must, Necessitate, Obruk, Promise, Sonties, Synallagmatic, Tie, Wattle

Oblique(ly) Askance, Askew, Asklent, Asquint, Athwart, Awry, Cross, Diagonal, Perverse, Separatrix, Skew, Slanting, Solidus, Squint, Virgule

▷ **Oblique** may indicate an anagram

Obliterate(d) Annul, Blot, Dele(te), Efface, Expunge, Exterminate, Rase, Rast, Raze, Wipe

Oblivion, Oblivious Forgetful, Lethe, Limbo, Nirvana, Obscurity

Oblong Rectangular

Obnoxious Foul, Horrid, Offensive, Pestilent, Repugnant, Septic

Obscene(ly), Obscenity Bawdy, Blue, Fescennine, Gross, Hard-core, Indecent, Lewd, Lubricious, Paw(paw), Porn(o), Salacious, Smut, Vulgar

Obscure, Obscurity Abstruse, Anheires, Becloud, Befog, Blend, Cloud, Cobweb, Conceal, Cover, Darken, Deep, Dim, Disguise, Eclipse, Encrypt, Envelop, Filmy, Fog, Hermetic, Hide, Mantle, Mist, Murk, Nebular, Night, Nubecula, Obfuscate, Opaque, Oracular, Overcloud, Overshade, Overshadow, Recherché, Recondite, Tenebrific, Twilit, Unclear, ➤ VAGUE, Veil, Vele, Wrap

▷ **Obscure(d)** may indicate an anagram

Obsequious Bootlicker, Brown nose, Fawn, Fulsome, Grovelling, Menial, Parasitic, Pig, Servile, Slimy, Sycophantic, Tantony, Toady

Observance, Observant, Observation Adherence, Alert, Attention, Comment, Custom, Empirical, Espial, Eyeful, Holy, Honour, Lectisternium, ➤ NOTICE, Obiter dicta, Percipient, Recce, Remark, Right, Rite, Ritual, Vising

Observatory Atalaya, Greenwich, Herstmonceux, Hurstmonceux, Lookout, Mount Palomar, Tower

Observe(d), Observer Behold, Bystander, Celebrate, Commentator, Detect, Espy, Eye, Heed, Keep, Mark, NB, Note, Notice, Obey, Onlooker, Optic, Regard(er), Remark, Rite, Scry, See, Sight, Spectator, Spial, Spot, Spy, Study, Take, Twig, View, Voyeur, Witness

Obsess(ed), Obsession, Obsessive Besot, Bug, Craze, Dominate, Fetish, Fixation, Hang-up, Haunt, Hobbyhorse, Hooked, Idée fixe, Infatuation, Mania, Monomania, Necrophilia, Neurotic, One-track, Preoccupy, Thing

Obsolete, Obsolescent Abandoned, Antique, Archaic, Dated, Dead, Defunct, Disused, Extinct, Latescent, Obs, Outdated, Outworn, Passé

Obstacle Barrage, Barrier, Boyg, Cheval de frise, Chicane, Dam, Drag, Dragon's teeth, Drawback, Gate, Handicap, Hindrance, Hitch, Hurdle, Node, Oxer, Remora, Rock, Sandbank, Snag, Stimie, Stumbling-block, Stymie

Obstetrics Gynaecology, Midwifery, Tocology, Tokology

Obstinacy, Obstinate Asinine, Buckie, Bullish, Contumacious, Cussed, Dour, Froward, Headstrong, Inflexible, Intractable, Intransigent, Mule, Persistent, Perverse, Pervicacious, Pig-headed, Recalcitrant, Refractory, Restive, Resty, Self-will, Stiff(-necked), Stubborn, Wilful

Obstreperous Noisy, Truculent, Unruly

Obstruct(ion) Bar, Block, Bottleneck, Clog, Crab, Cross, Cumber, Dam, Embolus, Fil(l)ibuster, Hamper, Hedge, Hinder, Hurdle, Ileus, Impede, Let, Obstacle, Sab(otage), Snooker, Stall, Stap, Stonewall, Stop, Stymie, Sudd, Thwart, Trammel, Trump

Obtain Achieve, Acquire, Cop, Exist, Gain, Get, Land, Pan, Prevail, Procure, Realise, Secure, Succeed, Wangle, Win

Obtrude, Obtrusive Expel, Impose, Loud, Prominent, Push, Sorn, Thrust

Obtuse Blunt, Dense, Dull, Purblind, Stupid, Thick

Obverse Complement, Cross, Face, Front, Head

Obviate Forestall, Preclude, Prevent

Obvious Apparent, Axiom, Blatant, Brobdingnag, Clear, Distinct, Evident, Flagrant, Frank, Kenspeck(le), Manifest, Marked, Open(ness), Overt, Palpable, Patent, Pikestaff, Plain, Pronounced, Salient, Self-evident, Transparent, Truism, Visible

Occasion Call, Cause, Ceremony, Encheason, Event, Fete, Field day, Nonce, ➤ OPPORTUNITY, Reason, Ride, Tide, Time

Occasional(ly) Casual, Chance, Daimen, Intermittent, Irregular, Motive, Orra, Periodic, Sometimes, Sporadic, While

Occident(al) West, Western(er)

Occlude, Occlusion Absorb, Clog, Coronary, Embolism, Obstruct

Occult(ist) Angekkok, Arcane, Art, Esoteric, I-ching, Magic, Mysterious

Occupant, Occupation, Occupy(ing) Absorb, Activity, Avocation, Beset, Business, Busy, Denizen, Embusy, Employ, Engage, Engross, Hold, In, Incumbent, Indwell, Inhabitant, Inmate, Involve, Line, Metier, People, Profession, Pursuit, Resident, Runrig, Sideline, Squat, Stay, Tenancy, Tenant, Tenure, Thrift, Trade, Upon, Use, Vocation, Walk of life

Occur(rence) Arise, Be, Betide, Betime, Case, Event, Fall, Happen, Incident, Instance, Outbreak, Outcrop, Pass, Phenomenon

Ocean(ic), Oceania Abssal, Abundance, Antarctic, Arctic, Atlantic, Blue, Deep, Hadal, Herring-pond, Indian, Melanesia, Micronesia, Pacific, Pelagic, Polynesia, Sea(way), Waves

Och aye Troggs

Ochre Keel, Ruddle, Sienna

Octave Diapason, Eight, Ottava, Utas

Octopus Cephalopod, Devilfish, Paper nautilus, Polyp, Poulp(e), Scuttle, Squid

Octoroon Mestee, Mestizo, Mustee

Od Energy, Force

Odd (person), Oddity Anomaly, Bizarre, Card, Cure, Curio, Droll, Eccentric, Erratic, Gink, Impair, Imparity, Offbeat, Orra, Outré, Paradox, Parity, Peculiar, Queer, Quiz, Random, Rare, Remote, Rum, Screwball, Singular, ➤ STRANGE, Uneven, Unmatched, Unusual, Weird, Whims(e)y

▷ **Odd(s)** may indicate an anagram or the odd letters in words

Odd job man Joey, Orraman, Rouster, Smoot

Odds, Oddments Bits, Carpet, Chance, Gubbins, Handicap, Line, Price, SP, Tails, Variance

Ode Awdl, Dit, Epicede, Epicedium, Epinicion, Epinikion, Genethliacon, Horatian, Hymn, Lay, Lyric, Monody, Paeon, Pindaric, Poem, Sapphic, Song, Stasimon, Threnody, Verse

Odin One-eyed, Woden

Odium, Odious Comparison, Disestimation, Disgrace, Foul, Hatred, Heinous, Invidious, Repugnant, Stigma

Odorous, Odour Air, BO, Flavour, Funk, Hum, Opopanax, Perfume, Quality, Redolence, Sanctity, Scent, Smell

Odourless Silent

Odyssey Epic, Journey, Wandering

Oedipus Complex, Parricide

Oeillade Glance, Leer, Ogle, Wink

Oesophagus Crop

Oestrogen, Oestrus Frenzy, Heat, Mestranol, Must, Rut, Stilb(o)estrol

Of (me) About, Among, Aus, By, De, From, My, Re

▷ **Of** may indicate an anagram

Of course Certainly, Natch, Yes

Off Absent, Agee, Ajee, Away, Discount, Distance, Far, From, High, Inexact, Licence, Odd, Reasty, Reesty, Relache, Start

▷ **Off** may indicate an anagram

Offal Cagmag, Carrion, Chitterling, Entrails, Fry, Gralloch, Gurry, Ha(r)slet, Heart, Innards, Kidney, Lamb's fry, Lights, Liver, Numbles, Sweetbread, Tripe

Off-beat Zoppo

Off-colour Pale, Seedy, Wan

▷ **Off-colour** may indicate an anagram

Offence Attack, Crime, Delict, Delinquency, Distaste, Fault, Huff, Hurt, Lapse, Miff, Misprision, Outrage, Peccadillo, Pip, Pique, Piracy, Regrate, Sedition, ➤ SIN, Summary, Trespass, Umbrage

Offend(ed), Offender Affront, Anger, Annoy, Bridles, Culprit, Default, Disoblige, Displease, Distaste, Hip, Huff, Hurt, Hyp, Infringe, Inveigh, Miffy, Miscreant, Nettle, Nonce, Nuisance, Peeve, Provoke, Sin(ner), Stray, Twoccer, Violate, Wrongdoer

Offensive Affront, Aggressive, Alien, Attack, Bombardment, Campaign, Cruel, Embracery, Execrable, Eyesore, Foul, Hedgehog, Hedgepig, Indelicate, Miasmic, Nasty, Noisome, Obnoxious, Obscene, Peccant, Personal, Push, Putrid, Rank, Repugnant, ➤ RUDE, Scandalous, Scurrilous, Sortie, Storm, Ugly, Unbecoming

Offer(ing) Alms, Altarage, Anaphora, Bid, Bode, Bouchée, Cadeau, Corban, Deodate, Dolly, Epanophora, Extend, Gift, Godfather, Hold, Inferiae, Oblation, Overture, Peddle, Plead, Potla(t)ch, Present, Propine, ➤ PROPOSAL, Propose, Propound, Sacrifice, Shewbread, Shore, S(h)raddha, Stand, Submit, Tender, Volunteer, Votive, Xenium

Offhand Airy, Banana, Brusque, Casual, Cavalier, Curt, Extempore, Impromptu, Indifferent

Office(s) Agency, Bedelship, Box, Branch, Broo, Bucket shop, Bureau, Buroo, Caliphate, Chair, Complin(e), Crown, Daftar, Dataria, Dead-letter, Den, Evensong, Foreign, Function, Holy, Home, Job, Lats, Left luggage, Mayoralty, Ministry, Missa, Mistery, Mudiria, Mutessarifat, Mystery, Nocturn, Nones, Obit, Oval, Papacy, Patent, Personnel, Place, Plum, Portfolio, Position, Post, Prelacy, Prime, Provosty, Regency, Register, Registry, Rite, See, Seraskierate, Shogunate, Sinecure, Situation, Tenebrae, Terce, Ticket, Tierce, Tol(l)booth, Tribunate, Vespers, Yamen

Officer(s) Acater, Adjutant, Admiral, Ag(h)a, Agistor, Aide, Apparitor, Bailiff, Beatty, Bimbashi, Black Rod, Blimp, Blue Rod, Bombardier, Bos(u)n, Brass-hat, Brigadier, Bumbailiff, Capt(ain), Catchpole, Catchpoll, Cater, Centurion, Chamberlain, Chancellor, CIGS, Colonel, Commander, Commodore, Compliance, Constable, Cop(per), Co-pilot, Cornet, Coroner, Counter-round, Cursitor, Darogha, Datary, Deacon, Decurion, Ensign, Equerry, Exciseman, Exon, Filacer, Filazer, Flap, Flying, Gallant, Gen(eral), GOC, Group, Gunner, Havildar, Hayward, Hetman, Ima(u)m, Infirmarian, Intendant, Jamadar, Janty, Jauntie, Jaunty, Jemadar, Jemidar, Jonty, Jurat, Lictor, Lt, Marshal, Mate, NCO, Number one, Oxon, Petty, Pilot, PO, Posse, Proctor, Provost, Provost-marshal, Purser, Pursuivant, Quartermaster, Remembrancer, Returning, Samurai, Sbirro, Schout, Second mate, Serang, Sewer, Sexton, Sheriff, Silver-stick, Skipper, SL, SM, Speaker, Staff, Striper, Sub(altern), Suba(h)dar, Subchanter, Sublieutenant, Supercargo, Tahsildar, Tidewaiter, Tindal, Tipstaff, Treasurer, Tribune, Usher, Varlet, Waldgrave, Warden, Wardroom, Warrant, Yeoman

Official(s), Officious Aga, Agent, Amban, Amtman, Atabeg, Atabek, Attaché, Authorised, Beadle, Bossy, Bureaucrat, Catchpole, Censor, Chamberlain, Chinovnik, Claviger, Commissar, Commissioner, Consul, Count, Dean, Ealdorman, Ephor, Equerry, Escheater, Executive, Fonctionnaire, ➤ FORMAL, Functionary, Gauleiter, Hayward, Incumbent, Intendant, Jack-in-office, Jobsworth, Keeper, Landdrost, Lictor, Mandarin, Marplot, Marshal, Mayor, MC, Meddlesome, Mirza, Mueddin, Mukhtar, Nazir, Notary, Ombudsman, Omlah, Palatine, Plenipotentiary, Polemarch, Poohbah, Postmaster, Pragmatic, Proctor, Procurator, Prog, Proveditor, Silentiary, Staff, Steward, Suffete, Suit, Syndic, Timekeeper, Tribune, Valid, Veep, Verderer, Verger, Whiffler, Woodward

Off-putting Dehortative, Discouraging, Manana, Negative, Procrastination, Rebarbative, Repellent, Yips

Offset Balance, Cancel, Compensate, Counter(act), Counterbalance

Offshoot Bough, Branch, Limb, Lye, Member, Outgrowth, Plant, Scion, Sien, Swarm

Offspring Boy, Burd, Chick, Children, Daughter, Descendant, Family, Fry, Get, Girl, Heir, Procreation, Product, Progeny, Seed, Sient, Son, Spawn

Offstage Wings

Often Frequent, Habitual, Repeated

▷ **Often** may indicate 'of ten'

Ogee Cyma, Moulding, Talon

Ogle Eliad, Eye, Glance, Leer, Oeillade

Ogre(ss) Baba yaga, Boyg, Brute, Eten, Etten, Fiend, Giant, Monster, Orc

Ohio Buckeye

Oil(y), Oil producer Aj(o)wan, Aleuritis, Anele, Anoint, Apiezon®, Argan, Attar, Balm, Banana, Bath, Beech-mast, Ben, Benne, Benni, Bergamot, Bittern, Bone, BP, Bribe, Brilliantine, Cajeput, Cajuput, Camphire, Camphor, Canola, Carapa, Carron, Carvacrol, Castor, Chaulmoogra, Chaulmugra, Chrism, Citronella grass, Clove, Coal, Coconut, Cod-liver, Cohune, Colza, Copra, Corn, Cotton-seed, Creasote, Creosote, Croton, Crude, Diesel, Dittany, Elaeis, Essence, Essential, Eucalyptus, Eugenol, Evening primrose, Extra virgin, Fatty, Fixed, Fuel, Fusel, Gingelli, Gingelly, Gingili, Golomynka, Good, Groundnut, Guttiferae, Heavy, Jojoba, Kerosene, Kerosine, Lamp, Lavender, Linalo(o)l, Linseed, Lipid, Lubricant, Lumbang, Macassar, Magilp, Megilp, Menthol, Midnight, Mineral, Mirbane, Moringa, Multigrade, Mustard, Myrbane, Myrrhol, Naphtha, Neat's-foot, Neem, Neroli, Nim, Oint, Oiticica, Oleo, Olive, Ottar, Otto, Palm, Paraffin, Parathion, Patchouli, Pellitory, Picamar, Pomade, Poon, Pristane, Pulza, Pyrrole, Ramtil, Rape, Rapeseed, Retinol, Ricinus, Rose, Rosin, Rusa, Safrole, Sassafras, Savin(e), Sebum, Semsem, Sesame, Shale, Sleek, Slick, Slum, Smalmy, Smarmy, Smeary, Sperm, Spike(nard), Stand, Star-anise, Sunflower, Tall(ow), Tolu, Train, Tung, Turpentine, Ulyie, Ulzie, Unction, Vanaspati, Vegetable, Virgin, Vitriol, Volatile, Whale, Wintergreen, Yolk

Oilcake Poonac

Oilcan Pourie

Oilcloth American, Lino

Oilman Driller, Prospector, Rigger, Texan

Oil painting Master, Titian

Ointment Balm, Basilicon, Boracic, Boric, Cerate, Cream, Nard, Pomade, Pomatum, Salve, Spikenard, Unguent, Vaseline®, Zinc

OK Agree(d), Approve, Authorise, Clearance, Copacetic, Copesettic, Hunky-dory, Initial, Kosher, Right(o), Sanction, Sound, U, Vet

Okra Bhindi, Lady's fingers

Old(er) Ae(t), Aged, Aine(e), Ancient, Antique, Auld, Bean, Decrepit, Dutch, Fogram, Former, Gaffer, Geriatric, Glory, Gray, Grey, Hills, Hoary, Immemorial, Methusaleh, Moore, Nestor, Nick, O, OAP, Obsolete, Off, Ogygian, One-time, Outworn, Palae-, Passé, Primeval, Rugose, Sen(escent), Senile, Senior, Shot, Stale, Trite, Venerable, Veteran, Victorian(a)

Old boy, Old girl Alumnae, Alumnus, OB

Old days Once, Past, Yore

Old English OE

Old-fashioned Aging, Ancient, Antediluvian, Arch(aic), Arriere, Bygone, Corn(y), Dated, Dowdy, Fuddy-duddy, Medieval, No tech, Obsolete,

Ogygian, Outmoded, Passé, Primeval, Quaint, Relic, Retro, Rinky-dink, Schmaltzy, Shot, Square, Steam, Stick-in-the-mud, Traditional, Uncool, Vieux jeu, Worm-eaten

Old maid Biddy, Spinster

Old man, Old woman Anile, Aunty, Bodach, Burd, Cailleach, Crow, Faggot, Fantad, Fantod, Fogey, Fogramite, Fogy, Fussy, Gammer, Geezer, Grannam, Greybeard, Greyhen, Husband, Kangaroo, Luckie, Lucky, Methuselah, Mort, Mzee, OAP, Oom, Presbyte, Trout, Wife, Wight, Woopie, Wrinkly

Old-timer Hourglass, Sundial, Veteran

Olid Fetid, Foul, High, Rancid, Rank

Olio Hash, Medley, Mess, Potpourri, Stew

Olive (grove), Olivine Cerulein, Drupe, Dunite, Gethsemane, Olea(ster), Peridot, Queen

Oliver Cromwell, Goldsmith, Hardy, Noll, Protector, Twist

Olympian, Olympus Asgard, Athlete, Celestial, Elis, Pantheon, Quadrennium, Zeus

Omelette Crepe, Foo yong, Foo yung, Frittata, Fu yung, Pancake, Spanish, Tortilla

Omen Abodement, Absit, Augury, Auspice, Foreboding, Forewarning, Freet, Freit, Portent, Presage, Prodrome, Sign, Token, Warning

Omentum Caul, Epiploon

Ominous Alarming, Baleful, Bodeful, Dire, Dour, Forbidding, Grim, Inauspicious, Oracular, Sinister, Threatening

Omission, Omit Aph(a)eresis, Apocope, Apospory, Apostrophe, Caret, Disregard, Drop, Elide, Elision, Ellipse, Ellipsis, Failure, Haplography, Haplology, Lipography, Loophole, Miss, Neglect, Nonfeasance, Oversight, Paral(e)ipomenon, Senza, Skip

Omnibus Anthology, Coach, Collection

Omniscient Encyclopedia

Omnivorous Pantophagous

On (it) About, Agreed, An, An't, At, Atop, By, Game, In, Leg, O', Of, Over, Pon, Re, Tipsy, Up(on)

▷ **On** may indicate an anagram

On account of Over

▷ **On board** may indicate chess, draughts, or 'SS' around another word

Once(r) Ance, ➤ AT ONCE, Bradbury, Earst, Erst(while), Ever, Ex, Fore, Former, Jadis, Oner, Onst, Secular, Sole, Sometime, Whilom

One(self) A, Ace, Ae, Alike, An(e), Any, Body, Chosen, Eeny, Ego, Ein, Individual, Integer, Me, Monad, Per se, Single(ton), Singular, Solo, Tane, Un, Unit(y), Unitary, United, Yin, You

One-act-er Playlet

One-eared Monaural

One-eyed Arimasp(ian), Cyclops

One-man band Moke

One o'clock 1 am, ➤ NNE

One-rayed Monact

Onerous Arduous, Exacting, Tedious, Weighty

Onion(s) Bengi, Bonce, Bulb, Chibol, Chive, Cibol, Cive, Eschalot, Head, Ingan, Jibbons, Leek, Lyonnaise, Moly, Pearl, Ramp, Ramson, Rocambole, Ropes, Scallion, Scilla, Shal(l)ot, Spanish, Spring, Squill, Sybo(e), Sybow

Onlooker Bystander, Kibitzer, Rubberneck, Spectator, Witness

Only Allenarly, Anerly, But, Except, Just, Meer, Merely, Nobbut, Seul, Singly, Sole

Onset Affret, Attack, Beginning, Charge, Dash, Rush, ➤ START, Thrust

Onslaught Attack, Dead-set, Onset, Raid, Spreagh, Storm

On time Pat, Prompt, Punctual

Onus Burden, Charge, ➤ DUTY, Responsibility

Onward Advance, Ahead, Away, Forth, Forward, Progress

Oodles Heaps, Lashings, Lots, Slather

Oolite Roestone

Oomph Energy, It, SA, Verve

Ooze Drip, Exhale, Exude, Gleet, Mud, Percolate, Pteropod(a), Seep, Sew, Sipe, Slime, Slob, Spew, Spue, Sweat, Sype, Transude

Opal(escent) Cymophanous, Fire, Gem, Girasol, Girosol, Hyalite, Hydrophane, Potch

Opaque, Opacity Dense, Dull, Leucoma, Obscure, Obtuse, Onycha, Roil, Thick

Open(er), Opening, Openness Adit, Ajar, Antithesis, Anus, Apert(ure), Apparent, Apse, Bald, Bare, Bat, Bole, Breach, Break, Broach, Buttonhole, Candid, Cardia, Cavity, Champaign, Chance, Chasm, Chink, Circumscissile, Clear, Crevasse, Dehisce, Deploy, Dispark, Door, Dup, Embrasure, Exordium, Expansive, Eyelet, Fair, Fenestra, Fissure, Fistula, Flue, Fontanel(le), Foramen, Frank, Free, Gambit, Gap, Gaping, Gat, Gate, Give, Glasnost, Glottis, Guichet, Gullwing, Hagioscope, Hatch, Hatchback, Hiatus, Hilus, ➤ HOLE, Inaugural, Interstice, Intro, Key, Lacy, Lance, Lead, Loid, Loophole, Loose, Machicolation, Manhole, Meatus, Micropyle, Mofette, Moongate, Mouth, Oillet, Oscule, Osculum, Ostiole, Ostium, Overture, Patent, Peephole, Pert, Pervious, Pick(lock), Placket, Plughole, Pore, Port(age), Porta, Porthole, Preliminary, Premiere, Prise, Pro-am, Public, Pylorus, Receptive, Rent, Riva, Room, Scuttle, Scye, Sesame, Sicilian, Sincere, Slit, Spare, Spirant, Squint, Start, Stenopaic, Stoma, Thereout, Touchhole, Trapdoor, Trema, Trou, Truthful, Unbar, Unbolt, Unbutton, Uncork, Undo, Unfurl, Unhasp, Unlatch, Unscrew, Untie, Vent, Vulnerable, Window

Open air Alfresco, Sub divo, Sub Jove

Opera Aida, Ariadne, Ballad, Bouffe, Burletta, Comic, ENO, Ernani, Falstaff, Faust, Fedora, Fidelio, Glyndebourne, Grand, Hansel and Gretel, Horse, Idomineo, Iolanthe, Light, Lohengrin, Lulu, Met, Musical, Nabucco, Norma, Oater, Oberon, Onegin, Orfeo, Otello, Parsifal, Pastorale, Patience,

Pinafore, Rigoletto, Ruddigore, Savoy, Scala, Seria, Singspiel, Soap, Space, Tell, The Met, Threepenny, Tosca, Turandot, Verismo, Work, Zarzuela

Opera-glasses Jumelle

Opera-lover Wagnerite

Opera-singer Baritone, Bass, Contralto, Diva, Savoyard, Soprano

Operate, Operation, Operative Act(ion), Activate, Actuate, Agent, Artisan, Attuition, Caesarean, Campaign, Conduct, Couching, Current, Detective, Exercise, Function, Game, Hobday, Keystroke, Manipulate, Mechanic, Overlord, Practice, Run, Sortie, Strabotomy, Ure, Valid, Work

Operator Agent, Conductor, Dealer, Manipulator, Nabla, Sparks, Surgeon

Opiate, Opium Dope, Drug, Hop, Laudanum, Meconin, Narcotic, Religion, Soporific, Thebaine

Opinion, Opinionative Attitude, Belief, Bet, Consensus, Cri, Dictum, Dogma, Doxy, Entêté, Esteem, Feeling, Guess, Judgement, Mind, Private, Public, Pulse, Say, Second, Sense, Sentence, Sentiment, Tenet, Utterance, View, Viewpoint, Voice, Vox pop, Vox populi

Opossum Lie, Marmose, Phalanger, Tarsipes, Yapo(c)k

Oppidan Cit, Townsman, Urban

Opponent(s) Adversary, Antagonist, Anti, E-N, Enemy, E-S, Foe, Gainsayer, N-E, N-W, S-E, S-W, W-N, W-S

Opportune, Opportunist, Opportunity Appropriate, Apropos, Break, Carpetbagger, ➤ CHANCE, Day, Facility, Favourable, Go-go, Heaven-sent, Occasion, Opening, Pat, Room, Seal, Seel, Sele, Snatcher, Tide, Timely, Timous, Window

Oppose(d), Opposing, Opposite, Opposition Against, Agin, Anti, Antipathy, Antipodes, Antiscian, Antithesis, Antithetic, Antonym, Argue, At, Au contraire, Averse, Battle, Black, Breast, Colluctation, Combat, Confront, Contradict, Contrary, Converse, Counter, Diametric, Dissent, Distance, E contrario, Face, Foreanent, Fornen(s)t, Hinder, Hostile, Impugn, Inimical, Inverse, Militate, Noes, Object, Overthwart, Polar, Reaction, Reluct, Repugn, Resist, Retroact, Reverse, Rival, Shadow, Subtend, Syzygy, Teeth, Terr, Thereagainst, Thwart, Toto caelo, Traverse, V, Versus, Vis-a-vis, Withstand

Oppress(ion), Oppressive Airless, Bind, Burden, Close, Crush, Despotic, Incubus, Jackboot, Onerous, Overpower, Persecute, Ride, Stifling, Sultry, Tyrannise

Opprobrium Disgrace, Envy, Odium, Scandal

Oppugn Attack, Criticise

Opt, Option(al) Alternative, ➤ CHOICE, Choose, Default, Elect, Facultative, Fine, Menu, Pick, Plump, Select, Soft, Voluntary, Votive, Wale, Zero(-zero)

Optic(al), Optics Fibre, Lens, Prism, Reticle, Visual

Optimism, Optimist(ic) Chiliast, Expectant, Hopeful, Morale, Pangloss, Pollyanna, Rosy, Sanguine, Upbeat, Utopiast, Yea-sayer

Opulent Abundant, Affluent, Moneyed, Rich, Wealthy

Opus Piece, Study, Work

Or Au, Either, Ere, Gold, Ossia, Otherwise, Sol

Oracle(s), Oracular Delphi, Dodonian, Mirror, Prophet, Pythian, Pythoness, Sage, Seer, Sibyl(line), Thummim, Urim, Vatic

Oral Acroamatic, Sonant, Spoken, Verbal, Viva, Viva voce, Vocal

Orange An(n)atta, Annatto, Arnotto, Aurora, Bergamot, Bigarade, Blood, Blossom, Chica, Clockwork, Croceate, Flame, Flamingo, Fulvous, Jaffa, Kamala, Kamela, Kamila, Karaka, Mandarin, Mock, Naartje, Nacarat, Nartjie, Navel, Osage, Pig, Roucou, Ruta, Satsuma, Seville, Shaddock, Tangerine, Tenné, Ugli, Ulsterman

Orang-utan Ape, Monkey, Satyr

Orate, Oration Address, Eloge, Elogium, Elogy, Eulogy, Harangue, Panegyric, Speech

Oratorio, Orator(y) Boanerges, Brompton, Brougham, Cantata, Cicero, Creation, Demosthenes, Diction, Elijah, Hwyl, Isocrates, Morin, Nestor, Prevaricator, Proseucha, Proseuche, Rhetor, Samson, Spellbinder, Stump, Tub-thumper, Windbag, Yarra-banker

Orb Ball, Eyeball, Firmament, Globe, Mound, Pome, Sphere

Orbit Apse, Apsis, Circuit, Dump, Eccentric, Ellipse, Eye, Path, Periastron, Perigee, Perihelion, Perilune, Periselenium, Revolution, Stationary

Orcadian Hoy

Orchard Arbour, Grove, Holt

Orchestra(te), Orchestration Ensemble, Gamelan, Hallé, LPO, LSO, Ripieno, Score, Symphony

Orchid Adam and Eve, Adder's mouth, Arethusa, Bee, Bird's nest, Bog, Burnt-tip, Calanthe, Calypso, Cattleya, Coalroot, Cymbidium, Disa, Epidendrum, Fly, Fragrant, Frog, Helleborine, Lady, Lady's slipper, Lady's tresses, Lizard, Man, Marsh, Military, Monkey, Musk, Naked lady, Odontoglossum, Oncidium, Puttyroot, Salep, Slipper, Snakemouth, Swamp pink, Twayblade, Vanda, Vanilla

Ord Beginning, Point

Ordain Arrange, Command, Decree, Destine, Enact, Induct, Japan, Priest

Ordeal Corsned, Disaster, Preeve, Test, ➤ TRIAL

Order(ed), Orderly, Orders Acoemeti, Adjust, Affiliation, Alphabetical, Apollonian, Apple-pie, Arrange, Array, Attendant, Attic, Avast, Bade, Bath, Batman, Battalia, Bed, Behest, Benedictine, Bespoke, Bid, Book, Call, Canon, Category, Caveat, CB, Chaprassi, Charter, Cheque, Chuprassy, Class, Coherent, Command(ment), Committal, Compensation, Composite, Corinthian, Cosmos, Court, Decorum, Decree, Demand, Dictate, Diktat, Direct(ion), Directive, Dispone, Distringas, Dominican, Doric, DSO, Edict, Embargo, Enclosed, Enjoin, En règle, Establishment, Eutaxy, Feldsher, Fiat, Firman, Form(ation), Franciscan, Fraternity, Freemason, Garnishee, Garter, Ginkgo, Habeas corpus, Heast(e), Hecht, Hest, Holy, Indent, Injunction, Interdict, Ionic, Irade, Kilter, Kosmos, Language, Mail, Mandamus, Mandate, Marching, Marshal, Masonic, Medjidie, Merit, Methodical, Mittimus, Monastic, Monitor, Neatness, Nunnery, OBE, Official, OM, Orange, Ord, Ordain, Organic, Pecking, Postal, Precedence, Premonstrant, Prescribe, Preservation, Pyragyrite, Rank,

Receiving, Règle, Regular, Restraining, Right, Rule, Ruly, Series, Settle, Shipshape, Short, Side, Standing, State, Statutory, Stop(-loss), Subpoena, Summons, Supersedere, System, Tabulate, Taxis, Tell, Thistle, Tidy, Trim, Tuscan, Ukase, Uniformity, Writ

▷ **Ordering** may indicate an anagram

Ordinal Book, Number, Second, Sequence

Ordinance Byelaw, Decree, Edict, Law, Prescript, Rite, Statute

Ordinary Average, Banal, Bog standard, Canton, Chevron, Comely, Common (or garden), Commonplace, Cot(t)ise, Everyday, Fess(e), Flanch, Flange, Folksy, Grassroots, Hackneyed, Mediocre, Middling, Mundane, ➤ NORMAL, O, OR, Plain, Prosy, Pub, Saltier, Saltire, Simple, Tressure, Trivial, Usual, Workaday, Your

Ordnance Artillery, Cannon, Guns, Supply

Ordure Cess, Dung, Fertiliser, Manure

Ore Alga, Babingtonite, Bauxite, Bornite, Calamine, Calaverite, Cerusite, Chalcocite, Chalcopyrite, Coffinite, Coin, Copper, Crocoite, Element, Galenite, Glance, Haematite, Hedyphane, Horseflesh, Ilmenite, Iridosmine, Ironstone, Limonite, Mat, Melaconite, Middlings, Mineral, Minestone, Niobite, Oligist, Peacock, Phacolite, Pitchblende, Proustite, Psilomelane, Pyragyrite, Pyromorphite, Realgar, Schlich, Seaweed, Slug, Smaltite, Sphalerite, Stephanite, Stilpnosiderite, Stream-tin, Tenorite, Tetrahedrite, Tin, Wad(d)

Organ(ic), Organs Anlage, Apollonicon, Archegonium, Barrel, Biogenic, Calliope, Carpel, Chemoreceptor, Chord, Claspers, Clave, Console, Cort's, Ctene, Ear, Echo, Exteroceptor, Feeler, Fin, Fundus, Gill, Glairin, Gonad, Hammond®, Hapteron, Harmonium, House, Imine, Isomere, Kerogen, Kidney, Lien, Liver, Means, Media, Medulla, Melodion, Ministry, Nasal, Natural, Nectary, Nephridium, Newspaper, Oogonia, Ovipositor, Palp, Pancreas, Parapodium, Part, Photophore, Photoreceptor, Pipe, Placenta, Plastid, Portative, Positive, Prothallus, Pulmones, Pyrophone, Radula, Receptor, Recit, Regal, Relict, Sang, Saprobe, Sense, Sensillum, Serra, Spinneret, Spleen, Sporangium, Sporophore, Stamen, Steam, Stratocyst, Swell, Syrinx, Tentacle, Thymus, Tongue, Tonsil, Tool, Tympanum, Uterus, Viscera, Viscus, Vitals, Voice, Wurlitzer®

Organise(d), Organisation, Organiser Activate, Anatomy, ➤ ARRANGE, Association, Brigade, Caucus, Collect, Comecon, Company, Coordinate, Design, Embody, Entrepreneur, Fascio, Firm, Impresario, Infrastructure, Jaycee, Logistics, Machine, Mafia, Marshal, Mobilise, Orchestrate, Outfit, Personal, Quango, Rally, Regiment, Rosicrucian, Run, Setup, Soroptimist, Stage, Steward, System, Tidy, Together, UN

▷ **Organise(d)** may indicate an anagram

Organism Aerobe, Agamic, Being, Biont, Biotic, Cell, Chimeric, Chlamydia, Ciliate, Clade, Coral, Diplont, Ecad, Entity, Epizoon, Eucaryote, Euglena, Eukaryote, Germ, Halobiont, Halophile, Heplont, Holophyte, Homeotherm, Incross, Infauna, Infusoria(n), Lichen, Medusa, Meroplankton, Microbe, Moneron, Morphology, Nekton, Neuston,

Paramecium, Pathogen, Phenetics, Plankter, Plankton, Protist, Protozoan, Radiolarian, Saprobe, Streptococcus, Symbiont, Torula, Volvox

Organ-stop Bourdon, Clarabella, Diapason, Gamba, Nasard, Principal, Pyramidon, Quint, Salicet

Organ-tuner Reed-knife

Orgy Bacchanalia(n), Binge, Bust, Carousal, Dionysian, Feast, Revel, Saturnalia, Spree, Wassail

Orient(al) Adjust, Annamite, Chinoiserie, Dawn, Dayak, E, East(ern), Fu Manchu, Hindu, Levant, Leyton, Malay, Mongolian, Shan, Sunrise, Tatar, Thai, Tibetan, Turk(o)man

Orifice Aperture, Gap, Hole, Nare, Opening, Pore, Spiracle, Trema, Vent

Origen's work Tetrapla

Origin(al), Originate, Originating Abo, Adam, Arise, Beginning, Birth, Come, Cradle, Creation, Derive, Editio princeps, Elemental, Emanate, Epicentre, Etymon, Extraction, First, Firsthand, Focus, Found, Generic, Genesis, Genetical, Germ, Grow, Hatch, Incunabula, Innovate, Invent, Master, Mother, Nascence, Natality, New, Novel, Ord, Primal, Primary, Primigenial, Primordial, Pristine, Prototype, Provenance, Rise, Root, Seminal, Source, Spring, Start, Ur, Ylem, Zoism

Oriole Firebird, Hangbird

Orison Blessing, Prayer

Ormer Abalone, Haliotis

Ornament(al), Ornamentation Acroter(ia), Adorn, Anaglyph, Antefix, Anthemion, Aplustre, Arabesque, Bahuti, Ball-flower, Barbola, Baroque, Barrette, Bead, Bedeck, Bez(z)ant, Billet, Boss, Bracelet, Breloque, Broider, Bugle, Bulla, Cartouche, Chase, Clock, Cockade, Crocket, Curin, Curlicue, Decorate, Decoration, Diamanté, Diglyph, Dog's-tooth, Doodad, Embellish, Emblem(a), Enrich, Epaulet(te), Epergne, Fallal, Fandangle, Figuration, Figurine, Filagree, Filigrain, Filigree, Fleuret, Fleurette, Fleuron, Florid, Fret, Fretwork, Frill, Furbelow, Furnish, Gadroon, Gaud, Gingerbread, Gorget, Griff(e), Guilloche, Gutta, Heitiki, Illustrate, Inlay, Knotwork, Labret, Lambrequin, Leglet, Mantling, Mense, Millefleurs, Mordent, Moresque, Motif, Nail-head, Netsuke, Nicknackery, Niello, O, Okimono, Ovolo, Palmette, Parure, Paua, Pawa, Pectoral, Pendant, Picot, Pipe, Pompom, Pompo(o)n, Pounce, Pralltriller, Prettify, Prunt, Purfle, Rel(l)ish, Rocaille, Rococo, Spangle, Tassel, Tettix, Tiki, Tool, Torque, Torsade, Tracery, Trappings, Trimming, Trinket, Triquetra, Turn, Wally, Water-leaf, Whigmaleerie, Whigmaleery

Ornate Baroque, Churrigueresque, Dressy, Elaborate, Fancy, Florid, Flowery

Ornithologist Audubon, Birdman

Orotund Bombastic, Grandiose, Pompous, Rhetorical, Sonant

Orphan Annie, Foundling, Ward

Orpiment Arsenic, Zarnich

Orpington Buff, Hen

Ort Bit, Crumb, Morsel, Remnant

Orthodox Cocker, Conventional, Hardshell, Proper, Sound, Standard

Orthorhombic Enstatite

Ortolan Bird, Bunting, Rail

Oscar Award, O, Wilde

Oscillate Fluctuate, Librate, Rock, Seiche, Squeg, Swing, Vibrate, Waver

Osier Reed, Sallow, Willow

Osmium Os

Osprey Fish-hawk, Ossifrage, Pandion

Osseous Bony, Hard, Skeletal, Spiny

Ostensibly Apparent, External, Seeming

Ostentation, Ostentatious Camp, Display, Dog, Eclat, Epideictical, Extravagant, Fantoosh, Flamboyant, Flash(y), Flaunt, Florid, Flourish, Garish, Gaudy, Highfalutin(g), Parade, Pomp, Pretence, Puff, ➤ SHOW(ING), Side, Splash, Swank, Tacky, Tulip

Ostracise, Ostracism Banish, Blackball, Boycott, Cut, Exclude, Exile, Potsherd, Snub, Taboo

Ostrich Em(e)u, Estrich, Estridge, Nandoo, Nandu, Ratite, Rhea, Struthio(nes)

Othello Moor, Morisco

Other(wise), Others Additional, Aka, Alia, Alias, Allo-, Besides, Different, Distinct, Else, Et al, Etc, Excluding, Former, Further, Rest, Significant

Other things Alia

▷ **Otherwise** may indicate an anagram

Otiose Idle, Indolent, Ineffective, Lazy, Needless, Superfluous

Otis Bustard

Otter Edal, Paravane, Tarka

Otto Attar, Chypre, Mahratta

Ottoman Osmanli, Porte, Turk

Oubliette Dungeon, Pit, Prison

Ouch Brooch, Ornament, Ow

Ought All, Should

Ouida Ramee

Ounce Cat, Liang, Oz, Panther, Tael, Uncial

Our(selves) Us, We

Oust Depose, Dislodge, Eject, Evict, Expel, Fire, Supplant, Unnest

Out Absent, Aglee, Agley, Asleep, Aus, Begone, Bowl, Dated, En ville, Exposed, External, Forth, Haro, Harrow, Hors, Oust, Skittle, Striking, Stump, Taboo, Uit, Unfashionable, Up, York

▷ **Out** may indicate an anagram

Out and out Absolute, Arrant, Sheer, Stark, Teetotal, Thorough, Totally, Utter

Outback Bundu

Outbreak Epidemic, Eruption, Explosion, Plague, Putsch, Rash, Recrudescence

Outburst Access, Blurt, Bluster, Boutade, Evoe, Explosion, Fit, Flaw, Furore, Fusillade, Gush, Gust, Paroxysm, Passion, Salvo, Storm, Tantrum, Tumult, Volley

Outcast Cagot, Discard, Exile, Exul, Ishmael, Leper, Mesel, Pariah, Rogue

Outcome Aftermath, Consequence, Dénouement, Effect, Emergence, End, Event, ➤ RESULT, Sequel, Upshot

Outcrop Basset, Blossom, Crag, Creston, Inlier, Mesa, Spur, Tarpit

Outcry Bray, ➤ CLAMOUR, Howl, Hue, Protest, Racket, Steven, Uproar, Utas

Outdated Archaic, Dinosaur, Effete, Feudal, Fossil, Obsolete, Outmoded, Passé, Square

Outdo Beat, Cap, Picnic, Surpass, Top, Trump, Worst

Outdoor(s) Alfresco, External, Garden, Open air, Plein-air

Outer External, Extrogenous, Magpie, Top

Outfit(ter) Catsuit, Ensemble, Equipage, Fitout, Furnish, Get-up, Haberdasher, Habit, Kit, Rig, Samfoo, Samfu, Strip, Suit, Team, Trousseau, Weed(s)

Outflow Anticyclone, Discharge, Effluence, Eruption, Surge

Outgoing Egression, Exiting, Extrovert, Open, Retiring

Outgrowth Ala(te), Aril, Bud, Enation, Epiphenomenon, Exostosis, Offshoot, Root-hair, Sequel, Trichome

Outhouse Lean to, Privy, Shed, Skilling, Skipper, Stable

Outing Excursion, Jaunt, Junket, Picnic, Sortie, Spin, Spree, Treat, Trip, Wayzgoose

Outlandish Barbarous, Bizarre, Exotic, Foreign, Peregrine, Rum

Outlaw Allan-a-Dale, Attaint, Badman, Ban, Bandit(ti), Banish, Exile, Fugitive, Hereward, Horn, Proscribe, Robin Hood, Rob Roy, Ronin, Tory, Waive

Outlay Cost, Expense, Mise

Outlet Débouché, Egress, Estuary, Exit, Femerell, Market, Opening, Outfall, Sluice, Socket, Tuyere, Tweer, Twier, Twire, Twyer(e), Vent

Outline Adumbration, Aperçu, Circumscribe, Configuration, Contorno, Contour, Delineate, Digest, ➤ DRAFT, Footprint, Layout, Note, Perimeter, Plan, Profile, Relief, Scenario, Schematic, Shape, Silhouette, Skeletal, Skeleton, Sketch, Summary, Syllabus, Synopsis, T(h)alweg, Trace

Outlook Casement, Perspective, Prospect, View, Vista

Outmoded Wasm

▷ **Out of** may indicate an anagram

Out of date Corny, Obs, Passé, Scrap, Square, Worn

Out of form Amorphous, Awry

Out of order Fritz

Out of sorts Cachectic, Nohow, Peevish, Poorly

▷ **Out of sorts** may indicate an anagram

Out of tune Discordant, Flat, Scordato, Scordatura

Outpost Colony, Picquet

Outpour(ing) Effuse, Flood, Flow, Gush, Libation, Stream, Torrent

Output Data, Get, Produce, Production, Turnout, Yield
▷ **Output** may indicate an anagram
Outrage(ous) Affront, Atrocity, Desecrate, Disgust, Egregious, Enorm(ity), Flagrant, Insult, OTT, Rich, Sacrilege, Scandal, Shocking, Ungodly, Violate
▷ **Outrageously** may indicate an anagram
Outright Clean, Complete, Entire, Point-blank, Utter
Outset Beginning, Start
Outshine Eclipse, Excel, Overshadow, Surpass
Outside Ab extra, Crust, Exterior, External, Front, Furth, Hors, Periphery, Rim, Rind, Rine, Surface
Outsider Alien, Bolter, Bounder, Cad, Extern, Extremist, Foreigner, Incomer, Oustiti, Pariah, Ring-in, Stranger, Stumer, Unseeded, Upstart
Outsize Capacious, Giant, Gigantic, Huge, OS
Outskirts Edge, Fringe, Periphery, Purlieu
Outspoken Bluff, Blunt, Broad, Candid, Explicit, Forthright, Frank, Plain, Rabelaisian, Round, Vocal
Outstanding Ace, Beaut(y), Belter, Billowing, Bulge, Chief, Eminent, Especial, Exceptional, Extant, First, Fugleman, Highlight, Humdinger, Impasto, Jut, Lulu, Marked, Matchless, Oner, Owing, Paragon, Phenomenal, Prince, Prize, Prominent, Promontory, Prosilient, Proud, Relief, Relievo, Salient, Signal, Special, Squarrose, Star, Stellar, Strout, Superb, Tour de force, Unpaid, Unsettled
Outstrip Best, Cap, Cote, Distance, Exceed, Overtake
Outward Efferent, Extern(e), External, Extrinsic, Extrorse, Extrovert, Posticous, Postliminary, Superficial
Outwit Baffle, Best, Circumvent, Dish, Euchre, Fox, Over-reach, ➤ THWART, Trick
Outwork Demilune, Jetty, Moon, Tenail(le), Tenaillon
Outworn Decrepit, Obsolete, Used
Oval Cartouche, Ellipse, Henge, Navette, Ooidal
Ovary Oophoron
Ovation Applause, Cheer, Standing
Oven(-like) Aga®, Calcar, Convection, Cul-de-four, Dutch, Furnace, Haybox, Horn(it)o, Kiln, Lear, Leer, Lehr, Lime kiln, Microwave, Muffle, Oast, Oon, Stove
Over Above, Across, Again, Atop, C, Clear, Done, Finished, Hexad, Left, Maiden, Of, On, Ore, Ort, Owre, Sopra, Spare, Superior, Surplus, Uber, Yon
Overact Burlesque, Emote, Ham, Hell, Hoke
Overall(s) Boiler suit, Denims, Dungarees, Dust-coat, Fatigues, Smicket, Smock, Tablier
Overbearing Arrogant, Dogmatic, Domineering, High-muck-a-muck, Imperious, Insolent, Lordly
Overbid Gazump
Overcast Cloudy, Lowering, Sew, Sombre
Overcharge Clip, Extort, Fleece, Gyp, OC, Rack-rent, Rook, Rush, Soak, Sting

Overcoat Benjamin, Benny, British warm, ➤ COAT, Crombie, Dolman, Grego, Inverness, Joseph, Paletot, Pos(h)teen, Prince Albert, Raglan, Redingote, Spencer, Tabard, Taglioni, Ulster, Warm, Wooden, Wrap-rascal

Overcome Beat, Bested, Conquer, Convince, Defeat, Kill, Master, Mither, Prevail, Quell, Speechless, Subjugate, Surmount, Vanquish, Win

Overcrowd Congest, Jam, Pack

Overdo(ne) Exceed, Ham, Hokey, Hokum, OTT, Percoct, Tire

Overdraft Red

▷ **Overdrawn** may indicate 'red' outside another word

Overdress(ing) Dudism, Flossy, Overall

Overdue Behindhand, Belated, Excessive, Late

Overeat(ing) Binge, Gorge, Hypertrophy, Satiate

Overemphasize Rub in, Stress

Overfeed Gorge, Sate, Stuff

Overflow Lip, Nappe, Ooze, Redound, Spillage, Surfeit, Teem

Overfull Brimming, Hept

Overgrow(n) Ivy'd, Jungle, Ramp(ant), Rank, Rhinophyma

Overhang(ing) Beetle, Bulge, ➤ JUT, Project, Shelvy

Overhaul Bump, Catch, Overtake, Recondition, Revision, Service, Strip

Overhead(s) Above, Aloft, Ceiling, Cost, Exes, Hair(s), Headgear, Oncost, Rafter, Upkeep, Zenith

Overhear Catch, Eavesdrop, Tap

Overindulge(nt) Crapulent, Crass, Pig

Overjoy Elate, Thrill

Overland Portage

Overlap(ping) Correspond, Equitant, Imbricate, Incubous, Kern(e), Limbous, Obvolute, Tace, Tasse

Overlay Ceil, Smother, Stucco, Superimpose, Veneer

Overlearned Pedantic

Overload Burden, Plaster, Strain, Surcharge, Tax

Overlook Condone, Disregard, Excuse, Forget, Miss, Pretermit, Superintend

Overlord Excess, Invasion

Overlying Incumbent, Jessant, Pressing

Overmuch Excessive, Surplus, Too, Undue

Overplay Ham, Hoke

Overpower(ing) Crush, Evince, Mighty, Onerous, Oppress, Overwhelm, Subdue, Surmount, Swelter, Whelm

Overpraise Adulate

Over-refined Dainty, Nice, Pernickety, Precious

Overrule Abrogate, Disallow, Veto

Overrun Exceed, Extra, Infest, Inundate, Invade, Swarm, Teem

Overseas Abroad, Colonial, Outremer

Oversee(r) Baas, Boss, Captain, Care, Deputy, Direct, Eyebrow, Foreman, Grieve, Handle, Induna, Periscope, Steward, Supercargo, Survey(or)

Oversentimental Byronic, Slushy

Overshadow Cloud, Dominate, Eclipse, Obscure, Outclass

Overshoe Arctic, Galosh, Sandal, Snowboot

Oversight Blunder, Care, Error, Gaffe, Lapse, Neglect, Parablepsis

Overstate(ment) Embroider, Exaggerate, Hyperbole

Overstrained Epitonic

Overt Manifest, Patent, Plain, Public

Overtake Catch, For(e)hent, Lap, Leapfrog, Overget, Overhaul, ➤ PASS, Supersede

Overthrow Dash, Defeat, Demolish, Depose, Down, Labefact(at)ion, Ruin, Smite, Stonker, Subvert, Supplant, Unhorse, Vanquish, Whemmle, Whommle, Whummle, Worst

Overture Advance, Carnival, Egmont, Hebrides, Intro, Leonora, Offer, ➤ OPENING, Prelude, Propose, Sinfonia, Toccata, Toccatella, Toccatina

Overturn(ing) Catastrophe, Quash, Reverse, Tip, Topple, Up(set), Whemmle

Overvalue Exaggerate, Salt

Overweening Bashaw, Cocky, Excessive, Imperious, Presumptuous

Overweight Sunk

Overwhelm(ed), Overwhelming Accablé, Assail, ➤ CRUSH, Inundate, KO, Mind-boggling, Overcome, Scupper, Smother, Submerge, Swamp

Overwork(ed) Fag, Hackneyed, Ornament, Slog, Stale, Supererogation, Tax, Tire, Toil

Overwrought Frantic, Hysterical, Ore-rested, Ornate, Rococo

Ovid Naso

Ovum Egg, Oosphere, Seed

Owe(d), Owing Attribute, Due, OD

Owen Glendower

Owl(s) Barn, Barred, Blinker, Boobook, Brown, Bubo, Bunter, Eagle, Elegant, Fish, Glimmergowk, Hawk, Hoo(ter), Horned, Jenny, Little, Long-eared, Longhorn, Madge, Moper, Mopoke, Mopus, Night, Ogle, Parliament, Ruru, Saw-whet, Scops, Screech, Snowy, Strich, Striges, Strigiformes, Tawny, Wood

Own(er), Owning, Ownership Admit, Agnise, Domain, Dominium, Have, Hold, Mortmain, Nain, Of, Possess, Proper, Proprietor, Recognise, Use

Ox(en) Anoa, Aquinas, Aurochs, Banteng, Banting, Bison, Bonas(s)us, Buffalo, Bugle, Bullock, Cat(t)alo, Fee, Gaur, Gayal, Gyal, Kouprey, Mart, Musk, Neat, Ovibos, Rother, Sapi-utan, S(e)ladang, Steare, Steer, Taurus, Ure, Urus, Yak, Yoke, Zebu

Oxford (group) Buchmanism, OU, Shoe

Oxhead Aleph

Oxidation, Oxide Alumina, Anatase, Ceria, Erbium, Eremacausis, Gothite, Gummite, Holmia, Kernite, Lithia, Magnesia, Nitrous, Psilomelane, Quicklime, Rutile, Samarskite, Strontia, Thoria, Zaffer, Zaffre

▷ **Oxtail** may indicate 'x'

Oxygen (and lack of) Anoxia, Epoxy, Liquid, Lox, Loxygen, O

Oyer Hearing, Trial

Oyster (bed), Oyster-eater Avicula, Bivalve, Bush, Cul(t)ch, Kentish, Lay, Mollusc, Native, Ostrea, Ostreophage, Pandore, Pearl, Plant, Prairie, Scalp, Scaup, Seed(ling), Spat, Spondyl, Vegetable

Oyster-catcher Sea-pie

Oyster-plant Gromwell, Salsify

Oz Amos, Australia

Ozone Air, Atmosphere, Oxygen

Pp

P Papa, Parking, Penny, Piano, Prince

PA Aide

Pabulum Aliment, Cheer, Food, Fuel, Nourishment

Pace, Pacemaker Canter, Clip, Cracking, Dog-trot, Easter, Gait, Jog-trot, Lope, Measure, Pari passu, Pioneer, ➤ RATE, Snail's, Spank, Speed, Stroll, Tempo, Tramp, Tread, Trot

Pachyderm Armadillo, Elephant, Hippo, Mastodon, Rhino

Pacific, Pacify Appease, Bromide, Conciliate, Dove, Ease, Irenic, Lull, Mild, Moderate, Ocean, Placid, Quiet, Serene, Soothe, Subdue, Sweeten, Tranquil

Pacifist CO, Conciliator, D(o)ukhobor

Pack(age), Packed, Packing Bale, Blister, Box, Bubble, Bundle, Cards, Compress, Congest, Cram, Crate, Crowd, Cry, Deck, Dense, Dunnage, Embox, Entity, Excelsior, Fardel, Floe, Gasket, Gaskin, Glut, Hamper, Hunt, Jam, Kennel, Knapsack, Load, Matilda, Pair, ➤ PARCEL, Pikau, Rout, Rucksack, Set, Shiralee, Steeve, Stow, Suits, Tamp, Tread, Troop, Truss, Wad, Wolf, Wrap

Packet Boat, Bundle, Liner, Mailboat, Mint, Parcel, Roll, Sachet, Steamboat, Wage

Pack-horse Sumpter

Packman Chapman, Hawker, Hiker, Pedlar, Tinker

Pact Agreement, Alliance, Bargain, Bilateral, Cartel, Contract, Covenant, Locarno, ➤ TREATY, Warsaw

Pad(ding) Batting, Bombast, Brake, Bustle, Compress, Crash, Cushion, Dabber, Dossil, Enswathe, Expand, Falsies, Filler, Flat, Frog, Hassock, Horse, Launch, Leg-guard, Lily, Nag, Numnah, Paw, Ped, Pillow, Pincushion, Plastron, Pledget, Plumper, Pouf(fe), Protract, Pulvillus, Stuff, Sunk, Tablet, Thief, Touch, Tournure, Tylopod, Tympan, Velour(s), Velure, Wad, Wase

Paddington Bear, Station

Paddle(-foot) Canoe, Dabble, Doggy, Oar, Pinniped, Seal, Side-wheel, Spank, Splash, Wade

Paddock Field, Frog, Meadow, Park

Paddy Fury, Ire, Irishman, Mick, Pat(rick), Pet, Rag, Rage, Tantrum, Temper, Wax

Padre Chaplain, Cleric, Father, Monk, Priest

Paean Hymn, Ode, Praise, Psalm

Pagan Animist, Atheist, Gentile, Gentoo, Godless, Heathen, Idolater, Infidel, Odinist, Paynim, Saracen

Page(s), Pageboy Bellboy, Bellhop, Bleep, Boy, Buttons, Flyleaf, Folio, Foolscap, Gate-fold, Groom, Haircut, Hornbook, Leaf, Messenger, Moth,

Octavo, P, Pane, PP, Quarto, Ream, Recto, Ro, Servant, Sheet, Side, Squire, Tear sheet, Tiger, Title, Varlet, Verso, Web, Yellow

Pageant Cavalcade, Pomp, Spectacle, Tattoo, Triumph

Pagoda Temple, To

Pah Pish, Tush, Umph

▶ **Paid** see PAY

Pail Bucket, Kettle, Leglan, Leglen, Leglin, Piggin

Pain(ful), Pains Ache, Aggrieve, Agony, Ake, Algesis, Angina, Anguish, Arthralgia, Bad, Bale, Bitter, Bore, Bot(t), Bother, Colic, Cramp, Crick, Distress, Dole, Doleur, Dolour, Dool(e), Dysmenorhoea, Dysury, Excruciating, Fibrositis, Gip, Grief, Gripe, Gyp, Harrow, Heartburn, ➤ HURT, Ill, Kink, Laborious, Mal, Mastalgia, Mastodynia, Migraine, Misery, Mulligrubs, Myalgia, Neuralgia, Nociceptive, Pang, Persuant, Pest, Prick, Pungent, Rack, Raw, Referred, Sair, Sciatica, Smart, Sore, Sorrow, Sten(d), Sting, Stitch, Strangury, Stung, Teen(e), Tene, Throe, Torment, Tormina, Torture, Twinge, Wrench, Wring

▷ **Pain** may indicate bread (French)

Painkiller Aminobutene, Analgesic, Bute, Cocaine, Distalgesic, Enkephalin, Meperidine, Metopon, Morphine, Number, Pethidine

Painlessness Analgesia

Painstaking Assiduous, Careful, Diligent, Elaborate, Exacting, Sedulous, Studious, Thorough

Paint(ed), Painting Abstract, Acrylic, Action, Airbrush, Alla prima, Aquarelle, Arcimboldo, Art autre, Art deco, Artificial, Art nouveau, Barbizon, Bice, Blottesque, Camaieu, Canvas, Cellulose, Chiaroscuro, Clair-obscure, Clobber, Coat, Colour, Cubism, Dadaism, Daub, Dayglo, Decorate, Depict, Diptych, Distemper, Duco, Eggshell, Emulsion, Enamel, Encaustic, Fard, Fauvism, Finery, Flemish, Fresco, Fucus, Genre, Gild, Gloss, Gouache, Grease, Grisaille, Hard-edge, Impasto, Impressionism, Intimism(e), Intonaco, Limn, Magilp, Matt, Megilp, Miniate, Miniature, Modello, Naive, Nihonga, Nocturne, Oaker, Ochre, Oil, Old Master, Oleo(graph), Op art, Orphism, Paysage, Pict, Picture, Pigment, Pinxit, Plein air, Pointillism(e), Portray, Poster, Post-Impressionism, Predella, Primitive, Quadratura, Raddle, Rosemaling, Roughstuff, Scumble, Secco, Sfumato, Sien(n)ese, Stencil, Stereochrome, Stipple, Suprematism, Tablature, Tachism(e), Tall-oil, Tanka, Tempera, Tenebrism, Thangka, Tondo, Ukiyo-e, Umber, Umbrian, Vanitas, Veduta, Vorticism, War

Painted woman Courtesan, Harlot, Pict, Tart

Painter ➤ ARTIST, Colourist, Cubist, Decorator, Gilder, Illusionist, Impressionist, Limner, Miniaturist, Paysagist, Plein-airist, Pre-Raphaelite, Primitive, Sien(n)ese

Pair(ing) Brace, Couple(t), Duad, Duo, Dyad(ic), Fellows, Geminate, Jugate, Link, Match, Mate, Ocrea, Pigeon, Pr, Span, Synapsis, Syndyasmian, Syzygy, Tandem, Thummim, Twa(e), Tway, Two, Urim, Yoke

Paisley Orange, Shawl

Pal Ally, Amigo, Bud(dy), China, Chum, Comrade, Crony, Cully, Mate

Palace Alhambra, Basilica, Blenheim, Buckingham, Court, Crystal, Edo, Elysee, Escorial, Escurial, Fontainebleau, Gin, Holyrood, Hotel, Istana, Lambeth, Lateran, Louvre, Mansion, Nonsuch, Palatine, Pitti, Quirinal, Sans Souci, Schloss, Seraglio, Serail, Shushan, Topkapi, Trianon, Tuileries, Valhalla, Vatican, Versailles

Paladin Champion, Charlemagne, Defender, Douzeper, Fièrabras, Ganelon, ➤ KNIGHT, Ogier, Oliver, Orlando, Rinaldo, Roland

Palanquin Doolie, Litter, Palkee, Palki, Sedan

Palatable, Palate Dainty, Relish, Roof, Sapid, Savoury, Soft, Taste, Toothsome, Uranic, Uraniscus, Uvula, Velum

Palatial Ornate, Splendid

Palatine Officer

Palaver Chatter, Debate, Parley, Powwow, ➤ TALK

Pale, Paling Ashen, Blanch, Bleach, Cere, Dim, Etiolate(d), Fade, ➤ FAINT, Fence, Ghostly, Haggard, Insipid, Lily (white), Livid, Mealy, Ox-fence, Pastel, Peelie-wally, Picket, Sallow, Shilpit, Stang, Verge, Wan, Whey-faced, White, Wishy-washy

Paleography Diplomatics

Paleolithic Acheulean, Acheulian, Chellean, Gravettian, Madelenian, Magdalenian, Perigordian, Strepyan

Palestine, Palestinian Amorite, Gadarene, Intifada, Israel, Pal, PLO, Samaria

Palette Board, Cokuloris

Palindrome, Palindromic Cancrine, Sotadic

Palisade Barrier, Fence, Fraise, Stacket, Stockade

Pall Bore, Cloy, Damper, Glut, Mantle, Satiate, Shroud

Palladium Defence, Pd, Safeguard

Pallas Athene

Pallet Bed, Cot, Couch, Mattress, Tick

Palliate, Palliative Alleviate, Anetic, Ease, Extenuate, Lessen, Mitigate, Reduce, Sedative

Pallid Anaemic, Ashen, Insipid, Pale, Wan, Waxy

Palm Accolade, Areca, Assai, Atap, Babassu, Betel, Buriti, Burrawang, Bussu, Cabbage, Calamus, Carnauba, Carna(h)uba, Chamaerops, Chiqui-chiqui, Coco, Cohune, Conceal, Coquito, Corozo, Corypha, Date (tree), Doom, Doum, Elaeis, Euterpe, Fan, Feather, Fob, Foist, Gomuti, Gomuto, Groo-groo, Gru-gru, Hand, Ita, Itching, Ivory, Jip(p)i-Jap(p)a, Jipyapa, Jupati, Kentia, Kittul, Laurels, Loof, Looves, Macahuba, Macaw, Macoya, Moriche, Nikau, Nipa, Oil, Palmyra, Paxiuba, Peach, Pupunha, Raffia, Raphia, Rat(t)an, Royal, Sabal, Sago, Sugar, Talipat, Talipot, Thenar, Toddy, Triumph, Troelie, Troolie, Trooly, Trophy, Vola, Washingtonia, Wax, Wine, Zatia

Palmer Lilli, Pilgrim

Palmerston Pam

Palmistry Ch(e)irognomy

Palm-leaf Frond
Palpable Evident, Gross, Manifest, Patent, Plain
Palpitate Flutter, Pulsate, Throb, Twitter, Vibrate
Palsy Bell's, Cerebral, Paralysis, Shakes
Paltry Bald, Cheap, Exiguous, Mean, Measly, Peanuts, Pelting, Petty, Poor, Puny, Scalled, Sorry, Tin(-pot), Tinny, Trashy, Trifling, Two-bit, Vile, Waff, Whiffet
Pamper(ed) Cocker, Coddle, Cosher, Cosset, Cuiter, Feather-bed, Gratify, High-fed, ➤ INDULGE, Mollycoddle, Pet, Spoon-fed
Pamphlet Brochure, Catalogue, Leaflet, Notice, Sheet, Tract
Pan Agree, Auld Hornie, Bainmarie, Balit, Basin, Betel(-pepper), Braincase, Chafer, Dent, Dial, Drip, Goat-god, Goblet, God, Ice-floe, Iron, Karahi, Ladle, Nature-god, Pancheon, Panchion, Patella, Patina, Peter, Poacher, Prospect, Roast, Salt, Search, Skillet, Slag, Slate, Spider, Vessel, Wo(c)k, Work
Panacea All-heal, Azoth, Catholicon, Cure(-all), Elixir, Ginseng, Remedy, Tutsan
Panache Bravura, Crest, Flair, Paz(z)azz, Piz(z)azz, Plume, Pzazz, Show, Talent
Pancake Blin(i), Blintz(e), Burrito, Crêpe (suzette), Drop(ped)-scone, Flam(m), Flapjack, Flaune, Flawn, Fraise, Fritter, Froise, Pikelet, Poppadum, Quesadilla, Slapjack, Suzette, Taco, Tortilla, Tostada, Waffle
Panda Bear-cat, Chi-chi, Chitwah, Giant, Red
Pandarus Go-between
Pandemonium Inferno
Pander Broker, Indulge, Pimp, Procurer, Toady
Pane Glass, Light, Panel, Quarrel, Quarry, Sheet
Panegyric Eulogy, Laudation, Praise, Tribute
Panel(ling) Board, Cartouche, Dashboard, Fa(s)cia, Gore, Hatchment, Inset, Instrument, Jury, Mandorla, Mimic, Orb, Patch(board), Rocker, Screen, Skreen, Solar, Stile, Stomacher, Tablet, Valance, Volet, Wainscot
Pang Achage, Ache, Qualm, Spasm, Stab, Twinge, Wrench
Pangolin Ant-eater, Manis
Panhandle(r) Beggar, W. Virginia
Panic Alar(u)m, Amaze, Consternation, Fear, Flap, Flat-spin, Fright, Funk, Guinea-grass, Millet, Raggee, Raggy, Ragi, ➤ SCARE, Scarre, Stampede, Stampedo, Stew, Tailspin, ➤ TERROR
Panicle Thyrse
Panjandrum Bashaw
Pannier Basket, Cacolet, Corbeil, Dosser, Skip, Whisket
Panoply Armour, Array, Pomp
Panorama, Panoramic Range, Scenery, Veduta, View, Vista
Pansy Gay, Heart's-ease, Kiss-me, Nance, Powder-puff, Queer, Viola
Pant(s) Bags, Breeches, Capri, Cargo, Chaps, Chinos, Culottes, Deck, Dhoti, Drawers, Fatigues, Flaff, Gasp, Gaucho, Harem, Long johns, Longs,

Parachute, Pech, Pedal-pushers, Pegh, Puff, Slacks, Smalls, Stovepipe, Sweat, Throb, Toreador, Trews, Trousers, Wheeze, Yearn

Pantaloon Columbine, Dupe, Pants

Pantheism Idolatry, Immanency

Panther Bagheera, Black, Cat, Cougar, Jaguar, Leopard, Pink

Panties Briefs, Knickers, Scanties, Step-ins, Undies

Pantomime Charade, Cheironomy, Dumb-show, Farce, Galanty, Harlequinade, Play

Pantry Buttery, Closet, Larder, Spence, Stillroom

Pap Dug, Mush, Nipple, Teat, Udder

Papal, Papist Catholic, Clementine, Concordat, Guelf, Guelph, Pontifical, RC, Roman, Vatican

Paper(s), Papery Allonge, Art, Atlas, Ballot, Baryta, Bible, Bond, Broadsheet, Broadside, Bromide, Brown, Bumf, Bumph, Carbon, Cartridge, Cellophane®, Chad, Chiyogami, Cigarette, Colombier, Command, Confetti, Cream-laid, Cream-wove, Crepe, Crown, Cutch, Daily, Decorate, Demy, Document, Dossier, Elephant, Emery, Emperor, Essay, Exam, File, Filter, Final, Flock, Folio, Foolscap, Fourdrinier, FT, Galley, Garnet, Gem, Glass(ine), Glumaceous, Graph, Greaseproof, Green, Guardian, Hieratica, India, Jesus, Journal, Kent cap, Kraft, Kutch, Laid, Linen, Litmus, Manil(l)a, Mirror, MS, Munimenti, Music-demy, News(print), Note, Onion-skin, Order, Page, Papillote, Papyrus, Parchment, Pickwick, Position, Post, Pot(t), Pravda, Press, Print, Quair, Quarto, Quire, Rag, Ramee, Rami(e), Ream, Retree, Rhea, Rice, Rolling, Royal, Saxe, Scent, Scotsman, Scrip, Sheaf, Sheet, Slipsheet, Sugar, Sun, Tabloid, Taffeta, Tap(p)a, TES, Test, Thesis, Tiger, Tissue, Toilet, Torchon, Touch, Tracing, Treatise, Turmeric, Vellum, Voucher, Waste, Wax(ed), Web, Whatman, White, Willesden, Wove, Wrapping, Writing, Zine

Paperback Limp(back)

Paper-cutting, Paper-folding Decoupage, Kirigami, Origami, Psaligraphy

Papier-mâché Flong

Par Average, Equate, Equivalent, ➤ NORMAL, Scratch

Parable Allegory, Fable, Proverb

Parabola Arc, Curve, Hyperbola

Parachute, Parachutist Aigrette, Drogue, Float, Jump, Para, Parabrake, Red Devil, Silk, Skyman, Thistledown, Umbrella

Parade (ground) Air, Arcade, Cavalcade, Church, Display, Dress, Drill, Easter, Emu, Flaunt, Gala, Hit, Identification. Procession, Identity, Maidan, March-past, Pageantry, Pomp, Prom(enade), Show, Sick, Ticker tape

Paradise Arcadia, Avalon, Bliss, Eden, Elysium, Garden, Heaven, Lost, Malaguetta, Nirvana, Park, Regained, Shangri-la, Svarga, Swarga, Swerga, ➤ UTOPIA

Paradox(ical) Absurdity, Cantor's, Contradiction, Dilemma, Electra, Gilbertian, Koan, Olber's, Puzzle, Russell's, Zeno's

Paraffin Earthwax, Kerosene, Kerosine, Liquid, Ozocerite, Ozokerite, Photogen(e), Propane

Paragon Model, Non(e)such, Pattern, Pearl, Phoenix, Rose
Paragraph (mark) Balaam, Note, Passage, Piece, Pilcrow
Parakeet Parrot, Popinjay, Rosella
Parallel Analog, Collimate, Corresponding, Equal, Even, Forty-ninth, Like
Parallelogram Rhomb
Paralysis, Paralyse Apoplexy, Cataplexy, Cramp, Curarise, Cycloplegia, Diplegia, Halt, Hemiplegia, Infantile, Monoplegia, Numbness, Palsy, Paraplegia, Paresis, Polio, Quadriplegia, Scram, Shock, Shut, Spastic, Spina bifida, Stun
Paramilitary SAS, Sena
Paramount Chief, Dominant, Greatest, Overall, Premier, ➤ SUPREME, Topless, Utmost
Paramour Franion, Gallant, Leman, Lover, Mistress, Thais
Paranormal Clairvoyant, ESP, Spiritual, Telekinesis
Parapet (space) Bartisan, Bartizan, Battlement, Brisure, Bulwark, Crenel, Flèche, Machicolation, Merlon, Rampart, Redan, Surtout, Terreplein, Top, Wall
Paraphernalia Belongings, Equipment, Gear, Trappings
Parasite, Parasitic Ascarid, Autoecious, Babesiasis, Bilharzia, Biogenous, Biotroph, Bladder-worm, Bloodsucker, Bonamia, Bot, Candida, Coccus, Conk, Copepod, Cryptosporidium, Cryptozoite, Dodder, Ectophyte, Endamoeba, Endophyte, Entophyte, Entozoon, Epiphyte, Epizoon, Filarium, Flea, Giardia, Gregarinida, Haematozoon, Hair-eel, Heartworm, Heteroecious, Hook-worm, Ichneumon, Inquiline, Isopod, Kade, Ked, Lackey, Lamprey, Leech, Licktrencher, Liverfluke, Louse, Lungworm, Macdonald, Mallophagous, Mistletoe, Monogenean, Nematode, Nit, Orobanche, Pinworm, Plasmodium, Puccinia, Rafflesia, Rhipidoptera, Rickettsia, Roundworm, Schistosoma, Scrounger, Shark, Smut-fungus, Sponge(r), Sporozoa(n), Strepsiptera, Strongyle, Strongyloid, Stylops, Sucker, Symphile, Tapeworm, Tick, Toady, Toxoplasma, Trematode, Trencher-friend, Trencher-knight, Trichina, Tryp(anosoma), Vampire, Viscum, Worms
Parasol Awning, Brolly, En tout cas, Sunshade, Umbrella
Parcel Allocate, Allot, Aret, Bale, Bundle, Holding, Lot, Package, Packet, Sort, Wrap
Parch(ed) Arid, Bake, Dry, Graddan, Roast, Scorched, Sere, Thirsty, Torrid
Parchment Diploma, Forel, Mezuzah, Papyrus, Pell, Pergameneous, Roll, Roule, Scroll, Sheepskin, Vellum
Pard Leopard, Pal, Partner
Pardon(able), Pardoner Absolve, Amnesty, Anan, Assoil, Clear, Condone, Eh, Excuse, ➤ FORGIVE, Grace, Mercy, Qu(a)estor, Release, Remission, Remit, Reprieve, Venial, What
Pare Flaught, Flay, Peel, Shave, Skive, Sliver, Strip, Whittle
Parent(al) Ancestral, Father, Forebear, Genitor, Maternal, Mother, Paternal, Storge
Parenthesis Aside, Brackets, Innuendo

Parhelion Sun-dog

Pariah Ishmael, Leper, Outcast, Pi(e)dog, Pyedog

Paris(ian), Parisienne Abductor, Athene, Elle, Gai, Gay, Grisette, Lutetian, Maillotin, Midinette, Trojan

Parish District, Flock, Kirkto(w)n, Parischan(e), Parishen, Parochin(e), Peculiar, Province, Title

Parity Smithsonian

Park(ing) Algonquin, Battery, Brecon Beacons, Business, Common, Daintree, Dales, Dartmoor, Death Valley, Enclosure, Etosha, Everglades, Exmoor, Fiordland, Fun, Garage, Grand Canyon, Green, Grounds, Hwange, Hyde, Jasper, Kakadu, Kalahari Gemsbok, Katmai, Kejionkujik, Kobuk Valley, Kruger, Lake District, Lamington, Lung, Mammoth Cave, Mansfield, Mesa Verde, Mount Aspiring, Mount McKinley, Mount Rainier, Mungo, Nahanni National, Nairobi, Northumberland, Osterley, P, Paradise, Peak District, Phoenix, Pitch, Prater, Preserve, Rec, Riding Mountain, Safari, Sanctuary, Sandown, Science, Sequoia, Serengeti, Shenandoah, Snowdonia, Stop, Theme, Tsavo, Valet, Wildlife, Wood Buffalo, Yard, Yellowstone, Yosemite

Parker Dorothy, Nos(e)y

Parkleaves Tutsan

Parley Confer, Discourse, Palaver, Speak, Tret

Parliament Addled, Althing, Barebones, Black, Boule, Bundestag, Commons, Congress, Cortes, Council, Cross-bench, Dail, Diet, Drunken, D(o)uma, Eduskunta, Folketing, House, Imperial, Knesset, Lack-learning, Lagt(h)ing, Landst(h)ing, Lawless, Legislature, Lok Sabha, Long, Lords, Majlis, Merciless, Mongrel, Odelsting, Rajya Sabha, Reichstag, Riksdag, Rump, St Stephens, Sanhedrin, Seanad, Seanad Eireann, Sejm, Short, Stannary, States-general, Stirthing, Stormont, Stort(h)ing, Thing, Tynwald, Unicameral, Unlearned, Useless, Volkskammer, Westminster

Parliamentarian Cabinet, Fairfax, Ireton, Leveller, Member, MP, Roundhead, Whip

Parlour Beauty, Funeral, Lounge, Massage, Salon, Snug

Parnassus Museum, Verse

Parody Burlesque, Lampoon, Mock, Piss-take, Satire, Sendup, Skit, Spoof, Travesty

Parole Pledge, Promise, Trust, Word

Paronychia Agnail, Felon, Whitlow

Paroxysm Fit, Rapture, Spasm, Subintrant, Throe

Parricide Cenci

Parrot Amazon, Cockatoo, Conure, Copy, Flint, Green leek, Imitate, Kaka(po), Kea, Lorikeet, Lory, Lovebird, Macaw, Mimic, Nestor, Owl, Parakeet, Paroquet, Poll(y), Popinjay, Psittacine, Quarrion, Repeat, Rosella, Rote, Stri(n)gops, T(o)uraco

Parrot-bill Glory-pea

Parry Block, Counter, Defend, Dodge, Forestall, Parade, Riposte, Sixte, Tac-au-tac, Thwart, Ward

Parsee Zoroastrian

Parsimonious, Parsimony Cheese-paring, Mean, Narrow, Near(ness), Niggardly, Stingy, Tight

Parsley Apiol, Kecks, Kex, Pot-herb

Parsnip Buttered, Buttery, Dill, Masterwort, Sium, Skirret

Parson Clergyman, Cleric, Minister, Non juror, Pastor, Priest, Rector, Rev, Sky-pilot, Soul-curer, Yorick

Part(ing) Accession, Aliquot, Antimere, Area, Aught, Bulk, Bye, Cameo, Character, Chunk, Component, Constituent, Crack, Cue, Dislink, Diverge, Dole, Element, Episode, Escapement, Farewell, Fascicle, Fork, Fraction, Goodbye, Half, Instalment, Lathe, Lead, Leave, Leg, Lill, Lilt, Lines, List, Member, Parcel, ➤ PIECE, Portion, Proportion, Pt, Quota, Rape, Ratio, Region, Rive, Role, Scena, Scene, Secondo, Section, Sector, Segment, Separate, Sever, Shade, Share, Shed, Sleave, Sle(i)ded, ➤ SOME, Spare, Split, Stator, Sunder, Tithe, Unit, Vaunt, Walk on, Wrench

Partake(r) Allottee, Eat, Participate, Share

Parthogenesis Thelytoky

Partial(ity), Partially Biased, Ex-parte, Fan, Favour, Halflins, Imbalance, Incomplete, One-sided, Predilection, Slightly, Unequal, Weakness

Participate Engage, Join, Partake, Share

Particle(s) Alpha, Anion, Antineutron, Antiproton, Atom, Baryon, Beta, Bit, Boson, Corpuscle, Curn, Dander, Delta, Deuteron, Effluvium, Fermion, Fleck, Fragment, Gemmule, Gluon, Grain, Granule, Graviton, Hadron, Higgs, Hyperon, Ion, J, Jot, Kaon, Lambda, Lemail, Lemel, Lepton, Meson, Micelle, Microsome, Mite, Molecule, Muon, Neutrino, Neutron, Nobiliary, Parton, Photon, Pion, Plasmagene, Platelet, Positron, Prion, Proton, Quark, Radioactivity, Shower, Sigma, Sinter, Smithereen, Speck, Strange, Subatom, Tachyon, Tardyon, Tau neutrino, Tauon, Thermion, Tittle, Virion, W, Whit, WIMP, X-hyperon, Z

Parti-coloured Fancy, Motley, Piebald, Pied, Variegated

Particular Choosy, Dainty, ➤ DETAIL, Endemic, Especial, Essential, Express, Fiky, Fog, Fussy, Item, Itself, London fog, Nice, Niffy-naffy, Own, Pea-souper, Peculiar, Pernickety, Pet, Point, Prim, Proper, ➤ RESPECT, Special, Specific, Stickler, Strict, Stripe

Partisan Adherent, Axe, Biased, Carlist, Champion, Devotee, Factional, Fan, Irregular, Partial, Provo, Sider, Spear, Supporter, Yorkist

Partition(ed) Abjoint, Bail, Barrier, Brattice, Bretasche, Bulkhead, Cloison, Cubicle, Diaphragm, Dissepiment, Division, Hallan, Mediastinum, Parpane, Parpen(d), Parpent, Parpoint, Perpend, Perpent, Replum, ➤ SCREEN, Scriene, Septum, Tabula, Wall, With

Partlet Hen, Overlaid

Partner(ship) Accomplice, Ally, Associate, Butty, Cahoot(s), Coachfellow, Colleague, Comrade, Confederate, Consort, Couple, Dutch, Escort, E-W, Firm, Gigolo, Mate, N-S, Pal, Pard, Sidekick, Silent, Sleeping, Sparring, Spouse, Stablemate, Stand, Symbiosis

▷ **Part of** may indicate a hidden word

Partridge Bird, Chik(h)or, Chuka, Chuker, Covey, Quail, Tinamou, Ynambu

Party Acid house, Alliance, Apparat, Assembly, At-home, Ba'ath, Ball, Band, Barbecue, Bash, Beano, Bee, Bloc, Blowout, Body, Bottle, Bunfight, Bust, Camp, Carousal, Carouse, Caucus, Celebration, Clambake, Cocktail, Commando, Communist, Concert, Conservative, Contingent, Cookie-shine, Cooperative, Coterie, Cult, Democratic, Detail, Ding, Discotheque, Do, Drum, Faction, Falange, Federalist, Fest, Fête champêtre, Fête Galante, Fianna Fáil, Fine Gael, Funfest, Gala, Gang, Garden, Green, Greenback, Guelf, Guelph, Hen, High heels, Hoedown, Hooley, Hootenannie, Hootenanny, Hoot(a)nannie, Hoot(a)nanny, Housewarming, Hurricane, Irredentist, Jol(lities), Junket, Junto, Kettledrum, Kitchen tea, Klat(s)ch, Knees-up, Kuomintang, L, Labour, Launch, Lib, Liberal, Low heels, Luau, Mallemaroking, Mollie, National, Neck-tie, Octobrist, Opposition, Person, Plaid, Progressive, Prohibition, Pyjama, Rave, Rave-up, Razzle(-dazzle), Reception, Republican, Revel, Ridotto, Rocking, Rort, Rout, SDP, Search, Sect, Set, Shindig, Shine, Shivoo, Shower, Shower tea, Side, Smoker, SNP, Soc(ialist), Social, Social Democratic, Soiree, Spree, Squad(rone), Stag, Symposium, Tailgate, Tea, Third, Thrash, Tory, Treat, Ultramontane, Unionist, Wafd, Warehouse, Whig, Whoop-de-do(o), Wingding, Working

Partygoer Raver, Socialite

Party-piece Solo

Parvenu Arriviste, Upstart

Pascal Blaise, Pressure

Pash Crush, Devotion

Pasha Achmed, Dey, Emir, Ismet

Pass(ed), Passing, Pass on, Past Ago, Agon, Aorist, Approve, Arise, Before, Behind, Bernina, Beyond, Bolan, Botte, Brenner, Brief, By, Bygone, Chal(l)an, Chilkoot, Chine, Chit(ty), Clear, Col, Cote, Cross, Cursory, Death, Defile, Delate, Demise, Diadron, Die, Disappear, Double, Elapse, Emit, End, Ensue, Ephemeral, Exceed, Exeat, Faena, Foist, Forby, Forgone, Former, Gap, Gate, Gha(u)t, Glencoe, Glide, Go, Gulch, Halse, Hand, Happen, Hause, Impart, Impermanent, In transit, Jark, Khyber, Kloof, Lap, Lead, Long syne, Mesmerism, Migrate, Moravian Gate, Mount Cenis, Nek, Notch, Nutmeg, Nye, Occur, Oer, OK, Okay, Oke, Omit, Overhaul, Overshoot, Overslaugh, Overtake, Pa, Palm, Participle, Perish, Permeate, Permit, Poll, Poort, Predicament, Preterit(e), Proceed, Propagate, Pun(c)to, Qualify, Railcard, Reach, Reeve, Refer, Relay, Retroactive, Retrospect, Roncesvalles, St Bernard, St Gotthard, Sanitation, Scissors, Senile, Serve, Shipka, Simplon, Since, Skim, Skip, Skirt, Slap, Sling, Snap, Spend, State, Thermopylae, Thread, Through, Ticket, Tip, Transient, Transilient, Transitory, Transmit, Transude, Travel, Triptyque, Troop, Veronica, Vet, Visa, Visé, Wall, Wayleave, Weather, While, Wrynose, Yesterday, Yesteryear, Ygoe

Passable Adequate, Fair, Navigable, Tolerable

Passage Adit, Aisle, Alley(way), Alure, Apostrophe, Arcade, Archway, Arterial, Atresia, Cadenza, Caponier(e), Career, Channel, Chute, Citation,

Clause, Close, Coda, Conduit, Corridor, Creep, Crossing, Crush, Cundy, Dead-end, Deambulatory, Defile, Drake, Drift, Duct, Eel-fare, Episode, Excerpt, Extract, Fare, Fat, Fistula, Flat, Flight, Flue, Gallery, Gangway, Gap, Gat, Gate, Ginnel, Gut, Hall, Head, Inlet, Journey, Kyle, Lane, Lapse, Larynx, Loan, Lobby, Locus, Meatus, Melisma, Mona, Movement, Northeast, Northwest, Para(graph), Path, Pend, Pericope, Phrase, Pore, Portion, Prelude, Prose, Ride, Rite, Ritornell(o), Route, Sailing, Shaft, Shunt, Slap, Slype, Snicket, Sprue, Strait, Street, Stretta, Stretto, Subway, Sump, Thirl, Thorough(fare), Tour, Trachea, Trance, Transe, Transit(ion), Travel, Tunnel, Undercast, Unseen, Ureter, Voyage, Way, Windpipe

▷ **Passage of arms** may indicate 'sleeve'

Passé Corny, Dated, Ex, Obsolete

Passenger Cad, Commuter, Fare, Pillion, Rider, Slacker, Steerage, Straphanger, Traveller, Voyager, Wayfarer

Passion(ate), Passionately Anger, Appetite, Ardour, Con fuoco, Fervour, Fire, Flame, Frampold, Fury, Gust, Heat, Hot, Hunger, Hwyl, Ileac, Iliac, Intense, Ire, Irish, Kama, Love, Lust, Mania, Obsession, Oestrus, Rage, Stormy, Sultry, Torrid, Violent, Warm, Wax, Wrath, Yen, Zeal

Passion-fruit Water-lemon

Passive (stage) Apathetic, Dormant, Inert, Pathic, Patient, Pupa, Supine, Yielding

Pass out Faint, Graduate, Swoon

Passover Agadah, Haggada, Omer, Pesach

Passport Access, Clearance, Congé(e), Key, Laissez-passer, Nansen, Navicert, Sea-letter, Visa

Password Code, Countersign, Logon, Nayword, Parole, Sesame, Shibboleth, Tessera, Watchword

▶ **Past** see PASS

Pasta Agnolotti, Cannelloni, Capelletti, Conchiglie, Durum, Farfal, Farfel, Fedelini, Fettuc(c)ine, Fusilli, Lasagna, Lasagne, Linguini, Macaroni, Manicotti, Noodles, Orzo, Penne, Perciatelli, Ravioli, Rigatoni, Spaghetti, Spaghettina, Tagliarini, Tagliatelle, Tortelli(ni), Vermicelli, Ziti

Paste, Pasty Ashen, Batter, Beat, Botargo, Boule, Bridie, Cerate, Clobber, Cornish, Dentifrice, Dough, Electuary, Fake, Filler, Fondant, Frangipane, Glue, Guarana, Harissa, Knish, Lute, Magma, Marzipan, Masala, Mastic, Miso, Mountant, Pale, Pallid, Putty, Pâté, Patty, Pearl-essence, Pie, Piroshki, Pirozhki, Poonac, Punch, Rhinestone, Slip, Slurry, Spread, Strass, Tahina, Tahini, Tapenade, Taramasalata, Wan

Pastern Hobble, Knee, Tether

Pastiche Cento, Collage, Medley, Patchwork, Potpourri

Pastille Jujube, Lozenge

Pastime Diversion, Game, Hobby, Recreation, Seesaw, Sport

Past master Champion, Expert, Historian, Pro

Past midnight 1 am

Pastor(al) Arcadia, Bucolic, Curé, Eclogue, Endymion, Idyl(l), Minister, Priest, Rector, Rural, Shepherd, Simple

Pastry Apfelstrudel, Baclava, Baklava, Bouchée, Calzone, Choux, Clafoutis, Croustade, Cruller, Crust, Danish, Dariole, Dough, Eclair, Empanada, Feuilleté, Filo, Flaky, Flan, Frangipane, Gougère, Hamantasch, Millefeuille, Pie, Phyllo, Pie-crust, Pirog, Piroshki, Pirozhki, Profiterole, Puff, Quiche, Rug(g)elach, Samosa, Shortcrust, Strudel, Tart, Turnover, Vol-au-vent

Pasture Alp, Eadish, Eddish, Feed, Fell, Fodder, Grassland, Graze, Herbage, Kar(r)oo, Lair, Lare, Lea, Lease, Leasow(e), Leaze, Ley, Machair, Mead(ow), Pannage, Potrero, Raik, Rake, Soum, Sowm, Tie, Transhume, Tye

▶ **Pasty** see PASTE

Pat Apt, Bog-trotter, Butter, Clap, Dab, Glib, Lump, Print, Prompt, Rap, Slap, Tap

Patch(y) Bed, Bit, Cabbage, Clout, Cobble, Cooper, Court plaster, Cover, Friar, Fudge, ▶ MEND, Mosaic, Nicotine, Pasty, Piebald, Piece, Plaque, Plaster, Pot, Purple, Solder, Tingle, Tinker, Vamp, Variegated

Patchwork Cento, Miscellany, Mosaic, Piecing

Pate, Pâté Crown, Paste, Rillettes, Taramasalata, Terrine

Patent(ed) Breveté, Copyright, Evident, Licence, License, Obvious, Overt, Plain, Rolls

Pater(nity) Father, Filiation, Walter

Paterfamilias Coarb, Master

Path(way) Aisle, Allée, Alley, Arc, Berm, Berme, Boreen, Borstal(l), Bridle, Causeway, Causey, Clickstream, Course, Eclipse, Flight, Gate, Ginnel, Glide, Lane, Ley, Locus, Orbit, Pad, Parabola, Primrose, Ride, Ridgeway, Route, Runway, Sidewalk, Spurway, Stie, Sty(e), Swath(e), Track, Trail, Trajectory, Trod, Walkway, ▶ WAY, Xystus

Pathan Pakhto, Pakhtu, Pashto, Pashtu, Pushto(o), Pushtu

Pathetic(ally) Doloroso, Drip, Forlorn, Piteous, Poignant, Sad, Touching

Pathfinder Compass, Explorer, Guide, Pioneer, Scout

Pathological Diseased, Morbid, Septic

Pathos Bathos, Pity, Sadness, Sob-stuff

Patience Calm, Endurance, Forbearance, Fortitude, Indulgence, Monument, Solitaire, Stoicism, Virtue

Patient(s) Calm, Case, Clinic, Forbearing, Grisel(da), Grisilda, Invalid, Job, Long-suffering, Passive, Resigned, Stoic, Subject, Ward

Patois Argot, Cant, Dialect, Jargon, Jive, Lingo, Scouse

Patriarch Aaron, Abuna, Catholicos, Elder, Isaac, Levi, Maron, Methuselah, Nestor, Noah, Pope, Simeon, Venerable

Patrician Aristocrat, Noble, Senator

Patrick Mick, Paddy, Pat, Spens

Patrimony Ancestry, Estate, Heritage

Patriot(ic), Patriotism Cavour, Chauvinist, DAR, Emmet, Flag-waving, Flamingant, Garibaldi, Hereward, Irredentist, Jingoism, Loyalist, Maquis, Nationalist, Tell

Patrol Armilla, Guard, Outguard, Picket, Piquet, Prowl-car, Scout, Sentinel, Turm

Patron(age), Patronise(d), Patronising Advowson, Aegis, Auspices, Benefactor, Business, Champion, Client, Customer, Donator, Egis, Fautor, Maecenas, Nepotic, Protector, Protégé, Provider, Shopper, ➤ SPONSOR, Stoop, Stoup

Patsy Dupe, Hendren, Scapegoat, Stooge

Patter Backchat, Cant, Jargon, Lingo, Mag, Rap, S(c)htick, Schtik, Spiel

Pattern(ed) Argyle, Bird's eye, Blueprint, Broché, Check, Chladni figure, Clock, Design, Dévoré, Diaper, Dog's tooth, Draft, Egg and dart, Epitome, Example, Exemplar, Fiddle, Figuration, Format, Fractal, Fret, Gestalt, Grain, Grammadion, Herringbone, Holding, Hound's tooth, Intarsia, Matel(l)asse, Matrix, Meander, ➤ MODEL, Mosaic, Norm, Paisley, Paradigm, Paragon, Pinstripe, Plan, Pompadour, Precedent, Prototype, Quincunx, Stencil, Symmetry, Syndrome, Tala, Tangram, Tattersall, Template, Tessella, Tessera, Tracery, Tread, Type, Willow

Patty Bouchée, Pie

Paul Jones, Oom, Pry, Revere, Robeson, S, St

Pauline Day-boy, Perils

Paunch Belly, Corporation, Gut, Kite, Kyte, Pod, Rumen, Tripe, Tum

Pauper Bankrupt, Beggar, Have-not, Mendicant, Penniless

Pause Break, Breakpoint, Breather, Caesura, Cessation, Cesura, Comma, Desist, Er, Fermata, Hesitate, Interkinesis, Interval, Limma, Lull, Pitstop, ➤ RESPITE, Rest, Selah, Stop, Tacet, Time out

Pave(ment), Paving Causeway, Clint, Diaper, Granolith, Path, Roadside, Set(t), Sidewalk, Travolator, Trottoir

Pavilion Ear, Gazebo, Jingling Johnny, Kiosk, Marquee, Tent

Paw Maul, Mitt, Pad, Pat, Pud, Pug

Pawky Dry, Humorous, Shrewd, Sly

Pawn(shop) Agent, Betel, Chessman, Counter, Derby, Dip, Gage, Gallery, Hanging, Hock, Hostage, Leaving-shop, Lumber, Mont-de-piété, Monti di pieta, Pan, Passed, Peacock, Piece, Pignerate, Pignorate, Pledge, Pop, Security, Siri, Spout, Tiddleywink, Tool, Wadset, Weed

Pawnbroker, Pawnee Hockshop, Lumber, Moneylender, Nunky, Sheeny, Uncle, Usurer

Pax Peace, Truce

Pay(master), Payment, Paid, Pay off, Pay out Advertise, Agterskot, Amortise, Annat, Annuity, Ante, Arles, Basic, Batta, Blench, Bonus, Bukshee, Bukshi, Cashier, Cens, Cheque, COD, Commute, Compensate, Consideration, Damage, Defray, Disburse, Discharge, Dividend, Down, Dub, Emolument, Endow, Escot, Farm, Fee, Finance, Foot, Fork out, Fund, Gale, Gate, Give, Grassum, Grave, Han(d)sel, Hazard, Hire, Hoot(oo), HP, Imburse, Leads and legs, Lobola, Lobolo, Mail, Meet, Merchet, Metayage, Mise, Modus, Overtime, Payola, Pension, Pittance, Pony, Prebendal, Premium, Primage, Pro, Pro forma, Purser, Quarterage, Quit(-rent), Ransom, Refund, Remuneration, Rent, Requite, Residual, Respects, Royalty, Salary, Satisfaction, Scot, Screw, Scutage, Settle, Severance, Shell, Sick, Sink, Sold(e), Soul-scat, Soul-scot, ➤ SPEND, Square, Stipend, Strike,

Stump, Sub, Subscribe, Sweetener, Table, Take-home, Tar, Tender, Token, Tommy, Treasure, Treat, Tribute, Truck, Unpurse, Usance, Veer, Wage, Wardcorn, X-factor

Pea(s) Carling, Chaparral, Chickling, D(h)al, Desert, Dholl, Garbanzo, Goober, Hastings, Legume, Mangetout, Marrowfat, Pigeon, Passiform, Pulse, Rounceval, Split, Sugar

Peace(ful), Peace-keeper, Peace organisation, Peace symbol Ahimsa, Ataraxy, Calm, Ease, Frith, Halcyon, Interceder, Irenic(on), King's, Lee, Lull, Nirvana, Olive, Pacific, Pax, Queen's, Quiet, Repose, Rest, Salem, Serene, Sh, Shalom, Siesta, Still, Tranquil, Truce, UN

Peacemaker ACAS, Arbitrator, Conciliator, Mediator, Trouble-shooter

Peach Blab, Cling, Clingstone, Dish, Dob, Freestone, Inform, Laetrile, Malakatoone, Melocoto(o)n, Nectarine, Oner, Quandang, Shop, Sneak, Split, Squeak, Stunner, Tattle, Tell, Victorine

Peachum Polly

Peacock Coxcomb, Dandy, Fop, Junonian, Muster, Paiock(e), Pajock(e), Payock(e), Pavo(ne), Pawn, Pown, Sashay

Peak(y) Acme, Aiguille, Alp, Apex, Ben, Comble, Communism, Crag, Crest, Darien, Drawn, Eiger, Gable, Gannett, Horn, Matterhorn, Mons,
➤ MOUNTAIN, Nib, Nunatak, Optimum, Pale, Pin, Pinnacle, Rainier, Sallow, Snowdon, Spire, Top, Tor, Visor, Widow's, Zenith

Peal Carillon, Chime, Clap, Toll, Triple

Peanut(s) Arnut, Chickenfeed, Goober, Groundnut, Monkey-nut, Pittance

Pear Aguacate, Alligator, Anchovy, Anjou, Asian, Avocado, Bartlett, Bergamot, Beurré, Blanquet, Catherine, Carmelite, Colmar, Conference, Cuisse-madame, Jargonelle, Muscadel, Muscatel, Musk, Nelis, Perry, Poperin, Poppering, Poprin, Prickly, Pyrus, Queez-maddam, Seckel, Seckle, Warden, William

Pearl(s), Pearly Barocco, Barock, Baroque, Cultured, Gem, Jewel, Mabe, Margaret, Margaric, Nacrous, Olivet, Orient, Prize, Rope, Seed, String, Sulphur, Unio(n)

Pear-shaped Obconic, Pyriform

Peasant Bonhomme, Boor, Bumpkin, Chouan, Churl, Clodhopper, Contadino, Cossack, Cottar, Cott(i)er, Fellah(s), Fellahin, Hick, Jungli, Kern(e), Kisan, Kulak, M(o)ujik, Muzhik, Raiyat, Roturier, Rustic, Ryot, Swain, Tyrolean, Whiteboy, Yokel

Peat Moss-litter, Sod, Turbary, Turf, Yarfa, Yarpha

Pebble(s), Pebbly Banket, Calculus, Cobblestone, Dreikanter, Gallet, Gooley, Gravel, Psephism, Pumie, Pumy, Scree, Shingle

Peccadillo Mischief, Misdemeanour, Offence

Peck Bill, Bushel, Dab, Forpet, Forpit, Gregory, Kiss, Lip, Lippie, Nibble, Tap

Pecksniff Charity

Peculiar(ity) Appropriate, Characteristic, Distinct, Eccentric, Especial, Exclusive, Ferly, Funny, Idiosyncratic, Kink, Kooky, Odd, Own, Proper, Queer, Quirk, Singular, ➤ SPECIAL, Specific, Strange, Unusual

▷ **Peculiar** may indicate an anagram

Pedagogue Academic, B.Ed, Teacher

Pedal Bike, Chorus, Cycle, Lever, P, Rat-trap, Soft, Treadle, Treddle

Pedal-coupler Tirasse

Pedant(ic) Casaubon, Chop logic, Dogmatic, Dryasdust, Elucubrate, Intellectual, Lucubrate, Pedagogue, Pernickety, Pompous, Precisian, Quibbler, Scholastic, Sesquipedalian

Peddle, Pedlar Bodger, Boxwallah, Camelot, Chapman, Cheapjack, Colporteur, Drummer, Duffer, Hawk, Huckster, Jagger, Packman, Pedder, Pether, Sell, Smouch, Smouse(r), Sutler, Tallyman, Tink(er), Yagger

▷ **Peddling** may indicate an anagram

Pedestal Acroter(ion), Dado, Pillar, Support

Pedestrian Banal, Commonplace, Dull, Ganger, Hack, Hike, Itinerant, Jaywalker, Laborious, Trite, Mundane, Walker

Pedigree(s) Ancestry, Blood, Breeding, Descent, House, Lineage, Phylogeny, Stemma(ta), Stirps, Thoroughbred

Pediment Fronton

Peduncle Scape, Stalk

Peek Eye, Glance, Glimpse, Peep

Peel(er) Bark, Bobby, Candied, Decorticate, Exfoliate, Flype, Pare, PC, Rind, Rine, Scale, Shell, Skin, ➤ STRIP, Tiff, Zest

▷ **Peeled** may indicate outside letter(s) to be removed from a word

Peep(er) Cheep, Cook, Glance, Gledge, Keek, Kook, Lamp, Nose, Peek, Pink, Pry, Squeak, Squint, Spy, Stime, Styme, Voyeur

Peer(age), Peers Archduke, Aristocrat, Backwoodsman, Baron(et), Burke, Coeval, Daimio, Doucepere, Douzeper(s), Duke, Earl, Egal, Elevation, Equal, Eyeball, Gynt, Lord, Match, Noble, Paladin, Peregal, Pink, Rank, Scry, Squint, Stare, Stime, Styme, Toot, Tweer, Twire

Peerless Matchless, Nonpareil, Supreme

Peevish(ness) Capernoited, Captious, Crabby, Cross, Doddy, Frabbit, Frampal, Frampold, Franzy, Fretful, Lienal, Moody, Nattered, Petulant, Pindling, Protervity, Shirty, Sour, Teachie, Te(t)chy, Testy

Peewit Lapwing, Peewee

Peg Cheville, Cleat, Cotter-pin, Die, Fix, Freeze, Knag, Leg, Margaret, Nail, Nog, Pin, Piton, Snort, Spigot, Spile, Square, Stengah, Stinger, Support, Tap, Tee, Thole, Tholepin, Thowel, Toggle, Tot, Woffington

Pegboard Solitaire

Pelagic Deep-sea, Marine, Oceanic

Pelf Lucre, Mammon, Money, Notes, Riches

Pelican Alcatras, Bird, Crossing, Golden Hind, LA, Louisiana, Steganopode

Pellagra Maidism

Pellet Bolus, Buckshot, Bullet, Pill, Prill, Slug

Pelt Assail, Clod, Fleece, Fur, Hail, Hide, Hie, Lam, Pepper, Random, Shower, Skin, Squail, Stone

Peltast Soldier, Targeteer

Pelvis Ilium

Pen Ballpoint, Bamboo, Bic®, Biro®, Cage, Calamus, Cartridge, Confine, Coop, Corral, Crawl, Cru(i)ve, Cub, Data, Enclosure, Fank, Farm, Fold, Fountain, Gladius, Hen, Highlighter, Hoosegow, J, ➤ JAIL, Keddah, Kraal, Lair, Light, Mew, Mure, Piggery, Pound, Quill, Ree, Reed, Ring, Rollerball, Scribe, Stell, Stie, Stir, Sty(e), Stylet, Stylo, Stylograph, Stylus, Swan, Tank, Write

▷ **Pen** may indicate a writer

Penal(ize) Cost, Fine, Gate, Handicap, Huff, Mulct, Punitive, Servitude

Penalty Abye, Amende, Cost, Eric, Fine, Forfeit, Han(d)sel, Huff, Pain, Price, Punishment, Sanction, Wide

Penance Atonement, Shrift

Penates Lares

Pence D, P, Peter's

Penchant Predilection

Pencil Beam, Ca(l)m, Charcoal, Chinagraph®, Crayon, Caum, Draft, Draw, Fusain, Grease, Keelivine, Keelyvine, Lead, Outline, Propelling, Stump, Styptic

Pendant Albert, Chandelier, Drop, Girandole, Laval(l)ière, Necklace, Poffle

Pending Imminent, In fieri, Unresolved, Until

Pendragon Uther

Pendulous, Pendulum Dewlap, Foucault's, Metronome, Noddy, One-way, Swing, Wavering

Penetrate, Penetrating, Penetration Acumen, Acuminate, Bite, Bore, Cut, Enpierce, Enter, Imbue, Impale, Incisive, Indent, Indepth, Infiltrate, Insight, Into, Intrant, Lance, Permeate, Pierce, Probe, Sagacious, Shear, Touch, Thrust, X-ray

Penguin Aeroplane, Anana, Auk, Emperor, Fairy, Gentoo, King, Korora, Macaroni, Rock-hopper

Penicillin Fleming

Peninsula Alaska, Alte, Antarctic, Arabian, Ards, Arm, Avalon, Baja California, Balkan, Banks, Bataan, Boothia, Cape, Cape Cod, Cape Verde, Chalcidice, Chersonese, Chukchi, Coromandel, Crimea, Deccan, Delmarva, East Cape, Eyre, Florida, Freycinet, Gallipoli, Gaspé, Gower, Iberia(n), Indo-China, Istria, Jutland, Kamchatka, Kathiawar, Kintyre, Kola, Kowloon, Labrador, Leizhou, Lleyn, Luichow, Malay, Melville, Neck, Nova Scotia, Otago, Palmer, Peloponnese, Promontory, Scandinavian, Sinai, Spit, Spur, The Lizard, Tasman, Wilson's Promontory, Wirral, Yorke, Yucatan

Penis Archie, Cor(e)y, Dick, Dildo(e), Dipstick, Dong, Ferret, Giggle(stick), Horn, Jack, John Thomas, Knob, Mojo, Pecker, Peezle, Percy, Phallus, Pillicock, Pintle, Pisser, Pizzle, Plonker, Prick, Rod, Roger, Shaft, Stiffy, Tonk, Tool, W(h)ang, Willie, Willy, Winkle, Yard, Zeppelin

Penitent(iary) Calaboose, Clink, Contrite, Gaol, Jail, Jug, Prison, Repenter, Stir

Pennant, Pennon Banner, Bunting, Fane, Flag, Guidon, Streamer

Penniless Bankrupt, Boracic, Broke, Bust, Poor, Skint, Strapped

Penny Bean, Cartwheel, Cent, Copper, D, Dreadful, P, Sen, Sou, Sterling, Stiver, Win(n), Wing

Pension(er) Allowance, Ann(at), Annuitant, Board, Chelsea, Cod, Cor(r)ody, Gratuity, Half-board, Payment, Retire, Serps, Stakeholder, Stipend, Superannuation

Pensive Dreamy, Moody, Musing, Thoughtful, Triste

Pentateuch T(h)orah

Pentecost Whit(sun)

Penthouse Cat, Lean-to, Roof

Peon Peasant, Serf, Slave, Ticca

Peony Moutan

People Bods, Body, Chosen, Commons, Demos, Ecology, Enchorial, Folk, Fraim, Gens, Guild, Human, Inhabit, Janata, Kin, Land, Lapith, Lay, Man(kind), Men, Mob, Nair, Nation(s), Nayar, One, Personalities, Phalange, Populace, Public, Punters, Race, Settle, Society, Souls, Tribe, Volk

Pep Buck, Dash, Enliven, Gism, Go, Jism, Jissom, Stamina, Verve, Vim

Pepper Alligator, All-spice, Ava, Bird, Black, Capsicum, Cayenne, Chilli, Condiment, Cubeb, Devil, Dittander, Dittany, Ethiopian, Green, Guinea, Jalapeno, Jamaica, Kava, Malaguetta, Matico, Negro, Paprika, Pelt, Pim(i)ento, Piper, Red, Riddle, Sambal, Spice, Sprinkle, Szechwan, Tabasco®, Yaqona, Yellow

Peppercorn Nominal

Peppermint Bull's Eye, Humbug, Pandrop

Per By, Each, Through

Perambulate, Perambulator Buggy, Expatiate, Pedestrian, Pram, Stroller, Wagon, Walker

Perceive, Perception, Perceptive Acumen, Albert, Anschauung, Apprehend, Clairvoyance, Clear-eyed, Cryptaesthetic, Descry, Dianoia, Discern, Divine, ESP, Extrasensory, Feel, Insight, Intelligence, Intuit(ion), Kinaesthesia, Notice, Observe, Pan(a)esthesia, Remark, ➤ SEE, Sense, Sensitive, Sentience, Shrewd, Tact, Taste, Tel(a)esthesia, Telegnosis

Percentage Agio, Commission, Contango, Cut, Proportion, Royalty, Share, Vigorish

Perch(ing) Aerie, Alight, Anabis, Bass, Comber, Eyrie, Fish, Fogash, Gaper, Insessorial, Lug, Perca, Pole, Roost, Ruff(e), Seat, Serranid, ➤ SIT, Zingel

Percolate, Percolation Filter, Infiltrate, Leach, Ooze, Osmosis, Permeate, Seep, Sipe, Soak, Strain, Sype

Percussion (cap) Amorce, Idiophone, Impact, Knee, Knock, Thump, Timbrel

Perdition Ades, Hades

Peremptory Absolute, Decisive, Haughty, Imperative, Imperious

Perennial Continual, Enduring, Flower, Livelong, Perpetual, Recurrent

Perfect, Perfection(ist) Absolute, Accomplish, Accurate, Acme, Apple-pie, Bloom, Complete, Consummation, Cross-question, Dead, Develop, Finish, Flawless, Fulfil, Full, Holy, Ideal(ist), Impeccable, Intact, It, Mint, Par, Paragon, Past, Peace, Pedant, Practice, Pure, Refine, Soma, Sound,

Spot-on, Stainless, Sublime, Thorough, Three-pricker, Unblemished, Unqualified, Utopian, Utter, Whole, Witeless

Perfidy Betrayal, Falsehood, Treachery, Treason

Perforate(d), Perforation, Perforator Cribrate, Cribrose, Drill, Eyelet, Hole, ➤ PIERCE, Prick, Punch, Puncture, Riddle, Trephine, Trocar

Perforce Necessarily, Needs

Perform(ed), Performer, Performing Achieve, Act(or), Appear, Artist(e), Basoche, Busk, Chansonnier, Discharge, Do, Enact, Entertainer, Execute, Exert, Exhibit, Fancy Dan, Fulfil, Function, Geek, Hand, Headliner, Hersall, Implement, Interlocutor, Majorette, Make, Moke, On, Player, Praxis, Recite, Render, Ripieno, Sword-swallower, Throw, Vaudevillian, Virtuoso

Performance Accomplishment, Achievement, Act, Bravura, Broadcast, Command, Concert, Dare, Deed, Demonstration, Discharge, Entracte, Execution, Gas, Gig, Hierurgy, Holdover, Hootenanny, Matinee, Operation, Perpetration, Première, Recital, Rehearsal, Rendering, Rendition, Repeat, Rigmarole, Scene, Show, Solo, Stunt, Turn

Perfume (box) Aroma, Attar, Bergamot, Cassolette, Chypre, Civet, Cologne, Enfleurage, Fragrance, Frangipani, Incense, Ionone, Lavender (water), Linalool, Myrrh, Opopanax, Orris, Orrisroot, Patchouli, Patchouly, Pomander, Potpourri, Redolence, ➤ SCENT, Terpineol

Perfunctory Apathetic, Careless, Cursory, Indifferent, Token

Perhaps A(i)blins, Belike, Haply, Happen, May(be), Peradventure, Percase, Perchance, Possibly, Relative, Say, Yibbles

▷ **Perhaps** may indicate an anagram

Perigee Apsis, Epigeum

Peril(ous) ➤ DANGER, Hazard, Jeopardy, Precarious, Risk, Threat, Yellow

Perimeter Boundary, Circuit, Circumference, Limits

Period(ic) Acheulian, AD, Age, Annual, Aurignacian, Azilian, Cambrian, Carboniferous, Chalcolithic, Chukka, Chukker, Climacteric, Curse, Cycle, Day, Devonian, Diapause, Dot, ➤ DURATION, Eocene, Epoch, Floruit, Full-stop, Glacial, Grace, Hercynian, Holocene, Horal, Interregnum, Jurassic, Kalpa, Lesson, Liassic, Limit, Meantime, Meanwhile, Mesolithic, Middle Kingdom, Miocene, Monthly, Neolithic, Neozoic, Octave, Olde-worlde, Oligocene, Ordovician, Paleolithic, Permian, Phanerozoic, Phoenix, Pleistocene, Pliocene, Protohistory, Quarter, Quarternary, Regency, Rent, Riss, Romantic, Season, Session, Silurian, Span, Spell, Stage, Stop, Term, Tertiary, Trecento, Triassic, Trimester, Usance

Periodic(al) Catamenia, Comic, Digest, Economist, Etesian, Journal, Liassic, Listener, Mag, New Yorker, Organ, Paper, Phase, Publication, Punch, Rambler, Regency, Review, Solutrean, Solutrian, Spectator, Strand, Stretch, Tatter, Tract

Peripatetic Gadabout, Itinerant, Promenader, Travelling

Periphery Ambit, Bounds, Fringe, Outskirts, Surface

Periscope Eye(-stalk)

Perish(able), Perished, Perishing Brittle, ➤ DIE, End, Ephemeral, Expire, Fade, Forfair, Fungibles, Icy, Tine, Tint, Transitory, Tyne, Vanish

Periwinkle Apocynum, Blue, Myrtle

Perjure(d) Forswear, Lie, Mansworn

Perk(s), Perky Brighten, Chipper, Freshen, Jaunty, LV, Perquisite

Perm(anent) Abiding, Durable, Eternal, Everlasting, Fixed, Full-time, Indelible, ➤ LASTING, Marcel, Stable, Standing, Stative, Wave

Permeate Infiltrate, Leaven, Osmosis, Penetrate, Pervade, Seep

Permission, Permit(ted) Allow, Authorise, Carnet, Chop, Clearance, Congé(e), Copyright, Enable, Grant, Lacet, Laisser-passer, Latitude, Leave, Legal, Let, Liberty, Licence, License, Lief, Luit, Nihil obstat, Ok(e), Pace, Pass, Placet, Power, Pratique, Privilege, Sanction, Stamp-note, Suffer, Ticket, Triptyque, Visa, Vouchsafe, Way-leave, Wear

Pernicious Evil, Harmful, Lethal, Noisome, Pestilent, Wicked

Pernickety Fikish, Niggly

Peroration Pirlicue, Purlicue

Peroxide Bleach, Blonde, Colcothar

Perpendicular Aplomb, Apothem, Atrip, Cathetus, Erect, Normal, Orthogonal, Plumb, Sheer, Sine, ➤ UPRIGHT, Vertical

Perpetrate Commit, Effect, Execute

Perpetual Constant, Eternal, Incessant, Sempiternal

Perplex(ed), Perplexity Anan, Baffle, Bamboozle, Beset, Bewilder, Bother, Buffalo, Bumbaze, Cap, Confound, Confuse, Feague, Floor, Flummox, Knotty, Mystify, Nonplus, Out, Puzzle, Quizzical, Stump, Tangle, Tickle, Tostication

Perquisite Ap(p)anage, Emolument, Extra, Gratuity, ➤ PERK, Tip

Perrier Stoner

Perry Mason

Persecute, Persecution Afflict, Annoy, Badger, Crucify, Dragon(n)ades, Harass, Haze, Intolerant, Oppress, Pogrom, Ride, Torture

Persevere, Perseverance Assiduity, Continue, Fortitude, Insist, Patience, Persist, Plug, Stamina, Steadfastness, Stick, Stickability, Tenacity

Persia(n) Babee, Babi, Bahai, Cyrus, Farsi, Iran(ian), Mazdean, Mede, Pahlavi, Parasang, Parsee, Pehlevi, Pushtu, Samanid, Sassanid, Sohrab, Xerxes, Zoroaster

Persimmon Kaki

Persist(ence), Persistent Adhere, Assiduity, Chronic, Continual, Diligent, Doggedness, Endure, Importunate, Labour, Longeval, Lusting, Persevere, Press, Sedulous, Sneaking, Stick, Tenacity, Urgent

Person(s), Personal Alter, Being, Bird, Bod(y), Chai, Chal, Chi, Cookie, Entity, Everymen, Figure, Fish, Flesh, Head, Human, Individual, One, Own, Party, Passer-by, Private, Quidam, Selfhood, Sod, Soul, Specimen, Tales

Personage, Personality Anima, Celeb(rity), Character, Charisma, Dignitary, Ego, Grandee, Identity, Noble, Notability, Panjandrum, Presence, Sama, Seity, Sel, Self, Sell, Star, Tycoon

Personified, Personification, Personify Embody, Incarnate, Prosopop(o)eia, Represent

Personnel Employees, Hands, Liveware, Staff

Perspective Attitude, Distance, Point of view, Proportion, View, Vista

Perspicacious Astute, Discerning, Keen, Shrewd

Perspiration, Perspire, Perspiring Aglow, Forswatt, Glow, Hidrosis, Sudor, Suint, Sweat, Swelter

Persuade(d), Persuasion, Persuasive Cajole, Coax, Cogent, Conviction, Convince, Disarm, Eloquent, Faith, Feel, Forcible, Geed, Get, Induce, Inveigle, Move, Plausible, ➤ PREVAIL, Religion, Soft sell, Suborn, Truckled, Wheedle, Winning

Pert(ness) Bold, Cocky, Dicacity, Flippant, Forward, Fresh, Impertinent, Insolent, Jackanapes, Minx, Saucy, Tossy

Pertain Belong, Concern, Relate, Touch

Pertinacious Dogged, Obstinate, Persistent, Stickler, Stubborn

Pertinent Apropos, Apt, Fit, Germane, Relevant, Timely

Perturb(ation) Aerate, Confuse, Dismay, Disturb, Dither, State, Trouble, Upset, Worry

Peru(vian) Inca, PE, Quechua(n), Quichua(n)

Peruse Examine, Inspect, Read, Scan, ➤ STUDY

Pervade, Pervasion, Pervasive(ness) Diffuse, Drench, Immanence, Permeate, Saturate

Perverse, Perversion, Pervert(ed) Aberrant, Abnormal, Algolagnia, Awry, Cam(stairy), Camsteary, Camsteerie, Cantankerous, ➤ CONTRARY, Corrupt, Cussed, Deviate, Distort, Donsie, False, Gee, Kam(me), Kinky, Licentious, Misuse, Nonce, Paraphilia, Refractory, Sadist, Sicko, Stubborn, Thrawn, Traduce, Unnatural, Untoward, Uranism, Warp(ed), Wayward, Wilful, Wrest, Wry

▷ **Perverted** may indicate an anagram

Pessimism, Pessimist(ic) Alarmist, Crapehanger, Crepehanger, Cynic, Defeatist, Doomwatch, Doomy, Doubter, Fatalist, Jeremiah, Killjoy, Negative

Pest(er) Badger, Bedbug, Blight, Bot, ➤ BOTHER, Brat, Breese, Bug, Disagreeable, Dim, Earbash, Fly, Fowl, Harass, Irritate, Mither, Mouse, Nag, Nudnik, Nuisance, Nun, Pize, Plague, Rotter, Scourge, Tease, Terror, Thysanoptera, Vermin, Weevil

Pesticide DDT, Derris, Heplachlor, Mouser, Permethrin, Synergist, Warfarin

Pestilence, Pestilent Curse, Epidemic, Evil, Lues, Murrain, Noxious, Pernicious, Plague

Pet Aversion, Cade, Canoodle, Caress, Chou, Coax, Cosset, Dandle, Daut(ie), Dawt(ie), Dod, Dort, Ducky, Favourite, Fondle, Glumps, Hamster, Huff, Hump, Ire, Jarta, Jo, Lallygag, Lapdog, Miff, Mouse, Neck, Pique, Rabbit, Smooch, Snog, Spat, Strum, Sulk(s), Tantrum, Teacher's, Tiff, Tout, Towt, Umbrage, Virtual, Yarta

Petal Ala, Keels, Labellum

Petard Firework, Squib

Peter Aumbry, Bell, Dwindle, Grimes, Pan, Principle, Quince, Quint, Rabbit, Safe, Saint, Sellers, Simon, Simple, Wane, Weaken

Petite Dainty, Mignon, Small

Petition(er) Appeal, Beg, Boon, Crave, Entreaty, Orison, Plaintiff, Postulant, Prayer, Representation, Round robin, Solicit, Sue, Suit(or), Suppli(c)ant, Vesper

Pet-name Hypocorisma, Nickname, So(u)briquet

Petrel Bird, Nelly, Prion, Stormbird

Petrify(ing) Fossilise, Frighten, Lapidescent, Niobe, Numb, Ossify, Scare, Terrify

Petrol(eum) Cetane, Diesel, Esso®, Ethyl, Fuel, Gas, High-octane, Ligroin, Maz(o)ut, Octane, Olein, Rock-tar, Unleaded

Petticoat Balmoral, Basquine, Crinoline, Female, Filabeg, Fil(l)ibeg, Jupon, Kilt, Kirtle, Phil(l)abeg, Phil(l)ibeg, Placket, Sarong, Shift, Underskirt, Wylie-coat

Pettifogger Lawmonger

Petty, Pettiness Baubling, Bumbledom, Childish, Little, Mean, Minor, Narrow, Niggling, Nyaff, One-horse, Parvanimity, Picayunish, Pimping, Puisne, Shoestring, Small, Stingy, Tin, Trivial, Two-bit

Petulance, Petulant Fretful, Huff, Moody, Peevish, Perverse, Procacity, Sullen, Toutie, Waspish

Pew Box, Carrel, Chair, Seat, Stall

Pewter Trifle, Tutenag

Phalanger Cus-cus, Honey-mouse, Opossum, Petaurist, Possum, Tait, Tarsipes, Tuan

Phalanx Cohort, Coterie, Legion

Phalarope Lobe-foot

Phallus Linga(m), Penis, Priapus

Phantasist, Phantasm Apparition, Chimera, Spectre, Werewolf

Phantom Apparition, Bogey, Bugbear, Eidolon, Idol, Incubus, Maya, Shade, Spectre, Tut, Wraith

Pharaoh Amenhotep, Cheops, Egyptian, Rameses, Thutmose, Tut, Tutankhamen, Tutankhamun, Tyrant

Pharisee Formalist, Humbug, Hypocrite, Nicodemus

Pharmacist ➤ CHEMIST, Dispenser, MPS, Preparator

Phase Cycle, Form, Period, Post-boost, REM, Stage, State, Synchronise

Pheasant Argus, Bird, Junglefowl, Mona(u)l, Nide, Nye, Tragopan

Phenol Orcine, Orcinol, Resorcin, Xylenol

Phenomenon Blip, Effect, Event, Flying saucer, Marvel, Miracle, Mirage, Paranormal, Psi, Synergy

Phial Bologna, Bottle, Flask

Phil, Philip Fluter, Macedonia, Pip

Philander(er) Flirt, Lothario, Playboy, Toyer, ➤ TRIFLE, Wolf, Womaniser

Philanthropist, Philanthropy Altruist, Benefactor, Carnegie, Charity, Coram, Donor, Nobel, Rockefeller, Samaritan, Shaftesbury, Tate, Wilberforce

Philately Timbromania

Phileas Fogg

▶ **Philip** see PHIL

Philippic Diatribe, Invective, Tirade

Philippine(s) Bisayan, Igorot, Moro, PI, RP, Tagalog, Visayan

Philistine, Philistinism Artless, Ashdod, Barbarian, Foe, Gaza, Gath, Gigman, Goliath, Goth, Lowbrow, Podsnappery, Vandal

Philology Linguistics, Semantics, Speechcraft

Philosopher, Philosophy Abelard, Academist, Activism, Ahimsa, Amiel, Anacharsis, Anaxagoras, Anaximander, Anaximenes, Anthrosophy, Antinomianism, Antiochian, Antiochene, Antisthenes, Apemanthus, Apollonius, Aquinas, Aristippus, Aristotle, Atomist, Attitude, Aver, Averr(h)oism, Avicenna, Ayer, Bacon, Bentham, Bergson, Berkeley, Boethius, Bosanquet, Callisthenes, Campanella, Cartesian, Casuist, Chrysippus, Cicero, Cleanthes, Comte, Comtism, Confucius, Cracker-barrel, Croce, Cynic, Cyreniac, Deipnosophist, Democritus, Deontology, Descartes, Dewey, Diderot, Diogenes, Eclectic, Eleatic, Emerson, Empedocles, Empiricism, Engels, Epicurus, Epistemology, Erasmus, Erigena, Ethics, Euhemerus, Existentialism, Foucault, Godwin, Gymnosophist, Harrison, Hegel, Heidegger, Heraclitus, Herbart, Herder, Hobbes, Hobbism, Holist, Hume, Hypatia, I Ching, Ideology, -ism, Kaizer, Kant, Kierkegaard, Leibniz, Leucippus, Locke, Lucretius, Mach, Malthus, Marcuse, Marxism, Materialism, Megarian, Mencius, Meng-tse, Menippus, Metaphysician, Mill, Monism, Montesquieu, Neoplatonism, Neoteric, Nietzsche, Nominalist, Occamist, Occam's razor, Ockhamist, Old Moore, Opinion, Ortega, Paine, Parmenides, Pascal, Peripatetic, Plato, Plotinus, Plutarch, Populism, Positivism, Protagoras, Pyrrho, Pythagoras, Renan, Rosminian, Rousseau, Russell, Sage, Sankhya, Sartre, Sceptic, Schelling, Schoolman, Schopenhauer, Scotus, Seneca, Sensist, Smith, Socrates, Sophist, Spencer, Spinoza, Steiner, Stoic, Swedenborg, Taine, Taoism, Thales, Theosophy, Thomist, Transcendentalism, Ultraism, Vedanta, Weil, Whitehead, Wittgenstein, Wolf, Xenocrates, Xenophanes, Xenophon, Yoga, Yogi, Zeno

Philosophic(al) Rational, Resigned, Thoughtful, Tranquil

Philtre Aphrodisiac, Charm, Drug, Hippomanes, Potion

Phlegm(atic) Calm, Composed, Pituita(ry), Pituite, Stolid, Unperturbed, Unruffled

Phloem Leptome

Phobia Aversion, Dread, Fear, Thing

Phoebe, Phoebus Apollo, Artemis, Day-star, Deaconess, Moon, Selene, Sol, Sun

Phoenix Fum, Fung, Paragon, Self-begotten

Phone Bell, Blower, Call, Cellular, Dial, Intercom, Mobile, Ring

Phonetic Oral, Palaeotype, Spoken, Symbol

▷ **Phonetically** may indicate a word sounding like another

Phon(e)y Bogus, Charlatan, Counterfeit, Fake, Impostor, Poseur, ➤ SHAM, Specious, Spurious

▷ **Phony** may indicate an anagram

Phosphate Monazite, Torbernite, Vivianite, Wavellite, Xenotime

Phosphor(escent), Phosphorus Briming, Foxfire, Luminescent, Noctilucent, P, Pyrosome, Sarin, Tabun

Photo(copy), Photograph(ic), Photography, Photo finish Ambrotype, Angiogram, Calotype, Close-up, Composite, Contre-jour, Daguerrotype, Diazo, Duplicate, Enprint, Exposure, Ferrotype, Film, Flash, Headshot, Heliotype, Hologram, Infra-red, Kallitype, Kirlian, Kodak®, Microdot, Microfilm, Monochrome, Mugshot, Negative, Opaline, Panel, Picture, Positive, Print, Resorcin, Rotograph, Rotogravure, Sepia, Shoot, Shot, Shutterbug, Snap, Still, Take, Talbotype, Time-lapse, Tintype, Topo, Trimetrogon, Vignette, Woodburytype, X-ray

Photographer Brandt, Cameraman, Cameron, Cartier-Bresson, Daguerre, Paparazzo, Schlierin, Talbot

Phrase Buzzword, Catch(word), Cliché, Comma, Expression, Heroic, Laconism, Leitmotiv, Locution, Mantra, Phr, Refrain, Riff, Slogan, Tag, Term

Phrygian Midas

Phthisis Decay, TB

Phylactery Amulet, Talisman, Tefillin, Tephillin

Phyllopod Brine-shrimp

Physic(s) Cryogenics, Culver's, Cure, Dose, Kinematics, Medicine, Nuclear, Nucleonics, Particle, Purge, Remedy, Rheology, Science, Thermodynamics

Physical Bodily, Carnal, Corpor(e)al, Material, Natural, Tangible

Physician Allopath, Doctor, Galen, Hakim, Harvey, Hippocrates, Internist, Leech, Linacre, Lister, Medic(o), Mesmer, Mindererus, Paean, Paracelsus, Practitioner, Quack, Roget, Therapist, Time

Physicist Alfren, Ampere, Angstrom, Appleton, Archimedes, Avogadro, Becquerel, Bohr, Born, Bose, Bragg, Brewster, Carnot, Cockcroft, Coulomb, Crookes, Curie, Dalton, Davisson, Debye, Einstein, Faraday, Fermi, Galileo, Gauss, Geiger, Giorgi, Hahn, Hawking, Heaviside, Heisenberg, Henry, Hertz, Huygens, Joliot-Curie, Josephson, Joule, Kirchhoff, Landau, Lawe, Lodge, Lorentz, Mach, Marconi, Newton, Oersted, Ohm, Oppenheimer, Pauli, Pic(c)ard, Planck, Popov, Reaumur, Ro(e)ntgen, Scientist, Stark, Torricelli, Van Allen, Volta, Young

Physiognomist, Physiognomy Face, Features, Lavater

Physiologist Pavlov

Physiotherapist Masseur

Physique Body, Build, Figure

Pi, Pious Devotional, Devout, Fraud, Gallio, God-fearing, Godly, Holy, Mid-Victorian, Sanctimonious, Savoury, Smug, Zaddik

Pianist Anda, Hambourg, Hess, Hofmann, Liszt, Morton, Pachmann, Padarewski, Tatum, Vamper, Virtuoso

Piano Bechstein, Celesta, Celeste, Concert grand, Cottage, Flugel, Forte, Grand, Honkytonk, Keyboard, Overstrung, P, Player, Softly, Steinway, Stride, Upright

Piano-maker Erard

Picaroon Brigand, Corsair, Pirate, Rogue

Piccadilly Whist

Piccolo Ottavino

Pick(er), Picking, Pick up Break, Choice, ➤ CHOOSE, Cream, Cull, Elite, Flower, Gather, Glean, Hack, Hopper, Mattock, Nap, Nibble, Oakum, Plectrum, Pluck, Plum, Select, Single, Sort, Steal, Strum, Tong, Wale

▷ **Picked** may indicate an anagram

Picket Demonstrate, Pale, Palisade, Protester, Stake, Tether, Tie

Pickings Harvest, Profits, Scrounging, Spoils

Pickle(r) Achar, Brine, Cabbage, Caper, Chow-chow, Chutney, Corn, Cure, Dilemma, Dill, Eisel, Esile, Gherkin, Girkin, Jam, Kimchi, Marinade, Marinate, Mess, Mull, Olive, Onion, Peculate, Peregrine, Piccalilli, ➤ PLIGHT, Samp(h)ire, Scrape, Souse, Vinegar, Wolly

Picklock Oustiti, Peterman

Pick-me-up Bracer, Drink, Restorer, Reviver, Tonic

Pickpocket Adept, Bung, Cly-faker, Cutpurse, Dip, Diver, Fagin, File, Nipper, Wire

Pick-up Arrest, Light o'love, Truck, Ute

Picnic Alfresco, Braaivleis, Clambake, Fun, Outing, Push-over, Spread, Wase-goose, Wayzgoose

Picture(s) Anaglyph, Arpillera, Art, Bambocciades, Bitmap, Canvas, Collage, Cyclorama, Decoupage, Depict, Describe, Diptych, Drawing, Drypoint, Emblem, Epitome, Etching, Film, Flick, Fresco, Gouache, Graphic, Histogram, Icon, Identikit®, Imagery, Inset, Kakemono, Landscape, Likeness, Lithograph, Montage, Motion, Movie, Movy, Mugshot, Myriorama, Oil, Photo, Photomosaic, Photomural, Pin-up, Pix, Plate, Polyptych, Portrait, Predella, Prent, Presentment, Print, Retraitt, Retrate, Scene, Shot, Slide, Snapshot, Stereogram, Stereograph, Still-life, Table(au), Talkie, Transfer, Transparency, Vanitas, Vision, Vraisemblance

Picturesque Idyllic, Scenic

Pidgin Chinook jargon, Creole, Fanagalo, Fanakalo, Tok Pisin

Pie(s) Anna, Banoffee, Battalia, Bridie, Chewet, Cottage, Custard, Easy, Flan, Hash, Humble, Madge, Mess, Pandowdy, Pastry, Pasty, Patty, Périgord, Pica, Piet, Pirog, Pizza, Pyat, Pyet, Pyot, Quiche, Resurrection, Shepherd's, Shoofly, Spoil, Squab, Star(ry)-gazy, Tart, Tarte tatin, Turnover, Tyropitta, Umble, Vol-au-vent, Warden

▷ **Pie** may indicate an anagram

Piebald Calico, Dappled, Motley, Pied, Pinto, Skewbald

Piece(s) Add, Bishop, Bit, Blot, Cameo, Cannon, Charm, ➤ CHESSMAN, Chip, Chunk, Coin, Companion, Component, Concerto, Crumb, Domino, End, Extract, Flitters, Fragment, Frust, Goring, Haet, Hait, Hunk, Item, Join, Mammock, Mite, Money, Morceau, Morsel, Nip, Novelette, Oddment,

Off-cut, Ort, Part, Party, Patch, Pawn, Peso, Pistareen, ➤ PORTION, Recital, Scliff, Scrap, Section, Set, Shard, Sherd, Skliff, Slice, Sliver, Sou, Speck, Stub, Swatch, Tait, Tate, Tile, Toccata, Truncheon, Wedge

Pièce de resistance Star-turn

Piecemeal, Piecework Gradually, Intermittent, Jigsaw, Serial, Tut

Pie-crust Coffin, Lid, Pastry

Pied-à-terre Nest, Pad

Pieman Shepherd

Pier(s) Anta, Groyne, Jetty, Jutty, Landing, Mole, Plowman, Quay, Slipway, Swiss roll, Wharf

Pierce(d), Piercer, Piercing Accloy, Awl, Broach, Cleave, Dart, Drill, Endart, Fenestrate(d), Gimlet, Gore, Gride, Gryde, Hull, Impale, Jag, Keen, Lance, Lancinate, Lobe, Move, Needle, Penetrate, Perforate, Pike, Poignant, Punch, Puncture, Riddle, Rive, Shrill, Skewer, Slap, Sleeper, Spear, Spike, Spit, Stab, Steek, Stiletto, Sting, Thirl, Thrill(ant)

Piety Devotion, Purity, Sanctity

Piffle Bilge, Codswallop, Hogwash, Tommy-rot, Twaddle

Pig(s), Pigskin Anthony, Babe, Babirusa, Barrow, Bartholomew, Bessemer, Bland, Boar, Bonham, Bush, Captain Cooker, Doll, Duroc, Elt, Farrow, Fastback, Football, Gadarene, Gilt, Glutton, Gride, Grumphie, Guffie, Guinea, Gus, Ham, Hog, Ingot, Iron, Javelina, Kentledge, Kintledge, Lacombe, Landrace, Large black, Large white, Lingot, Long, Napoleon, Peccary, Policeman, Pork(er), Razorback, Rosser, Runt, Saddleback, Shoat, Shot(e), Shott, Slip, Snowball, Sounder, Sow, Squealer, Suid(ae), Tamworth, Tayassuid, Tithe, Toe, Vietnamese pot-bellied, Warthog, Yelt

Pig-disease Bullnose

Pigeon Archangel, Barb, Bird, Cape, Carrier, Clay, Cropper, Culver, Dove, Fantail, Goura, Gull, Homer, Homing, Horseman, Jacobin, Kuku, Manumea, Nun, Owl, Passenger, Peristeronic, Pouter, Ringdove, Rock(er), Roller, Ront(e), Ruff, Runt, Scandaroon, Solitaire, Spot, Squab, Squealer, Stock-dove, Stool, Talkie-talkee, Tippler, Tumbler, Turbit, Wonga-wonga, Zoozoo

Pigeonhole Classify, Compartment, File, Postpone, Shelve, Slot, Stereotype

Pigeon-house Columbary, Cote, Dovecot(e)

Pig-food Mast, Swill

Pig-iron Kentledge, Kintledge

Pigment(ation) Anthoclore, Anthocyan(in), Argyria, Betacyanin, Bilirubin, Biliverdin, Bister, Bistre, Bronzing, Cappagh-brown, Carmine, Carotene, Carotenoid, Carotin, Carotinoid, Chlorophyll, Chrome, Chromogen, Cobalt, Colcothar, Colour, Dye, Etiolin, Flavin(e), Fucoxanthin, Gamboge, Gossypol, Haem, H(a)emocyanin, H(a)emoglobin, Hem(e), Iodopsin, Lamp-black, Lithopone, Liverspot, Lutein, Luteolin, Madder, Melanin, Naevus, Nigrosine, Ochre, Opsin, Orpiment, Paris-green, Phthalocyanine, Phycoerythrin, Phycoxanthin, Phytochrome, Porphyrin, Pterin, Quercetin, Realgar, Red lead, Respiratory, Retinene, Rhiboflavin, Rhodopsin, Sepia,

Sienna, Sinopia, Smalt, Tapetum, Tempera, Terre-verte, Tincture, Umber, Urochrome, Verditer, Viridian, Xanthophyll, Xanthopterin

Pigtail Braid, Cue, Plait, Queue

Pi jaw Cant

Pike Assegai, Crag, Dory, Fogash, Gar(fish), Ged, Gisarme, Glaive, Hie, Holostei, Javelin, Lance, Luce, Partisan, Pickerel, Ravensbill, Scafell, Snoek, Spear, Speed, Spontoon, Vouge, Walleyed

▶ **Pilaster** see PILLAR

Pile(d), Piles, Piling Agger, Atomic, Bing, Bomb, Camp-sheathing, Camp-shedding, Camp-sheeting, Camp-shot, Clamp, Cock, Column, Crowd, Deal, Down, Emerods, Farmers, Fender, Fig, Floccus, Fortune, Hair, Heap, Hept, Historic, Hoard, Load, Lot, Marleys, Mass, Nap, Post, Pyre, Raft, Reactor, Ream(s), Rouleau, Shag, ▶ STACK, Starling, Stilt, Trichome, Upheap, Voltaic, Wealth, Windrow, Wodge

Pile-driver Tup

Pilfer(ing) Crib, Filch, Finger, Maraud, Miche, Nick, Peculate, Pickery, Pickle, Pinch, Plagiarise, Plunder, Purloin, Snitch, ▶ STEAL

Pilgrim(age) Aske, Childe Harold, Expedition, Fatima, Hadj(i), Hajj(i), Loreto, Lourdes, Mecca, Palmer, Pardoner, Reeve, Scallop-shell, Shrine, Voyage, Yatra

Pill Ball, Bitter, Bolus, Caplet, Capsule, Dex, Doll, Dose, Globule, Lob, Medicine, Number nine, Peel, Pellet, Pilula, Pilule, Placebo, Poison, Protoplasmal, Sleeping, Spansule, Tablet, Troche, Trochisk, Upper

Pillage Booty, Devastate, Plunder, Ransack, Rapine, Ravage, Razzia, Robbery, Sack, Spoil

Pillar(ed), Pillars Anta, Apostle, Atlantes, Baluster, Balustrade, Boaz, Canton, Caryatides, Cippus, Columel, Column, Eustyle, Gendarme, Hercules, Herm, Impost, Islam, Jachin, Lat, Man, Modiolus, Monolith, Newel, Obelisk, Pedestal, Peristyle, Pier, Post, Respond, Stalactite, Stalagmite, Stoop, Telamon, Trumeau

Pillion Cushion, Pad, Rear

Pillory Cang(ue), Cippus, Crucify, Jougs, Little-ease, Pelt, Satirise, Slam

Pillow(case) Bear, Beer, Bere, Bolster, Cod, Cushion, Headrest, Pad

Pilot Ace, Airman, Auto(matic), Aviator, Captain, ▶ CONDUCT, Experimental, George, Govern, Guide, Hobbler, Lead, Lodesman, Palinure, Palinurus, Pitt, Prune, Shipman, Steer, Test, Tiphys, Trial, Usher, Wingman

Pimento Allspice

Pimp Apple-squire, Bludger, Fleshmonger, Hoon, Mack, Pandarus, Pander, Ponce, Procurer, Solicit, Souteneur

Pimpernel Scarlet, Wincopipe, Wink-a-peep

Pimple, Pimply Blackhead, Botch, Gooseflesh, Grog-blossom, Hickey, Horripilation, Papula, Plook, Plouk, Pock, Pustule, Quat, Rumblossom, Rum-bud, Spot, Uredinial, Wen, Whelk, Whitehead, Zit

Pin Bayonet, Belaying, Bolt, Brooch, Cotter, Dowel, Drawing, Drift, Fasten, Fid, Firing, Fix, Gam, Gudgeon, Hairgrip, Hob, Joggle, Kevel, Needle, Nog,

Panel, Peg, Pivot, Preen, Rivet, Rolling, Safety, SCART, Scatter, Shear, Skewer, Skittle, Skiver, Spike, Spindle, Split, Staple, Stump, Swivel, Thole, Thumbtack, Tre(e)nail, U-bolt, Woolder

Pinafore Apron, Brat, HMS, Overall, Pinny, Save-all, Tire

Pince-nez Nose-nippers

Pincers Chela, Claw, Forceps, Forfex, Nipper, Tweezers

Pinch(ed) Arrest, Bit, Bone, Chack, Constrict, Cramp, Crisis, Emergency, Gaunt, Misappropriate, Nab, Nick, Nim, Nip, Peculate, Peel, Pilfer, Pocket, Pook(it), Prig, Pugil, Raft, Rob, Scrimp, Scrounge, Skimp, Smatch, Snabble, Snaffle, Sneak, Sneap, Sneeshing, Snuff, Squeeze, ➤ STEAL, Swipe, Tate, Tweak, Twinge

Pine(s), Pining Arolla, Bristlecone, Celery, Cembra, Chile, Cone, Conifer, Cypress, Dwine, Droop, Earn, Erne, Fret, Ground, Hone, Hoop, Huon, Jack, Jeffrey, Kauri, Languish, Languor, Loblolly, Long, Longleaf, Monkey-puzzle, Picea, Pitch, Radiata, Scotch, Scots, Softwood, Spruce, Starve, Stone, Sugar, Tree, Umbrella, Urman, Waste, Yearn

Pineapple Anana, Bomb, Bromelia, Grenade, Pina, Poll, Sorosis, Tillandsia

Ping Knock, Whir(r)

Pinguin Anana(s)

Pinion Fetter, Penne, Pinnoed, Secure, Shackle, Wing

Pink Blush, Carolina, Castory, Clove, Colour, Coral, Dianthus, Emperce, Gillyflower, Knock, Lake, Lychnis, Moss, Oyster, Peak, Perce, Pierce, Pompadour, Pounce, Rose(ate), Salmon, Scallop, Shell, Shocking, Shrimp, Spigelia, Spit, Stab, Tiny

Pinnacle Acme, Apex, Crest, Crown, Height, Needle, Summit

Pinniped Seal

Pin-point Focus, Identify, Isolate, Localise

Pint Jar, Log

Pintail Duck, Smeath, Smee(th)

Pin-up Cheesecake, Star

Pioneer Baird, Bandeirante, Blaze, Boone, Colonist, Emigrant, Explore, Fargo, Fleming, Frontiersman, Harbinger, Innovator, Lead, Marconi, Oecist, Pathfinder, Rochdale, Sandgroper, Spearhead, Settler, Trail-blazer, Trekker, Voortrekker, Wells

Pious Craw-thumper

▶ **Pious** see PI

Pip Ace, Acinus, Blackball, Bleep, Hip, Hump, Phil, Pyrene, Seed, Star

Pipe(s), Piper, Pipeline, Piping Antara, Aorta, Aulos, Balance, Barrel, Blub, Bong, Broseley, Bubble, Call, Calumet, Cheep, Cherrywood, Chibouk, Chibouque, Chillum, Churchwarden, Clay, Conduit, Corncob, Crane, Cutty, Downcomer, Drain, Dry riser, Duct, Dudeen, Dudheen, Ell, Exhaust, Faucet, Fistula, Flue, Flute, Gage, Gedact, Gedeckt, Hod, Hogger, Hooka(h), Hose, Hubble-bubble, Hydrant, Kalian, Kelly, Mains, Manifold, Marsyas, Meerschaum, Mirliton, Montre, Narghile, Nargile(h), Narg(h)il(l)y, Oat(en), Oboe, Peace, Pepper, Pibroch, Piccolo, Pied, Pifferaro, Pitch, Poverty, Pule, Qanat, Quill, Recorder, Ree(d), Rise,

Sack-doudling, Salicional, Sennit, Serpent, Shalm, Shawm, Shrike, Siphon, Skirl, Sluice, Soil, Squeak, Stack, Standpipe, Stummel, Syrinx, Tibia, Tootle, Trachea, Tube, Tubule, Tweet, U-bend, Uillean(n), Union, Uptake, Waste, Water(-spout), Weasand, Whistle

Pipefish Sea-adder

Pipe-laying Graft

Pipit Bird, Skylark, Titlark

Pippin Apple, Orange, Ribston

Pipsqueak Nobody

Piquancy, Piquant Pungent, Racy, Relish, Salt, Sharp, Spicy, Tangy

Pique Dod, Huff, Resentment, Titillate

Piracy, Pirate, Piratical Algerine, Barbarossa, Blackbeard, Boarder, Bootleg, Brigand, Buccaneer, Buccanier, Cateran, Condottier, Conrad, Corsair, Crib, Dampier, Fil(l)ibuster, Flint, Hijack, Hook, Kidd, Lift, Loot, Picaro(on), Pickaroon, Plagiarise, Plunder, Rakish, Rover, Sallee-man, Sallee-rover, Sea-king, Sea-rat, Sea-robber, Silver, Smee, Steal, Teach, Viking, Water-rat, Water-thief

Piranha Caribe, Characinoid, Piraya

Pistillate Female

Pistol Air, Ancient, Automatic, Barker, Colt®, Dag, Derringer, Gat, ➤ GUN, Hackbut, Horse, Luger®, Pepperbox, Petronel, Revolver, Rod, Shooter, Starter, Starting, Very, Water, Weapon

Piston Four-stroke, Plunger, Ram, Trunk

Pit(ted) Abyss, Alveolus, Antrum, Catch, Cave, Cesspool, Chasm, Cloaca, Colliery, Crater, Den, Depth, Depression, Dungmere, Ensile, Fossa, Fovea, Foxhole, Hangi, Heapstead, Hell, Hole, Hollow, Inferno, Khud, Lacunose, Mark, Match, ➤ MINE, Mosh, Orchestra, Parterre, Pip, Play, Pock, Pock-mark, Punctate, Putamen, Pyrene, Ravine, Scrobicule, Silo, Soakaway, Solar plexus, Stone, Sump, Tar, Trap, Trou-de-loup

Pitch(ed) Absolute, Asphalt, Atilt, Attune, Bitumen, Coal-tar, Concert, Crease, Diamond, Dive, Ela, Elect, Encamp, Erect, Establish, Fever, Fling, Fork, Ground, Intonation, Key, Labour, Length, Level, Lurch, Maltha, Neume, Patter, Peck, Perfect, Pight, Pin, Plong(e), Plunge, Pop, Resin, Rock, Ruff(e), Scend, Seel, Send, Shape, Sling, Slope, Spiel, Stoit, Tar, Tessitura, Tilt, Tone, Tonemic, Tonus, Tune, Wicket

Pitchblende Cleveite

Pitcher(-shaped) Ascidium, Aryt(a)enoid, Bowler, Cruse, Ewer, Jug, Steen, Urceolus

Pitchfork Hurl, Toss

Pitfall Danger, Hazard, Trap

Pith(y) Ambatch, Aphorism, Apo(ph)thegm, Core, Down, Essence, Gnomic, Hat-plant, Heart, Marrow, Medulla, Moxa, Nucleus, Rag, Succinct, Terse

Pithead Broo, Brow, Minehead

Pithless Thowless

Pitiless Flint-hearted, Hard, Ruthless

Piton Rurp

Pitt Chatham

Pity, Piteous, Pitiful Ah, Alack, Alas, Commiseration, ➤ COMPASSION,
Mercy, Pathos, Rue, Ruth(ful), Seely, Shame, Sin, Sympathy

Pivot(al) Ax(i)le, Central, Focal, Fulcrum, Gooseneck, Gudgeon, Kingbolt,
Revolve, Rotate, Slue, ➤ SWIVEL, Trunnion, Turn, Wheel

Pixie Brownie, Elf, Fairy, Gremlin, Sprite

Pizza Calzone, Pepperoni

Placard Affiche, Bill, Playbill, Poster

Placate Propitiate

Place Aim, Allocate, Berth, Bro, Decimal, Deploy, Deposit, Fix, Habitat,
Hither, Howf, Identify, Impose, ➤ IN PLACE OF, Install, Job, Joint,
Juxtapose, Lay, Lieu, Locality, Locate, Locus, Pitch, Plat, Plaza, Point, Posit,
➤ POSITION, Put, Realm, Region, Scene, Second, Set, Site, Situate,
Situation, Spot, Stead, Sted(e), Stedd(e), Stratify, Town, Vendome

Placid Cool, Easy, Easy-osy, Quiet, Tame, Tranquil

Plagiarise, Plagiarist Copy, Crib, Lift, Pirate, Steal

Plague (spot) Annoy, Bane, Bedevil, Black death, Boil, Bubonic, Burden,
Curse, Dog, Dun, Goodyear, Goujeers, Harry, Infestation, Locusts, Lues,
Murrain, Murran, Murrin, Murrion, Pest, Pester, Pox, Press, Scourge, Tease,
Token, Torture, Try, Vex

Plaid Maud, Roon, Tartan, Wales

Plain(s) Abraham, Archimedes, Artless, Ascetic, Bald, Banat, Bare, Blatant,
Broad, Campo, Candid, Carse, Chryse, Clavius, Clear, Cook, Dowdy,
Downright, Dry, Evident, Explicit, Flat, Girondist, Homely, Homespun,
Inornate, Kar(r)oo, Lande, Langrenus, Llano, Lombardy, Lowland, Maidan,
Manifest, Marathon, Mare, Monochrome, Nullarbor, Obvious, Oceanus
Procellarum, Olympia, ➤ ORDINARY, Outspoken, Overt, Pampa(s),
Paramo, Patent, Pikestaff, Playa, Polje, Prairie, Ptolemaeus, Purbach,
Sabkha(h), Sabkha(t), Sailing, Salisbury, Savanna(h), Secco, Sharon,
Simple, Sodom, Spoken, Steppe, Tableland, Tundra, Vega, Veldt, Visible

Plainsman Llanero

Plainsong Ambrosian, Chant

Plaint(ive) Complaint, Dirge, Lagrimoso, Lament, Melancholy, Sad, Whiny

Plaintiff Doe, Impeacher, Litigant, Suer

Plait Braid, Crimp, Cue, Frounce, Furbelow, Goffer, Pigtail, Plica, Queue,
Ruche, Sennit, Splice

Plan(ned), Planner, Planning Aim, Angle, Arrange, Architect,
Axonometric, Blueprint, Budget, Chart, Complot, Contrive, Dart,
Deliberate, Design, Desyne, Device, Devise, Diagram, Draft, Drawing,
Elevation, Engineer, Format, Hang, Ichnography, Idea, Intent, Lay(out),
Map, Marshall, Mastermind, Outline, Pattern, Pipe-dream, Plat, Plot, Ploy,
Policy, Premeditate, Prepense, Procedure, Programme, Project, Projet,
Proposal, Protraction, Scenario, Schedule, Scheme, Spec(ification),
Stratagem, Strategy, Subterfuge, System, Town, Wheeze

Plane Aero(dyne), Air, ➤ AIRCRAFT, Airliner, Airship, Bandit, Boeing,
Bomber, Bus, Camel, Canard, Cartesian, Chenar, Chinar, Comet,

Concorde, Crate, Dakota, Datum, Delta-wing, Even, Facet, Fault, Fillester, Fillister, Flat, Glider, Gotha, Hurricane, Icosahedron, Icosohedra, Jack, Jet, Jointer, Jumbo, Level, MIG, Mirage, Mosquito, Moth, Octagon, Platanus, Polygon, Rocket, Router, Shackleton, Shave, Smooth, Sole, Spitfire, Spokeshave, STOL, Surface, Sycamore, Taube, Thrust, Trainer, Tree, Trident, Viscount

Plane figure Endecagon, Hendecagon

Planet(ary) Alphonsine, Ariel, Asteroid, Body, Cabiri, Ceres, Chiron, Constellation, Earth, Eros, Hyleg, Inferior, Jovian, Jupiter, Mars, Mercury, Moon, Neptune, Pluto, Psyche, Quartile, Saturn, Sphere, Starry, Sun, Superior, Terrestrial, Uranus, Venus, Vista, Vulcan, World

Plangent Mournful

Plank Board, Chess, Duckboard, Garboard, Plonk, Sarking, Slab, Spirketting, Straik, Strake, Stringer, Wood

Plankton Neuston, Pelagic, Seston, Spatfall

Plant (part) Annual, Anther, Bed, Biennial, Biota, Cultigen, Cultivar, Dibble, Ecad, Embed, Endogen, Enrace, Epiphyte, Establish, Factory, Fix, Growth, Herbarium, Insert, Instil, Inter, Labiate, Land, Machinery, Ornamental, Sere, Shrub, Sow, Succulent, Tree, Weld, Works

PLANTS

3 letters:	Yarr	Murva	Exogen
Dal	**5 letters:**	Musci	Gnetum
Kex	Ajwan	Orpin	Hyssop
Meu	Anise	Orris	Iberis
Pia	Aroid	Oshac	Knawel
Rue	Benni	Panax	Madder
Set	Blite	Sedge	Mallow
Til	Boree	Sedum	Medick
Udo	Buchu	Spink	Mimosa
Urd	Bucku	Tetra	Moorva
Yam	Bugle	Timbo	Nerium
4 letters:	Calla	Urena	Nettle
Alga	Canna	**6 letters:**	Nuphar
Aloe	Clary	Acacia	Orchis
Anil	Clote	Acorus	Orpine
Deme	Cress	Ajowan	Pachak
Fern	Fouat	Alisma	Phloem
Forb	Fouet	Alpine	Protea
Herb	Gemma	Arnica	Rattle
Ixia	Glaux	Bablah	Reseda
Kali	Gorse	Betony	Retama
Loco	Guaco	Burnet	Rubber
More	Hosta	Cactus	Sesame
Nard	Inula	Cassia	Silene
Ombu	Jalap	Catnep	Smilax
Rhus	Kenaf	Cnicus	Spider
Sego	Kudzu	Cosmea	Spurge
Sola	Lathe	Cosmos	Spurry
Sunn	Lotus	Croton	Squill
Taro	Lurgi	Datura	Styrax
Thea	Medic	Derris	Teasel
Vine	Morel	Dodder	Thrift

Tulipa
Tutsan
Yarrow
7 letters:
Alkanet
All-good
Allseed
Alyssum
Brinjal
Burdock
Caltrop
Cardoon
Carduus
Carline
Cat's ear
Chervil
Dasheen
Dioecia
Dittany
Ephedra
Filaree
Fly-trap
Freesia
Frogbit
Gentian
Gerbera
Haemony
Henbane
Ipomoea
Isoetes
Lantana
Lucerne
Lychnis
Mahonia
Melilot
Mercury
Mullein
Nemesia
Nigella
Nonsuch
Opuntia
Palmiet
Pareira
Petunia
Ragwort
Rhodora
Ruellia
Saffron
Salfern
Salsola
Sampire
Sanicle
Scandix
Setwall
Skirret

Spignel
Spiraea
Spurrey
Stapela
Syringa
Tagetes
Thallus
Triffid
Tritoma
Vanilla
Vervain
Zedoary
8 letters:
Acanthus
Agrimony
Angelica
Arenaria
Asphodel
Bindi-eye
Buckbean
Buplever
Camomile
Canaigre
Centaury
Costmary
Diandria
Dielytra
Dumbcane
Fluellin
Fumitory
Geophite
Gesnaria
Gnetales
Gromwell
Hag-taper
Henequen
Hepatica
Hibiscus
Larkspur
Lavender
Mandrake
Monstera
Oleander
Opopanax
Plumbago
Psilotum
Putchock
Ratsbane
Roly-poly
Samphire
Scammony
Self-heal
Silphium
Sparaxis
Spergula

Stapelia
Staragen
Starwort
Tamarisk
Tritonia
Tuberose
Tuckahoe
Wait-a-bit
9 letters:
Adderwort
Andromeda
Arrowroot
Artemisia
Aubrietia
Bald-money
Brooklime
Broom-rape
Butterbur
Colocasia
Coltsfoot
Cordaites
Coreopsis
Coriander
Dittander
Erythrina
Euphorbia
Eyebright
Fenugreek
Germander
Groundsel
Herb-paris
Horse-tail
Liver-wort
Lousewort
Mare's-tail
Moneywort
Moschatel
Patchouli
Pimpernel
Portulaca
Rocambole
Screwpine
Spearmint
Spearwort
Spikenard
Stone-crop
Sweet-gale
Tomatillo
Tormentil
Wake-robin
Wincopipe
Wolf's bane
10 letters:
Alexanders
Angiosperm

Aspidistra
Astralagus
Dyer's-broom
Earth-smoke
Five-finger
Fraxinella
Fritillary
Goat-sallow
Goats-thorn
Goat-willow
Goldilocks
Icosandria
Maidenhair
Mignonette
Parkleaves
Rest-harrow
Salicornia
Touch-me-not
Tropophyte
Yellowroot
11 letters:
Acidanthera
Bears-breech
Bristle-fern
Callitriche
Convolvulus
Dusty-miller
Hurtleberry
Loosestrife
Meadowsweet
Nancy-pretty
Schizophyte
Sempervivum
Thallophyte
12 letters:
Adam's flannel
Epacridaceae
Midsummer-men
Morning glory
Parsley-piert
Pasqueflower
Phytobenthos
Resurrection
Southernwood
Water-soldier
13 letters:
Townhall clock
14 letters:
Chincherinchee
Lords and ladies
Shepherd's purse

Plantagenet Angevin, Broom
Plantain Ribwort, Waybread

Plantation Arboretum, Bosket, Bosquet, Estate, Grove, Hacienda, Pen, Pinetum, Ranch, Tara, Vineyard
Plant disease Anthracnose, Bunt, Club-root, Curlytop, Frogeye, Rosette
Planted In
Planter Dibber, Farmer, Settler, Trowel
Plaque Calculus, Plateau, Scale
Plasma Dextran
Plaster(ed) Bandage, Blotto, Cake, Cataplasm, Clam, Clatch, Compo, Court, Daub, Diachylon, Diachylum, Drunk, Emplastrum, Fresco, Gesso, Grout, Gypsum, Intonaco, Leep, Lit, Mud, Mustard, Oiled, Parge(t), Poultice, Render, Scratch-coat, Screed, Secco, Shellac, Sinapism, Smalm, Smarm, Smear, Sowsed, Staff, Stookie, Stucco, Teer
Plastic Bakelite®, Cel(luloid), Ductile, Fablon®, Fictile, Fluon, Formica®, Ionomer, Laminate, Loid, Lucite, Melamine, Perspex®, Plexiglas®, Pliant, Polyethylene, Polystyrene, Polythene, Polyvinyl, PVC, Styrene, Teflon®, Urea-formaldehyde, Vinyl, Wet-look, Yielding
▷ **Plastic** may indicate an anagram
Plastic surgeon, Plastic surgery McIndoe, Neoplasty
Plate(d), Platelet, Plating Acierage, Ailette, Angle, Anode, Armadillo, Armour, Ashet, Baffle, Bakestone, Baleen, Batten, Brass, Butt, Chamfrain, Chape, Chrome, Coat, Coccolith, Copper, Cramper, Cribellum, Dasypus, Denture, Disc, Dish, Electro, Elytron, Elytrum, Enamel, Entoplastron, Fashion, Fine, Fish, Flatware, Foil, Frog, Frons, Futtock, Glacis, Gula, Home, Hot, Illustration, L, Lame, Lamella, Lamina, Lanx, Mazarine, Nail, Nef, Nickel, Notum, Ortho, Osteoderm, Paten, Patina, Patine, Pauldron, Peba, Petri, Plaque, Platter, Pleximeter, Poitrel, Prescutum, Print, Race, Riza, Rove, Salamander, Scale, Scute, Scutum, Seg, Selling, Sheffield, Shield, Silver, Slab, Soup, Spoiler, Squama, Stencil, Stereo(type), Sternite, Strake, T, Tablet, Tace, Tasse(l), Terne, Tin(ware), Torsel, Trade, Trencher, Trophy, Tuill(ett)e, Tymp, Urostegite, Vassail, Vessail, Vessel, Wall, Web, Whirtle, Wortle
Plateau Altiplano, Deccan, Fjeld, Highland, Highveld, Horst, Kar(r)oo, La Mancha, Langres, Mat(t)o Grosso, Mesa Verde, Meseta, Nilgiris, Ozark, Paramo, Piedmont, Puna, Tableland
Platform Almemar, Bandstand, Barbette, Base, Bema, Bier, Catafalque, Catwalk, Crane, Dais, Deck, Dolly, Drilling, Emplacement, Entablement, Estrade, Exedra, Exhedra, Flake, Footpace, Foretop, Gangplank, Gantry, Gauntree, Gauntry, Hustings, Kang, Machan, Pallet, Perron, Plank, Podium, Predella, Programme, Pulpit, Raft, Rig, Rostrum, Round-top, Scaffold, Shoe, Soapbox, Sponson, ➤ STAGE, Stand, Stereobate, Stoep, Stylobate, Tee, Thrall, Ticket, Top, Traverser, Tribune, Turntable
Platinum Pt, Ruthenium, Sperrylite
Platitude Bromide, Cliché, Truism
Platocephalus Flat-headed
Platonic, Platonist Academician, Ideal, Spiritual
Platoon Company, Squad, Team

Platter Dish, EP, Graal, Grail, Lanx, LP, Plate, Record, Salver, Trencher

Platypus Duckbill, Duck-mole, Water mole

Plausible, Plausibility Cogent, Credible, Fair, Glib, Oil, Probable, Proball, Sleek, Smooth, Specious

Play(ing) Accompany, Active, Amusement, Antic, Antigone, Brand, Candida, Caper, Charm, Chronicle, Clearance, Crucible, Curtain-raiser, Daff, Dandle, Docudrama, Drama, Echo, Endgame, Escapade, Everyman, Extended, Fair, Finesse, Frisk, Frolic, Fun, Gamble, Gambol, Game, Ghosts, Hamlet, Holiday, Inside, Interlude, Jam, Jape, Jest, Jeu, Kinderspiel, Laik, Lake, Latitude, Lear, Leeway, Licence, Long, Macbeth, Mask, Masque, Medal, Melodrama, Miracle, Monodrama, Morality, Mousetrap, Mummers, Mysteries, Nativity, Nurse, Oberammergau, Parallel, Passion, Perform, Personate, Portray, Prank, Pretend, Recreation, Represent, Riff, Rollick, Romp, Room, Rope, RUR, Saw, Sketch, Sport, Stage, Strain, Stroke, Strum, Tolerance, Tonguing, Toy, Tragedy, Trifle, Tweedle, Twiddle, Two-hander, Vamp, Vent, Word

▷ **Play** may indicate an anagram

Playback Echo, Repeat, Replay

Player(s) Actor, Athlete, Back, Black, Brass, Bugler, Busker, Cast, CD, Centre, Colt, Defenceman, E, East, ENSA, Equity, Fiddle, Flanker, Fullback, Gary, Goalie, Half, Harlequin, Hooker, Juke-box, Kest, Linebacker, Lineman, Lion, Lock, Longstop, Lutanist, Lutenist, Man, Midfield, Mid-on, Mime, Musician, N, Nero, North, Onside, Orpheus, Pagliacci, Participant, Pianola®, Pitcher, Pone, Pro, Prop, Quarterback, Rover, S, Scrape, Scratch, Seagull, Secondo, Seed, Shortstop, Side, South, Split end, Stand-off, Stereo, Strolling, Super, Sweeper, Team, Thespian, Troubador, Troupe, Upright, Virtuosi, W, West, White, Wing

Playfair Code

Playfellow Actor, Chum, Companion

Playful Arch, Coy, Frisky, Humorous, Kittenish, Ludic, Merry, Piacevole, Scherzo, Skittish, Sportive

Playgirl Actress, Electra

Playground Close, Garden, Park, Rec(reational), Theatre, Tot lot, Yard

Playhouse Amphitheatre, Cinema, Theatre, Wendy

Playsuit Rompers

Playwright Aeschylus, Albee, Arden, Ayckbourn, Barrie, Barry, Beaumarchais, Beaumont, Beckett, Behan, Bellow, Bennett, Besier, Bolt, Brecht, Chekhov, Congreve, Corneille, Coward, Dekker, Delaney, ➤ DRAMATIST, Dramaturge, Dramaturgist, Drinkwater, Euripides, Fletcher, Fry, Gems, Genet, Goldoni, Gorky, Harwood, Hay, Ibsen, Jonson, Marlowe, Massinger, Menander, Miller, Molière, Mortimer, O'Casey, Odets, O'Neill, Orton, Osborne, Pinero, Pinter, Pirandello, Priestley, Racine, Rattigan, Scriptwriter, Shaw, Sheridan, Sherry, Simpson, Sophocles, Stoppard, Storey, Strindberg, Synge, Tate, Terence, Thespis, Travers, Vanbrugh, Webster, Wesker, Wilde

Plea Appeal, Claim, Defence, Entreaty, Excuse, Exoration, Orison, Placitum, Prayer, Rebuttal, Rebutter, Rogation, Suit

Plead(er) Answer, Argue, Beg, Entreat, ➤ IMPLORE, Intercede, Litigate, Moot, Vakeel, Vakil

Please(d), Pleasant, Pleasing, Pleasure(-seeker) Aggrate, Agreeable, Alcina, Algolagnia, Amene, Amuse, Arride, Bitte, Braw, Cheerful, Chuffed, Comely, Comfort, Content, Cute, Delice, Delight, Do, Euphonic, Fair, Felicitous, Fit, Flatter, Fun, Genial, Glad, Gladness, Gratify, Hedonism, Jammy, Joy, Kama, Kindly, Lepid, List, Oblige, Piacevole, Primrose path, Prithee, Prythee, Satisfy, Suit, Tasty, Tickle, Treat, Vanity, Voluptuary, Will, Winsome, Wrapped, Xanadu List

Pleasure-garden, Pleasure-ground Lung, Oasis, Park, Policy, Ranelagh, Tivoli

Pleat Accordion, Box, Crimp, Fold, French, Frill, Goffer, Gusset, Kick, Knife, Plait, Pranck(e), Prank, Sunburst, Sunray

Pleb(eian) Common, Homely, Laic, Ordinary, Roturier

Pledge Affidavit, Arles, Band, Betroth, Bond, Borrow, Bottomry, Dedicate, Deposit, Earnest(-penny), Engage, Fine, Gage, Guarantee, Hypothecate, Hock, Impignorate, Mortgage, Oath, Pass, Pawn, Pignerate, Pignorate, Plight, Propine, Sacrament, Security, Stake, Surety, Teetotal, Toast, Troth, Undertake, Vow, Wad, Wed

Pleiades Alcyone, Celaeno, Electra, Maia, Merope, Sterope, Taygete

Plentiful, Plenty Abounding, Abundance, Abundant, Ample, Bags, Copious, Copy, Easy, Excess, Foison, Fouth, Ful(l)ness, Fushion, Galore, Goshen, Lashings, Lots, Oodles, Pleroma, Profusion, Quantity, Riches, Rife, Routh, Rowth, Scouth, Scowth, Slue, Sonce, Sonse, Umpteen

Plenum Spaceless

Pliable, Pliant Amenable, Flexible, Limber, Limp, Lithe, Malleable, Plastic, Supple, Swack, Swank

▶ **Pliers** see PLY

Plight Betrothal, Case, Misdight, Peril, Pickle, Pledge, State, Troth

Plimsoll(s) Dap, Gutty, Gym-shoe, Line, Mutton-dummies, Sandshoe, Tacky

Plinth Acroter, Base, Block, Stand

Plod(der) Drudge, Ploughman, Traipse, Tramp, Trog, Trudge

Plonk Rotgut, Wine

Plop Cloop, Drop, Fall, Plap, Plump

Plot(s) Allotment, Babington, Bed, Brew, Carpet, Chart, Cliché, Connive, Conspiracy, Conspire, Covin, Covyne, Engineer, Erf, Erven, Frame-up, Graph, Gunpowder, Imbroglio, Intrigue, Locus, Lot, Machination, Map, Meal-tub, Odograph, Pack, Patch, Plan, Plat, Rye-house, Scenario, ➤ SCHEME, Sect(ion), Shot, Site, Story, Taluk, Terf, Turf, Web

Plotter Artist, Cabal, Camarilla, Catesby, Conspirator, Engineer, Oates, Schemer

Plough(man), Ploughed Arable, Ard, Arval, Big Dipper, Bull tongue, Chamfer, Charles's wain, Dipper, Disc, Ear, Earth-board, Ere, Fail, Fallow,

Farmer, Feer, Flunk, Gadsman, Gang, Great bear, Harrow, Lister, Middlebreaker, Middlebuster, Piers, Pip, Push, Rafter, Rib, Rive, Rove, Scooter, Septentrion(e)s, Sill, Sow, Till(er), Triones

Plough-cleaner Pattle, Pettle

Ploughshare Co(u)lter, Sock

Ploughwise Boustrophedon

Plover Bud, Lapwing, Pretincole, Prostitute, Stand, Tewit, Wing

Plowman Piers

Ploy Brinkmanship, Dodge, Manoeuvre, Stratagem, Strike, Tactic, Wile

Pluck(ing), Plucky Avulse, Bare, Carphology, Cock, Courage, Deplume, Epilate, Evulse, Floccillation, Gallus, Game, ➤ GRIT, Guts, Loot, Mettle, Pick, Pinch, Pip, Pizzicato, Plectron, Plectrum, Ploat, Plot, Plunk, Pook(it), Pouk(it), Pull, Race, Scrappy, Snatch, Spin, Spirit, Spunk, Summon, Tug, Twang, Tweak, Tweeze, Yank

Plug Ad, Banana, Block, Bung, Caulk, Chew, Commercial, Dam, DIN, Dook, Dossil, Dottle, Douk, Fipple, Fother, Hype, Jack, Lam, Operculum, Pessary, Prod, Promote, Publicity, Ram, Recommendation, Spark(ing), Spile, Spiling, Stop(per), Stopple, Strobili, Suppository, Tampion, Tap, Tompion, Tent, Wander, Wedge

Plum Bullace, Cherry, Choice, Damson, Gage, Greengage, Ground, Japanese, Kaki, Mammee-sapota, Marmalade, Maroon, Mirabelle, Mussel, Myrobalan, Naseberry, Persimmon, Proin(e), Pruin(e), Prune, Quetsch, Raisin, Sapodilla, Sebesten, Victoria

Plumage, Plume Aigrette, Crest, Egret, Feather, Hackle, Panache, Preen, Ptilosis, Quill

Plumb(er) Bullet, Dredge, Fathom, Lead(sman), Perpendicular, Plummet, Sheer, Sound, Test, True, Vertical

Plumbago Graphite

Plummet Dive, Drop, Lead, ➤ PLUNGE

Plump(er) Bold, Bonnie, Bonny, Buxom, Chubbed, Choose, Chubby, Dumpy, Embonpoint, Endomorph, Fat, Fleshy, Flop, Fubsy, Full, Lie, Opt, Plonk, Plop, Podgy, Portly, Roll-about, Rotund, Round, Sonsie, Sonsy, Soss, Souse, Squab, Squat, Stout, Swap, Swop, Tidy, Well-fed

Plunder(er) Berob, Booty, Depredate, Despoil, Devastate, Escheat, Fleece, Forage, Freebooter, Gut, Harry, Haul, Herriment, Herryment, Hership, Loot, Maraud, Peel, Pill(age), Privateer, ➤ RANSACK, Rape, Rapparee, Ravine, Reave, Reif, Reive, Rieve, Rifle, Rob, Sack, Scoff, Shave, Skoff, Spoil(s), Spoliate, Sprechery, Spuilzie, Spuly(i)e, Spulzie, Swag

Plunge Demerge, Dive, Douse, Dowse, Duck, Enew, Immerge, Immerse, La(u)nch, Nose-dive, Plummet, Raker, Send, Sink, Souse, Swoop, Thrust

Plural Multiply, Pl

Plus Addition, And, Gain, More, Positive

Plush(ed) Die, Luxurious, Smart, Tint, Velour, Velvet

Pluto(crat), Plutonic Abyssal, Dis, Hades, Hypogene, Nob, Pipeline, Underground

Plutonium Pu

Ply, Plier(s) Bend, Birl, Cab, Exercise, Exert, Gondoliers, Importune, Layer, Practise, Run, Trade, Wield

▷ **Plying** may indicate an anagram

PM Addington, Afternoon, Attlee, Autopsy, Bute, Cabinet-maker, Disraeli, Gladstone, Melbourne, Major, Peel, Pitt, Portland, Premier, ➤ PRIME MINISTER, Salisbury, Taoiseach

Pneumonia Visna

Poach Cook, Encroach, Filch, Lag, Steal, Trespass

Pochard Duck, Scaup

Pocket Air, Appropriate, Bag, Bin, Cavity, Cly, Cup, Enclave, Fob, Glom, Hideaway, Jenny, Misappropriate, Patch, Placket, Pot, Pouch, Purloin, Purse, Sac, Sky, Slash, Sling, Steal, Take

Pod(s) Babul, Bean, Belly, Carob, Chilli, Dividivi, Gumbo, Lomentum, Neb-neb, Okra, Pipi, Pregnant, Siliqua, Tamarind, Vanilla

Poem(s), Poetry Acrostic, Aeneid, Alcaic, Anthology, Awdl, Ballad(e), Beowulf, Bestiary, Byliny, Caccia, Canzone, Cargoes, Cento, Choliamb, Choriamb, Cicada, Cinquain, Complaint, Concrete, Decastich, Dit(t), Divan, Dizain, Doggerel, Duan, Dunciad, Eclogue, Elegy, Elene, Epic(ede), Epigram, Epilogue, Epithalamium, Epode, Epopee, Epopoeia, Epos, Epyllion, Erotic, Fifteener, Finlandia, Gauchesco, Georgic, Ghazal, Graveyard, Haikai, Haiku, Heptastich, Hexastich, Hokku, Hull, Hypermeter, Idyll, If, Iliad, Imagism, Jazz, Lay, Limerick, Logaoedic, London, Mahabharata, Melic, Metaphysical, Metre, Monostich, Nostos, Ode, Palinode, Paracrostic, Parnassus, Pastoral, Penill(ion), Pentastich, Poesy, Prelude, Prothalamion, Purana, Qasida, Quatrain, Quire, Rat-rhyme, Renga, Rhapsody, Rime, Rondeau, Rondel, Rubai(yat), Rune, Scazon (iambus), Senryu, Sestina, Sijo, Sirvente, Song, Sonnet, Spondee, Stanza, Stornello, Symphonic, Tanka, Telestich, Temora, Tercet, Tone, Triolet, Tristich, Verse, Versicle, Villanelle, Voluspa, Voluspe, Waka

Poet(s) Bard(ling), Cyclic, Elegist, Georgian, Iambist, Imagist, Laureate, Layman, Lyrist, Maker, Meistersinger, Metaphysical, Metrist, Minnesinger, Minstrel, Monodist, Odist, Parnassian, PL, Pleiade, Poetaster, Rhymer, Rhymester, Rhymist, Rymer, Scald, Scop, Skald, Smart, Sonneteer, Spasmodic, Thespis, Tragic, Troubadour, Trouvère, Trouveur

POETS			
2 letters:	Hood	**5 letters:**	Eliot
AE	Hugo	Arion	Frost
3 letters:	Hunt	Auden	Gower
Gay	Lake	Blair	Griot
Poe	Lang	Blake	Heine
4 letters:	Omar	Burns	Hesse
Abse	Ovid	Byron	Homer
Blok	Owen	Cadou	Horne
Cory	Pope	Carew	Hulme
Dyer	Rowe	Cinna	Iqbal
Gray	Rumi	Clare	Keats
Gunn	Tate	Dante	Keyes
Hogg	Vega	Donne	Lewis

Logue	Lowell	Orpheus	
Lorca	Milton	Pushkin	
Lucan	Morris	Ronsard	
Makar	Motion	Russell	Traherne
Marot	Ossian	Sassoon	Tyrtaeus
Meyer	Pindar	Service	Verlaine
Moore	Racine	Shelley	Whittier
Nashe	Sappho	Sitwell	**9 letters:**
Noyes	Seaman	Skelton	Aeschylus
Plath	Shanks	Southey	Bunthorne
Pound	Sidney	Spender	Coleridge
Prior	Tagore	Spenser	Euripides
Rilke	Thomas	Statius	Goldsmith
Rishi	Trench	Terence	Lamartine
Sachs	Villon	Thomson	Lucretius
Tasso	Virgil	Vaughan	Marinetti
Theon	Waller	Whitman	Masefield
Yeats	**7 letters:**	**8 letters:**	Quasimodo
Young	Addison	Anacreon	Shenstone
6 letters:	Alcaeus	Betjeman	Simonides
Arnold	Aretino	Browning	Sophocles
Austin	Ariosto	Campbell	Stevenson
Barham	Beddoes	Catullus	Swinburne
Barnes	Belleau	Cavalier	**10 letters:**
Belloc	Bridges	Cummings	Baudelaire
Brecht	Caedmon	Cynewulf	Chatterton
Brooke	Campion	Davenant	Cumberland
Butler	Chapman	Day Lewis	Drinkwater
Clough	Chaucer	De la Mare	Fitzgerald
Cowper	Collins	Hamilton	Longfellow
Crabbe	Corinna	Kynewulf	Propertius
Dowson	Cynwulf	Langland	Tannhauser
Dryden	Emerson	Leopardi	Theocritus
Dunbar	Flaccus	Lovelace	Wordsworth
Ennius	Flecker	Mallarmé	**11 letters:**
George	Heredia	Menander	Apollinaire
Glycon	Herrick	Petrarch	Asclepiades
Goethe	Hopkins	Rossetti	Maeterlinck
Graves	Housman	Schiller	**12 letters:**
Hesiod	Juvenal	Shadwell	Archilochian
Horace	Layamon	Stephens	Aristophanes
Hughes	Martial	Suckling	**14 letters:**
Landor	Marvell	Taliesin	Dante Alighieri
Larkin	Mistral	Tennyson	**15 letters:**
Lawman	Newbolt	Thompson	Ettrick Shepherd

Poetaster Della-Cruscan

Poetess Ingelow, Orinda

Poet laureate Motion, PL

▶ **Poetry** see POEM

Poignant Acute, Biting, Haunting, Keen, Pungent, Stirring, Touching

Point(ed), Pointer, Points Ace, Acro-, Aculeate, Aim, Antinode, Antler, Apex, Aphelion, Apogee, Appui, Apse, Apsis, Bar, Barb, Bisque, Boiling, Breaking, Brownie, Calk, Cape, Cardinal, Cash, Centre, Choke, Clou, Clue, Colon, Comma, Cone, Conic, Corner, Cover, Crisis, Crux, Cultrate, Curie, Cusp, Cursor, Cuss, Decimal, Degree, Detail, Direct, Dot, E, Epanodos,

Epee, Fang, Fastigiate, Feature, Fitch(e), Focal, Focus, Foreland, Freezing, Fulcrum, Germane, Gist, Gnomon, Hastate, Head, Hinge, Home-thrust, Index, Indicate, Indicator, Ippon, Jester, Keblah, Kiblah, Kip(p), Knub, Lagrangian, Lance, Lead, Limit, Lizard, Locate, Locus, Mark, Melting, Metacentre, Moot, Mucro, N, Nail, Nasion, Neb, Needle, Neel, Ness, Nib, Node, Nodus, Nombril, Now, Nub, Obelion, Obelisk, Opinion, Ord, Particle, Peak, Perigee, Perihelion, Perilune, Pin, Pinnacle, Place, Power, Pressure, Prong, Prow, Punctilio, Punctual, Punctum, Ras, Rhumb, Rhumbline, S, Saturation, Scribe, Seg(h)ol, Set, Shaft, Sheva, Show, Shy, Silly, Socket, Sore, Spearhead, Spicate, Spick, Spike, Spinode, Spinulose, Stage, Star, Sticking, Stigme, Stiletto, Sting, Stipule, Strong, Sum, Tacnode, Talking, Taper, Technicality, Tine, ➤ TIP, Tongue, Trig, Triple, Turning, Urde(e), Urdy, Use, Vane, Vantage, Verge, Verse, Vertex, Vowel, W

Pointless Blunt, Curtana, Flat, Futile, Inane, Inutile, Muticous, Otiose, Stupid, Vain

Point of honour Pundonor

Poise Aplomb, Balance, Composure, P, Serenity

Poison(er), Poisoning, Poisonous Abron, Aconite, Acrolein, Adamsite, Aflatoxin, Aldrin, Antiar, Apocynum, Aqua-tofana, Arsenic, Aspic, Atropia, Atropin(e), Bane, Barbasco, Belladonna, Borgia, Botulism, Brom(m)ism, Brucine, Cacodyl, Cadaverine, Calabar-bean, Cicuta, Colchicine, Coniine, Cowbane, Curare, Curari, Cyanide, Cyanuret, Datura, Daturine, Deadly nightshade, Digitalin, Dioxin, Dumbcane, Echidnine, Embolism, Emetin(e), Envenom, Ergotise, Gelsemin(in)e, Gila, Gossypol, Hebenon, Hebona, Hemlock, Henbane, Hydragyrism, Hydrastine, Hyoscyamine, Iodism, Lead, Limberneck, Lindane, Lobeline, Malevolent, Mandragora, Mezereon, Miasma, Mineral, Monkshood, Muscarine, Mycotoxin, Nerve gas, Neurine, Neutron, Noxious, Obeism, Ouabain, Ourali, Ourari, Paraquat®, Phallin, Phalloidin, Phosphorism, Picrotoxin, Pilocarpine, Plumbism, Ptomaine, Py(a)emia, Raphania, Ratsbane, Rot, Safrole, Samnitis, Santonin, Sapraemia, Sassy wood, Saturnism, Saxitoxin, Septic(aemia), Solanine, Solpuga, Soman, Stibium, Stonefish, Strophanthus, Strychnine, Sugar of lead, Surinam, Tanghin, Tanghinin, Tetro(do)toxin, Thebaine, Thorn-apple, Timbo, Toxaphene, Toxic, Toxicology, Toxin, Trembles, Tropine, Tutu, Upas, Urali, Uroshiol, Venefic, Venin, Venom(ous), Veratridine, Veratrin(e), Viperous, Virous, Virulent, Wabain, Warfarin, Wolfsbane, Woorali, Woorara, Wourali, Yohimbine

Poke, Poky Bonnet, Broddle, Garget, Itchweed, Jab, Meddle, Mock, Nousle, Nudge, Nuzzle, Ombu, Peg, Pick, Pote, Pouch, Powter, ➤ PRISON, ➤ PROD, Prog, Proke, Punch, Root(le), Rout, Rowt, Stab, Thrust

Poker (work) Bugbear, Curate, Draw, Game, High-low, Mistigris, Penny ante, Pyrography, Red-hot, Salamander, Strip, Stud(-horse), Tickler, Tine

Poland PL, Sarmatia

Polar, Pole Anode, Antarctic, Arctic, Boom, Bowsprit, Bum(p)kin, Caber, Celestial, Copernicus, Cowl-staff, Cracovian, Crossbar, Extremity, Fishgig, Flagstaff, Flagstick, Geomagnetic, Janker, Kent, Liberty, Lug, Magnetic, Mast, N, Nadir, Negative, Nib, North, Periscian, Po, Polack, Punt, Quant,

Racovian, Range, Ricker, Ripeck, Rood, Ry(e)peck, S, Shaft, Slav, South, Spar, Sprit, Staff, Stang, Starosta, Stilt, Sting, Stobie, Telegraph, Thyrsos, Thyrsus, Topmast, Totem, Vegetal, Zenith

▷ **Polar** may indicate with a pole

Polecat Ferret, Fitch, Fitchet, Foulmart, Foumart, Weasel

Polemic(al) Argument, Controversy, Debate, Eristic(al)

Police(man), Policewoman Babylon, Bear, Beast, Bizzy, Black and Tans, Blue, Bluebottle, Bobby, Bog(e)y, Bull, Busy, Carabinero, Carabiniere, Centenier, Cheka, Chekist, CID, Constable, Cop(per), Cotwal, Crusher, Detective, Druzhinnik, Filth, Flatfoot, Flattie, Flic, Flying Squad, Force, Fuzz, Garda, Gendarme, Gestapo, Gill, G-man, Guard, Gumshoe, Harmanbeck, Heat, Hermandad, Inspector, Interpol, Jamadar, Jemadar, John Hop, Keystone, Kotwal, Limb, Military, Met(ropolitan), Mountie, Mulligan, Nabman, Nark, Ochrana, Officer, OGPU, Ovra, PC, Peeler, Peon, Pig, Polis, Polizei, Posse (comitatus), Prefect, Puppy-walker, Ranger, Redbreast, Redcap, Regulate, RIC, Riot, Robert, Rosser, Rozzer, RUC, Sbirro, SC, Secret, Securitate, Securocrat, Sepoy, Shamus, Sleeping, Slop, Smokey, Sowar(ry), Special, Stasi, Super, Sureté, Sweeney, T(h)anadar, The Bill, The Law, Thirdborough, Thought, Trap, Vigilante, Walloper, Wolly, Woodentop, Zaptiah, Zaptieh, Zomo

Police car Black Maria, Panda, Patrol, Prowl

Police station Copshop, Lock-up, Tana, Tanna(h), Thana(h), Thanna(h), Watchhouse

Policy Assurance, Ballon d'essai, CAP, Comprehensive, Course, Demesne, Endowment, Expedience, Insurance, Knock for knock, Laisser-faire, Lend-lease, Line, Method, Open-sky, Plank, Platform, Practice, Programme, Pork-barrel, Revanchism, Scorched earth, Stop-go, Tack, Tactics, Ticket

Polish(ed), Polisher Beeswax, Black, Blacklead, Bob, Buff, Bull, Burnish, Chamois, Complaisant, Edit, Elaborate, Elegant, Emery, Enamel, Finish, French, Furbish, Gentlemanly, Glass, Gloss, Heelball, Hone, Inland, Lap, Lustre, Nail, Perfect, Planish, Polite, Refinement, Refurbish, Rottenstone, Rub, Sand, Sandblast, Sandpaper, Sejm, Sheen, Shellac, Shine, Slick, Supercalender, Urbane, Veneer, Wax

Polite Civil, Courteous, Genteel, Grandisonian, Mannered, Suave, Urbane, Well-bred

Politic(al), Politics Apparat, Body, Chartism, Civic, Diplomacy, Discreet, Expedient, Falange, Leftism, Poujadism, Public, Radicalism, Rightism, Statecraft, Tactful, Wise

Politician(s) Bright, Carpet-bagger, Catiline, Chesterfield, Demo(crat), Diehard, Disraeli, Eden, Green, Guelph, Independent, Ins, Isolationist, Laski, Left, Legislator, Liberal, MEP, MP, Parnell, Polly, Rad, Rep, Senator, Socialist, Statesman, Statist, Tadpole, Taper, TD, Tory, Trotsky, Unionist, Veep, Warhorse, Whig, Wilberforce

Poll Ballot, Bean, Canvass, Count, Cut, Deed, Dod, Election, Exit, Gallup, Head, Humlie, Hummel, MORI, Nestor, Not(t), Opinion, Parrot, Pineapple, Pow, Scrutiny, Straw, Votes

▷ **Poll** may indicate a first letter

Pollack Fish, Lob, Lythe

Pollard Doddered

Pollen, Pollinated Anemophilous, Beebread, Dust, Errhine, Farina, Fertilised, Witch-meal, Xenia

Pollenbrush Scopa

Pollex Thumb

Pollster Psephologist

Pollute(d), Pollutant, Pollution Adulterate, Contaminate, Defile, Dirty, File, Foul, Impure, Infect, Miasma, Nox, Rainout, Soil, Soilure, Stain, Sully, Taint, Violate

Polly Flinders, Parrot, Peachum

Polo Chukka, Marco, Mint, Navigator

Polonium Po

Poltergeist Apport, Ghost, Spirit, Trouble-house

Poltroon Coward, Craven, Dastard, Scald, Scaramouch

Polyandry Nair

Polygraph Lie-detector

Polymath Knowall, Toynbee

Polymer Isotactic, Lignin, Oligomer, Resin, Silicone, Tetramer, Trimer

Polymorphic Multiform, Proteus, Variform

Polynesian Moriori, Tahitian, Tongan

Polyp(s) Alcyonaria, Hydra, Nematophore, Obelia, Sea-anemone, Tumour

Polyphony Counterpoint

Polyzoan Sea-mat

Pom Choom

Pomander Pounce(t)-box

Pommel Beat, Knob, Pound, Pummel

Pomp(ous) Big, Bombastic, Budge, Ceremonial, Display, Dogberry, Euphuistic, Fustian, Grandiloquent, Grandiose, Heavy, Highfalutin(g), High-flown, High-muck-a-muck, High-sounding, Hogen-mogen, Inflated, Orotund, Ostentatious, Pageantry, Parade, Pretentious, Solemn, Splendour, Starchy, State, Stilted, Stuffy, Turgid

Pom-pom Ball, Tassel

Ponce Pander, Solicit, Souteneur

Poncho Ruana

Pond(s) Dew, Dub, Hampstead, Lakelet, Pool, Pound, Puddle, Slough, Stank, Stew, Tank, Turlough, Vivarium, Viver

Ponder(ous) Brood, Cogitate, Contemplate, Deliberate, Heavy, Laboured, Mull, Muse, Perpend, Poise, Pore, Reflect, Ruminate, ➤ THINK, Vise, Volve, Weight(y), Wonder

Poniard Bodkin, ➤ DAGGER, Dirk, Stiletto

Pontiff, Pontifical, Pontificate Aaron, Aaronic, Antipope, Dogmatise, Papal

Pontoon Blackjack, Bridge, Caisson, Chess, Game, Vingt-et-un

Pony Canuck, Cayuse, Dartmoor, Exmoor, Garran, Garron, Gen(n)et, GG, Griffin, Griffon, Gryfon, Gryphon, Jennet, Mustang, New Forest, Polo, Pownie, Shanks', Sheltie, Shetland, Show, Tangun, Tat(too), Welsh

Poodle Barbet, Swan

Pooh Bah, Bear, Pugh, Winnie, Yah

Pool Backwater, Bank, Bethesda, Billabong, Bogey hole, Cenote, Cess, Collect, Combine, Dub, Dump, Flash, Flow, Jackpot, Kitty, Lido, Lin(n), Meer, Mere, Mickery, Milkvah, Milkveh, Moon, Natatorium, Piscina, Piscine, Plash, Plesh, Plunge, ➤ POND, Reserve, Snooker, Spa, Stank, Sump, Tank, Tarn, Wave

Poor(ly) Bad, Bare, Base, Bijwoner, Breadline, Buckeen, Bywoner, Catchpenny, Conch, Cronk, Destitute, Gritty, Hard-up, Have-nots, Hopeless, Humble, Hungry, Ill(-off), Impecunious, Indigent, Lazarus, Lean, Low, Low-downer, Meagre, Mean, Needy, Obolary, Pauper, Peaky, Poxy, Roinish, Rop(e)y, Roynish, Sad, Scrub, Shabby, Shitty, Sober, Sorry, Sub, Thin, Third-rate, Trashy, Undeserving, Unwell

▷ **Poor** may indicate an anagram

Poorhouse Union, Workhouse

Pooter Nobody, Nonentity

Pop (off), Popper, Popping Bang, Brit, Burst, Cloop, Crease, Die, Father, Fr, Gingerbeer, Hip-hop, Hock, Insert, Lumber, Mineral, Nip, Pater, Pawn, Pledge, Population, Press-stud, Punk, Sherbet, Soda, Splutter, Weasel

▷ **Pop** may indicate an anagram

Pope(s) Adrian, Alexander, Atticus, Boniface, Clement, Dunciad, Eminence, Fish, Great Schism, Gregory, Hildebrand, Holiness, Innocent, Joan, Leo, Papa, Pius, Pontiff, Ruff(e), Schism, Theocrat, Tiara, Urban, Vatican, Vicar of Christ

Pop-gun Bourtree-gun

Popinjay Barbermonger, Coxcomb, Dandy, Fop, Macaroni, Prig, Skipjack

Poplar Abele, Aspen, Balsam, Cottonwood, Lombardy

Poppet Valve

Poppy Argemone, Bloodroot, California, Chicalote, Coquelicot, Corn, Diacodin, Eschscholtzia, Flanders, Horned, Iceland, Matilija, Mawseed, Opium, Papaver, Ponceau, Prickly, Puccoon, Rhoeadales, Shirley, Tall, Welsh

Poppycock Bosh, Nonsense, Rubbish

Popular(ity) Common, Demotic, General, Heyday, Hit, In, Laic, Lay, Mass, Plebeian, Prevalent, Public, Successful, Tipped, Trendy, Vogue

Population, Populace Catchment, Census, Demography, Inhabitants, Malthusian, Mass, Mob, ➤ PEOPLE, Public, Universe

Porcelain Arita, Bamboo, Belleek®, Blanc-de-chine, Celadon, Chelsea, China, Coalport, Crackle(ware), Dresden, Eggshell, Famille, Goss, Hard-paste, Hizen, Imari, Jasper, Jasper(ware), Limoges, Lithophane, Minton, Parian, Sèvres, Softpaste, Spode, Sung

Porch Galilee, Lanai, Stoa, Stoep, Veranda(h)

Porcupine Hedgehog, Urson

Pore Browse, Hole, Hydrathode, Lenticel, Muse, Ostium, Outlet, Ponder, Stoma, Study

Porgy Braise, Scup(paug)

Pork Bacon, Boar, Brawn, Chap, Crackling, Flitch, Griskin, Ham, Pancetta, Scrapple, Spare-rib

Porn(ography) Erotica, Hard, Hard-core, Rhyparography, Soft, Soft-core

Porous Cellular, Permeable, Pumice, Sponge

Porpoise Bucker, Dolphin, Mereswine, Pellach, Pellack, Pellock, Phocaena, Sea pig, Sea swine

Porridge Berry, Bird, Brochan, Brose, Busera, Crowdie, Drammach, Drammock, Gaol, Grits, Grouts, Gruel, Hominy, Kasha, Mahewu, Mealie pap, Oaten, Oatmeal, Parritch, Pease-brose, Polenta, Pottage, Praiseach, Sadza, Samp, Sentence, Skilly, Stirabout, Stretch, Sup(p)awn, Time, Ugali

Porridge stick Thible, Thivel

Port(s) Beeswing, Carry, Cinque, Entrepot, Free, Gate, ➤ HARBOUR, Haven, Hithe, Hythe, Larboard, Left, Manner, Mien, Parallel, Tawny, Treaty, Wine

PORTS

3 letters:	Vigo	Ostia	Gdynia
Abo	Wick	Pusan	Harbin
Ayr	**5 letters:**	Rabat	Havana
Goa	Arhus	Salto	Hobart
Hué	Aqaba	Sidon	Iloilo
Rio	Arica	Split	Inchon
Rye	Aulis	Surat	Kisumu
4 letters:	Barry	Tampa	Lobito
Acre	Basra	Tunis	Lubeck
Aden	Batum	Turku	Madras
Akko	Belem	Visby	Malaga
Amoy	Brest	Yalta	Manila
Apia	Cadiz	**6 letters:**	Mobile
Baku	Cairo	Aarhus	Nantes
Bari	Colon	Abadan	Naples
Cobh	Dilli	Agadir	Narvik
Cork	Dover	Albany	Nassau
Deal	Dubai	Ancona	Nelson
Dill	Eilat	Bastia	Odense
Elat	Emden	Batumi	Odessa
Hilo	Galle	Bergen	Ostend
Hull	Genoa	Bilbao	Padang
Icel	Haifa	Bootle	Quincy
Kiel	Izmir	Boston	Ragusa
Kobe	Jaffa	Bremen	Recife
Lima	Jedda	Burgas	Rimini
Oban	Jidda	Calais	Rostov
Omsk	Kerch	Callao	Smyrna
Oran	Kochi	Canton	St Malo
Perm	Larne	Cochin	Tacoma
Pula	Leith	Danzig	Venice
Puri	Lulea	Darwin	Whitby
Said	Malmo	Dieppe	**7 letters:**
Suez	Mocha	Elblag	Abidjan
Tyre	Osaka	Galata	Ajaccio

Antibes	Okayama	Harfleur	Fishguard
Antwerp	Palermo	Holyhead	Fleetwood
Augusta	Piraeus	Honolulu	Fremantle
Bristol	Rangoon	Istanbul	Gallipoli
Buffalo	Rapallo	Kanazawa	Gateshead
Catania	Rosario	Murmansk	Gravesend
Cologne	Rostock	Nagasaki	Inhambane
Colomba	Runcorn	Newhaven	Las Palmas
Conakry	Salerno	Paramibo	Newcastle
Corinth	Seattle	Penzance	Rotterdam
Dunedin	Seville	Pevensey	Schleswig
Dunkirk	Stettin	Plymouth	Sheerness
Ephesus	Swansea	Ramsgate	Stavanger
Esbjerg	Tampico	San Diego	Stornoway
Foochow	Tangier	Sandwich	Stranraer
Funchal	Taranto	Schiedam	Tarragona
Geelong	Trieste	Shanghai	Trondheim
Grimsby	Tripoli	Syracuse	Volgograd
Harwich	Ushuaia	Valencia	**10 letters:**
Incheon	**8 letters:**	Veracruz	Alexandria
Iquique	Acapulco	Yokohama	Bratislava
Iquitos	Alicante	**9 letters:**	Casablanca
Karachi	Arbroath	Anchorage	Charleston
Kinsale	Batangas	Annapolis	Chittagong
Kowloon	Benghazi	Angostura	Hammerfest
Latakia	Bordeaux	Archangel	Launceston
Le Havre	Boulogne	Baltimore	Queenstown
Legaspi	Brindisi	Cartagena	**11 letters:**
Lorient	Calcutta	Cherbourg	Southampton
Marsala	Flushing	Dartmouth	Trincomalee
Messina	Freetown	Dubrovnik	Vladivostok
Milazzo	Geropiga	Ellesmere	**12 letters:**
Mombasa	Greenock	Esperance	Barranquilla
Munster	Hamilton	Famagusta	Buenaventura

Portend, Portent(ous) Augur, Bode, Dire, Omen, Phenomenon, Presage, ➤ WARN(ING)

Porter Ale, Bearer, Bellboy, Bummaree, Caddie, Caddy, Cole, Concierge, Coolie, Doorman, Door-keeper, Dvornik, Entire, Ham(m)al, Hamaul, Humper, Janitor, October, Ostiary, Red-cap, Stout

Portfolio Holding

Portico Colonnade, Decastyle, Distyle, Dodecastyle, Exedra, Loggia, Narthex, Parvis(e), Porch, Prostyle, Stoa, Veranda(h), Xystus

Portion Ann(at), Bit, Deal, Distribute, Dole, Dose, Dotation, Fragment, Helping, Heritage, Hunk, Jointure, Lot, Modicum, Nutlet, Ounce, ➤ PART, Piece, Ratio, Scantle, Scantling, Section, Segment, Serving, Share, Size, Slice, Something, Tait, Taste, Tate, Tittle, Tranche, Wodge

Portland Bill, Cement, Stone

Portly Ample, Corpulent, Gaucie, Gaucy, Gawcy, Gawsy, Stout

Portmanteau Bag, Combination, Holdall, Valise

Portrait(ist) Depiction, Drawing, Eikon, Icon, Ikon, Image, Kit-cat, Lely, Likeness, Painting, Retraitt, Retrate, Sketch, Vignette

Portray(al) Caricature, Depict, Describe, Feature, Image, Limn, Paint, Render, Represent, ➤ SHOW

Portsmouth Pompey

Portugal, Portuguese Lusitania(n), Macanese, Senhor

Pose(r), Poseur Aesthete, Affect(ation), Arabesque, Asana, Ask, Contrapposto, Drape, Lotus, Masquerade, Model, Place, Plastique, Posture, Pretend, Problem, Propound, Pseud, Sit, Stance, Sticker, Tickler

Poseidon Earthshaker

Posh Grand, Ornate, Ritzy, Swanky, Swish, U

Position Asana, Attitude, Bearing(s), Emplacement, Enfilade, F(o)etal, Foothold, Grade, Instal, Lay, Lie, Location, Locus, Lodg(e)ment, Lotus, Missionary, Mudra, Office, Pass, Peak, Place, Plant, Point, Pole, Post, Seat, Set(ting), Site, Situ, Stance, Standing, Standpoint, Station, Status, Syzygy, Tagmeme, Thesis, Tierce, Viewpoint

Positive, Positivist Absolute, Anode, Assertive, Categorical, ➤ CERTAIN, Comte, Definite, Emphatic, Plus, Print, Sure, Thetic, Upbeat, Yang, Yes

Posse Band, Mob, Vigilantes

Possess(ed), Possession, Possessive Apostrophe, Asset, Aver, Bedevil, Belonging(s), Demonic, Driven, Energumen, Estate, Have, Haveour, Haviour, Heirloom, His, Hogging, Know, Lares (et) penates, Mad, Obsessed, Occupation, ➤ OWN, Sasine, Seisin, Sprechery, Usucap(t)ion, Vacant, Worth

Possible, Possibility, Possibly Able, Contingency, Feasible, Likely, Maybe, Mayhap, Peradventure, Perchance, Perhaps, Posse, Potential, Prospect, Resort, Viable, Will

▷ **Possibly** may indicate an anagram

Possum Burramys, Cataplexy, Opossum, Ringtail, Sugar glider, Sugar squirrel, Tait

Post(s) Affix, After, Assign, Bitt, Bollard, Carrick bitt, Command, Correspondence, Dak, Dawk, Delivery, Dragon's teeth, Emily, Finger, Flagpole, Hurter, Jamb, King, Last, Listening, Log, Mail, Mast, Newel, Observation, Outstation, Pale, Paling, Parcel, Penny, Picket, Pile, Piling, Piquet, Placard, Place, Plant, Plum, Pole, Position, Presidio, Puncheon, Queen, Quintain, Quoin, Registered, Remit, Residency, RM, Seat, Send, Spile, Staff, Staging, Stake, Station, Stell, Stoop, Stoup, Studdle, Tom, Trading, Upright, Vacancy, Winning

Postcard(s) Deltiology

Poster Advertisement, Affiche, Bill, Broadsheet, Placard, Sender

Posterior Behind, Bottom, Jacksie, Jacksy, Later, Lumbar, Pygal, Rear, Tail

Post-free Franco

Postman, Postmaster, Postwoman Carrier, Courier, Emily, Hill, Messenger, Nasby, Pat, Portionist, Sorter

Postmark Frank

Post mortem Autopsy, Enquiry, Necropsy

Postpone(ment) Adjourn, Contango, Defer, Delay, Frist, Long-finger, Moratorium, Mothball, Pigeon-hole, Postdate, Prorogue, Reprieve, Shelve, Stay, Suspend, Withhold

Postulant Candidate, Novice

Postulate Assert, Assume, Claim, Propound

Posture Affectation, Asana, Attitude, Decubitus, Deportment, Mudra, Pose, Pretence, Site, Stance, Vorlage

Posy Bouquet, Buttonhole, Corsage, Nosegay, Tuzzi-muzzy

Pot(s), Potting, Potty Abridge, Aludel, Bankroll, Basil, Belly, Cafetière, Cannabis, Casserole, Ca(u)ldron, Ceramic, Chamber, Chanty, Chatti, Chatty, Chimney, Cocotte, Crewe, Crock(ery), Crucible, Cruse(t), Delf(t), Dixie, Ewer, Flesh, Gage, Gallipot, Ganja, Gazunder, Grass, Hash(ish), Helmet, Hemp, In off, Inurn, Jardinière, Jordan, Kettle, Kitty, Lobster, Lota(h), Maiolica, Majolica, Marijuana, Marmite, Melting, Ming, Olla, Olpe, Pan, Pat, Pipkin, Planter, Pocket, Poot, Posnet, ➤ POTTERY, Pout, Prize, Samovar, Shoot, Skillet, Steamer, Skeet, Stomach, Tajine, Tea, Test, Throw, Trivet, Tureen, Urn, Vial, Ware, Wok

Potash Kalinite, Polverine, Sylvine, Sylvite

Potassium K, Kalium, Saleratus, Saltpetre

Potation Dram, Drink

Potato(es) Batata, Chat, Couch, Datura, Duchesse, Fluke, Hashbrowns, Hog, Hole, Hot, Jersey, Kumara, Lyonnaise, Mash, Murphy, Peel-and-eat, Pratie, Praty, Roesti, Seed, Solanum, Stovies, Tatie, Tattie, Teddy, Tuber, Ware, Yam

Pot-bearer Trivet

Pot-bellied Kedge, Kedgy, Kidge, Paunchy, Portly, Stout

Potboiler Hob

Pot-boy Basil, Ganymede, Scullion

Potent(ate) Dynamic, Emperor, Huzoor, Influential, Kinglet, Mogul, Nawab, Panjandrum, Powerful, Ruler, Squirearch, Sultan

Potential Action, Capacity, Making(s), Manqué, Possible, Promise, Resting, Scope, Viable

▷ **Potentially** may indicate an anagram

Pothole(r) Giant's kettle, Spelunker

Pot-house Shebeen, Tavern

Potion Dose, Draught, Drink, Dwale, Mixture, Philtre, Tincture

Pot-pourri Hotchpotch, Medley, Pasticcio, Salmi

Potsherd Ostracon, Ostrakon

Pottage Berry

Potter Cue, Dabbity, Dacker, Daidle, Daiker, Dibble, Dilly-dally, Dodder, Etruscan, Fettle, Fiddle, Footer, Footle, Fouter, Gamesmanship, Idle, Mess, Minton, Muck, Niggle, One-upmanship, Plouter, Plowter, Spode, Thrower, Tiddle, Tink(er), Troke, Truck, Wedgwood

▷ **Potter** may indicate a snooker-player

Pottery Agatewear, Bank, Bisque, Celadon, Ceramet, Ceramic, China, Creamware, Crock, Crouch-ware, Dabbity, Delf(t), Encaustic, Etruria, Faience, Flatback, Gombroon, Granitewear, Hollowware, Jomon, Majolica, Ming, Raku, Satsuma, Scroddled, Sgraffito, Slab, Slipware, Smalto, Spode, Spongeware, Stoneware, Sung, Ware, Wedgwood®, Wemyss, Whieldon

Pouch(ed) Bag, Brood, Bum-bag, Bursa, Caecum, Cheek, Cisterna, Codpiece, Diverticulum, Fanny pack, Gill, Jockstrap, Marsupial, Poke, Purse, Sac, Scrip, Scrotum, Spleuchan, Sporran

Poultice Application, Cataplasm, Embrocation, Epithem(a), Lenient, Plaster

Poultry Dorking, Fowl, Gallinaceous, Poot, Pout, Welsummer

Poultry disease Keel

Pounce Claw, Jump, Lunge, Powder, Sere, Souse, Sprinkle, Swoop, Talon

Pound(er) Ache, As, Bar, Bash, Batter, Beat, Bombard, Bradbury, Bray, Broadpiece, Bruise, Contund, Coop, Drub, Embale, Enclosure, Ezra, Fold, Green, Hammer, Hatter, Imagist, Intern, Iron man, Jail, Kiddle, Kidel, Kin, Knevell, L, Lam, Lb, Lock, Mash, Nevel, Nicker, Oncer, One-er, Oner, Pale, Pen, Penfold, Pestle, Pin, Pindar, Pinfold, Powder, Pulverise, Pun, Quop, Rint, Smacker, Sov(ereign), Stamp, Strum, Thump, Tower, Weight

Pour Birl(e), Bucket, Cascade, Circumfuse, Decant, Diffuse, Flood, Flow, Jaw, Jirble, Libate, Rain, Seil, Shed, Sile, Skink, Spew, Stream, Teem, Turn, Vent, Weep, Well

Pout Blain, Brassy, Fish, Mope, Mou(e), Scowl, Sulk, Tout, Towt

Poverty Beggary, Dearth, Deprivation, Illth, Indigence, ➤ LACK, Need, Penury, Poortith, Squalor, Want

Powder(ed), Powdery Amberite, Araroba, Baking, Ballistite, Boracic, Calamine, Chalk, Cosmetic, Crocus, Culm, Cuttlefish, Dentifrice, Dover's, Dust, Explosive, Floury, Glaucous, Goa, Gregory, Grind, Kohl, Levigate, Lithia, Lupulin, Meal, Moust, Mu(i)st, Pemoline, Pollen, Pounce, Pruinose, Pulver, Pulvil, Rachel, Rochelle, Rottenstone, Rouge, Saleratus, Seidlitz, Seme(e), Sherbet, Silver iodide, Smeddum, Spode, Spodium, Talc(um), Thimerosal, Toner, Tooth, Triturate, Zein

Power(ful), Powers Ability, Able, Aeon, Aggrandisement, Amandla, Arm, Attorney, Autarchy, Authority, Axis, Big, Chakra, Cham, Charisma, Clairvoyance, Clout, Cogency, Command, Corridor, Cube, Danger, Despotic, Diadem, Dioptre, Dominion, Effective, Eminence, Empathy, Empery, Energy, Eon, Exponent, Facility, Faculty, Flower, Force, Force majeure, Hefty, Hegemony, High, Hildebrandic, Horse, Hp, Hydroelectric, Hot, Imperium, Influence, Kami, Kilowatt, Log, Logarithm, Lusty, Mana, Mastery, Megalomania, Might, Mogul, Motive, Movers and shakers, Muscle, Nature, Nth, Od-force, Omnificent, Omnipotent, P, Panjandrum, Plenipotency, Posse, Potency, Prepollence, Prepotent, Puissant, Punch, Regime, Siddhi, Sinew, Soup, Stamina, Steam, Stiff, Strength, ➤ STRONG, Supercharge, Supreme, Suzerain, Teeth, Telling, Throne, Tycoon, Tyrone, Valency, Vigour, Vis, Volt, Vroom, Water, Watt, Wattage, Weight, Wind

Powerless Diriment, Downa-do, Hamstrung, Helpless, Impotent, Impuissant, Incapable, Unable, Unarmed, Weak

Powwow Confab, Conference, Council, Meeting

Pox Orf, Pize

Practical, Practicable Active, Doable, Joker, Pragmatic, Realist(ic), Realpolitik, Sensible, Useful, Viable, Virtual

Practice, Practise, Practitioner Abuse, Custom, Do, Drill, Enure, Exercise, General, Group, Habit, Inure, Ism, Keep, Knock-up, Meme, Nets, Operate, Order, Ply, Policy, Praxis, Private, Prosecution, Pursuit, Rehearsal, Rehearse, Restrictive, Rite, Rut, Sharp, Test-run, Trade, Tradition, Train, Trial, Ure, Usage, Use

Pragmatic, Pragmatist Ad hoc, Busy, Dogmatic, Humanist, Meddling, Officious, Realist

Prairie IL, Illinois, Llano, Plain, Savanna, Steppe, Tundra, Veldt

Prairie dog Whippoorwill, Wishtonwish

Praise(worthy) Acclaim, Adulation, Alleluia, Allow, Anthem, Applause, Belaud, Bless, Blurb, Bouquet, Butter, Carol, Citation, CL, Commend(ation), Compliment, Dulia, Encomium, Envy, Eulogise, Eulogium, Eulogy, Exalt, Extol, Gloria, Glory, Herry, Hery(e), Hosanna, Hype, Incense, Laud, Lip service, Lo(o)s, Meritorious, Panegyric, Rap, Roose, Tribute

Pram Carriage, Cart, Scow

Prance Brank, Canary, Caper, Cavort, Galumph, Gambol, Jaunce, Jaunse, Prank(le), Swagger, Tittup, Trounce

Prang Accident, Crash, Smash, Whale

Prank(s) Attrap, Bedeck, Bedizen, Caper, Dido, Escapade, Fredaine, Frolic, Gaud, Jape, Lark, Mischief, Rag, Reak, Reik, Rex, Rig, Spoof, Trick, Vagary

Praseodymium Pr

Prat Bottom, ➤ STUPID PERSON

Prate Babble, Boast, Haver, Talk

Prattle Babble, Blat(her), Chatter, Gab(nash), Gas, Gibber, Gossip, Gup, Lalage, Patter, Yap

Prawn Scampi, Shrimp

Pray(ing) Appeal, Beg, Beseech, Daven, ➤ ENTREAT, Impetrate, Intone, Invoke, Kneel, Mantis, Solicit, Wrestle

Prayer (book), Prayers Act, Amidah, Angelus, Ardas, Ave (Maria), Bead, Bede, Bene, Breviary, Collect, Common, Confiteor, Cry, Cursus, Daven, Deus det, Devotion, Eleison, Embolism, Entreaty, Epiclesis, Euchologion, Geullah, Grace, Hail Mary, Hallan-shaker, Imam, Intercession, Invocation, Kaddish, Khotbah, Khotbeh, Khutbah, Kol Nidre, Kyrie, Kyrie eleison, Lauds, Litany, Lord's, Lychnapsia, Ma(c)hzor, Mantis, Mat(t)ins, Mincha(h), Missal, Musaf, Novena, Orant, Orarium, Orison, Our Father, Paternoster, Patter, Petition, Phylactery, Placebo, Plea, Proseucha, Proseuche, Puja, Requiem, Requiescat, Rogation, Rosary, Secret, Shema, Siddur, Stations of the Cross, Suffrage, Te igitur, Tenebrae, Triduum, Yizkov

▷ **Prayer** may indicate one who begs

Preach(er) Ainger, Boanerges, Devil-dodger, Donne, Ecclesiastes, Exhort, Evangelist, Gospeller, Graham, Holy Roller, Itinerant, Knox, Lecture, Mar-text, Minister, ➤ MORALISE, Patercove, Postillate, Predicant, Predicate, Predikant, Priest, Prophet, Pulpiteer, Rant, Spintext, Spurgeon, Teach

Preamble Introduction, Preface, Proem, Prologue

Precarious Dangerous, Parlous, Perilous, Risky, Uncertain, Unsteady

Precaution Care, Guard, Fail-safe, In case, Prophylaxis, Safeguard

Precede(nce), Precedent Antedate, Example, Forego, Forerun, Herald, Pas, Predate, Preface, Priority, Protocol

Precept Adage, Canon, Commandment, Maxim, Motto, Saw

Precinct(s) Ambit, Area, Banlieue, Close, Courtyard, District, Environs, Peribolos, Region, Temenos, Verge, Vihara

Precious Adored, Chary, Chichi, Costly, Dear, Dearbought, Ewe-lamb, La-di-da, Murr(h)a, Owre, Precise, Rare, Valuable

Precipice Bluff, Cliff, Crag, Krans, Kran(t)z, Sheer

Precipitate, Precipitation, Precipitous Abrupt, Accelerate, Cause, Deposit, Hailstone, Headlong, Impetuous, Launch, Lees, Pellmell, Pitchfork, Rash, Sca(u)r, Sheer, Shoot, Sleet, Snowflake, Start, ➤ STEEP

Precis Abstract, Aperçu, Epitome, Résumé, Summary

Precise(ly), Precisian, Precision Absolute, Accurate, Dry, Exact, Explicit, Minute, Nice(ty), Particular, Perfect, Plumb, Prig, Prim, Punctilious, Spang, Specific, Starchy, Stringent, Tight, Very

Preclude Bar, Debar, Estop, Foreclose, Hinder, Impede, Prevent

Precocious Advanced, Bratpack, Forward, Premature

Preconception Ideating

Precursor Avant-courier, Forerunner, Harbinger

Predator(y) Carnivore, Eagle, Fox, Glede, Harpy-eagle, Jackal, Kestrel, Kite, Lycosa, Marauder, Predacious, Puma, Tanrec, Tarantula, Tenrec

Pre-dawn Antelucan, Ante lucem

Predecessor Ancestor, Forebear, Foregoer

Predestined Doomed, Fated, Tramway

Predicament Box, Dilemma, Embroglio, Hobble, Hole, Jam, Pass, Peril, Pickle, Plight, Quandary, Scrape, Spot

Predict(ion), Predictable, Predictor Augur, Belomancy, Bet, Divination, Forecast, Foreshow, Foretell, Forsay, Horoscope, Nap, Necromancy, Portend, Presage, Previse, Prognosis, Prophecy, Prophesy, Regular, Soothsayer

Predilection Fancy, Liking, Prejudice, Taste, Tendency

Predisposition Aptitude, Inclination, Parti-pris, Tendency

Predominate Abound, Govern, Overshadow, Prevail, Reign

Pre-eminence, Pre-eminent Arch, Foremost, Palm, Paramount, Primacy, Supreme, Topnotch, Unique

Pre-empt Enter

Preen Perk, Primp, Prink, Prune

Prefab(ricated) Quonset

Preface Foreword, Herald, Intro, Preamble, Precede, Proem, Prolegomenon, Usher

Prefect Prepositor

Prefer(ence), Preferred Advance, Choose, Elect, Faard, Faurd, Favour, Incline, Lean, Predilect(ion), Prefard, Priority, Proclivity, Promote, Sooner, Stocks, Taste, Will

Prefix Eka, Introduce, Name

Pregnancy, Pregnant Big, Clucky, Cyesis, Ectopic, Enceinte, Fertile, Gestation, Gravid(a), Great, Heavy, Knocked-up, Pseudocyesis

Prehistoric Ancient, Azilian, Beakerfolk, Brontosaurus, Cambrian, Clovis, Cro-magnon, Eocene, Folsom, Primeval, Primitive, Pteranodon, Pterodactyl(e), Pterosaur, Saurian, Sinanthropus, Titanosaurus, Trilith(on)

Prejudice(d) Bias, Discrimination, Down, Derry, Illiberal, Impede, Injure, Insular, Intolerance, Partiality, Parti pris, Preoccupy, Prepossession, Racism

Prelate Cardinal, Churchman, Exarch, Monsignor, Odo, Priest

Preliminary Draft, Exploration, Heat, Initial, Introductory, Precursory, Previous, Prodrome, Prolusion, Rough, Title-sheet

Prelude Entree, Forerunner, Intrada, Overture, Proem(ial), Ritornell(e), Ritornello

Premature Early, Precocious, Pre(e)mie, Premy, Previous, Slink, Untimely, Untimeous

Premeditate Anticipate, Foresee, Plan

Premier Chief, Leader, Main, PM, ➤ PRIME MINISTER, Tojo

Premise(s) Assumption, Datum, Epicheirema, Ground, Hypothesis, Inference, Lemma, Postulate, Property, Proposition, Reason

Premium Ap, Bond, Bonus, Discount, Grassum, Pm, Reward, Scarce

Premonition Hunch, Omen, Presentiment, Prodromal, Warning

Preoccupation, Preoccupied, Preoccupy Absorb, Abstracted, Distrait, Engross, Hang-up, Intent, Obsess, Thing

Prepaid Pro-forma, Sae

Prepare(d), Preparation Address, A la, Arrange, Attire, Boun, Bowne, Busk, Calver, Cock, Concoct, Cooper, Countdown, Decoct, Did, Do, Dress, Edit, Forearm, Game, Groom, Ground, Inspan, Key, Lay, Legwork, Lotion, Measure, Mobilise, Parascene, Prime, Procinct, Prothesis, Provide, Psych, ➤ READY, Rehearsal, Ripe, Set, Spadework, Stand-to, Suborn, Train, Truss, Warm-up, Yare

▷ **Prepare(d)** may indicate an anagram

Preponderance, Preponderant, Preponderate Important, Majority, Outweigh, Paramount, Prevalence, Sway

Preposition Premise

Prepossessing, Prepossession Attractive, Fetching, Predilection, Winsome

Preposterous Absurd, Chimeric, Foolish, Grotesque, Unreasonable

▷ **Preposterous** may indicate a word reversed

Pre-Raphaelite Rossetti

Prerequisite Condition, Essential, Necessity, Sine qua non

Prerogative Faculty, Franchise, Liberty, Privilege, Right

Presage Abode, Foresight, Omen, Portend, Presentiment, Prophesy

Presbyter(ian) Berean, Blue, Cameronian, Covenanter, Elder, Knox, Macmillanite, Moderator, Sacrarium, Whig(gamore)

Prescient Clairvoyant, Fly

Prescribe Appoint, Assign, Dictate, Enjoin, Impose, Ordain, Rule, Set

Prescription Cipher, Decree, Direction, Formula, Medicine, R, Rec, Receipt, Ritual, Specific

Presence Aspect, Bearing, Closeness, Company, Debut, Hereness, Shechinah, Shekinah, Spirit

Present(ed), Presenter, Presently Anchorman, Anon, Assists, Award, Bestow, Bonsela, Boon, Bounty, Box, Cadeau, Congiary, Coram, Current, Debut, Dee-jay, DJ, Deodate, Donate, Dotal, Douceur, Dower, Endew, Endow, Endue, Enow, Etrenne, Existent, Fairing, Feature, Front-man, Gie, ➤ GIFT, Give, Going, Grant, Gratuity, Hand, Here, Hodiernal, Introduce, Inst, Largess(e), Linkman, MC, Mod, Nonce, Now, Nuzzer, Porrect, Potlach, Pr, Produce, Proffer, Pro-tem, Put, Render, Show, Slice, Tip, Today, Vee-jay, Xenium, Yeven

Preserve(d), Preservative, Preserver Bottle, Burnettize, Can, Chill, Confect, Corn, Creosote, Cure, Dehydrate, Dry, Eisel, Embalm, Fixative, Formaldehyde, Formalin, Freeze, Guard, Hair, Hesperides, Jam, Jerk, Keep, Kinin, Kipper, Konfyt, Kyanise, ➤ MAINTAIN, Marmalade, Mummify, Pectin, Peculiar, Piccalilli, Pickle, Pot, Powellise, Salt, Salve, Saut, Souse, Store, Stuff, Tanalized, Tar, Tin, Vinegar, Waterglass

Preside(nt) Abe, Adams, Banda, Carter, Chair, Childers, Cleveland, Coolidge, Coty, Dean, Director, Eisenhower, Ford, Garfield, Grant, Harding, Harrison, Hoover, Ike, Kennedy, Kruger, Lead, Lincoln, Madison, Moderator, Nixon, P, Peron, Polk, Pr(a)eses, Prexy, Roosevelt, Sa(a)dat, Speaker, Superintendent, Supervisor, Taft, Tito, Truman, Tyler, Veep, Washington

Press(ed), Pressing, Pressure Acute, Aldine, Armoire, Atmospheric, Bar, Bench, Blackmail, Bramah, Button, Cabinet, Clarendon, Clothes, Coerce, Cram, Crease, Crimp, Critical, Crowd, Crush, Cupboard, Dragoon, Drill, Dun, Duress, Duresse, Enslave, Exigent, Force, Fourth estate, Goad, Greenmail, Gutter, Hasten, Head, Heat, Herd, Hie, Hug, Hustle, Hydraulic, Impact, Important, Importune, Inarm, Iron, Isobar, Jam, Knead, Lie, Lobby, Mangle, Megabar, Microbar, Mill, Minerva, Newspapers, Obligate, Onus, Osmotic, PA, Pascal, Peer, Persist, Piezo-, Ply, Prease, Printing, Psi, Pump, ➤ PUSH, Ram, Record, Recruit, Reporter, Ridge, Roll, Rounce, Rush, Samizdat, Screw, Scrooge, Scrouge, Scrowdge, Scrum, Serr(e), Sit, Speed, Spur, Squash, Squeeze, Stop, Straint, Stress, Tension, Thlipsis, Threap, Threep, Throng, Throttle, Torr, Tourniquet, ➤ URGE, Urgence, Urgency, Vapour, Vice, Waid(e), Wardrobe, Weight, Wring

Press-gang Force, Impress, Shanghai

Pressman Ed, Reporter, PRO, Twicer

Prestidigitate(r) Conjure, Juggle, Legerdemain, Magician, Palm

Prestige, Prestigious Cachet, Credit, Distinguished, Fame, Influence, Kudos, Notable, Status

Presume, Presumably, Presumption, Presumptuous Allege, Arrogant, Audacity, Believe, Bold, Brass, Cocksure, Cocky, Doubtless, ➤ EXPECT, Familiar, Gall, Impertinent, Insolent, Liberty, Outrecuidance, Pert, Probably, Suppose, Uppish, Whipper-snapper

Pretence, Pretend(er), Pretext Act, Affect(ation), Afflict, Assume, Blind, Bluff, Charade, Charlatan, Claim, Cover, Cram, Dissemble, Dissimulate, Excuse, Feign, Feint, Gondolier, Hokum, Humbug, Hypocrisy, Impostor, Jactitation, Lambert Simnel, Let-on, Make-believe, Malinger, Masquerade, Obreption, Old, Parolles, Perkin Warbeck, Pose, Profess, Pseud(o), Quack, Sham, Simulate, Stale, Stalking-horse, Subterfuge, Suppose, Warbeck, Young

Pretension, Pretentious(ness) Arty, Bombast, Fantoosh, Fustian, Gaudy, Grandiose, High-falutin(g), Kitsch, La-di-da, Orotund, Ostentatious, Overblown, Paraf(f)le, Pompous, Pseud(o), Sciolism, Showy, Snobbish, Squirt, Tat, Tinhorn, Uppity

Pretty Becoming, Chocolate-box, Comely, Cute, Dish, Decorate, Elegant, Fair(ish), Fairway, Inconie, Incony, Keepsaky, Moderately, Pass, Peach, Picturesque, Primp, Quite, Sweet, Twee, Winsome

Prevail(ing) Dominate, Endure, Go, Induce, Persist, Persuade, Predominant, Preponderate, Reign, Ring, Triumph, Victor, Win

Prevalent Catholic, Common, Dominant, Endemic, Epidemic, Obtaining, Rife, Widespread

Prevaricate, Prevarication Equivocate, Hedge, Lie, Runaround, Stall, Whittie-whattie

Prevent(ive) Avert, Bar, Debar, Deter, Embar, Estop, Foreclose, Forfend, Help, Impound, Inhibit, Keep, Let, Obstruct, Obviate, Preclude, Prophylactic, Stop, Theriac, Trammel

Preview Sneak, Trailer, Vernissage

Previous(ly) Afore, Already, Before, Earlier, Ere(-now), Fore, Former, Hitherto, Once, Prior

Prey Booty, Feed, Kill, Pelt, Plunder, Predate, Proul, Prowl, Quarry, Raven, Ravin(e), Soyle, Spreagh, Victim

Price(d), Price-raising Appraise, Assess, Charge, Consequence, Contango, ➤ COST, Dearth, Due, Evens, Expense, Fee, Fiars, Hire, Limit, List, Market, Packet, Quotation, Quote, Rate, Regrate, Reserve, Song, Starting, Street value, Unit, Upset, Value, Vincent, Weregild, Wergeld, Wergild, Worth, Yardage

Prick(ed), Prickle, Prickly Acanaceous, Accloy, Argemone, Arrect, Bearded, Brakier, Bramble, Brog, Bunya, Cactus, Cloy, Cnicus, Echinate, Goad, Gore, Hedgehog, Hedgepig, Impel, Inject, Jab, Jook, Juk, Kali, Penis, Pierce, Prod, Puncture, Rubus, Ruellia, Seta, Setose, Smart, Spinate, Stab, Star-thistle, Stimulus, Sting, Tattoo, Tatu, Teasel, Thistle, Thorn, Tingle, Urge

Prickly heat Miliaria

Prickly-pear Opuntia, Tuna

Pride Bombast, Brag, Conceit, Elation, Esprit de corps, Glory, Hauteur, Hubris, Inordinate, Lions, London, Machismo, Plume, Preen, Purge, Triumphalism, Vainglory, Vanity

Priest(ess), Priests Aaron, Abaris, Abbess, Abbot, Ananias, Annas, Archimandrite, Bacchae, Bacchantes, Baptes, Becket, Bonze, Brahmin, Cardinal, Clergyman, Cleric, Cohen, Concelebrant, Corybant(es), Curé, Dalai Lama, Druid, Eli, Elisha, Fetial, Flamen, Fr, Habacuc, Habakkuk, Hero, Hieratic, Hierophant, High, Io, Jethro, Lack-Latin, Lama, Laocoon, Levite, Lucumo, Mage, Magus, Mambo, Marabout, Metropolitan, Missionary, Monsignor, Mufti, Norma, Oratorian, Padre, Papa, Pastor, Patercove, Patrico, Pawaw, Presbyter, Père, Pontifex, Pontiff, Pope, Powwow, Pr, Preacher, Prelate, Prior(ess), Pythia, Rabbi, Rebbe, Rev, Sacerdotal, Savonarola, Seminarian, Shaman, Shaveling, Sky pilot, Tohunga, Vicar, Vivaldi, Worker, Zadok

Prig Dandy, Fop, Humbug, Nimmer, Pilfer, Prude, Puritan

Prim Demure, Mun, Neat, Old-maidish, Preceese, Precise, Proper, Starchy

Primacy, Primate Ape, Aye-aye, Bandar, Bigfoot, Biped, Bishop, Bush baby, Cardinal, Ebor, Gibbon, Hanuman, Hominid, Jackanapes, King-kong, Loris, Macaque, Magot, Mammal, Marmoset, ➤ MONKEY, Orang, Pongid, Potto, Prosimian, Quadruman, Ramapithecus, Rhesus, Sifaka

Prima donna Diva, Patti, Star

Prim(a)eval Ancient, Prehistoric, Primitive

Prime(r), Primary, Priming Arm, Basic, Bloom, Cardinal, Charging, Chief, Choice, Claircolle, Clearcole, Clerecole, Detonator, Donat, Donet, Election, Enarm, First, Flower, Heyday, Mature, Original, Paramount, Peak, Radical, Remex, Supreme, Thirteen, Tip-top, Totient, Totitive, Valuable, Windac, Windas, Ylem

Prime Minister Asquith, Attlee, Baldwin, Begin, Bute, Canning, Chamberlain, Chatham, Dewan, Disraeli, Diwan, Eden, Grey, Home, Leaderene, North, Peel, Pitt, PM, Premier, Shastri, Tanaiste, Taoiseach, Thatcher, Walpole

Primitive Aborigine, Amoeba, Antediluvian, Arabic, Archaic, Barbaric, Caveman, Crude, Early, Evolué, Fundamental, Naive, Neanderthal, Neolithic, Old, Persian, Pro, Prothyl(e), Protyl(e), Radical, Rudimentary, Savage, Subman, Turkish, Uncivilised, Ur

Primordial Blastema, Fundamental, Original

Primrose, Primula League, Oenothera, Onagra, Ox-lip, Pa(i)gle, Rosebery, Vicar, Yellow

Prince(ly) Ahmed, Albert, Ameer, Amir, Amphitryon, Anchises, Atheling, Barnmecide, Black, Cadmus, Caliph, Chagan, Charming, Crown, Czarevich, Elector, Equerry, Eugene, Florizel, Fortinbras, Gaekwar, Guicowar, Hal, Highness, Hospodar, Huzoor, Igor, Inca, Infante, Khan, Ksar, Lavish, Lucumo, Margrave, Meleager, Merchant, Mir, Mirza, Nawab, Nizam, Noble, Otto, P, Pendragon, Porphyrogenite, Potentate, Rainier, Rajah, Rana, Ras, Rasselas, Ratoo, Ratu, Regal, RH, Rupert, Serene, Sharif, Shereef, Sherif, Siegfried, Student, Tengku, Tsar(evich), Tunku, Upper Roger

Princess Andromache, Andromeda, Anne, Ariadne, Begum, Czarevna, Czarista, Danae, Di(ana), Electra, Electress, Eudocia, Europa, Hermione, Hesione, Ida, Imogen, Infanta, Iseult, Isolde, Jezebel, Maharanee,

Maharani, Pocahontas, Procne, Rani, Regan, Tou Wan, Tsarevna, Tsarista, Turandot

Principal Arch, Capital, Central, ➤ CHIEF, Decuman, Especial, First, Foremost, Head, Leading, Main(stay), Major, Mass, Protagonist, Ringleader, Staple, Star

Principality Andorra, Lichtenstein, Monaco, Wales

Principle(s), Principled Animistic, Anthropic, Archimedes, Axiom, Basis, Brocard, Canon, Carnot, Code, Criterion, Cui bono, Cy pres, D'Alembert's, Doctrine, Dogma, Element, Entelechy, Essential, Fermat's, Gause's, Generale, Germ, Honourable, Huygen's, Key, Law, Le Chatelier's, Logos, Methodology, Organon, Ormazd, Ormuzd, Pauli-exclusion, Peter, Platform, Pleasure, Precept, Prescript, Rationale, Reason, Rudiment, Rule, Sakti, Seed, Shakti, Summum bonum, Spirit, Tenet, Theorem, Ticket, Yang, Yin

Prink Beautify, Bedeck, Dress

Print(er), Printing Baskerville, Batik, Benday, Bromide, Calotype, Caveman, Caxton, Chromo, Cibachrome, Cicero, Collotype, Dab, Dot matrix, Elzevir, Engrave, Etching, Fine, Flexography, Font, Gravure, Gurmukhi, Gutenberg, Heliotype, Impress, Incunabula, Ink-jet, Intaglio, Italic, Laser, Letterpress, Line, Lino-cut, Lithograph, Logotype, Lower-case, Monotype®, Moon, Off-line, Offset, Oleo, Oleograph, Opaline, Plate, Positive, Press, Publish, Report, Reproduction, Rotogravure, Samizdat, Serigraph, Ship, Silk-screen, Small, Smoot, Splash, Stamp, Stenochrome, Stonehand, Strike, Thermal, Typesetter, Whorl, Woodcut, Xerography, Zincograph

Printing-press Rounce

Prior(ity) Abbot, Afore, Antecedent, Earlier, Former, Hitherto, Monk, Overslaugh, Pre-, Precedence, Prefard, Preference, Previous, Privilege, Triage

▶ **Prise** see PRIZE

Prism(s), Prismatic Catadioptric, Iriscope, Nicol, Periaktos, Rhombohedron, Spectrum, Teinoscope, Wollaston

Prison Albany, Alcatraz, Bagnio, Barracoon, Bastille, Bin, Bird, Bridewell, Brig, Brixton, Cage, Can, Cell, Chillon, Chok(e)y, Clink, Club, College, Confine, Cooler, Coop, Counter, Dartmoor, Dungeon, Durance, Fleet, Fotheringhay, Gaol, Glass-house, Guardhouse, Guardroom, Gulag, Hokey, Holloway, Hoos(e)gow, Hulk(s), Internment, ➤ JAIL, Jug, Kitty, Limbo, Lob's pound, Lock-up, Logs, Lumber, Marshalsea, Massymore, Maze, Newgate, Nick, Oflag, Open, Panopticon, Pen, Penitentiary, Pentonville, Pit, Poke(y), Pound, Quad, Quod, Rasp-house, Reformatory, Roundhouse, Scrubs, Shop, Sing-sing, Slammer, Spandau, Stalag, Stir, Strangeways, The Leads, Tol(l)booth, Tower, Tronk, Wandsworth

Prisoner Canary-bird, Captive, Collegian, Collegiate, Con(vict), Detainee, Detenu, Inmate, Internee, Lag, Lifer, Political, POW, Trustee, Trusty, Yardbird, Zek

Pristine Fire-new, Fresh, New, Original, Unmarked, Unspoiled

Private(ly) Ain, Aside, Atkins, Auricular, Buccaneer, Byroom, Clandestine, Close, Closet, Confidential, Enisle(d), Esoteric, Homefelt, Hush-hush, In camera, Individual, Inner, Intimate, Non-com, Own, Personal, Piou-piou, Poilu, Proprietary, Pte, Rank(er), Retired, Sanction, Sapper, Secret, Several, ➤ SOLDIER, Sub rosa, Tommy

Privateer(s) Buccaneer, Corsair, Freebooter, Marque(s), Pirate

Privation Hardship, Penury, Want

Privileg(ed) Birthright, Blest, Charter, Curule, Enviable, Exempt, Favour, Franchise, Freedom, Indulgence, Liberty, Mozarab, Nomenklatura, Octroi, Patent, Prerogative, Pryse, Regale, Regalia, Right, Sac

Privy Apprised, Can, Closet, Intimate, Jakes, John, Loo, Necessary, Reredorter, Secret, Sedge, Siege

Prize(s), Prizewinner Acquest, Apple, Archibald, Assess, Award, Best, Booby, Booker, Bravie, Capture, Champion, Consolation, Creach, Cup, Dux, Efforce, ➤ ESTEEM, Force, Garland, Goncourt, Grice, Honour, Jackpot, Jemmy, Lever, Lot, Money, Nobel, Palm, Pearl, Pewter, Pie, Plum, Plunder, Pot, Pulitzer, Purse, Ram, Reprisal, ➤ REWARD, Scalp, Ship, Spreaghery, Sprechery, Stakes, Tern, Treasure, Trophy, Turner, Value

Pro Aye, Coach, For, Harlot, Moll, Paid, Tramp, Yea, Yes

Probable, Probability Apparent, Belike, Ergodic, Feasible, Likely, Possible

Probation(er) Novice, Novitiate, Stibbler, Test, Trainee, Trial

Probe Antenna, Bore, Cassini, Delve, Dredge, Explore, Fathom, Feeler, Fossick, Inquire, Investigate, Pelican, Poke, Pump, ➤ SEARCH, Seeker, Sound, Space, Stylet, Tent, Thrust, Tracer

Probity Honour, Integrity, Justice

Problem(s) Acrostic, Boyg, Brainteaser, Crux, Dilemma, Egma, Enigma, Facer, Glitch, Handful, Hang-up, Headache, Hitch, Hurdle, Indaba, Knot(ty), Koan, Miniature, Musive, Net, Nuisance, Obstacle, Pons asinorum, Poser, Quandary, Question, Re, Rebus, Riddle, Rider, Snag, Sorites, Sum, Teaser, Thing, Tickler, Toughie, Tsuris, Yips

Proboscis Haustellum, Promuscis, Snout, Trunk

Proceed(s), Proceeding, Procedure Acta, Afoot, Algorithm, Continue, Course, Drill, Emanate, Fand, Flow, Fond, Goes, Haul, Issue, MO, Machinery, March, Mechanics, Mine, Modal, Move, On, Pass, Practice, Praxis, Process, Profit, Punctilio, Pursue, Put, Rake, Return, Rite, Routine, Sap, Steps, System, Take, Use, Yead(s), Yede, Yeed

Process(ion) Acromion, Action, Ala, Ambarvalia, Axon, Ben Day, Bessemer, Catalysis, Cortège, Demo, Haber, Handle, Markov, Method, Moharram, Mond, Motorcade, Muharram, Open hearth, Pageant, Parade, Paseo, Photosynthesis, Pipeline, Pomp, Recycle, Series, Skimmington, Solway, Speciation, String, Train, Treat, Trial

Proclaim, Proclamation Announce, Annunciate, Ban, Blaze, Blazon, Boast, Broadsheet, Cry, Edict, Enounce, Enunciate, Herald, Indiction, Kerygma, Oyez, Preconise, Profess, Publish, Ring, Shout, Trumpet, Ukase

Procrastinate, Procrastinating Defer, Delay, Dilatory, Dilly-dally, Linger, Pettifog, Postpone, Shelve, Temporise, Vacillate

Procreate Beget, Engender, Generate, Initiate
Procrustean Conformity
Proctor Agent, Monitor, Prog, Proxy
Procurator, Procure(r) Achieve, Aunt, Crimp, Earn, Get, Induce, Naunt, Obtain, Pander, Pilate, Pimp, Sort, Suborn
Prod Egg, Goad, Impel, Jab, Job, Jog, Nudge, Poke, Pote
Prodigal Costly, Lavish, Profligate, Unthrift, Wanton, Wasteful, Waster
Prodigious, Prodigy Abnormal, Amazing, Huge, Immense, Monster, Monument, Mozart, Phenomenal, Portentous, Tremendous, Wonder, Wonderwork, Wunderkind
Produce(r), Producing Afford, Breed, Cause, Create, Crop, Ean, Edit, Effect, Engender, Evoke, Exhibit, Extend, Fruit, Generate, Get, Grow, Impresario, Issue, Kind, Make, Offspring, Onstream, Originate, Output, Propage, Propound, Raise, Son, Stage, Supply, Teem, Throw, Wares, Whelp, Yield
▷ **Produces** may indicate an anagram
Product(ion), Productive(ness), Productivity Actualities, Apport, Artefact, Ashtareth, Ashtaroth, Astarte, Bore, Coefficient, Drama, Fecund, Fertile, Fruit, Genesis, Harvest, Output, Outturn, Profilic, Result, Rich, Show, Speiss, Uberous, Uberty, Waste, Work, Yield
▷ **Production** may indicate an anagram
Proem Pre, Preface, Foreword, Overture
Profane, Profanation, Profanity Coarse, Coprolalia, Desecrate, Impious, Irreverent, Sacrilege, Unholy, Violate
Profess(ed), Professor Absent-minded, Academic, Adjoint, Admit, Asset, Challenger, Claim, Declare, Disney, Emeritus, Higgins, Hodja, Kho(d)ja, Know-all, Ostensible, Own, Practise, Pundit, Regent, Regius, RP, STP
Profession(al) Admission, Assurance, Buppy, Business, Career, Creed, Expert, Métier, Practitioner, Pretence, Pursuit, Regular, Salaried, Skilled, Trade, Vocation, Yuppie
Proffer Give, Present, Proposition, Tender
Proficiency, Proficient Adept, Alert, Dan, Expert, Forte, Past master, Practised, Skill, Technique
Profile Analysis, Contour, Half-face, Loral, Outline, Silhouette, Sketch, Statant, T(h)alweg, Vignette
Profit(able), Profiteer, Profits Advantage, Arbitrage, Asset, Avail, Benefit, Boot, Bunce, Cere, Clear, Divi(dend), Economic, Edge, Emoluments, Exploit, Fat, Gain, Graft, Gravy, Grist, Income, Increment, Issue, Jobbery, Juicy, Leech, Lucrative, Makings, Melon, Milch cow, Mileage, Moneymaker, Net, Pay(ing), Perk, Rake-off, Return, Reward, Royalty, Spoils, Use, Usufruct, Utile, Utility, Vail
Profligate Corinthian, Corrupt, Degenerate, Dissolute, Extravagant, Lecher, Libertine, Lorel, Losel(l), Oatmeal, Rakehell, Reprobate, Roué, Spend-all, Wastrel
Profound Altum, Bottomless, Complete, Deep, Intense, Recondite
Profuse, Profusion Abundant, Copious, Excess, Free, Galore, Lavish, Liberal, Lush, Quantity, Rank, Rich, Two-a-penny

Progenitor, Progenitrix Ancestor, Ma, Predecessor, Sire, Stock

Progeny Children, Descendants, Fruit, Issue, Offspring, Seed

Prognosis Forecast, Prediction

Prognosticate, Prognostication Augur, Foretell, Omen, Predict, Prophesy

Program(ming) language, Programmer Ada, Algol, Applet, BIOS, Basic, Bloatware, Boot, Bot, Cancelbot, CU See Me, Cobol, Columbus, Debugger, Dictionary, Est, Firmware, Fortran, Freeware, Inputter, Java®, Linker, LISP, Logo, PROLOG, PROM, Package, Pascal, Router, Screensaver, Search engine, Shell, Spreadsheet, Telnet, Utility, Web browser, Web crawler

Programme Agenda, Broadcast, Card, Code, Docusoap, Event, Fly-on-the-wall, Infotainment, Linear, ➤ PDL, Prank, Playbill, Schedule, Scheme, Sked, Soap, Software, Syllabus, System, Telecast, Telethon, Timetable

Progress(ive), Progression ➤ ADVANCE, Afoot, Arithmetic, Avant garde, Course, Fabian, Flow, Forge, Forward, Gain, Geometric, Go, Growth, Headway, Incede, Liberal, Move, Onwards, Paraphonia, Pilgrim's, Prosper, Rack, Rake's, Reformer, Roll, Run, Sequence, Series, Step, Vaunce, Way, Yead, Yede, Yeed

Prohibit(ion), Prohibitionist Ban, Block, Debar, Dry, Embargo, Estop, Forbid, Hinder, Index, Interdict, Noli-me-tangere, Prevent, Pussyfoot, Taboo, Tabu, Veto

Project(ile), Projecting, Projection, Projector Aim, Ammo, Assignment, Astrut, Ball, Ballistic, Beetle, Bullet, Butt, Buttress, Cam, Cast, Catapult, Cinerama®, Cog, Conceive, Condyle, Conic, Console, Corbel, Crossette, Coving, Cutwater, Denticle, Diascope, Discus, Eaves, Echinus, Elance, Enterprise, Episcope, Excrescence, Exsert, Extrapolate, Fet(ter)lock, Flange, Gair, Gore, Guess, Hangover, Hoe, Inion, Jut, Kern, Knob, Ledge, Lobe, Lug, Malleolus, Manhattan, Mercator, Mitraille, Mollweide, Mutule, Nab, Nose, Nunatak(er), Olecranon, Orillion, Outcrop, Outjut, Overhang, Overhead, Oversail, Peters, Pitch, Planetarium, Polyconic, Pork barrel, Prickle, Promontory, ➤ PROTRUDE, Proud(er), Raguly, Rocket, Sail, Salient, Sally, Scaw, Scheme, Screen, Shelf, Shrapnel, Skaw, Snag, Snout, Spline, Sponson, Sprocket, Spur, Squarrose, Stereopticon, Tang, Tappet, Tenon, Throw, Toe, Tracer, Trippet, Trunnion, Tusk, Umbo, Undertaking, Villus, Vitascope

Prolapse Procidence

Proletarian, Proletariat People, Plebeian, Popular

Proliferate Expand, Increase, Multiply, Propagate, Snowball

Prolific Abounding, Fecund, Fertile, Fruitful, Profuse, Teeming

Prolix(ity) Lengthy, Prosaic, Rambling, Rigmarole, Verbose, Wire-draw, Wordy

Prologue Introduce, Preface

Prolong(ed) Extend, Lengthen, Protract, Sostenuto, Spin, Sustain

Prom(enade) Alameda, Boulevard, Cakewalk, Catwalk, Crush-room, Esplanade, Front, Mall, Parade, Paseo, Pier, Sea-front, Stroll, ➤ WALK

Prometheus Fire

Promethium Pm

Prominence, Prominent Antitragus, Blatant, Bold, Colliculus, Condyle, Conspicuous, Egregious, Emphasis, Featured, Gonion, Important, Insistent, Manifest, Marked, Salient, Signal, Teat, Toot, Tragus

Promiscuous, Promiscuity Casual, Free, Indiscriminate, Light, Motley, Pell-mell, Slapper, Whoredom

Promise, Promising Accept, Augur, Avoure, Behest, Behight, Behote, Bode, Coming, Covenant, Engagement, Foretaste, Guarantee, Hecht, Hest, Hete, Hight, IOU, Likely, Manifest, Parole, Pledge, Plight, Pollicitation, Potential, Recognisance, Recognizance, Rosy, Sign, Sponsor, Swear, Tile, Undertake, Vow, Warranty, Word

Promised land Beulah, Canaan, Israel

Promissory note IOU, PN

Promontory Bill, Cliff, Foreland, Headland, Hoe, Hogh, Mull, Naze, Nose, Ness, Peak, Spit

Promote(r), Promotion Adman, Advance, ➤ ADVERTISE, Aggrandise, Aid, Assist, Blurb, Boost, Campaign, Dog and pony show, Elevate, Encourage, Foment, Foster, Further, Help, Hype, Increase, Make, Prefer, Promulgate, Provoke, Queen, Rear, Remove, Run, Sell, Sponsor, Spruik, Stage, Step, Tendencious, Tendentious, Upgrade, Uplead, Uprate

Prompt(er), Promptly, Promptness Actuate, Alacrity, Autocue®, Believe, Celerity, Chop-chop, Cue, Egg, Expeditious, Frack, Idiot-board, Immediate, Incite, Inspire, Instigate, Move, Pernicious, Premove, Punctual, Quick, Ready, Speed(y), Spur, Stimulate, Sudden, Tight, Tit(e), Titely, Tyte, Urgent

Promulgate Preach, Proclaim, Publish, Spread

Prone Apt, Groof, Grouf, Grovel, Liable, Lying, Prostrate, Recumbent, Subject, Susceptible

Prong Fang, Fork, Grain, Peg, Tang, Tine

Pronghorn Cabrie, Cabrit

Pronoun Personal, Reciprocal, Relative

Pronounce(d), Pronouncement Adjudicate, Affirm, Articulate, Assert, Conspicuous, Clear, Declare, Dictum, Enunciate, Fiat, Marked, Opinion, Palatalise, Pontificate, Recite, Utter, Vocal, Voice, Vote

Pronto PDQ

Pronunciation Betacism, Cacoepy, Delivery, Diction, Etacism, Itacism, Orthoepy, Phonetics, Plateasm, Proclitic, Received, Rhotacism, Sound

Proof Apagoge, Argument, Bona fides, Confirmation, Evidence, Firm, Foundry, Galley, Positive, Preif(e), Probate, Pull, Quality, Refutation, Remarque, Resistant, Revision, Secure, Strength, Test, Tight, Token, Trial, Upmake, Validity

Prop Airscrew, Bolster, Buttress, Crutch, Dog-shore, Fulcrum, Leg, Loosehead, Misericord(e), Punch(eon), Rance, Rest, Shore, Sprag, Spur, Staff, Stay, Stempel, Stemple, Stilt, Stoop, Stoup, Stull, ➤ SUPPORT, Tighthead, Underpin

Propaganda, Propagandist Agitprop, Ballyhoo, Brainwashing, Chevalier, Doctrine, Promotion, Psyop, Psywar, Publicity, Slogan

Propagate, Propagator Dispread, Generate, Graft, Hatch, Increase, Produce, Promulgate, Provine, Spread, Tan-bed

Propel(ler) Airscrew, Ca', Drive, Fin, Launch, Leg, Lox, ➤ MOVE, Oar, Paddle, Pedal, Project, Push, Rotor, Row, Screw, Throw

Propensity Aptness, Bent, Inclination, Penchant, Tendency

Proper(ly) Ain, Convenance, Correct, Decent, Decorous, Due, En règle, Ethical, ➤ FIT, Genteel, Governessy, Kosher, Noun, Ought, Own, Pakka, Pathan, Prim, Pucka, Pukka, Puritanic, Seemly, Suitable, Tao, Trew, True, Well

Property Assets, Attribute, Aver, Belongings, Chattel, Chose, Contenement, Demesne, Des res, Dowry, Effects, Enclave, Escheat, Escrow, Estate, Fee, Feu, Flavour, Fonds, Freehold, Goods, Hereditament, Hotchpot, Inertia, Jointure, Leasehold, Living, Means, Paraphernalia, Peculium, Personal, Personalty, Premises, Private, Public, Quale, Quality, Stock, Stolen, Theft, Time-share, Trait, Usucapion, Usucaption

Prophesy, Prophet(ess), Prophetic Amos, Augur, Bab, Balaam, Calchas, Cassandra, Daniel, Divine, Deborah, Elias, Elijah, Elisha, Ezekiel, Ezra, Fatal, Fatidical, Forecast, Foretell, Germancer, Habakkuk, Haggai, Hosea, Is, Isa, Is(a)iah, Jeremiah, Joel, Jonah, Mahdi, Mahound, Major, Malachi, Mani, Mantic, Micah, Minor, Mohammed, Mormon, Mopsus, Moses, Nahum, Nathan, Nostradamus, Obadiah, Ominous, Oracle, Portend, Predictor, Prognosticate, Pythoness, Seer, Sibyl, Tiresias, Vatic, Vaticinate, Voluspa, Zephaniah, Zoroaster, Zwickau

Prophylactic, Prophylaxis Inoculation, Preventive, Serum, Vaccine, Variolation

Propitiate Appease, Atone, Pacify, Reconcile, Sop

Propitious Benign, Favourable, Lucky

Proponent Advocate, Backer, Partisan

Proportion(ate) Commensurable, Dimension, Portion, Pro rata, Quantity, Quota, Ratio, Reason, Regulate, Relation, Sine, Size, Soum, Sowm

Proposal, Propose Advance, Bid, Bill, Eirenicon, Feeler, Irenicon, Mean, Motion, Move, Nominate, Offer, Overture, Plan, Pop, Proffer, Propound, Recommend, Resolution, Scheme, Slate, Submission, ➤ SUGGEST, Table, Tender, Volunteer, Woot, Would

Proposition Axiom, Corollary, Deal, Disjunction, Ergo, Hypothesis, Lemma, Overture, Pons asinorum, Porism, Premise, Premiss, Rider, Sorites, Spec, Superaltern, Theorem, Thesis

Propound Advocate, Purpose, State

Proprietor, Propriety Correctitude, Decorum, Etiquette, Grundy, Keeper, Lord, Master, Owner, Patron, Rectitude

Prosaic Common, Drab, Flat, Humdrum, Tedious, Workaday

Proscenium Forestage

Proscribe Exile, Outlaw

Prose, Prosy Haikai, Polyphonic, Saga, Stich, Verbose, Version, Writing

Prosecute, Prosecutor, Prosecution Allege, Avvogadore, Charge, Fiscal, Furtherance, Indict, Practise, Public, Sue, Wage

Proselytise(r), Proselytism Indoctrination, Propagandism, Souper

Prospect(or) Explore, Forty-niner, Fossick, Look-out, Mine, ➤ OUTLOOK, Panorama, Perspective, Pleases, Reefer, Scenery, Search, Sourdough, View, Vista, Visto, Wildcatter

Prosper(ity), Prosperous Blessed, Blossom, Boom, Fair, Flourish, Heyday, Mérimée, Palmy, ➤ SUCCEED, Thee, Thrift, Thrive, Up, Warison, Wealth, Welfare, Well-to-do

Prostitute Brass, Bulker, Callet, Catamite, Chippie, Cockatrice, Cocotte, Debase, Dell, Dolly-mop, Doxy, Fille de joie, Harlot, Hetaera, Hetaira, Ho, Jailbait, Loose woman, Madam, Magdalen(e), Moll, Mutton, Plover, Pole-cat, Pro, Punk, Quail, Rent-boy, Road, Rough trade, Scrubber, Slap, Stew, Streetwalker, Strumpet, Tart, Trull, Venture, Whore

Prostrate, Prostration Collapse, Exhausted, Fell, Flat, Ko(w)tow, Laid, Obeisance, Overcome, Procumbent, Prone, Repent, Throw

Protactinium Pa

Protean Amoebic, Fusible, Variable

Protect(ed), Protection, Protector Adonise, Aegis, Alexin, Arm, Asylum, Auspice, Bastion, Bestride, Bield, Buckler, Chaffron, Chamfrain, Chamfron, Charm, Cherish, Cloche, Coat, Cocoon, Coleor(r)hiza, Conserve, Cover, Covert, Cromwell, Cushion, Danegeld, Defend, Defilade, Degauss, Egis, Entrenchment, Escort, Estacade, Faun, Flank, Gobo, Groundsheet, Guard(ian), Gumshield, Hedge, House, Hurter, Inalienable, Indemnify, Insure, Keckle, Keep, Kickback, Mac(k)intosh, Mail, Male, Mollycoddle, Mother, Muniment, Noll, Nosey, Orillion, Overall, Parados, Patent, Patron, Pomander, Preserve, Rabbit's foot, Redome, Safeguard, Sandbag, Save, Schanse, Schan(t)ze, Screen, Scug, Shadow, Sheathing, Sheeting, Shelter, ➤ SHIELD, Skug, Splashback, Splashboard, Splasher, Starling, Sunscreen, Tribute, Tutelar, Umbrella, Vaccine, Ward(ship), Warhead, Warrant, Weatherboard, Weatherstrip, Wing

Protégé Pupil, Tutee, Ward

Protein Abrin, Actin, Actomyosin, Adipsin, Alanine, Albumen, Albumin, Aleuron(e), Allergen, Amandine, Analogon, Angiotensin, Antibody, Avidin, Bradykinin, Calmodulin, Capsid, Capsomere, Caseinogen, Ceruloplasmin, Collagen, Complement, Conchiolin, Conjugated, Cytokine, Dystrophin, Elastin, Enzyme, Factor VIII, Ferritin, Fibrin, Fibrinogen, Fibroin, Flagellin, Gelatin, Gliadin, Glob(ul)in, Gluten, Haemoglobin, Haptoglobin, Histone, Hordein, Immunoglobulin, Incaparina, Interferon, Interleukin, Lactalbumin, Lectin, Legumin, Leptin, Leucin(e), Luciferin, Lysin, Meat, Myogen, Myoglobin, Mucin, Myosin, Opsin, Opsonin, Ovalbumin, Pepsin(e), Phaseolin, Prion, Prolamin(e), Protamine, Proteose, Prothrombin, Quorn®, Renin, Repressor, Ribosome, Sclerotin, Sericin, Serum albumin, Serum globulin, Single-cell, Spectrin, Spongin, Soya, Tempeh, Toxalbumin, Transferrin, Tropomyosin, Troponin, Tubulin, Vitellin, Zein

Protest(er) Andolan, Aver, Avouch, Clamour, Come, Démarche, Demo, Demonstrate, Demur, Deprecate, Dharna, Dissent, Expostulate, Gherao, Hartal, Inveigh, Lock-out, Luddite, March, Object, Outcry, Picket, Plea, Refus(e)nik, Remonstrate, Sit-in, Squawk, Squeak, Squeal, Work-to-rule

Protestant Amish, Anabaptist, Anglo, Calvin, Congregationalism, Covenanter, Cranmer, Dissenter, Evangelic, Gospeller, Huguenot, Independent, Lady, Lutheran, Mennonite, Methodist, Moravian, Nonconformist, Oak-boy, Orangeman, Pentecostal, Pietism, Prod, Puritan, Stundist, Swaddler, Wesleyan

Protocol Agreement, Code, Convention, Etiquette, Point-to-Point

Proton Nucleon

Protoplasm(ic) Cytode, Sarcode

Prototype Exemplar, Model, Original, Pattern

Protozoa(n) Am(o)eba, Foraminifer, Giardia, Globigerina, Gregarine, Heliozoan, Infusoria, Leishmania, Moner(a), Moneron, Radiolaria, Rhizopod, Thrichomonad, Trypanosome, Vorticella

Protract(ed) Delay, ➤ EXTEND, Lengthen, Livelong, Prolong

Protrude, Protrusion Bulge, Exsert, Jut, Pop, Pout, Project, Strout, Tel

Protuberance, Protuberant Apophysis, Bulge, Bump, Condyle, Gibbous, Hump, Knap, Knob, Malleolus, Node, Papillose, Papule, Spadix, Swelling, Tragus, Tuber, Venter

Proud Arrogant, Boaster, Cocky, Conceited, Dic(k)ty, Elated, Flush, Haughty, Haut, Level, Lordly, Orgulous, Superb, Vain

Prove(d) Apod(e)ictic, Argue, Ascertain, Assay, Attest, Authenticate, Aver, Confirm, Convince, Evince, Justify, ➤ PROOF, ➤ SHOW, Substantiate, Test

Proverb Adage, Axiom, Byword, Gnome, Maxim, Paroemia, Saw

▷ **Proverbial** may refer to the biblical Proverbs

Provide(d), Provident Afford, Allow, Arrange, Besee, Bring, Cater, Compare, Conditional, Endow, Equip, Far-seeing, Fend, Find, Furnish, Generate, Give, If, Maintain, Proviso, Purvey, Serve, So, Sobeit, ➤ SUPPLY

Province, Provincial(ism) Acadia, Alberta, Anjou, Antwerp, Area, Connacht, District, Eparchy, Eritrea, Exclave, Eyalet, Forte, Gascony, Hebel, Henan, Hubei, Iloilo, Insular, Jiangsu, Jiangxi, Jilin, Land, Leinster, Liaoning, Lusitania, Manitoba, Maritime, Mofussil, Munster, Narrow, Nome, Normandy, Oblast, Ontario, Palatinate, Pale, Patavinity, Picardy, Realm, Regional, R(h)aetia, Rural, Sanjak, Satrapy, Shoa, Sircar, Subah, Suburban, Territory, Tyrol, Ulster, Vilayet

Provision(s) Acates, A(p)panage, Board, Fodder, Jointure, Larder, Proggins, Scran, Skran, Stock, Supply, Suttle, Viands, Viaticum, Victuals

Proviso, Provisional Caution, Caveat, Clause, Condition, Interim, IRA, On trial, Reservation, Salvo, Temporary, Tentative

Provocation, Provocative, Provoke Agacant, Alluring, Egg, Elicit, Erotic, Exacerbate, Excite, Flirty, Harass, Incense, Induce, Instigate, Irk, Irritate, Needle, Nettle, Occasion, Pique, Prompt, Raise, Sedition, Spark, Stimulate, Tar, Tease, Vex, Wind up

Provost Dean, Keeper, Marshal, Warden

Prow Bow, Cutwater, Fore, Nose, Prore, Stem

Pro-war Hawk

Prowess Ability, Bravery, Forte, Fortitude

Prowl(er) Hunt, Lurch, Lurk, Mooch, Prole, Ramble, Roam, Rove, Snoke, Snook, Snowk, Tenebrio, Tom

Proxime accessit Next best

Proximity Handiness

Proxy Agent, Attorn, Deputy, PP, Regent, Sub, Surrogate, Vicar, Vice

Prude(nce), Prudent, Prudery Bluenose, Canny, Caution, Circumspect, Comstocker, Conservative, Discreet, Discretion, Foresight, Frugal, Grundyism, Metis, Mrs Grundy, Politic, Prig, Prissy, Provident, Sage, Sensible, Sparing, Strait-laced, Strait-lacer, Thrifty, Vice-nelly, Victorian, Ware, Wary, Well-advised, Wise

Prune(r) Bill-hook, Dehorn, Lop, Plum, Proign, Proin(e), Reduce, Reform, Secateur, Sned, Thin, Trim

Prunella Hedge-sparrow, Self-heal

Prurient Avaricious, Itchy, Lewd, Obscene

Prussia(n) Blue, Junker, Pruce, Spruce, Westphalian

Pry Ferret, Force, Lever, Meddle, Nose, Paul, Peep, Question, Search, Snoop, Toot

Psalm Anthem, Cantate, Chant, Chorale, Hallel, Hymn, Introit, Jubilate, Metrical, Miserere, Neck-verse, Paean, Proper, Ps, Song, Tone, Tract, Venite

Pseudo Bogus, Mock, Sham, Spurious

Pseudonym Aka, Alias, Allonym, Anonym, Pen-name, Stage-name

Pshaw Chut, Pooh, Tilley-valley, Tilly-fally, Tilly-vally

Psyche Ego, Self, Soul, Spirit, Superego

Psychiatrist, Psychologist Adler, Alienist, Clare, Coué, Ellis, Freud, Headshrinker, Jung, Laing, Reich, Shrink, Trick-cyclist

Psychic ESP, Lodge, Medium, Seer, Telekinesis

Psychology, Psychologist Behaviourism, Clinical, Depth, Eysenck, Gestalt, Piaget

Ptarmigan Rype

Ptomaine Neurine

Pub Bar, Boozer, Free-house, Gin-palace, Houf(f), House, Howf(f), Inn, Joint, Local, Pothouse, Potshop, Shanty, Tavern, Tiddlywink

Puberty Adolescence, Hebetic, Teens

Pubescence Tomentum

Public Apert, Bar, Civil, Common, Demos, General, Inn, Lay, Limelight, National, Open, Overt, Populace, State, Vulgar, World

Publican Ale-keeper, Bung, Host, Landlord, Licensee, Tapster, Taverner

Publication Announcement, Broadsheet, Edition, Exposé, Issue,
➤ JOURNAL, Lady, Mag, Organ, Pictorial, Samizdat, Tabloid, Tatler, Tract, Tribune, Yearbook

Publicist, Publicity Ad(vert), Airing, Ballyhoo, Coverage, Exposure, Flack, Glare, Hype, Leakage, Limelight, Plug, PRO, Promotion, Propaganda, Réclame, Spin-doctor, Splash

Publish(ed), Publisher, Publicise Air, Blaze, Cape, Delator, Desktop, Disclose, Edit, Evulgate, Issue, Noise, OUP, Out, Pirate, Plug, Post, Print(er), Proclaim, Propagate, Release, Run, Vanity, Vent, Ventilate

Puck Disc, Elf, Lob, Sprite, Squid

Pucker(ed) Cockle, Contract, Gather, Plissé, Purse, Ruck, Shir(r), Wrinkle

Pud Fin, Paw

Pudding Afters, Black, Blancmange, Brown Betty, Cabinet, Charlotte, Christmas, Clootie dumpling, College, Custard, Dessert, Drisheen, Duff, Dumpling, Eve's, Flummery, Fritter, Fromenty, Frumenty, Furme(n)ty, Furmity, Haggis, Hasty, Kugel, Mealie, Milk, Nesselrode, Panada, Pandowdy, Parfait, Pease, Plum, Popover, Rice, Roly-poly, Sowens, Sponge, Spotted dick, Stickjaw, Stodge, Suet, Summer, Sundae, Sweet, Tansy, Tapioca, Umbles, White hass, White hause, White hawse, Yorkshire, Zabaglione

Puddle Collect, Dub, Flush, Pant, Plash, Plouter, Plowter, Pool, Sop

Puff(ed), Puffer, Puffy Advertise, Blouse, Blow, Blowfish, Blurb, Bouffant, Breath, Chuff, Chug, Drag, Encomist, Eulogy, Exsufflicate, Fag, Flaff, Flatus, Fluffy, Fuff, Globe-fish, Grampus, Gust, Hype, Lunt, Pech, Pegh, Pluffy, Plug, Powder, Recommend, Skiff, Slogan, Steam, Swell, Toke, Waff, Waft, Waif, Whiff, Whiffle

Puffin Rockbird, Sea-parrot, Tammie Norie, Tam Noddy

Pug(ilist) Belcher, Boxer, Bruiser, Carlin, Fancy, Fistic, Monkey

Pugnacious Aggressive, Belligerent, Combative

Puke Retch, Sick, Vomit

Pukka Authentic, Genuine, Real, True

Pulchritude Beauty, Cheese-cake, Grace

Pull (up) Adduce, Attraction, Crane, Drag, Draw, Force, Haul, Heave, Heeze, Hook, ➤ INFLUENCE, Lug, Mousle, Pluck, Rein, Ring, Rove, Rug, Saccade, Sally, Sole, Soole, Sowl(e), Stop, Tit, Tow, Trice, Tug, Undertow, Yank, Wrest

Pulley Block, Capstan, Idle(r), Jack-block, Swig, Trice, Trochlea, Truckle

Pullover Jersey, Jumper, Sweater, Sweatshirt

Pullulate Teem

➤ **Pull up** see PULL

Pulp Cellulose, Chyme, Chymify, Crush, Flong, Kenaf, Marrow, Mash, Mush, Pap, Paste, Pomace, Pound, Puree, Rot, Rubbish, Squeeze, Squidge

Pulpit(e) Ambo(nes), Lectern, Mimbar, Minbar, Pew, Rostrum, Tent, Tub, Wood

Pulsate Beat, Palpitate, Quiver, Throb, Vibrate

Pulse Alfalfa, Beat, Calavance, Caravance, Chickpea, D(h)al, Dholl, Dicrotic, Garbanzo, Gram, Groundnut, Ictus, Lentil, Lucerne, Pea, Rhythm, Sain(t)foin, Soy beans, Sphygmus, Sync, Systaltic, Systole, Throb

Pulverise Calcine, Comminute, Contriturate, Demolish, Grind, ➤ POUND, Powder

Puma Catamount, Cougar, Panther

Pummel(ling) Beat, Drub, Fib, Nevel, Pound, Tapotement, Thump

▷ **Pummelled** may indicate an anagram

Pump Bellows, Bowser, Centrifugal, Compressor, Cross-question, Drive, Elicit, Filter, Force, Grease-gun, Grill, Heart, Heat, Hydropult, Inflate, Knee-swell, Nodding-donkey, Parish, Piston, Pulsometer, Question, Shoe, Stirrup, Stomach, Suction, Water

Pumphandle Sweep

Pumpkin Cashaw, Gourd, Quash

Pun Calembour, Clinch, Equivoque, Paragram, Paronomasia, Quibble, Ram

Punch(ed) Antic, Biff, Blow, Boff, Bolo, Box, Bradawl, Bumbo, Card, Check, Chop, Clip, Dry-beat, Fib, Fid, Fist(ic), Glogg, Haymaker, Hit, Hook, Horse, Jab, Key, Knobble, Knubble, KO, Lander, Mat, Milk, Nail set, Nubble, One-er, Perforate, Pertuse, Planter's, Plug, Poke, Polt, Pommel, Pounce, Prod, Pummel, Rabbit, Roundhouse, Rumbo, Slosh, Sock, Sting(o), Sucker, Suffolk, Sunday, Swop, Upper-cut, Wap, Wind, Zest

Punctilious Exact, Formal, Nice, Particular, Picked, Precise, Prim, Stickler

Punctual(ity) Politesse, Prompt, Regular

Punctuate, Punctuation (mark) Bracket, Colon, Comma, Emphasize, Interabang, Interrobang, Interrupt, Mark, Semicolon

Puncture(d) Bore, Centesis, Criblé, Cribrate, Deflate, Drill, Flat, Hole, Lumbar, Perforate, Pierce, Prick

Pundit Expert, Guru, Oracle, Sage, Savant, Swami, Teacher

Pungency, Pungent Acid, Acrid, Acrolein, Alum, Ammonia, Bite, Bitter, Caustic, Hot, Mordant, Nidorous, Piquant, Poignant, Point, Racy, Salt, Spice, Sting, Tangy, Witty

Punish(ed), Punishing, Punishment Amerce, Attainder, Baffle, Bastinado, Beat, Birch, Brasero, Cane, Capital, Cart, Castigate, Chasten, Chastise, Come-uppance, Commination, Corporal, Cucking-stool, Dam(nation), Defrock, Desert(s), Detention, ➤ DISCIPLINE, Fine, Flog, Gantlope, Gate, Gauntlet, Gruel, Hellfire, Hiding, Horsing, Imposition, Impot, Interdict, Jankers, Jougs, Keelhaul, Knout, Laldie, Laldy, Lambast(e), Lines, Log, Marmalise, Necklace, Nemesis, Pack-drill, Pandy, Penalise, Penance, Penology, Perdition, Picket, Pillory, Pine, Rap, Reprisal, Retribution, Ruler, Scaffold, Scath, Scourge, Sentence, Six of the best, Smack, Smite, Spif(f)licate, Stocks, Strafe, Straff, Strap, Strappado, Swinge(ing), Talion, Toco, Toko, Tophet, Treadmill, Trim, Tron, Trounce, Tumbrel, Tumbril, Visit, War(r)ison, Whip, Ywrake, Ywroke

▷ **Punish** may indicate an anagram

Punk Inferior, Neer-do-well, Nobody, Touchwood, Worthless

Punnet Basket, Thug

Punt(er), Punting Antepost, Back, Bet, Gamble, Kent, Kick, Pound, Quant, Turfite

Puny Frail, Inferior, Petty, Reckling, Runtish, Scram, Shilpit, Sickly, Small, Weak

Pup(py) Cub, Whelp

Pupa Chrysalis, Nymph, Obtect

Pupil Abiturient, Apple, Apprentice, Boarder, Cadet, Catechumen, Disciple, Etonian, Eyeball, Follower, Gyte, Junior, L, Monitor, Prefect, Protégé(e), Scholar, Senior, Student, Tutee, Ward

▷ **Pupil** may refer to an eye

Puppet(eer) Bunraku, Creature, Doll, Dummy, Faineant, Fantoccini, Glove, Guignol, Jack-a-lent, Judy, Marionette, Mawmet, Mommet, Motion(-man), Pageant, Pawn, Pinocchio, Promotion, Punch(inello), Quisling, Rod, Tool

Purchase, Purchasing Bargain, Buy, Coff, Compulsory, Earn, Emption, Get, Grip, Halliard, Halyard, Hold, Layaway, ➤ LEVERAGE, Louisiana, Parbuckle, Secure, Shop, Toehold

Pure, Purity Absolute, Cando(u)r, Cathy, Chaste, Chiarezza, Clean(ly), Cosher, Fine, Good, Holy, Immaculate, Incorrupt, Innocent, Intemerate, Inviolate, Kathy, Kosher, Lily, Lilywhite, Maidenhood, Me(a)re, Net(t), Pristine, Quintessence, Sanctity, Sheer, Simon, Simple, Sincere, Snow-white, Stainless, True, Unalloyed, Vertue, Virgin, Virtue, White

Puree Coulis, Fool

Purgative, Purge Aloes, Aloetic, Araroba, Cacoon, Calomel, Cascara, Cassia, Castor-oil, Catharsis, Cholagogue, Colquintida, Croton, Delete, Diacatholicon, Diarrh(o)ea, Drastic, Elaterin, Eliminate, Eluant, Emetic, Enos®, Erase, Evacuant, Exonerate, Expiate, Gleichschaltung, Hiera-picra, Ipecacuanha, Ipomoea, Jalap, Laxative, McCarthyism, Picra, Relaxant, Scour, Senna, Soil, Turbith, Turpeth, Wahoo

Purification, Purifier, Purify(ing) Absolve, Bowdlerise, Catharsis, Clay, Clean(se), Depurate, Dialysis, Distil, Edulcorate, Elution, Exalt, Expurgate, Filter, Fine, Gas-lime, Lustre, Lustrum, Refine, Retort, Samskara, Sanctify, Scorify, Scrub, Try

Puritan(ical) Bible belt, Bluenose, Digger(s), Ireton, Ironsides, Pi, Pilgrim, Precisian, Prude, Prynne, Roundhead, Seeker, Traskite, Waldenses, Wowser, Zealot

Purl(er) Cropper, Eddy, Fall, Knit, Ripple, Stream

Purloin Abstract, Appropriate, Lift, Nab, Pilfer, Snaffle, Steal

Purple Amarantin(e), Assai, Aubergine, Chlamys, Corkir, Cudbear, Dubonnet, Eminence, Golp(e), Heather, Imperial, Indigo, Korkir, Lilac, Magenta, Mallow, Mauvin(e), Mulberry, Murrey, Orcein, Orcin(e), Orcinol, Pance, Pansy, Plum, Pompadour, Pontiff, Porporate, Proin(e), Puce, Puke, Punic, Rhodopsin, Royal, Solferino, Tyrian, Violet, Visual

Purport Bear, Claim, Drift, Feck, Mean, Tenor

Purpose Advertent, Aim, Avail, Cautel, Design, Ettle, Goal, Here-to, ➤ INTENT, Mean(ing), Meant, Mint, Motive, Object, Plan, Point, Raison d'être, ➤ REASON, Resolution, Resolve, Sake, Telic, Telos, Tenor, Use

Purposeless Dysteleology, Otiose

Purr Curr, Rumble

Purse Ad crumenam, Bag, Bung, Caba, Clutch, Crease, Crumenal, Fisc, Fisk, Long Melford, Pocket, Prim, Privy, Prize, Pucker, Spleuchan, Sporran, Wallet, Whistle

▷ **Pursed** may indicate one word within another

Pursue(r), Pursuit Alecto, Business, Chase, Chivvy, Course, Dog, Follow, Hobby, Hot-trod, Hound, Hunt, Practice, Practise, Proceed, Prosecute, Quest, Scouring, Stalk, Trivial

Purulent Mattery

Purvey(or) Cater, Provide, Provisor, Sell, Supply

Pus Empyema, Matter, Purulence, Quitter, Quittor

Push (in) Barge, Birr, Boost, Bunt, Detrude, Drive, Edge, Effort, Elbow, Fire, Horn, Hustle, Impulse, Invaginate, Jostle, Nose, Nudge, Nurdle, Obtrude, Pitchfork, Plod, Ply, Press, Promote, Propel, Railroad, Ram, Sell, ➤ SHOVE, Snoozle, Subtrude, Thrust, Urge

Pushchair Baby buggy®, Buggy, Stroller

Pushover Doddle, Soda

Pusillanimous Coward, Timid, Weak, Yellow

Puss(y) Amentum, ➤ CAT, Catkins, Face, Galore, Hare, Mouth, Rabbit, Septic

Pussyfoot Dry, Equivocate, Inch, Paw, Steal, TT

Put (off; on; out; up) Accommodate, Add, Bet, Cup, Daff, Defer, Dish, Do, Don, Douse, Implant, Impose, Incommode, Inn, Lade, Lodge, Lump, Oust, Pit, Place, Plonk, Set, Smore, Station, Stow

Put away Sheathe, Store, Stow

Put down Abase, Demean, Disparage, Floor, Humiliate, Land, Write

▷ **Put off** may indicate an anagram

Putrefaction, Putrefy(ing), Putrid Addle, Bitter, Corrupt, Decay, Fester, Olid, Rot, Sepsis, Septic

Putt(ing) Gobble, Green, Hash, Sink, ➤ STUPID PERSON

Putter Chug, Club

Put together Assemble, Compile, Synthesize

Puzzle(r) Acrostic, Baffle, Bemuse, Bewilder, Chinese, Confuse, Conundrum, Crossword, Crux, Egma, Elude, Enigma, Fox, Glaik, Gravel, Intrigue, Jigsaw, Kittle, Logogriph, Mind-bender, Monkey, Mystify, Nonplus, Perplex, Ponder, Pose(r), Rebus, Riddle, Sorites, Sphinx, Stick(l)er, Stump, Tangram, Tickler

Pygmy Atomy, Dwarf, Negrillo, Negrito, Pyknic, Thumbling

Pyjamas Jimjams

Pyramid Cheops, Chephren, Frustum, Stack, Teocalli

Pyre Bale(-fire), Bonfire, Brasero, Darga, Gha(u)t

Pyrenean Basque

Pyrites Mispickel, Mundic

Pyrotechnics Arson, Fireworks

Pyroxene Aegirine, Aegirite, Diopside

Pyrus Service-tree

Pythagoras Samian

Pythian (seat) Delphic, Tripod

Python Anaconda, Diamond, Kaa, ➤ SNAKE, Zombi(e)

Q q

Q Koppa, Quebec, Question

QC Silk

Qua As

Quack Charlatan, Crocus, Dulcamara, Empiric, Fake, ➤ IMPOSTOR, Katerfelto, Mountebank, Pretender, Saltimbanco

Quad(rangle) Close, Compluvium, Court, Em, En, Horse, Pane

Quadrilateral Trapezium

Quadrille Dance, Lancers, Matador(e), Pantalon

Quaff Carouse, Drink, Imbibe

Quagmire Bog, Fen, Imbroglio, Marsh, Morass, Swamp, Wagmoire

Quail Asteria, Bevy, Bird, Blench, Bob-white, Button, Caille, Colin, Flinch, Harlot, Hen, Quake, Shrink, Tremble

Quaint Naive, Odd, Old-world, Picturesque, Strange, Twee, Wham, Whim(sy)

Quake(r), Quaking Aminadab, Broad-brim, Dither, Dodder, Fox, Friend, Fry, Hicksite, Obadiah, Penn, Quail, Seism, Shake(r), Shiver, Trepid, ➤ TREMBLE, Tremor

Qualification, Qualified, Qualify Able, Adapt, Capacitate, Caveat, Competent, Condition, Degree, Diplomatic, Entitle, Graduate, Habilitate, Meet, Pass, Proviso, Restrict, Temper, Versed

Quality Aroma, Attribute, Body, Calibre, Cast, Charisma, Essence, Fabric, Fame, Five-star, Flavour, Grade, Inscape, It, Long suit, Mystique, Premium, Property, Q, Quale, Reception, Sort, Standard, Stature, Substance, Suchness, Thew, Thisness, Timbre, Virgin, Virtu(e), Water, Worth

Qualm Compunction, Misgiving, Scruple

Quandary Dilemma, Fix, Predicament

Quantity ➤ AMOUNT, Analog(ue), Batch, Bundle, Capacity, Deal, Dose, Feck, Fother, Hundredweight, Intake, Jag, Lock, Lot, Mass, Measure, Melder, Myriad, Nonillion, Number, Ocean(s), Operand, Parameter, Parcel, Peck, Plenty, Posology, Pottle, Qs, Qt, Quire, Quota, Quotient, Ream, Scalar, Slather, Slew, Slue, Sum, Surd, Tret, Vector, Warp, Whips

Quantum Graviton

Quarantine Isolate

Quarrel(some) Affray, Aggress, Altercate, Arrow, Barney, Barratry, Barretry, Bate, Bicker, Brabble, Brattle, Brawl, Breach, Breeze, Broil, Brulyie, Brulzie, Cagmag, Cantankerous, Carraptious, Caterwaul, Chance-medley, Chide, Clash, Combative, Contretemps, Difference, Disagree, Dispute, Eristic, Estrangement, Exchange, Feisty, Fracas, Fractious, Fratch(et)y, Fray, Hassle, Issue, Jar, Outcast, Outfall, Pugnacious, Ragbolt, Row, Spat, Squabble, Tiff, Vendetta, Wap, Whid, Wrangle

Quarry Chalkpit, Game, Mine, Pit, Prey, Scabble, Scent, Stone pit, Victim

Quarter(ing), Quarters Airt, Barrio, Billet, Canton(ment), Casern(e), Chinatown, Clemency, Close, Coshery, District, Dorm, E, Enclave, Fardel, Focsle, Forpet, Forpit, Fourth, Ghetto, Ham(s), Harbour, Haunch, Latin, Medina, ➤ MERCY, N, Note, Oda, Pity, Point, Principium, Quadrant, Region, S, Season, Sector, Tail, Trimester, W, Wardroom, Warp

Quarter-day LD

▷ **Quarterdeck** may indicate a suit of cards

Quartet Foursome, Mess, Tetrad

Quartz Agate, Amethyst, Buhrstone, Cacholong, Cairngorm, Chalcedony, Citrine, Flint, Jasp(er), Morion, Onyx, Plasma, Prase, Rubasse, Silex, Silica, Smoky, Stishovite, Tiger-eye, Tonalite

Quash Abrogate, Annul, Quell, Recant, Scotch, Subdue, Suppress, Terminate, Void

Quaver Shake, Trill, Vibrate, Warble

Quay Bund, Levee, Wharf

Queasy Delicate, Nauseous, Squeamish

Quebec Q

Queen(ly) Adelaide, African, Alcestis, Alexandra, Anna, Anne, Artemesia, Atossa, Balkis, Beauty, Bee, Begum, Bess, Boadicea, Boudicca, Brunhild(e), Camilla, Candace, Card, Caroline, Cleopatra, Dido, Drag, Drama, Eleanor(a), Ellery, Ena, ER, Esther, FD, Gertrude, Guinevere, Hatshepset, Hatshepsut, Hecuba, Helen, Hermione, Hippolyta, HM, Isabel, Ishtar, Isolde, Jocasta, Juno, Leda, Maam, Mab, Maeve, Marie Antoinette, Mary, Matilda, May, Maya, Medb, Mobled, Monarch, Nance, Nefertiti, Omphale, Pance, Pansy, Parr, Paunce, Pawnce, Pearly, Penelope, Persephone, Phaedram, Prince, Proserpina, Qu, R, Ranee, Rani, Regal, Regina(l), Sara, Semiramis, Sheba, Sultana, Titania, Victoria, Virgin, Warrior

Queen Anne Mrs Morley

Queer(ness) Abnormal, Berdash, Bizarre, Crazy, Cure, Curious, Fey, Fie, Fifish, Gay, Nance, Nancy, ➤ ODD, Outlandish, Peculiar, Pervert, Poorly, Quaint, Rum, Spoil, Uranism, Vert

Quell Alegge, Allay, Calm, Quiet, Repress, Subdue, Suppress

Quench Assuage, Cool, Extinguish, Satisfy, Slake, Slo(c)ken, Sta(u)nch, Yslake

▶ **Query** see Question

Quest Goal, Graal, Grail, Hunt, Pursuit, Venture

Question(ing), Questionnaire Appose, Ask, Bi-lateral, Catechise, Chin, Contest, Conundrum, Cross-examine, Debrief, Direct, Dispute, Dorothy Dixer, Doubt, Erotema, Eroteme, Erotesis, Examine, Grill, Heckle, Impeach, Impugn, Indirect, Innit, Interpellation, Interrogate, Interview, Koan, Leading, Maieutic, Matter, Oppugn, Pop, Probe, Problem, Pump, Q, Qu, Quare, Quiz, Rapid-fire, Refute, Rhetorical, Riddle, Speer, Speir, Survey, Suspect, Tag, Teaser, Vexed, What, Worksheet

Questionable Ambiguous, Dubious, Fishy, Socratic

Question-master Interrogator, Torquemada, Ximenes

Queue Braid, Breadline, Cercus, Crocodile, Cue, Dog, File, ➤ LINE, Pigtail, Plait, Plat, Tail(back), Track

Quibble(r) Balk, Carp, Carriwitchet, Casuist, Cavil, Chicaner, Dodge, Elenchus, Equivocate, Nitpick, Pedantry, Pettifoggery, Prevaricate, Pun, Quiddity, Quillet, Sophist

Quiche Flan, Tart

Quick(en), Quickening, Quicker, Quickly, Quickness Accelerate, Acumen, Adroit, Agile, Alive, Allegr(ett)o, Animate, Apace, Breakneck, Breathing, Brisk, Celerity, Chop-chop, Citigrade, Cito, Con moto, Core, Cracking, Cuticle, Dapper, Deft, Enliven, Existent, Expeditious, Express, Fastness, Festination, Foothot, Gleg, Hasten, Hie, High-speed, Hotfoot, Impulsive, Jiffy, Keen, Lickety-split, Living, Mercurial, Mistress, Mosso, Nailbed, Nimble, Pdq, Piercing, Piu mosso, Post-haste, Prestissimo, Presto, Prompt, Pronto, Rapid, Rath(e), Rough and ready, Schnell, Sharp, Skin, Smart, Snappy, Snort, Sodain(e), Soon, Spry, Streamline, Sudden, Swift, Swith, Tout de suite, Trice, Veloce, Vital, Vite, Vivify, Wikiwiki, Yare

Quicksand Flow, Syrtis

Quicksilver Mercury

Quid Chaw, Chew, L, Nicker, Plug, Pound, Quo, Sov, Tertium, Tobacco

Quid pro quo Mutuum, Tit-for-tat

Quiescence, Quiescent Calm, Di(o)estrus, Inactive, Inert, Latent, Still

Quiet(en), Quietly Accoy, Allay, Appease, Barnacle, Calm, Compose, Conticent, Doggo, Ease, Easeful, Easy, Encalm, Entame, Gag, Grave, Kail, Laconic, Loun(d), Low, Low-profile, Lown(d), Lull, Meek, Mp, Muffle, Mute, P, Pacify, Pauciloquent, Pause, Peace, Piano, QT, Reserved, Sedate, Settle, Sh, Shtoom, Silence, Sitzkrieg, Sly, Sober, Soothe, Sotto voce, Still, Stum(m), Subdued, Tace, Tranquil, Wheesht, Whish, Whisht, Whist

Quill Calamus, Feather, Float, Plectre, Plectron, Plectrum, Plume, Remex

Quillwort Isoetes

Quilt(ed), Quilting Comfort(er), Counterpane, Cover, Doona®, Duvet, Echo, Eiderdown, Futon, Kantha, Matel(l)asse, Patchwork, Trapunto

Quince Bael, Bel, Bhel, Japonica

Quinine China, Crown-bark, Kina, Quina, Tonic

Quinsy Angina, Cynanche, Garget, Squinancy

Quintessence Heart, Pith

Quintet Pentad, Trout

Quip Carriwitchet, Crack, Epigram, Gibe, Jest, Jibe, Joke, Taunt, Zinger

Quirk Concert, Foible, Idiosyncrasy, Irony, Kink, Twist

Quisling Collaborator, Traitor

Quit(s) Abandon, Absolve, Ap(p)ay, Cease, Desert, Even(s), Go, Leave, Meet, Resign, ➤ STOP

Quite Actually, All, Ap(p)ay, Clean, Dead, Enow, Fairly, Fully, Precisely, Real, Right, Sheer, Very

Quiver(ing) Aspen, Quake, Shake, Sheath, The yips, Tremble, Tremolo, Tremor, Tremulate, Trepid, Vibrant, Vibrate

Qui vive Go-go

Quixote, Quixotic Don, Errant, Impractical

Quiz Bandalore, Catechism, Examine, Interrogate, I-spy, Mastermind, Oddity, Probe, Question, Smoke, Trail, Yo-yo

Quizzical Curious, Derisive, Odd, Queer, Socratic

Quod Can, Clink, Jail, Prison

Quoit Disc(us), Disk, Ring

Quondam Once, Sometime, Whilom

Quorum Minyan

Quota Proportion, Ration, Share

Quotation, Quote(d) Adduce, Citation, Cite, Co(a)te, Duckfoot, Epigraph, Evens, Extract, Instance, Name, Price, Recite, Reference, Say, Soundbite, Tag, Verbatim, Wordbite

Quoth Co, Said

Quotient Intelligence, Kerma, Quaternion, Ratio, Respiratory

R r

R Arithmetic, King, Queen, Reading, Recipe, Right, Romeo, Run, Writing

Rabbi Dayan, Mashgiah, Rebbe

Rabbit Angora, Astrex, Brer, Buck, Bun(ny), Chat, Con(e)y, Cottontail, Daman, Dassie, Doe, Harp, Hyrax, Jack, Klipdas, Marmot, Muff, Nest, Novice, Oarlap, Patzer, Prate, Rattle, Rex, Snowshoe, Tapeti, Terricole, Waffle, Yak, Yap, Yatter

Rabble Canaille, Clamjamphrie, Clanjamfray, Colluvies, Crowd, Doggery, Herd, Hoi-polloi, Horde, Legge, Mob, Raffle, Rag-tag, Rascaille, Rascal, Riff-raff, Rout, Scaff-raff, Shower, Tag, Tagrag

Rabelaisian Pantagruel, Panurge

Rabid, Rabies Extreme, Frenzied, Hydrophobia, Lyssa, Mad, Raging, Virulent

Raccoon Coati, Panda, Procyon

Race(course), Racing, Race meeting Aintree, Ascot, Autocross, Boat, Boskop, Breed, Broose, Brouze, Bumping, Career, Catadrome, Caucus, Cesarewitch, Chantilly, Chase, Classic, Cone, Contest, Corso, Country, Course, Current, Cursus, Dash, Derby, Dogs, Doncaster, Drag, Dromos, Enduro, Epsom, Event, Fastnet, Flapping, Flat, Flow, Generation, Ginger, Goodwood, Grand Prix, Handicap, Hare and hounds, Harness, Herrenvolk, Hippodrome, Human(kind), Hurry, Inca, Indy, Indy Car, Kermesse, Kind, Lampadedromy, Lampadephoria, Le Mans, Leat, Leet, Leger, Lick, Lignage, Line(age), Longchamps, Man, Marathon, Master, Meets, Mile, Motocross, ➤ NATIONAL, Newmarket, Nursery, Oaks, Obstacle, One-horse, Paceway, Palio, Paper chase, Pattern, Plate, Pluck, Point-to-point, Pursuit, Rallycross, Rallying, Rapids, Rat, Redcar, Regatta, Relay, Rill, Rod, Ronne, Roost, Sack, Selling, St Leger, Scramble, Scratch, Scud, Scurry, Seed, Shan, Slalom, Slipstream, Sloot, Sluit, Speedway, Sprint, Stakes, Steeplechase, Stem, Stirp(s), Stirpes, Stock, Strain, Streak, Strene, Sweepstake, Taste, Tear, Three-legged, Tide, Torpids, Towcester, Tribe, TT, Turf, Two-horse, Velodrome, Volsungs, Walk-over, Waterway, Whid, Wincanton

Racehorse, Racer Eclipse, Filly, Hare, Maiden, Plater, Red Rum, Steeplechaser, Trotter

Raceme Corymb, Panicle

Racial (area) Apartheid, Colour, Ethnic, Ghetto, Quarter

Rack Bin, Cloud, Cratch, Drier, Flake, Frame, Hack, Hake, Pulley, Roof, Stretcher, Toast, Torment, Torture

Racket(eer) ➤ BAT, Bassoon, Battledore, Bloop, Brattle, Caterwaul, Chirm, Clamour, Crime, Deen, Din, Discord, Earner, ➤ FIDDLE, Gyp, Hubbub, Hustle, ➤ NOISE, Noisiness, Protection, Ramp, Rort, Sokaiya, Stridor, Swindle, Tumult, Uproar, Utis

Racy Ethnic, Piquant, Pungent, Ribald, Salty, Spicy, Spirited
Rad Rem
Radar Angel, AWACS, DEW line, Doppler, Gee, Lidar, Loran, Monopulse, Rebecca-eureka, Shoran, Teleran®
Raddle Hurdle, Ochre, Red
Radial Quadrant, Rotula, Spoke
Radiance, Radiant Actinic, Aglow, Aureola, Beamish, Brilliant, Glory, Glow, Happy, Lustre, Refulgent, Sheen
Radiate, Radiating, Radiation, Radiator Actinal, Air-colour, Beam, Bremsstrahlung, Cherenkov, Effuse, Emanate, Fluorescence, Glow, Heater, Infrared, Isohel, Laser, Millirem, Pentact, Photon, Pulsar, Quasar, Rem(s), Rep, Roentgen, ➤ SHINE, Sievert, Spherics, Spoke, Stellate, SU, Sun, Ultra violet, Van Allen
Radical Allyl, Amide, Amyl, Aryl, Benzoyl, Bolshevist, Bolshie, Butyl, Calumba, Cetyl, Dyad, Ester, Extreme, Fundamental, Gauchist, Glyceryl, Glycosyl, Innate, Isopropyl, Leftist, Leveller, Ligand, Maximalist, Methyl, Montagnard, Nitryl, Oxonium, Parsnip, Phenyl, Phosphonium, Pink, Propyl, Red, Revolutionary, Rhizocaul, Root, Rudiment, Sulfone, Sulphone, Trot(sky), Uranyl, Vinyl, Whig, Xylyl
Radio Boom-box, CB, Cellular, Citizen's band, Crystal set, Ether, Gee, Loudspeaker, Marconigraph, Receiver, Reflex, Set, Simplex, Sound, Tranny, Transceiver, Transmitter, Transponder, Walkman®, Wireless
Radioactive, Radioactivity Actinide, Americium, Astatine, Bohrium, Cobalt 60, Emanation, Hot, Nucleonics, Steam, Thorium, Uranite
Radiogram Cable, Telegram, Wire
Radish Charlock, Mooli, Runch
Radium Ra
Radius Schwarzschild
Radon Rn
Raffia Rabanna
Raffle(s) Burglar, Draw, Lottery, Sweepstake
Raft Balsa, Catamaran, Float, Kontiki, Life, Pontoon
Rafter Barge-couple, Beam, Chevron, Jack, Joist, Ridge, Spar, Timber
Rag(ged), Rags Bait, Bate, Clout, Coral, Deckle, Dud(s), Duddery, Duddie, Duster, Fent, Figleaf, Glad, Guyed, Haze, Kid, Lap(pie), Lapje, Mop, Paper, Red, Remnant, Revel, Rivlins, Roast, Rot, S(c)hmatte, Scold, Scrap, ➤ SHRED, Slate, Slut, Splore, Tat(t), Tatter(demalion), Tatty, Taunt, ➤ TEASE, Tiger, Tongue, Uneven
▷ **Rag(ged)** may indicate an anagram
Rage, Raging ➤ ANGER, Ardour, Bait, Bate, Bayt, Chafe, Conniption, Explode, Fashion, Fierce, Fit, Fiz(z), Fume, Furibund, Furore, Fury, Gibber, Go, Ire, Mode, Paddy(-whack), Passion, Pelt, Pet, Rabid, Ramp, Rant, Road, Snit, Storm, Tear, Temper, Ton, Utis, Wax, Wrath
Raglan Sleeve
Ragout Compot, Goulash, Haricot, Stew

Rag-picker Bunter

Raid(er) Assault, Attack, Bodrag, Bust, Camisado, Chappow, Commando, Do, For(r)ay, Imburst, Incursion, Inroad, Inrush, Invade, Jameson, Maraud, March-treason, Mosstrooper, Pict, Pillage, Plunder, Ransel, Razzia, Reive, Sack, Scrump, Skrimp, Skrump, Smash-and-grab, Sortie, Spreagh, Storm, Viking

Rail(er), Railing Abuse, Amtrack, Arm, Arris, Balustrade, Ban, Banister, ➤ BAR, Barre, Barrier, Bird, Bullhead, Cloak, Conductor, Coot, Corncrake, Criticise, Dado, Fender, Fiddle, Fife, Flow, Gush, Insult, Inveigh, Metal, Neckerchief, Notornis, Parclose, Picture, Plate, Post, Pulpit, Rag, Rate, Rave, Rung, Scold, Slang-whang, Slate, Snash, Sneer, Sora, Soree, Spar, Taffrail, Taunt, Thersites, Towel, Train, Vituperation, Weka

Raillery Badinage, Banter, Chaff, Persiflage, Sport

Railroad, Railway Amtrak, BR, Bulldoze, Cable, Coerce, Cog, Cremaillière, Dragoon, El, Elevated, Funicular, GWR, Inclined, L, Light, Lines, LMS, LNER, Maglev, Metro, Monorail, Rack, Rack and pinion, Rly, Road, Rollercoaster, Ropeway, ROSCO, Ry, Scenic, SR, Switchback, Telpher-line, Track, Train, Tramline, Tramway, Tube, Underground

Railwayman Driver, Guard, NUR, Stephenson, Stoker

Raiment Apparel, Clothes, Garb, Ihram

Rain(y) Acid, Brash, Deluge, Drizzle, Hyad(e)s, Hyetal, Mistle, Mizzle, Oncome, Onding, Onfall, Pelt, Pluviose, Pluvious, Pour, Precipitation, Right, Roke, Scat, Seil, Serein, Serene, Shell, Shower, Sile, Skiffle, Skit, Smir(r), Smur, Soft, Spat, Spet, Spit, Storm, Thunder-plump, Virga, Weep, Wet

Rainbow(-maker) Arc, Bifrost, Bruise, Iris, Spectroscope, Sunbow, Water-gall, Weather-gall

Raincoat Burberry®, Gaberdine, Mac, Mino, Oils(kins), Waterproof

Raingauge Ombrometer, Udometer

Rain-maker Indra

Raise(d), Raising Advance, Aggrade, Attollent, Boost, Build, Cat, Coaming, Cock, Collect, Elate, ➤ ELEVATE, Emboss, Enhance, Ennoble, Erect, Escalate, Exalt, Fledge, Grow, Heave, Heezie, Heft, High, Hike, Hoist, Increase, Jack, Key, Leaven, Lift, Mention, Overcall, Perk, Rear, Regrate, Repoussé, Revie, Rouse, Saleratus, Siege, Sky, Snarl, Sublimate, Upgrade, Weigh

Rake, Rakish Casanova, Comb, Corinthian, Dapper, Dissolute, Enfilade, Jaunty, Lecher, Libertine, Lothario, Raff, Reprobate, Rip, Roué, Scan, Scour, Scowerer, Scratch, Strafe, Swash-buckler, Swinge-buckler, Wagons

Rale Crepitus, Rattle

Rally, Rallying-point Autocross, Autopoint, Badinage, Banter, Demo, Gather, Jamboree, Meeting, Mobilise, Monte Carlo, Muster, Oriflamme, Persiflage, Recover, Rely, Rest, Risorgimento, Roast, Rouse, Scramble

Ralph Imp, Nader, Rackstraw

Ram Aries, Battering, Buck, Bunt, Butter, Corvus, Crash, Drive, Hidder, Hydraulic, Mendes, Pun, Sheep, Stem, Tamp, Tup, Wether

Ramble(r), Rambling Aberrant, Aimless, Digress, Incoherent, Liana, Liane, Rigmarole, Roam, Rose, Rove, Skamble(-skamble), Sprawl, Stray, Vagabond, Wander

Rameses Pharaoh

Ramp Bank, Gradient, Helicline, Incline, Slipway, Slope

Rampage Fury, Spree, Storm

Rampant Lionel, Predominant, Profuse, Rearing, Rife

▷ **Rampant** may indicate an anagram or a reversed word

Rampart Abat(t)is, Brisure, Butt, Defence, Fortification, Parapet, Terreplein, Vallum, Wall

Ramrod Gunstick

Ramshackle Decrepit, Heath Robinson, Rickety, Rickle

Ranch Bowery, Corral, Farm, Hacienda, Spread

Rancid Frowy, Reast(y), Reest(y), Sour, Turned

Rancour Gall, Hate, Malice, Resentment, Spite

Rand Border, R, Roon

Random Accidental, Aleatoric, Arbitrary, ➤ AT RANDOM, Blind, Casual, Desultory, Fitful, ➤ HAPHAZARD, Harvest, Hit-or-miss, Indiscriminate, Scattershot, Sporadic, Stochastic

▷ **Random(ly)** may indicate an anagram

Range(r), Rangy Align, Ambit, Andes, Atlas, AZ, Ballpark, Band, Bowshot, Carry, Cheviot, Compass, Cotswolds, Course, Diapason, Dispace, Dolomites, Err, ➤ EXTENT, Flinders, Gamut, Glasgow, Gunshot, Hamersley, Helicon, Himalayas, Ken(ning), Ladakh, Leggy, Limit, Line, Long, Massif, Middleback, ➤ MOUNT, Orbit, Oven, Palette, Point-blank, Purview, Rake, Reach, Register, Repertoire, Rifle, Roam, Scale, Scope, Sc(o)ur, Selection, Short, Sierra, Sloane, Spectrum, Sphere, Stove, Strzelecki, Tape, Tessitura, Teton, Texas, Tier, Urals, Waldgrave, Woomera

Rank(s) Arrant, Ayatollah, Begum, Brevet, Caste, Category, Cense, Classify, Cornet, Degree, Dignity, Downright, Earldom, Estate, Etat(s), Grade, Graveolent, Gross, High, Hojatoleslam, Hojatolislam, Majority, Olid, Parage, Place, Range, Rate, Rooty, Row, Seigniorage, Sergeant, Serried, Shoulder-strap, Sort, ➤ STATION, Status, Taxi, Tier, ➤ TITLE, Titule, Utter, Viscount

Rankle Chafe, Gall, Irritate, Nag

Ransack Fish, Loot, Pillage, Plunder, Rifle, Ripe, Rob, Rummage

Ransom King's, Redeem, Release, Rescue

Rant(er), Ranting Bombast, Declaim, Fustian, Ham, Harangue, Rail, Rodomontade, Scold, Spout, Spruik, Stump, Thunder, Tub-thump

Rap(ped) Blame, Censure, Clour, Gangsta, Halfpenny, Knock, Ratatat, Shand, Strike, Swapt, Tack, Tap

Rapacious Accipitrine, Esurient, Exorbitant, Greedy, Harpy, Kite, Predatory, Ravenous, Ravine

Rape Abuse, Assault, Belinda, Cole-seed, Colza, Creach, Creagh, Date, Deflower, Despoil, Gangbang, Hundred, Lock, Lucretia, Navew, Oilseed, Plunder, Stuprate, Thack, Violate

Rapid(ity), Rapidly Chute, Dalle, Express, Fast, Meteoric, Mosso, Presto, Pronto, Quick-fire, Riffle, Sault, Shoot, Speedy, Suckle, Swift, Veloce, Wildfire

Rapier Sword, Tuck

Rappel Abseil

Rapport Accord, Affinity, Agreement, Harmony

Rapprochement Detente, Reconciliation

Rapt Riveted

Raptor Stooper

Rapture, Rapturous Bliss, ➤ DELIGHT, Ecstasy, Elation, Joy, Trance

Rare, Rarity Blue moon, Curio, Earth, Geason, Infrequent, Intemerate, One-off, Rear, Recherché, Scarce, Seeld, Seld(om), Singular, ➤ UNCOMMON, Uncooked, Underdone, Unusual

Rarefied Thin

Rascal(ly) Arrant, Bad hat, Cad, Cullion, Cur, Devil, Gamin, Hallian, Hallion, Hallyon, ➤ KNAVE, Limner, Loon, Low, Rip, Rogue, Scallywag, Scamp, Scapegrace, Schelm, Skeesicks, Skellum, Skelm, Smaik, Spalpeen, Tinker, Toe-rag, Varlet, Varmint, Villain

Rash(er) Acne, Bacon, Brash, Collop, Daredevil, Eruption, Erysipelas, Exanthem(a), Fast, Foolhardy, Harum-scarum, ➤ HASTY, Headlong, Hives, Hotspur, Impetigo, Impetuous, Imprudent, Impulsive, Lardo(o)n, Lichen, Madbrain, Madcap, Miliaria, Morphew, Nettle, Outbreak, Overhasty, Precipitate, Purpura, Reckless, Roseola, Rubella, Sapego, Serpigo, Spots, Tetter, Thoughtless, Unheeding, Unthinking, Urticaria

Rasp(er) File, Grate, Odontophore, Risp, Rub, Scrape, Scroop, Xyster

Raspberry Berate, Bronx-cheer, Etaerio, Razz

Rastafarian Dread

Rat(s), Ratty Agouta, Bandicoot, Blackleg, Blackneb, Boodie, Brown, Bug-out, Cane, Cur, Defect, Desert, Fink, Footra, Foutra, Geomyoid, Gym, Heck, Hydromys, Informer, Kangaroo, Maori, Mole, Moon, Norway, Pack, Poppycock, Potoroo, Pshaw, Pup(py), Rice, Rodent, Roland, Rot(ten), Scab, Shirty, Squeal, Stinker, Turncoat, Vole, Water, Whiskers

Rat-catcher Cat, Ichneumon, Mongoose, Pied Piper

Rate, Rating Able, Appreciate, Assess, Base, Bit, Castigate, Cess, Classify, Count, Credit, Deserve, Erk, Estimate, Evaluate, Exchange, Grade, Hearty, ISO, MPH, Octane, OS, Pace, Percentage, Rag, Red, Refresh, Reproof, Rocket, Row, Sailor, Scold, ➤ SET, ➤ SPEED, Standing, TAM, Tax, Tempo, Upbraid, Value, Water, Wig, World-scale

Rather Degree, Gey, Instead, Lief, Liever, Loor, More, Prefer, Pretty, Some(what), Sooner

Ratify Approve, Confirm, Pass, Sanction, Validate

Ratio Albedo, Aspect, Bypass, Compression, Cosine, Fraction, Gyromagnetic, Loss, Neper, Pi, Poisson's, Proportion, PE, Sin(e), Tensor, Trigonometric

Ration(s) Allocate, Apportion, Compo, Dole, Etape, Iron, K, Quota, Restrict, Scran, Share, Size

Rational Dianoetic, Level-headed, Logical, Lucid, Matter-of-fact, Sane, Sensible, Sine, Sober, Tenable

Rationale Motive

Rattle (box) Chatter, Clack, Clank, Clap, Clatter, Clitter, Conductor, Crescelle, Crotalaria, Death, Demoralise, Disconcert, Gas-bag, Hurtle, Jabber, Jangle, Jar, Maraca, Natter, Nonplus, Rale, Rap, Reel, Rhonchus, Ruckle, Shake, Sistrum, Sunn, Tirl, Upset

Raucous Guttural, Hoarse, Loud, Strident

Ravage Depredation, Desecrate, Despoil, Havoc, Pillage, Prey, Ruin, Sack, Waste

Rave, Raving Boil, Enthuse, Praise, Redwood, Redwud, Storm, Ta(i)ver, Tear

Ravel Disentangle, Explain, Involve, Snarl, Tangle

Raven(ous) Black, Corbel, Corbie, Corvine, Croaker, Daw, Grip, Hugin, Munin, Unkindness

Ravine Arroyo, Barranca, Barranco, Canada, Chasm, Chine, Clough, Coulee, Couloir, Dip, Flume, Ghyll, Gorge, Grike, Gulch, Gully, Kedron, Khor, Khud, Kidron, Kloof, Lin(n), Nal(l)a, Nallah, Nulla(h), Pit

Ravish Constuprate, Debauch, Defile, Devour, Rape, Stuprate, Transport, Violate

Raw Brut, Chill, Coarse, Crude, Crudy, Damp, Fresh, Greenhorn, Natural, Recruit, Rude, Uncooked, Wersh

Raw-boned Gaunt, Lanky, Lean, Randle-tree

Ray(ed) Actinic, Alpha, Beam, Beta, Canal, Cathode, Cosmic, Delta, Diactine, Dun-cow, Eagle, Electric, Fish, Gamma, Grenz, Guitarfish, Homelyn, Manta, Medullar, Monactine, Polyact, R, Radius, Re, Roentgen, Roker, Röntgen, Sawfish, Sea-devil, Sephen, Shaft, Skate, Stick, Sting, Stingaree, Tetract, Thornback, Torpedo

Rayon Acetate, Faille, Viscose

Raze Annihilate, Bulldoze, Demolish, Destroy, Level

Razor(-maker) Cut-throat, Occam, Safety

Razorbill Murre

Razor-fish Solen

Razz Raspberry

RE Sappers

Re About, Rhenium, Touching

Reach(ed) Ar(rive), Attain, Boak, Boke, Carry, Come, Get out, Hent, Hit, Key-bugle, Lode, Octave, Peak, Raught, Rax, Retch, Ryke, Seize, Stretch, Touch, Win

Reach-me-downs Slop-clothing

React(or), Reaction(ary) Allergy, Answer, Anaphylaxis, Backlash, Backwash, Behave, Blimp, Blowback, Bourbon, Breeder, Bristle, ➤ CANDU, Catalysis, Chain, Convertor, Core, Counterblast, Dibasic, Diels-Adler, Falange, Fast(-breeder), Feedback, Flareback, Furnace, Gut, Hydrolysis, Imine, Interplay, Junker, Kickback, Knee-jerk, Magnox, Neanderthal, Nuclear, Outcry, Oxidation, Photolysis, Pile, Reciprocate, Recoil, Redox,

Repercussion, Respond, Reversible, Rigid, Sensitive, Solvolysis, Spallation, Sprocket, Swing-back, Thermal, Tokamak, Vaccinia

▷ **Reactionary** may indicate reversed or an anagram

Read(ing) Bearing, Browse, Decipher, Decode, Exegesis, Grind, Grounden, Haftarah, Haphtarah, Interpret, Learn, Lection, Lesson, Lu, Maftir, Maw, Pericope, Peruse, Pore, Rad, Rennet-bag, Scan, See, Solve, Stomach, ➤ STUDY, Vell, Ycond

Reader ABC, Alidad(e), Bookworm, Editor, Epistoler, Lay, Lector, Primer, Silas Wegg, Taster

Readiest, Readily, Readiness, Ready Alacrity, Alamain, Alert, Amber, Apt, Atrip, Available, Boun, Bound, Brass, Cash, Conditional, Dough, Eager, Early, Eftest, Fettle, Fit, Forward, Game, Go, Keyed, Lolly, Masterman, Money, Predy, Prepared, Present, Prest, Primed, Prompt, Reckoner, Ripe, Set, Soon, Spot, Turnkey, Usable, Willing, Yare

Readjust Mend, Regulate, Retrue

Readymade Bought, Precast, Prepared, Prêt-à-porter, Slops, Stock, Store

Reagent Ninhydrin, Reactor, Titrant

Real, Reality, Realities, Really Actual, Bona-fide, Coin, Deed, Dinkum, Dinky-di(e), Earnest, Echt, Ens, Entia, Entity, Essence, ➤ GENUINE, Honest, Indeed, McCoy, McKoy, Naive, Ontic, Royal, Simon Pure, Sooth, Sterling, Substantial, Tangible, Tennis, Thingliness, True, Verismo, Very, Virtual

Realgar Rosaker, Zarnec, Zarnich

Realise, Realisation, Realism, Realistic Achieve, Attain, Attuite, Cash, Embody, Encash, Fetch, Fruition, Fulfil, Learn, Practical, Sell, Sense, Understand

▶ **Realities, Reality** see REAL

Realm Dominion, Field, Kingdom, Land, Region, Special(i)ty, UK

Ream Bore, Foam, Froth, Paper, Rime, Screed

Reap(er) Binder, Crop, Death, Earn, Gather, Glean, Harvest, Scythe, Shear, Sickleman, Solitary, Stibbler

Reappear(ance) Emersion, Materialise, Recrudesce

Rear(ing) Aft, Back(side), Baft, Behind, Bring-up, Bunt, Cabré, Derrière, Foster, Haunch, Hind, Loo, Nousell, Nurture, Prat, ➤ RAISE, Serafile, Serrefile, Tonneau

Rearrange(ment) Adjust, Anagram, Ectopia, Reorder

Reason(ing), Reasonable A fortiori, Analytical, Apagoge, A priori, Argue, Argument, Basis, Call, Cause, Colour, Consideration, Deduce, Expostulate, Fair, Ground(s), Ijtihad, Inductive, Intelligent, Logic, Logical, Logistics, Mind, Moderate, Motive, Noesis, Plausible, Petitio principii, Point, Pretext, Pro, Proof, Purpose, Rational(e), Sanity, Sense, Sensible, Settler, Syllogism, Synthesis, Think, Why, Wit

Reave Despoil, Reif, Rob, Spoil

Rebate Diminish, Lessen, Refund, Repayment

Rebecca Sharp

Rebel(lion), Rebellious Aginner, Apostate, Arian, Beatnik, Bolshy, Boxer, Cade, Contra, Croppy, Danton, Diehard, Emeute, Fifteen, Forty-five,

Frondeur, Glendower, Hampden, Hereward the Wake, Iconoclast, Insurgent, Insurrection, IRA, Jacobite, Jacquerie, Kick, Luddite, Mutine(er), Mutiny, Oates, Putsch, Recalcitrant, Recusant, Resist, Revolt, Rise, Scofflaw, Sedition, Spartacus, Steelboy, Straw, Tai-ping, Ted, Titanism, Tyler, Venner, Warbeck, Whiteboy, Zealot

▷ **Rebellious** may indicate a word reversed

Rebirth Palingenesis, Renaissance, Revival, Samsara

Rebound Backfire, Bounce, Cannon, Recoil, Repercussion, Ricochet

Rebuff Check, Cold-shoulder, Noser, Quelch, Repulse, Retort, Rubber, Sneb, Snib, Snub

Rebuke Admonish, Berate, Check, Chide, Earful, Lecture, Neb, Objurgate, Rap, Rate, Razz, Reproof, Reprove, Reprimand, Rollick, Scold, Slap, Slate, Snub, Strop, Threap, Threep, Tick off, Trim, Tut, Upbraid, Wig

Rebut Disprove, Refute, Repulse, Retreat

Recalcitrant Mulish, Obstinate, Unruly, Wilful

Recall(ing) Annul, Eidetic, Encore, Evocative, Reclaim, Recollect, Redolent, Remember, Remind, Reminisce, Repeal, Retrace, Revoke, Total, Withdraw

Recant(ation) Disclaim, Palinode, Retract, Revoke

Recap(itulate), Recapitulation Epanodos, Summarise

Recapture Rescue

▷ **Recast** may indicate an anagram

▶ **Recce** see RECONNAISSANCE

Recede Decline, Ebb, Lessen, Regress, Shrink, Withdraw

Receipt(s) Acknowledge, Chit, Docket, Recipe, Revenue, Take, Voucher

Receive(d), Receiver Accept, Accoil, Admit, Antenna, Assignee, Bailee, Dipole, Dish, Donee, Ear, Fence, Get, Grantee, Greet, Hydrophone, Inherit, Pernancy, Phone, Pocket, Radio, Reset, Roger, Set, Take, Tap, Transistor

Recent(ly) Alate, Current, Fresh, Hot, Late, Modern, New, Yesterday, Yestereve, Yesterweek

Receptacle Ash-tray, Basket, Bin, Bowl, Box, Ciborium, Container, Cyst, Hell-box, Monstrance, Reliquary, Relique, Sacculus, Spermatheca, Tank, Thalamus, Tidy, Tore, Torus

Reception, Receptive Accoil, At home, Bel-accoyle, Couchée, Court, Durbar, Greeting, Infare, Kursaal, Levée, Open, Ovation, Ruelle, Saloon, Sensory, Soirée, Teleasthetic, Welcome

Recess(ion) Alcove, Antrum, Apse, Apsidal, Apsis, Bay, Bole, Bower, Break, Closet, Columbarium, Corrie, Cove, Croze, Dinette, Ebb, Embrasure, Exedra, Fireplace, Grotto, Hitch, Inglenook, Interval, Loculus, Mortise, ▶ NICHE, Nook, Oriel, Outshot, Rabbet, Rebate, Respite, Rest, Slump, Withdrawal

▷ **Recess** may indicate 'reversed'

Rechabite TT

Réchauffé Hachis, Hash, Salmi

Recidivist Relapser

▷ **Recidivist** may indicate 'reversed'

Recipe Dish, Formula, Prescription, R, Receipt, Take

Recipient Assignee, Beneficiary, Disponee, Grantee, Heir, Legatee, Receiver

Reciprocal, Reciprocate Corresponding, Elastance, Exchange, Inter(act), Mutual, Repay, Return

Recital, Recitation(ist), Recite(r) Ave, Declaim, Diseuse, Enumerate, Litany, Monologue, Parlando, Quote, Reading, Reel, Relate, Rhapsode, Say, Sing, Tell

Reckless(ness) Blindfold, Careless, Catiline, Desperado, Devil-may-care, Gadarene, Harum-scarum, Hasty, Headfirst, Headlong, Hell-bent, Madcap, Perdu(e), Ramstam, Rantipole, ➤ RASH, Slapdash, Temerity, Ton-up, Wanton, Wildcat

▷ **Reckless** may indicate an anagram

Reckon(ing) Assess, Calculate, Cast, Census, Computer, Consider, Count, Date, Doomsday, Estimate, Fancy, Figure, Number, Rate, Settlement, Shot, Tab

Reclaim(ed), Reclamation Assart, Empolder, Impolder, Innings, Novalia, Polder, Recover, Redeem, Restore, Swidden, Tame, Thwaite

Recline Lean, Lie, Lounge, Rest

Recluse Anchor(et), Anchorite, Ancress, Eremite, Hermit, Solitaire

Recognise(d), Recognition Accept, Acknow(ledge), Admit, Anagnorisis, Appreciate, Ascetic, Cit(ation), Exequatur, Identify, Isolated, Ken, ➤ KNOW, Nod, Oust, Own, Reward, Salute, Scent, Wat, Weet

Recoil Backlash, Bounce, Kick(back), Quail, Rebound, Redound, Repercussion, Resile, Reverberate, Shrink, Shy, Spring, Start

Recollect(ion) Anamnesis, Memory, Pelmanism, Recall, ➤ REMEMBER, Reminisce

▷ **Recollection** may indicate an anagram

Recommend(ation) Advise, Advocate, Counsel, Direct, Endorse, Nap, Promote, Rider, Suggest, Testimonial, Tip, Tout

Recompense Cognisance, Deodand, Deserts, Expiate, Guerdon, Pay, Remunerate, Repayment, Requite, Restitution, Reward

Reconcile(d) Adapt, Adjust, Affrended, Atone, Harmonise, Henotic, Make up, Mend

Recondite Difficult, Esoteric, Mystic, Obscure, Occult, Profound

Reconnaissance, Reconnoitre Case, Investigate, Recce, Scout, Survey

Reconstitute, Reconstitution Diagenesis

Reconstruction Perestroika

Record(er), Record company, Recording Album, Ampex, Analogue, Annal(ist), Archive, Archivist, Aulos, Bench-mark, Black box, Book, Campbell-Stokes, Can, Cartulary, Casebook, CD, Chart, Chronicle, Clog-almanac, Coat(e), Daybook, Diary, Disc, Document, Dossier, Eloge, Elpee, EMI, Enter, Entry, EP, Estreat, Ever, Filater, File, Film, Flight, Flute, Form, Forty-five, Gram, Hansard, Helical scan, Hierogrammat, History, Indie, Journal, Lap-chart, Ledger, List, Log, Logbook, LP, Mark, Memento, Memo(randum), Memorial, Memorise, Meter, Mind, Minute, Mono,

Noctuary, Notate, Notch, Note, Odometer, Pass book, Platter, Playback, Pressing, Public, Quipo, Quipu, Quote, Regest, Register, Release, Roll, Score(board), Seven-inch, Seventy-eight, Shellac, Single, Spectogram, Sphygmogram, Tally, Tape, Thirty-three, Trace, Track, Transcript, Twelve-inch, VERA, Vid(eo), Vote, Wax, Wisden, Write

Record-holder Champion, Sleeve

Record-player DJ, Stereo

Recount Describe, Enumerate, ➤ NARRATE, Relate, Tell

Recourse Access, Resort

Recover(y) Amend, Clawback, Comeback, Convalescence, Cure, Dead cat bounce, Lysis, Over, Perk, Rally, Reclaim, Recoup, Redeem, Regain, Repaint, Replevin, Replevy, Repo(ssess), Rescript, Rescue, Resile, ➤ RETRIEVE, Revanche, Salvage, Salve, Upswing

Recreate, Recreation Diversion, Hobby, Palingenesia, Pastime, Play, Revive, Sport

Recriminate, Recrimination Ruction

Recruit(s) Attestor, Bezonian, Choco, Conscript, Crimp, Draft, Employ, Engage, Enlist, Enrol, Headhunt, Intake, Muster, Nignog, Nozzer, Rookie, Sprog, Volunteer, Wart, Yobbo

Rectangle, Rectangular Matrix, Oblong, Quad, Square

Rectify Adjust, Amend, Dephlegmate, Redress, Regulate, ➤ REMEDY, Right

Recto Ro

Rector R

Rectum Tewel

Recuperate Convalesce, Rally, Recover

Recur(rent), Recurring Chronic, Quartan, Quintan, Recrudesce, Repeated, Repetend, Return

▷ **Recurrent** may indicate 'reversed'

Red(den), Redness Admiral, Alizarin, Angry, Archil, Ashamed, Auburn, Beet, Bilirubin, Blush, Bolshevik, Brick, Burgundy, C, Carmine, Castory, Cent, Cerise, Cherry, Chica, Choy-root, Chrome, Cinnabar, Claret, Coccineous, Commo, Communist, Congo, Coquelicot, Coral, Corallin(e), Corkir, Cramesy, Cromosin, Cuprite, Cyanin, Damask, Debit, Duster, Embarrassed, Eosin, Eric, Erik, Erythema, Florid, Flush, Geranium, Gory, Grog-blossom, Gu(les), Guly, Hat, Herring, Incarnadine, Indian, Inflamed, Infra, Inner, Intertrigo, Jacqueminot, Keel, Kermes, Korkir, Lac-lake, Lake, Lateritious, Left(y), Lenin, Letter, Magenta, Maoist, Marxist, Menshevik, Miniate, Minium, Modena, Murrey, Neaten, Orchel, Orchilla-weed, Orseille, Oxblood, Phenol, Pillar-box, Plethoric, Pompeian, Ponceau, Pyrrhous, Raddle, Radical, Raw, Realgar, Rhodamine, Rhodopsin, Ridinghood, Roan, Rosaker, Rose, Rot, Rouge, Roy, Rubefy, Rubella, Rubescent, Rubicund, Rubric, Ruby, Ruddle, Rufescent, Russ(e), Russet, Russian, Rust(y), Rutilant, Sang-de-boeuf, Sanguine, Sard, Sericon, Setter, Solferino, Stammel, Tape, Tidy, Titian, Trot, Trotsky, Turacin, Turkey, Tyrian, Venetian, Vermeil, Vermilion, Vermily, Vinaceous, Wallflower, Wine

▷ **Red** may indicate an anagram

Redcoat Rust, Soldier

Redeem, Redemption Cross, Liberate, Mathurin, Ransom, Retrieve, Salvation, Save

Red-faced Coaita, Florid, Flushed

Red-head Auburn, Blue(y), Carroty, Commissar, Mao, Rufus

Red herring Soldier

Redirect Sublimate

▷ **Rediscovered** may indicate an anagram

Redolent Aromatic, Fragrant, Reeking, Suggestive

Redoubtable Stalwart

Redress Amends, Offset, Recompense, Rectify, Remedy, Right

Redshank Gambet, Totanus

Redskin Indian, Tomato

Red spot Tika

Reduce(r), Reduced, Reduction Abatement, Allay, Alleviate, Amortize, Attenuate, Beggar, Beneficiate, Clip, Commute, Condense, Contract, Cut, Cutback, Damping, Debase, Decimate, Decrease, Decrement, Demote, Deplete, Detract, Devalue, Diminish, Diminuendo, Discount, Downsize, Draw-down, Epitomise, Foreshorten, Grind, Kinone, ➤ LESSEN, Lite, Markdown, Mitigate, Moderate, Palliate, Pot, Pulp, Put, Quinol, Razee, Remission, Retrench, Rundown, Scant, Shade, Shorten, Shrinkage, Slash, Strain, Taper, Telescope, Thin, Weaken, Write-off

Redundancy, Redundant Frill, Needless, Otiose, Pleonasm, Superfluous, Surplus

Redwood Amboyna, Mahogany, Sanders, Wellingtonia

Reed Arundinaceous, Calamus, Oboe, Papyrus, Pipe, Quill, Raupo, Rush, Sedge, Seg, Sley, Spear, Sudd, Syrinx, Thatch, Twill, Whistle

Reef Atoll, Barrier, Bombora, Cay, Coral, Fringing, Great Barrier, Key, Knot, Lido, Motu, Sca(u)r, Skerry, Witwatersrand

Reefer Cigarette, Jacket, Joint

Reek Emit, Exude, Stink

Reel Bobbin, Dance, Eightsome, Hoolachan, Hoolican, Pirn, Spin, Spool, Stagger, Strathspey, Sway, Swift, Swim, Totter, Wheel, Whirl, Wintle

Refectory Frater

Refer Advert, Allude, Assign, Cite, Direct, Mention, Pertain, Relate, Renvoi, Renvoy, See, Submit

Referee Arbiter, Commissaire, Mediate, Oddsman, Ref, Umpire, Voucher, Whistler, Zebra

Reference Allusion, Apropos, Character, Coat, Index, Innuendo, Mention, Passion, Quote, Regard, Renvoi, Respect, Retrospect, Testimonial

Referendum Mandate, Plebiscite, Vox populi

Refill Replenish

Refine(d), Refinement, Refiner(y) Alembicate, Attic, Catcracker, Couth, Cultivate, Culture, Distinction, Elaborate, Elegance, Exility, Exquisite,

Genteel, Grace, Nice, Nicety, Polish(ed), Polite, Précieuse, Pure, Rare(fy),
Recherché, Saltern, Sift, Smelt, Spirituel, Subtilise, Try, U, Urbane, Veneer
Reflect(ing), Reflection, Reflective, Reflector Albedo, Blame, Cat's eye,
Catoptric, Cats-eye, Chew, Cogitate, ➤ CONSIDER, Echo, Glass, Glint,
Image, Meditate, Mirror, Muse, Ponder, Ruminate, Spectacular,
Speculum, Symmetrical, Tapetum, Thought
Reflex Babinski, Bent, Cancrizans, Re-entrant, Single-lens, Tic
Reform(er) Amend, Apostle, Beveridge, Bloomer, Calvin, Chartism,
Chastise, Correct, Enrage, Fry, Ghandi, Gradualism, Howard, Hussite,
Improve, Knox, Lollard, Luther, Meiji, Melanchthon, Mend, Mucker, New
Deal, PR, Progressionist, Protestant, Proudhon, Puritan, Rad(ical), Really,
Recast, Reclaim, Reconstruction, Rectify, Regenerate, Resipiscence,
Ruskin, Satyagraha, Savonarola, Syncretise, Transmute, Tyndale, Young
Turk
▷ **Reform(ed)** may indicate an anagram
Reformatory Borstal, Magdalen(e)
Refractive, Refractor(y) Anaclastic, Firestone, Obstinate, Perverse, Prism,
Recalcitrant, Refringe, Restive, Stubborn, Sullen, Wayward
Refrain Abstain, Alay, Avoid, Bob, Burden, Chorus, Desist, Epistrophe, Fa-la,
Forbear, Hemistich, Repetend, Ritornello, Rumbelow, Rum(p)ti-iddity,
Rum-te-tum, Spare, Tag, Tirra-lirra, Tirra-lyra, Undersong, Wheel
Refresh(er), Refreshment Air, Bait, Be(a)vers, Cheer, Elevenses, Enliven,
Food, Nap, New, Nourishment, Refection, Reflect, Refocillate,
Reinvigorate, Renew, Repast, Restore, Revive, Seltzer, Shire, Slake, Water
Refrigerator Chill, Cooler, Esky®, Freezer, Fridge, Ice-box, Minibar, Reefer
Refuge Abri, Asylum, Bolthole, Dive, Fastness, Funkhole, Girth, Grith,
Harbour, Haven, Hideaway, Hole, Holt, Home, Hospice, Oasis, Port, Reefer,
Resort, Retreat, Sheet-anchor, ➤ SHELTER, Soil, Stronghold
Refugee DP, Escapist, Fugitive, Grenzganger, Huguenot
Refund Clawback
▷ **Refurbished** may indicate an anagram
Refusal, Refuse Attle, Bagasse, Ba(u)lk, Bilge, Bin, Black, Bran, Brash,
Breeze, Brock, Bull, Bunkum, Chaff, Clap-trap, Crane, Crap, Cul(t)ch,
Debris, Decline, Denay, Deny, Disown, Draff, Drivel, Dross, Dunder, Dung,
Eighty-six, Fag-end, Fenks, Fiddlesticks, Finks, Flock, Frass, Garbage, Gob,
Guff, Hards, Hurds, Husk, Interdict, Jib, Junk, Knickknackery, Knub,
Lay-stall, Leavings, Litter, Lumber, Marc, Megass(e), Midden, Mullock,
Mush, Nay(-say), Nill, No, Nould, Nub, Offal, Off-scum, Orts, Pellet,
Pigwash, Punk, Radwaste, Raffle, Rape(cake), Rat(s), Rebuff, Recrement,
Recusance, Red(d), Redargue, Reest, Regret, Reneg(u)e, Renig, Rot,
➤ RUBBISH, Ruderal, Scaff, Scrap, Scree, Scum, Sewage, Shant, Sordes,
Spurn, Sullage, Sweepings, Swill, Tinpot, Tip, Toom, Tosh, Trade, Trash,
Tripe, Trock, Troke, Trumpery, Twaddle, Unsay, Utter, Wash, Waste,
Wastrel
▷ **Re-fused** may indicate an anagram
Refutation, Refute Deny, Disprove, Elench(us), Rebut, Redargue, Refel

Regain Recover, Revanche

▶ **Regal** see ROYAL

Regalia ➤ CIGAR, Mound, Orb, Sceptre

Regard(ing) As to, Attention, Care, Consider, ➤ ESTEEM, Eye, Gaum, Look, Observe, Odour, Pace, Rate, Re, Respect, Revere, Sake, Steem, Value, Vis-à-vis

Regardless Despite, Heedless, Irrespective, Notwithstanding, Rash, Uncaring, Willy-nilly

Regatta Head of the river, Henley

Regent Interrex, Ruler, Viceroy

Regent's Park Zoo

Reggae Ska

Regicide Ireton, Macbeth

Regime(n) Administration, Control, Diet(etics), Method, Reich

Regiment Black Watch, Buffs, Colour(s), Discipline, Greys, Ironsides, Lifeguard, Monstrous, Nutcrackers, Organise, RA, RE, REME, Rifle, Royals, Tercio, Tertia

▷ **Regiment** may indicate an anagram

Region Arctogaea, ➤ AREA, Belt, Brittany, Bundu, Camargue, Chiasma, Climate, Clime, District, E, End, Hinterland, Hundred, Midi, Offing, Pargana, Part, Pergunnah, Piedmont, Province, Quart(er), Realm, Refugium, Ruthenia, Sector, Stannery, Subtopia, Tagma, Territory, Tetrarchate, Tract, Tundra, Umbria, Vaud, Weald, Zone

Register(ing), Registration Actuarial, Almanac, Annal, Cadastral, Cadastre, Calendar, Cartulary, Census, Check-in, Diptych, Enlist, Enrol, Enter, Index, Indicate, Inscribe, Inventory, Ledger, List, Log, Matricula, Menology, Note, Notitia, Park, Patent, Read, Record, Reg(g)o, Roll, Roule, Score, Soprano, Terrier, Voice

Registrar Actuary, Greffier, Recorder

Regress(ion) Backslide, Recidivism, Revert

Regret(ful), Regrettable Alack, Alas, Apologise, Deplore, Deprecate, Ewhow, Forthwink, Ichabod, Lackaday, Lament, Mourn, Otis, Pity, Remorse, Repentance, Repine, ➤ RUE, Ruth, Sorrow, Tragic

Regular(ity), Regularly Clockwork, Constant, Custom, Episodic, Even, Giusto, Goer, Habitual, Habitué, Hourly, Insider, Methodic, Nine-to-five, Normal, Often, Orderly, Orthodox, Patron, Peloria, Periodic, Rhythmic, Routine, Set, Smooth, ➤ STANDARD, Stated, Statutory, Steady, Strict, Symmetric, Uniform, Usual, Yearly

Regulate, Regulation, Regulator Adjust, Appestat, Bye-law, Code, Control, Correction, Curfew, Customary, Direct, Gibberellin, Governor, Guide, Logistics, Metrostyle, Order, Ordinance, Police, Rule, Snail, Square, Standard, Statute, Stickle, Sumptuary, Thermostat, Valve

Regulus Matte

Rehabilitate, Rehabilitation Cure, Orthotics, Physio(therapy), Repone

Rehearsal, Rehearse Drill, Dry-run, Dummy-run, Practice, Practise, Preview, Recite, Repeat, Trial

Reichenbach Falls, Od

Reign Era, Govern, Meiji, Prevail, Raine, Realm, Restoration, ➤ RULE

Reimburse(ment) Indemnity, Recoup, Redress, Repay

Rein(s) Bearing, Check, Control, Curb, Free, Lumbar, Restrain

Reindeer Caribou, Moss, Tarand

Reinforce(ment) Aid, Augment, Bolster, Boost, Brace, Buttress, Cleat, Line, Plash, Pleach, Recruit, Reserve, ➤ STRENGTHEN, Support, Tetrapod, Underline

Reinstate Repone

Reinvigorate Recruit

Reiterate(d), Reiteration Battology, Emphasize, Plug, Ostinato, ➤ REPEAT

Reject(ion) Abhor, Abjure, Athetise, Bin, Blackball, Cast, Deny, Dice, Discard, Disclaim, Disdain, Diss, Flout, Frass, Jilt, Kest, Kill, Knock-back, Ostracise, Oust, Outcast, Outtake, Pip, Plough, Rebuff, Recuse, Refuse, Reny, Reprobate, Repudiate, Repulse, Scout, Scrub, Spet, Spin, Spit, ➤ SPURN, Sputum, Thumbs-down, Turndown, Veto

Rejoice, Rejoicing Celebrate, Exult, Festivity, Gaude, Glory, Joy, Maffick, Sing

Rejoin(der), Rejoined Answer, Counter, Relide, Reply, Response, Retort, Reunite

Rejuvenation Shunamitism

Relapse Backslide, Deteriorate, Recidivism, Regress, Revert, Sink

Relate(d), Relation(ship), Relative Account, Affair, Affine, Affinity, Agnate, Akin, Allied, Antibiosis, Appertain, Associate, Brer, Brisure, Cognate, Commensal, Concern, Connection, Connexion, Consanguinity, Coosen, Cousin, Coz, Deixis, Eme, Enate, German(e), Granny, Heterogeneous, Homologous, Impart, Industrial, Item, Kin, Link, Love-hate, Mater, Material, Matrix, Mutualism, Narrative, Osculant, Pertain, Pi, Plutonic, Privity, ➤ PROPORTION, Public, Rapport, Rapprochement, Ratio, Reciprocity, Recite, Recount, Rede, Refer(ence), Relevant, Respect(s), Sib(b), Sibbe, Sibling, Sine, Sybbe, Syntax, Tale, Tell, Who

Relating to Of

Relax(ation), Relaxant, Relaxed Abate, Atony, Autogenics, Calm, Chalone, Com(m)odo, Contrapposto, Degage, Detente, Diversion, Downbeat, Ease, Easy-going, Flaccid, Gallamine, Icebreaker, Laid-back, Leisured, ➤ LOOSEN, Mitigate, Peace, Relent, Relief, Remit, Rest, Slacken, Sleep, Toneless, Unbend, Unknit, Untie, Unwind

▷ **Relaxed** may indicate an anagram

Relay(er) Convey, Race, Shift, Tell, Telstar, Torch-race

▷ **Relay(ing)** may indicate an anagram

Release Abreact, Announcement, Bail, Catharsis, Clear, Day, Death, Deliver(y), Desorb, Disburden, Discharge, Disclose, Disimprison, Dismiss, Disorb, Emancipate, Enfree, Excuse, Exeem, Exeme, Extricate, Exude, Free, ➤ LIBERATE, Manumit, Moksa, Parole, Quietus, Quittance, Relinquish,

Ripcord, Spring, Tre corde, Unconfine, Undo, Unhand, Unloose, Unpen, Unshackle, Untie

Relegate Banish, Consign, Demote, Exile, Stellenbosch

Relent Bend, Mollify, Soften, Yield

Relentless Cruel, Hard, Pitiless, Rigorous, Stern

Relevance, Relevant Ad rem, Applicable, Apposite, Apropos, Apt, Germane, Material, Pertinent, Point, Valid

▶ **Reliable, Reliance** see RELY

Relic Antique, Ark, Artefact, Fossil, Leftover, Memento, Neolith, Remains, Sangraal, Sangrail, Sangreal, Souvenir, Survival

Relict Survivor, Widow

Relief, Relieve(d) Aid, Air-lift, Allay, Allegeance, Alleviate, Alms, Anaglyph, Anastatic, Anodyne, Assistance, Assuage, Bas, Beet, Beste(a)d, Bete, Cameo, Cavo-relievo, Comfort, Cure, Détente, Ease(ment), Emboss, Emollient, Free, Grisaille, High, Let-up, Lighten, Lucknow, Mafeking, Palliate, Phew, Pog(e)y, Reassure, Redress, Remedy, Replacement, Repoussé, Reprieve, ▶ RESCUE, Respite, Rid, Spell, Stand-in, Stiacciato, Succour, Tondo, Toreutics, Wheugh, Whew, Woodcut

Religion, Religious (sect) Baha'i, Biblist, Bogomil, Camaldolite, Carthusian, Celestine, Christadelphian, Cistercian, Coenobite, Congregant, Creed, Culdee, Denomination, Devout, Doctrine, Druse, Druz(e), Faith, Gilbertine, God-squad, Gueber, Guebre, Hadith, Hare Krishna, Has(s)id, Hieratic, Hospital(l)er, Ignorantine, Islam, Ismaili, Jain(a), Jansenism, Jehovah's Witness, Jesuit, Jewry, Judaism, Lamaism, Loyola, Lutheran, Mahatma, Manichee, Mazdaism, Mazdeism, Missionary, Missioner, Mithraism, Mormonism, Nun, Opium, Pantheist, Parsism, Pi, Piarist, Pietà, Postulant, Progressive, Reformation, Sabbatarian, Sabian, Sacramentarian, Santeria, Scientology®, Serious, Shaker, Shamanism, Shango, Shinto(ism), Sikhism, Sodality, Sons of Freedom, Spike, Sunna, Taoism, Theatine, Theology, Tractarianism, Tsabian, Utraquist, Voodooism, Whore, Zabian, Zarathustric, Zealous, Zend-avesta, Zoroaster

Religious book Bible, Koran, Missal, NT, OT, Sefer, Tantra, Targum, T(h)orah

Relinquish Abdicate, Cede, Discard, Drop, Forlend, Waive(r), Yield

Reliquary Chef, Encolpion, Encolpium, Tope

Relish(ing) Botargo, Catsup, Chow-chow, Condiment, Enjoy, Flavour, Gentleman's, Gout, Gust(o), Ketchup, Lap(-up), Lust, Opsonium, Palate, Sapid, Sar, Sauce, Savour, Seasoning, Tang, Tooth, Worcester sauce, Zest

Reluctant Averse, Backward, Chary, Circumspect, Grudging, Laith, Loth, Nolition, Renitent, Shy, Unwilling

Rely, Reliance, Reliant, Reliable Addiction, Authentic, Bank, Confidence, Constant, ▶ COUNT, Dependent, Found, Hope, Jeeves, Lean, Loyal, Mensch, Presume, Pukka, Rest, Safe, Secure, Solid, Sound, Sponge, Stand-by, Staunch, Trustworthy, Trusty, Unfailing

Remain(der), Remaining, Remains Abide, Ash(es), Balance, Bide, Continue, Corse, Dreg(s), Dwell, Embers, Estate, Exuviae, Fag-end, Kreng,

Last, Late, Lave, Left, Lie, Locorestive, Manet, Nose, Oddment, Orts, Other, Outstand, Relic(ts), Persist, Reliquae, Remnant, Residue, Rest, Ruins, Scourings, Scraps, Stay, Stick, Stub, Surplus, Survive, Tag-end, Talon, Tarry, Wait

Remark Aside, Barb, Bromide, Comment(ary), Descry, Dig, Generalise, Mention, Noise, ➤ NOTE, Notice, Obiter dictum, Observe, Platitude, Reason, Sally, Shot, State

Remarkable, Remarkably Arresting, Beauty, Bodacious, Conspicuous, Egregious, Extraordinary, Heliozoan, Legendary, Lulu, Mirable, Notendum, Noteworthy, Phenomenal, Rattling, ➤ SIGNAL, Singular, Some, Striking, Tall, Unco, Visible

Remedial, Remedy Aid, Antacid, Antibiotic, Antidote, Antiodontalgic, Arcanum, Arnica, Azoth, Bach, Basilicon, Calomel, Catholicon, Corrective, Cortisone, ➤ CURE, Drug, Elixir, Femiter, Feverfew, Fumitory, Ginseng, Heal, Ipecac, Leechdom, Medicate, Medicine, Moxa, Nosode, Nostrum, Palliative, Panacea, Panpharmacon, Paregoric, Poultice, Repair, Rectify, Redress, Salutory, Salve, Simillimum, Simple, Specific, Taraxacum, Therapeutic, Tonga, Treatment, Tutsan

Remember(ing), Remembrance Bethink, Commemorate, Con, Mention, Mem, Memorial, Memorise, Mneme, Recall, Recollect, Remind, Reminisce, Retain, Rosemary, Souvenir

▷ **Remember** may indicate RE-member, viz. Sapper

Remind(er) Aftertaste, Aide-memoire, Bookmark, Evocatory, Evoke, Jog, Keepsake, Mark, Memento, Memo, Mnemonic, Mnemotechnic, Monition, Nudge, Phylactery, Prod, Prompt, Souvenir, Token

Reminiscence(s), Reminiscent Ana, Evocative, Memory, Recall, Recollect, Remember, Retrospect

Remiss Careless, Derelict, Lax, Lazy, Negligent, Tardy

Remission Abatement, Absolution, Acceptilation, Indulgence, Pardon, Pause

Remit Excuse, Forward, Pardon, Postpone

Remnant Butt, End, Fent, Heeltap, Left-over, Odd-come-short, Offcut, Relic, ➤ REMAINDER, Rump, Trace, Vestige

Remonstrate Argue, Complain, Expostulate, Protest, Reproach

Remorse Angst, Ayenbite, Breast-beating, Compunction, Contrition, Had-i-wist, Pity, ➤ REGRET, Rue, Ruing, Ruth, Sorrow

Remote Aloof, Aphelion, Backveld, Backwater, Backwood, Bullamakanka, Bundu, ➤ DISTANT, Forane, Inapproachable, Insular, Irrelevant, Jericho, Long(inquity), Out(part), Outback, Scrub, Secluded, Shut-out, Slightest, Surrealistic, Unlikely, Withdrawn

Remount(s) Remuda

Removal, Remove(d) Abduct, Ablation, Abstract, Apocope, Asport, Banish, Blot, Circumcision, Clear, Couch, Declassify, Dele(te), Depilate, Depose, Detach, Detract, Dishelm, Dislodge, Dispel, Doff, Efface, Eject, Eloi(g)n, Emend, Eradicate, Erase, Esloyne, Estrange, Evacuate, Evict, Exalt, Excise, Extirpate, Far, Flit, Huff, Nick, Redline, Remble, Razee, Rid, Scratch,

Sequester, Shift, Spirit, Sublate, Subtract, Supplant, Transfer, Transport, Unperson, Unseat, Uproot

Remuneration Pay, Return, Reward, Salary, Solde

Remus Uncle

Renaissance Awakening, Cinquecento, Quattrocento, Revival

Rend Cleave, Harrow, Lacerate, Rip, Rive, Rupture, Tear

Render(ing) Construe, Deliver, Do, Gie, Give, Interpretation, Make, Melt, Pebble-dash, Plaster, Provide, Recite, Represent, Restore, Setting, Tallow, Try, Yeve

Rendezvous Date, Meeting, Philippi, Tryst, Venue

Rendition Account, Delivery, Interpretation, Translation

Rene Descartes

Renegade, Renege Apostate, Default, Defector, Deserter, Rat(ton), Traitor, Turncoat

▷ **Renegade** may indicate a word reversal

Renew(al) Instauration, Neogenesis, Palingenesis, Refresh, Replace, Resumption, Retrace, Revival, Urban

Rennet Steep, Vell

Renounce, Renunciation Abandon, Abdicate, Abjure, Abnegate, Disclaim, Disown, For(e)go, For(e)say, Forfeit, Forisfamiliate, Forsake, Forswear, Kenosis, Recede, Relinquish, Renay, Retract, Sacrifice

Renovate, Renovation Instauration, Refurbish, Renew, Repair, Restore, Revamp

Renown(ed) Fame, Glory, Illustrious, Kudos, Lustre, Notoriety, Prestige

Rent Broken, Charge, Cornage, Crack, Cranny, Cuddeehih, Cuddy, Division, Economic, Farm, Fee, Fissure, Gale, Gavel, Ground, ➤ HIRE, Lease, Let, Mail, Occupy, Quit-rent, Rack, Rip, Rived, Riven, Screed, Slit, Split, Stallage, Tare, Tithe, Tore, Torn, Tythe

Reorientate Rabat

Repair(er), Reparation Amend(s), Anaplasty, Botch, Cobble, Damages, Darn, Doctor, Fettle, Fitter, Go, Haro, Harrow, ➤ MEND, Overhaul, Patch, Recompense, Redress, Refit, Reheel, Remedy, Renew, Repoint, Resort, Restore, Retouch, Satisfaction, Stitch, Ulling, Vamp, Volery

Repartee Backchat, Badinage, Banter, Persiflage, Rejoinder, Retort, Riposte, Wit

Repast Bever, Collection, Food, Meal, Tea, Treat

Repay(ment) Avenge, Compensate, Quit, Refund, Requite, Retaliate, Reward, Satisfaction

Repeal Abrogate, Annul, Cancel, Rescind, Revoke

Repeat(edly), Repetition, Repetitive Again, Alliteration, Anadiplosis, Anaphora, Battology, Belch, Bis, Burden, Burp, Copy, Ditto(graphy), Duplicate, ➤ ECHO, Echolalia, Encore, Epanalepsis, Epistrophe, Epizeuxis, Eruct, Facsimile, Habitual, Harp, Image, Imitate, Ingeminate, Iterate, Iterum, Leit-motiv, Merism, Ostinato, Palillogy, Parrot, Passion, Perpetuate, Playback, Polysyndeton, Recite(r), Redo, Refrain, Regurgitate, Reiterate, Renew, Rep, Repetend, Rerun, Retail, Rondo, Rosalia, Rote,

Same(y), Screed, Segno, Symploce, Tautology, Tautophony, Thrum, Verbigerate

Repel(lent) Estrange, Harsh, Offensive, Rebarbative, Reject, Repulse, Revolt, Squalid, Turn-off, Ug(h), Ward

Repent(ant), Repentance Metanoia, Penitent, Regret, Rue, Yamim Nora'im

Repercussion Backlash, Backwash, Effect, Impact, Recoil

Repertoire, Repertory Company, Depot, Rep, Store

▶ **Repetition** see REPEAT

Replace(ment), Replaceable, Replacing Change, Deputise, Diadochy, For, Pre-empt, Raincheck, Refill, Replenish, Restore, Stand-in, Substitute, Supersede, Supplant, Surrogate, Taxis, Transform, Transliterate, Understudy

Replay Action, Instant, Iso(lated), Segno

Replenish Refill, Refresh, Revictual, Stock, Supply, Top

Replete, Repletion Awash, Full, Gorged, Plenitude, Plethora, Sated, Satiation

Replica Clone, Copy, Duplicate, Facsimile, Image, Repetition, Spit

Reply Accept, Answer, Churlish, Duply, Rejoinder, Rescript, Response, Retort, Surrebut, Surrejoin

Report(er) Account, Announce, Bang, Bulletin, Bruit, Clap, Columnist, Comment, Commentator, Correspondent, Court, Cover, Crack, Crump, Cub, Debrief, Disclose, Dispatch, Explosion, Fame, Fireman, Grapevine, Hansard, Hearsay, Jenkins, Journalist, Legman, Libel, News, Newshawk, Newshound, Newsman, Noise, Pop, Pressman, Protocol, Relate, Relay, Repute, Return, Rumour, Sitrep, Sound(bite), State(ment), Stringer, Tale, ➤ TELL, Thesis, Transcribe, Tripehound, Troop, Update, Whang

▷ **Reported** may indicate the sound of a letter or word

Repose Ease, Kaif, Kef, Kif, Lie, Lig, Peace, Relax, ➤ REST, Serenity

Repository Ark, Cabinet, Container, Genizah, Reservoir, Sepulchre, Vault

Reprehend Blame, Censure, Criticise, Rebuke, Warn

Represent(ation), Representative Agent, Ambassador, Anaconic, Caricature, Commercial, Cross-section, Delegate, Depict, Deputation, Describe, Display, Drawing, Drummer, Effigy, Elchee, Eltchi, Emblem, Embody, Emissary, Example, Figurative, Image, John Bull, Lobby, Map, Mimesis, Mouthpiece, MP, Personate, Personify, Portray, Proportional, Rep, Resemble, Salesman, Senator, Spokesman, Stand-in, Steward, Symbolic, Syndic, Tableau, Tiki, Typical, Vakeel, Vakil, Vehicle

▷ **Represented** may indicate an anagram

Repress(ed) Check, Curb, Pent, Quell, Sneap, Stifle, Subjugate, Withhold

Reprieve Delay, Postpone, Relief, Respite

Reprimand Bounce, Carpet, ➤ CENSURE, Chide, Dressing-down, Earful, Jobe, Lace, Lecture, Rating, Rebuke, Reproof, Rocket, Rollicking, Slate, Strafe, Targe, Tick off, Tongue-lashing, Wig

Reprint Copy, Paperback, Replica

Reprisal(s) Marque, Retaliation, Revenge

Reproach Blame, Braid, Byword, Chide, Discredit, Dispraise, Exprobate, Gib, Mispraise, Odium, Opprobrium, Rebuke, Ronyon, Runnion, Scold, Shend, Sloan, Stigma, Taunt, Truant, Upbraid, Upcast, Yshend

Reprobate Outcast, Rascal, Scallywag, Scamp

Reprocess Re-make

Reproduce(r), Reproduction, Reproductive (organ) Amphimixis, Ape, Apomixis, Archegonium, Carpel, Clone, Copy, Counterfeit, Depict, Edition, Etch, Eugenics, Gamogenesis, Gemmate, Isospory, Megaspore, Meristematic, Mono, Multiply, Oogamy, Ozalid®, Parthogenesis, Phon(e)y, Propagate, Pullulation, Refer, Replica, Roneo®, Schizogony, Seminal, Simulate, Spermatia, Stereo, Syngamy, Syngenesis

▷ **Reproduce** may indicate an anagram

Reproof, Reprove Admonish, Berate, Chide, Correction, Correption, Lecture, Rate, Rebuff, Rebuke, Scold, Sloan, Tut, Upbraid

Reptile, Reptilian Agamid, Alligarta, Alligator, Base, Basilisk, Caiman, Cayman, Chameleon, Chelonian, Creeper, Crocodile, Diapsid, Dicynodont, Dinosaur, Goanna, Herpetology, Lacertine, Lizard, Mamba, Pteranodon, Pterodactyl, Rhynchocephalian, Sauroid, ➤ SNAKE, Squamata, Synapsid, Tegu(exin), Thecodont, Therapsid, Tortoise, Tuatara, Tuatera, Turtle, Worm

Republic Afghanistan, Albania, Algeria, Andorra, Angola, Argentina, Azerbaijan, Banana, Bangladesh, Bashkir, Bashkortostan, Belarus, Belau, Belorussia, Benin, Bolivia, Bosnia-Herzegovina, Botswana, Bukavu, Bulgaria, Burundi, Byelorussia, Cambodia, Cameroon, Cape Verde, Chad, Chechen, Chechnya, Chile, Colombia, Comoros, Costa Rica, Croatia, Cuba, Czech, Dagestan, Djibouti, Dominica(n), Ecuador, Egypt, Eire, El Salvador, Est(h)onia, Fiji, Finland, Gabon, Gambia, Ghana, Guatemala, Guinea(-Bissau), Guyana, Haiti, Honduras, Hungary, Iceland, Indonesia, Ingush, Iran, Israel, Italy, Kalmuck, Kalmuk, Karelian, Kazak(h)stan, Khakass, Khmer, Kiribati, Komi, Kyrgyzstan, Latvia, Laos, Lebanon, Liberia, Lithuania, Macedonia, Madagascar, Malagasy, Malawi, Maldives, Mali, Malta, Mauritania, Mauritius, Mexico, Moldova, Mongolia, Montenegro, Mordvinian, Mozambique, Myanma(r), Namibia, Nauru, Nicaragua, Niger, Nigeria, Palau, Panama, Paraguay, Peru, Philippines, R, Romania, Rwanda, San Marino, Second, Senegal, Serbia, Sierra Leone, Sinn Fein, Slovakia, Slovenia, Somalia, Sri Lanka, State, Sudan, Surinam, Switzerland, Syria, Tajikistan, Tanzania, Togo, Tunisia, Turkey, Turkmenistan, UAR, Ubang-Shari, Udmurtia, Ukraine, Uruguay, Vanuatu, Venezuela, Vietnam, Weimar, Yemen, Yugoslavia, Zaire, Zambia, Zimbabwe

Republican Antimonarchist, Democrat, Fenian, Fianna Fail, Girondist, IRA, Iraqi, Leveller, Montagnard, Mugwump, Plato, Red, Sansculotte, Sansculottic, Sinn Fein, Whig

Repudiate Abjure, Deny, Discard, Disclaim, Disown, Ignore, Recant, Reject, Renounce, Repel

Repugnance, Repugnant Abhorrent, Alien, Disgust, Distaste, Fulsome, Horror, Loathing, Revulsion

Repulse, Repulsive Grooly, Lo(a)th, Off-putting, Rebut, Rebuff, Refel, Refuse, Repel, Repugnant, Slimy, Squalid, Ugly, Vile

Reputable, Reputation, Repute(d) Bubble, Dit, Estimate, Fame, Good, Izzat, Loos, Los, Name, Note, Notoriety, Odour, Opinion, Prestige, Putative, Regard, Renown, Said, Sar, ➤ STANDING, Stink, Trustworthy

Request Adjure, Appeal, Apply, Ask, Desire, Entreaty, Invite, Petition, Plea, Prayer, Solicit

Requiem Agnus dei, Mass

Require(d), Requirement Charge, Crave, De rigueur, Desire, Enjoin, Exact, Expect, Incumbent, Lack, Necessity, Need, Prerequisite

Requisite, Requisition Commandeer, Due, Embargo, Essential, Indent, Necessary, Needful, Order, Press

Rescind Abrogate, Annul, Recant, Remove, Repeal

Rescue Aid, Air-sea, Deliver, Free, Liberate, Ransom, Recover, Recower, Redeem, Regain, Relieve, Reprieve, Retrieve, Salvage, Salvation, ➤ SAVE

Research(er) Boffin, Delve, Dig, Enquiry, Explore, Fieldwork, Investigate, Legwork, Market, Operational, Pioneer, Sus(s)

Resemblance, Resemble, Resembling Affinity, Apatetic, Approach, Assonant, Likeness, Similitude, -oid, -opsis, Replica, Simulate

Resent(ful), Resentment Anger, Bridle, Choler, Cross, Dudgeon, Grudge, Indignation, Ire, Malign, Miff, Pique, Rankle, Smart, Spite, Umbrage

Reservation, Reserve(d), Reservist(s) Aloof, Arrière-pensée, Backlog, Bashful, Book, By, Caveat, Cold, Demiss, Detachment, Distant, Earmark, Engage, Ersatz, Except, Fall-back, Fort Knox, Hold, Husband, Ice, Introvert, Layby, Landwehr, Locum, Nature, Nest-egg, Proviso, Qualification, Reddendum, Res, Rest, Restraint, Retain, Reticence, Retiring, Rez, Salvo, Sanctuary, Save, Scruple, Special, Stand-by, Stand-offishness, Stash, Stock(pile), TA(men), Uncommunicate, Understudy, Warren, Waves, Withhold

Reservoir Basin, Cistern, G(h)ilgai, Gilgie, Repository, Stock, Sump, Tank

Reset Taxis

Reside(nce), Resident Abode, Address, Amban, Chequers, Commorant, Consulate, Denizen, Dwell, Embassy, Establishment, Expatriate, Exurbanite, Gremial, Guest, Home, Indweller, Inholder, Inmate, Intern, Ledger, Lei(d)ger, Lieger, Lodger, Metic, Pad, Parietal, Resiant, Settle, Sojourn, Stay, Tenant, Villager, Yamen

Residual, Residue Ash, Astatki, Calx, Caput, Chaff, Cinders, Crud, Draff, Dregs, Expellers, Greaves, Leavings, Mazout, Mortuum, Remainder, Remanent, Remnant, Slag, Slurry, Snuff, Vinasse

Resign(ed), Resignation Abandon, Abdicate, Demit, Fatalism, Heigh-ho, Leave, Meek, ➤ QUIT, Reconcile, Stoic, Submit

Resilience, Resilient Bounce, Buoyant, Elastic, Flexible, Recoil

Resin Acaroid, Agila, Alkyd, Amber, Amine, Amino, Anime, Arar, Asaf(o)etida, Bakelite®, Balsam, Benjamin, Benzoin, Bursera, Cannabin, Caranna, Carauna, Charas, Cholestyramine, Churrus, Colophony, Conima, Copai(ba), Copaiva, Copal(m), Coumarone, Courbaril, Dam(m)ar,

Dammer, Dragon's blood, Elemi, Epoxy, Frankincense, Galbanum, Galipot, Gambi(e)r, Gamboge, Glyptal, Guaiacum, Gum, Hasheesh, Hashish, Hing, Jalapin, Kino, Lac, Ladanum, Lignaloes, Mastic, Melamine, Myrrh, Olibanum, Opopanax, Phenolic, Podophyllin, Polycarbonate, Polyester, Polymer, Propolis, Retinite, Roset, Rosin, Rosit, Rozet, Rozit, Sagapenum, Sandarac(h), Saran, Scammony, Shellac, Storax, Styrax, Synthetic, Takamaka, Taxin, Urea, Xylenol

Resist Bristle, Buck, Contest, Defy, Face, Fend, Gainstrive, Impede, Oppose, Redound, Reluct, Stand, ➤ WITHSTAND

Resistance, Resistant, Resistor Barretter, Bleeder, Ceramal, Cermet, Chetnik, Coccidiostat, Drag, Element, Friction, Hostile, Immunity, Impediment, Klendusic, Klepht, Maquis, Maraging, Megohm, Microhm, Obstacle, Ohm, Passive, Pull, R, Reluctance, Renitent, Resilient, Rheostat, Satyagraha, Stability, Stand, Stonde, Stubborn, Tough

Resolute, Resolution Analysis, Bold, Cast-iron, Courage, Decided, Decision, Denouement, Determined, ➤ FIRM, Fortitude, Granite, Grim, Grit, Hardiness, Insist, Pertinacity, Promotion, Rede, Resolve, Stable, Stalwart, Staunch, Stout, Strength, Sturdy, Tenacity, Unbending, Valiant, Willpower

Resolve(d), Resolver Analyse, Calculate, Decide, Declare, ➤ DETERMINE, Deux et machina, Factorise, Fix, Hellbent, Intent, Nerve, ➤ PURPOSE, Settle, Steadfast, Tenacity, Vow

▷ **Resolved** may indicate an anagram

Resonance, Resonant Canorous, Electromer, Orotund, Ringing, Sonorous, Timbre, Vibrant

Resort Centre, Dive, Etaples, Expedient, Frame, Frequent, Haunt, Hove, Hydro, Invoke, Lair, Las Vegas, Last, Morecambe, Nassau, Pau, Pis aller, Rapallo, Recourse, Repair, Riviera, Southend, Spa(w), Use

▷ **Resort(ing)** may indicate an anagram

Resound(ing) Echo, Plangent, Reboant, Reboation, Reverberate, Ring

Resource(s), Resourceful Assets, Beans, Bottom, Chevisance, Clever, Faculty, Funds, Gumption, Ingenious, Input, Inventive, Means, Sharp, Stock-in-trade, ➤ VERSATILE, Wealth

Respect(ed), Respectable, Respectful Admire, Ahimsa, Aspect, Behalf, Consider, Decent, Deference, Devoir, Duty, Esteem, Gigman, Homage, ➤ HONOUR, Kempt, Latria, Obeisant, Officious, Pace, Particular, Preppy, Prestige, Proper, Reference, Regard, Relation, Reputable, Revere, S(t)irrah, Sir, U, Venerate, Wellborn, Well-thought-of, Wise, Worthy

Respirator, Respire, Respiration Artificial, Blow, Breathe, Exhale, Gasmask, Inhale, Iron lung, Pant, Snorkel

Respite Break, Breather, Interval, Leisure, Pause, Reprieve, Rest, Stay, Truce

Respond, Response, Responsive Amenable, Answer, Antiphon, Comeback, Conditioned, Echo, Feedback, Flechman, Immune, Kyrie, Litany, Nastic, Pavlovian, Photonasty, React(ion), Reflex, Reply, Rheotaxis, Rise, Synapte, Syntonic, Tender, Thigmotropic, Tic, Tropism, Warm

Responsibility, Responsible Answerable, Baby, Blame, Buck, Charge, Culpable, Dependable, Diminished, Duty, Incumbent, Instrumental, Liable, Mea culpa, Onus, Pigeon, Sane, Solid, Trust

Rest (day) Anchor, Alt, Avocation, Balance, Bed, Beulah, Break, Breather, Calm, Catnap, Cetera, Comma, Depend, Dwell, Ease, Easel, Etc, Feutre, Fewter, Gite, Halt, Inaction, Jigger, Lave, Lean, Lie, Lie-in, Light, Lodge, Loll, Lound, Lyte, Nap, Nooning, Others, Pause, Quiescence, Quiet, Relache, Relax, Rely, Remainder, Repose, Requiem, Respite, Sabbath, Siesta, ➤ SLEEP, Sloom, Slumber, Spell, Spider, Stopover, Support, Surplus, Y-level

Re-start Da capo

Restaurant, Restaurateur Automat, Beanery, Bistro, Brasserie, Cabaret, Cafe, Canteen, Chophouse, Commissary, Diner, Eatery, Estaminet, Greasy spoon, Grill, Grub shop, Maxim's, Noshen, Padrone, Rathskeller, Rotisserie, Slap-bang, Takeaway, Taqueria, Taverna, Teahouse, Tearoom, Teashop, Trattoria

Rest-home Aggie, Hospice

Resting-place Bed, Couch, Dharmsala, Gite, Grave, Inn, Khan, Serai, She'ol, Stage

Restitute, Restitution Amends, Apocatastasis, Reparation, Restore, Return

Restive, Restless(ness) Chafing, Chorea, Fikish, Free-arm, Itchy, Jactitation, Toey, Unsettled

▷ **Restless** may indicate an anagram

Restoration, Restorative, Restore(d) Cure, Descramble, Heal, Mend, Pentimento, Pick-me-up, Redeem, Redintegrate, Redux, Regenerate, Rehabilitate, Rejuvenate, Remedial, Renew, Repone, Restitute, Revamp, Revive, Stet, Tonic

Restrain(ed), Restraint Abstinence, Ban, Bate, Bit, Bottle, Branks, Bridle, Cage, Chain, Chasten, ➤ CHECK, Cohibit, Compesce, Confinement, Contain, Control, Cramp, Curb, Dam, Decorum, Detent, Dry, Duress, Embargo, Enfetter, Freeze, Halt, Hamshackle, Handcuffs, Harness, Heft, Hinder, Hopple, Impound, Inhibit, Jess, Lid, Low-key, Manacle, Measure, Mince, Moderation, Muzzle, Quiet, Rein, Repress, Restrict, Ritenuto, Shackle, Sober, Sobriety, Squeeze, Stay, Stent, Stint, Straitjacket, Temper, Tether, Tie, Trash

Restrict(ed), Restriction Band, Bar, Bind, Bit, Cage, Catch, Chain, Closet, Condition, Cord, Corset, Cramp, Curb, DORA, Fence, Fold, Gate, Ground, Guard, Hamper, Hidebound, Hobble, Inhibit, Intern, Kennel, Let, ➤ LIMIT, Lock, Mere, Narrow, Net, Nick, Pale, Parochial, Pen, Pent, Pier, Pin, Pot-bound, Private, Proscribed, Qualify, Regulate, Rein, Rope, Scant, Seal, Section, Selected, Shackle, Snare, Squeeze, Stenopaic, Stint, Stop, Straiten, Tether, Tie

Restructure, Restructuring Perestroika

Result(s) Aftermath, Ans(wer), Bring, Causal, Consequence, Effect, Emanate, End, Ensue, Entail, Event, Eventuate, Finding, Fruict, Fruits,

Issue, Karmic, Lattermath, ➤ OUTCOME, Outturn, Pan, Proceeds, Quotient, Sequel, Side-effect, Sum, Upshot, Wale

Resume, Résumé Continue, Pirlicue, Purlicue, Summary

Resurrect(ion) Anabiosis, Rebirth, Revive, Zomb(ie)

Resuscitate(d) Quicken, Redivivus, Restore, Revive

Retail(er) Chandler, Dealer, ➤ NARRATE, Sell, Shopkeeper, Tell

Retain(er), Retains Brief, Contain, Deposit, Fee, Hold, Keep, Panter, Pantler, Reserve, Retinue, Servant

Retaliate, Retaliation Avenge, Counter, Lex talionis, Quit(e), Redress, Repay, Reprisal, Requite, Retort, Talion

Retard(ed) Arrest, Brake, Encumber, Hinder, Slow

Retch Boak, Bock, Boke, Cowk, Gap, Heave, Keck, Reach, Vomit

Reticence, Reticent Clam, Coy, Dark, Reserve, Restraint, Secretive, Shy, Taciturn

Reticule, Reticulum Bag, Carryall, Dragnet, Lattice, Net

Retina Detached, Fovea, Macula lutea

Retinue Company, Cortège, Equipage, Following, Meiney, Meinie, Meiny, Sowarry, Suite

Retire(d), Retirement, Retiring Abed, Aloof, Baccare, Backare, Backpedal, Blate, Bowler-hat, Cede, Coy, Depart, Ebb, Emeritus, Essene, Former, Leave, Lonely, Modest, Mothball, Nun, Outgoing, Pension, Private, Quit, Recede, Recluse, Reserved, Resign, Retract, Retreat, Retrocedent, Roost, Rusticate, Scratch, Shy, Superannuate, Unassertive, Withdraw

▷ **Retirement** may indicate 'bed' around another word, or word reversed

Retort Alembic, Comeback, Courteous, Quip, Repartee, ➤ REPLY, Retaliate, Riposte, Still

Retract(ion) Disavow, Epanorthosis, Palinode, Recall, Recant, Renounce, Revoke

Retreat Abbey, Arbour, Ashram(a), Asylum, Backwater, Bower, Bug, Cell, Cloister, Convent, Crawfish, Dacha, Departure, Donjon, Girth, Grith, Hermitage, Hideaway, Hide-out, Hole, Interstadial, Ivory-tower, Katabasis, Lair, Lama(sery), Mew, Monastery, Nest, Neuk, Nook, Recede, Recoil, Recu(i)le, Redoubt, Reduit, Refuge, Retire, Retraite, Right-about, Rout, Shelter, Skedaddle, Stronghold, Withdraw

Retribution Come-uppance, Deserts, Nemesis, Revenge, Reward, Utu, Vengeance

Retrieve(r), Retrieval Access, Bird-dog, Field, Gundog, Labrador, Read-out, Recall, Recoup, Recover, Redeem, Rescue, Salvage

Retroflex Cacuminal

Retrograde Backward, Decadent, Decline, Hindward, Rearward, Regrede

Retrospect(ive) Contemplative, Ex post facto, Hindsight, Regardant

Return(s) Agen, Bricole, Census, Comeback, Day, Dividend, Elect, Er, Extradite, Gain, Pay, Profit, Rebate, Rebound, Recur, Redound, Regress, Reject, Render, Rent, Repay, Replace, Reply, Requital, Respond, Restore, Retour, Revenue, Reverse, Revert, Riposte, Takings, Tax, ➤ YIELD

Rev Gun, Minister

Reveal(ing), Revelation Advertise, Air, Apocalyptic, Bare, Betray, Bewray, Confess, Descry, Disclose, Discover, Discure, ➤ DIVULGE, Epiphany, Exhibit, Explain, Expose, Giveaway, Hierophantic, Impart, Indicate, Ingo, Kythe, Leak, Manifest, Open, Satori, ➤ SHOW, Spill, Tell-tale, Unclose, Uncover, Unfold, Unheal, Unmask, Unveil

Revel(ling), Reveller, Revelry Ariot, Bacchanalia, Bend, Carnival, Carouse, Comus, Corybant, Dionysian, Feast, Gloat, Glory, Joy, Merriment, Orgy, Rant, Rejoice, Riot, Roister, Rollicks, Rout, Saturnalia, Splore, Swig, Upsee, Ups(e)y, Wallow, Wassail, Whoopee

Reveller Bacchant, Birler, Guisard, Guiser, Maenad, Orgiast, Silenus

Revenant Fetch, Ghost, Spectre

Revenge(ful) Aftergame, Avenge, Commination, Goel, Grenville, Montezuma's, Reprise, Requite, Retaliation, Revanche, Ultion, Utu, Vindictive

Revenue Capital, Finance, Fisc(al), Fisk, Income, Inland, Jag(h)ir, Jaghire, Prebend, Rent, Taille, Tax, Turnover, Zamindar, Zemindar

Reverberate Echo, Recoil, Reflect, Repercuss, Resound

Revere(nce) Admire, Awe, Bostonian, Dread, Dulia, Esteem, Hallow, Hery, Homage, ➤ HONOUR, Hyperdulia, Latria, Obeisance, Paul, Respect, Venerate

Reverie Dream(iness), Fantasy, Memento

Revers Lap(p)el

Reversal, Reverse, Reversing, Reversion Antithesis, Antonym, Arsy-versy, Atavism, Back(slide), Change-over, Chiasmus, Counter(mand), Escheat, Evaginate, Exergue, Flip, Inversion, Misfortune, ➤ OPPOSITE, Overturn, Palindrome, Pile, Regress, Revoke, Rheotropic, Switchback, Tails, Throwback, Transit, Turn, Un-, Undo, U-turn, Verso, Vice versa, Volte-face

Revert Annul, Backslide, Regress, Relapse, Resort, Retrogress, Return

Review(er) Appeal, Censor, Critic, Critique, Editor, Feuilleton, Footlights, Inspect, Judicial, Magazine, March-past, Notice, Pan, Recapitulate, Repeat, Revise, Rundown, Spithead, Summary, Survey, Write-up

▷ **Review** may indicate an anagram or a reversed word

Revile, Reviling Abuse, Execrate, Inveigh, Rail, Rayle, Vilify

Revise(r), Revision Alter, Amend, Correct, Diaskeuast, Edit, Peruse, Reappraise, Reassess, Recense, Reform, Rev, Update

▷ **Revise(d)** may indicate an anagram

Revival, Revive, Revivify, Reviving Araise, Enliven, Gothic, Rally, Reanimate, Reawake(n), Rebirth, Redintegrate, Refresh, Rekindle, Renaissance, Renascent, Renew, Renovate, Restore, Resurrect, Resuscitate, Risorgimento, Romantic, Rouse, Wake

Revoke Abrogate, Cancel, Countermand, Negate, ➤ RECALL, Repeal, Rescind

Revolt(ing), Revolution(ary) Agitator, Agitprop, Anarchist, Apostasy, Appal, Bloodless, Bolivar, Bolshevik, Bolshevist, Boxer, Bulldog, Cade,

Castro, Chartist, Che, Circle, Commune, Coup d'etat, Cultural, Cycle, Danton, Dervish, Disgust, Emeute, Emmet, Engels, Enrage, February, Fenian, Foul, Girondin, Girondist, Glorious, Guevara, Gyration, Industrial, Inqilab, ➤ IN REVOLT, Insurgent, Insurrection, Intifada, Jacquerie, IRA, Jacobin, Komitaji, Lap, Lenin, Marat, Marx, Maypole, Minimalist, Mountain, Mutiny, Nihilist, Orbit, Outbreak, Poujadist, Putsch, Radical, ➤ REBEL(LION), Red, Reformation, Riot, Rise, Robespierre, Roll, Rotation, Round, Run, Sandinista, Sansculotte(rie), Sedition, Spartacus, Thermidor, Trot(sky), Twist, Up(rise), ➤ UPRISING, Villa, Wat Tyler, Whirl, Wolfe Tone, Young Turk, Zapata

▷ **Revolutionary** may indicate 'reversed'

Revolve(r), Revolving Carrier, Catherine wheel, Centrifuge, Colt®, Gat, Girandole, Grindstone, ➤ GUN, Gyrate, Iron, Klinostat, Lathe, Maelstrom, Peristrephic, Pistol, Pivot, Roller, Rotate, Rotifer, Rotor, Roundabout, Run, Tone, Turn(stile), Turntable, Turret, Wheel, Whirl(igig), Whirlpool

Revue Follies

Reward Albricias, Bonus, Bounty, Compensate, Consideration, Desert, Emolument, Fee, Guerdon, Head money, Meed, Payment, Premium, Price, Prize, Profit, Purse, Recompense, Reguerdon, Remuneration, Requital, Requite, S, Shilling, Wage, War(r)ison

Reworking Rifacimento

Rex Priam, R

Reynolds Joshua, PRA

Rhapsodic, Rhapsody Ecstasy, Epic, Music, Unconnected

Rhea Em(e)u, Nandoo, Nandu, Ostrich

Rhenium Re

Rhesus Bandar, Macaque, Monkey

Rhetoric(al) Anaphora, Apophasis, Aureate, Bombast, Chiasmus, Eloquence, Enantiosis, Epistrophe, Erotema, Eroteme, Erotesis, Euphemism, Hendiadys, Oratory, Paral(e)ipsis, Peroration, Pleonasm, Syllepsis, Trivium

Rhino Blunt, Bread, Cash, Lolly, Loot, ➤ MONEY, Tin

Rhinoceros Baluchitherium, Keitloa

Rhodes, Rhodesia(n) Cecil, Ridgeback, Scholar, Zimbabwe

Rhodium Rh

Rhubarb Pie-plant, Rhapontic, Rheum, Rot, Spat

Rhyme(r), Rhyming Assonance, Clerihew, Closed couplet, Couplet, Crambo, Cynghanedd, Doggerel, Eye, Feminine, Head, Internal, Masculine, Measure, Nursery, Perfect, Poetry, Rondel, Runic, Sight, Slang, Slant, Tercet, Terza-rima, Thomas, Triple, ➤ VERSE, Virelay

Rhythm(ic) Agoge, Alpha, Asynartete, Backbeat, Beat, Beta, Bo Diddley beat, Breakbeat, Cadence, Circadian, Duple, In-step, Meter, Movement, Oompah, Pyrrhic, Rubato, Sdrucciola, Singsong, Sprung, Swing, Syncopation, Tala, Talea, ➤ TEMPO, Time, Voltinism

Rib(bed), Ribbing, Rib-joint Bar, Chaff, Cod, Costa, Cross-springer, Dutch, Eve, False, Floating, Futtock, Groin, Intercostal, Lierne, Nervate, Nervular,

Nervure, Ogive, Persiflage, Rally, Spare, Springer, Sub-Costa, Tease, Tierceron, Tracery, True, Wife

Ribald(ry) Balderdash, Coarse, Scurrilous, Smut, Sotadic, Vulgar

Ribbon Band, Bandeau, Blue, Bow, Braid, Caddis, Caddyss, Cordon, Fattrels, Ferret, Fillet, Grosgrain, Hatband, Infula, Pad, Petersham, Radina, Rein, Soutache, Taenia, Tape, Teniate, Tie, Torsade

Ribless Ecostate

Rice Arborio, Basmati, Brown, Elmer, Entertainer, Indian, Kedgeree, Patna, Pilaf, Pilau, Pilaw, Reis, Risotto, Sushi, Twigs, Wild

Rich(es) Abounding, Abundant, Affluent, Amusing, Bonanza, Comic, Copious, Croesus, Dives, Edmund, Edwin, Fat, Feast, Fertile, Flush, Fruity, Full, Golconda, Haves, Heeled, High, Loaded, Lush, Luxurious, Mammon, Moneybags, Moneyed, Nabob, Oberous, ➤ OPULENT, Plenteous, Plush, Plutocrat, Rolling, Sumptuous, Toff, Vulgarian, ➤ WEALTHY, Well-heeled, Well-to-do

Richard Angevin, Burbage, Dick(y), Lionheart, Rick, Roe

Richthofen Red Baron

Rick (burning) Goaf, Sprain, Swingism, Wrench

Rickets, Rickety Dilapidated, Rachitis, Ramshackle, Shaky, Unsound

▷ **Rickety** may indicate an anagram

Rickshaw Pedicab

Ricochet Boomerang, Glance, Rebound

Rid Clear, Deliver, Ditch, Eliminate, Eradicate, Free, Obviate, Offload, Purge

Riddle Boulter, Charade, Colander, Dilemma, Enigma, Koan, Logogriph, Pepper, Perforate, Permeate, Puzzle, Screen, Searce, Search, Sieve, Sift, Siler, Sorites, Strain, Tems(e), Trommel

Ride, Riding Annoy, Bareback, Bestride, Bruise, Canter, Coast, Cycle, District, Division, Drive, Equitation, Field, Hack, Harass, Haute école, Hitchhike, Merry-go-round, Mount, Pick-a-back, Piggyback, Postil(l)ion, Rape, Revere's, Roadstead, Rollercoaster, Sit, Spin, Stang, Switchback, Third, Trot, Weather, Welter, Wheelie, White-knuckle

Rider Addendum, Adjunct, Appendage, Attachment, Cavalier, Charioteer, Codicil, Condition, Corollary, Equestrian, Eventer, Godiva, Guidon, Haggard, Horseman, Jockey, Lochinvar, Postil(l)ion, Proviso, PS, Revere, Walkyrie

Ridge Alveolar, Anthelix, Antihelix, Arete, Arris, As(ar), Balk, Bank, Baulk, Berm, Bur(r), Carina, Chine, Clint, Crease, Crest, Crista, Cuesta, Darling Range, Drill, Drum(lin), Dune, Esker, Fret, Gonys, Gyrus, Hammock, Hoe, Hogback, Horst, Hummock, Keel, Knur(l), Ledge, Linch, Lynchet, Mid-ocean, Missionary, Nek, Promontory, Ramp, Rand, Raphe, Razor-back, Reef, Rib, Rig, Rim, Sastruga, Screw-thread, Serac, Serpentine, Sowback, Torus, Varix, Verumontanum, Vimy, Wale, Weal, Whelp, Whorl, Windrow, Withers, Yardang, Zastruga

Ridicule, Ridiculous Absurd, Badinage, Bathos, Chaff, Cockamamie, Deride, Derisory, Egregous, Foolish, Gibe, Gird, Guy, Haze, Jibe, Josh, Laughable, Ludicrous, Mimic, Mock, Paradox, Pasquin, Pillory, Pish,

Pooh-pooh, Raillery, Rich, Roast, Satire, Scoff, Scout, Screwy, Sight, Silly, Skimmington, Taunt, Travesty

Ridinghood Nithsdale, Red

Riding-master RM

Riding-school Manège

Rife Abundant, Manifest, Numerous, Prevalent

Riffle Rapid

Riff-raff Canaille, Hoi polloi, Mob, Populace, Rag-tag, Scaff, Scum, Trash

Rifle Air, Armalite®, Bone, Browning, Bundook, Burgle, Carbine, Chassepot, Enfield, Enfield musket, Express, Garand, ➤ GUN, Kalashnikov, Loot, Martini®, Mauser®, Minié, Pilfer, Ransack, Repeater, Rob, Springfield, Winchester®

Rift Altercation, Chasm, Crevasse, Fault, Fissure, Gap, Gulf, Split

Rig(ging) Accoutre, Attire, Bermuda, Drilling, Equip, Feer, Gaff, Get-up, Gunter, Hoax, Jack-up, Manipulate, Marconi, Martingale, Outfit, Panoply, Ratline, Ropes, Schooner, Sport, Stack, Swindle, Tackle, Trull

▷ **Rigged** may indicate an anagram

Right(en), Rightness, Rights Accurate, Advowson, Angary, Appropriate, Appurtenance, Befit, Blue-pencil, BNP, Bote, Champart, Civil, Claim, Competence, Conjugal, Conservative, Copyhold, Cor(r)ody, ➤ CORRECT, Coshery, Cure, Curtesy, Customer, De jure, Dexter, Direct, Divine, Doctor, Droit, Due, Easement, Eminent domain, Emphyteusis, Equity, Esnecy, Estover, Ethical, Exactly, Faldage, Farren, Fascist, Feu, Fire-bote, Fitting, Franchise, Free-bench, Freedom, Germane, Gunter, Haybote, Infangthief, Interest, Isonomy, Iure, Junior, Jural, Jus, Leet, Legit, Letters patent, Liberty, Lien, Maritage, Meet, Moral, Naam, Ninepence, Off, Offhand, Offside, OK, Okay, Oke, Okey-dokey, Ortho-, Oughtness, Paine, Passant, Pat, Ploughbote, Pose, Postliminy, Prerogative, Primogeniture, Priority, Prisage, Privilege, Proper, R, Rain, Reason, Recourse, Rectify, Rectitude, Redress, Remainder, Remedy, Repair, Rt, Sac, Sake, Side, Soc, Squatter's, Starboard, Stillicide, Tao, Terce, Ticket, Title, Trivet, True, Turbary, User, Usucap(t)ion, Usufruct, Venville, Vert, Warren

Right-angle(d) Orthogonal

Righteous(ness) Devout, Good, Just, Moral, Pharisee, Prig, Rectitude, Tzaddik, Virtuous

Right-hand Dexter, E, Far, Recto, RH, Ro

Right-winger Falangist

Rigid(ity) Acierated, Catalepsy, Craton, Extreme, Fixed, Formal, Hidebound, Inflexible, Renitent, Set, Slavish, Starch(y), Stern, Stiff, Stretchless, Strict, Stringent, Tense, Turgor

Rigmarole Nonsense, Palaver, Paraphernalia, Protocol, Riddlemeree, Screed

Rigorous, Rigour Accurate, Austere, Cruel, Exact, Firm, Hard, Inclement, Iron-bound, Stern, Strait, Strict, Stringent

Rile Anger, Annoy, Harry, Irritate, ➤ NETTLE, Vex

▷ **Rile(y)** may indicate an anagram

Rill Purl, Sike

Rim Atlantic, Border, Chimb, Chime, Edge, Felloe, Felly, Flange, ➤ LIP, Margin, Strake, Verge

Rime Crust, Frost, Hoar, Rhyme, Rhythm

Rind Bark, Peel, Skin

Ring(ed), Ringing, Rings Angelus, Annulus, Anthelion, Arcus, Arena, Band, Bangle, Bell, Broch, Brogh, Call, Cartel, Cartouche, Change, Chime, Circinate, Circle, Circlet, Circus, Claddagh, Clam, Clang, Clink, Coil, Collet, Cordon, Corral, Corrida, Crawl, Cricoid, Cringle, Cromlech, Cycle, Cyclic, Dial, Dicyclic, Ding, Disc, Dohyo, Dong, D(o)uar, Draupnir, Echo, Encircle, Encompass, Engagement, Enhalo, Enlace, Environ, Enzone, Eternity, Fainne, Fairlead(er), Fairy, Ferrule, Fisherman, Fistic(uffs), Gimmal, Gird(le), Girr, Gloriole, Groin, Grom(m)et, Grummet, Guard, Gyges, Gymmal, Gyre, Halo, Hob, ➤ HOOP, Hoop-la, Ideal, Inorb, Inner, Involucre, Jougs, Jow, Karabiner, Kartell, Keeper, Key, Knell, Knock-out, Kraal, Link, Loop, Luned, Lute, Manacle, Manilla, Magpie, Marquise, Newton's, Nibelung, O, Orb, Outer, Pappus, Peal, Pele, Pen, Phone, Ping, Piston, Prize, Puteal, Quoit, Resonant, Resound, Round, Rove, Rundle, Runner, Scrunchy, Signet, Snap-link, Sound, Spell, Split, Stemma, Stemme, Surround, Swivel, Syndicate, Tang, Tattersall, Terret, Territ, Thimble, Ting, Tingle, Tink, Tinnitius, Tintinnabulate, Toe, Toll, Toplady, Tore, Torques, Torret, Torus, Travelling, Tree, Turret, Tweed, Varvel, Vervel, Vice, Wagnerian, Washer, Wedding, Welkin, Withe, Woggle, Zero

Ring-dance Carol

Ring-leader Bell-wether, Fugleman, Instigator

Ringlet Curl(icue), Lock, Tendril, Tress

Ringmaster Wagner

Ringworm Serpigo, Tinea

Rinse Bathe, Cleanse, Douche, Sind, Sine, Swill, Synd, Syne, Tint, Wash

Riot(er), Riotous(ly), Riots Anarchy, Brawl, Clamour, Demo, Deray, Gordon, Hilarious, Hubbub, Luddite, Medley, Melee, Orgy, Pandemonium, Peterloo, Porteous, Profusion, Quorum, Rag, Rebecca, Rebel, Roister, Rout, Rowdy, Ruffianly, Swing, Tumult

▷ **Rioters, Riotous** may indicate an anagram

Rip(ping) Basket, Buller, Cur, Grand, Handful, Horse, Lacerate, Rent, Rep, Splendid, Tear, Tide, Topnotch, To-rend, Unseam

Ripe, Ripen(ing) Auspicious, Full, Mature, Mellow, Rathe, Ready

Riposte Repartee, Retaliate, Retort

Ripple Bradyseism, Fret, Overlap, Purl, Undulation, Wave, Wavelet, Wrinkle

▷ **Rippling** may indicate an anagram

Rise(r), Rising Advance, Appreciate, Ascend, Assurgent, Bull, Butte, Cause, Easter, Eger, Elevation, Emerge, Emeute, Eminence, Erect, Escalate, Hance, Hauriant, Haurient, Heave, Hike, Hill, Hummock, Hunt's up, Improve, Increase, Insurgent, Intumesce, Jibe, Knap, Knoll, Lark, Levee, Levitate, Lift, Mount, Mutiny, Orient, Peripety, Putsch, Rear, Resurgent, Resurrection, ➤ REVOLT, Saleratus, Scarp, Soar, Stand, Stie, Sty, Surface,

Surge, Tor, Tower, Transcend, Up, Upbrast, Upburst, Upgo, Uprest, Upsurge, Upswarm, Upturn, Well

Risk(y) Actuarial, Adventure, Back, Calculated, Chance, Compromise, ➤ DANGER, Daring, Dice, Dicy, Emprise, Endanger, Fear, Gamble, Game, Hairy, Hazard, Imperil, Jeopardy, Liability, Peril, Precarious, Security, Spec, Unsafe, Venture

Risorgimento Renaissance

Risqué Blue, Racy, Salty, Scabrous, Spicy

Rissole(s) Cecils, Croquette, Faggot, Quennelle, Veggieburger

Rite(s) Asperges, Bora, Ceremony, Exequies, Initiation, Liturgy, Nagmaal, Obsequies, Powwow, Ritual, Sacrament, Sarum use, Superstition, York

Ritual Agadah, Arti, Ceremony, Chanoyu, Customary, Formality, Haggada, Lavabo, Liturgy, Rite, Sacring, Seder, Social, Use

Rival(ry), Rivals Absolute, Acres, Aemule, Compete, Emulate, Emule, Envy, Fo(n)e, ➤ MATCH, Needle, Opponent, Touch, Vie

River Ea, Estuary, Flood, Flower, Fluvial, Ord, Potamic, R, Riverain, Runner, Stream, Tributary, Waterway

RIVERS

2 letters:	Aire	Kwai	Ural
Ob	Alma	Lahn	Vaal
Po	Alph	Lech	Wear
3 letters:	Amur	Lena	Xero
Aar	Arno	Liao	Yalu
Aln	Aran	Lune	Yare
Axe	Aude	Maas	Yate
Ayr	Avon	Main	Yuan
Bug	Back	Meta	Yuen
Cam	Beni	Milk	**5 letters:**
Dee	Dart	Mino	Abana
Don	Deva	Mole	Acton
Ems	Doon	Nene	Adige
Esk	Dove	Neva	Afton
Exe	Earn	Nile	Agate
Fal	Ebbw	Nith	Aisne
Fly	Ebro	Oder	Argun
Han	Eden	Ohio	Avoca
Inn	Eder	Oise	Boyne
Lee	Elbe	Ouse	Chari
Lot	Erne	Oxus	Clyde
Nar	Esla	Prut	Congo
Red	Eure	Ruhr	Cross
San	Gila	Saar	Dasht
Tay	Gota	Soar	Desna
Tet	Huon	Spey	Douro
Ure	Idle	Styx	Drava
Usk	Isar	Swan	Duero
Wye	Iser	Taff	Eblis
4 letters:	Isis	Tarn	Firth
Abus	Juba	Tees	Fleet
Abzu	Kama	Teme	Forth
Acis	Kill	Test	Green
Adur	Kura	Tyne	Havel

Indre	Arzina	Teviot	Shannon
Indus	Barcoo	Thames	Swannee
Isere	Bio-bio	Ticino	Thomson
James	Calder	Tigris	Ucayali
Jumna	Canton	Tugela	Uruguay
Kasai	Crouch	Tyburn	Vistula
Kenga	Cydnus	Ubangi	Waikato
Lethe	Danube	Wabash	Welland
Liard	Dawson	Wairau	Yangtse
Loire	Donets	Wensum	Yenisey
Marne	Duddon	Wharfe	Zambesi
Meuse	Durack	Yarrow	**8 letters:**
Minho	Finlay	Yellow	Anderson
Mosel	Fraser	**7 letters:**	Blue Nile
Mulla	Gambia	Acheron	Canadian
Namoi	Ganges	Aruwimi	Cherwell
Negro	Granta	Chagres	Chindwin
Niger	Hodder	Cocytus	Clarence
Onega	Hudson	Damodar	Columbia
Oreti	Humber	Darling	Daintree
Peace	Irtysh	Derwent	Demerara
Pearl	Irwell	Dnieper	Dneister
Pecos	Itchen	Dubglas	Dordogne
Pelly	Japura	Durance	Flinders
Piave	Javari	Ettrick	Franklin
Pison	Javary	Fitzroy	Gascoyne
Plate	Jhelum	Garonne	Godavari
Rance	Jordan	Genesee	Klondike
Rhine	Kennet	Gironde	Kootenay
Rhone	Kolyma	Guapore	Maeander
Rogue	Komati	Huang He	Mahanadi
Seine	Liffey	Hwangho	Menderes
Shire	Mamoré	Iguassu	Missouri
Snake	Medway	Irawadi	Mitchell
Snowy	Mekong	Kanawha	Pactolus
Somme	Mersey	Krishna	Paraguay
Spree	Mohawk	Lachlan	Rio Negro
Staff	Morava	Limpopo	Suwannee
Stour	Murray	Lualaba	Torridge
Swale	Neckar	Madeira	Toulouse
Tagus	Orange	Manning	Victoria
Tamar	Orwell	Maranon	Wanganui
Tapti	Ottawa	Maritsa	Windrush
Teign	Pahang	Mataura	**9 letters:**
Terek	Parana	Meander	Ashburton
Tiber	Pripet	Moselle	Billabong
Tisza	Rakaia	Orinoco	Crocodile
Trent	Ribble	Orontes	Euphrates
Tweed	Riffle	Pechora	Irrawaddy
Volga	Rother	Pharpar	Mackenzie
Volta	Sabine	Potomac	Magdelana
Weser	Saluda	Rubicon	Murchison
Yaqui	Santee	Sabrina	Porcupine
Yarra	Severn	Salinas	Qu'Appelle
Yukon	Struma	Salween	Rangitata
6 letters:	Sutley	Salzach	Rio Grande
Amazon	Swanee	Sanders	Santa Cruz
Angara	Tarsus	Senegal	White Nile

10 letters:	Rangitaiki	Lesser Slave	
Blackwater	Rangitikei	Mississippi	
Courantyne	St Lawrence	Yellowstone	
Housatonic	**11 letters:**	**12 letters:**	
Phlegethon	Cooper Creek	Guadalquivir	Saskatchewan

River-bank, Riverside Brim, Carse, Riparian

River-bed Thalweg

River-mouth Firth, Frith

Rivet Bolt, Clinch, Clink, Concentrate, Fasten, Fix, Pean, Peen, Stud, Transfix

Rivulet Beck, Brook, Burn, Gill, Rill, Runnel, Strand

RNA Riboromal, Ribozyme

Roach Fish, Red-eye

Road(side) A, A1, Anchorage, Arterial, Autobahn, Autostrada, Ave(nue), B, Beltway, Boulevard, Burma, Carriageway, Causeway, Cloverleaf, Corduroy, Corniche, Course, Escape, Expressway, Fairway, Feeder, Foss(e) Way, Freeway, Highway, Kerb, Lane, Loan, Loke, Mall, Metal, M1, Motorway, Parkway, Path, Pike, Rd, Relief, Ride, Ring, ➤ ROUTE, Service, Shoulder, Shunpike, Slip, Spur(way), St(reet), Switchback, Thoroughfare, Tobacco, Toby, Trunk, Turning, Turnpike, Underpass, Verge, Via, Way

Road-keeper Way-warden

Road-maker Drunkard, Macadam, Navigator, Telford, Wade

Roam Extravagate, Peregrinate, Rake, Ramble, Rove, Stray, Wander, Wheel

Roan Barbary, Bay, Horse, Leather, Schimmel

Roar(ing) Bawl, Bell(ow), Bluster, Boom, Boys, Cry, Forties, Guffaw, Laugh, Roin, Rote, Rout, Royne, Thunder, Tumult, Vroom, Wuther, Zoom

Roast Barbecue, Bake, Baste, Birsle, Brent, Cabob, Cook, Crab, Crown, Decrepitate, Grill, Kabob, Pan, Ridicule, Scathe, Scald, Sear, Slate, Tan, Torrefy

Rob(bed), Robber(y) Abduct, Bandalero, Bandit, Barabbas, Bereave, Blag, Brigand, Burgle, Bust, Cabbage, Cacus, Cateran, Clyde, Dacoit, Dakoit, Daylight, Depredation, Despoil, Do, Drawlatch, Fake, Filch, Fleece, Flimp, Footpad, Gilderoy, Heist, Hership, Highjack, Highwayman, Hijack, Hold-up, Hustle, Ladrone, Larceny, Latrocinium, Latron, Loot, Mill, Mosstrooper, Pad, Pandoor, Pandour, Pinch, Piracy, Plunder, Procrustes, Rapine, Reave, Reft, Reive, Rieve, Rifle, Roberdsman, Robertsman, Roll, Rover, Roy, Rubbet, Rustler, Sack, Sciron, Screw, Short change, Sinis, Skinner, Smash and grab, Snaphaunch, Spoliation, ➤ STEAL, Steaming, Stick-up, Sting, Swindle, Thief, Toby, Turn-over, Turpin

Robe(s) Alb, Amice, Amis, Attrap, Camis, Camus, Cassock, Chimer, Chrisom(-cloth), Christom, Dalmatic, Dolman, ➤ DRESS, Gown, Ihram, Kanzu, Khalat, Khilat, Kill(a)ut, Kimono, Mantle, Parament, Parliament, Pedro, Peplos, Pontificals, Regalia, Rochet, Saccos, Sanbenito, Soutane, Sticharion, Stola, Stole, Talar, Tire, Vestment, Yukata

Robert Bob(by), Bridges, Browning, Burns, Cop, Flic, Peel, Rab, Rob

Robin Adair, Bird, Cock, Day, Goodfellow, Hob, Hood, Puck(-hairy), Ragged, Redbreast, Reliant, Round, Ruddock, Starveling, Wake

Robot Android, Automaton, Cyborg, Dalek, Golem, Nanobot, Puppet, RUR, Telechir

Robust Hale, Hardy, Healthy, Hearty, Iron, Sound, Stalwart, Sthenic, Stout, Strapping, Sturdy, Vigorous

Roc Bird, Ruc, Rukh

Rock(er), Rocking, Rocks, Rocky Ages, Agitate, Astound, Country, Cradle, Heavy metal, Marciano, Punk, Quake, Reggae, Rip-rap, Sally, ➤ SHAKE, Shoogle, Showd, Stun, Sway, Swee, Swing, Ted, Teeter, Totter, Unstable, Unsteady

TYPES OF ROCK AND ROCK FORMATIONS

2 letters:	Trass	Diamond	Elvanite
Aa	Uluru	Diorite	Eutaxite
3 letters:	Wacke	Eucrite	Fahlband
Gem	**6 letters:**	Fastnet	Ganister
Gib	Aplite	Felsite	Hepatite
Jow	Banket	Granite	Hornfels
Tor	Basalt	Greisen	Idocrase
4 letters:	Dacite	Lorelei	Inchcape
Bell	Diapir	Marlite	Laterite
Crag	Dunite	Minette	Lopolith
Gang	Flaser	Molasse	Mesolite
Glam	Flysch	Moraine	Mudstone
Jura	Fossil	Needles	Mylonite
Lava	Gabbro	Nunatak	Obsidian
Lias	Gangue	Olivine	Peperino
Noup	Gibber	Ophites	Petuntse
Reef	Gneiss	Outcrop	Phyllite
Sill	Gossan	Outlier	Pisolite
Sima	Gozzan	Peridot	Plutonic
Trap	Hyboid	Picrite	Plymouth
Tufa	Inlier	Remanie	Porphyry
Tuff	Kingle	Rhaetic	Psammite
Zoic	Masada	Sinking	Psephite
5 letters:	Norite	Spilite	Ragstone
Ayers	Oolite	Syenite	Regolith
Brash	Pelite	Thulite	Rhyolite
Calpe	Pluton	Tripoli	Rocaille
Chair	Pumice	Wenlock	Roe-stone
Chalk	Rognon	**8 letters:**	Saxatile
Chert	Sarsen	Adularia	Saxonite
Cliff	Schist	Aegirine	Scorpion
Craig	Sinter	Andesite	Sunstone
Elvan	Skerry	Aphanite	Taconite
Flint	Sklate	Basanite	Tarpeian
Geode	S. Peter	Brockram	Tephrite
Glass	Stonen	Burstone	The Olgas
Krans	Synroc	Calcrete	Tonalite
Magma	Tephra	Calc-tufa	Trachyte
Nappe	**7 letters:**	Calc-tuff	Trappean
Scalp	Aquifer	Ciminite	Xenolith
Scree	Boulder	Diabasic	**9 letters:**
Shale	Breccia	Dolerite	Anticline
Slate	Clastic	Dolomite	Argillite
Solid	Cuprite	Eclogite	Batholite
Stone	Cyanean	Eklogite	Bentonite

Bluestone	Mortstone	**10 letters:**	
Buhrstone	Mugearite	Ailsa Craig	
Claystone	Natrolite	Amygdaloid	**11 letters:**
Cockhorse	Neocomian	Camptonite	Agglomerate
Colluvium	Nunatakkr	Epidiorite	Amphibolite
Cornstone	Ophiolite	Foundation	Annabergite
Dalradian	Ottrelite	Granophyre	Anorthosite
Eddystone	Pegmatite	Greenstone	Carbonatite
Edinburgh	Petrology	Hypabyssal	Geanticline
Evaporite	Phonolite	Ignimbrite	Halleflinta
Firestone	Phosphate	Kersantite	Lamprophyre
Flowstone	Pleonaste	Kimberlite	Monchiquite
Gannister	Protogine	Lherzolite	Napoleonite
Gibraltar	Quartzite	Limburgite	Nephelinite
Goslarite	Reservoir	Novaculite	Phillipsite
Granulite	Sandstone	Palagonite	Pyroclastic
Greensand	Saprolite	Peridotite	Sedimentary
Greystone	Scablands	Permafrost	Symplegades
Greywacke	Schistose	Phenocryst	**12 letters:**
Hornstone	Siltstone	Rupestrian	Babingtonite
Impactite	Soapstone	Schalstein	Granodiorite
Intrusion	Tachylyte	Serpentine	Grossularite
Ironstone	Theralite	Sparagmite	Slickenslide
Laccolite	Tinguaite	Stinkstone	Stromatolite
Laccolith	Toadstone	Stonebrash	Syntagmatite
Limestone	Travertin	Stonehenge	Thunderstone
Meteorite	Variolite	Syntagmata	**13 letters:**
Migmatite	Vulcanite	Teschenite	Hypersthenite
Monadnock	Whinstone	Touchstone	**14 letters:**
Monocline	Whunstane	Travertine	Roche
Monzonite	Zechstein	Troctolite	moutonnée

Rock-boring Pholas
Rock-cress Arabis
Rocket Arugula, Booster, Capsule, Carpet, Congreve, Delta, Drake, Dressing down, Engine, Flare, Jato, Onion, Posigrade, Reprimand, Reproof, Retro, SAM, Skylark, Soar, Sounding, Stephenson, Thruster, Tourbillion, Upshoot, V1, Vernier, Warhead, Weld
Rock-living Rupicoline, Saxatile, Saxicoline, Saxicolous
Rock-pipit Sea-lark
▷ **Rocky** may indicate an anagram
Rococo Baroque, Fancy, Ornate, Quaint
Rod(like), Rods Aaron's, Bar, Barbel(l), Barre, Birch, Caduceus, Caim, Came, Can, Cane, Cue, Cuisenaire, Dipstick, Divining, Dowser, Drain, Ellwand, Fasces, Firearm, Fisher, Fly, Fuel, Gun, Handspike, Jacob's staff, Kame, Laver, Linchpin, Lug, Moses, Napier's bones, Newel, Notochord, Perch, Pin, Pistol, Piston, Pitman, Pointer, Pole, Pontie, Pontil, Ponty, Probang, Puntee, Punty, Raddle, Rhabdoid, Rhabdus, Rood, Scollop, Shaft, Spindle, Spit, Stadia, Stair, Stanchion, Staple, Stave, Stay-bolt, Stick, Strickle, Switch, Tie, Triblet, Tringle, Trocar, Twig, Urochord, Ventifact, Verge, Virgate, Virgulate, Wand, Withe
Rod-bearer Lictor
Rodent Acouchi, Acouchy, Ag(o)uti, Bandicoot, Bangsring, Banxring, Beaver, Biscacha, Bizcacha, Bobac, Bobak, Boomer, Capybara, Cavy,

Chickaree, Chincha, Chinchilla, Civet, Coypu, Cricetus, Dassie,
Deer-mouse, Delundung, Dormouse, Fieldmouse, Gerbil(le), Glires,
Glutton, Gnawer, Gopher, Ham(p)ster, Hog-rat, Hutia, Hyrax, Jerboa, Jird,
Lemming, Marmot, Mouse, Murid, Mus, Musk-rat, Musquash, Ochotona,
Ondatra, Paca, Porcupine, Potoroo, Rat, Ratel, Ratton, Renegade,
Runagate, Sciurine, Sewellel, Shrew, Spermophile, Springhaas,
Springhase, Squirrel, Taira, Tuco-tuco, Tucu-tuco, Vermin, Viscacha, Vole

Roderick Random, Usher

Rodomontade Bluster, Boast, Bombast, Brag, Gas

Roe Caviar(e), Coral, Fry, Melt, Milt(z), Pea, Raun, Rawn

Roger Ascham, Bacon, Jolly, OK, Rights

Rogue, Roguish(ness) Arch, Bounder, Charlatan, Chiseller, Drole,
Dummerer, Elephant, Espiegle(rie), Ganef, Ganev, Ganof, Gonif, Gonof,
Greek, Gypsy, Hempy, Herries, Imp, Knave, Latin, Limmer, Panurge,
Picaresque, Picaroon, Poniard, Rapparee, Riderhood, Savage, Scamp,
Schellum, Schelm, Skellum, Sleeveen, Slip-string, Swindler, Varlet, Villain

Roil Agitate, Annoy, Churn, Provoke, Vex

Roister(er) Blister, Carouse, Ephesian, Revel, Rollick, Scourer, Scowrer,
Swashbuckler, Swinge-buckler

Role Bit, Cameo, Capacity, Function, Metier, ➤ PART, Prima-donna, Title

Roll(ed), Roller, Roll-call, Rolling, Rolls Absence, Bagel, Bap, Barrel,
Beigel, Billow, Bolt, Bridge, Brioche, Butterie, Chamade, Comber,
Convolv(ut)e, Cop, Court, Croissant, Cylinder, Dandy, Drum, Electoral,
Enswathe, Eskimo, Even, Fardel, Fardle, Flatten, Furl, Go, Inker, Involute,
Labour, List, Lurch, Makimono, Mangle, Mano, Matricula, Motmot,
Moving, Muster, Notitia, Opulent, Paradiddle, Patent, Paupiette, Piano,
Pipe, Platen, Rafale, Ragman, Ra(p)scal(l)ion, Record, Reef, Reel, Register,
Ren, Revolute, Revolve, Rhotacism, Road, Rob, Roster, Rota, Rotifer,
Roulade, Rouleau, RR, Rub-a-dub, Rumble, Run, Sausage, Schnecken,
Snap, Somersault, Spool, Spring, Sway, Swell, Swiss, Table, Taxi, Temple,
Tent, Terrier, Toilet, Tommy, Trill, Trindle, Trundle, Victory, Volume,
Volutation, Wad, Wallow, Wamble, Waul, Wave, Wawl, Web, Welter,
Western, Wince, Wrap

Rollick(ing) Frolic, Gambol, Romp, Sport

▷ **Rollicking** may indicate an anagram

Roman Agricola, Agrippa, Candle, Calpurnia, Catholic, Cato, Consul, CR,
Crassus, Decemviri, Decurion, Empire, Flavian, Galba, Holiday, Italian,
Jebusite, Latin, Maecenas, Papist, Patrician, PR, Quirites, Raetic, RC,
Retarius, Rhaetia, Road, Scipio, Seneca, Sulla, Tarquin, Tiberius, Type,
Uriconian

Romance, Romantic (talk) Affair, Amorous, Byronic, Casanova, Catalan,
Dreamy, Fancy, Fantasise, Fib, Fiction, Gest(e), Gothic, Invention, Ladin(o),
Ladinity, Langue d'oc(ian), Langue d'oil, Langue d'oui, Lie, Neo-Latin,
Novelette, Poetic, Quixotic, R(o)uman, Stardust, Tale

▶ **Romanian** see RO(U)MANIAN

Romanov Nicholas

▶ **Romany** see GYPSY

Romeo Casanova, Montagu, Swain

Romp(ing) Carouse, Escapade, Fisgig, Fizgig, Frisk, Frolic, Hoyden, Randy, Rig, Sport, Spree

Ron Glum, Moody

Rondo Rota

Rontgen R, X-ray

Roo Joey

Roof (edge), Roofing Belfast, Bell, Ceil, Cl(e)ithral, Cover, Curb, Divot, Dome, Drip, Eaves, French, Gable, Gambrel, Hardtop, Hip(ped), Home, Imperial, Jerkin-head, Leads, Mansard, Monopitch, Palate, Pavilion, Pop-top, Porte-cochère, Rigging, Saddle, Shingle, Skirt, Tectiform, Tectum, Teguila, Thatch, Thetch, Tiling, Top, Uraniscus

Roof-climber Stegopholist

Roofless Hypaethral, Upaithric

Rook Bird, Castle, Cheat, Crow, Fleece, Fool, R, Swindle

Rookie Beginner, Colt, Galoot, Greenhorn, Nignog, Novice, Recruit, Tyro

Room(s), Roomy Antechamber, Anteroom, Apadana, Apartment, Attic, Ben, Berth, Bibby, Boudoir, Bower, But, Cabin(et), Camarilla, Camera, Capacity, Casemate, CC, Ceiling, Cell, Cellar, Cenacle, Chamber, Changing, Chaumer, Closet, Cockloft, Commodious, Compartment, Conclave, Consulting, Cubicle, Cuddy, Cutting, Delivery, Digs, Divan, Dojo, Dressing, Durbar, Elbow, End, Ex(h)edra, Extension, Foyer, Gap, Garret, Genizah, Kiva, Kursaal, Lab, Latitude, Laura, Lavra, Lebensraum, Leeway, Library, Locker, Lodge, Loft, Loo, Lounge, Margin, Megaron, Misericord(e), Oda, Orderly, Oriel, Pad, Palm Court, Parlour, Parvis, Penetralia, Pentice, Pentise, Powder, Private, Projection, Public, Pump, Recovery, Recreation, Rest, Robing, Rumpus, Sacristy, Salon, Sanctum, Scope, Scriptorium, Shebang, Single, Sitkamer, Snug, Solar, Solarium, ➤ SPACE, Spence, Still, Strong, Studio, Study, Suite, Tap, Twin, Ullage, Utility, Vestry, Voorkamer, Waiting, Ward, Zeta

Roost(er) Cock, Perch, Siskin, Sit

Root(ing), Roots Calumba, Cassava, Cheer, Contrayerva, Costus, Cube, Delve, Deracinate, Derris, Dig, Eddo, Elacampane, Eradicate, Eringo, Eryngo, Etymic, Extirpate, Fibrous, Foundation, Gelseminine, Ginseng, Grass, Grout, Grub, Heritage, Horseradish, Hurrah, Irradicate, Jalap, Jicama, Licorice, Mandrake, Mangold, Mishmee, Mishmi, Mooli, More, Myall, Nousle, Nuzzle, Orris, Pachak, Poke, Prop, Pry, Putchock, Putchuk, Race, Radish, Radix, Repent, Rhatany, Rhizic, Rhizoid, Rhizome, Scorzonera, Senega, Setwall, Snuzzle, Source, Square, Stock, Tap, Taro, Tuber, Tulip, Turbith, Turnip, Turpeth, Vetiver, Yam, Zedoary

Rootless Psilotum

Rope(s) Abaca, Ba(u)lk, Backstay, Becket, Bind, Bobstay, Boltrope, Brail, Breeching, Bunt-line, Cable, Cablet, Colt, Cord, Cordon, Cringle, Downhaul, Earing, Fake, Fall, Foresheet, Forestay, Funicular, Futtock-shroud, Gantline, Grist, Guide, Guy, Halliard, Halser, Halter,

Halyard, Hawser, Hawser-laid, Headfast, Inhaul, Jack-stay, Jeff, Jump, Kernmantel, Knittle, Ladder, Lanyard, Lasher, Lashing, Lasso, Line, Longe, Lunge, Mainbrace, Mainsheet, Marlin(e), Messenger, Mooring, Nettle, Noose, Oakum, Outhaul, Painter, Parbuckle, Pastern, Prolonge, Prusik, Rawhide, Reef point, Riata, Roband, Robbin, Rode, Runner, Sally, Seal, Selvagee, Sennit, Sheet, Shroud, Sinnet, Span, Spancel, Spun-yarn, Stay, Sternfast, Stirrup, String, Sugan, Swifter, Tackle, Tether, Tie, Timenoguy, Tippet, Tow(line), Trace, Trail, Triatic, Triatic stay, Vang, Wanty, Warp, Widdy

Rosalind Ganymede

Rosary Beads, Mala, Paternoster

Rose(-red), Rosie, Rosy Albertine, Amelanchier, Aurorean, Avens, Bear's-foot, Blooming, Bourbon, Breare, Briar, Brier, Cabbage, Canker, China, Christmas, Compass, Damask, Dog, Eglantine, Eglatère, England, Floribunda, Geum, Guelder, Hybrid, Jacque, Jacqueminot, Lal(age), Lancaster, Lee, Moss, Multiflora, Musk, Noisette, Opulus, Peace, Petra, Pink, Promising, Pyrus, Rambler, Red(dish), Remontant, Rhodo-, Rugosa, Snowball, Sprinkler, Standard, Tea, Tokyo, Tudor, Whitethorn, York

Rose-apple Jamboo, Jambu

Rose-bay Oleander

Rosette Buttonhole, Chou, Cockade, Favour, Patera, Rosula

Rosin Colophony, Resin, Roset, Rosit, Rozet, Rozit

Rosinante Jade

Roster List, Register, Scroll, Table

Rostrum Ambo, Bema, Lectern, Podium, Pulpit, Tribune

Rot(ten), Rotting Addle, Baloney, Boo, Bosh, Botrytis, Bull, Caries, Carious, Corrode, Corrupt, Daddock, Decadent, ➤ DECAY, Decompose, Degradable, Dotage, Dry, Eat, Erode, Fester, Foul, Kibosh, Manky, Mildew, Noble, Nonsense, Poppycock, Poxy, Punk, Putid, Putrefy, Putrid, Rail, Rancid, Rank, Rat, Ret, Rust, Sapropel, Septic, Sour, Squish, Twaddle, Wet

Rotate(r), Rotation Gyrate, Pivot, Pronate, Rabat(te), Reamer, Revolve, Roll, Selsyn, Trundle, Turn, Wheel, Windmill

Rote Heart, Memory, Recite, Routine

Rotor Impeller

▶ **Rotten** see ROT

▷ **Rotten** may indicate an anagram

Rotter Cad, Knave, Stinker, Swine

Rotund Chubby, Corpulent, Plump, Round, Stout

Rotunda Pantheon

Roué Debauchee, Decadent, Libertine, Profligate, Rake(-shame), Rip

Rouge Blush, Raddle, Redden, Reddle, Ruddy

Rough(en), Roughly, Roughness About, Approximate, Asper(ate), Burr, C, Ca, Choppy, Circa, Coarse, Craggy, Crude, Frampler, Grained, Gross, Gruff, Gurly, Gusty, Hard, Harsh, Hispid, Hoodlum, Hooligan, Impolite, Imprecise, Incondite, Inexact, Irregular, Jagged, Karst, Keelie, Kokobeh, Muricate, Push, Ragged, Ramgunshoch, Raspy, Raucle, Rip, Risp, Robust,

Row, Rude, Rugged, Rusticate, Rusty, Scabrid, Sea, Shaggy, Sketchy, Some, Spray, Spreathe, Squarrose, Stab, Strong-arm, Swab, Tartar, Tearaway, Ted, Textured, Uncut, Violent, Yahoo

Roughage Ballast, Bran, Fodder

Rough breathing Asper, Rale, Wheeze

Roughcast Harl

▷ **Roughly** may indicate an anagram

Roulette Russian

Ro(u)manian, Rumanian R(o)uman, Ro, Vlach, Wal(l)achian

Round(ness) About, Ammo, Ball, Beat, Bombe, Bout, Cartridge, Catch, Circle, Complete, Cycle, Dome, Doorstep, Figure, Full, Global, Globate, Hand, Jump-off, Lap, Leg, Milk, O, Oblate, Orb, Orbicular, Ought, Patrol, Peri-, Pirouette, Plump, Quarter-final, Rev, Ring, Robin, Roly-poly, Ronde, Rondure, Rota, Rotund, Route, Routine, Rundle, Rung, Salvo, Sandwich, Sellinger's, Semi-final, Shot, Skirt, Slice, Sphaer, Sphere, Spherical, Spiral, Step, Table, Tour, Tubby, U-turn

▷ **Round** may indicate a word reversed

Roundabout Ambages, Approximately, Bypass, Carousel, Circuit, Circumambient, Circumbendibus, Circus, Devious, Eddy, ➤ INDIRECT, Peripheral, Rotary, Tortuous, Turntable, Waltzer, Whirligig

Round building Tholos, Tholus

Round-mouth Hag

Round-up Collate, Corner, Corral, Gather, Herd, Rodeo, Spiral

Roup Auction, Croak, Pip, Roop

Rouse, Rousing Abrade, Abraid, Abray, Amo(o)ve, Animate, Beat, Bestir, Emotive, Enkindle, Firk, Flush, Hearten, Heat, Innate, Kindle, Send, Stimulate, Suscitate, Unbed, Waken, Whip

Rousseau Emile

Rout Clamour, Debacle, Defeat, Drub, Fleme, Flight, Hubbub, Hurricane, Rabble, Retreat, Rhonchal, Snore, Thiasus, Upsee, Upsey, Upsy, Vanquish, Whoobub

Route Avenue, Causeway, Course, Direction, Itinerary, Line, Path, Road, Track, Trade, Via, Way

Routine Automatic, Drill, Everyday, Grind, Groove, Habitual, Jogtrot, Pattern, Perfunctory, Pipe-clay, Red tape, Rota, Rote, Round, Rut, S(c)htick, Schtik, Treadmill, Workaday

Rove(r), Roving Discursive, Enrange, Gad, Globetrotter, Marauder, Nomad, Proler, Prowl, Ralph, Range, ➤ ROAM, Slub(b), Stray, Vagabond, Varangarian, Viking, Wander

Row(er) Align, Altercation, Arew, Argue, Argument, Bank, Barney, Bedlam, Bobbery, Bow, Brattle, Cannery, Colonnade, Death, Debate, Deen, Din, Dispute, Dust-up, Feud, File, Fireworks, Food, Fyle, Hullabaloo, Line(-up), Noise, Oar, Paddle, Parade, Peripteral, Pull, Quarrel, Rammy, Range, Rank, Raunge, Rew, Rhubarb, Rotten, Ruction, Rumpus, Scene, Scull, Series, Set, Shindig, Shindy, Shine, Skid, Spat, Splore, Stern, Street, Stridor, Stroke, Stushie, Sweep, Terrace, Tier, Tiff, Torpid, Wetbob, Wherryman

Rowan Ash, Quicken
Rowdy, Rowdiness Hooligan, Loud, Noisy, Rorty, Rough, Roughhouse, Ruffian, Scourer, Skinhead, Stroppy, Unruly, Uproarious
Roy Rob
Royal(ty), Royalist Academy, Angevin, Basilical, Battle, Bourbon, Emigré, Exchange, Fee, Hanoverian, Imperial, Imposing, Inca, Kingly, Majestic, Malignant, Palatine, Payment, Pharaoh, Plantagenet, Prince, Purple, Queenly, Regal, Regis, Regius, Regnal, Sail, Sceptred, Society
Rub(bing), Rubber(y), Rub out Abrade, Attrition, Balata, Buff, Buna®, Bungie, Bungy, Bunje(e), Bunjie, Bunjy, Butyl, Calk, Calque, Camelback, Caoutchouc, Chafe, Cold, Condom, Corrade, Corrode, Crepe, Cul(t)ch, Destroy, Dunlop®, Ebonite, Efface, Elastic, Elastomer, Embrocate, Emery, Erase, Factice, Fawn, Foam, Fray, Fret, Friction, Fridge, Frottage, Fudge, Funtumia, Gall, Galoch, Goodyear®, Grate, Graze, Grind, Guayule, Gutta-percha, Hevea, Hale, India, Inunction, Irritate, Isoprene, Lagos, Latex, Leather, Masseur, Negrohead, Neoprene, Nuzzle, Obstacle, Para, Polish, Pontianac, Pontianak, Safe, Sandpaper, Scour, Scrub, Scuff, Seringa, Silastic®, Sorbo®, Stroke, Towel, Trace, Ule, Vulcanite, Wild, Wipe, Xerotripsis
▷ **Rubbed** may indicate an anagram
Rubbish Bull, Bunkum, Clap-trap, Debris, Dre(c)k, Drivel, Fiddlesticks, Garbage, Grot, Grunge, Hogwash, Kak, Landfill, Leavings, Mullock, Nonsense, Phooey, Raffle, ➤ REFUSE, Stuff, Tinpot, Tip, Tom(fool), Tosh, Twaddle
Rubbish heap Dump, Lay-stall, Sweepings, Toom
Rubble Brash, Debris, Detritus, Moellon, Remains, Riprap, Talus
Rubidium Rb
Ruby Agate, Balas, Cuprite, Pigeon's blood, Port, Red, Star
Ruck Furrow, Scrum, Wrinkle
Rucksack Backpack, Bergen
Ruction Ado, Fuss, Quarrel
Rudder Budget, Helm, Steerer
Ruddy Bally, Bloody, Florid, Flashy, Red, Roseate, Rubicund, Sanguine
Rude Abusive, Barbaric, Bestial, Bumpkin, Callow, Churlish, Coarse, Discourteous, Elemental, Goustrous, Green, Ill-bred, Impolite, Indecorous, Inficete, Ingram, Ingrum, Insolent, Ocker, Offensive, Peasant, Raw, Risque, Rough, Simple, Surly, Unbred, Uncomplimentary, Uncourtly, Unlettered, Unmannered, Vulgar
Rudiment(ary), Rudiments ABC, Absey, Anlage, Beginning, Element, Embryo, Foundation, Germ(en), Inchoate, Vestige
Rudolph Hess, Reindeer
Rue(ful) Boulevard, Dittany, Harmala, Harmel, Herb of grace, Mourn, Regret, Repent, Ruta, Sorry
Ruff Collar, Crest, Fraise, Frill, Partlet, Pope, Ree, Trump
Ruffian Apache, Bashi-bazouk, Brute, Bully, Cut-throat, Desperado, Goon(da), Highbinder, Hoodlum, Hooligan, Keelie, Larrikin, Lout,

Miscreant, Mohock, Myrmidon, Phansigar, Plug-ugly, Raff, Rowdy, Sweater, Tearaway, Thug, Toe-ragger, Trailbaston, Tumbler

Ruffle(d) Bait, Dishevel, Falbala, Flounce, Fluster, Fret, ➤ FRILL, Gather, Irritate, Jabot, Peplum, Rouse, Rumple, Ruche, Shirty, Tousle

▷ **Ruffle** may indicate an anagram

Rug Afghan, Bearskin, Carpet, Drugget, Ensi, Flokati, Gabbeh, Hearth, Herez, Heriz, Kelim, K(h)ilim, Kirman, Lap robe, Mat, Maud, Numdah, Oriental, Prayer, Runner, Rya, Scatter, Travelling

Rugby (player) Back, Fifteen, Forward, Harlequin, Lion, Pack, Quin, RU, Scrum, Sevens, Threequarter, Wing

Rugged Craggy, Harsh, Knaggy, Rough, Strong

Ruin(ed), Ruins Annihilate, Blast, Blight, Carcase, Corrupt, Crash, Crock, Damn, Decay, Defeat, Demolish, Despoil, Destroy, Devastate, Disfigure, Dish, Dogs, Doom, Downcome, Downfall, End, Fordo, Hamstring, Heap, Hell, Insolvent, Inure, Kaput(t), Kibosh, Loss, Mar, Overthrow, Petra, Pot, Puckerood, Ravage, Reck, Relic, Scotch, Scupper, Scuttle, Shatter, Sink, Smash, ➤ SPOIL, Stramash, Subvert, Undo, Unmade, Ur, Violate, Whelm, Woe, Wrack

▷ **Ruined** may indicate an anagram

Rule(r), Rules, Ruling Abbasid, Algorithm, Align, Ameer, Amir, Ardri(gh), Aristocrat, Arret, Article, Atabeg, Atabek, Autocrat, Bajayet, Bajazet, Ban, Bey, Bretwalda, Britannia, Burgrave, Bylaw, Bosman, Caesar, Caliph, Canon, Caractacus, Catapan, Caudillo, Chagan, Cham, Chandragupta, Cheops, Chogyal, Club-law, Code, Condominium, Control, Cosmocrat, Criterion, Czar, Decree, Dergue, Despot, Dewan, Dey, Dictator, Diwan, Doge, Domineer, Dominion, Duce, Dynast, Elector, Emir, Emperor, Empire, Estoppel, Ethnarch, Etiquette, Exarch, Fatwa, Feint, Fetwa, Fleming's, Formation, Formula, Fuhrer, Gaekwar, Gaikwar, Genghis Khan, Gerent, Golden, Govern, Govern-all, Ground, Heptarch, Herod, Hierarch, Home, Hyleg, Inca, Jackboot, Jamshid, Jamshyd, K, Kabaka, Kaiser, Khan, Khedive, King, Law, Lesbian, Lex, Liner, Maharaja, Majority, Mameluke, Manchu, Matriarchy, Maxim, McNaghton, Mede, Meteyard, Method, Mikado, Ministrate, Mir, Mistress, Mogul, Monarchy, Motto, Mpret, Mudir, Naismith's, Nawab, Negus, Netiquette, Nizam, Norm(a), Oba, Ochlocratic, Oligarchy, Omayyad, Oppress, Ordinal, Padishah, Parallel, Pasha, Pendragon, Pharaoh, Pie, Plantocracy, Plutocracy, Plumb, Potentate, Precedent, Precept, Prescript, Prester John, Prevail, Prince, Principate, Principle, Pye, Queen, Queensberry, R, Raine, Raj(ah), Rajpramukh, Rana, Realm, Rector, Regal, Regent, Regula, Reign, Rex, Ring, Rubric, Sachem, Sagamore, Saladin, Sassanid, Satrap, Scammozzi's, Shah, Shaka, Sheik, Sherif, Shogun, Sirdar, Slide, Sophi, Sophy, Souldan, Sovereign, Squier, Squire, Stadtholder, Standard, Statute, Stratocracy, Sultan, Sutra, Suzerain, Swaraj, Sway, Synarchy, Tamerlane, Tetrarch, Thearchy, Three, Thumb, Toparch, Tsar, T-square, Tycoon, Tyrant, Umayyad, Vali, Wali, Wield, Zamorin

Rule-book Code, Pie, Pye

Rum(mer) Abnormal, Bacardi, Bay, Cachaca, Demerara, Eerie, Eery, Glass, Grog, Island, Jamaica, Odd(er), Peculiar, Quaint, Queer, Strange, Tafia, Weird

▶ **Rumanian** see R(O)UMANIAN

Rumble, Rumbling Borborygmus, Brool, Curmurring, Drum-roll, Groan, Growl, Guess, Lumber, Mutter, Rumour, Thunder, Tonneau, Twig

Ruminant, Ruminate Antelope, Cabrie, Camel, Cavicornia, Champ, Chew, Contemplate, Cow, Gemsbok, Goat, Meditate, Merycism, Pecora

Rummage Delve, Fish, Foray, Jumble, Powter, Ransack, Root, Rootle, Scavenge, Search, Tot

Rummy Canasta, Cooncan, Game, Gin, Queer

Rumour Breeze, Bruit, Buzz, Canard, Cry, Fame, Furphy, ➤ GOSSIP, Grapevine, Hearsay, Kite, Noise, On-dit, Pig's-whisper, Report, Repute, Say-so, Smear, Talk, Underbreath, Unfounded, Vine, Voice, Whisper, Word

Rump Arse, Bottom, Buttocks, Croup(e), Croupon, Crupper, Curpel, Derriere, Parliament, Podex, Pygal, Steak, Uropygium

Rumple Corrugate, Crease, Mess, Tousle, Wrinkle

Rumpus Commotion, Riot, Row, Ruction, Shindig, Shindy, Shine, Stushie, Tirrivee, Uproar

Run(ning), Run away, Run into, Runny, Runs Admin(ister), Arpeggio, Bleed, Bolt, Break, Bunk, Bye, Career, Chase, Coop, Corso, Course, Cresta, Current, Cursive, Cut, Dash, Decamp, Direct, Double, Drive, Escape, Extra, Fartlek, Flee, Flit, Flow, Fly, Follow, Gad, Gallop, Gauntlet, Go, Hare, Haste(n), Hennery, Hie, Idle, Jog, Ladder, Lauf, Leg, Lienteric, Lope, Manage, Marathon, Melt, Mizzle, Molt, Neume, Now, On, On-line, Operate, Pace, Pelt, Ply, Pour, Purulent, R, Race, Renne, Rin, Romp, Roulade, Rounder, Ruck, Scapa, Scamper, Scarper, Schuss, Scud, Scutter, Scuttle, See, Sequence, Shoot, Single, Skate, Skedaddle, Ski, Skid, Skitter, Slalom, Slide, Smuggle, Spew, Split, Spread, Sprint, Sprue, Squitters, Stampede, Straight, Streak, Stream, Taxi, Tear, Tenor, Trickle, Trill, Trot

Runaway Drain, Easy, Escapee, Fugue, Fugitive, Refugee

Run down Asperse, Belie, Belittle, Calumniate, Denigrate, Derelict, Dilapidated, Infame, Knock, Low, Obsolesce(nt), Poorly, Rack, Résumé, Scud, Tirade, Traduce

Rune, Runic Ash, Futhark, Futhorc, Futhork, Kri, Ogham, Spell, Thorn, Wen, Wyn(n)

Rung Crossbar, Roundel, Rundle, Stave, Tolled, Tread

Runner(s) Atalanta, Bean, Blade, Bow Street, Carpet, Coe, Courser, Deserter, Emu, Field, Geat, Gentleman, Gillie-wetfoot, Harrier, Hatta, Hencourt, Internuncio, Lampadist, Leg bye, Legman, Messenger, Miler, Milk, Mohr, Mousetrap, Nurmi, Owler, ➤ RUN(NING), Sarmentum, Scarlet, Series, Slipe, Smuggler, Stolon, Stream, Trial

▷ **Running, Runny** may indicate an anagram

Runt Dilling, Oobit, Oubit, Reckling, Scalawag, Scrog, Smallest, Titman, Woobut, Woubit

Run through Impale, Pierce, Rehearsal

Runway Airstrip, Drive, Slipway, Strip, Tarmac®

Run wild Lamp, Rampage
Rupee(s) Lac, Lakh, Re
Rupert Bear
Rupture Breach, Burst, Crack, Hernia, Rend, Rhexis, Rift, Split
Rural Agrarian, Agrestic, Boo(h)ai, Bucolic, Boondocks, Country, Forane, Georgic, Mofussil, Platteland, Praedial, Predial, Redneck, Rustic, Sticks, The Shires, Wops-wops
Ruse Artifice, Decoy, Dodge, Engine, Hoax, Pawk, Stratagem, ➤ TRICK
Rush(ed) Accelerate, Barge, Bolt, Bustle, Career, Charge, Dart, Dash, Eriocaulon, Expedite, Faze, Feese, Feeze, Feze, Fly, Frail, Friar, Gad, Gold, Hare, Hasten, High-tail, ➤ HURRY, Hurtle, Jet, Juncus, Lance, Leap, Luzula, Moses, Onset, Palmiet, Pellmell, Phase, Pheese, Pheeze, Phese, Plunge, Precipitate, Railroad, Rampa(u)ge, Rash, Rayle, Reed, Rip, Scamp(er), Scirpus, Scour, Scud, Scurry, Sedge, Spate, Speed, Stampede, Star(r), Streak, Streek, Surge, Swoop, Swoosh, Tear, Thrash, Thresh, Tilt, Torrent, Tule, Viretot, Zap, Zoom
Rusk Zwieback
Russell AE, Bertrand, Jack
Russet Rutile
Russia(n), Russian headman, Russian villagers Apparatchik, Ataman, Belorussian, Beria, Bolshevik, Boris, Boyar, Byelorussian, Circassian, Cossack, D(o)ukhobor, Dressing, Esth, Igor, Ivan, Kabardian, Kalmuk, Kalmyck, Leather, Lett, Mari, Menshevik, Minimalist, Mir, Muscovy, Octobrist, Osset(e), Red, Romanov, Rus, Russ(niak), Russki, Ruthene, Salad, Serge, Slav, Stakhanovite, SU, Thistle, Udmurt, Uzbeg, Uzbek, Vladimir, Vogul, Yuri, Zyrian
Rust(y) Aeci(di)um, Brown, Corrode, Cor(ro)sive, Erode, Etch, Ferrugo, Iron-stick, Maderise, Oxidise, Rubiginous, Soare, Stem, Teleutospore, Telium, Uredine, Uredo, Verdigris
Rust-fungus Aecidiospore
Rustic Arcady, Bacon, Bor(r)el(l), Bucolic, Bumpkin, Chawbacon, Churl, Clodhopper, Clown, Corydon, Damon, Doric, Forest, Georgic, Hayseed, Hick, Hillbilly, Hind, Hob, Hobbinoll, Hodge, Homespun, Idyl(l), Pastorale, Peasant, Pr(a)edial, Put(t), Rube, Rural, Strephon, Swain, Villager, Villatic, Yokel
▷ **Rustic** may indicate an anagram
Rusticate Banish, Seclude
Rustle(r), Rustling Abactor, Crinkle, Duff, Fissle, Frou-frou, Gully-raker, Poach, Speagh(ery), Sprechery, Steal, Stir, Susurration, Swish, Thief, Whig
Rust-proof Zinced
Rut Channel, Furrow, Groove, Heat, Routine, Track
Ruth Babe, Compassion, Mercy, Pity, Remorse
Ruthenium Ru
Rutherfordium Rf
Ruthless Brutal, Cruel, Fell, Hard, Hardball
Rye Gentleman, Grain, Grass, Spelt, Whisky

S s

S Ogee, Saint, Second, Sierra, Society, South, Square
SA It, Lure
Sabbatarian Wee Free
Sabbath Juma, Lord's Day, Rest-day, Shabbat, Sunday, Witches
Sabbatical Leave
Sabine Horace, Women
Sable Black, Jet, Negro, Pean, Zibel(l)ine
Sabotage, Saboteur Destroy, Frame-breaker, Ratten, Spoil, Wrecker
Sabre, Sabre rattler Jingo, Sword, Tulwar
Sabrina Severn
Sac Allantois, Amnion, Aneurism, Aneurysm, Bag, Bladder, Bursa, Caecum,
  Cisterna, Cyst, Follicla, Pericardium, Pod, Scrotum, Tylose, Tylosis, Vesica,
  Yolk
Sack(cloth), Sacking Bag, Bed, Boot, Bounce, Budget, Burlap, Can, Cashier,
  Chasse, Congé, Congee, Dash, Depredate, Despoil, Discharge, Doss, Fire,
  Gunny, Havoc, Jute, Knap, Loot, Mailbag, Maraud, Mitten, Pillage,
  Plunder, Poke, Push, Rapine, Reave, Road, Rob, Sanbenito, Sherris, Sherry,
  Spoliate, Vandalise
▷ **Sacks** may indicate an anagram
Sacrament Baptism, Communion, Confirmation, Eucharist, Extreme
  unction, Housel, Lord's supper, Matrimony, Nagmaal, Orders, Penance,
  Promise, Ritual, Unction, Viaticum
Sacred, Sacred place Adytum, Churinga, Hallowed, Heart, Hierurgy, Holy,
  Ineffable, Nine, Padma, Pietà, Sacrosanct, Sanctum, Taboo, Temenos
Sacrifice Alcestic, Cenote, Forego, Gambit, Hecatomb, Holocaust,
  Immolate, Iphigenia, Isaac, Lay down, Molech, Moloch, Oblation,
  ➤ OFFERING, Relinquish, Sati, Suovetaurilia, Supreme, Surrender, Suttee,
  Taurobolium, Tophet, Vicarious, Victim
Sacrilege, Sacrilegious Blaspheme, Impiety, Profane, Violation
Sacristan, Sacristy Diaconicon, Sceuophylax, Sexton
Sacrosanct Inviolable
Sad(den), Sadly, Sadness Alas, Attrist, Blue, Con dolore, Dejected,
  Desolate, Disconsolate, Dismal, Doleful, Dolour, Downcast, Drear, Dull,
  Dumpy, Heartache, Lovelorn, Low, Lugubrious, Mesto, Oh, Plangent,
  Sorry, Tabanca, Tear-jerker, Threnody, Tragic, Triste, Tristesse, Unhappy,
  Wan, Wo(e)begone
Saddle (bag, girth, pad) Alforja, Aparejo, Arson, Burden, Cantle, Cinch,
  Col, Crupper, Demipique, Lumber, Numnah, Oppress, Pack, Panel,
  Pigskin, Pilch, Pillion, Seat, Sell(e), Shabrack, Side, Stock, Tree, Western
Saddle-bow Arson
Saddler Whittaw(er)

Sadie Thompson

Sadism, Sadistic Algolagnia, Cruel

▷ **Sadly** may indicate an anagram

Safari Expedition, Hunt

Safe(ty) Allright, Almery, Ambry, Coolgardier, Copper-bottomed, Delouse, GRAS, Harmless, Impunity, Inviolate, Keister, Night, Peter, Reliable, Roadworthy, Sanctuary, Secure, Sound, Strong-box, Strongroom, Sure, Worthy

Safeguard Bulwark, Caution, Ensure, Fail-safe, Frithborh, Fuse, Hedge, Palladium, Protection, Register, Ward

Saffron Crocus, Yellow

Sag(gy) Decline, Dip, Droop, Hang, Hogged, Lop, Slump, Swayback, Wilt

Saga Aga, Chronicle, Edda, Epic, Icelandic, Laxdale, Legend, Odyssey, Volsunga

Sagacity Commonsense, Depth, Elephant, Judgement, Sapience, Wisdom

Sage Abaris, Aquinian, Bactrian, Bias, Carlyle, Cheronian, Chilo(n), Clary, Cleobulus, Confucius, Counsellor, Greybeard, Hakam, Herb, Imhotep, Maharishi, Mahatma, Malmesbury, Manu, Mirza, Orval, Pandit, Periander, Philosopher, Pittacus, Rishi, Salvia, Savant, Seer, Solon, Thales, Wiseacre

Sage-brush Nevada

Sahib Pukka

Said Co, Emir, Port, Quo(th), Related, Reputed, Spoken, Stated

▷ **Said** may indicate 'sounding like'

Sail(s) Bunt, Canvas, Circumnavigate, Coast, Cloth, Course, Cross-jack, Cruise, Fan, Fore-and-aft, Gaff(-topsail), Genoa, Head, Jib, Jut, Lateen, Leech, Luff, Lug, Moonraker, Muslin, Navigate, Parachute spinnaker, Peak, Ply, Rag, Reef, Rig, Ring-tail, Royal, Sheet, Spanker, Spencer, Spinnaker, Spritsail, Square, Staysail, Steer, Studding, Stun, Suit, Top-hamper, Top(-gallant), Van, Vela, Wardrobe, Yard

Sailor(s) AB, Admiral, Anson, Argonaut, Blue-jacket, Boatman, Boatswain, Bosun, Budd, Commodore, Crew, Deckhand, Drake, Evans, Galiongee, Gob, Grommet, Hat, Hearties, Helmsman, Hornblower, Jack, Janty, Jauntie, Jaunty, Jonty, Khalasi, Killick, Killock, Kroo(boy), Krooman, Kru(boy), Kruman, Lascar, Leadsman, Limey, Loblolly boy, Lt, Lubber, Mariner, Matelot, Matlo(w), Middy, MN, Nelson, Noah, Oceaner, OS, Popeye, Powder monkey, Privateer, Rating, RN, Salt, Seabee, Sea-dog, Sea-lord, ➤ SEAMAN, Serang, Shellback, Sin(d)bad, Stowaway, Submariner, Tar, Tarp(aulin), Tarry-breeks, Tindal, Triton, Waister, Water-dog

Saint(ly), Saints Agatha, Agnes, Aidan, Alban, Alexis, Alvis, Ambrose, Andrew, Anselm, Anthony, Asaph, Audrey, Augustine, Barbara, Barnabas, Bartholomew, Basil, Bees, Benedict, Bernard, Boniface, Brandan, Brendan, Bridget, Canonise, Canonize, Catharine, Cecilia, Chad, Christopher, Clement, Columba(n), Crispian, Crispin(ian), Cuthbert, Cyr, David, Denis, Denys, Diego, Dominic, Dorothea, Dunstan, Dymphna, Elmo, Eloi, Elvis, Eulalie, Francis, Genevieve, George, Giles, Gertrude, Hagiology, Hallowed,

Helena, Hilary, Hilda, Hugh, Ignatius, James, Jerome, John, Joseph, Jude, Kentigern, Kevin, Kilda, Latterday, Lawrence, Leger, Leonard, Linus, Loyola, Lucy, Luke, Malo, Margaret, Mark, Martha, Martin, Matthew, Michael, Monica, Mungo, Nicholas, Ninian, Odyl, Olaf, Oswald, Pancras, Patrick, Patron, Paul(inus), Peter, Pillar, Plaster, Polycarp, Quentin, Regulus, Ride, Rishi, Roch, Ronan, Roque, Rosalie, Rule, S, Sebastian, Severus, Simeon, Simon, SS, St, Stanislaus, Stephen, Swithin, Templar, Teresa, Thecia, Theresa, Thomas, Tobias, Ursula, Valentine, Veronica, Vincent, Vitus, Walstan, Wilfred, William, Winifred

St Anthony's Fire Ergotism, Erysipelas

St Elmo's Fire Corposant

St James Scallop-shell

St John's bread Carob

St Lucia WL

St Paul's Wren-ch

St Vincent WV

Sake Account, Behalf, Cause, Drink

Sal Volatile

Salacious, Salacity Lewd, Lust, Obscene, Scabrous

Salad Caesar, Calaloo, Calalu, Chef's, Chicon, Cos, Cress, Cucumber, Days, Endive, Escarole, Fennel, Finnochio, Finoc(c)hio, Frisée, Fruit, Greek, Guacamole, Lamb's lettuce, Lettuce, Lovage, Mesclum, Mesclun, Mixture, Niçoise, Purslane, Radicchio, Radish, Rampion, Rocket, Rojak, Russian, Slaw, Tabbouleh, Tabbouli, Tomato, Waldorf

▷ **Salad** may indicate an anagram

Salamander Axolotl, Ewt, Hellbender, Lizard, Menopome, Mole, Mudpuppy, Olm, Proteus, Spring-keeper

Salami, Salami technique Fraud, Peperoni

Salary Emolument, Fee, Hire, Pay, Prebend, Screw, Stipend, ➤ WAGE

Sale(s) Auction, Cant, Clearance, Fire, Garage, Market, Outroop, Outrope, Raffle, Retail, Roup, Subhastation, Turnover, Venal, Vendue, Vent, White, Wholesale

Saleroom Pantechnicon

Salesman Agent, Assistant, Bagman, Broker, Buccaneer, Bummaree, Counterhand, Drummer, Huckster, Loman, Pedlar, Rep, Retailer, Tallyman, Tout, Traveller

Salient Coign, Jut, Projection, Prominent, Redan, Spur

Saliva Drool, Parotid, Ptyalism, Sial(oid), Slobber, Spawl, Spit(tle), Sputum

Sallow Adust, Pallid, Pasty, Sale, Sauch, Wan

Sally Aunt, Boutade, Charge, Dash, Escape, Excursion, Flight, Foray, Issue, Jest, Mot, Pleasantry, Quip, Sarah, Sortie, Witticism

Salmagundi Mess

Salmon Alevin, Atlantic, Baggit, Blue-cap, Blueback, Boaz, Chinook, Chum, Cock, Coho(e), Dog, Grav(ad)lax, Grilse, Humpback, Kelt, Keta, Kipper, Kokanee, Lax, Ligger, Lox, Masu, Mort, Nerka, Oncorhynchus,

Ouananiche, Par(r), Peal, Pink, Quinnat, Redfish, Rock, Samlet, Shedder, Skegger, Smelt, Smolt, Smout, Smowt, Sockeye, Sparling, Spirling, Sprod

Salon, Saloon Barrel-house, Car, Hall, Honkytonk, Lounge, Pullman, Sedan, Shebang, Tavern

Salt(s), Salty AB, Alginate, Aluminate, Andalusite, Aspartite, Attic, Aurate, Azide, Bath, Bicarbonate, Bichromate, Borate, Borax, Brackish, Brine, Bromate, Bromide, Capr(o)ate, Caprylate, Carbamate, Carbonate, Carboxylate, Cerusite, Chlorate, Chlorite, Chromate, Citrate, Complex, Corn, Cure(d), Cyanate, Cyclamate, Datolite, Deer lick, Dithionate, Double, Enos, Epsom, Ferricyanide, Formate, Glauber, Glutamate, Halite, Halo-, Health, Hydrochloride, Iodide, Ioduret, Isocyanide, Lactate, Lake-basin, Lithate, Liver, Magnesium, Malate, Malonate, Manganate, Matelot, Microcosmic, Monohydrate, Mucate, Muriate, Nacl, Nitrate, Nitrite, Oleate, Osm(i)ate, Oxalate, Palmitate, Pandermite, Perchlorate, Periodate, Phosphate, Phthalate, Picrate, Piquancy, Plumbite, Potassium, Powder, Propionate, Pyruvate, Rating, Resinate, Rochelle, Rock, Sailor, Sal ammoniac, Sal volatile, Salify, Saut, Sea-dog, Seafarer, Seasoned, Sebate, Selenate, Smelling, Soap, Sodium, Stannate, Stearate, Suberate, Succinate, Sulfite, Sulphate, Sulphite, Sulphonate, Tannate, Tartrate, Tellurate, Thiocyanate, Thiosulphate, Titanate, Tungstate, Uranin, Urao, Urate, Vanadate, Water-dog, Wit(ty), Xanthate

Salt meat Mart

Saltpetre Caliche, Chile, Nitre

Salt-water Sea

Salubrious Healthy, Sanitary, Wholesome

Salutary Beneficial, Good, Wholesome

Salutation, Salute Address, Ave, Banzai, Barcoo, Bid, Cap, Cheer, Command, Coupé(e), Curtsey, Embrace, Feu de joie, Fly-past, Genuflect, Greet, Hail, Hallo, Halse, Homage, Honour, Jambo, Kiss, Present, Salaam, Salvo, Sieg Heil, Toast, Tribute, Wassail

Salvador Dali

Salvage Dredge, Lagan, Ligan, Reclaim, Recover, Recycle, Rescue, Retrieve, Tot

Salvation(ist) Booth, Redemption, Rescue, Soterial, Yeo

Salve Anele, Anoint, Assuage, Ave, Lanolin(e), Lotion, Ointment, Remedy, Saw, Tolu, Unguent

Salver Tray, Waiter

Salvo Fusillade, Salute, Volley

Sal volatile Hartshorn

Sam Browse, Uncle, Weller

Samara Ash-key

Samarium Sm

Same(ness) Ae, Agnatic, Contemporaneous, Do, Egal, Equal, Ib(id), Ibidem, Id, Idem, Identical, Identity, Ilk, Iq, Like, One, Thick(y), Thilk, Uniform, Ylke

Samovar Urn

Samoyed Dog, Uralian, Uralic

Sample Biopsy, Blad, Browse, Example, Foretaste, Handout, Muster, Pattern, Pree, Prospect, Quadrat, Scantling, Specimen, Swatch, Switch, ➤ TASTE, Transect, Try

Samuel Pepys, Smiles

Samurai Ronin

▷ **Sam Weller** may indicate the use of 'v' for 'w' or vice versa

Sanctify Consecrate, Purify, Saint

Sanctimonious Banbury, Devout, Pi, Righteous, Saintly

Sanction Allow, Appro, Approbate, Approof, Approve, Authorise, Bar, Countenance, Endorse, Imprimatur, Mandate, OK, Pass, Pragmatic, Ratify, Sustain

Sanctities, Sanctity Halidom, Holiness, Hollidam, Sonties

Sanctuary, Sanctum Adytum, Asylum, By-room, Cella, Ch, Church, Frithsoken, Frithstool, Girth, Grith, Holy, Lair, Naos, Oracle, Penetralia, Preserve, Refuge, Sacellum, Sacrarium, ➤ SHELTER, Shrine, Temple

Sand(bank), Sandbar, Sands, Sandy Alec, Alex, Areg, Arena(ceous), Arenose, Arkose, As, Atoll, Bar, Barchan(e), Bark(h)an, Beach, Caliche, Dene, Desert, Down, Dudevant, Dune, Dupin, Eremic, Erg, Esker, Gat, George, Ginger, Goodwin, Grain, Granulose, Hazard, Loess, Machair, Nore, Oil, Overslaugh, Podsol, Podzol, Portlandian, Psammite, Ridge, Sabulous, Sawney, Seif, Shelf, Shoal, Shore, Tee, Time, Tombolo

Sandal(s) Alpargata, Calceamentum, Chappal, Espadrille, Flip-flop, Ganymede, Geta, Huarache, Jelly, Patten, Pump, Talaria, Thong, Zori

Sandalwood Algum, Almug, Chypre, Pride, Santal

Sandarac Arar

Sander Pike-perch

Sandhurst RMA

Sand-loving Ammophilous, Psammophil

Sandpiper Bird, Knot, Ree, Ruff, Sandpeep, Stint, Terek

Sandstone Arkose, Dogger, Fa(i)kes, Flysch, Grit, Hassock, Kingle, Quartzite, Red

Sandstorm Haboob, Tebbad

Sandwich Bruschetta, Butty, Club, Croque-monsieur, Cuban, Doorstep, Earl, Hamburger, Island, Open, Roti, Round, Sarney, Sarnie, Smorbrod, Smorgasbord, Smorrebrod, Sub, Submarine, Thumber, Toastie, Triple-decker, Twitcher, Victoria

▷ **Sandwich(es)** may indicate a hidden word

Sane, Sanity Compos mentis, Formal, Healthy, Judgement, Rational, Reason, Sensible, Wice

Sangfroid Aplomb, Cool, Poise

Sanguine Confident, Hopeful, Optimistic, Roseate, Ruddy

Sanitary Hygienic, Salubrious, Sterile

Sanskrit Purana, Ramayana, Sutra, Upanishad

Santa Claus Abonde, Kriss Kringle

Sap Benzoin, Bleed, Cremor, Drain, Enervate, Entrench, Ichor, Juice, Laser, Latex, Lymph, Mine, Mug, Pulque, Ratten, Resin, Roset, Rosin, Rozet, Rozit, Secretion, Soma, Sura, Swot, Undermine, Weaken

Sapid Flavoursome, Savoury, Tasty

Sapience, Sapient Discernment, Sage, Wisdom

Sapling Ash-plant, Ground-ash, Plant, Tellar, Teller, Tiller, Youth

Sapper(s) Miner, RE

Sapphire Star

Sappho Lesbian

Sapwood Alburnum

Sarah Battle, Gamp, Sal

Sarcasm, Sarcastic Biting, Cutting, Cynical, Derision, Irony, Mordacious, Mordant, Pungent, Quip, Sarky, Satire, Sharp, Snide, Sting, Wisecrack

Sardine Fish, Sard

Sardonic Cutting, Cynical, Ironical, Scornful

Sargasso Ore, Sea(weed)

Sark Chemist, CI, Shirt

Sarong Sulu

Sash Baldric(k), Band, Belt, Burdash, Cummerbund, Obi, Scarf, Window

Sassaby Tsessebe

Sassenach English, Lowlander, Pock-pudding

Satan Adversary, Apollyon, Arch-enemy, Cram, ➤ DEVIL, Eblis, Lucifer, Shaitan

Satchel Bag, Scrip

Sate(d), Satiate Glut, Replete, Sad, Surfeit

Satellite Adrastea, Ananke, Ariel, Astra, Atlas, Attendant, Belinda, Bianca, Callisto, Calypso, Camenae, Carme, Charon, Communications, Comsat®, Cordelia, Cressida, Deimos, Desdemona, Despina, Dione, Disciple, Early bird, Echo, Enceladus, Explorer, Europa, Follower, Galatea, Galilean, Ganymede, Geostationary, Helene, Henchman, Himalia, Hyperion, Iapetus, Intelsat, Io, Janus, Larissa, Metis, Mimas, Miranda, Moon, Mouse, Nereid, Oberon, Ophelia, Orbiter, Pan, Pandora, Pasiphae, Phobos, Phoebe, Portia, Prometheus, Puck, Rhea, Rosalind, Sinope, Sputnik, Syncom, Telesto, Telstar, Tethys, Thalassa, Tiros, Titan, Titania, Triton

▶ **Satin** see SILK

Satire, Satirical, Satirist Arbuthnot, Archilochus, Burlesque, Butler, Candide, Chaldee, Dryden, Horace, Iambographer, Juvenal, Lampoon, Lash, Lucian, Menippean, Mockery, Pantagruel, Parody, Pasquil, Pasquin(ade), Pope, Raillery, Sarky, Sotadic, Spoof, Squib, Swift, Travesty

Satisfaction, Satisfactory, Satisfy(ing) Agree, Ah, Ap(p)ay, Appease, Atone, Change, Compensation, Complacent, ➤ CONTENT, Defrayment, Enough, Feed, Fill, Fulfil, Glut, Gratify, Indulge, Jake, Liking, Meet, OK, Pacation, Palatable, Pay, Please, Propitiate, Qualify, Redress, Repay, Replete, Sate, Satiate, Serve, Settlement, Slake, Square, Suffice, Well

Saturate(d) Drench, Glut, Imbue, Impregnate, Infuse, Permeate, ➤ SOAK, Sodden, Steep, Waterlog

Saturn God, Kronos, Lead, Planet, Rocket

Satyr Faun, Leshy, Lesiy, Libertine, Marsyas, Pan, Silen(us), Woodhouse, Woodwose

Sauce, Saucy Alfredo, Arch, Allemanse, Baggage, Béarnaise, Béchamel, Bolognese, Bordelaise, Bourguignonne, Bread, Brown, Caper, Carbonera, Catchup, Catsup, Chasseur, Chaudfroid, Cheek, Chilli, Condiment, Coulis, Cranberry, Cream, Custard, Dapper, Dip, Dressing, Enchilada, Espagnole, Fenberry, Fondue, Fu yong, Fu yung, Gall, Garum, Gravy, Hard, Hoison, Hollandaise, Horseradish, HP, Impudence, Ketchup, Lip, Malapert, Marinara, Matelote, Mayonnaise, Melba, Meunière, Mint, Mirepoix, Mole, Mornay, Mousseline, Nam pla, Nerve, Newburg, Nuoc mam, Oxymal, Oyster, Panada, Parsley, Passata, Peart, Pert, Pesto, Piri-piri, Pistou, Ravigote, Relish, Remoulade, Rouille, Sabayon, Sal, Salpicon, Salsa, Sambal, Sass, Satay, Shoyu, Soja, Soubise, Soy, Soya, Sue, Supreme, Sweet and sour, Stroganoff, Tabasco®, Tamari, Tartar(e), Tomato, Tossy, Velouté, Vinaigrette, White, Worcester, Worcestershire

Sauceboat-shaped Scaphocephalate

Saucepan Chafer, Goblet, Skillet, Stockpot

Saucer Ashtray, Discobolus, UFO

Sauna Bath, Sudatorium, Sudorific

Saunter Amble, Dander, Lag, Mosey, Promenade, Roam, Shool, Stroll

Sausage(s) Andouillette, Banger, Black pudding, Boerewors, Bologna, Bratwurst, Cervelat, Cheerio, Chipolata, Chorizo, Cumberland, Devon, Drisheen, Frankfurter, Knackwurst, Knockwurst, Liver(wurst), Mortadella, Pep(p)eroni, Polony, Salami, Sav(eloy), Snag(s), String, White pudding, Wiener(wurst), Wienie, Wurst, Zampone

Sausage-shaped Allantoid

Savage Ape, Barbarian, Boor, Brute, Cannibal, Cruel, Feral, Fierce, Grim, Gubbins, Immane, Inhuman, Maul, Sadistic, Truculent, Vitriolic, Wild

Savanna Plain, Sahel

Savant Expert, Sage, Scholar

Save, Saving(s) Bank, Bar, Besides, But, Capital, Conserve, Deposit, Economy, Except, Hain, Hoard, Husband, ISA, Layby, Keep, Nest egg, Nirlie, Nirly, PEPS, Preserve, Put by, Reclaim, Redeem, Relieve, Reprieve, ➤ RESCUE, Reskew, Sa', Salt, Salvage, Scrape, Scrimp, Shortcut, Slate club, Spare, Stokvel, Succour, TESSA, Unless

Saviour Deliverer, Jesu(s), Messiah, Redeemer

Savour(ed), Savoury Aigrette, Bouchée, Canapé, Essence, Fag(g)ot, Flavour, Olent, Ramekin, Relish, Resent, Sair, Sapid, Sar, Smack, Starter, Tang, ➤ TASTE, Vol au vent

Savoy Cabbage, Opera

Saw Adage, Aphorism, Apothegm, Back, Band, Beheld, Bucksaw, Buzz, Chain, Circular, Cliché, Compass, Coping, Cross-cut, Crown, Cut, Dictum, Dovetail, Frame, Fret, Gang, Gnome, Grooving, Hack, Jig, Keyhole,

Legend, Maxim, Met, Motto, Panel, Paroemia, Pitsaw, Proverb, Ribbon,
Rip, Sash, Saying, Scroll, Serra, Slogan, Spied, Stadda, Sweep, Tenon,
Trepan, Trephine, Whip, Witnessed

Sawbones Surgeon

Saxon Cedric, Hengist, Wend

Say(ing) Adage, Agrapha, Aphorism, Apophthegm, Apostrophise,
Articulate, Axiom, Beatitude, Bromide, Byword, Cant, Catchphrase, Cliché,
Declare, Dict(um), Eg, Enunciate, Epigram, Express, Fadaise, Gnome,
Impute, Logia, Logion, ➤ MAXIM, Mean, Mot, Mouth, Observe, Predicate,
Pronounce, Proverb, Put, Quip, Recite, Rede, Relate, Remark, Report,
Saine, Saw, Sc, Sententia, ➤ SPEAK, Suppose, Utter, Voice, Word

▷ **Say** may indicate a word sounding like another

Scab(by) Blackleg, Crust, Eschar, Leggism, Leprose, Mangy, Rat, Scald, Scall,
Sore

Scabbard Frog, Pitcher, Sheath, Tsuba

Scabies Itch, Psora

Scabrous Harsh, Rough

Scaffold(ing), Scaffolder Gallows, Gantry, Hoarding, Putlock, Putlog, Rig,
Spiderman, Stage

Scald Blanch, Burn, Leep, Ploat, Plot

Scale, Scaly Analemma, Ascend, Balance, Baumé, Beaufort, Binet- Simon,
Bismar, Brix, Bud, Burnham, Celsius, Centigrade, Ceterach, Chromatic,
➤ CLIMB, Desquamate, Diatonic, Douglas, Elo, Escalade, Fahrenheit,
Flake, Furfur, Gamme, Gamut, Ganoid, Gauge, Gunter's, Kelvin, Ladder,
Lamina, Layer, Leaf, Lepid, Lepidote, Leprose, Libra, Ligule, Likert,
Lodicule, Loricate, Major, Mercalli, Minor, Mohs, Munsell, Natural,
Nominal, Octad, Ordinal, Palea, Palet, Patagium, Peel, Pentatonic,
Pholidosis, Placoid, Plate, Platform, Ramentum, ➤ RANGE, Rankine,
Réaumur, Regulo, Richter, Scan, Scarious, Scincoid, Scurf, Scutellate, Shin,
Skink, Sliding, Speel, Squama, Squame(lla), Submediant, Tegmentum,
Tegula, Tonal, Tron(e), Tridymite, Vernier

Scallop(ed) Bivalve, Clam, Coquille, Crenate, Escalop, Frill, Gimp, Mush,
Vandyke

Scallywag Rascal, Scamp, Skeesicks

Scalp Cut, Scrape, Skin, Trophy

Scalpel Bistoury, Knife

Scamp Fripon, Imp, Limb, Lorel, Lorrell, Losel, Lozell, Neglect, ➤ RASCAL,
Reprobate, Rip, Rogue, Scallywag, Skeesicks

Scamper Gambol, Lamp, Run, Scurry, Skedaddle, Skelter

Scan(ning), Scanner CAT, CT, Examine, Helical, OCR, Peruse, PET, Rake,
Raster, Scrutinise, SEM, SPET, Survey, Tomography, Ultrasound, Vet

Scandal(ous), Scandalise Belie, Canard, Commesse, Disgrace, Gamy,
Hearsay, Muck-raking, Opprobrium, Outrage, Shame, Slander, Stigma,
Watergate

Scandinavian Dane, Finn, Laplander, Lapp, Nordic, Norseland, Runic,
Swede, Varangian, Viking

Scandium Sc

Scant(y) Bare, Brief, Exiguous, Ihram, Jejune, Jimp, Poor, Scrimpy, Short, Shy, Slender, Spare, Sparse, Stingy

Scapegoat Butt, Fall-guy, Hazazel, Joe Soap, Patsy, Stooge, Target, Victim, Whipping-boy

Scapula Blade, Omoplate

Scar(face) Al, Blemish, Cheloid, Cicatrix, Cliff, Craig, Epulotic, Hilum, Keloid, Leucoma, Leukoma, Mark, Pockmark, Stigma, Ulosis, Wipe

Scarab Beetle, Gem

Scarce(ly), Scarcity Barely, Dear, Dearth, Famine, Few, Hardly, Ill, Lack, Rare, Scanty, Seldom, Short, Strap, Uncommon, Want

Scare(mongering), Scaring Alarmist, Alert, Amaze, Fleg, Fright, Gally, Gliff, Hairy, Panic, Startle

Scarecrow Bogle, Bugaboo, Dudder, Dudsman, Gallibagger, Gallibeggar, Gallicrow, Gallybagger, Gallybeggar, Gallycrow, Malkin, Mawkin, Potato-bogle, Ragman, S(h)ewel, Tattie-bogle

Scarf Babushka, Belcher, Cataract, Comforter, Cravat, Curch, Doek, Dupatta, Fichu, Hai(c)k, Haique, Hyke, Lambrequin, Madras, Mantilla, Muffettee, Muffler, Neckatee, Nightingale, Orarium, Pagri, Palatine, Rail, Rebozo, Sash, Screen, Stole, Tallith, Tippet, Trot-cosy, Trot-cozy, Vexillum

Scarifier Scuffler

Scarlet Cinnabar, Crimson, Pimpernel, Ponceau, Red, Vermilion

Scarper Bunk, Run, Shoo, Welsh

Scat Aroint, Dropping

Scathe, Scathing Mordant, Sarcastic, Savage, Severe, Vitriolic

Scatter(ed), Scattering Bestrew, Broadcast, Diaspora, Disject, Dispel, ➤ DISPERSE, Dissipate, Flurr, Litter, Rout, Scail, Skail, Sow, Sparge, Splutter, Sporadic, Spread, Sprinkle, Squander, Straw, Strew

Scatterbrain(ed) Dippy, Ditsy

Scavenge(r) Dieb, Forage, Hunt, Hy(a)ena, Jackal, Rake, Ratton, Rotten, Scaffie, Sweeper, Totter

Scenario Outline, Plot, Script

Scene(ry) Arena, Boscage, Coulisse, Decor, Flat(s), Landscape, Locale, Prop, Prospect, Set, Sight, Site, Sketch, Stage, Tableau, Tormenter, Tormentor, Venue, View

Scent Aroma, Attar, Chypre, Cologne, Essence, Fragrance, Frangipani, Fumet(te), Gale, Moschatel, Nose, Odour, Orris, Ottar, Otto, Perfume, Sachet, Smell, Spoor, Vent, Waft, Wind

Scentless Anosmia

Sceptic(al) Cynic, Doubter, Incredulous, Infidel, Jaundiced, Nihilistic, Pyrrho(nic), Sadducee

Schedule Agenda, Calendar, Itinerary, Prioritise, Programme, Register, Slot, Table, Timetable

Scheme(r), Scheming Concoct, Conspire, Crafty, Cunning, Dare, Darien, Dart, Decoct, Devisal, Diagram, Dodge, Draft, Gin, Honeytrap, Intrigue,

Jezebel, Machiavellian, Machinate, Manoeuvre, Nostrum, ➤ PLAN, Plat, Plot, Project, Purpose, Racket, Ruse, Stratagem, System, Table, Wangle, Wheeze

Schism(atic) Disunion, Division, Heterodox, Rent, Split

Schizo(phrenia) Catatonic, Dementia praecox

Schmaltz Goo, Slush

Schmieder S

Schmuck Gunsel

Scholar Abelard, Academic, Alumni, Atticus, BA, Bookman, Boursier, Catachumen, Clergy, Clerisy, Clerk, Commoner, Demy, Disciple, Erasmus, Erudite, Etonian, Exhibitioner, Extern(e), Externat, Goliard, Graduate, Grecian, Hafiz, Inkhorn, Literate, Littérateur, MA, Mal(l)am, Masorete, Occam Ulama, Pauline, Plutarch, Polymath, Pupil, Rhodes, Sap, Savant, Schoolboy, Sizar, Soph, ➤ STUDENT, Tabardar, Taberdar, Taberder, Tom Brown

Scholarship Bursary, Education, Erudition, Exhibition, Grant, Learning, Lore, Mass, Rhodes

School Academy, Ampleforth, Approved, Ashlan, Barbizon, Bauhaus, Benenden, Bluecoat, Boarding, Charm, Charterhouse, Chartreux, Chautauqua, Choir, Church, Classical, Composite, Comprehensive, Conservative, Conservatoire, Conservatory, Correspondence, Crammer, Cult, Dada, Dame, Day, Direct grant, Dojo, Downside, Drama, Drill, Driving, Educate, Elementary, Essenes, Eton, Exercise, Fettes, Finishing, Flemish, Frankfurt, Gam, Giggleswick, Gordonstoun, Grade, Grammar, Grant-aided, Grant-maintained, Group, Gymnasien, Gymnasium, Harrow, Hedge, High, Historical, Honour, Hospital, Hostel, Independent, Infant, Institute, Integrated, Intermediate, Junior, Kailyard, Kaleyard, Kant, Kindergarten, Lancing, Loretto, Lower, LSE, Lycée, Madrassah, Magnet, Maintained, Manchester, Mannheim, Marlborough, Middle, Night, Normal, Nursery, Oundle, Palaestra, Parnassian, Parochial, Pensionnat, Perse, Pod, Poly, Porpoises, Prep, Preparatory, Primary, Progymnasium, Public, RADA, RAM, Ramean, Reformatory, Repton, Residential, Roedean, Rossall, Rydal, Sabbath, Sadducee, Satanic, Scandalous, Sciences, Scul, Scull(e), Secondary(-modern), Sect, Seminary, Shoal, Slade, Special, State, Stonyhurst, Stowe, Style, Summer, Sunday, Teach, Tonbridge, Trade, ➤ TRAIN, Tutor, Upper, Wellington, Whales, Winchester, Yeshiva

Schoolboy, Schoolgirl Carthusian, Coed, Colleger, East, Etonian, Fag, Miss, Monitor, Oppidan, Petty, Stalky, Wykehamist

School-leaver Abiturient

Schoolmaam, Schoolman, Schoolmaster, Schoolmistress Beak, Dominie, Duns, Holofernes, Miss, Occam, Orbilius, Pedagogue, Pedant, Sir, Squeers, Teacher, Ursuline

Schooner Glass, Hesperus, Prairie, Ship, Tern

Science Anatomy, Anthropology, Art, Atmology, Axiology, Biology, Botany, Chemistry, Dismal, Eth(n)ology, Exact, Geology, Life, Noble,

Nomology, Ology, Optics, Pedagogy, Physics, Rocket, Skill, Social, Soil, Sonics, Stinks, Tactics, Technics, Technology

Science fiction Cyberpunk

Scientist Alchemist, Anatomist, Archimedes, Aston, Astronomer, Atomist, Boffin, BSc, Cavendish, Copernicus, Curie, Dalton, Davy, Einstein, Expert, Faraday, Fourier, FRS, Galileo, Geodesist, Harvey, Heaviside, Kennelly, Lodge, Lovell, Newton, Oersted, Pascal, Pasteur, Pauli, Piccard, Potamologist, Reaumur, Volta

Scimitar Acinaciform, Sword

Scintillate Dazzle, Emicate, Gleam, Glitter, ➤ SPARKLE

Scion Graft, Imp, Offspring, Sprig, Sprout

Scissors Clippers, Criss-cross, Cutters, Forfex, Nail, Shears

Scoff Belittle, Boo, Chaff, Deride, Dor, Eat, Flout, Food, Gall, Gibe, Gird, Gobble, ➤ JEER, Mock, Rail, Rib, Ridicule, Scaff, Scorn, Sneer, Taunt

Scold(ing) Admonish, Berate, Callet, Catamaran, Chastise, Chide, Clapperclaw, Do, Earful, Flite, Flyte, Fuss, Jaw(bation), Jobation, Lecture, Nag, Objurgate, Philippic, Rant, Rate, ➤ REBUKE, Reprimand, Reprove, Revile, Rouse on, Row, Sas(s)arara, Sis(s)erary, Slang, Slate, Termagant, Tick-off, Tongue-lash, Trimmer, Upbraid, Virago, Wig, Xant(h)ippe, Yaff, Yankie, Yap

Sconce Candlestick, Crown, Forfeit, Head, Ice, Nole

Scone Drop, Girdle

Scoop Bale, Dipper, Exclusive, Gouge, Grab, Hollow, Ladle, Lap, Pale, Shovel, Trowel

Scope Ambit, Diapason, Domain, Elbow-room, Extent, Freedom, Gamut, Ken, Latitude, Leeway, Purview, Range, Remit, Room, Rope, Scouth, Scowth, Size, Sphere

Scorch(er) Adust, Blister, Brasero, ➤ BURN, Char, Destroy, Frizzle, Fry, Parch, Scouther, Scowder, Scowther, Sear, Singe, Soar, Speed, Swale, Swayl, Sweal, Sweel, Torrefy, Torrid, Wither

Score Apgar, Bill, Birdie, Bye, Capot, Chase, Conversion, Count, Crena, Debt, Eagle, Etch, Groove, Hail, Honours, Ingroove, Ippon, Law, Make, Music, Net, Notation, Notch, Partitur(a), Peg, Pique, Point, Record, Repique, Rit(t), Rouge, Run, Rut, Scotch, Scratch, Scribe, Scrive, Set, Single, Spare, Stria, String, Sum, Tablature, ➤ TALLY, Twenty, Vocal, Waza-ari, Win

Score-board, Score-sheet Card, Telegraph

▷ **Scoring** may indicate an anagram

Scorn(ful) Arrogant, Bah, Contempt, Contumely, Deride, Despise, Dis(s), Disdain, Dislike, Flout, Geck, Haughty, Insult, Meprise, Mock, Opprobrium, Putdown, Rebuff, Ridicule, Sarcastic, Sardonic, Sarky, Scoff, Scout, Sdaine, Sdeigne, Sneer, Spurn, Wither

Scorpion Chelifer, False, Father-lasher, Pedipalp(us), Vinegarroon, Whip

Scot(sman), Scots(woman), Scottish Angus, Antenati, Berean, Bluecap, Caledonian, Celt, Clansman, Covenanter, Duni(e)wassal, Dunniewassal, Erse, Gael, Highland, Ian, Jock, Kelt, Kiltie, Kitty, Knox, Laird, Lallan(s), Lot,

Lowland, Luckie, Lucky, Mac, Mon, Peght, Pict, Ross, Sandy, Sawn(e)y, Stuart, Teuchter, Torridonian

Scotch(man) Censor, Distiller, Glenlivet®, Notch, Score, Scratch, Thwart, Usquebaugh, Whisky

Scot-free Wreakless

Scotland Alban(y), Albion, Caledonia, Lallans, Lothian, NB, Norland, Scotia

Scoundrel Cur, Knave, Reprobate, Scab, Smaik, Varlet, ➤ VILLAIN

Scour Beat, Depurate, Full, Holystone, Purge, Quarter, Scrub

▷ **Scour** may indicate an anagram

Scourge Bible-thumper, Cat, Discipline, Knout, Lash, Pest, ➤ PLAGUE, Scorpion, Whip, Wire

Scout Akela, Beaver, Bedmaker, Colony, Disdain, Explorer, Flout, Guide, Outrider, Pathfinder, Pickeer, Pioneer, Reconnoitre, Rover, Runner, Scoff, Scorn, Scourer, Scurrier, Scurriour, Sixer, Spyal, Talent, Tenderfoot, Tonto, Vedette, Venture

Scowl(ing) Frown, Glower, Gnar, Lour, Lower, Sullen

Scrabble Paw

Scrag(gy) Bony, Dewitt, Ewe-necked, Neck, Scrawny

Scram Begone, Hence, Scat, Shoo

Scramble Addle, Clamber, Encode, Grubble, Hurry, Mêlée, Mix, Motocross, Muss(e), Scamble, Sprattle, Sprawl, Swerve

Scrap(s), Scrappy Abandon, Abrogate, ➤ BIT, Cancel, Conflict, Discard, Dump, ➤ FIGHT, Fisticuffs, Fragment, Fray, Iota, Jot, Mêlée, Mellay, Morceau, Morsel, Odd, Off-cut, Ort, Ounce, Patch, Piece, Pig's-wash, Rag, Rase, Raze, Remnant, Scarmoge, Scissel, Scissil, Scrub, Set-to, Shard, Sherd, Shred, Skerrick, Skirmish, Snap, Snippet, Spall, Tait, Tate, Tatter, Titbit, Trash, Truculent, Whit

Scrap book Album, Grangerism

Scrap box Tidy

Scrape(r) Abrade, Agar, Bark, Clat, Claw, Comb, Curette, D and C, Escapade, Grate, Graze, Harl, Hoe, Hole, Jar, Kowtow, Lesion, Lute, Predicament, Racloir, Rake, Rasorial, Rasp, Rasure, Raze, Razure, Saw, Scalp, Scart, Scrat(ch), Scroop, Scuff, Shave, Skimp, Skive, Squeegee, Strake, Strigil, Xyster

Scraping noise Curr, Scroop

Scrap merchant Didakai, Didakei, Diddicoi, Diddicoy, Didicoi, Didicoy, Gold-end-man, Totter

Scratch(ed) Annul, Cancel, Cla(u)t, Claw, Curry, Devil, Efface, Eradicate, Erase, Graze, Nick, Par, Periwig, Quit, Race, Rase, Rasp, Rast, Root, Satan, Scarify, Scart, Scrab(ble), Scram(b), Scrape, Scrattle, Scrawm, Scrub, Spag, Tease, Teaze, Wig

▷ **Scratch(ed)** may indicate an anagram

Scrawl Doodle, Scribble

Scream(er) Bellow, Cariama, Caterwaul, Comedian, Comic, Cry, Eek, Headline, Hern, Kamichi, Laugh, Priceless, Primal, Riot, Scare-line, Screech, Seriema, Shriek, Skirl, Squall, Sutch, Yell

Scree Bahada, Bajada, Eluvium, Talus

Screech(ing) Cry, Screak, Screich, Screigh, Scriech, Scritch, Skreigh, Skriech, Skriegh, Ululant, Whoot

Screed Megillah, Ms, Tirade

Screen Abat-jour, Arras, Backstop, Blind(age), Brise-soleil, Camouflage, Chancel, Check, Chick, Cinerama®, Cloak, Cornea, Coromandel, Cover, Cribble, Curtain, Dodger, Eyelid, Festoon-blind, Fire, Glib, Gobo, Grille, Hallan, Hide, Hoard, Hoarding, Iconostas(is), Jube, Lattice, Mantelet, Mask, Nonny, Obscure, Organ, Over-cover, Parclose, Part-off, Partition, Pella, Purdah, Radar, Riddle, Road, Sconce, Scope, ➤ SHADE, Shelter, Shield, Shoji, Show, Sift, Silver, Small, Smoke, Split, Sunblock, Televise, Touch, Transenna, Traverse, Umbrella, VDU, Vet, Windbreak, Windshield, Winnow

Screw Adam, Allen, Archimedes, Butterfly, Coach, Countersunk, Dungeoner, Extort, Grub, Interrupted, Jailer, Jailor, Lag, Lead, Levelling, Machine, Miser, Monkey-wrench, Niggard, Phillips®, Prop(ellor), Salary, Skinflint, Spiral, Thumb(i)kins, Twist, Vice, Worm

Screwdriver Pozidriv®

Scribble Doodle, Pen, Scrawl

Scribe Clerk, Ezra, Mallam, Scrivener, Sopherim, Tabellion, Writer, WS

Scrimmage Bully, Maul, Mêlée, Rouge, Scrap, Skirmish, Struggle

Script Book, Gurmukhi, Hand, Hiragana, Italic, Jawi, Kana, Libretto, Linear A, Linear B, Lines, Lombardic, Miniscule, Nagari, Nastalik, Nastaliq, Ogam, Ronde, Scenario, Screenplay, Writing

Scripture(s), Scriptural version Adi Granth, Agadah, Antilegomena, Avesta, Bible, Gemara, Gematria, Gospel, Granth (Sahib), Guru Granth, Haggada(h), Hermeneutics, Hexapla, Holy book, Holy writ, Koran, K'thibh, Lesson, Lotus Sutra, Mishna(h), OT, Rig-veda, Smriti, Tantra, Targum, Testament, Upanishad, Veda, Vedic, Verse, Vulgate

Scrofula Crewels, Cruel(l)s, King's evil, Struma

Scroll(-work) Cartouche, Dead Sea, Makimono, Megillah, Mezuza(h), Parchment, Pell, Roll, Roul(e), Sefer Torah, Turbinate, Vitruvian, Volume, Volute

Scrooge Blagueur, Miser

Scrounge(r) Blag, Bludge(r), Borrow, Bot, Cadge, Forage, Freeload, Layabout, Ligger, Scunge, Sponge

Scrub(ber) Cancel, Chaparral, Cleanse, Dele(te), Gar(r)igue, Loofa(h), Luffa, Masseur, Negate, Pro, Rub, Scour, Tart

▷ **Scrub** may indicate 'delete'

Scruff(y) Dog-eared, Grubby, Nape, Raddled, Tatty, Uncombed, Untidy

Scrum Maul, Mob, Rouge, Ruck

Scrummy, Scrumptious Delectable, Delicious, Toothy, Yum-yum

Scrunt Carl

Scruple(s), Scrupulous Compunction, Conscience, Doubt, Meticulous, Nicety, Precise, Punctilious, Qualm, Queasy, Righteous, Stickle

Scrutinise, Scrutiny Check, Docimasy, Examine, Observe, Peruse, Pore, Pry, ➤ SCAN, Study

Scud East, Scoot, Spark, Spindrift, Spoom, Spoon, Spray

Scuff Brush, Shuffle

Scuffle Bagarre, Brawl, Scarmage, Skirmish, Struggle, Tussle

▷ **Scuffle** may indicate an anagram

Scull Oar, Row

Sculpt(ure) Acrolith, Aeginetan, Bas-relief, Boast, Bronze, Calvary, Canephor(a), Canephore, Canephorus, Carve, Chryselephantine, Della-robbia, Figure, Kore, Kouros, Mobile, Nude, Pergamene, Pieta, Relievo, Sc, Shape, Stabile, ➤ STATUARY, Topiary

Sculptor Arp, Artist, Bartholdi, Bernini, Canova, Cellini, Daedalus, Della Robbia, Donatello, Giacometti, Gibbons, Gill, Hepworth, Klippel, Landseer, Michelangelo, Myron, Nollekens, Paclozzi, Phidias, Pisano, Praxiteles, Pygmalion, Rodin, Scopas, Stevens, Wheeler

Scum Confervoid, Dregs, Dross, Epistasis, Glass-gall, Kish, Legge, Mantle, Mother, Rabble, Sandiver, Scorious, Slag, Slime, Spume, Sullage

Scupper Drain, Ruin, Scuttle, Sink

Scurf, Scurvy Dander, Dandriff, Dandruff, Furfur, Horson, Lepidote, Leprose, Scabrous, Scall, Scorbutic, Whoreson, Yaws, Yaw(e)y

Scurrilous Fescennine, Profane, Ribald, Sotadic, Thersites, Vulgar

Scurry Beetle, Hurry, Scamper, Scutter, Skedaddle, Skelter

Scut Fud, Tail

Scute Plate

Scuttle Abandon, Dan, Hod, Purdonium, Scoop, Scrattle, Scupper, Sink, Wreck

Scythe Bushwhacker, Cut, Hook, Sickle, Sieth, Snath(e), Snead, Sneath, Sned

Sea(s) Adriatic, Aegean, Amundsen, Andaman, Arabian, Arafura, Aral, Azov, Baltic, Banda, Barents, Beaufort, Bellingshausen, Benthos, Bering, Billow, Biscay, Black, Blue, Bosp(h)orus, Brine, Briny, Caribbean, Caspian, Celebes, Celtic, Ceram, Channel, China, Chukchi, Coral, Dead, Ditch, Drink, Euripus, Euxine, Flores, Galilee, Greenland, Head, Herring-pond, High, Hudson Bay, Icarian, Inland, Ionian, Irish, Japan, Kara, Labrador, Laptev, Ler, Ligurian, Main, Mare, Marmara, Med, Mediterranean, Nordenskjold, North, Norwegian, ➤ OCEAN, Offing, Offshore, Oggin, Okhotsk, Pelagic, Philippine, Polynya, Quantity, Red, Ross, Sargasso, Seven, Skagerrak, South, South China, Spanish main, Strand, Sulu, Tasman, Tethys, Thalassic, Tiberias, Tide, Timor, Tyrrhenian, Water, Weddell, White, Yellow, Zee

Sea-anemone Actinia, Zoantharia

Sea-bear Fur-seal, Otary, Seal, Seecatchie

Sea-beast Ellops, Manatee

Sea-bream Carp, Fish, Porgie, Porgy, Tai

Sea-cow Dugong, Lamantin, Manatee, Rhytina, Sirenian

Sea-cucumber Bêche-de-mer, Trepang

Sea-dog Salt, Tar

Sea-ear Abalone, Paua

Sea-fight Naumachy

Seafood Crab, Crevette, ➤ FISH, Lobster, Prawn, Shrimp, Zooplankton

Sea-front, Seaside Beach, Coast(line), Esplanade, Littoral, Orarian, Prom(enade)

Sea-god Neptune, Nereus, Triton

Sea-green Glaucous, Incorruptible, Robespierre

Sea-horse Hippocampus, Hippodame, Lophobranchiate, Morse, Pipefish, Tangie

Seal(s), Seal box Airtight, Appose, Bachelor, Bladdernose, Bull(a), Cachet, Cap, Caulk, Chesterfield, Chop, Clinch, Close, Cocket, Common, Consign, Crab-eater, Cylinder, Eared, Earless, Elephant, Emblem, Fob, Fur, Gasket, Great, Greenland, Harbour, Harp, Hermetic, Hooded, Hudson, Impress, Jark, Lute, Monk, Obsign, O-ring, Otary, Phoca, Pinnipedia, Pintadera, Pod, Privy, Proof, Ringed, Rookery, Sea-bear, Sealch, Sealgh, Seecatch(ie), Selkie, Sigil, Signet, Silkie, Silky, Size, Skippet, Solomon's, Sphragistic, Stamp, Wafer, Washer, Weddell, Whitecoat, Womb, Zalophus

Sea-legs Balance, Pleons

Sea-level Geoid

Sea-lily Crinoid, Palmatozoa

Seam Commissure, Fell, French, Furrow, Join, Layer, Sew, Suture, Welt

Seaman, Seamen AB, Crew, Jack, Lascar, Lubber, Mariner, OD, Ordinary, PO, RN, ➤ SAILOR, Salt, Swabby, Tar

Sea-mat Flustra, Hornwrack

Sea-matiness Gam

Sea-monster Kraken, Merman, Wasserman

Sea-mouse Bristle-worm

Séance Communication, Session, Sitting

Sea-parrot Puffin

Sear Brand, Burn, Catch, Cauterise, Frizzle, Parch, Scath(e), Scorch, Singe, Wither

Search(ing) Beat, Comb, Dragnet, Examine, Ferret, ➤ FORAGE, Fossick, Frisk, Grope, Home, Hunt, Indagate, Inquire, Jerk, Jerque, Kemb, Manhunt, Perscrutation, Probe, Proll, Prospect, Proul, Prowl, Quest, Rake, Rancel, Ransack, Ransel, Ranzel, Ravel, Ripe, Root, Rootle, Rummage, Scan, Scour, Scur, Sker, Skirr, Snoop, Strip, Thumb, Trace, Zotetic

Sea-rover Norseman, Viking

Sea-serpent, Sea-snake Ellops, Hydrophidae, Phoca

▶ **Seaside** see SEA-FRONT

Sea-slug Bêche-de-mer, Trepang

Sea-snail Neritidae

Season(able), Seasonal, Seasoned, Seasoning Accustom, Age, Aggrace, Autumn, Betimes, Christmas, Close, Condiment, Devil, Dress, Duxelles, Easter, Enure, Etesian, Fall, Fennel, Festive, Flavour, G(h)omasco, Garlic,

Growing, Hiems, High, In, Inure, Lent, Marjoram, Master, Mature, Nutmeg, Open, Paprika, Pepper, Powellise, Practised, Ripen, Salt, Sar, Seal, Seel, Sele, Silly, Solstice, Spice, Spring, Summer(y), Tahini, Ticket, Tide, Time, Whit, Winter

Sea-squirt Ascidian, Cunjevoi

Seat Backside, Banc, Banquette, Bench, Bleachers, Booster, Borne, Bottom, Box, Bucket, Bum, Buttocks, Canapé, Centre, Chair, Coit, Couch, Creepie, Croup(e), Croupon, Cushion, Davenport, Deckchair, Derriere, Dick(e)y, Dicky, Ejector, Epicentre, Faldistory, Faldstool, Foundation, Fud, Fundament, Gradin, Hall, Home, Hot, Houdah, Howdah, Humpty, Hurdies, Jump, Knifeboard, Love, Marginal, Marquise, Mercy, Misericord, Natch, Nates, Ottoman, Palanquin, Palfrey, Perch, Pew, Pillion, Pit, Pouffe, Ringside, Rumble, Rumble-tumble, Rump, Saddle, Safe, Sedes, Sedilium, See, Sell, Settee, Settle, Siege, Sliding, Sofa, Squab, Stool, Strapontin, Subsellium, Sunk(ie), Sunlounger, Synthronus, Throne, Tonneau, Woolsack

Sea-urchin Asteria, Echinus, Pluteus, Whore's egg

Sea-vampire Manta

Sea-wall Bulwark, Dyke, Groyne

Sea-weed Agar, Alga(e), Arame, Badderlock, Bladderwort, Bladderwrack, Carrag(h)een, Ceylon moss, Conferva, Coralline, Chondrus, Cystocarp, Desmid, Diatom, Dulse, Enteromorpha, Fucus, Gulfweed, Heterocontae, Kelp, Kilp, Kombu, Laminaria, Laver, Nori, Nullipore, Oarweed, Ore, Peacock's tail, Porphyra, Redware, Rockweed, Sargasso, Seabottle, Sea-furbelow, Sea-lace, Sea-lettuce, Sea-mat, Sea-moss, Sea-tangle, Seaware, Sea-whistle, Sea-wrack, Tang, Ulva, Varec(h), Vraic, Wakame, Wakane, Ware, Wrack

Sea-worm Palolo, Spunculid

Secede, Secession(ist) Adullamite, Antiburgher, Defy, Desert, Dissident, Flamingant, Sever, Splinter

Seclude, Seclusion Cloister, Incommunicado, Isolate, Maroon, Nook, Privacy, Purdah, Retreat, Secret, Sequester, Solitude

Second(ary), Seconds Abet, Alternative, Another (guess), Appurtenance, Assist, Back(er), Beta, Coming, Comprimario, Deuteragonist, Flash, Friend, Imperfect, Indirect, Inferior, Instant, Jiffy, Latter, Lesser, Minor, Mo(ment), Nature, Other, Pig's-whisper, Runner-up, Sec, Shake, Share, Side(r), Sight, Silver, Split, Subsidiary, Support, Tick, Trice, Twinkling, Wind

Second-best Worsted

▶ **Second-class** see SECOND-RATE

Second earth Antichthon

Second-hand Hearsay, Reach-me-down, Re-paint, Tralatitious, Used

Second-rate, Second-class B, Inferior, Mediocre

Second-sight Deuteroscopy, Divination, Tais(c)h

Second tine Bay, Bez

Second-year student Semi(e)(-bajan), Sophomore

Secrecy, Secret(s), Secretive Apocrypha, Arcana, Arcane, Arcanum, Backstairs, Cabbalistic, Cagey, Clam, Clandestine, Closet, Code, Conventicle, Covert, Cryptadia, Cryptic, Crypto, Dark, Dearn, Dern, Deep, Devious, Esoteric, Hidden, Hidling, Hidlin(g)s, Hole and corner, Hugger-mugger, Hush-hush, Hushy, Inly, Inmost, Latent, Mysterious, Mystical, Mystique, Oyster, Petto, ➤ PRIVATE, Privity, Privy, QT, Rune, Scytale, Shelta, Silent, Sly, State, Stealth, Sub rosa, Trade, Unbeknown, Undercover, Underhand, Undescried, Unknown, Unre(a)d, Unrevealed, Untold

Secretary Aide, Amanuensis, Chancellor, Chronicler, CIS, Desk, Desse, Famulus, Minuteman, Moonshee, Munshi, Notary, Permanent, Scrive, Social, Stenotyper, Temp

Secretary-bird Messenger, Serpent-eater

Secrete, Secretion Aequorin, Allomone, Autacoid, Cache, Castor, Chalone, Cuckoo-spit, Discharge, Emanation, Exude, Hide, Hormone, Juice, Lac, Lerp, Melatonin, Mucus, Musk, Osmidrosis, Resin, Rheum, Saliva, Sebum, Secern, Smegma, Spit(tle), Trypsin

➤ **Secret society** see SECT

Sect(arian), Secret society Abelite, Adamite, Amish, Anabaptist, Assassin, Babee, Babi, Bahai, Bigendian, Brahmin, Cabal, Cainite, Calixtine, Camorra, Cathar, Clan, Clapham, Crypto, Cult, Danite, Darbyite, Dissenter, Docate(s), Donatist, Druse, Druze, Dunkard, Dunker, Ebionite, Essene, Gheber, Ghebre, Giaour, Gnostic, Group, Gueber, Guebre, Gymnosophist, Harmonist, Harmonite, Hauhau, Hillmen, Illuminati, Jacobite, Jansenist, Karaite, Karmathian, Little-endian, Lollard, Macedonian, Macmillanite, Mandaean, Marcionite, Maronite, Monothelite, Montanist, Moonie, Mormon, Mucker, Muggletonian, Nazarine, Order, Partisan, Perfectionist, Pharisee, Philadelphian, Phrygian, Picard, Plymouthite, Porch, Rappist, Ribbonism, S(h)aiva, Sabbatian, Sabian, Sadducee, School, Seekers, Senus(s)i, Sex, Shaker, Shia(h), Therapeutae, Tunker, Unitarian, Valdenses, Vaudois, Wahabee, Wahabi(i)te, Waldenses, Yezdi, Yezidee, Yezidi, Zen, Zezidee

Section, Sector Caesarian, Chapter, Classify, Conic, Cross, Cut, Division, Ellipse, Eyalet, Gan, Hyperbola, Lith, Metamere, Mortice, Movement, Octant, Outlier, Passus, ➤ PIECE, Platoon, Private, Public, Segment, Severy, Slice, Stage, Ungula, Unit, Zone

Secular Earthly, Laic, Non-CE, Profane, Temporal, Worldly

Secure, Security Anchor, Assurance, Bag, Bail, Band, Bar, Batten, Belay, Bolt, Bond, Bottomry, Calm, Catch, Cement, Chain, Cheka, Cinch, Clamp, Clasp, Clench, Clinch, Close, Cocoon, Collateral, Consols, Debenture, Dunnage, Engage, Ensure, Equity, Establishment, Fasten, Fastness, Fortify, Frap, Gilt, Grith, Guarantee, Guy, Hypothec, Immune, Indemnity, Invest(ment), Knot, Lace, Land, Lash, Latch, Lien, Lock, Long-dated, Longs, Medium-dated, Mortgage, Nail, National, Obtain, Patte, Pin, Pledge, Pot, Pre-empt, Preference, Protect, Quad, Rope, Rug, ➤ SAFE, Safety, Settle, Snell, Snug, Sound, Stable, Stanchion, Staple, Staylace,

Stock, Strap, Sure(ty), Tack, Take, Tie, Tight, Trap, Trice, Warrant, Watertight, Wedge, Win

Sedan Battle, Brougham, Chair, Jampan(i), Jampanee, Litter, Palanquin, Palkee, Palki, Saloon

Sedate Calm, Cool, Decorous, Dope, Douce, Drug, Sad, Serene, Staid, Stand

Sedative Amytal®, Anodyne, Aspirin, Barbitone, Bromide, Chloral, Depressant, Hypnic, Lenitive, Lupulin, Meprobamate, Metopryl, Miltown, Narcotic, Nembutal®, Opiate, Paraldehyde, Pethidine, Phenobarbitone, Premed(ication), Scopolamine, Seconal®, Soothing, Thridace, Veronal

Sedentary Inactive, Sessile, Stationary

Sedge Carex, Chufa, Seg, Xyris

Sediment Alluvium, Chalk, Deposit, Dregs, F(a)eces, Fecula, Foots, Grounds, Lees, Molasse, Placer, Residue, Salt, Sapropel, Silt, Sludge, Terrigenous, Till, Varve, Warp

Sedition, Seditious Incitement, Insurrection, Revolt, Riot, Treason

Seduce(r), Seductive Allure, Betray, Bewitch, Bribe, Cuckold-maker, Debauch, Dishonour, Entice, Honeyed, Honied, Jape, Lothario, Luring, Mislead, Pull, Siren, Slinky, Tempt, Trepan, Undo, Wrong

▷ **Seduce** may indicate one word inside another

See(ing) Acknow, Barchester, Behold, Bishopric, C, Consider, Deek, Descry, Diocesan, Discern, Durham, Ecce, Ely, Episcopal, Eye, Glimpse, Holy, La, Lo, Meet, Norwich, Notice, Observe, Papal, Perceive, Realise, Remark, Rumble, Since, Sodor and Man, Spae, Spot, Spy, Truro, Twig, Understand, V, Vatican, Vid(e), View, Vision, Visit, Voila, Witness, York

Seed(s), Seedy Achene, Argan, Arilli, Arillode, Ash-key, Bean, Ben, Best, Bonduc, Cacoon, Caraway, Carvy, Cebadilla, Cevadilla, Chickpea, Coriander, Corn, Cum(m)in, Dragon's teeth, Embryo, Endosperm, Ergot, Favourite, Germ, Grain, Gritty, Issue, Ivory-nut, Kernel, Lomentum, Mangy, Miliary, Nucellous, Nut, Offspring, Ovule, Pea, Pinon, Pip, Poorly, Poppy, Sabadilla, Scuzz, Semen, Seminal, Sesame, Shabby, Silique, Sorus, Sow, Sperm, Spore, Zoosperm

Seed-case Aril, Bur(r), Husk, Pea(s)cod, Pod, Testa, Theca

Seed-leaf Cotyledon

Seedsman Driller, Nurseryman, Sower

Seek(er) Ask, Beg, Busk, Chase, Court, Endeavour, Pursue, Quest, Scur, Search, Skirr, Solicit, Suitor

Seem(ingly) Appear, Look, Ostensible, Purport, Quasi, Think

Seemly Comely, Decent, Decorous, Fit, Suitable

Seep Dribble, Exude, Leak, Ooze, Osmose, Percolate

Seer Auspex, Eye, Melampus, Nahum, Observer, Oculiform, Onlooker, Prescience, Prophet, Sage, Sibyl, Soothsayer, T(e)iresias, Witness, Zoroaster

Seesaw Bascule, Teeter(-totter), Tilt, Vacillate, Wild mare

Seethe(d) Boil, Bubble, Churn, Ferment, Simmer, Smoulder, Sod

Segment Antimere, Arthromere, Cut, Division, Gironny, Gyronny, Intron, Lacinate, Lobe, Merome, Merosome, Metamere, Pig, Prothorax, Scliff,

Share, Shie, Skliff, Somite, Split, Sternite, Syllable, Tagma, Telson, Urite, Uromere

Segregate, Segregation Apartheid, Exile, Insulate, Intern, ➤ ISOLATE, Jim Crow, Seclude, Separate

Seidlitz Powder, Rochelle

Seismic Terremotive

Seismograph Tromometer

Seize, Seizure Angary, Apprehend, Areach, Arrest, Attach(ment), Bag, Bone, Capture, Claw, Cleek, Cly, Collar, Commandeer, Confiscate, Distrain, Distress, For(e)hent, ➤ GRAB, Grip, Hend, Impound, Impress, Maverick, Na(a)m, Nab, Nap, Nim, Poind, Possess, Pot, Raid, Replevy, Rifle, Sequestrate, Smug, Tackle, Wingding

Seldom Infrequent, Rare, Unoften

Select(ing), Selection, Selector Assortment, Bla(u)d, Cap, Casting, Choice, Choose, Classy, Cull, Darwinism, Discriminate, Draft, Draw, Eclectic, Edit, Elite, Excerpt, Exclusive, Extract, Favour, Garble, Inside, K, Nap, Natural, Pericope, ➤ PICK, Pot-pourri, Prefer, Recherché, Sample, Seed, Single, Sort, Stream, Tipster, Triage, UCCA

Selenium Se, Zorgite

Self Atman, Auto, Character, Ego, Person, Psyche, Seity, Sel, Soul

Self-confidence Aplomb, Ego

Self-contained Absolute, Reticent, SC, Taciturn

Self-contradictory Absurd, Irish

Self-control, Self-discipline Ascesis, Encraty, Modesty, Patience, Restraint, Temper(ance)

▶ **Self-defence** see MARTIAL (ARTS)

Self-esteem Amour-propre, Conceit, Confidence, Egoism, Pride

Self-evident Axiom, Manifest, Obvious, Patent, Truism, Truth

Self-existence Solipsism

Self-fertilisation, Self-origination Aseity, Autogamy

Self-governing Autonomy, Idior(r)hythmic, Kabele, Kebel, Puritanism, Swaraj

Self-help Smiles

Self-important, Self-indulgent, Self-interested Aristippus, Arrogant, Conceited, Immoderate, Jack-in-office, Licentious, Narcissistic, Pompous, Pragmatic, Profligate, Solipsist, Sybarite

Selfish(ness) Avaricious, Egoist, Greedy, Hedonist, Mean, Solipsism

Selfless(ness) Non-ego, Tuism

Self-limiting Kenotic

▶ **Self-origination** see SELF-FERTILISATION

Self-pollinating Cl(e)istogamic

Self-possession Aplomb, Composure, Cool, Nonchalant

Self-satisfied, Self-satisfaction Complacent, Narcissism, Smug, Tranquil

Self-service Automat, Buffet, Cafeteria, Supermarket

Self-sufficiency Absolute, Autarky, Complete

Self-taught Autodidact

Sell(er), Selling Apprize, Auction, Barter, Bear, Betray, Catch, Chant, Chaunt, Cope, Dispose, Do, Flog, Go, Hard, Have, Hawk, Hustle, Inertia, Knock down, Market, Menage, Merchant, Peddle, Purvey, Push, Pyramid, Realise, Rep, Retail, Ruse, Simony, Stall-man, Sugging, ➤ TRADE, Vend

Selvage Border, Edge, Roon

Semantics Onomasiology

Semaphore Signal, Tic-tac

Semblance Aspect, Likeness, Sign, Verisimilitude

Semen Jis(so)m, Milt

Semi-conductor Germanium

Seminar(y) Class, Colloquium, Group, Theologate, Tutorial

Semi-paralysis Dyaesthesia

Semitic Accadian, Akkadian, Ammonite, Amorite, Arab, Aramaic, Chaldean, Geez, Jewish

Senate Council, Curia, Seanad (Eireann)

Senator Antiani, Cicero, Elder, Legislator, Solon

Send, Sent Consign, ➤ DESPATCH, Disperse, Emit, Entrance, Issue, Launch, Order, Post, Rapt, Ship, Transmit, Transport

Send back Refer, Remit, Remand, Return

Send down Lower, Rusticate

Send up Chal(l)an, Lampoon, Promote

Senegal SN

Senescence Age

Senile, Senility Caducity, Dementia, Disoriented, Doddery, Doitit, Dotage, Eild, Eld, Gaga, Nostology, Twichild

Senior Aîné, Doyen, Elder, Father, Grecian, Mayor, Père, Primus, Superior, Upper

Senor(a) Caballero, Don(a), Hidalga, Hidalgo

Sensation(al) Acolouthite, Anoesis, Aura, Blood, Commotion, Emotion, Empfindung, Feeling, Gas, Lurid, Melodrama, Pyrotechnic, Shock-horror, Shocker, Splash, Stir, Styre, Synaesthesia, Thrill, Tingle, Vibes, Wow, Yellow

Sense, Sensual Acumen, Aura, Carnal, Coherence, Common, Dress, Faculty, Feel, Gross, Gumption, Gustation, Hearing, Horse, Idea, Import, Instinct, Intelligence, Lewd, Meaning, Olfactory, Palate, Rational, Receptor, Rumble-gumption, Rumgumption, Rum(m)el-gumption, Rum(m)le-gumption, Sight, Sixth, Slinky, Smell, Sybarite, Synesis, Taste, Touch, Voluptuary, Voluptuous, Wisdom, Wit

Senseless Absurd, Anosmia, Illogical, Mad, Numb, Stupid, Stupor, Unconscious, Unwise

Sensible Aware, Dianoetic, Prudent, Raisonné, Rational, Sane, Solid, Well-balanced

Sensitive, Sensitivity Algesia, Alive, Allergic, Atopy, Delicate, Erethism, Erogenous, Hypaesthesia, Keen, Nesh, Nociceptive, Orthochromatic,

Passible, Sympathetic, Tactful, Tender, Thermaesthesia, Thin-skinned, Ticklish

Sensor Palpi

Sentence(s) Assize, Bird, Carpet, Clause, Commit, Condemn, Custodial, Death, Decree(t), Deferred, Doom, Fatwah, Indeterminate, Judgement, Life, Matrix, Paragraph, Period(ic), Porridge, Predicate, Rap, Rheme, Rune, Stretch, Suspended, Swy, Tagmene, Verdict, Versicle

Sententious Concise, Gnomic, Laconic, Pithy, Pompous, Terse

Sentiment(al), Sentimentality Byronism, Corn, Cornball, Drip, Feeling, Goo, Govey, Gucky, Gush, Maudlin, Mawkish, Mind, Mush, Opinion, Romantic, Rose-pink, Rosewater, Saccharin, Schmaltzy, Sloppy, Smoochy, Soppy, Spoony, Tear-jerker, Traveller, Treacly, Twee, View, Weepy, Yucky

Sentry Custodian, Guard, Jaga, Picket, Sentinel, Vedette, Vidette, Watch

Separate(d), Separation, Separately Abstract, Asunder, Atmolysis, Avulsion, Comma, Cull, Cut, Decollate, Decompose, Decouple, Deglutinate, Demerge, Detach, Dialyse, Diastasis, Diazeuxis, Diremption, Disally, Discerp, Disconnect, Discrete, Dissociate, Distance, Distinct, Disunite, Divide, Division, Divorce, Eloi(g)n, Elute, Elutriate, Esloin, Estrange, Filter, Hive, Hyphenate, Insulate, Intervene, Isolate, Laminate, Lease, Legal, Monosy, Part, Piece, Prescind, Ramify, Red(d), Scatter, Schism, Screen, Scutch, Secern, Sever, Several, Shed, Shore, Shorn, Sift, Sleave, Sle(i)ded, Solitary, Sort, ➤ SPLIT, Steam-trap, Stream, Sunder, Sundry, Tems(e), Tmesis, Try, Twin(e), Unclasp, Winnow, Wrench, Yandy

Sepia Cuttle, Ink

Seppuku Hara-kiri, Hari-kari

Septic Poisonous, Rotting

Septimus Small

Septum Mediastinum

Sepulchral, Sepulchre Bier, Cenotaph, Charnel, Crypt, Funeral, Monument, Pyramid, Tomb, Vault, Whited

Sequel After-clap, Consequence, Effect, Outcome, Suite

Sequence Agoge, Algorithm, Byte, Chronological, Continuity, Continuum, Fibonacci, Intron, Line, Order, Program(me), Run, Seriatim, Series, Succession, Suit, Suite, Train, Vector

Sequester, Sequestrate Confiscate, Esloin, Esloyne, Impound, Isolate, Retire, Seclude, Separate

Sequin Paillette, Zecchino

Sequoia Redwood

Seraph Abdiel, ➤ ANGEL

Serb(ian) Chetnik

Sere Arid, ➤ DRY, Scorch, Wither

Serenade(r) Aubade, Charivari, Horning, Minstrel, Nocturne, Shivaree, Sing-song, Wait, Wake

Serene, Serenity Calm, Composed, Placid, Repose, Sangfroid, Sedate, Smooth, ➤ TRANQUIL

Serf(dom) Adscript, Bondman, Ceorl, Churl, Helot, Manred, ➤ SLAVE, Thete, Thrall, Vassal, Velle(i)nage

Serge Russian, Say

Sergeant Buzfuz, Cuff, Drill, Havildar, Kite, ➤ NCO, Platoon, RSM, Sarge, SL, SM, Staff, Technical, Troy

Serial Episode, Feuilleton, Heft, Livraison

Series Balmer, Catena, Chain, Concatenation, Continuum, Course, Cycle, Cyclus, Enfilade, Engrenage, En suite, Episode, Fibonacci, Fourier, Gradation, Harmonic, Homologous, Line, Links, Maclaurin's, Partwork, ➤ PROGRESSION, Rest, Rubber, Run, Sequence, Ser, Sitcom, String, Succession, Suit, Taylor's, Train, World

Serious(ly) Critical, Earnest, Grave, Gravitas, Important, Major, Momentous, Pensive, Sad, Serpentine, Sober, Solemn, Sombre, Staid, Straight(-faced), Very

Sermon Address, Discourse, Gatha, Homily, Lecture, Preachment, Spital

Serow Goral, Thar

Serpent(ine) Adder, Amphisbaena, Anguine, Apepi, Apophis, Asp, Aspic(k), Basilisk, Boa, Cockatrice, Dipsas, Firedrake, Midgard, Nagas, Ouroboros, Peridotite, Retinalite, Sea-snake, Shesha, ➤ SNAKE, Traitor, Uraeus, Viper

Serrate(d) Diprionidian, Saw, Scallop, Serried

Serum Antilymphocyte, Antitoxin, ATS, Fluid, Humoral, Opsonin, Senega

Serval Bush-cat

Servant, Server Attendant, Ayah, Batman, Bearer, Bedder, Bedmaker, Boots, Butler, Boy, Caddie, Chaprassi, Cook, Chuprassy, Daily, Domestic, Dromio, Drudge, Employee, Factotum, Famulus, Flunkey, Footboy, Footman, Friday, Gehazi, G(h)illie, Gip, Gully, Gyp, Haiduk, Handmaid, Helot, Henchman, Heyduck, Hireling, Iras, Jack, Jeames, Khansama(h), Khidmutgar, Khitmutgar, Lackey, Lazy Susan, Maid, Major-domo, Man, Man Friday, Menial, Minion, Myrmidon, Nethinim, Obedient, Page, Pantler, Person, Postman, Retainer, Retinue, Scout, Scrub, Scullion, Servitor, Sewer, Skip, Soubrette, Steward, Tapsman, Tendance, Theow, Thete, Tiger, Tweeny, Underling, Vails, Vales, Valet, Varlet, Vassal, Waiter, Wash-rag, Weller

Serve, Service Ace, Act, Active, Amenity, Answer, Arriage, Asperges, Assist, ATS, Attendance, Avail, Benediction, Candlemas, Cannonball, Ceefax®, China, Civil, Communion, Community, Complin(e), Corvée, Credo, Devotional, Dinnerset, Dish, Do, Dow, Duty, Employ, Evensong, Fault, Fee, Feudal, Forward, ➤ FUNCTION, Further, Go, Help, Helpline, Hour, Ka(e), Let, Line, Ling, Lip, Litany, Liturgy, Mass, Mat(t)ins, Memorial, Minister, Ministry, Missa, National, Nocturn, Nones, Oblige, Office, Oracle, Overhaul, Pass, Pay, Pottery, Prime, Proper, Public, RAF, Requiem, Rite, RN, Room, Sacrament, Secret, Senior, Sext, Shuttle, Silver, Social, Sorb, Stead, Sted, Sue, Tableware, Tea, Tenebrae, Trental, Uncork, Under-arm, Use, Utility, Vespers, Wait, Waiterage, Watch-night, Worship

Service-book Hymnal, Hymnary, Missal, Triodion

▷ **Serviceman** may indicate a churchman

Servile, Servility Abasement, Base, Crawling, Knee, Lickspittle, Menial, Obsequious, Slavish, Slimy, Suck-hole, Sycophantic, Truckle

Serving Helping, Heuristic, Portion

Servitude Bondage, Domination, Peonism, Slavery, Thrall, Yoke

Sesame Gingelly, Gingili, Grapple-plant, Jinjilli, Semsem, Til

Session(s) Bout, Meeting, Nightshift, Petty, Quarter, Round, Séance, Sederunt, Settle, Sitting, Term

Set(ting) (down; in; off; out; up) Adjust, Appoint, Arrange, Batch, Bent, Bezel, Boun, Cake, Case, Cast, Chaton, Class, Claw, Clique, Cliveden, Closed, Coagulate, Cock, Cockshy, Collection, Collet, Comp(ositor), Companion, Compose, Congeal, Context, Coterie, Couvert, Crew, Crystal, Decline, Decor, Diorama, Dispose, Earnest, Earth, Environment, Establish, Fit, Flagstone, Flat(s), Found, Garniture, Geal, Gel, Genome, Group, Harden, Ilk, Incut, Jee, Jeel, Jell(y), Kit, Laid, Land, Lay, Leg, Locale, Locate, Lot, Mandelbrot, Milieu, Mise en scène, Monture, Mournival, Nest, Occident, Ordinate, Parure, Physique, Pitch, Place(ment), Plant, Plaste, Ply, Posed, Posit, Put, Radio, Ready, Receiver, Relay, Rigid, Rooted, Rubber, Scenery, Series, Showcase, Sink, Solidify, Squad, Stand, Stationed, Stede, Stell, Stick, Stiffen, Still, Stream, Suit, Suite, Surround, Synchronize, Tar, Tea, Team, Teeth, Telly, Till, Trigger, Tube, Venn (diagram), Weather, Wide-screen, Yplast

Setback Checkmate, Hiccup, Jolt, Relapse, Retard, Retreat, Reversal, Scarcement, Sickener, Tes, Vicissitude

Setter Cement, Comp, Dog, Gordon, Gundog, Irish, Pectin, Red, Smoot, Sphinx, Trend

Settle(d), Settler, Settlement Adjust, Agree, Alight, Appoint, Arrange, Ascertain, Ausgleich, Avenge, Balance, Bandobast, Bed, Bench, Boer, Bundobust, Bustee, Camp, Clear, Clench, Clinch, Colonial, Colonise, Colony, Compose, Compound, Compromise, Crannog, Decide, Defray, Determine, Diktat, Discharge, Dorp, Dowry, Ekistics, Encamp, Endow, Ensconce, Entail, Establish, Feeze, Fix, Foot, Foreclose, Gravitate, Gridironer, Guilder, Illegitimate, Jointure, Kibbutz, Land, Ledge, Light, Lyte, Merino, Mission, Moshav, Nahal, Nest, Nestle, Oecist, Oikist, Opt, Outpost, Pa(h), Pakka, Pale, Patroon, Pay, Pheazar, Peise, Penal, Perch, Pheese, Pheeze, Phese, Pilgrim, Pioneer, Placate, Planter, Populate, Presidio, Pucka, Pueblo, Pukka, Rancheria, Rancherie, Readjust, Reduction, Reimburse, Remit, Reside, Resolve, Rest, Sate, Satisfaction, Secure, Sedimentary, Shagroon, Smoot, Sofa, Solve, Square, State, Still, Subside, Taurus, Township, Ujamaa, Utu, Vest(ed), Voortrekker

▷ **Settlement** may indicate an anagram

▷ **Settler** may indicate a coin

Set upon Assail, Attack, Sick

Seven(th) Ages, Days, Dials, Great Bear, Hebdomad, Hepta-, Hills, Nones, Pleiad(es), S, Sages, Seas, Septenary, Septimal, Sins, Sisters, Sleepers, Stars, Wonders, Zeta

Seventy S

Sever Amputate, Cut, Detach, Divide, Sunder

Several Divers, Many, Multiple, Some, Sundry

Severe(ly), Severity Acute, Bad, Chronic, Cruel, Dour, Draconian, Drastic, Eager, Extreme, Grave, Grievous, Gruel(ling), Hard, ➤ HARSH, Ill, Inclement, Morose, Penal, Rhadamanthine, Rigo(u)r, Roundly, Serious, Sharp, Snell(y), Sore, Spartan, Stern, Strict

Sew(ing) Baste, Cope, Embroider, Fell, Machine, Mitre, Overlock, Run, Seam, Seel, Stitch, Tack, Whip

Sewage, Sewer Cesspool, Cloaca, Culvert, Dorcas, ➤ DRAIN, Effluence, Jaw-box, Jaw-hole, Mimi, Needle, Privy, Shore, Soil, Sough, Soughing-tile, Waste

Sex(y) Bed-hopping, Coupling, Erotic, Favours, Female, Gam(ic), Gender, Hump, Incest, Intercourse, Kind, Libidinous, Libido, Lingam, Lumber, Male, Mate, Nookie, Oomph, Oral, Paedophilia, Pederasty, Phat, Priapean, Race, Randy, Raunchy, Rut(ish), Salacious, Screw, Sect, Steamy, Sultry, Teledildonics, Venereal, Venery, VI, Voluptuous

Sex appeal It, Oomph, SA

Sexcentenarian Shem

Sexless Agamogenetic, N, Neuter

Sextet Over, Six

Sexton Blake, Fossor, Sacristan, Shammes, Warden

Seychelles SY

Sh P, Quiet

Shabby Base, Buckeen, Dog-eared, Down-at-heel, Fusc(ous), Grotty, Mean, Moth-eaten, Oobit, Oorie, Oubit, Ourie, Outworn, Owrie, Raunch, Scaly, Scruffy, Seedy, Shoddy, Squalid, Tatty, Worn, Woubit

Shack Hideout, Hut

Shackle(s) Bilboes, Bind, Bracelet, Chain, Entrammel, Fetter(lock), Hamper, Irons, Manacle, Restrict, Tie, Trammel, Yoke

Shad Allice, Allis, Fish, Twait(e)

Shaddock Grapefruit, Pomelo

Shade(d), Shades, Shading, Shadow, Shady Adumbrate, Arbour, Awning, Blend, Blind, Bongrace, Bowery, Brocken spectre, Buff, Cast, Chiaroscuro, Chroma, Cloche, Cloud, Cross-hatch, Degree, Dis, Dog, Dubious, Eclipse, Eye, Five o'clock, Galanty, Gamp, Ghost, Gradate, Gray, Hachure, Hell, Herbar, Hint, Hue, Inumbrate, Larva, Lee, Mezzotint, Nuance, Opaque, Overtone, Parasol, Phantom, Presence, Ray-Bans®, Satellite, Screen, Shroud, Sienna, Silhouette, Silvan, Skia-, Soften, Spectre, Spirit, Stag, Sunglasses, Swale, Swaly, Tail, Tinge, Tint, Tone, Ugly, Umbra(tile), Umbrage(ous), Underhand, Velamen, Velar(ium), Velum, Visor

Shadowless Ascian

Shaft Arbor, Arrow, Barb, Barrow-train, Beam, Capstan, Cardan, Chimney, Column, Crank, Cue, Disselboom, Dolly, Drive, Fil(l), Fust, Incline, Journal, Limber, Loom, Mandrel, Mandril, Moulin, Parthian, Passage, Pile, Pit, Pitch,

Pole, Propellor, Ray, Scape, Scapus, Shank, Snead, Spindle, Staff, Stale, Steal(e), Steel, Stele, Stulm, Sunbeam, Thill, Tige, Trave, Upcast, Winze, Winning

Shag Cronet, Hair, Intercourse, Nap, Pile, Scart(h), Skart(h), Tire, Tobacco

Shaggy Ainu, Comate, Hairy, Hearie, Hirsute, Horrid, Horror, Rough, Rugged, Shock, Shough, Tatty, Untidy

Shah Ruler, Sophi, Sophy

Shake(n), Shakes, Shaky Ague(-fit), Astonish, Brandish, Coggle, Concuss, Dabble, Dick(e)y, Didder, Dither, Dodder, ➤ DT'S, Feeble, Groggy, Hod, Hotch, Jar, Jiggle, Joggle, Jolt, Jounce, Judder, Jumble, Milk, Mo, Nid-nod, Press flesh, Quake, Quiver, Quooke, Rattle, Rickety, Rickle, ➤ ROCK, Rouse, Shimmer, Shiver, Shock, Shog, Shoogle, Shudder, Succuss(ation), Tremble, Tremolo, Tremor, Tremulous, Trill(o), Undulate, Vibrate, Vibrato, Wag, Wobble, Wonky

▷ **Shake** may indicate an anagram

Shakedown Blackmail, Chantage, Pallet

Shakespeare Bard, Will, WS

Shale Blaes, Fa(i)kes, Kerogen, Rock, Till, Torbanite

Shall Sal

Shallot C(h)ibol, Onion, Scallion, Sybo(e), Sybow

Shallow(s) Ebb, Flat, Fleet, Flew, Flue, Justice, Neritic, Shoal, Slight, Superficial

Sham Apocryphal, Bluff, Bogus, Braide, Charade, Counterfeit, Deceit, Fake, ➤ FALSE, Hoax, Idol, Impostor, Mimic, Mock, Phony, Pinchbeck, Postiche, Pretence, Pseudo, Repro, Snide, Spurious

Shamble(s) Abattoir, Butchery, Mess, Shuffle, Totter, Tripple

Shame(ful), Shame-faced Abash, Aidos, Contempt, Crying, Degrade, Discredit, Disgrace, Dishonour, Embarrass, Fie, Gross, Hangdog, Honi, Humiliate, Ignominy, Infamy, Inglorious, Modesty, Mortify, Pity, Pudor, Pugh, Shend, Sin, Slander, Stain, Stigma, Yshend

Shameless Audacious, Brash, Immodest, Ithyphallic

Shampoo(ing) Massage, Tripsis, Wash

Shandy Drink, Sterne, Tristram

Shanghai Abduct, Kidnap, Trick

Shank Leg, Shaft, Steal(e), Steel, Steil, Stele, Strike

Shanty, Shanty town Boatsong, Bothy, Bustee, Cabin, Dog-hole, Favela, Forebitter, Hutment, Lean-to, Pondok, Shack, Song

Shape(d), Shapely, Shaping Blancmange, Boast, Bruting, Cast, Contour, Face, Fashion, Figure, Form, Format, Geoid, Gnomon, Headquarters, Hew, Holohedron, Jello, Model, ➤ MOULD, Pendentive, Ream, Rhomb(us), Scabble, Sculpt, Spile, Tromino, Whittle, Wrought, Zaftig, Zoftig

Shapeless Amorphous, Chaos, Dumpy, Indigest, Vague

Shard Fragment, Sliver, Splinter

Share(d), Shares Allocation, Allotment, Apportion, Blue-chip, Bovate, Cahoots, Co, Cohabit, Coho(e), Common, Contango, Culter, Cut,

Divi(dend), Divide, Divvy, Dole, Dutch, Equity, Finger, Impart, Interest, Kaffer, Kaf(f)ir, Lion's, Market, Moiety, Ordinary, Oxgang, Oxgate, Oxland, Parcener, ➤ PART, Partake, Participate, Plough, Portion, Prebend, Pref(erred), Preference, Pro rata, Quarter, Quota, Ration, Rug, Rundale, Scrip, Security, Shr, Slice, Snack, Snap, Sock, Split, Stock, Teene, Tranche, Whack

Shareholder Stag

Shark Angel, Basking, Beagle, Blue, Bonnethead, Carpet, Cestracion, Cow, Demoiselle, Dog(fish), Hammerhead, Houndfish, Huss, Lemonfish, Loan, Mackerel, Mako, Noah, Nurse, Penny-dog, Plagiostomi, Porbeagle, Requiem, Rhin(e)odon, Rigg, Sail-fish, Sea-ape, Sharp, Shovelhead, Smoothhound, Squaloid, Swindler, Thrasher, Thresher, Tiger, Tope, Usurer, Whale, Wobbegong, Zygaena

Sharkskin Shagreen

Sharp(er), Sharpen(er), Sharpness Abrupt, Accidental, Acerose, Acidulous, Acrid, Aculeus, Acumen, Acuminate, Acute, Alert, Angular, Arris, Bateless, Becky, Bitter, Brisk, Cacuminous, Cheat, Clear, Coticular, Cutting, Dital, Edge(r), Fine, Gleg, Grind, Hone, Hot, Keen, Kurtosis, Massé, Oilstone, Peracute, Piquant, Poignant, Pronto, Pungent, Razor, Rogue, Rook, Set, Shrewd, Snap, Snell, Sour, Spicate, Strop, Swindler, Tart, Tomium, Vivid, Volable, Whet

Sharpshooter Bersaglier, Franc-tireur, Sniper, Tirailleur, Voltigeur

Shatter(ing) Astone, Break, Brisance, Craze, Dash, Explode, Shiver, Smash, Smithereen, Splinter, Unnerve

Shave(r), Shaving(s) Barb(er), Excelsior, Grain, Moslings, Pare, Plane, Pogonotomy, Poll, Raze, Scrape, Skive, Sliver, Splinter, Swarf, Todd, Tonsure, Whittle

Shaw Artie, Green, Spinn(e)y, Wood

Shawl Afghan, Buibui, Cashmere, Chuddah, Chuddar, Dopatta, Dupatta, Fichu, Kaffiyeh, Mantilla, Maud, Paisley, Partlet, Prayer, Serape, Stole, Tallith, Tonnag, Tozie, Tribon, Whittle, Wrap(per), Zephyr

She A, Hoo

Sheaf Aplustre, Bundle, Folder, Gait, Garb(e), Gerbe, Mow, Shock, Thr(e)ave

Shear(er), Shears Clip, Cut, Fleece, Greasy, Poll, Ring(er), Shave, Snips, Trim

Sheath Axolemma, Capsule, Case, Cocoon, Coleorhiza, Condom, Cover, Fingerstall, Glume, Myelin, Neurilemma, Neurolemma, Oc(h)rea, Perineurium, Periosteum, Quiver, Rhinotheca, Scabbard, Spathe, Thecal, Thumbstall, Vagina, Volva

Sheave Bee, Clevis

Shed(der), Shedding Autotomy, Barn, Cast, Cho(u)ltry, Coducity, Depot, Discard, Doff, Drop, Effuse, Exuviate, Hangar, Hovel, Hut, Infuse, Lair, Lean-to, Linhay, Linny, Mew, Moult, Pent, Potting, Salmon, Shippen, Shippon, Shuck, Skeo, Skillion, Skio, Slough, Sow, Spend, Spent, Spill, Tilt, Tool

Sheen Glaze, Gloss, Luminance, Lustre, Patina, Schiller, Shine

Sheep(ish) Ammon, Ancon(es), Aoudad, Argali, Bell(wether), Bharal, Bident, Bighorn, Black, Blackface, Blate, Broadtail, Burhel, Burrel(l), Caracul, Cheviots, Coopworth, Corriedale, Cotswold, Coy, Crone, Dinmont, Down, Drysdale, Embarrassed, Ewe, Exmoor, Fank, Fat-tailed, Flock, Fold, Hampshire, Hangdog, Herdwick, Hidder, Hirsel, Hog(g), Hogget, Jacob, Jemmy, Jumbuck, Karakul, Kent, Lamb, Lanigerous, Leicester, Lincoln, Lo(a)ghtan, Loghtyn, Marco Polo, Merino, Mor(t)ling, Mouf(f)lon, Mountain, Muflon, Mug, Mus(i)mon, Mutton, Oorial, Ovine, Perendale, Ram, Rambouillet, Romeldale, Romney Marsh, Rosella, Shearling, Shorthorn, ➤ SHY, Soay, Southdown, Suffolk, Sumph, Swaledale, Teeswater, Teg(g), Texel, Theave, Trip, Tup, Udad, Urial, Wensleydale, Wether, Woollyback, Yow(e), Yowie

Sheep disease Braxy, Dunt, Gid, Hoove, Louping-ill, Orf, Rubbers, Scrapie, Sturdy, Swayback, Variola, Water-brain, Wildfire, Wind

Sheepdog Collie, Huntaway, Maremma

Sheepfold Fank, Pen

Sheepskin Basan, Caracul, Karakul, Mouton, Roan, Wool

Sheeptrack Terracette

Sheer Absolute, Clear, Main, Mere, Peekaboo, Plumb, Pure, Simple, Stark, Steep, Swerve, Thin, Utter

Sheet(s) Balance, Cere-cloth, Cerement, Charge, Chart, Crime, Cutch, Dope, Expanse, Film, Folio, Foolscap, Heft, Leaf, Membrane, Nappe, Out-hauler, Page, Pot(t), Pour, Proof, Prospectus, Ream, Rope, Sail, Scandal, Shroud, Stern, Stratus, Taggers, Tarpaulin(g), Tear, Tentorium, Terne, Thunder, Time, Web, Winding

Sheet-anchor Letter-weight, Paperweight

Sheet-iron Taggers, Terne(plate)

Sheikdom Bahrein, Dubai

Shekel Mina, Sickle

Sheldrake Bergander

Shelf, Shelve(s) Bank, Bar, Bracket, Continental, Counter, Credence, Delay, Étagère, Hob, Ledge, Leeboard, Mantle, Overmantel, Postpone, Rack, Retable, Shunt, Sidetrack, Sill, Spinsterhood, Whatnot, Windowsill

Shell(ed), Shellfish Abalone, Acorn-shell, Ambulacrum, Ammo, Argonaut, Balamnite, Balanus, Bivalve, Blitz, Boat, Bombard, Buckie, Camera, Capiz, Capsid, Carapace, Cartridge, Casing, Chank, Chelonia, Chitin, Clam, Clio, Cochlea, Cockle, Cohog, Conch, Copepoda, Cover, Cowrie, Cowry, Crab, Crustacea, Cuttlefish, Dariole, Deerhorn, Dentalium, Dop, Drill, Escallop, Foraminifer, Framework, Frustule, Globigerina, Haliotis, Hull, Husk, Hyoplastron, Isopoda, Lamp, Langouste, Limacel, Limpet, Lorica, Lyre, Malacostraca, Mollusc, Monocoque, Moreton Bay bug, Mother-of-pearl, Mussel, Murex, Nacre, Nautilus, Ormer, Ostracod, Ostrea, Oyster, Paua, Pawa, Peag, Peak, Pea(s)cod, Pecten, Pereia, Periostracum, Periwinkle, Pipi, Pipsqueak, Plastron, Pod, Projectile, Purple, Putamen, Quahog, Razor, Sal, Scalarium, Scallop, Scollop, Sea-ear, Sea-pen, Shale, Sheal, Sheel, Shiel, Shill, Shock, Shot, Shrapnel, Shuck, Sial, Smoke-ball, Spend,

Star, Stomatopod, Stonk, Straddle, Strafe, Stromb(us), Swan-mussel, Test(a), Thermidor, Toheroa, Top, Torpedo, Trivalve, Turbo, Turritella, Tusk, Univalve, Valency, Venus, Wakiki, Wampum, Whelk, Whiz(z)bang, Winkle, Xenophya, Yabbie, Yabby, Zimbi

Shelled Cracked, Kernel

▷ **Shelled** may indicate an anagram

Shell money Wakiki, Wampum, Zimbi

Shelter Abri, Anderson, Asylum, Awn, Awning, Belee, Bender, Bield, Blockhouse, Booth, Bunker, Butt, Cab, Carport, Casemate, Cot(e), Cove, Covert, Coverture, Defence, Dripstone, Dug-out, Fall-out, Garage, Gunyah, Harbour, Haven, Hithe, Hospice, Hostel, House, Hovel, Humpy, Hut, Kipsie, Lee, Loun, Lound, Lown, Lownd, Mai mai, Morrison,
➤ REFUGE, Retreat, Roof, Sanctuary, Scog, Sconce, Scoog, Scoug, Screen, Scug, Shed, Shiel(ing), Shroud, Skug, Succah, Sukkah, Summerhouse, Tent, Testudo, Tortoise, Tupik, Twigloo, Umbrage, Weather, Wheelhouse, Wi(c)kiup, Wickyup, Wil(t)ja, Windbreak

Shemozzle Debacle

Shenanigan Antic

Shepherd(ess) Abel, Acis, Amaryllis, Amos, Bergère, Bo-peep, Chloe, Clorin, Conduct, Corin, Corydon, Cuddy, Daphnis, Dorcas, Drover, Endymion, Escort, Ettrick, German, Grubbinol, Gyges, Herdsman, Hobbinol, Lindor, Marshal, Menalcas, Padre, Pastor(al), Pastorella, Phebe, Sheepo, Strephon, Tar-box, Thenot, Thyrsis, Tityrus

Sheriff Bailiff, Deputy, Grieve, Land-dros(t), Shireman, Shirra, Shrievalty, Viscount

Sherry Amoroso, Cobbler, Cyprus, Doctor, Fino, Gladstone, Jerez, Manzanilla, Oloroso, Sack, Solera, Whitewash, Xeres

Sherwood Anderson, Forest

Shibboleth Password

Shield(-shaped) Ablator, Achievement, Aegis, Ancile, Armour, Arms, Bodyguard, Box, Buckler, Canadian, Cartouche, Clypeus, Defend, Escutcheon, Fence, Gobo, Guard, Gyron, Hatchment, Heat, Hielaman, Insulate, Mant(e)let, Pavis(e), Pelta, Protect, Riot, Rondache, Screen, Scute, Scutum, Sternite, Targe(t), Thyroid, Visor

Shift(er), Shifty Amove, Astatic, Blue, Budge, Change, Chemise, Core, Cymar, Devious, Displace, Doppler, Evasive, Expedient, Fend, Graveyard, Hedging, Landslide, Linen, Move, Night, Nighty, Red, Relay, Remove, Ruse, Scorch, Shirt, Shovel, Shunt, Simar(re), Slicker, Slip(pery), Spell, Stagehand, Stint, Tour, Transfer, Tunic, Turn, Vary, Veer, Warp

▷ **Shift(ing)** may indicate an anagram

Shilling Bob, Deaner, Falkiner, Hog, S, Teston

Shilly-shally Whittie-whattie

Shimmer(ing) Chatoyant, Glint, Glitter, Iridescence, Shine

▷ **Shimmering** may indicate an anagram

Shin Clamber, Climb, Cnemial, Leg, Shank, Skink, Swarm

Shindig, Shindy Bobbery, Row, Rumpus, Shivoo, Uproar

Shine(r) → Ships and boats

Shine(r), Shining, Shiny Aglow, Beam, Buff, Burnish, Deneb, Effulge, Excel, Flash, Gleam, Glisten, Gloss, ➤ GLOW, Irradiant, Japan, ➤ LAMP, Leam, Leme, Lucent, Luminous, Lustre, Mouse, Nitid, Phosphoresce, Polish, Radiator, Relucent, Resplend, Rutilant, Skyre, Sleek, Twinkle, Varnish

Shingle(s), Shingly Beach, Chesil, Cut, Dartre, Dartrous, Gravel, Herpes, Herpetic, Shale, Stone, Zona, Zoster

Shinpad Greave

Shinty Caman, Camanachd

▷ **Shiny** may indicate a star

Ship(ping) Boat, Container, Convoy, ➤ DISPATCH, Embark, Export, Gravy, Her, Hulk, Jolly, Keel, Man, MV, Post, Privateer, Prize, Prow, Raft, Ram, Sail, She, SS, Tall, Tub, Vessel, Weather

SHIPS AND BOATS

1 letter:	Coble	Borley	Schuit
Q	Coper	Bounty	Schuyt
3 letters:	Crare	Caique	Settee
Ark	Dandy	Carack	Slaver
Cat	Dingy	Carvel	Tartan
Cog	Drake	Castle	Tender
Cot	Ferry	Coaler	Tonner
Dow	Funny	Cobble	Torpid
Hoy	Keteh	Cooper	Trader
Red	Laker	Crayer	Whaler
4 letters:	Liner	Cutter	Wherry
Argo	Moses	Decker	Zebeck
Bark	Oiler	Dingey	**7 letters:**
Brig	Pinky	Dinghy	Belfast
Buss	Pinto	Dogger	Bidarka
Cock	Prore	Droger	Bumboat
Dhow	Razee	Dromon	Capital
Dory	Sabot	Drover	Caravel
Duck	Scoot	Dugout	Carrack
Grab	Screw	Frigot	Carract
Koff	Scull	Galiot	Carrect
Nina	Shell	Galley	Catboat
Pink	Skiff	Gay-you	Clipper
Pont	Sloop	Hooker	Coaster
Pram	Tramp	Jigger	Collier
Prau	U-boat	Launch	Coracle
Proa	Umiak	Lorcha	Counter
Ro-ro	Whiff	Lugger	Currach
Saic	Xebec	Masula	Curragh
Scow	Yacht	Nuggar	Dredger
Snow	Zabra	Packet	Drifter
Tern	Zebec	Pedalo	Drogher
Trow	**6 letters:**	Pequod	Dromond
Yawl	Argosy	Pinkie	Factory
Zulu	Banker	Pirate	Felucca
5 letters:	Barque	Pitpan	Flyboat
Aviso	Bateau	Pulwar	Frigate
Barge	Bawley	Puteli	Gabbard
Broke	Beagle	Randan	Gabbart
Camel	Bethel	Sampan	Galleon
Canoe	Bireme	Sandal	Galliot

Galloon	Bilander	Dahabiyeh	
Geordie	Billyboy	Dromedary	
Gondola	Cabotage	First-rate	
Gunboat	Corocore	Freighter	
Jetfoil	Corocoro	Frigatoon	
Liberty	Corvette	Hydrofoil	
Lymphad	Dahabieh	Klondiker	
Masoola	Faldboat	Klondyker	
Mistico	Foldboat	Lapstreak	Windjammer
Monitor	Galleass	Leviathan	**11 letters:**
Mudscow	Galliass	Lightship	Barquentine
Oomiack	Gallivat	Mayflower	Bellerophon
Patamar	Hoveller	Minelayer	Berthon-boat
Pelican	Indiaman	Monoxylon	Cockleshell
Pinnace	Ironclad	Outrigger	Dreadnought
Piragua	Longboat	Peter-boat	Merchantman
Pirogue	Longship	Shear-hulk	Minesweeper
Polacca	Mackinaw	Sheer-hulk	Penteconter
Polacre	Mary Rose	Steamboat	Quinquereme
Pontoon	Masoolah	Submarine	Side-wheeler
Revenge	Massoola	Vaporetto	Skidbladnir
Shallop	Merchant	Whale-back	Submersible
Sharpie	Monohull	Whaleboat	Supertanker
Steamer	Pinafore	**10 letters:**	Three-decker
Stew-can	Savannah	Brigantine	Three-master
Tartane	Schooner	Golden Hind	Torpedo boat
Titanic	Shanghai	Hydroplane	**12 letters:**
Trireme	Showboat	Icebreaker	Fore-and-after
Tugboat	**9 letters:**	Knockabout	Great Eastern
Vedette	Bucentaur	Paddleboat	Marie Celeste
Victory	Catamaran	Quadrireme	Stern-wheeler
Vidette	Cutty Sark	Santa Maria	**14 letters:**
8 letters:	Dahabeeah	Trekschuit	Ocean
Acapulco	Dahabiyah	Triaconter	greyhound

Shipmate Crew, Hearty, Sailor

Shipping line P and O

Ship's biscuit Dandyfunk, Dunderfunk

Shipshape Apple-pie, Neat, Orderly, Tidy, Trim

Shipwreck Split

Shire County

Shirk(er) Cuthbert, Dodge, Evade, Funk, Malinger, Mike, Pike, Poler, Scrimshank, Skive, Skrimshank, Slack, Soldier

Shirt Boiled, Brown, Calypso, Camese, Camise, Chemise, Choli, Cilice, Dasheki, Dashiki, Dick(e)y, Dress, Fiesta, Garibaldi, Grandad, Hair, Hawaiian, Jacky Howe, Kaftan, Kaross, K(h)urta, Nessus, Non-iron, Parka, Partlet, Polo, Red, Safari, Sark, Serk, Shift, Smock, Stuffed, Subucula, T

Shiva Destroyer

Shiver(ing), Shivers, Shivery Aguish, Break, Chitter, Crumble, Dash, Dither, Fragile, Frisson, Grew, Grue, Malaria, Oorie, Ourie, Owrie, Quake, Quiver, ➤ SHAKE, Shatter, Shrug, Shudder, Smash, Smither, Smithereens, Splinter, Timbers, Tremble

▷ **Shiver(ed)** may indicate an anagram

Shoal Bar, Fish, Quantity, Reef, Run, School, Shallows, Shelf, Tail

Shock(ed), Shocker, Shocking Aghast, Agitate, Appal, Astound, Astun, Awhape, Bombshell, Brunt, Bunch, Consternate, Culture, Defibrillate, Disgust, Dorlach, Dreadful, Drop, Earthquake, ECT, Egregious, Epiphenomenon, Fleg, Floccus, Forelock, Gait, Galvanism, Hair, Horrify, Impact, Infamous, Jar, Jolt, Live, Mane, Mop, Outrage, Putrid, Recoil, Revolt, Rick(er), Scandal(ise), Seismic, Shaghaired, Shake, Sheaf, Shilling, Shook, Stagger, Start(le), Stitch, Stook, Stound, Stun, Trauma, Turn

Shock-absorber Buffer, Oleo, Snubber

▷ **Shocked** may indicate an anagram

Shod Calced

Shoddy Cagmag, Catchpenny, Cheapjack, Cheap, Cloth, Cowboy, Gimcrack, Imitation, Oorie, Ourie, Owrie, Rag-wool, Ropy, Schlock, ➤ SHABBY, Tatty, Tawdry, Tinny

Shoe(s) Accessory, Arctic, Athletic, Ballet, Balmoral, Bauchle, Boot, Brake, Brogan, Brogue, Brothel creepers, Buskin, Calceate, Calk(er), Calkin, Casuals, Caulker, Cawker, Chopin(e), Clog, Co-respondent, Court, Creeper, Dap, Espadrille, Flattie, Galoche, Galosh, Gatty, Geta, Ghillie, Golosh, Gumshoe, High-low, Hush-puppies®, Jandal®, Kletterschue, Kurdaitcha, Loafer, Mary-Janes®, Mocassin, Moccasin, Muil, Mule, Open-toe, Oxford, Oxonian, Panton, Patten, Peeptoe, Plate, Plimsole, Plimsoll, Poulaine, Pump, Rivlin, Rope-soled, Rubbers, Rullion, Sabaton, Sabot, Saddle, Safety, Sandal, Sandshoe, Sannie, Scarpetto, Skid, Skimmer, Slingback, Slip-on, Slipper, Sneaker, Sock, Soft, Solleret, Spike, Stoga, Stogy, Suede, Tie, Track, Trainer, Upper, Vamp(er), Veld-schoen, Veldskoen, Vesskoen, Vibram®, Vibs, Wedgie, Welt, Winkle-picker, Zori

Shoeless Barefoot, Discalced

Shoemaker Blacksmith, Clogger, Cobbler, Cordiner, Cordwainer, Cosier, Cozier, Crispi(a)n, Farrier, Leprechaun, Sachs, Smith, Snob, Soutar, Souter, Sowter, Sutor

Shoe-string Cheap, Lace, Pittance

Shoe-toe Poulaine

Shoo Away, Begone, Hoosh, Off, Scat(ter), Voetsek

Shoot(er), Shooting Ack-ack, Airgun, Arrow, Bine, Bostryx, Braird, Breer, Bud, Bulbil, Catapult, Chit, Cyme, Dart(le), Delope, Discharge, Drib, Elance, Enate, Eradiate, Film, Fire, Germ, Germain(e), Germen, Germin(ate), Glorious twelfth, ➤ GUN, Gunsel, Head-reach, Hurl, Imp, Layer, Limb, Loose, Offset, Photograph, Pluff, Plug, Poot, Pop, Pot, Pout, Ramulus, Rapids, Ratoon, Riddle, Rod, Rove, Runner, Septembriser, Skeet, Snipe, Spire, Spirt, Spout, Spray, Sprout, Spurt, Spyre, Start, Stole, Stolon, Strafe, Sucker, Tellar, Teller, Tendril, Tiller, Turion, Twelfth, Twig, Udo, Vimen, Wand, Weapon, Wildfowler

Shop(s) Atelier, Arcade, Betray, Boutique, Bucket, Buy, Chain, Charity, Chippy, Closed, Coffee, Co-op, Corner, Dairy, Delicatessen, Denounce, Duddery, Duka, Emporium, Factory, Galleria, Gift, Grass, Inform, Luckenbooth, Machine, Mall, Market, Parlour, Patisserie, Precinct, PX,

Retail, RMA, Salon, Shebang, Spaza, Store, Studio, Superette, Supermarket, Thrift, Tuck, Union, Warehouse, Works

Shopkeeper British, Butcher, Chemist, Gombeen-man, Greengrocer, Grocer, Haberdasher, Hosier, Ironmonger, Merchant, Newsagent, Provisioner, Retailer, Stationer

Shoplift(er) Boost, Heist

Shore Bank, Beach, Buttress, Coast, Coste, Eustatic, Landfall, Littoral, Offing, Prop, Rance, Rivage, Seaboard, Strand, Strandline, Support

Short(en), Shortly Abbreviate, Abridge, Abrupt, Anon, Apocope, Brief, Brusque, Commons, Compendious, Concise, Contract, Crisp, Cross, Curt, Curtail, Curtal, Diminish, Drink, Eftsoons, Epitomise, Ere-long, Fubsy, Inadequate, Lacking, Laconical, Light, Limited, Low, Mini, Near, Nip, Nutshell, Pudsey, Punch, Pyknic, Reduce, Reef, Scanty, Scarce, Shrift, Shy, Soon, Sparse, Spirit, Squab, Squat, Staccato, Stint, Stocky, Strapped, Stubby, Succinct, Syncopate, Systole, Taciturn, Teen(s)y, Terse, Tight, Tot, Towards, Transient, Wee

Shortage Dearth, Deficit, Drought, Famine, Lack, Need, Paucity, Scarcity, Sparsity, Wantage

Short circuit Varistor

Shortcoming Weakness

Shorthand Gregg, Outline, Phonographic, Pitman, Speedwriting®, Stenotypy, Tachygraphy, Tironian, Triphone

Short-headed Brachycephal

Short-lived Ephemeral, Fragile, Meson, Transitory

Shorts Bermuda, Board, Boxer, Briefs, Culottes, Hot pants, Kaccha, Lederhosen, Plus-fours, Stubbies®, Trunks

Short-sight Myopia, Myosis

Short-winded Breathless, Concise, Puffed, Purfled, Pursy, Succinct

Shot(s) Aim, All-in, Ammo, Approach, Attempt, Backhand, Ball, Barrage, Bisque, Blank, Blast, Bricole, Bull, Bullet, Burl, Canna, Cartridge, Case, Chain, Chatoyant, Chip, Crack, Dink, Dolly, Dram, Draw, Drop, Dunk, Exhausted, Forehand, Gesse, Glance, Go, Grape, Guess, Gun-stone, Hook, Jump, Langrage, Langrel, Langridge, Longjenny, Magpie, Marksman, Massé, Matte, Mulligan, Multi-coloured, Noddy, Parthian, Parting, Passing, Pelican, Pellet, Phiff, Photo, Pop, Pot, Puff, Rid, Round, Salvo, Scratch, Shy, Sighter, Silk, Six, Slam-dunk, Slap, Slice, Slug, Sped, Spell, Spent, Square cut, Stab, Still, Throw, Tonic, Tracking, Trial, Try, Turn, Volley, Warning

Should Ought

Shoulder(-blade) Carry, Cold, Crossette, Epaule, Hard, Hump, Omohyoid, Omoplate, Pick-a-back, Roadside, Scapula, Shouther, Spald, Spall, Spaul(d), Speal, Spule, Tote, Withers

Shout(er), Shouting Barrack, Bawl, Bellow, Boanerges, Call, Claim, Clamour, Cry, Din, Exclaim, Heckle, Hey, Hoi(cks), Holla, Holla-ho(a), Holler, Hollo, Holloa, Hooch, Hosanna, Howzat, Hue, Rah, Rant, Root,

Round, Sa sa, Treat, Trumpet, Vociferate, Whoop, Yell(och), Yippee, Yoohoo

Shove Barge, Birr, Elbow, Jostle, Push, Ram, Spoon, Thrust

Shovel Backhoe, Dustpan, Hat, Main, Peel, Power, Scoop, Shool, Spade, Steam, Trowel, Van

Show(ing), Shown, Showy Anonyma, Appearance, Bench, Betray, Brummagem, Burlesque, Cabaret, Circus, Come, Con, Cruft's, Demo(nstrate), Depict, Diorama, Display, Do, Dressy, Effeir, Endeictic, Epideictic, Establish, Evince, ➤ EXHIBIT, Expo, Extravaganza, Facade, Fair, Fangled, Farce, Flamboyant, Flash, Flaunt, Galanty, Game, Garish, Gaudy, Gay, Give, Glitz(y), Gloss, Horse, Indicate, Jazzy, Kismet, Light, Loud, Manifest, Matinée, Meritricious, Musical, Naumachy, Ostensible, Ostentatious, Pageant, Pantomime, Parade, Performance, Phen(o), Point, Pomp, Portray, Pretence, Pride, Project, Prominence, Prove, Pseudery, Puff, Raree, Razzmatazz, Represent, Reveal, Revue, Road, Roll-out, Rushes, Screen, Sight, Sitcom, Slang, Soap, Son et lumière, Specious, Spectacle, Splay, Stage, Stunt, Talk, Tamasha, Tattoo, Tawdry, Telethon, Theatrical, Uncover, Usher, Vain, Variety, Vaudeville, Veneer, Wear, Wild west, Zarzuela

Showdown Confrontation, Crunch

Shower Douche, Exhibitor, Flurry, Hail, Indicant, Indicator, Meteor, Party, Pelt, Pepper, Precipitation, Rain, Scat, Scouther, Scowther, Skit, Snow, Spat, Spet, Spit, Splatter, Spray, Sprinkle, Ticker tape

▷ **Showers** may indicate an anagram

Showgirl Evita, Nanette

▷ **Showing, Shown in** may indicate a hidden word

Showman Bailey, Barnum, Goon, Lord Mayor, MC, Ringmaster

Show-off Exhibitionist, Extrovert, Sport, Swagger, Swank

Showpiece Flagship

Show-place Exhibition, Olympia, Pavilion, Theatre

Shrapnel Fragment, Shell, Splinter

Shred Clout, Filament, Grate, Julienne, Mammock, Mince, Mummock, Rag, Screed, Swarf, Tag, Ta(i)ver, Tatter, Thread, To-tear, Wisp

Shrew Bangsring, Banxring, Callet, Fury, Hellcat, Kate, Marabunta, Nag, Otter, Pygmy, Show, Solenodon, Sondeli, Sorex, Spitfire, Tana, Termagant, Tree, Trull, Tupaia, Virago, Vixen, Xant(h)ippe, Yankie

Shrewd Acute, Arch, Argute, Artful, Astucious, Astute, Callid, Canny, Clued-up, Cute, File, Gnostic, Gumptious, Judicious, Knowing, Pawky, Politic, Sagacious, Sapient(al), Wily, Wise

Shriek Cry, Scream, Scrike, Shright, Shrike, Shrill, Shritch, Skirl, Yell

Shrift Attention, Penance, Short

Shrike Bird, Butcher-bird

Shrill Argute, High, Keen, Reedy, Screech, Sharp, Treble

Shrimp(s) Fairy, Krill, Mantis, Midge, Opossum, Potted, Prawn, Runt, Small, Squill(a), Stomatopod

Shrine Adytum, Altar, Dagoba, Dargah, Delphi, Fatima, Feretory, Harem, Holy, Joss house, Kaaba, Marabout, Naos, Pagoda, Reliquary, Scrine, Scryne, Stupa, Tabernacle, Temple, Tope, Vimana, Walsingham

Shrink(age), Shrinking, Shrunk Alienist, Blanch, Blench, Boggle, Cling, Compress, Constringe, Contract, Cour, Cower, Creep, Crine, Cringe, Dare, Decrew, Depreciate, Dread, Dwindle, Flinch, Funk, Gizzen, Less, Nirl, ➤ PSYCHIATRIST, Pycnosis, Quail, Recoil, Reduce, Sanforised, Shrivel, Shy, Sphacelate, Violet, Wince, Wizened

Shrivel(led) Cling, Crine, Desiccate, Dry, Nirl, Parch, Scorch, Scrump, Sear, Shrink, Skrimp, Skrump, Tabid, Welk, Wither, Wizened, Writhled

Shropshire Salop

Shroud(s) Chuddah, Chuddar, Cloak, Cloud, Conceal, Cover, Futtock, Grave-cloth, Rigging, Screen, Sheet, Sindon, Turin, Winding-sheet, Wrap

Shrub Aalii, Acacia, Alhagi, Andromeda, Arboret, Arbutus, Aucuba, Azalea, Barberry, Beautybrush, Bottlebrush, Brere, Brush, Buaze, Buazi, Buckthorn, Buddleia, Bullace, ➤ BUSH, Camellia, Caper, Cascara, Clianthus, Cola, Coprosoma, Coyotillo, Crossandra, Cytisus, Daphne, Epacris, Fatsia, Feijoa, Firethorn, Frutex, Fynbos, Gardenia, Garrya, Gorse, Harhback, Hebe, Henna, Hibiscus, Hop-tree, Horizontal, Inkberry, Jaborandi, Jasmine, Jessamine, Jetbread, Jojoba, Joshua tree, Juniper, Kat, Lantana, Laurustine, Lavender, Lignum, Manoao, Maqui(s), Matico, Melaleuca, Mesquit, Mimosa, Mistletoe, Monte, Myrica, Myrtle, Nabk, Ninebark, Ocotillo, Olea(cea), Parkleaves, Patchouli, Pituri, Plant, Poinsettia, Privet, Protea, Pyracantha, Pyxie, Qat, Rhatany, Rhododendron, Rhus, Rock rose, Romneya, Rue, Ruta, Salal, Savanna(h), Savin(e), Senna, Shadbush, Shallon, Skimmia, Southernwood, Spekboom, Spicebush, Steeplebush, Sumach, Supplejack, Sweetsop, Tamarisk, Tea-tree, Thyme, Titi, Toyon, Tutsan, Tutu, Undergrowth, Wahoo, Waratah, Ya(u)pon, Yupon, Zamia

Shrug Discard, Toss

Shudder(ing) Abhor, Ashake, Frisson, Grew, Grise, Grue, Jerk, Quake, Shake, Spasm, Tremble

Shuffle Dodge, Drag, Hedge, Make, Mix, Palter, Riffle, Scuff, Shamble, Shauchle, Stack

Shun Attention, Avoid, Eschew, Evade, Forbear, Ignore, Ostracise, Secede, ➤ SPURN

Shunt Move, Shelve, Shuttle, Side-track

Shut(s), Shut (down; in; out; up) Bar, Close, Confined, Coop, Debar, Embar, Emure, Fasten, Fend, Impale, Impound, Latch, Lay-off, Lock, Rid, Scram, Seal, Shet, Spar, Steek, Telescope, Tine, To

Shutter(s) Blind, Dead-lights, Douser, Jalousie, Louvre, Persiennes, Shade

Shuttle Alternate, Commute, Drawer, Flute, Go-between, Shoot, Shunt, Space, Tat(t), Weave

Shy Bashful, Blate, Blench, Cast, Catapult, Chary, Coy, Deficient, Demure, Farouche, Flinch, Funk, Heave, Jerk, Jib, Laithfu', Lob, Mim, Rear, Recoil,

Reserved, Sheepish, Shrinking, Skeigh, Start, Thraw, Throw, Timid, Tongue-tied, Toss, Try, Violet, Verecund, Willyard, Willyart, Withdrawn

Siamese Seal-point, T(h)ai

Siberian Chukchi, Ostiak, Ostyak, Samo(y)ed, Tungus, Yakut

Sibilant Hissing, Whistling

Sibling Brother, Kin, Sister

Sibyl Oracle, Prophetess, Seer, Soothsayer, Witch

Sicilian Sicanian, Trinacrian

Sick(en), Sickening, Sickly, Sickness Aegrotat, Affection, Ague, Ail, Bad, Bends, Cat, Chalky, Colic, Chunder, Crapulence, Crook, Delicate, Disorder, Donsie, Gag, Icky, Ill, Infection, Maid-pale, Mal, Mawkish, Morbid, Nauseous, Pale, Peaky, Pestilent, Plague, Puly, Puna, Queachy, Queasy, Queechy, Radiation, Regorge, Repulsive, Retch, Shilpit, Soroche, Spue, Squeamish, Travel, Twee, Uncle Dick, Valetudinarian, Virus, Vomit, Wamble-cropped, Wan

Sick bay San

Sickle(-shaped) Falcate, Falx, Hook, Scythe

Side Abeam, Airs, Beam, Border, Camp, Distaff, Edge, Effect, Eleven, English, Epistle, Facet, Flank, Flip, Gunnel, Hand, Hypotenuse, Iliac, Lateral, Lee(ward), Left, Off, On, OP, Pane, Part, Partisan, Party, Port, Pretension, Profile, Prompt, Rave, Reveal, Right, Rink, Silver, Slip, Spear, Starboard, Swank, ➤ TEAM, Windward, Wing, XI

Sideboard(s) Beauf(f)et, Buffet, Cellaret, Commode, Credence, Credenza, Dresser, Whiskers

Side-effect, Side-issue Offshoot, Secondary, Spin-off

Side-line Hobby, Lye, Siding, Spur

Side-step Crab, Dodge, Evade, Hedge, Maori, Volt

Side-track Distract, Divert, Shunt

Sidewalk Crab, Footpath, Pavement

Sideways Askance, Indirect, Laterally, Laterigrade, Oblique

Siding Alliance, Byway, Lie, Lye, Spur

Sidle Edge, Passage

Siege (work) Alamo, Beleaguer, Beset, Blockade, Gherao, Investment, Ladysmith, Leaguer, Obsidional, Perilous, Poliorcetic, Ravelin, Surround

Siesta Nap, Noonday, Nooning

Sieve, Sift(ing) Analyse, Bolt(er), Boult(er), Bunting, Colander, Coliform, Cribble, Cribrate, Cribrose, Cullender, Eratosthenes, Ethmoid, Filter, Riddle, Screen, Searce, Separate, Siler, Strain, Sye, Tamis, Tammy, Tems(e), Trommel, Try, Winnow

Sigh Exhale, Heave, Lackaday, Long, Moan, Sough, Suspire, Welladay

Sight(ed) Aim, Barleycorn, Bead, Conspectuity, Eye(ful), Eyesore, Glimpse, Ken, Long, Oculated, Prospect, Range, Riflescope, Scene, Scotopia, Second, See, Short, Spectacle, Taish, Vane, ➤ VIEW, Visie, Vision, Vista

Sight-screen Eyelid

Sightseer, Sightseeing Lionise, Observer, Rubberneck, Tourist, Tripper, Viewer

Sign, Signing Ache, Ale-stake, Ampassy, Ampersand, Aquarius, Archer, Aries, Arrow, Auspice, Autograph, Badge, Balance, Beck, Brand, Bull, Bush, Call, Cancer, Capricorn, Caract, Caret, Chevron, Clue, Coronis, Crab, Cross, Cue, Dactylology, Diacritic, Di(a)eresis, Diphone, DS, Earmark, Emblem, Endeixis, Endorse, Endoss, Enlist, Evidence, Exit, Fascia, Fish, Gemini, Gesture, Goat, Grammalogue, Hallmark, Hamza(h), Harbinger, Hex, Hieroglyphic, Hint, Ideogram, Indian, Indicate, Indication, Indicium, Initial, Inscribe, Ivy-bush, Leo, Lexigram, Libra, Logogram, Neume, Nod, Notice, Obelisk, Obelus, Omen, Phraseogram, Pisces, Presa, Presage, Prodromus, Radical, Ram, Rest, Sagittarius, Sain, Scorpio, Segno, Semeion, Shingle, Show, Sigil, Sigla, Signal, Subscribe, Superscribe, Symbol, Symptom, Syndrome, Tag, Taurus, Tic(k)tac(k), Tilde, Token, Trace, Triphone, Twins, Umlaut, V, Virgo, Warning, Waymark, Word, Zodiac

Signal(ler) Alarm, Aldis lamp, Alert, Amber, Assemble, Baud, Beacon, Bell, Bleep, Bugle, Buzz, Chamado, Code, Compander, Compandor, Cone, Cue, Detonator, Diaphone, Distress, Earcon, Flag, Flagman, Flare, Flash, Gantry, Gesticulate, Gong, Griffin, Gun, Harmonic, Heliograph, Heliostat, Herald, Hooter, Horse and hattock, Icon, Important, Interrupt, Mark, Mase, Megafog, Message, Modem, Morse, Navar, NICAM, Notation, Noted, Output, Password, Peter, Pinger, Pip, Pulsar, Radio, Renowned, Reveille, Robot, Salient, Semaphore, Semiology, Singular, Smoke, SOS, Squawk, Taps, Target, Tchick, Telegraph, Teles(e)me, Thumb, Tic(k)-tac(k), Time, Troop, Video, Very, Waff, Waft, Wave, Wave-off, Wigwag

Signature Alla breve, Autograph, By-line, Digital, Hand, John Henry, John Hancock, Key, Mark, Onomastic, Specimen, Time

Signet Ring, Seal, Sigil, Sphragistics

Significance, Significant Cardinal, Consequence, Emblem, Impact, Important, Indicative, Key, Magnitude, Matter, Meaningful, Moment(ous), Noted, Noteworthy, Paramount, Pith, Pregnant, Salient, Special, Telling

Signify Bemean, Denote, Imply, Indicate, Intimate, Matter, ➤ MEAN, Represent

Sign language Ameslan, Semaphore, Tic(k)tac(k)

Sikh(ism) Granth, Kaccha, Kangha, Kara, Kesh, Khalsa, Kirpan, Mazhbi, Nanak, (Ranjit) Singh

Silas Uncle, Wegg

Silence(r), Silent Amyclaean, Clam, Clamour, Conticent, Gag, Hesychastic, Hist, Hush, Hushkit, Mim(budget), Muffler, Mum(p), Mumchance, Mute, Obmutescent, Omertà, Quench, Quiesce, ➤ QUIET, Reticence, Shtoom, Shush, Speechless, Still, Sulky, Tace(t), Tacit(urn), Throttle, Wheesh(t), Whis(h)t

Silhouette Contour, Outline, Planform, Profile, Shape, Skyline

Silica(te) Albite, Analcite, Andalusite, Chabazite, Chert, Cristobalite, Datolite, Diopside, Dioptase, Float-stone, Hiddenite, Humite, Iolite, Kieselguhr, Kyanite, Monticellite, Montmorillonite, Olivine, Opal,

Penninite, Pinite, Rhodonite, Saponite, Scapolite, Silex, Staurolite, Tridymite, Tripoli, Ultrabasic, Vermiculite, Zeolite

Silicon Chip, Si

Silk(y), Silk screen Alamode, Atlas, Barathea, Brocade, Bur(r), Charmeuse®, Chenille, Chiffon, Cocoon, Corn, Crape, Crepe, Duchesse, Dupion, Faille, Filature, Filoselle, Florence, Florentine, Flosh, Floss, Flox, Foulard, Gazar, Gazzatum, Georgette, Gimp, Glossy, KC, Kincob, Lustrine, Lustring, Lutestring, Makimono, Marabou(t), Matelasse, Mercery, Ninon, Oiled, Organza, Ottoman, Paduasoy, Parachute, Peau de soie, Pongee, Prunella, Prunelle, Prunello, Pulu, Raw, Samite, Sars(e)net, Satin, Schappe, Sendal, Seric, Sericeous, Serigraph, Shalli, Shantung, Sien-tsan, Sleave, Sle(i)ded, Sleek, Smooth, Spun, Surah, Tabaret, Tabby, Taffeta, Tasar, Thistledown, Tiffany, Tram, Tulle, Tussah, Tusseh, Tusser, Tussore, Velvet

Silkworm (eggs) Bombyx, Eria, Graine, Sericulture, Tussore

Sill Ledge, Threshold

Silly, Silliness Absurd, Anserine, Brainless, Buffer, Crass, Cuckoo, Daft, Ditsy, Divvy, Dumb, Fatuous, Folly, Fool, Footling, Frivolous, Goopy, Goosey, Gormless, Idiotic, Imbecile, Inane, Inept, Infield(er), Liminal, Mid-off, Mid-on, Mopoke, Puerile, Season, Simple, Soft(y), Spoony, ➤ STUPID, Tripe, Wacky

▷ **Silly** may indicate relating to a sill

Silt Alluvium, Deposit, Dregs, Land, Lees, Residue, Sullage, Varve

Silver(skin) Ag, Albata, Alpac(c)a, Arg(ent), Argyria, Cardecue, Cerargyrite, German, Grey, Lunar, Nickel, One-legged, Paktong, Pegleg, Piastre, Plate, Plateresque, Stephanite, Sterling, Sycee, Thaler

▷ **Silver** may indicate a coin

Silversmith Demetrius, Lamerie, Plater

Simian Apelike, Catar(r)hine

Similar(ity) Analog(ue), Analogical, Corresponding, Etc, Equivalent, Homoeoneric, Homogeneous, Homologous, Homonym, Kindred, ➤ LIKE, Parallel, Resemblance, Samey

Similitude Parable

Simmer Bubble, Seethe, Stew

Simon Bolivar, Cellarer, Magus, Peter, Pure, Simple

Simper Bridle, Giggle, Smirk

Simple(r), Simplicity, Simplify, Simply Aefa(u)ld, Afa(w)ld, Arcadian, Artless, Austere, Bald, Bare, Basic, Crude, Doddle, Doric, ➤ EASY, Eath(e), Elegant, ESN, Ethe, Fee, Folksy, Gomeral, Gotham, Green, Herb(alist), Herborist, Homespun, Idyllic, Incomposite, Inornate, Jaap, Japie, Mere, Moner(on), Naive(té), Naked, Niaiserie, One-fold, Open and shut, Ordinary, Paraphrase, Pastoral, Peter, Plain, Pleon, Provincial, Pure, Reduce, Rustic, Saikless, Sapid, Semplice, Sheer, Silly, Simon, Spartan, Stupid, Tout court, Woollen

Simpleton Abderite, Airhead, Cokes, Cuckoo, Duffer, Flat, Fool, Gomeral, Gomeril, Greenhorn, Juggins, Spoon, ➤ STUPID PERSON, Wiseacre, Zany

Simulate, Simulating Affect, Anti, Feign, Pretend

Simultaneous Coinstantaneous, Contemporaneous, Synchronous, Together

Sin(ful) Aberrant, Accidie, Acedia, Anger, Avarice, Besetting, Bigamy, Covetousness, Crime, Deadly, Debt, Envy, Err, Evil, Folly, Gluttony, Hamartiology, Harm, Hate, Impious, Lapse, Lust, Misdeed, Misdoing, Mortal, ➤ OFFENCE, Original, Peccadillo, Piacular, Pride, Scape, Scarlet, Sine, Sloth, Transgress, Trespass, Unrighteous, Venial, Vice, Wicked, Wrath, Wrong

Sinai Horeb, Mount

Since Ago, As, Meantime, Seeing, Sens, Sinsyne, Sith(en), Whereas

Sincere(ly), Sincerity Bona-fide, Candour, Earnest, Entire, Frank, Genuine, Heartfelt, Honest, Open, Real(ly), True, Verity, Whole-hearted

Sinclair Lewis, Upton

Sinecure Bludge, Commendam

Sinew Fibre, Ligament, Nerve, String, Tendon

▶ **Sinful** see SIN

Sing(ing) Barbershop, Bel canto, Bhajan, Carol, Chant, Cheep, Chorus, Coloratura, Cough, Croon, Crow, Doo-wop, Gorgia, Hum, Inform, Intone, Karaoke, Kirtan, La-la, Lilt, Melic, Parlando, Peach, Pen(n)illion, Pipe, Rand, Rant, Rap, Scat, Second(o), Solmization, Sprechgesang, Sprechstimme, Squeal, Tell, Thrum, Trill, Troll, Vocalise, Warble, Yodel

Singe Burn, Char, Scorch

Singer Alto, Balladeer, Bard, Baritone, Bass, Bing, Bird, Callas, Canary, Cantabank, Cantatrice, Cantor, Car, Carreras, Caruso, Castrato, Chaliapin, Chanteuse, Chantor, Chazan, Cher, Chorister, Coloratura, Comprimario, Crooner, Dawson, Diva, Dylan, Ella, Falsetto, Gleemaiden, Gleeman, Haz(z)an, Kettle, Lark, Lauder, Lead, Lind, Lorelei, Lulu, Mathis, Melba, Minstrel, Oscine, Patti, Pitti, Qawwal, Robeson, Sinatra, Siren, Snitch, Songstress, Soprano, Soubrette, Stoolie, Succentor, Swan, Tatiana, Tenor, Torch, Treble, Troubador, Vocalist, Voice, Wait, Warbler

Single, Singly Ace, Aefa(u)ld, Aefawld, Alone, Azygous, Bachelor, Celibate, Discriminate, EP, Exclusive, Feme sole, Matchless, Monact, Mono, Odd, One-off, Only, Pick, Run, Sole, Solitary, Spinster, Unattached, Uncoupled, Unique, Unwed, Versal, Yin

Single-cell Protista

Single-chambered Monothalamous

Singlestick Sword

Singlet Tunic, Vest

Singular Curious, Especial, Exceptional, Extraordinary, Ferly, Odd, Once, One, Peculiar, Queer(er), Rare, ➤ UNIQUE, Unusual

Singultus Hiccup

Sinister Bend, Dark, Dirke, Evil, L, Left, Lh, Louche, ➤ OMINOUS

Sink(ing), Sunken Basin, Bog, Cower, Delapse, Depress, Descend, Devall, Dip, Down, Drain, Drink, Drop, Drown, Ebb, Flag, Founder, Gravitate, Hole, Immerse, Invest, Jawbox, Lagan, Laigh, Lapse, Ligan, Merger, Pot,

Prolapse, Put(t), Relapse, Sag, Scupper, Scuttle, Set, Settle, Shipwreck, Steep-to, Sty, Submerge, Subside, Swag, Swamp

Sinner Evildoer, Malefactor, Offender, Reprobate, Trespasser

Sinuous Curvy, Ogee, Snaky, Wavy, Winding

Sinus Cavity, Recess

Sip(ping) Delibate, Haporth, Libant, Sample, Sowp, Sup, Taste, Tiff(ing)

Siphon Draw, Rack, Soda, Suck, Transfer

Sir Dan, Dom, K, Kt, Lord(ing), Sahib, Signor, Sirrah, Stir, Stirra(h), Tuan

Sire Beget, Father

Siren Alarm, Alert, Diaphone, Hooter, Houri, Leucosia, Ligea, Lorelei, Mermaid, Oceanides, Parthenope, Salamander, Teaser, Temptress, Vamp

Sirenian Dugong, Lamantin, Manatee, Manati, Sea-cow

Sirloin Backsey

Sirree Bo

Sisal Agave

Siskin Aberdevine, Bird, Finch

Sister(s) Anne, Beguine, Minim, ➤ NUN, Nurse, Religeuse, Sib, Sibling, Sis, Sob, Soul, Swallow, Titty, Ursuline, Verse, Weird

Sisyphean Uphill

Sit(ter), Sitting Bestride, Clutch, Dharna, Duck, Gaper, Lit de justice, Model, MP, Perch, Pose, Reign, Represent, Roost, Séance, Sejeant, Session, Squat

Site, Siting Area, Camp, Feng shui, Greenfield, Home-page, Location, Lot, Pad, Place, Plot, Rogue, Silo, Spot, Stance

Situation Berth, Cart, Case, Catch, Catch-22, Cliff-hanger, Contretemps, Cow, Dilemma, Galère, Hole, Job, Lie, Lurch, Matrix, Niche, No-win, Office, Plight, Position, Post, Scenario, Set-up, Showdown, Status quo, Strait, Where

Six(th) Digamma, Hexad, Prime, Senary, Sestette, Sextet, Sice, Size, Vau, VI

Six counties NI

Six days Hexa(e)meron

Six feet Fathom

Sixpence Bender, Kick, Slipper, Tanner, Tester(n), Testril(l), Tizzy, VID, VIP, Zack

Sixteen Sweet

Sixty Degree, Threescore

Size(able) Amplitude, Area, Bulk, Calibre, Countess, Demy, ➤ EXTENT, Format, Girth, Glair, Glue, Gum, Imperial, Measure, Physique, Pot(t), Princess, Proportion, Tempera, Tidy

Sizzle Fry, Hiss, Scorch

Skate(r), Skating Blade, Choctaw, Cousins, Curry, Dean, Figure, Fish, In-line, Maid, Mohawk, Rock(er), Roller, Rollerblade®, Runner

Skedaddle Shoo, Vamoose

Skein Hank, Hasp

Skeleton, Skeletal Anatomy, Atomy, Axial, Bones, Cadaverous, Cadre, Cage, Coenosteum, Corallum, Framework, Key, Ossify, Outline, Scenario, Sclere

Sketch Cameo, Character, Charade, Croquis, Delineate, Diagram, Draft, ➤ DRAW, Ebauche, Esquisse, Illustration, Limn, Line, Maquette, Modello, Outline, Pencilling, Playlet, Pochade, Précis, Profile, Skit, Summary, Thumbnail, Trick, Vignette, Visual

Skew Agee, Ajee, Oblique, Sheer, Squint, Swerve, Veer

Skewer Brochette, Prong, Spit, Transfix

Ski(ing) Aquaplane, Glide, Glissade, Hot-dog, Langlauf, Nordic, Schuss, Super G, Telemark, Vorlage, Wedeln

Skid Aquaplane, Jackknife, Side-slip, Slew, Slide, Slip, Slither, Spinout

▷ **Skidding** may indicate an anagram

Skiff Canoe, Dinghy, Outrigger

Skill(ed), Skilful Ability, Able, Ace, Adept, Address, Adroit, Art, Bravura, Canny, Chic, Competence, Craft, Deacon, Deft, Dextrous, Expertise, Facility, Feat, Finesse, Flair, Gleg, Hand, Handicraft, Handy, Hend, Hot, Ingenious, Knack, Know-how, Knowing, Lear(e), Leir, Lere, Masterly, Masterpiece, Mean, Mistery, Mystery, Mystique, Practised, Proficient, Prowess, Quant, Resource, Savvy, Science, Skeely, Sleight, Tactics, Technic, Technique, Touch, Trade, Trick, Versed, Virtuoso

Skim Cream, Despumate, Flit, Glide, Graze, Plane, Ream, Scan, Scud, Scum, Skiff, Skitter

Skimp Restrict, Scamp, Scrimp, Stint

Skin(s) Agnail, Armour, Bark, Basan, Basil, Box-calf, Calf, Callus, Case, Cere, Chevrette, Coat, Corium, Cortex, Cuticle, Cutis, Deacon, Derm(a), Dermatome, Dermis, Dewlap, Disbark, Ectoderm, Enderon, Epicanthus, Epicarp, Epidermis, Eschar, Excoriate, Exterior, Fell, Film, Flaught, Flay, Flench, Flinch, Forel, Hangnail, Hide, Jacket, Kip, Kirbeh, Leather, Membrane, Nebris, Pachyderm, Parfleche, Peau, Peel, Pell, Pellicle, Pelt, Perinychium, Plew, Plu(e), Prepuce, Pteryla, Rack, Rind, Scarskin, Serosa, Shell, Shoder, Spetch, Strip, Tegument, Tulchan, Veneer, Water-bouget

Skin disease, Skin trouble Boba, Boil, Buba, Causalgia, Chloasma, Chloracne, Cowpox, Cyanosis, Dartre, Dermatitis, Dermatosis, Dyschroa, EB, Ecthyma, Erysipelas, Exanthem(a), Favus, Flay, Framboesia, Gum rash, Herpes, Hives, Ichthyosis, Impetigo, Leishmaniasis, Livedo, Lupus vulgaris, Mal del pinto, Mange, Miliaria, Morula, Patagium, Pemphigus, Pinta, Pityriasis, Prurigo, Psoriasis, Pyoderma, Rash, Ringworm, Rosacea, Rose-rash, Sapego, Scabies, Sclerodermia, Scurvy, Seborrhoea, Serpigo, Strophulus, Tetter, Tinea, Vaccinia, Verruca, Verruga, Vitiligo, Xanthoma, Yaws, Yawy

Skinflint Dryfist, Miser, Niggard, Pinch-gut, Scrooge, Tightwad

Skinful Drunk, Sausage

Skinhead Not, Punk, Scalp

Skink Seps

Skinny Barebone, Bony, Dermal, Emaciate, Lean, Scraggy, Thin, Weed

Skint Broke, Ghat, Penniless, Stony

Skip(ped), Skipper Boss, Caper, Captain, Cavort, Drakestone, Elater, Frisk, Hesperian, Jump, Jumping-mouse, Lamb, Luppen, Miss, Omit, Patroon, Ricochet, Saury, Scombresox, Spring, Tittup, Trounce(r)

Skirl Humdudgeon, Pibroch, Pipe, Screigh

Skirmish(er) Brush, Dispute, Escarmouche, Fray, Pickeer, Spar, Tirailleur, Velitation

Skirt(ing) Bases, Bell, Border, Bouffant, Cheongsam, Circle, Coat, Crinoline, Culotte(s), Dado, Dirndl, Edge, Fringe, Fustanella, Fustanelle, Girl, Gore, Harem, Hobble, Hoop, Hug, Hula, Kilt, Lamboys, Lava-lava, Marge, Mini, Mopboard, Pareo, Pareu, Pencil, Peplum, Piu-piu, Plinth, Puffball, Ra-ra, Rim, Sarong, Sidestep, Tace, Tail, Taslet, Tasse(t), Tonlet, Tutu, Wraparound

Skit Lampoon, Parody, Sketch

Skittish Curvetting, Frisky, Restless

Skittle(s) Bayle, Bowl, Kail(s), Kayle, Kingpin, Ninepin, Pin, Spare

Skive Scrimshank, Shirk

Skivvy Drudge, Slave

Skrimshank Bludge, Skive

Skulk Lurk, Mooch, Shool

Skull Bregma(ta), Calvaria, Cranium, Head, Malar, Obelion, Occiput, Pannikell, Phrenology, Scalp, Sinciput

Skullcap Ya(r)mulka, Yarmulke, Zucchetto

Skunk Atoc, Atok, Hognosed, Polecat, Teledu, Zoril(lo)

Sky(-high) Air, Azure, Blue, Canopy, Carry, E-layer, Element, Empyrean, Ether, Firmament, Heaven, Lift, Loft, Mackerel, Occident, Octa, Welkin

Sky-diver Para

Skylark Aerobatics, Bird

Skylight Abat-jour, Aurora, Comet, Lunette, Star

Skyline Horizon, Rooftops

Sky-pilot Chaplain, Vicar

Slab Briquette, Bunk, Cake, Chunk, Dalle, Hawk, Ledger, Marver, Metope, Mihrab, Mud, Plank, Sclate, Sheave, Slate, Slice, Stela, Stelene, Tab, Tile

Slack(en), Slackness Abate, Careless, Crank, Dilatory, Dross, Ease, Easy-going, Idle, Lax(ity), Loose, Malinger, Nerveless, Relax, Release, Remiss, Shirk, Skive, Slow, Surge, Unscrew, Veer

Slag Calx, Cinder, Dross, Scoria, Sinter

Slake Abate, Cool, Quench, Refresh, Satisfy

Slam Crash, Criticise, Dad, Grand, Pan(dy), Sock, Swap, Swop, Vole, Wap

Slander(ous) Asperse, Backbite, Calumny, Defame, Derogatory, Disparage, Libel, Malediction, Malign, Missay, Mud, Obloquy, Sclaunder, Smear, Traduce, Vilify, Vilipend

Slang Abuse, Argot, Back, Berate, Cant, Colloquial, Ebonics, Flash, Jargon, Lingo, Nadsat, Rhyming, Slate, Zowie

Slant(ing) Angle, Asklent, Atilt, Bevel, Bias, Brae, Cant, Careen, Chamfer, Clinamen, Diagonal, Escarp, Oblique, Prejudice, Slew, ➤ SLOPE, Splay, Talus, Tilt, Virgule

Slap Clatch, Clout, Cuff, Pandy, Sclaff, Scud, Skelp, Smack, Spat, Twank

Slapdash Careless, Hurried, Random

Slash(ed) Chive, Cut, Gash, Jag, Laciniate, Leak, Oblique, Rash, Rast, Reduce, Scorch, Scotch, Separatrix, Slit, Solidus, Wee

Slat(s) Fish, Jalousie, Louvre

Slate, Slaty Cam, Countess, Credit, Criticise, Decry, Double, Duchess, Duchy, Enter, Griseous, Imperial, Killas, Knotenschiefer, Lady, Marchioness, Pan, Peggy, Princess, Queen, Rag(g), Roof, Schalstein, Shingle, Slat, Small, Tomahawk, Viscountess

Slater Hellier, Insect

Slattern Bag, Besom, Drab, Drazel, Frump, Mopsy, Sloven, Slummock, Traipse, Trapes, Trollop

Slaughter(house), Slaughterer Abattoir, Bleed, Bloodshed, Butcher, Carnage, Decimate, Hal(l)al, Holocaust, Jhatka, Kill, Mactation, ➤ MASSACRE, Sc(h)ehita(h), Schochet, Scupper, Shambles, Shechita(h), Smite

Slav Bohunk, Croat, Czech, Kulak, Polabian, Serb, Sorb, Wend(ic)

Slave(ry), Slaves Addict, Aesop, Aida, Androcles, Barracoon, Blackbird, Bond, Bond(s)man, Bondwoman, Bordar, Boy, Caliban, Coffle, Contraband, Drudge, Drug, Dulocracy, Esne, Galley, Gibeonite, Helot, Hierodule, Mameluke, Maroon, Minion, Odali(s)que, Odalisk, Peasant, Pr(a)edial, Rhodope, Serf, Servitude, Spartacus, Terence, Theow, Thersites, Thete, Thrall, Topsy, Vassal, Villein, White, Yoke

Slave-driver, Slave-owner Assam, Task-master

Slaver Bespit, Dribble, Drivel, Drool, Slobber, Spawl

Slay(er), Slaying Destroy, Execute, Ghazi, ➤ KILL, Mactation, Murder, Quell, Slaughter, Saul

Sleazy Flimsy, Scuzzy, Seamy, Sordid, Squalid, Thin

Sled(ge), Sleigh(-ride) Bob, Dray, Hurdle, Hurly-hacket, Kibitka, Komatik, Lauf, Luge, Polack, Pulk(h)(a), Pung, Skidoo®, Slipe, Stoneboat, Tarboggin, Toboggan, Travois

Sleek Bright, Shine, Silky, Smarm, Smooth, Smug

Sleep(er), Sleepiness, Sleeping, Sleepy Beauty, Bed, Bivouac, Blet, Car, Catnap, Coma, Couchette, Crash, Cross-sill, Cross-tie, Dormant, Dormient, Doss, Doze, Drowse, Endymion, Epimenides, Gum, Hibernate, Hypnology, Hypnos, Kip, Lethargic, Lie, Morpheus, Nap, Narcolepsy, Nod, Over, Paradoxical, Petal, REM, Repast, Repose, Rest, Rip Van Winkle, Sandman, Shuteye, Skipper, Sloom, Slumber, Snooz(l)e, Somnolent, Sopor(ose), Sownd, Swone, Tie, Torpid, Twilight, Wink, Zizz

Sleeping place Bed, Cot, Dormitory, Kang

Sleepless Wake-rife, Wauk-rife

Sleep-walking Noctambulation

Sleet Graupel, Hail

Sleeve (opening) Arm(hole), Batwing, Bishop's, Bush, Collet, Cover, Dolman, Gigot, Gland, Leg-o'-mutton, Liner, Magyar, Manche, Querpo, Raglan, Sabot, Scye, Slashed

▶ **Sleigh** see SLED

Sleight Artifice, Conjury, Cunning, Dodge, Legerdemain, Trick

Slender(ness) Asthenic, Ectomorph, Elongate, Exiguity, Exility, Fine, Flimsy, Gracile, Jimp, Leptosome, Loris, Skinny, Slight, Slim, Spindly, Styloid, Svelte, Sylph, Tenuous, Waif

Sleuth Bloodhound, Detective, Dick, Eye, Lyam(-hound), Lime-hound, Lyme(-hound)

Slew Number, Skid, Slide, Twist

Slice Cantle, Chip, Collop, Cut, Doorstep, Fade, Frustrum, Piece, Rasure, Round, Sector, Segment, Share, Sheave, Shive, Slab, Sliver, Tranche, Wafer, Whang

▷ **Slice of** may indicate a hidden word

Slick Adroit, Glim, Oil, Smooth, Suave

Slide Chute, Cursor, Diapositive, Drift, Glissando, Hirsle, Ice-run, Illapse, Lantern, Mount, Pulka, Schuss, Skid, Skite, Slip, Slither, Snowboard, Transparency

Slight(ly) Affront, Belittle, Cold shoulder, Cut, Detract, Disparage, Disregard, Facer, Flimsy, Halfway, Insult, Neglect, Nominal, Pet, Petty, Rebuff, Remote, ▶ SLENDER, Slim, Slimsy, Slur, Small, Sneaking, Snub, Subtle, Superficial, Sylphine, Thin, Tiny

Slim Jimp, Macerate, Reduce, Slender, Slight, Sylph, Tenuous, Thin

Slime, Slimy Glair, Glit, Guck, Gunk, Mother, Muc(o)us, Oily, Ooze, Sapropel, Slake, Sludge, Uliginous

Sling Balista, Catapult, Drink, Fling, Hang, Parbuckle, Prusik, Support, Toss, Trebuchet

Slink Lurk, Skulk, Slope

Slip(ped), Slipping, Slips Boner, Cutting, Disc, Docket, Drift, EE, Elapse, Elt, Engobe, Error, Faux pas, Fielder, Form, Freudian, Glide, Glissade, Infielder, Label, Landslide, Lapse, Lath, Lauwine, Mistake, Muff, Nod, Oversight, Parapraxis, Petticoat, Prolapse, Ptosis, Quickset, Rejection, Relapse, Run, Scape, Sc(h)edule, Scoot, Set, Shim, Sin, Ski, Skid, Skin, Skite, Slade, Slidder, Slide, Slither, Slive, Spillican, Stumble, Surge, Ticket, Trip, Tunicle, Underskirt, Unleash

Slipper Baboosh, Babouche, Babuche, Calceolate, Carpet, Eel, Mocassin, Moccasin, Moyl, Mule, Pabouche, Pampootie, Pantable, Pantof(f)le, Panton, Pantoufle, Pump, Rullion, Runner, Ski, Sledge, Sneaker, Sock

Slippery Foxy, Glid, Icy, Lubric, Shady, Shifty, Skidpan, Slick

Slipshod Careless, Hurried, Jerry, Lax, Slapdash, Slatternly, Sloppy, Toboggan

▷ **Slipshod** may indicate an anagram

Slit Cut, Cranny, Fent, Fissure, Fitchet, Gash, Loop, Pertus(at)e, Placket, Race, Rit, Scissure, Spare, Speld(er), Vent

Slithy Tove

Sliver Flake, Fragment, Moslings, Rove, Shaving, Slice, Splinter, Trace

Slob(ber) Drool, Lout, Slaver, Smarm, Wet

Sloe Blackthorn, Slae

Slog(ger) Drag, Strike, Swot, Traipse, Tramp, Trape, Trudge, Yacker, Yakka, Yakker

Slogan Amandla, Byword, Catchword, Jai Hind, Mot(to), Phrase, Rallying-cry, Slughorn(e), Warcry, Watchword

Sloop Cutter, Hoy, Ship

Slop(s) Cop(per), Gardyloo, Jordeloo, Muck, Policeman, Rossers, Rozzers, Schmaltz, Sop, Spill, Swill

Slope(s), Sloping Acclivity, Angle, Bahada, Bajada, Bank, Batter, Bevel, Borrow, Borstal(l), Brae, Breast, Chamfer, Cuesta, Declivity, Delve, Diagonal, Fla(u)nch, Glacis, Grade, Gradient, Heel, Hill, Incline, Kant, Lean, Nursery, Oblique, Pent, Periclinal, Pitch, Rake, Ramp, Rollway, Scarp, Schuss, Scrae, Scree, Shelve, Sideling, Skewback, Slant, Slippery, Slipway, Splay, Steep, Stoss, Talus, Tilt, Verge, Versant, Weather

Sloppily, Sloppy Lagrimoso, Lowse, Madid, Mushy, Remiss, Schmaltzy, Slapdash, Slipshod, Sloven, Slushy, Untidy

▷ **Sloppy** may indicate an anagram

Slosh(y) Dowse, Fist, Splash, Wet

Slot(ted) Groove, Hasp, Hesp, Hole, Key, Keyway, Mortice, Mortise, Seat, Slit, Swanmark, Time

Sloth(ful) Accidie, Acedia, Ai, Bradypus, Edentate, Ground, Idle, Inaction, Indolent, Inertia, Lazy, Lie-abed, Megatherium, Mylodon, Slugabed, Sweer(t), Sweered, Sweir(t), Three-toed, Unau

Slot machine One-armed bandit, Pokey, Pokie

Slouch Mooch, Mope, Slump

Slough(ing) Cast, Despond, Ecdysis, Eschar, Exuviae, Lerna, Marsh, Morass, Paludine, Shed, Shuck, Swamp

Sloven(ly) Careless, D(r)aggle-tail, Dag(gy), Frowsy, Grobian, Jack-hasty, Ratbag, Slaister, Slammakin, Slammerkin, Slattern, Sleazy, Slipshod, Slubberdegullion, Slubberingly, Slummock, Untidy

Slow(ing), Slower, Slowly Adagio, Allargando, Andante, Brady, Brake, Broad, Calando, Crawl, Dawdle, Deliberate, Dilatory, Dull, Dumka, ESN, Flag, Gradual, Inchmeal, Lag, Langram, Larghetto, Largo, Lash, Lassu, Late, Leisurely, Lentando, Lento, Lifeless, Loiter, Meno mosso, Obtuse, Pedetentous, Rall(entando), Rein, Reluctant, Retard, Ribattuta, Ritardando, Ritenuto, Slack, Slug, Sluggish, Snaily, Solid, Stem, Tardigrade, Tardive, Tardy

Slow-match Portfire

Sludge Gunge, Mire, Muck, Sapropel

Slug(s) Ammo, Bêche-de-mer, Blow, Bullet, Cosh, Drink, Limaces, Limax, Linotype®, Mollusc, Nerita, Pellet, Shot, Snail, Trepang

Sluggard Drone, Lazy, Lie-abed, Lusk, Unau

Slug(gish) Dilatory, Drumble, Idler, Inert, Jacent, Lacklustre, Laesie, Languid, Lazy, Lentor, Lethargic, Lug, Phlegmatic, Saturnine, Sleepy, ➤ SLOW, Stagnant, Tardy, Torpid, Unalive

Sluice Aboideau, Aboiteau, Drain, Gutter, Koker, Penstock, Rinse, Sasse

Slum Basti, Bustee, Busti, Ghetto, Pavela, Rookery, Shanty, Slurb, Warren

Slumber Doze, Drowse, Nap, Nod, Sleep, Sloom, Snooze

Slump Decrease, Depression, Deteriorate, Dip, Flop, Recession, Sink, Slouch

Slur(ring) Defame, Drawl, Innuendo, Opprobrium, Slight, Smear, Synaeresis, Tie

Slush Bathos, Boodle, Bribe, Drip, Money, Mush, Pap, Slop, Sposh, Swash

Slut Dollymop, Draggle-tail, Dratchell, Drazel, Floosie, Harlot, Slattern, Sow, Tart, Traipse, Trapes, Trollop

Sly Christopher, Clandestine, Coon, Covert, Cunning, Foxy, Leery, Peery, Reynard, Shifty, Sleeveen, Stealthy, Subtle, Tinker, Tod, Tricky, Weasel, Wily

▷ **Slyly** may indicate an anagram

Smack(er) Buss, Cuff, Flavour, Foretaste, Fragrance, Hooker, Kiss, Lander, Lips, Pra(h)u, Relish, Salt, Saut, Skelp, Slap, Slat, Smatch, Smouch, Soupçon, Spank, Spice, Splat, Tack, ➤ TANG, Taste, Thwack, Tincture, Trace, X, Yawl

Small (thing) Ateleiosis, Atom, Bantam, Beer, Bittie, Bitty, Centesimal, Curn, Denier, Dinky, Drib, Elfin, Few, Fry, Grain, Haet, Ha'it, Half-pint, Handful, Holding, Insect, Ion, Leet, Lilliputian, Limited, Lite, ➤ LITTLE, Lock, Low, Meagre, Measly, Midget, Mignon, Miniature, Minikin, Minute, Mite, Modest, Modicum, Peerie, Peewee, Petit(e), Petty, Pigmean, Pigmy, Pink(ie), Pinky, Pint-size, Pittance, Pocket, Poky, Poujadist, Rap, Reduction, Runt, S, Santilla, Scattering, Scrump, Scrunt, Scut, Shrimp, Skerrick, Slight, Slim, Smattering, Smidge(o)n, Smidgin, Smithereen, Smout, Soupçon, Sprinkling, Spud, Stim, Stunted, Tad, Thin, Tidd(l)y, Tiny, Titch(y), Tittle, Tot(tie), Totty, Trace, Trivial, Unheroic, Wee, Weedy, Whit

Smallest Least, Minimal, Runt

Smallholder, Smallholding Croft, Nursery, Rundale, Share-cropper, Stead

Small-minded(ness) Parvanimity, Petty

Smallness Exiguity, Paucity

Smallpox Alastrim, Variola

Smarm(y) Oil, Unctuous

Smart(en), Smartest Ache, Acute, Alec, Astute, Best, Bite, Chic, Classy, Clever, Cute, Dandy, Dapper, Dressy, Elegant, Flash, Flip, Fly, Groom, Kookie, Kooky, Natty, Neat, Nifty, Nip, Nobby, Pac(e)y, Pacy, Posh, Preen, Primp, Prink, Pusser, Raffish, Rattling, Ritzy, Saucy, Slick, Sly, Smoke, Smug, Snappy, Soigné(e), Spiff, Sprauncy, Sprightly, Spruce, Sprush, Spry, Sting, Swagger, Sweat, Swish, Tiddley, Tippy, Titivate, Toff, U

Smash(ed), Smasher, Smashing Atom, Bingle, Brain, Break, Crush, Demolish, Devastate, Dish, Forearm, High, Jarp, Jaup, Kaput, Kill, Lulu,

Shatter, Shiver, Slam, Squabash, Stave, Super, Terrific, Tight, To-brake,
➤ WRECK

Smear Assoil, Besmirch, Blur, Cervical, Clam, Daub, Defile, Denigrate,
Discredit, Drabble, Enarm, Gaum, Gorm, Lick, Oil, Pap(anicolaou), Pay,
Plaster, Slairg, Slaister, Slather, Slime, Slubber, Slur, Smalm, Smarm,
Smudge, Sully, Teer, Traduce, Wax

Smell(ing), Smelly Aroma, Asafoetida, BO, Caproate, Effluvium,
Empyreuma, Fetor, F(o)etid, Fug, Gale, Gamy, Graveolent, Guff, Hing,
Honk, Hum, Mephitis, Miasm(a), Musk, Nidor, Niff, Nose, Odour, Olent,
Olfact(ory), Osmatic, Perfume, Pong, Ponk, Pooh, Rank, Redolent, Reech,
Reek, Sar, Savour, ➤ SCENT, Sniff, Snifty, Snook, Snuff, Steam, Stench,
Stifle, Stink, Tang, Whiff

Smelt(ing) Atherinidae, Melt, Salmon, Scoria, Speiss

Smile(s), Smiling Agrin, Beam, Cheese, Favour, Gioconda, Grin, Rictus,
Self-help, Simper, Smirk

Smirk Grimace, Simper

Smite, Smitten Assail, Enamoured, Hit, Strike, Strook

Smith Adam, Farrier, FE, Forger, Mighty, Stan, Vulcan, Wayland

Smithy Forge, Smiddy

Smock Blouse, Chemise, Drabbet, Gather, Shift, Slop, Smicket

Smoke(r), Smoking, Smoky Blast, Bloat, Censer, Chain, Chillum,
➤ CIGAR(ETTE), Cure, Fog, Fuliginous, Fume, Funk, Gasper, Hemp,
Incense, Indian hemp, Inhale, Kipper, Latakia, Lum, Lunt, Manil(I)a,
Nicotian, Pother, Pudder, Puff, Reech, Reek, Reest, Roke, Smeech, Smeek,
Smoor, Smoulder, Smudge, Snout, Toke, Vapour, Viper, Whiff, Wreath

Smoke-hating Misocapnic

Smoking-room Divan

Smollett Tobias

➤ **Smooch** see SMOUCH

Smooth(e), Smoother, Smoothly Bland, Brent, Buff, Chamfer, Clean,
Clockwork, Dress, Dub, Easy, Even, Fettle, File, Flat, Fluent, Glabrous,
Glare, Glassy, Glib, Goose, Iron, Legato, Level, Levigate, Linish, Mellifluous,
Oil, Plane, Plaster, Rake, Roll, Rub, Sand(er), Satiny, Scrape, Sleek, Slick,
Slickenslide, Slur, Smug, Snod, Sostenuto, Streamlined, Suave,
Swimmingly, Terete, Terse, Trim, Urbane

Smooth-haired Lissotrichous

Smother Burke, Choke, Muffle, Oppress, Overlie, Smoor, Smore, Stifle,
Suppress

Smouch Cheat, Kiss, Lallygag, Lollygag, Neck

Smoulder Burn, Seethe

Smudge Blur, Dab, Offset, Slur, Smear, Smooch, Stain

Smug Complacent, Conceited, Goody-two-shoes, Neat, Oily, Pi,
Self-satisfied, Trim

Smuggle(d), Smuggler, Smuggling Bootleg, Contraband, Donkey, Fair
trade, Gunrunning, Moonshine, Mule, Owler, Rum-runner, Run, Secrete,
Steal, Traffic

Smut(ty) Bawdy, Blight, Blue, Brand, Burnt-ear, Coom, Filth, Grime, Racy, Soot, Speck

Smut-fungus Basidia, Ustilago

Snack Bever, Bhelpuri, Bite, Brunch, Butty, Canapé, Chack, Crudités, Elevenses, Entremets, Gorp, Meze, Nacket, Nibble, Nocket, Nooning, Nuncheon, Pie, Popcorn, Rarebit, Refreshment, Samo(o)sa, Sandwich, Savoury, Tapa, Taste, Vada, Voidee, Wada, Zakuska

Snaffle Bit, Bridoon, Grab, Purloin

Snag Catch, Contretemps, Drawback, Hindrance, Hitch, Impediment, Knob, Nog, Obstacle, Remora, Rub, Snubbe, Stub, Tear

Snail Brian, Cowrie, Cowry, Dodman, Escargot, Gasteropod, Helix, Hodmandod, Limnaea, Lymnaea, Nautilus, Nerite, Roman, Slow, Slug, Strombus, Unicorn-shell, Univalve, Wallfish, Whelk

Snake Adder, Aesculapian, Amphisbaena, Anaconda, Anguine, Anguis, Apod(e), Asp, Bandy-bandy, Berg-adder, Blacksnake, Blind, Blue-racer, Boa, Boma, Boomslang, Brown, Bull, Bush-master, Camoodi, Carpet, Cerastes, Clotho, Coachwhip, Cobra, Coluber, Congo, Constrictor, Copperhead, Coral, Corn, Cottonmouth, Cribo, Crotalidae, Daboia, Death-adder, Dendrophis, Diamond(-back), Dipsas, Dugite, Elaps, Ellops, Fer-de-lance, Garter, Glass, Grass, Habu, Hamadryad, Hognose, Homorelaps, Hoop, Horned viper, Horsewhip, Hydra, Indigo, Jararaca, Jararaka, Joe Blake, Kaa, K(a)rait, King (cobra), Lachesis, Langaha, Mamba, Massasauga, Meander, Milk, Mocassin, Moccasin, Mulga, Naga, Naia, Naja, Ophidian, Pipe, Pit-viper, Plumber's, Puff-adder, Python, Racer, Rat, Rattler, Reptile, Ribbon, Ringhals, Ringneck, Rinkhals, River jack, Rock, Sand viper, Seps, ➤ SERPENT, Sidewinder, Slowworm, Smooth, Spitting, Squamata, Sucuruju, Surucucu, Taipan, Takshaka, Thirst, Thread, Tiger, Timber rattlesnake, Tree, Uraeus, Vasuki, Viper, Water (moccasin), Whip, Wind, Worm

Snake-charmer Lamia

Snake-in-the-grass Peacher, Rat, Traitor

Snake-root Senega

Snap(per), Snappy, Snap up Autolycus, Bite, Break, Brittle, Camera, Click, Crack, Curt, Edgy, Fillip, Girnie, Glom, Gnash, Hanch, Knacker, Knap, Photo, Photogene, Snack, Snatch, Spell, Still, Tetchy, Vigour

Snare Bait, Benet, Engine, Entrap, Gin, Grin, Hook, Illaqueate, Inveigle, Net, Noose, Rat-trap, Springe, Toil, ➤ TRAP, Trapen, Trepan, Web, Weel, Wire

Snarl(ing) Chide, Complicate, Cynic, Enmesh, Gnar(l), Gnarr, Growl, Grumble, Knar, Knot, Snap, Tangle, Yirr

Snatch Claucht, Claught, Excerpt, Fragment, Grab, Kidnap, Nip, Pluck, Race, Rap, Rase, Raunch, Refrain, Snippet, Song, Spell, Strain, Take, Tweak, Wrap, Wrest

▷ **Snatch** may indicate the first letter of a word

Snazzy Cat

Snead Snath

Sneak Area, Carry-tale, Clipe, Clype, Inform, Lurk, Mumblenews, Nim, Peak, Scunge, Skulk, Slip, Slyboots, Snitch, Snoop, Split, Steal, Stoolie, Tell(-tale)

Sneer(ing) Critic, Cynical, Fleer, Gibe, Jeer, Scoff, Smirk, Snide

Sneeze (at), Sneezing Atishoo, Neese, Neeze, Ptarmic, Scorn, Sternutation

Snick Click, Cut, Edge, Glance

Snicker Snigger, Titter, Whinny

Snide Shand, Bitchy

Sniff Inhale, Nose, Nursle, Nuzzle, Scent, Smell, Snivel, Snort, Snuffle, Vent, Whiff

Snigger Giggle, Laugh, Snicker, Snirtle, Titter, Whicker

Snip(pet) Bargain, Cert, Clip, Cut, Piece, Sartor, Snatch, Snick, Tailor

Snipe(r) Bird, Bushwhacker, Criticise, Franc-tireur, Gutter, Heather-bleat(er), Heather-bluiter, Heather-blutter, Scape, Shoot, Walk, Wisp

Snitch Conk, Konk, Nose

Snivel Blubber, Snotter, Snuffle, Weep, Whine

Snob(bery), Snobbish Cobbler, Crispin, High-hat, Scab, Side, Snooty, Soutar, Souter, Sowter, Toffee-nose, Vain, Vamp

Snooker Pool, Stimie, Stimy, Stym(i)e

Snoop(er) Meddle, Nose, Pry, Tec

Snooty Bashaw, Snob(bish)

Snooze Calk, Caulk, Dove, Doze, Nap, Nod, Sleep

Snore, Snoring Rhonchus, Rout, Snort, Stertorous, Zz

Snort(er) Drink, Grunt, Nare, Nasal, Roncador, Snore, Toot

Snot(ty) Mucoid

Snout Bill, Boko, Cigar, Informer, Muzzle, Nose, Nozzle, Proboscis, Schnozzle, Tinker, Tobacco, Wall

Snow(storm), Snowy Brig, Buran, Cocaine, Coke, Corn, Cornice, Crud, Firn, Flake, Flurry, Graupel, Half-pipe, Heroin, Mogul, Neve, Nival, Niveous, Oncome, Onding, Sastruga, Stall, White-out, Wintry, Wreath, Zastruga

Snowball Accelerate, Cramp-bark, Cumulative, Guelder-rose, Increase, Magnify, Opulus, Pelt, Rose

Snowdrop Avalanche

Snowflake Leucojum

Snow-goose Wav(e)y

Snowman Abominable, Eskimo, Junkie, Sherpa, Yeti

Snowshoe Racket, Racquet

Snub Cut, Diss, Go-by, Lop, Pug, Quelch, Rebuff, Reproof, Retroussé, Short, Slap, Slight, Sloan, Sneap, Snool, Wither

Snuff(le) Asarabacca, Dout, Errhine, Extinguish, Maccaboy, Ptarmic, Pulvil, Rappee, Smother, Snaste, Sneesh(an), Sniff, Snift, Snush, Tobacco, Vent

Snuffbox Mill, Mull

Snug(gle) Burrow, Cose, ➤ COSY, Couthie, Couthy, Croodle, Cubby, Cuddle, Embrace, Lion, Neat, Nestle, Nuzzle, Rug, Snod, Tight, Trim

So Ergo, Forthy, Hence, Sae, Sic(h), Sol, Therefore, This, Thus, True, Very, Yes

Soak Bate, Bath(e), Beath, Bewet, Bloat, Blot, Buck, Cree, Deluge, Drench, Drink, Drook, Drouk, Drown, Drunk, Duck, Dunk, Embay, Embrue, Fleece, Grog, Imbrue, Infuse, Lush, Macerate, Marinate, Mop, Oncome, Permeate, Rait, Rate, Ret(t), Saturate, Seep, Sipe, Sog, Sop, Souce, Souse, Sows(s)e, Steep, Sype, Thwaite, Toper, Wet

Soap(y) Cake, Carbolic, Castile, Flake, Flannel, Flattery, Green, Lather, Metallic, Moody, Pears®, Saddle, Saponaceous, Saponin, Sawder, Slime, Soft, Suds, Sudser, Sugar, Syndet, Tall-oil, Toheroa, Windsor

Soapstone Steatite, Talc

Soar(ing) Ascend, Essorant, Fly, Glide, Hilum, Rise, Tower, Zoom

Sob (stuff) Blub(ber), Boohoo, Goo, Gulp, Lament, Singult, Snotter, Wail, Weep, Yoop

Sober(sides) Abstemious, Calm, Demure, Pensive, Sedate, Staid, Steady, TT

Sobriquet Byname, Cognomen, Nickname, To-name

So-called Alleged, Nominal, Soi-disant

Sociable, Sociability Affable, Cameraderie, Chummy, Cosy, Extravert, Folksy, Friendly, Genial, Gregarious

Social(ise) Hobnob, Hui, Mingle, Mix, Musicale, Phatic, Tea-dance, Yancha

Socialism, Socialist Champagne, Chartist, Dergue, Fabian, Fourierism, ILP, International, Lansbury, Left(y), Marxism, Nihilism, Owen(ist), Owenite, Pinko, Red, Revisionist, Sandinista, Spartacist, Utopian, Webb

Socialite Deb

Society Affluent, Association, Beau monde, Body, Broederbond, Building, Camorra, Carbonari, Class, Club, College, Company, Conger, Co-op, Culture, Danite, Defenders, Dorcas, Eleutheri, Elks, Fabian, Fashion, Foresters, Freemans, Freemasons, Friendly, Friends, Glee club, Grotian, Group, Guilds, Haut monde, Hetairia, High, Illuminati, Institute, Invincibles, Ku-klux-klan, Kyrle, Law, Linnean, Lodge, Mafia, Malone, Mau-mau, Oddfellows, Oratory, Order, Permissive, Phi Beta Kappa, Plunket, Plural, Pop, Provident, Ribbonism, Rosicrucian, Rotary, S, School, Secret, Soc, Soroptomist, Sorority, Stakeholder, Tammany, Toc H, Ton, Tong, Triad, U, World

Sock(s) Argyle, Argyll, Biff, Bobby, Bootee, Hose(n), Slosh, Strike, Tabi

Socket Acetabulum, Alveole, Budget, Gudgeon, Hollow, Hosel, Hot shoe, Jack, Nave, Ouch, Pod, Port, Power-point, Strike, Torulus

Sock-eye Nerka, Salmon

Socrates, Socratic Ironist, Maieutics, Sage

Sod Clump, Delf, Delph, Divot, Gazo(o)n, Mool, Mould, Mouls, Scraw, Sward, Turf

Soda, Sodium Acmite, Arfvedsonite, Baking, Barilla, Bicarb, Caustic, Club, Cream, La(u)rvikite, Na, Natrium, Natron, Reh, Saleratus, Splash, Trona, Washing

Sofa Canapé, Chesterfield, Couch, Daybed, Divan, Dos-à-dos, Dosi-do, Ottoman, Settee, Squab, Tête-à-tête

So far As, Until, Yonder

Soft(en), Softener, Softening, Softly Amalgam, Anneal, B, BB, Blet, Boodle, Casefy, Cedilla, Cree, Dim, Dolcemente, Doughy, Emolliate, Emollient, Flabby, Gentle, Hooly, Humanise, Intenerate, Lash, Lax, Lenient, Limp, Low, Malacia, Malax(ate), Mardarse, Mardie, Mease, Mellow, Melt, Mild, Milksop, Mitigate, Modulate, Mollify, Mollities, Morendo, Mulch, Mush(y), Mute, Neale, Nesh, Option, P, Palliate, Pastel, Piano, Plushy, Porous, Propitiate, Rait, Rate, Relent, Scumble, Sentimental, Silly, Slack, Squashy, Squidgy, Squishy, Sumph, Talcose, Temper, ➤ TENDER, Tone, Velvet, Weak

Softness Lenity

Software Firewall, Firmware, Groupware, Middleware, Parser, Payware, Shareware, Spreadsheet, Stiffware, Vaccine, Windows

Sog(gy) Sodden

Soil(ed), Soily Acid, Adscript, Agronomy, Alluvium, Bedraggle, Chemozem, Clay, Defile, Desecrate, Dinge, Dirt(y), Discolour, Earth, Edaphic, Glebe, Grey, Grimy, Ground, Gumbo, Hotbed, Humus, Illuvium, Lair, Land, Latosol, Loam, Loess, Lome, Loss, Mire, Mo(u)ld, Mool, Mud, Peat, Ped, Pedalfer, Pedocal, Pedology, Phreatic, Planosol, Podsol, Podzol, Pure, Regar, Regur, Rendzina, Root-ball, Sal, Smudge, Smut, Solonchak, Solonetz, Solum, Soot, Stain, Stonebrash, Sully, Tarnish, Tash, Terrain, Terricolous, Tilth, Tschernosem, Udal, Umber, Yarfa, Yarpha

Soirée Drum, Levee, Musicale

Sojourn Abide, Respite, Stay, Tarry

Sol G, Soh, Sun

Solace Cheer, Comfort

Solar(ium) Heliacal, Tannery

Sold Had

Solder Blaze, Join, Spelter, Tin, Weld

Soldier(s) Achilles, Alpini, Ant, Anzac, Army, Arna(o)ut, Askari, Atkins, ATS, Banner, Bashi-Bazouk, Battalion, Bersaglier(e), Bluff, Bod, Bombardier, Borderer, Botha, Brave, Brigade, Buff-coat, Buff-jerkin, Butter-nut, Cadet, Caimac(am), Campaigner, Cannon-fodder, Car(a)bineer, Car(a)binier, Cataphract, Centinel(l), Centonel(l), Chasseur, Chindit, Chocko, Choco, Cohort, Colonel, Colours, Commando, Confederate, Contingent, Cornet, Corp(s), Cossack, Curassier, Detail, Dog-face, Doughboy, Draftee, Dragoon, Dugout, Emmet, Engineer, Enomoty, Evzone, Fag(g)ot, Federal, Fencibles, Fighter, Flanker, Foederatus, Foot, Forlorn-hope, Fugleman, Fusilier, Fuzzy-wuzzy, Fyrd, Gallo(w)glass, Galoot, GI, Gippo, Goorkha, Grenadier, Grunt, Guardee, Guardsman, Guerilla, Gurkha, Gyppo, Hackbuteer, Hobbler, Hoplite, Hussar, Immortal, Impi, Inf(antry), Iron Duke, Ironside, Irregular, Jackman, Janissary, Janizary, Jawan, Joe, Johnny Reb(el), Kaimakam, Kern(e), Kitchener, Knight, Lancer, Landsknecht, Lansquenet, Lashkar, Leatherneck, Legionary, Legionnaire, Levy, Line, Linesman, Lobster, Maniple, Martinet, Men-at-arms, Miles (gloriosus), Militiaman, Miner, Minuteman, Musketeer, Nahal, Naik, Nasute, Nizam, Non-com, OR, Orderly, Palatine, Palikar, Pandoor, Pandour, Paratroop, Partisan, Peltast, Peon, Perdu(e), Persevere, Phalanx, Pikeman, Piou-piou,

Pistoleer, Platoon, Poilu, Pongo, Post, Private, Rajput, Ranger, Rank(er), Rat-tail, Reb, Redcoat, Reformado, Regiment, Regular, Reiter, Reservist, Retread, Rifleman, Rutter, Sabre, Sammy, Samurai, SAS, Sebundy, Sentinel, Sepoy, Serviceman, Signaller, Silladar, Snarler, So(d)ger, Soldado, Sowar(ee), Sowarry, Spearman, Squaddie, Squaddy, Stalhelm(er), Stormtrooper, Strelitz, Subaltern, Swad(dy), Sweat, Targeteer, Templar, Terrier, Timariot, Tin, Tommy, Train-band, Trencher, Trooper, Troops, Turco(pole), Uhlan, Unknown, Velites, Vet(eran), Volunteer, Warhorse, Warmonger, Warrior, Yardbird, Zouave

▷ **Soldiers** may indicate bread for boiled eggs

Sole, Solitaire, Solitary Alone, Anchoret, Anchorite, Clump, Fish, Incommunicado, Lemon, Lonesome, Megrim, Merl, Meunière, Monkish, Only, Pad, Palm, Patience, Pelma, Planta(r), Plantigrade, Platform, Recluse, Scaldfish, Single(ton), Skate, Slip, Smear-dab, Tap, Thenar, Unique, Vibram®, Vola

Solemn Agelast, Austere, Devout, Earnest, Grave, Gravitas, Majestic, Owlish, Po-faced, Sacred, Sedate, Serious, Sober, Sobersides

Solent Lee

Solicit Accost, Approach, Ask, Attract, Bash, ➤ BEG, Canvass, Cottage, Importun(at)e, Plead, Ply, Speer, Speir, Tout, Woo

Solicitor Attorney, Avoué, Beggar, Canvasser, Hallanshaker, Law-agent, Lawyer, Notary, SL, Tout, Writer to the Signet, WS

Solid(arity), Solidify Cake, Chunky, Clot, Clunky, Compact, Comradeship, Concrete, Cone, Congeal, Consolidate, Cube, Cylinder, Dense, Enneahedron, Firm, Foursquare, Freeze, Frustrum, Fuchsin(e), Gel, Hard, Holosteric, Impervious, Merbromin, Octahedron, Pakka, Petrarchan, Platonic, Polyhedron, Prism, Pucka, Pukka, Robust, Set, Stilbene, Sublimate, Substantial, Tetrahedron, Thick, Unanimous

Solipsism Egotism, Panegoism

Solitude Privacy, Seclusion

Solo Aria, Cadenza, Cavatine, Concertante, Lone, Monodrama, Monody, Ombre, One-man, Scena, Variation

Solon Sage

So long Cheerio, Ciao, Goodbye, Tata

Solstice Tropic

Soluble Alkaline, Surfactant

Solution Acetone, Alkali, Ammonia, ➤ ANSWER, Austenite, Benedict's, Collodion, Dakin's, Dobell's, Eclairassement, Elixir, Emulsion, Eusol, Fehling's, Key, Leachate, Limewater, Lixivium, Lye, Oleoresin, Rationale, Ringer's, Rinse, Saline, Solid, Solvent, Suspensoid, Tincture, Titrate

▷ **Solution** may indicate an anagram

Solve(d), Solver Assoil, Casuist, Clear, Crack, Decode, Loast, Loose, Read(er), Troubleshoot, Unclew, Unriddle

Solvent Acetaldehyde, Acetone, Alcahest, Aldol, Alkahest, Anisole, Aqua-regia, Banana oil, Cleanser, Decalin, Diluent, Dioxan(e), Eluant, Eleunt, Ether, Funded, Furan, Hexane, Ligroin, Megilp, Menstruum,

Methanol, Methylal, Naphtha, Paraldehyde, Picoline, Protomic, Pyridine, Sound, Stripper, Terebene, Terpineol, Tetrachloromethane, Thiophen, Toluene, Toluol, Trike, Trilene, Turpentine

Sombre Dark, Drab, Drear, Dull, Gloomy, Grave, Morne, Subfusc, Subfusk, Sullen, Triste

Some Any, Arrow, Ary, Certain, Few, Divers, One, Part, Portion, Quota, These, They, Wheen

▷ **Some** may indicate a hidden word

Somebody Dignitary, Name, Notable, One, Person, Quidam, Someone, ➤ VIP

Somehow Somegate

▷ **Somehow** may indicate an anagram

Somersault Flip(-flap), Flip-flop, Handspring, Pitchpole, Pitchpoll

Something Aliquid, Chattel, Matter, Object, Summat, Whatnot

Sometime(s) Erstwhile, Ex, Former, Occasional, Off and on, Quondam

Somewhat Bit, -ish, Mite, Partly, Quasi, Quite, Rather

Somewhere Somegate

Son Boy, Disciple, Epigon(e), Fils, Fitz, Lad, Lewis, M(a)c, Offspring, Prodigal, Progeny, Scion

Song Air, Anthem, Antistrophe, Aria, Art, Aubade, Ayre, Ballad, Ballant, Ballata, Barcarol(l)e, Belter, Berceuse, Bhajan, Blues, Brindisi, Burden, Burthen, Calypso, Cancionero, Canticle, Cantilena, Canzona, Canzone, Canzonet(ta), Carmagnole, Carol, Catch, Cavatina, Chanson, Cha(u)nt, Come-all-ye, Corn-kister, Descant, Dirge, Dithyramb, Ditty, Epithalamion, Epithalamium, Fado, Fit, Flamenco, Folk, Forebitter, Glee, Gorgia, Gradual, Hillbilly, Hum, Hymeneal, Hymn, Internationale, Jug(-jug), Lay, Lied(er), Lilt, Lullaby, Lyric, Madrigal, Magnificat, Marseillaise, Matin, Melic, Melisma, Melody, Mento, Noel, Number, Oat, Paean, Pane, Patter, Pennillion, Plaint, Prick, Prothalamion, Prothalamium, Psalm, Qawwali, Rap, Recitativo, Relish, Rhapsody, Rispetto, Roulade, Roundelay, Rune, Scat, Secular, Serenade, Shanty, Siren, Sirvente, Skolion, Spiritual, Stave, Strain, Strophe, Swan, Taps, Tenebrae, Theme, Torch, Trill, Tune, Volkslied, Warble, Wassail, Waulking, Yodel, Yodle

Songbook Cancionero, Hymnal, Kommersbuch, Libretto, Psalter

Songsmith, Songwriter Dowland, Espla, Foster, Kern, Minot, Zappa

Sonnet Amoret, Italian, Petrarch(i)an, Shakespearean, Shakespearian, Spenserian

Sonometer Monochord

Soon(er) Anon, Directly, Erelong, OK, Oklahoma, Presently, Shortly, Tight, Timely, Tit(ely), Tite, Tyte

Soot(y) Colly, Coom, Crock, Fuliginous, Grime, Lampblack, Smut, Speck

Soothe, Soothing Accoy, Allay, Anetic, Appease, Assuage, Bucku, Calm, Compose, Demulcent, Emollient, Irenic, Lenitive, Lull, Mellifluous, Mollify, Pacific, Paregoric, Poultice, Quell, Rock

Soothsayer Astrologer, Augur, Calchas, Chaldee, Divine, Forecaster, Haruspex, Melampus, Oracle, Picus, Prophet, Pythoness, ➤ SEER, Shipton, Tiresias

Sop Appease, Berry, Douceur, Rait, Ret, Sponge

Sophist(ic) Casuist, Elenchic, Quibbler

Sophisticate(d) Blasé, Boulevardier, City slicker, Civilised, Cosmopolitan, Couth, Doctor, High-end, Patrician, Polished, Sative, Slicker, Svelte, Urbane, Worldly

▷ **Sophoclean** may indicate Greek (alphabet, etc)

Soporific Barbiturate, Bromide, Drowsy, Halothane, Hypnotic, Lullaby, Narcotic, Opiate, Sedative, Tedious

Soppiness, Soppy Maudlin, Schwarmerei, Sloppy, Slushy

Soprano Castrato, Crespin, Descant, Lind, Treble

Sorcerer, Sorceress, Sorcery Angakok, Ashipu, Circe, Conjury, Diablerie, Hoodoo, Kadaitcha, Kurdaitcha, Lamia, Mage, Magic(ian), Magus, Medea, Merlin, Morgan le Fay, Mother Shipton, Necromancer, Obi, Pishogue, Shaman, Sortilege, Voodoo, Warlock, Witch, Wizard

Sordid Base, Scungy, Seamy, Sleazy, Squalid, Vile

Sore(ly), Sores Abrasion, Bitter, Blain, Boil, Canker, Chancre, Chap, Chilblain, Cold, Dearnly, Felon, Gall, Impost(h)ume, Ireful, Kibe, Quitter, Quittor, Raw, Rupia(s), Saddle, Sair, Shiver, Sitfast, Surbate, Ulcer(s), Whitlow, Wound

Sore throat Garget, Prunella, Quinsy, Tonsillitis

Sorrel Hetty, Oca, Soar(e), Sore, Sourock

Sorrow(ful) Affliction, Distress, Dole, Dolour, ➤ GRIEF, Lament, Misery, Nepenthe, Penance, Pietà, Remorse, Rue, Triste, Wae, Waugh, Wirra, Woe, Yoop

Sorry Ashamed, Contrite, Miserable, Oops, Penitent, Pitiful, Poor, Regretful, Relent, Wretched

▷ **Sorry** may indicate an anagram

Sort(ing) Arrange, Breed, Brand, Category, Character, Classify, Collate, Drive, Grade, ➤ KIND, Nature, Pranck(e), Prank, Sift, Species, Stamp, Tidy, Triage, Type, Variety

Sortie Attack, Foray, Mission, Outfall, Raid, Sally

▶ **Sorts** see OUT OF SORTS

So-so Average, Indifferent, Mediocre, Middling

So to speak Quasi

▷ **So to speak** may indicate 'sound of'

Sotto voce Murmur, Whisper

▶ **Soubriquet** see SOBRIQUET

Sough Rustle, Sigh

Soul(ful) Alma, Ame, Anima, Animist, Atman, Ba, Brevity, Deep, Eschatology, Expressive, Heart, Inscape, Larvae, Manes, Person, Psyche, Saul, Shade, Spirit

Sound(ed), Soundness, Sound system Accurate, Acoustic, Affricate, Amphoric, Audio, Bay, Bleep, Blow, Boing, Bong, Cacophony, Chime, Chord, Clam, Clang, Clop, Clunk, Continuant, Dental, Dolby®, Echo, Euphony, Fast, Fathom, Fere, Fettle, Fit, Hale, Harmonics, Healthy, Hearty, Hi-fi, Ich-laut, Inlet, Knell, Kyle, Labiodental, Lucid, McMurdo, Mersey, Milford, Mouillé, Music, Narrow, ➤ NOISE, Onomatopaeia, Oompah, Orthodox, Palatal, Palato-alveolar, Pamlico, Peal, Pectoriloquy, Phone(me), Phonetic, Phonic, Plap, Plink, Plonk, Plop, Plosion, Plumb, Plummet, Plunk, Probe, Puget, Quadraphonic(s), Quadrophonic(s), Rale, Rational, Real, Ring, Roach, Robust, Rong, Rumble, Rustle, Sabin, Safe, Sane, Scoresby, Solid, Sonance, Sone, Souffle, Sough, Sowne, Stereo, Strait, Swish, Tamber, Tannoy®, Thorough, Timbre, Tone, Trig, Trumpet, Twang, Ultrasonic(s), Unharmed, Valid, Voice, Vowel, Wah-wah, Well, Whole(some), Whump

Sounder Lead

Soundproof Deaden

Sound-track Dubbing, Stripe

Soup Alphabet, Avgolemono, Bird's nest, Bisk, Bisque, Borsch, Bouillabaisse, Bouillon, Brewis, Broth, Burgoo, Chowder, Cock-a-leekie, Consommé, Garbure, Gazpacho, Gomb(r)o, Gruel, Gumbo, Hoosh, Julienne, Kail, Kale, Madrilene, Marmite, Mess, Minestrone, Mock turtle, Mulligatawny, Oxtail, Pot(t)age, Pot-au-feu, Primordial, Puree, Ramen, Rubaboo, Sancoche, Shchi, Shtchi, Skilligalee, Skilligolee, Skilly, Skink, Stock, Tattie-claw, Toheroa, Turtle, Vichyssoise

▷ **Soup** may indicate an anagram

Soupçon Thought, Touch

Sour(puss) Acerb, Acescent, Acid, Acidulate, Alegar, Bitter, Citric, Crab, Esile, Ferment, Moody, Stingy, ➤ TART, Turn, Verjuice, Vinegarish

Source Authority, Basis, Bottom, Centre, Database, Derivation, Egg, Fons, Font, Fount, Fountain-head, Germ, Head-stream, Mine, Mother, Origin, Parent, Pi, Pion, Provenance, Quarry, Reference, Rise, Riverhead, Root, Seat, Seed, Spring, Springhead, Urn, Well, Wellhead, Wellspring, Widow's cruse, Ylem

Sour milk Curds, Smetana, Whey, Whig, Yogh(o)urt

Souse Duck, Immerse, Pickle, Plunge, Soak, Spree, Steep

South(ern), Southerner Austral, Dago, Decanal, Decani, Dixieland, Meridian, S

South African Bantu, Caper, Grikwa, Griqua, Hottentot, Kaf(f)ir, SA, Springbok, Swahili, Xhosa, ZA, Zulu

South American Araucanian, Arawak, Argentino, Aymara, Bolivian, Carib, Chibcha, Chilean, Galibi, Guarani, Inca, Jivaro, Mam, Mapuchi, Mochica, Quechua, SA, Tapuyan, Tupi

Southwark Boro'

Souvenir Keepsake, Memento, Relic, Remembrance, Scalp, Token, Trophy

Sovereign(ty), Sovereign remedy Anne, Autocrat, Bar, Condominium, Couter, Dominant, ER, Goblin, Haemony, Harlequin, Imperial, Imperium,

James, King, L, Liege, Nizam, Pound, Quid, Royalty, Ruler, Shiner, Supreme, Swaraj, Synarchy, Thick'un, Thin'un

Soviet Circassian, Council, Estonian, Russian, Supreme, Volost

Sow(ing) Catchcrop, Elt, Foment, Gilt, Inseminate, Plant, Scatter, Seed, Sprue, Strew, Yelt

Soya Tempe(h)

Spa Baden, Baden-Baden, Bath, Evian, Harrogate, Hydro, Kurhaus, Kursaal, Leamington, Vichy

Space(d), Spacing Abyss, Acre, Area, Areola, Bay, Bracket, Breathing, C(o)elom, Cellule, Compluvium, Concourse, Contline, Crookes, Cubbyhole, Deep, Diastema, Distal, Distance, Elbow-room, Esplanade, Ether, Expanse, Extent, Footprint, Forecourt, Gap, Glade, Goaf, Gob, Gutter, Hair, Headroom, Homaloid, Inner, Interstice, Kerning, Killogie, Lacuna, Lair, Lebensraum, Legroom, Logie, Lumen, Lung, Machicolation, Maidan, Metope, Mihrab, Muset, Musit, Orbit, Outer, Peridrome, Plenum, Pomoerium, Priest hole, Quad, ➤ ROOM, Ruelle, Sheets, Spandrel, Spandril, Step, Storage, Tympanum, Ullage, Vacuole, Vacuum, Vast, Vector, Void

Spacecraft, Space agency, Space object, Spaceship, Space station Apollo, Capsule, Explorer, Galileo, Giotto, Lander, LEM, Mariner, MIR, Module, NASA, Orbiter, Pioneer, Probe, Quasar, Salyut, Shuttle, Skylab, Soyuz, Sputnik, Starship, Tardis, Vostok, Voyager

Space walk EVA

Spade Breastplough, Caschrom, Cas crom, Castrato, Detective, Graft, Loy, Negro, Paddle, Pattle, Pettle, Pick, S, Shovel, Slane, Spit, Suit, Tus(h)kar, Tus(h)ker, Twiscar

Spain E, Iberia

Spalpeen Sinner

Span Age, Arch, Attention, Bestride, Bridge, Chip, Ctesiphon, Extent, Life, Range

Spangle(d) Avanturine, Aventurine, Glitter, Instar, O, Paillette, Sequin

Spaniard, Spanish Alguacil, Alguazil, Barrio, Basque, Cab, Caballero, Carlist, Castilian, Catalan, Chicano, Dago, Don, Fly, Grandee, Hidalgo, Hispanic, Jose, Main, Mestizo, Mozarab, Pablo, Señor, Spic(k), Spik

Spaniel Blenheim, Clumber, Cocker, Crawler, Creep, Dog, Fawner, Maltese, Papillon, Placebo, Skip-kennel, Springer, Sussex, Tibetan, Toad-eater

Spank(ing) Cob, Paddywhack, Rapid, Scud, Slap, Slipper, Sprack

Spanner Arc, Box, Bridge, Clapper, Key, Torque, Wrench

Spar Barytes, Blue John, Boom, Bowsprit, Box, Cauk, Cawk, Fight, Gaff, Iceland, Jib-boom, Mainyard, Martingale, Mast, Nail-head, Outrigger, Rafter, Rail, Ricker, Shearleg, Sheerleg, Snotter, Spathic, Sprit, Steeve, Stile, Triatic, Yard

Spare, Sparing Angular, Cast-off, Dup(licate), Economical, Free, Frugal, Gash, Gaunt, Hain, Lean, Lenten, Other, Pardon, Reserve, Rib, Save, Scant, Slender, Stint, Subsecive, Thin

Spark Animate, Arc, Beau, Blade, Bluette, Dandy, Flash, Flaught, Funk, Ignescent, Kindle, Life, Muriel, Scintilla, Smoulder, Spunk, Trigger, Zest

Sparkle(r), Sparkling Aerated, Coruscate, Diamanté, Effervesce, Elan, Emicate, Fire, Fizz, Flicker, Frizzante, Glint, Glisten, Glitter, Pétillant, Scintillate, Seltzer, Seltzogene, Spangle, Spritzig, Spumante, Twinkle, Verve, Witty, Zap

Sparrow Bird, Isaac, Junco, Mossie, Passerine, Piaf, Prunella, Spadger, Speug, Sprug, Titling

Sparrow-grass Asparagus, Sprue

Sparse Meagre, Rare, Scant, Thin

Spartan(s) Austere, Basic, Enomoty, Hardy, Helot, Laconian, Lysander, Menelaus, Severe, Valiant

Spasm(odic) Blepharism, Chorea, Clonus, Cramp, Crick, Fit(ful), Hiccup, Hippus, Intermittent, Irregular, ➤ JERK, Kink, Laryngismus, Nystagmus, Paroxysm, Periodical, Start, Tetany, Throe, Tonic, Tonus, Trismus, Twinge, Twitch

▷ **Spasmodic** may indicate an anagram

Spastic Athetoid, Clonic, Jerky

Spat(s) Bicker, Brattle, Gaiters, Legging, Quarrel, Shower, Tiff

Spate Flood, Sluice, Torrent

Spatter Disject, Ja(u)p, Scatter, Splash, Spot, Sprinkle

▷ **Spattered** may indicate an anagram

Spawn(ing), Spawning place Anadromous, Blot, Fry, Progeny, Propagate, Redd, Roud, Seed, Spat, Spet, Spit

Speak(er), Speaking Address, Articulate, Broach, Chat, Cicero, Collocuter, Communicate, Converse, Coo, Declaim, Dilate, Discourse, Diseur, Dwell, Effable, Elocution, Eloquent, Expatiate, Express, Extemporise, Filibuster, Intercom, Intone, Inveigh, Jabber, Jaw, Lip, Loq, Mang, Mention, Mina, Mike, Mouth, Mouthpiece, Nark, Open, Orate, Orator, Palaver, Parlance, Parley, Pontificate, Prate, Preach, Prelector, Rhetor, ➤ SAY, Sayne, Spout, Spruik, Squawk box, Stump, Talk, Tannoy®, Tongue, Trap, Tweeter, Utter, Voice, Waffle, Witter, Word

Speakeasy Fluent, Shebeen

Spear Ash, Asparagus, Assagai, Assegai, Dart, Gad, Gavelock, Gig, Gungnir, Hastate, Impale, Javelin, Lance(gay), Launcegaye, Leister, Morris-pike, Partisan, Pierce, Pike, Pilum, Skewer, Spike, Trident, Trisul(a), Waster

Spear-rest Feutre, Fewter

Special Ad hoc, Constable, Designer, Distinctive, Extra, Important, Notable, Notanda, Particular, Peculiar, Specific

Specialise, Specialist(s) Authority, Concentrate, Connoisseur, Consultant, ENT, Expert, Illuminati, Maestro, Major, Quant, Recondite, Technician

Species Class, Genre, Genus, Kind, Strain, Taxa

Specific(ally), Specified, Specify As, Ascribe, Assign, Concretize, Cure, Define, Detail, Explicit, Full-blown, Itemise, Medicine, Namely, Precise, Remedy, Sp, Special, State, Stipulate, The, Trivial

Specimen(s) Example, Exempla, Imago, Model, Sample, Slide, Swab, Topotype

Specious False, Glib, Hollow, Plausible, Spurious

Speck(le) Atom, Bit, Dot, Fleck, Floater, Freckle, Muscae volitantes, Particle, Peep(e), Pip, Spreckle, Stud

Spectacle(d), Spectacles, Spectacular Arresting, Barnacles, Bifocals, Blazers, Blinks, Bossers, Cheaters, Colourful, Epic, Escolar, Giglamps, Glasses, Goggles, Nose-nippers, Oo, Optical, Outspeckle, Pageant, Pince-nez, Pomp, Preserves, Raree-show, Scene, Show, Sight, Son et lumière, Sunglasses, Tamasha, Tattoo

Spectator(s) Bystander, Dedans, Etagère, Eyer, Gallery, Gate, Groundling, Kibitzer, Observer, Onlooker, Standerby, Witness

Spectograph Aston

Spectral, Spectre Apparition, Boggle, Bogy, Eidolon, Empusa, Ghost, Idola, Iridal, Malmag, Phantasm, Phantom, Phasma, Spirit, Spook, Tarsier, Walking-straw, Wraith

Spectrum Iris, Rainbow, Sunbow, Sundog, Visible

Speculate, Speculative, Speculator Arbitrage, Bear, Better, Bull, Conjecture, Flier, Flyer, Gamble, Guess, Ideology, If, Imagine, Meditate, Notional, Operate, Pinhooker, Shark, Stag, Theoretical, Theorise, Theory, Thought, Trade, Wonder

Speech, Speech element Accents, Address, Argot, Articulation, Bunkum, Burr, Delivery, Dialect, Diatribe, Diction, Direct, Dithyramb, English, Eulogy, Free, Gab, Glossolalia, Harangue, Idiolect, Idiom, Indirect, Jargon, Keynote, Lallation, ➤ LANGUAGE, Lingua franca, Litany, Monologue, Morph(eme), Motherese, Oral, Oration, Parabasis, Parle, Peroration, Phasis, Philippic, Prolocution, Prolog(ue), Reported, Rhetoric, Sandhi, Screed, Sermon, Side, Slang, Soliloquy, Talk, Tirade, Tongue, Vach, Visible, Voice

Speech defect, Speech disease Dysarthria, Dysphasia, Dysphoria, Echolalia, Idioglossia, Lisp, Palilalia, Paralalia, Paraphasia, Pararthria, Psellism, Stammer, Stutter

Speechless Alogia, Dumb, Dumbstruck, Inarticulate, Mute, Silent

Speed(ily), Speedy Accelerate, Alacrity, Amain, Amphetamine, Apace, Bat, Belive, Belt, Breakneck, Burn, Celerity, Clip, Dart, Despatch, DIN, Dispatch, Expedite, Fangy, Fast, Fleet, Further, Gait, Gallop, Goer, Gun, Haste, Hie, Hotfoot, Hypersonic, Induce, Knot, Lick, Mach, Merchant, MPH, ➤ PACE, Phase, Pike, Post-haste, Pronto, Race, Rapidity, Rate, RPS, Scorch, Scud, Scurr, Skirr, Soon, Spank, Split, Stringendo, Supersonic, Swift, Tach, Tear, Tempo, V, Velocity, Vroom, Whid, Wing

Speedwell Brooklime, Fluellin, Germander, Veronica

Spelaean Troglodyte

Spelk Skelf, Splinter

Spell(ing) Abracadabra, Bewitch, Bout, Cantrip, Charm, Conjuration, Do, Elf-shoot, Enchantment, Entrance, Fit, Go, Gri(s)-gri(s), Hex, Incantation, Innings, Jettatura, Juju, Knur, ➤ MAGIC, Need-fire, Nomic, Orthography,

Period, Philter, Philtre, Pinyin, Relieve, Ride, Romaji, Run, Rune, Scat, Shot, Signify, Snap, Snatch, Sorcery, Sp, Spasm, Splinter, Stint, Stretch, Tack, Tour, Trick, Turn, Weird, Whammy, Witchcraft

Spelling-book ABC, Grimoire

Spencer Topcoat, Tracy, Vest

Spend(ing) Anticipate, Birl, Blue, Boondoggling, Consume, Deplete, Disburse, Exhaust, Fritter, Live, Outlay, Pass, Pay, Splash, Splurge, Ware

Spendthrift Prodigal, Profligate, Profuser, Scattergood, Wastrel

Spent Consumed, Dead, Done, Expended, Stale, Tired, Used, Weak

Sperm Seed, Semen

Spew Eject, Emit, Gush, Spit, Vomit

Sphagnum Moss, Peat

Sphere, Spherical Armillary, Celestial, Discipline, Element, Field, Firmament, Globe, Mound, Orb(it), Planet, Prolate, Province, Realm, Theatre, Wheel

Sphinx Hawk-moth, Oracle, Riddler

Spice, Spicy Amomum, Anise, Aniseed, Aryl, Cardamom, Cassareep, Cassaripe, Cinnamon, Clove, Clow, Coriander, Cubeb, Cum(m)in, Dash, Devil, Garam masala, Ginger, Mace, Malaguetta, Marjoram, Masala, Myrrh, Nutmeg, Oregano, Paprika, Peppercorn, Pimento, Piperic, Piquant, Salsa verde, Season, Stacte, Staragen, Tamal(e), Tamara, Tansy, Tarragon, Taste, Turmeric, Vanilla, Variety

Spick Dink, Neat, Spike, Tidy

Spicule Sclere, Tetract

Spider(s) Anancy, Ananse, Arachnid, Aranea, Araneida, Arthrapodal, Attercop, Bird, Bobbejaan, Cardinal, Cheesemite, Chelicerate, Citigrade, Diadem, Epeira, Epeirid, Ethercap, Ettercap, Funnel-web, Harvester, Harvestman, Hunting, Huntsman, Jumping, Katipo, Lycosa, Mite, Money, Mygale, Orb-weaver, Pan, Phalangid, Podogona, Pycnogonid, Red, Redback, Rest, Ricinulei, Saltigrade, Solifugae, Solpuga, Spinner, Strap, Tarantula, Telary, Trapdoor, Violin, Water, Wolf

Spiderwort Tradescantia

Spiel Spruik

Spignel Baldmoney, Meu

Spigot Plug

Spike(d) Barb, Brod, Calk, Calt(h)rop, Chape, Cloy, Crampon, Ear, Fid, Foil, Gad, Goad, Grama, Herissé, Impale, Lace, Locusta, Marlin(e), Nail, ➤ PIERCE, Point, Pricket, Prong, Puseyite, Rod, Sharp, Shod, Skewer, Spadix, Spear, Spicate, Spicule, Strobiloid, Tang, Thorn, Tine

Spill(age) Divulge, Drop, Fidibus, Jackstraw, Lamplighter, Leakage, Let, Overflow, Overset, Scail, Scale, Shed, Skail, Slop, Stillicide, Taper, Tumble

Spin(ner), Spinning Arachne, Birl, Cribellum, Cut, Dextrorse, DJ, Flat, Flip, Gimp, Googly, Gymp, Gyrate, Gyre, Hurl, Lachesis, Mole, Nun, Peg-top, Pirouette, Precess, Prolong, Purl, Rev(olve), Ride, Rotate, Screw, Sinistrorse, Slide, Spider, Stator, Strobic, Swirl, Swivel, Throstle, Tirl, Toss, Trill, Twirl, Twist, Wheel, Whirl, Work

Spinach Florentine, Orach(e)

Spinal (chord), Spine, Spiny Acromion, Aculeus, Areole, Backbone, Barb, Chine, Coccyx, Column, Doorn, Epidural, Muricate, Myelon, Notochord, Ocotillo, Prickle, Quill, Rachial, Ray, R(h)achis, Thorn, Tragacanth

Spindle(-shanks), Spindly Arbor, Bobbin, Fusee, Fusiform, Fusil, Pin, Scrag, Staff

▶ **Spine** see SPINAL

Spinel Balas, Picotite

Spineless Muticous, Timid, Weak

Spinn(e)y Shaw

Spinning-wheel Chark(h)a

Spinster Discovert, Feme sole, Old maid, Tabby

Spiral Cochlea, Coil, Dextrorse, Gyrate, Helical, Helix, Inflationary, Logarithmic, Loxodromical, Screw, Scroll, Sinistrorse, Tailspin, Turbinate, Volute, Whorl, Wind

Spire Broach, Flèche, Peak, Shaft, Steeple

Spirit(ed) Ahriman, Akvavit, Alcohol, Angel, Animation, Aqua vitae, Aquavit, Arak, Arch(a)eus, Ardent, Ariel, Arrack, Asmoday, Blithe, Bogle, Brandy, Bravura, Brio, Buggan(e), Buggin, Cant, Cherub, Courage, Creature, Crouse, Daemon, Dash, Deev, Deva, Distillation, Div, Djinn(i), Domdaniel, ▶ DRINK, Dryad, Duende, Duppy, Dybbuk, Eblis, Eidolon, Elan, Element(al), Emit, Empusa, Entrain, Esprit, Essence, Ethos, Eudemon, Faints, Familiar, Feints, Feisty, Feni, Fenny, Fetich(e), Fetish, Fettle, Fight, Firewater, Gamy, Geist, Geneva, Genie, Genius, ▶ GHOST, Ghoul, Ginger, Ginn, Gism, Glendoveer, Go, Grappa, Gremlin, Grit, Grog, Gumption, Gytrash, Heart, Hollands, Huaca, Imp, Incubus, Indwelt, Jann, Jinn(i), Jinnee, Jism, Ka, Kachina, Kelpie, Kindred, Kirsch, Kobold, Larva, Lemur(e), Liquor, Lively, Loki, Manes, Manito(u), Mare, Marid, Metal, Meths, Methyl(ated), Mettle, Mindererus, Mobbie, Mobby, Morale, Nain rouge, Nis, Nix, Nobody, Numen, Ondine, Orenda, Panache, Paraclete, Pecker, Pep, Peri, Pernod®, Petrol, Phantom, Pluck(y), Pneuma, Poltergeist, Pooka, Poteen, Presence, Proof, Psyche, Puck, Python, Racy, Rakshos(a), Rosicrucian, Ruin, Rum(bullion), Rye, Samshoo, Samshu, Schnapps, Seraph, Shade, Shadow, Shaitan, She'ol, Short, Smeddum, Spectre, Spright, Sprite, Spunk, Steam, Strunt, Surgical, Sylph, Tafia, Tangie, Taniwha, Team, Tequila, Tokoloshe, Ton, Turps, Undine, Verve, Vigour, Vim, Vodka, Voodoo, Weltgeist, White, Wili, Witblits, Wood, Wraith, Zeitgeist, Zephon, Zing

Spiritless Craven, Dowf, Insipid, Languid, Meek, Milksop, Poor, Tame, Vapid

Spirit-level Vial

Spiritual Aerie, Aery, Coon-song, Ecclesiastic, Ethereous, Eyrie, Eyry, Incorporeal, Negro, Planchette

Spirt Gush, Jet, Rush

Spit(ting), Spittle Barbecue, Broach, Chersonese, Dead ringer, Dribble, Drool, Emptysis, Eructate, Expectorate, Fuff, Gob, Golly, Gooby, Grill,

Hawk, Impale, Jack, Lookalike, Peninsula, Ras, Ringer, Rotisserie, Saliva, Skewer, Slag, Spade(ful), Spawl, Sputter, Sputum, Tombolo, Yesk, Yex

Spite(ful) Grimalkin, Harridan, Irrespective, Malevolent, Malgrado, Malice, Mau(l)gre, Petty, Pique, Rancour, Spleen, Venom, Waspish

Spitfire Cacafogo, Cacafuego, Wildcat

Spittoon Cuspidor(e)

Spiv Lair, Rorter

Splash Blash, Blue, Dabble, Dash, Dog, Drip, Feature, Flouse, Fl(o)ush, Gardyloo, Jabble, Ja(u)p, Jirble, Paddle, Plap, Plop, Plowter, Sket, Slosh, Soda, Sozzle, Spairge, Spat(ter), Spectacle, Splat(ch), Splatter, Splodge, Splosh, Splotch, Spray, Spree, Squatter, Swash, Swatter, Water, Wet

Splay(ed) Flew, Flue, Patte(e), Spread

Spleen Acrimony, Bite, Lien, Melt, Milt(z), Pip, Wrath

Splendid, Splendour Ah, Braw, Brilliant, Bully, Capital, Champion, Clinker, Dandy, Eclat, Effulgent, Excellent, Fine, Finery, Gallant, Garish, Glitterand, Glittering, Glorious, Glory, Gorgeous, Grand(eur), Grandiose, Ha, Heroic, Lustrous, Mooi, Noble, Palatial, Panache, Pomp, Proud, Radiant, Rich, Ripping, Stunning, Super(b), Wally

Splice Braid, Join, Knit, Wed

▷ **Spliced** may indicate an anagram

Splint Brace, Cal(l)iper, Splenial

Splinter(s) Bone-setter, Breakaway, Flinder, Fragment, Matchwood, Shatter, Shiver, Skelf, Sliver, Spale, Spall, Speel, Spelk, Spicula, Spill

Split Axe, Banana, Bifid, Bifurcate, Bisect, Break, Chasm, Chine, Chop, Clint, Clove(n), Crack, Crevasse, Cut, Departmentalise, Disjoin, Distrix, ➤ DIVIDE, Division, Divorce, End, Fissile, Fissure, Grass, Lacerate, Partition, Red(d), Rift(e), Rip, Rive, Ryve, Schism, Scissor, Segregate, Separate, Septemfid, Sever, Share, Skive, Slit, Sliver, Spall, Spalt, Speld, Tattle, Tmesis, Told, To-rend, To-tear, Wedge

▷ **Split** may indicate a word to become two; one word inside another; or a connection with Yugoslavia

Splodge, Splotch Blot, Drop, Splash

Splurge Binge, Indulge, Lavish, Spend, Splash, Spree

Splutter Chug, Expectorate, Fizz, Gutter, Spray, Stammer

Spoil(s), Spoilt Addle, Agrise, Agrize, Agryze, Blight, Blunk, Booty, Bribe, Coddle, Corrupt, ➤ DAMAGE, Dampen, Deface, Defect, Deform, Dish, Foul, Hames, Harm, Impair(ed), Indulge, Loot, Maderise, Maltreat, Mar, Mardy, Muck, Mutilate, Mux, Pamper, Pet, Pickings, Pie, Plunder, Prize, Queer, Rait, Rate, Ravage, Ret, Rot, Ruin, Scupper, Spuly(i)e, Swag, Taint, Tarnish, Vitiate, Winnings

▷ **Spoil(ed), Spoilt** may indicate an anagram

Spoilsport Damper, Party pooper, Wet blanket, Wowser

Spoke(s) Concentric, Radius, Ray, Rung, Said, Sed, Strut

▷ **Spoken** may indicate the sound of a word or letter

Spokesman Foreman, Mouthpiece, Orator, Prophet, Representative

Spoliation, Spoliative Devastation, Pillage, Plunder, Predatory, Reif

Sponge(r), Spongy Ambatch, Argentine, Battenburg, Bum, Cadge, Cake, Diact, Diploe, Fozy, Free-loader, Glass-rope, Hexact, Lig, Lithistid(a), Loofa(h), Madeira, Madeleine, Mooch, Mop, Mouch, Mump, Parasite, Parazoa, Pentact, Porifera(n), Quandong, Rhabdus, Sarcenchyme, Scambler, Schnorrer, Scrounge, Shark, Shool, Siphonophora, Smell-feast, Sooner, Sop, Sucker, Swab, Sycophant, Tetract, Tiramisu, Tylote, Velamen, Venus's flowerbasket, Wangle, Wipe, Zimocca, Zoophyte

Sponsor(ship) Aegis, Angel, Backer, Egis, Finance, Godfather, Godparent, Gossip, Guarantor, Lyceum, Patron, Surety

Spontaneous Autonomic, Gratuitous, Immediate, Impromptu, Impulsive, Instant, Intuitive, Natural, Ultroneus, Unasked

Spoof Chouse, Cozenage, Deception, Delusion, Fallacy, ➤ HOAX, Imposture, Ramp, Swindle, Trick

Spook(s), Spooky CIA, Eerie, Fantom, Frightening, Ghost, Phantom, Shade

Spool Bobbin, Capstan, Pirn, Reel, Trundle

Spoon(ful), Spoon-shaped Apostle, Canoodle, Cochlear, Dollop, Dose, Gibby, Labis, Ladle, Mote, Neck, Rat-tail, Runcible, Scoop, Scud, Server, Spatula, Sucket, Woo, Wooden

Spoonerism Marrowsky, Metathesis

Spoor Trace, Track, Trail

Sporadic Fitful, Isolated, Occasional, Patchy

Spore (case) Conidium, Fungus, Glomerule, Lenticel, Seed, Sorus, Telium, Uredinium

Sporran Pock

Sport(s), Sporting, Sportive Aikido, Amusement, Angling, Aquatics, Autocross, Blood, Bonspiel, Breakaway, Brick, By-form, Contact, Curling, Cyclo-cross, Daff, Dalliance, Dally, Deviant, Drag-racing, Field, Freak, Frisky, Frolic, Fun, ➤ GAME, Gent, Gig, In, Joke, Karate, Kickboxing, Korfball, Laik, Lake, Langlauf, Lark, Merimake, Merry, Morph, Mutagen, Octopush, Orienteering, Pal, Paragliding, Parasailing, Parascending, Paraskiing, Polo, Recreate, Rogue, RU, Shinny, Shinty, Skijoring, Spectator, Speed-skating, Speedway, Squash, Steeplechase, Sumo, Tournament, Tourney, Toy, Trampolining, Wakeboarding, Water polo, Wear, Weightlifting, Windsurfing, Wrestling

▷ **Sport(s)** may indicate an anagram

Sportsman, Sportsmen All-rounder, Athlete, Blue, Corinthian, Hunter, Nimrod, Pentathlete, Pitcher, Shamateur, Shikaree, Shikari

Spot(s), Spotted, Spotting, Spotty Ace, Acne, Areola, Areole, Baily's beads, Bausond, Bead, Beauty, Blackhead, Blain, Blemish, Blind, Blip, Blob, Blot, Blotch(ed), Blur, Brind(l)ed, Carbuncle, Caruncle, Cash, Check, Cloud, Colon, Comedo, Corner, Curn, Cyst, Dance, Dapple(-bay), Dick, Discern, Discover, Dot, Drop, Eruption, Espy, Eye, Facula, Fleck, Floater, Fogdog, Foxed, Freak, Furuncle, G, Gay, Gricer, Gräfenberg, Guttate, High, Hot, Jam, Leaf, Lentago, Location, Loran, Macle, Mackle, Macul(at)e, Mail, Meal, Measly, Microdot, Milium, Moil, Mole, Morbilli, Mote, Muscae volitantes,

Note, Ocellar, Ocellus, Paca, Papule, Paraselene, Pardal, Parhelion, Patch, Peep(e), Penalty, Petechia, Pied, Pimple, Pin, Pip, Place, Plook, Plouk, Pock, Punctuate, Pupil, Pustule, Quat, Radar, Rash, Recognise, Red, Rose-drop, Scotoma, Skewbald, Smut, Soft, Speck(le), Speculum, Splodge, Spy, Stigma, Sully, Taint, Touch, Weak, Whelk, Whitehead, X, Zit

Spotless Immaculate, Virginal

Spotlight Baby, Brute

Spot on To a t

Spouse Companion, Consort, F(i)ere, Hubby, Husband, Mate, Oppo, Partner, Pheer, Pirrauru, Wife, Xant(h)ippe

Spout(er) Adjutage, Erupt, Gargoyle, Geyser, Grampus, Gush, Impawn, Jet, Mouth, Nozzle, Orate, Pawn, Pourer, Raile, Rote, Spurt, Stream, Stroup, Talk, Tap, Vent

Sprain(ed) Crick, Reckan, Rick, Stave, Strain, Wrench, Wrick

Sprat Brit, Fish, Garvies, Garvock

Sprawl Loll, Scramble, Sprangle, Spread, Stretch, Urban

Spray Aerosol, Aigrette, Atomiser, Buttonhole, Corsage, Egret, Hair, Posy, Rose, Rosula, Shower, Sparge, Spindrift, Splash, Spoondrift, Sprent, Sprig, Sprinkle, Spritz, Strinkle, Syringe, Twig

▷ **Spray** may indicate an anagram

Spread(ing), Spreader Air, Apply, Banquet, Bestrew, Blow-out, Branch, Bush, Butter, Carpet, Centre, Contagious, Couch, Coverlet, Coverlid, Deploy, Diffract, Diffuse, Dilate, Disperse, Dissemination, Distribute, Divulge, Drape, Dripping, Elongate, Expand, Extend, Fan, Feast, Flare, Guac(h)amole, Honeycomb, Jam, Lay, Marge, Multiply, Nutter, Oleo, Open, Overgrow, Paste, Perfuse, Pervade, Pâté, Patent, Patulous, Picnic, Propagate, Radiate, Ran, Run, Scale, Set, Sheet, Slather, Smear, Smorgasbord, Sow, Span, Speld, Spelder, Spillover, Splay, Sprawl, Spray, Straw, Stretch, Strew, Strow, Suffuse, Teer, Unfold, Unguent, Widen, Wildfire

▷ **Spread** may indicate an anagram

Spree Bat, Beano, Bender, Binge, Bum, Bust, Carousal, Frolic, Jag, Jamboree, Juncate, Junket, Lark, Loose, Splore, Randan, Rantan, Razzle(-dazzle), Revel, Rouse, Tear, Ups(e)y

Sprig Brad, Branch, Cyme, Nail, Sien, Spray, Syen, Twig, Youth

Sprightly Agile, Airy, Chipper, Jaunty, Mercurial

Spring(s), Springtime, Springy Aganippe, Alice, Arise, Bolt, Bounce, Bound, Box, Bunt, Cabriole, Caper, Capriole, Castalian, Cavort, Cee, Coil, Dance, Elastic, Eye, Fount(ain), Germinate, Geyser, Grass, Hair, Helix, Hippocrene, Hop, Hot, Jump, Leap, Lent, Lep, Litt, Low-water, May, Originate, Persephone, Pierian, Pounce, Prance, Primavera, Resilient, Ribbon, Rise, Season, Skip, Snap, Spa, Spang, Spaw, Stem, Sulphur, Thermae, Thermal, Trampoline, Vault, Vaute, Vawte, Voar, Ware, Waterhole, Well(-head), Whip, Winterbourne

▷ **Spring(y)** may indicate an anagram

Springbok Amabokoboko

Springless Telega

Springtail Apterygota

Sprinkle(r) Asperge, Aspergill(um), Bedash, Bedrop, Bescatter, Caster, Dredge, Dust, Hyssop, Lard, Pouncet, Rose, Scatter, Shower, Sow, Spa(i)rge, Spatter, Splash, Spray, Spritz, Strinkle

Sprint(er) Burst, Dash, Race, Rash, Run, Rush, Wells

Sprite Apsaras, Croquemitaine, Echo, Elf, Fairy, Fiend, Genie, Goblin, Gremlin, Hobgoblin, Ondine, Puck, Spirit, Troll, Trow, Umbriel, Undine

Sprout Braird, Breer, Bud, Burgeon, Chit, Crop, Eye, Germ(inate), Grow, Pullulate, Shoot, Spire, Tendron, Vegetate

Spruce Dapper, Engelmann, Natty, Neat, Norway, Picea, Pitch-tree, Prink, Shipshape, Sitka, Smart, Spiff, Tidy, Tree, Trim, Tsuga

Spry Active, Agile, Constance, Dapper, Nimble, Volable

Spud Murphy, Potato, Spade, Tater, Tatie

Spume Eject, Foam, Froth, Lather, Spet, Spit

Spunk Courage, Grit, Pluck, Tinder

Spur Accourage, Activate, Calcar(ate), Encourage, Fame, Fire, Goad, Heel, Incite, Limb, Lye, Needle, Prick, Rippon, Rowel, Shoot, Spica, Stimulus, Strut, Stud, Tar, Urge

Spurge (tree) Candelilla, Euphorbia, Kamala, Poinsettia, Ricinus

Spurious Adulterine, Apocryphal, Bogus, Counterfeit, Dog, Phoney, Pseudo, Sciolism

▷ **Spurious** may indicate an anagram

Spurn Despise, Disdain, Ignore, Jilt, Reject, ➤ SCORN, Shun

Spurt Burst, Geyser, Jet, Outburst, Pump, Spout

Sputter Fizzle, Spit, Splutter, Stutter

Spy, Spies Agent, Beagle, Caleb, CIA, Descry, Dicker, Emissary, Fink, Informer, Keeker, Mata Hari, MI, Mole, Mouchard, Nark, Nose, Operative, Pimp, Plant, Pry, Recce, Scout, See, Setter, Shadow, Sinon, Sleeper, Spetsnaz, Spook, Tout, Wait

Spyhole Eyelet, Judas-hole, Oillet, Peephole

Squab Chubby, Cushion, Obese

Squabble Argue, Bicker, Quarrel, Rhubarb, Row, Scrap

Squad(ron) Band, Blue, Company, Crew, Death, Drugs, Escadrille, Firing, Flying, Fraud, Hit, Nahal, Platoon, Red, Snatch, Vice, Wing

Squalid, Squalor Abject, Colluvies, Dinge, Dingy, Filth, Frowsy, Grungy, Poverty, Scuzzy, Seedy, Sleazy, Slum(my), Slurb, Sordid

Squall Blast, Blow, Commotion, Cry, Drow, Flaw, Flurry, Gust, Sumatra, Wail, Yell, Yowl

Squander Blow, Blue, Fritter, Frivol, Mucker, Slather, Splash, Splurge, Ware, ➤ WASTE

Square(d), Squares Agree, Anta, Ashlar, Ashler, Bang, Belgrave, Berkeley, Block, Bribe, Chequer, Compone, Compony, Corny, Deal, Dinkum, Even(s), Fair, Fog(e)y, Forty-nine, Fossil, Four, Gobony, Grey, Grosvenor, Leicester, Level, Magic, Meal, Nasik, Neandert(h)aler, Nine, Norma, Old-fashioned,

Palm, Passé, Pay, Perfect, Piazza, Place, Plaza, Platz, Quad(rangle), Quadrate, Quarry, Quits, Red, Rood, S, Set(t), Sloane, Solid, Squier, Squire, Straight, T, Tee, Times, Traditionalist, Trafalgar, Unhip

Squash Adpress, Butternut, Conglomerate, Crush, Gourd, Kia-ora, Knead, Marrow, Mash, Oblate, Pattypan, Press, Pulp, Silence, Slay, Slew, Slue, Squidge, Suppress, Torpedo

Squat(ter) Bywoner, Crouch, Croup(e), Dumpy, Fubby, Fubsy, Hunker, Pudsey, Pyknic, Rook, Ruck, Sit, Spud, Stubby, Swatter, Usucaption

Squaw Kloo(t)chman

Squawk Complain, Cry, Scrauch, Scraugh

Squeak(er) Cheep, Creak, Peep, Pip, Scroop, Shoat, Squeal

Squeal(er) Blow, Eek, Howl, Inform, Pig, Screech, Sing, Sneak, Tell, Wee

Squeamish(ness) Delicate, Disgust, Nervous, Prudish, Queasy, Reluctant

Squeeze Bleed, Chirt, Coll, Compress, Concertina, Constrict, Cram, Crowd, Crush, Dispunge, Exact, Express, Extort, Hug, Jam, Mangle, Milk, Preace, Press, Sandwich, Sap, Scrooge, Scrouge, Scrowdge, Scruze, Shoehorn, Squash, Squish, Sweat, Thrutch, Wring

Squelch Gurgle, Squash, Squish, Subdue

Squib Banger, Damp, Firework, Lampoon

Squid Calamari, Calamary, Cephalopod, Ink-fish, Loligo, Mortar, Nautilus, Octopus

Squiffy Drunk, Tiddley

▷ **Squiggle** may indicate an anagram

Squint(ing) Boss-eyed, Cast, Cock-eye, Cross-eye, Glance, Gledge, Glee, Gley, Heterophoria, Louche, Proptosis, Skellie, Skelly, Sken, Squin(n)y, Strabism, Swivel-eye, Vergence, Wall-eye

Squire Armiger(o), Beau, Donzel, Escort, Hardcastle, Headlong, Land-owner, Scutiger, Swain, Western

Squirm(ing) Reptation, Twist, Wriggle, Writhe

Squirrel, Squirrel's nest Aye-aye, Boomer, Bun, Cage, Chickaree, Chipmuck, Chipmunk, Dray, Drey, Flickertail, Fox, Gopher, Grey, Ground, Hackee, Hoard(er), Meerkat, Petaurist, Phalanger, Red, Sciuroid, Sewellel, Skug, S(o)uslik, Spermophile, Taguan, Vair, Zizel

Squirt(er) Chirt, Cockalorum, Douche, Jet, Scoosh, Scoot, Skoosh, Spirt, Spout, Spritz, Urochorda, Wet, Whiffet, Whippersnapper

Sri Lanka Ceylon, CL, Serendip, Vedda

St Saint, Street

Stab Bayonet, Crease, Creese, Effort, Go, Gore, Guess, Jab, Knife, Kreese, Kris, Lancinate, Pang, Pierce, Pink, Poniard, Prick, Prong, Stick, Stiletto, Wound

Stabilise(r), Stability Aileron, Balance, Emulsifier, Even, Maintain, Peg, Permanence, Plateau, Poise, Steady

Stable(s) Augean, Balanced, Byre, Constant, Durable, Firm, Livery, Manger, Mews, Poise, Secure, Solid, Sound, Stall, Static(al), Steadfast, Steady, Stud, Sure

Stableman Groom, Lad, Ostler

Stachys Betony

Stack Accumulate, Chimney, Clamp, Cock, End, Funnel, Heap, Lum, ➤ PILE, Rick, Shock, Staddle

Stadium Arena, Ballpark, Bowl, Circus, Circus Maximus, Coliseum, Hippodrome, Velodrome

Staff Alpenstock, Ash-plant, Bato(o)n, Bourdon, Burden, Caduceus, Cane, Crook, Crosier, Cross(e), Crozier, Crutch, Cudgel, Entourage, Equerry, Etat-major, Faculty, Ferula, Ferule, Flagpole, Linstock, Lituus, Mace, Omlah, Personnel, Pike, Pole, Rod, Runic, Sceptre, Skeleton, Stave, Stick, Taiaha, Tapsmen, Thyrsus, Truncheon, Verge, Wand, Workers, Workforce

Stag Brocket, Buck, Deer, Imperial, Line, Male, Party, Royal, Rutter, Ten-pointer, Wapiti

Stage Act, Anaphase, Apron, Arena, Bema, Boards, Catasta, Chrysalis, Committee, Diligence, Dog-leg, Estrade, Fargo, Fit-up, Grade, Juncture, Key, Landing, Leg, Level, Metaphase, Milestone, Moment, Mount, Oidium, Phase, Phasis, Pier, Pin, Platform, Point, Prophase, PS, Puberty, Report, Rostrum, Scene, Sensorimeter, Sound, Stadium, Step, Stor(e)y, Subimago, Theatre, Thrust, Transition, Trek, Yuga

Stage-coach Diligence, Thoroughbrace

Stagecraft Pinafore

Stagger(ed) Alternate, Amaze, Astichous, Awhape, Daidle, Falter, Floor, Lurch, Recoil, Reel, Rock, Shock, Stoiter, Stot(ter), Stumble, Sway, Teeter, Thunderstricken, Thunderstruck, Titubate, Tolter, Totter, Wamble, Wintle

▷ **Staggered** may indicate an anagram

Stagirite, Stagyrite Aristotle

Stagnant, Stagnation Foul, Inert, Scummy, Stasis, Static

Staid Decorous, Demure, Formal, Grave, Matronly, Prim, Sad, Sober

Stain(er) Aniline, Bedye, Besmirch, Blemish, Blot, Blotch, Discolour, Dishonour, Dye, Embrue, Ensanguine, Eosin, Fox, Gram's, Grime, Imbrue, Iodophile, Keel, Maculate, Mail, Meal, Mote, Slur, Smirch, Smit, Soil, Splodge, Splotch, Stigma, Taint, Tarnish, Tinge, Tint, Woad

Stair(case), Stairs Apples, Apples and pears, Caracol(e), Cochlea, Companionway, Escalator, Flight, Perron, Rung, Spiral, Step, Tread, Turnpike, Vice, Wapping

Stake Ante, Bet, Claim, Gage, Holding, Impale, Impone, Interest, Lay, Loggat, Mark, Mise, Paal, Pale, Paliform, Paling, Palisade, Peel, Peg, Pele, Picket, Pile, Play, Post, Pot, Punt, Rest, Revie, Risk, Septleva, Spike, Spile, Stang, Stob, Sweep, Tether, Vie, Wager

Stalactite Dripstone, Helictite, Lansfordite, Soda straw

Stale Aged, Banal, Flat, Fozy, Frowsty, Hackneyed, Handle, Hoary, Mouldy, Musty, Old, Pretext, Rancid, Urine, Worn

▷ **Stale** may indicate an obsolete word

Stalemate Deadlock, Dilemma, Hindrance, Impasse, Standoff, Zugswang

Stalk(s) Anthophore, Bun, Cane, Follow, Funicle, Garb(e), Ha(u)lm, Keck(s), Kecksey, Keksye, Kex, Pedicel, Pedicle, Peduncle, Petiole, Petiolule,

Phyllode, Pursue, Scape, Seta, Shaw, Spear, Spire, Stem, Sterigma, Stipe(s), Stride, Strig, Strut, Stubble, Stump, Trail, Yolk

Stalking-horse Stale

Stall(s) Arrest, Bay, Booth, Box, Bulk, Crib, ➤ DELAY, Floor, Flypitch, Hedge, Kiosk, Loose-box, Orchestra, Pen, Pew, Prebendal, Seat, Shamble, Sideshow, Stand, Stasidion, Temporise, Trap, Traverse, Travis, Trevis(s)

Stallion Cooser, Cuisser, Cusser, Entire, ➤ HORSE, Stag, Staig, Stonehorse, Stud

Stalwart Anchor-man, Buirdly, Firm, Manful, Robust, Sturdy, Valiant

Stamen(ed) Androecium, Octandria, Polyandria

Stamina Endurance, Fibre, Fortitude, Guts, Last, Stamen, Stay, Steel

Stammer(ing) Balbutient, Hesitate, Hum, Psellism, Stumble, ➤ STUTTER, Waffle

Stamp(s), Stamped Appel, Cast, Character, Date(r), Die, Enface, Frank, Impress, Imprint, Incuse, Label, Mint, Pane, Penny black, Perfin, Philately, Pintadera, Press(ion), Rubber, Seal, Seebeck, Signet, Spif, Strike, Swage, Tête-bêche, Touch, Trading, Trample, Tromp, Type

Stamp-collecting Philately, Timbrology, Timbrophily

Stampede Debacle, Flight, Panic, Rampage, ➤ RUSH

Stance Attitude, Pose, Position, Posture

Stand(ing), Stand up Apron, Arraign, Attitude, Base, Be, Bear, Bide, Binnacle, Bipod, Bristle, Brook, Canterbury, Caste, Confrontation, Crease, Dais, Degree, Dock, Dree, Easel, Etagère, Face, Foothold, Freeze, Gantry, Gueridon, Hob, Insulator, Klinostat, Last, Lectern, Nef, Odour, One-night, Ovation, Place, Plant, Podium, Pose, Position, Pou sto, Prestige, Promenade, Protest, Rack, Rank, Regent, Remain, Represent, Repute, Rise, Stall, Statant, Station, ➤ STATUS, Stay, Stillage, Stock, Stool, Straddle, Straphang, Stroddle, Strut, Table, Tantalus, Terrace, ➤ TREAT, Tree, Tripod, Trivet, Upright, Whatnot

Standard(s) Banner, Base, Basic, Benchmark, Bogey, Canon, Classic(al), Cocker, Colour(s), Criterion, Eagle, English, Ethics, Examplar, Example, Exemplar, Flag, Ga(u)ge, Gold, Gonfalon, Labarum, Level, Living, Model, Norm(a), Normal, Numeraire, Old Glory, Par, Parker Morris, Pennon, Principle, Rate, Regular, Rod, Rose, Routine, ➤ RULE, Staple, Sterling, Stock, Time, Touchstone, Tricolour, Troy, Usual, Valuta, Vexillum, Yardstick

Standard-bearer Alferez, Cornet, Ensign, Vexillary

Stand-by Adminicle, Reserve, Substitute, Support, Understudy

Stand-in Double, Locum, Sub(stitute), Surrogate, Temp, Understudy

Standish Miles

Stand-off(ish) Aloof, Remote, Reserved, Stalemate, Upstage

Standpoint Angle

Standstill Deadset, Halt, Jam

Stanley Baldwin, Knife, Rupert

Stannic Tin

Stanza Heroic, Ottava, Poem, Sixaine, Spenserian, Staff, Stave, Tetrastich, Verse

Staple Basic, Bread, Chief, Maize, Pin

Star(s) Achernar, Acrux, Agena, Aldebaran, Algol, Alioth, Alkaid, Alpha, Altair, Andromeda, Antares, Aquila, Arcturus, Argo, Aster(isk), Auriga, Barnard's, Bellatrix, Beta(crucis), Betelgeuse, Betelgeuze, Big Dipper, Binary, Body, Bootes, Brown dwarf, Calaeno, Canopus, Capella, Carbon, Carina, Cassiopeia, Castor, Celebrity, Centaurus, Cepheus, Ceres, Chamber, Circinus, Circumpolar, Columba, Comet, Constant, Constellation, Cygnus, Cynosure, Dark, Delphinus, Delta, Deneb(ola), Dolphin, Dorado, Draco, Dubhe, Dwarf, Epsilon, Equuleus, Esther, E(s)toile, Evening, Falling, Feature, Film, Fixed, Fomalhaut, Fornax, Galaxy, Gamma, Grus, Headline, Hero, Hesperus, Hexagram, Hyad(e)s, Idol, Indus, Lead, Lion, Little Dipper, Lode, Lucifer, Lupus, Lyra, Megrez, Mensa, Merak, Merope, Meteor(ite), Mira, Mizar, Mogen David, Morning, Movie, Mullet, Neutron, Norma, North, Nova, Octans, Ophiuchus, Orion's belt, Pavo, Pegasean, Pentacle, Pentagram, (The) Pointers, Personality, Phecda, Phoenix, Phosphor(us), Pip, Pleiades, Plough, Pointer, Polar, Polaris, Pole, Pollux, Praesepe, Principal, Procyon, Proxima centaur, Proximo, Psyche, Pulsar, Pulsating, Puppis, Quasar, Radio, Red dwarf, Red giant, Regulus, Rigel, Rigil, Sabaism, Saturn, Scorpius, Serpens, Shell, Shine, Shooting, Sidereal, Sirius, Sol, Solomon's seal, Sothis, Spangle, Spica, Starn(ie), Stellar, Stern, Sterope, Supergiant, Supernova, Synasty, Theta, Top-liner, Triones, Uranus, Ursa, Variable, Vedette, Vega, Vela, Venus, Vesper, Virgo, Volans, Wagon(er), Waggoner, Whale, White dwarf, Wolf-Rayet, Zeta

Starboard Right

Starch(y), Starch producer Amyloid, Arrowroot, Cassava, Ceremony, Congee, Conjee, Coontie, Coonty, Cycad, Farina, Fecula, Formal, Glycogen, Manioc, Maranta, Pentosan, Stamina, Statolith, Tapioca, Tous-les-mois

Stare Eyeball, Fisheye, Gape, Gapeseed, Gawp, Gaze, Goggle, Gorp, Look, Outface, Peer, Rubberneck

Starfish Asterid, Asteroid(ea), Bipinnaria, Brittlestar, Ophiurid, Radiata

Star-gaze(r), Star-gazing Astrodome, Astronomy, Copernicus

Stark Apparent, Austere, Bald, Bare, Gaunt, Harsh, Naked, Nude, Sheer, Stiff, Utterly

Starling Bird, Murmuration, Pastor, Stare

Star of Bethlehem Chincherinchee, Chinkerinchee

Start(ed), Starter Ab ovo, Abrade, Abraid, Abray, Activate, Actuate, Begin, Boggle, Broach, Bug, Chance, Commence, Crank, Create, Dart, Ean, Embryo, Face-off, False, Fire, Flinch, Float, Flush, Flying, Found, Gambit, Gan, Genesis, Getaway, Gun, Handicap, Hot-wire, Impetus, Imprimis, Incept(ion), Initiate, Instigate, Institute, Intro, Jerk, Jump, Jump-off, Kick-off, L, Lag, Launch, Lead, Off, Offset, Onset, Ope(n), Ord, Origin, Outset, Preliminary, Prelude, Proband, Put-up, Reboot, Resume, Roll, Rouse, Scare, Set off, Shy, Slip, Snail, Spring, Spud, String, Wince

▷ **Start** may indicate an anagram or first letter(s)

Startle, Startling Alarm, Bewilder, Disturb, Flush, Frighten, Magical, Scare

Starvation, Starve(d), Starving Anorexia, Anoxic, Bant, Clem, Cold, Deprive, Diet, Famish, Inanition, Macerate, Perish, Pine, Undernourished

▷ **Starving** may indicate an 'o' in the middle of a word

State(s) Affirm, Alabama, Alaska, Alle(d)ge, Andorra, Aread, Arizona, Ark(ansas), Arrede, Assert, Assever, Attest, Aver, Avow, Bahar, Belize, Benin, Brunei, Buffer, California, Carolina, Case, Chad, Cite, Client, Colorado, Commonwealth, Condition, Confederate, Conn(ecticut), Country, Dakota, Declare, Del(aware), Dependency, Dubai, Durango, Emirate, Empire, Ethiopia, Federal, Fettle, Fla, Flap, Florida, Free, Ga, Georgia, Ghana, Gulf, Habitus, Hawaii, Honduras, Humour, Ia, Idaho, Illinois, Indiana, Iowa, Jamahiriya, Jumhouriya, Kansas, Kentucky, Land, Louisiana, Madras, Maine, Malawi, Maryland, Mass(achusetts), Md, Me, Mess, Mi(chigan), Minnesota, Mississippi, Missouri, Montana, Mysore, Name, Nation, NC, Nebraska, Nevada, New Hampshire, New Jersey, New Mexico, New York, Nirvana, NY, Ohio, Oklahoma, Oman, Oregon, Orissa, Pa, Palatinate, Papal, Parana, Pennsylvania, Perak, Plight, Police, Predicament, Predicate, Premise, Pronounce, Protectorate, Punjab, Puppet, Realm, Reich, Republic, RI, Satellite, Say, Sikkim, Sorry, Sparta, Standing, Tabasco, Tamil Nadu, Tasmania, Tennessee, Texas, Threeness, Togo, Travancore, Trucial, UK, Union, United, US, Ut, Utah, Va, Venezuela, Vermont, Victoria, Virginia, Washington, Welfare, Wis(consin), Wyoming

▷ **Stated** may indicate a similar sounding word

Stately (home) August, Dome, Grand, Imposing, Noble, Regal

Statement Account, Affidavit, Aphorism, Assertion, Attestation, Avowal, Bill, Bulletin, Communiqué, Deposition, Dictum, Diktat, Encyclical, Evidence, Expose, Factoid, Invoice, Jurat, Manifesto, Mission, Outline, Pleading, Press release, Profession, Pronouncement, Proposition, Quotation, Release, Remonstrance, Report, Sentence, Soundbite, Sweeping, Testimony, Truism, Utterance, Verb

Stateroom Bibby, Cabin

Statesman American, Attlee, Botha, Briand, Bright, Canning, Clarendon, Diplomat, Disraeli, Draco, Elder, Flaminius, Franklin, Georgian, Gladstone, Gracchi, Grotius, Guy, Kissinger, Kruger, Lafayette, Lie, North, Politician, Politico, Seneca, Smuts, Stein, Talleyrand, Tasmanian, Thiers, Walpole, Wealsman, Yankee

Static Electricity, Inert, Maginot-minded, Motionless, Stationary

Station(s) Action, Berth, Birth, Camp, Caste, CCS, Crewe, Deploy, Depot, Dressing, Euston, Filling, Fire, Garrison, Halt, Hill, Ice, Lay, Location, Marylebone, Outpost, Panic, Pitch, Place, Plant, Point, Police, Polling, Post, Power, Quarter, Rank, Relay, Rowme, Seat, Service, Sit, Space, Stance, Stand, Status, Stond, Tana, Tanna(h), Terminus, Thana(h), Thanna(h), Tracking, Victoria, Waterloo, Waverley, Weather

Stationary Immobile, Fasten, Fixed, Parked, Sessile, Stable, Static

Stationery-case Papeterie

Statistic(ian), Statistics Actuary, Fermi-Dirac, Figure, Gradgrind, Graph, Lod, Number, Percentage, Vital

Statuary, Statue(tte) Acrolith, Bronze, Bust, Colossus, Discobolus, Effigy, Figure, Figurine, Idol, Image, Galatea, Kore, Kouros, Liberty, Memnon, Monument, Oscar, Palladium, Pietà, Sculpture, Sphinx, Stonework, Tanagra, Torso, Xoanon

Stature Growth, Height, Inches, Rank

Status Caste, Class, ➤ POSITION, Quo, Rank, Standing

Statute Act, Capitular, Chapter 7, Chapter 11, Decree, Edict, Law, Novels

Staunch Amadou, Leal, Resolute, Steady, Stem, Stout, Styptic, Watertight

Stave Break, Dali, Forestall, Lag, Slat, Stanza, Ward

Stay(s) Alt, Avast, Bide, Bolster, Cohab(it), Corselet, Corset, Embar, Endure, Fulcrum, Gest, Guy, Hawser, Indwell, Jump, Lie, Lig, Linger, Manet, Moratorium, Piers, Prop, ➤ REMAIN, Reprieve, Restrain, Settle, Sist, Sleepover, Sojourn, Stem, Strut, Sustain, Tarry

Stay-at-home Indoor, Tortoise

STD Aids, Herpes, Telephone, VD

Steadfast Constant, Firm, Implacable, Resolute, Sad, Stable

Steady Andantino, Ballast, Beau, Boyfriend, Composer, Constant, Even, Faithful, Firm, Girlfriend, Measured, Regular, Stabilise, Stable, Unswerving

Steak Carpet-bag, Chateaubriand, Chuck, Fillet, Flitch, Garni, Mignon, Minute, Porterhouse, Rump, Slice, T-bone, Tenderloin, Tournedos

Steal(ing) Abstract, Bag, Bandicoot, Bone, Boost, Cabbage, Cly, Condiddle, Convey, Creep, Crib, Duff, Embezzle, Filch, Glom, Grab, Half-inch, Heist, Hotting, Kidnap, Knap, Lag, Liberate, Lift, Loot, Mag(g), Mahu, Mill, Naam, Nam, Nap, Nick, Nim, Nip, Nym, Peculate, Pilfer, Pillage, Pinch, Plagiarise, Plunder, Poach, Prig, Proll, Purloin, Ram-raid, Remove, Rifle, Rob, Rustle, Scrump, Skrimp, Smug, Snaffle, Snatch, Sneak, Snitch, Souvenir, Swipe, Take, Theft, Thieve, Tiptoe, TWOC, Whip

Stealth(y) Art, Catlike, Covert, Cunning, Furtive, Obreption, Surreptitious

Steam(ed), Steamy Boil, Condensation, Fume, Gaseous, Het, Humid, Mist, Porn, Radio, Roke, Sauna, Spout, Vapor, Vapour

Steamer, Steamboat Kettle, Showboat, Side-wheeler, SS, Str, Tramp

Steam-hammer Ram

Steed Charger, Horse, Mount

Steel(y) Acierate, Adamant, Bethlehem, Blade, Blister, Bloom, Brace, Carbon, Crucible, Maraging, Martensite, Metal, Nickel, Pearlite, Ripon, Rolled, Sorbite, Stainless, Structural, Sword, Toledo, Tool, Tungsten, Vanadium, Wootz

Steelyard Bismar

Steep Abrupt, Arduous, Brent, Embay, Expensive, Hilly, Krans, Krantz, Kranz, Macerate, Marinade, Marinate, Mask, Precipice, Precipitous, Rapid, Rate, Rait, Ret, Saturate, Scarp, ➤ SHEER, Soak, Sog, Souse, Stey, Stickle

Steeple(jack) Spiderman, Spire, Turret

Steer(er), Steering Ackerman, Airt, Buffalo, Bullock, Cann, Castor, Con(n), Cox, Direct, ➤ GUIDE, Helm, Navaid, Navigate, Ox, Pilot, Ply, Rudder, Stot, Whipstaff, Zebu

Stem Alexanders, Arrow, Axial, Bine, Bole, Caudex, Caulicle, Caulome, Check, Cladode, Cladophyll, Confront, Corm, Culm, Dam, Epicotyl, Floricane, Ha(u)lm, Kex, Pedicle, Peduncle, Pin, Pseudaxis, Rachis, Rhizome, Rise, Sarment, Scapus, Seta, Shaft, Shank, Sobole(s), Spring, Stalk, Staunch, Stipe, Stolon, Stopple, Sympodium, Tail

Stench F(o)etor, Funk, Miasma, Odour, Smell, Stink, Whiff

Stencil Copy, Duplicate, Mimeograph®, Pochoir

Stenographer, Stenography Amanuensis, Secretary, Shorthand, Typist

Step(s) Act, Balancé, Chassé, Choctaw, Corbie, Dance, Démarche, Echelon, Escalate, Flight, Fouetté, Gain, Gait, Goose, Grecian, Greece, Grees(e), Greesing, Grese, Gressing, Griece, Grise, Grize, Halfpace, Lavolt, Measure, Move, Notch, Pace, Pas, Pas de souris, Phase, Pigeon's wing, Raiser, Ratlin(e), Rattlin(e), Rattling, Roundel, Roundle, Rung, Shuffle, Slip, Stage, Stair, Stalk, Stile, Stope, Stride, Toddle, Trap, Tread, Unison, Waddle, Walk, Winder

Stephen Martyr, Stainless

Stepmother Novercal

Stepney Spare

Steppe Llano, Plain

Stereotype(d) Ritual

Sterile, Sterilise(r), Sterility Acarpous, Aseptic, Atocia, Autoclave, Barren, Dead, Fruitless, Impotent, Infertile, Neuter, Pasteurise, Spay

Sterling Excellent, Genuine, Pound, Silver, Sound

Stern Aft, Austere, Counter, Dour, Flinty, Grim, Hard, Implacable, Iron, Isaac, Nates, Poop, Rear, Relentless, Rugged, Stark, Strict, Tailpiece

Steroid Anabolic, Androsterone, Cortisone, Dexamethasone, Ergosterol, Fusidic, Predruso(lo)ne, Spironolactone, Testosterone

Sterol Stigmasterol

Stertorous Snore

Stet Restore

Stevedore Docker, Dockhand, Longshoreman, Stower, Wharfinger

Stevenson RLS, Tusitala

Stew(ed), Stews Bagnio, Bath, Blanquette, Boil, Bordel(lo), Bouillabaisse, Bouilli, Braise, Bredie, Brothel, Burgoo, Carbonade, Casserole, Cassoulet, Cholent, Chowder, Coddle, Colcannon, Compot(e), Daube, Flap, Fuss, Goulash, Haricot, Hash, Hell, Hot(ch)pot(ch), Irish, Jug, Lobscouse, Maconochie, Matapan, Matelote, Mulligan, Navarin, Olla podrida, Osso bucco, Paddy, Paella, Pepperpot, Pot-au-feu, Pot-pourri, Ragout, Ratatouille, Salmi, Sass, Scouse, Seethe, Simmer, Slumgullion, Squiffy, Stie, Stove, Stovies, Sty, Succotash, Sweat, Swelter, Tajine, Tzimmes, Zarzuela

Steward Butler, Cellarer, Chamberlain, Dewan, Factor, Hind, Malvolio, Manciple, Maormor, Mormaor, Official, Oswald, Panter, Purser, Reeve, Seneschal, Shop, Sommelier, Waiter

▷ **Stewed** may indicate an anagram

Stibnite Antimony, Kohl

Stick(ing) (out), Sticks, Sticky, Stuck Adhere, Agglutinant, Aground, Ash, Atlatl, Attach, Bamboo, Bastinado, Bat, Baton, Bauble, Bayonet, Bludgeon, Bond, Boondocks, Caman, Cambrel, Cammock, Cane, Celery, Cement, Chalk, Clag, Clam(my), Clarty, Clave, Cleave, Cling, Clog, Club, Cocktail, Cohere, Coinhere, Crab, Crosier, Cross(e), Crozier, Crummack, Crummock, Cue, Distaff, Divining-rod, Dog, Dure, Endure, Fag(g)ot, Firewood, Flak, Founder, Fuse, Gad(e), Gaid, Gambrel, Gelatine, Glair, Gliadin, Glit, Glue, Goad, Goo, Gore, Ground-ash, Gum, Gunge, Gunk, Harpoon, Hob, Hurley, Immobile, Impale, Inhere, Isinglass, Jab, Jam, Jut, Kid, Kierie, Kindling, Kip, Kiri, Knitch, Knobkerrie, Ko, Lance, Lathee, Lath(i), Lentisk, Limy, Lug, Message, Molinet, Orange, Parasitic, Paste, Penang-lawyer, Persist, Phasmid, Piceous, Piolet, Pierce, Plaster, Pogo, Pole, Posser, Protrude, Protuberant, Pugol, Quarterstaff, Rash, Ratten, Rhubarb, Rhythm, Rod, Ropy, Shillela(g)h, Shooting, Size, Smudge, Spear, Spurtle, Squail(er), Staff, Stand, Stang, Stob, Stodgy, Supplejack, Swagger, Switch, Swizzle, Swordstick, Tacamahac, Tack(y), Tally, Tar, Thick, Throwing, Truncheon, Trunnion, Vare, Viscid, Viscous, Waddy, Wait, Walking, Wand, Woolder, Woomera(ng)

Sticker Araldite®, Barnacle, Bur, Glue, Label, Limpet, Partisan, Poster, Slogan

Stickler Poser, Problem, Purist, Rigid, Rigorist, Tapist

Stiff, Stiffen(er), Stiffening, Stiffness Anchylosis, Angular, Ankylosis, Baleen, Bandoline, Brace, Buckram, Budge, Corpse, Corpus, Dear, Defunct, Expensive, Formal, Frore(n), Frorn(e), Gammy, Goner, Gut, Hard, Mort, Myotonia, Petrify, Pokerish, Prim, Ramrod, Rigid, Rigor, Rigor mortis, Sad, Set, Shank-iron, Size, Solid, Starch, Stark, Stay, Steeve, Stieve, Stilted, Stoor, Stour, Stowre, Sture, Unbending, Whalebone, Wigan, Wooden

Stifle Crush, Dampen, Funk, Muffle, Scomfish, Smore, Smother, Stive, Strangle

Stigma(tise) Blemish, Brand, Carpel, Discredit, Note, Slur, Smear, Spot, ➤ STAIN, Wound

Stile Gate, Steps, Sty

Stiletto Bodkin, Heel, Knife

Still Accoy, Airless, Alembic, Assuage, Becalm, Calm, Check, Current, Doggo, Ene, Even(ness), Howbe, However, Hush, Illicit, Inactive, Inert, Kill, Languid, Limbec(k), Lull, Motionless, Nevertheless, Patent, Peaceful, Photograph, Placate, Placid, Pose, Quiescent, Quiet, Resting, Silent, Snapshot, Soothe, Stagnant, Static, Stationary, Though, Yet

Stilt Avocet, Bird, Poaka, Prop, Scatch

Stilted Formal, Pedantic, Stiff, Unruffled, Wooden

Stimulant, Stimulate, Stimulus Activate, Adrenaline, Antigen, Arak, Arouse, Auxin, Caffeine, Cinder, Clomiphene, Coca, Coramine, Cue, Dart, Digitalin, Digoxin, Egg, Energise, Evoke, Excitant, Fillip, Fuel, Galvanize, Ginger, Goad, Hormone, Incite, Innerve, Irritate, Jog, Key, K(h)at, Kick, L-dopa, Mneme, Motivate, Nikethamide, Oestrus, Oxytocin, Paraphilia, Pemoline, Pep, Philtre, Pick-me-up, Piquant, Pituitrin, Prod, Promote, Provoke, Psych, Qat, Rim, Roborant, ➤ ROUSE, Rowel, Rub, Sassafras, Sensuous, Spur, Sting, Stir, Tannin, Tar, Theine, Tickle, Titillate, Tone, Tonic, Upper, Whet(stone), Wintergreen

Sting(ing) Aculeate, Barb, Bite, Cheat, Cnida, Goad, Nematocyst, Nettle(tree), Overcharge, Perceant, Piercer, Poignant, Prick, Pungent, Rile, Scorpion, Sephen, Smart, Spice, Stang, Stimulus, Surcharge, Tang, Trichocyst, Urent, Urtica

Sting-ray Sephen, Trygon

Stingy Cheeseparing, Chintzy, Close, Costive, Hard, Illiberal, Mean, Miserly, Narrow, Near, Nippy, Parsimonious, Snippy, Snudge, Tight-arse, Tight(wad)

▷ **Stingy** may indicate something that stings

Stink(er), Stinking, Stinks Abroma, Atoc, Atok, Brock, Cacodyl, Crepitate, Desman, Fetor, Foumart, Guff, Heel, Hellebore, Malodour, Mephitis, Miasma, Ming, Niff, Noisome, Rasse, Reek, Rich, Science, ➤ SMELL, Sondeli, Stench, Teledu

Stinkbird Hoa(c)tzin

Stint Chore, Economise, Limit, Scantle, Scamp, Scrimp, Share, Skimp

Stipend Ann(at), Annexure, Pay, Prebend, Remuneration, Salary, Wages

Stipulate, Stipulation Clause, Condition, Covenant, Insist, Provision, Proviso, Rider, Specify

Stipule Ocrea

Stir(red), Stirring Accite, Admix, Ado, Afoot, Agitate, Amo(o)ve, Animate, Annoy, Bother, Bustle, Buzz, Can, Churn, Cooler, Excite, Foment, Furore, Fuss, Gaol, Hectic, Impassion, Incense, Incite, Inflame, Insurrection, Intermx, Jee, Jog, Kitty, Limbo, Live, ➤ MIX, Move, Noy, Poss, Pother, ➤ PRISON, Prod, Provoke, Quad, Quatch, Quetch, Quinche, Qui(t)ch, Quod, Rabble, Rear, Roil, Rouse, Roust, Rummage, Rustle, Sod, Steer, Styre, Swizzle, To-do, Upstart, Wake

▷ **Stir(red), Stirring** may indicate an anagram

Stirrup (guard) Bone, Footrest, Footstall, Iron, Stapes, Tapadera, Tapadero

Stitch Bargello, Baste, Blanket, Blind, Buttonhole, Cable, Chain, Couching, Crochet, Embroider, Feather, Fell, Florentine, Garter, Gathering, Herringbone, Insertion, Knit, Lazy daisy, Lock, Moss, Needle, Overcast, Overlock, Petit point, Rag, Running, Saddle, Satin, Sew, Slip, Spider, Stab, Stay, Steek, Stem, Stockinette, Stocking, Straight, Sutile, Suture, Tack, Tent, Topstitch, Vandyke, Whip

Stock(ed), Stocks, Stocky Aerie, Aery, Amplosome, Blue-chip, Bouillon, Bree, Breech, Brompton, But(t), Carry, Cattle, Choker, Cippus, Congee, Conjee, Court-bouillon, Cravat, Debenture, Endomorph, Equip, Fumet,

Fund, Graft, Handpiece, He(a)rd, Hilt, Hoosh, Inventory, Kin, Laughing, Line, Little-ease, Locuplete, Omnium, Pigeonhole, Preferred, Pycnic, Race, Ranch, Rep(ertory), Replenish, Reserve, Rolling, Scrip, Seed, Shorts, Soup, Squat, Staple, Steale, Steelbow, Stirp(e)s, ➤ STORE, Strain, Stubby, Supply, Surplus, Talon, Team, Tie, Utility

Stockade Barrier, Eureka, Zare(e)ba, Zereba, Zeriba

Stocking(s) Fishnet, Hogger, Hose, Leather, Moggan, Netherlings, Nylons, Seamless, Sheer, Sock, Spattee, Tights

Stockman, Stockbroker Broker, Jobber, Neatherd

Stodge, Stodgy Dull, Filling, Heavy

Stoic(al) Impassive, Job, Logos, Patient, Philosophical, Porch, Seneca(n), Spartan, Stolid, Zeno

Stoke(r), Stokes Bram, Coal-trimmer, Fire(man), Fuel, S, Shovel

Stole(n) Bent, Epitrachelion, Hot, Maino(u)r, Manner, Manor, Nam, Orarion, Orarium, Reft, Scarf, Staw, Tippet

Stolid Deadpan, Dull, Impassive, Phlegmatic, Po(-faced), Thickset, Wooden

Stomach(ic) Abdomen, Abomasum, Accept, Appetite, Belly, Bible, Bingy, Bonnet, Bread-basket, Brook, C(o)eliac, Corporation, Epigastrium, Epiploon, Fardel-bag, Gaster, Gizzard, Gut, Heart, Jejunum, King's-hood, Kite, Kyte, Manyplies, Mary, Maw, Mesaraic, Midriff, Omasum, Paunch, Potbelly, Propodon, Proventriculus, Psalterium, Pylorus, Read, Rennet, Reticulum, Rumen, Stick, Swagbelly, ➤ SWALLOW, Tripe, Tum, Urite, Vell, Venter, Wame, Wem, Zingiber

Stomach-ache Colic, Colitis, Collywobbles, Giardiasis, Gripe, Gutrot, Mulligrubs

Stone(d), Stone age, Stones, Stony Blotto, Drunk, Pelt, Rocking, Sermon

TYPES OF STONE

2 letters:	Opal	Kenne	Wacke
St	Plum	Lapis	Wyman
3 letters:	Ragg	Logan	**6 letters:**
Gem	Sard	Menah	Amazon
Hog	Skew	Metal	Ashlar
Pit	Slab	Mocha	Ashler
Rag	Soap	Niobe	Baetyl
Tin	Tile	Paste	Bezoar
4 letters:	**5 letters:**	Prase	Brinny
Bath	Agate	Pumie	Cobble
Blue	Amber	Quern	Coping
Celt	Balas	Quoin	Cultch
Door	Beryl	Quoit	Dolmen
Flag	Black	Rubin	Flusch
Hone	Chalk	Rufus	Fossil
Horn	Chert	Rybat	Gibber
Iron	Coade	Scone	Gooley
Jasp	Culch	Scree	Goolie
Kerb	Drupe	Slate	Gravel
Lias	Flint	Sneck	Humite
Lime	Gooly	Stela	Jargon
Lode	Grape	Stele	Jasper
Onyx	Jewel	Topaz	Kidney

Kingle	Moabite	Elf-arrow	
Ligure	Niobean	Endocarp	
Lithic	Olivine	Essonite	
Menhir	Parpane	Ganister	
Metate	Parpend	Girasole	Gannister
Muller	Parpent	Lapidate	Greensand
Nutlet	Peridot	Megalith	Hessonite
Oamaru	Perpend	Menamber	Hoarstone
Paving	Perpent	Monolith	Lithiasis
Pebble	Petrous	Nephrite	Paleolith
Pot-lid	Pudding	Omphalos	Pipestone
Pumice	Purbeck	Onychite	Rubicelle
Pyrene	Putamen	Parpoint	Scagliola
Rip-rap	Rosetta	Petrosal	Trilithon
Sarsen	Sardine	Phengite	Turquoise
Scarab	Sarsden	Portland	Ventifact
Summer	Scaglia	Precious	**10 letters:**
Tanist	Schanse	Rollrich	Adamantine
7 letters:	Schanze	Sapphire	Alectorian
Asteria	Smaragd	Sardonyx	Aragonites
Avebury	Tektite	Scalpins	Chalcedony
Blarney	Telamon	Schantze	Draconites
Bologna	Tripoli	Tonalite	Enhydritic
Boulder	Urolith	Voussoir	Foundation
Breccia	**8 letters:**	**9 letters:**	Gastrolith
Callais	Aerolite	Alabaster	Grey-wether
Chuckie	Aerolith	Asparagus	Kimberlite
Curling	Amethyst	Cairngorm	Lherzolite
Girasol	Asteroid	Carnelian	Lithophyte
Granite	Baguette	Cholelith	Rhinestone
Hyacine	Cabochon	Chondrite	**11 letters:**
Hyalite	Calculus	Cornelian	Peristalith
Jargoon	Cinnamon	Crossette	**12 letters:**
Lia-fail	Cromlech	Dichroite	Carton-pierre
Lithoid	Ebenezer	Firestone	Philosopher's

Stone-crop Orpin(e), Sedum, Succulent

Stone-pusher Sisyphus

Stone-thrower Bal(lista), Catapult, David, Mangonel, Onager, Perrier, Sling, Trebuchet

Stone-wall(er) Block, Mule, Revet

Stone-worker Jeweller, Knapper, Sculptor

Stooge Butt, Cat's-paw, Feed

Stook(s) Sheaf, Stack, Thr(e)ave

Stool Buffet, Coppy, Cracket, Creepie, Cricket, Cucking, Curule, Cutty, Faeces, Hassock, Milking, Piano, Pouf(fe), Seat, Sir-reverence, Step, Stercoral, Sunkie, Taboret, Tripod, Turd

Stoop Bend, Condescend, C(o)urb, Daine, Deign, Incline, Porch, Slouch

Stop(page), Stopper, Stopping Abort, An(n)icut, Arrest, Avast, Bait, Bide, Blin, Block, Brake, Buffer, Bung, Canting-coin, ➤ CEASE, Cessation, Check, Cheese, Cholestasis, Clarabella, Clarino, Clarion, Clog, Close, Colon, Comma, Conclude, Cork, Coupler, Cremo(r)na, Cremorne, Cromorna, Cut, Deactivate, Debar, Demurral, Desist, Deter, Devall, Diaphone,

Discontinue, Dit, Dolce, Dot, Dulciana, Embargo, End, Field, Fifteenth, Flue, Flute, Foreclose, Fr(a)enum, Freeze, Gag, Gamba, Gemshorn, Glottal, Gong, Halt, Hamza(h), Hartal, Hinder, Hitch, Ho, Hold, Hoy, Intermit, Ischuria, Jam, Kibosh, Let-up, Lill, Lin, Lute, Media, Mutation, Nasard, Oboe, Obturate, Occlude, Oppilate, Organ, Outspan, Pause, Period, Piccolo, Pit, Plug, Point, Poop, Preclude, Prevent, Principal, Prorogue, Punctuate, Quash, Quint, Quit, Racket, Red, Reed, Refrain, Register, Rein, Remain, Request, Salicet, Scotch, Screw-top, Semi-colon, Sese, Sesquialtera, Sext, Sist, Solo, Spigot, Stall, Stanch, Standstill, Stash, Stasis, Station, Staunch, Stay, Stive, Strike, Subbase, Subbass, Suppress, Suspend, Tamp(ion), Tenuis, Terminate, Toby, Toho, Truck, Voix celeste, Vox angelica, Vox humana, Waldflute, Waldhorn, When, Whistle, Whoa

Stopgap Caretaker, Gasket, Gaskin, Interim, Makeshift, Temporary

Storage, Store(house) Accumulate, Arsenal, Backing, Barn, Bin, Bottle, Bunker, Buttery, Cache, Cell, Cellar, Chain, Clamp, Coop, Cootch, Cupboard, Cutch, Deli, Dene-hole, Department(al), Depository, Depot, Dime, Discount, Dolia, Elevator, Emporium, Ensile, Entrepot, Etape, Fund, Garner, Genizah, Girnal, Glory hole, Go-down, Granary, Groceteria, ➤ HOARD, Hold, House, Humidor, Husband, Hypermarket, Imbarn, Larder, Lazaretto, Magazine, Mart, Mattamore, Memory, Mine, Morgue, Mothball, Mow, Multiple, Nest-egg, Off-licence, Pantechnicon, Pantry, Pithos, Provision, Rack(ing), RAM, Repertory, Reposit, ROM, Sector, Shop, Silage, Silo, Spence, Spooling, Stack, Stash, Stock, Stockroom, Stow, Supermarket, Supply, Tack-room, Tank, Thesaurus, Tithe-barn, Tommy-shop, Volutin, Warehouse

▶ **Storey** see STORY

Stork Adjutant, Antigone, Argala, Bird, Jabiru, Marabou(t), Marg, Saddlebill, Wader, Wood

Stork's bill Erodium

Storm(y) Ablow, Adad, Assail, Attack, Baguio, Blizzard, Bluster, Bourasque, Buran, Calima, Charge, Cyclone, Devil, Dirty, Dust, Enlil, Expugn, Furore, Gale, Gusty, Haboob, Hurricane, Magnetic, Monsoon, Onset, Oragious, Rage(ful), Raid, Rain, Rampage, Rant, Red spot, Rugged, Rush, Shaitan, Snorter, Squall, Sumatra, Tea-cup, Tebbad, Tempest, Tornade, Tornado, Tropical, Unruly, Weather, Willy-willy, Wroth, Zu

▷ **Stormy** may indicate an anagram

Story, Storey, Stories Account, Allegory, Anecdote, Apocrypha, Arthuriana, Attic, Bar, Basement, Baur, Bawr, Biog, Chestnut, Clearstory, Clerestory, Cock and bull, Conte, Cover, Decameron, Edda, Epic, Episode, Etage, Exclusive, Exemplum, Fable, Fabliau, Fib, Fiction, Flat, Floor, Gag, Geste, Ghost, Hard-luck, Heptameron, Hitopadesa, Horror, Idyll, Iliad, Jataka, Lee, Legend, Lie, Mabinogion, Marchen, Mezzanine, Myth(os), Mythus, Narrative, Nouvelle, Novel(la), Oratorio, Parable, Pentameron, Plot, Rede, Report, Romance, Rumour, Saga, Scoop, Script, Serial, SF, Shaggy dog, Shocker, Sob, Spiel, Spine-chiller, Splash, Stage, Success, Tale, Tall, Tier, Triforium, Upper, Version, Yarn

Story-teller Aesop, Fibber, Griot, Liar, Munchausen, Narrator, Raconteur, Shannachie, Tusitala

Stoup Benitier, Bucket, Vessel

Stout(ness) Ale, Burly, Chopping, Chubby, Embonpoint, Endomorph, Entire, Fat, Fubsy, Hardy, Humpty-dumpty, Lusty, Manful, Milk, Obese, Overweight, Porter, Portly, Potbelly, Robust, Stalwart, Stalworth, Sta(u)nch, Strong, Stuggy, Sturdy, Substantial, Tall

Stove Baseburner, Break, Calefactor, Cockle, Cooker, Furnace, Gasfire, Oven, Primus®, Potbelly, Range, Salamander

Stow Cram, Flemish (down), Load, Pack, Rummage, Stash, Steeve

Strabismus Squint

Straddle Bestride, Strodle

Strafe Bombard, Shell, Shoot

Straggle(r), Straggly Estray, Gad, Meander, Ramble, Rat-tail, Spidery, Sprawl, Stray, Wander

Straight(en), Straightness Align, Bald, Beeline, Correct, Die, Direct, Downright, Dress, Frank, Gain, Het(ero), Honest, Lank, Legit, Level, Normal, Rectilineal, Rectitude, Righten, Sheer, Slap, Tidy, True, Unbowed, Unlay, Upright, Veracious, Virgate

Straight edge Lute, Ruler

Straightforward Candid, Direct, Easy, Even, Forthright, Honest, Level, Jannock, Plain sailing, Pointblank, Simple

Straight-haired Leiotrichous

Strain(ed), Strainer, Straining Agonistic, Ancestry, Aria, Breed, Carol, Clarify, Colander, Distend, Drawn, Effort, Exert, Filter, Filtrate, Fit, Fitt(e), Force, Fray, Fytt(e), Intense, Kind, Melody, Milsey, Molimen, Music, Note, Overtask, Passus, Percolate, Pressure, Pull, Rack, Raring, Reck(an), Retch, Rick, Seep, Seil(e), Set, Shear, Sieve, Sift, Sile, Stape, Start, Stock, Streak, Stress, Stretch, Sye, Tamis, Tammy, Tax, Tenesmus, Tense, Tension, Threnody, Try, Vein, Vice, Work, Wrick

Strait(s) Bass, Bering, Bosp(h)orus, Canso, Channel, Condition, Cook, Crisis, Cut, Dardanelles, Davis, Denmark, Euripus, Formosa, Foveaux, Gat, Gibraltar, Gut, Hormuz, Hudson, Johor, Juande Fuca, Kattegat, Korea, Kyle, Little Belt, Lombok, Magellan, Malacca, Menai, Messina, Narrow, Otranto, Palk, Predicament, Solent, Sound, St, Sunda, Taiwan, Torres

Straiten(ed) Impecunious, Impoverish, Poor, Restrict

Strait-laced Blue-nosed, Narrow, Primsie, Puritan, Stuffy

Strand(ed) Abandon, Aground, Bank, Beach, Desert, Fibre, Haugh, Hexarch, Isolate, Lock, Maroon, Neaped, Ply, Rice, Rope, Shore, Sliver, Thread, Three-ply, Tress, Wisp

Strange(ness), Stranger Alien, Aloof, Amphitryon, Curious, Eerie, Exotic, Foreign, Fraim, Frem(d), Fremit, Frenne, Funny, Guest, Malihini, New, Novel, Odd(ball), Outlandish, Outsider, Quare, Queer, Rum, S, Screwy, Selcouth, Singular, Tea-leaf, Uncanny, Unco, Unked, Unket, Unkid, Unused, Unusual, Weird, Wondrous

▷ **Strange** may indicate an anagram

Strangle Choke, Garotte, Jugulate, Suppress, Throttle

Strap(ping) Band, Barber, Beat, Bowyangs, Brail, Braw, Breeching, Browband, Crupper, Cuir-bouilli, Curb, Girth, Halter, Harness, Jess, Larrup, Lash, Ligule, Lorate, Lore, Manly, Martingale, Nicky-tam, Pandy, Rand, Rein, Robust, Sling, Spider, Strop, Surcingle, T-bar, Tab, Taws(e), Thong, Throatlash, Throatlatch, Trace, Tump-line, Wallop

Stratagem, Strategist, Strategy Artifice, Coup, Deceit, Device, Dodge, Fetch, Finesse, Fraud, Masterstroke, Maximum, Minimax, Plan, ➤ RUSE, Scheme, Sleight, Tactic(s), Tactician, Trick, Wile

Stratum, Strata Bed, Coal Measures, Kar(r)oo, Layer, Neogene, Permian, Schlieren, Seam, Syncline

Straw(s), Strawy Balibuntal, Boater, Buntal, Chaff, Cheese, Halm, Hat, Haulm, Hay, Insubstantial, Last, Leghorn, Nugae, Oaten, Panama, Parabuntal, Pedal, Stalk, Stramineous, Strammel, Strummel, Stubble, Trifles, Wisp, Ye(a)lm

Strawberry Birthmark, Fragaria, Hautbois, Hautboy, Potentilla

Stray Abandoned, Chance, Depart, Deviate, Digress, Err, Forwander, Foundling, Maverick, Meander, Misgo, Pye-dog, Ramble, Roam, Sin, Straggle, Streel, Traik, Unowned, Waff, Waif, Wander

Streak(ed), Streaker, Streaky Archimedes, Bended, Blue, Brindle, Comet, Flaser, Flash, Fleck, Freak, Hawked, Highlights, Lace, Layer, Leonid, Mark, Merle, Mottle, Race, Run, Schlieren, Seam, Striate, Striga, Strip(e), Vein, Venose, Vibex, Waif, Wake, Wale

Stream Acheron, Anabranch, Arroyo, Beam, Beck, Bogan, Bourne, Burn, Course, Current, Driblet, Fast, Flow, Flower, Freshet, Gulf, Gush, Headwater, Influent, Jet, Kill, Lade, Lane, Leet, Logan, Pokelogan, Pour, Pow, Rill, River, Rivulet, Rubicon, Run, Runnel, Sike, Streel, Syke, Tide-race, Tributary, Trickle, Watercourse

Streamer Banderol(e), Bandrol, Banner(all), Bannerol, Pennon, Pinnet, Ribbon, Vane

Streamline(d), Streamliner Clean, Fair, Fairing, Simplify, Sleek, Slim

Street Alley, Ave(nue), Bowery, Broad, Carey, Carnaby, Cato, Causey, Cheapside, Civvy, Close, Corso, Court, Crescent, Downing, Drive, Easy, Fleet, Gate, Grub, Harley, High(way), Lane, Meuse, Mews, One-way, Parade, Paseo, Queer, Road, Side, Sinister, St, Strand, Terrace, Thoroughfare, Threadneedle, Throgmorton, Wall, Wardour, Watling, Way, Whitehall

Street arab Mudlark

Streetcar Desire, Tram

Strength(en), Strengthening Afforce, Bant, Beef, Brace, Brawn, Build, Confirm, Consolidate, Enable, Energy, Foison, Force, Forte, Fortify, Freshen, Grit, Herculean, Horn, Intensity, Iron, Line, Main, Man, Might, Munite, Muscle, Nerve, ➤ POWER, Prepotence, Pre-stress, Proof, Reinforce, Roborant, Sinew, Spike, Stamina, Steel, Sthenia, ➤ STRONG, Stoutness, Tensile, Thews, Titration, Unity, Vim

Strenuous Arduous, Effort, Exhausting, Hard, Laborious, Vehement

Strephon Rustic, Wooer

Stress(ed) Accent, Arsis, Birr, Brunt, Emphasis, Ictus, Impress, Italicise, Marcato, Orthotonesis, Oxytone, Proof, PTSD, Rack, Ram, RSI, Sforzando, Strain, Taut, Tense, ➤ TENSION, Try, Underline, Underscore, Urge

Stretch(able), Stretched, Stretcher, Stretching Belt, Brick, Crane, Distend, Draw, Ectasis, Eke, Elastic, Elongate, Expanse, Extend, Extensile, Farthingale, Fib, Frame, Give, Gurney, Lengthen, Litter, Narrows, Outreach, Pallet, Pandiculation, Porrect, Procrustes, Prolong, Protend, Pull, Rack, Rax, ➤ REACH, Sentence, Shiner, Spell, Spread, Strain, Taut, Tend, Tense, Tensile, Tenter, Term, Time, Tract, Tractile, Tree, Trolley

Striate Lineolate, Vein

Stricken Beset, Hurt, Overcome, Shattered

Strict Dour, Harsh, Literal, Medic, Narrow, Orthodox, Penal, Puritanical, Rigid, Rigorous, Severe, Spartan, Stern, Strait(-laced)

Stride Gal(l)umph, Leg, Lope, March, Pace, Piano, Stalk, Sten, Straddle, Stroam, Strut, Stump

Strident Brassy, Grinding, Harsh, Raucous, Screech

Strife Bargain, Barrat, Colluctation, Conflict, Conteck, Contest, Discord, Disharmony, Dissension, Feud, Food, Friction, Ignoble, Scrap(ping), Sturt

Strike(r), Striking, Strike out Affrap, Air, Alight, Annul, Appulse, Arresting, Attitude, Backhander, Baff, Band, Bandh, Bang, Bash, Bat, Baton, Batsman, Batter, Beat, Belabour, Better, Biff, Black, Bonanza, Buff, Buffet, Bund(h), Butt, Catch, Cane, Chime, Chip, Clap, Clash, Clatch, Clip, Clock, Clout, Club, Cob, Collide, Coup, Cue, Cuff, Dad, Dent, Dev(v)el, Ding, Dint, Dismantle, Distingué, Douse, Dowse, Dramatic, Drive, Dush, Eclat, Evenement, Fet(ch), Fillip, Firk, Fist, Flail, Flog, Frap, Get, Gowf, Hail, Hartal, ➤ HIT, Horn, Hour, Hunger, Ictus, Illision, Impact, Impinge, Impress, Jarp, Jaup, Jole, Joll, Joule, Jowl, Knock, Lam, Lambast, Laser, Lay(-off), Lightning, Match, Notable, Noticeable, Out, Pash, Pat(ter), Pean, Peen, Pein, Pene, Percuss, Picket, Pize, Plectrum, Pronounced, Pummel, Punch, Ram, Rap, Remarkable, Roquet, Salient, Scrub, Shank, Sideswipe, Sitdown, Sit-in, Slam, Slap, Slat, Slog, Slosh, Smack, Smash, Smite, Sock, Souse, Sowce, Sowse, Spank, Stayaway, Stop(page), Stub, Swap, Swat, Swinge, Swipe, Swop, Sympathy, Tan, Tapotement, Tat, Thump, Tip, Tonk, Walk-out, Wallop, Wap, Whack, Whap, Whomp, Whop, Wick, Wildcat, Wipe, Wondrous, Zap

Strike-breaker Blackleg, Fink, Rat, Scab

String(s), Stringy Band, Beads, Bowyang, Cello, Chalaza, Chanterelle, Cord, Cosmic, Creance, Cremaster, Drill, Enfilade, Fiddle, Fillis, G, Gut, Henequin, Heniquin, Hypate, Keyed, Lace, Lag, Lichanos, Macramé, Mese, Necklace, Nete, Nicky-tam, Paramese, Pledget, Proviso, Quint, Ripcord, Rope, Second, Series, Shoe(-tie), Sinewy, Straggle, Strand, Sympathetic, Team, Tendon, Thairm, Tough, Train, Trite, Viola, Violin

String-course Moulding, Table

Stringent Extreme, Rigid, Severe, Strict, Urgent

Strip(ped), Stripper, Striptease Airfield, Armband, Band, Bare, Bark, Batten, Belt, Bereave, Casparian, Comic, Cote, Defoliate, Denude, Deprive, Derobe, Despoil, Devest, Disbark, Dismantle, Dismask, Disrobe, Divest, Drag, Ecdysiast, Ecdysis, Ecorché, Fannel(l), Fiche, Flaught, Flay, Fleece, Flench, Flense, Flinch, Flounce, Flype, Gaza, Goujon, Hatband, Infula, Jib, Label, Lardon, Lath, Ledge, Linter, List, Littoral, Loading, Median, Mobius, Panhandle, Peel, Pillage, Pluck, Pull, Puttee, Puttie, Rand, Raunch, Raw, Ribbon, Ring-bark, Roon, Royne, Rumble, Rund, Runway, Screed, Scrow, Shear, Shed, Shuck, Skin, Slat, Slit, Sliver, Spellican, Spilikin, Spill(ikin), Splat, Splent, Spline, Splint, Splinter, Spoil, Straik, Strake, Strap, Streak, Strop, Swath, Sweatband, Tack, Tee, Thong, Tirl, Tirr, Uncase, Undress, Unfrock, Unrig, Unrip, Unvaile, Valance, Widow, Zone

Stripe(d) Band, Bausond, Candy, Chevron, Cingulum, Cove, Endorse, Lance-jack, Laticlave, Line, List, ➤ NCO, Ombré, Pale, Pirnie, Pirnit, Slash, Straik, Strake, Streak, Stroke, Tabaret, Tabby, Tiger, Tragelaph(us), Vitta, Weal

Strive, Striving Aim, Aspire, ➤ ATTEMPT, Contend, Endeavour, Enter, Kemp, Labour, Nisus, Pingle, Press, Strain, Struggle, Toil, Try, Vie

Stroke Apoplex(y), Backhander, Bat, Blow, Boast, Breast, Butterfly, Caress, Carom, Chip, Chop, Counterbuff, Coup, Coy, Crawl, Dash, Dint, Dog(gy)-paddle, Drear(e), Drere, Dropshot, Effleurage, Estrarnazone, Exhaust, Feat, Flick, Fondle, Foozle, Forehand, Glance, Hairline, Hand(er), Ictus, Inwick, Jenny, Jole, Joll, Joule, Jowl, Knell, Knock, Lash, Like, Line, Loft, Loser, Massé, Oarsman, Oblique, Odd, Off-drive, Outlash, Palp, Paw, Pot-hook, Pull, Put(t), Reverso, Roquet, Rub, Scart, Sclaff, Scoop, Seizure, Sixte, Smooth, Solidus, Strike, Stripe, Sweep, Swipe, Tact, Tittle, Touk, Trait, Trudgen, Trudgeon, Tuck, Virgule, Wale, Whang

Stroll(er), Strolling Ambulate, Bummel, Dander, Daun(d)er, Dawner, Flanerie, Flaneur, Idle, Lounge, Ramble, Saunter, Stravaig, Stray, Toddle, Walk, Walkabout, Wander

Strong Able, Brawny, Cast-iron, Doughty, Durable, F, Fit, Forceful, Forcible, Forte, Hale, Hercules, Humming, Husky, Intense, Mighty, Nappy, Pithy, Pollent, Potent, Powerful, Pungent, Racy, Rank, Robust, Samson, Solid, Stalwart, Stark, Steely, ➤ STRENGTH, Sthenic, Stiff, Stout, Str, Strapping, Sturdy, Substantial, Suit, Tarzan, Thesis, Thickset, Trusty, Vegete, Vehement, Vigorous, Violent, Well-set, Ya(u)ld

Stronghold Acropolis, Aerie, Bastion, Castle, Citadel, Eyrie, Fastness, Fortress, Keep, Kremlin, Redoubt, Tower

Strontium Sr

Strop Leather, Sharpen, Strap

Struck Aghast, Raught, Smitten

Structural, Structure Allotrope, Anatomy, Armature, Analysis, Building, Compage(s), Edifice, Erection, Fabric, Fairing, Format(ion), Formwork, Frame, Ice-apron, Lantern, Mole, Organic, Palmation, Pediment, Pergola, Phloem, Physique, Retinaculum, Shape, Skeleton, Sponson, Sporocarp, Squinch, Starling, Stylobate, Syntax, System, Tectonic, Texas, Texture, Trochlea, Undercarriage

Struggle Agon(ise), Agonistes, Buckle, Camp, Chore, Conflict, Contend, Contest, Cope, Debatement, Effort, Endeavour, Fight, Flounder, Grabble, Grapple, Kampf, Labour, Luctation, Mill, Pingle, Rat-race, Scrape, Scrimmage, Scrum, Scrummage, Scuffle, Sprangle, ➤ STRIVE, Toil, Tug, Tussle, Vie, War(sle), Wrestle

▷ **Struggle** may indicate an anagram

Strum Thrum, Tweedle, Vamp

Strumpet Cocotte, Harlot, Hiren, Lorette, Paramour, Succubus, Wench

Strut(ter), Strutting Bracket, Brank, Bridging, Cock, Dolphin striker, Flounce, Haught(y), Kingrod, Longeron, Martingale boom, Member, Nervure, Peacock, Pown, Prance, Prop, Scotch, Shore, Spur, Stalk, Stretcher, Strunt, Swagger, Swank, Tall-boom, Tie-beam

Stuart Anne, James, Pretender

Stub(by) Butt, Counterfoil, Dout, Dowt, Dumpy, Squat, Stob, Stocky

Stubble Ar(r)ish, Bristle, Designer, Hair, Ill-shaven, Stump

Stubborn(ness) Adamant, Bigoted, Contumacious, Cussed, Diehard, Entêté, Hard(-nosed), Hidebound, Intransigent, Inveterate, Moyl(e), Mulish, Mumpsimus, Obdurate, Obstinate, Opinionated, Ornery, Ortus, Pertinacious, Perverse, Recalcitrant, Reesty, Refractory, Rigwiddie, Rigwoodie, Self-willed, Stiff, Tenacious, Thrawn, Wrong-headed

Stuck Fast, Glued, Jammed, Set, Stopped, Wedged

Stuck-up Chesty, Highty-tighty, Hoity-toity, La(h)-di-da(h), Proud, Sealed, Vain

Stud(ded) Boss, Cooser, Cripple, Cu(i)sser, He-man, Knob, Nail, Race, Rivet, Seg, Set, Sire

Student(s) Alphabetarian, Alumnus, Apprentice, Bajan, Bejant, Bursch(en), Cadet, Catachumen, Class, Coed, Commoner, Dan, Dig, Disciple, Dresser, Dux, Exhibitioner, Extensionist, Form, Fresher, Freshman, Gownsman, Graduand, Gyte, Kommers, Kyu, ➤ LEARNER, Magistrand, Mature, Nomologist, NUS, Opsimath, Ordinand, Oxonian, Peking duck, Pennal, Plebe, Poll, Preppy, Pupil, Reader, Sap, ➤ SCHOLAR, Self-taught, Semi, Seminar, Seminarian, Shark, Sizar, Sizer, Smug, Softa, Soph(omore), Sophister, Swot, Templar, Tosher, Trainee, Tuft, Tutee, Wedge, Wonk, Wrangler, Year

Studio Atelier, Bottega, Gallery, Pinewood, Workshop

Study, Studied, Studies, Studious Analyse, Bone, Brown, Carol, Classics, Con(ne), Conscious, Consider, Cram, Den, Dig, Etude, Feasibility, Field, Learn, Lucubrate, Media, Mug, Mull, Muse, Perusal, Peruse, Pore, Post-doctoral, Probe, Read, Recce, Reconnoitre, Research, Reverie, Revise, Sanctum, Sap, Scan, Scrutinise, Specialize, Stew, Take, Time and motion, Typto, Voulu, Wonk

Stuff(iness), Stuffing, Stuffy Airless, Canvas, Close, Cloth, Codswallop, Cram, Crap, Dimity, Farce, Feast, Fiddlesticks, Fill, Force, Forcemeat, Frows(t)y, Frowzy, Fug, Gear, Gobble, Gorge, Guff, Havers, Hooey, Horsehair, Lard, Line, Linen, ➤ MATERIAL, Matter, No-meaning, Nonsense,

Overeat, Pad, Pang, Panne, Pompous, Ram, Replete, Rot, Sate, Scrap, Sob, Stap, Steeve, Stew, Taxidermy, Trig, Upholster, Wad, Youth

Stultify Repress, Ridicule, Smother

Stumble Blunder, Err, Falter, Flounder, Founder, Lurch, Peck, Snapper, Stoit, Titubate, Trip

Stump(ed), Stumps, Stumpy Butt, Clump, Fag-end, Floor, More, Nog, Nonplus, Orate, Runt, Scrag, Snag, Snooker, Squab, St, Staddle, Stob, Stock, Stool, Stub(ble), Stud, Tortillon, Tramp, Truncate, Wicket

Stun(ning), Stunned Astonish, Astound, Awhape, Bludgeon, Concuss, Cosh, Daze, Dazzle, Deafen, Donnard, Donnert, Dove, Drop-dead, Glam, KO, Shell-shocked, Shock, Stoun, Stupefy

Stunner Belle, Bobby-dazzler, Cheese, Cosh, KO, Peach, Taser®

Stunt(ed) Aerobatics, Confine, Droichy, Dwarf, Feat, Gimmick, Hot-dog, Hype, Jehad, Jihad, Loop, Nirl, Puny, Ront(e), Runt, Ruse, Scroggy, Scrub(by), Scrunt(y), Stub, Trick, Wanthriven

Stupefaction, Stupefy(ing) Amaze(ment), Assot, Benumb, Dozen, Dumbfound, Etherise, Fuddle, Hocus, Narcoses, Numb, Stonne, Stun

Stupid (person) Abderian, Abderite, Airhead, Analphabet, Anserine, Asinico, Asinine, Ass, Auf, Baeotian, Bampot, Barmpot, Becasse, Beccaccia, Berk, Besotted, Bete, Blockhead, Blockish, Bob, Bobb(y), Boeotian, Bonehead, Booby, Boodle, Boofhead, Bozo, Braindead, Brute, Buffer, Buffoon, Bumbo, Burk, Cake, Calf, Capocchia, Changeling, Charlie, Chick, Chipochia, Chowderhead, Chump, Clod(pole), Clodpoll, Clot, Clunk, Cod, Cokes, Cony, Coof, Coot, Crackpot, Crass, Cretin, Cuckoo, Cuddie, Cuddy, Cully, Daft, Daw, Dense, Desipient, Dick(e)y, Dickhead, Dill, Dim(wit), Dimwit, Dipstick, Dizzard, Doat, Doddipoll, Doddypoll, Dodipoll, Dodkin, Dolt, Donkey, Donnard, Donnart, Donner(e)d, Donnert, Dork, Dote, Dotterel, Dottipoll, Dottle, Dottrell, Drongo, Dubbo, Dull(ard), Dumbbell, Dumb-chick, Dumbo, Dunce, Dunderhead, Dunderpate, Dweeb, Eejit, Fatuous, Featherbrain, Featherhead, Flat, Flathead, Fog(e)y, Fon, Fool(ish), Fozy, Gaby, Gaga, Galah, Gaupus, Geck, Gelt, Git, Goat, Gobshite, Golem, Gomeral, Gomeril, Goof, Goofball, Goofy, Goon, Goop, Goose(-cap), Gormless, Gothamite, Gouk, Gowk, Gross, Gubbins, Gull, Gump, Gunsel, Half-wit, Hammerheaded, Hash, Haverel, Headbanger, Hoser, Idiot, Ignaro, Ignoramus, Imbecile, Inane, Ingram, Ingrum, Insensate, Insipient, Insulse, Jackass, Jay, Jerk, Jobernowl, Josser, Juggins, Klutz, Knucklehead, Lamebrain, Leather-head, Liripipe, Liripoop, Lob, Log, Loggerhead, Looby, Loony, Lown(e), Lummox, Lunkhead, Lurdane, Lurden, Mafflin(g), Malt-horse, Meathead, Mindless, Mome, Mong, Moon-calf, Moron, Muggins, Mutt, Muttonhead, Nana, Natural, Neddy, Nerd, Nerk, Nidget, Nig-nog, Nincompoop, Nincum, Ninny(-hammer), Nit(wit), Noddy, Nong, Noodle, Numpty, Nurd, Oaf, Obtuse, Ocker, Omadhaun, Ouph(e), Owl, Oxhead, Palooka, Patch, Pea-brain, Pillock, Pinhead, Plonker, Poon, Poop, Pot-head, Prat, Prune, Put(t), Putz, Quo-he, Rook, Sap, Schlemiel, Schlemihl, Schlep, Schmo(e), Schmock, Schmuck, Schnook, Scogan, Scoggin, Shatterbrain, Shot-clog, Silly, Simon, Simp(leton), Snipe, Softhead, Sot, Spoon, Stock, Stot, Stupe, Sucker,

Sumph, Ta(i)ver, Thick, Thickhead, Thickie, Thicko, Thimblewit, Tom-noddy, Tony, Torpid, Tosser, Touchstone, Tumphy, Turkey, Turnip, Twerp, Twit, Twp, Vacuous, Waldo, Wally, Want-wit, Warb, Wazzock, Wiseacre, Woodcock, Wooden(head), Yap, Yo-yo, Zany, Zombie

Stupidity Goosery, Hebetude, Thickness, Torpor

Stupor Catatony, Coma, Daze, Dwa(u)m, Fog, Lethargy, Narcosis, Trance

Sturdy Burly, Dunt, Gid, Hardy, Hefty, Lubbard, Lubber, Lusty, Stalwart, Staunch, Steeve, Stieve, Strapping, Strong, Thickset, Turnsick, Vigorous

Sturgeon Beluga, Ellops, Fish, Huso, Osseter, Sevruga, Sterlet

Stutter Hesitate, Stammer

Sty Frank, Hovel, Pen

Stye Eyesore, Hordeolum

Style(s), Stylish Adam, A la, Band, Barocco, Barock, Baroque, Biedermeier, Burin, Call, Cantilena, Carry-on, Chic, Chinoiserie, Class, Cultism, Cut, Dapper, Dash, Decor, Decorated, Diction, Directoire, Dub, Elan, Elegance, Empire, Entitle, Euphuism, Execution, Face, Farand, ➤ FASHION, Finesse, Flamboyant, Flossy, Form(at), Genre, Gnomon, Gongorism, Grace, Hair-do, Hand, Hip, Intitule, Lapidary, Manner, Marivaudage, Mod(e), Modish, New, Nib, Nifty, Old, Panache, Pattern, Pen, Perm, Phrase, Pistil, Pointel, Port, Preponderant, Probe, Rakish, Rank, Regency, Rococo, Romanesque, Silk, Snazzy, Snorty, Spiffy, Swish, Taste, Term, Title, Ton, Tone, Touch, Tuscan, Uncial, Vogue, Way

Stymie Thwart

Styptic Alum, Amadou, Matico, Sta(u)nch

Suave Bland, Oily, Smooth, Unctuous, Urbane

Sub Advance, Due, Submarine, Subordinate, Under

Sub-atomic Mesic

Subconscious Inner, Instinctive, Not-I, Subliminal, Suppressed

Sub-continent India

Subdivision Arm, Oblast, Sanjak, Wapentake

Subdominant Fah

Subdue(d) Abate, Adaw, Allay, Chasten, Conquer, Cow, Dant(on), Daunt(on), Dominate, Entame, Lick, Low-key, Master, Mate, Mute, ➤ QUELL, Quieten, Reduce, Refrain, Slow, Sober, Suppress, Tame, Under

Subfusc, Subfusk Dim, Dressy, Dusky, Evening, Sombre

Subhuman Bestial

Subject(s), Subjection, Subject to Amenable, Art, Bethrall, Caitive, Case, Citizen, Core, Cow, Enthrall, Gist, Hobby, Hobby-horse, Inflict, Liable, Liege(man), Matter, National, On, Overpower, PE, People, Poser, RE, RI, Serf, Servient, Servitude, Slavery, Sitter, Snool, Submit, Suit, ➤ THEME, Thirl, Thrall, Topic, Under, Vassal

Subjugate Enslave, Master, Oppress, Overcome, Reduce, Repress, Suppress

Sublieutenant Cornet

Sublimate(r) Aludel, Cleanse, Suppress, Transfer

Sublime August, Empyreal, Grand, Great, Lofty, Majestic, Outstanding, Perfect, Porte, Splendid

Submarine Diver, Innerspace, Nautilus, Pig-boat, Polaris, Sub, U-boat, Undersea

▷ **Submarine** may indicate a fish

Submerge(d) Dip, Dive, Drown, Embathe, Engulf, Imbathe, Lemuria, Overwhelm, Ria, Sink, Take, Whelm

Submissive, Submit Acquiesce, Bow, Capitulate, Comply, Defer, Docile, Knuckle, Meek, Obedient, Obtemperate, Passive, Pathetic, Refer, Render, Resign, Snool, Stoop, Succumb, Truckle, ➤ YIELD

Subordinate Adjunct, Dependent, Flunky, Inferior, Junior, Minion, Myrmidon, Offsider, Postpone, Secondary, Servient, Stooge, Subject, Subservient, Surrender, Under(ling), Underman, Under-strapper, Vassal

Subscribe(r), Subscription Abonnement, Approve, Assent, Conform, Due, Pay, Sign(atory), Signature, Undersign, Underwrite

Subsequent(ly) Anon, Consequential, Future, Later, Next, Postliminary, Since, Then

Subservient Kneel, Obedient, Obsequious

Subside, Subsidence, Subsidy Abate, Adaw, Aid, Assuage, Bonus, Diminish, Ebb, Grant, Sink, Sit, Swag

Subsidiary Auxiliar(y), By(e), Junior, Secondary, Side, Spin-off, Succursal

Subsist(ence) Batta, Bread-line, Dole, Keep, Live, Maintain, Rely, Survive

Substance, Substantial Ambergris, Antithrombin, Antitoxin, Blocky, Body, Calyx, Cermet, Chalone, Chemzyne, Chitin, Chromatin, Colloid, Considerable, Content, Ectoplasm, Elemi, Essential, Excipient, Exudate, Fabric, Fixative, Getter, Gist, Gluten, Gossypol, Gravamen, Guanazolo, Hearty, Hefty, Indol, Inhibitor, Iodophor, Isatin(e), Isomer, Lecithin, Leucotriene, Linin, Material, Matter, Meaning, Meat(y), Mineral, Mole, Morphogen, Orgone, Phlogiston, Polymer, Protyl(e), Quid, Reality, Resin, Sense, Solid, Stuff, Sum, Surfactant, Tabasheer, Tabashir, Tangible, Tusche, Viricide

Substandard Infra dig, Off, Poor, Schlo(c)k, Second, Small

▶ **Substantial** see SUBSTANCE

Substantiate Confirm, Prove, Strengthen, Support

Substantive Direct, Noun

Substitute, Substitution Acting, Carborundum®, Change, Changeling, Commute, Creamer, Deputy, Dextran, Emergency, Ersatz, -ette, Euphemism, Exchange, Fill-in, Improvise, Instead, Lieu(tenant), Locum, Makeshift, Metonymy, Pinch-hit, Proxy, Regent, Relieve, Replace, Represent, Reserve, Resolution, Ringer, Seth, Stand-in, Stead, Stopgap, Subrogate, Succedaneum, Surrogate, Switch, Swop, Understudy, Vicar(ial), Vicarious

Substructure Base, Foundation, Keelson, Platform, Podium

Subterfuge Artifice, Chicane, Evasion, Hole, Ruse, Strategy, Trick

Subterranean Concealed, Sunken, Underground, Weem

Subtle(ty) Abstruse, Alchemist, Crafty, Fine(spun), Finesse, Ingenious, Nice, Sly, Thin, Wily

Subtle difference Nuance

Subtract(ion) Commission, Deduct, Discount, Sum, Take, Tithe, Withdraw

Suburb Banlieue, Environs, Exurbia, Faubourg, Outskirts, Purlieu, Subtopia

Subversion, Subvert Fifth column, Overthrow, Reverse, Sabotage, Sedition, Treasonous, Undermine, Upset

Subway Metro, Passage, Tube, Underground

Succeed, Success(ful) Accomplish, Achieve, Arrive, Blockbuster, Boffo, Breakthrough, Contrive, Coup, Eclat, Effective, Efficacious, Fadge, Felicity, Flourish, Follow, Fortune, Gangbuster, Go, Hit, Hotshot, Inherit, Killing, Landslide, Luck, Manage, Masterstroke, Mega, Offcome, Pass, Prevail, Prosper, Purple patch, Reach, Replace, Riot, Score, Seal, Seel, Sele, Socko, Speed, Tanistry, Triumph, Up, Up and coming, Upstart, Vault, Weather, Win, Wow, Wunderkind

Succession Apostolic, Chain, Line, Order, Reversion, Sequence, Seriatim, Series, Suite

Successor Co(m)arb, Deluge, Descendant, Ensuite, Epigon(e), Heir, Incomer, Inheritor, Khalifa, Next, Syen

Succinct Brief, Cereus, Compact, Concise, Houseleek, Laconic, Short

Succour Aid, Assist, Help, Minister, Relieve, Rescue, Sustain

Succulent Cactus, Echeveria, Juicy, Lush, Rich, Saguaro, Sappy, Spekboom, Tender, Toothy

Succumb Capitulate, Fall, Go under, Surrender, Yield

Such Like, Sae, Sike, Similar, That

Suck(er), Sucking Absorb, Acetabular, Acetabulum, Amphistomous, Antlia, Aphis, Aspirator, Ass, Bull's eye, Culicidae, Dracula, Drink, Dupe, Fawn, Fellatio, Gnat, Graff, Graft, Gull, Haustellum, Haustorium, Hoove, Lamia, Lamprey, Leech, Liquorice, Mammal, Monotremata, Mouth, Mug, Osculum, Patsy, Plunger, Remora, Rook, Shoot, Siphon, Slurp, Smarm, Spire, Spyre, Straw, Surculus, Swig, Sycophant, Tellar, Teller, Tick, Tiller, Toad-eater, Turion, Vampire

Suckle Feed, Mother, Nourish, Nurse, Nurture

Suction Adhere, Pump, Siphon

Sud(s) Foam, Sapples

Sudanese Mahdi, Nuba

Sudden(ly) Abrupt, Astart, Astert, Extempore, Ferly, Fleeting, Foudroyant, Hasty, Headlong, Impulsive, Overnight, Rapid, Slap, Sodain, Subitaneous, Swap, Swop, Unexpected

Sue Ask, Beseech, Dun, Entreat, Implead, Implore, Petition, Pray, Process, Prosecute, Woo

Suede Split

Suffer(er), Suffering Abide, Aby(e), Ache, Affliction, Agonise, Auto, ➤ BEAR, Brook, Calvary, Cop, Die, Distress, Dree, Endurance, Endure, Feel, Gethsemane, Golgotha, Grief, Hardship, Have, Incur, Let, Luit, Martyr, Pain, Passible, Passion, Passive, Patible, Patience, Pellagrin, Permit, Pine,

Plague, Purgatory, Stand, Stomach, Sustain, Thole, Tolerate, Toll, Torment, Trial, Tribulation, Undergo, Use, Victim

Suffering remnant Macmillanite

Suffice, Sufficient Adequate, Ample, Basta, Do, Due, Enow, Enough, Satisfy, Serve

Suffocate Asphyxiate, Choke, Smoor, Smore, Smother, Stifle, Strangle, Throttle

Suffrage(tte) Ballot, Feminist, Franchise, Vote

Suffuse Colour, Glow, Imbue, Saturate, Spread

Sugar(y), Sugar cane Aldohexose, Aldose, Amygdalin, Arabinose, Barley, Blood, Brown, Candy, Cane, Caramel, Carn(e), Cassonade, Caster, Cellobiose, Cellose, Chaptalise, Daddy, Demerara, Deoxyribose, Dextrose, Disaccharide, Flattery, Fructose, Fucose, Furanose, Galactose, Gallise, Glucose, Glucosoric, Goo(r), Granulated, Grape, Gur, Heroin, Hexose, Honeydew, Iced, Icing, Inulin, Invert, Jaggary, Jaggery, Jagghery, Lactose, Laevulose, Loaf, Lump, Maltose, Manna, Mannose, Maple, Money, Monosaccharide, Muscovado, Palm, Panocha, Pentose, Penuche, Raffinose, Rhamnose, Ribose, Saccharine, Saccharoid, Simple, Sis, Sorbose, Sorg(h)o, Sorghum, Sparrow, Spun, Sweet, Trehala(se), Triose, Xylose

Sugar-daddy Lyle, Tate

Suggest(ion), Suggestive Advance, Advice, Advise, Connote, Cue, Hint, Idea, Imply, Innuendo, Insinuate, Intimate, Mention, Modicum, Moot, Posit, Prompt, Proposal, Propound, Provocative, Racy, Raise, Recommend, Redolent, Reminiscent, Risqué, Smacks, Soft core, Suspicion, Touch, Trace, Wind, Wrinkle

Suicide Felo-de-se, Hara-kiri, Hari-kari, Kamikaze, Lemming, Lethal, Sati, Seppuku, Suttee

Suit Action, Adapt, Agree, Answer, Appropriate, Become, Befit, Beho(o)ve, Bequest, Beseem, Birthday, Boiler, Cards, Case, Clubs, Conform, Courtship, Diamonds, Dittos, Do, Drapes, Dress, Effeir, Effere, Etons, Fadge, Fashion, Fit, G, Garb, Gee, Gree, Hearts, Hit, Jump, Long, Lounge, Major, Mao, Match, Minor, Monkey, Orison, Outcome, Paternity, Petition, Plaint, Plea, Please, Point, Prayer, Process, Pyjama, Quarterdeck, Queme, Romper(s), Safari, Sailor, Salopettes, Samfoo, Samfu, Satisfy, Serve, Shell, Siren, Spades, Strong, Sunday, Supplicat, Tailleur, Three-piece, Track, Trouser, Trumps, Twin, Two-piece, Uniform, Wet, Zoot

Suitable Apposite, Appropriate, Apt, Becoming, Capable, Congenial, Consonant, Convenance, Convenient, Due, Expedient, ➤ FIT, Giusto, Keeping, Meet, Opportune, Relevant, Seasonal, Seemly, Very, Worthy

Suite Allemande, Apartment, Chambers, Ensemble, Entourage, Hospitality, Lounge, Nutcracker, Partita, Retinue, Rooms, Serenade, Set, Tail, Three-piece, Train, Two-piece

Suitor Beau, John Doe, Gallant, Lover, Petitioner, Pretender, Suppli(c)ant, Swain

Sulk(y), Sulkiness B(r)oody, Dod, Dort, Gee, Glout(s), Glower, Glum, Grouchy, Grouty, Grumps, Huff, Hump, Jinker, Mardy, Maungy, Mope, Mulligrubs, Mump, Pet, Pique, Pout, Spider, Strunt, Stunkard, Sullen, Tout(ie), Towt

Sullen Dorty, Dour, Farouche, Glum(pish), Grim, Moody, Peevish, Stunkard, Sulky, Surly

Sully Assoil, Bedye, Besmirch, Blot, Defile, Glaur(y), Smear, Smirch, Soil, Tarnish, Tar-wash

Sulphate, Sulphide Alum, Alunite, Bluestone, Bornite, Copperas, Coquimbite, Glance, Pyrites, Zarnec, Zarnich

Sulphur Baregine, Brimstone, Hepar, Oleum, S, Stannite, Thionic

Sultan(a), Sultanate Brunei, Caliph, Emir, Hen, Kalif, Oman, Osman, Padishah, Roxane, Saladin, Soldan, Tippoo, Tipu

Sultry Humid, Sexy, Smouldering, Steamy, Tropical

Sum(s), Sum up Add(end), Aggregate, All, Amount, Arsmetric, Bomb, Connumerate, Encapsulate, Foot, Number, Perorate, Plumule, ➤ QUANTITY, Re-cap, Refund, Solidum, Total, Vector

Summarize, Summary Abridge, Abstract, Aperçu, Bird's eye, Brief, Compendium, Condense, Conspectus, Digest, Docket, Epitome, Gist, Instant, Minute, Offhand, Outline, Overview, Precis, Recap, Resume, Résumé, Round-up, Syllabus, Synopsis, Tabloid, Tabulate, Tabulation, Wrap-up

Summer(time) Aestival, BST, Computer, Estival, Indian, Lintel, Luke, Prime, Solstice, St Luke's, St Martin's, Totter

Summerhouse Belvedere, Chalet, Conservatory, Folly, Gazebo

Summit Acme, Acri-, Apex, Brow, Climax, Conference, ➤ CREST, Crown, Height, Hillcrest, Jole, Peak, Pike, Pinnacle, Spire, Vertex, Vertical, Yalta

Summon(s) Accite, Arrière-ban, Azan, Beck(on), Call, Cist, Cital, Citation, Command, Convene, Drum, Evoke, Garnishment, Gong, Hail, Invocation, Muster, Order, Page, Post, Preconise, Rechate, Recheat, Reveille, Signal, Sist, Ticket, Warn, Warrant, Whoop, Writ

Sumo Makunouchi

Sump Bilge, Drain, Pool, Sink

Sumpter Led horse, Pack-horse

Sumptuous Expensive, Palatial, Rich(ly), Superb

Sun(-god), Sunlight, Sunny, Sunshine Amen-Ra, Amon-Ra, Apollo, Aten, Bright, Cheer, Day(star), Dry, Earthshine, Glory, Heater, Helio(s), Helius, Horus, Mean, Midnight, New Mexico, Parhelion, Phoebean, Photosphere, Ra, Radiant, Rays, Re, Rising, Shamash, Sol(ar), Soleil, Sonne, Surya, Svastika, Swastika, Tabloid, Tan, Titan, UV

Sunbathe Apricate, Bask, Brown, Tan

Sunbeam Car, Ray

Sunburn Bronze, Combust, Peeling, Tan

Sunday Advent, Best, Cantate, Care, Carle, Carling, Dominical, Easter, Fig, Jubilate, Judica, Laetare, Lost, Low, Mid-Lent, Mothering, Orthodox, Palm, Passion, Quadragesima, Quasimodo, Quinquagesima, Refection,

Refreshment, Remembrance, Rogation, Rose, Rush-bearing, S, Septuagesima, Sexagesima, Stir-up, Tap-up, Trinity, Whit

Sunday school SS

Sunder Divide, Divorce, Part, Separate, Sever, Split

Sundew Drosera, Eyebright

Sundial Analemma, Gnomon, Solarium

Sundry Divers, Several, Various

Sunflower Kansas, KS

Sunglasses Shades

▶ **Sun-god** see SUN

▶ **Sunken** see SINK

Sunrise, Sun-up Aurora, Dawn, East

Sunshade Awning, Brise-soleil, Canopy, Chi(c)k, Cloud, Parasol, Umbrella

Sunspot Facula, Freckle, Macula

Sunstroke Heliosis, Siriasis

Sunwise Deasi(u)l, Deasoil, Deis(h)eal, Eutropic

Sun-worshipper Heliolater

Sup Dine, Eat, Feast, Sample, Sip, Swallow

Super A1, Arch, Extra, Fab(ulous), Great, Grouse, Ideal, Lulu, Paramount, Superb, Terrific, Tip-top, Tops, Walker-on, Wizard

Superadded Advene

Superb A1, Fine, Concours, Grand, Great, Majestic, Splendid, Top-notch

Supercilious Aloof, Arrogant, Bashaw, Cavalier, Haughty, Lordly, Snide, Sniffy, Snooty, Snotty, Snouty, Superior

Superficial Cosmetic, Cursenary, Cursory, Exterior, Facile, Glib, Outside, Outward, Overlying, Perfunctory, Shallow, Sketchy, Skindeep, Smattering, Veneer

▷ **Superficial(ly)** may indicate a word outside another

Superfluous, Superfluity Cheville, De trop, Extra, Lake, Mountain, Needless, Otiose, Pleonastic, Redundant, Spare, Unnecessary

Superhuman Bionic, Herculean, Heroic, Supernatural

Superintend(ent) Boss, Director, Foreman, Guide, Janitor, Oversee(r), Preside, Sewer, Surveillant, Warden, Zanjero

Superior(ity) Abbess, Abeigh, Above, Advantage, Aloof, Atop, Better, Choice, Condescending, Custos, De luxe, Dinger, Eminent, Excellent, Exceptional, Finer, Herrenvolk, Liege, Mastery, Nob, Over, Paramount, Predominance, Prestige, Pretentious, Superordinate, Supremacy, Swell, Top(-loftical), Transcendent(al), U, Udal, Upper(most), Uppish, Upstage

Superlative Best, Exaggerated, Peerless, Supreme, Utmost

Superman Batman, Bionic, Titan, Ubermensch

Supermarket Co-op, GUM, Self service, Store

Supernatural Divine, Eerie, Fey, Fie, Fly, Gothic, Mana, Paranormal, Sharp, Siddhi, Unearthly

Supernumerary Additional, Corollary, Extra, Mute, Orra

Supersede Replace, Stellenbosch, Supplant

Superstition Aberglaube, Abessa, Fable, Freet, Myth, Uncertainty

Superstructure Mastaba(h)

Supertonic Ray

Supervise(d), Supervision, Supervisor Administer, Chaperone, Check, Direct, Engineer, Foreman, Grieve, Handle, Honcho, Invigilate, Manager, Officiate, Overman, Oversee(r), Probation, Shopwalker, Targe, Under, Walla(h)

Supine Inactive, Inert, Lying, Protract

Supper Dinner, ➤ DRINK(ER), Hawkey, Hockey, Horkey, Last, Meal, Nagmaal, Repast, Soirée

Supplant Displace, Exchange, Replace, Substitute, Supersede

Supple Compliant, Leish, Limber, Lissom(e), ➤ LITHE, Loose, Loose-limbed, Pliable, Souple, Wan(d)le, Wannel, Whippy

Supplement(ary) Addend(um), Addition, And, Annex(e), Appendix, Auxiliary, Colour, Eche, Eke, Extra, Paralipomena, Postscript, Relay, Ripienist, Ripieno, Weighting

Supplicant, Supplicate Beg, Entreat, Importune, Invoke, Petition, Request, Schnorr, Sue

Supplier, Supplies, Supply Accommodate, Advance, Afford, Cache, Cater, Commissariat, Contribute, Crop, Endue, Equip, Feed, Fill, Find, Fit, Foison, Fund, Furnish, Give, Grist, Heel, Holp(en), Indue, Issue, Lend, Lithely, Mains, Materiel, Plenish, Ply, ➤ PROVIDE, Provision, Purvey, RASC, Retailer, Serve, Source, Stake, Stock, ➤ STORE, Vintner, Yield

Support(er), Supporting Abacus, Abet, Abutment, Adherent, Adminicle, Advocate, Aficionado, Aid, Aidance, Aliment(ative), Ally, Ammunition, Anchor, Ancillary, Andiron, Anta, Appui, Arch, Arm, Assistant, Axle, Back-up, Back(bone), Baculum, Baluster, Bankroll, Banister, Barrack, Barre, Base, Batten, Beam, Bear, Belt, Bibb, Bier, Bolster, Boom, Bouclée, Bra, Brace, Bracket, Brassiere, Breadwinner, Breast-summer, Bridge, Bridgeboard, Buttress, Chair, Champion, Chaptrel, Clientele, Column, Confirm, Console, Corbel, Corbel-table, Cornerstone, Cross-beam, Crutch, Dado, Diagrid, Dog-shore, Easel, Encourage, Endorse, Endow, Espouse, Fan, Favour, Fid, Finance, Flying buttress, Fly-rail, Footrest, Footstool, For, Gamb, Gantry, Garter, Girder, Glia, Grass roots, Harpin(g)s, Headrest, Help, Henchman, Horse, Hound, Idealogue, Impost, Income, Instantiate, Ite, Jack, Jockstrap, Joist, Keep, Kingpost, Knee, Knighthead, Lectern, Leg, Lierne, Lifebelt, Lifebuoy, Lobby, Loper, Loyalist, Mahlstick, Mainstay, Maintain, Makefast, Miserere, Misericord(e), Monial, Mortsafe, Nervure, Neuroglia, -nik, Nourish, Paranymph, Parawalker, Partisan, Partizan, Partners, Patronage, Pedestal, Pessary, Pier, Pillar, Pin, Plinth, Poppet, Post, Potent, Prop, Proponent, Prop-root, PTA, Purlin(e), Purlins, Pylon, Raft, Reinforce, Relieve, Respond, Rest, Rind, Rod, Roof-plate, Root, Royalist, Rynd, Samaritan, Sanction, Sawhorse, Second, Shore, Skeg, Skeleton, Skewput, Skid, Sleeper, Sling, Snotter, Socle, Solidarity, Splat, Splint, Sponson, Sprag, Spud, Staddle, Staff, Staging, Stalwart, Stanchion, Stay, Steady, Stem(pel), Step, Stirrup, Stool, Stringer, Strut, Stylobate, Subscribe, Subsidy, Succour, Suffragist, Summer, Suppedaneum,

Suspender, Sustain, Tailskid, Tee, Telamon, Tendril, Third, Tie, Tige, Torsel, Trabecula, Tress(el), Trestle, Tripod, Trivet, Truss, Underlay, Underpin, Understand, Unipod, Uphold, Upkeep, Viva, Waterwings, Y-level, Zealot

Suppose(d), Supposition An, Assume, Believe, Expect, Guess, Hypothetical, Idea, If, Imagine, Imply, Opine, Presume, Putative, Sepad, Theory

Suppress(ion) Abolish, Adaw, Burke, Cancel, Censor, Clampdown, Crush, Ecthlipsis, Elide, Elision, Gleichschaltung, Mob(b)le, Quash, Quell, Quench, Restrain, Silence, Smother, Squash, Stifle, Submerge, Subreption

Suppurate, Suppuration Diapyesis, Discharge, Exude, Fester, Maturate, Ooze, Pus, Pyorrhoea, Rankle

Supreme, Supremacy, Supremo Baaskap, Caudillo, Consummate, Kronos, Leader, Napoleon, Overlord, Paramount, Peerless, Regnant, Sovereign, Sublime, Sudder, Top, Utmost

Surcharge Addition, Extra, Tax

Surd Voiceless

Sure(ly) Assured, Ay, Bound, Cert(ain), Confident, Definite, Doubtless, Firm, Know, Pardi(e), Pardy, Perdie, Positive, Poz, Safe, Secure, Shoo-in, Sicker, Syker, Uh-huh, Yes

Surety Bail, Guarantee, Mainprise, Security, Sponsional

Surf(er) Breach, Breaker, Rollers, Rote, Sea, Waxhead

▷ **Surfer** may indicate programming

Surface Appear, Area, Arise, Camber, Day, Dermal, Dermis, Emerge, Epigene, Exterior, External, Face, Facet, Flock, Macadam, Meniscus, Outcrop, Outward, Patina, Pave, Plane, Reveal, Rise, Salband, Side, Skin, Soffit, Superficies, Tar-seal, Tarmac®, Texture, Top, Toroid

Surf-boat Masoola(h), Masula

Surfeit(ed) Blasé, Cloy, Excess, Glut, Overcloy, Plethora, Satiate, Stall, Staw

Surge Billow, Boom, Drive, Gush, Onrush, Seethe, Sway, Swell

Surgeon Abernethy, BCh, BS, CHB, CM, Doctor, Lister, Medic, Operator, Orthopod, Plastic, Sawbones, Tang, Vet(erinary)

Surgery Facelift, Keyhole, Knife, Laparotomy, Medicine, Op, Open-heart, Osteoplasty, Plastic, Prosthetics, Reconstructive, Repair, Ta(g)liacotian

Surly Bluff, Cantankerous, Chough, Chuffy, Churl(ish), Crusty, Cynic, Glum, Gruff, Grum, Grumpy, Rough, Sullen, Truculent

Surmise Guess, Imagine, Infer, Presume, Suppose

Surmount Beat, Climb, Conquer, Crest, Master, Overcome, Scan, Superate, Tide, Transcend

Surname Cognomen, Patronymic

Surpass Bang, Beat, Best, Cap, Ding, Eclipse, Efface, Exceed, Excel, Outdo, Outgun, Out-Herod, Outshine, Outstrip, Overtop, Transcend

Surplice Cotta, Ephod, Rochet, Vakass

Surplus Excess, Extra, Glut, Lake, Mountain, Out-over, Over, Overcome, Remainder, Rest, Spare, Surfeit

Surprise(d), Surprising Alert, Amaze, Ambush, Arrah, Astonish, Bewilder, Blimey, Boilover, Bombshell, Caramba, Catch, Confound, Coo, Cor,

Crick(e)y, Crikey, Criminé, Cripes, Criv(v)ens, Dear, Eye-opener, Gadso, Gee, Gemini, Geminy, Gemony, Gobsmacked, Golly, Gordon Bennett, Gosh, Ha, Hah, Hallo, Hech, Heh, Hello, Ho, Jeepers, Jeez(e), Lawks, Lordy, Lummy, Marry, Musha, My, Obreption, Och, Odso, Oops, Open-mouthed, Overtake, Pop-eyed, Really, Shock, Singular, Spot, Stagger, Startle, Strewth, Struth, Stun, Sudden, Treat, Turn-up, Uh, Whew, Whoops, Wonderment, Wow, Wrongfoot, Yikes, Yow, Zinger, Zowie

Surrealist Bizarre, Dali, Ernst, Grotesque, Magritte, Miro

Surrender Capitulate, Cave-in, Cession, Enfeoff, Fall, Forfeit, Handover, Hulled, Kamerad, Naam, Recreant, Release, Relinquish, Remise, Rendition, Submit, Succumb, Waive, ➤ YIELD

Surreptitious Clandestine, Covert, Fly, Furtive, Secret, Sly, Underhand

Surrey Carriage, Sy

Surrogate Agent, Depute, Deputy, Locum, Proxy

Surround(ed), Surrounding(s) Ambient, Architrave, Background, Bathe, Bego, Beset, Bundwall, Circumvallate, Circumvent, Compass, Doughnutting, Ecology, Embail, Encase, ➤ ENCIRCLE, Enclave, Enclose, Encompass, Enfold, Environ, Enwrap, Fence, Gherao, Gird, Hedge, Impale, Invest, Mid, Orb, Orle, Outflank, Outside, Perimeter, Setting, Wall

Surtees Jorrocks, Sponge

Surveillance, Survey(ing), Surveyor Behold, Cadastre, Case, Conspectus, Domesday, Doomwatch, Espial, Examination, Eye, Geodesy, Groma, Look-see, Once-over, Ordnance, Poll, Recce, Reconnaissance, Regard, Review, Scan, Scrutiny, Stakeout, Straw poll, Supervision, Terrier, Theodolite, Triangulate, Vigil, Watch

Survival, Survive, Surviving, Survivor Cope, Endure, Extant, Hibakusha, Last, Leftover, Outdure, Outlast, Outlive, Outwear, Persist, Relic(t), Ride, Street-wise, Viability, Warhorse, Weather

Susan Lazy

Susceptible, Susceptibility Anaphylaxis, Liable, Receptive, Vulnerable

Suspect, Suspicion, Suspicious Askance, Breath, Dodgy, Doubt, Dubious, Fishy, Grain, Guess, Hint, Hunch, Jalouse, Jealous, Leery, Misdeem, Misdoubt, Misgiving, Mistrust, Modicum, Notion, Paranoia, Queer, Scent, Smatch, Soupçon, Thought, Tinge, Whiff

▷ **Suspect, Suspicious** may indicate an anagram

Suspend(ed), Suspense, Suspension Abate, Abeyance, Adjourn, Anabiosis, Cliffhanger, Colloid, Dangle, Defer, Delay, Freeze, Ground, ➤ HANG, Hydraulic, Intermit, Mist, Moratorium, Nailbiter, Pensile, Poise, Prorogue, Reprieve, Respite, Rusticate, Sideline, Sol, Swing, Tenterhooks, Truce, Withhold

▷ **Suspended** may indicate 'ice' (on ice) at the end of a down light

Sussex Rape

Sustain(ed), Sustaining, Sustenance Abide, Aliment, Bear, Constant, Depend, Endure, Food, Keep, Last, Maintain, Nutriment, Pedal, Prolong, Sostenuto, Succour, Support, Tenuto

Sutler Vivandière

Suture Lambda, Pterion, Stitch

Suzanne, Suzie Lenglen, Wong

Svelte Lithe, Slender, Slim

Swab Dossil, Dry, Mop, Pledget, Scour, Sponge, Stupe, Tampon, Tompon, Squeegee, Wipe

Swaddle Bind, Envelop, Swathe, Wrap

Swag Booty, Encarpus, Festoon, Haul, Loot, Maino(u)r, Manner, Matilda, Shiralee, Toran(a)

Swagger(er), Swaggering Birkie, Bluster, Boast, Brag, Bragadisme, Bravado, Bucko, Cock, Crow, Jaunty, Matamore, Nounce, Panache, Pra(u)nce, Roll, Roist, Rollick, Roul, Royster, Ruffle, Side, Strive, Swank, Swash(-buckler)

Swain Amoretti, Beau, Churl, Corin, Damon, Hind, Lover, Rustic, Shepherd, Strephon, Wooer

Swallow(able), Swallowing Aerophagia, Ariel, Barn, Bird, Bolt, Consume, Deglutition, Devour, Down, Drink, Eat, Endue, Englut, Engulf, Esculent, Glug, Gobble, Gula, Gulp, Hirundine, Incept, Ingest, Ingulf, Ingurgitate, Itys, Lap, Martin, Martlet, Progne, Quaff, Shift, Sister, Slug, Stomach, Swig, Take

Swamp(y) Bog, Bunyip, Cowal, Deluge, Dismal, Drown, Engulf, Everglade, Flood, Inundate, Lentic, Lerna, Lerne, Loblolly, Mar(i)sh, Morass, Muskeg, Okavango, Okefenokee, Overrun, Overwhelm, Paludal, Quagmire, Slash, Slough, Sudd, Uliginous, Urman, Vlei, Vly

Swan(s) Avon, Bewick's, Bird, Black, Cob, Cygnet, Cygnus, Game, Leda, Lindor, Mute, Pen, Seven, Seward, Song, Stroll, Trumpeter, Whooper

Swank(y) Boast, Lugs, Pretentious, Side, Style

Swan-song Finale, Last air

Swap, Swop ➤ BARTER, Chop, Commute, Exchange, Scorse, Switch, Trade, Truck

▷ **Swap(ped)** may indicate an anagram

Sward Grass, Green, Lawn, Sod, Turf

Swarm(ing) Abound, Alive, Bike, Bink, Byke, Cast, Cloud, Crowd, Flood, Geminid, Host, Hotter, Infest, Pullulate, Rife, Shin, Shoal, Throng

Swarthy Dark, Dusky, Melanotic

Swash Swig, Swill

Swash-buckler Adventurer, Boaster, Braggart, Gascon, Swordsman

Swastika Filfot, Fylfot, Gamma(dion), Hakenkreuz

▶ **Swat** see SWOT

Swathe Bind, Enfold, Enroll, Swaddle, Wrap

Sway(ing) Careen, Carry, Command, Diadrom, Domain, Dominion, Flap, Fluctuate, Govern, Hegemony, Influence, Lilt, Oscillate, Prevail, Reel, Reign, Rock, Roll, Rule, Shog, Shoogle, Swag, Swale, Swee, Swing(e), Teeter, Titter, Totter, Vacillate

Swear(ing), Swear word Attest, Avow, Coprolalia, Curse, Cuss, Depose, Execrate, Jurant, Juratory, Oath, Pledge, Plight, Rail, Sessa, Tarnal, Tarnation, Verify, Vow

6

Sloppy Joe, Woolly

Swede Nordic, Rutabaga, Scandinavian, Turnip

Sweeney Police, Todd

Sweep(er), Sweeping(s) Besom, Broad, Broom, Brush, Chimney, Clean, Curve, Debris, Detritus, Expanse, Extensive, Lash, Libero, Lottery, Net, Oars, Police-manure, Range, Scud, Sling, Snowball, Soop, Sooterkin, Stroke, Surge, Swathe, Vacuum, Waft, Wide

Sweepstake Draw, Gamble, Lottery, Raffle, Tattersall's, Tombola

Sweet(s), Sweetener, Sweetmeat Adeline, Afters, Alcorza, Aldose, Amabile, Aspartame, Bombe, Bonbon, Bonus, Brandyball, Bribe, Bull's eye, Burnt-almonds, Butterscotch, Candy, Candyfloss, Caramel, Chaptalise, Charming, Choc(olate), Cloying, Comfit, Confect(ion), Confetti, Confiserie, Confit, Conserve, Crème, Cute, Cyclamate, Dessert, Dolce, Dolly, Douce(t), Dowset, Dragée, Dulcet, Elecampane, Flummery, Fondant, Fool, Fragrant, Fresh, Fudge, Glucose, Glycerin, Gob-stopper, Goody, Gum(drop), Gundy, Hal(a)vah, Halva, Honey(ed), Humbug, Ice, Icky, Indican, Jelly baby, Jelly bean, Jube, Jujube, Kiss, Lavender, Licorice, Liquorice, Lollipop, Lolly, Lozenge, Luscious, Marchpane, Marshmallow, Marzipan, Melodious, Mint, Mousse, Muscavado, Nectared, Noisette, Nonpareil, Nougat, Pastille, Pea, Peardrop, Pet, Pie, Praline, Pud(ding), Redolent, Rock, Romic, Saccharin(e), Scroggin, Seventeen, Sillabub, Sixteen, Solanine, Soot(e), Sop, Sorbet, Spice, Split, Stickjaw, Sucrose, Sugar, Syllabub, Syrupy, Tablet, Taffy, Tart, Thaumatin, Toffee, Torte, Trifle, Truffle, Twee, Uses, William, Winsome, Xylitol

Sweetbread Bur(r), Inchpin, Pancreas

Sweetheart Amoret, Amour, Beau, Dona(h), Dowsabel(l), Doxy, Dulcinea, Flame, Follower, Honey(bunch), Honeybun, Jarta, Jo(e), Lass, Leman, Lover, Masher, Neaera, Peat, Romeo, Steady, Toots(y), True-love, Valentine, Yarta, Yarto

Sweet-seller Butcher, Confectioner

Swell(ing) Adenomata, Ague-cake, Anasarca, Aneurysm, Apophysis, Bag, Bellying, Berry, Billow, Blab, Blister, Bloat, Blow, Boil, Boll, Bolster, Botch, Braw, Bubo, Bulb, Bulge, Bump, Bunion, Capellet, Carnosity, Cat, Chancre, Chilblain, Clour, Cratches, Cyst, Dandy, Desmoid, Diapason, Dilate, ➤ DISTEND, Dom, Don, Ectasia, Eger, Elephantiasis, Enhance, Entasis, Epulis, Excellent, Farcy-bud, Frog, Gall, Gathering, Gent, Goiter, Goitre, Gout, Grandee, Ground, H(a)ematoma, Heave, Heighten, Hove, Hydrocele, Increase, Inflate, Intumesce, Kibe, L, Lampas(se), Lampers, Louden, Lump, Macaroni, Mouse, Nodule, Odontoma, Oedema, OK, Onco-, Ox-warble, Parotitis, Plim, Plump, Protrude, Proud, Pulvinus, Rise, Roil, Scirrhus, Scleriasis, Sea, Splenomegaly, Strout, Struma, Stye, Surge, Teratoma, Toff, Torulose, Tuber(cle), Tumescence, Tumour, Tympany,

Upsurge, Varicocele, Venter, Wallow, Warble, Wen, Whelk, Windgall, Xanthoma

▷ **Swelling** may indicate a word reversed

Swelter(ing) Perspire, Stew, Sweat, Tropical

Swerve, Swerving Bias, Broach, Careen, Deflect, Deviate, Lean, Sheer, Shy, Stray, Swing, Warp, Wheel

Swift(ly) Apace, Bird, Dean, Dromond, Fleet, Flock, Hasty, Martlet, Newt, Nimble, Presto, Prompt, Quick, ➤ RAPID, Slick, Spanking, Velocipede, Wight

Swig Drink, Gulp, Nip, Scour, Swill, Tighten

Swill Guzzle, Leavings, Rubbish, Slosh, Swash

▷ **Swilling** may indicate an anagram

Swim(ming) Bathe, Bogey, Bogie, Crawl, Dip, Float, Naiant, Natatorial, Paddle, Reel, Run, Skinny-dip, Soom, Synchro(nized), Trudgen, Whirl

▷ **Swim** may indicate an anagram

Swimmer Bather, Cichlid, Duckbill, Duckmole, Dugong, Frogman, Leander, Pad(d)le, Paidle, Planula, Pleopod, Pobble, Terrapin, Trudgen, Webb

▷ **Swimmer** may indicate a fish

Swimming costume Bathers, Bikini, Cossie, Maillot, Monokini, One-piece, Tanga, Trunks

Swindle(r) Beat, Bucket-shop, Bunco, Bunkosteerer, Cajole, Champerty, ➤ CHEAT, Chouse, Con, Defraud, Diddle, Do, Escroc, Fiddle, Finagle, Fineer, Fleece, Fraud, Gazump, Goose-trap, Gip, Graft, Grifter, Gyp, Hocus, Hustler, Leg, Leger, Long-firm, Magsman, Mulct, Nobble, Peter Funk, Plant, Racket, Ramp, Rig, Rogue, Scam, Sell, Shark, Sharper, Shicer, Shyster, Skelder, Skin, Sting, Stitch-up, Stumer, Suck, Swiz(z), Trick, Twist, Two-time

Swine(herd) Boar, Brute, Cad, Eumaeus, Gadarene, Heel, Hog, Peccary, Pig, Pork, Rotter, Sounder, Sow, Sybotic

Swing(er), Swinging Colt, Dangle, Flail, Hang, Hep, Kip(p), Lilt, Metronome, Mod, Music, Oscillate, Pendulate, Pendulum, Rock, Rope, Shoogie, Shuggy, Slew, Swale, Sway, Swee, Swerve, Swey, Swipe, Trapeze, Vibratile, Voop, Wave, Wheel, Whirl, Yaw

Swipe(s) Backhander, Beer, Haymaker, Steal, Strike, Tap-lash

Swirl Eddy, Purl, Swoosh, Tourbill(i)on, Twist, Whirl

▷ **Swirling** may indicate an anagram

Swish Cane, Frou-frou, Rustle, Smart, Whir, Whisper

Swiss Genevese, Ladin, Roll, Tell, Vaudois

Switch Birch, Change, Convert, Dimmer, Dip, Exchange, Hairpiece, Knife, Replace, Retama, Rocker, Rod, Scutch, Thyristor, Time, Toggle, Trip, Twig, Wave, Zap

Switzerland CH, Helvetia

Swivel Caster, Pivot, Root, Rotate, Spin, Terret, Territ, Torret, Turret, Wedein

Swiz Chiz(z)

Swollen Blown, Bollen, Bulbous, Full, Gourdy, Gouty, Incrassate, Nodose, Puffy, Tumid, Turgescent, Turgid, Varicose, Ventricose, Vesiculate

Swoon Blackout, Collapse, Deliquium, Dover, Dwa(l)m, Dwaum, Faint

Swoop Descend, Dive, Glide, Plummet, Souse

▶ **Swop** see SWAP

Sword(-like), Swordplay Andrew Ferrara, Anelace, Angurvadel, Anlace, Arondight, Balisarda, Balmung, Bilbo, Blade, Brand, Brandiron, Broad(sword), Caliburn, Cemitare, Claymore, Colada, Curtal-ax, Curtana, Curtax, Cutlass, Daisho, Damascene, Damaskin, Damocles, Dance, Dirk, Duranda(l), Durindana, Ensate, Ensiform, Epée, Espada, Estoc, Excalibur, Falchion, Faulchi(o)n, Firangi, Foil, Forte, Fox, Gladius, Glaive, Gleave, Glorious, Hanger, Joyeuse, Katana, Kendo, Khanda, Kirpan, Kris, Kukri, Kusanagi, Mandau, Merveilleuse, Mimming, Montanto, Morglay, Nothung, Philippan, Rapier, Rosse, Sabre, Samurai, Schiavone, Schlager, Scimitar, Semita(u)r, Shabble, Shamshir, Sharp, Sigh, Simi, Skene-dhu, Smallsword, Spadroon, Spirtle, Spit, Spurtle(blade), Steel, Toasting-iron, Toledo, Tuck, Tulwar, Waster, Whinger, Whiniard, Whinyard, White-arm, Xiphoid, Yatag(h)an

Sword-bearer, Swordsman, Swordswoman Aramis, Athos, Blade, Brenda(n), D'Artagnon, Fencer, Frog, Gladiator, Porthos, Selictar, Spadassin, Spadroon, Spartacus, Swashbuckler, Zorro

Sword-dancer Matachin

Swordfish Espada, Istiophorus, Xiphias

Sword-swallower Samite

Swot Dig, Grind, Kill, Mug, Smug, Stew, Strike, Swat

Sybarite Aristippus, Epicure, Hedonist, Voluptuary

Sycamore Acer, Maple, Plane, Tree

Sycophant Brown-nose, Claqueur, Crawler, Creeper, Damocles, Fawner, Lickspittle, Parasite, Pickthank, Placebo, Toad-eater, Toady, Yesman

Syllabary Hiragana, Kana, Katakana

Syllable(s) Acatalectic, Anacrusis, Aretinian, Om, Tonic

Syllabus Program(me), Prospectus, Résumé, Summary, Table

Syllogism Argument, Conclusion, Deduction, Epicheirema

Sylph Ariel, Nymph

Symbol(ic), Symbols, Symbolism, Symbolist Acrophony, Agma, Allegory, Ampersand, Aniconic, Ankh, Apostrophus, Aramanth, Asterisk, Cachet, Caret, Cedilla, Character, Chord, Choropleth, Cipher, Clef, Colon, Crest, Daffodil, Decadent, Del, Descriptor, Diesis, Dingbat, Double-axe, Eagle, Emblem, Emoticon, Eng, Equal, Grapheme, Hash, Heitiki, Hieroglyph, Hierogram, Hiragana, Ichthus, Icon, Ideogram, Index, Kalachakra, Kanji, Length mark, Logo(gram), Logograph, Mandala, Mark, Menorah, Metaphor, Mezuzah, Minus, Mogen David, Moral, Motif, Mystical, Nabla, Nominal, Notation, Obelus, One, Ouroborus, Paragraph, Pentacle, Phonetic, Phraseogram, Pi, Pictograph, Plus, Presa, Redon, Rose, Rune, Segno, Semicolon, Semiotic, Shamrock, Sigla, Sign, Slur, Smiley, Star of David, Status, Svastika, Swastika, Syllabogram, Tag, Talisman,

Thistle, Tiki, Tilde, Token, Totem, Trademark, Triskele, Triskelion, Type, Uraeus, Yoni

Symmetric(al), Symmetry Balance, Digonal, Diphycercal, Even, Harmony, Isobilateral, Radial, Regular

Sympathetic, Sympathise(r), Sympathy Approval, Commiserate, Compassion, Condole(nce), Condone, Congenial, Crypto, Empathy, Fellow-traveller, Humane, Par, Pity, Rapport, Ruth, Side, Vicarious

Symphony Concert, Eroica, Fifth, Jupiter, Manfred, Music, New World, Opus, Pastoral, Sinfonia, Unfinished

Symposium Assembly, Conference, Synod

Symptom(s) Epiphenomenon, Feature, Indicia, Merycism, Mimesis, Prodrome, Semiotic, Sign, Syndrome, Token, Trait, Withdrawal

Synagogue Beit Knesset, Beth Knesseth, Shul, Temple

Synchronise(r) Coincide, Genlock, Tune

Syncopated, Syncopation Abridged, Breakbeat, Revamp, Zoppa, Zoppo

Syndicate Associate, Cartel, Combine, Mafioso, Pool, Ring

Syndrome Adams-Stokes, Asperger's, Carpal tunnel, Characteristic, China, Chronic fatigue, Cushing's, Down's, Empty nest, Fragile X, Hutchinson-Gilford, Jerusalem, Korsakoff's, Locked-in, Marfan, ME, Menières, Munchhausen's, Nonne's, Pattern, Postviral, Premenstrual, Reiter's, Reye's, Sezary, Sjogren's, Stevens-Johnson, Stockholm, Stokes-Adams, Temperomandibular, TMJ, Tourette's, Toxic shock, Turner's, Wag the Dog, Wernicke-Korsakoff, Wobbler

Synod Assembly, Conference, Convocation

Synonym(ous) Comparison, Reciprocal

Synopsis Abstract, Blurb, Conspectus, Digest, Outline, Résumé, Schema, ➤ SUMMARY

Syntax Grammar

Synthesis Amalgam, Fusion, Merger

Synthesizer Moog®, Vocoder

Synthetic Ersatz, Fake, False, Mock, Polyamide, Spencerian

Syphilis Chancre, Lues

Syrian Aramaean, Aramaic, Druse, Druz(e), Hittite, Hurrian, Levantine, Phoenician

Syringe(s) Douche, Flutes, Harpoon, Hypo, Needle, Reeds, Spray, Squirt, Wash

Syrup Capillaire, Cassis, Cocky's joy, Corn, Diacodion, Diacodium, Flattery, Grenadine, Linctus, Maple, Molasses, Moskonfyt, Orgeat, Quiddary, Rob, Sorghum, Sugar, Treacle

System(atic) ABO, Bertillon, Binary, Braille, Code, Copernican, Cosmos, Course, Decimal, Delsarte, Dewey (Decimal), Economy, Eocene, Ergodic, Establishment, Feudal, Giorgi, Harvard, Iastic, Life-support, Limbic, Linear, Madras, ➤ METHOD, Metric, Microcosm, Miocene, Nervous, Network, Nicam, Notation, Octal, Order, Organon, Permian, Pleiocene, Process, Ptolemaic, Regime, Regular, Root, Scientific, SI, Solar, Sonar, Stanislavski, Structure, Studio, Ternary, Theory, Tommy, Trias(sic), Universe

T t

T Bone, Junction, Potence, Tau-cross, Tango, Tee, Time

Tab Bill, Check, ➤ LABEL, Ring-pull, Tally

Tabby Blabbermouth, Brindled, ➤ CAT, Gossip, Mottled, Spinster, Striped, Trout

Tabitha Gazelle

Table(-like) Alphonsine, Altar, Board, Bradshaw, Breakfast, Calendar, ➤ CHART, Console, Contingency, Counter, Credence, Credenza, Desk, Diagram, Dinner, Dolmen, Dressing, Drop-leaf, Ephemeris, Food, Gateleg, Glacier, Graph, Green-cloth, Gueridon, High, Index, Key, League, ➤ LIST, Mahogany, Matrix, Mensa(l), Mesa, Monopode, Occasional, Pembroke, Periodic, Piecrust, Pier, Plane, Platen, Pool, Prothesis, Pythagoras, Reckoner, Refectory, Roll, Round, Rudolphine, Slab, Spoon, Stall, Stone, Taboret, Tabular, Te(a)poy, Tea, Tide, Times, Trestle, Trolley, Twelve, Washstand, Water, Workbench

Table-land Barkly, Kar(r)oo, Mesa, Plateau, Puna

Table-list Memo, Menu

Tablet Abacus, Album, Aspirin, Caplet, Eugebine, Medallion, Opisthograph, Osculatory, Ostracon, Ostrakon, ➤ PAD, ➤ PILL, Plaque, Slate, Stele, Stone, Tombstone, Torah, Triglyph, Triptych, Troche, Trochisk, Ugarit

Table-talker Deipnosophist

Table-turner Tartar

Table-ware China, Cutlery, Silver

Taboo, Tabu Ban(ned), Bar, Blackball, Forbidden, No-no, Non dit, Unclean

Tacit, Taciturn(ity) Implicit, Laconic, Mumps, Silent, Understood

Tack Baste, Beat, Brass, Cinch, Clubhaul, Cobble, Gybe, Leg, Martingale, Nail, Saddlery, Salt-horse, ➤ SEW, Sprig, Stirrup, Veer, White-seam, Yaw, Zigzag

Tackle Accost, Approach, Attempt, Beard, Bobstay, Burton, Claucht, Claught, Clevis, Clew-garnet, Collar, Dead-eye, Garnet, Gear, Haliard, Halyard, Harness, Jury-rig, Rig, Rigging, Scrag

Tact, Tactful Delicacy, Diplomacy, Diplomatic, Discreet, Discretion, Politic, Savoir-faire

Tactic(s) Audible, Hardball, Manoeuvre, Masterstroke, Plan, Ploy, Salami, Shock, ➤ STRATEGY, Strong-arm

Tactless(ness) Blundering, Brash, Crass, Gaffe, Gauche, Indelicate

Tadpole Polliwig, Polliwog, Pollywig, Pollywog, Porwiggle

Taffy Thief, Toffee, Welshman

Tag Aglet, Aiguillette, Cliché, Dog, End, Epithet, ➤ FOLLOW, Kabaddi, Kimball, Label, Price, Quote, Remnant, Tab, ➤ TICKET, Treasury

Tail, Tailpiece Apocopate, ➤ APPENDAGE, Bob, Brush, Caudal, Cercal, Cercus, Coda, Colophon, Cue, Dock, Empennage, Fan, Fee, Floccus, ➤ FOLLOW, Fud, Liripoop, Parson's nose, Pole, Pope's nose, PS, Queue, Rumple-bane, Seat, Scut, Stag, Stern, Telson, ➤ TIP, Train, Uropygium, Uro(some), Women

Tailless Acaudal, An(o)urous, Fee-simple

Tail-lobes Anisocercal

Tailor(ed) Bespoke, Bushel, Cabbager, Couturier, Cutter, Darzi, Durzi, Epicene, Feeble, Nine, Outfitter, Pick-the-louse, Pricklouse, Sartor, Seamster, Snip, Starveling, Style, Whipcat, Whipstitch

▷ **Tailor** may indicate an anagram

Taint(ed) Besmirch, Blemish, Fly-blown, High, Infect, Leper, Off, Poison, ➤ SPOIL, Stain, Stigma, Trace, Unwholesome

Taiwan RC

Take(n), Take in, Taking(s), Take over Absorb, ➤ ACCEPT, Adopt, Assume, Attract, Bag, Beg, Bite, Bone, Borrow, Bottle, ➤ CAPTURE, Catch, Cop, Coup, Detract, Dishy, Distrain, Exact, Expropriate, Get, Grab, Haul, Hent, House, Howe, Huff, Incept, Ingest, Mess, Nick, Occupy, Pocket, Quote, R, Rec, Receipt, Receive, Recipe, Rob, Seise, Sequester, Ship, Smitten, Snatch, Sneak, ➤ STEAL, Stomach, Subsume, Swallow, Sweet, Swipe, Toll, Trump, Turnover, Usurp, Wan, Winsome, Wrest

Take away, Take off Aph(a)eresis, Asport, Carry-out, Deduct, Dock, Doff, Esloin, Exenterate, Expropriate, Jato, Parody, Parrot, Press-gang, Shanghai, Skit, Subtract, Vertical, VTO(L)

Take care Guard, See, Tend, Watch

▷ **Taken up** may indicate reversed

Take part Act, Engage, Side

Talbot House Toc H

Talc Potstone, Rensselaerite, Soapstone, Steatite

Tale(s) Allegory, Blood, Boccaccio, Conte, Decameron, Edda, Fable, Fabliau, Fairy, Fiction, Gag, Geste, Hadith, Iliad, Jataka, Jeremiad, Legend, Lie, Mabinogion, Maise, Ma(i)ze, Marchen, Mease, Milesian, Narrative, Odyssey, Pentameron, Rede, Saga, Sandabar, Score, Sinbad, Sind(a)bad, Spiel, ➤ STORY, Tradition, Travellers', Weird

Tale-bearer, Tale-teller Gossip, Grass, Informer, Sneak, Tattler, Tusitala

Talent(ed) Accomplishment, Aptitude, Bent, Dower, Faculty, Flair, Genius, Gift, Knack, Nous, Prodigy, Schtick, Strong point, Versatile, Virtuoso, W(h)iz(z), Whiz-kid

Talion Reprisal

Talisman Amulet, Charm, Saladin, Sampo, Telesm

Talk, Talker, Talks Ana, Articulate, Babble, Bibble-babble, Blab, Blague, Blat, Blether-skate, Cant, Chat, Chinwag, Chirp, Circumlocution, Colloquy, Commune, Confabulate, Confer, Converse, Coo, Cross, Descant, Dialog(ue), Diatribe, Dilate, Discourse, Diseur, Dissert, Earbash, Earful, Express, Filibuster, Froth, Gab, Gabble, Gabnash, Gas, Gibber, Gossip, Grandiloquence, Guff, Harp, Imparl, Jabber, Jargon, Jaw, Jazz, Korero, Lip,

Logorrhoea, Macrology, Mang, Maunder, Mince, Monologue, Motormouth, Nashgab, Noise, Omniana, Palabra, Palaver, Parlance, Parley, Patter, Pawaw, Pep, Perorate, Phraser, Pidgin, Pillow, Pitch, Potter, Powwow, Prate, Prattle, Prose, Ramble, Rap, Rigmarole, Rote, SALT, Shop, Slang(-whang), Small, Soliloquy, ➤ SPEAK, Spiel, Spout, Sweet, Table, Turkey, Twaddle, Twitter, Unbosom, Up(s), Utter, Vocal, Waffle, Witter, Wongi, Wrangle, Yabber, Yack, Yak, Yammer, Yap, Yalta, Yatter

Talkative Chatty, Fluent, Gabby, Garrulous, Gash, Glib, Loquacious, Vocular, Voluble

Tall Etiolated, Exaggerated, Hie, High, Hye, Lanky, Lathy, Leggy, Lofty, Long, Procerity, Randle-tree, Tangle, Taunt, Tower, Towery

Tallboy Chest, Dresser

Tallow Greaves, Hatchettite, Wax

Tally ➤ AGREE, Census, Correspond, Count, Match, Nickstick, Notch, Record, ➤ SCORE, Stick, Stock, Tab, Tag

Talon Claw, Ogee, Single

Talus Scree

Tamarind Assam

Tamasha Fuss, To-do

Tame Amenage, Break, Docile, Domesticate, Mansuete, Meek, Mild, Safe, Snool, Subdue

Tammany Hall, Sachem

Tamp, Tampon Plug

Tamper(ing) Bishop, Cook, Doctor, Fake, Fiddle, Meddle, Medicate, Monkey, Nobble, Phreaking

Tam-tam Gong

Tan(ned), Tanned skin, Tanning Adust, Bablah, Babul, Bark, Basil, Beige, Bisque, Bronze, ➤ BROWN, Catechu, Insolate, Lambast, Leather, Neb-neb, Paste, Pipi, Puer, Pure, Spank, Sun, Tenné, Umber, Valonea, Val(l)onia, Ybet

Tandem Duo, Random

Tang Relish, Smack, Taste

Tangent Ratio, Slope, Touching

Tangible Concrete, Palpable, Plain, Solid, Tactual

Tangle Alga, Badderlock, Burble, Dulse, Embroil, Entwine, Fank, Fankle, Heap, Implication, Ket, ➤ KNOT, Labyrinth, Laminaria, Lutin, Mat, Mix, Nest, Oarweed, Ore, Pleach, Perplex, ➤ RAVEL, Sea-girdle, Seaweed, Skean, Skein, Snarl, Taigle, Taut(it), Tawt, Thicket, Varec

▷ **Tangled** may indicate an anagram

Tank Amphibian, Aquarium, Centurion, Cesspool, Challenger, Chieftain, Cistern, Feedhead, Float, Flotation, Gasholder, Header, Keir, Kier, Mouse, Panzer, Pod, ➤ RESERVOIR, Ripple, Septic, Sherman, Sponson, Sump, Think, Tiger, Valentine, Vat, Vivarium, Whippet

Tankard Blackjack, Pewter, Pot, Stein

Tanker Bowser, Lorry, Oiler

Tanner(y) Bender, Kick, Solarium, Sunbather, Sunshine, Tawery, Tester(n), 'Vld', Zack

Tannin Catechu

Tantalise Entice, Tease, Tempt, Torture

Tantalum Ta

Tantivy Alew, Halloo

Tantrum Paddy, Pet, Rage, Scene, Tirrivee, Tirrivie

Tap(ping), Taps Accolade, Bibcock, Blip, Broach, Bug, Cock, Col legno, Drum, Faucet, Flick, Hack, Milk, Mixer, Paracentesis, Pat, Patter, Percuss, Petcock, ➤ RAP, Spigot, Stopcock, Stroup, Tack, Tat, Tit, Touk, Tuck

Tape DAT, ➤ DRINK, Ferret, Finish, Incle, Inkle, Insulating, Magnetic, Masking, Measure, Metal, Paper, Passe-partout, Perforated, Punched, Record, Red, Scotch, Sticky, Ticker, Video

Taper(ed), Tapering Diminish, Fastigiate, Featheredge, Fusiform, Lanceolate, Narrow, Nose, Subulate, Tail

Tapestry Alentous, Arras(ene), Bayeux, Bergamot, Crewel-work, Dosser, Gobelin, Hanging, Oudenarde, Tapet

Tapeworm Hydatid, Measle, Scolex, Taenia, Teniasis

Tapioca Cassava, Yuca, Yucca

Tapir Anta, S(e)ladang

Tar, Tar product AB, Bitumen, Coal, Creosote, Egg, Gladwellise, Gob, Indene, Maltha, Matelot, Matlo, Mineral, Naphtha, Needle, OS, Parcel, Pay, Picamar, Picene, Pine, Pitch, Rating, Retene, Sailor, Salt, Uintahite, Uintaite, Wood, Xylol

Tardy Behindhand, Dilatory, Late, ➤ SLOW

Tare Tine, Vetch

Target ➤ AIM, Blank, Butt, Cockshy, End, Hit, Home, Hub, Inner, Magpie, Mark, Motty, ➤ OBJECT, Outer, Pelta, Pin, Prey, Prick, Quintain, Sitter, Tee, Victim

Tariff List, Rate, Zabeta

Tarnish Discolour, Soil, Stain, Sully, Taint

Taro Arum, Coc(c)o, Dasheen, Eddo

Tarot Arcana

Tarpaulin Weathercloth

Tarragon Staragen

Tarry Bide, Dally, Leng, ➤ LINGER, Stay, Sticky

Tarsier Malmag

Tarsus Saul

Tart Acetic, Acid, Bakewell, Broad, Charlotte, Cocotte, Croquante, Cupid, Dariole, Doxy, Duff, Flam(m), Flan, Flawn, Harlot, Hussy, Jade, Lemony, Mirliton, Moll, Mort, Nana, ➤ PIE, Pinnace, Piquant, Pro, Quean, Quiche, Quine, ➤ SHARP, Slapper, Slut, Sour, Stew, Strumpet, Tatin, Tramp, Treacle, Trull, Unsweet

Tartan Argyle, Maud, Plaid, Set(t), Trews

Tartar Argal, Argol, Beeswing, Crust, Hell, Plaque, Rough, Scale, Tam(b)erlane, Zenocrate

Tashkent Uzbek

Task Assignment, Aufgabe, ➤ CHORE, Duty, Errand, Exercise, Fag, Imposition, Mission, Ordeal, Pensum, Stint, Thankless, Vulgus

Tasmania Apple Isle

Tassel Pompom, Toorie, Tourie, Tuft

Taste(ful), Tasty Acquired, Aesthetic, Appetite, Degust, Delibate, Discrimination, ➤ EAT, Fashion, Flavour, Form, Gout, Gust, Hint, Lick, Palate, Penchant, Pica, Pree, Refinement, Relish, ➤ SAMPLE, Sapor, Sar, Savour, S(c)hme(c)k, Sip, Smack, Smatch, Snack, Stomach, Soupçon, Succulent, Tang, Titbit, Toothsome, ➤ TRY, Vertu, Virtu

Tasteless Appal, Fade, Flat, Insipid, Stale, Vapid, Vulgar, Watery, Wearish, Wersh

Tat, Tatter, Tatty Rag, Ribbon, Roon, Scrap, Shred, Tag, Tan, Untidy

Tattie-bogle Scarecrow

Tattle(r) Blab, Chatter, ➤ GOSSIP, Prate, Rumour, Sneak, Snitch, Totanus, Willet

Tattoo Drum, Moko, Rataplan, Row-dow, Tat

Tatum Art

Taught Up

Taunt Dig, Fling, Gibe, Gird, ➤ JEER, Rag, Ridicule, Twight, Twit

Taut Stiff, Tense

Tavern Bar, Bodega, Bousing-ken, Bush, Fonda, ➤ INN, Kiddleywink, Kneipe, Mermaid, Mitre, Mughouse, Pothouse, Shebeen, Taphouse

Taw Alley, Ally, Marble

Tawdry Catchpenny, ➤ CHEAP, Flashy, Gaudy, Sleazy, Tatty, Tinsey

Tawny Brindle, Dusky, Fawn, Fulvous, Mulatto, Port, Tan

Tawse Cat, Lash, Thong, Whip

Tax(ing), Taxation ACT, Aid, Agist, Alms-fee, Assess, Capitation, Carucage, Cense, Cess, ➤ CHARGE, Corporation, Council, Custom, Danegeld, Direct, Duty, Energy, EPT, Escot, Escuage, Exact, Excise, Exercise, Gabelle, Geld, Gift, Head, Hidage, Impose, Imposition, Impost, Impute, Indirect, Inheritance, IR, Jaghir(e), Jagir, Land, Levy, Likin, Lot, Murage, Octroi, Operose, Overwork, Pavage, PAYE, Peter-pence, Poll, Poundage, Primage, Property, Proportional, PT, Purchase, Rate, Road, Rome-pence, Scat(t), Scot (and lot), Scutage, Sess, SET, Skat, Stent, Streetage, Taille, Tallage, Talliate, Task, Teind, Tithe, Toilsome, Toll, Tonnage, Tribute, Try, VAT, Wattle, Wealth, Weary, White rent, Window, Withholding, Zakat

Tax area Tahsil, Talooka, Taluk(a)

Tax-collector, Taxman Amildar, Cheater, Exciseman, Farmer, Gabeller, Inspector, IR(S), Publican, Stento(u)r, Tithe-proctor, Tollman, Undertaker, Zemindar

Taxi Cab, Hackney, Samlor

Taxidermist Venus

▶ **Taxman** see TAX-COLLECTOR

TB Scrofula

TE Lawrence, Ross, Shaw

Tea Afternoon, Assam, Beef, Black, Bohea, Brew, Brick, Bush, Cambric, Camomile, Ceylon, Cha, Chamomile, Chanoyu, China, Chirping-cup, Congo(u), Cream, Cuppa, Darjeeling, Earl Grey, Grass, Green, Gunfire, Gunpowder, High, Hyson, Indian, Jasmine, K(h)at, Kitchen, Labrador, Lapsang, Lapsang Souchong, Leaves, Ledum, Marijuana, Maté, Oolong, Orange pekoe, Oulong, Paraguay, Pekoe, Pot, Qat, Red-root, Rooibos, Russian, Senna, Souchong, Switchel, Tay, Thea, Theophylline, Twankay, Yerba (de Maté)

Teach(er), Teaching (material), Teachings Acharya, Adjoint, Agrege, AMMA, Apostle, Barbe, Beale, BEd, Bhagwan, Buss, Catechist, Chalkface, ➤ COACH, Con(ne), Didactic, Didascalic, Docent, Doctrine, Dogma, Dominie, Dressage, Edify, ➤ EDUCATE, EIS, ELT, Explain, Faculty, Froebel, Gerund-grinder, Gooroo, Gospel, Governess, Guru, Head, Heuristic, Hodja, Inculcate, Indoctrinate, Inform, Instil, Instruct, Ism, Kho(d)ja, Lair, Lancasterian, Larn, Lear(e), Lecturer, Leir, Lere, Maam, Maggid, Magister, Maharishi, Mahavira, Mallam, Marker, Marm, Master, Maulvi, Mentor, Miss, Mistress, Molla(h), Monitor, Montessorian, Moola(h), Moovi(e), Mufti, Mullah, Munshi, Mystagogue, PT, Paedotribe, Pedagogue, Pedant, Pr(a)efect, Preceptor, Prof, Privat-docent, Rabbi, Realia, Rebbe, Rhetor, Scholastic, Schoolman, Scribe, Sensei, Show, Sir, Smriti, Socrates, Sophist, Staff, Starets, Staretz, Sunna, Supply, Swami, Tantra, Train(er), Tutelage, Tutor, Usher

Teach-in Seminar

Teahouse Sukiya

Team Colts, Crew, Dream, Ecurie, Eleven, Equipe, Fifteen, Outfit, Oxen, Panel, Possibles, Probables, Relay, Scrub, ➤ SIDE, Span, Squad, Squadron, Staff, Troupe, Turnout, Unicorn, United, XI

Tea-party Boston, Bunfight, Cookie-shine, Drum, Kettledrum, Shine

Teapot Billycan, Cadogan, Samovar

Tear(s), Tearable, Tearful, Tearing Beano, Claw, Crocodile, Drop, Eye-drop, Eye-water, Greeting, Hurry, Lacerate, Laniary, Pelt, Ranch, Rash, Reave, ➤ REND, Rheum, Rip, Rive, Rume, Screed, Shred, Snag, Split, Spree, Tire, Wet, Worry, Wrench, Wrest

Tearaway Get, Hothead, Ned

Tear-jerker Onion

Tear-pit Crumen, Larmier

Tease, Teasing Arch, Backcomb, Badinage, Bait, Banter, Chap, Chiack, Chip, Chyack, Cod, Grig, Guy, Hank, Imp, Ironic, Itch, Josh, Kemb, Kid, Mag, Nark, Persiflage, ➤ RAG, Raillery, Rally, Razz, Rib, Rot, Strip, ➤ TANTALISE, Toaze, Torment(or), Twilly, Twit

Teasel Dipsacus, Valerian

Teat Dug, Dummy, Mamilla, Mastoid, Nipple, Pap, Soother, Tit

Tea-time Chat

Teaze Gig, Moze

Technetium Tc

Technical, Technician, Technique Adept, Alexander, Artisan, Brushwork, College, Delphi, Execution, Kiwi, Manner, ➤ METHOD, Operative, Salami, Science

Technology, Technological State of the art, Stealth

Ted(dy) Bodgie, Dexter, Ducktail, Moult, Widgie, Yob

Tedium, Tedious Boring, Chore, Deadly, Drag, Dreich, Dull, Ennui, Heaviness, Long, Longspun, Monotony, Operose, Prosy, Soul-destroying, ➤ TIRING, Wearisome, Yawn

Tee Hub, Umbrella

Teem(ing) Abound, Bustling, Empty, Great, Pullulate, Swarm

Teenager Adolescent, Bobbysoxer, Junior, Juvenile, Minor, Mod, Rocker, Sharpie

➤ **Teeth** see TOOTH

Teething ring Coral

Teetotal(ler) Abdar, Blue Ribbon, Nephalist, Rechabite, Temperate, TT, Water-drinker, Wowser

Telecommunications Cellnet®, Vodafone®

Telegram, Telegraph Bush, Cable, Ems, Grapevine, Greetings, Message, Moccasin, Telex, Wire

Telepathy, Telepathic Clairvoyance, ESP, Seer

Telephone Ameche, ATLAS, Bell, Blower, BT, Call, Cellphone, Centrex, Cordless, Dial, GRACE, Handset, Horn, Intercom, Line, Lo-call®, Mercury, Pay-station, Pdq, Ring, STD, Touch-tone, Vodafone®, Wire

Teleprinter Creed

Telescope Altazimuth, Binocle, Cassegrain(ian), Collimator, Coudé, Finder, Galilean, Glass, Gregorian, Heliometer, Hubble, Intussuscept, Newtonian, Palomar, Radio, Reflector, Refractor, Schmidt, Shorten, Spyglass, Stadia, Terrestrial, Tube

Teletext® Ceefax®, Oracle®

Television, Telly Box, Digital, Diorama, Goggle box, ITV, MAC, PAL, RTE, Set, Small screen, Tube, ➤ TV, Video

Tell Acquaint, Announce, Apprise, Archer, Beads, Blab, Clipe, Clype, Compt, Direct, ➤ DISCLOSE, Divulge, Grass, Impart, Inform, ➤ NARRATE, Noise, Notify, Number, Recite, Recount, Relate, Report, Retail, Rumour, Sneak, Snitch, Spin, Teach, William

Tellurium Te

Temerity Cheek, Gall, Impertinence, Imprudence, Impudence, Incaution, Rashness, Recklessness

Temper, Temperate Abstemious, Abstinent, Allay, Anneal, Assuage, Attune, Balmy, Bile, Blood, Calm, Choler, Comeddle, Continent, Dander, Delay, Ease, Fireworks, Flaky, Irish, Leaven, ➤ MILD, Mitigate, Moderate, Modify, ➤ MOOD, Neal, Paddy, Paddywhack, Pet, Rage, Season, Sober, Soften, Spitfire, Spleen, Strop, Swage, Tantrum, Techy, Teen, Teetotal, Tetchy, Tiff, Tone, Trim, Tune

Temperament(al) Bent, Blood, Crasis, Disposition, Kidney, Mettle, Moody, ➤ NATURE, Over-sensitive, Prima donna

Temperance Moderation, Pledge, Rechabite

Temperature Absolute, Celsius, Centigrade, Chambré, Curie, Fahrenheit, Fever, Flashpoint, Heat, Heterothermal, Hyperthermia, Kelvin, Regulo, Room, T, Weed, Weid

Tempest(uous) Bourasque, Euraquilo, Euroclydon, Gale, High, Marie, ➤ STORM(Y)

Temple, Temple gate Adytum, Amphiprostyle, Capitol, Chapel, Church, Delphi, Delubrum, Ephesus, Fane, Gompa, Gurdwara, Haffet, Haffit, Heroon, Inner, Mandir(a), Masjid, Middle, Monopteron, Monopteros, Mosque, Museum, Naos, Pagod(a), Pantheon, Parthenon, ➤ SHRINE, Shul(n), Teocalli, Teopan, Torii, Vihara, Wat

Tempo Agoge, Rate, ➤ RHYTHM, Rubato

Temporary Acting, Caretaker, Cutcha, Ephemeral, Hobjob, Interim, Kutcha, Locum, Makeshift, Pro tem, Provisional, Short-term, Stopgap, Temp, Transient, Transitional

Tempt(ation), Tempting, Tempter, Temptress Allure, Apple, Bait, Beguile, Beset, Dalilah, Decoy, Delilah, ➤ ENTICE, Eve, Groundbait, Impulse, Lure, Providence, Satan, Seduce, Siren, Snare, Tantalise, Tice, Test, Trial

Ten Commandments, Decad, Dectet, Decury, Denary, Googol, 10, Iota, Tera-, Tribes, X

Tenacious, Tenacity Clayey, Determined, Dogged, Fast, Guts, Hold, Intransigent, Persevering, Persistent, Resolute, Retentive, Sticky

Tenancy, Tenant(s) Censuarius, Cosherer, Cottar, Cotter, Cottier, Dreng, Feuar, Feudatory, Homage, Ingo, Inhabit, Leaseholder, Lessee, ➤ LODGER, Metayer, Occupier, Rentaller, Renter, Shorthold, Sitting, Socager, Socman, Sokeman, Suckener, Tacksman, Valvassor, Vassal, Vavasour, Visit

Tend Care, Dress, Herd, Incline, Lean, Liable, Nurse, Prone, Run, Shepherd, Verge

Tendency Apt, Bent, Bias, Conatus, Drift, Import, Militant, Penchant, Proclivity, Propensity, Trend

Tender(iser), Tenderly, Tenderness Affettuoso, Amoroso, Bid, Bill, Coin, Con amore, Crank, Ding(h)y, Dingey, Fond, Frail, Gentle, Green, Humane, Jolly-boat, Legal, Nesh, Nurse, ➤ OFFER, Papain, Pinnace, Prefer, Present, Proffer, Proposal, Quotation, Red Cross, Sair, Shepherd, ➤ SOFT, Sore, SRN, Submit, Sympathy, Tendre

Tenderfoot Babe, Chechacho, Chechako, Cub, Greenhorn, Innocent

Tenderloin Psoas, Undercut

Tendon Achilles, Aponeurosis, Hamstring, Leader, Paxwax, Sinew, String, Vinculum, Whitleather

Tendril(led) Capreolate, Cirrose, Cirrus, Tentacle

Tenement(s) Land, Rook, Tack

Tenet Adiaphoron, Creed, ➤ DOCTRINE, Dogma

Tenfold Decuple

Tennis LTA, Real, Set, Sphairistike, Wimbledon

Tenon Cog, Dovetail, Lewis

Tenor Course, ➤ DRIFT, Effect, Gigli, Gist, Purport, Singer, T, Timbre, Trial, Vein

Tense Aor, Aorist, Case, Clench, Drawn, Edgy, Electric, Essive, Imperfect, Keyed up, Mood(y), Nervy, Overstrung, Past, Perfect, Pluperfect, Preterite, Rigid, Stiff, Stressed(-out), Strict, T, ➤ TAUT, Uptight

Tensing Sherpa

Tension Isometrics, Isotonic, Nerviness, Premenstrual, ➤ STRAIN, Stress, Stretch, Surface, Tone, Yips

Tent Bell, Bivvy, Cabana, Douar, Duar, Kedar, Kibitka, Marquee, Oxygen, Pavilion, Probe, Ridge, Shamiana(h), Shamiyanah, Shelter, Tabernacle, Teepee, Tepee, Tipi, Top, Topek, Trailer, Tupek, Tupik, Wigwam, Y(o)urt

Tentacle Actinal, Cirrate, Feeler, Hectocotylus, Horn, Lophophore

Tentative Empirical, Experimental, Gingerly, Peirastic

Tent-dweller, Tent-maker Camper, Indian, Kedar, Omar, St Paul

Tenth Disme, Teind, Tithe

Ten Thousand Toman

Tenuous Frail, Slender, Slight, Thin, Vague

Tenure Blench, Burgage, Copyhold, Cottier(ism), Drengage, Fee-farm, Feu, Frankalmoi(g)n(e), Gavelkind, Leasehold, Manorial, Occupation, Raiyatwari, Rundale, Runrig, Ryotwari, Socage, ➤ TERM, Vavasory, Venville, Zemindar

Tepid Laodicean, Lukewarm

Terbium Tb

Terete Centric(al)

Term(s), Terminal, Termly Anode, Buffer, Cathode, Coast, Coste, Designate, Desinant, Distal, ➤ EPITHET, Euphemism, Expression, Final, Gnomon, Goal, Half, Hilary, Inkhorn, Lent, Michaelmas, ➤ PERIOD, Sabbatical, Semester, Session, Stint, Stretch, Trimester, Trimestrial, Trinity, Ultimatum, ➤ WORD, Zeroth

Termagant Jade, Shrew, Shrow, Spitfire, Vixen

Terminate, Termination, Terminus Abort, Axe, Conclude, Depot, Desinent, Earth, ➤ END, Expiry, ➤ FINISH, Goal, Liquidate, Naricorn, Railhead, Suffix

Termite Duck-ant

Tern Egg-bird, Scray, Three

Terrace Barbette, Beach, Bench, Linch, Lynchet, Perron, Shelf, Stoep, Tarras, Undercliff, Veranda(h)

Terra-cotta Tanagra

Terrain Area, Landscape, Tract

Terrapin Diamondback, Emydes, Emys, Slider, Turtle

Terrible, Terribly Awful, Deadly, Fell, Frightful, Ghastly, Horrible, Much, Odious, Very

Terrible person Humgruffi(a)n, Ivan, Ogre

Terrier Aberdeen, Airedale, Apsos, Australian, Black and tan, Border, Boston, Bull, Catalogue, Griffon, Kerry blue, Lakeland, Maltese, Manchester, Norfolk, Norwich, Pinscher, Pit bull, Ratter, Register, Scottie, Sealyham, Silky, Skye, TA, Tibetan, Welsh, West Highland, Yorkshire

Terrific, Terrified, Terrify Affright, Aghast, Agrise, Agrize, Agryze, Appal, Awe, Enorm, Fear, Fine, Fley, Gast, Helluva, Huge, Overawe, ➤ PETRIFY, Scare, Superb, Unman, Yippee

Territory Abthane, Ap(p)anage, Colony, Domain, Dominion, Duchy, Emirate, Enclave, Exclave, Goa, Lebensraum, Manor, Margravate, No-man's-land, Northern, Nunavut, Panhandle, Principate, Protectorate, Province, Realm, ➤ REGION, Sphere, Sultanate, Ter(r), Trust, Yukon

Terror Bugaboo, Bugbear, Eek, ➤ FEAR, Fright, Holy, Panic, Skrik

Terrorist Alarmist, Anarchist, Bogeyman, Bomber, Bully, Cagoulard, Desperado, Dynamitard, Eta, Grapo, Hijacker, Ku Klux Klan, Mau-mau, Maximalist, Mountain, Nightrider, Nihilist, Pirate, PLO, Provo, Robespierre

Terry Ellen, Towel

Terse Abrupt, Brusque, Curt, Laconic, Pithy, Precise, Succinct

Tertiary Cainozoic, Eocene, Miocene, Oligocene, Palaeogene, Pliocene

Test(er), Testing Acid, Alpha, Ames, Amniocentesis, Apgar, Appro, Assay, Audition, Bench, Bender, Beta, Breathalyser®, Brinell, Candle, Canopy, Check, Chi-square, Cloze, Conn(er), Coomb's, Criterion, Crucial, Crucible, Crunch, Dick, Docimastic, Driving, Dummy-run, Eprouvette, Examine, Exercise, Experiment, Field, International, Litmus, Mann-Whitney, Mantoux, Means, MOT, Mug, Neckverse, Objective, Oral, Ordalian, ➤ ORDEAL, Pale, Pap, Papanicolaou, Patch, Paternity, Performance, Personality, PH, Pilot, Pree, Preeve, Preif, Preve, Probe, Projective, Proof, Prove, Proving-ground, Pyx, Quiz, Rally, Reagent, Rorschach, SAT, Scalogram, Schick's, Schilling, Screen, Showdown, Shroff, Significance, Sixpence, Skin, Smear, Sound, Stanford-Binet, Tempt, Touch, Touchstone, Trier, Trior, Try, Viva, Wassermann's, Wilcoxon, Zack

Testament Bible, Heptateuch, Hexateuch, New, Old, Pentateuch, Scripture, Septuagint, Tanach, Targum, Will

Testicle(s) Ballocks, Balls, Bollocks, Bollix, Cojones, Gool(e)y, Goolie, Knackers, Monorchid, Nuts, Ridgel, Ridgil, Rig(gald), Rocks, Stone

Testify, Testimonial, Testimony Character, Chit, Declare, Depone, Deposition, ➤ EVIDENCE, Rap, Scroll, Viva voce, Witness

Testy, Tetchy Cross, Narky, Peevish, Ratty

Tetanus Lockjaw

Tête-a-tête Collogue, Confab, Hobnob, Twosome

Tether Cord, Endurance, Noose, Picket, Seal, Stringhalt, ➤ TIE

Tetrahedrite Fahlerz, Fahlore

Tetrarchy Iturea

Tetrasyllabic Paeon

Tetrode Resnatron

Teuton(ic) Erl-king, German, Goth, Herren, Vandal

Texas Ranger

Text(s), Textbook ABC, Body, Brahmana, Codex, Donat, Ennage, Harmony, Libretto, Mandaean, Mezuzah, Octapla, Op-cit, Philology, Plain, Pyramid, Quran, Responsa, Rubric, S(h)astra, Script, Shema, ➤ SUBJECT, Sutra, Tefillin, Tephillin, Tetrapla, Thesis, Topic, Tripitaka, Typography, Upanis(h)ad, Variorium, Vulgate, Zohar

Textile Cloth, Fabric, Mercy

Texture Constitution, Feel, Fiber, Fibre, Grain, Wale, Weave, Woof

Thai(land) Karen, Lao(s), Shan, Siam

Thallium Tl

Thames Father, Tamesis

Than And

Thank(s), Thankful, Thanksgiving Appreciate, Collins, Deo gratias, Gloria, Grace, Gramercy, Grateful, Gratitude, Kaddish, Mercy, Roofer

Thankless Ingrate, Vain

That (is), That one As, Cestui, Das heisst, Dh, Exists, How, Ie, Ille, Namely, Que, Sc, Such, Thence, Thon(der), What, Which, Yon, Yt

Thatch(er), Thatching At(t)ap, Hair, Heard, Hear(i)e, Hele, Hell, Mane, PM, Reed, Straw, Thack, Theek, Wig

Thaw Debacle, Defreeze, Defrost, ➤ MELT, Melt-water, Relax

▷ **Thaw** may indicate 'ice' to be removed from a word

The Der, Die, El, Il, La, Le, Los, T', Ye, Ze

Theatre, Theatrical(ity) Abbey, Adelphi, Broadway, Camp, Cinema, Coliseum, Criterion, Drama, Everyman, Field, Gaff, Gaiety, Globe, Grand Guignol, Haymarket, Hippodrome, Histrionic, House, Kabuki, La Scala, Legitimate, Lyceum, Mermaid, National, Noh, Odeon, Odeum, OUDS, Palladium, Panache, Playhouse, Political, Rep(ertory), Shaftesbury, Sheldonian, Shop, Stage, Stoll, Straw-hat, Street, Touring, Vic, Windmill, Zarzuela

Theatregoer Circle, Gallery, Gods, Pit, Stalls

Theft Appropriation, Burglary, Heist, Kinchinlay, Larceny, Maino(u)r, Manner, Pilfery, Plunder, Ram-raid, Robbery, Stealth, Stouth(rief), Touch

Their Her

Theist Believer, Unitarian

Them 'Em, Hem, Tho

Theme Crab canon, Donnée, Fugue, Idea, Leitmotiv, Lemma, Lemmata, ➤ MELODY, Motif, Peg, Question, ➤ SUBJECT, Text, Topic, Topos

Then(ce) Away, Next, Since, So, Syne, Thereupon, Tho

▷ **The northern** may indicate t'

Theodolite Diopter, Dioptre, Groma

Theologian, Theologist, Theology Abelard, Aquinas, Calvin, Christology, Colet, DD, Divine, Erastus, Eschatology, Eusebius, Exegetics, Hase, Irenics, Jansen, Kierkegaard, Knox, Mullah, Newman, Niebuhr, Origen, Paley, Pelagius, Pusey, Rabbi, Religious, Schoolman, Softa, STP, Tertullian, Ulema, Universalist

Theorem, Theoretical, Theorist, Theory Academic, Bayes(ian), Bernouilli's, Binomial, Bohr, Chaos, Darwinian, Dependency, Dictum, Domino, Dow, Einstein, Epigenesist, Gödel's, Guess, Holism, Hypothesis, Ideal, Ideology, Ism(y), James-Lange, Kinetic, Laingian, Lamarckism, Lemma, Monism, Notion, Poynting, Probability, Proof, Pure, Pythagoras, Quantum, Qunatity, Relativity, Speculative, Steady state, System, Tachyon, TOE, Vulcanist, Wasm, Wholism, Wolfian

Therapeutic, Therapy Aura-Soma, Aversion, Behaviour, Bowen, Cognitive, Curative, Dianetics, Electric shock, Electroconvulsive, Gene, Gestalt, Group, Logop(a)edics, Looyenwork, Occupational, Osteopathy, Physical, Primal, Radiation, Radio, Reflexology, Reichian, Reiki, Relaxation, Rolfing, Sanatory, Scientology®, SHEN, Shiatsu, Shiatzu, Shock, Speech

There(after), Thereby, Thereupon Ipso facto, Thither, Thon, Upon, Y, Yonder

Therefore Argal, Ergo, Forthy, Hence, So, Why

Thermometer Aethrioscope, Centesimal, Glass, Pyrometer, Wet and dry bulb

Thermoplastic Cel(luloid), Resin

Thesaurus Dictionary, Lexicon, Roget, Treasury

These Thir

Theseus Champion

Thesis Argument, Dissertation, Theme

Thespian ➤ ACTOR, Ham, Performer

Thessalonian Lapith

They A

Thick(en), Thickening, Thickener, Thickness, Thickset Abundant, Algin, Burly, Bushy, Callosity, Callus, Clavate, Cloddy, Cruddle, Curdle, Dense, Dextrin(e), Dumose, Engross, Grist, Grume, Guar, Gum, Hyperostosis, Incrassate, Inspissate, Kuzu, Liaison, Panada, Roux, Sclerosis, ➤ SOLID, Soupy, Squat, Stumpy, ➤ STUPID, Thieves, This, Thixotropic, Waulk, Wooden, Xantham

Thick-coated Atheromatous

Thicket Bosk, Brake, Brush, Cane-brake, Chamisal, Coppice, Copse, Dead-finish, Greve, Grove, Macchie, Maquis, Queach, Reedrand, Reedrond, Salicetum, Shola

Thick-lipped Labrose

Thick-skinned Armadillo, Callous, Pachyderm, Tough

Thief, Thieves, Thievish Abactor, Autolycus, Blood, Chummy, Coon, Corsair, Cutpurse, Dismas, Dysmas, Filcher, Flood, Footpad, Freebooter, Furacious, Ganef, Gestas, Heist, Hotter, Huaquero, Iceman, Jackdaw, Kiddy, Kondo, Larcener, Light-fingered, Limmer, Looter, Mag, Montith, Nip(per), Nuthook, Pad, Peculator, Pilferer, Pirate, Plagiarist, Poacher, Prig, Raffles, River-rat, ➤ ROBBER, Rustler, Shark, Shop-lifter, Sneak, Sticky fingers, Taffy, Taker, Tea-leaf, Thick

Thigh Femoral, Ham, Haunch, Hock, Meros

Thin(ner) Acetone, Attenuate, Bald, Bony, Cull, Dilute, Ectomorph, Emaciated, Enseam, Fine, Fine-drawn, Flimsy, Gaunt, Hair('s-)breadth, Inseam, Lanky, Lean, Mawger, Puny, Rackabones, Rangy, Rare, Rarefied, Reedy, Scant, Scraggy, Scrannel, Scrawny, Sheer, Sieve, Skeletal, Skimpy, Skinking, Slender, Slim, Slimline, Slink, ➤ SPARE, Sparse, Spindly, Stilty, Stringy, Subtle, Taper, Tenuous, Turps, Wafer, Washy, Waste, Watch, Water(y), ➤ WEAK, Weedy, Whirtle, Wiry, Wispy, Wortle, Wraith

Thing(s) Alia, Article, Chattel, Chose, Doodah, Doofer, Entia, Fetish, Fixation, It, Item, Jingbang, Job, Material, Matter, ➤ OBJECT, Obsession, Paraphernalia, Phobia, Res, Tool, Whatnot

Thingummy Dingbat, Dinges, Doodah, Doofer, Doohickey, Gubbins, Whatsit, Yoke

Think(er), Thinking Associate, Believe, Brain, Brood, Casuistry, Cogitate, Consider, Contemplant, ➤ CONTEMPLATE, Deem, Deliberate, Descartes, Dianoetic, Esteem, Fancy, Fear, Ghesse, Gnostic, Guess, Hegel, Hold, ➤ IMAGINE, Judge, Lateral, Meditate, Mentation, Muse, Opine, Pensive, Philosopher, Phrontistery, Ponder, Pore, Presume, Rational, Reckon, Reflect, Reminisce, Ruminate, Trow, Ween

Thin-skinned Sensitive

Third, Third rate Bronze, C, Eroica, Gamma, Gooseberry, Interval, Mediant, Picardy, Quartan, Tertius, Tierce, Trisect

Third man Abel, Lime

Thirst(y) ➤ CRAVE, Dives, Drought, Drouth, Dry, Hydropic, Nadors, Pant, Polydipsia, Thrist

Thirteen Baker's dozen, Long dozen, Riddle, Unlucky

Thirty Lambda

Thirty nine books All-OT, OT

This Hic, Hoc, The, Thick, Thilk, Thir

Thistle Canada, Carduus, Carline, Cnicus, Echinops, Musk, Safflower, Sow, Star, Thrissel, Thristle

This year Ha

Thomas Aquinas, Arnold, Christadelphian, De Quincey, Didymus, Doubting, Dylan, Erastus, Hardy, Loco, Parr, Rhymer, Tompion, True, Turbulent

Thong Babiche, Jandal®, Lash, Latchet, Leather, Lore, Riem, Shoe-latchet, ➤ STRAP, Taws(e), Whang, Whip

Thor Thunderer

Thorax Chest, Peraeon, Pereion, Throat

Thorium Th

Thorn(y) Acantha, Bael, Bel, Bhel, Bramble, Briar, Coyotillo, Doom, Edh, Eth, Irritation, Jerusalem, Mahonia, Mayflower, Nabk, Nebbuk, Nebe(c)k, ➤ NEEDLE, Prickle, Slae, Spine, Spinescent, Spinulate, Trial, Wagn'bietjie, Ye, Zare(e)ba, Zariba, Zeriba

Thorn-apple Jimpson-weed

Thornless Inerm

Thorough(ly) A fond, Complete, Even-down, Firm, Fully, Ingrained, Inly, Out, Out and out, Painstaking, Pakka, Pucka, Pukka, Ripe, Sound, Strict, Total, Tout à fait, Up

Thoroughbred Arab, Bloodstock, Pedigree

Thoroughfare Avenue, Broadway, Causeway, Freeway, Highway, Parkway, ➤ ROAD, Street

Those Thaim, Them, Tho, Yon

Thou M, Mil

Though Albe, Albeit, All-be, Ever, Tho, Whenas

Thought(ful), Thoughtfulness Avisandum, Broody, Cerebration, Cogitation, Concept, Considerate, Contemplation, Dianoetic, Idea, Innate, Kind, Maieutic, Mind, Musing, Opinion, Pensée, Pensive, Philosophy, Reflection, Rumination

Thoughtless Blindfold, Careless, Heedless, Inconsiderate, Pillock, ➤ RASH, Remiss, Reckless, Scatter-brained, Vacant

Thousand(s) Chiliad, Gorilla, K, Lac, Lakh, M, Millenary, Millennium, Plum, Toman

Thracian Spartacus

Thrall Captive, Esne, Serf, Slave

Thrash(ing) ➤ BEAT, Belabour, Belt, Bepelt, Binge, Bless, Cane, Dress, Drub, Flail, Flog, Jole, Joll, Joule, Jowl, Lace, Laldie, Laldy, Lambast, Larrup, Lather, Leather, Lick, Marmelise, Paste, Ploat, Quilt, Slog, Smoke, Strap-oil, Swat, Targe, Towel, Trim, Trounce, Whale, Whap

Thread, Threadlike Ariadne, Bottom, Buttress, Chalaza, Chromatid, Chromatin, Chromosome, Clew, Clue, Cop(pin), Cord, Eel-worm, End, Fibre, Filament, File, Filiform, Filose, Filoselle, Gossamer, Heddle, Ixtle, Lace, Lap, Lingel, Lingle, Link, Lisle, Lurex®, Meander, Mycellum, Nematode, Nematoid, Organzine, Pearlin(g), Pick, Plasmodesm, Ravel, Reeve, Sacred, Seton, ➤ STRAND, Suture, Tassel, Tendril, Theme, Thrid, Thrum, Trace, Tram, Trundle, Tussore, Twine, Warp, Watap, Weft, Whitworth, Whitworth screw, Wick, ➤ WIND, Wisp, Worm

Threadbare Hackneyed, Napless, Shabby, Worn

Threadworm Nemathelminth, Strongyl, Vinegar-eel

Threat(en), Threatened, Threatening Baleful, Blackmail, Bluster, Comminate, Face, Fatwa, Fraught, Greenmail, Greymail, Hazard, Impend, Imperil, Loom, ➤ MENACE, Minacious, Minatory, Mint, Omen, Overcast, Overhang, Parlous, Peril, Portent, Ramp, Shore, Strongarm, Ugly, Veiled, Warning

Three, Threefold, Three-wheeler, Thrice Graces, Har, Harpies, Jafenhar, Leash, Muses, Musketeers, Pairial, Pair-royal, Prial, T.i.d, Ter, Tern, Terzetta, Thrice, Thridi, Tid, Tierce, Tray, Trey, Triad, Tricar, Triennial, Trifid, Trigon, Trilogy, Trinal, Trine, Trinity, Trio, Triple, Triptote, Troika

Three-D(imensional) Lenticular, Stereopsis

Three-day Triduan, Triduum

Threehalfpence Dandiprat, Dandyprat

Three-handed Cutthroat

Three hundred B, Carpet

Three-legged IOM, Triskele, Triskelion

Threepence, Threepenny bit Tickey, Tray, Trey, Treybit

Three-year old Staggard

Threnody Dirge, Epicede, ➤ LAMENT

Thresh Beat, Flail, Separate

Threshold Cill, Doorstep, Limen, Liminal, Sill, Verge

▶ **Thrice** see THREE

Thrift(y) Economy, Frugal, Husbandry, Oeconomy, Sea-grass, Sea-pink, Virtue

Thrill(er), Thrilling Atingle, Delight, Dindle, Dinnle, Dirl, Dread, Emotive, ➤ ENCHANT, Excite, Film noir, Frisson, Gas, Jag, Kick, Perceant, Plangent, Pulsate, Pulse, Quiver, Sensation, Thirl, Tinglish, Tremor, Vibrant, Whodunit

Thrive Batten, Blossom, Boom, Do, Fl, ➤ FLOURISH, Flower, Grow, Mushroom, ➤ PROSPER, Succeed, Thee

Throat(y) Craw, Crop, Deep, Dewlap, Fauces, Gorge, Gular, Gullet, Guttural, Jugular, Maw, Pereion, Pharynx, Prunella, Quailpipe, Roopit, Roopy, Strep, Swallet, Thrapple, Thropple, Throttle, Weasand, Wesand, Whistle, Windpipe

Throb(bing) Beat, Palpitate, Pant, Pit-a-pat, Pulsate, Quop, Stang, Tingle, Vibrato

▷ **Throbbing** may indicate an anagram

Throe(s) Agony, Pang, Paroxysm

Throne Bed-of-justice, Cathedra, Episcopal, Gadi, Rule, Seat, See, Siege, Tribune

Throng(ing) Crowd, Flock, Host, Press, Resort, Swarm

Throttle ➤ CHOKE, Gar(r)otte, Gun, Mug, Scrag, Silence, Stifle, Strangle, Strangulate, We(a)sand

Through, Throughout Along, Ana, By, Dia-, During, Everywhere, Over, Passim, Per, Pr, Sempre, Sic passim, To, Trans, Via, Yont

▶ **Throw(n)** see TOSS

Throwback Atavism, Echo

Throw-out, Throw-up Bin, Cast-off, Chunder, Egesta, Jettison, Puke, Spew, Squirt, Squit

Thrush Aphtha, Bird, Chat, Fieldfare, Hermit, Mavis, Missel, Mistle, Pitta, Prunella, Redwing, Sprue, Veery

Thrust, Thruster Aventre, Bear, Boost, Botte, Burn, Detrude, Dig, Drive, Elbow, Exert, Extrude, Flanconade, Foin, ➤ FORCE, Hay, Imbroc(c)ata, Impulse, Job, Lunge, Montant(o), Obtrude, Oust, Pass, Passado, Peg, Perk, Pitchfork, Poke, Potch(e), Pote, Probe, Propel, Pun, Punto, ➤ PUSH, Put, Remise, Repost, Run, Shove, Single-stock, Sock, Sorn, Stap, Stick, Stoccado, Stoccata, Stock, Stuck, Thrutch, Tilt, Tuck

Thud Drum, Dump, Flump, Phut, Plod, Thump

Thug(s) Goon(da), Gorilla, Gurrier, Hoodlum, Loord, Ninja, Ockers, Phansigar, Roughneck, SS, Strangler, Ted, Tityre-tu, Tsotsi
Thule Ultima
Thulium Tm
Thumb Green, Hitch, Midget, Ovolo, Pollex, Scan, Tom
Thump(ing) Blow, Bonk, Cob, Crump, Drub, Dub, Hammer, Knevell, Knock, Nevel, Oner, Paik, ➤ POUND, Pummel, Slam, Slosh, Swat, Swingeing, Thud, Tund
Thunder(ing), Thunderstorm Bolt, Boom, Clap, Donnerwetter, Foudroyant, Foulder, Fulminate, Intonate, Lei-king, Pil(l)an, Raiden, ➤ ROAR, Rumble, Summanus, Tempest, Thor, Tonant
Thursday Chare, Maundy, Sheer, Shere
Thus Ergo, Sic, So, Therefore
Thwart Baffle, Balk, ➤ CROSS, Dish, Foil, Frustrate, Hamstring, Hogtie, Obstruct, Outwit, Pip, Prevent, Scotch, Snooker, Spike, Spite, Stonker, Stymie, Transverse
Thy Yourn
Tiara Cidaris, Crownet
Tiberius Gracchus
Tibetan Lamaist, Naga, Sherpa, Sitsang
Tic Vocal
Tick, Tick off Acarida, Acarus, Beat, ➤ CHIDE, Click, Cr, ➤ CREDIT, Deer, HP, Idle, Instant, Jar, Ked, Mattress, Mile, Mo, Moment, Ricinulei, Second, Strap, Worm
Ticket(s) Billet, Bone, Brief, Carnet, Complimentary, Coupon, Docket, Dream, Label, Meal, Parking, Pass, Pass-out, Platform, Raincheck, Return, Season, Single, Stub, Supersaver, ➤ TAG, Tempest, Tessera(l), Tyburn
Ticket-seller Scalper
Tickle, Ticklish Amuse, Delicate, Divert, Excite, Gratify, Gump, ➤ ITCH, Kittle, Queasy, Thrill, Titillate
Tiddler Brit, Tom
Tide, Tidal Current, Drift, Eagre, Easter, Eger, Estuary, Flood, High, Low, Marigram, Neap, Roost, Sea, Seiche, Slack water, Spring, Trend, Wave
Tide-gate Aboideau, Aboiteau, Weir
Tidings Gospel, ➤ NEWS, Rumour, Word
Tidy Comb, Considerable, Curry, Fair, Fettle, Kempt, Large, Neat, ➤ ORDER, Pachyderm, Predy, Preen, Primp, Red(d), Slick, Snug, Sort, Spruce, Trim
Tie, Tying Ascot, Attach, Barcelona, Berth, Bind, Black, ➤ BOND, Bootlace, Bow, Bowyang, Cable, Cope, Cravat, Cup, Dead-heat, Drag, Draw, Frap, Halter, Handicap, Harness, Holdfast, Kipper, ➤ KNOT, Lash, Level, Ligament, Ligate, Ligature, Link, Marry, Match, Moor, Oblige, Obstriction, Oop, Oup, Overlay, Raffia, Restrain, Rod, Scarf, School, Score draw, Shackle, Shoelace, Shoestring, Sleeper, Slur, Solitaire, Soubise, Splice, Stake, Strap, String, Tether, Trice, Truss, Unite, White
Tier Bank, Gradin(e), Knotter, Layer, Rank, Stage, Storey

Tierce Leash, Tc

Tiff Bicker, Contretemps, Difference, Dispute, Feed, Feud, Huff, Miff, Skirmish, Spat, Squabble

Tiger Bengal, ➤ CAT, Clemenceau, Demoiselle, Lily, Machairodont, Machairodus, Margay, Paper, Sabre-tooth, Smilodon, Tasmanian, Woods

Tight(en), Tightness, Tights Boozy, Bosky, Brace, Close(-hauled), Constriction, Cote-hardie, ➤ DRUNK, Fishnet, Fleshings, High, Hose, Jam, Leggings, Lit, Loaded, Maillot, Mean, Merry, Niggardly, Oiled, Pang, Phimosis, Pickled, Pinch(penny), Plastered, Prompt, Proof, Rigour, Snug, Squiffy, Stenosis, ➤ STINGY, Strict, Stringent, Swift, Swig, Taut, Tense, Tipsy, Trig, Woozy

Tightrope(-walker) Aerialist, Blondin, Equilibrist, Funambulist

Tightwad Cheapskate, ➤ MISER, Scrooge

Tile(d), Tiles Antefix, Arris, Azulejo, Dalle, Derby, Encaustic, ➤ HAT, Imbrex, Imbricate, Lid, Ostracon, Ostrakon, Peever, Quarrel, Quarry, Rag(g), Rooftop, Sclate, Shingle, Slat, ➤ SLATE, Tegula, Tessella, Tessera, Titfer, Topper, Wall, Wally

Till Cashbox, Checkout, Coffer, Ear, Eulenspiegel, Farm, Hasta, Hoe, Husband, Lob, Peter, ➤ PLOUGH, Set, Unto

Tiller Gardener, Helm, Ploughman, Wheel

Tilt Awning, Bank, Camber, Cant, Cock, Dip, Heel, Hut, Joust, Just, ➤ LIST, Quintain, Rock, Tip, Unbalance

Timber Apron, Batten, Beam, Carapa, Chess, Coulisse, Cross-tree, Cruck, Dwang, Elmwood, Flitch, Four-by-two, Futchel, Futtock, Greenheart, Intertie, Iroko, Ironwood, Joist, Knee, Knighthead, Lauan, Ligger, Lintel, Log, Lumber, Nothofagus, Plank-sheer, Purlin(e), Putlock, Putlog, Pyengadu, Radiata, Ramin, Rib, Rung, Sandalwood, Sapele, Satinwood, Scantling, Shook, Sissoo, Skeg, Softwood, Souari, Stemson, Stere, Sternson, Straddle, Stull, Stumpage, Summer, Transom, Trestletree, Wale, ➤ WOOD, Yang

Timbre Clang, Klang(farbe), ➤ TENOR, Tone

Time(s), Timer Access, Agoge, Apparent, Bird, BST, Chronic, Chronometer, Chronon, Clock, Closing, Connect, Core, Counter, Date, Day, Decade, Dimension, Double, Duple, Duration, Early, Eastern, Egg-glass, Enemy, Eon, Epoch, Equinox, Era, Extra, Father, Forelock, Free, Gest, Healer, Horologe, Hour, Hourglass, Hr, Idle, Injury, Innings, Instant, Interlude, Jiff, Juncture, Kalpa, Lay-day, Lead, Lean, Leisure, Life, Lighting-up, Lilac, Mean, Menopause, Metronome, Mountain standard, Multiple, Nonce, Nones, Occasion, Oft, ➤ ON TIME, Part, Period, Pinger, Porridge, Post, Prelapsarian, Prime, Quality, Question, Quick, Reaction, Real, Reaper, Seal, ➤ SEASON, Seel, Semeion, Serial, Session, Shelf-life, Sidereal, Sight, Sith(e), Solar, Space, Span, Spare, Spell, Spin, Split, Standard, Stoppage, Stopwatch, Stound, Stownd, Stretch, Summer, Sundown, Sythe, T, Tem, Tempo, Tempore, Tense, Thief, Thunderer, Tick, Tid, Tide, Triple, Turnaround, Two-four, Universal, Usance, While, X, Yonks, Zero

Time-keeper Ben, Clock, Hourglass, Ref, Sand-glass, Sundial, Ticker, Tompion, Watch

Timeless Eternal, Nd, Undying

Timely Appropriate, Apropos, Happy, Opportune, Pat, Prompt

Time-server Prisoner, Trimmer

Timetable Bradshaw, ➤ CHART, Schedule

Timid, Timorous Afraid, Aspen, Bashful, Blate, Chicken, Cowardly, Eerie, Eery, Faint-hearted, Fearful, Hare, Hen-hearted, Milquetoast, Mous(e)y, Mouse, Pavid, Pigeon-hearted, Pusillanimous, Quaking, ➤ SHY, Shrinking, Skeary, Sook, Yellow

Timothy Cat's-tail, Grass, Phleum

Tin(ned), Tinfoil, Tinny Argentine, Britannia metal, Can, Cash, Debe, Dixie, Maconochie, ➤ MONEY, Moola(h), Ochre, Plate, Rhino, Sn, Stannary, Stannic, Tain, Tole

Tincture Arnica, Bufo, Chroma, Elixir, Fur, Infusion, Laudanum, Metal, Or, Sericon, Sol, Spice, Taint, Tenné, Vert

Tinder Amadou, Faggot, Fuel, Funk, Punk, Spark, Spunk, Touchwood

Tine Antler, Bay, Cusp, Grain, Prong, Surroyal, Trey

Tinge Dye, Eye, Flavour, Gild, ➤ HUE, Taint, Tincture, Tone, Touch

Tingle, Tingling Dinnle, Dirl, Paraesthesia, Prickle, Thrill, Throb, Tinkle

Tinker Bell, Caird, Coster, Didicoy, Didikoi, ➤ FIDDLE, Gypsy, Mender, Pedlar, Potter, Prig, Putter, Repair, Sly, Snout, Tamper, Tramp, Traveller

Tinkle Pink

Tinsel(ly) Clinquant, Gaudy, Glitter, O, Spangle

Tint Colour, Henna, Hue, Pigment, ➤ STAIN, Tinct, Tinge, Woad

Tiny Atto-, Baby, Diddy, Dwarf, Ha'it, Infinitesimal, Itsy-bitsy, Lilliputian, Minikin, Minim, Mite, Negligible, Petite, Small, Smidgeon, Teeny, Tim, Tine, Toy, Wee

Tip, Tipping Apex, Arrowhead, Asparagus, Backshish, Baksheesh, Batta, Beer-money, B(u)onamono, Bonsel(l)a, Cant, Cert, Chape, Counsel, Coup, Cowp, Crown, Cue, Cumshaw, Douceur, Dump, Extremity, Fee, Felt, Ferrule, Filter, Forecast, Glans, Gratillity, Gratuity, Heel, ➤ HINT, Hunch, Inkle, Iridise, Lagniappe, Largess(e), List, Mess, Middenstead, Nap, Noop, Ord, Perk, Perquisite, Point, Pointer, Pour, Previse, Suggestion, Summit, Tag, Tail, Tilt, Toom, Touch, Tronc, Vail, Vales, Whisper, Wrinkle

Tippet Cape, Fur, Scarf

Tipple Bib, Booze, ➤ DRINK, Paint, Pot, Poteen

Tipster Prophet, Tout

Tipsy Bleary, Boozy, Bosky, ➤ DRUNK, Elevated, Moony, Nappy, Oiled, On, Rocky, Screwed, Slewed, Slued, Squiffy, Wet

▷ **Tipsy** may indicate an anagram

Tiptoe Digitigrade

Tirade Diatribe, Invective, Jobation, Laisse, Philippic, Rand, Rant, Screed, Slang

Tire(d), Tiredness, Tiring All-in, Beat, Bore, Bushed, Caparison, Dress, Drowsy, ➤ EXHAUST, Fag, Fatigue, Flag, Fordid, Fordod, Forjeskit, Frazzle, Gruel, Irk, Jade, Lassitude, Limp, ME, Poop, Puggled, ➤ ROBE, Rubber, Sap, Shagged, Sicken, Sleepry, Sleepy, Swinkt, Tax, Tedious, Wabbit, Wappend, Weary, Wrecked

Tiresome Boring, Humdrum, Pill, Tedious

Tirl Rattle, Risp, Strip, Turn

➤ **Tiro** see TYRO

Tissue Adenoid, Adhesion, Aerenchyma, Aponeurosis, Archesporium, Callus, Cartilage, Cementum, Chalaza, Cheloid, Chlorenchyma, Coenosarc, Collagen, Collenchyma, Commissure, Connective, Cortex, Diploe, Epimysium, Epineurium, Epithelium, Eschar, Fabric, Fascia, Flesh, Gamgee, Gauze, Gleba, Glia, Gum, Heteroplasia, Histogen, Histoid, Infarct, Keloid, Mesophyll, Myocardium, Neuroglia, Lamina, Lies, Ligament, Luteal, Medulla, ➤ MEMBRANE, Meristem, Mole, Myelin(e), Nucellus, Pack, Pannus, Paper, Papilla, Parenchyma, Perimysium, Perinephrium, Perineurium, Perisperm, Phellogen, Phloem, Pith, Plerome, Polyarch, Primordium, Prothallis, Pterygium, Pulp, Radula, Sarcenet, Sars(e)net, Scar, Sclerenchyma, Sequestrum, Sinew, Somatopleure, Stereome, Stroma, Submucosa, Suet, Tarsus, Tela, Tendon, Tonsil, Tunica, Vascular, Velum, Web, Xylem

Tit, Tit-bit(s) Analecta, Currie, Curry, Delicacy, Dug, Nag, Nipple, Pap, Quarry, Sample, Scrap, Snack, Teat, Tug, Twitch, Zakuska

Titan(ic), Titaness Atlas, Colossus, Cronos, Enormous, Giant, Huge, Hyperion, Kronos, Leviathan, Liner, Oceanus, Phoebe, Prometheus, Rhea, Themis, Vast

Titanium Sagenite, Ti

Tit for tat Deserts, Revenge, Talion

Tithe Disme, Dyzemas, Frankpledge, Teind, Tenth

Titian Abram, Auburn

Titillate Delight, Excite, Tickle

Titivate Primp

Title Abbe, Ag(h)a, Antonomasia, Appellative, Bahadur, Baroness, Baronet, Bart, Bretwalda, Calif, Caliph, Caption, Charta, Claim, Conveyance, Count(ess), Courtesy, Credit, Dan, Datin, Datuk, Dauphin, Dayan, Deeds, Devi, Dom, Don, Dowager, Dub, Duchess, Duke, Earl, Effendi, Epithet, Esquire, Excellency, Frau(lein), Gospodin, Gyani, Hafiz, Handle, Header, Heading, Headline, Hon, Interest, Kalif, Kaliph, Kaur, King, Lady, Lala, Lemma, ➤ LIEN, Lord, Marchesa, Marchese, Marquess, Marquis, Masthead, Maulana, Memsahib, Meneer, Mevrou, Milord, Mirza, Mr(s), Name, Nomen, Padishah, Peerage, Pir, Polemarch, Prefix, Prince(ss), Queen, ➤ RANK, Reb, ➤ RIGHT, Rubric, Sahib, Sama, San, Sayid, Senhor(a), Senor(a), Shri, Sir, Son, Sowbhagyawati, Sri, Torrens, Tycoon, V

Title-holder Cartouche, Champion, Landlord, Noble

Titmouse Bird, Mag, Reedling, Tit

Titter Giggle, Snigger, Tehee

Tittle Jot

Titus Oates

Tizz(y) Pother, Spin, Tanner, Testril, Vld

TNT Explosive, Trotyl

To(wards) At, Beside, Inby, Onto, Shet, Shut, Till

Toad(y) Bootlicker, Bufo, Bumsucker, Cane, Clawback, Crawler, Fawn, Frog, Horned, Jackal, Jenkins, Knot, Lackey, Lickspittle, Midwife, Minion, Natterjack, Nototrema, Paddock, Parasite, Pipa, Placebo, Platanna, Puddock, Sook, Spade-foot, Surinam, Sycophant, Tuft-hunter, Xenopus, Yesman

Toadstool Amanita, Death-cap, Death-cup, ➤ FUNGUS, Grisette, Paddock-stool, Parrot, Sulphur tuft

Toast Bacchus, Bell, Birsle, Brindisi, ➤ BROWN, Bruschetta, Bumper, Cheers, Chin-chin, Crostini, Crouton, French, Gesundheit, Grace-cup, Grill, Health, Iechyd da, Kiaora, L'chaim, Lechayim, Loyal, Melba, Pledge, Propose, Prosit, Round, Scouther, Scowder, Scowther, Sentiment, Sippet, Skoal, Slainte, Soldier, Sunbathe, Zwieback

Toastmaster MC, Symposiarch

Tobacco, Tobacco-field Alfalfa, Bacchi, Baccy, Bird's eye, Broadleaf, Burley, Canaster, Capa, Caporal, Cavendish, Chew, Dottle, Honeydew, Killikinnick, Kinnikinick, Latakia, Mundungus, Nailrod, Navy-cut, Negro-head, Nicotine, Niggerhead, Perique, Pigtail, Plug, Quid, Régie, Returns, Shag, Sneesh, Snout, Snuff, Stripleaf, Turkish, Twist, Vega, Virginia, Weed

Toboggan Sled(ge), Sleigh

Toby Dog, Highwayman, Jug

Tocsin Alarm, Siren

Today Hodiernal, Now, Present

Toddle(r) Baim, Gangrel, Mite, Tot, Totter, Trot, Waddle

Toddy Arrack, ➤ DRINK, Sura

To-do Sensation, Stir

Toe Dactyl, Digit, Hallux, Hammer, Piggy, Pinky, Pointe, Poulaine, Prehallux, Tootsie

Toff Nob, Nut, Swell

Toffee Butterscotch, Caramel, Cracknel, Gundy, Hard-bake, Hokey-pokey, Humbug, Tom-trot

Together Among, At-one, Atone, Attone, Gathered, Infere, ➤ JOINT, Pari-passu, Sam, Unison, Wed, Y, Yfere, Ysame

Toggle Fastener, Netsuke

Togs Clothes, Gear, Rig, Strip

Toil(s) Drudge, Fag, Industry, ➤ LABOUR, Mesh, Net, Seine, Sisyphus, Sweat, Swink, Tela, Tew, Trap, Travail, Tug, Web, Wrest, ➤ WORK, Yacker, Yakka, Yakker

Toilet Can, Coiffure, John, Lat(rine), Lavatory, Loo, Pot, Powder room, WC

Token Buck, Counter, Coupon, Disc, Double-axe, Emblem, Gift, Indication, ➤ MEMENTO, Nominal, Portend, Seal, Sign, Signal, Symbol, Symptom, Tessera, Valentine

Tolerable Acceptable, Bearable, Mediocre, Passable, So-so

Tolerance, Tolerant, Tolerate(d) Abear, Abide, ➤ ALLOW, Bear, Brook, Endure, Hack, Had, Latitude, ➤ LENIENT, Lump, Mercy, Permit, Stand, Stick, Stomach, Studden, Suffer, Support, Thole, Wear

Toll Chime, Customs, Due, Duty, Excise, Joll, Joule, Jowl, Octroi, Pierage, Pike, Pontage, Rates, ➤ RING, Scavage, Streetage, Tariff, Tax

Tom(my) Atkins, Bell, Bowling, Bread, Brown, ➤ CAT, Collins, Edgar, Gib, Grub, Gun, He-cat, Jerry, Jones, Mog(gy), Nosh, Peeping, Private, Pte, Puss, Ram-cat, Sawyer, Snout, Soldier, Stout, Thos, Thumb, Tiddler, Tucker

Tomato Beef(steak), Cherry, Husk, Love-apple, Plum, Strawberry, Tamarillo, Wolf's peach

Tomb(stone) Burial, Catacomb, Catafalque, Cenotaph, Cist, Coffin, Dargah, Durgah, Grave, Hypogeum, Kistvaen, Marmoreal, Mastaba, Mausoleum, Megalithic, Monument, Pyramid, ➤ SEPULCHRE, Sepulture, Serdab, Shrine, Speos, Tholos, Tholus, Through-stone, Treasury, Vault

Tombola Draw, Lottery, Raffle

Tomboy Gamine, Gilpey, Gilpy, Hoyden, Ladette, Ramp, Romp

Tome ➤ BOOK, Volume

Tomfoolery Caper, Fandangle, Shenanigan

Tomorrow Future, Manana, Morrow

Tompion Watchman

Tom Snout Tinker

Ton C, Chic, Hundred, T

Tone, Tonality Brace, Fifth, Harmonic, Inflection, Key, Klang, Ninth, Partial, Qualify, ➤ SOUND, Strain, Temper, Tenor, Timbre, Trite, Whole

Tong(s) Curling, Lazy

Tongue Brogue, Burr, Chape, Clack, Clapper, Doab, Final, Forked, Glossa, Glossolalia, Jinglet, ➤ LANGUAGE, Langue(tte), Lap, Ligula, Lill, Lingo, Lingulate, Mother, Organ, Radula, Ranine, Rasp, Red rag, Spit, Tab, Voice

Tongue-twister Jaw-breaker, Shibboleth

Tonic Bracer, C(h)amomile, Doh, Key, Mease, Medicinal, Mishmee, Mishmi, Oporice, Pick-me-up, Quassia, Refresher, Roborant, Sarsaparilla, Solfa

▷ **Tonic** may indicate a musical note

Tonsil, Tonsillitis Amygdala, Antiaditis, Quinsy

Tonsure(d) Epilate, Haircut, Peel, Pield

Tony Bête, Fool, Smart

Too Als(o), Besides, Eke, Excessive, Item, Likewise, Moreover, Oer, Over, Overly, Plus, Troppo

Took Naam, Nam, Set, Stole, Wan, Won

Tool Adze, Aiguille, Auger, Awl, Ax(e), Beetle, Bevel, Billhook, Bit, Broach, Brog, Bur(r), Burin, Calipers, Catspaw, Chisel, Clippers, Dibber, Dibble, Die, Dolly, Drawknife, Drawshave, Eatche, Elsin, Eolith, Facer, Fid, File, Float,

Float-stone, Former, Fraise, Froe, Frow, Gad, Gimlet, Go-devil, Grattoir, Graver, Hammer, Hardy, Hob, Hoe, ➤ IMPLEMENT, Insculp, ➤ INSTRUMENT, Iron, Jackhammer, Jemmy, Jointer, Laster, Loggerhead, Loom, Lute, Marlin(e)spike, Microlith, Moon-knife, Muller, Oustiti, Outsiders, Palaeolith, Pattle, Pawn, Penis, Percussion, Pestle, Pick, Picklock, Pitchfork, Piton, Plane, Pliers, Plunger, Pricker, Property, Prunt, Punch, Puncheon, Rabble, Rasp, Ripple, Router, Sander, Saw, Scalpel, Scauper, Scissors, Scorper, Scraper, Screwdriver, Scriber, Scutch, Seamset, Shoder, Sickle, Slater, Spanner, Spirit-level, Spitsticker, Spokeshave, Strickle, Strike, Strimmer®, Swage, Swingle, Swipple, Tjanting, Triblet, Trowel, Try square, Tweezers, Twibill, Upright, Wimble, Wrench

Toot(er) Blow, Horn, Trumpet

Tooth(ed), Toothy, Teeth Bicuspid, Bit, Buck, Bunodont, Canine, Carnassial, Chactodon, Cog, Crena(te), Ctenoid, Cusp, Dentin(e), Dentures, Egg, Eye, Fang, Gam, Gat, Gnashers, Grinder, Heterodont, Incisor, Ivory, Joggle, Laniary, Milk, Molar, Nipper, Odontoid, Pawl, Pearly gates, Pectinate, Peristome, Phang, Plate, Pre-molar, Prong, Ratch, Scissor, Secodont, Sectorial, Serration, Set, Snaggle, Sprocket, Sweet, Trophi, Tush, Tusk, Uncinus, Upper, Wallies, Wang, Wiper, Wisdom, Zalambdodont

Toothache, Tooth troubles Caries, Odontalgia

Toothless Edentate, Gummy, Pangolin

Toothpaste Dentifrice

Top(drawer; hole; line; notcher), Topmost, Topper Ace, Acme, A1, Apex, Apical, Altissimo, Behead, Best, Better, Big, Blouse, Blouson, Brow, Bustier, Cacumen, Cap, Capstone, Ceiling, Coma, Cop, Coping, Corking, ➤ CREST, Crista, Crown, Culmen, Decollate, Diabolo, Dog, Dome, Drawer, Dreid(e)l, Elite, Execute, Finial, Gentry, Gyroscope, Hard, Hat, ➤ HEAD, Height, Hummer, Imperial, Lid, Nun, One-er, Optimate, Orb, ➤ PEAK, Peerie, Peery, Peg, Peplos, Peplus, Pinnacle, Pitch, Replenish, Ridge, Roof, Sawyer, Secret, Shaw, Shirt, Skim, Slay, Star, Summit, Superate, Superb, Supernal, Supreme, Supremo, Surface, Tambour, Targa, Teetotum, Texas, Tile, Trash, T-shirt, Turbinate, Up(most), Uppermost, V, Vertex

▷ **Top** may indicate first letter

Topaz Citrine, Colorado, Oriental, Pycnite

Topcoat Finish, Overcoat, Ulster

Tope(r) Boozer, Bouser, Dagaba, Dagoba, ➤ DRUNK, Sot, Tosspot

Topic(al) Head, Item, Motion, Subject, Text, ➤ THEME

Top-knot Tuft

Topping Grand, Icing, Meringue, Pepperoni, Piecrust, Streusel

Topple Oust, Overbalance, Overturn, Tip, Upend, ➤ UPSET

Topsy Parentless

Topsy-turvy Careen, Cockeyed, Inverted, Summerset, Tapsalteerie, Tapsleteerie

Torch Brand, Cresset, Flambeau, Lamp, Lampad, Link, Plasma, Tead(e), Wisp

Torch-bearer Usherette

Toreador Escamillo, Matador, Picador, Torero

Torment(ed), Tormentor Agony, Anguish, Bait, Ballyrag, Bedevil, Butt, Cruciate, Crucify, Curse, Distress, Excruciate, Frab, Grill, Harass, Hell, Martyrdom, Molest, Nag, Nettle, Pang, Pine, Plague, ➤ RACK, Sadist, Tantalise

Tornado Twister, Waterspout

Torpedo Bangalore, Bomb, Ray, Weapon

Torpedo-guard Crinoline

Torpid, Torpor Comatose, Dormant, Languid, Lethargic, Sluggish, Slumbering

Torrent Flood, Spate

Torrid Amphiscian, Hot, Sultry, Tropical

Torsk Cusk

Tortilla Pancake, Taco

Tortoise Chelonia, Emydes, Emys, Galapagos, Hic(c)atee, Kurma, Pancake, Snapping-turtle, Terrapin, Testudo, Timothy, Turtle

Tortoiseshell Epiplastra, Hawksbill, Testudo

Tortuous Ambagious, Twisty, Winding

▷ **Tortuous** may indicate an anagram

Torture, Torture chamber, Torture instrument Agonise, Auto-da-fé, Bastinade, Bastinado, Boot, Bootikin, Catasta, Crucify, Engine, Excruciate, Flageolet, Fry, Gadge, Gyp, Iron maiden, Knee-cap, Naraka, Persecute, Pilliwinks, Pine, Pinniewinkle, Pinnywinkle, ➤ RACK, Sadism, Scaphism, Scarpines, Scavenger, Strappado, Tantalise, Thumbscrew, Tumbrel, Tumbril, Water, Wheel, Wrack

▷ **Tortured** may indicate an anagram

Torturer Torquemada

Torus Disc, Stellarator

Tory Abhorrer, Blimp, Blue, C, Right, Tantivy, Unionist

Toss, Throw(n) Abject, Bandy, Bounce, Buck, Bung, Buttock, Cant, Canvass, Cast, Catapult, ➤ CHUCK, Crabs, Cross-buttock, Dad, Daud, Deal, Disconcert, Elance, Estrapade, Falcade, ➤ FLING, Flip, Flump, Flutter, Flying (head)-mare, Gollum, Haunch, Heave, Hipt, Hoy, ➤ HURL, Jact(it)ation, Jaculation, Jeff, Jump, Lance, Lob, Loft, Pash, Pitch, Purl, Round-arm, Seamer, Shy, Slat, Sling, Unhorse, Unseat, Upcast

Toss-up Cross and pile, Heads or tails

Tot Add, Babe, Bairn, ➤ CHILD, Dop, Dram, Infant, Mite, Nightcap, Nip(per), Nipperkin, Slug, Snifter, Snort, Tad

Total, Toto Absolute, Aggregate, All(-out), Amount, Balance, Be-all, ➤ COMPLETE, Entire, Gross, Lot, Sum, Tale, Tally, Unqualified, Utter, Whole

Totalitarian Autocrat, Despot, Etatiste, Fascist

Tote Bear, ➤ CARRY, Yomp

Totem Fetish, Icon, Image, Pole

Tottenham Hotspur

Totter Abacus, Daddle, Daidle, Didakai, Didakei, Didicoi, Did(d)icoy, Halt, Ragman, Rock, ➤ STAGGER, Swag, Sway, Topple, Waver

Touch(ed), Touching, Touchy Accolade, Adjoin, Anent, Badass, Barmy, Cadge, Captious, Carambole, Caress, Carom, Common, Concern, Connivent, Contact, Contiguous, Emove, ➤ FEEL, Finger, Finishing, Flick, Fondle, Haptic, Huffy, ➤ IN TOUCH, J'adoube, Liaison, Libant, Loan, Loco, Midas, Miffy, Nie, Nigh, Nudge, Pathetic, Potty, Re, Sense, Skiff, Soft, Sore, Spice, ➤ SPOT, Tactile, Tactual, Tag, Tap, Taste, Tat, Tickle, Tig, Tinderbox, Trace, Trait, Vestige

Touchline Tangent

Touchstone Basanite, Criterion, Norm, Standard

Touchwood Monk, Punk, Spunk, Tinder

Tough(en) Adamantine, Anneal, Apache, Arduous, Ballsy, Burly, ➤ HARD, Hard-boiled, Hardy, Heavy duty, He-man, Hood, Husky, Indurate, Knotty, Leathern, Leathery, Nut, Pesky, Rambo, Rigwiddie, Rigwoodie, Roughneck, Sinewy, Spartan, Steely, Stiff, String, Sturdy, Teuch, Thewed, Tityre-tu, Virile

Toupee Hairpiece, Rug, Tour, ➤ WIG

Tour(er), Tourist Barnstorm, Circuit, Cook's, Emmet, Excursion, Grand, Grockle, GT, Holiday-maker, Itinerate, ➤ JOURNEY, Lionise, Mystery, Outing, Posting, Roadie, Rubberneck, Safari, ➤ TRAVEL, Trip(per), Viator, Whistle-stop

Tourmaline Schorl, Zeuxite

Tournament Basho, Carousel, Drive, Event, Jereed, Jerid, Joust, Just, Plate, Pro-am, Round robin, Royal, Tilt, Tourney, Wimbledon

Tourniquet Garrot, Throttle, Torcular

Tousle Dishevel, Rumple

Tout Barker, Laud, Ply, Praise, Runner, Solicit, Toot

Tow(ing) Button, Fibre, ➤ HAUL, Pull, ➤ ROPE, Skijoring, Stupe, Track

➤ **Towards** see TO

Towel Dry, Jack, Nappy, Roller, Rub, Sanctuary, Tea, Terry, Turkish

Tower Atalaya, Babel, Barbican, Bastille, Bastion, Belfry, Bell, Bloody, Brattice, Brettice, Brogh, Campanile, Conning, Control, Cooling, Donjon, Dungeon, Edifice, Eiffel, Fortress, Garret, Giralda, Gopura(m), Guérite, Ivory, Keep, Leaning, Loom, Maiden, Martello, Minar(et), Monument, Mooring, Mouse, Nuraghe, Nurhag, Overtop, Peel, Pinnacle, Pound, Pylon, Rear, Rise, Rolandseck, Sail, Sears, Shot, Sikhara, Silo, Ski-lift, Space Needle, Specula, Spire, Stealth, Steeple, ➤ TURRET, Tête-de-pont, Tractor, Tugboat, Victoria, Water, Yagura, Ziggurat, Zikkurat

Town, Township Boom, Borgo, Borough, Bourg, Burg(h), City, Conurbation, County, Deme, Dormitory, Dorp, Favella, Garrison, Ghost, Ham(let), Intraurban, Market, Municipal, Nasik, One-horse, Podunk, Pueblo, Satellite, Shanty, Tp, Twin, Urban, Wick

Townee, Townsman Cad, Cit(izen), Dude, Freeman, Oppidan, Philister, Resident

Town hall Prytaneum

Toxaemia Eclampsia

Toxic, Toxin Abrin, Antigen, Botulin, Coumarin, Curare, Deadly, Dioxan, Eclampsia, Lethal, Muscarine, Phenol, Phenothiazine, Psoralen, Sepsis, Serology, Venin, Venomous

Toy Bauble, Bull-roarer, Cockhorse, Dally, Dandle, Doll, Executive, Faddle, Finger, Flirt, Frisbee®, Gewgaw, Golly, Gonk, Kaleidoscope, Kickshaw, Knack, Pantine, Peashooter, Plaything, Praxinoscope, Rattle, Skipjack, Taste, Teddy, Thaumatrope, ➤ TRIFLE, Trinket, Tu(r)ndun, Whirligig, Yoyo

Trace Atom, Cast, Derive, Describe, Draft, Dreg, Draw, Echo, Footprint, Ghost, ➤ HINT, Mark, Outline, Relic, Relict, Remnant, Scintilla, Semblance, Sign, Smack, Soupçon, Strap, ➤ TOUCH, Track, Vestige, Whit

Tracery Filigree

Track(er), Tracking, Trackman Aintree, B-road, Band, Caterpillar®, Circuit, Course, DOVAP, Dog, Ecliptic, El, Fast, Fettler, Footing, Gaudy dancer, Hunt, Ichnite, Ichnolite, Lane, Line, Loipe, Loopline, Monitor, Monza, ➤ PATH, Persue, Piste, Pug, Pursue, Race, Raceway, Rail, Railway, Rake, Ridgeway, Route, Run, Rut, Siding, Sign, Slot, Sonar, Speedway, Spoor, Tan, ➤ TRAIL, Trajectory, Tram, Tread, Trode, Tug(boat), Wake, Way

Tract(able), Tracts Area, Belt, Bench, Clime, Common, Dene, Enclave, Flysheet, Lande, Leaflet, Monte, Moor, ➤ PAMPHLET, Prairie, Province, Purlieu, Pusey, Region, Taluk, Tawie, Terrain, Wold

Tractarian(ism) Newman, Oxford movement, Pusey(ism)

Tractor Cat, Caterpillar®, Pedrail, Tower

Trade(r), Tradesman, Trading Arb(itrageur), Banian, Banyan, Bargain, Barter, Bun(n)ia, Burgher, Business, Cabotage, Calling, Carriage, Chaffer, Chandler, Chapman, Cheapjack, Coaster, Comanchero, ➤ COMMERCE, Coster, Costermonger, Crare, Crayer, Deal(er), Easterling, Errand, Exchange, Factor, Free, Handle, Hosier, Hot, Importer, Indiaman, Industry, Insider, Ironmonger, Jobber, Legrolling, Line, Merchant, Métier, Middleman, Mister, Monger, Outfitter, Ply, Rag, Retailer, Scalp, Sell, Simony, Slave, Stallenger, Stallinger, Stationer, Sutler, ➤ SWAP, Traffic, Trant, Truck, Union, Vend, Wholesaler, Wind

Trademark Brand, Chop, Idiograph, Label, Logo

Trade union ASLEF, Syndicalism, UNISON, USDAW

Trading money, Trading post Cabotage, Fort, Wampum

Tradition(s), Traditional(ist) Ancestral, Classical, Convention, Custom(ary), Hadith, Heritage, Legend, Lore, Misoneist, Old guard, Old-school, Pharisee, Pompier, Practice, Purist, Time-honoured, Trad, Tralaticious, Tralatitious

Traduce Abuse, Asperse, Defame, Impugn, Malign, Smear, Vilify

Traffic, Traffic pattern Barter, Broke, Cabotage, Clover-leaf, Commerce, Contraflow, Deal, Negotiate, Passage, Run, Smuggle, Trade, Truck, Vehicular

Tragedian, Tragedy, Tragic Aeschylus, Buskin, Calamity, Cenci, Corneille, Dire, ➤ DRAMA, Euripides, Macready, Melpomene, Oedipean, Oresteia, Otway, Pathetic, Seneca, Sophoclean, Thespian, Thespis

Trail(er), Trailing Abature, Bedraggle, Caravan, Creep, Drag, Draggle, Follow, Ipomaea, Lag, Liana, Liane, Nature, Oregon, Path, Persue, Preview, Promo(tion), Pursue, Repent, Runway, Scent, Shadow, Sign, Sleuth, Slot, Spoor, Stream, Streel, Trace, ➤ TRACK, Trade, Traipse, Trape, Trauchle, Trayne, Troad, Vapour, Vine, Virga, Wake

Train(er), Training Advanced, APT, BR, Breed, Caravan, Cavalcade, Coach, Commuter, Condition, Cortège, Diesel, Direct, Discipline, Dressage, Drill, Drive, Educate, Entourage, Enure, Epicyclic, Eurostar®, Exercise, Fartlek, Flier, Freightliner®, Fuse, Gear, Ghan, Ghost, Gravy, Grounding, GWS, Handle(r), Instruct, Intercity®, Interval, Jerkwater, Journey, Liner, Link, LMS, LNER, Loco, Longe, Lunge, Maglev, Mailcar, Mein(e)y, Meinie, Mentor, Nurture, Nuzzle, Pack, Paddy, PE, Potty, Practise, ➤ PREPARE, Procession, PT, Puffer, Puff-puff, Queue, Rattler, Rehearse, Retinue, Roadwork, Rocket, Ry, Sack, ➤ SCHOOL, Series, Sinkansen, Sloid, Sloyd, Sowarree, Sowarry, Special, SR, Steer, String, Suite, Tail, ➤ TEACH, Tire, Tirocinium, Track shoe, Trail, Tube, Wagon

▷ **Train(ed)** may indicate an anagram

Trainee ➤ APPRENTICE, Cadet, Learner, Rookie, Rooky

Train-spotter Gricer

Trait Characteristic, Feature, Knack, Ph(a)enotype, Strain, Thew, Trick

Traitor Betrayer, Casement, Dobber-in, Joyce, Judas, Nid(d)ering, Nid(d)erling, Nithing, Proditor, Quisling, Renegade, Reptile, Tarpeian, Traditor, Treachetour, Turncoat, Viper, Wallydraigle, Weasel

Trajectory Parabola, Track

▷ **Trammel** may indicate an anagram

Tramp, Trample Bog-trotter, Bum, Caird, Clochard, Clump, Derelict, Dero, Dingbat, Dosser, Estragon, Footslog, Freighter, Gadling, Gook, Hike, Hobo, Knight of the road, Overrun, Override, Pad, Piker, Plod, Poach, Potch(e), Rover, Scorn, Ship, Splodge, Sundowner, Swagman, ➤ TINKER, Toe-rag(ger), Track, Traipse, Tread, Trek, Trog, Tromp, Truant, Trudge, Tub, Vagabond, Vagrant, Weary Willie

Trampoline Trampet(te)

Trance Catalepsy, Cataplexy, Goa, Narcolepsy

Tranquil(lity) Ataraxy, Calm, Composure, Halcyon, Lee, Quietude, Sedate, ➤ SERENE

Tranquillise(r) Appease, Ataraxic, Ataractic, ➤ CALM, Diazepam, Downer, Hypnone, Hypnotic, Librium®, Nervine, Nitrazepam, Oxazepam, Placate, Satisfy, Soothe, Still, Valium®

Transaction(s) Affair, Agio, Brokerage, Deal, Escrow, Fasti, Tr

Transcend(ent), Transcendental(ist) Excel, Mystic, Overtop, Surpass, Thoreau

Transcribe, Transcript Copy, Tenor, ➤ TRANSLATE, Transume

Transfer Alien, Alienate, ➤ ASSIGN, Attorn, Calk, Cede, Communize, Consign, Convey(ance), Crosstalk, Decal, Demise, Devolve, Download, Exchange, Explant, Mancipation, Metathesis, Mortmain, On-lend, Pass,

Reassign, Redeploy, Remit, Remove, Repot, Second, Settlement, Uproot, Virement

▷ **Transferred** may indicate an anagram

Transfix Impale, Rivet, ➤ SKEWER, Spear, Spit

Transform(ation), Transformer Alter, Balun, Change, Lorentz, Metamorphism, Metamorphose, Metamorphosis, Metaplasia, Metastasis, Morphing, Permute, Rectifier, Sea change, Tinct, Toupee, Transmogrify, Wig

▷ **Transform(ed)** may indicate an anagram

Transfusion Apheresis

Transgress(ion) Encroach, Err, Infringe, Offend, Overstep, Peccancy, ➤ SIN, Violate

Transient, Transit(ion), Transitory Brief, Ephemeral, Fleeting, Fly-by-night, Fugacious, Hobo, Metabasis, Passage, Passing, Provisional, Seque, T, Temporary

Translate, Translation, Translator Calque, Crib, Construe, Convert, Coverdale, Explain, Free, Horse, Interpret, Key, Linguist, Metaphrase, Paraphrase, Pinyin, Polyglot, Reduce, Render, Rendition, Rhemist, Targum, Tr, Transcribe, Transform, Trot, Unseen, Version(al), Vulgate, Wycliffe

▷ **Translate(d)** may indicate an anagram

Transmigrate, Transmigration Exodus, Metempsychosis, Passage, Trek

Transmit(ter), Transmitted, Transmission Air, Band, Beacon, ➤ BROADCAST, Carry, CB, Communicate, Consign, Contagion, Convection, Convey, Forward, Gearbox, Gene, Heredity, Impart, Intelsat, Manual, Microphone, Modem, Nicol, Permittivity, Propagate, Racon, Radiate, Radio, Receiver, Simulcast, Sonabuoy, Tappet, Telecast, Telegony, Telemetry, Teleprinter, Televise, Telex, Tiros, Traduce, Traject, Tralaticious, Tralatitious, UART, Uplink, Upload, Walkie-talkie

Transparent, Transparency Adularia, Clear, Crystal(line), Diaphanous, Dioptric, Glassy, Glazed, Hyaloid, Iolite, Leno, Limpid, Lucid, Luminous, Patent, Pellucid, Sheer, Slide, Tiffany

Transpire Happen, Occur

Transplant Allograft, Anaplasty, Graft, Repot, Reset, Shift

Transport(ed), Transporter, Transportation Argo, Bear, Bike, Broomstick, BRS, Bus, Cargo, Carract, ➤ CARRY, Cart, Charm, Convey, Delight, Ecstasy, Eloin, Enrapt, Enravish, Entrain, Esloin, Estro, Freight, Haul(age), Helicopter, Jerrican, Joy, Kurvey, Maglev, Monorail, Palanquin, Pantechnicon, Public, Put, Rape, Rapine, Rapture, Roadster, Shuttle, Ship, Sledge, Supersonic, Tote, Trap, Tuktuk, Waft, Wheels, Wireway

Transpose, Transposition Anagram, Commute, Convert, Invert, Metathesis, Shift, Spoonerism, Switch, Tr

▷ **Transposed** may indicate an anagram

Transubstantiate, Transubstantiation Capernaite

Transverse Across, Diagonal, Obliquid, Thwart

Transvestite Berdache, Berdash, Eonist

Tranter Dolly

Trap(s), Trapdoor, Trappings Ambush, ➤ BAGGAGE, Bags, Belongings, Booby, Buckboard, Bunker, Carriage, Catch, Clapnet, Corner, Cru(i)ve, Deadfall, Decoy, Dogcart, Eelset, Emergent, Ensnare, Entrain, Fall, Fit-up, Fly, Flypaper, Frame-up, Fyke, Gig, Gin, Gob, Grin, Hatch, Jinri(c)ksha(w), Keddah, Kettle, Kheda, Kiddle, Kidel, Kipe, Kisser, Knur(r), Lime, ➤ LUGGAGE, Lure, Mesh, Mouth, Net, Nur(r), Paraphernalia, Pitfall, Plant, Pot, Poverty, Putcheon, Putcher, Quicksand, Radar, Regalia, Sand, Scruto, ➤ SNARE, Speed, Spell, Spider, Springe, Stake-net, Stench, Sting, Tangle, Toil, Tonga, Trou-de-loup, U, U-bend, Vampire, Web, Weel, Weir, Wire

Trapezist Leotard

Trapper Carson

Trash(y) Bosh, Deface, Dre(c)k, Garbage, Junk, Kitsch, Pulp, ➤ RUBBISH, Schlock, Scum, Tinpot, Vandalise, Worthless

Trauma Insult, Shock

Travel(ler), Travelling Backpack, Bagman, Commercial, Commute, Crustie, Crusty, Drive, Drummer, Fare, Fellow, Fly, Fogg, Gipsen, Gipsy, Gitano, Globe-trotter, Go, Gulliver, Gypsy, Hike, Interrail, Itinerant, Journey, Long-haul, Marco Polo, Meve, Migrant, Motor, Move, Mush, Nomad, Passepartout, Peregrination, Peripatetic, Pilgrim, Ply, Polo, Range, Rep, Ride, Rom(any), Rove, Safari, Sail, Salesman, Samaritan, ➤ TOUR, Trek, Tripper, Tsigane, Viator, Voyage, Wayfarer, Wend, Wildfire, Zigan

Traverse Cross, Quest, Trace

Travesty Burlesque, Charade, Distortion, Parody, Show, Skit

Trawl Drag-net, Hose-net, Net

Tray Antler, Carrier, Case, Charger, Coaster, Gallery, Joe, Lazy Susan, Plateau, ➤ SALVER, Tea, Trencher, Voider

Treacherous, Treachery Deceit, Delilah, Fickle, Ganelon, Guile, Insidious, Knife, Medism, Perfidious, Punic, Quicksands, Serpentine, Sleeky, Snaky, Trahison, Traitor, ➤ TREASON, Two-faced, Viper

Treacle Blackjack, Butter, Molasses

Tread Clamp, Clump, Dance, Pad, Step, Stramp, Track, Trample

Treason Betrayal, Insurrection, Lèse-majesté, Lese-majesty, Perduellion, Sedition, ➤ TREACHERY

Treasure(r), Treasury Banker, Bursar, Cache, Camerlengo, Camerlingo, Cherish, Chest, Cimelia, Coffer, Ewe-lamb, Exchequer, Fisc(al), Fisk, Godolphin, Golden, Heritage, Hoard, Montana, Palgrave, ➤ PRIZE, Procurator, Purser, Relic, Riches, Steward, Thesaurus, Trove

Treat, Treatment Action, Acupuncture, Allopathy, Antidote, Archilowe, Arenation, Aromatherapy, Balneotherapy, Beano, Besee, Capitulate, Care, Chemotherapy, Chiropractic, Condition, Course, Cryotherapy, Cupping, Cure, Deal, Detox(ification), Dialysis, Do, ➤ DOCTOR, Dose, Dress, Dutch, Enantiopathy, Entertain, Facial, Fango, Figuration, Foment, Handle, Holistic, Homeopathy, Hydrotherapy, Immunotherapy, Jin shin do, Kenny, Manage, Medicate, Moxibustion, Naturopathy, Negotiate, Opotherapy, Osteopathy, ➤ OUTING, Pasteur, Pedicure, Physic, Pie,

Probiotics, Process, Prophylaxis, Psychoanalysis, Psychotherapy, Radiotherapy, Shout, Shrift, Smile, ➤ STAND, Tablet, Tebilise®, Thalassotherapy, Therapy, Titbit, Traction, Usance, Use, Vet
▷ **Treated** may indicate an anagram
Treatise Almagest, Commentary, Didache, Discourse, Monograph, Pandect, Summa, Tract(ate), Upanishad, Vedanta
Treaty Agreement, Alliance, Assiento, Concordat, Covenant, Entente, Lateran, Maastricht, ➤ PACT, Protocol, Utrecht
Treble Castrato, Choirboy, Chorist(er), Pairial, Soprano, ➤ TRIPLE, Triune
Tree Actor, ➤ ANCESTRY, Axle, Beam, Boom, Bottle, Conifer, Corner, Deciduous, Decision, Dendrology, Descent, Family, Fault, Fringe, Gallows, Grove, Hang, Hardwood, Jesse, Nurse, Pedigree, Pole, Sawyer, Shoe, Softwood, Staddle, Summer, Timber, Tyburn, ➤ WOOD

TREES

2 letters:	Dika	Ackee	Kokum
Bo	Dita	Afara	Larch
Ti	Eugh	Alamo	Lemon
3 letters:	Gean	Alder	Lilac
Ash	Hule	Alnus	Lotus
Asp	Jack	Anona	Mahoe
Bay	Kaki	Areca	Mahua
Bel	Kiri	Argan	Mahwa
Ben	Kola	Aspen	Mamey
Box	Lime	Beech	Maple
Elm	Lote	Belah	Matai
Fir	Mako	Birch	Melia
Gum	Ming	Bodhi	Motte
Ita	Mott	Boree	Mulga
Jak	Mowa	Butea	Mvule
Koa	Nipa	Cacao	Myall
Mot	Ombu	Carap	Ngaio
Nim	Palm	Cedar	Nyssa
Oak	Pine	Ceiba	Opepe
Sal	Plum	China	Osier
Tea	Poon	Cocoa	Palas
Til	Rata	Cocus	Palay
Ule	Rhus	Coral	Panax
Wax	Rimu	Elder	Pecan
Yew	Shea	Fagus	Pinon
4 letters:	Silk	Fever	Pipal
Acer	Sloe	Flame	Pipul
Aloe	Sorb	Guava	Plane
Amla	Tawa	Hakea	Quina
Arar	Teak	Hazel	Ramin
Atap	Teil	Hevea	Roble
Bael	Titi	Holly	Rowan
Bhel	Toon	Iroko	Sabal
Bito	Tung	Jambu	Saman
Bosk	Tutu	Jarul	Sassy
Cade	Upas	Judas	Scrog
Coco	Yang	Karri	Silva
Cola	**5 letters:**	Kauri	Smoke
Dali	Abele	Khaya	Sumac
Dhak	Abies	Kiaat	Taxus

Thorn	Gidjee	Samaan	Durmast
Thuja	Gingko	Sapele	Geebung
Thuya	Ginkgo	Sapium	Genipap
Tilia	Gnetum	Sapota	Gluinap
Tsuga	Gopher	Saxaul	Hickory
Tuart	Glinap	She-oak	Holm-oak
Tulip	Guango	Sinder	Jipyapa
Vitex	Gurjun	Souari	Kumquat
Wahoo	Gympie	Spruce	Lacquer
Wilga	Illipe	Stemma	Lagetto
Xylem	Illipi	Storax	Lentisk
Yacca	Jarool	Sumach	Logwood
Yulan	Jarrah	Sunder	Lumbang
Zaman	Joshua	Sundra	Madrono
Zamia	Jujube	Sundri	Mahaleb
6 letters:	Kamala	Tamanu	Manjack
Abroma	Kamela	Tewart	Marasca
Acacia	Karaka	Titoki	Margosa
Alerce	Karite	Tooart	Mazzard
Angico	Kowhai	Totara	Mesquit
Annona	Laurel	Tupelo	Moringa
Antiar	Lebbek	Waboom	Morrell
Arbute	Linden	Wandoo	Pereira
Arolla	Locust	Wicken	Pimento
Balsam	Longan	Willet	Platane
Banyan	Loquat	Willow	Pollard
Baobab	Lucuma	Witgat	Populus
Bilian	Macoya	Yarran	Quassia
Bombax	Mallee	Zamang	Quicken
Bonsai	Manuka	**7 letters:**	Quillai
Bo-tree	Mastic	Ailanto	Quinain
Buriti	Mimosa	Amboina	Radiata
Carapa	Mopane	Arbutus	Rampike
Carica	Mopani	Avodire	Redwood
Cashew	Myrtle	Bebeeru	Rock elm
Cembra	Nutmeg	Bilimbi	Saksaul
Cerris	Obeche	Bilsted	Sandbox
Chaste	Orange	Bubinga	Saouari
Chenar	Padauk	Buck-eye	Sapling
Cherry	Padouk	Bursera	Sausage
Chinar	Pagoda	Cajeput	Sequoia
Citron	Papaya	Cajuput	Seringa
Coffee	Pawpaw	Calamus	Service
Cordon	Peepul	Camphor	Shittah
Cornel	Pepper	Camwood	Sourgum
Cornus	Platan	Canella	Soursop
Deodar	Pomelo	Catalpa	Spindle
Diana's	Poplar	Champac	Sundari
Dragon	Popple	Champak	Varnish
Durian	Protea	Chayote	Wallaba
Durion	Puriri	Coquito	Witchen
Emblic	Quince	Corylus	Wych-elm
Feijoa	Red-bud	Corypha	Xylopia
Fustet	Ricker	Cumquat	Zelkova
Fustic	Roucou	Daddock	**8 letters:**
Gallus	Rubber	Dagwood	Aguacate
Garjan	Sabicu	Dogwood	Algaroba
Gidgee	Sallow	Dryades	Aquillia

Bangalow	Rambutan	Krummholz	
Basswood	Rangiora	Kurrajong	
Benjamin	Rewa-rewa	Lancewood	
Blackboy	Sago-palm	Lemonwood	
Blimbing	Sandarac	Macadamia	Ilang-ilang
Bountree	Santalum	Mockernut	Jaboticaba
Bourtree	Sapindus	Monkeypot	Jippi-jappa
Breadnut	Sapucaia	Naseberry	Letter-wood
Brigalow	Sea grape	Nux vomica	Lilly-pilly
Calabash	Simaruba	Paloverde	Macrocarpa
Cinchona	Soapbark	Paperbark	Manchineel
Cinnamon	Softwood	Paulownia	Mangabeira
Cocoplum	Sourwood	Persimmon	Mangosteen
Coolabah	Sweet gum	Pistachio	Marblewood
Coolibah	Sweetsop	Pitch-pine	Palisander
Dendroid	Sycamine	Poinciana	Paper birch
Dracaena	Sycamore	Ponderosa	Pohutukawa
Espalier	Sycomore	Pontianac	Quercitron
Flittern	Tamarack	Quebracho	Ribbonwood
Fraxinus	Tamarind	Rauwolfia	Sandalwood
Garcinia	Tamarisk	Rose-apple	Sappanwood
Ghost-gum	Taxodium	Sapodilla	Silverbell
Gnetales	Umbrella	Sassafras	Sneezewood
Guaiacum	Whitegum	Satinwood	Strawberry
Hagberry	Ygdrasil	Star-anise	Turpentine
Hornbeam	**9 letters:**	Stinkwood	Witch-hazel
Huon-pine	Agila-wood	Tacamahac	Witgatboom
Igdrasil	Ailantous	Terebinth	Woollybutt
Ironbark	Albespine	Toothache	Yellowwood
Ironwood	Azedarach	Torchwood	Ylang-ylang
Jelutong	Bilimbing	Wagenboom	**11 letters:**
Kingwood	Bitternut	Whitebeam	Appleringie
Laburnum	Blackbutt	Whitewood	Cabbage-palm
Lacebark	Bolletrie	Yggdrasil	Chaulmougra
Lecythis	Boobialla	Zebrawood	Chokecherry
Loblolly	Bully-tree	**10 letters:**	Cryptomeria
Magnolia	Burrawary	Arbor Vitae	Dipterocarp
Mahogany	Butternut	Blackbully	Eriodendron
Makomako	Caliatour	Bulletwood	Flamboyante
Mangrove	Caliature	Calamondin	Fothergilla
Manna-ash	Candlenut	Calliature	Leatherwood
Mesquite	Carambola	Candle-wood	Lignum vitae
Mulberry	Casuarina	Cannonball	Liquidambar
Ocotillo	Cherimoya	Chamaerops	Maceranduba
Oiticica	Chincapin	Chaulmugra	Pomegranate
Oleaceae	Chinkapin	Cheesewood	Purpleheart
Oleaster	Coachwood	Chinaberry	Shittimwood
Palmetto	Cordyline	Chinquapin	Sitka spruce
Pichurim	Courbaril	Cottonwood	**12 letters:**
Pinaster	Cupressus	Cowrie-pine	Hercules' club
Pyinkado	Evergreen	Eucalyptus	Liriodendron
Quandang	Flame-leaf	Fiddlewood	Mammee-sapota
Quandong	Greenwood	Flamboyant	Masseranduba
Quantong	Hackberry	Flindersia	Monkey-puzzle
Quillaia	Ivory palm	Frangipani	Washingtonia
Quillaja	Jacaranda	Green-heart	**13 letters:**
Raintree	Kahikatea	Hackmatack	Paper-mulberry

Tree-climber, Tree-dweller Monkey, Opossum, Sciurus, Squirrel, Unau

Tree disease Dutch elm, Waldsterben

Tree-man Ent

Tree-moss Usnea

Tree-paeony Moutan

Tree-pecker Picus

Tree-shrew Tana

Trefoil Hop, Lotos, Lotus

Trek Hike, Journey, Odyssey, Safari, Yomp

Trellis Espalier, Lattice, Pergola, Treillage, Treille

Tremble, Trembling, Tremor Aftershock, Butterfly, Dither, Dodder, Hotter, Judder, Palpitate, Quail, Quake, Quaver, Quiver, Seismal, ➤ SHAKE, Shiver, Shock, Shudder, Stound, Temblor, Trepid, Twitchy, Vibrate, Vibration, Vibratiuncle, Vibrato, Wobble, Wuther, Yips

Tremendous Big, Enormous, Howling, Immense, Marvellous

Tremolo Bebung, Trillo

➤ **Tremor** see TREMBLE

Tremulous Dithering, Hirrient, Quaking, Shaky, Timorous

Trench(er) Boyau, Cunette, Cuvette, Delf, Delph, Dike(r), ➤ DITCH, Dyke(r), Encroach, Fleet, Foss(e), Foxhole, Fur(r), Furrow, Grip, Gullet, Gutter, Leat, Line, Mariana, Moat, Oceanic, Outwork, Rill, Rille, Ring-dyke, Salient, Sap, Shott, Slip, Sod, Sondage

Trenchant Acid, Cutting

Trend(y) Bent, Bias, Chic, Climate, Drift, Fashion, Hep, In, Mainstream, Newfangled, Pop, Posey, Rage, Style, Swim, Tendency, Tendenz, Tenor, Tide, Tonnish

Trespass(ing) Encroach, Errant, Hack, Impinge, Infringe, Offend, Peccancy, Sin, Trench, Wrong

Tress(es) Curl, Lock, Ringlet, Switch, Tallent

Trestle Sawhorse

Trial Adversity, Affliction, Appro, Approbation, Approval, Assize, Attempt, Bane, Bernoulli, Bout, Corsned, Cross, Court-martial, Cow, Dock, Essay, ➤ EXPERIMENT, Field, Fitting, Hearing, Nuremberg, Pilot, Pree, Ordeal, Probation, Proof, Rehearsal, Scramble, Taste

Triangle(d), Triangular Acute, Bermuda, Cosec, Deltoid, Equilateral, Eternal, Gair, Golden, Gore, Gyronny, Isosceles, Obtuse, Pascal's, Pedimental, Pyramid, Rack, Right-angled, Scalene, Similar, Trigon, Tromino, Warning

Trias(sic) Bunter, Keuper, Muschelkalk, Rhaetic

Tribe, Tribal, Tribesmen Amalekite, Ammonites, Ashanti, Asher, Benjamin, Celt, Cherokee, Clan(nish), Creek, Dan, Dinka, Dynasty, Edomites, Family, Gad, Gens, Gentes, Gentilic, Goth, Hapu, Helvetii, Hittite, Horde, Hottentot, Ibo, Iceni, Israelite, Jat, Kaffir, Kenite, Kurd, Lashkar, Levi, Masai, Moabite, Mongol, Moro, Naga, Naphtali, Nation, Nervii, Ngati, Ostrogoths, Pathan, Phyle, ➤ RACE, Reuben, Riff, Rod, Sakai,

Salian, Senones, Senussi, Sept, Shawnee, Silures, Simeon, Tasaday, Teuton, Trinobantes, Vandals, Wolof, Wyandot(te), X(h)osa

Tribune, Tribunal Aeropagus, Bema, Bench, ➤ COURT, Divan, Forum, Hague, Industrial, Leader, Platform, Rienzi, Rota, Star-chamber

Tributary Affluent, Bogan, Branch, Creek, Fork

Tribute Cain, Citation, Commemoration, Compliment, Deodate, ➤ DUE, Epitaph, Festschrift, Gavel, Heriot, Homage, Kain, Memento, Ode, Panegyric, Peter's pence, ➤ PRAISE, Rome-penny, Scat(t), Tax, Toast, Wreath, Wroth

Trice Flash, Instant

Trichosanthin Q

Trick(s), Trickery, Trickster, Tricky Antic, Art, Artifice, Attrap, Bamboozle, Begunk, Book, Bunco, Bunko, Cantrip, Capot, Catch, Cheat, Chicane(ry), Chouse, Claptrap, Cog, Confidence, Coyote, Crook, Davenport, Deception, Deck, Delicate, Delude, Device, DO, ➤ DODGE, Dupe, Elf, Fard, Fetch, Fiddle, Finesse, Flam, Flim-flam, Fob, Fox, Fraud, Fun, Game, Gaud, Gleek, Glike, Guile, Hoax, Hocus(-pocus), Hoodwink, Hornswoggle, Hum, Illude, Illusion, Illywhacker, Jadery, Jockey, John, Kittle, Knack, Lark, Mislead, Monkey, Nap, Nasruddin, Palter, Parlour, Pass, Pawk, Pleasantry, Pliskie, Prank, Prestige, Put-on, Ramp, Raven, Reak, Reik, Rex, Rig, Roughie, Ruse, Scam, Sell, Set-up, Shanghai, Shavie, Shenanigan, Shifty, Shill, Skin-game, Skite, Skul(l)duggery, Skylark, Sleight, Slight, Slinter, Spoof, Stall, Stint, Subterfuge, Sug, Swiftie, Thimble-rig, Three-card, Ticklish, Trap, Tregetour, Trump, Turn, Tweedler, Undercraft, Underplot, Vole, Wangle, Wheeze, Wile, Wrinkle

▷ **Trick** may indicate an anagram

Trickle Drib(ble), Driblet, Leak, Rill, Seep

Trickless Misère

Triclinic Anorthic

Trident Fork, Plane, Trisul(a)

Trifle(s), Trifling Bagatelle, Banal, Baubee, Bibelot, Birdseed, Bit, Cent, Chickenfeed, Coquette, Dabble, Dalliance, ➤ DALLY, Denier, Desipient, Do, Doit, Faddle, Falderal, Fallal, Fattrell, Fewtril, Fiddle, Fig, Fingle-fangle, Flamfew, Fleabite, Flirt, Folderol, Fool, Footle, Fribble, Frippery, Fritter, Frivol, Gewgaw, Idle, Iota, Kickshaw, Knick-knack, Luck-penny, Mite, Nick-nacket, Niff-naff, Nothing, Nugae, Nugatory, Nyaff, Palter, Peanuts, Peddle, Peppercorn, Petty, Philander, Picayune, Piddle, Piffle, Pin, Pingle, Pittance, Play, Potty, Quiddity, Quiddle, Slight, Smatter, Song, Sport, Stiver, Straw, Sundry, Sweet Fanny Adams, Tiddle, Toy, Trinket, Trivia, Whifflery, Whim-wham, Whit

Trig Neat, Sech, Tosh, Trim

Trigger Detent, Hair, Instigate, Pawl, Precipitate, Start

Trill(ed), Triller, Trilling Burr, Churr, Hirrient, Quaver, Ribattuta, Roll, Staphyle, Trim, Twitter, Warble

Trilobite Olenellus, Olenus, Paradoxide

Trim(mer), Trimming Ballast, Bleed, Braid, Bray, Chipper, Clip, Dapper, Dinky, Dress, Ermine, Face, Falbala, Fettle, File, Froufrou, Garnish, Garniture, Gimp, Guimpe, Macramé, Macrami, Marabou, Neat, Net(t), Ornament, Pare, Passament, Passement(erie), Pipe, Plight, Posh, Preen, Proign, Pruin(e), Proyn(e), Prune, Robin, Ruche, Sax, Sett, Shipshape, Smirk, Smug, Sned, Snod, ➤ SPRUCE, Straddle, Stroddle, Strodle, Stylist, Svelte, ➤ TIDY, Time-server, Torsade, Trick, Whippersnipper, Wig

Trinidadian Carib

Trinitarian, Trinity Mathurin(e), Triad, Trimurti, Triune

Trinket Bauble, Bibelot, Bijou(terie), Charm, Fallal, Nicknack, Toy, Trankum

Trio Catch, Graces, Skat

Trip(per) Cruise, Dance, Day, Ego, Errand, ➤ FALL, Field, Flight, Flip, Guilt, Head, High, Journey, Junket, Kilt, Link, Outing, Power, Ride, Round, Run, Sail, Sashay, Spin, Spurn, ➤ STUMBLE, Tour, Trek, Voyage

▷ **Trip** may indicate an anagram

Tripe Abracadabra, Bosh, Caen, Entrails, Rot

Triple, Triplet Codon, Hemiol(i)a, Sdrucciola, Ternal, Tiercet, Treble, Trifecta, Trilling, Trin(e), Tripling

Tripod Cat, Cortina, Highhat, Oracle, Triangle, Trippet, Trivet

Triptych Volet

Trishaw Cycle

Trite Banal, Boilerplate, Corny, Hackneyed, Hoary, Novelettish, Rinky-dink, Stale, Stock, Time-worn

Triton Eft, Evet, Ewt, Trumpet-shell

Triumph(ant) Cock-a-hoop, Codille, Cowabunga, Crow, Exult, Glory, Impostor, Killing, Oho, Olé, Ovation, Palm, Victorious, ➤ WIN

Triumvir Caesar, Crassus, Pompey

Trivet Tripod, Trippet

Trivia(l) Adiaphoron, Bagatelle, Balaam, Bald, ➤ BANAL, Frippery, Frothy, Futile, Idle, Light, Minutiae, Nitpicking, Paltry, Pap, Peppercorn, Pettifoggery, Petty, Picayune, Piffling, Shallow, Small, Small beer, Small fry, Snippety, Squirt, Squit, Toy(s)

Trochee Choree

Troglodyte Ape, Caveman, Hermit, Spelean, Wren

Trojan Agamemnon, Dardan, Iliac, Priam, Teucrian, Troic

Troll Gnome, Rove, Trawl, Warble

Trolley Brute, Cart, Dolly, Gurney, Shopping, Tea, Truck, Trundler

► **Trollop** see LOOSE WOMAN

Trombone Posaune

Troop(s), Trooper Band, BEF, Brigade, Company, Depot, Detachment, Guard, Horde, Midianite, Militia, Pultan, Pulton, Pultoon, Pultun, SAS, School, Sowar, State, Storm, Tp, Turm(e)

Troopship Transport

Trophy Adward, Ashes, ➤ AWARD, Belt, Cup, Emmy, Memento, Palm, ➤ PRIZE, Scalp, Schneider, Spoils, Tourist, TT

A_____

Tropic(al) Cancer, Capricorn, Derris, Jungle, Neogaea, Sultry

Trot(ter), Trot out Air, Crib, Crubeen, Job, Jog, Passage, Pettitoes, Piaffe, Pony, Ranke, Red(-shirt), Rising, Tootsie

Troth Perfay, Troggs

Trotsky Entr(y)ism, Leon

Troubador Blondel, Griot, Manrico, Minstrel, Singer, Sordello

Trouble(s), Troublemaker, Troublesome Ache, Ado, Affliction, Aggro, Agitate, Ail, Alarm, Annoy, Bale, Barrat, ➤ BOTHER, Brickle, Burden, Care, Coil, Concern, Debate, Disaster, Disquiet, Distress, Disturb, Dog, Dolour, Eat, Esclandre, Exercise, Fash, Fashious, Firebrand, Fossick, Gram(e), Grief, Hag-ride, Harass, Harry, Hassle, Hatter, Heat, Heist, Hellion, Hot water, Howdyedo, Hydra, Inconvenience, ➤ IN TROUBLE, Jam, Kiaugh, Mess, Moil, Molest, Noy, Perturb, Pester, Plague, Poke, Reck, Rub, Shake, Shtuck, Soup, Spiny, Stir, Storm, Sturt, Tartar, Teen, Teething, Thorny, Tine, Toil, Trial, Tsouris, Tsuris, Turn-up, Tyne, Unsettle, Vex, ➤ WORRY

Trouble-free Gallio

Trouble-shooter Ombudsman

▷ **Troublesome** may indicate an anagram

Trough Back, Bed, Bucket, Buddle, Channel, Chute, Culvert, Graben, Hod, Hutch, Manger, Stock, Straik, Strake, Syncline, Troffer, Tundish, Tye

Trounce ➤ BEAT, Hammer, Thump

Trousers Bags, Bell-bottoms, Bloomers, Capri pants, Churidars, Clam-diggers, Continuations, Cords, Corduroys, Cossacks, Culottes, Daks, Drainpipe, Drawers, Ducks, Eel-skins, Flannels, Flares, Galligaskins, Gaskins, Gauchos, Hipsters, Inexpressibles, Innominables, Jeans, Jodhpurs, Kaccha, Lederhosen, Longs, Loons, Moleskins, Oxford bags, Palazzos, Pantaloons, Pants, Pedal pushers, Pegtops, Plus-fours, Reach-me-downs, Salopettes, Shalwar, Ski pants, Slacks, Strides, Strossers, Sweatpants, Trews, Trouse, Unmentionables, Unutterables, Utterless

Trout Aurora, Brook, Brown, Bull, Coral, Finnac(k), Finnock, Fish, Gillaroo, Herling, Hirling, Peal, Peel, Phinnock, Pogies, Quintet, Rainbow, Sewen, Sewin, Speckled, Splake, Steelhead, Togue, Whitling

Trow Faith, Meseems

Trowel Float

Troy Ilium, Sergeant, T, Weight

Truant Absentee, AWOL, Dodge, Hooky, Kip, Miche, Mitch, Mooch, Mouch, Wag

Truce Armistice, Barley, Ceasefire, Fainites, Fains, Interlude, Pax, Stillstand, Treague, Treaty

Truck Bakkie, Bogie, Business, Cattle, Cocopan, Dealings, Dolly, Dumper, Forklift, Haul, Journey, ➤ LORRY, Low-loader, Pallet, Pick-up, Tipper, Trolley, Ute, Utility, Van

Trudge Footslog, Jog, Lumber, Pad, Plod, Stodge, Stramp, Taigle, Traipse, Trash, Trog, Vamp

True Accurate, Actual, Apodictic, Constant, Correct, Exact, Factual, Faithful, Genuine, Honest, Indubitable, Leal, Literal, Loyal, Platitude, Plumb, Pure, Real, Realistic, Sooth, Very

Truffle Tuber, Tuberaceae

Trug Basket, Wisket

Truly Certes, Fegs, Forsooth, Indeed, Verily, Yea

Trump(s), Trumpet(er) Agami, Alchemy, Alchymy, Bach, Blare, Blast, Bray, Buccina, Bugle(r), Call, Card, Clarion, Conch, Cornet, Corona, Crow, Daffodil, Elephant, Fanfare, Hallali, Honours, ➤ HORN, Invent, Jew's, Last, Lituus, Lur(e), Lurist, Manille, Marine, Megaphone, ➤ NO TRUMP, Proclaim, Ram's-horn, Resurrect, Ruff, Salpingian, Salpinx, Satchmo, Sennet, Shofar, Shophar, Slug-horn, Surpass, Tantara, Tantarara, Tar(at)antara, Theodomas, Tiddy, Triton, Triumph

Trumpery Fattrels, Jimcrack, Paltry, Trashy

Truncate(d) Abrupt, Cut, Dock, Shorten

Truncheon Billie, Billy, Blackjack, Cosh, Night-stick

Trundle Hump, Trill, Troll

Trunk(s) Aorta(l), A-road, Bole, Body, Box, Bulk, But(t), Carcase, Chest, Coffer, Hose, Imperial, Log, Peduncle, Pollard, Portmanteau, Portmantle, Proboscis, Ricker, Road, Saratoga, Shorts, STD, Stock, Stud, Synangium, Torso, Valise, Wardrobe

Truss ➤ BIND, Ligate, Oop, Oup, Sheaf, Tie, Upbind

Trust(y), Trusting, Trustworthy Affy, Authentic, Belief, Care, Cartel, Charge, Combine, Confide, Credit, Dependable, Discretionary, ➤ FAITH, Fiduciary, Gullible, Honest, Hope, Investment, Leal, Lippen, Loyal, National, NT, Reliable, Reliance, Rely, Repose, Reputable, Staunch, Tick, Trojan, Trow, True, Trump, Unit

Trustee Agent, Executor, Fiduciary, Tr

Truth(ful), Truism Accuracy, Alethic, Axiom, Bromide, Cliché, Cold turkey, Dharma, Dialectic, ➤ FACT, Facticity, Forsooth, Gospel, Home, Honesty, Idea(l), Naked, Pravda, Reality, Sooth, Veridical, Verity

Try(ing) Aim, Approof, Assay, Attempt, Audition, Bash, Bid, Birl, Burden, Burl, Conative, Contend, Crack, Effort, Empiric(utic), ➤ ENDEAVOUR, Essay, Examine, Experiment, Fand, Fish, Fling, Foretaste, Go, Harass, Hard, Hear, Importunate, Irk, Offer, Ordalium, Practise, Pree, Prieve, ➤ SAMPLE, Seek, Shot, Sip, Stab, Strain, Strive, Taste, Tax, Tempt, Test, Touchdown, Whirl

Tryst Date, Rendezvous

Tsar(ist) Alexis, Emperor, Godunov, Octobrist, Ruler

TT Rechabite

Tub, Tubbiness, Tub-thumper Ash-leach, Back, Bath, Boanerges, Bran, Corf, Cowl, Dan, Diogenes, Endomorph, Firkin, Keeve, Kid, Kieve, Kit, Pin, Podge, Pudge, Pulpit, Tun, Vat, Wash

Tuba Bombardon, Euphonium

Tube Arteriole, Artery, Barrel, Blowpipe, Bronchus, Burette, Calamus, Canaliculus, Cannula, Capillary, Casing, Catheter, Cathode-ray, Conduit,

Crookes, Digitron, Diode, Discharge, Duct, Electron, Epididymis, Eustachian, Fallopian, Fistule, Fulgurite, Geissler, Grommet, Hose, Iconoscope, Image(orthicon), Inner, Kinescope, Klystron, Macaroni, Malpighian, Matrass, Metro, Nixie, Oval, Oviduct, Pentode, Pilot-static, ➤ PIPE, Pipette, Pitot, Pneumatic, Pollen, Promethean, Salpinx, Saucisse, Saucisson, Schnorkel, Shadow-mask, Sieve, Siphon, Siphonostele, Siphuncle, Skelp, Skiatron, Sleeve, Snorkel, Spaghetti, Speaking, Spout, Staple, Static, Strobotron, Swallet, Teletron, Television, Test, Tetrode, Thyratron, Tile, Torpedo, Trachea, Triniscope, Trocar, Trunk, Tunnel, Tuppenny, U, Ureter, Urethra, Vacuum, Vas, Vein, Vena, Venturi, Video

Tuber(s) Arnut, Arracacha, Bulb, Chufa, Coc(c)o, Dasheen, Earth-nut, Eddoes, Mashua, Oca, Potato, Salep, Taproot, Taro, Yam

Tuberculosis Consumption, Crewels, Cruel(l)s, Decline, Lupus, Phthisis, Scrofula

Tuck Dart, Friar, Gather, Grub, Kilt, Pin, Pleat, Scran

Tuesday Hock, Shrove

Tuft(ed) Amentum, Beard, C(a)espitose, Candlewick, Catkin, Cluster, Coma, Comb, Cowlick, Crest, Dollop, Flaught, Floccus, Goatee, Hassock, Pappus, Penicillate, Quiff, Scopate, Shola, Tait, Tassel, Toorie, Toupee, Tourie, Tussock, Tuzz, Whisk

Tug Drag, Haul, Jerk, Lug, Pug, ➤ PULL, Rive, Ship, Sole, Soole, Sowl(e), Tit, Tow, Towboat, Yank

Tui Poebird

Tully Cicero

Tumble, Tumbler Acrobat, Cartwheel, Drier, Fall, ➤ GLASS, Pitch, Popple, Purl, Realise, Spill, Stumble, Topple, Trip, Twig, Voltigeur, Welter

▷ **Tumble** may indicate an anagram

Tumbledown Decrepit, Dilapidated, Ramshackle, Rickle, Ruinous

Tumbril Caisson

Tummy Belly, Colon, Mary, Paunch, Pod

Tummy-ache Colic, Gripe, Tormina

Tumour Adenoma, Anbury, Angioma, Angiosarcoma, Astrocytoma, Burkitt('s) lymphoma, Cancer, Carcinoid, Carcinoma, Carcinosarcoma, Chrondoma, Condyloma, Crab(-yaws), Dermoid, Encanthis, Encephaloma, Enchondroma, Endothelioma, Epulis, Exostosis, Fibroid, Fibroma, ➤ GROWTH, Ganglion, Gioblastoma, Glioma, Granuloma, Grape, Gumma, Haemangioma, Haematoma, Hepatoma, Lipoma, Lymphoma, Medullablastoma, Melanoma, Meningioma, Mesothelioma, Metastasis, Mole, Myeloma, Myoma, Myxoma, Neoplasm, Neuroblastoma, Neuroma, Osteoclastoma, Osteosarcoma, Retinoblastoma, Scirrhous, Seminoma, Thymoma, -oma, Oncology, Osteoma, Papilloma, Polypus, Sarcoma, Steatoma, Struma, Talpa, Teratoma, Wart, Wen, Wilms, Windgall, Wolf, Xanthoma, Yaw

Tumult Brattle, Brawl, Coil, Deray, Ferment, Fracas, Hirdy-girdy, Hubbub, Reird, Riot, ➤ ROAR, Romage, Rore, Stoor, Stour, Stowre, Stramash, Tew, ➤ UPROAR

Tumulus Barrow, Mote, Motte

Tun Cask, Keg

Tune(s), Tuneful, Tuner Adjust, Air, Aria, Canorous, Carillon, Catch, Choral, Dump, Etude, Fork, Harmony, Hornpipe, Jingle, Key, Maggot, Measure, Melisma, ➤ MELODY, Old Hundred, ➤ OUT OF TUNE, Peg, Port, Potpourri, Raga, Rant, Ranz-des-vaches, Signature, Snatch, Song, Spring, Strain, Sweet, Syntonise, Temper, Theme, Tone, Tweak

Tungstate, Tungsten Scheelite, W, Wolfram

Tunic Ao dai, Caftan, Chiton, Choroid, Cote-hardie, Dalmatic, Dashiki, Gymslip, Hauberk, Kabaya, Kaftan, Kameez, K(h)urta, ➤ SINGLET, Tabard, Toga

Tunnel Bore, Channel, Condie, Countermine, Culvert, Cundy, Gallery, Head, Mine, Qanat, Simplon, Stope, Subway, Syrinx, Tube, Underpass, Wind, Wormhole

Tunny Bonito, Tuna

Turban Bandanna, Hat, Mitral, Pagri, Puggaree, Puggery, Puggree, Sash, Scarf

Turbid Cloudy, Dense, Drumly, Roily

Turbine Francis

Turbulence, Turbulent Becket, Bellicose, Buller, Factious, Fierce, Rapids, Stormy

▷ **Turbulent** may indicate an anagram

Turf Caespitose, Clod, Divot, Earth, Fail, Feal, Flaught, ➤ GRASS, Greensward, Peat, Screw, ➤ SOD, Sward

Turk(ish) Anatolian, Bashaw, Bashkir, Bey, Bimbashi, Bostangi, Byzantine, Caimac(am), Crescent, Effendi, Gregory, Horse(tail), Irade, Kaimakam, Kazak(h), Kurd, Mameluke, Mutessarif(at), Omar, Osman(li), Ottamite, Ottoman, Ottomite, Rayah, Scanderbeg, Selim, Seljuk(ian), Seraskier, Spahi, Tatar, Timariot, Usak, Uzbeg, Uzbek, Yakut

Turkey, Turkey-like Anatolia, Brush, Bubbly(-jock), Curassow, Eyalet, Flop, Gobbler, Norfolk, Sultanate, Talegalla, TR, Trabzon, Vulturn

Turmeric Curcumine

Turmoil Chaos, Din, Ferment, Stoor, Stour, Tornado, Tracasserie, Tumult, ➤ UPROAR, Welter

▷ **Turn(ing)** may indicate an anagram

Turn(ing), Turned away, Turned up, Turns Acescent, Act, Addle, Advert, Antrorse, Apostrophe, Apotropaic, Avert, Bank, Become, Bend, Buggins, Bump, Canceleer, Cancelier, Caracol(e), Careen, Cartwheel, Cast, Chainé, Chandelle, Change, Char(e), Chore, Christiana, Christie, Christy, Churn, Cock, Coil, Crank(le), Cuff, Curd(le), Curve, Defect, Deflect, Demi-volt(e), Detour, Deviate, Dig, Digress, Divert, Ear, Earn, Elbow, Evert, Fadge, Flip, Go, Gruppetto, Hairpin, Handbrake, Head-off, Hie, High, Hinge, Hup, Immelmann, Influence, Innings, Intussuscept, Invert, Jar, Jink, Keel, Kick, Laeotropic, Lot, Luff, Mohawk, Number, Obvert, Parallel, Parry, Penchant, Pivot, Plough, Pronate, Prove, PTO, Quarter, Quersprung, Rebut, Refer, Refract, Remuage, Retroflex, Retroussé, Retrovert, Rev, Revolt, Ride, Riffle,

Rocker, Roll, Root, ➤ ROTATE, Rote, Roulade, Rout, Routine, Screw, Secund, Sheer, ➤ SHOT, Shout, Sicken, Slew, Slue, Solstice, Sour, ➤ SPELL, Spin, Spot, Sprain, Star, Start, Step, Swash, Swing, Swivel, Telemark, Three-point, Throw, Tiptilt, Tirl, Torque, Transpose, Trend, Trick, Trochilic, Turtle, Twiddle, Twist, U, Uey, Up, Veer, Versed, Version, Vertigo, Volta, Volte-face, Wap, Warp, Wedein, Wend, Went, ➤ WHEEL, Whelm, Whirl, Whorl, Wimple, Wind, Wrest, Zigzag

Turn-coat Apostate, Cato, Defector, Quisling, Rat, Renegade, Tergiversate, Traitor

Turner Axle, Lana, Lathe, Painter, Pivot, Rose-engine, Spanner, Worm, Wrench

Turning point Crisis, Crossroads, Landmark

Turnip(-shaped) Bagie, Baggy, Hunter, Napiform, Navew, Neep, Rutabaga, ➤ STUPID PERSON, Swede, Tumshie

Turnkey Gaoler, Jailer

Turn-out Eventuate, Gathering, Product, Rig, Splay, Style

Turn over Capsize, Careen, Flip, Inversion, Production, PTO, Somersault, TO, Up-end

Turnpike Highway, Toll

Turnstile Tourniquet

Turntable Rota, Rotator

Turpentine Galipot, Rosin, Thinner, Turps

Turquoise Bone, Ligure, Odontolite

Turret(ed) Barmkin, Bartisan, Garret, Louver, Louvre, Pepperbox, Sponson, ➤ TOWER, Turriculate

Turtle, Turtle head Bale, Calipash, Calipee, Chelone, Green, Hawksbill, Inverted, Leatherback, Loggerhead, Matamata, Mossback, Mud, Musk, Ridley, Snapper, Soft-shelled, Stinkpot, Terrapin, Thalassian

Tusk Gam, Horn, Ivory, Tooth, Tush

Tusker Dicynodont, Elephant, Mastodon

Tussle Giust, Joust, Mêlée, Scrimmage, Scrum, Scuffle, Skirmish, Touse, Touze, Towse, Towze, Tuilyie, Wrestle

Tussock Hassock, Niggerhead, Tuft

Tut(-tut) Och, Pooh

Tutelary Guardian, Protector

Tutor Abbé, Aristotle, Ascham, Bear, ➤ COACH, Crammer, Don, Instruct, Leader, Preceptor, Répétiteur, Supervisor, Teacher

Tuxedo DJ

TV Baird, Box, Cable, Digital, Idiot-box, Lime Grove, Monitor, PAL, SECAM, Sky, Tele, Telly, Tube, Video

Twaddle Blether, Drivel, Rot, Slipslop, Tripe

Twang Nasal, Pluck, Plunk, Rhinolalia

Tweak Pluck, Twiddle, Twist, Twitch

Tweed(y) Donegal, Harris®, Homespun, Lovat, Raploch

Tweet Chirrup

Twelfth, Twelve Apostles, Dozen, Epiphany, Glorious, Grouse, Midday, Midnight, N, Night, Noon, Ternion, Twal

Twenty, Twenty-sided Icosahedron, Score, Vicenary, Vicennial, Vicesimal, Vigesimal

Twenty-five Quartern

Twenty-four Thr(e)ave

Twerp Pipsqueak

▶ **Twice** see TWO

Twice-yearly Biennial, Equinox

Twiddle Fidget

Twig(s) Besom, Birch, Cotton, Cow, Dig, Grasp, Kow, Osier, Realise, Reis, Rice, Rumble, Sarment, See, Sprig, Sticklac, Switch, Understand, Wand, Wattle, Wicker, Withe

Twilight Cockshut, Crepuscular, Demi-jour, Dusk, Gloam(ing), Gotterdämmerung

Twill Chino

Twin(s) Asvins, Castor, Coetaneous, Didymus, Dioscuri, Ditokous, Dizygotic, Double, Fraternal, Gemel, Identical, Isogeny, Kindred, Macle, Monozygotic, Pigeon-pair, Pollux, Siamese, Tweedledee, Tweedledum

Twine Braid, Coil, Cord, Inosculate, Packthread, Sisal, Snake, String, Twist, Wreathe

Twinge Pang, Scruple, Stab

Twinkle, Twinkling Glimmer, Glint, Mo(ment), ➤ SPARKLE, Starnie, Trice

Twirl Spin, Swivel, Tirl, Trill, Twiddle, Twizzle, Whirl

▷ **Twirling** may indicate an anagram

Twist(ed), Twister, Twisting, Twisty Anfractuous, Askant, Askew, Becurl, Bought, Card-sharper, Chisel, Coil, Contort, Convolution, Crinkle, Crinkum-crankum, Crisp, Cue, Curl(icue), Cyclone, Deform, Detort, Distort, ➤ DODGE, Garrot, Helix, Imposture, Kink, Mat, Möbius strip, Oliver, Pandanaceous, Plait, Quirk, Raddle, Ravel, Rick, Rogue, Rotate, Rove, Skew, Slew, Slub(b), Slue, Snarl, Spin, Spiral, Sprain, Squiggle, Squirm, Swivel, Tendril, Torc, Tornado, Torque, Torsade, Torsion, Torticollis, Tortile, Turn, Tweak, Twiddle, Twine, Twirl, Valgus, Volvulus, Warp, Welkt, Wigwag, Wind, Wound-wrap, Wrast, Wreathe, Wrench, Wrest, Wrethe, Wrick, Wriggle, Wring, Writhe, Wry, Zigzag

▷ **Twisted, Twisting** may indicate an anagram

Twit, Twitter Chaff, Cherup, Chirrup, Dotterel, Gear(e), Giber, ➤ JEER, Stupid, Taunt, Warble

Twitch(ing), Twitchy Athetosis, Clonic, Grass, Jerk, Life-blood, Start, Subsultive, Tic, Tig, Tit, Tweak, Twinge, Vellicate, Yips

Two(some), Twice Bice, Bis, Bisp, Both, Brace, Couple(t), Deuce, Double, Duad, Dual, Duet, Duo, Dyad, ➤ PAIR, Swy, Tête-à-tête, Twain, Twins, Twister

Two-edged Ancipitous

Two-faced Dihedral, Dorsiventral, Hypocritical, Janus, Redan

Two-gallon Peck
Two-headed Amphisbaenic, Dicephalous
Two hundred H
Two hundred and fifty E, K
Two-master Brig
Two-rayed Diactinal
Two-sided Bilateral, Equivocatory
Two thousand Z
Two-up Kip, Swy
Tycoon Baron, Magnate, Plutocrat, Shogun
Type(s) A, Agate, Aldine, Antimony, Antique, B, Balaam, Baskerville,
   Bembo, Black-letter, Bodoni, Body, Bold face, Bourgeois, Braille, Brand,
   Brevier, Brilliant, Canon, Caslon, Category, Character, Chase, Cicero,
   Clarendon, Class, Columbian, Cut, Egyptian, Elite, Elzevir, Em, Emblem,
   Emerald, English, Face, Font, Form(e), Fount, Fraktur, Fudge, Garamond,
   Gem, Genre, Gent, Gothic, Great primer, Gutenberg, Hair, Ilk, Image,
   Kern(e), Key, Kidney, Kind, Ligature, Longprimer, Minion, Modern, Moon,
   Mould, Non-pareil, Norm, Old style, Old-face, Paragon, Pattern, Pearl,
   Peculiar, Pi, Pica, Pie, Plantin, Point, Primer, Print, Quad(rat), Roman,
   Ronde, Ruby, Sanserif, Semibold, Serif, ➤ SORT, Sp, Species, Stanhope,
   Style, Times, Tissue, Version
▷ **Type of** may indicate an anagram
Typewriter Golfball, Portable, Stenograph
Typhoon Cyclone, Hurricane, Monsoon, Tornado, Wind
Typical Average, Characteristic, Classic, Normal, Representative, Standard,
   Symbolic, True-bred, Usual
Typist Audio, Printer, Temp
Tyrannise(d) Domineer, Lord, Under
Tyrant, Tyranny, Tyrannical Absolutism, Autocrat, Caligula, Despot,
   Dictator, Drawcansir, Gelon, Herod, Lordly, Nero, Oppressor, Pharaoh,
   Sardanapalus, Satrap, Stalin, Totalitarian, Tsar, Yoke
Tyre Balloon, Cross-ply, Michelin, Pericles, Radial, Recap, Remould, Retread,
   Sidewall, Slick, Snow, Spare, Tread, Tubeless, Whitewall
Tyro Beginner, Ham, ➤ NOVICE, Rabbit, Rookie, Rooky, Starter
Tyrolese R(h)aetian

U u

U, U-type Gent, Unicorn, Universal, Uranium
Ubiquitous Everywhere, Omnipresent
Udder Bag, Dug
Ugandan Obote
Ugly Cow, Customer, Eyesore, Foul, Gorgon, Gruesome, Hideous, Homely, Huckery, Loth, Mean, Ominous, Plain
Ugrian Ostiak, Ostyak, Samo(y)ed, Vogul
Ukase Decree
Ukraine Ruthene, UR
Ulcer(ous) Abscess, Aphtha, Canker, Chancroid, Decubitus, Duodenal, Gastric, Helcoid, Noma, Peptic, Phagedaena, Rodent, Rupia, Sore, Wolf
Ulster NI, Overcoat, Raincoat, Ulad
Ulterior External, Hidden
Ultimate Absolute, Basic, Deterrent, Eventual, Final, Furthest, Last, Maximum, So, Supreme, Thule
Ultra Drastic, Extreme, Radical
Ultra-republican Leveller
Ulysses Bloom, Grant, Odysseus
Umbellifer Angelica, Arnut, Car(r)away, Dill, Honewort, Pig-nut, Seseli
Umbrage Offence, Pique, Resentment, Shade
Umbrella(-shaped) Bumbershoot, Chatta, Gamp, Gingham, Gloria, Mush(room), Parasol, Sunshade, Tee
Umbria Eugubine, Iguvine
Umpire Arb(iter), Byrlawman, Daysman, Decider, Judge, Oddjobman, Odd(s)man, Overseer, Referee, Rule, Stickler, Thirdsman
Unabashed Bare-faced, Brazen, Shameless
Unable Can't, Incapable
Unaccented Atonic, Proclitic
Unacceptable Non-U, Not on, Out, Stigmatic
Unaccompanied A cappella, Alone, High-lone, Secco, Single, Solo, Solus
Unaccustomed Desuetude, New
Unadorned Bald
Unadulterated Sincere
Unaffected Artless, Genuine, Homely, Natural, Plain, Sincere, Unattached
Unaided Solo
Unaltered Constant, Same
Unanswerable Erotema, Irrefragable, Irrefutable
Unarguable Erotema
Unarmed Inerm, Naked, Vulnerable
Unashamed Blatant, Brazen

Unassigned Adespota, Anonymous

Unattached Freelance

Unattractive Drac(k), Lemon, Plain, Plug-ugly, Rebarbative, Seamy, Ugly

Unattributable Anon

Unauthentic Plagal

▷ **Unauthentic** may indicate an anagram

Unavail(able), Unavailing Bootless, Futile, Ineluctable, Lost, No use, Off, Vain

Unavoidable Inevitable, Necessary, Perforce

Unaware Heedless, Ignorant, Incognisant, Innocent

Unbalanced Asymmetric, Deranged, Doolalli, Doolally, Loco, Lopsided, Uneven

Unbearable Bassington, Intolerable

Unbeaten All-time

Unbecoming, Unbefitting Improper, Infra dig, Shabby, Unfitting, Unseemly, Unsuitable, Unworthy

Unbelievable, Unbeliever Agnostic, Atheist, Cassandra, Doubter, Giaour, Heathen, Incredible, Infidel, Pagan, Painim, Paynim, Sceptic, Tall, Zendik

Unbent Relaxed

Unbiased Fair, Impartial, Just, Neutral, Objective, Unattainted

Unblemished Spotless, Vestal

Unblinking Alert, Astare, Fearless

Unborn Future, Unbred

Unbowed In-kneed, Resolute

Unbreakable Infrangible, Inviolate

Unbridled Fancy free, Footloose, Lawless, Uncurbed, Unrestricted, Unshackled, Untramelled

Unburden Confide, Offload, Relieve, Unload

Uncanny Eerie, Eldritch, Extraordinary, Geason, Rum, Spooky, Weird

Uncastrated Stone

Uncertain(ty) Blate, Broken, Chancy, Chary, Contingent, Delicate, Dicey, Dither, Doubtful, Dubiety, Hesitant, Iffy, Indeterminate, Indistinct, Irresolute, Peradventure, Queasy, Risky, Slippery, Tentative, Vor

▷ **Uncertain** may indicate an anagram

Unchangeable, Unchanged, Unchanging As is, Enduring, Eternal, Idempotent, Immutable, Monotonous, Stable

Uncharacteristic Atypical

Uncharged Neutral, Neutron

Unchaste Corrupt, Immodest, Immoral, Impure, Lewd, Wanton

Unchecked Rampant

Uncivil(ised) Barbaric, Benighted, Boondocks, Discourteous, Disrespectful, Giant-rude, Heathen, Impolite, Military, Rude, Rudesby

Uncle Abbas, Afrikaner, Arly, Bob, Dutch, Eme, Nunky, Oom, Pawnbroker, Pop-shop, Remus, Sam, Tio, Tom, Usurer, Vanya

Unclean Defiled, Dirty, Impure, Obscene, Ordure, Squalid, Tabu, T(e)refa(h)

Unclear Ambitty, Hazy, Nebulous, Obscure
Unclothed Bald, Nude
Uncloven Soliped
Uncommitted Laodicean
Uncommon Rare, Strange, Unusual
▷ **Uncommon(ly)** may indicate an anagram
Uncommunicative Tight-lipped
Uncompanionable Threesome
Uncomplimentary Blunt
Uncomprehending Anan, Ignorant
Uncompromising Hardshell, Intransigent, Rigid, Strict, Ultra
Unconcealed Open, Pert
Unconcerned Bland, Careless, Casual, Cold, Indifferent, Insouciant, Nonchalant, Strange
Unconditional Absolute, Free, Pure
Unconnected Asyndetic, Detached, Disjointed, Off-line
Unconscious(ness) Asleep, Catalepsy, Cold, Comatose, Instinctive, Non-ego, Subliminal, Trance, Under
Unconsidered Impetuous, Rash
Uncontrolled Atactic, Free, Incontinent, Loose, Wild
Unconventional Beatnik, Bohemian, Drop-out, Eccentric, Gonzo, Heretic, Heterodox, Informal, Irregular, Offbeat, Original, Outlandish, Outré, Raffish, Unorthodox
▷ **Unconventional** may indicate an anagram
Unconverted Neat
Unconvincing Farfet(ched), Lame, Thin
Uncoordinated Asynergia, Ataxic, Awkward, Clumsy
Uncorrect Stet
Uncouth(ness) Backwoodsman, Bear, Crude, Gothic, Inelegant, Rube, Rude, Rugged, Uncivil
Uncover(ed) Bare, Disclose, Expose, Inoperculate, Open, Peel, Reveal, Shave, Shill, Shuck, Uncap
Unction, Unctuous(ness) Anele, Balm, Chrism, Extreme, Ointment, Oleaginous, Ooze, Smarm, Soapy
Uncultivated, Uncultured Artless, Bundu, Fallow, Ignorant, Philistine, Rude, Tramontane, Wild
Undamaged Intact, Sound, Whole
Undated Sine die
Undecided Doubtful, Non-committal, Pending, Open-ended, Pendulous, Uncertain, Wavering
Undefiled Chaste, Clean, Pure, Virgin
Undeniable Fact, Incontestable, Irrefutable
Under Aneath, Below, Beneath, Hypnotized, Sotto, Sub-, Unconscious
Underarm Axilla, Lob

Underburnt Samel

Under-butler Bread-chipper

Undercarriage Bogie

Undercoat Base, Primer

Undercooked Rare, Raw, Samel

Undercover Espionage, Secret, Veiled

Undercurrent Acheron, Undertone, Undertow

Underdevelopment Ateleiosis

Underdog Cerberus, Loser, Victim

▶ **Undergarment** see UNDERWEAR

Undergo Bear, Dree, Endure, Sustain

Undergraduate Fresher, L, Pup, Sizar, Sophomore, Student, Subsizar

Underground (group) Basement, Catacomb, Cellar, Hell, Hypogaeous, Irgun, Kiva, Macchie, Maquis, Mattamore, Metro, Phreatic, Pict, Plutonia, Pothole, Secret, Souterrain, Subsoil, Subterranean, Subway, Tube

Undergrowth Brush, Chaparral, Firth, Frith, Scrub

Underhand Dirty, Haunch, Insidious, Lob, Oblique, Secret, Sinister, Sly, Sneaky, Surreptitious

Underlease Subtack

Underline Emphasise, Insist

Underling Bottle-washer, Cog, Inferior, Jack, Menial, Munchkin, Subordinate

Underlying Subjacent

Undermine Erode, Fossick, Sap, Subvert, Tunnel, Weaken

Undernourished Puny, Starveling

Underpass Simplon, Subway

Underside Soffit

Understand(able), Understanding Accept, Acumen, Agreement, Apprehend, Capeesh, Clear, Comprehend, Conceive, Concept, Cotton-on, Deal, Dig, Enlighten, Entente, Exoteric, Fathom, Follow, Gather, Gauge, Gaum, Gorm, Grasp, Have, Head, Heels, Insight, Ken, Kind, Knowhow, Learn, Omniscient, Pact, Rapport, Rapprochement, Realise, Savey, Savvy, See, Sole, Substance, Tolerance, Tumble, Twig, Uptak(e), Wisdom, Wit

Understatement Litotes, M(e)iosis

Understood Implicit, OK, Perspicuous, Roger, Tacit, Unspoken

Understudy Deputy, Double, Stand-in, Sub

Undertake, Undertaking Attempt, Contract, Covenant, Enterprise, Guarantee, Pledge, Promise, Scheme, Shoulder, Warranty

Undertaker Entrepreneur, Mortician, Obligor, Sponsor, Upholder

Under-ten Unit, Yarborough

Undertone Murmur, Rhubarb, Sotto voce

Underwater Demersal

Underwear Balbriggan, Bloomers, Bodice, Body, Bra(ssiere), Briefs, Broekies, Camiknickers, Camisole, Chemise, Combs, Dainties, Frillies,

Girdle, Innerwear, Jump, Linen, Lingerie, Linings, Long Johns, Pantalets, Pantaloons, Panties, Petticoat, Scanties, Semmit, Slip, Smalls, Stays, Step-ins, Subucula, Suspenders, Tanga, Teddy, Thermal, Underdaks, Undergarments, Underpants, Undershirt, Underthings, Undies, Unmentionables, Vest, Wyliecoat, Y-fronts®

Underworld Chthonic, Criminal, Hell, Lowlife, Mafia, Shades, Tartar(e), Tartarus, Tartary

Underwrite, Underwritten Assure, Endorse, Guarantee, Insure, Lloyds, PS

Undeserving Immeritous

Undesirable Kibitzer

Undeveloped Backward, Depauperate, Green, Inchoate, Latent, Ridgel, Ridgil, Ridgling, Rig, Riggald, Riglin(g), Rudimentary, Seminal

Undifferentiated Thalliform, Thallus

Undigested Crude

Undignified (end) Disaster, Foot, Improper, Infra dig, Unseemly

Undiluted Neat, Pure, Sheer

Undiminished Entire, Intact, Whole

Undiplomatic Brusque, Tactless

Undisciplined Hothead, Rule-less, Rulesse, Sloppy, Unruly, Wanton

Undisclosed Hidden, In petto

Undisguised Apert, Clear, Plain

Undistinguished Plebeian

Undivided Aseptate, Complete, Entire, Indiscrete

Undo(ing) Annul, Defeat, Destroy, Downfall, Dup, Poop, Poupe, Release, Ruin, Unravel

Undoctored Neat

Undone Arrears, Left, Postponed, Ran, Ruined

Undoubtedly Certes, Positively, Sure

Undress(ed) Bare, Disrobe, En cuerpo, Expose, Négligé, Nude, Nue, Peel, Querpo, Raw, Rough, Self-faced, Spar, Strip, Unapparelled

Undulate, Undulating Billow, Nebule, Ripple, Roll, Wave

▷ **Unduly** may indicate an anagram

Undyed Greige

Undying Amaranthine, Eternal

Unearth(ly) Astral, Dig, Discover, Disentomb, Exhumate, Indagate

Unease, Uneasiness, Uneasy Angst, Anxious, Creeps, Inquietude, Itchy, Malaise, Restive, Shy, Tense, The willies, Uptight, Windy, Womble-cropped

Unedifying Idle

Unembarrassed Blasé, Dégagé

Unemotional Bland, Cool, Iceberg, Matter-of-fact, Sober, Stolid

Unemployed, Unemployment Drone, Idle, Latent, Lay-off, Redundant

Unending Chronic, Eternal, Lasting, Sempiternal

Unenlightened Ignorant, Nighted

Unenthusiastic Damp, Tepid

Unenveloped Achlamydeous

Unequal(led) Aniso-, Disparate, Non(e)such, Scalene, Unjust

Unerring Dead, Exact, Precise

Unestablished Free

Unethical Amoral, Corrupt, Immoral

Uneven(ness) Accident, Blotchy, Bumpy, Irregular, Jaggy, Patchy, Ragged, Scratchy

▷ **Unevenly** may indicate an anagram

Unexpected(ly) Abrupt, Accidental, Adventitious, Fortuitous, Inopinate, Snap, Sodain(e), Sudden, Turn-up, Unawares, Unwary

Unexperienced Strange

Unexplained Obscure

Unfading Evergreen, Immarcescible

Unfailing Sure

Unfair Bias(s)ed, Crook, Dirty, Inclement, Invidious, Mean, Partial

Unfaithful Disloyal, Godless, Infidel, Traitor

Unfamiliar New, Quaint, Strange

Unfashionable Cube, Dowdy, Passe, Square

▷ **Unfashionable** may indicate 'in' to be removed

Unfavourable Adverse, Ill, Poor, Untoward

Unfeeling Adamant, Callous, Cold, Cruel, Dead, Hard, Inhuman(e), Insensate, Robotic

Unfinished Crude, Inchoate, Raw, Scabble, Scapple, Stickit

Unfit(ting) Disabled, Faulty, Ill, Impair, Inept, Outré, Tref(a), Unable

▷ **Unfit** may indicate an anagram

Unfixed Isotropic, Loose

Unflinching Fast, Staunch

Unfold Deploy, Display, Divulge, Evolve, Interpret, Open, Relate, Spread

Unforced Voluntary

Unforeseen Accident, Sudden

Unfortunate(ly) Accursed, Alack, Alas, Hapless, Ill-starred, Luckless, Shameless, Unlucky

Unfounded Groundless

Unfriendly Aloof, Antagonistic, Asocial, Chill(y), Cold, Fraim, Fremd, Fremit, Hostile, Icy, Remote, Surly

Unfruitful Abortive, Barren, Sterile

Unfulfilled Manqué

Ungainly Awkward, Gawkish, Uncouth, Weedy

Ungodliness, Ungodly Impiety, Pagan, Perfidious, Profane

Ungracious Cold, Offhand, Rough, Rude

Ungrammatical Anacoluthia

Ungrateful Ingrate, Snaky

Unguent Nard, Pomade, Salve

Ungulate Antelope, Dinoceras, Eland, Equidae, Hoofed, Moose, Rhino, Ruminantia, Takin, Tapir, Tylopoda

Unhappily, Unhappy, Unhappiness Blue, Depressed, Disconsolate, Dismal, Doleful, Down-hearted, Downcast, Dysphoria, Glumpish, Love-lorn, Lovesick, Miserable, Sad, Sore, Tearful, Unlief, Upset

▷ **Unhappily** may indicate an anagram

Unharmed Safe, Scatheless

Unharness Outspan

Unhealthy Bad, Clinic, Diseased, Epinosic, Insalubrious, Morbid, Noxious, Peaky, Prurient, Sickly

Unholy Profane, Wicked

Uniat Maronite

Unicorn Coin, Monoceros, Moth, Myth, Narwhal

Unidentified Anon, Anonym(ous), Incognito, Ligure

Unification, Unify(ing) Henotic, Integrate, Risorgimento, Unite

Uniform Abolla, Battledress, Consistent, Dress, Equable, Equal, Even, Flat, Forage-cap, Homogeneous, Identical, Khaki, Kit, Livery, Regimentals, Regular, Rig, Robe, Same, Sole, Standard, Steady, Strip, Unvaried

Unimaginative Banausic, Literalistic, Pedestrian, Pooter

Unimpaired Entire, Intact, Sound

Unimportant Cog, Fiddling, Footling, Frivolous, Idle, Immaterial, Inconsequent, Inconsiderable, Insignificant, MacGuffin, Makeweight, Minnow, Minutiae, Negligible, Nugatory, Peripheral, Petty, Small-time, Trifling, Trivia(l)

Unimpressible Cynical

Uninformed Ingram

Uninhabited Bundu, Deserted, Lonely

Uninhibited Bold, Raunchy

Uninspired Humdrum, Pedestrian, Pompier, Tame

Unintelligent Dumb, Obtuse, Stupid

Unintelligible Arcane, Code, Greek

Unintentional Inadvertent

Uninterested, Uninteresting Apathetic, Bland, Dreary, Dry, Dull, Incurious, Nondescript

Uninterrupted Constant, Incessant, Running, Steady

Uninvited Gatecrasher, Interloper, Intruder, Sorner, Trespasser

Union(ist) Affiance, Allegiance, Alliance, Anschluss, Association, Bed, Benelux, Bond, Combination, Concert, Covalency, Craft, Credit, Diphthong, Economic, Enosis, Ensemble, Equity, EU, European, Fasciation, Federal, Federation, Fusion, Group, Guild, Heterogamy, Impanation, Industrial, Knight of labour, Liaison, Link-up, Marriage, Match, Merger, Nuptials, NUM, NUR, NUS, NUT, Parabiosis, Pearl, RU, Rugby, Samiti, Sex, Sherman, Solidarity, Splice, Sponsal, Student, Soviet, Symphysis, Syngamy, Synizesis, Synostosis, Synthesis, Teamsters,

➤ TRADE UNION, TU, U, UNISON, USDAW, Uxorial, Verein, Wedding, Wedlock, Wield, Zollverein, Zygosis

Unique(ness) Alone, A-per-se, Hacceity, Inimitable, Lone, Matchless, Nonesuch, Nonpareil, Nonsuch, Only, One-off, Peerless, Rare, Singular, Sole, Sui generis

Unisex(ual) Epicene, Hermaphrodite

Unison Chorus, Harmony, One, Sync

Unit Abampere, Ace, Amp, Angstrom, Bar, Barn, Baud, Becquerel, Bit, Byte, Cadre, Candela, Cell, Centimorgan, Centipoise, Chaldron, Chronon, Codon, Congius, Corps, Coulomb, Crith, Cusec, Dalton, Daraf, Darcy, Debye, Degree, Denier, Derived, Dessiatine, DIN, Detachment, Dioptre, Division, Dobson, Dol, Dyne, Echelon, Ecosystem, Electron, Element, Em, En, Energid, Ensuite, Erg, Erlang, Farad, Fermi, Flight, Fresnel, Gal, Gauss, GeV, Gigabit, Gilbert, Glosseme, Gram, Gray, Hartree, Henry, Hertz, Hide, Ion, Item, Jansky, Joule, K, Kelvin, Kilderkin, Kilerg, Kilowatt, Lambert, Langley, Last, League, Lexeme, Lumen, Lux, Maceral, Magneton, Man-hour, Maxwell, Measure, Megabyte, Megahertz, Megaton, Megawatt, Metre, Mho, Micella, Micelle, Microcurie, Microinch, Micron, Mil, Module, Mole, Monad, Morgan, Morgen, Morpheme, Mutchkin, Neper, Nepit, Nest, Newton, Nit, Octa, Oersted, Ohm, Okta, Organ, Parasang, Pascal, Pennyweight, Phoneme, Phot, Pixel, Poise, Poundal, Ploughgate, Probit, Protoplast, RA, Radian, Rem, Remen, Rep, Ro(e)ntgen, Rutherford, Sabin, Second, Semeion, Sememe, SI, Siemens, Sievert, Singleton, Slug, Sone, Steradian, Stilb, Stoke(s), Syllable, Syntagm(a), TA, Tagmeme, Terabyte, Tesla, Therblig, Therm, Tog, Token, Torr, Vanity, Var, Volt, Watt, Weber, Wing, Yrneh

Unitarian Arian, Paulian, Socinian

Unite(d) Accrete, Bind, Coalesce, Combine, Concordant, Connate, Connect, Consolidate, Consubstantiate, Covalent, Fay, Federal, Federate, Fuse, Gene, Injoint, Join, Kingdom, Knit, Lap, Link, Marry, Meint, Meng, Ment, Merge, Meynt, Ming, Nations, Oop, Oup, Siamese, Solid, States, Tie, ➤ WED, Weld, Yoke

United Ireland Fine Gael

United Kingdom Old Dart, UK

Unity Harmony, One, Solidarity, Sympathy, Togetherness

Univalent Monatomic

Universal, Universe All, Catholic, Cosmos, Creation, Ecumenic(al), Emma, General, Global, Infinite, Macrocosm, Maddala, Microcosm, Sphere, U, World(wide)

University Academe, Academy, Alma mater, Aston, Berkeley, Bonn, Brown, Campus, Civic, College, Columbia, Cornell, Exeter, Gown, Harvard, Ivy League, Open, OU, Oxbridge, Pennsylvania, Princeton, Reading, Redbrick, St Andrews, Sorbonne, Varsity, Yale

Unjust(ified) Groundless, Inequity, Iniquitous, Invalid, Tyrannical

Unkempt Dishevelled, Raddled, Shaggy

Unknown Agnostic, Anon, A.N.Other, Hidden, Ign, Incog(nito), N, Nobody, Noumenon, Occult, Quantity, Secret, Soldier, Strange, Symbolic, Tertium quid, Warrior, X, Y

Unleavened Azymous

Unless Nisi, Save, Without

Unliable Exempt

Unlicensed Illicit

Unlike(ly) Difform, Disparate, Dubious, Improbable, Inauspicious, Long shot, Outsider, Remote, Tall, Unlich

Unlimited Almighty, Boundless, Indefinite, Measureless, Nth, Universal, Vast

Unload Disburden, Discharge, Drop, Dump, Jettison, Land

Unlock(ed) Bald

Unlucky Donsie, Hapless, Ill(-starred), Inauspicious, Infaust, Jonah, Misfallen, S(c)hlimazel, Stiff, Thirteen, Untoward, Wanchancie, Wanchancy

Unman Castrate

Unmannerly Crude, Discourteous, Impolite, Rude

Unmarried Bachelor, Common-law, Single, Spinster

Unmask Expose, Rumble

Unmatched Bye, Champion, Orra, Unique

Unmentionable(s) Bra, Foul, ➤ UNDERWEAR, Undies

Unmindful Heedless, Oblivious

Unmistakable Clear, Manifest, Plain

Unmitigated Absolute, Arrant, Sheer, Ultra

Unmixed Me(a)re, Neat, Nett, Pure, Raw, Straight

Unmoved, Unmoving Adamant, Doggo, Firm, Serene, Static, Stolid

Unnamed Anon

Unnatural Abnormal, Affected, Cataphysical, Contrived, Eerie, Flat, Geep, Irregular, Strange

▷ **Unnaturally** may indicate an anagram

Unnecessary Extra, Gash, Gratuitous, Needless, Otiose, Redundant, Superfluous

Unnerve, Unnerving Discouraging, Eerie, Rattle

Unobserved Backstage, Sly, Unseen

Unobtrusive Low profile

Unoccupied Empty, Idle, Vacant, Void

Unofficial Wildcat

Unoriginal Banal, Copy, Derivative, Imitation, Plagiarised, Slavish

Unorthodox Heretic, Heterodox, Maverick, Off-the-wall, Unconventional

Unpaid Amateur, Brevet, Hon(orary), Voluntary

Unpaired Azygous, Bye

Unpalatable Acid, Bitter, Unsavoury

Unparalleled Supreme, Unique

Unpartitioned Aseptate

Unperturbed Bland, Calm, Serene

Unpleasant, Unpleasant person Creep, God-awful, Grim, Grotty, Horrible, Icky, Invidious, Nasty, Obnoxious, Odious, Offensive, Painful, Pejorative, Rebarbative, Shady, Shitty, Shocker, Sticky, Toerag, Wart

Unpopular Hat(e)able

Unpractical Futile, Orra

Unpredictable Aleatory, Dicy, Erratic, Maverick, Wild card

Unprepared Ad lib, Extempore, Impromptu, Unready

Unpretentious Quiet

Unprincipled Amoral, Dishonest, Irregular, Reprobate

Unproductive Arid, Atokal, Atokous, Barren, Dead-head, Eild, Fallow, Futile, Lean, Poor, Shy, Sterile, Yeld, Yell

Unprofitable Bootless, Fruitless, Lean, Thankless

Unprogressive Inert, Square

Unprotected Exposed, Nude, Vulnerable

Unpublished Inedited

Unpunctual Tardy

Unqualified Absolute, Entire, Outright, Profound, Pure, Quack, Sheer, Straight, Thorough, Total, Utter

Unquestionably, Unquestioning Absolute, Certain, Doubtless, Implicit

Unravel Construe, Disentangle, Feaze, Fray, Solve

Unready Unripe

Unreal(istic) Eidetic, En l'air, Escapist, Fake, Fancied, Illusory, Mirage, Oneiric, Phantom, Phon(e)y, Pseudo, Romantic, Sham, Spurious

Unreasonable, Unreasoning Absurd, Bigot, Extreme, Illogical, Irrational, Misguided, Perverse, Rabid

Unrecognised Incognito, Inconnu, Invalid, Thankless, Unsung

Unrefined Coarse, Common, Crude, Earthy, Gur, Rude, Vul(g), Vulgar

Unrehearsed Extempore, Impromptu

Unrelenting Implacable, Remorseless, Severe, Stern

Unreliable Dodgy, Erratic, Fickle, Flighty, Fly-by-night, Shonky, Unstable, Wankle, Wonky

Unremitting Dogged, Intensive

Unresponsive Cold, Frigid, Nastic, Rigor

Unrest Ferment

Unrestrained Free, Hearty, Homeric, Immoderate, Incontinent, Lax, Lowsit, Rampant, Wanton, Wild

Unreturnable Ace

Unrighteousness Adharma

Unrivalled Nonesuch

Unromantic Classic(al), Mundane

Unruffled Calm, Placid, Serene, Smooth, Tranquil

Unruly Anarchic, Bodgie, Buckie, Camstairy, Camsteary, Camsteerie, Exception, Lawless, Obstreperous, Ragd(e), Raged, Ragged, Rampageous, Rattlebag, Riotous, Tartar, Turbulent, Turk, Wanton, Wayward

▷ **Unruly** may indicate an anagram

Unsafe Deathtrap, Fishy, Insecure, Perilous, Precarious, Vulnerable

Unsatisfactory, Unsatisfying Bad, Lame, Lousy, Meagre, Rocky, Thin, Wanting

Unsavoury Epinosic

Unscramble Decode, Decrypt

Unscrupulous Rascally, Slippery

Unseasonable, Unseasoned Green, Murken, Raw, Untimely

Unseat Depose, Dethrone, Oust, Overset, Overthrow, Throw

Unseemly Coarse, Improper, Indecent, Indign, Untoward

Unselfish Altruist, Generous

Unsent Square

Unsettled Homeless, Hunky, Indecisive, Nervous, Outstanding, Queasy, Restive

▷ **Unsettled** may indicate an anagram

Unsexy N, Neuter

Unsheltered Bleak, Exposed, Homeless

Unsightly Hideous, Repulsive, Ugly

Unsinning Impeccable, Pure

Unskilled Awkward, Dilutee, Gauche, Green, Inexpert, Rude

Unsmiling Agelastic

Unsociable Anchoretic, Grouchy, Solitary

Unsophisticated Alf, Boondocks, Boonies, Bushie, Direct, Faux-naif, Hillbilly, Homebred, Homespun, Inurbane, Jaap, Jay, Naive, Rube

Unsound Barmy, Infirm, Invalid, Shaky, Wildcat, Wonky

▷ **Unsound** may indicate an anagram

Unsparing Severe

Unspeakable Dreadful, Ineffable, Nefandous

Unspecific General, Generic, Vague

Unspoiled, Unspoilt Innocent, Natural, Perfect, Pristine, Pure

Unspoken Silent, Tacit

Unstable, Unsteady Anomic, Astatic, Bockedy, Casual, Crank, Crank(y), Dicky, Erratic, Fluidal, Groggy, Infirm, Insecure, Labile, Rickety, Shifty, Slippy, Tickle, Tottery, Totty, Variable, Wambling, Wankle, Wobbly

Unstated Concordat, Tacit, Unknown

▶ **Unsteady** see UNSTABLE

Unstressed Enclitic

▷ **Unstuck** may indicate an anagram

Unsubstantial Aeriform, Airy, Flimsy, Paltry, Shadowy, Slight, Thin, Yeasty

Unsuccessful Abortive, Futile, Manqué, Vain

Unsuitable Impair, Improper, Inapt, Incongruous, Inexpedient, Malapropos, Unfit

Unsupported Astylar, Floating, Unfounded

Unsure Tentative

Unsurpassed All-time, Best, Supreme

Unsuspecting Credulous, Innocent, Naive

Unsweetened Brut, Natural

Unsymmetrical Heterauxesis(m), Irregular, Lopsided

Unsympathetic Short shrift

Unthinking Mechanical

Untidy Daggy, Dowd(y), Frowzy, Litterbug, Ragged, Scruff(y), Slipshod, Slovenly, Tatty

▷ **Untidy** may indicate an anagram

Untie Free, Undo, Unlace

Until Hasta

Untilled Fallow

Untiring Assiduous

Untold Secret, Umpteen, Unred, Unread, Vast

Untouchable Burakumin, Dalit, Harijan, Immune, Sealed

Untouched Intact, Pristine, Inviolate, Virgin

▷ **Untrained** may indicate 'BR' to be removed

Untried New, Virgin

Untrue, Untruth Apocryphal, Eccentric, Faithless, False(hood), Lie, Prefabrication, Unleal

Untrustworthy Dishonest, Fickle, Shifty, Sleeky, Tricky

Untypical Anomalous, Isolated, Unusual

Unused, Unusable Impracticable, New, Over, Wasted

Unusual(ly) Abnormal, Atypical, Extra(ordinary), Freak, New, Novel, Odd, Particular, Rare, Remarkable, Singular, Special, ➤ STRANGE, Unique, Untypical, Unwonted

▷ **Unusual** may indicate an anagram

Unutterable Ineffable

Unvarying Constant, Eternal, Stable, Static, Uniform

Unveil Expose, Honour

Unvoiced Surd

Unwanted De trop, Exile, Gooseberry, Nimby, Outcast, Sorn

Unwed Celibate, Single

Unwelcome, Unwelcoming Frosty, (Persona) Non grata, Icy, Lulu, Obtrusive

Unwell Ailing, Crook, Dicky, Ill, Impure, Poorly, Seedy, Toxic

Unwholesome Miasmous, Morbid, Noxious

Unwieldy Cumbersome

Unwilling(ness) Averse, Disinclined, Intestate, Loth, Nolition, Nolo, Perforce, Reluctant

Unwind Relax, Straighten, Unreave, Unreeve
▷ **Unwind** may indicate an anagram
Unwise Foolish, Ill-advised, Impolitic, Imprudent, Inexpedient, Injudicious
Unwitting Accidental, Nescient
Unwonted Inusitate
Unworkable Impossible, Inoperable
Unworried Carefree
Unworthy Below, Beneath, Indign, Inferior
Unwritten Verbal
Unyielding Adamant, Eild, Firm, Inexorable, Intransigent, Obdurate, Rigid, Steely, Stubborn, Tough
Unyoke Outspan
Up(on), Upper, Uppish A, Afoot, Antidepressant, Arrogant, Astir, Astray, Astride, Cloud-kissing, Euphoric, Heavenward, Hep, Horsed, Incitant, Off, On, Primo, Range, Ride, Riding, Skyward, Speed, ➤ UPPER CLASS, Vamp, Ventral
Up-anchor Atrip, Weigh
Upbeat Anacrusis, Arsis
Upbraid Abuse, Rebuke, Reproach, Reprove, Scold, Twit
Upcountry Anabasis, Inland
Update Renew, Report
Upheaval Cataclysm, Eruption, Seismic, Stir
▷ **Upheld** may indicate 'up' in another word
Uphill Arduous, Borstal, Sisyphean
Uphold Assert, Defend, Maintain
Upholstery Lampas, Moquette, Trim
Upkeep Support
Upland Downs, Wold
Uplift Boost, Edify, Elate, Elevation, Exalt, Hoist, Levitation, Sky
Upper class, Upper crust Aristocrat, County, Crachach, Nobility, Patrician, Posh, Sial, Top-hat, Tweedy, U
Upright(s), Uprightness Aclinic, Anend, Apeak, Apeek, Aplomb, Arrect, Erect, Goalpost, Honest, Jamb, Joanna, Merlon, Mullion, Orthograde, Perpendicular, Piano, Pilaster(s), Post, Rectitude, Roman, Splat, Stanchion, Stares, Stile, Stud, Vertical, Virtuous
Uprising Incline, Intifada, Rebellion, Revolt, Tumulus
Uproar(ious) Ballyhoo, Bedlam, Blatancy, Brouhaha, Charivari, Clamour, Collieshangie, Commotion, Cry, Din, Dirdam, Dirdum, Durdum, Emeute, Ferment, Flaw, Fracas, Furore, Garboil, Hell, Hoopla, Hubbub(oo), Hullabaloo, Hurly(-burly), Katzenjammer, Noise, Noyes, Outcry, Pandemonium, Racket, Raird, Reird, Riotous, Ruckus, Roister, Romage, Rowdedow, Rowdydow(dy), Ruction, Rumpus, Stramash, Turmoil, Whoobub
Uproot Eradicate, Evict, Outweed, Supplant, Weed

Upset(ting) Aggrieve, Alarm, Bother, Capsize, Catastrophe, Choked, Coup, Cowp, Crank, Derange, Dip, Discomboberate, Discombobulate, Discomfit, Discomfort, Discommode, Disconcert, Dismay, Disquiet, Distraught, Disturb, Dod, Eat, Fuss, Inversion, Keel, Miff, Nauseative, Offend, Overthrow, Overturn, Perturb, Pip, Pother, Purl, Rattle, Rile, Ruffle, Rumple, Sad, Seel, Shake, Sore, Spill, Tapsalteerie, Tip, Topple, Trauma, Undo

▷ **Upset** may indicate an anagram; a word upside down; or 'tes'

Upshot Outcome, Result, Sequel

Upside down Inverted, Resupinate, Tapsie-teerie, Topsy-turvy

Upstart Buckeen, Jumped-up, Mushroom, Parvenu

▷ **Upstart** may indicate 'u'

Upstream Thermal

Upsurge Thrust, Waste

Uptake Shrewdness, Understanding, Wit

Up to Till, Until

Up-to-date Abreast, Contemporary, Current, Mod, New-fashioned, Right-on, State-of-the-art, Swinging, Topical, Trendy

Upwards Acclivious, Aloft, Antrorse, Cabré

Uranium Pitchblende, U

Urban Civic, Megalopolis, Municipal, Town

Urbane Civil, Debonair, Townly

Urchin Arab, Brat, Crinoid, Crossfish, Cystoid, Echinoidea, Echinus, Gamin, Gutty, Heart, Mudlark, Nipper, Ragamuffin, Sand-dollar, Sea-egg, Spatangoidea, Spatangus, Street-arab, Townskip

Urge, Urgent Admonish, Ca, Coax, Constrain, Crying, Dire, Drive, Egg, Enjoin, Exhort, Exigent, Goad, Hard, Hie, Hoick, Hunger, Hurry, Id, Impel, Impulse, Incense, Incite, Insist(ent), Instance, Instigate, Itch, Kick, Libido, Nag, Peremptory, Persuade, Press(ing), Prod, Push, Set on, Spur, Strong, Wanderlust, Whig, Yen

▷ **Urgent** may indicate 'Ur-gent', viz. Iraqi

Uriah Hittite, Humble, Umble

Urinal Bog, John, Jordan, ➤ LAVATORY, Loo, Pissoir

Urinate, Urine Chamber-lye, Emiction, Enuresis, Lant, Leak, Micturition, Pee, Piddle, Piss, Slash, Stale, Strangury, Tiddle, Widdle

Urn(s) Cinerarium, Ewer, Grecian, Olla, Ossuary, Samovar, Storied, Vase

Us 's, UK, Uns, We

Usage, Use(d), Utilise Application, Apply, Avail, Boot, Consume, Custom, Deploy, Dow, ➤ EMPLOY, Ex, Exercise, Exert, Exploit, Flesh, Habit, Hand-me-down, Inured, Manner, Ply, Practice, Sarum, Spent, Sport, Tradition, Treat, Ure, Wield, With, Wont

Useful Asset, Availing, Commodity, Dow, Expedient, Invaluable

Useless Base, Bung, Cumber, Dead-wood, Dud, Empty, Futile, Gewgaw, Idle, Inane, Ineffective, Lame, Lemon, Otiose, Plug, Sculpin, Sterile, Swap, US, Vain, Void, Wet

Usher Black Rod, Chobdar, Commissionaire, Conduct(or), Doorman, Escort, Herald, Huissier, Macer, Rod, Show, Steward

Usual Common, Customary, Habit(ual), Natural, Normal, Ordinary, Rule, Solito, Typical, Wont

Usurer, Usury Gombeen, Loanshark, Moneylender, Note-shaver, Shark, Uncle

Usurp(er) Abator, Arrogate, Encroach, Invade

Ut As, Doh, Utah

Utah Ut

Utensil(s) Chopsticks, Colander, Cookware, Corer, Fish-kettle, Fork, Gadget, Implement, Instrument, Knife, Mandolin(e), Ricer, Skillet, Spatula, Spoon, Things, Tool, Zester

▶ **Utilise** see USE

Utilitarian Benthamite, Mill, Practical, Useful

Utility Elec(tricity), Gas, Water

Utmost Best, Extreme, Farthest, Maximum

Utopia(n) Adland, Cloud-cuckoo-land, Ideal, Pantisocracy, Paradise, Perfect, Shangri-la

Utter(ance), Uttered, Utterly Absolute, Accent, Agrapha, Agraphon, Arrant, Cry, Dead, Deliver, Dictum, Dog, Downright, Ejaculate, Enunciate, Express, Extreme, Glossolalia, Issue, Judgement, Lenes, Lenis, Most, Oracle, Pass, Phonate, Pronounce, Pure, Quo(th), Rank, Rattle, Remark, Saw, ➤ SAY, Sheer, Stark, State, Syllable, Tell, Vend, Vent, Very, Voice

Uvula Staphyle

V v

V Anti, Bomb, Del, Five, Nabla, See, Sign, Verb, Verse, Versus, Victor(y), Volt, Volume

Vacancy, Vacant Blank, Empty, Glassy, Hole, Hollow, Inane, Place, Space, Vacuum

Vacation Holiday, Leave, Non-term, Outing, Recess, Trip, Voidance

Vaccination, Vaccine Antigen, Cure, HIB, Jenner, Sabin, Salk, Serum, Subunit

Vacillate, Vacillating Dither, Feeble, Hesitate, Shilly-shally, Trimmer, Wabble, Wave(r)

Vacuous Blank, Empty, Toom, Vacant

Vacuum Blank, Cleaner, Dewar, Emptiness, Magnetron, Nothing, Plenum, Thermos®, Void

Vade-mecum Ench(e)iridion, Notebook

Vagabond Bergie, Gadling, ➤ GYPSY, Hobo, Landlo(u)per, Rapparee, Romany, Rover, Runagate, Tramp

Vagrant Beachcomber, Bum, Bummer, Caird, Crusty, Dosser, Drifter, Gangrel, Gang-there-out, Goliard, Gypsy, Hobo, Landlo(u)per, Lazzarone, Nomad, Patercove, Rinthereout, Rogue, Romany, Scatterling, Strag, Straggle, Stroller, Swagman, Tinker, ➤ TRAMP, Truant

Vague(ness) Amorphous, Bleary, Blur, Confused, Dim, Equivocal, Hazy, Ill-headed, Indeterminate, Indistinct, Loose, Mist, Nebulous, Shadowy, Woolly-minded

▷ **Vaguely** may indicate an anagram

Vain Bootless, Coxcomb, Coxcomical, Egoistic, Empty, Fruitless, ➤ FUTILE, Hollow, Idle, Proud, Strutting, Useless, Vogie

Vainglory Panache

Valance Pand, Pelmet

Vale Addio, Adieu, Cheerio, Coomb, Dean, Dedham, Dene, Ebbw, Enna, Glen, Ta-ta, Tempé, Valley

Valedictory Apopemptic, Farewell

Valentine Card, Sweetheart

Valerian All-heal, Cetywall, Setuale, Setwale, Setwall

Valet Aid, Andrew, Jeames, Jeeves, Man, Passepartout, Servant, Skip-kennel

Valetudinarian Hypochondriac, Invalid

Valiant Brave, Doughty, Resolute, Stalwart, Wight

Valid(ate) Confirm, Establish, Just, Legal, Sound

Valise Bag, Case, Dorlach, Satchel

Valkyrie Brynhild

Valley Ajalon, Aosta, Baca, Barossa, Bekaa, Bolson, Clough, Comb(e), Coomb, Cwm, Dale, Dargle, Dean, Defile, Dell, Den, Dene, Dingle, Dip, Gehenna, Ghyll, Glen, Graben, Great Glen, Great Rift, Hanging, Haugh, Heuch, Hollow, Hope, Humiliation, Hutt, Ladin, Lagan, Lallan, Nemean, Olympia, Ravine, Rhondda, Ria, Rift, San Fernando, Silicon, Slack, Slade, Strath(spey), Tempe, Tophet, Trossachs, Umbria, Valdarno, Vale, Vallambrosa, Water

Valour Bravery, Courage, Heroism, Merit, Prowess

Valuable, Valuation, Value Appraise, Appreciate, Apprize, Assess(ment), Asset, Bargain, Calibrate, Checksum, Cherish, Cop, Cost, CIF, Equity, Esteem, Estimate, Face, Intrinsic, Limit, Market, Modulus, Nominal, Nuisance, Omnium, Ph, Place, Precious, Price, Prize, Prys, Quartile, Rarity, Rate, Rating, Regard, Respect, Salt, Sentimental, Set, Steem, Stent, Store, Surrender, Taonga, Treasure, Valuta, ➤ WORTH

Valueless Bum, Fig, Mare's nest, Orra, Useless, Worthless

Valve Air, Ball, Bicuspid, Bleed, Butterfly, Check, Clack, Cock, Dynatron, Flip-flop, Gate, Magnetron, Mitral, Non-return, Pentode, Petcock, Piston, Poppet, Puppet, Resnatron, Safety, Seacock, Semilunar, Shut-off, Sleeve, Sluice, Stopcock, Tap, Tetrode, Thermionic, Throttle, Thyratron, Triode, Ventil, Vibroton

Vamoose Abscond, Decamp, Scat, Scram

Vamp Adlib, Charm, Rehash, Seduce, Siren, Strum, Twiddle

Vampire Bat, Dracula, False, Ghoul, Lamia, Lilith, Pontianak

Van(guard) Advance, Box-car, Brake, Camper, Cart, Dormobile®, Forefront, Foremost, Front, Head, Kombi®, Lead, Leader(s), Lorry, Loudspeaker, Panel, Pantechnicon, Removal, Spearhead, Truck, Wagon, Ute

Vanadium V

Vandal(ise), Vandalism Desecrate, Hooligan, Hun, Loot, Pillage, Ravage, Rough, Sab(oteur), Sack, Saracen, Skinhead, Slash, Trash

Vandyke Beard, Painter

Vane Fan, Web, Wing

Vanessa Butterfly

Vanish(ed) Cease, Disappear, Disperse, Dissolve, Evanesce(nt), Evaporate, Extinct, Faint(ed), Mizzle, Slope, Unbe

Vanity Amour-propre, Arrogance, Ego, Esteem, Futility, Pomp, Pretension, Pride, Self-esteem

Vanquish Beat, Conquer, Floor, Master, Overcome

Vantage (point) Ascendancy, Coign(e), Height

Vaporise, Vapour Boil, Cloud, Fog, Fume, Halitus, Iodine, Miasma, Mist, Reek, Roke, ➤ STEAM, Steme, Water

Variable Amphoteric, Cepheid, Diverse, Fickle, Fluctuating, Inconstant, Omniform, Parametric, Protean, Twistor, Versatile

▶ **Variance, Variant, Variation** see VARY

Varicose Haemorrhoids

▶ **Varied, Variety** see VARY

▷ **Varied** may indicate an anagram

Variegate(d) Dappled, Flecked, Fretted, Motley, Mottle, Pied, Rainbow, Skewbald, Tissue

▷ **Variety of** may indicate an anagram

Various Divers(e), Manifold, Multifarious, Separate, Several, Sundry

Various years Vy

Varlet Cad, Knave

Varnish(ing) Arar, Bee-glue, Copal, Cowdie-gum, Dam(m)ar, Desert, Dope, Dragon's-blood, Glair, Japan, Lacquer, Lentisk, Nail, Nibs, Resin, Shellac, Spirit, Tung-oil, Tung-tree, Vernis martin, Vernissage

Vary(ing), Variable, Variance, Variant, Variation, Varied, Variety Ablaut, Aelotropy, Alter, Assortment, Breed, Brew, Change, Chequered, Colour, Contrapuntal, Counterpoint, Daedal(e), Dedal, Discrepancy, Diversity, Enigma, Farraginous, Form, Iid, Inconsistent, Isochor, Isopleth, Line, Medley, Mix, Morph, Morphosis, Multifarious, Multiplicity, Mutable, Nuance, Olio, Orthogenesis, Partita, Remedy, Smorgasbord, Sort, Species, Spice, Sport, Stirps, Strain, Timeserver, Tolerance, Var, Versiform, Version, Vl, Wane, Wax, X, Y, Z

Vase Bronteum, Canopus, Diota, Hydria, Jardiniere, Kalpis, Lecythus, Lekythos, Murr(h)a, Portland, Pot, Potiche, Stamnos, Urn, Vessel

Vassal Client, Feoffee, Lackey, Liege, Man, Manred, Servant, Vavaso(u)r

Vast(ness) Big, Cosmic, Enormous, Epic, Extensive, Huge(ous), Immense, Mighty, Ocean, Prodigious

Vat Back, Barrel, Blunger, Chessel, Copper, Cowl, Cuvee, Fat, Girnel, Keir, Kier, Tank, Tub, Tun

Vatican Rome, V

Vaudeville Zarzuela

Vaughan Silurist

Vault(ed), Vaulting Arch, Barrel, Cavern, Cellar, Chamber, Clear, Cross, Crypt, Cul-de-four, Cupola, Dome, Dungeon, Fan, Firmament, Fornicate, Groin, Hypogeum, Jump, Kiva, Leap(frog), Lierne, Palm, Pend, Pendentive, Pole, Rib, Safe, Sepulchre, Severy, Shade, Souterrain, Tomb, Wagon, Weem

▷ **Vault** may indicate an anagram

Vaunt Boast, Brag, Crow

Veal Escalope, Fricandeau, Galantine, Scallop, Schnitzel

Vector, Vector operator Dyad, Nabla, Phasor

Veer Bag, Boxhaul, Broach, Deviate, Gybe, Swerve, Tack, Turn, Wear, Yaw

Vegetable(s) Alexanders, Allium, Artichoke, Asparagus, Aubergine, Beans, Beet(root), Brassica, Broccoli, Cabbage, Calabrese, Calaloo, Calalu, Cardoon, Carrot, Castock, Cauliflower, Celeriac, Celery, Chard, Choko, Chufa, Cocoyam, Colcannon, Cole, Collard, Coulis, Courgette, Crout, Custock, Daikon, Endive, Escarole, Eschalot, Fennel, Flora, Greens, Guar, Hastings, Inert, Ingan, Jicama, Kale, Kohlrabi, Kumara, Kumera, Lablab, Leek, Legume(n), Lettuce, Macedoine, Mangel(-wurzel), Mangetout, Mangold, Marrow(-squash), Mirepoix, Mooli, Navew, Neep, Oca, Okra, Okro, Olitory, Onion, Orach(e), Parsnip, Pea(se), Plant, Potato, Pottage,

Pratie, Primavera, Pulse, Pumpkin, Quinoa, Radicchio, Radish, Rapini, Ratatouille, Rocambole, Root, Rutabaga, Sabji, Salad, Salsify, Samphire, Sauce, Sauerkraut, Savoy, Scorzonera, Shallot, Sium, Skirret, Spinach(-beet), Spinage, Sprouts, Spud, Squash, Succotash, Swede, Sweet potato, Taro, Tomato, Tonka-bean, Triffid, Turnip, Udo, Yam, Zucchini

Vegetable extract Solanine

Vegetarian Herbivore, Maigre, Meatless, Parev(e), Parve, Pythagorean, Vegan, Veggie

Vegetate, Vegetator, Vegetation Alga, Cover, Flora, Greenery, Herb, Maquis, Quadrat, Scrub, Stagnate, Sudd, Transect

Vehemence, Vehement(ly) Amain, Ardent, Fervid, Frenzy, Heat, Hot, Intense, Violent

Vehicle Ambulance, Amtrack, Artic, Articulated, ATV, Autocycle, Autorickshaw, Brancard, Brake, Buggy, Bus, Cab, Car, Caravan, Carry-all, Cart, Channel, Chariot, Conveyance, Crate, Curricle, Cycle, Dennet, Dog-cart, Dormobile®, Dray, Dune buggy, Estate car, Fiacre, Float, Gharri, Gharry, Gladstone, Go-cart, Go-kart, Growler, Half-track, Hansom, Hatchback, Hearse, Hovercraft, Jeep®, Jeepney, Jingle, Jinker, Jitney, Juggernaut, Kago, Kart, Koneka, Land Rover, Landau, Launch, LEM, Limber, Litter, Lorry, Machine, Means, Medium, Minibus, Minicab, Minivan, Norimon, Pedicab, Penny-farthing, People carrier, Perambulator, Phaeton, Pick-up, Quad, Ricksha(w), Runabout, Samlor, Sand-yacht, Scow, Shay, Sidecar, Skibob, Skidoo®, Sled(ge), Sleigh, Sno-Cat®, Snowmobile, Snowplough, Soyuz, Spider, Stanhope, Station wagon, Steam-car, Sulky, Surrey, Tarantas(s), Taxi, Tempera, Three-wheeler, Tipcart, Tip-up, Tonga, Tracked, Tractor, Trailer, Tram, Transporter, Trap, Tricar, Tricycle, Trishaw, Troika, Trolley, Truck, Tuk tuk, Tumble-car(t), Tumbril, Turbo, Two-wheeler, Unicycle, Ute, Utility, Vahana, Velocipede, Vespa, Volante, Wagon, Wheelbarrow

Veil Burk(h)a, Calyptra, Chad(d)ar, Chador, Chuddah, Chuddar, Cover, Curtain, Envelop, Hejab, Hijab, Humeral, Kalyptra, Kiss-me, Lambrequin, Mantilla, Mist, Obscure, Purdah, Scene, Veale, Volet, Weeper, Wimple, Yashmak

Vein Artery, Basilic, Coronary, Costa, Epithermal, Fahlband, Gate, Innominate, Jugular, Ledge, Lode, Mainline, Media, Midrib, Mood, Nervure, Percurrent, Portal, Postcava, Precava, Pulmonary, Rake, Rib, Saphena, Sectorial, Stockwork, Stringer, Style, Varicose, Varix, Vena, Venule

Vellum Cutch, Kutch, Parchment

Velocity Muzzle, Radial, Rate, Speed, Terminal, V

Velvet Bagheera, Chenille, National, Panné, Pile, Three-pile, Velour, Velure

Venal Corruptible, Mercenary, Sale

Vend(or) Hawk, Pedlar, Rep, Sell, Sutler

Vendetta Feud

Veneer Facade, Gloss, Varnish

Venerable Aged, August, Bede, Guru, Hoary, Sacred, Sage

Venerate, Veneration Adore, Awe, Douleia, Dulia, Hallow, Homage, Idolise, Latria, Revere, Worship

Venereal NSU, VD

Venery Chase

Venetian Blind, Doge, Gobbo, Polo

Vengeance, Vengeful Erinyes, Reprisal, Ultion, Vindictive, Wannion, Wrack, Wreak

Venom(ous) Gall, Gila, Jamestown-weed, Jim(p)son-weed, Poison, Rancour, Spite, Toxic, Virus

Vent Aperture, Belch, Chimney, Emit, Express, Fumarole, Issue, Ostiole, Outlet, Solfatara, Spiracle, Undercast, Wreak

Venter Uterus

Ventilate, Ventilator Air, Air-brick, Air-hole, Discuss, Express, Louvre, Plenum, Shaft, Voice, Windsail, Windway, Winze

Venture(d) Ante, Chance, Dare, Daur, Durst, Flutter, Foray, Handsel, Hazard, Opine, Presume, Promotion, Risk, Spec, Throw

Venue Bout, Locale, Place, Tryst, Visne

Venus Cohog, Cytherean, Hesper(us), Love, Lucifer, Morning-star, Primavera, Quahog, Rokeby, Vesper

Venus fly-trap Dionaea

Veracity, Veracious Accurate, Factual, Sincere, Truth(ful)

Veranda(h) Balcony, Gallery, Lanai, Patio, Porch, Sleep-out, Stoep, Stoop, Terrace

Verb(al) Active, Auxiliary, Conative, Copula, Infinitive, Intransitive, Irregular, Passive, Phrasal, Preterite, Stative, Transitive, Vb, Word-of-mouth

Verbascum Mullein

Verbena Vervain

Verbose, Verbosity Padding, Prolix, Talkative, Wordy

Verdant Lush

Verdict Decision, Judg(e)ment, Open, Opinion, Pronouncement, Resolution, Ruling

Verdigris Aeruginous, Patina

Verge Border, Brink, ➤ EDGE, Hard shoulder, Incline, Rim

Verger Beadle, Pew-opener

Verify Affirm, Ascertain, Check, Confirm, Crosscheck, Prove, Validate

Verily Yea

Verisimilitude Artistic, Authenticity, Credibility

Verity Fact, Sooth, Truth

Vermifuge Cow(h)age, Cowitch

Vermilion Cinnabar, Minium, Red

Vermin(ous) Carrion, Catawampus, Lice, Mice, Ratty, ➤ RODENT, Scum

Vermouth French, It(alian), Martini®

Vernacular Common, Dialect, Idiom, Jargon, Lingo, Native, Patois

Veronica Hebe, Speedwell

Verruca Wart

Versatile Adaptable, All-rounder, Flexible, Handy, Protean, Resourceful

Verse(s), Versed Acatalectic, Adonic, Alcaics, Alexandrine, Amphigory, Archilochian, Asclepiad, Asynartete, Awdl, Ballad, Beatitude, Blad, Blank, Blaud, Burden, Canto, Catalectic, Cinquain, Comus, Dimiter, Dithyramb, Ditrochee, Doggerel, Duan, Elegiac, Epic, Epigram, Epode, Epos, Fabliau, Fescennine, Fit, Free, G(h)azal, Ghazel, Glyconic, Gnomic, Goliardic, Haikai, Heroic, Hexameter, Hokku, Hudibrastic(s), Huitain, Hymn, Ionic, Jingle, Kyrielle, Laisse, Leonine, Lyric, Macaronic, Madrigal, Meter, Miurus, Mock-heroic, Monometer, Neck, Nonsense, Octameter, Octastich, Octave, Ottava rima, Pantoum, Pantun, Pennill(ion), Pentameter, Pindaric, Poem, Poesy, Prosody, Pythian, Quatrain, Renga, Rhopalic, ➤ RHYME, Rhyme-royal, Riding-rhyme, Rime, Rondeau, Rondel, Rove-over, Rubai(yat), Sapphic, Saturnian, Scansion, Scazon, Senarius, Septenarius, Serpentine, Sestina, Sestine, Sijo, Sirvente, Sixaine, Song, Spasm, Stanza, Stave, Stiches, Stornello, Strain, Strophe, Tanka, Tercet, Terza rima, Terzetta, Tetrameter, Tetrastich, Tiercet, Tract, Triad, Trimeter, Tripody, Tristich, Up, V, Vers, Versicle, Vers libre

Versed sine Sagitta

Versifier Lyricist, Poetaster, Rhymer, Rhymester

Version Account, Authorised, Cover, Edition, Form, Paraphrase, Rede, Rendering, Rendition, Revision, Translation

Vertebra(e), Vertebrate Agnathan, Amniote, Amphioxus, Ascidian, Atlas, Axis, Bone, Centrum, Cervical, Chordae, Dorsal, Gnathostome, Ichthyopsida, Lamprey, Lumbar, Sauropsida, Spondyl, Tetrapod, Tunicata, Vermis

Vertex Apex, Crest, Crown, Summit, Zenith

Vertical Apeak, Apeek, Atrip, Erect, Lapse, Ordinate, Perpendicular, Plumb, Sheer, Standing, Stemmed, Stile, Upright

Vertigo Dinic, Dizziness, Fainting, Giddiness, Megrim, Nausea, Staggers, Whirling

Verve Dash, Energy, Go, Panache, Vigour

Very (good, well) A1, Ae, Assai, Awfully, Bonzer, Boshta, Boshter, Dashed, Def, Ever, Extreme(ly), Fell, Frightfully, Gey, Grouse, Heap, Hellova, Helluva, Highly, Jolly, Light, Mighty, Molto, Much, OK, Opt, Precious, Precise, Purler, Real, Self same, So, Sore, Stinking, Très, Utter, V, VG, Way

Vesicle Ampul, Bladder

Vespers Evensong, Placebo, Sicilian

Vessel Alcarraza, Aludel, Amphora, Ampulla, Aorta, Argyle, Argyll, Ark, Artery, Aspersorium, Autoclave, Barge, Bark, Bathyscaph(e), Beaker, Bicker, Bin, Blood, ➤ BOAT, Bouget, Bowl, Bucentaur, Bucket, Buss, Calabash, Calandria, Canteen, Carafe, Carboy, Cask, Casserole, Cat, Cauldron, Chalice, Chatty, Ciborium, Coaster, Cog(ue), Colander, Container, Coolamon, Copper, Corvette, Costrel, Cot(t), Cowl, Craft, Crare, Crayer, Cresset, Crewe, Crock, Crucible, Cruet, Cruiser, Cucurbit,

Cullender, Cup, Cupel, Cuvette, Cyathus, Dandy, Decanter, Deep-sinker, Destroyer, D(h)ow, Dinghy, Dish, Dixie, Dogger, Dolium, Dredger, Drifter, Elutor, Etna, Fat, Felucca, Figuline, Flagon, Flagship, Font, Frigate, Frigot, Galiot, Galleass, Galleon, Galley, Galliass, Galliot, Gallipot, Gallivat, Goblet, Goglet, Gourd, Grab, Gurglet, Humpen, Hydrofoil, Jardinière, Jerrican, Jugular, Keel, Ketch, Kettle, Lachrymatory, Laver, Longboat, Lorcha, Lota(h), Mazer, Monteith, Mortar, Mudscow, Noggin, Obo, Oiler, Olpe, Pan(cheon), Panchion, Pannikin, Patamar, Pig, Pinnace, Pitcher, Pokal, Polacca, Privateer, Quart, Receptacle, Retort, Round, Rumkin, Saic(k), Saique, Sampan, Sconce, Scoop, She, Shell, ➤ SHIP, Shippo, Sinusoid, Situla, Skin, Smack, Snow, Steamer, Stean(e), Steen, Stoop, Stoup, Tankard, Tanker, Tappit-hen, Tassie, Tazza, Terreen, Triaconter, Troopship, Trough, Tub, Tureen, Urn, Utensil, Varix, Vas(e), Vat, Vein, Vena, Venule, Vial, Wherry, Xebec, Zabra, Zulu

Vest Beset, Confer, Gilet, Modesty, Semmit, Singlet, Skivvy, Spencer, Sticharion, String, Undercoat, Waistcoat

Vestibule Anteroom, Atrium, Entry, Exedra, Foyer, Hall, Lobby, Narthex, Porch, Portico, Pronaos, Tambour

Vestige Hint, Mark, Mention, Shadow, Sign, Trace

Vestment Alb, Chasuble, Cotta, Dalmatic, Ephod, Fannel, Fanon, Garb, ➤ GARMENT, Mantelletta, Omophorion, Pallium, Parament, Ph(a)elonian, Pontificals, Raiment, Rational, Rochet, Rocquet, Sakkos, Sticharion, Stole, Surplice, Tunic(le)

Vestry Sacristy

Vet(ting), Veterinary, Vets Check, Doc(tor), Examine, Inspect, OK, Screen, Veteran, Zoiatria, Zootherapy

Vetch Ers, Fitch, Locoweed, Tare, Tine

Veteran BL, Expert, GAR, Master, Old sweat, Old 'un, Oldster, Old-timer, Retread, Seasoned, Soldier, Stager, Stalwart, Stalworth, Vet, War-horse

▷ **Veteran** may indicate 'obsolete'

Veto Ban, Debar, Negative, Pocket, Reject, Taboo, Tabu

Vex(ed) Anger, Annoy, Bother, Chagrin, Debate, Fret, Gall, Grieve, Harass, Irritate, Mortify, Pester, Rankle, Rile, Sore, Spite, Tease, Torment, Trouble

Vexation(s) Barrator, Chagrin, Drat, Grief, Nuisance, Pique, Spite, Trouble

Vexillum Web

Via By, Per, Through

Viable Economic, Going, Healthy, Possible

Viand Cate

Vibrant Energetic, Plangent, Resonant

Vibrate, Vibration(s) Atmosphere, Diadrom, Dinnle, Dirl, Flutter, Fremitus, Hotter, Jar, Judder, Oscillate, Pulse, Quake, Resonance, Seiche, Shimmy, Shudder, Thrill, Throb, Tingle, Tremble, Tremor, Trill, Twinkle, Wag, Whir(r)

Viburnum Opulus

Vicar Bray, Elton, Incumbent, Pastoral, Plenarty, Primrose, Rector, Rev(erend), Trimmer

Vice Clamp, Crime, Deputy, Eale, Evil, Greed, Iniquity, Instead, Jaws, Regent, Second (in command), ➤ SIN

Vice-president Croupier, Veep

Viceroy Khedive, Nawab, Provost, Satrap, Willingdon

Vichy water Eau

Vicinity Area, Environs, Hereabouts, Locality, Neighbourhood, Region

Vicious Flagitious, Hotbed

Victim Abel, Butt, Casualty, Dupe, Frame, Host, Lay-down, Mark, Martyr, Nebbich, Neb(b)ish, Pathic, Patsy, Prey, Quarry, Sacrifice, Scapegoat

Victor(y) Banzai, Beater, Cadmean, Captor, Champ(ion), Conqueror, Conquest, Epinicion, Epinikion, Flagship, Fool's mate, Gree, Gris, Hugo, Jai, Kobe, Landslide, Lepanto, Ludorum, Mature, Nike, Palm, Philippi, Pyrrhic, Runaway, Scalp, Signal, Triumph, VE (day), Vee, Vic, Walkover, Win(ner)

Victoria(n) Aussie, Plum, Prig, Station

Victualler Caterer, Grocer, Purveyor, Supplier

Video Minitel, Pixelation, Promo, Scratch, Vera

Vie Compete, Contend, Emulate, Strive

Vienna Wien

Vietnamese Cham

View(er) Aim, Angle, Aspect, Belief, Bird's eye, Cineaste, Consensus, Consider, Cosmorama, Dekko, Dogma, Doxy, Endoscope, Eye, Facet, Gander, Glimpse, Grandstand, Idea, Introspect, Kaleidoscope, Landscape, Notion, Opinion, Optic®, Outlook, Pan, Panorama, Point, Private, Profile, ➤ PROSPECT, Scan, Scape, Scene(ry), See, Sight, Slant, Specular, Standpoint, Stereoscope, Synop(sis), Tenet, Thanatopsis, Theory, Veduta, Vista, Visto, Watch, Witness, Worm's eye

Viewpoint Attitude, Belvedere, Grandstand, Perspective, Sight

Vigil, Vigilant(e) Awake, Aware, Deathwatch, Eve, Lyke-wake, Pernoctate, Wake, Wake-rife, Wary, Watch, Whitecap

Vignette Print, Profile, Sketch

Vigorous(ly), Vigour Athletic, Billy-o, Birr, Blooming, Con brio, Drastic, Elan, Emphatic, Energetic, Flame, Forceful, Furioso, Go, Green, Heart(y), Heterosis, Lush, Lustihood, Lusty, P, Pep, Pith, Potency, Punchy, Racy, Rank, Robust, Round, Rude, Spirit, Sprack, Sprag, Sthenic, Stingo, Strength, Strong, Thews, Tireless, Tone, Trenchant, Vegete, Vim, Vitality, Vivid, Zip

▷ **Vigorously** may indicate an anagram

Viking Dane, Norseman, Rollo

Vile Base, Corrupt, Depraved, Dregs, Durance, Earthly, Mean, Offensive, Scurvy, Vicious

Vilify Smear

Villa Bastide, Chalet, Dacha, House

Village Aldea, Auburn, Burg, Clachan, Dorp, Endship, Global, Gram, Greenwich, Hamlet, Kainga, Kampong, Kraal, Mir, Pueblo, Rancheria, Rancherie, Shtetl, Thorp(e), Vill, Wick

Villain(y) Baddy, Bluebeard, Bravo, Crim(inal), Crime, Dastard, Dog, Heavy, Iago, Knave, Macaire, Miscreant, Mohock, Nefarious, Ogre, Rogue, Scelerat, Scoundrel, Tearaway, Traitor

Villein Bordar, Churl, Serf

Vim Go, Vigour, Vitality, Zing

Vincent Van Gogh

Vindicate, Vindication Absolve, Acquit, Apologia, Avenge, Clear, Compurgation, Darraign(e), Darrain(e), Darrayn, Defend, Deraign, Justify

Vindictive Hostile, Malevolent, Repay(ing), Spiteful

Vine(yard) Ampelopsis, Ayahuasco, Balloon, Bine, Chateau, Clos, Colocynth, Cru, Cubeb, Cypress, Dodder, Domaine, Grapery, Hop, Kangaroo, Kudzu, Lawyer, Matrimony, Muskmelon, Naboth's, Sarsaparilla, Stephanotis, Supplejack, Turpeth, Vitis, Yam

Vinegar Acetic, Alegar, Balsam, Eisel(l), Esile, Oxymel, Tarragon, Wine

Vintage Classic, Crack, Cru, Old, Quality

Viola, Violet African, Alto, Amethyst, Archil, Dame's, Dog, Dog's tooth, Gamba, Gentian, Gridelin, Ianthine, Indole, Ionone, Kiss-me, Mauve, Orchil, Pansy, Parma, Prater, Saintpaulia, Shrinking, Tenor

Violate, Violating, Violation Abuse, Breach, Contravene, Defile, Fract, Infraction, ➤ INFRINGE, March-treason, Outrage, Peccant, Rape, Ravish, Stuprate, Transgress, Trespass

Violence, Violent(ly) Amain, Attentat, Berserk, Brutal, Drastic, Extreme, Fierce, Flagrant, Force, Frenzied, Furious, Heady, Het, High, Hot, Mighty, Onset, Rage, Rampage, Rampant, Rough, Rude, Severe, Slap, Stormy, Ta(r)tar, Tearaway, Thuggery, Tinderbox, Vehement, Vie

➤ **Violet** see VIOLA

Violin(ist), Violin-maker, Violin-shaped Alto, Amati, Cremona, Fiddle, Griddle, Gu(e), Guarneri(us), Guarnieri, Kit, Kubelik, Leader, Luthier, Nero, Paganini, Pandurate, Rebeck, Rote, Stradivarius

VIP Bashaw, Bigshot, Bigwig, Brass, Cheese, Cob, Effendi, Envoy, Imago, Magnate, Magnifico, Mugwump, Nabob, Nib, Nob, Pot, Snob, Someone, Swell, Tuft, Tycoon, Worthy

Viper Asp, Gaboon, Pit, Rattlesnake, Russell's, Saw-scaled, ➤ SNAKE, Traitor, Villain

Virago Amazon, Battle-axe, Beldam(e), Harpy, Shrew

Virgil Maro

Virgin(al), Virginity Celibate, Chaste, Cherry, Intact, Maiden, Maidenhead, Maidenhood, May, New, Pietà, Pucel(l)age, Pucelle, Pure, Queen, Snood, Tarpeia, Vestal

Virginia(n) Creeper, Tuckahoe, Va, Wade

Virile, Virility Energetic, Machismo, Macho, Manly, Red-blooded

Virtu Curio

Virtue, Virtuous Angelic, Assay-piece, Attribute, Cardinal, Caritas, Charity, Chastity, Continent, Dharma, Efficacy, Ethical, Excellent, Faith, Fortitude, Good, Grace, Hope, Justice, Moral(ity), Patience, Plaster-saint, Prudence, Qua, Say-piece, Temperance, Upright, Worth

Virtuosity, Virtuoso Artist, Excellence, Executant, Maestro, Savant

Virulent Acrimonious, Deadly, Hostile, Malign, Noxious, Toxic, Vitriolic, Waspish

Virus Antigen, Arbovirus, Bacteriophaze, Capsid, Contagium, Coxsackie, EB, Ebola, Echo, Epstein-Barr, Germ, Granulosis, Hantavirus, Herpes, HIV negative, HIV positive, Lassa, Latent, Lentivirus, Michelangelo, Parvo(virus), Pathogen, Picornavirus, Polyoma, Prophage, Reovirus, Retrovirus, Rhabdovirus, Rhinovirus, Ross River, Rotavirus, Shingles, Slow, Street, SV40, Varicella, Zoster

Visa Transit

Viscera Bowels, Entrails, Giblets, Guts, Harigal(d)s, Haslet, Innards, Omentum, Umbles, Vitals

Viscount Vis

Viscous (liquid), Viscosity Glaireous, Gluey, Gummy, Slab, Sticky, Stoke, Tacky, Tar, Thick

Visible Clear, Conspicuous, Evident, Explicit, Obvious

Visigoth Asaric

Vision(ary) Aery, Aisling, Apparition, Bourignian, Double, Dream(er), Emmetropia,.Fancy, Idealist, Image, Kef, Moonshine, Mouse-sight, Mystic, Ocular, Phantasm(a), Phantom, Pholism, Photopia, Romantic, Seeing, Seer, Sight, Stereo, Tunnel, Twenty-twenty

Visit(or) Affliction, Alien, Caller, ET, Event, First-foot, Frequent, Gam, Guest, Habitue, Haunt, Kursaal, See, Sightseer, Stranger, Take

Visor, Vizor Eyeshade, Mesail, Mezail, Umbrel, Umbr(i)ere, Umbril, Vent(ayle)

Vista Enfilade, Outlook, Scene, View

Visual(ise) Envisage, Ocular, Optical, Visible

Vital(ity) Central, Critical, Crucial, Energy, Esprit, Essential, Existent, Foison, Gusto, Indispensable, Key, Kick, Life-blood, Linchpin, Lung, Mites, Momentous, Oomph, Organ, Pizzazz, Salvation, Sap, Viable, Vigour, Zing, Zoetic

Vitals Numbles, Umbles, Viscera

Vitamin(s) A, Aneurin, Axerophthol, B, Bioflavonoid, Biotin, C, Calciferol, Calcitriol, Citrin, Cobalamin, D, E, Ergocalciferol, H, Inositol, K, Linoleic, Menadione, Menaquinone, Niacin, P, Pan(to)thenol, Phylloquinone, Phytonadione, Pyridoxine, Retinol, Riboflavin, Ribose, Thiamin(e), Tocopherol, Torulin, Tretinoin

Vitiate(d) Flaw(ed)

Vitreous Glassy, Hyaline

Vitriol(ic) Acid, Acrimonious, Biting, Caustic, Mordant

Vituperate Abuse, Berate, Castigate, Censure, Defame, Inveigh, Lash, Rail, Scold

Viva Oral

Vivacity, Vivacious Animation, Brio, Esprit, Exuberant, Spirit, Verve

Vivid Bright, Brilliant, Dramatic, Eidectic, Fresh, Graphic, Keen, Live, Pictorial, Picturesque, Sharp, Violent

Vixen Catamaran, Harridan, Shrew, Virago

Viz Sc, Videlicet

Vizier Pheazar, Wazir

▶ **Vizor** see VISOR

Vocabulary Glottochronology, Idiolect, Idioticon, Jargon, (Kata)kana, Lexicon, Lexis, Meta-language, Nomenclator, Wordbook

Vocal(ist) Articulate, Eloquent, Minstrel, Oral, Singer

Vocation Call, Métier, Mission, Priesthood, Profession, Shop

Vociferous(ly) Clamant, Loud, Ore rotundo, Strident

Vogue Chic, Day, ▶ FASHION, Mode, Rage, Style, Ton

Vogul Ugrian, Ugric

Voice(d) Active, Air, Alto, Ancestral, Contralto, Countertenor, Edh, Emit, Eth, Express, Falsetto, Glottis, Harp, Mouth, Opinion, Passive, Phonic, Pipe, Presa, Quill, Say, Sonant, Soprano, Speak, Spinto, Sprechstimme, Steven, Syrinx, Tais(c)h, Tenor, Throat, Tone, ▶ TONGUE, Treble, Utter

Voiceless Aphonia, Aphony, Dumb, Edh, Eth, Mute, Silent, Tacit

Void Abyss, Annul, Belch, Defeasance, Defecate, Diriment, Empty, Evacuate, Gap, Hollow, Inane, Invalid, Irritate, Lapse, Nullify, Quash, Space, Vacuum

Volatile Explosive, Latin, Live(ly), Mercurial, Temperamental, Terpene

Volcanic, Volcano Aa, Agglomerate, Amygdale, Andesite, Aniakchak, Antisana, Aragats, Ararat, Askja, Aso(san), Cameroon, Chimborazo, Citlaltépetl, Cone, Conic, Corcovado, Cotopaxi, Demavend, Egmont, El Misti, Erebus, Etna, Fuji, Fumarole, Haleakala, Hekla, Hornito, Ice, Idocrase, Igneous, Ignimbrite, Iliamna, Ischia, Iwo Jima, Katmai, Kauai, Kazbek, Kilimanjaro, Krakatoa, Lassen Peak, Maui, Mauna Kea, Mauna Loa, Mayon, Misti, Mofette, Montserrat, Mount Katmai, Mount St Helens, Mud, National Park, Nyamuragira, Nyiragongo, Obsidian, Olympus Mons, Paricutin, Pele, Pelée, Plinian, Popocatepetl, Pozz(u)olana, Pumice, Puy, Puzzolana, Ruapehu, St Helens, Salse, Soffioni, Solfatara, Soufrière Hills, Stromboli, Tambora, Taraniki, Tangariro, Thira, Tolima, Trass, Tuff, Vesuvius, Warrumbungle Range

Vole Arvicola, Musquash, Ondatra

Volition Velleity, Will

Volley Barrage, Boom, Broadside, Platoon, Salvo, Tirade, Tire

Volt(age) BeV, Bias, HT

Voltaire Arouet

Volte face U-turn

Voluble Fluent, Glib

Volume Band, Barrel, Book, Bushel, Capacity, CC, Code(x), Content, Cubage, Gallon, Hin, Loudness, Mass, Ml, Omnibus, Peck, Pint, Quart, Quart(o), Roll, Roul(e), Size, Space, Stere, Tome, Vol

Voluntary, Volunteer Enlist, Fencible, Free, Honorary, Offer, Postlude, Reformado, Spontaneous, Tender, Tennessee, Terrier, TN, Ultroneous, Yeoman

Voluptuary, Voluptuous Carnal, Hedonist, Luscious, Sensuist, Sensuous, Sybarite

Volute Helix, Roll

Vomit(ing) Anacatharsis, Barf, Boak, Boke, Cascade, Cat, Chunder, Disgorge, Egist, Egurgitate, Emesis, Haematemesis, Honk, Keck, Parbreak, Posset, Puke, Ralph, Retch, Rolf, Spew, Upchuck

Voodoo Charm, Jettatura, Kurdaitcha, Obeah, Sorcery, Zombi(e)

Voracious, Voracity Bulimia, Edacity, Gluttony, Greed, Ravenous, Serrasalmo

Vortex Charybdis, Eddy, Gyre, Whirlpool

Votary Adherent, Cenobite, Devotee, Disciple, Fan, Nun, Swinger, Zealot

Vote(r), Votes, Voting Aye, Ballot, Block, Card, Casting, Choose, Colonist, Coopt, Cross, Division, Donkey, Fag(g)ot, Floating, Franchise, Informal, Nay, No, Opt, People, Placet, Plebiscite, Plump, Poll, Postal, Pot-wabbler, Pot-waller, Pot-walloner, Pot-walloper, Pot-wobbler, PR, Referendum, Return, Scrutiny, Side, Straw(-poll), Suffrage, Swinging, Tactical, Ten-pounder, Theta, Ticket, Transferable, Voice, X, Yea, Yes

Vote-catcher Pork

Vouch(er), Vouchsafe Accredit, Assure, Attest, Chit, Coupon, Endorse, Gift, Guarantee, Luncheon, Meal-ticket, Receipt, Ticket, Token, Warrant

Voussoir Quoin, Wedge

Vow Behight, Behot(e), Earnest, Ex voto, Hecht, Hest, Nuncupate, ➤ OATH, Pledge, Plight, Promise, Swear, Troth, Vum

Vowel(s) Ablaut, Anaptyxis, Aphesis, Breve, Cardinal, Diphthong, Indeterminate, Monophthong, S(c)hwa, Seg(h)ol, Svarabhakti, Triphthong

Voyage(r) Anson, Course, Cruise, Launch, Passage, Peregrinate, Sinbad, Travel

Voyeur Scopophiliac

VTOL Convertiplane

Vulcan(ite) Blacksmith, Ebonite, Fire, Mulciber, Wayland

Vulgar(ian) Banausic, Barbaric, Blatant, Blue, Brassy, Buffoon, Canaille, Cheap, Cit, Coarse, Common, Crude, Demotic, Flash, Forward, Gaudy, General, Gent, Heel, Hussy, Ignorant, Indecent, Laddish, Lewd, Low(-life), Naff, Obscene, Ostentatious, Pandemian, Plebeian, Popular, Proletarian, Raffish, Riff-raff, Scaff, Tacky, Tawdry, Threepenny, Tiger, Tink, Upstart, Vulg

Vulnerable Exposed, Open, Susceptible, Unguarded

Vulture Aasvogel, Bird, Buzzard, California (condor), Condor, Culture, Falcon, Gallinazo, Gier, Griffon, Gripe, Grype, Lammergeier, Lammergeyer, Ossifrage, Predator, Turkey, Urubu, Zopilote

W w

W Watt, West, Whisky, Women

Wad(ding) Batting, Lump, Pad, Pledget, Roll, Swab, Wodge

Waddle Toddle, Waggle

Waddy Club, Cowboy, Stick

Wade(r), Wading Antigropelo(e)s, Curlew, Dikkop, Egret, Flamingo, Gallae, Grallatorial, Greenshank, Heron, Ibis, Jacksnipe, Limpkin, Paddle, Phalarope, Plodge, Sarus, Seriema, Shoebill, Splodge, Stilt(bird), Terek, Virginia

Waesucks Ewhow, O(c)hone

Wafer Biscuit, Cracker, Crisp, Gaufer, Gaufre, Gofer, Gopher, Host, Papad, Seal

Waff Flap, Flutter, Wave

Waffle Adlib, Blather, Equivocate, Gas, Gaufer, Gaufre, Gofer, Gopher, Hedge, Poppycock, Prate, Rabbit

Waft(ing) Airborne, Aura, Blow, Drift, Float

Wag(gish), Waggle Arch, Card, Comedian, Joker, Lick, Nod, Rogue, Shake, Sway, Wit(snapper), Wobble

Wage(s) Ante, Fee, Hire, Living, Meed, Pay, Practise, Prosecute, Salary, Screw

Wage-earner Breadwinner, Employee, Proletariat(e)

Wager Back, ➤ BET, Gamble, Lay, Pascal's, Stake, Wed

Wagon(er) Ar(a)ba, Aroba, Bootes, Boxcar, Brake, Buckboard, Buggy, Caisson, Carriage, Cart, Cattle truck, Chuck, Cocopan, Conestoga, Corf, Covered, Dray, Flatcar, Fourgon, Gambo, Hopper, Hutch, Low-loader, Mammy, Paddy, Palabra, Patrol, Plaustral, Rave, Reefer, Rubberneck, Shandry, Station, Tartana, Telega, Tender, Trap, Trekker, Truck, Van, Wain

Waif Arab, Foundling, Jetsam, Stray, Weft

Wail(er) Banshee, Bawl, Blubber, Howl, Keen, Lament, Moan, Skirl, Threnody, Threnos, Ululate, Vagitus, Wah-wah, Yammer

Wain Cart, Dray, Wagon

Waist(band) Belt, Cummerbund, Girdlestead, Hour-glass, Middle, Midship, Obi, Sash, Shash, Wasp, Zoster

Waistcoat Gilet, Jerkin, Lorica, MB, Sayon, Vest, Weskit

Wait(er) Abid(e), Ambush, Bide, Butler, Buttle, Commis, Delay, Expect, Flunkey, Frist, Garçon, Hesitate, Hover, Interval, Khidmutgar, Linger, Lurch, Maitre d', Maitre d'hôtel, Omnibus, Pannier, Pause, Remain, Serve(r), Sommelier, Stay, Steward, Suspense, Taihoa, Tarry, Tend(ance), Tray, Won

Waitress Hebe, Miss, Mousme(e), Nippy, Server

Waive Abandon, Defer, Overlook, Postpone, Relinquish, Renounce

Wake(n) Abrade, Abraid, Abray, Aftermath, Alert, Animate, Arouse, Astern, Deathwatch, Excite, Hereward, Keen, Prod, Rear, ➤ ROUSE, Train, Wash

Waldo Emerson

Wale(r) Prop, Ridge, Weal

Wales Cambria, Cymru, Dyfed, Principality

Walk(er), Walking, Walkabout, Walkway Alameda, Alley, Alure, Amble, Arcade, Berceau, Birdcage, Cloister, Clump, Constitutional, Dander, Dauner, Esplanade, EVA, Expatiate, Frescade, Gait, Gallery, Ghost, Go, Gradient, Gressorial, Heel and toe, Hike, Hump, Lambeth, Leg, Lumber, Mainstreeting, Mall, Mince, Mosey, Pace, Pad, Pasear, Paseo, Passage, Path, Ped, Perambulate, Pergola, Pipe-opener, Prance, Prom(enade), Rack, Ramble, Rampart, Sashay, Shamble, Sidle, Space, Stalk, Step, Striddle, Stroll, Strut, Stump, Terrace, Toddle, Tramp, Trash, Travolator, Tread, Trog, Trudge, Turn, Wend, Widow's, Xyst

Walk-over Doddle, Pie, Scratch

Wall Antonine, Bail, Bailey, Barrier, Berlin, Berm, Cavity, Chinese, Countermure, Curtain, Dado, Dam, Dike, Dry-stone, Enceinte, Epispore, Exine, Fail-dike, Fronton, Gable, Great, Hadrian's, Hanging, Head, Immure, Intine, Mahjongg, Mani, Merlon, Myocardium, Parapet, Parie(te)s, Parietal, Parpane, Parpen(d), Parpent, Parpoint, Partition, Party, Pericarp, Perpend, Perpent, Pleuron, Qibla, Retaining, Revet(ment), Roman, Roughcast, Septum, Severus, Side, Somatopleure, Spandrel, Spandril, Street, Tariff, Trumeau, Vallum, Wa', Wailing, Zooecia

Wallaby Brusher, Dama, Kangaroo, Pademelon, Pad(d)ymelon, Quokka, Tammar

Wallaroo Euro

Wall-covering Anaglypta®, Arras, Burlap, Lincrusta, Paper, Tapestry, Tapet

Waller Fats, Mason

Wallet Billfold, Case, Notecase, Pochette, Purse, Scrip

Wallflower Crucifer, Dowd(y), Pariah

Wall-game Eton, Mahjongg

Wallop Bash, Baste, Batter, Beat, Biff, Clout, Cob, ➤ HIT, Lam, Lounder, Polt, Pound, Slog, Strap, Swinge, Tan, Tat, Trounce

Wallow(ing) Bask, Flounder, Luxuriate, Revel, Roll, Splash, Swelter, Tolter, Volutation, Welter

Wall-painting Fresco, Graffiti, Grisaille

Wall-plate Tassel, Torsel

Wall-support Beam, Foundation, Pier, Rear-arch, Rere-arch

Walnut Black, Hickory, Juglans

Walrus Morse, Moustache, Pinniped, Rosmarine, Sea-horse, Tash

Walter Bruno, Mitty, Pater, Scott

Waltz Anniversary, Boston, Dance, Hesitation, Rotate, Valse

Wampum Peag, Shell-money

Wan Pale, Pallid, Pasty, Sanguine, Sorry

Wanchancy Unlucky

Wand Baton, Caduceus, Rod, Runic, Stick, Thyrse, Thyrsus, Vara, Vare

Wander(er), Wandering Aberrance, Bedouin, Berber, Bum, Caird, Delirious, Desultory, Deviate, Digress, Divagate, Drift, Errant, Estray, Evagation, Excursive, Expatiate, Gad(about), Grope, Hobo, Jew, Landloper, Maunder, Meander, Meandrian, Mill, Moon, Nomad(e), Odysseus, Pedder, Peregrine, Peripatetic, Rache, Ramble, Range, Ratch, Roamer, Romany, Room, Rove, Solivagant, Stooge, Straggle, Stravaig, Stray, Streel, Stroam, Stroll, Swan, Ta(i)ver, Tramp, Troll, Tuareg, Vagabond, Vagrant, Vague, Waif, Wend, Wheel, Wilder, Wolves

▷ **Wandering** may indicate an anagram

Wane Decline, Decrease, Diminish, Ebb

Wangle Arrange, Finagle, Trick

Want(ing), Wants Absence, Conative, Covet, Crave, Dearth, Defect, Deficient, Derth, Desiderata, ➤ DESIRE, Destituetion, Envy, Hardship, Indigent, Itch, Lack, Long, Mental, Need, Penury, Require, Scarceness, Scarcity, Shortfall, Shy, Void, Wish, Yen

Wanton(ness) Bona-roba, Cadgy, Chamber, Cocotte, Deliberate, Demirep, Filly, Flirt-gill, Gammerstang, Giglet, Giglot, Gillflirt, Hussy, Jay, Jezebel, Jillflirt, Lewd, Licentious, Loose, Nice, Protervity, Roué, Slut, Smicker, Sportive, Sybarite, Toyish, Twigger, Unchaste, Wayward

Wap Blow, Knock, Strike

War(fare) Ares, Armageddon, Arms, Attrition, Baron's, Bate, Battle, Biological, Bishop, Chemical, Civil, Clash, Cod, Cold, Combat, Conflict, Crescentade, Crimean, Crusade, Emergency, Feud, ➤ FIGHT, Flame, Food, Fray, Germ, Gigantomachy, Guer(r)illa, Gulf, Hostilities, Hot, Hundred Years', Internecine, Jehad, Jenkin's Ear, Jihad, Jugurthine, Krieg, Mars, Mexican, Napoleonic, Opium, Peloponnesian, Peninsular, Price, Psychological, Punic, Roses, Seven Years', Six Day, Spam, Star, Stoush, Sword, Terrapin, Trench, Vietnam, World

Warble(r) Carol, Chiff-chaff, Chirl, Fauvette, Peggy, Rel(l)ish, Trill, Vibrate, Yodel, Yodle

War-chant, War-cry Alalagmos, Haka, Slogan

Ward (off) Artemus, Averruncate, Care, Casual, Charge, Defend, District, Fend, Guard, Maternity, Nightingale, Oppose, Parry, Protégé, Pupil, Soc, Soken, Vintry, Wear, Weir

Warden Caretaker, Concierge, Constable, Curator, Custodian, Game, Guardian, Keeper, Meter maid, Ranger, Septimus, Spooner, Steward, Traffic

Warder Beefeater, Gaoler, Guardian, Keeper, Screw, Turnkey, Twirl

Wardrobe Almirah, Closet, Clothes, Garderobe, Outfit, Vestuary

Ware(s) Arretine, Beware, Biscuit, Cameo, Canton, China, Etruria, Faience, Goods, Lustre, Merchandise, Palissy, Samian, Shippo, Truck

Warehouse Data, Depository, Entrepôt, Freight-shed, Go-down, Hong, Store

▶ **Warfare** see WAR

War-game Kriegs(s)piel

War-god Ares, Mars, Tiu, Tiw, Tyr

Warhead Atomic, Supremo

Warhorse Charger, Destrier, Fighter

Wariness, Wary Ca'canny, Cagey, Careful, Cautel, Caution, Chary, Discreet, Distrust, Guarded, Leery, Mealy-mouthed, Prudent, Sceptical, Vigilant

Warlike Battailous, Bellicose, Gung-ho, Lachlan, Martial, Militant

Warlord Haw-haw, Kitchener, Shogun

Warm(er), Warming, Warmth Abask, Admonish, Air, Ardour, Balmy, British, Calefacient, Calid(ity), Chambré, Cordial, Empressement, Enchafe, Fervour, Foment, Genial, Global, Glow, ➤ HEAT, Hot, Incalescent, Kang, Lew, Logic, Loving, Muff, Muggy, Mull, Tepid, Thermal, Toast, Toasty

Warm-blooded Homothermal, Homothermic, Homothermous, Idiothermous

Warmonger Hawk

Warn(ing) Admonish, Alarum, Alert, Amber, Aposematic, Apprise, Beacon, Bleep, Buoy, Caution, Caveat, Commination, Cone, Counsel, Document, Early, En garde, Example, Fore, Foretoken, Gardyloo, Garnishment, Harbinger, Heads up, Hoot, Horn, Klaxon, Larum, Lesson, Light, Maroon, Monition, Nix, Nota bene, Notice, Omen, Pi-jaw, Premonitory, Portent, Presage, Prodromal, Scarborough, Sematic, Shore, Signal, Tattler, Threat, Tip-off, Token, Vigia, Vor

Warner Alarm, Fore, Plum, Siren

Warp(ed) Bias, Buckle, Cast, Contort, Distort, Kam, Kedge, Pandation, Time, Twist, Weft

Warpath Rampage

▷ **Warped** may indicate an anagram

Warrant Able, Authorise, Caption, Certificate, Detainer, Distress, Guarantee, Justify, Mittimus, Permit, Precept, Royal, Search, Sepad, Swear, Transire, Vouch, Warn

Warren Burrow, Colony, Hastings

Warrior Achilles, Agamemnon, Ajax, Amazon, Anzac, Berserk(er), Brave, Crusader, Eorl, Fianna, Fighter, Geronimo, Ghazi, Heimdall, Housecarl, Impi, Myrmidon, Nestor, Samurai, Soldier, Tatar, Unknown, Warhorse, Zulu

Warship Battleship, Castle, Cog, Corvette, Cruiser, Destroyer, Drake, Dromon(d), Invincible, Man-o-war, Mine-layer, Monitor, Privateer, Ram

Wart(y) Anbury, Blemish, Muricate, Plantar, Tuberous, Verruca, Wen

Warwick Kingmaker

▶ **Wary** see WARINESS

Was Erat, Existed, Past

Wash(ed), Washer, Washing, Wash out Ablution, Affusion, Alluvion, Bath, Bay(e), Bidet, Bur(r), Calcimine, Circlip, Clean(se), Cradle, D, Dashwheel, Dele(te), Dip, Edulcorate, Elute, Enema, Fen, Flush, Freshen, Gargle, Grommet, Grummet, Irrigate, Kalsomine, Lap, ➤ LAUNDER, Lave, Leather, Lip, Lotion, Marsh, Maundy, Mop, Nipter, Pan, Pigswill, Poss, Purify, Rinse,

Scrub, Shampoo, Shim, Sind, Sloosh, Sluice, Soogee, Soojee, Soojey, Squeegie, Sujee, Swab, Synd, Tie, Twin tub, Tye, Wake

Washbasin, Washtub, Washhouse Copper, Lavabo, Steamie

Washerman, Washerwoman Dhobi, Laundress

Washington Wa

Wasn't Nas, Wasna

Wasp(ish) Bembex, Bink, Bite, Chalcid, Cuckoo-fly, Cynipidae, Cynips, Digger, Fig, Fretful, Gall(-fly), Hornet, Horntail, Hoverfly, Irritable, Marabunta, Mason, Miffy, Muddauber, Paper, Peevish, Pompilid, Potter, Seed, Solitary, Spider, Vespa, Yellow jacket

Wasp's nest Bike, Bink, Byke

Wassail Carouse, Pledge, Toast

Wast Wert

Wastage, Waste(d), Wasting, Wasteland Atrophy, Blue, Cesspit, Cirrhosis, Consume, Contabescent, Crud, Decay, Dejecta, Desert, Detritus, Devastate, Dilapidate, Dissipate, Dross, Dung, Dwindle, Dwine, Dystrophy, Effluent, Egesta, Emaciate, Erode, Estrepe, Exhaust, Expend, Exudate, Flue, Forpine, Fritter, Garbage, Gash, Gob, Gunge, Haggard, Havoc, Hazardous, Knub, Lavish, Loose, Lose, Loss, Marasmus, Misspent, Moor, Moulder, Muir, Mullock, Mungo, Novalia, Nub, Nuclear, Offal, Ordure, Pellagra, Phthisis, Pine, Prodigalise, Radioactive, Ravage, Recrement, Red tape, ➤ REFUSE, Reif, Rubble, Ruderal, Schappe, Scissel, Scoria, Scrap, Sewage, Slag, Slurry, Spend, Spill, Spoil(age), Squander, Sullage, Syntexis, Tabes, Tailing, Thin, Ureal, Urine, Uropoiesis, Vast, Wanze, Wear, Wilderness, Yearn

▷ **Wasted** may indicate an anagram

Wastrel Profligate, Scattergood, Spend-all, Spendthrift, Stalko, Vagabond

Watch(er) Analog(ue), Analogon, Argus, Await, Bark, Bird-dog, Black, Clock, Coastguard, Cock-crow, Digital, Dog, Espy, Fob, Glom, Gregory, Guard, Half-hunter, Huer, Hunter, Kettle, Latewake, Lo, Look, Morning, Nark, Neighbourhood, Night, Note, Nuremberg egg, Observe, Patrol, Pernoctation, Posse, Quartz, Regard, Repeater, Rolex®, Scout, Sentinel, Sentry, Shadow, Spectate, Spotter, Stemwinder, Surveillance, Tend, Ticker, Timepiece, Timer, Tompion, Tout, Turnip, Vedette, ➤ VIGIL, Voyeur, Wait, Wake

Watch-chain Albert, Slang

Watch-control Escapement

Watchful(ness) Alert, Aware, Care, Ira, Jealous, Vigilant, Wary

Watchman Bellman, Charley, Charlie, Chok(e)y, Cho(w)kidar, Guard, Sentinel, Sentry, Speculator, Tompion, Viewer

Watch-tower Atalaya, Barbican, Beacon, Mirador, Sentry-go

Watchword Cry, Password, Shibboleth, Slogan

Water(ed), Waters, Watery Adam's ale, Amrit, Apollinaris, Aq(ua), Aquatic, Aqueous, Barley, Bayou, Bedabble, Broads, Brook, Burn, Canal, Cancer, Chresard, Chuck, Deaw, Demersal, Dew, Dill, Dilute, Dribble, Eau, Ebb, Echard, Element, Ennerdale, Epilimnion, Euphotic, Evian®, Flood, Ford,

Water-sprite Kelpie, Kelpy, Nix(ie), Nixy, Tangie, Undine, Water-nymph

Water supply Dewpond, H, Hydrant, Spring, Tank, Tap

Waterway Aqueduct, Canal, Channel, Culvert, Ditch, Igarapé, Illinois, Intracoastal, Lode, River, Sound, Straight, Suez

Water-wheel Noria, Pelton, Sakia, Saki(y)eh

Wattle(s) Acacia, Boree, Dewlap, Gills, Mimosa, Mulga, Sallow, Snot

Wave(d), Waves, Wavy Alfven, Alpha, Beachcomber, Beam, Beck, Beta, Billow, Bore, Brain, Brandish, Breaker, Carrier, Circular polarisation, Clapotis, Comber, Complex, Crenulate, Crest, Crime, Crimp, Cymotrichous, De Broglie, Decuman, Delta, Dumper, Finger, Flap, Flaunt, Float, Flote, Gesticulate, Gravity, Groundswell, Gyrose, Heat, Hertzian, Internal, Lee, Long, Marcel, Medium, Mexican, Nebule, New, Oundy, Peristalsis, Perm(anent), Plunger, Primary, Radar, Radiation, Radio, Rayleigh, Repand, Ripple, Roller, Sastrugi, Sea, Secondary, Seiche, Seismic, Shock, Short, Sine, Sky, Snaky, Soliton, Sound, Spiller, Squiggle, Standing, Stationary, Stream, Surf, Surge, Sway, Tabby, Theta, Tidal, Train, Transverse, Tsunami, Undate, Unde, Undulate, Vermicular, Waffle, Waft, Wag, Waive, Wash, Waw, Whitecap, White-horse, Wigwag

▷ **Wave(s)** may indicate an anagram

Wave-band Channel

Wave-detector Coherer

Wavelength Band, De Broglie

Waver(ing) Dither, Falter, Flag, Gutter, Hesitate, Oscillate, Stagger, Sway, Swither, Teeter, Vacillate, Waffle, Wet, Wow

Wax(ed), Waxing, Waxy Adipocere, Ambergris, Appal, Bate, Candelilla, Carna(h)uba, Cere, Ceresin, Cerumen, Cobbler's, Cutin, Effuse, Enseam, Gr(e)aves, Grow, Heelball, Honeycomb, Increase, Increscent, Inseam, Ire, Japan, Kiss, Lecithin, Lipide, Livid, Lost, Lyrical, Mineral, Montan, Mummy, Ozocerite, Ozokerite, Paraffin, Parmacitie, Pela, Petroleum, Propolis, Pruina, Rage, Seal, Spermaceti, Suberin, Tallow, Tantrum, Temper, Vegetable, Yielding

Waxwing Cedar-bird, Icarus

Way(s), Wayside Access, Agate, Appian, Autobahn, Avenue, Borstal(l), Bypass, Companion, Course, Crescent, Direction, Door, Draw, E, Each, Entrance, Family, Fashion, Flaminian, Foss(e), Gate, Habit, Hatch, Hedge, High, Hither, How, Lane, Manner, Means, Method, Milky, Mo, Mode, N, Pass, Path, Permanent, Pilgrim's, Procedure, Railroad, Regimen, Ridge, ➤ ROAD, Route, S, Sallypost, St(reet), Style, System, Thoroughfare, Thus, Trace, Trail, Troade, Turnpike, Underpass, Untrodden, Via, W, Wise

Wayfarer Commuter, Piepowder, Pilgrim, Traveller, Voyager

Waylay Accost, Ambuscade, Ambush, Beset, Buttonhole, Molest, Obstruct

Way-out Advanced, Bizarre, Egress, Esoteric, Exit, Exotic, Extreme, Offbeat, Trendy

Wayward Capricious, Disobedient, Errant, Erratic, Loup-the-dyke, Obstreperous, Perverse, Stray, Unruly, Wilful

We I and I, Oo, Us

Weak(er), Weaken(ing), Weakest, Weakness Achilles' heel, Acrasia, Antimnemonic, Aphesis, Appal, Arsis, Asthenia, Blot, Brickle, Brittle, Cachexia, Cataplexy, Chink, Cripple(d), Debile, Debilitate, Decrease, Delay, Dilute, Disable, Effete, Emasculate, Enervate, Enfeeble, Entender, Fade, Faible, Failing, Faint, Fatigue, Feeble, Fissile, Flag, Flaw, Flimsy, Foible, Fragile, Frail(tee), Frailty, Give, Gone, Ham, Hamartia, Helpless, Honeycomb, Impair, Impotence, Infirm, Knock-kneed, Labefaction, Lassitude, Leptosomatic, Low, Milk and water, Myasthenia, Namby-pamby, Pale, Pall, Paresis, Paraparesis, Puny, Push-over, Pusillanimous, Reckling, Reduce, Simp, Slack, Thesis, Thin, Tottery, Unable, Underdog, Undermine, Unnerve, Unstable, Vapid, Velleity, Vessel, Vulnerability, W, Water(y), Wish(y)-wash(y), Wuss(y)

Weakling Dilling, Drip, Milksop, Nerd, Reed, Softie, Wuss

Weal Ridge, Stripe, Wealth, Welfare, Welt, Whelk

Wealth(y) Abundance, Affluence, Bullion, Croesus, Fat-cat, Fortune, Golconda, Jet-set, Klondike, Klondyke, Loaded, Lolly, Mammon, Means, Mine, Mint, Moneyed, Nabob, Opulence, Ore, Pelf, Plutocrat, Reich, Rich, Ritzy, Solid, Substance, Treasure, Untold, Well-heeled, Well-off, Well-to-do

Wean Ablactation, Bairn, Spain, Spane, Spean

Weapon Airgun, Arbalest, Arblast, Arm, Armalite®, Arquebus(e), Arrow, Arsenal, Assegai, Ataghan, Backsword, Baton, Battleaxe, Bayonet, Bazooka, Bill, Binary, Bludgeon, Bolo, Bondook, Broadsword, Caliver, Calthrop, Caltrap, Caltrop, Carbine, Catapult, Cestus, Club, Co(e)horn, Cosh, Cudgel, Culverin, Cutlass, Dag(ger), Dart, Derringer, Doodlebug, Dragoon, Elf-arrow, Enfield, Estoc, Excalibur, Flail, Flintlock, Forty-five, Fougade, Fougasse, Gad(e), Gaid, Gingal(l), Gisarme, Glaive, Grenade, Halberd, Halbert, Harpoon, Harquebus, Hoplology, Howitzer, Javelin, Jingal, Knuckleduster, Kris, Life-preserver, Longbow, Machete, Mangonel, Matchet, Maurikigusari, Mauser®, Maxim, Missile, Morgenstern, Mortar, Munition, Musket, Nuke, Nunchaku (sticks), Orgue, Partisan, Petronel, Pilum, Pistol, Quarterstaff, Revolver, Rifle, Sabre, Saker, Sandbag, Sarbacane, Shotgun, Sidearm, Skean-dhu, Skene-dhu, Snickersnee, Sparke, Sparth, Spat, Spontoon, Sten, Stiletto, Sting, Stinkpot, Sword, Taiaha, Taser®, Tomboc, Torpedo, Trebuchet, Trident, Truncheon, V1, Vou(l)ge, Whirl-bat, Whorl-bat

Wear(ing), Wear Out Abate, Ablative, Abrade, Attrition, Chafe, Corrade, Corrode, Deteriorate, Detrition, Efface, Erode, Erosion, Fashion, For(e)spend, Fray, Frazzle, Fret, Garb, Impair, In, Pack, Scuff, Sport, Stand, Tedy

▷ **Wear** may indicate the NE (eg Sunderland)

Weariness, Wearisome, Weary Beat, Bejade, Bore, Cloy, Dog-tired, Ennui, Ennuyé, Exhaust, Fag, Fatigate, Fatigue, Harass, Hech, Irk, Jade, Lacklustre, Lassitude, Pall, Puny, Ramfeezle, Sleepy, Spent, Tire, Trash, Try, Tucker, Wabbit, Worn

Weasel Beech-marten, Cane, Delundung, Ermine, Ferret, Glutton, Grison, Kolinsky, Marten, Mink, Mustela, Pekan, Polecat, Stoat, Taira, Tayra, Vermin, Whitrick, Whitterick, Whit(t)ret, Wolverine, Woodshock

Weather, Weather forecast Atmosphere, Cyclone, Discolour, Ecoclimate, Elements, Endure, Met, Sky, Stand, Survive, Tiros, Undergo, Withstand

Weathercock Barometer, Fane, Vane

Weave(r), Weaves, Weaving Arachne, Basket, Cane, Complect, Entwine, Finch, Heald, Heddle, Interlace, Lace, Lease, Leno, Lion, Loom, Marner, Plain, Raddle, Ripstop, Rya, Shuttle, Sparrow, Spider, Splice, Taha, Texture, Throstle, Tissue, Tweel, Twill, Twine, Wabster, Waggle, Webster, Zigzag

Weaver-bird Amadavat, Avadavat, Quelea, Rice-bird, Taha

Web(bing), Web-footed, Web-site Aranea, Food, Fourchette, Infomediary, Internet, Mat, Maze, Mesh(work), Offset, Palama, Palmate, Palmiped, Patagium, Pinnatiped, Skein, Snare, Tela, Tissue, Toil, Totipalmate, World Wide

Webster Spider, Weaver

Wed(ding), Wedlock Alliance, Bet, Diamond, Espousal, Golden, Hymen, Join, Knobstick, Link, Marriage, Marry, Mate, Meng(e), Me(i)nt, Meynt, Ming, Nuptials, Pair, Penny, Ruby, Shotgun, Silver, Spousal, ➤ UNION, Unite, White, Y

Wedge Chock, Chunk, Cleat, Cotter, Cuneal, Doorstop, Feather, Forelock, Gagger, Gib, Jack, Jam, Key, Niblick, Prop, Quoin, Scotch, Shim, Sphenic, Stick, Trig, Vomerine, Whipstock

Wedgwood Benn, China®

Wednesday Ash, Midweek, Spy

Wee Leak, Little, Pee, Sma(ll), Tiny, Urinate

Weed(y) Adderwort, Alga, Allseed, Anacharis, Arenaria, Bedstraw, Bell-bind, Blinks, Burdock, Carpetweed, Charlock, Chickweed, Chlorella, Cigar(ette), Cissy, Clover, Cockle, Colonist, Coltsfoot, Corncockle, Couch, Daisy, Dallop, Darnel, Dock, Dollop, Dulse, Elodea, Ers, Fag, Fat hen, Femitar, Fenitar, Fucoid, Fumitory, Groundsel, Helodea, Hoe, Indian, Joe-pye, Knapweed, Knawel, Knot-grass, Lemna, Mare's-tail, Marijuana, Matfelon, Mayweed, Nard, Nettle, Nipplewort, Nostoc, Oxygen, Pearlwort, Pilewort, Piri-piri, Plantain, Potamogeton, Purslane, Ragi, Ragwort, Reate, Rest-harrow, Ruderal, Runch, Sagittaria, Sargasso, Scal(l)awag, Scallywag, Senecio, Sorrel, Spurge, Spurrey, Sudd, Sun-spurge, Swine's-cress, Tansy, Tare, Thistle, Tine, Tobacco, Tormentil, Twitch, Ulotrichale, Ulva, Vetch, Wartcress, Widow's, Winnow, Yarr

Weedkiller Arsenic, Atrazine, Dalapon, Diquat, Diuron, Herbicide, Paraquat®, Simazine

Week(ly) Hebdomadary, Holy, Orientation, Ouk, Oulk, Passion, Periodical, Sennight

Weekend K, Sat, Sun

Weep(er), Weepy, Wept Bawl, Blubber, Cry, Grat, Greet, Lachrymose, Lament, Loser, Maudlin, Niobe, Ooze, Pipe, Sob, Wail

Weevil Anthonomous, Boll, Bug, Curculio, Diamond-beetle, Grain, Insect, Rice, Seed

Weft Roon, Shot, Texture, Warp, Woof

Weigh(ing), Weigh down, Weight(y) All-up, Arroba, Artal, As, Atomic, Avoirdupois, Balance, Bantam, Baric, Bob, Bulk, Burden, Candie, Candy, Cantar, Carat, Catty, Cental, Centner, Clove, Consider, Count, Counterpoise, Cruiser, Ct, Dead, Decagram(me), Deliberate, Derham, Dirham, Dirhem, Drail, Dumbbell, Emphasis, Equivalent, Feather, Fother, G, Gerah, Grain, Gram, Heft, Importance, Impost, Incumbent, Journey, Kandy, Kantar, Kat(i), Katti, Kerb, Khat, Kin, Kip, Last, Libra, Lisp(o)und, Load, Mark, Massive, Maund, Metage, Mina, Mna, Molecular, Moment, Mouse, Nail, Obol, Oke, Onerous, Oppress, Ounce, Overpoise, Oz, Pease, Peaze, Peise, Peize, Perpend, Peyse, Pikul, Plummet, Poise, Ponderal, Pood, Pound, Preponderance, Prey, Pud, Pudge, Quintal, Recul, Rod, Rotolo, Scruple, Seer, Semuncia, Ser, Sinker, Sit, Slang, Slung-shot, Stone, Stress, Talent, Tare, Throw, Tical, Tod, Tola, Ton(nage), Tonne, Tophamper, Troy, Trutinate, Unce, Unmoor, Welter, Wey, Wt

Weighing machine Bismar, Scales, Steelyard, Tron(e)

Weightless Agravic

Weight-lifter Crane, Lewis, Windlass

Weir Cauld, Dam, Garth, Kiddle, Kidel, Lasher, Pen, Watergate

Weird Bizarre, Curious, Dree, Eerie, Eery, Eldritch, Kookie, Offbeat, Spectral, Strange, Supernatural, Taisch, Uncanny, Zany

Welch, Welsh Abscond, Cheat, Default, Embezzle, Levant, Rat, Reneg(ue), Renig, Skedaddle, Weasel

Welcome, Welcoming Aloha, Ave, Bel-accoyle, Ciao, Embrace, Entertain, Glad-hand, Greet, Haeremai, Halse, Hallo, Hello, Hospitable, How, Hullo, Receive, Reception, Salute

Weld(ing) Arc, Join, Merge, Sinter, Unite

Welfare Advantage, Alms, Benison, Ha(y)le, Heal, Health, Sarvodaya, Weal

Welkin Firmament, Sky

Well (done) Artesian, Atweel, Aweel, Bien, Bore(hole), Bravo, Cenote, Development, Dry hole, Euge, Famously, Fine, Fit, Gasser, Good, Gosh, Gusher, Hale, ➤ HEALTHY, Hot, Inkpot, Law, My, Namma hole, Odso, Oh, Oil, Phreatic, Potential, So, Source, Spa, Spring, Sump, Surge, Um, Upflow, Zemzem

Well-being Atweel, Bien-être, Comfort, Euphoria, Euphory, Good, Health, Welfare

Well-bred Genteel

Well-built Sturdy, Tight

Well-covered Chubby, Padded

Well-curb Puteal

Welles Orson

Wellington Gumboot, Iron Duke, Nosey

Well-known Famous, Illustrious, Notorious, Notour, Prominent

Well-off Affluent, Far, Rich, Wealthy

Well part Bucket, Shadoof, Shaduf

Wells Bombardier, Fargo

Well-wisher Friend

▶ **Welsh** see WELCH

Welshman Briton, Brittonic, Brython, Cake, Cambrian, Celtic, Cog, Cym(ric), Cymry, Dai, Emlyn, Evan, Fluellen, Gareth, Harp, Idris, Ifor, Keltic, P-Celtic, P-Keltic, Rabbit, Rarebit, Rees, Rhys, Sion, Taffy, Tudor, W

Wen Cyst, Talpa, Tumour, Wart

Wench Blowze, Court, Gouge, Girl, Hussy, Maid, Ramp, Rig, Smock, Strumpet

Wend Meander, Sorb, Steer

Wendy Darling, House

Went Left

Werewolf Loup-garou, Lycanthrope, Nazi, Turnskin, Vampire

Wesleyan Epworth, Methodist

West(ern), Westerly Ang mo, Favonian, Hesperian, Mae, Movie, Oater, Occidental, Ponent, Spaghetti, Sunset, W, Wild

West African Kroo, Wolof

▷ **West end** may indicate 't' or 'W1'

West Indian Carib, Creole, Jamaican, Taino

Westminster SW1

Wet(ting) Bedabble, Bedraggled, Clammy, Daggle, Damp, Dank, Dew, Dip, Douse, Dowse, Drench, Drip(ping), Drook, Drouk, Embrue, Enuresis, Feeble, Humect, Humid, Hyetal, Imbue, Irrigate, Madefy, Madid, Marshy, Moil, Moist(en), Molly, Namby-pamby, Pee, Rainy, Ret(t), Roral, Roric, Runny, Saturate, Shower, Simp(leton), Sipe, Sluice, ▶ SOAK, Sodden, Sopping, Sour, Steep, Urinate, Wat, Wee, Wimpy, Wringing

Whack(ed) Belt, Bemaul, Biff, Deadbeat, Joll, Joule, Jowl, Lambast, Lounder, Swish, Thump

Whale(meat), Whaling Baleen, Beaked, Beluga, Blower, Blubber, Blue, Bottlehead, Bottlenose, Bowhead, Cachalot, Calf, Cetacea(n), Cete, Cowfish, Dolphin, Fall, Fin(back), Finner, Gam, Glutton, Grampus, Greenland, Grey, Humpback, Killer, Kreng, Leviathan, Manatee, Minke, Monodon, Mysticeti, Odontoceti, Paste, Physeter, Pilot, Pod, Porpoise, Right, Rorqual, School, Scrag, Sea-canary, Sea-unicorn, Sei, Social, Sperm, Sulphur-bottom, Thrasher, Toothed, Toothless, White, Zeuglodon(t)

▷ **Whale** may indicate an anagram

Whaler Ahab, Harpooner, Ship, Specksioneer, Specktioneer, Waister

Whales' meat Clio

Wham Bang, Collide

Whang Blow, Flog, Thrash, Whack

Wharf(inger) Dock(er), Jetty, Key, Landing, Pier, Quay, Roustabout, Rouster, Staith(e)

What Anan, Eh, How, Pardon, Que, Siccan, That, Which

Whatnot, What's-its-name Dinges, Dingus, Doings, Etagère, Gismo, Jiggamaree, Jiggumbob, Thingamy, Thingumajig, Thingumbob, Thingummy, Timenoguy

Wheat Amelcorn, Blé, Bulg(h)ur, Cracked, Durum, Einkorn, Emmer, Federation, Fromenty, Frumenty, Furme(n)ty, Furmity, Grain, Hard, Mummy, Rivet, Sarrasin, Sarrazin, Seiten, Semolina, Sharps, Spelt, Triticum

Wheatsheaf Bale, Gerbe, Stook

Wheedle Banter, Barney, Blandish, Cajole, Coax, Cog, Cuiter, Cuittle, Flatter, Inveigle, Tweedle, Whilly(whaw)

Wheel(er) Balance, Bedel, Bevel, Bogy, Buff(ing), Caracol(e), Caster, Castor, Catherine, Circle, Cistern, Crown, Cycle, Daisy, Disc, Driving, Emery, Escape, Felloe, Felly, Ferris, Gear, Helm, Hurl, Idle(r), Kick, Mortimer, Nabob, Nose, Paddle, Pedal, Pelton, Perambulator, Pinion, Pivot, Planet, Potter's, Prayer, Pulley, Ratchet, Rhomb, Roll, Rotate, Roulette, Rowel, Sheave, Spinning, Sprocket, Steering, Stepney, Trindle, Trochus, Trolley, Trundle, ➤ TURN, Tympan(um), Water, Wharve, Wire, Worm, Zoetrope

Wheelbarrow Monotroch

Wheelhouse Caravan, Paddle-box

Wheel-hub Axle, Nave

Wheelman Cyclist, Ixion

Wheelwright Spokesman

Wheeze Asthma, Jape, Joke, Pant, Ploy, Rale, Reak, Reik, Rhonchus, Ruse, Stridor, Trick, Whaisle, Whaizle

Whelk Buckie, Limpet, Shellfish, Stromb, Triton

Whelp Bear, Bra(t)chet, Pup

When(ever) Although, As, If, Once, Though, Time

Where(abouts) Location, Neighbourhood, Place, Site, Vicinity, Whaur, Whither

Wherefore Cause, Reason, Why

Whereupon So, When

Wherewithal Finance, Means, Money, Needful, Resources

Wherry Barge, Rowboat

Whet(stone) Coticular, Excite, Hone, Sharpen, Stimulate

Whether Conditional, If

Whey Whig

Which(ever), Which is Anyway, As, QE, Whatna, Whilk, Who

Whiff Breath, Cigarette, Gust, Puff, Redolence, Smatch, Sniff, Trace, Waft

Whig Adullamite, Jig, Rascal, Tory, Whey

While Although, As, Interim, Since, Space, Span, Though, Throw, Time, When, Whenas, Yet

Whim(s), Whimsical, Whimsy Bizarre, Caprice, Conceit, Crotchet, Fad, Fancy, Fey, Flisk, Kicksy-wicksy, Kink, Notion, Quaint, Quirk, Tick, Toy, Vagary

Whimper Cry, Grizzle, Mewl, Pule, Snivel, Whine

Whin Furze, Gorse, Ulex

Whine, Whinge Cant, Carp, Complain, Cry, Grumble, Kvetch, Mewl, Moan, Peenge, Pule, Snivel, Whimper, Yammer

Whinny Neigh, Nicker, Whicker

Whip(ped), Whip out, Whipping Beat, Braid, Brede, Bullwhack, Bullwhip, Cat, Chabouk, Chantilly, Chastise, Chief, Cilium, Colt, Crop, Drive, Flagellate, Flagellum, Feague, Firk, Flay, Hide, Jambok, Knout, K(o)urbash, Larrup, ➤ LASH, Limber, Quirt, Rawhide, Riem, Scourge, Sjambok, Slash, Steal, Strap-oil, Swinge, Switch, Taw, Thong, Three-line, Trounce, Welt, Whap, Whop

Whippersnapper Dandiprat, Dandyprat, Pup, Squirt

Whirl(ing) Circumgyrate, Dervish, Eddy, Gyrate, ➤ IN A WHIRL, Pivot, Reel, Spin, Swing, Swirl, Vortex, Vortical, Whirry

Whirlpool Eddy, Gulf, Gurge, Maelstrom, Moulin, Swelchie, Vorago, Vortex, Weel, Wiel

Whirlwind Cyclone, Dust devil, Eddy, Tornado, Tourbillion, Typho(o)n, Vortex, Willy-willy

Whisk Chowri, Chowry, Swish, Switch, Whid, Whip

Whisker(s) Beard, Beater, Burnsides, Cat's, Dundreary, Hackle, Hair, Moustache, Mutton-chop, Samuel, Side(-boards), Side-burns, Vibrissa

Whisk(e)y Alcohol, Barley-bree, Barley-broo, Barley-broth, Bond, Bourbon, Canadian, Cape Smoke, Corn, Cratur, Creature, Fife, Fire-water, Hokonui, Hoo(t)ch, Irish, Malt, Monongahela, Moonshine, Morning, Mountain dew, Nip, Peat-reek, Pot(h)een, Ragwater, Red eye, Rye, Scotch, Sourmash, Spunkie, Tanglefoot, Usquebaugh, Wheech, Whiss

▷ **Whisky** may indicate an anagram

Whisper Breath(e), Bur(r), Hark, Hint, Innuendo, Murmur, Rumour, Round, Rustle, Sigh, Stage, Susurrus, Tittle, Undertone

Whist Hush, Quiet, Sh, Solo

Whistle(r) Blow, Calliope, Feedback, Hiss, Marmot, Penny, Ping, Pipe, Ref, Siffle(ur), Sowf(f), Sowth, Steam, Stop, Stridor, Swab(ber), Tin, Toot, Tweedle, Tweet, Warbler, Wheeple, Wheugh, Whew, Wolf

Whit Atom, Doit, Figo, Haet, Iota, Jot, Particle, Pentecost, Point, Red cent

White(n), Whitener, Whiteness Agene, Agenise, Alabaster, Albedo, Albescent, Albino, Albugineous, Albumen, Argent, Ashen, Bakra, Blameless, Blanch, Blanco, Bleach, Buckra, Cam, Calm, Camstone, Candid, Candour, Canescent, Canities, Caucasian, Caum, Chinese, Christmas, Cliffs, Collar, Company, Dealbate, Egg, Elephant, Ermine, European, Fang, Fard, Feather, Flag, Flake, Glair, Gwen(da), Gwendolen, Honorary, Hore, House, Innocent, Ivory, Lie, Lily, Livid, Man, Mealy, Niveous, Opal, Oyster, Pakeha, Pale(face), Pallor, Paper, Pearl, Poor, Pure, Redleg, Russian, Sclerotic, Selborne, Sheep, Snow(y), Taw, Vitiligo, Wan, Wedding

Whitefish Menominee

Whitefriars Alsatia

Whitehall Ministry

Whitehead Milium

White horses Skipper's daughters

White man Ba(c)kra, Buckra, Caucasian, Gub(bah), Haole, Honkie, Honky, Larney, Mzungu, Occidental, Ofay, Pakeha, Paleface, Redleg, Redneck, WASP

Whitewash Calcimine, Excuse, Kalsomine, Lime, Skunk, Trounce

Whitlow Ancome, Felon, Panaritium, Paronychia

Whitsun Pinkster, Pinxter

Whittle Carve, Pare, Sharpen

Whizz Wheech

Who As, Doctor

Whodunit Mystery

Whole, Wholehearted, Wholeness, Wholly All, Eager, Entire(ty), Entity, Fully, Hale, Intact, Integer, Integrity, Largely, Lot, Sum, Systemic, Thoroughly, Total, Unbroken, Uncut

Wholesale(r) Cutprice, En bloc, Engrosser, Jobber, Sweeping

Wholesome Clean, Good, Healthy, Physical, Sound

Whoop(er), Whooping cough Alew, Celebrate, Chincough, Crane, Cry, Excite, Kink(cough), Kink-hoast, Pertussis, Swan

Whoopee Carouse, Evoe, Hey-go-mad, Roister

Whoosh Birr, Swish

Whopper, Whopping Barn, Crammer, Huge, Immense, Jumbo, Lie, Lig, Oner, Out and outer, Scrouger, Slapper, Slockdolager, Soc(k)dalager, Soc(k)dolager, Soc(k)doliger, Soc(k)dologer, Sogdolager, Sogdoliger, Sogdologer, Tale, Taradiddle

Whore Drab, Harlot, Loose woman, Pinnace, Pro, Quail, Road, Strumpet, Tart

Whorl Corolla, Eucyclic, Spiral, Swirl, Verticil, Volute

Why Reason, Yogh

Wick Farm, Rush, Snaste, Vill(age)

Wicked(ness) Adharma, Atrocity, ➤ BAD, Candle, Criminal, Cru(i)sie, Crusy, Depravity, Devilish, Evil, Facinorous, Flagitious, Goaty, Godless, Heinous, Immoral, Impious, Improbity, Iniquity, Lantern, Nefarious, Night-light, Ponerology, Pravity, Rush, Satanic, Scelerate, Sin(ful), Taper, Turpitude, Unholy, Vile

▷ **Wicked** may indicate containing a wick

Wicker(work) Basketry, Sale, Seal

Wicket Gate, Hatch, Pitch, Square, Sticky, Stool, Stump, Yate

Wicket-keeper Stumper

Wide, Widen(ing), Width Abroad, Ample, Bay, Broad, Dilate, Drib, Eclectic, Expand, Extend, Far, Flanch, Flange, Flare, Flaunch, Ga(u)ge, General, Miss, Prevalent, Roomy, Spacious, Spread, Sundry, Sweeping, Vast

Wide-awake Alert, Fly, Hat, Wary, Watchful

Widespread Diffuse, Epidemic, Extensive, General, Pandemic, Panoramic, Prevalent, Prolate, Routh(ie), Sweeping

Widow(ed) Black, Dame, Dowager, Golf, Grass, Jointress, Relict, Sati, Sneerwell, Suttee, Vidual, Viduous, Whydah-bird, Widdy

Wield Brandish, Control, Exercise, Handle, ➤ MANIPULATE, Ply

Wife, Wives Bride, Concubine, Consort, Devi, Dutch, Enid, Feme, Feme covert, Fiere, Frau, Haram, Harem, Harim, Helpmate, Helpmeet, Hen, Kali, Kickie-wickie, Kicksy-wicksy, Kloo(t)chman, Lakshmi, Mate, Memsahib, Missis, Missus, Mrs, Mummer's, Partner, Pirrauru, Potiphar's, Rib, Seraglio, Spouse, Squaw, Trouble and strife, Ux(or), W

Wig Bagwig, Bob(wig), Brutus, Buzz-wig, Campaign, Carpet, Cauliflower, Caxon, Chevelure, Chide, Cockernony, Dalmahoy, Full-bottomed, Gizz, Gregorian, Hair(piece), Heare, Jas(e)y, Jazey, Jiz, Major, Periwig, Peruke, Postiche, Ramil(l)ie(s), Rate, Reprimand, Rug, Scold, Scratch, Sheitel, Spencer, Targe, Tie, Toupee, Toupet, Tour

Wiggle, Wiggly Jiggle, Scoleciform, Wobble, Wriggle

Wight Man, Vectis

Wigwam Te(e)pee

Wild Aberrant, Agrestal, Barbarous, Berserk, Bundu, Bush, Chimeric, Crazy, Earl, Errant, Erratic, Farouche, Feral, Frantic, Frenetic, Haggard, Hectic, Lawless, Mad(cap), Manic, Meshugge, Myall, Natural, Rampant, Raver, Riotous, ➤ SAVAGE, Unmanageable, Unruly, Violent, Warrigal, West, Woolly

▷ **Wild(ly)** may indicate an anagram

Wild beast Eyra, Sapi-utan, Scrubber

Wildcat Lion, Manul, Ocelot, Strike, Tiger

Wilderness Bush, Desert, Ruderal, Sinai, Solitude, Waste

Wild goose Chase, Greylag

Wild oats Haver

Wile, Wily Art, Artifice, Artful, Astute, Braide, ➤ CUNNING, Deceit, Foxy, Peery, Ruse, Shifty, Shrewd, Slee, ➤ SLY, Spider, Stratagem, Streetwise, Subtle, Trick, Versute, Wide

Wilful Deliberate, Headstrong, Heady, Obstinate, Recalcitrant, Wayward

Will, Willing(ly) Alsoon, Amenable, Bard, Bequeath, Bewildered, Bill(y), Complaisant, Compliant, Conation, Content, Desire, Devise, Fain, Free, Game, Hay, Leave, Legator, Lief, Lieve, Living, Obedient, On, Please, Prone, Purpose, Ready, Receptive, Scarlet, Soon, Spirit, Swan, Testament, Testate, Volition, Voluntary, Volunteer, Way, Wimble

▷ **Will** may indicate an anagram

William(s) Bill(y), Conqueror, Occam, Orange, Pear, Rufus, Silent, Sweet, Tell, Tennessee

Will o' the wisp Friar's lantern, Ignis-fatuus, Jack o'lantern, Min min, Nightfire, Rush

Willow(ing), Willowy Crack, Lissom(e), Lithe, Osier, Poplar, Pussy, Salix, Sallow, Sauch, Saugh, Supple, Twilly, Weeping, Withy

Willpower Determination, Strength

Willy-nilly Nolens volens, Perforce

Wilt Decline, Droop, Fade, Flag, Sap, Shalt, Wither

Wiltshireman Moonraker

▶ **Wily** see WILE

Wimple Gorget, Meander, Ripple, Turn

▷ **Wimple** may indicate an anagram

Win(ner), Winning Achieve, ➤ BEAT, Capot, Champion, Conquer, Cup, Cute, Decider, Disarming, Dormie, Dormy, Earn, Endearing, First, Gain, Gammon, Hit, Jackpot, Land, Laureate, Lead, Medallist, Motser, Motza, Nice, Pile, Pot, Prevail, Profit, Purler, Rubicon, Shoo-in, Slam, Snip, Success, Sweet, Take, ➤ TRIUMPH, Up, Vellet, Velvet, Victor(y), Vole, Wrest

Wince Blench, Cringe, Flinch, Recoil

Winch Crab, Crane, Jack, Windlass

Winchester® Rifle

Wind(y) Aeolian, Air, Airstream, Anabatic, Anti-trade, Aquilo(n), Argestes, Auster, Baguio, Bend, Berg, Bise, Blore, Blow, Bluster, Bora, Boreas, Bourasque, Brass, Breeze, Brickfielder, Buran, Burp, Buster, Cape doctor, Carminative, Caurus, Chili, Chill, Chinook, Coil, Colic, Corus, Crank, Curl, Cyclone, Downwash, Draught, Draw, Dust devil, Easterly, Etesian, Euraquilo, Euroclydon, Eurus, Favonian, Favonius, Fearful, Firn, Flatulence, Flatus, Flaw, Fo(e)hn, G(h)ibli, Gale, Gas, Gregale, Gust, Haboob, Harmattan, Heaves, Hurricane, Hurricano, Kamseen, Katabatic, K(h)amsin, Levant(er), Libecc(h)io, Libs, Meander, Meltemi, Mistral, Monsoon, Nervous, Nor(th)wester(ly), Noreast, Norther, Noser, Notus, Pampero, Ponent, Poop, Puna, Purl, Quill, Reeds, Reel, Rip-snorter, Roll, Samiel, Sciroc, Scirocco, Screw, Sea, Second, Serpentine, Shimaal, Simoom, Simoon, Sirocco, Slant, Snake, Snifter, Snorter, Solano, Solar, Sough, Souther, Spiral, Spool, Squall, Stellar, Sumatra, Tail, Thread, Throw, Tornado, Tourbillon, Trade, Tramontana, Trend, Turn, Twaddle, Twine, Twister, Typhoon, Vayu, Veer, Ventose, Volturnus, Waffle, Weave, Wester, Whirlblast, White squall, Williwaw, Willy-willy, Winch, Woold, Wrap, Wreathe, Wrest, Wuthering, Zephyr(us), Zonda

Windbag Balloon, Drogue, Prattler, Whoopee cushion, Zeppelin

Windfall Bonanza, Buckshee, Caduac, Fortune, Godsend, Manna

Windflower Anemone

Winding(s) Ambages, Anfractuous, Creeky, Evagation, Link, Sinuous, Spiral, Tortuous, Twisty

Windlass Whim, Winch

Windmill Post, Smock, Whirligig

Window(s) Bay, Bow, Casement, Catherine-wheel, Companion, Compass, Day, Deadlight, Dormer, Dream-hole, Eye, Eyelids, Fanlight, Fenestella, Fenestra, French, Gable, Garret, Glaze, Guichet, Jalousie, Jesse, Judas, Lancet, Lattice, Launch, Loop-light, Lozen, Lucarne, Lunette, Luthern, Lychnoscope, Marigold, Mezzanine, Mirador, Monial, Mullion, Oculus, Oeil-de-boeuf, Ogive, Orb, Oriel, Ox-eye, Pane, Pede, Picture, Porthole, Quarterlight, Rosace, Rose, Sash, Sexfoil, Spyhole, Storm, Transom, Trellis, Ventana, Weather, Wicket, Windock, Winnock

Window-bar, Window-fastening Astragal, Espagnolette

Windpipe Bronchus, Gular, Throat, Trachea, Weasand

Windscale Beaufort

Windsock Drogue, Sleeve

Windswept Scud

Wind-up End, Fright, Liquidate, Span

Windward Ahold, Aloof, Laveer, Luff, Up

Wine Alicant, Amontillado, Amoroso, Anjou, Anker, Asti, Auslese, Bacharach, Bardolino, Barley, Barolo, (Cabernet) Sauvignon, Barsac, Bastard, Beaujolais, Beaune, Biddy, Bin, Bishop, Blanc, Bombo, Bordeaux, Brut, Bubbly, Bucellas, Bull's blood, Burgundy, Cabernet, Canary, Catawba, Cava, Chablis, Chambertin, Champers, Chardonnay, Charneco, Chateau, Chianti, Claret, Comet, Constantia, Cowslip, Cup, Cuvée, Dao, Dessert, Dubonnet®, Eiswein, Elderberry, Espumoso, Essence, Essencia, Falernian, Fendant, Fortified, Frascati, Genevrette, Gewürztraminer, Ginger, Gladstone, Gluhwein, Graves, Hermitage, Hippocras, Hoccamore, Hochheimer, Hock, It, Jerepigo, Johannisberger, Kabinett, Lambrusco, Languedoc, Liebfraumilch, Lisbon, Log-juice, Loll-shraub, Loll-shrob, Macon, Madeira, Malaga, Malmsey, Malvasia, Malvesie, Malvoisie, Manzanilla, Marcobrunner, Margaux, Marsala, Medoc, Meersault, Merlot, Mirin, Mocker, Montilla, Montrachet, Mosel(le), Mountain, Mull, Muscadel, Muscadet, Muscadine, Muscat(el), Must, Negus, Niersteiner, Noisy, Nuits Saint Georges, Oenology, Oenomel, Ordinaire, Orvieto, Palm, Peter-see-me, Piece, Piesporter, Piment, Pinot noir, Pinot(age), Pipe, Plonk, Plotty, Pomerol, Pommard, Port, Pouilly-Fousse, Pouilly-Fume, Pradikat, Prisage, Race, Red, Resinata, Retsina, Rhenish, Rhine, Riesling, Rioja, Rosé, Rosy, Rudesheimer, Sack, Sangaree, Sangria, Sauterne, Sauvignon, Scuppernong, Sec, Sekt, Shiraz, Soave, Spätlese, Sparkling, Spumante, Steinberger, St Emilion, Straw, Stum, Supernaculum, Syrah, Table, Tarragona, Tent, Toddy, Tokay, Trockenbeernauslese, Tun, Tutu, Valpolicella, Vat, Verdelho, Vermouth, Vin ordinaire, Vin(o), Vinho verde, Vintage, Vouvray, White, Xeres, Zinfandel

Wine-cellar, Wine-shop Bistro, Bodega, Vault, Vaut(e)

Wine-glass Flute

Wine-making Gallising, Remuage

Wing(ed), Winger, Wings, Wing-like Aerofoil, Ala(r), Alula, Annexe, Appendage, Arm, Bastard, ➤ BIRD, Branch, Canard, Cellar, Corium, Coulisse, Delta, Dipteral, El(l), Elevon, Elytral, Elytriform, Elytron, Elytrum, Fender, Flap, Flew, Flipper, Forward, Halteres, Hurt, Left, Limb, Parascenia, Parascenium, Patagium, Pennate, Pennon, Pinero, Pinion, Pip, Pterygoid, Putto, Right, Rogallo, Sail, Scent-scale, Segreant, Seraphim, Sweepback, Sweptback, Sweptwing, Swift, Swingwing, Tailplane, Tectrix, Tegmen, Transept, Van, Vol(et), Wound(ed)

Winged sandals Talaria

▷ **Winger** may indicate a bird

Wing-footed Aliped, Fleet, Swift

Wingless Apteral

Wink Bat, Condone, Connive, Flicker, Ignore, Instant, Nap, Nictitate, Pink, Twinkle

Winnie Pooh

Winnow Fan, Riddle, Separate, Sift, Van, Wecht

Winsome Bonny, Engaging, Gay, Pleasant

Winter, Wintry Bleak, Brumal, Cold, Dec, Fimbul, Frigid, Frore, Hibernate, Hiemal, Hiems, Hodiernal, Jasmine, Nuclear, Snowy

Winter cherry Chinese lantern

Wintergreen Sarcodes

Winter pear Nelis

Winter-sport Ski

Wipe (out), Wiping Abolish, Abrogate, Absterge, Amortise, Cancel, Cleanse, Demolish, Destroy, Deterge, Dicht, Dight, Expunge, Hanky, Mop, Nose-rag, Null, Purge, Raze, Sponge, Tersion, Tissue

Wire(s), Wiry Aerial, Barb(ed), Cable, Chicken, Coil, Earth, Filament, Filar, File, Heald, Heddle, High, Lean, Lecher, Live, Marconigram, Mil, Nichrome®, Nipper, Pickpocket, Razor, Sinewy, Snake, Spit, Staple, Stilet, Strand, String, Stylet, Telegram, Thoth, Thread

Wireless (operator), Wireless part Baffle, Set, Sparks, Valve

Wise(acre), Wisdom Advisedly, Athena, Athene, Canny, Depth, Ernie, Gothamite, Hep, Hindsight, Judgement, Learned, Long-headed, Lore, Manner, Mimir, Minerva, Norman, Oracle, Owl, Philosopher, Philosophy, Politic, Polymath, Prajna, Profound, Prudence, Sagacity, Sage, Salomonic, Sapience, Savvy, Shrewd, Sophia, Smartie, Solon, Wice

Wisecrack Dig, One-liner

Wise man Balthazar, Caspar, Heptad, Melchior, Nestor, Sage, Sapient, Seer, Solomon, Swami, Thales, Worldly

Wish(es) Crave, Death, Desiderate, ➤ DESIRE, Hope, List, Long, Pleasure, Precatory, Regards, Velleity, Want, Yearn

Wishbone Furcula, Marriage-bone, Merrythought, Skipjack

Wishy-washy Bland, Feeble, Insipid, Irresolute, Milksop, Weak, Wheyey

Wisp(y) Cirrate, Frail, Scrap, Shred, Virga, Wase

Wit(s), Witticism, Witty Acumen, Attic, Badinage, Banter, Brevity, Commonsense, Concetto, Cunning, Dry, Epigram, Esprit, Estimation, Eutrapelia, Eutrapely, Facetious, Fantasy, Hartford, Humour, Imagination, Intelligence, Irony, Jest, Jeu d'esprit, Joke, Marbles, Marinism, Memory, Mind, Mot, Mother, Native, Nous, Pawky, Pun, Repartee, Rogue, Sally, Salt, Saut, Sconce, ➤ SENSE, Shaft, Smart, Videlicet, Viz, Wag, Weet, Wisecrack, Word-play

Witch(craft) Broomstick, Cantrip, Carline, Circe, Coven, Craigfluke, Crone, Cutty Sark, Ensorcell, Galdragon, Glamour, Goety, Gramary(e), Gyre-carlin, Hag, Hecat(e), Hex, Lamia, Magic, Medea, Myal(ism), Night-hag, Obeahism, Obiism, Pythoness, Salem, Selim, Sibyl, Sieve, Sorceress, Speller, Sycorax, Trout, Valkyrie, Vaudoo, Vilia, Voodoo, Weird, Wicca

Witch-doctor Boyla, Medicine man, Mganga, Pawaw, Powwow, Sangoma, Shaman

Witch-hazel Fothergilla, Platan(e), Winter-bloom
Witch-hunter McCarthy
With And, By, Con, Cum, Hereby, In, Mit, Of, W
Withdraw(al), Withdrawn Abdicate, Alienate, Aloof, Cold turkey, Detach, Disengage, Distrait, Enshell, Evacuate, Inshell, Introvert, Offish, Palinode, Preserve, Recant, Recoil, Repair, Resile, Reticent, Retire, Retract(ion), Retreat, Revoke, Revulsion, Scratch, Secede, Sequester, Shrink, Shy, Subduct, Unreeve, Unsay
Wither(ed), Withering, Withers Arefy, Atrophy, Burn, Corky, Die, Droop, Dry, Evanish, Fade, Forpine, Googie, Languish, Marcescent, Miff, Nose, Scram, Sere, Shrink, Shrivel, Welk, Welt
Withershins Eastlin(g)s
▷ **With gaucherie** may indicate an anagram
Withhold(ing) Abstain, Conceal, Curt, Deny, Detain, Detinue, Hide, Keep, ➤ RESERVE, Trover
Within Enclosed, Endo-, Indoors, Inside, Interior, Intra
With it Hep, Hip, Syn, Trendy, W
Without Bar, Beyond, Ex, Lack(ing), Less, Minus, Orb, Outdoors, Outside, Sans, Save, Sen, Senza, Sine, X
▷ **Without** may indicate one word surrounding another
▷ **Without restraint** may indicate an anagram
Without stimulus Nastic
Withstand Brave, Contest, Defy, Endure, Oppose, Resist
Witness Attest, Bystander, Deponent, Depose, Expert, Evidence, Hostile, Jehovah's, Martyr, Material, Muggletonian, Observe, Obtest, Onlooker, Proof, ➤ SEE, Testament, Teste, Testify, Testimony
Witness-box Peter, Stand
▶ **Witticism** see WIT
Wizard (priest) Archimage, Carpathian, Conjuror, Expert, Gandalf, Hex, Magician, Merlin, Oz, Prospero, Shaman, Sorcerer, Super, Warlock, ➤ WITCH-DOCTOR
Wizen(ed) Dehydrate, Dry, Sere, Shrivel, Sphacelate, Wither
Woad Anil, Dye, Indigo, Isatis, Pastel, Pastil
Wobble, Wobbling Chandler's, Coggle, Precess, Quaver, Rock, Shoggle, Shoogle, Totter, Tremble, Trillo, Wag, Waggle, Walty, Waver
Wodehouse Plum
Woe(ful) Alack, Alas, Bale, Bane, Distress, Doole, Dule, Ewhow, Gram, Grief, Jeremiad, Lack-a-day, Misery, Pain, Plague, ➤ SORROW, Tribulation
Wolf(-like) Akela, Assyrian, Cancer, Casanova, Coyote, Cram, Dangler, Earth, Engorge, Fenrir, Fenris, Gorge, Grey, Ise(n)grim, Lobo, Lone, Lothario, Lupine, Luster, Lycanthrope, MI, Michigan, Pack, Prairie, Red, Rip, Roué, Rout, Rye, Scoff, Sea, Strand, Tasmanian, Thylacine, Tiger, Timber, Wanderer, Were, Whistler
Wolfram Tungsten
Wolf's bane Aconite, Friar's-cap

Wolseley Sir Garnet

Woman(hood), Women Anile, Bellibone, Besom, Biddy, Bimbo, Bint, Boiler, Broad, Cailleach, Callet, Chai, Chapess, Citess, Crone, Cummer, Dame, Daughter, Doe, Dona(h), Dorcas, Drab, Eve, F, Fair, ➤ FEMALE, Feme, Flapper, Floozy, Frail, Frow, Gammer, Gimmer, Gin, Girl, Gyno-, Harpy, Harridan, Inner, Jade, Lilith, Madam(e), Mademoiselle, Peat, Tedesca, Tottie, Totty, -gyny, Hen, Her, Jane, Lady, Lorette, Maenad, Mary, Miladi, Milady, Mob, Mort, Ms, Muliebrity, Pandora, Pict, Piece, Placket, Popsy, Quean, Queen, Ramp, Rib, Ribibe, Ronyon, Rudas, Runnion, Sabine, Sakti, Scarlet, Shakti, She, Skirt, Sort, Squaw, Tail, Tib, Tiring, Tit, Trot, Umfazi, Vahine, Wahine, Wifie

Womaniser Casanova, Lady-killer, Poodle-faker, Wolf

Womb Belly, Matrix, Metritis, Side, Uterus, Ventricle

Women's club, Women's lib S(h)akti, Soroptimist

Won Chon, W

Wonder(s) Admire, Agape, Amazement, AR, Arkansas, Arrah, Awe, Colossus, Ferly, Grape-seed, Marle, ➤ MARVEL, Meteor, Mirabilia, Miracle, Muse, Nine-day, Phenomenon, Prodigy, Speculate, Stupor, Suppose, Surprise, Wheugh, Whew, Wow

Wonderful(ly) Amazing, Bees' knees, Bitchin(g), Chinless, Ferly, Gee-whiz, Gramercy, Épatant, Fantastic, Far-out, Geason, Glorious, Great, Lal(l)apalooza, Magic, Mirable, Old, Purely, Ripping, Smashing, Sublime

Wonder-worker Thaumaturgist, Thaumaturgus

Wonky Cockeyed

Wont(ed) Accustomed, Apt, Custom, Habit, Shan't, Used

Woo(er) Address, Beau, Carve, Court, Seduce, Suitor, Swain

Wood(en), Woodland, Woody Afrormosia, Agalloch, Agila, Alburnum, Alerce, Algum, Almug, Amboina, Ash, Balsa, Bamboo, Basswood, Batten, Bavin, Baywood, Beam, Beaver, Beech, Beef, Bent, Birnam, Blockboard, Board, Bocage, Boord(e), Boscage, Bowl, Box, Brassie, Brazil, Briarwood, Bulletwood, Bushveld, Caatinga, Calamander, Caliature, Cam, Cambium, Campeachy, Canary, Candlewood, Carapa, Carr, Cask, Cedar, Channel, Chipboard, Chittagong, Clapboard, Conductor, Coppice, Copse, Cord, Coromandel, Coulisse, Dead, Deadpan, Deal, Dingle, Drive, Dunnage, Duramen, Eaglewood, Ebony, Elm, Eugh, Fathom, Fiddlewood, Fire, Firth, Fish, Forest, Frith, Fruitwood, Funk, Furious, Fustic, Fustet, Fustoc, Gaboon, Gambrel, Gantry, Gapó, Gauntree, Gopher, Green, Greenheart, Grove, Gumwood, Hackmatack, Hanger, Hard, Harewood, Heartwood, Heben, Hickory, Holt, Hornbeam, Hurst, Hyle, Igapó, Iroko, Iron, Isle, Jarool, Jarrah, Jarul, Joist, Kindling, Kingwood, Kip, Knee, Kokra, Laburnum, Lana, Lath, Lignum(-vitae), Lime, Log(gat), Lumber, Mad, Mahogany, Maple, Matchwood, Mazer, Meranti, Miombo, Myall, Nemoral, Nemorous, Nettle-tree, Obeche, Offcut, Opepe, Orache, Orange, Palisander, Pallet, Palmyra, Partridge, Pimento, Plane, Poplar, Pulpwood, Punk, Pyengadu, Pyinkado, Quebracho, Raddle, Ramin, Rata, Red, Rock, Rosewood, Rowan, Sabele, Sabicu, Sandal, Sanders(wood), Sapan, Sapele, Sappan, Sapucaia, Sapwood, Satinwood, Shagbark, Shaw, Shawnee,

Shittim, Silvan, Sissoo, Slat, Slippery elm, Soft, Southern, Spinney, Splat, Spline, Splint, Sponge, Spoon, Stink, Stolid, Summerwood, Sylvan, Taiga, Tamarack, Tangle, Thorn, Three-ply, Timber, Touch, Treen, Trees, Tulip, Twiggy, Vert, Waboom, Wald, Wallaba, Walnut, Wenge, Wild, Xylem, Xyloid, Yang, Zante

▷ **Wood** may indicate an anagram (in sense of mad)

Wood-carver Bodger, Gibbons, Whittler

Woodchuck Bobac, Marmot

Woodcock Becasse, Beccaccia, Snipe

Woodlouse Isopod, Oniscus, Slater

Woodman Ali (Baba), Forester, Hewer, Logger, Lumberjack

Woodpecker Bird, Flicker, Hickwall, Picarian, Rainbird, Sapsucker, Saurognathae, Witwall, Woodwale, Yaffle

Wood-pigeon Bird, Cushat, Que(e)st, Qu(o)ist

Wood-sorrel Oca

Wood-tar Furan, Furfuran

Woodwind Bassoon, Clarinet, Cornet, Flute, Oboe, Piccolo, Pipe, Recorder, Reed

Woodwork(er) Sloid, Sloyd, Tarsia, Termite

Woodworm Gribble, Termes

Wookey Stalactite

Wool(len), Woolly Alpaca, Angora, Aran, Ardil, Bainin, Barège, Beige, Berlin, Botany, Bouclé, Calamanco, Cardi(gan), Cas(s)imere, Cashmere, Clip, Cotton, Crutchings, Daglock, Doeskin, Dog, Doily, Doyley, Down, Drugget, Duffel, Fadge, Fingering, Fleece, Flock, Frib, Frieze, Fuzz, Glass, Guernsey, Hank, Hause-lock, Hogget, Indumentum, Jaeger, Jersey, Kashmir, Ket, Lanate, Laniferous, Lanigerous, Lanose, Lock, Loden, Merino, Mineral, Mortling, Moul, Mullein, Noil(s), Nun's-veiling, Offsorts, Oo, Pashm, Pelage, Persian, Qiviut, Rock, Rolag, Sagathy, Saxon, Say, Shalloon, Shetland, Shoddy, Skein, Slip-on, Slipe, Slub, Spencer, Staple, Steel, Strouding, Swansdown, Tamise, Tammy, Thibet, Three-ply, Tod, Tricot, Tweed, Vicuna, Virgin, Wire, Worcester, Yarn, Zephyr, Zibel(l)ine

Wool-gatherer Argo, Dreamer

Wool-holder, Woolsack Bale, Distaff

Woolly-bear Tiger-moth, Woubit

Wool-oil Yolk

Wooster Bertie

Woozy Drunk, Vague, Woolly

Worcester Wigorn

Word(s), Wording, Wordy Appellative, Bahuvrihi, Buzz, Claptrap, Code, Comment, Dick, Dit(t), Enclitic, Epos, Etymon, Faith, Ghost, Grace, Hard, Heteronym, Hint, Hyponym, ➤ IN A WORD, ➤ IN TWO WORDS, Key, Last, Lexeme, Lexicon, Lexis, Logia, Logos, Lyrics, Mantra, Message, Morpheme, Mot, Neologism, News, Nonce, Nonsense, Noun, Oracle, Order, Palabra, Paragram, Parole, Paroxytone, Perissology, Phrase, Pledge, Portmanteau, Prolix, Promise, Rhematic, Rumour, Saying, Selah,

Semantics, Signal, Subtitle, Surtitle, Term, Tetragram, Text, Verb, Verbiage, Verbose, Warcry, Weasel, Wort, Written

Word-blindness Alexia, Dyslexia

Word-play Charade, Paronomasia, Pun

Work(er), Working(-class), Workman(ship) Act(ivate), Ant, Appliqué, Artefact, Artel, Artifact, Artificer, Artisan, Beaver, Bee, Blue-collar, Bohunk, Boondoggle, Business, Casual, Char, Chore, Claim, Clock, Coolie, Corvée, Darg, Do, Dog, Dogsbody, Droil, Drudge, Drug, Dung, Earn, Effect, Effort, Erg(ataner), Ergatoid, Erg-nine, Ergon, Ergonomics, Erg-ten, Em, Eta, Evince, Exercise, Exploit, Factotum, Facture, Fat, Fettler, Field, Floruit, Fret, ➤ FUNCTION, Fuller, Gastarbeiter, Gel, Go, Graft, Grind, Grisette, Hand, Harness, Hat, Hobo, Horse, Hunky, Industry, Innards, Job, Journeyman, Kolhoznik, Labour, Laid, Luddite, Lump, Man, Manipulate, Meng, Midinette, Mine, Ming, Moider, Moil, Moonlight, Movement, Navvy, Neuter, Oeuvre, On, Op, Opera(tion), Operative, Operator, Opus, Opusc(u)le, Ouvrier, Ox, Parergon, Peasant, Peg, Pensum, Peon, Ply, Potboiler, Practise, Production, Prole(tariat), Prud'homme, Pursuit, Red-neck, Rep, Ride, Roughneck, Rouseabout, Roustabout, Run, Samiti, Satisfactory, Scabble, Scapple, Serve, Service, Situation, Slogger, Smithy, Social, Staff, Stakhanovite, Stevedore, Stint, Strive, Sweat, Swink, Take, Tamper, Task, Temp, Tenail(le), Tenaillon, Termite, Tew, Tick, Till, Toccata, Toil, Toreutic, Travail, Treatise, Trojan, TU, Tut, Typto, Uphill, Wage plug, Walla(h), Wark, White-collar, Wobblies, Yacker, Yakka, Yakker

Workable Feasible, Practical

Work-basket, Workbox Caba(s), Nécessaire

Workhouse Spike, Union

▷ **Working** may indicate an anagram

Working-party Bee, Quilting-bee, Sewing-bee, Squad

Works, Workshop Atelier, Engine, Factory, Forge, Foundry, Garage, Hacienda, Innards, Lab, Mill, Plant, Shed, Shop, Skylab, Smithy, Studio

Workshy Sweer(ed), Sweert, Sweir(t)

World(ly) Carnal, Chthonic, Cosmopolitan, Cosmos, Dream, Earth, Fourth, Ge, Globe, Kingdom, Lay, Mappemond, Microcosm, Mondaine, Mondial, Mundane, Orb, Oyster, Planet, Possible, Secular, Sensual, Society, Sphere, Temporal, Terra, Terrene, Terrestrial, Third, Universe, Vale, Welt

Worm(-like), Worms, Wormy Acorn, Anguillula, Annelid, Annulata, Apod(e), Apodous, Arrow, Articulata, Ascarid, Bilharzia, Bladder, Bob, Bootlace, Brandling, Bristle, Caddis, Caseworm, Catworm, Capeworm, Cestode, Cestoid, Clamworm, Dew, Diet, Diplozoon, Edge, Enteropneust, Fan, Filander, Filaria, Fluke, Gilt-tail, Gordius, Guinea, Hair-eel, Hairworm, Heartworm, Helminth, Hemichordata, Hookworm, Horsehair, Inchworm, Leech, Liver-fluke, Lob, Lumbricus, Lytta, Merosome, Nematoda, Nematode, Nemertea, Nereid, Night-crawler, Oligochaete, Paddle, Palmer, Palolo, Paste-eel, Peripatus, Piper, Planarian, Platyhelminth, Polychaete, Ragworm, Ribbon, Sabella, Schistosome, Scoleciform, Scolex, Seamouse, Serpula, Servile, Sipunculacea, Sipunculoidea, Stomach, Strawworm, Strongyl(e), Taenia, Tag-tail, Tenioid, Teredo, Termite,

Threadworm, Tiger tail, Tongue, Toxocara, Trematode, Trichin(ell)a, Trichina, Trichinosed, Triclad, Tube, Tubifex, Turbellaria, Vermiform, Vinegar, Wheat-eel, Wheatworm, Whipworm

Wormkiller Anthelmintic, Santonin

Wormwood Absinth, Appleringie, Artemisia, Mugwort, Santonica

Worn(-out) Attrite, Bare, Decrepit, Detrition, Effete, Epuisé, Exhausted, Forfairn, Forfoughten, Forjaskit, Forjeskit, Frazzled, Old, On, Passé, Raddled, Rag, Seedy, Shabby, Shot, Spent, Stale, Tired, Traikit, Trite, Used, Weathered, Whacked

Worried, Worrier, Worry Agonise, Annoy, Anxiety, Badger, Bait, Beset, Bother, Care(worn), Cark, Chafe, Concern, Deave, Deeve, Distress, Disturb, Dog, Eat, Exercise, Feeze, Frab, Fret, Fuss, Harass, Harry, Hyp, Inquietude, Knag, Nag, Perturb, Pester, Pheese, Pheeze, Phese, Pingle, Pium, Rile, Sool, Stew, Tew, Touse, Towse, Trouble, Vex, Wherrit, Worn

▷ **Worried** may indicate an anagram

Worse(n) Adversely, Degenerate, Deteriorate, Exacerbate, Impair, Inflame, Pejorate, Regress, War(re), Waur

Worship(per) Adore, Adulation, Angelolatry, Autolatry, Bless, Churchgoer, Cult, Deify, Douleia, Dulia, Epeolatry, Fetish, Glorify, Gurdwara, Idolise, Latria, Lionise, Liturgics, Lordolatry, Mariolatry, Oncer, Orant, Praise, Puja, Revere, Sabaism, Sakta, Service, Shacharis, Shakta, Synaxis, Thiasus, Vaishnava, Venerate, Votary, Wodenism

Worst Beat, Best, Defeat, Get, Nadir, Outdo, Overpower, Pessimum, Rock-bottom, Scum, Severest, Throw, Trounce

Worsted Caddis, Caddyss, Challis, Coburg, Genappe, Lea, Ley, Serge, Shalli, Tamin(e), Whipcord

▷ **Worsted** may indicate an anagram

Wort Laser, Parkleaves, Plant, Tutsan

Worth(while), Worthy Admirable, Asset, Be, Cop, Deserving, Eligible, Estimable, Feck, ➤ MERIT, Notable, Substance, Tanti, Use, Value, Virtuous, Wealth

Worthless (person) Base, Beggarly, Bodger, Bootless, Bum, Catchpenny, Cheapjack, Crumb, Cypher, Damn, Docken, Dodkin, Doit, Doitkin, Draffish, Draffy, Dreck, Dross, Fallal, Footra, Fouter, Foutre, Frippery, Gimcrack, Gingerbread, Glop, Gubbins, Javel, Jimcrack, Left, Light, Lorel, Lorrell, Losel, Lozell, Manky, Mare's nest, Mud, Nugatory, Nyaff, Obol, Orra, Otiose, Paltry, Pin, Poxy, Punk, Raca, Rag, Rap, Rubbishy, Scabby, Scum, Shinkin, Sorry, Straw, Tinhorn, Tinpot, Tinsel, Tittle, Toerag, Trangam, Trashy, Trumpery, Tuppenny, Twat, Two-bit, Twopenny, Useless, Vain, Vile, Waff, Wanworthy, Wauff

Wotchermean Anan

Would be Assumed, Pseudo, Soi-disant

Wouldn't Nould(e)

Wound(ed) Battery, Bite, Bless, Blighty, Bruise, Chagrin, Coiled, Crepance, Cut, Dere, Engore, Ganch, Gash, Gaunch, Gore, Harm, Hurt, Injury, Lacerate, Lesion, Maim, Molest, Mortify, Offend, Pip, Sabre-cut, Scab, Scar,

Scath, Scotch, Scratch, Shoot, Snaked, Snub, Sore, Stab, Sting, Trauma, Twined, Umbrage, Vuln, Vulnerary, Walking, Wing, Wint

Woven Knitted, Pirnit, Textile, Wattle

Wow Amaze, Howl, My, Success

Wrack Destroy, Downfall, Kelp, Ore, Torment, Varec(h), Vengeance

Wraith Apparition, Fetch, Ghost, Phantom, Shadow, Spectre

Wrangle, Wrangling Argie-bargie, ➤ ARGUE, Altercate, Bandy, Bicker, Brangle, Broil, Dispute, Haggle, Mathematical, Rag, Vitilitigation

Wrap(per), Wrapping, Wrap up Amice, Amis, Bind, Bubble, Bundle, Cellophane®, Cere, Clingfilm, Cloak, Clothe, Cocoon, Conclude, Emboss, Enfold, Enrol(l), Ensheath(e), Envelop(e), Foil, Folio, Furl, Hap, Hem, Kimono, Kraft, Lag, Lap, Mail, Muffle, Negligee, Parcel, Roll, Rug, Shawl, Sheath(e), Stole, Swaddle, Swathe, Tinfoil, Tsutsumu, Velamen, Wap, Wimple

Wrasse Conner, Cunner, Parrot-fish

Wrath Anger, Cape, Fury, Ire, Passion, Vengeance

Wreak Avenge, Indulge, Inflict

Wreath(e) Adorn, Anadem, Chaplet, Coronal, Crown, Entwine, Festoon, Garland, Laurel, Lei, Torse, Tortile, Twist

Wreathe(d) Hederated

Wreck(age), Wrecked, Wrecker Crab, Debris, Demolish, Devastate, Flotsam, Founder, Goner, Hesperus, Hulk, Lagan, Ligan, Luddite, Mutilate, Ruin(ate), Sabotage, Shambles, Shatter, Sink, Smash, Subvert, Torpedo, Trash, Wrack

▷ **Wrecked** may indicate an anagram

Wren Architect, Bird, Hannah, Jenny, Kinglet, Rifleman-bird, Sailor

Wrench Allen, Fit, Jerk, Lug, Mole, Monkey, Pin, Pull, Socket, Spanner, Sprain, Stillson®, Strain, Tear, Twist, Windlass, Wrest

Wrestle(r), Wrestling All-in, Antaeus, Arm, Basho, Catch-as-catch-can, Clinch, Flying mare, Folding-press, Grapple, Haystacks, Indian, Judo, Makunouchi, Milo, Ozeki, Palaestral, Pancratium, Rikishi, Sambo, Stable, Struggle, Sumo, Sumotori, Tag, Tag (team), Tussle, Wraxle, Writhe, Yokozuna

Wretch(ed) Blackguard, Blue, Caitiff, Chap-fallen, Cullion, Forlorn, Git, Hapless, Lorn, Measly, Miser, Miserable, Peelgarlic, Pilgarlick, Pipsqueak, Poltroon, Poor, Punk, Rat, Scoundrel, Scroyle, Seely, Snake, Unblest, Wo(e)

▷ **Wretched** may indicate an anagram

Wriggle Hirsle, Shimmy, Squirm, Twine, Wiggle, Writhe

Wring(er) Drain, Extort, Mangle, Screw, Squeeze, Twist

Wrinkle(d), Wrinkly Clue, Cockle, Corrugate, Crease, Crepy, Crimpy, Crow's-foot, Crumple, Fold, Frounce, Frown, Frumple, Furrow, Gen, Groove, Headline, Hint, Idea, Line, Lirk, Plissé, Pucker, Purse, Ridge, Rimple, Rivel, Rop(e)y, Ruck(le), Rugose, Rumple, Runkle, Seamy, Shrivel, Sulcus, Time-worn, Tip

Wrist Carpus, Radialia, Shackle-bone

Writ(s) Capias, Certiorari, Cursitor, Dedimus, Distringas, Elegit, Fieri facias, Filacer, Habeas corpus, Holy, Injunction, Latitat, Law-burrows, Mandamus, Mittimus, Noverint, Praemunire, Process, Replevin, Scirefacias, Significat, Subpoena, Summons, Supersedeas, Tolt, Venire, Warrant

Write(r), Writing Allograph, Annotator, Apocrypha, ➤ AUTHOR, Automatic, Ballpoint, Biographer, Biro®, Bloomsbury Group, Boustrophedon, Calligraphy, Clerk, Collectanea, Columnist, Creative, Cuneiform, Diarist, Dite, ➤ DRAMATIST, Draft, Elohist, Endorse, Endoss, Engross, Epigrammatise, Epistle, ➤ ESSAYIST, Expatiate, Festschrift, Fist, Form, Formulary, Freelance, Ghost, Gongorism, Graffiti, Grammatology, Graphite, Hack, Hairline, Hand, Hieratic, Hiragana, Indite, Ink, Inkslinger, Inscribe, Join-hand, Jot(tings), Journalese, Journalist, Journo, Kalakana, Kaleyard School, Kana, Kanji, Katakana, Keelivine, Keelyvine, Leader, Lexigraphy, Lexis, Linear A, Lipogram, Litterateur, Longhand, Lucubrate, Marivaudage, Minoan, Mirror, Ms(s), Nesk(h), Nib, Notary, Notate, Novelese, ➤ NOVELIST, Paragraphia, Pasigraphy, Pen, Pencil, Penmanship, Penne, Pentel®, Pinyin, Planchette, ➤ POET, Polemic, Pot-hook, Proser, Pseudepigrapha, Quill, Roundhand, Samizdat, Sanskrit, Sci-fi, Scissorer, Scratch, Screed, Screeve, Scribe, Scrip(t), Scripture, Scrivener, Scrow, Scytale, Secretary, Shaster, Shastra, Style, Subscript, Superscribe, Sutra, Syllabary, Syngraph, Tantra, Transcribe, Treatise, Tushery, Uncial, Wordsmith

WRITERS

3 letters:	Opie	Gorky	Powys
APH	Ovid	Gosse	Quipu
Eco	Pope	Greer	Reade
Lee	Saki	Grimm	Renan
Paz	Sand	Hardy	Rilke
Poe	Shaw	Henty	Sagan
RLS	Snow	Hesse	Scott
4 letters:	Ward	Heyer	Shute
Amis	West	Homer	Spark
Asch	Zola	Ibsen	Stark
Aymé	**5 letters:**	Innes	Stein
Bede	Acton	James	Swift
Bolt	Albee	Joyce	Synge
Cary	Auden	Kafka	Twain
Cree	Ayres	Lewis	Verne
Dahl	Bates	Lodge	Waugh
Gide	Blake	Lorca	Wells
Hope	Caine	Makar	Wilde
Hugo	Camus	Mason	Woolf
Hunt	Corvo	Milne	Yates
King	Crane	Munro	Yonge
Lamb	Defoe	Musil	**6 letters:**
Loos	Doyle	Nashe	Ambler
Loti	Dumas	Ouida	Arnold
Lyly	Eliot	Pater	Artaud
Mann	Ellis	Paton	Asimov
More	Genet	Pliny	Austen
Nash	Gogol	Pound	Balzac

Baring	Smiles	Pushkin	
Barrie	Steele	Ransome	
Belloc	Sterne	Rostand	Trollope
Bellow	Storey	Saroyan	Turgenev
Borges	Thomas	Sassoon	Voltaire
Borrow	Updike	Shelley	Williams
Braine	Virgil	Simenon	**9 letters:**
Bronte	Walton	Sitwell	Aeschylus
Buchan	Wilder	Surtees	Ainsworth
Bunyan	**7 letters:**	Terence	Blackmore
Butler	Addison	Thoreau	Boccaccio
Capote	Aldrich	Tolkien	Burroughs
Cicero	Aretino	Tolstoy	Cervantes
Conrad	Beckett	Travers	Dos Passos
Corpus	Bennett	Wallace	Du Maurier
Cowper	Bentley	Walpole	Edgeworth
Cronin	Boileau	Wharton	Goldsmith
Daudet	Boswell	Whitman	Hawthorne
Dryden	Burgess	**8 letters:**	Hemingway
Engels	Carlyle	Andersen	Isherwood
Fowles	Chaucer	Beaumont	Lermontov
France	Chekhov	Browning	Linklater
Gibbon	Cobbett	Caldwell	Mackenzie
Goethe	Colette	Caroline	Madariaga
Graves	Collins	Chandler	Mansfield
Greene	Coppard	Childers	Oppenheim
Heller	Corelli	Christie	Pasternak
Hobbes	Cranmer	Constant	Priestley
Hughes	Deeping	De la Mare	Santayana
Huxley	Dickens	Disraeli	Sholokhov
Jerome	Drabble	Faulkner	Steinbeck
Jonson	Dreiser	Fielding	Stevenson
Le Fanu	Durrell	Flaubert	Thackeray
London	Emerson	Forester	Wodehouse
Lucian	Fenelon	Goncourt	**10 letters:**
Lytton	Forster	Inkerman	Ballantyne
Mailer	Gissing	Ishiguro	Chesterton
Malory	Golding	Kingsley	Dostoevsky
Mannin	Haggard	Lawrence	Fitzgerald
Miller	Herbert	Mannheim	Galsworthy
Milton	Hichens	Meredith	Mandeville
Morgan	Johnson	Naipaaul	Maupassant
Nerval	Kipling	Perrault	Richardson
Onions	Lardner	Plutarch	**11 letters:**
Orwell	Marryat	Rabelais	Machiavelli
Proust	Maugham	Rattigan	Maeterlinck
Purana	Mauriac	Remarque	Shakespeare
Racine	Mérimée	Rousseau	**12 letters:**
Runyon	Mitford	Salinger	Aristophanes
Ruskin	Moravia	Schiller	Solzhenitsyn
Sapper	Murdoch	Smollett	**13 letters:**
Sayers	Nabokov	Stendhal	Chateaubriand
Sewell	Peacock	Taffrail	Sackville-West

Write-off Amortise, Annul, Cancel, Scrap

Writhe, Writhing Athetosis, Contort, Curl, Scriggle, Squirm, Twist, Wriggle

▷ **Writhing** may indicate an anagram

Writing-case Kalamdan

Writing-room Scriptorium

Wrong Aggrieve, Agley, Amiss, Astray, Awry, Bad, Chout, Delict, Disservice, Err, Fallacious, False, Harm, Ill, Immoral, Improper, Incorrect, Injury, Mischief, Misintelligence, Misled, Mistake(n), Misuse, Nocent, Offbase, Offend, Peccadillo, Perverse, Sin(ful), Tort, Transgress, Unethical, Unright, Unsuitable, Withershins, Wryly, X

▷ **Wrong** may indicate an anagram

Wrong opinion Cacodoxy

Wrought (up) Agitated, Beaten, Carved, Created, Excited, Filigree, Freestone, Shaped

Wrung Twisted, Withers

Wry Askew, Contrary, Devious, Distort, Droll, Grimace, Ironic

Wryneck Iynx, Jynx, Torticollis, Yunx

Wycliffian Lollard

Wyoming Wy

X x

X(-shaped) Buss, By, Chi, Christ, Cross, Decussate, Drawn, Kiss, Ten, Times, Unknown, X-ray

Xant(h)ippe Battle-axe, Dragon

Xenon Xe

Xerophyte, Xerophytic Cactus, Cereus, Mesquite, Tamaricaceae, Tamarisk

Xhosan Caffre, Kaf(f)ir

Ximenes Cardinal

X-ray Angiogram, Cholangiography, Emi-Scanner, Encephalogram, Encephalograph, Fermi, Grenz, Mammogram, Plate, Pyelogram, Radioscopy, Rem, Roentgen, Sciagram, Screening, Skiagram, Tomography, Venogram

Xmas Noel, Yuletide

Xylophone Marimba, Sticcado, Sticcato

Y y

Y Samian, Unknown, Yankee, Yard, Year, Yen, Yttrium

Yacht Britannia, Dragon, Ice, Keelboat, Land, Maxi, Sailboat, Sand

Yachtsman, Yachtsmen Chichester, RYS

Yak Gup, Talk

Yale® Key, Lock

Yam Batata, Camote, Dioscorea, Diosgenin, Kumara

Yank(ee) Bet, Carpetbagger, Hitch, Jerk, Jonathan, Lug, Northerner, Pluck, Pull, Rug, Schlep(p), So(o)le, Sowl(e), ➤ TUG, Tweak, Twitch, Wrench, Wrest

▷ **Yank** may indicate an anagram

Yap Bark, Yelp

Yard Area, CID, Close, Court, Farm-toun, Garden, Haw, Hof, Kail, Mast, Measure, Patio, Ree(d), Scotland, Spar, Sprit, Steel, Stick, Stride, Y, Yd

Yarn(s) Abb, Berlin, Bouclé, Caddice, Caddis, Chenille, Clew, Clue, Cop, Cord, Crewel, Fib, Fibroline, Fingering, Genappe, Gimp, Gingham, Guimp(e), Gymp, Homespun, Jaw, Knittle, Knot, Lay, Lea, Ley, Line, Lisle, Lurex®, Marl, Merino, Nylon, Organzine, Orlon®, Ply, Rigmarole, Ripping, Saxony, Sennit, Sinnet, Skein, Story, Strand, Tale, Taradiddle, Thread, Thrid, Thrum(my), Tram, Warp, Weft, Woof, Wool, Worsted, Zephyr

Yarrow Milfoil

Yashmak Veil

Yaw(s) Boba, Buba, Deviate, Framboesia, Lean, Morula, Tack, Veer

Yawn(ing) Boredom, Chasmy, Fissure, Gant, Gape, Gaunt, Greys, Hiant, Oscitation, Pandiculation, Rictus

Yea Certainly, Truly, Verily, Yes

Year(ly), Years A, Age, Anno, Annual, Astronomical, Common, Dot, Equinoctial, Financial, Fiscal, Gap, Indiction, Julian, Leap, Light, Lunar, PA, Platonic, Riper, Sabbatical, Sidereal, Solar, Sothic, Summer, Sun, Tax, Time, Towmon(d), Towmont, Twelvemonth

Yearbook Annual

Yearling Colt, Hogget, Stirk, Teg

Yearn(ing) Ache, Ake, Aspire, Brame, Burn, Crave, Curdle, Desire, Erne, Greed, Hanker, Hone, ➤ LONG, Nostalgia, Pant, Pine, Sigh

▷ **Yearning** may indicate an anagram

Year's end Dec

Yeast Barm, Bees, Brewer's, Ferment, Flor, Leaven, Saccharomycete, Torula, Vegemite®

Yell Cry, Hue, Shout, Skelloch, Tiger, Waul, Yoick

Yellow(ish) Abram, Amber, Anthoclore, Auburn, Back, Beige, Buff, Cadmium, Canary, Chicken, Chrome, Citrine, Cowardly, Craven,

Zoroastrian Gabar, Gheber, Ghebre, Gueber, Guebre, Magus, Mazdaist, Mazdean, Ormazd, Ormuzd, Parsee, Parsi
Zulu Chaka, Impi, Inkatha, Matabele, Niger, Shaka, Warrior
Zut Crimini

Curcumin(e), Etiolin, Fallow, Fever, Filemot, Flavescent, Flavin(e), Flavon, Flaxen, Fulvous, Gamboge, Gold, Icteric, Isabel(le), Jack, Jaundiced, Lammer, Lemon(y), Lupulin, Lutein, Lutescent, Mustard, Nankeen, Naples, Oaker, Ochery, Ochre(y), Or(eide), Oroide, Pages, Peril, Pink, Primrose, River, Saffron, Sallow, Sear, Spineless, Straw, Sulphur, Tawny, Topaz, Tow, Vitelline, Weld, Xanthous, Yolk
Yellowhammer Bunting, Yeldring, Yeldrock, Yite, Yoldring
Yellow-wood Gopher
Yelp Cry, Squeal, Whee, Ya(w)p
Yemeni Saba, Sabean, Sheba
Yen Desire, Itch, Longing, Urge, Y, Yearn
Yeoman Beefeater, Exon, Goodman, Goodwife, Salvation
Yep OK, Yes
Yes Ay(e), Da, Indeed, Ja, Jokol, Nod, OK, Oke, Quite, Sure, Truly, Uh-huh, Wilco, Yea, Yokul, Yup
Yesterday Démodé, Eve, Hesternal, Pridian
Yet But, Even, How-be, Moreover, Nay, Nevertheless, Now, Still, Though
Yeti Abominable snowman, Sasquatch
Yew Taxus
Yibbles A(i)blins
Yield(ing) Abandon, Afford, Bend, Bow, Breed, Capitulate, Catch, Cede, Come, Comply, Concede, Crack, Crop, Defer, Dividend, Docile, Ductile, Easy, Elastic, Facile, Flaccid, Flexible, Give, Harvest, Interest, Knuckle, Meek, Meltith, Mess, Output, Pan, Pay, Pliant, Produce, Relent, Render, Return, Sag, Soft, ➤ SUBMIT, Succumb, Surrender, Susceptible, Truckle
Yodel Song, Warble
Yoga, Yogi Bear, Bhakti, Fakir, Hatha, Maha, Raja, Sid(d)ha
Yoghurt Madzoon, Matzoon
Yoke Bow, Cang(ue), Collar, Couple, Harness, Inspan, Jugal, Pair, Span
Yokel Boor, Bumpkin, Chaw(-bacon), Clumperton, Hayseed, Hick, Jake, Jock, Peasant, Rustic
Yolk Parablast, Vitellicle, Vitellus, Yellow
Yon(der) Distant, Further, O'erby, Thae, There, Thether, Thither
Yore Agone, Olden, Past
Yorick Sterne
York(shire), Yorkshireman Batter, Bowl, Ebor, Pudding, Ridings, Tyke
Yorker Tice
You One, Sie, Thee, Thou, Usted, Ye
Young (person), Youngster, Youth(ful) Adolescent, Amorino, Bodgie, Boy, Boyhood, Brigham, Bub, Buckie, Ch, Chick, Chicken, Child, Chile, Cockerel, Cockle, Colt, Comsomol, Cornstalk, Cub, DJ, Early, Ephebe, Ephebus, Esquire, Flapper, Fledgling, Foetus, Fry, Gigolo, Girl, Gunsel, Halfling, Hebe, Hobbledehoy, Immature, Imp, Infant, Issue, Junior, Juvenal, Juvenesce, Juvenile, Keral, Kid, Kiddo, Kiddy, Kipper, Knave-bairn, Komsomol, Lad, Lamb, Latter-day, Less, Litter, Little, Loretta,

Minor, Misspent, Mod, Mormon, Nance, Neanic, Neophyte, Nestling, (Pre-)pubescent, New, Nipper, Nymph, Plant, Progeny, Protégé(e), Punk, Pup, Sapling, Scent, Scion, Shaver, Skinhead, Slip, Son, Spawn, Sprig, Springal(d), Stripling, Swain, Syen, Ted, Teenager, Teens, Teenybopper, Toyboy, Vernal, Whelp, Whippersnapper, Yippy, Yoof, Yopper, Younker, Yumpie, Yuppie

Younger, Youngest Baby, Benjamin, Cadet, Last born, Less, Minimus, Seneca, Wallydrag, Wallydraigle, Yr

Your(s) Thee, Thine, Thy

Yo-yo Bandalore

Ytterbium Yb

Yttrium Y

Yucky Gooey, Grooly, Sickly, Sticky

Yugoslav Croat(ian), Serb, Slovene

Yukon YT

Yuletide Advent, Dec, Noel, Xmas

Z z

Z Izzard, Izzet, Zambia, Zebra

Zamenhof Esperanto

Zander Fogash, Sander

Zany Bor(r)el, Comic, Cuckoo, Idiotic, Mad

Zeal(ous) Ardour, Bigotry, Devotion, Eager, Enthusiasm, Evangelic, Fervour, Fire, Perfervid, Study

Zealot Bigot, Devotee, Fan(atic), St Simon, Votary

Zebra Convict, Quagga

Zenith Acme, Apogee, Height, Pole, Summit

Zeno Colonnade, Elea, Stoic

Zeolite Analcime, Analcite

Zephyr Breeze, Wind

Zeppelin Airship, Balloon, Dirigible

Zero Absolute, Blob, Cipher, Ground, Nil, Nothing, Nought, O, Z

Zest Condiment, Crave, Élan, Gusto, Pep, Piquancy, Relish, Spice, Tang, Zap

Ziegfeld Flo

Zigzag Crémaillère, Crinkle-crankle, Dancette, Feather-stitch, Indent, Ric-rac, Slalom, Stagger, Tack, Traverse, Yaw

Zinc Blende, Gahnite, Mossy, Sherardise, Spelter, Sphalerite, Tutenag, Tutty, Willemite, Wurtzite, Zn

Zip(per) Dash, Energy, Fastener, Fly, Go, Oomph, Presto, Stingo, Vim, Vivacity, Whirry, Zero

Zircon Hyacinth, Jacinth, Jargo(o)n

Zirconium Baddeleyite, Zr

Zither Cithara, Kantela, Kantele, Koto

Zodiac(al) Aquarius, Archer, Aries, Bull, Cancer, Capricorn, Counter-glow, Crab, Fish, Gemini, Gegenschein, Goat, Horoscope, Leo, Libra, Lion, Ophiuchus, Pisces, Ram, Sagittarius, Scales, Scorpio(n), Taurus, Twins, Virgin, Virgo, Watercarrier

Zola Budd, Emile, Nana, Realism

Zombie Catatonic, Dolt, Robot

Zone Anacoustic, Area, Band, Belt, Benioff, Buffer, Canal, Climate, Collision, Convergence, Crumple, Drop, Ecotone, End, Enterprise, Erogenous, Exclusion, F layer, Free, Fresnel, Frigid, Hot, Impact, No-fly, Precinct, ➤ REGION, Rift, Ring, Sahel, Smokeless, Temperate, Time, Torrid, Tundra, Twilight

Zoo Bedlam, Circus, Menagerie, Vivarium, Whipsnade

Zoologist, Zoology Biologist, Botanist, Cetology, Naturalist

Zoom Close-up, Speed